Philosophy After Marx

Historical Materialism Book Series

The Historical Materialism Book Series is a major publishing initiative of the radical left. The capitalist crisis of the twenty-first century has been met by a resurgence of interest in critical Marxist theory. At the same time, the publishing institutions committed to Marxism have contracted markedly since the high point of the 1970s. The Historical Materialism Book Series is dedicated to addressing this situation by making available important works of Marxist theory. The aim of the series is to publish important theoretical contributions as the basis for vigorous intellectual debate and exchange on the left.

The peer-reviewed series publishes original monographs, translated texts, and reprints of classics across the bounds of academic disciplinary agendas and across the divisions of the left. The series is particularly concerned to encourage the internationalization of Marxist debate and aims to translate significant studies from beyond the English-speaking world.

For a full list of titles in the Historical Materialism Book Series available in paperback from Haymarket Books, visit:
www.haymarketbooks.org/category/hm-series

Philosophy After Marx

100 Years of Misreadings and the Normative Turn in Political Philosophy

Christoph Henning

Translated by
Max Henninger

Haymarket Books
Chicago, IL

First published in 2014 by Brill Academic Publishers, the Netherlands

Published in paperback in 2015 by
Haymarket Books
P.O. Box 180165
Chicago, IL 60618
773-583-7884
www.haymarketbooks.org

ISBN: 978-1-60846-476-0

Trade distribution:
In the US, Consortium Book Sales, www.cbsd.com
In Canada, Publishers Group Canada, www.pgcbooks.ca
In the UK, Turnaround Publisher Services, www.turnaround-psl.com
In Australia, Palgrave Macmillan, www.palgravemacmillan.com.au
In all other countries, Publishers Group Worldwide, www.pgw.com

Cover design by Ragina Johnson.

This book was published with the generous support of
Lannan Foundation and the Wallace Global Fund.

Printed in Canada by union labor.

10 9 8 7 6 5 4 3 2 1

Library of Congress Cataloging-in-Publication data is available.

GCC/IBT

FSC
www.fsc.org
MIX
Paper from
responsible sources
FSC® C103567

Contents

Sandblasting Marx

By Fredric Jameson. This review of the German original of the present volume appeared in New Left Review, *II/55.*

A Marx revival seems to be under way, predating the current disarray on Wall Street, even though no clear-cut political options yet seem to propose themselves. Sensible opportunists have welcomed any sign of sympathy for Marxian positions, without wanting to alienate the new converts (or returning fellow-travellers). The big ideological issues – anarchism, the party, economic planning, social classes – are still mainly avoided, on the grounds that they remind too many people of Communist propaganda. Such a reminder is unwanted, not so much because it is accompanied by the memory of deaths and violence (memory is fragile in postmodernity) as simply and less dramatically because such topics now appear boring.

On the face of it, then, it does not seem plausible to welcome a book which, somewhat in the Althusserian vein of yesteryear, implacably denounces the idealistic deviations and doctrinal errors, the ideological misappropriations and misguided revisions of thinkers widely supposed to have some Marxian pedigree or relevance for younger would-be Marxists today. Christoph Henning's *Philosophie nach Marx* is a comprehensive, six-hundred page indictment of everyone from Kautsky to present-day left liberals of Habermasian or Rawlsian stripe, and it is well worth standing up to its innumerable provocations. It is a tireless catalogue of what I will call Marx-avoidance, which for all its unremitting zeal remains oddly non-partisan. Henning does not seem to speak from any easily identifiable political or ideological position, although his philosophical bias would seem to be a kind of Wittgensteinian Kantianism, appropriate enough for this intellectual operation.

The reader needs to be warned, however, that the word 'theory', now generally taken, at least in the West, to signify post-structuralism or Frankfurt School Hegelianism and quizzed for its exhaustion or demise, or attacked for its perniciously elitist abstraction, is used quite differently here, as a term for Marx's work itself, whose object according to Henning was *bürgerliche Gesellschaft* – by which he means not civil society (that fatigued war-horse to which left liberals and radical democrats alike still appeal), but rather capitalism as such: a system to be confronted in its totality, rather than from any purely political or philosophical, or even from any narrowly economic, perspective. Henning's emphasis, however, remains focused on Marx's work itself, whose 'content and character have rarely been adequately grasped either by its enemies or its defenders'. This perspective will occasionally remind us of Horkheimer's plaintive confession: 'I pledge allegiance to critical theory; that means that I can tell what is false, but cannot define what is correct'. But such frankness, hoping to convert seeming weakness into aggressive counter-attack, does not exempt the Frankfurt School from the force of Henning's critical juggernaut; on the contrary, it will become one of its principal targets.

Henning's critical panorama divides into two unequal segments: the first covers the fate of 'Marxism' or Marxist theory from the death of Marx to the October Revolution. This is familiar ground, but Henning's analysis of the respective shortcomings of social-democratic and communist theory has interesting new things to tell us. The second and longer part of *Philosophie nach Marx* sets out from the 'social philosophy' of the late nineteenth and early twentieth centuries, and brings us up to the present, with a wide-angle view of its successors today, where Henning distinguishes four dominant schools: Habermas, Rawls, normative 'economic ethics' and neo-pragmatism. But although his review of all this is roughly chronological, it avoids any purely historical account by organising its material around nine systematic *Kernpunkte* or 'key points' – an awkward formula which might better have been rendered as Althusserian *problématiques*, or versions of the medieval 'crux' around which debates traditionally revolved, pressing on an unresolved conceptual dilemma.

This is an excellent framework, but before we outline it, the limits of Henning's enterprise need to be indicated. For one thing, the social philosophy canvassed in its second part is, with the exception of Rawls, exclusively German. It is true, of course, that the only foreign intellectual scene with which English-speaking intellectuals are generally familiar, in its broad outlines and principal players, is French. The richness of Italian or German intellectual life is mostly a closed book to them, with the exception of a few well-known stars, who collaborate with such provincialism by reorienting their footnotes and references around an Anglophone sociology or philosophy that has become hegemonic. Here the theoretically minded reader will miss discussions of Foucault and Derrida, Deleuze and Badiou, Agamben and Negri, Rorty and Giddens. This is a matter for regret, since it would have been good to have a review of these thinkers in the Henning manner, which, however truly damaging or unremittingly negative, is never basely partisan in the fashion of Althusserian denunciations of old (or even of the perhaps still related anti-theoretical inquisitions and denunciations of the present).

Particularly in the area of sociology, on the other hand, the English-language reader will discover unfamiliar references: the philosopher Rudolf Eucken (1846–1926), for example, or René Koenig (1906–92), founder of the Cologne school of sociology, whose critique of sociological discourse is fundamental for Henning. But they will readily imagine their own equivalents, for the debates are everywhere analogous. (One could think of such transpositions as a literary historian might of the unfamiliar formal patterns of a history of music or the visual arts, whose very non-translatability may yield insight into the dynamics of comparable but dissimilar historical processes.) In any case the names of Kautsky and Habermas, or Heidegger and Horkheimer, are central enough in the history of ideas to warrant attention in their own contexts, however local these may seem to a parochially Anglophone 'West'.

Henning's handling of the concept of social philosophy also needs a gloss. It includes everything from straightforward political and economic manifestos of the early years of revolutionary or parliamentary Marxism, through the sociology of Weber and Luhmann, all the way to outright (or 'pure') philosophy, in Heidegger and Adorno, since the latter is as implicitly political and social as the former is philosophical. Indeed the book's basic argument is that social and political analyses have been sapped and vitiated by their 'ontologisation', that is to say, by their translation and above all sublimation into purely philosophical arguments and issues. This is Henning's version of the more frequent and vulgar reproach of 'idealism', which has become something of a ritual insult. Henning does seem to have a philosophical basis for his own bias against philosophy; it is, as has been suggested, a discreet Wittgensteinian Kantianism. In short, the corpus will consist of the social sciences, as they impinge on philosophy (or at least on thought), and philosophy and its contemporary acolyte theories, as these encroach on the social sciences. If the latter seem to have a pronouncedly philosophical cast, is this to be attributed to German intellectual traditions antithetical to either British empiricism or a younger American pragmatism? If so, that would be yet another reason to work through these unfamiliar German materials.

To be sure, social philosophy is a latecomer – sociology itself only really emerges as a discipline at the very end of the nineteenth century, with Weber and Durkheim. There will therefore be a welcome and extended prologue dealing with the more overt fortunes of Marxism itself, in social democracy, communism and Marxist economics, before we reach 'bourgeois' developments. Henning's non-partisan but implacable critique of Marxism's own native traditions (no one is spared) gives his book a breadth and variety of targets that mark it out as far more ambitious than any of the usual polemics.

We may now outline an inventory of his *Kernpunkte,* organised by roman numerals. Unsurprisingly, the immediate debates in the first heyday of social democracy turned on social reproduction (i) and the falling rate of profit (ii). That both issues are still with us in the age of globalisation should be plain, but can be documented by the frequency and intensity of the word 'crisis', in all its various meanings, in every kind of public discourse today, in which Marx is 'repressed' by a naturalisation of the business cycles that 'ontologises' them, to use Henning's language (I would rather say it flattens them out, de-dialecticises them, and turns them into non-dialectical 'laws' or regularities). The notion of a 'falling rate of profit', meanwhile, leads to standard denunciations of Marx's distinction between price and value, and an excuse to leave Marxist economics behind forever.

With Bolshevism the centre of gravity moves towards politics as such, which means that the third nodal point or crux will centre on the theory of imperialism (iii), involving not merely the arc from Soviet foreign policy to theories of globalisation, but also Lenin's and Hilferding's discussions of finance capital. The more purely political emphasis of Lenin and Stalin 'de-economises and re-ideologises' Marx's original problematic (Trotsky and Mao are given short shrift).

Thus abandoned to the professional economists, Marx is ready for burial at the hands of pre- and post-Marxist economists alike – from Smith to Keynes and Friedman, many a nominally Marxist economist covertly endorsing some of these non-Marxian paradigms. Here the crucial nodal point (iv) is the theory of money itself, which takes us back again to the opening chapters of *Capital*; while the accompanying non-Marxist developments in sociology founder, in all their variety of thematics – from Weber to Luhmann – on the fundamental crux of social classes (v).

With these now classical moves and positions established, the reader has been prepared to confront the seemingly more modern, or at least twentieth-century, developments that start with the name of Martin Heidegger. The second part of the book will be accompanied by new *Kernpunkte*: vi, Hegel and Marx; vii, Marx's Critique of Religion; viii, Marx and Ethics; and ix, Marx and Law. But they will also be organised in a supplementary fashion around theses proposed by René Koenig that reinforce the 'anti-philosophical' bias of Henning's approach to his more modern texts. Koenig's eight theses are summarised as follows: (i) social philosophy is an alienating reaction against Marxism; (ii) as a reaction, it remains thereby secretly bound to Marxism; (iii) its origins lie in a Hegelian dialectic shorn of its negativity; (iv) it transforms an idealist philosophy of identity into an existential one; (v) it short-circuits historical origins into modes of being, and thinking into Being; (vi) it problematises theory *in toto*, generating a crisis in philosophy; (vii) a loss of objectivity and scientificity ensues; and (viii) in their place comes an empty 'politics' of identity and self-affirmation. This last displacement can also be characterised as decisionism, fundamental to all forms of existentialism, and attributable to Fichte, who becomes the true villain of the story, rather than Hegel. In this tale of decline and fall, Heidegger occupies a privileged position by reason of the crucial role played in it by Henning's term 'ontologisation', by which we may take him to mean, simply, turning a problem or a theory into philosophy; or perhaps one should say, a philosophy, for reasons that will shortly become apparent.

I have never placed much faith in that solitary footnote to *History and Class Consciousness*, at the very end of *Sein und Zeit*, which is supposed to document Heidegger's direct engagement with Lukács's work of a few years before. Lucien Goldmann's early argument to this effect always struck me as far-fetched, an exercise in wishful thinking meant essentially to appropriate Heidegger for the Marxian tradition (for Henning, to be sure, Lukács himself is highly ambiguous, always on the point of lapsing into 'philosophy', but generally too intelligently Marxian to succumb irrevocably), though discussion is certainly possible, not so much about the left National Socialist elements as about the implicit concept of revolution in general in Heidegger. But I do not think the *Seinsfrage* in his work, after the *Kehre*, is particularly incompatible with Marxism, which has proved compatible with so many other 'philosophies', inasmuch as it is not – here I agree with Henning – itself a philosophy.

But therein lies the problem with Henning's slogan, for the ontology of the pre-*Kehre* Heidegger was a phenomenology of the life-world; and if Marx's object of study is taken to be *bürgerliche Gesellschaft* in the most general sense, as the dynamics of capital on all its levels, then Marxism has an obligation to include that phenomenology, to which the 'pragmatic' Heidegger certainly made a fundamental contribution, if we divest it of its anthropological pretensions (the Ur-Germanic etymologies) and its oversimplified diagnoses of technology. His critique of modernity, whether 'irrationalist' or not, is as ambiguous as all such visions, from Burke and the Romantics on down, as Raymond Williams memorably demonstrated in *Culture and Society*. Its ethical and decisionist moments then remain open to analysis, and will receive their appropriate attention at other stages in Henning's book.

For the philosophising of social themes – let us rather from now on say, of the varied features and manifestations of capitalism – will not take only such narrowly ontological and existentialising forms. It will also have Hegelian variants, particularly in the traditions of the Frankfurt School (among whom, as Henning rightly notes, Habermas is not to be numbered). It is of course outrageous that his very limited comments on Adorno are included, not under the rubric of philosophy, but of religion; although his subtle reading of the works of the 'school' as a whole centres on Pollock's evacuation of Marxian economics in the name of an essentially political shift towards a theory of state capitalism. Without any mention of Marx's essay on the 'Jewish question', Henning's discussion of the relationship to religion is incomplete, to say the least. Yet I do agree with Henning's provocative conclusion that the Marx of *Capital* has no interest in religion whatsoever. The critique of fetishism is the analysis of an illusion or a mirage, important for its structural findings, but not as the social diagnosis of a pathology that can be treated in and of itself – rather its causes must be made to disappear, with the end of the capitalist dynamics of commodity production.

Yet from another perspective this quite proper dismissal of the political significance of religion might well be taken to signal the return of that wholesale rejection of the superstructures which characterised so-called orthodox Marxism and which it was the task of a more contemporary 'Western' and 'philosophised' or 'ontologised' Marxism to restore. Is this simply the result of an Althusserian separation of the levels, or does it lapse back into the old 'materialist' dismissal of all of what were considered so many 'idealisms', from philosophy and religion all the way to ethics and the law? Politics has already been set to one side with a dismissal of its primacy in Leninism, as a displacement. As for culture in general, in whatever form, it is excluded altogether from this book. Above all, there is to be no immanent critical practice of philosophy or anything else, as if this invariably assumed that to identify a faulty idea or ideology was enough to change a society.

This is thus only in part a repudiation of 'pan-Marxism', as the Chinese call it – that is, of Marxism as a philosophy of everything, or philosophy *tout court*, the old 'dialectical materialism'. It is also, if more implicitly, a repudiation of the political fantasies and self-aggrandisement of intellectuals themselves, even if the argument never descends to the *ad hominem* levels to be found in the Bourdieu school – Bourdieu is himself attacked in passing. But perhaps it is better to grasp Henning's procedures in a dialectical manner. He himself frequently describes Marx's rectification of the Hegelian dialectic (in Hegel's spirit) as an insistence on 'the difference and yet identity of two realms of being, a unity of opposites'. The model is not that of a reflection, or base-and-superstructure, but rather of metabolism – clearly the more fundamental linguistic figure in Marx's thinking. What Henning will therefore deplore as an absence of 'theory' is the lack of any explanation of the metabolic production of one phenomenon (a faulty concept, say) from out of another one (for example, the structure of the commodity).

I myself conclude that if autonomous philosophising, and the illusion that the critique of the faulty concept will modify its structural origin, is to be rejected, the alternative is not best formulated in Henning's language – less philosophising and more 'theory' – but ought rather to call for more philosophising, that is to say, less non-Marxian philosophising and more dialectics as such. We may take as an example what has been stigmatised as the re-entry of a bad Hegelianism into recent Marxian thinking, namely so-called Capitalogic and a resurrected 'theory of value', to be found respectively in Helmut Reichelt's pathbreaking *Zur logischen Struktur des Kapitalbegriffs bei Karl Marx* (1970), Hans-Georg Backhaus's *Dialektik der Wertform* (1997), and Christopher Arthur's *The New Dialectic and Marx's Capital* (2002) – a body of work seeking to show that Marx simplified his own thought in the changes he made to the second edition of *Capital* and thereby made less accessible the properly dialectical nature of his notion of value as the quantity of labour power, and so the origin of the famous fetishism of commodities. Here value becomes a historically unique phenomenon in which a unity-and-difference of the ideal and the material only becomes visible through a dialectical lens.

Henning seems to think little enough of these 'theological subtleties', and this is not the place to pursue them further. But there ensues an interesting consequence, namely that the formation of value can be understood 'philosophically' as well as 'theoretically' (in Henning's sense) or 'dialectically' (in mine). That many of the processes described in *Capital* are survivals, extensions and expansions of the process Marx called 'alienation' in his early writings seems unquestionable, as Stanley Moore's unjustly neglected *Three Tactics: The Background in Marx* (1963) has shown. The fundamental question is rather whether we should still call them that, whether we should still use this philosophical (or idealistic or metaphysical) word for the later 'mature' work. Althusser proposed building a firewall against such usage by positing the famous 'epistemological break'. The Hegelian Marxists however have mostly delighted in this continuity and taken it as an excuse to do the very thing Althusser feared, erecting an existential psychology or even a philosophy or a metaphysics on its basis (Heidegger, indeed, singling out the concept of alienation for ontological approval in his post-war *Letter on Humanism*).

But if the propensity to ontologisation and philosophising is to be named, I propose to call it thematisation. For the minute one thematises such a phenomenon, a process of autonomisation sets in which turns it into the founding term for a new and semi-autonomous complex of concepts – call it a philosophy, if you like, or a 'world-picture' (Heidegger), an ideology or a worldview. These new thematisations then most often serve as the point of departure for a *Kulturkritik*, that is to say, a wholesale diagnosis of what is wrong with modern society, its culture, its psychology or subjectivity, its mode of living. Rather than call these discourses attacks on modernity, critiques of it, and the like, as is so often done, it is better to recognise them as a specific discursive form or genre, which passes itself off as an analysis of contemporary (or modern) society that could be viewed as a scientific proposition. Something like this can also happen to the Capitalogicians when they absolutise the diagnosis of fetishism and brandish, as I often do myself, Marx's own word *Verdinglichung* or reification. Any of these features of capitalism, when named in such a way as to lend itself to a terminology, can give rise to an idealistic hypostasis in the form of this or that culture critique; and it seems to me precisely this to which Henning so often and so properly objects. His labour has uncovered a rich and varied field of just such language pathologies for us to explore and to 'theorise' from a Marxist perspective.

I pass over the valuable concluding sections, which trenchantly dissect a variety of social democratic or 'Third Way' revisionisms, from Habermas or Rawls to business-philosophical and neo-pragmatist versions of their normative philosophies in Germany. For it is the Marxist deviations from Marx that are of most interest, rather than the outright and unabashed 'post-Marxisms', even if the critique of a return to norms and even to a kind of natural law – whatever function these may on occasion serve as buffers against the hegemony of the free market and its depredations – is probably always salutary and bears repeating worldwide.

Yet one cannot entirely endorse the programme with which the book concludes. Henning enumerates four basic features of the various misreadings – intentional or otherwise – of Marxist theory, today and yesterday. These are (1) a substitution of nature for society as Marx's basic object of study; (2) a misunderstanding of the way in which Marx uses the term 'law', as in the laws of capitalism; (3) a retranslation of Marx back into a philosophical discourse; and (4) an interpretation of the ensuing naturalistic world-view 'according to the hermeneutics of a *Lebensphilosophie*', as the expression of a praxis. Henning's identification of his project with Kant is intended to validate his work as a 'critique' that sets limits to what Marxism can do (as well as to celebrate its indispensable achievements). His invocation of Wittgenstein supposes an ambition to cleanse its language of false problems and hypostasised solutions. This worthy task has the advantage of taking us back to the economic essentials without which Marx is not Marxist. But I must necessarily feel, as would any 'culture worker', that too much is being abandoned in this project, and not only in cultural analysis itself.

There is also the political, about which it can certainly be asserted that *Capital* has little enough to do with politics and has no political lessons to offer. Yet Marx was, like Lenin, a political strategist (and tactician) of genius, and it does not matter that several distinct and sometimes even antithetical strategies can be detected in his own positions at various historical stages. *Capital* is a book about capitalism; politics, on the other hand, has to do with the ways in which socialism might be achieved (and constructed). But this does not mean that our judgements on *Capital* are unpolitical. On the contrary, and without wanting to fall into the error of the substitution of the political for the economic which Henning describes here, such judgements and the analyses of its typical misreadings themselves – the omissions and repressions, the displacements and substitutions – are necessarily political acts.

Chapter One
Introduction

1.1 The problem

The number of publications devoted to a thinker is generally considered an index of his relevance. For this reason, philosophical works often begin by referring to recent publications that point out a problem worthy of further investigation. The German book market aside, there has not recently been any dearth of reputable publications on Karl Marx.[1] While there have also been a number of new German books on Marx, they tend to leave a stale aftertaste of political rearguard action.[2]

But then, things often work out differently when it comes to Marx. The problem he addressed was not textual, but real: Marx dealt with the terrible condition of the human world. One need only think of the numerous famines in the midst of affluence, the tolerated environmental disasters and the worldwide persistence of social conflict to see that little has changed. The topicality of Karl Marx is better revealed by the phenomena of the real world than by the number of publications devoted to him. One need do no more than peruse daily newspapers to encounter headlines on the rising number of unemployed people, the growing

1. Recent publications in English include Bermann 1999, Itoh 1999, Wheen 1999, Perelmann 2000, Boudin 2001, Dussel 2001, Lee-Lampshire 2001, Oihshi 2001, Renton 2001, Arthur 2002, Brenner 2002, Campbell 2002, Desai 2002, Eatwell 2002, Martin 2002, Megill 2002, Rockmore 2002, Sullivan 2002, Wolff 2002, Antonio 2003.

2. The Cold War of theory is perpetuated by Thomas 1993, Khella 1995, Löw 1996, Löw 2001, Kelpanides 1999, Schöler 1999, Gerhardt 2001, Backes 2002 and *Bild Dresden* 2002. I have reviewed some of the works published after completion of my book manuscript (M. Berger 2003, Iorio 2003, Kittsteiner 2003, Postone 2003, Heinrich 2004, H.-J. Lenger 2004 and Derrida 2004); see Henning 2004a, Henning 2005.

state deficit, ever new cuts to workers' benefits, tax cuts for corporations, recurring environmental scandals, explosive economic crises (such as those recently experienced in Asia, Argentina and Brazil) and the slow death of Africa as caused by the debt crisis and AIDS, with the pharmaceutical industry playing a prominent role in the latter.[3] Armed conflicts are raging the world over, often in places where divergent economic interests clash, and we have recently begun to witness the erosion of painstakingly achieved international legal standards not just through war[4] but also, to cite just one other example, through corruption.[5] All this is set to the persistent tune of the global privatisation of education, pension schemes and healthcare, on the one hand, and of the constantly increasing volume and mobility of monetary flows, on the other. Meanwhile, inequality both within and between nations is on the rise the world over.

What does this have to do with Marx? All these phenomena can be explained by means of Marx's theory. They represent the everyday behaviour of the globally active and anarchic capitalist economic system. This makes Marx's theories more relevant than ever.[6] Not only does Marx allow us to understand the interrelatedness of the phenomena mentioned; his theory also provides us with the instruments for deciphering the mechanisms that operate behind them. These mechanisms are something other than what we encounter when perusing the newspaper; they are the objects of a scientific discipline, namely political economy. It was by engaging with the field of political economy that Marx was able to note an acceleration of capitalist growth, periodic crises of the global economy and a tendency toward social polarisation. These mechanisms allow us to *explain* the processes whose manifestations the newspaper headlines merely describe.

Yet if our pre-theoretical perception of social reality demonstrates the relevance of Marx, whichever way we look,[7] why is this not reflected in German social philosophy? 'Because socialism has died' – that is the usual answer. But to say this is to give proof of one's own 'lazy reason',[8] since the political model of the collapsing Soviet states in no way resembled an 'association of free human beings'.[9] Why should the decline of an

3. Werner 2001, pp. 106, 226.
4. Habermas 2003a.
5. Henning 2005.
6. 'Marx's theories have never been more relevant' (Rockmore 2002, p. xii; Wolff 2002).
7. The German edition of the *Financial Times* featured a portrait of Marx with the caption: 'Marx would surely have endorsed the globalisation of politics' ('Gegen die Allmacht Washingtons', *Financial Times Deutschland*, 22 August 2002). German weekly *Deutsches Allgemeine Sonntagsblatt* wrote: 'Had Marxism not died, then it ought now to triumph' ('*Marx und die Banken*', 10 March 2000; see Sichtermann 1990, Ziegler 1992, Cassidy 1997, Hobsbawm 1998, H. Lohmann 2001, p. 137; W. Winkler 2003). In 2001 Moritz Leuenberger opened the 31st World Economic Forum with a quotation from Marx and praised him as an early globaliser, as reported in *Financial Times Deutschland*, 25 January, 'Weltsozialforum als Alternative').
8. Kant 1998, A 689 f.
9. *MECW* 1, pp. 192 f.; *MECW* 35, pp. 88 f. The aim was to achieve individuals' 'all-round development' (*MECW* 5, p. 292) – not the development of man *qua* isolated individual, but the 'return of man to himself as a social (i.e., human) being' (*MECW* 3, p. 296; see Fromm 1963).

empire that suppressed virtually every emancipatory idea prompt us to close the book on Marx? A mode of thinking that consists, at heart, in criticising existing conditions can never be so closely entwined with something existent as to share in its decline – as the history of Judaeo-Christian religion has proven often enough. There must be other reasons for the fact that Marxist thought, once so central, continues to lie dormant 25 years after the fall of the Berlin Wall and despite the return of turbocapitalism.[10]

One of these reasons is related to the history of theory: as a school of thought, Marxism exhausted itself long before 1989. On one side of the Iron Curtain, there was dogmatic 'historical materialism' and the mantra-like reiteration of its dictums; on the other, there was Western Marxism, diluted into 'cultural criticism'. Both had long ceased to be theoretically sustainable. Prodded once, these Marxisms collapsed. There could, in any case, be no question of latching onto such 'atrophied stages' of Marxism today.[11] We can only return to Marxian theory itself, as found in Marx's own texts. But there is a problem. In order to access Marx's theory, we first need to work our way through the fatal history of the reception of his texts – the history not only of their political, but also of their theoretical reception. Failing this, we are left with reissues of one or another problematic Marxist narrative, on the basis of which Marx's texts are subjected to *ex ante* interpretation. The perpetuation of assessments of Marx's thought that were already questionable prior to 1989 is evident not just in strategies for justifying the refusal to say anything more about Marx, but also in attempts to keep him alive within theoretical memory – attempts that do more to prevent than to promote a renewed reading of his texts.[12]

The purpose of this work consists, therefore, in overcoming the barriers-to-reception and immanent distortions that Marxian thought has inherited, at least to the extent that these can be grasped theoretically. It is only in this way that Marxian thought can, once more, be made fruitful for social theory. The present work is a first step in this direction. It addresses one part of the problem, to which it can offer only a limited solution. It seeks to achieve its aim by engaging with two questions:

1) Given Marx's obvious relevance to pre-theoretical considerations, how are we to understand the fact that the theories of contemporary social science and social philosophy typically shy away from Marx?

---

10. Fehrmann 1997, Luttwak 1999.

11. The concept of 'atrophied stages' [*Schwundstufen*] is culled from a pathogenesis of Kantianism (Marquard 1954). On the 'crisis of Marxism', see Althusser 1978, Kallscheuer 1986 and the vivid account of Koenen 2001; see also Korsch 1935.

12. Veteran Marxists often recycle older arguments. See, for example, Steigerwald 1996, Backhaus 1997, Stieler 1997, Haug 2001 or Kurz 2001. Honneth 1999a; 2002 and Wildt 1997; 2002 also persist in reading Marx the way they have always done, that is, normativistically. Economists likewise resort to old arguments (Nutzinger 1999, Heinrich 2001, Gerlach 2003). 'A "positive" reconstruction of Marxian theory needs therefore to be preceded by an examination of this reception history' (Stephan 1974, p. 111; a similar argument is formulated in Rockmore 2002, pp. xiv, 1 ff.). 'Old ideas give way slowly; for they are more than abstract logical forms and categories. They are habits … deeply engrained attitudes of aversion and preference' (Dewey 2008, p. 14).

2) What are the consequences of this 'excluded centre',[13] or of the absence of Marxian insights, for the character of contemporary social philosophy?

Engagement with these questions will eventually yield systematic prospects for a considered and critical understanding of philosophy. It is from this that the present work derives its title. I chose to restrict the material by which I engage with my two questions in two ways: only *theories* are considered, and these theories have mainly been formulated *in German*. These two restrictions are arbitrary, but justified by the very nature of my subject. It is only on such a basis that a methodically precise procedure becomes possible. The approach is presented in section 1.4. The structure of the work follows from it, and is briefly presented for the reader's orientation (section 1.5). While more will be said below about Marx's absence from contemporary theories (in section 1.3, by way of introduction), the *objective* reasons for this absence are not discussed as such, due to my methodological choice to analyse theories only. I will, however, begin by expanding somewhat on my initial remarks about real phenomena, since it is from them that the present work derives its plausibility and motivational force (section 1.2).

1.2 Retaining Marx? A preliminary account of his theory

> The real question posed by the watershed of 1989 is... not the one everyone is talking about ('Why has socialism failed?'). The question ought rather to be: Why were several generations of communists and left-wing intellectuals able to perceive the state socialism of the most backward regions... as a step forward by comparison to the industrialised nations and their highly developed capitalism?[14]

The present work is intended as a work of philosophy. It does not claim to provide a distinct politico-economic analysis of the present. Nevertheless, *every* socio-philosophical account works from preliminary notions on the basis of which it has already interpreted the social world.[15] The hermeneutical 'prejudice' from which the present work begins is a worldview based on common sense. It contains roughly the following assumptions:

Today, it is a country's economic situation that determines the fate of politicians. Culture and education are dependent on economic facts. The better-off dispose of militarily fortified residential complexes not just in Brazil, South Africa and Israel, but also in the USA and England.[16] I depart from many contemporary approaches in taking this as pre-theoretical evidence that Marx's statements are highly relevant to the present. Since

13. Johannes 1995.
14. Schneider 1992, p. 15.
15. Henning 2001b.
16. For similar observations, see, for example, Philipps 1990, Chomsky 1993, S. George 1995, UNDP 1996, Forrester 1997, Gray 1999, Soros 1999, Klein 2001, Kraus 2001, Chossudovsky 2002, Ziegler 2002, Worldwatch 2003.

1989 in particular, it has become clear that capitalism has not ceased to exist. *Everything* is subordinated to the logic of the market, including areas formerly exempt from it, such as transportation, healthcare, welfare, culture and education. In the USA, there are jobs that are insufficient, by themselves, for earning a living.[17] At the same time, incomes are rising rapidly in the upper tiers of society.[18] The trend toward unequal development is a clear one, and even the word 'class' is being used widely again ('two-class medical system', 'first class' travel, and such like).[19] Yet the presupposition that Marx is relevant to our present is supported not just by *economic* facts. Marx also pointed out two problems the 'system' of capitalism encounters in its relationship with its 'environment'. Such problems are also becoming increasingly evident today. This is true in a threefold sense:

- First, there is social nature. According to Marx, the disadvantaged classes will eventually oppose the capitalist economic system. In fact, much recent history (such as the current second wave of revolution in the Caucasus or in certain South-American countries) cannot be understood without reference to conflicts between social groups with divergent political aims.
- Second, there is individual nature. It is exposed to the dominant capitalist culture.[20] While the symptoms shift constantly, the causes of many modern psychopathologies cannot be understood without reference to the conditions in which they develop, and these include economic conditions.[21] This is true even of racist and patriarchal tendencies or socio-psychological defects such as those analysed by Freud and Sennett at the outset and the close of the twentieth century.[22]
- Finally, there is ecological nature, the chief victim of economic growth.[23]

17. Ehrenreich 2001.

18. Kienbaum 2003.

19. According to Werkstadt 2003, Germans dispose of 14,600 billion euros worth of assets after taxes. The lower half of the population owns 4.5 percent of this sum, whereas the upper half own 42.3 percent. There are 365,000 Germans with more than one billion euros worth of monetary assets. A person is considered poor when they earn half the average income; 10.9 percent of West-German citizens fall into this category, 66 percent more than during the 1970s. The tax burden is also being redistributed: in 1960, wage earners contributed 11.8 percent of total taxes; in 2000, they contributed 35.4 percent, or three times as much. The share of total taxes represented by income tax has fallen from 31.1 percent in 1960 to 2.7 percent in 2000 (see below, sections 2.4.6; 3.2.3. Henceforth, I will refer to sections by numbers only.)

20. Claessens 1973.

21. Henning 2008.

22. Freud 1900, Sennett 2000; see Reich 1929, Brückner 1972, Holzkamp 1975, Dahmer 1994, Honneth 1994 and 2002a.Everyday phenomena such as the rising levels of classroom violence are cases in point.

23. 'Capitalist production . . . develops technology, and the combining together of various processes into a social whole, only by sapping the original sources of all wealth – the soil and the labourer' (*MECW* 35, pp. 507 f.; see also pp. 53 f.; *MECW* 3, p. 272 and elsewhere; see Fetscher 1985, pp. 110 ff.; 1999, pp. 123 ff.; Grundmann 1991).

It comes as no surprise, from Marx's point of view, that these three 'environments' have found and continue to find the courage to revolt by means of various social movements. The point of attack chosen by Marx's theory was apologetic economic liberalism, which ignores social differences theoretically, thereby exacerbating them practically. This very school of economic thought has exercised an enormous influence on the leading economic powers and the international economic institutions controlled by them, the IMF and the World Bank[24] – resulting in veritable laboratory conditions for the application of Marxian theories.[25] But there is more: following the historical doldrums of the 1990s, 11 September 2001 has heralded the return of a full-blown world politics.[26] Powerful economic interests are visibly at work within it. And the enemies of capitalism have also long since made their return, from Seattle to Porto Alegre.[27]

To what preliminary understanding of Marx's theories are we resorting, when such phenomena are taken to confirm those theories? We are resorting to the approach that assumes the centre of force of modern-day developments lies not in religion, morality, art, politics or philosophy, but in bourgeois society, whose form is shaped by a specific set of economic procedures, the 'capitalist mode of production'.[28] This mode of production is premised on ownership of the means of production by one part of the population, while another part of the population works for the property-owning classes or, to put this more specifically, produces surplus value. Such a manner of looking at things is far from economistic, because it treats the economy as embedded in a social context – after all, the object of Marxian theory is bourgeois society. However, the capitalist economy operates according to laws that are so powerful as gradually to impose themselves upon the basic structure of society,[29] shaping even 'spheres' once relatively remote from economic affairs – such as science, religion, art and politics – in accordance with the exigencies of the market.[30] The mechanism of the capitalist economy, which perpetually regulates itself by means of crises, is increasingly causing these economised areas of society to be exposed to permanent crisis like the others.

---

24. Huffschmid 1999, pp. 98 ff.

25. 'But in theory it is assumed that the laws of capitalist production operate in their pure form. In reality there exists only approximation; but, this approximation is the greater, the more developed the capitalist mode of production and the less it is adulterated and amalgamated with survivals of former economic conditions' (*MECW* 37, p. 174).

26. Ross 2002.

27. On the critique of globalisation (3.3.6), see Altvater 1996, Hirsch 1996, Martin 1996, Gruppe 1997, Loccumer Initiative 1997, Zugehör 1998, Todd 1999, Starr 2000, Appelt 2001, Biermann 2001, Cassen 2002, Grefe 2002, Löwy 2002, Mander 2002 and Walk 2002. See also (from unexpected quarters) Krugmann 1999, Stiglitz 2002 and Wilke 2001, pp. 7 ff.

28. *MECW* 35, p. 8.

29. *MECW* 6, pp. 482 ff.

30. Bröckling 2000.

In what sense does this preliminary account of Marxian theory[31] allow us to interpret the phenomena we encounter when perusing the newspaper as confirmations? According to Marx, the chief motive behind the capitalist economy is the realisation of profit.[32] For the owner of capital, the value-producing agent is human labour; he therefore needs to obtain as much labour as possible, and for as low a price as possible. When workers are too few in number or too expensive from the point of view of the profit motive, the capitalist economy may go into crisis – and, with it, all of society. It should be noted that the crisis does not consist in the economy producing too few goods, but in the propertied classes obtaining too little profit.

The national debt, capital flight, high unemployment and the burdens with which employees continue to be saddled all fit this picture. And everyone is familiar with the phenomenon of working hours rising constantly: sixty-hour weeks are no longer unusual, not just for shopkeepers and doctors, but also for white-collar workers and even interns. The average working life will, in all probability, grow longer. Today's political measures aim primarily to cheapen the 'labour factor' and create the best possible tax conditions for corporations. So much for point (a). Points (b) and (c) are also borne out by the facts:

An approach that assumes the inherent logic of numerous 'value spheres' to be increasingly influenced and distorted by economic imperatives provides explanatory approaches for many of the psychopathologies referred to above. If some value spheres are important for the development of a stable personality (time spent with one's family and attention received from it, appreciation shown by one's social environment, opportunities for broad cultural activity), then psychic instabilities come as no surprise.[33] Marx called this 'alienation'.[34] Finally, the ecological crisis and recent political upheavals result partly from the fact that the capitalist economy is expanding constantly – and must in fact do so, according to Marx. It trespasses every limit, from the 'limits to growth'[35] to the limits of national politics[36]. It is no longer out of the ordinary, where economic gain requires intervention in another country's affairs, for imperial wars of aggression to ensue.[37] But war is not necessarily required: similar results can be achieved, according to Marx, by the opening of markets.[38] These observations – the list could be

31. For introductions to Marxian theory, see, for example, W. Blumenberg 1962; Singer 1980; Euchner 1983, H. Lohmann 2000, Callinicos 1995, Eagleton 1997, Fetscher 1999.

32. *MECW* 37, p. 255.

33. Henning 2008.

34. *MECW* 3, pp. 271 f.

35. Meadows 1972.

36. Beck 1999, Habermas 2001.

37. Marx and Engels penned analyses of military strategy that were published in the *New York Tribune* and elsewhere (see Volumes 8–14 of their *Collected Works*).

38. 'The cheap prices of commodities are the heavy artillery with which it batters down all Chinese walls, with which it forces the barbarians' intensely obstinate hatred of foreigners to capitulate' (*MECW* 6, p. 488). It is not just raw materials and purchasing power that lure capitalists into other countries, but also – and especially – cheap labour power (Sassen 1988).

extended – have not been rendered analytically inconsequential by the fact that the twentieth century has seen the communist alternative discrediting itself irremediably. Yet there is nothing in contemporary social theory that corresponds to this insight, except a major lacuna.

1.3 The lacuna in contemporary social theory

The critique of progress is in vogue in contemporary theory. But it tends to remain inconsequential. Some authors' habit of resorting to out-of-the-way sources meets with appreciation, but as a rule, citing books published more than twenty years ago is considered an aberration. Yet this says more about the literature cited than about those citing it: if works of social philosophy date so quickly, the reason could be that many of them were written to be 'topical'.

This, however, discredits the notion of an automatic progress of knowledge within the humanities.[39] Assuming the existence of such progress is problematic. It would seem that certain sets of problems are sometimes left unattended to. This would explain the recurrent phenomena of renaissances and rediscoveries.[40] In the humanities, neglect of certain problems is usually due less to a 'refutation' than to a change in theoretical fashion. This is strikingly evident in the treatment received by Marxism. The days when one still dealt directly with Marxists were also the ones when Marxian theories were engaged with most seriously.[41] Positions formulated in older works may, in some cases, have been corrected since, and it would be negligent to ignore such corrections. Mostly, however, it is a case of a near-universal failure to meet erstwhile standards of debate. Thus later 'results' are by no means automatically superior to earlier ones.

Marx has largely disappeared from the stage of philosophy since 1989: he has been declared definitively dead by his critics.[42] His place has been taken, within the socio-philosophical literature published in Germany since the 1990s, by the rise of normative principles. Discussions turned on whether the newly unified country required a new constitution, on how to conceptualise the hierarchy of norms within the 'postnational constellation' formed by the new nation state and the new Europe, on how human rights

39. Things are different in the experimental sciences, which allow for unambiguous falsification and the exact specification of results. Absent a veritable paradigm shift, and aside from the formation of schools of thought (evident here as elsewhere), each author does in fact build on the work of his predecessors.

40. Levy 1927, Riedel 1972, Sandbote 2001.

41. Thus German philosophers once penned serious works on Marx: see, for example, Löwith 1965, Henrich 1961, Apel 1962, Fleischer 1970, K. Hartmann 1970, Bubner 1972, pp. 44 ff.; Steinvorth 1977 or Arndt 1985.

42. Conway 1987, Pilgrim 1990, Liessmann 1992, Negt 1992, Aronson 1995, Manuel 1995; see also the early example of Benoist 1970.

and 'justice' might be grounded philosophically, and such like.[43] As rewarding as such normative reflections are, they cannot *replace* inquiries into the material base. When a normativistically restricted point of view takes the place of the former social theory, super-normativism results.[44]

Due to the phenomena mentioned (the rising number of economic, social and political conflicts, the dismantling of welfare security and the Machiavellian reordering of global relations), this kind of normative social philosophy is becoming increasingly untenable. Would escaping the ivory tower not require a socio-theoretical reflection on the real preconditions of successful coexistence? 'Normativity' can never be more than one aspect of these preconditions, namely their moral or legal expression.

No one has any quarrel with 'human rights' or other fundamental norms. But *talk* of such norms is embedded in social contexts. These contexts were the theme of empirically substantive political economy, which had learned from Hegel that every determinate moral precept 'holds with regard to' (Emil Lask) a determinate being – namely, is formulated and imposed. This is why it is difficult not to sound ideological when speaking about what *ought* to be without ever referring to what *is*. Reflections of this kind are, however, largely absent from contemporary German social philosophy. This can already be seen from the reactions provoked simply by *recalling* such a mode of philosophical reasoning. With regard to human rights, Marx's 'view of the totality' entailed little more than interpreting existing norms not according to their internal logic or in a way that remains immanent to the field of law, but in such a way as to situate them in their real contexts. Today, this approach is rejected even on the most fundamental level, that of categories.[45]

Yet this leads only to *philosophy* remaining on the normative level – unnecessarily. This is why the present work examines the lacuna I have referred to from several angles and with an eye to the genesis of certain theories. The widespread willingness to pick up on previously neglected theoretical currents from other countries, evident since 1989,

43. Ebeling and Henrich 1993, Habermas 1998, Brunkhorst 1999a, Druwe 1999, Gosepath 1999. Government commissions opened up new fields of inquiry for ethical thinkers (Türcke 1989, Taureck 1992, Pieper 1998, Kettner 2000, Thurnherr 2000).

44. In 'normative monism', not only is everything else ignored, but it is 'deduced' from morality, which is taken to be 'fundamental'. The term 'normative foundation' (Fraser and Honneth 2003, pp. 7 ff.; Stekeler 2003, p. 7; Popitz 1980) is symptomatic of this.

45. *MECW* 3, pp. 159 ff.; see Brenkert 1986, Maihofer 1992 and the contrary position of G. Lohmann 1999. Rentsch 1999, pp. 52 ff. interprets this as an attack on ethics. 'The legitimation [of human rights] is to be separated from, say, the debate on economic requirements' (Höffe 1998, p. 31). In Habermas 2003a, p. 33, consideration of normativity's internal history precludes taking real factors into account: 'Functions such as the geostrategic securing of spheres of power and resources, which such a politics ought also to fulfil, may invite an approach oriented toward the critique of ideology. But [!] such conventional explanations trivialise the break with norms that the United States felt bound by until now. This break would have been unthinkable a year and a half ago' (see Habermas 1984–7, Vol. 2, p. 396 f.). No connection is made between what is and what ought to be. 'Here, the downgrading of "being" with regard to "normativity" is so pronounced... as to amount to the declaration that one is not interested in being' (Mannheim 1964d, p. 331).

clearly indicates the lacuna's existence. Rohrmoser[46] accounts for this state of affairs by reference to the suddenness with which Marxist thinking, formerly so dominant, was vanquished. Pending critical engagement with this development, it is too early to speak of 'post-Marxism', according to Rohrmoser.[47] It does in fact seem likely that one reason why attempts to work through theoretical Marxism and anti-Marxism have been so few and far between is that a critique of this theoretical history would have to involve criticism of many of one's *own* contributions – both in the East and in the West. What last presented itself as Marxism was imbued with the numerous crystallisations of a decades-long history of interpretation and reinterpretation. The requisite clean-up work will be undertaken in the present work. But differently from what Rohrmoser and Becker believe, this will amount to clearing the way back to Marx, or to an approach that takes account of politico-economic considerations, including within philosophy.

1.4 On the method employed in this study

1.4.1 *The choice to work with texts only*

As a philosophical work, the present study is concerned primarily with texts. The name 'Marx' may prompt expectations of a critique of ideology formulated on the basis of political economy. But there are several reasons why relating philosophical ideas to real social being is something that will *not* be done here. To begin with, such an undertaking would be premature, since Marxian theory, whose justification is what is at issue, has itself been employed in this way, and would thus be presiding over its own trial. Moreover, such an approach would provoke the objection that it is 'reductionist'. What would be problematic about such an approach would not be the actual act of tracing philosophical notions back to social reality; this act is fundamental to science.[48] It would, however, be inopportune to engage in it in an *uncontrolled* manner. For despite many ventures in this direction, we still lack a comprehensive theory of the social 'base'. Nor will the present work be able to provide such a theory. Yet this very absence is in need of explanation. Thus the present work raises the question of *why* such a theory is currently missing. It does so in a specific way.

This study treats the texts it discusses as something extrinsic, since it does not prematurely relate them back to a social base. But it does not engage with these texts in a purely immanent way, either. Rather, it examines them in order to learn something about a certain theoretical function, thus engaging in an 'immanent functional interpretation'.[49]

46. Rohrmoser 1994, pp. 55 ff.
47. See W. Becker 1996, p. 43.
48. Mannheim 1936, p. 17.
49. Karl Mannheim provided a methodological reflection on this procedure. He speaks of the 'sense of function' of theories, which is made apparent through immanent functional interpretation (Mannheim 1926, pp. 395 ff.). 'In this case, sociology's outside view does not serve to leave

Texts are analysed with an eye to the function they have performed within the reception of Marx, the Marxist tradition or critiques of Marx. To what extent do they need to be seen as performing the function of *avoiding Marx*, and what alternative 'worldview' do they convey? The texts are not analysed for their own sake, but with an eye to contemporary social philosophy and the reasons for the meagreness of its offerings. In other words, the present work is by no means merely historical; it is strongly oriented to the present.

Genetic considerations cannot detract from a theory's validity in and of themselves. To do this, one has to move beyond historicisation and engage with issues of validity. When, however, there is evident confusion on the level of validity – meaning, in the case of theories, within their arguments or the way they refer to their objects – a theoretico-genetic approach may very well contribute to elucidating the *origin* of these ambiguities.[50] Thus the historicisation of contemporary philosophy *qua* critique does not remain extrinsic to its object. For it may contribute to explaining the sometimes bizarrely distorted ways in which our present circumstances are perceived today.

In this way, certain circumstances related to the history of theory are elucidated. These circumstances are not the *causes* of historical development; they are themselves a symptom. Yet investigating the history of ideas is worthwhile even if it does not tell us much about real causes. While processes appertaining to the history of ideas never play out in the lofty realm of pure spirit, and cannot be fully explained in terms of their intrinsic features, theory does dispose of its own temporality, or of a 'relative autonomy'. Those who *distinguish* between superstructure and base, thought and being, theory and reality, as I do in this book, may not be able to make inferences about social reality directly from theoretical problems, or *vice versa*. But an approach that examines the history of ideas and knows its own limits will at least be able to shed light effectively on instances of inertia, or on the *failure* of ideas to respond to real developments. Holism, or a commitment to the totality, is preserved to the extent that a variety of theoretical influences and fields are considered – a totality *within* theory.

1.4.2 *The focus on German-language texts*

Having opted for a textual approach, there remain a great many further options from which to choose. An additional selective focus is required, therefore. For this reason, my genealogy of receptions of Marx and my critique of contemporary philosophy focus on

---

behind the sphere of 'the mental' altogether [it is not eliminatively reductionist]. Rather, it is only by abandoning immanent interpretation that meaningful [theoretico-genetic] premises are revealed...When a mental content is treated as a function of its underlying meaningful context of being, it assumes a new meaning' (Mannheim 1964c, p. 397). It is a question of 'determining the systematic presuppositions by which different... currents of thought go about processing a... fact' (Mannheim 1964d, p. 325).

50. 'The tradition of all dead generations weighs like a nightmare on the brain of the living' (*MECW* 11, p. 103).

the context of the German-speaking world.[51] And not without reason: a philosophical perspective *must*, in fact, devote itself specifically to the German-speaking world: the 'three sources of Marxism' (as Lenin put it) – French socialism, English political economy and German philosophy – drifted apart again after Marx. Today's Anglophone political economy often has little to offer except reductive models. It falls back behind classical political economy, in terms of what it has to say. Attempts to 'reconstruct' Marx on such thin ice often lead to open rejection, or at least distortions, of Marx.[52]

French theoretical currents, with their relatively pronounced political inflection, have tended towards a focus on surface phenomena that are immediately relevant to politics and culture, and this has meant that little attention has been devoted to the underlying structures. While this has rendered the spectrum of the symbolic newly accessible to social theory, it has also resulted in theorists increasingly losing sight of the *foundations* of the symbolic. Postmodern critiques and reconstructions of Marx have involved the argument that Marx was not a fictionalist, or that he had not yet understood that only surface reflections in fact exist, and the like. This severe loss of substance has even been *welcomed* as 'anti-essentialism'.[53]

Thus non-German traditions boast their own 'atrophied stages' of the reception of Marx. International philosophical discourse would benefit greatly from individual linguistic communities critically tending to their own theoretical fields before tossing the fruits on the global market. In the present work, I set out to do this for the German-speaking world. Lenin already considered not philosophy, but *German* philosophy the third 'source of Marxism'. To be sure, Marxism long had its most powerful catalyst in German social democracy – and this in itself would justify the focus on German-language texts. But the Germans, a metaphysical people, have a difficult relationship to politics, and so they soon began reading Marx 'intellectually' again: he was *re-philosophised*.

---

51. Reference to non-German or international literature is made when formulating a critique of German authors. The third chapter also examines two dominant influences on post-1989 German philosophy, John Rawls and pragmatism.

52. Thus 'analytical Marxism' (Cohen 1979, Roemer 1981 and 1986, Ball 1989, Nielsen 1989, Paris 1993) 'makes sense' of Marx (Elster 1986) by reconstructing him on the basis of utilitarian models, which Marx himself had criticised (*MECW* 5, pp. 408 ff.; *MECW* 35, p. 604 f.) K. Müller 1988, Hunt 1993, and others have pointed out critically that this may easily yield 'No Sense' (Mandel 1989). On the US debate, see Guibaut 1983, Bonde 1987, Diggins 1992, Lloyd 1997; in the present work, sections 3.2, 3.4; a more in-depth account can be found in Henning 2005.

53. Derrida 1994, p. 85 f. See similar statements in Debord 1967, Baudrillard 1993, Lyotard 1989, Castoriadis 1998 and Foucault 1991. Postmodern 'reconstructions' of Marx have been attempted by Laclau 1985, Callari 1995, Derrida 1994, jour-fixe 1999, Negri and Hardt 2000 and the US journal *Rethinking Marxism*. For comparisons with Marx's own approach, see Ryan 1982, Meistner 1990, Barrett 1991, Callari 1995, Marsden 1999; in the German-speaking world, Bonacker 2000 comes closest to this current; for critiques, see Descombes 1980, pp. 131 ff.; Frank 1984, Frank 1993, pp. 119 ff.; Ferry 1987, Jameson 1991, O'Neill 1995, Eagleton 1997, Fraser 1998. The *nouveaux philosophes* already tried to wind their way out of Marxism (Benoist 1970, Glucksmann 1976; see also Schiwy 1978, Altwegg 1986, pp. 108 ff.; Taureck 1988).

As is well known, Marx himself hailed from German idealism (from the 'Teutonic forests').[54] His familiarity with German idealism allowed him to work his way through it critically. But the fact that he continued to bear its mark often prompted German thinkers to jostle him back towards 'mind' or 'spirit'. Whoever wishes to interpret Marx philosophically would thus be well advised to pay attention to his German reception. In functional terms, the mentalisation or spiritualisation of Marx was also an avoidance of Marx – and an effective one. Theoretical Marxism's final, post-1989 implosion needs to be understood, in part, as a late effect of Marx's transposal to the field of philosophy.

In this respect, it is of relevance that the present work is not one of vulgar Marxism. It does not approach problems from outside, declaring every explicit critique of Marx and every implicit strategy of avoiding him an instance of 'bourgeois ideology', on the assumption that such ideology simply refutes itself. Rather, it engages with the relevant texts, examines their theoretico-strategic function[55] and attempts an immanent verification of whether or not this function is performed by the arguments offered. The only hope of freeing Marx from his inhibitive over-philosophisation consists in working one's way *through* philosophy. Philosophy must be thought through to the end – so as to end up in reality again. This is what links Marx to Kant and Wittgenstein.

Thus the decision to consider only German-language theories has a precise methodological purpose: what is at stake is the *critique of philosophy*. Even before German philosophy devoted itself to Marx, he was philosophised by other disciplines – politics, economics, sociology and theology. Thus the present critique of philosophy does not limit itself to works of academic philosophy, which after all does not choose its objects of inquiry freely; my study engages with the entire theoretical terrain on which Marx has been and continues to be read or not read, mentalised and criticised, and this terrain includes disciplines other than philosophy.

1.5 The structure of the study

The decline of orthodox Marxism, once so influential, is the appropriate occasion for attempting a revival of Marxian thought. But where to begin? Is there a virgin 'substance' by reference to which possible deviations can be identified? Such a substance exists only in the sense that we dispose of Marx's texts. They are well preserved, in no less than two complete editions (*Marx Engels Werke*, MEW, and *Marx Engels Gesamtausgabe*, MEGA). But there is hardly an innocent sentence to be found in them: the legacy of more than one hundred and fifty years in the history of the reception of Marx is so powerful that one can never be sure of understanding what he meant to say without being influenced

54. *MECW* 3, p. 177.

55. By no means does this function have to be intentional. Karl Mannheim already thought of the 'worldview totality' as 'atheoretical' (Mannheim 1964a, p. 98). A strategic orientation may be the result of an unconscious 'tendency'.

by one of the numerous applications of his ideas. Every author has arrived at Marx by one road or another, and they imbue what he has written with their own preconceptions. These preconceptions are all the less visible the more commonplace they have become, but they are frequently the main obstacle to understanding Marx. What is to be done? Instead of rushing to present a new Marx as the 'real' one to whom we ought to 'return', an approach frequently chosen and one that usually amounts to the reassertion of a traditional reading, the present work follows the opposite path of engaging in a destruction of the tradition's development [*Destruktion des Überlieferungsgeschehens*].[56]

This involves treating the various stages of reception as interpretations that build upon one another. While they may have missed the mark for a variety of reasons (including political reasons), they have, nonetheless, consolidated themselves and given rise to new interpretations. Marx is referred to only when a deviation from the meaning of his theories is evident at some nodal point in the history of his reception. Since systematic remarks on Marx would stall the flow of the account, they have been appended to the relevant chapters in the form of remarks on 'Key Elements of Marxian Theory'. This allows for the presentation of a substantial part of Marx's work, without forcing that work into the corset of a lustreless system. Instead, the explosive topicality that distinguishes Marxian theory from Marxism is revealed at the very points where the two diverge. This accords better with the spirit of criticism than the penning of a hermetic and antiquarian monograph.

The second and most voluminous chapter of the present work examines theoretical Marxism's progressive self-debilitation up until the fall of the Berlin Wall in 1989. It seeks to understand how Marx's thought, which is more topical than ever, was able to exhaust itself in such a way in the course of the history of its reception. In examining the German reception of Marx – both within Marxism and on the part of its enemies – special attention needs to be paid to the mentalisations and moralisations to which Marxian theory fell victim. Marx was labelled a philosopher, a moralist and even a theologian. The course followed by Marx's German reception shows that he was one of the hidden centres of social philosophy. While there were exceptions, it remains astounding to see how frequently the function of refuting or avoiding Marx has constituted one of the nuclei around which German thought tacitly revolved.[57] This is what eventually caused theoretical Marxism to implode: it *concurred* with too many mentalisations. There resulted a veritable eliminatory idealism: the social sciences lost sight of their very own object of inquiry, namely 'society' and its concretisation 'capitalism'. Alongside the temporary success of Marxism as a political movement, we thus find a 'history of decline', that of theory insofar as it was Marxist or responded to Marx. When political Marxism collapsed,

---

56. This expression is taken from the 'existential interpretation' of Martin Heidegger.

57. According to Negt, 'the 20th century intellectual situation' consists, in fact, of 'footnotes to Marx' (Negt and Kluge 1992, p. 271). Negt's phrase alludes to a statement about Plato by A.N. Whitehead.

there was no theoretical net to break theory's fall. We do, however, dispose of ruins that allow us to reconstruct this history.

The second chapter covers the period from the 1892 Erfurt Programme to the end of socialism in 1989. But its mode of presentation is not historical. The chapter is structured systematically, distinguishing between the discursive contexts of various disciplines that overlap temporally. Sections 2.1 to 2.6 are structured so as to draw attention to an *increasing withdrawal from reality*. It begins with the treatment Marx received on the level of political-party literature, which was concrete insofar as it was geared to practical issues (2.1, 2.2). Marx was then engaged with in increasingly abstract ways. Economic analysis (2.3) and its spinoff sociology (2.4) were still intended for concrete application, albeit in a mediated way. After discussing them, the chapter examines Marxism's transposal to the field of philosophy (2.5) and its ultimate mentalisation, that is, its theologisation (2.6). This process of progressive abstraction involved arguments from one sphere being appropriated by another, and these arguments were not always the best. Ironically, it was theology that succeeded in *preserving* Marx's 'memory' after socialism, and it was able to do so precisely because of its lack of concern for practical matters (3.3.2).

The structure for which I have opted is meant to do justice to the fact that while the various disciplines often engage with similar issues, each functions according to its own particular grammar. If one follows Hegel in thinking of philosophy as the 'spirit of the times', then philosophy must look beyond its own nose. The second chapter shows that in dealing with Marx, philosophy often employed *topoi* adopted uncritically from the proto-philosophical disciplines. These *topoi* are difficult to criticise in a purely 'philosophical' way; in criticising patterns of reception, one needs to engage with the grammar of the proto-philosophical disciplines in which distortions of Marx originated, rectifying them *there*.

The shorter third chapter examines contemporary political philosophy. The post-mortal prolongation of the critique of philosophy beyond 1989, the moment of Marx's 'second death',[58] shows the German tendency to mentalise real phenomena has further waxed in strength since the disappearance of Marxism *qua* critical interlocutor. For as long as it faced Marxist opponents, German thought was forced not to elide social reality altogether. And it was confronted with the Marxist critique of philosophy, which raised the question of what made the philosophical statements advanced possible *as* statements. To the extent that it now lacks such a critical interlocutor (one who is at the same time its equal), contemporary philosophy has grown more grandiose, and hence more uncritical. The third chapter attempts to reconstitute the kind of critique that has been lost. In criticising some of the main currents of contemporary political philosophy (3.1–3.4), in-depth historical analysis has proven an invaluable tool. Uncovering – and hence exposing to criticism – the idealist premises of contemporary philosophy requires consideration of their theoretico-historical background. Thus ignorance of theory turns

58. Liessmann 1992.

out, in the course of analysis, to be a product of history; certain assumptions can be shown to underlie it. These background assumptions – such as the well-known claim that the welfare state has 'settled' class issues – usually originate in a single discipline and seldom stand up to empirical verification.

The reappropriation of Marxian thought provides the present work with a framework for criticising today's normative social philosophy. In breaking down barriers of reception, it also seeks to facilitate further productive recourse to Marx. Thus the fourth chapter's systematic conclusion has no ready-made 'new philosophy' to present. Instead, it attempts to revive a traditional discipline, one for which the names of Marx and Kant have long stood: *critique*. Critique refuses to be reduced to abstract formulas – except the one that apposite criticism ought to be both concrete and substantive.[59] Thus even systems theory, which takes itself to be above this world, contains central claims that depend on a specific historical constellation, one that has not existed since 1989.[60]

This issue, that of external consistency, is precisely the one that any critique that wants to be effective ought to treat as its point of attack. Such a critique is less in need of 'normative' than of valid *substantive* arguments. By virtue of this conclusion, a negative and critical one as far as the scope of social philosophy is concerned, the fourth chapter enacts a return to the meaning of philosophy as defined by Kant and Wittgenstein: philosophy *as such* is unable to make substantive claims about the world. Marx already knew this; his intellectual origins lay in German idealism and he needed considerable time to disentangle himself from it.[61] Philosophy after Marx limits itself to a critique of other philosophies and proto-philosophies. To do so, it must open itself up to the world and the empirical sciences without abandoning itself to them. For here lie the proto-philosophical ideologemes by which philosophies are so often deluded. As the present work makes clear, there remains plenty of work for philosophy to do.

It remains to point out some technical details. The footnotes, sometimes quite extensive, contain no additional arguments; they simply serve to illustrate the reflections developed in the main text. They indicate literature that contains similar reflections, as well as other passages in the present work. Some tables have been included to clarify complex economic phenomena; these tables serve no purpose but that of making the basic structure of what is being said more transparent. The term 'economy' always refers to the thing itself, whereas 'economics' refers to theories *about* the economy. Quotations from Marx are not intended as substantive proofs; their purpose is simply to allow the reader to verify where and in what manner Marx formulated particular claims.

---

59. On the criterion of substantiveness, see Lask 1902, p. 43; Carnap 1928, §7; Demmerling 1998, p. 82: Stekeler 1995, p. 282 f.

60. Luhmann 1971; see sections 2.4.6, 2.5.6.

61. *MECW* 1, pp. 220 f.

Chapter Two
Marx Yesterday: A Genealogy of Misconceptions

This chapter examines the fate of Marxian theory from the point of view of the history of theory, taking as its time frame the century after the death of Engels in 1895 and the years up to the watershed of 1989. The chapter proceeds as follows: section 2.1 examines how Marx was received within the first Marxist mass party, German Social Democracy and its various currents. The starting point is the empiricist fallacy contained in the 1892 'Erfurt Programme' (2.1.1). The Programme misinterpreted Marx's theory as an empirical description, thereby failing to grasp its internal complexity. Thus only two options remained: adjusting the theory to a reality that seemed constantly to be changing in fundamental ways (2.1.2, revisionism) or holding on to the theory at the cost of refusing to confront it with reality (2.1.4, orthodoxy). This involved orthodoxy subjecting society – which was the object of Marx's theories, including his economic theories – to a naturalist reduction. The revisionist reaction consisted in a transposal to the field of ethics. Two 'retrospective considerations' reveal this fatal rupture's frequently overlooked prelude in economic theory and the theoretical situation in which it resulted (2.1.5, 2.1.6).

The next section examines another crucial aspect of the history of Marx's history, namely Marxian theory's transfiguration into Marxism-Leninism (2.2). It is here that the 'primacy of politics' originates, an approach that further diverted attention from Marx's economic theories (2.2). While Leninist political theory reinforced the notion of the autonomy of political groups within society (2.2.1), the violent and dictatorial implementation of this concept (2.2.2, 2.2.3) involved a reversal of the way theory had hitherto been understood. In order to act effectively, one needs to define the possibilities for action precisely. This function of theory was revised under communism: theory went from being a critical corrective of practice to becoming one of its instruments (2.2.4). This is another instance of the object of inquiry 'society' being dissolved dualistically into technique and ethics: on the one hand, there developed a mechanistic theory of crisis, while on the other, there emerged a political voluntarism, evident not just in Lenin and Stalin, but also in Trotsky (2.2.5). Yet while the primacy of politics now made economic considerations seem less pertinent, it was itself based on certain economic premises. These departed considerably from Marx's theories. Marx was abandoned via the proclamation of a new, monopolistic stage of development. A retrospective consideration examines what this entailed for economic theory (2.2.6).

The next section (2.3) looks directly at how Marx was engaged with (or not engaged with) economic theory. In functional terms, the neoclassical reorganisation of the economic principles invoked by the radical workers' movement can be read as a reaction to Marxism (2.3.1). Starting now from different principles, theory no longer confronted Marx on the level of content, but on that of categories. Economic 'refutations of Marx' are really ways of avoiding Marx, since the new basic concepts no longer allow one to grasp his claims adequately (2.3.2). The Marxist departure from Marx's theories discussed in sections 2.1 and 2.2 led to a situation in which significant currents of theoretical Marxism accepted these new theoretical principles even though they were irreconcilable with those of classical economics, on the basis of which Marx had formulated his arguments (2.3.3). This was a crucial step toward the later implosion of Marxism. Thus the departure from Marxian theory was twofold: the general ignorance of economic theory evident in German Marxism was compounded, within those currents that had not yet abandoned economic thinking, by the adoption of non-Marxian theoretical foundations.[1] This was why Marxism was not able properly to play the role of acting as the critical corrective to 'bourgeois' social theory. Thus the latter, and the neoclassical paradigm in particular, exercised a hegemonic influence on other disciplines (2.3.4), as will be seen later. The section on economic theory's concluding 'retrospective consideration' focuses on monetary issues as an exemplary case of how Marxian theory departs from bourgeois approaches to economic and social theory. The example of money is significant because critical theory and attempts to revive Marxism *qua* 'value-form analysis' do not take Marx's notion of money as their starting point; instead, they start from a neoclassical notion that has been transposed to philosophy via the theories of Simmel.

Neoclassical economics' desociologisation of economic theory was paralleled by a de-economisation of sociology (section 2.4). The dualism of technique and ethics evident from Bernstein and Kautsky onward – a dualism that resulted from the disintegration

1. Due to the 'primacy of politics', German Marxists reacted only to developments in the English-speaking world when it came to matters of economic theory. These developments will thus be examined in their own right, to the extent that they are relevant to our topic.

of what was formerly a unified theoretical project – was taken up by certain schools of sociology. In economics, one encounters a dualism of abstract, model-oriented neoclassical theories, on the one hand, and moralistic but largely atheoretical historical narratives, on the other; similarly, in sociology, the theorisation of sterile, closed-circuit systems coexists with the theorisation of moral epiphenomena, without any connection being made between the two (2.4.1). In theoretical terms, this consolidated the loss of 'society' *qua* object of inquiry. It turns out that this loss is the price to be paid for avoiding Marx. After some conjecture about the socio-structural factors that may have played into this loss of theoretical substance (2.4.2), I provide a sketch of the specifically German phenomenon of excessive emphasis on normativity, evident on both sides of the dualism (2.4.3). Here, we find a first transfiguration of theories about ethics into theories that are themselves ethically prescriptive. This ambiguity continues to be evident in the current usage of the term 'normative theory' – after all, the history of theory is never just historical.

Next, an analysis of sociological approaches to Marx is used to elucidate the functional role which theoretical avoidance of Marx has played in the development of the theoretical constellation just described (2.4.4). The anti-sociological dualism of technology and ethics – which may also appear as one of nature and mind, explication [*Erklären*] and comprehension [*Verstehen*], or work and interaction – consolidated itself in the technocracy school, the influence of whose specific appropriation of Marx extends to Habermas, whom it prompted to assume an anti-Marxian stance. It is with an eye to this reception history that the school is analysed in its own right (2.4.5). The considerations to be found in the section on sociology are rendered more concrete in the concluding example, which addresses a question that is of central importance to sociology: that of society's socio-structural division into classes and the history of the disappearance of this perspective. The latter phenomenon is often interpreted, overhastily, as a disappearance of the object (classes) itself. Analysis of the relevant theoretical history yields a different result, however (2.4.6).

The philosophical backdrop to this tendency – that of conclusions about social reality being drawn from the history of theories – is discussed in the section on social philosophy (2.5). Social philosophy can only be interpreted in functional terms, as a response to Marxian hypotheses, after one has recognised the ways in which it is mediated by other, pre-philosophical developments: the technicistic underdetermination of the economic base (2.1.1/2.1.4, 2.2), which was 'compensated' for by elements as diverse as neoclassical economics (2.3), technocracy (2.4.5) and systems theory (2.4.6, 2.5.6), provoking a backlash in the form of attempts to formulate an ethics-based counterphilosophy. This counterphilosophy can be seen as a way of supplementing the underdetermined base by a normative superstructure, upon which attention is then focused (this is what I call 'normativism'). Given that the counterphilosophy often lacked any connection to theories of the base, it could also, however, be seen as substituting for them (this is what I call 'supernormativism'). Once ethics is considered the foundation of 'society', intratheoretical ethicisation becomes idealist and supernormativist social philosophy (2.5 and 4.4).

The hypothesis that German social philosophy's response to Marx rendered it idealist and tendentially irrationalist is not new. I begin by presenting one of its more moderate variants, that of René König (2.5.1). In order to explicate my use of the term 'idealist' and explain more precisely from whence the 'tradition of all dead generations' derives its power to determine philosophical thinking (1.4.1), I then reconstruct those aspects of the history of philosophy that continue to exercise a marked influence on German social philosophy (2.5.2). My analysis of some of the main exponents of twentieth-century social philosophy reveals the ongoing influence of German idealism: Rudolf Eucken (2.5.3), Martin Heidegger (2.5.5) and Niklas Luhmann (2.5.6) are examined with an eye to their idealism and philosophised understanding of Marx. This also serves to highlight the dilemma that every attempt to return to Marx is faced with today: theoretical Marxism has concurred not only with technicistically reductionist notions of the economic base (2.3.3), but also with their complement, moralist-idealist overemphasis on the superstructure.

This, in any case, is what emerges from my analysis of Georg Lukács's thought, which was important not only for critical theory's understanding of Marx, but also for that of Heidegger (2.5.4). Following this analysis, the section's retrospective consideration is completed by a systematic investigation of Marx's relationship to Hegel. One can only invoke Marx to argue against German Hegelianisations and mentalisations if one recognises that Marx's relationship to Hegel was, primarily, a critical one (2.5.7).

Technicistically reductionist notions of the economic base and the complementary philosophisation of the superstructure are also to be found in critical theory (2.6). Pollock's economic theories turn on the notion of an inescapable, hermetic 'system', a notion informed by both neoclassical economics and Leninism (2.6.2). Horkheimer's philosophical premises (2.6.1) were vitalist and Adorno's aspirations (2.6.3) religious. The affinity with theology evident in several authors associated with critical theory raises the question of to what extent such theologisation is compatible with Marx's theories. In order to answer this question, attention is directed at Marx's critique of religion, which is systematically reviewed (2.6.4). At first, the critique of religion was an intermediate stage for Marx; in his later work, it became an instrument of political critique (2.6.5). It focused less on religion as such than on the theologisation of social philosophy, which critical theory revived. By contrast, whenever professional twentieth-century theologians have picked up on elements of Marx's thought, it was his critique of religion, and of the ways in which religion may be instrumentalised, to which they turned. This can be seen especially clearly in the cases of Karl Barth and Paul Tillich (2.6.6). The only critical theorist who was aware of this link between theology and materialism was Walter Benjamin, who is thus examined in a concluding section (2.6.7). Ironically, it was theology that finally put an end to speculative thought, thus creating the possibility of a return to reality and practice.

2.1 Marx in the theory of Social Democracy

2.1.1 *The Erfurt Programme*

Looking back on Social Democracy, Walter Benjamin formulated the following judgement: 'The conformism which has marked the Social Democrats from the beginning attaches not only to their political tactics but to their economic views as well. It is one reason for the eventual breakdown of their party'.[1] This statement by an important German-speaking Marxist amounts to a fundamental critique. Now, German Social Democracy is a political party like any other, which is to say it is free to choose its political tactics and economic notions as it sees fit. Those who subscribe to other notions are free to join some other party. Social Democracy was, however, faced with a special problem, and it is precisely this problem that Benjamin alludes to: Social Democracy was the political embodiment of Marxism. During his lifetime, Marx intervened whenever the Party subscribed to notions that diverged from his own. Even decades after his death, the Party continued to relate its ideas back to Marx: it was constrained either to prove that its current tactics accorded with Marxian theories, or that those theories contained errors or were limited in their applicability. This was true, in any case, for as long as Social Democracy did not break fully with Marx.[2] But even then, Marx remained one the most stimulating authors from the Party's tradition; to see this, one need think only of the theories developed by the 'Young Socialists' (*Jungsozialisten* or *Jusos*). Even Eduard Bernstein, the founder of 'revisionism' whose theories underwent a renaissance during the 1970s, thought of himself as a Marxist; after all, he had been a confidant of Engels and had later administered his estate. Thus the first sedimentation of Marx's writings, to which the archaeology of Marx exegeses must turn, is to be found in the way Marx's reception was channelled by the political fate of the mass party SPD (*Sozialdemokratische Partei Deutschlands*, German Social Democratic Party). In keeping with the principle of examining texts only, and, more specifically, those texts that provide insight into how certain developments became possible, I will engage with texts by those authors who devoted themselves to fundamental theoretical issues and who may be considered representative. The two most important such authors are Eduard

1. Benjamin 2003, p. 393.

2. The 1959 Godesberg Programme makes no reference whatsoever to Marx: 'Democratic socialism' is rooted in 'Christian ethics, humanism, and classical philosophy' (Abendroth 1969, p. 129). A co-author of the Programme recalls: 'We ... spent considerable time discussing whether or not we wanted to continue subscribing to Marx in principle, taking note of the major errors and outdated elements of his teachings while further developing what remains fruitful in his true, empirical doctrine. In the end, we found this distinction was not very helpful and told ourselves our task consisted primarily in attending to what was new in the twentieth century' (Weisser 1976, p. 105). It would have been quite possible to do this in a Marxist way. 'After more than half a century, the theory of democratic socialism has marked the triumph of revisionism' (Gneuss in Labedz 1965, p. 50; see also Bernstein 1976, p. 13).

Bernstein (1850–1932) and Karl Kautsky (1854–1938): they shaped Social Democracy's programme during its first period of major popularity.

Bernstein and Kautsky penned the 1891 Erfurt Programme, which is widely seen as marking the breakthrough of Marxism within the workers' movement.[3] The Party's 1875 founding document, the Gotha Programme, had been sharply criticised by Marx.[4] When the SPD was declared a legal party again in 1890 and could resume its parliamentary work, it gave itself an openly Marxist programme for the first time. This was so important to the movement that it was even considered a new edition of the *Manifesto of the Communist Party*.[5] However, the four-page programme was penned at a time when the third volume of Marx's *Capital* (edited and published by Engels in 1894) had not yet appeared, much less Marx's early writings, which remained unpublished until the 1930s.

Nevertheless, the Programme was like a fanfare inaugurating Marxism's great success.[6] It is representative of what Marxism was taken to be at the time, and one should not forget that the elderly Engels gave it his blessing. Recognition of its content would later become a point of contention in the controversy between revisionists and orthodox Marxists. The Programme begins with the following statements:

> The economic development of bourgeois society leads by natural necessity to the downfall of small industry, whose foundation is formed by the worker's private ownership of his means of production. It separates the worker from his means of production, and converts him into a propertyless proletarian, while the means of production become the monopoly of a relatively small number of capitalists and large landowners.[7]

Hegel had already been constrained to admit[8] that bourgeois society had become the powerhouse of modern development, notwithstanding the fact that it yielded chaotic results and social inequality.[9] Marx radicalised this diagnosis. It is taken up in the Erfurt Programme, albeit it in a popularised form. What is it, exactly, that is lost in the course of this popularisation? To anticipate the answer to this question: the Programme mis-

3. On the genesis of the Erfurt Programme, see *MECW* 27, pp. 217 ff.; Miller 1964, pp. 179 ff.; Grebing 1966, p. 10 f.; Abendroth 1969, pp. 28 ff.; Beyer 1975, Lehnert 1983, pp. 80 ff.; Fricke 1987, pp. 214 ff; see also *MECW* 24, p. 340.

4. *MECW* 24, pp. 75 ff.

5. Thus Lenin wrote in 1899: 'We are not in the least afraid to say that we want to imitate the Erfurt Programme; there is nothing bad in imitating what is good' (*Works* [*LW*] vol. 4, p. 235; see also A. Weiss 1965).

6. At the time, Engels rejoiced that Marx's critique had made a strong impact (*MECW* 49, pp. 264 ff.).

7. German Social Democratic Party 1904, p. 316.

8. Hegel 1991, §§ 182 ff.

9. '[C]ivil society affords a spectacle of extravagance and want as well as of...physical and ethical degeneration' (Hegel 1991, § 185). When 'civil society is in a state of unimpeded activity', the 'amassing of wealth is intensified', as is the 'dependence and distress of the class tied to work' (§ 243). 'It hence becomes apparent that despite an excess of wealth civil society is not rich enough, i.e. its own resources are insufficient to check excessive poverty and the creation of a penurious rabble' (§ 245; Haltern 1985).

interprets highly abstract Marxian propositions about the general logic of the process of production as descriptions of the immediate present – thereby abandoning them.[10] What is thereby lost is scientific depth. Let us consider some examples. Marx and Engels described the way bourgeois society's fundamental antagonism – the opposition between capitalism's two classes, labour and capital – absorbs earlier class oppositions: 'The lower strata of the middle class ... all these sink gradually into the proletariat'.[11] What was at issue here were the historical origins of the proletariat;[12] the passage from the Erfurt Programme quoted above reads as if it were a question of contemporary workers in small enterprises.[13]

By interpreting a statement on history as a description of the present, the Programme makes it possible to present the existence of modern-day middle classes as a refutation of Marx.[14] Similarly, Marx does not describe the expulsion of 'superfluous laborers' as a continuous process of 'forever greater growth', as the Programme would have it:

> Forever greater grows the number of proletarians, more gigantic the army of superfluous laborers, and sharper the opposition between exploiters and exploited. The class-struggle between the bourgeoisie and proletariat is the common mark of all industrial countries; it divides modern society into two opposing camps and the warfare between them constantly increases in bitterness.

Rather, he describes a *tendency* that does not become manifest except under certain conditions. If wages are high and profit expectations low, the capitalist will invest less and hence require fewer workers. In this case, workers will, indeed, be expelled from the production process.

Yet this expulsion has two consequences. First, unemployed persons are forced to take work for lower wages. This depresses wages, thereby increasing the profit expectations of the entrepreneur, which may, in turn, result in investment and new employment. Second, the entrepreneur will attempt to improve his productive technology. If he wants to make a greater profit, he needs either to cheapen the production process, or else produce more. A new method of production may further increase his chances of making a profit (see section 2.1.6). He will, therefore, be especially likely to invest when wages are low due to high unemployment. This may lead to ulterior positive developments on

10. This was due less to an insufficient sense of 'dialectics', as Western Marxism believed, than to a simplistic notion of economics (see Kautsky 1980; according to Mohl 1867, p. 9, both friend and foe felt that whoever had read this book no longer needed to read *Capital*). While Bernstein and Kautsky were personally familiar with Marx and Engels, they were neither philosophers, nor economists, nor politicians, but publicists.

11. *MECW* 6, p. 491.

12. *MECW* 35, pp. 176 ff.

13. The *Manifesto* is referring to 'the small tradespeople, shopkeepers, and retired tradesmen generally, the handicraftsmen and peasants' (*MECW* 6, p. 491), who owned means of production and were, therefore, not 'free workers'. The worker needs to take his labour power to market because it is all he owns (2.4.6).

14. Bernstein 1961, pp. 73 ff.; see sections 2.1.2, 2.4.7.

the labour market. Thus the number of unemployed people is far from increasing 'forever'; it may decrease during periods of economic upturn. 'Tendentially', or across business cycles, the number of newly created jobs will, however, be lower than that of the jobs made redundant by rationalisation, since an increase in the productivity of labour achieved by an improvement in productive technology reduces the labour intensity of the single product.[15] This tendency does not have to be in effect at every moment, but it does shape social relations over time. The tendential character of the Marxian laws is thoroughly misunderstood when those laws are taken as descriptions of momentary situations. While there can be no doubt that much has changed, the tendency can still be demonstrated to be at work today.[16] Only those who make its validity dependent on what appears to be happening at a particular moment will periodically declare it to have been 'refuted'.[17] The following passage also contains numerous reinterpretations: 'But all the advantages of this transformation are monopolized by capitalists and large landowners. For the prolateriate [sic] and the declining intermediate classes... it means a growing augmentation of the insecurity of their existence, of misery, oppression, enslavement, debasement, and exploitation'.[18]

The phrase 'increase in the insecurity of their existence' was added at the behest of Engels, since he was aware of how the situation of German workers had improved during the *Gründerzeit* period.[19] Yet expressions such as 'increase... of misery' are reminiscent of the theory of progressive immiseration defended by Malthus and others. While the early Marx subscribed to this theory,[20] he abandoned it soon after.[21] According to this

15. *MECW* 35, pp. 623 ff.
16. Sassen 1988, p. 136.
17. This is reminiscent of the following joke. One person asks another whether the indicator of a car is working. The reply: 'Working, not working, working, not working...' The respondent has obviously not understood the way an indicator works. 'The greater the social wealth, the functioning capital, the extent and energy of its growth, and, therefore, also the absolute mass of the proletariat and the productiveness of its labour, the greater is the industrial reserve army. The same causes which develop the expansive power of capital, develop also the labour-power at its disposal.... *This is the absolute general law of capitalist accumulation.* Like all other laws it is modified in its working by many circumstances' (*MECW* 35, p. 638). Goodwin 1972 develops this feedback phenomenon into a theory of the 'growth cycle', without taking account, however, of the influence of trade unions. Lederer 1931, on the other hand, explains unemployment by reference to monopolisation.
18. German Social Democratic Party 1904, p. 316. Compare this with Marx's original formulation: 'Along with the constantly diminishing number of the magnates of capital, who usurp and monopolize all advantages of this process of transformation, grows the mass of misery, oppression, slavery, degradation, exploitation; but with this too grows the revolt of the working class, a class always increasing in numbers, and disciplined, united, organized by the very mechanism of the process of capitalist production itself' (*MECW* 35, p. 750).
19. *MECW* 27, p. 223.
20. *MECW* 3, pp. 239 f.; *MECW* 6, p. 499.
21. *MECW* 9, pp. 214 f.; Abendroth 1969, p. 35; Rosdolsky 1977, pp. 282 ff.; Shaikh n.d. The 'entanglement of all peoples in the net of the world market' (*MECW* 35, p. 750) has caused poverty to increase the world over (Baratta 2002, p. 1086; U. Neumann 1999).

theory, workers only ever receive *subsistence level* wages. The assumption seemed easy to refute, since German workers had seen their standard of living improve around 1900. However, exploitation may increase even when real wages are on the rise; the mature Marx understood exploitation in terms of the *ratio* of productivity increases to wage increases. When productivity increases more rapidly than wages, as is to be expected (2.1.6), the capitalist obtains a higher share of surplus value from the labour he has purchased than before. Thus the rate of exploitation has risen despite the rise in wages.[22] Wage levels are not limited by the absolute minimum required for subsistence, but by labour power's variable value, which is determined by the goods required for its reproduction. Which goods are required and which are not is a question that is answered in the course of social conflicts. This implies the existence of a 'moral element',[23] of which the Erfurt Programme loses sight.

The concept of 'monopoly' is also blurred by an interpretation based on a semantics of what is immediately given. By definition, the capitalist class holds a monopoly on the means of production,[24] but this should not be confused with economic theory's more specific concept of monopoly. Aggressive pricing policies, enforced concentration and political or natural market barriers may lead to the temporary formation of monopolies within a sector of industry; these monopolies then eliminate competition within this industry for some time.[25] Yet competition remains the prerequisite of such a monopoly.[26] Economically speaking, 'the' means of production are not monopolised by 'one' group of capitalists, since inter-capitalist competition prevents capitalists from forming a homogeneous group. The historical and the economic concept of monopoly are confounded whenever 'monopoly' is interpreted as referring to a momentary state of affairs. This reductive approach can also be seen in Hilferding and Lenin, when they proclaim the 'new stage' of monopoly capitalism (2.2.6) – a proclamation that gave Marxists license to stop reading Marx (2.3.3).

In all the examples mentioned, simplification concerns one and the same aspect: this mode of representation knows only one level of analysis. What is being said, in effect, is: this is how it is, and this is how it will be. The key notion at work in this operation is 'natural necessity'. A necessity is proclaimed without being demonstrated, and it is claimed that this necessity plays out in a way similar to 'nature'. Invocation of such quasi-natural development alludes to Darwinism, which was experiencing its moment of triumph at the time when the Erfurt Programme was written. Kautsky subscribed temporarily to Darwinism, and Bernstein to the theories of Eugen Dühring.[27] Engels had

22. 3.2.2; *MECW* 35, p. 599 f.; Shaikh 1986c.
23. *MECW* 35, pp. 181, 225 f., 276 f., 536 f.; *MECW* 20, p. 8; *MECW* 24, p. 380.
24. *MECW* 5, p. 335; *MECW* 35, p. 243.
25. *MECW* 6, pp. 190 ff.; *MECW* 37, pp. 436, 608 ff.
26. *MECW* 6, pp. 195 f.; *MECW* 35, pp. 621 f.
27. On Bernstein, see Gay 1954, p. 193; Colletti 1971, Gustavson 1972, Meyer 1977, Carsten 1993 and Steger 1997. On Kautsky, see Lenin 1972a, Korsch 1929, Matthias 1957, Steenson 1978, Salvadori

already drawn comparisons between the development of nature and that of society.[28] Kautsky and Bernstein later proceeded to replace historical by natural historical development. Kautsky did so in his 1906 work *Ethics*, and Bernstein when he expressed his faith in a 'peaceful transition to socialism' [*friedliches Hineinwachsen in den Sozialismus*].[29] The shift of focus, from society to nature, created the possibility of closing ranks with social Darwinist tendencies (2.1.4).[30] The new 'concept' rendered superfluous the very political action that Marx had wanted to illuminate conceptually.[31] This was what Benjamin lamented in the opening quotation.

The changed concept of nature[32] implies a changed understanding of science. By his models, Marx meant neither to offer a faithful representation of the circumstances of his own time, nor to anticipate those of the future; his intention was that of analysing the forces that were at work behind contemporary appearances and manifested themselves in them. One does not need Hegel's *Logic* to distinguish between 'essence and appearance'. Simple examples suffice to show that many scientific disciplines operate on the basis of this distinction: we see the Sun rise every morning, and yet we know that in

---

1979, Kołakowski 1976, pp. 379 ff.; Vranitzky 1981, pp. 305 ff.; Mende 1985, Gilcher-Holtey 1986, Geary 1987, Schelz-Brandenburg 1992, Koth 1993 and Häupel 1993. On Marx's relation to Darwin, see Mozetic 1987, pp. 117 ff.; for general accounts, see Lichtheim 1961, McLellan 1979, and Howard 1989, pp. 65 ff.

28. *MECW* 25, pp. 313 ff.

29. The original German suggests an organic process, as '*Hineinwachsen*' literally means 'to grow into' [translator's note].

30. Bebel 1971, pp. 255 ff.; Woltmann 1899, Raddatz 1975, p. 288; Heyer 1982. In 1933, the residual SPD faction voted in favour of the law on euthanasia (Weingart 1988, Mosse 1990).

31. The Party's official interpretation of its own programme states: 'The capitalist social system has run its course... Irresistible economic forces lead with the certainty of doom to the shipwreck of capitalist production' (Kautsky 1971, p. 117) – and with it socialism: 'But socialist production must, and will, come. Its victory will have become inevitable as soon as that of the proletariat has become inevitable' (p. 191; for an early instance of this view, see Bebel 1971, pp. 343 ff., 372 ff.). Kautsky wants to avoid the impression that the exploited will reap the fruits of the social revolution without having to do anything in the meantime. But this is precisely the import of what he says: 'We consider the breakdown of the present social system to be unavoidable, because we know that the economic evolution inevitably brings on conditions that will compel the exploited classes to rise against this system of private ownership', since it leaves them 'no choice but to go down into degradation or to overthrow the system of private property' (p. 90). It seems that nothing needs to be done except await this political 'victory': 'Socialist production is, therefore, the natural result of a victory of the proletariat' (p. 191). And 'victory' seemed easy enough to achieve: 'Bourgeois society is preparing its own downfall so vigorously that we need only await the moment in which to pick up the power that falls from its grasp' (Bebel speaking at the 1891 Party Congress, quoted in Lehnert 1983, p. 83). First capitalism collapses, then power is seized, then there is socialism: everything plays out by natural necessity. But what has become of political practice, over and beyond the organisation of the party? Kautsky confirmed retrospectively that the road to practice had been obstructed by these theories: 'Bringing about the revolution... seemed to me to be... impossible. It could only be the work of immense historical events that the Party had no way of influencing' (in *Der Sozialist*, 5, 4, p. 55). 'To want to make a revolution is... folly' (Lassalle 1987, p. 198).

32. See *MECW* 35, p. 616; Schmidt 1960; Dahmer 1994.

fact the Earth revolves around the Sun.[33] One does not need to be a Hegelian to acknowledge this fact. Not even in the realm of nature does the distinction entail determinism, for the force of gravity has its counterpart in centrifugal force, so that objects do not have to stick to the ground as if made of stone. Properly understood, the law of gravity is not to be refuted simply by pointing out the existence of airborne butterflies. Theory and experience operate on different levels. Relating them to one another requires methodologically controlled mediations. Marx provided a highly abstract model of capitalism's general *modus operandi*. When proceeding methodologically from the abstract to the concrete, description of contemporary circumstances requires the progressive introduction of increasingly substantial specific conditions, namely those under which a given process plays out in each particular instance.[34]

These mediations are precisely what is lacking in the Erfurt Programme. Those who misunderstand the 'laws' presented by Marx as descriptions of the immediate phenomena of the present make those laws 'susceptible to empirical refutation'[35] as soon as other phenomena occur. This is true not only of Marx's statements on the concentration of capital and unemployment, but also of those on crises, the tendency of the rate of profit to fall, and the labour theory of value. Marx's approach was simple: the long-term interplay of forces can only be interpreted once their general logic has been understood. Because this approach involves such a high level of abstraction, the future cannot be predicted precisely. It is a matter, rather, of measuring the range of possibilities staked out by the laws in question. The political activity of the workers' movement needs to do justice to these possibilities by implementing effective strategies.[36] By contrast, the Erfurt Programme makes the activity of Social Democracy dependent on the crises predicted, crises that 'constantly become more comprehensive and more devastating'.[37] Because private ownership of the means of production has become 'incompatible with their appropriate application... and their full development, its 'transformation... into social ownership' represents the only possible remedy. How exactly this transformation was

33. Political economy 'has a parallel in the solar system which displays to the eye only irregular movements, though its law may none the less be ascertained' (Hegel 1991, note to § 189; see *MECW* 35, p. 321; Sheehan 1985). Talk of essence and appearance does not in itself constitute a 'dialectical method' (Simon-Schäfer 1974, p. 224).

34. *MECW* 28, p. 37; *MECW* 37, p. 27; see Hegel, *Werke* 4, p. 413 and *Werke* 16, p. 78; Sweezy 1970, pp. 11 ff.; Rosdolsky 1977, pp. 25 ff. and Euchner 1972, pp. 9 ff.; Eberle 1974 and Jánoska 1994.

35. Holzey 1994, p. 11.

36. Traditional interpretations of Marx were often more appropriate than the destructive postures of later academic Marxists. Rosa Luxemburg was one theorist who grasped the tendential character of the Marxian laws: 'The struggle of the average size enterprise against big Capital cannot be considered a regularly proceeding battle in which the troops of the weaker party continue to melt away directly and quantitatively. It should be rather regarded as a periodic mowing down of the small enterprises, which rapidly grow up again, only to be mowed down once more by large industry' (Luxemburg 1971a, p. 32; see also Bebel 1971, p. 380 f.). Problems arise only with the question of what this means for analysis and political practice. Some reductive interpretations are not the product of a philosophical 'error of interpretation', but of pragmatic considerations.

37. German Social Democratic Party 1904, p. 317.

to be brought about was considered a secondary issue, for the time being, the assumption being that the Party ought first to focus on political work and political education. Yet it was precisely the naturalised notion of transformation that gave the Party such faith in the 'historical necessity' it took to be its ally. The assumption was only plausible for as long as 'crises, conflicts, catastrophes'[38] did, indeed, occur as predicted. Marx felt the need to intensify his study of political economy after his own expectations of revolution had been disappointed twice (in 1848 and 1857). His own economic theory was a response to these disappointments. The theory Marx developed is precisely what is elided in the Erfurt Programme's prediction of future crises (see 2.1.5).

The rhetoric of crisis has virtually no effect on the Programme's concrete demands, which were formulated by Bernstein. The Programme demands, 'immediately', equal suffrage, democratic legislation, the replacement of the standing army by an 'armed nation', freedom of opinion, gender equality, the privatisation of religion, compulsory education and occupational safety measures; it also formulates demands related to the administration of justice and taxation. Now, these demands could just as well have been formulated without predicting crises and without a worldview based on the notion that the means of production will, one day, need to be socialised. In the Erfurt Programme, a pessimistic view of the economic future goes hand in hand with an optimistic assessment of what is politically possible. Marx was thinking of small, limited steps that would prepare the ground for larger steps. But the small steps could not replace the larger ones, for they were bound to provoke counterreactions in the medium term.[39]

Now, in the Erfurt Programme, one finds a peculiar gap between small steps and large steps, between the Programme's naturalised scenario of crisis and its liberal demands. Marx's general object of theoretical inquiry, 'society', vanished inside this gap (see 2.4.1). This can be seen in the way the Programme misconstrues its specific object of inquiry, 'Germany ca. 1900'. Notions of the autonomy of politics *vis-à-vis* the economy, and of the primacy of politics, were imposed upon the concrete circumstances of the time.[40]

---

38. The phrase was coined by Kautsky in 1902; quoted in Gay 1954, p. 238; see Hofmann 1979, p. 182.

39. *MECW* 20, pp. 5 ff., 144 ff.; *MECW* 23, p. 3 f. 'The practical daily struggle for reforms, for the amelioration of the condition of the workers within the framework of the existing social order, and for democratic institutions, offers Social Democracy the only means of engaging in the proletarian class struggle and working in the direction of the final goal – the conquest of political power and the suppression of wage labor. For Social Democracy there exists an indissoluble tie between social reforms and revolution. The struggle for reforms is the *means*; the social revolution, its *goal*' (Luxemburg 1971a, p. 52).

40. See 2.2.6, 2.3.3, 2.6.2. 'These are attempts to convince oneself and the party that 'present-day society is developing towards socialism' without asking oneself whether it does not thereby just as necessarily outgrow the old social order and whether it will not have to burst this old shell by force... One can conceive that the old society may develop peacefully into the new one in countries where the representatives of the people concentrate all power in their hands, where, if one has the support of the majority of the people... But in Germany where the government is almost omnipotent and the Reichstag and all other representative bodies have no real power, to advocate such a thing in Germany, when, moreover, there is no need to do so, means removing

Later developments within Social Democracy can be traced back to the choices made in the Erfurt Programme. The political course there charted stood in no relation to the demands formulated by the Party and the tactics applied by it, and this was felt to be a contradiction in need of resolution. One can distinguish three major currents that developed from this nodal point. 'Revisionism' (2.1.2) fully abandoned the rhetoric of crisis and socialisation: it revised the theoretical premises of Social-Democratic policies and provided those policies with an *ex post* foundation, a set of principles by which to justify the Party's practices as they had developed until then. This involved a thorough transformation of the theory-practice relation. The consequences can be traced all the way to twentieth-century philosophy. Certain lines of argument, such as the tendency to instrumentalise ethics for social theory, are still current today (2.4, 3.1). It was only when Social-Democratic policies lost their material foundation in political economy, with the latter being replaced by 'ethics', that 'normative foundations' began to be required – as a justification both for the policies and for the 'ethics'.

The second current, that of 'orthodoxy', attempted to gloss over the contradiction for as long as possible (2.1.4). Kautsky sought to demonstrate that Social Democracy's current tactics accorded with Marx's theories. Like revisionism, this current exercised a far-reaching influence; its approach proved useful whenever the need arose to demonstrate the 'Marxist' character of certain political practices. This involved a downright instrumentalisation of dialectics, which was often used to link what never belonged together, and which was, therefore, strongly fetishised. This was the case in socialist states as well as in Western Hegelian Marxism; whenever the latter's Marxist terminology seemed not to fit the given circumstances, it was justified not by means of a thorough analysis of the present, but by questionable borrowings from Hegel. A third current attempted to bring political practice into line with the goal of socialisation. Its exponents were unable to devote much attention to the specific circumstances under which the goal would have to be realised. Notwithstanding the differences between them, Rosa Luxemburg, Lenin and Trotsky can be seen as belonging to this current (see 2.2). It influenced not just actually-existing socialism, but also the radical elements of the student movement, left-wing terrorism and Third World communism.[41] None of these three currents can be

the fig-leaf from absolutism and becoming oneself a screen for its nakedness. In the long run such a policy can only lead one's own party astray' (Engels, *MECW* 27, p. 226; see also Kautsky 1893). 'If one thing is certain it is that our party and the working class can only come to power under the form of a democratic republic... But the fact that in Germany it is not permitted to advance even a republican party programme openly, proves how totally mistaken is the belief that a republic, and not only a republic, but also communist society, can be established in a cosy, peaceful way' (p. 227). The primacy of politics is even more evident in the draft programme, where there is talk not only of 'two hostile camps', but also of 'domination', 'degradation', 'dependence', and such like. Engels criticised the fact that this 'creates the false impression that this has been caused by the *political* domination of that gang of robbers', whereas what was at stake was 'an economic fact, which should be explained in economic terms' (p. 223).

41. McLellan 1979.

properly understood without consideration of the choices made within the Marxism of the Second International. Each current gave rise to new interpretations, but they all started from the one I have criticised in the Erfurt Programme. Let us consider the consequences within Social Democracy.

2.1.2 *Revisionism*

> The final goal, whatever it may be, is nothing to me; the movement everything.[42]

The years after 1890, during which German Social Democracy expanded consistently, saw the Party settle for the political options available in imperial Germany. What this meant, first and foremost, was that the Party's parliamentary faction strove to introduce pro-worker ideas into parliamentary debates while supporting the trade unions, which had also gained in strength.[43] The persistent threat of a new ban on the Party, combined with internal controversies over long-term political goals, led to Social Democracy's growing *commitment* to parliamentary politics. Despite its stubborn rejection by the upper classes and the temporarily non-compliant stance of its Reichstag faction, the Party was able, up until 1914, to achieve many improvements in the social and political situation of workers, thereby helping to modernise imperial Germany.[44] Yet the political recognition associated with these successes increasingly brought the Party's leaders into conflict with the radical rhetoric of their programme. Theory and practice no longer accorded with each other.

It was then that Eduard Bernstein, who had spent decades in exile and worked as the private secretary of Engels, set out to develop a new theory, one that started from the Party's actual practice and could be used to justify that practice. His programmatic work *Evolutionary Socialism* (first published in 1899), penned at the behest of August Bebel, states this purpose clearly: it was a question of 'co-ordinating theory and practice'.[45] Of course, the term 'theory' was used, here, in much the same way as Horkheimer[46] would later use it: what was meant was *Marx's* theory: 'German social democracy acknowledges to-day as the theoretical foundation of its activity the theory of society worked out by Marx and Engels and called by them scientific socialism'.[47] This foundation needed now to be 'corrected' on the basis of current practice: 'The mistakes of a theory can only be considered as overcome when they are recognised as such by the advocates of that

42. Bernstein 1897, p. 556.

43. 'The trade unions sought to organise their members in a solidary manner, fighting for improvements in wage levels and working conditions within the framework of bourgeois society' (Grebing 1972, p. 101).

44. Ullmann 1996, p. 206; Grebing 1966, p. 105; for general accounts, see Roth 1963, D. Groh 1973.

45. Bernstein 1961, p. 25.

46. Horkheimer 1988a.

47. Bernstein 1961, p. 1.

theory'.[48] Since 'scientific Socialism'[49] was, first and foremost, an economic theory, Bernstein was compelled to refute it on the terrain of 'pure science', in order then to propose alternative models for 'applied science'.[50] Yet what he refuted was not Marx's theory itself, but the simplified interpretation of it found in the Erfurt Programme (of which Bernstein was himself one of the authors): 'If society were constituted or had developed in the manner the socialist theory has hitherto assumed, then certainly the economic collapse would be only a question of a short span of time. Far from society being simplified as to its divisions compared with earlier times, it has been graduated and differentiated both in respect of incomes and of business activities'.[51]

Observations of this kind are presented as falsifying a theory that anticipates constant social polarisation and predicts imminent crises. Yet Marx held that description of a specific form of society requires the introduction of numerous intermediate levels of analysis. Confronting simple observations with a theory is possible only when both are situated on the same level. This is the case within the Erfurt Programme, but not with regard to Marx's statements on economic classes and crises. To Marx, science was necessary because mere momentary observations do *not* reveal the logic according to which a given phenomenon functions.[52] Bernstein gives short shrift to this point of view, by attributing it to Marx's entrapment in the snares of the dialectic.

Yet Marx is simply reiterating a basic tenet of the modern conception of science – whereas Bernstein abandons it. This attempt at a 'refutation' has since become a staple of the debate on Marx. It was rooted not just in the history of ideas,[53] but also in reality: following the 'great depression' of 1873 to 1896, the economy rebounded, including in Germany.[54] In fact, and for historical reasons, it did so especially rapidly in imperial Germany. The industrial revolution had been late to reach Germany, due mainly to the country's pre-1871 division into small states. Yet when it did begin, Germany was able quickly to apply the most up-to-date technologies. This allowed it to produce more cheaply than other countries, without having to invest more in development. The state also acted to foster growth – and it could afford to do so due to wartime profits. In Germany, a 'developing country', the transportation system was built by the state. State-owned railway and naval construction also provided some sectors of heavy industry with the additional advantages of guaranteed sales and monopolised market shares.[55]

48. Bernstein 1961, p. 26.
49. Bernstein 1961, p. 1; Engels, *MECW* 24, p. 325.
50. Bernstein 1961, p. 2.
51. Bernstein 1961, p. 49.
52. 'But all science would be superfluous if the outward appearance and the essence of things directly coincided' (*MECW* 37, p. 804; see also *MECW* 43, p. 68 f.). Marx is part of 'the great tradition of rational philosophy', as he seeks to describe reality 'as comprehensively and completely as possible' (Rohrmoser 1970, p. 60).
53. Colletti 1974; Gustavson 1972.
54. Rosenberg 1974, p. xxiv; Colletti 1971, p. 59; Mandel 1975, pp. 114 ff.; Ullmann 1995, p. 60.
55. Rosenberg 1955, Henning 1974, Fischer 1985, Hobsbawm 1987, Ullmann 1995, p. 95.

Bernstein offers some observations on the new economic boom. But he immediately interprets the state-driven growth as a qualitatively new stage in the logic of development.[56] In a later lecture, Bernstein presented graphs: Marxism had postulated gradual decline across a series of business cycles, he argued, when in fact the general tendency was one of greater growth.[57] The graphs are, however, unspecific. Marx would immediately have granted Bernstein that the 'wealth of society' had increased. After all, capitalism is characterised by constant growth: ever greater amounts of capital search for profitable investment opportunities; ever greater numbers of goods are produced and thrown onto the market (2.3.1). What declines tendentially, according to Marx, is the share of productivity growth represented by wages (that is, exploitation increases) and the rate of profit (2.1.6). Bernstein simplifies the theory, and thereby fails to do justice to it. He attributes to particular phenomena within the capitalist economy the *new* function of allowing for prosperity without crises. Specifically, he attributes a new significance to credit, joint-stock companies and cartels. What changes does he make to Marx's model?

According to Marx, *credit* comes about when 'idle capital'[58] in search of investment opportunities meets companies in search of money. The creditor (or the bank *qua* intermediate institution) obtains interest on this flow of capital; the interest corresponds to a portion of the profit made. Such reproductive credit is as old as capitalist banking.[59] Marx attributed to credit both a beneficial and a destructive effect on accumulation.[60]

---

56. Bernstein 1961, p. 79 f.

57. Bernstein 1976, p. 123.

58. *MECW* 37, pp. 73, 251, 317, 496 f.; Marx means disposable money capital that is not productively invested by its owner into his own industry, due to a lack of profitability.

59. This is why Bernstein thinks this idea is far from new (Bernstein 1961, p. 81). Consumer credit provided by banks is a recent innovation (such as payment of cars or houses by instalments), but where it takes the form of usury (*MECW* 37, p. 588), it is older than other forms of trade credit (deferral of payment) or state credit (debts incurred by the state to compensate for its budget deficit; see *MECW* 10, pp. 49 ff.; for a general account, see Pohl 1993, as well as 2.3.5).

60. Marx attributes 'two characteristics' to credit: on the one hand, 'the credit system accelerates the material development of the productive forces and the establishment of the world market'; on the other hand, it also 'accelerates the violent eruptions of this contradiction – crises' (*MECW* 37, p. 439). Credit renders capital more mobile: existing assets currently fixed (in A) can be used as securities to obtain money, which can then immediately be invested in another branch of industry (B). The amount of money seems to have doubled: the capital owner receives income from two investments of the same capital (minus interest). But one half (B) consists of debt that will, one day, have to be paid off. This capital is 'fictitious'; it functions, but only as negative capital (*MECW* 37, pp. 397, 462; *MECW* 1, p. 103 f.; Keynes considered the profit on capital B to be of central importance, since it seems to appear from nowhere). By 'acceleration' (*MECW* 37, p. 433), Marx means that capital can now move more swiftly from A to B than it could if it needed to wait until its turnover period has been completed. It does not have to wait for the production cycle of capital A to be completed. This is regulated by the equalisation of the rate of profit (*MECW* 37, p. 433). Moreover, credit already represents association in production, since it combines many small capitals into one large capital (p. 435). In order for it to benefit everyone, a political revolution would be required – Bernstein says nothing about this (Schimkowsky 1974, p. 194). Pending this revolution, the separation of money owners and entrepreneurs leads to capital being handled

Bernstein now attributes to them the *new* property of curbing the spread of a crisis, and nothing else:[61] when a company runs into difficulties, it can stay above water by means of credit and does not have to go bankrupt immediately. As true as this is, it should not tempt one to consider 'general commercial crises' unlikely.[62] For companies can still go bankrupt, and the consequences of such a bankruptcy may even be worse: if the bankrupt company has obtained substantial amounts of credit, this may spell ruin for the company's bank as well; and this, in turn, would lead to a chain reaction. As long as the profit motive remains the driving force behind the economy, credit cannot abolish the logic of the big fish eating the small. While credit may curb crises in the short term, as Bernstein rightly argues against Rosa Luxemburg, financial interdependence is also a factor that may cause a crisis to spread, since one link in the chain can drag the others down with it.[63] Credit accelerates capitalist growth by shortening turnover. But in doing so, it simultaneously reinforces the cause of crises.[64] This is to say nothing of the monetary crises that result from the anarchic character of the money market; their frequency has increased during the 1990s (2.3.5). Such monetary crises also show that the problem of crisis cannot be solved simply by expanding the credit system. Bernstein and Luxemburg turned the twofold character of credit into a distinction between good credit and bad credit.

The *joint-stock company* was also quick to make its appearance in capitalism. It leads to a diversification of capital sources: many small capitals unite to form a joint-stock company (or 'collective capitalist').[65] This special form of money lending eliminates the transaction costs of the banking and financial sector, but it is feasible only for long-term projects.[66] Joint-stock companies were also considered a dynamic factor by Marx: they allow for projects on a scale that individuals would hardly ever be able to finance, due to

---

irresponsibly: money is increasingly handled by 'pure adventurers' (*MECW* 37, p. 437). Casino capitalism becomes the 'purest and most colossal form of gambling and swindling' (p. 439), and what the 'speculating wholesale merchant risks' (p. 437) is social property – a familiar phenomenon in the day of globalised financial markets and national bankruptcies.

61. Bernstein 1961, p. 81.

62. Bernstein 1961, p. 80.

63. In 1897, Luxemburg emphasised the destructive role of credit in an argument directed against Bernstein: 'If it is true that crises appear as a result of the contradiction between the capacity for expansion, the tendency of production to increase, and the restricted consumption capacity [on the theory of underconsumption, see 2.1.5], then . . . credit is precisely the specific means of making this contradiction break out as often as possible. . . . Thus, far from being a means for the elimination or the attenuation of crises, credit is, on the contrary, a particularly forceful factor in the formation of crises' (Luxemburg 1971a, p. 61).

64. They increase the organic composition of capital (2.1.6; *MECW* 35, p. 621 f.; *MECW* 37, pp. 432 ff.; see also Fritsch 1968, pp. 100 ff.; Brunoff 1976, pp. 77 ff.; Kim 1999, pp. 70 ff.; 2.3.5).

65. *MECW* 35, p. 339.

66. 'Shareholder value' is more oriented toward short-term stock market return than long long-term profitability. Thus the New Economy bubble bursting, for example (Brenner 2002).

the amounts of capital required, and, in doing so, they contribute to centralisation.[67] Yet while they promote capitalist growth, they also have disadvantages: they pose a threat to smaller capitalists, since competition is rendered more arduous by the existence of such large companies,[68] and capital intensity within production increases tremendously.[69] Thus the character of joint-stock companies is also twofold. Yet Bernstein sees in them only a single and *new* force: one that does not lead to a 'centralisation of capital', but actually works to prevent it.[70] This contradicts the claim on social polarisation advanced in the Erfurt Programme.[71] Joint-stock companies are not, however, a new phenomenon. Nor does their existence refute that of centrifugal forces within the economy. On the contrary, they allow for additional concentration, since the capitalists dispose not only of their own capital, but also of additional borrowed capital. Marx speaks of the *simultaneous* 'attraction and repulsion' of capitals.[72] Bernstein considers only the 'splitting up of shares of property in centralised undertakings'.[73] In functional terms, this amounts to pulling the foundation of Marxist theory out from underneath it. With regard to cartels, Bernstein chooses to focus on their exact opposite, socialisation. Here, too, Bernstein turns a complex of mutually implicated and counteracting forces that work together to produce an overall tendency (not so much the famous 'concentration' as an increase in capital intensity within production) into an either/or dichotomy, whereupon he opts for

67. 'The world would still be without railways if it had had to wait until accumulation had got a few individual capitals far enough to be adequate for the construction of a railway. Centralisation, on the contrary, accomplished this in the twinkling of an eye, by means of joint-stock companies' (*MECW* 35, p. 622; see Shaikh 1983c).

68. 'One capitalist always kills many': *MECW* 35, p. 750.

69. While 'centralisation thus intensifies and accelerates the effects of accumulation, it simultaneously extends and speeds those revolutions in the technical composition of capital which raise its constant portion at the expense of its variable portion, thus diminishing the relative demand for labour' (*MECW* 35, p. 622). And it lowers the rate of profit – these are the two Marxian 'laws' (*MECW* 35, pp. 607 ff.; *MECW* 37, pp. 209 ff.).

70. Bernstein 1961, p. 44.

71. Bernstein 1961, p. 48. 'The shareholder takes the graded place in the social scale which the captains of industry used to occupy before the concentration of businesses' (p. 54). Rising numbers of shareholders do not amount to 'people's capitalism'. In the short term, share value can only rise for as long as new buyers continue to flock to the market. Participation by non-capitalist groups does not entail any attenuation of economic antagonism. 'The people who are losing their jobs are – shareholders' (W. Uchatius in *Die Zeit*, 23 March 2000). 'For workers, the purchase of shares amounts to a reduction in their real income [since the shares are either paid for out of this income or represent a part of the worker's wages] and entails the risk of suffering losses due to market fluctuations [one need think only of the shares issued by *Deutsche Telekom*]. Yet small shares are of special... importance to large shareholders. Even... minimal amounts of money can be mobilised to extend and intensify the process of production and exploitation, while the highly diversified nature of the capital sources makes it easier for large shareholders to control a joint-stock company. Moreover,... small shares, especially employees' shares, serve to bind workers to capitalist enterprises both ideologically and economically' (Becher 1976, p. 216 f.).

72. *MECW* 37, p. 207. 'At the same time portions of the original capitals disengage themselves and function as new independent capitals. Besides other causes, the division of property, within capitalist families, plays a great part in this' (*MECW* 35, p. 620).

73. Bernstein 1961, p. 44.

one of the two terms and considers the other obsolete. Bernstein tears apart the theoretical unity of Marx's work.[74]

Finally, *cartels* are agreements between entrepreneurs, typically within a single industry; the entrepreneurs agree to divide the market up between themselves by colluding on prices and dividing market segments between one another. Price competition is suppressed with the intention of keeping prices stable. When the state is involved, this is called interventionism or protectionism. Bernstein's reference to cartels is at odds with his claims regarding the spread of wealth: a sufficiently effective agreement is possible only between industry giants. Moreover, he attributes to cartels the power to attenuate crises, arguing that they are capable of 'preventing the anarchy of production'.[75] This is a correct description as far as the *response* to crises is concerned. But for this very reason, cartels cannot be a means of *preventing* crises. Measures such as scaling down productive capacity or reducing working hours are already an expression of crisis. When an entire branch of industry reduces its output (one of the 'remedial measures for overproduction'),[76] this presupposes not just a state-imposed protective tariff that eliminates foreign competition but also a massive sales crisis. The 'advantages of organisation' are, therefore, insufficient for preventing crisis; in fact, they presuppose it. In times of crisis, it is advantageous for large companies to *continue* their price war so as to rid themselves of troublesome competitors. And there are counteracting forces at work, here, as well.[77] Whatever happened to the tendencies toward repulsion to which Bernstein attributes such importance in the case of joint-stock companies? Bernstein passes over inter-capitalist competition by assuming that the 'advantages' are enjoyed collectively. This is a step toward later notions of a 'general cartel' or 'state monopoly capitalism' (2.2.6). But it misconstrues the character of society, which is more than the sum of individual interests.[78]

74. See Kautsky 1976, p. 80; Colletti 1974, p. 24.

75. Bernstein 1961, p. 89.

76. Bernstein 1961, p. 90.

77. Luxemburg notes correctly: 'What method do cartels employ to this end [holding back the fall of the rate of profit]? It is, essentially, that of keeping inactive a part of the accumulated capital... The remedy and the illness resemble each other... When the market outlets begin to shrink... then the forced partial idleness of capital will reach such dimensions that the remedy will itself be transformed into an illness... In the face of the increased difficulties of finding even a tiny place, each individual portion [of capital] will prefer to take its chances alone. At that time, the [employers'] organizations will burst like soap bubbles and give way to free competition' (Luxemburg 1971a, p. 64). 'And as soon as formation of capital were to fall into the hands of a few established big capitals,... the vital flame of production would be altogether extinguished. It would die out' (*MECW* 37, p. 258).

78. In Luxemburg's view (Luxemburg 1971a, p. 92), Bernstein's theory of capitalist adaptation was a 'theoretical generalization of the conception of the individual capitalist' (see 2.1.5, 2.3.2).

Joint-stock companies and cartels, monopolies and cooperatives:[79] according to Marx, all these cooperative forms of production *anticipate* socialisation.[80] Marx meant to show that the demand for the socialisation of the means of production is not utopian, but simply represents the implementation of a measure prepared by the 'old society' itself, although it cannot be implemented for as long as the barriers of the private capitalist mode of appropriation persist.[81] In making these points, Marx meant to encourage socialists to engage in political activity. Bernstein turns the political conclusion on its head by turning an anticipation of the future into a fully realised fact. In his work, actual political transformation is replaced by theoretical transformation. In Bernstein's considerations, class antagonism, which rests on property relations, is simply elided – and with it, the capitalist character of 'society'. Notwithstanding his critique of Hegelianism,[82] he thereby becomes a Hegelian himself: he blurs the boundaries between theory and reality, turning a theoretical possibility into a reality by abstracting from the problems associated with it.[83] This resembles the method for which Marx criticised the Young Hegelians, although in Bernstein's case, the method is rooted not in philosophy, but in a poorly developed economic theory. Marx's economic theory examines capitalism's 'natural laws of … movement',[84] the logic of its overall process.

In order to verify whether his observations really reflected something new and different, Bernstein would have had to choose a longer time frame. He ignores the degree of abstraction proper to Marx's theory, a theory that is all too easy to falsify when one misunderstands it as describing surface appearances.

To summarise: some of Bernstein's observations question the accuracy of the expectations formulated in the Erfurt Programme. There, Marxian propositions were already misunderstood as operating on the level of description and prediction. Bernstein's attempt

---

79. *MECW* 37, p. 438.

80. 'The capital, which in itself rests on a social mode of production and presupposes a social concentration of means of production and labour-power, is here directly endowed with the form of social capital (capital of directly associated individuals) … This is the abolition of the capitalist mode of production within the capitalist mode of production itself' (*MECW* 37, p. 432 f.; see *MECW* 35, p. 622).

81. 'No social order is ever destroyed before all the productive forces for which it is sufficient have been developed, and new superior relations of production never replace older ones before the material conditions for their existence have matured within the framework of the old society. Mankind thus inevitably sets itself only such tasks as it is able to solve, since closer examination will always show that the problem itself arises only when the material conditions for its solution are already present or at least in the course of formation' (*MECW* 29, p. 263; see *MECW* 6, p. 211). From this, Marx concluded, at the time: 'The capitalist stock companies, as much as the co-operative factories, should be considered as transitional forms from the capitalist mode of production to the associated one' (*MECW* 37, p. 438). Capitalism as a social relation is not 'a thing given direct from all eternity' (*MECW* 5, p. 39).

82. Bernstein 1961, pp. 47 ff.

83. Party disagreements have become less venomous, he writes (Bernstein 1961, p. 141). And democracy is defined – this is pure Hegelianism – as the 'suppression of class government' (p. 143 f.). But the definition is accurate in principle only.

84. *MECW* 35, p. 10.

to refute them historically or limit the scope of their applicability shows that he misunderstood their internal structure. By surrendering their analytic core, he ultimately does away with them altogether.[85] What are the consequences of this erroneous reading?

Bernstein wanted to adjust theory to practice. In doing so, he transformed practice: those elements of theory that transcended the immediate present having disappeared, he began calling more emphatically for tactics whose relevance had, until then, been limited, such as cooperatives or parliamentary work. Thus politics loses the corrective of theory, and retains only the function of pragmatically solving day-to-day problems. *This* social-democratic politics has lost the reflexive moment of Marxian theory.[86] The development had immediate consequences for Social-Democratic policy, and less immediate ones for the way Marx was understood. Within politics, there emerged the risk of a loss of standards by which to determine the way forward when new practical issues arise.[87] How ought the workers' party to position itself *vis-à-vis* small businessmen and peasants, *vis-à-vis* cartels, the state or colonialism? Revisionism turned everything that benefited the working population in the short term into a Social-Democratic position of principle, and it was able to do so successfully, since no reliable corrective existed.[88] This was why Social Democrats went on to speak out *in favour* of colonialism, expected cartels and protective tariffs to produce positive effects, and took an increasingly affirmative view of the monarchist state, which seemed favourably disposed towards them. Not only did they tolerate the social-Darwinist thinking evident in the military clubs of the period, but they in fact adopted it. Given this approach, it was quite clear that Social Democracy would side with the monarchist state in the case of war – 4 August 1914 came as no great surprise.[89]

---

85. 'Whether the Marxist theory of value is correct or not is quite immaterial to the proof of surplus labour' (Bernstein 1961, p. 35). 'The theory of value gives a norm for the justice or injustice of the partition of the product of labour just as little as does the atomic theory for the beauty or ugliness of a piece of sculpture' (p. 39). In fact, values differ from prices in that there exists no 'measure' that could be applied to them (p. 35). They can, however, be calculated. Price movements can only be explained consistently by assuming the existence of value, which functions as a kind of centre of gravity (Shaikh 1977; 1996, pp. 78 ff.). Marx engaged in value calculations as a matter of course (see 2.1.5, 2.1.6, 2.3.2).

86. 'This forgetting of the great, the principal considerations for the momentary interests of the day, this struggling and striving for the success of the moment regardless of later consequences, this sacrifice of the future of the movement for its present, may be "honestly" meant, but it is and remains opportunism, and "honest" opportunism is perhaps the most dangerous of all!' (Engels, *MECW* 27, p. 227).

87. The policies of the Kaiser also vacillated considerably (see Rosenberg 1955).

88. Revisionism later 'triumphed across the board' (Carlo Schmidt, in Bernstein 1976, p. 13; Meyer 1977, Miller 1983, Lehnert 1983, Freyberg 1989, Lösche 1992).

89. 'Germany's national capitalism has to mature fully before socialism can grow and wax in strength. As a socialist, I want to see Germany take not third or second, but first place' (Calwer's 1907 'Kolonialpolitik und Sozialdemokratie', quoted in Hofmann 1979, p. 180 f.; see Bernstein 1961, p. 175 f.; Fetscher 1973a, pp. 546 ff., 657 ff.). Michels 1978 attempted to derive from the Party's affirmative attitude toward the state a 'law' of oligarchisation (see Sternhell 1986). One may interpret such 'national socialism' (Naumann 1964, p. 218; see also Naumann 1905) as a precursor of National

The failure to distinguish between what benefited the German working class in the short term, from a pragmatic point of view, and the need to get a thorough theoretical grasp of the situation, from a distanced, scientific point of view, led to revisionism adopting *pro*-capitalist positions. Marxism had required a struggle against capital and the 'class state', since its theory postulated that no short-term improvement in the condition of the working classes can lead to significant long-term improvements for as long as bourgeois society continues to exist. Revisionism surrendered both. Politics always has a symbolic dimension – but how far will a symbol get us, when it lacks a material base? How to maintain the plausibility of the Party's programmatic claim that it was fending for the interests of the *déclassé* sections of the population? After all, setbacks and sacrifices were still the order of the day in the everyday life of the working class. Once Marx's material justification for Social-Democratic practice had been shelved, there remained a 'justification deficit'. Bernstein improvised an economic theory that attributed much greater importance to mental and moral factors.[90] Since, in his view, the economic sphere had become less susceptible to crises, while the possibilities for mastering crises by political means had improved, there seemed to have occurred an overall extension of the scope of what was politically possible.[91] It was now a question of using the state to master economic problems, ethics to formulate theoretical answers to new issues and parliament to try to develop political influence. *This* was the process that was now called 'socialism',[92] in a radical redefinition of a symbol of community long cherished by the *déclassé* sections of the population. Ethics was applied to social theory to the extent that a misinterpreted 'natural necessity' was rejected. In this way, Bernstein turned to democracy[93] and liberalism.[94] But this amounted to grossly overestimating the possibilities for democracy in imperial Germany. Social Democracy condemned itself to insignificance, at least for the time being. The theoretical primacy of politics led ultimately to Social-Democratic

---

Socialism proper (Dahrendorf 1967b, Sternhell 1986, Lauermann 1998). This hypothesis is to be distinguished from the absurd postulation of a 'causal nexus' (Ernst Nolte). The 1920 agreement between Ebert and Noske, which Sebastian Haffner characterised as having sealed the fate of the Weimar Republic, was an extension of this tendency.

90. Bernstein, who knew England well, was consulted by Max Weber about the 'Protestant ethic' (Lenk 1986, p. 220). Bernstein and Weber share a theoretical tendency to account for phenomena in mental terms (2.4.6). It may be noted in passing that Norbert Elias inquired into court society as a degenerating form that postponed its decline by means of symbolism. 'Thus one needs to explore the objective reality that lies beyond symbols before one can judge whether that reality's symbolic representation is appropriate or ideological' (Baumgart 1991, p. 150).

91. Bernstein 1961, p. 14 f.

92. Bernstein 1961, pp. 200 ff.; Habermas 1990a, pp. 213 ff.

93. Bernstein 1961, pp. 142 ff.

94. Bernstein 1961, pp. 148 ff. According to Laclau 1996, 'Socialism' is an 'empty signifier' only when it is deliberately emptied of all theoretical content. 'There is actually no real liberal thought which does not also belong to the elements of the ideas of socialism' (Bernstein 1961, p. 151). Thus socialism is rendered superfluous as a political current in its own right. Habermas followed in Bernstein's footsteps by fleshing out critical theory's implicit liberalism (Habermas 1990a, p. 228).

statism. On the road from Lassalle to Bernstein and Lenin (2.2.3), Marx was *bypassed*.[95] This reconfiguration of the foundations of theory had consequences that we will encounter again: the abandonment of Marxian theories and the proclamation of a new era in Lenin (2.2.6), technicist interpretations of Marx (2.4.5), the dismissal of a conveniently reconfigured dialectic and the counter-movement provoked by this dismissal (2.5.7).

2.1.3 *Neo-Kantianism: a fortunate coincidence*

As far as providing socialism with an ethical 'foundation' was concerned, revisionism benefited from a fortunate coincidence: academic ethical theory had increasingly discovered its interest in socialism. There was nothing objectionable in this; what is questionable, however, is the way ethics was *opposed* to Marx. Friedrich Albert Lange had already directed philosophy's attention to the 'worker question'; tellingly, he did so midway between the founding of Lassalle's and that of Bebel's workers' party (1863 and 1869, respectively).[96] Other neo-Kantians, Hermann Cohen in particular, began to engage with socialism. Many reached the surprising conclusion that there was a direct trajectory leading from Kant to socialism: 'Apply Kant's words practically, and you are socialists; give them an economic foundation, and you have socialism'.[97] Considering the reservations against socialism and the sense of professional distinction that were widespread within the academic élite of the period, this is a remarkably open-minded statement. Such open-mindedness was not unusual among neo-Kantians: Kurt Eisner, Paul Natorp, Karl Vorländer, and Max Adler expressed similar views. Whether these authors were led from Kant to socialism via materialism (Lange), epistemology (Max Adler), ethics (Cohen, Staudinger) or the philosophy of history (Conrad Schmidt) is a secondary issue. What matters is that significant sections of the educated middle class were prepared to cooperate peacefully with workers.[98] Thus Natorp, who was based in Marburg, wrote:

---

95. 'The state becomes the lever by which to institute socialism' (Renner 1918, p. 12). Fischer 1992, pp. 168 ff. equates 'socialism' with 'statism' – and rightly so, at least to the extent that one is talking about the Social Democrats of the time and the actually-existing socialism of later years. Incidentally, the authors of the draft of the Erfurt Programme distanced themselves from 'so-called state socialism' (*MECW* 27, pp. 226 f.). Bernstein published Lassalle's works (Lassalle 1892). One cannot 'place the blame on Marx and Engels, who were two of the most ardent critics of Lassalleanism and social democratic statism' (Schneider 1992, p. 161; see 2.2.6).

96. Lange 1865. Lange influenced Bernstein, via the work of Karl Höchberg (*MECW* 45, pp. 394 ff.). Both in his ethics and in his politics, Lassalle tended to take Fichte as his starting point (see 2.5.2, 3.1.5). On political Fichteanism, see Henning 1999.

97. Poggi 1904, Vorländer 1926, p. 226; Holzey 1994, p. 237. 'The idea of the realisation of humanity's end becomes ... the idea of socialism' (Cohen 1907, p. 320).

98. The bourgeoisie does not constitute an erratic bloc: members of the academic élite may come from the property-owning bourgeoisie (Simmel, Horkheimer) but they do not automatically belong to it *qua* members of the administrative élite, so that only very proximate conclusions can be drawn from their bourgeois background (Bourdieu 1984, Kocka 1988, Gall 1991, Hartmann 2002). Extreme bureaucratisation and the fact that systemic transformations tend, by and large, to acccommodate existing élites made socialism attractive to intellectuals.

> The goal I see before me is that of giving the inevitable class struggle a peaceful form by promoting thorough education among the mass of the people... This requires an effort to approach the organised working class and establish a level-headed dialogue based on scholarship and education.[99]

From Marx's perspective, such dialogue is by no means undesirable. Even the prospect of revolution in 1848 had not stopped him from viewing a bourgeois revolution, and hence liberalism, as necessary conditions for communism. Nor did Marx ever oppose such an alliance policy in later years. He welcomed the small steps to be achieved in this way as educating and empowering workers ('reality must itself strive towards thought').[100] Meanwhile, in the other camp, A.F. Lange felt it was important to create spaces for workers to express themselves freely, without attempting to refute their worldview or influence them in any other way.[101] Maintaining this was quite permissible in systematic terms: Kant had posited that the human world is irreducibly biperspectival. While natural processes can be interpreted from the point of view of the natural sciences, without recourse to higher powers, it remains the case that everyone needs to engage with the question of ends and make moral decisions. Kant's position is not an ontological 'dualism', but a methodological perspectivism that involves the epistemological decision to put ultimate, unanswerable questions last. Kant does not distinguish between worlds, but between perspectives. Far from being the result of an insufficiently thorough reflection, as Hegel objected, this is, in fact, a *comprehensive* description of the basic human situation (4.2.1). Karl Vorländer recognised the advantages of Kant's clear-cut methodological distinction: Kant's ethics 'do not preclude... a strictly causal conception of history. On the contrary, it is precisely because Kant distinguishes methodologically between the ideal and the real that he was able to combine an idealist pure ethics with an essentially realist philosophy of history and society'.[102]

Before ethics is applied, one needs a clear understanding of to what exactly one is applying it. Ethics cannot itself produce the conditions of its application. Every ethical judgement requires a prior *material* definition of its object. It is, therefore, not possible to play Kant out against Marx; their arguments operate on different levels. Thus Cohen had no difficulty describing Kant as 'the true and genuine founder of German socialism',[103] while simultaneously confessing that 'in soc. dem., I still prefer to follow the classics

---

99. Natorp said this before his university department in 1894 – quoted in Holzey 1994, p. 14.

100. *MECW* 3, p. 183. Marx's warning that premature socialisation merely generalises scarcity (*MECW* 5, p. 49) is well known. 'In the same measure, however, as the popular understanding increases regarding the untenableness of the existing order and the necessity of its radical change, the power of resistance decreases on the part of the ruling classes... This cross effect is evident; hence, everything that promotes it must be welcome' (Bebel 1971, p. 253). Reforms of the educational system are, therefore, always highly political affairs.

101. 'The workers ought to attend to the affairs of their social estate themselves' (Lange, quoted in Holzey 1994, p. 125).

102. Vorländer 1926, p. 16; see also Holzey 1994, p. 86; Fetscher 1973a, pp. 244 ff.

103. Cohen 1974, p. 112; also quoted in Sandkühler 1974, p. 70; see Holzey 1994, pp. 26, 147 f.

rather than any variant of revisionism'.[104] In systematic terms, there is not much to be learned from Kant's philosophy about whether or not Marx's theories are justified. Those theories have to stand on their own footing. Until now, only Austro-Marxism's short spring was able to render this constellation fruitful.[105] The interests of otherwise independent groups converged. Different backgrounds might have led to political coalitions, rather than stoking conflict.

What was it that seemed to German Social Democracy to argue *against* such an ethics? Perhaps aftereffects of Lassalle's theory of the 'one reactionary mass'[106] were to blame for the German Social Democrats' refusal to reach 'concrete compromises with bourgeois parties'. Later (as in 1914 and 1959), this meant that cooperation was conceivable only as a break with past principles (principles that had not, however, been derived from Marx). The theoretical conflict between ethics and the economy only arises when the two perspectives are brought too close together theoretically. Bernstein – neither an economist nor a philosopher – was the first to believe that Kant could be used to refute Marx.[107] Bernstein believed Kant's ethics could *replace* socialism's scientific foundation, which he believed had been falsified.[108] This attack on socialism's theoretical substance provoked socialists to take a regrettably hostile stance toward Bernstein's political views, which were simply the views of a liberal and a democrat.

Socialists engaged in a stubborn defence of what Bernstein had been right to criticise: the naturalised evolutionary concepts of the Erfurt Programme. Later, and for all their mutual antagonism, Kautsky and Luxemburg would agree on one point: if capitalism was not doomed by 'natural necessity', then the socialist project was at risk – *therefore* capitalism had to be doomed. With the development of this fundamentalist 'party science', orthodoxy took shape.[109]

---

104. A letter quoted in Holzey 1994, p. 12.

105. See, for instance, Adler 1928. See also Sandkühler 1970, Bottomore 1978, Leser 1985, Pfabigam 1982, and Mozetič 1987.

106. Abendroth 1969, p. 36; see *MECW* 49, pp. 261 ff.

107. 'Kant against Cant' in Bernstein 1961, pp. 200 ff.

108. Thus Alfred Schmidt's and Iring Fetscher's synoptic account of the matter (in Holzey 1994, pp. 39, 124).

109. The 'law of collapse', a bugbear invented by Bernstein, informed a variety of political strategies, as did its negation (Kautsky 1976, Groh 1973, Kurz 1994a; see 2.1.5). 'Bernstein began his revision of Social Democracy by abandoning the theory of capitalist breakdown. The latter, however, is the cornerstone of scientific socialism, and the with the removal of this cornerstone, Bernstein must also reject the whole socialist doctrine.... But the class struggle of the proletariat cannot be carried on without a definite final aim' (Luxemburg 1971a, p. 123 f.). Neither East-German philosophy nor even Sandkühler were able to extricate themselves from this naturalist apology: ethical socialism was accused of 'class betrayal' (1974, pp. v, xxiii; on East-German philosophy, see Wrona 1979, Sass 1980, Kapferer 1990, Wilharm 1990, Eichler 1996 and Rauh 2001). 'But, that we are ceaselessly approaching the beginning of the end, the period of the final crises of capitalism, follows precisely from the same phenomena which provisionally condition the absence of crises' (Luxemburg 1971a, p. 69). In Luxemburg's case, this conviction rested on a theory of underconsumption (2.1.5).

2.1.4 *Orthodoxy*

Darwin's theory leads to socialism.[110]

In today's party democracies, political parties have little use for theory. They need to make concrete decisions that cannot be deduced from any ready-made theory. They tend, rather, to require a specialist knowledge of certain political fields, in addition to a practical knowledge of how to turn the rules of the political game to their advantage.[111] Within party programmes and propaganda, theory serves to win new members or voters; it needs, therefore, to be as simple, plausible and punchy as possible. In the case of the Social Democracy of the 1890s, it was a different matter, for a variety of reasons. Science had played a major role in the Party's history, and so the Party continued to aspire to a practice that could be justified in terms of scientific insights.[112] In addition to this, the years of illegality had left an urgent need for internal debate.

Third and last, the precondition of today's lack of need for theory was not yet fulfilled: the context in which Social Democracy operated was not that of a party democracy, but that of a monarchy with a constitutional veneer. It was necessary to engage with the basic question of whether or not one wanted to help maintain this state form. The dilemma was already formulated by Thomas More: ought one to participate in what is bad, for the sake of small improvements and at the cost of being corrupted, or ought one to opt for a more consistent but palpably inefficient stance of total refusal?[113] As a political party, Social Democracy had placed itself on the terrain of legitimacy, like it or not, and in doing so, it had effected a retroactive legitimation of this terrain. The Party had nevertheless been declared illegal, and the ban had increased its popularity by revealing the resoluteness with which Social Democrats struggled to establish an alternative social order. This delicate issue became acutely topical in the uncertain situation that followed the lifting of the ban, when the Social Democrats were accepted back into legitimacy as a major party.

The Erfurt Programme attempted a neat separation of politics from economics.[114] The Party positioned itself on the terrain of legality for the time until its anticipated rise to power; once it had won its hoped-for electoral victory, it would itself decide what was

---

110. Virchow 1877.

111. Aside from their constitutional programmes, which dated rapidly (Uertz 1981), the German Christian Democrats (*Christlich Demokratische Union*, CDU) operated without a programme for decades. It was only when they became the opposition party that they set up commissions charged with penning party programmes again.

112. One might attribute this scientism to the spirit of the times. But socialist movements have tended to be the originators, rather than the victims, of scientism. The movements that formulated bourgeois interests in terms of natural science, such as Haeckel's Monist League (Hartmann 1993) or the Eucken League (Eucken 1925; see 2.4.5), were *countermovements*.

113. More 1516 opted for a 'third way' (Giddens 1994) and imagined an island where he could make everything anew. Kautsky (1888, 1947) was fascinated by this idea.

114. 'The working class ... cannot transfer ownership of the means of production to society in its entirety without first taking political power' (quoted in Abendroth 1969, p. 96).

right and what was not. It would effect 'social revolutions' without ever breaking the law.[115] Yet this tactic presupposed that such an electoral victory was possible in principle, that it would eventually be achieved, and that a parliamentary majority would constitute a power base sufficient for acting in the way envisaged. The Erfurt Programme attempted to offer a scientific justification for these presuppositions by showing that the proletariat was growing constantly, since the intermediate social classes were increasingly dissolving, and that capitalism would soon experience crises that would radicalise the proletariat; it also proposed constitutional changes ('*direct legislation by the people*'). These very presuppositions were now being challenged within the Party: the first two points were challenged by the revisionists, the third by the left of the Party. The left insisted that, under the general conditions of capitalism, every state was a 'class state' that would never allow for what was being proposed. Moreover, under the specific conditions of imperial Germany, parliament lacked the powers required for implementing the envisaged political measures (such as socialisation); it lacked even the powers required for implementing the requisite constitutional changes.[116]

The Party's programmatic spokesman, Karl Kautsky, had to respond to this situation. Thus theory became a political issue within the Party. Kautsky's commentary on the Erfurt Programme had stressed the necessity of a 'catechism of Social Democracy'.[117] To Kautsky, the greatest risk was that the coherence of the Marxist worldview might suffer. Accordingly, his main objection to Bernstein was that 'the question of the final goal of our politics . . . is intimately bound up with the question of organisation and propaganda'.[118] Bernstein was putting both at risk: in Kautsky's view, he had not understood the function of theory, which was necessary for obtaining the support of the proletariat, and which needed, therefore, to be as unified and coherent as possible. This is the reason why one classic analysis defines 'Kautskyanism' as an 'ideology of integration'.[119] Kautsky defended the 'truths' of the Erfurt Programme for reasons that are politically understandable. But he held that in matters of theory, it is not enough to merely present the results of research, without justification and discussion.[120] After all, Bernstein had, indeed, identified certain of its weak points, although he had benefited mainly from the Erfurt Programme's tendency to draw premature empiricist conclusions that were all

115. Kautsky 1907. While its goals were different, the NSDAP pursued a similar tactic until 1933.

116. Luxemburg 1971a, pp. 111 ff.; Engels, *MECW* 27, p. 226; see also Abendroth 1969, pp. 42 ff.; Freyberg 1975, pp. 30 ff.; Grebing 1970, pp. 108 ff.; Hofmann 1979, pp. 176 ff.; Kołakowski 1976, pp. 415 ff.; Vranicki 1983, pp. 294, 326; and 2.2.3.

117. Robert C. Tucker in Kautsky 1971, p. 2.

118. Kautsky 1976, p. 184.

119. Matthias 1957. Gramsci had something similar in mind, but in his case, differently from Kautsky, this was perceived as an advantage (Laclau 1985, p. 60; Anderson 1979; 2.5.4).

120. 'Whoever declares these aims [those of the Socialist Party] to be false should show in what respect the teachings of Socialist political economy are false' (p. 111). This is precisely what happened.

too easy to refute. These very conclusions were now reiterated by Kautsky. He corrected Bernstein on economic points of detail, but retained the expectation of imminent crises.[121] He does add that these crises are not sufficient for a painless transition to the socialism rendered possible by the existence of large firms, since the 'subjective factor' of proletarian struggle is also required. But he argues that the growing proletariat's will to struggle also develops by 'natural necessity'.[122] And so everything turns on this prognosis.

Kautsky succeeded one last time in qualifying Bernstein's objections and integrating them into the Party's worldview: the tactic proposed by Bernstein is plausible, he argues, during times of prosperity, but not during times of crisis.[123] But there remained the fundamental problem that German Social Democracy was beginning to face in matters of theory, and which had provoked revisionism in the first place: theory had become a core element of the Social-Democratic self-conception, but the goal of implementing a practice guided by theory was no longer being met. Kautsky acknowledged this state of affairs and blamed it on a lack of able theorists.[124] And yet he contributed to the situation himself by remodelling Marx's theory into a worldview.

Marx's economic theory had not intended to *establish* the practice of the workers' movement; it was not in a position to demonstrate the need for a social-democratic party. Instead, it wanted to provide the existing movement with indications on how it might conduct its struggle in the most effective manner.[125] His economic theory bears on politics only in a mediated way, and by no means does someone have to *believe* it for them to be able to engage in socialist politics. But this was precisely what Kautsky used it for. Since it was not suited to his purpose, he had to take it 'with a pinch of salt'.[126] Marxism's frequently noted character as a 'church' begins with Kautsky. Within orthodoxy, identity is established by reference to a text that is read literally – just as in 'scholasticism'.[127] It is not understanding Marx's analyses that matters, but whether one understands *oneself* to be a Marxist. To be sure, Marx's works allow for various applications – all the more so when their abstract character is acknowledged. How a given

121. Laclau 1985, p. 51.

122. Kołakowski 1976, p. 387 f., pointedly formulates Kautsky's rejection of the neo-Kantians: '[The neo-Kantians'] position was that Marx had shown that socialism was an objective necessity, and they held that awareness of this fact must be supplemented by the socialist norm of value. Kautsky contended that Marx had shown socialism to be an objective necessity, and that one factor in this necessary process was the proletariat's awareness and approval of that necessity: this awareness and approval were inevitable, and nothing more was required'. Practice was elided in both versions of the argument.

123. Kautsky 1976, p. 163.

124. Kautsky 1976, pp. 10, 33.

125. Rosenberg 1937, Fleischer 1970.

126. Kautsky 1976, p. 51.

127. Kautsky 1976, pp. 11, 33.

proposition is to be applied cannot be determined in advance; its application is never unambiguous.[128]

Pluralism, however, is something political parties often cannot permit themselves. This is all the more true when a party is constrained by outside pressure, perhaps even military pressure, to act in a unified way in order to survive. Lenin was Kautsky's legitimate heir, insofar as he made a virtue out of this necessity. He translated several works by Kautsky. When he later attacked him sharply,[129] what was at issue was interpretational sovereignty in a concrete situation, not the *principle* by which to interpret Marx.[130] The principle remained the same: Leninism also required Marxian theory and political practice to be 'reconciled' dogmatically, especially when the revolutionary surge began to ebb. This was done within theory, as in any other orthodoxy. Theory was expected to smooth over any contradictions between itself and practical reality. It attempted this by 'scientifically' predicting historical development, which, it was assumed, would ultimately confirm Marxism. Thus the Marxist philosophy of history was born: Kautsky interpreted Marxism as the 'materialist conception of history'.[131]

Marx's historical investigations were materialist to the extent that his analysis involved consideration of the degree to which the forces and relations of production had developed.[132] But by no means did it provide a *philosophy* of history that purported to say anything about the future course of history, on a level far removed from concrete analysis.[133] Marx explicitly *objected* to the 'all-purpose formula of a general historico-philosophical theory whose supreme virtue consists in being supra-historical'.[134] While it is true that the young Marx was unable to suppress, within his considerations on history, the occasional speculative aside,[135] it was precisely his insight into the inadequacy of such constructs that drove him to formulate critiques of Hegelian philosophy and political economy. Marx's early writings share with Kautsky's polemical writings the feature of

---

128. The laws of the economy merely provide the framework within which history plays out – thus the *Eighteenth Brumaire* (*MECW* 11) and *Capital* (*MECW* 35) do not contradict one another. Marx's historical analyses examine special circumstances, so they are ill-suited to being used as laws by which to analyse other phenomena, as attempted by Lenin 1917 with regard to the 'commune' and Thalheimer 1974 with regard to 'Bonapartism' (see Lohmann 1980, p. 261, on Schelling).

129. Lenin 1972a.

130. It was precisely because revolution became an article of faith, in Kautsky, that it was lost sight of: 'Our task is not to organize the revolution but to organize ourselves for the revolution; not *to make* the revolution but to take advantage of it' (quoted in Laclau and Mouffe 1985, p. 22). It was this, more than anything else, against which Lenin took a stand by emphasising self-activity (2.2.1).

131. Kautsky 1927, 1947.

132. Cohen 1978.

133. The statements from the 1857 'Preface' to 'A Contribution to the Critique of Political Economy' (*MECW* 29, pp. 261–5), later turned into dogmas, are heuristic-methodological instructions, written down 'not for publication but for self-clarification' (p. 261); they are not 'historical materialism' *qua* philosophy of history (2.6.6, Excursus).

134. *MECW* 24, p. 201; *MECW* pp. 18, 28.

135. *MECW* 3, pp. 167 f., 186 f., 296 f.

being political propaganda. This largely accounts for occasional exaggerations of the role to be played by those that these writings were meant to encourage.[136] However, Marx's intention was that of formulating a *call* to coordinated action by pointing out a historical option, whereas for Kautsky it was a matter of *preventing* overhasty action by positing a development that would occur anyhow and of necessity.

This could not but alter the character of theory: in Marx, theory is deliberately kept open to practice, whereas in Kautsky, it covers the past, the present and the future and is, therefore, self-contained. Marx aimed at critical reflection conducted in the midst of political processes and with the purpose of analysing and *correcting* those processes.[137] Kautsky aimed at a 'worldview' by which to *legitimate* the practice of Social Democracy, which had become problematic to the Party's members: a worldview according to which capitalism is bound, by natural necessity, to reach its downfall, whereas socialism is bound for victory. But this philosophy of history was itself ahistorical. With achievement of the ultimate goal considered certain, more thorough analysis of the situation and the fine-tuning of political strategy could be dispensed with.[138] Economics became economism, a dogmatisation of heuristic principles *qua* philosophy of history. In Kautsky, nature takes the place of an analysis of society and its contingent history. Kautsky derives ethics[139] and even democracy from social 'impulses'. Kautsky was a Darwinist before he became a Marxist, and he remained a Darwinist.[140]

This had been encouraged by none other than Engels.[141] He already viewed the 'materialistic treatment of history'[142] as an ideological buttress, justifiable in terms of a 'dialectics of nature'.[143] His popular breviaries indicated the path that humanity needed to follow during the 'ascent of man from the kingdom of necessity to the kingdom of freedom'.[144] Engels begins by stating that the 'compulsory laws of competition . . . work themselves out . . . as inexorable natural laws'.[145] This formulation still accords with Marx; it does

---

136. Fleischer 1993 considers this 'political rhetoric'. A proper understanding of Marx requires a hermeneutics of genre (2.2.3, 2.4.6, 2.6.6). The use of the present tense in vistas of the political future ('The expropriators are expropriated': *MECW* 35, p. 750) is reminiscent of stage directions. When it is interpreted one-dimensionally, as a prediction, the impression is created that what is at stake is a preordained process that only the initiated know about. Lenin – an admirer of Kautsky until 1914 – still numbered among those who laid claim, without further justification, to such special knowledge ('The Marxist doctrine is omnipotent because it is true': *LW* 19, p. 23).

137. *MECW* 4, p. 35 f.; *MECW* 5, p. 48 f.

138. Cf. Groh 1973, Fetscher 1973a, pp. 680 ff. and 99 ff. Critical theory affirms the philosophy of history to this day (Horkheimer 1993, Negt 1972, Behrens 1997, 2.6.3).

139. Kautsky 1906.

140. Kautsky 1880, Kautsky 1947, Kautsky 1921, pp. 21 ff.; Häupel 1993, p. 60. Löwith's substitution of history with nature (Löwith 1983a) overlooked the fact that Darwin, Marxism and the *völkisch* movement had already transposed history into nature (2.6.6).

141. Colletti 1971, p. 62.

142. *MECW* 24, p. 304; *MECW* 27, pp. 202 ff.

143. *MECW* 25.

144. *MECW* 24, p. 324.

145. *MECW* 24, p. 311 f.

not deny the 'anarchy of production'.[146] Engels is referring to economic, not to historical laws. They do not determine the course of history, but merely define the range of possibilities available to politics: the laws 'work, despite anarchy, in and through anarchy'.[147] The statement '[i]t is the Darwinian struggle of the individual for existence transferred from Nature to society with intensified violence'[148] merely describes the basic situation of capitalism.[149] Yet Engels's abolition of the rule of nature occurs by means of a fatalist, Spinozian 'acknowledgement of necessity': he believes scientific socialism's task is that of identifying independently existing developments and states of affairs, on the model of the natural sciences, which have transformed the destructive forces of nature into a boon. History becomes a component of natural history, whose course is preordained.[150]

Engels viewed the course of history as having been *predetermined* by the expansion of the proletariat[151] and the 'political and intellectual bankruptcy' of the bourgeoisie.[152] What was the 'dialectic' supposed to do for this historico-philosophical prophecy? Kautsky held that '[t]he method is what is decisive in Marxist socialism, not the results'.[153] Lukács still considered this orientation toward method the hallmark of 'orthodox Marxism',[154] although he simultaneously strove to 'return to Marx' and marginalised Engels.[155] In Marx, the dialectic functioned as a familiar model that could be used to describe a situation in which two contrary phenomena can be traced back to the same cause.[156] By contrast, Engels believed that it could be used to discover 'laws' – even in history. Differently from Marx, who limited himself, in his conception of dialectics, to clear-cut descriptions of social phenomena, the late Engels interpreted it as a doctrine concerning natural processes, and he considered history an aspect of nature: 'Nature is

---

146. *MECW* 24, p. 313.
147. *MECW* 24, p. 311.
148. *MECW* 24, p. 313.
149. Darwin encountered the notion of 'survival of the fittest' in Adam Smith: 'It was in the discussion of such social formations as language and morals, law and money, that in the eighteenth century the twin conceptions of evolution and the spontaneous formation of an order were a last clearly formulated, and provided the intellectual tools which Darwin and his contemporaries were able to apply to biological evolution' (Hayek 1973, p. 23).
150. 'Active social forces work exactly like natural forces: blindly, forcibly, destructively, so long as we do not understand, and reckon with, them. But, when once we understand them, when once we grasp their action, their direction, their effects, it depends only upon ourselves to subject them more and more to our own will, and, by means of them, to reach our own ends' (Engels, *MECW* 24, p. 319 f.). Yet when Marx stated that history 'is the true natural history of man' (*MECW* 3, p. 337), what he meant was that nature has little to teach us about socialised man (Callinicos 1995, pp. 82 ff.).
151. *MECW* 24, p. 320.
152. *MECW* 24, p. 322.
153. Kautsky 1976, p. 17.
154. Lukács 1971, pp. 1 ff.
155. Lukács, pp. 131 ff.
156. It is a method of presentation, not a law of thought or even of being (*MECW* 35, p. 19; Steinvorth 1977, Hunt 1993). Lenin assumed the legacy of Kautsky by adhering to naturalism in epistemology (Lenin 1972) and to the Hegelian dialectic in politics (Lenin 1961).

the proof of dialectics'; 'Nature works dialectically and not metaphysically'.[157] Kautsky is thus quite justified in appealing to the authority of Engels when he defines dialectics as follows: 'The driving force of all development is the struggle of opposites'.[158] Yet what is impossible to overlook, both in Kautsky and in Lukács, is their uncertainty as to what exactly this method is supposed to consist in. The formulas about the 'view of totality' and the 'relation to the whole'[159] are nothing but set phrases, so long as they are not implemented in the form of concrete analyses (see 2.5.4).

The quarrel between Kautsky and Bernstein turned on the question of which of the two had licence to interpret Engels as he saw fit. Yet despite all of his naturalising tendencies, the late Engels still viewed the revolution as inevitable (as '[t]he proletariat seizes political power'),[160] since he took the state, in its present form, to be 'the official representative of capitalist society'.[161] Thus the quarrel over who was Engels's legitimate successor could not break out until after the death of Engels in 1895. The subsequent history of the Social-Democratic Party was, by and large, uninfluenced by Marxian theory. To be sure, reference was still made to Marx, but this was usually done only for the purpose of presenting one's own arguments and strategies. The arguments employed usually followed the course set by Bernstein and Kautsky. For example, Kurt Schumacher presented a theoretical rehabilitation of the state that corresponded to the way in which Ebert had co-opted the state practically – or, perhaps, been co-opted by it.[162] Some party programmes, such as that of 1925, upheld the spirit of Erfurt and made reference to Marx, in addition to endorsing trade-union struggle.[163] But the post-1914 split in the workers' movement and the hostile policy of the communists meant that initial efforts to build an 'economic democracy' in Germany petered out quickly.[164] Once again, the Social Democrats were forced to form political alliances with liberal and nationalist forces. The Weimar Republic's institutional structure may have allowed for greater political leeway, but the Social Democracy of the period lacked both an electoral majority and a clearly defined model for action. Soon after the catastrophe of the Third Reich, Social Democracy began to adopt revisionist programmes. Let us therefore conclude our review of Social Democracy's theoretical history and sum up. We will go on to encounter a number of functional effects of the course set by Social Democracy later in this study.

The various positions evident in the Marxism of the Second International go back to a one-dimensional conception of society. Different ways of knowing are strung together and distinguished from one another in purely temporal terms, by reference to their 'pre-

157. *MECW* 24, p. 301.
158. Kautsky 1976, p. 23. Quoting Engels (*MECW* 26, p. 384), Kautsky also says 'that the world is not to be comprehended as a complex of readymade *things*, but as a complex of *processes*'.
159. Lukács 1971, p. 12 f.
160. *MECW* 24, p. 320.
161. *MECW* 24, p. 318.
162. Schumacher 1920.
163. Abendroth 1969.
164. Naphtali 1928.

condition', their 'movement' and their 'ultimate goal'. The naturalist Erfurt Programme was both incapable of ordering the various elements of Marxian theory and unable to use this theory to provide orientation to extra-scientific political practice. Thus Bernstein felt compelled to *reproach* Marx, and Kautsky believed himself capable of *reconciling* him with the facts, while Lenin thought of himself as the *executor* of Marx's theories. They all shared the belief that they were dealing with a 'knowledge' that predicts the course of history and constitutes an instrument for achieving political success. Strategies that consisted in using Kant to supplement and complement this objectivism, in the manner of the neo-Kantians, or in disrupting it by resorting to Hegel as an 'antidote', as later attempted by communist dissidents and unorthodox Western Marxists (see sections 2.5.4, 2.5.7), perpetuated the misconception associated with 'scientific socialism' *qua* self-contained system of propositions, a system developed by the late Engels and by Kautsky. When Marx became aware of this dogmatisation, he insisted he was not a Marxist.[165]

The process by which Marxism was stripped of its economic content and dogmatised set the course for later theoretical developments. Thus Bernstein became the founding father of postwar Social Democracy. He, not Lukács or Lenin,[166] was the father of Western Marxism, whose occasional rhetorical radicalism was usually based on *philosophical* considerations. Marx's critical theory[167] became a moral creed, one that now needed to be provided with 'normative foundations'. As for the discursive amalgamation of Marxism and the dialectic, it goes back to orthodoxy.[168] Where material analysis was neglected, the dialectic was especially quick to degenerate into a mere fetish; this was the case both in the East and the West (2.5.7). For want of more adequate concepts by which to explicate one's own theoretical foundations, the dialectic became a mere subterfuge.[169] Moreover, Marx's economics were misinterpreted as a philosophy of history (2.6.6) – usually as a technicist one (2.5.4). The legacy of this naturalisation was a faith in society's moral 'evolution' and in the unproblematic character of parliamentary democracy (3.1.5). It provoked a correction in the form of a stronger emphasis on 'ethics'. Thus it was somewhere between total determinism and total freedom that reflection went astray.[170]

---

165. Engels quoted Marx's statement '*je ne suis pas marxiste*' (*MECW* 27, p. 70).

166. Milner 1999, p. 31.

167. Bolte 1995.

168. Kautsky 1899, Rees 1998.

169. It should, however, be noted that Marx can be read and interpreted without consideration of issues related to the dialectic, issues that tended, in any case, to amount to diversionary manoeuvres (Anderson 1978; see 2.3.5, 2.5.7, 2.6.3). 'But such a perversion of words is merely a sophistical evasion for escaping from a difficult question' (Kant 1998, p. 351/A 257).

170. 'Critique of reductionism has apparently resulted in the notion of society as a totally open discursive field' (Stuart Hall, in Milner 1999, p. 53; see 4.3.2).

2.1.5 Key elements of Marxian theory I: the schemes of reproduction

This brings us to the end of our considerations on the development of post-Marxian thought within German Social Democracy. We have been able to concretise our preliminary concept of Marx's theory (1.3) *ex negativo*, by reference to an event that set the course for later theoretical developments, namely the split between Kautsky's reductive and naturalist reading of Marx and its excessively normative corollary in Bernstein – a split that was contrary to Marxian theory itself. This study's theoretical interludes on key elements of Marxian theory are intended to provide a more in-depth account of those elements, which are relevant to the issues discussed elsewhere, but cannot be fully discussed from the point of view of the history of ideas, and thus need to be presented separately. Two things are achieved by proceeding in this way. First, central components of Marx's work are presented in a new way, that is, with an eye to the history of their theoretical reception. Second, theoretical Marxism's deviations from Marxian theory, identified and discussed elsewhere, are made apparent once more, in a systematic way, and from the perspective of Marxian theory, in terms of *economics*.

How are the advantages of genuinely Marxian thought to be situated systematically? Within the context of modern philosophy, which operates in the Cartesian realms of nature and mind, the novelty of Marx's thought consists in its capacity to penetrate its object of inquiry, bourgeois society, both in factual and in conceptual terms.[171] To Marx, bourgeois society is the 'true focus and theatre of all history'.[172]

---

171. See Haltern 1985. Definitions of man have long vacillated between the concept of the animal and the concept of God; such vacillation is, in fact, still evident in twentieth-century philosophical anthropology. Modern society was simply passed over. Plessner 1928 still sought a 'concept' of man capable of uniting nature and mind, without ever mentioning society. Marx, to whom Plessner often refers (pp. 5, 10, 17, and so on) is read in naturalist terms (on Plessner's idealism, see Petrowizc 1992, pp. 49 ff.). Aristotle already reflected on man's character as a social being (*MECW* 28, 18), but the structures of the *polis* have changed fundamentally since antiquity.

172. *MECW* 5, p. 50. 'My inquiry led me to the conclusion that neither legal relations nor political forms could be comprehended whether by themselves or on the basis of a so-called general development of the human mind, but that on the contrary they originate in the material conditions of life, the totality of which Hegel, following the example of English and French thinkers of the eighteenth century, embraces within the term "civil society"; that the anatomy of this civil society, however, has to be sought in political economy' (*MECW* 29, p. 262). Althusser 1996, pp. 219 ff.; Althusser 1972, pp. 71 ff. and Brentel 1989 speak of a 'new object' of inquiry in Marx. This new object already announced itself in the 'three sources of Marxism' (as Lenin put it): French socialism analysed society mainly in political terms, while English political economy did so in economic terms and German philosophy with an eye to issues of principle. Kant's concept of autonomy generalised the 'principle' of bourgeois society as popularised by Rousseau, self-legislation, whereas Hegel provided this principle with institutional substance. Kant and Hegel effected a shift of emphasis vis-à-vis pre-bourgeois philosophy, but differed with regard to their definition of the liminal realms 'nature and mind': Kant distinguished between the two, whereas Hegel declared them to be 'identical' (2.5.2, 3.4.2, 4.2.2). This did not yield much insight into the new object of inquiry. Polanyi exposed the naturalism of classical political economy: 'As gradually the laws governing a market economy were apprehended, these laws were put under the authority of Nature herself. The law of diminishing returns was a law of plant physiology' (Polanyi 1944, p. 130). Marx criticised this

In describing his new object of inquiry, Marx resorted to expressions that were products of the old dualism – after all, this dualism is in no way 'suspended' by the new object.[173] Yet when Marx speaks of the 'spirit' or 'nature' of something, he does so with a denotative intent, since he is explicitly *not* dealing with 'Nature' or 'Spirit' as such.[174] He rejects both misconceived naturalisations of social relations and their opposite, the dissolution of political economy into a mere critique of categories.[175] Marx's allusions

---

naturalism, without falling back into an idealist account. German thought had difficulties grasping the new object of inquiry – perhaps because German society was a political 'latecomer' compared to other Western democracies (Plessner 1935). Operating with a dichotomy of *nature and mind*, German thought often failed to grasp the new object of inquiry. To this day, every deviation from the model of *mind* risks being branded 'naturalist' or 'objectivist' by those subscribing to the paradigm of mind, even before it has been properly engaged with, while the opposite camp unthinkingly categorises deviations from the nature paradigm as 'moralist' or 'utopian' and assumes that nothing more needs to be said about them. Yet the object of inquiry 'bourgeois society' and its centrepiece 'capitalism' refuse to fit into this binary scheme. Thus Marxophobia threatens to make theory lose hold of its object (on this, see 2.4.1).

173. Nature and mind are realms that need to be distinguished from one another, and no epistemological theory or dialectic can make it otherwise. There is, of course, a point of view from which they appear as 'one', namely the speculative or mystico-theological point of view. It represents a feat of abstract thinking that is hardly to be outdone (see the articles '*Einheit*' [unity] and '*Übergegensätzlichkeit*' [supercontrariety] in the *Historisches Wörterbuch der Philosophie*). Yet this perspective does not allow for the formulation of any substantive proposition about either of the two realms. The laws of logic literally dissolve into 'Nothing', as does every sphere of reference (see the article '*Nichts*' [Nothing] therein; see also 2.5.2).

174. 'Nothing is more characteristic of the spirit of capital [!] than the history of the English Factory Acts from 1833 to 1864' (*MECW* 35, p. 284; see Derrida 1994, p. 125 f.). 'In proportion as payments are concentrated at one spot, special institutions and methods are developed for their liquidation' (*MECW* 35, p. 148). 'So far therefore as labour is a creator of use value, is useful labour, it is a necessary condition, independent of all forms of society, for the existence of the human race; it is an eternal nature-imposed necessity, without which there can be no material exchanges between man and Nature, and therefore no life' (*MECW* 35, p. 53). '*Nature* is just as much the source of use values [...] as labor, which itself is only the manifestation of a force of nature, human labour power' (*MECW* 24, p. 81).

175. Marx did away with the naturalist 'illusion [...] that capitalist relations are the natural relations of every mode of production' (*MECW* 37, p. 862). 'Nature no more produces money than it does bankers or a rate of exchange' (*MECW* 29, p. 387; see Schmidt 1960, Schmied-Kowarzik 1984 and Dahmer 1994, who hardly mention the economy, however). Marx countered misconceived mentalisations (as today in Backhaus 1997, Bensch 1997, ISF 1999; see 2.3.5) by noting that he who takes 'these relations for principles, categories, abstract thoughts, has merely to put into *order* these thoughts, which are to be found alphabetically arranged at the end of every treatise on political economy. The economists' material is the active, energetic life of man; M. Proudhon's material is the dogmas of the economists' (*MECW* 6, p. 162). 'The *human character* of nature and of the nature created by history [!] – man's products – appears [in Hegel, wrongly] in the form that they are *products* of abstract mind and as such, therefore, phases of *mind – thought-entities*' (*MECW* 3, p. 332). Grasping an object categorically (and, by extension, epistemologically) is something that can only be done once the object has been grasped factually; the opposite course is not viable. Where German Marxism becomes an epistemological critique, it confuses cause and effect (Habermas 1971b, Sohn-Rethel 1977, Behrens 1993; see also Kallscheuer 1986).

always refer ultimately to bourgeois society, which is merely *limited* by 'nature' (such as by the productivity of the soil) and 'spirit'.[176]

Given the wealth and precision of determinations that Marx provided for his new object of inquiry, he can in no way be accused of 'conceptual paucity', confusion or imprecision.[177] Yet the mode of being proper to his object was, nonetheless, difficult to grasp. This emerges from the difficulties encountered by the German reception of Marx as discussed above: Kautsky related Marx's determinations of society to 'nature', and Bernstein's reaction to this consisted in ethicisation. *Both* factions miss the specific character of the Marxian object of inquiry by making it conform to the classic philosophical modes of being, nature and mind. Both factions were paradigmatic for the later reception of Marx. For example, 'naturalisation' is closely related to the theory of crisis. To remain plausible, the Erfurt Programme needed there to be *further* crises. It based its position not only on the *Manifesto of the Communist Party*, but also on the 'historical' passages in the first volume of *Capital*, where the tendencies toward social polarisation and economic concentration are invoked as the triggers (but not necessarily as the causes) of a possible political revolution. True, Marx used the expression 'law of Nature', but he did not do so in order to give in to naturalist fatalism; rather, he was concerned to guide political work along its proper path.[178]

There is an important passage in Marx that discusses the 'nature' of capitalist production and its susceptibility to crises: the reproduction schemes.[179] When Bernstein

---

176. 'Our desires and pleasures spring from society; we measure them, therefore, by society and not by the objects which serve for their satisfaction. Because they are of a social nature [sic!], they are of a relative nature' (*MECW* 9, p. 216; see *MECW* 21, pp. 56 ff.). By the same token, 'there enters into the determination of the value of labour-power a historical and moral element' (*MECW* 35, p. 181). This is the same as what is meant by the notion – somewhat overused today – of 'embeddedness' (as used by Polanyi).

177. Following Althusser, some allege that Marx 'did not fully grasp the status of his own theory' (Heinrich 2001, p. 46; Schmidt in Euchner 1972, pp. 30 ff.; Lohmann 1980, p. 201; Reichelt 2002). This was preceded by the fashion of presenting whatever had not been properly understood as 'dialectical' (Reichelt 1970). Understanding needs to be demonstrated by reference to the thing itself, not by reference to 'method'. This German confusion results from the problems discussed above (see 2.3.5).

178. 'But capitalist production begets, with the inexorability of a law of Nature, its own negation' (*MECW* 35, p. 751). It should be noted that this 'negation' is already present: in the form of the proletariat and in that of the socialisation of production under capital. By no means does this justify the conclusion that the attempt to bring about a political revolution must 'necessarily' be successful. Marx wanted to shed light on the working class, which was struggling to liberate itself (Helmut Fleischer). In doing so, he did not by any means elide subjective factors: 'The creation of a normal working-day is, therefore, the product of a protracted civil war, more or less dissembled, between the capitalist class and the working-class' (*MECW* 35, p. 303). But he also pointed out the limits of volition: 'The *will* of the capitalist is certainly to take as much as possible. What we have to do is not to talk about his *will*, but to enquire into his *power*, the *limits of that power*, and the *character of those limits*' (*MECW* 20, p. 105; see section 2.4.6).

179. *MECW* 35, pp. 565 ff.; *MECW* 36, pp. 390 ff., 488 ff.; *MECW* 41, pp. 484 ff.; *MECW* 28, pp. 329 ff.

began the revisionism debate, the reproduction schemes had already become the object of a wide-ranging controversy among Marxists. The controversy was prompted by the question of how capitalism would develop in Russia, where there was virtually no effective demand, due to the preponderance of agriculture; a question discussed in connection with this was that of the capitalist economy's overall prospects for survival.[180] The controversy turned mostly on the implications of Marx's model of dynamic equilibrium. The debate allows for a paradigmatic exposition of both naturalisation and its countertendency, ethicisation. The ontologisation of a model, its unmediated projection into reality, is always quick to produce misunderstandings. Such an ontologisation was evident on *both* sides of the debate on the interpretation of the reproduction schemes; the naturalist disproportionalists were as guilty of this as the harmonists, who believed in the need for a revisionist ethicisation of socialist theory. We need to consider this debate briefly.

A *pre*-Marxian argument commonly invoked to explain periodic economic crises is that formulated in the theory of underconsumption: crises are caused by a chronic lack of demand. Malthus deduced from this the necessity of a class that consumes without being productive; Luxemburg used underconsumption to account for imperialism, and even the twentieth century's Keynesian and welfare-state strategies for stimulating demand were indebted to this notion.[181] By contrast, Marx held that the phenomenon of an unsaleable stock of commodities is not so much a *cause* of crisis as an aspect of capitalism's normal way of functioning; in the case of a crisis, it becomes a symptom. In order to provide evidence for this position, Marx began by demonstrating, in his model of 'simple reproduction', that a closed, static economy principally allows for the sale of all commodities. This model is largely a fiction. It is not meant to describe a historical period of static reproduction; its purpose is to illustrate the fundamentally self-contained nature of reproduction using the simplest possible model. It was on this basis that Marx then demonstrated the possibility of permanent capitalist *growth*. In order to illustrate the basic character of the permanent circuit of reproduction whose possibility he intends to demonstrate, Marx abstracted from capitalism's long-term tendencies.[182] Marx divides

180. In reaction to the Russian works Tugan-Baranovsky 1894 and Bulgakov 1897, the participants in the debate argued over dynamic accumulation's long-term development. Important contributions to the debate include Lenin 1960, Hilferding 1981, Luxemburg 1951, Bauer 1913, Bukharin 1972 and Grossmann 1929. Even Pollock needs to be read with this background in mind (see 2.6.2). The debate has been documented in Rosdolsky 1969, pp. 524 ff. (see also pp. 63 ff., 279 ff.); Gustafsson 1972; Kühne 1976, pp. 192–286; Shaikh 1978 and 1988; Heinrich 1988; Howard 1989, pp. 106 ff., 165 ff., 269 ff.; and Mandel 1992, pp. 27 ff.

181. Bleaney 1976.

182. The rates of surplus value (s/v), of the organic composition of capital (c/v) and of profit (s/c+v) are treated as constant in both departments of production (differently from the discussion of the rate of profit, where these values are decisive). Moreover, the value of money is assumed to be stable (thus 'monetary crises' are excluded; they are discussed in the third volume; see 2.3.5), and it is also assumed that values are sold at their prices (on the so-called 'transformation

society into workers and capitalists only; within the economy, he distinguishes two departments: one produces means of production (I), the other means of consumption (II). If there is to be no crisis-threatening surplus or lack of goods and money, then the yearly product must be fully distributed between these four parties, and it needs to be distributed in such a way as to ensure that workers receive their wages while capitalists obtain consumable surplus value. The question that arises is whether such a form of reproduction, in which all commodities are sold, can persist in the long term, given an anarchic economy, or one that operates without any reliable knowledge of the future. After all, the producers are working on the basis of mere *estimates* of future demand. Marx's answer is yes – as long as certain conditions are fulfilled. The total value of the wages earned by workers and the surplus value consumed by capitalists within the industries producing means of production (Department I) needs to correspond to the total value required for means of production in industries producing means of consumption (Department II), and such a balanced exchange must in fact occur between the two departments.[183] This circuit can be represented as follows:[184]

problem', see 2.3.2). Credit-based financing is ignored, and with it the banking sector. The reason Marx leaves it aside is that he does not wish to explain reproduction on the basis of the financial sector, but rather the financial sector on the basis of reproduction. Banks operate on the basis of reproduction, not vice versa (Foley 1986a). The conditions assumed by Marx amount to an entrepreneur's paradise, yet one can already discern in them the possibility of serious crises. The purpose of Marx's abstract model is precisely to identify the source of such crises.

183. Such realisation of invested capital presupposes that the exchange values produced are use values to their buyers. In quantifying values, Marx assumed (in this context) that commodities are sold at their values. Some German Marxists prolong the debate on positivism by insisting that value cannot be quantified. More than anything else, this seems to be the result of a sort of vitalist dislike for figures. The controversial passages in the first chapter of *Capital* (*MECW* 35, pp. 45–93), which have often been considered in isolation and hence mystified (Reichelt 1970, 1996, 2002; Backhaus 1997; Haug 1978; Wolf 1985), are important for the entire work (*MECW* 35–37) and can only be fully understood on such a basis.

184. As always, the meaning of the variables is the following: C = commodity, M = money, c = the part of total capital represented by constant capital (outlays for means of production, including fixed capital, such as machines, and circulating capital, such as raw materials), v = the part of total capital expended for variable capital or wages, s = the surplus value obtained (the difference between the newly created value of the product and its price of production, the expenses for materials, machines and labour-power). The exchange of commodities for money (C–M) intersects with the opposite exchange, that of money for commodities (M–C) (*MECW* 29, pp. 323 ff.; *MECW* 36, pp. 31 ff.; here, I am following Shaikh 1984, p. 54). Marx defines production (P) as P... C' – M' – C'... P (*MECW* 36, p. 70). Production yields surplus value (M' minus M; turnover minus costs for renewed production), which the capitalist uses to maintain himself, and begins again as before. Surplus value is generated by the input factor labour-power, for labour-power is not sold at the value it produces, but at its own value, which corresponds to the amount of commodities labour-power requires to reproduce itself (see 2.3.1).

Table 1: Simple Reproduction

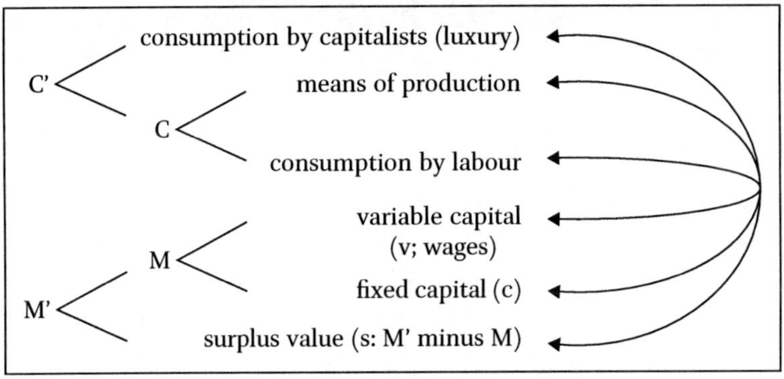

The formula for simple reproduction's condition of equilibrium is: vI + sI = cII (usually written as I (v+s) = II c). This is easy to understand if we consider the example of simple reproduction provided by Marx:[185]

> Department I (industry producing means of production):
> 4,000 cI + 1,000 vI + 1,000 sI = 6,000
>
> Department II (industry producing means of consumption):
> 2,000 cII + 500 vII + 500 sII = 3,000

500 vII, 500 sII and 4,000 cI are exchanged for the value produced in their *own* industry. Workers and capitals associated with the industry producing means of consumption use their income to purchase means of consumption, while the capitalists within Department I purchase means of production from their own industry. This leaves twice 2,000 value units out of the total value produced. This remaining value is realised by Department II purchasing means of production worth 2,000 from Department I, while Department I purchases means of consumption worth 2,000 from Department II. The result of this circular exchange can be represented as follows:

Table 2: vI + sI = cII

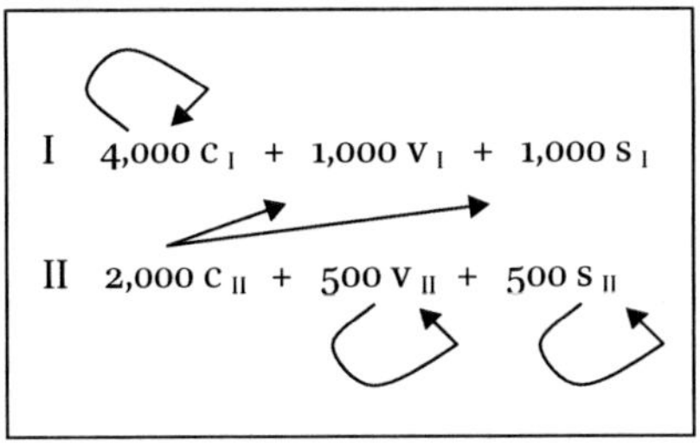

185. *MECW* 36, pp. 396, 401.

This model states that the total value produced in one period of production can be fully distributed among all parties involved. The model is not intended to state what neoclassical models of equilibrium state, namely that such equilibrium exists at all times; it is merely intended to state that such equilibrium *can* exist in principle. Even given the counterfactual assumption of a static economy, crises may result, since the condition of equilibrium is obtained only by means of permanent disequilibrium, due to the anarchic mechanisms of the market. 'Disproportions' *always* arise, but they may do so in two opposite ways: as underconsumption (an unsalable remainder of commodities persists in Department II) or as underinvestment (a surplus of produced durable goods, namely means of production). It is only by means of the perpetual balancing of disequilibria that equilibrium is achieved. Thus the model predicts a long-term stability that imposes itself by means of permanent disorder and crisis, not an idyllic and static equilibrium of the kind envisaged in neoclassical and monetarist economic theories (see 2.3.1).[186]

The model does not yet explain what is most important for understanding the capitalist mode of production: accumulation. After all, capitalism is characterised, first and foremost, by growth. The implication for the model here presented is that part of the surplus value obtained by the capitalists is not directly consumed by them, but reinvested. Following the model of simple reproduction, one can deduce underconsumption from this. *During this one year*, there results a demand gap with regard to consumer goods, since the capitalists cannot spend their additional investment in production for consumer goods. But to reason thusly would be to misinterpret the didactic model of simple reproduction as a historical 'stage' from which there is no way out. After the pre-Marxist theorists of underconsumption, who argued in this or a similar way,[187] it was mainly the leftist Social Democrat Rosa Luxemburg who picked up on this notion. In her view, the fact that accumulation is financed by surplus value entails a *permanent* demand gap that can only be bridged by 'third persons' – that is, by sections of the population that correspond to neither of the two poles labour and capital.[188] Luxemburg went on to

186. 'But this constant tendency to equilibrium, of the various spheres of production, is exercised, only in the shape of a reaction against the constant upsetting of this equilibrium. The *a priori* system on which the division of labour, within the workshop, is regularly carried out, becomes in the division of labour within the society, an *a posteriori*, nature-imposed necessity, controlling the lawless caprice of the producers, and perceptible in the barometrical fluctuations of the market-prices' (*MECW* 35, p. 361). Exchange is mediated by money; it is not barter. To the extent that it functions as a means of payment, money is still 'neutral' (*MECW* 35, pp. 145 ff.). This is a key point, in that it distinguishes Marx's theory from monetarist theories (such as those of Keynes, Friedman, Proudhon or Gesell), which assume that money is of primary importance for production. In Marx, money, interest and credit are understood on the basis of their role within production, not vice versa. The agents of the process described by Marx already dispose of money before they obtain more money (the capitalists use money to pay their workers before they have sold their product for money, and so on). Other functions of money can be accounted for on the basis of this time lag, without 'decoupling' them from production (*MECW* 37, pp. 461 ff.; see 2.3.5).

187. Malthus and Sismondi; see Bleaney 1976; Wright 1977; Shaikh 1978, 1983b.

188. 'Thus the immediate and vital conditions for capital and its accumulation is the existence of non-capitalist buyers of the surplus value' (Luxemburg 1913, p. 366).

characterise imperialism as the force that conquers additional sales markets (although production also occurs where those markets are located). And she deduces from this the coming 'collapse' of capitalism, arguing that since the capitalist dynamic will soon have done away with all third persons, the effects of underconsumption will be felt fully.[189]

However, it can be shown on the basis of Marx's extended reproduction schemes that this argument is as flawed as its precursors. This can already be appreciated by considering Marx's *terminological* choice to consider every additional investment 'consumption', namely demand; it is simply demand for a different sort of goods, namely means of production ('productive consumption').[190] An increase in demand will hardly reduce demand. The theorists of underconsumption commit the error of situating 'nature' at *too early* a point in the process. They consider the motive behind economic activity to consist only in the production and consumption of means of consumption, because this seems to correspond to human 'nature'.[191] Yet the motive behind *capitalist* economic activity is not the satisfaction of needs in itself, but the generation of profit – no matter whether it is achieved by producing and selling consumer goods or by producing and selling means of production. Luxemburg's theory of underconsumption results (like that of Hobson) from the fact that she considers the whole of Department I as a means by which to achieve the ends of Department II, rather than considering it as an economic sector in its own right.[192]

To postulate a *chronic* gap in the demand for means of consumption, in the manner of Luxemburg and her followers, is to overlook two features of Marx's model: the dynamic of value transfer (1) and the temporal dynamic (2).

As far as (1) is concerned, it is clear that whenever an unexpected increase in the demand for a certain good (iodine compounds, guns, and so on) leads to rapid accumulation, the capitalist demand for means of consumption will *decrease*.[193] This is simply a different way of saying that the demand for means of production and labour power *increases*. The disproportionality will balance out the following year, due to capital flowing from Department II, which has become relatively unprofitable, into Department I, which is more attractive.[194] Just as in the case of simple reproduction, constant

189. A similar argument can still be found in Sternberg 1926, Sweezy 1970 and Sweezy 1966.
190. *MECW* 28, p. 28; *MECW* 35, pp. 565 f. and elsewhere.
191. Shaikh 1978, p. 220.
192. Shaikh 1978, pp. 225 and 229 – Bulgakov represents the opposite extreme.
193. The plausibility of Luxemburg's argument rests on the fact that she assumes a static model of equilibrium and never ventures beyond this. Add sudden accumulation (a 'shock'), and the model will be bound to go into disequilibrium, if only temporarily. This simply means that the conditions of dynamic equilibrium differ from those of static equilibrium; it does not mean that there are no conditions of dynamic equilibrium (Mandel 1975, p. 28).
194. Mandel 1975, pp. 30 f. Marx explains the restoration of equilibrium by reference to a disequilibrium within the consumer goods industry: 'So long as this ... process of levelling ... lasts ... as much capital is supplied to the production of the latter as is withdrawn from other branches of production, until the demand is satisfied. Then the equilibrium is restored' (*MECW* 36, p. 339). Marx later discusses this phenomenon in terms of the formation of an average rate of profit (*MECW* 37,

disequilibria produce equilibrium in the long term and on average, the point being that the resulting equilibrium is *dynamic* (Shaikh speaks of 'turbulent dynamics').[195] Again, *both* sides may be left with unsold commodities. But the transfer of value between the two departments is more than simply a change of figures, since beyond the figures there lie specific use values.[196]

They cannot be *materially* transfered from Department II to Department I, because they would be depreciated in the case of non-realisation (consumer goods spoil and means of production are subject to wear and tear). Luxemburg's argument turns on the non-realisation of excess commodities. But in doing so, she elides the *dynamic* of extended reproduction. The single capitalist always has more disposable money than he is currently investing in production, and if he does not, he can borrow it.[197] Another possibility is that of the capitalists operating in Department II using their surplus value to purchase their own excess commodities and then withdrawing the amount they have spent from production the following year. Let us assume, then, that total values *could* simply be transferred between the two departments. Let us leave aside the money market, for the time being, and simply postulate that commodities can still be sold during the next productive cycle (stockpiling); only the expenses obviated by this are transferred. The following numerical examples are by no means intended to demonstrate the validity of the argument (they cannot do this, because they have been chosen randomly), but simply to illustrate its purpose. The first example illustrates the periodic disproportionality in *both* departments:

---

pp. 141 ff.). 'The most familiar type of transfer is that brought about by the formation of a general rate of profit. Industries with high organic compositions (C/Vs) will have prices of production above direct prices, while those with low C/V's will have prices of production below direct prices. Thus the formation of prices of production transfers surplus value from industries with low C/Y's to those with high ones' (Shaikh 1979, p. 48).

195. Shaikh 1994, p. 3.

196. The total values consist either of c (that is, they represent demand or supply with regard to means of production) or of v (the quantity of labour-power/wages – with wages only being spent on means of consumption, in this model). The values take the form of disposable money capital only when surplus value has successfully been realised. Not for the first time, we encounter, here, the significance of use values for the development of capital. There are cases in which there is an excess both of money and of commodities – due to the specific use value that value happens to be incorporated in. Thus high unemployment will not lead to excess money capital being used to create new employment for as long as such new employment does not sufficiently display the feature that makes it a use value for capital, namely that of creating surplus value, the anticipated rate of profit being too low (*MECW* 37, pp. 249 ff.).

197. Luxemburg charges Marx with neglecting the 'money form' (Luxemburg 1951, p. 121). But it had already been integrated in his model: 'The fact that the production of commodities is the general form of capitalist production implies the role which money is playing in it not only as a medium of circulation, but also as money-capital' (*MECW* 36, p. 494). Even if capital depreciates during a bad year, this does not prevent the capitalists from investing more of it the following year. Thus a transfer of value is possible.

Table 3: Synchronic Proportionality in Productive Cycle 1

(year 1)	I:	$1000\ c_I + 500\ v_I + 500\ s_I = 2000\ (+/-\ 0)$
	II:	$1000\ c_{II} + 500\ v_{II} + 500\ s_{II} = 2000\ (+/-\ 0)$

Here, the two departments are still proportional to one another (since c II = v I + s I). Let us now assume that for some extrinsic reason there is an expectation of additional demand for goods produced in Department I, without there being precise knowledge of when this demand will arise. Instead of 'eating up' all of their surplus value,[198] the capitalists operating in Department I now begin reinvesting part of it – say 60 percent – in their branch of industry, without making any changes to the organic composition of capital (2 c = 1 v).[199] Since the economy is not 'planned', several capitalists will engage in such reinvestment, each of them hoping to make a profit on the expected additional demand. Since Is no longer exchanges itself against means of consumption in the usual way, Department II is left with unsold commodities worth the amount accumulated in I. We thus have a surplus of 300 value units in Department II. We can express this as follows:

Table 4: Synchronic Disproportionality in Productive Cycle 1

(first year)	I:	$1000\ c_I + 500\ v_I + 200\ s_I = 1700$
	II:	$1000\ c_{II} + 500\ v_{II} + 500\ s_{II} = 2000$ (excess commodities: + 300)

Let us now also assume that these 300 unrealised value units can be transferred to Department I: Department II invests them in Department I, which has become the more profitable of the two departments. This would lead to the following increases in the values invested in Department I the following year: an increase of 200 cI and 100 vI (surplus value obtained in Department I during the first year), plus an additional increase of 200 cII and 100 vII (value transferred from Department II). The result is that the disproportion is reversed, since it is now Department I that can no longer sell all of its commodities, whereas demand exceeds supply in Department II (since c II = v I + s I):

Table 5: Diachronic Disproportionality in Productive Cycle 2

(second year)	I:	$1400\ c_I + 700\ v_I + 700\ s_I = 2800$ (excess commodities: + 600)
	II:	$800\ c_{II} + 400\ v_{II} + 400\ s_{II} = 1600$

198. *MECW* 35, p. 593.

199. Such accumulation would be nothing more than an extension of production, as opposed to its intensification, which would involve a change in the organic composition of capital, with a significant proportion of capital taking the form of c (*MECW* 37, pp. 209 ff.).

This is the case even if another 60 percent (420) are withdrawn from Is for the purposes of accumulation; Department I would still be saddled with an excess supply of 180 value units. To round off the example, let us make the additional assumption that the third year sees Department I transferring its 'superfluous' 600 value units into Department II, which is booming again, even as the capitalists in Department II seize the opportunity by accumulating 50 percent of their surplus value (200). The value increases in Department II would then be distributed thus:

Table 6: Diachronic Proportionality in Productive Cycle 3

(third year)	I:	$1400\ c_I + 700\ v_I + 700\ s_I = 2800$ (+/– 0)
	II:	$1400\ c_{II} + 700\ v_{II} + 700\ s_{II} = 2800$ (+/– 0)

At this point, equilibrium would have been restored, but with a growth of 40 percent as compared to at the outset. Should the third year also turn out to be one of additional demand (due, say, to the opening of a border), the new equilibrium will immediately be lost again. In reality, such moments of equilibrium will, therefore, only ever arise in the form of an 'accident',[200] or as intermediate stages. Nevertheless, they help us understand accumulation. Growth rates and disproportions are not irrational; rather, they vacillate turbulently around a dynamic equilibrium. While this dynamic equilibrium is seldom *visible* (which is why the above is not a description), it nevertheless represents the law (or 'essence') of phenomena within this analysis. In the real world, discrepancies between prices and values, international trade and the relatively autonomous dynamic of the financial sector (interest, rates of exchange, and so on) all come into play. This only makes it all the more important to understand the basic mechanism.

(2) Another feature of the dynamic of expanded reproduction consists in its temporal dilation, which we have so far ignored. A capitalist does not pay the expenses he incurs during a given year out of the income he receives during that same year: he uses his income from the *previous* year. However, the product of this year's investment will only be available and saleable at the end of the productive cycle (that is, *the following* year, in our model). Thus even our simple model involves at least three intertwined productive cycles.[201] This is another source of error in Luxemburg's calculation. The apparently 'superfluous' means of consumption that result from sudden accumulation are not exchanged against the consumption expenses of the same year, but against those of the following year. Thus the correct way to write the formula for the condition of equilibrium is $cII_n = vI_{n+1} + sI_{n+1}$, where 'n' denotes the year.[202] Examples can be provided for

200. *MECW* 36, p. 494.

201. Current investments depend on past profits and future expectations.

202. In order not to make the model too complicated, let us also assume that Ic and IIv and IIs are exchanged against the total value of the same year. These data can also be dynamised (in fact, they would have to be, if the model were to be perfected). This illustrates the model's enor-

this, too. Let us assume two departments that operate over a period of three years and whose relations of exchange do not balance each other synchronically, but do so diachronically ($cII_{n+1} = vI_{n+2} + sI_{n+2}$):

Table 7: Diachronic Balancing of Disproportionalities

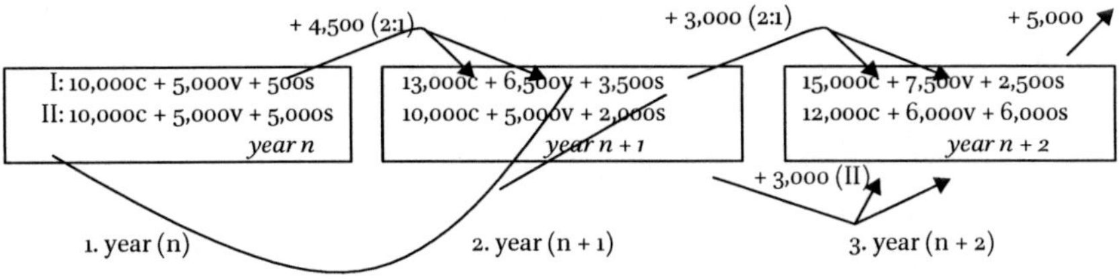

Here, we have a case of 'dynamic equilibrium', with the figures for the first year revealing considerable underconsumption, which balances out, however, as soon as we consider a longer time period. This does not even require any transfer of value. This is to say no more and no less than that, as far as *circulation* is concerned, long-term capitalist growth is possible. Yet by demonstrating that this is possible on principle, one also begins to see where *crises* may arise. 'This process is so complicated that it offers ever so many occasions for running abnormally'.[203] There may arise disproportions between Department I and Department II, resulting in the destruction of capital and in bottlenecks; the transfer of value may not succeed, so that commodities spoil; predictions of future demand may miss the mark at any time; and emergency money reserves may turn out to be insufficient, resulting in deferral of payments and bankruptcy – all this may happen by virtue of nothing more than the circulation of capital.[204]

This social model, which illustrates an possibility that (in principle) may play out in this way or in that, depending on the most varied contingencies, but which always asserts

---

mous complexity, which remains evident despite numerous simplifications. A model can always be made more complicated, but its purpose is to make things comprehensible by expressing them simply. Luxemburg rightly criticised the numerical experiments engaged in during the debate on Marx's reproduction schemes, by pointing out that mere mathematical possibilities are far from taking account of social conditions. It is a matter, however, of demonstrating that just such possibilities exist, and of describing their character ('The total movement of this disorder is its order': *MECW* 9, p. 208).

203. *MECW* 36, p. 495.

204. 'The fact that the production of commodities is the general form of capitalist production ... engenders certain conditions of normal exchange peculiar to this mode of production and therefore of the normal course of reproduction, whether it be on a simple or on an extended scale – conditions which change into so many conditions of abnormal movement, into so many possibilities of crises, since a balance is itself an accident owing to the spontaneous nature of this production' (*MECW* 36, p. 494; see Sweezy 1970, pp. 187 ff.). There are other types of crises. The Marxian theory of crisis does not consist of one theory alone; it comprises an entire set of phenomena (Mandel 1975; Wright 1977; Shaikh 1978; Perelman 1987).

itself in the form of crisis, was reductively interpreted as a natural process that develops either in one direction *or* in the other. In the Russian literature, the model become that of a mechanism that runs its course automatically;[205] in Kautsky and Luxemburg, it became the model of an automatic collapse. The link between crisis and growth was severed. Bulgakov developed the erroneous idea that capitalist growth involves Department I growing at the expense of Department II, with Department I uncoupling itself from Department II and consumption thus *decreasing* absolutely.[206] Tugan-Baranowsky's later vision of *production for the sake of production* anticipated the technocracy hypothesis.[207] The idea that machines might produce machines or even human beings is still invoked as a horrific vision within today's cinematic social imaginary.[208] What is correct in this idea is that the organic composition of capital, or the share of constant capital, does, in fact, increase over time. But this does not have to result in the relative growth of Department I, since similiar developments may occur in Department II – the rise in the organic composition of capital affects both departments.[209] The *relationship* between the two departments remains stable for as long as their rates of accumulation do not diverge too strongly. The equalisation of profit rates ensures that the rates of accumulation come to resemble one another.[210] For this reason, an absolute decrease in the production of consumer goods is more than just counterintuitive; in the long run, it is quite improbable.

Moreover, Tugan-Baranowsky forgets that machines, aside from their use value (that of producing other machines as well as the necessities of life), must also be bearers of *exchange value*. What stands in the way of the scenario of one worker operating every

---

205. Tugan-Baranovsky 1894, Bulgakov 1897, Lenin 1960.

206. Bulgakov 1897, pp. 161 f.; Rosdolsky 1977, p. 466; Luxemburg 1951, pp. 268 ff. Tugan-Baranowsky 1894 experimented with the Marxian schemes and concluded that no immanent disruptions can be deduced from them for as long as the proper proportions are maintained. He wrongly concluded from this that there could be crisis-free growth in reality. In doing so, he not only ontologised the model (Rosdolsky 1977, p. 464), but also misunderstood its purpose. Pointing out what distinguishes crises from a smoothly running process of reproduction is necessary only for understanding the causes of crises (see the critique formulated by G. Eckstein, in Luxemburg 1951, p. 487). The fact that the Russian Marxists, of all people, sought to demonstrate capitalism's resilience is due to the rivalry between them and the Populists, who neglected the role of capitalism in Russia, which was still far from having been fully industrialised (Rosdolsky 1977, p. 472 f. and 474 f.).

207. Tugan-Baranowsky 1905; see *MECW* 29, p. 366; *MECW* 35, pp. 587, 591; section 2.4.5.

208. The theme of the reproduction schemes is to be found even in the most popular sectors of the culture industry. See the films *Terminator, Blade Runner, Matrix, I Robot, Star Trek: Contact* or *Star Wars Episode II*, where C3PO, himself a robot, finds himself in a fully automated factory where machines produce machines. This is a frightening experience for him, since he enjoys a 'human' relationship with his constructor, Anakin Skywalker (see the motto of 1, as well as the character 'Cal' in *Alien IV*).

209. Rosdolsky 1977, pp. 475 f., 501 f.; Shaikh 1989b.

210. The absence of accumulation in Department II would lead to a relatively low organic composition in that department. This would increase the rate of profit vis-à-vis Department I (since the mass of surplus value is greater where variable capital makes up a greater share of total capital, a point I discuss below). This, in turn, would attract fresh capital (from both departments), thus leading to accumulation.

machine while the rest of humanity lives leisurely? A plethora of sales crises undergone by the producers of those very machines.[211] After all, the machines would not only have to satisfy a social need for use values; they would also have to lead to the creation of surplus value, or it would prove impossible to *realise* them on the scale required. But this is precisely what machines cannot do.[212] In other words, Tugan is not holding the mirror up to capitalism: he is presenting the dystopia of a planned economy. His misinterpretation results from an underdetermination of Marx's object of inquiry. He reduces the 'twofold character' of the capitalist economy (production and exchange)[213] to 'production for the sake of production',[214] or to its 'use-value aspect', without any consideration of the laws of exchange. This may have been due to the outside perspective from which Tugan was writing, as a Russian author.

The harmonist interpretation developed by Russian authors seemed to suggest that capitalism could function without crises in the long term. This was, however, a problematic conclusion for German socialists, since it rendered obsolete the rhetoric of crises associated with the Erfurt Programme. The *naturalisation* of capitalism's capacity to continue functioning now prompted an *ethicisation* of the critique of capitalism, as in Bernstein. It did so, in any case, for those who still wanted to continue criticising capitalism at all. The justification for demanding a different kind of society was now no longer framed in economic terms. Later Marxists such as Hilferding, Bukharin, the late Kautsky and Pollock believed the 'natural function' of well-proportioned production could be performed, in a compensatory manner, by the *state*. Thus it was no longer capitalism as such that was credited with an unlimited lifespan, but 'state capitalism' (see sections 2.2.7 and 2.6.2).[215] Here, too, political strategy needed to be adapted to an ostensibly new

211. The problem with any increasing preponderance of Department I is that while the whole construction would depend for its legitimation on popular consumption, the professed economic motive ('satisfaction of needs') would not accord well with the immense scale on which means of production would have to be produced. Nevertheless, the industry producing means of production would remain dependent on the sale of means of consumption, since the producers of means of consumption would purchase some of the means of production. This is why Marx speaks of the 'restricted consumption of the masses' as the 'ultimate reason for all real crises' (*MECW* 37, p. 483; a passage cited enthusiastically by Bernstein: 1961, p. 73 f.). Rosdolsky 1969 and Mandel 1975, who tend towards the theory of underconsumption, often quote other passages that suggest that the production of means of production cannot be delinked from the production of means of consumption, such that the former can expand at the expense of the latter only thanks to political coercion (as under Stalin): 'Besides ... continuous circulation takes place between constant capital and constant capital (even regardless of accelerated accumulation). It is at first independent of individual consumption because it never enters the latter. But this consumption definitely limits it nevertheless, since constant capital is never produced for its own sake but solely because more of it is needed in spheres of production whose products go into individual consumption' (*MECW* 37, p. 303 f.).

212. *MECW* 35, pp. 389 ff.

213. See *MECW* 35, p. 51.

214. *MECW* 35, p. 588.

215. The model 'state capitalism' was important for Hilferding 1981, Bukharin 1972 and Pollock 1941a (see 2.2.6) Those defending the theory of disproportion might have cited the draft of the

situation, albeit in a defeatist and escapist manner. Of course, harmonism also provoked criticism from within the Marxist camp.[216] Yet the opposing view, prominently defended by Luxemburg and Grossmann, did not so much do away with naturalisation as redefine the 'nature' at issue. Instead of crediting capitalism with an unlimited lifespan, Luxemburg and Grossmann simply formulated the law of its collapse.

Luxemburg also dealt with the extended reproduction schemes, although in her view, the capitalist dynamic was incapable of neutralising the effects of underconsumption. She explicitly rejected Marx's schemes, which had, at least, demonstrated the possibility of such a neutralisation.[217] While she was justified in drawing attention to underconsumption, she did not conceptualise it as a *periodically* arising disproportionality that is compensated for by cyclical underinvestment in the long term (the way Marx had done); instead, she wrongly took underconsumption to be a *chronic* deficit. The persistent expansion of both departments results in increased consumption by the capitalists – this is the profit motive that is so central to capitalism.[218] Thus the schemes demonstrate the rationality of this type of economy, from the point of view of individual capitalists.

Yet Rosa Luxemburg takes just this to be 'absurd': 'We are plainly running in circles [!]. From the capitalist point of view it is absurd to produce more consumer goods merely in order to maintain more workers, and to turn out more means of production merely to keep this surplus of workers occupied'.[219] The possibility of such a 'circular' motion – the circulation process of capital – was precisely what Marx set out to demonstrate. Luxemburg's economic thought resembles that of neoclassical economics, in that she fails to conceptualise anything other than a *static* equilibrium – with the difference that she takes such static equilibrium to bear within it the seeds of its own destruction.

Both naturalisations, harmonist and catastrophist, overlooked two things. First, both assumed that directly proportional production is possible *within capitalism*, thus falsely attributing to it the features of a 'planned economy'. This amounted to playing down the seriousness of disproportionalities, reducing them to mere errors of political planning. Moreover, both approaches considered only production and neglected distribution. This was to ignore the problem of realisation. But given the anarchy of the market, it is never

---

Erfurt Programme in support of their position: 'The absence of planning [!] inherent in the essence of capitalist production produces ever more prolonged crises that . . . further aggravate the situation of workers' (*MECW* 22, p. 596).

216. 'Rosa Luxemburg's book *The Accumulation of Capital*, whose central theme . . . involves stressing the idea of breakdown . . . can only be understood . . . as a reaction to the neo-harmonist interpretation of Marx's theory' (Rosdolsky 1977, p. 491).

217. Luxemburg 1951, pp. 114, 290 f. 'But because Rosa Luxemburg believed the Marxian reproduction schemes demonstrate the actual possibility of unfettered accumulation *ad infinitum*, and that Tugan, Hilferding and later Otto Bauer correctly derived this notion from the model, she abandoned the Marxian scheme, so as to rescue the notion of collapse that follows from the first volume of *Capital*' (Grossmann 1992, p. 281 f.).

218. *MECW* 36, p. 75; *MECW* 37, p. 255.

219. Luxemburg 1951, p. 132.

certain that products will be sold at all, not to speak of being sold at their values. Thus both approaches ended up being aporetic. The Marxian object of social analysis was lost between an *affirmative* naturalisation, whose criticism was ethical at best, and a catastrophism *negating* naturalisation.

The aporia was not resolved until Henryk Grossmann, the Frankfurt School's economist stepson and a vehement critic of Luxemburg, succeeded in doing so by showing how the problem of crises could be approached in a different way. The cause he traced the 'law of collapse' back to was, however, also related to the reproduction schemes. Otto Bauer and Nikolai Bukharin had developed a formula that identified conditions of equilibrium of dynamic growth. If growth occurs in accordance with these proportions, then its long-term continuation becomes conceivable. The formula is the following: v I + s I_α+ s I_γ = c II + s II_β.[220] Bauer provides an example:[221]

Table 8: Conditions of Equilibrium (Extended Reproduction)

I: 120,000	cI	+ 50,000 vI	+ 37,500 sγ	+ 10,000 sβ	+ 2,500 sα
II: 80,000	cII	+ 50,000 vII	+ 37,500 sγ	+ 10,000 sβ	+ 2,500 sα

The condition of equilibrium is met during the first year, since 50,000 vI + 37,500 s Iα + 2,500 s Iγ = 80,000 cII + 10,000 s IIγ. This formula for dynamic equilibrium did not require additional formalisation, since different rates of accumulation are required for different starting conditions and years, if the condition of equilibrium is to continue being met. Since these rates are not centrally planned, but can only be calculated *ex post* and as long-term averages, this is not a flaw.[222] The formula shows roughly what the structure of accumulation must look like when there is long-term growth. Thus accumulation loses its mysterious character. Yet the formula also lent itself to a 'harmonist' interpretation. While this suited the Austro-Marxist Bauer, it was not something that Bukharin, the theorist of the Communist International who had studied in Germany, or the German-Polish communist Grossmann were particularly interested in. The assumption of an economic

220. S Iγ denotes the portion of the surplus value created in Department I that is invested in additional vm, while sIα denotes the portion that is 'unproductively' consumed by capitalists. Both portions are exchanged for consumer goods. sIIβ denotes the *additional* constant capital (c) accumulated in Department II, on the basis of the surplus value there created (Mandel 1992, pp. 27 ff.; Bauer 1913, Bukharin 1972, p. 154 f.).

221. Bauer 1913, cited in Grossmann 1929, p. 247; see Rosdolsky 1977, pp. 499 f.; Mandel 1971, p. 279.

222. Eckstein 1913, p. 491. The basic misunderstanding of which both Grossman and Luxemburg are guilty concerns the rate of accumulation, which is not known at the outset, since it is an average and *ex post* figure. Single capitals can always resort to credit to invest more in production than production is currently yielding (such as when their profit expectations are high); other, more prudent capitals will reinvest only part of their surplus value. There is no guarantee that either strategy will be successful – both capitals may fail.

base that operates in a purely technical manner and without crises left socialists with only one option, that of a *moral* critique. Grossmann joined Luxemburg and Bukharin in objecting to the ethicisation of the critique of capitalism.[223]

Luxemburg's theory of underconsumption having proven erroneous,[224] there arose the difficult question of how a 'law of collapse' might be made to accord with Bauer's condition of equilibrium. To answer this question, Grossmann worked with Bauer's figures, which the latter had used to demonstrate stable growth. Bauer had supplemented Marx by integrating the rising organic composition of capital into his model, via the assumption that c increases by ten percent annually, whereas v increases by only five percent. Grossmann arrived at a 'law of collapse' by calculating the increase in accumulation as a percentage of *fixed capital*, rather than of surplus value.[225] Since surplus value's share of total value decreases constantly for as long as the organic composition of capital rises, there comes a point at which surplus value is insufficient for accumulation – the point of absolute crisis, which coincides with the thirty-fifth year, in this model.[226] It would, however, have been more realistic to calculate accumulation by reference to *surplus value*. In purely mathematical terms, this precludes any overextension of the system. Even Grossmann is still guilty of naturalising the reproduction schemes by attributing to capitalists a 'nomological' behaviour, by virtue of which they deprive themselves of their own mass of profit. By contrast, in Marx, the mass of profit *increases* in the long term, despite the fall in the rate of profit. A global decrease in the *mass* of surplus value would directly contradict the capitalist profit motive.[227] Thus it is not just the harmonists, but also the theorists of collapse, who naturalise the Marxian model, and in doing so, both commit factual errors and errors of interpretation. The theorists of collapse relegated the catastrophe to a future so remote that they, too, were forced to resort to ethics when it came to formulating their political strategy.[228] *Politically*, they gained little,

223. 'If one hopes capitalism will be overthrown purely by the political struggle of the masses, who have been schooled for socialism, then "the centre of gravity of the entire argument is shifted from the realm of economics to consciousness" [Bukharin]. Similarly, Luxemburg wrote: "With the assumption that capitalist accumulation has no economic limit, socialism loses its granite foundation of objective historical necessity. We then take flight into the mist of pre-Marxist systems and schools which sought to deduce socialism from the mere injustice and badness of the present-day world and from the mere revolutionary determination of the working class"' (Grossmann 1929, p. 108; see also p. 74; Grossmann is quoting Tugan-Baranowsky 1904, p. 274, and Luxemburg 1972, p. 42).

224. No one accepted this theory except Sternberg; even Mehring refused to endorse it.

225. Grossmann 1929, p. 117.

226. Grossmann 1929, p. 132.

227. It seems quite unlikely that an entrepreneur would knowingly ruin himself by spending more than he earns – yet Grossmann seems to be assuming just such behaviour. It is the system that is irrational, not its elements. Marx held that 'the absolute mass of the profit produced by it [capital], *can*... increase, and increase progressively, in spite of the progressive drop in the rate of profit. And this not only *can* be so. Aside from temporary fluctuations it *must* be so, on the basis of capitalist production' (*MECW* 37, p. 216).

228. Hence Kołakowski 1976, p. 411 f. (on Luxemburg); Mandel 1975, p. 31 (on Grossmann).

and as far as *theory* is concerned, it is quite clear that both currents were not guided by their object of inquiry, but attempted, rather, to arrive at the conclusion they thought politically desirable. If anything, this *obscured* Marx's economic theory. Once again, the object of inquiry 'society' is lost somewhere between nature and mind.[229] Grossmann had, however, redirected attention to an important Marxian theme: the tendency of the rate of profit to fall.[230]

2.1.6 Key elements of Marxian theory II: the falling rate of profit

While social phenomena – Marx's theme – involve conscious decisions, their consequences may, nevertheless, run contrary to original intentions, which is to say they escape the point of view of the participants.[231] Interpretation of the reproduction schemes was rendered especially difficult by their status. They result from aggregated individual acts, which is to say they are not the product of any particular volition; moreover, they impose themselves only in an anarchic manner and in the long term (2.4.6). The tendency of the rate of profit to fall as discussed in the third volume of *Capital* (chapters 13–15) involves the same dialectic of individual intentions and social consequences. It was only in this context that Marx began considering the exacerbation of crises, whereas he still treated disproportionality and valorisation crises as easily superable. The latter were mere cyclical phenomena, but the fall of the rate of profit was a development that intensified from one cycle to the next. The basis of this development is to be seen in the mechanisation and capitalisation of production as discussed in the first volume of *Capital*;[232] such mechanisation and capitalisation manifests itself in the rising 'organic composition of capital', that is, in a rise of the ratio c/v.[233]

While the individual capitalist initially incurs higher expenses due to his investment in additional, new machinery (constant capital), he also saves on wages while simultaneously cheapening his final product, which he can now produce on a larger scale.[234]

---

229. Incidentally, there were revolutionary and conservative variants both of the theory of underconsumption (Luxemburg vs. Malthus) and of harmonism (Hilferding vs. Lenin). See also 2.3.3 (Dobb vs. Gillmann) and 2.4.4.

230. Something that only Preiser 1924 had done before him; see Howard 1992, pp. 316 ff.

231. *MECW* 29, p. 275 f.; see Adam Smith's 'invisible hand' (Binswanger 1998, pp. 47 ff.; Koslowski 1982, p. 38; Hong 2002).

232. *MECW* 35, pp. 474 ff., 616 ff.; Shaikh 1983d, 1987f.

233. It is important to distinguish between capital's 'technical composition' (the ratio of machines to workers, in material terms), its 'value composition' (that is, its technical composition as expressed in value terms: c/v), its 'organic composition', which involves a temporal index, and its materialised composition (c/L, Shaikh 1986f). Expressed in monetary terms, a rise in the latter entails a rising capital/output ratio (K/Y). This can be used to demonstrate an increase in c/v, since K/Y is the monetary expression of such an increase. Price movements are almost exactly parallel in the two departments, with deviations of five percent (Shaikh 1989b, p. 3, following Juillard 1981; see Howard 1989, pp. 316 ff.; Howard 1992, pp. 128 ff., 316 f.).

234. Or: '[O]n average new methods of production embody higher amounts of fixed capital per unit output (at normal capacity). In microeconomic terms, this translates into the familiar propo-

Ultimately, this allows the individual capitalist to obtain a *greater* mass of surplus value. Can such a development lead to a *fall* in the rate of profit? Marx assumes that extended reproduction – permanent accumulation – is the normal scenario – once it has established itself, the capitalist economy *must* grow.[235] However, this growth process quickly reaches certain limits, and it does so long before the ecological limits to growth[236] become apparent. There are two such limits: the limited number of available workers[237] and the limited marketability of products at given prices. These limits entail two disadvantages for capital. On the one hand, 'full employment' and a given level of technological development preclude or severely curb additional accumulation. On the other hand, a job glut allows workers to exchange their labour-power *at a higher price*. Trade unions dispose of significant political power in such a situation (although this is not the cause of crises, as the theory of the 'profit squeeze' would have it).

There is another way of continuing to accumulate aside from simply expanding production: resorting to labour-saving measures ('intensification' of production),[238] and doing this constantly, not just during crises. Such labour-saving measures cheapen the product, since they decrease the wage bill. They increase the marketable volume of commodities while simultaneously making capital more independent of trade unions.[239] This is why it is *normal*, within a capitalist economy, for production to be rendered ever more capital-intensive in order to increase the mass of profit. This phenomenon is

---

sition that more advanced methods have higher average fixed costs, lower average variable costs, and lower average total cost (i.e. lower unit cost-price in the sense of Marx), at normal capacity utilisation' (Shaikh 1989a, p. 1).

235. For the individual capitalist, the necessity of growth results from competition. If he does not accumulate, he will lose market shares to his competitors, since he will eventually be forced to produce more expensively than they do. If his capital does not expand, it will soon contract (his income from surplus value decreases, forcing him eventually to use up his original capital stock; in addition to this, his monetary assets are depreciated by inflation, and his productive assets by obsolescence) – and this will always involve the risk of his being swept off the market altogether. For a society, a stationary economy would entail a constant decline in the disposable mass of surplus value, since commodity prices continue to fall on the world market. This would have a negative effect on social consumption (public services, infrastructure, culture); employment would decline, and so on. Thus striving for stasis would lead to atrophy. Consequently, growth must be the goal of every individual capitalist and of bourgeois politics (*MECW* 35, pp. 578 ff., 607 ff.).

236. Meadows 1972.

237. This was the situation in the Federal Republic of Germany during the early 1960s; it led to the import of additional labour power from abroad (the so-called 'guest workers'). Another way of responding to such a situation consists in the proletarisation of additional segments of the population, such as peasants (as in seventeenth-century England), children (as in nineteenth-century England, and almost everywhere in Africa, Asia and Latin America during the twenty-first century), women (in Germany, this occurred mainly during the Second World War) or, more recently, humanities scholars.

238. *MECW* 35, p. 412; *MECW* 36, p. 257; *MECW* 37, p. 230.

239. Initially, higher productivity allows for slightly higher wages. But the simultaneous expulsion of workers from the production process intensifies competition between workers and may lead to a decline in wage levels; this then increases the rate of surplus value. Wage levels are not so much a cause as one effect among others.

not limited to industrialisation during the dismal nineteenth century; we still witness it today, and on a daily basis. At every train station, we encounter ticket machines rather than ticket vendors.

It is not any particular historical constellation, such as the strength of the labour movement, that leads to the rise in the organic composition of capital; the cause is, rather, to be seen in the basic motive governing the capitalist economy *itself*, namely obtaining ever greater surplus value. Yet there is a problem associated with the capitalisation of production: machines never transfer more value to their products than they themselves contain[240] (in the reproduction schemes, this was expressed in the annual renewal of c). Thus the share of surplus-value-producing labour, or variable capital's share of total capital, v/(c+v), *decreases*.[241] This development has the effect of also decreasing the share of surplus value (s), even if the rate of exploitation (s/v) increases. Thus the rate of profit, s/(c+v), will fall as constant capital's share of total capital (c) increases at the expense of variable capital's share (v).[242] There are, however, counteracting influences, such as an increase in the rate of surplus value or the depreciation of constant capital through technological progress,[243] so that the law only ever imposes itself in the form of a tendency – a constant rise and fall is to be expected, although the *long-term* trend is one of decline.[244]

The complexity of this law consists in the fact that it expresses the ratio of two ratios to one another, or the relationship between the rate of surplus value (s/v, assumed to be 100 percent throughout the preceding examples) and the organic composition of capital (the ratio of dead labour to living labour, or of constant to variable capital – c/v). According to Marx, *both* ratios increase over time, since they are related to one another. Assuming a given extraction of absolute surplus value,[245] a higher rate of surplus value can be achieved through higher productivity, which, in turn, is achieved through the mechanisation and capitalisation of production (and which is thus also limited by them). Is it conceivable that the two ratios balance each other out? Many Marxists assumed this, thus interpreting the 'tendency' of the rate of profit to fall as a historical tendency that is ultimately attributable to *politics*. Some variants of ethicisation build upon this economic foundation, in particular the faith in the *political control* (regulation) of capitalism; first formulated by Lassalle, it was canonised by Bernstein and then given a rational form by Keynes. The conventional Marxist (not Marxian) interpretation of the formula for the rate of profit can be expressed in value magnitudes as follows:

240. *MECW* 35, pp. 389 ff.
241. *MECW* 35, pp. 616 ff.
242. *MECW* 37, pp. 209 ff.
243. *MECW* 37, pp. 230 ff.
244. *MECW* 37, pp. 239 ff.
245. *MECW* 35, pp. 509 ff.

Table 9: Conventional interpretation of the tendency of the rate of profit to fall

$$p = \frac{s}{c + v}$$ where p is the rate of profit, s is surplus value, c is constant and v is variable capital.

If we now divide the numerator and the denominator by v, we obtain the following result:

$$p = \frac{s/v}{(c/v) + 1}$$ where s/v denotes the rate of surplus value and c/v denotes the value composition of capital.

It seems to follow from this that, contrary to Marx's law, there is no determinism governing the development of the rate of profit. Both ratios may rise, but it does not follow from this that the rate of profit falls. If both ratios rise uniformly, the rate of profit rises initially, but then remains about the same (with 1 as the limit value).[246] If the numerator rises more rapidly, there results an *increase* in the rate of profit. This assumption was widespread even within Marxism, and one still encounters it today.[247]

While formally correct, this equation is based on several illusory assumptions. The two developments identified – a rise in the organic composition of capital and an increase in surplus value – appear to be able to balance each other out only for as long as one elides their characteristic, or more specifically, their *capitalist* context. In purely mathematical terms, it would seem that the ratio s/v (the rate of exploitation or surplus value) can increase infinitely – an illusion comparable to Tugan-Baranovsky's vision. In fact, however, the ratio is linked in several ways to the rate of surplus value: by the length of the working day, which cannot exceed 24 hours,[248] and by inter-capitalist competition, which may force each individual capital to lower its prices, to the extent that it is not already doing so freely.

246. If we take the formula for the rate of profit to be p = s/ (c+v) and assume v to remain constant while c and v increase uniformly, then the rate of profit seems, in fact, to rise continually. If all values = 1, then p = 50 percent; if c and s = 2, then p = 67 percent; if c and s = 100, then p reaches its limit value of 100 percent. Yet by assuming s and c increase in synchrony, we are simply eliminating the variable v, so that the original ratio s/c emerges ever more clearly (in our example: 1/1 = 1). However, this ratio reflects the organic composition of capital (v/c), since s depends on the existence of v, and the point is precisely that v decreases over time.

247. Sweezy 1970, pp. 123 ff.; Robinson 1966, Gillman 1958, Rolshausen 1970, Ott 1989, p. 24; more recently, Heinrich 2001, pp. 330, 339; Heinrich 2004, pp. 140 ff.; see also Henning 2004a; for a comprehensive account, see Howard 1989, pp. 316–36 and Howard 1992, pp. 128–45, 316–18.

248. Surplus value (s) can be calculated by subtracting the part of the total product required for the replacement of assets (machines, raw materials, labour-power), or by subtracting the labour time required for producing the commodities necessary for the reproduction of labour ('necessary' labour time) from total labour time. If we take the minimum unit of labour time to be one hour, with parts of hours counting as full hours, and if we then assume necessary labour time to amount only to the minimum of one hour, then we have the extreme case of the rate of profit rising to 23 (assuming a 24-hour workday).

Of course, to lower sales prices while prices of production remain constant is to narrow one's profit margin.[249] It can however be formally demonstrated that while the rate of surplus value may increase, its increase cannot compensate for the increase in the organic composition of capital – because the organic composition of capital is ultimately what determines the rate of surplus value. In other words, the rate of profit must fall in the long term because the increase in the organic composition of capital is the *dominant* tendency (Shaikh 1983a, p. 139; cf. Shaikh 1983b, 1989a and 1989b). To express this in a formula as well, we may write the following:

Table 10: Alternative interpretation of the tendency of the rate of profit to fall

$$p = \frac{s}{K}$$ where K = c + v = total advanced capital (constant and variable).

If we now divide the numerator and the denominator by L, where L = s + v (total living labour), we obtain the following result:

$$p = \frac{s}{L} \cdot \frac{L}{K}$$ where L/K = (s + v) / (c + v): the organic composition of capital.

If we now divide the numerator and the denominator of s/L by v, we obtain the following (because L = s + v):

$$p = \frac{s/v}{(s/v)+1} \cdot \frac{L}{K}$$

While the rate of surplus value can influence the equation, it cannot do so indefinitely; in fact, the more it increases, the *less* influence it exerts. It may increase almost to infinity without being able to influence the dominant tendency, since an increase in s/v causes (s/v) / (1 + s/v) to approach the limit value of 1.[250] Thus the rate of profit *does* depend on the organic composition of capital. But since K/L increases, L/K decreases, and with it p, the rate of profit. Applied to reality, this does not mean that 'collapse' would be the direct result, as Grossmann would have it (in an argument that amounted to an indirect

249. The determined nature of the rate of profit is taken account of formally by considering s as a share of total labour time, so that s/v becomes s/(v+s). An increase in surplus value leads to the limit value of 1.

250. A simple demonstration consists in inserting s = L – v (surplus value is the share of added labour that remains when wages have been subtracted) into the rate of profit (s / c + v). This gives us (L – v) / (c + v). An increase in the rate of profit (s/v) entails that s is increasing at the expense of v, the maximum being represented by s = L, since this would amount to v = 0. Even in this case (the best possible one from the capitalist's point of view), p = L/c holds true. If c/L increases, then L/c decreases. Thus the rate of profit is determined, in the long run, by the composition of capital (in this case, by the materialised composition of capital).

defense of Kautsky), since it is still possible for the *mass* of profit to increase.[251] To put this more accurately, the mass of profit will in fact increase *cyclically*.[252]

What this does mean, however, is that *vulnerability* to crises increases over time. Achieving an adequate profit requires the investment of ever greater masses of capital. Small capitalists (so-called 'small businesses') may find this increasingly difficult, as recurrent merger waves show. Wages have to be depressed ever further to arrest the fall in the rate of profit; more innovative technology is needed ever more urgently in order to be able to compete successfully. Yet this simply accelerates the fall in the rate of profit. While the rate of profit may recover during the crisis, it will have to rise to a higher level vis-à-vis the previous cycle, due to the changing organic composition of capital, and this means that any *additional* increase in the rate of profit will require an intensification of class struggle (such as by continuously depressing wages and welfare benefits). All of this corresponds to phenomena that no one alive today is unfamiliar with. On the contrary, high unemployment, rapid technological development, the ever greater mobility of capitals that seek ever more rapid returns, the persistent dismantling of social and ecological standards – all of these things have plainly come to be the rule rather than the exception. Thus appearances clearly *confirm* Marx's law.

Despite its astonishing clarity and great explanatory power, this idea has seldom been adequately received. In the majority of cases – as in the shift toward revisionism that was discussed above, and which persists to this day – the law was interpreted, at best, as a historical law that can be manipulated *politically*, like proportional reproduction.[253] *Reformist* politics has often sought to legitimate itself by pointing out that such political manipulation has occurred in the past and might be practised more thoroughly in the future. But how are we to understand this departure from Marxian theory? Of course, one reason for it would seem to be the fact that Marx never got around to publishing his theory in an adequate form.[254] Nevertheless, the most important ideas are there; they

---

251. There is no terminal crisis *qua* quasi-natural event: 'There is no final crisis until workers are sufficiently class conscious and organized to overthrow the system itself', Shaikh 1983a points out with reference to Cohen 1978, pp. 201 ff.

252. Marx's theory of the economic cycle is closely bound up with the rate of profit (Shaikh 1987, p. 117 f.; Shaikh 1989b, pp. 4 f.; Shaikh 1992, pp. 178 f.). The ideal type of a cycle can be described as follows. In a booming economy, the promising rate of profit leads to substantial investment, until the mass of profit stagnates due to the fall in the rate of profit. (If the rate of profit is ten percent in year n, 500,000 c + v will yield 50,000 s during that year, but if the rate of profit sinks to 9.5 percent in year n + 1, then 525,000 c + v will yield only 50,000 s during that year – accumulation has not been 'worthwhile'.) At this point, investment declines (or capital is transferred to other sectors, such as speculation) and the excess capital allows for a 'purging' crisis (2.3.3). Once the crisis breaks out, the rate of profit falls even further. Firms need to borrow money to get by, and this leads to higher interests rates, which may intensify the crisis to the point where banks collapse. Unemployment increases, which depresses wages. In combination with the depreciation of 'excess' capital and the elimination of numerous competitors, this causes the rate of profit to recover. The game starts over, albeit it with a higher organic composition than during the previous cycle.

253. Shaikh 1983a, p. 139 distinguishes between 'possibility' and 'necessity theories' of crisis.

254. Rosdolsky 1977, Schwarz 1978, Rojas 1991.

would only have had to be fleshed out further. Insistence on the 'natural necessity' of capitalism's collapse was not very helpful, no more than denial of such necessity, insofar as both sides refused to provide any reasons for their position.

The fact that 'bourgeois' economics did not follow Marx is hardly in need of explanation, but the same cannot be said of the half-hearted manner in which Marxist economists did so (2.3.3). A special feature of the law of the tendency of the rate of profit to fall is that Marx himself identified a wealth of 'counteracting influences',[255] whose relationship to the law is not immediately apparent. It seems to stand to reason that these counteracting influences might neutralise the law. One final reason lies in the fact that Marx's theory seems to be 'refuted' periodically by empirical observation, when the two are confronted in an unmediated manner, as in Bernstein.

It is only when looking more closely that one realises that in many cases, such observations do not necessarily refute Marx, but may in fact confirm him. Let us review some possible objections. The first question that can be asked is whether the development described by Marx does in fact exist. The classics already assumed this development to be a *fact*; they merely puzzled over its explanation. It is important to pay attention to what the law states in Marx. It does not state that the rate of profit can never rise, but only that its cyclical rise and fall reveals a long-term tendency to fall. Even this simple point was ignored by many of Marx's critics, who took a short-term rise in the rate of profit to constitute a refutation of Marx. The majority of economists assumes that the rate of profit does fall in the long term. What is controversial is how this fall ought to be explained.[256]

If one is to answer the question of whether or not the rate of profit falls in the long term, one also needs to know what exactly 'profit' is taken to mean, as this is decisive for the survey and interpretation of empirical figures (which are essential). Thus one needs, first of all, to distinguish between Marxist surplus value as it presents itself *prior* to any division into interest, accumulation, entrepreneurial profit and so on,[257] and profit as understood by the *individual* entrepreneur, that is net gain after all expenses – including those for sales, taxes and so on – have been deducted. If one fails to take account of the fact that Marx considers these deductions to be part of surplus value (the part that is not retained by the productive capitalist but passed on to commercial capital, banks, service providers and the state), then the significance of the figures is altered considerably and the import of Marx's categories is not properly grasped.[258]

255. *MECW* 37, pp. 230 ff.

256. The classical economists 'perceived the phenomenon and cudgelled their brains in tortuous attempts to interpret it' (*MECW* 37, p. 211; Shaikh 1978, p. 235). The 'fall of the profit rate is a fact' (Bernstein 1961, p. 42). Keynes called it the 'marginal efficiency of capital' (Keynes 1964, p. 135). See *Historical Materialism* 4/5 on the 'Brenner Debate'.

257. *MECW* 37, p. 212.

258. Shaikh 1978, p. 238 f.; Shaikh 1998. Here, we are touching upon the complex distinction between productive and unproductive labour (*MECW* 35, p. 510; *MECW* 36, pp. 133 ff., 137 f.; Mandel 1992, pp. 38 ff.). What is meant by this distinction is that from the capitalist point of view, only

Such negligence is exacerbated when, in addition to concepts immediately relevant to a given context being conflated with theoretical concepts, Marxist categories are mixed with neoclassical ones.[259] Another criticism to be made is that the value composition of capital does *not* rise, as fixed capital is depreciated due to it becoming available at ever lower prices – as Marx himself recognised[260] (this has become know as the 'Harrod neutrality' of technological progress). While such depreciation may curb the fall of the rate of profit, it cannot eliminate it in the long term, as the same effect leads to a depreciation of *commodities*, such that the monetary form of the organic composition of capital – the ratio of capital to output – rises after all. Moreover, the depreciation of consumer goods reduces the expenses associated with necessary labour (v). Thus both variables of the ratio c/v are affected.[261]

Another popular criticism is that the fall in the rate of profit is not caused by any mechanism inherent to accumulation but by an *external* influence. Here, the actual development of the rate of profit is ignored and the discussion is reduced to a zero sum game involving surplus value and wages. From this point of view, a fall in the rate of profit is possible only when the wage increases achieved thanks to the strength of the labour movements claim 'too large' a part of the productivity increase, at the expense of profit, whose rate, it is claimed, must then inevitably fall. Oddly enough, this argument, which is reminiscent of the threnodies to be heard periodically from entrepreneurs, has also been formulated by Marxist writers.[262] The argument resembles the misinterpretation of the categories 'productive labour' and 'profit' in that it amounts to a neoclassical downplaying of capitalism. Because production is largely ignored, the internal relationship between the 'factors of production' is lost. Wage levels and the 'capital rent' become variables confronting each other in isolation – variables that are determined only by *politics*. This creates the impression that wages are 'too high' not from the point of view of the individual entrepreneur, but from that of the entire economy. In Marx, wages can rise only if (which is to say, because) capital's rising organic composition increases productivity. Wage increases are one aspect of productivity increases; productivity increases are what make wage increases possible in the first place. Wage increases cannot make

---

labour that is performed for capital and in return for a wage produces (surplus) value. Other labour is either not productive (of value) (for example, services, which are paid for from surplus value and thus belong in the rubric of consumption), or it has not been subsumed under capital (such as housework), or both (Shaikh 1996, pp. 20 ff.). This does not mean that such labour is not given any moral recognition. After all, it is precisely the massive privatisation of formerly public services that makes 'voluntary' social work so crucial. Capital has an interest in 'civil society' receiving 'recognition', since capital profits from privatisation. A social critique that presents itself as being more radical because it is more pluralist is ultimately pro-capitalist (Fraser 1997; 3.2.3).

259. See 2.3.3; for comprehensive accounts, see 2.3.2, Shaikh 1978, p. 235; Shaikh 1996, pp. 38 ff.

260. *MECW* 37, p. 234.

261. There does not have to be any long-term disproportionality of the two departments. According to Juillard 1981, the variations in productivity amount to five percent.

262. Glyn 1972, Himmelweit 1974, Boddy 1975, Bowles 1983, Howard 1992, pp. 318 ff.; see also the debate on Shaikh 1978a in the *Cambridge Journal of Economics*, issue 4 of 1980.

excessive claims on productivity without clashing with the specifically *capitalist* valorisation motive that is the reason why mechanisation occurs in the first place.[263] Although it is basal, this international relationship between factors of production is overlooked even by Michael Heinrich, who may otherwise be considered the most competent German interpreter of Marx to have written during the last few years.

The purpose of the capitalistion of production is to achieve greater profit. While the increase in the productivity of labour associated with this allows for higher real wages, the rate of exploitation (s/v) may nevertheless rise as well, and will in fact do so under normal circumstances. Real wages tend to rise more slowly than productivity. It is true that in the case of a crisis, the mass of surplus value will decrease, but so will wages – both developments are *symptoms* of crisis. The impression that rising wages *cause* crises results from neglect of Marx's theory of the falling rate of profit; on this theory, the fall of the rate of profit is determined by the rising organic composition of capital.[264]

A final, related criticism is linked to the dialectic of individual intentions and social effects already mentioned above. The 'Okishio Theorem', often invoked to counter Marx, states that an individual capitalist will introduce new technology only when this promises an increase in *his* rate of profit and that the introduction of new technology must lead to a rise in the rate of profit across society as long as *all* capitalists behave in this way.[265] This fallacy, which elides the logic of society, rests on the harmonising notion of competition proper to neoclassical economics. Firms are perceived as passively accepting prices that develop 'naturally' on the market (as a result of supply and demand). If market prices were indeed to remain stable, the individual capitalist would obtain a higher profit by switching to a cheaper method of production. However, this account abstracts from the purpose of technological innovations as understood by Marx (and entrepreneurs): namely, to reduce not just prices of production, but also sales prices, in order to be able to compete more successfully. The producer whose cost price is lower will reduce his market price in order to be able to sell *more* of his product.[266]

---

263. *MECW* 35, pp. 599 f., 615 f.

264. The theorists of the 'profit squeeze' observed that the ratio of profits to wages sinks before the outbreak of crises, but they interpreted this as a cause, not as a symptom (Shaikh 1978, p. 237; 'profit' refers, here, to company profits). The increase in real wages does not exceed that of productivity. 'The tendency of the rate of profit to fall is bound up with a tendency of the rate of surplus value to rise, hence with a tendency for the rate of labour exploitation to rise. Nothing is more absurd, for this reason, than to explain the fall in the rate of profit by a rise in the rate of wages . . . The rate of profit does not fall because labour becomes less productive, but because it becomes more productive' (*MECW* 37, p. 238).

265. Okishio 1961; see Nakatani 1979, Roemer 1979, Bowles 1981, Parijs 1980, Howard 1992, pp. 138 and 145; see also Heinrich 2001, p. 339; King 1990, Vol. III; 2.3.3.

266. 'The battle of competition is fought by cheapening of commodities. The cheapness of commodities depends, *caeteris paribus*, on the productiveness of labour, and this again on the scale of production. Therefore, the larger capitals beat the smaller. It will further be remembered that, with the development of the capitalist mode of production, there is an increase in the minimum amount of individual capital necessary to carry on a business under its normal conditions' (*MECW* 35, p. 621; see Shaikh 1978a, pp. 47 ff.; see also 2.3.3).

In doing so, he makes an extra profit, but only for a short time, as his competitors will quickly follow suit and employ a similar technology – if need be, they will resort to industrial espionage – so as to be able to produce as cheaply as he does, or even more cheaply. This will *further* decrease the commodity's sales price. Yet the process involves not just a decrease in the commodity's observable price, but also a shift in the centre of gravity around which sales prices fluctuate, that is, the commodity's price of production. Along with the commodity's price of production, its value also changes; the commodity's value is determined by the amount of socially necessary labour time required to produce it, and this quantity of time has been reduced. When we consider this from the point of view of society as a whole, we see that the rate of profit will eventually fall as the rising organic composition of capital takes effect, notwithstanding the fact that individual capitals can temporarily increase the *mass* of their profits.

I return to these economic matters in section 2.3. Here, I have discussed them only so as to confront both the 'laws of collapse' that proliferated during Social Democracy's early years and the refutations of those 'laws' with Marx's own theory. Marx's fundamental theory of crisis, the 'law of the tendency of the rate of profit to fall', can be fully understood only by taking into account the law's complex social causes and effects. It is symptomatic that both Luxemburg[267] and Grossmann[268] rejected the falling rate of profit as an explanation of crisis (Luxemburg opined that capitalists would hang themselves before ceasing to accumulate because of a fall in the *rate* of profit). Marxism's subsequent naturalisations and the ethicisations that are their mirror image can be traced back to a failure to address the actual social object of inquiry – Luxemburg and Grossmann sought something more palpable, more *natural*. To others, Marx's long-term law was already too palpable and not *mental* enough; they 'overcame' it by turning to ethical criteria,[269] but also – and this is not as different as people tend to assume today – by turning to racist criteria (2.3.1).[270] The Marxian reference point, political economy, is absent in both approaches. Thus even publications from an early period of the Party's history and the efforts in economic theory that underlay those publications were characterised by a significant departure from Marx's own economic theory.

These two sections, devoted to exploring the Marxian system, have shown that Marx's texts contain substantive theories about bourgeois society that can be meaningfully interpreted. These theories describe laws that impose themselves within and by means of bourgeois society, strongly shaping that society's changing appearance. While these laws do not determine bourgeois society down to the last detail, they do stake out a range of possibilities whose relevance can be demonstrated by means of politico-

267. Luxemburg 1951.
268. Grossmann 1929, pp. 110, 197.
269. See Shaikh 1978, p. 236.
270. Heidegger 1956 blamed 'foreign' elements within the Party, and in particular 'Eastern European Jews' (p. 59 f., cited in Noske 1947, p. 27) for the German worker's loss of a 'healthy' attachment to 'his' state (p. 20).

economic analyses. Their political import is that engaging in politics – socialist politics – requires one to be well-informed. However, and as we have seen, the theoretical import of these economic laws was lost in their German reception; it was eroded between claims concerning a quasi-natural determinism (a 'nomological' collapse due to underconsumption or overaccumulation) and the opposite hypothesis that the economy can be given an ethical framework, which can then be 'normatively' modelled as one sees fit. We will re-encounter this dualism in most of the chapters that follow.

In the present chapter (2.1), the dualism has appeared in an area whose practical relevance is quite immediate, namely the Party political literature influenced by Bernstein's ethical revisionism, on the one hand, and Kautsky's naturalist orthodoxy, on the other. The next chapter returns to the methodology of the history of ideas in order to examine one of German Social Democracy's offspring, namely Lenin's Bolshevik Party, and its interpretive schemes such as the 'primacy of politics'. While these interpretive schemes did not originate in Germany, they were of central importance to the development of German theory.[271] We will see that Marxian theory, whose import was already lost in the developments discussed above, not only continued to be given a new thematic framework, but also displayed a 'changing function'.[272] A mode of thinking that operates within complex and dynamic socio-economic structures of development was replaced by a simplified rationale of domination. In functional terms, this led to a transformation of theory. Theory went from being a critical companion of politics to being an instrument by which to ideologically affirm a political voluntarism that was practised in a largely unreflected manner.

---

271. Linden 1992.
272. Lukács 1971, pp. 223 ff.; see Negt 1995, pp. 7 ff.

2.2 Marx in the theory of communism

> It was precisely because the conditions that Marx thought necessary for a successful proletarian revolution did exist in Germany that there was no desire to make it; and it was also because they did not exist in Russia that Lenin was able to seize power in the name of Marx and the proletariat.[1]

This chapter examines how Marxian theory was remodelled within a second major current of its reception history, communism, and more specifically within Leninism – which will be examined here to the extent that it became relevant to the reception of Marx in Germany. Originally, there was no substantive distinction between the terms 'communism' and 'socialism', even if Marxism-Leninism discussed the relationship between the two in terms of stages of development.[2] It is not the case that Marx and Engels invented communism, thereby departing from earlier currents that called themselves 'socialist'. Due to various differences, they broke with the communist 'League of the Just' (*Bund der Gerechten*) in the 1850s; in 1864, they began to support the more moderate 'International Workingmen's Association'.[3] It has become common practice to describe as communist those parties and states whose positions are more radical than those of social democrats, in that they strive not just to improve the condition of the labouring classes, but also to genuinely bring about a political revolution and socialise the means of production.

There have been 'left-deviating' tendencies for almost as long as there has been a labour movement organised according to social-democratic principles: witness Bakunin's break with the International and the 'wild youth' of the 1890s; the Independent Social

---

1. Plamenatz 1954, p. 187.

2. Leonhard 1962, pp. 244 ff.; Becher 1976, pp. 824 ff.; Lenin, *Works* (henceforth cited as: *LW*), pp. 29, 419 f. Ruben 1990 retains a modified version of this distinction, defining socialism as a form of society and communism as a form of state. Marx and Engels initially treated the two terms as synonymous (*MECW* 5, pp. 455), but then decided, for propagandistic reasons, to reserve the term 'communists' for a subset of socialists with which they identified; this is what distinguished them from the majority of socialists (*MECW* 6, pp. 497 ff.). 'The Communists do not form a separate party opposed to the other working-class parties... The Communists are distinguished from the other working-class parties [the socialists] by this only:... they always and everywhere represent the interests of the movement as a whole. The Communists, therefore, are... practically, the most advanced and resolute section of the working-class parties of every country, that section which pushes forward all others... The immediate aim of the Communists is the same as that of all other proletarian parties: formation of the proletariat into a class, overthrow of the bourgeois supremacy, conquest of political power by the proletariat' (*MECW* 6, p. 497 f.). The journal of the Bolsheviks was called 'Social Democrat'.

3. *MECW* 23, pp. 3 ff.; *MECW* 26, pp. 312 ff.; *MECW* 27, pp. 235 ff.; for historical accounts, see Rosenberg 1937 and Wheen 1999. Anti-totalitarian texts (Arendt 1951, Seidel 1968a, Nolte 1986, Maier 1996, Söllner 1999, Courtois 1998, Jesse 1999, Backes 2002) seldom trace communism back further than Marx, even though the notion of an economy based on common property was already familiar to Aristotle and Aquinas. The concept seems too strongly bound up with the names of Marx and Engels. On early socialism, see Ramm 1955, Vester 1970, Höppner 1975, Jonas 1976, Vol. 1, pp. 175–243; Opitz 1988, pp. 541–792; Euchner 1991.

Democratic Party of Germany (USPD), active around 1918; the Young Socialists, who defended the theory of 'state-monopoly capitalism' during the 1970s; and reunified Germany's Party of Democratic Socialism (PDS). All of these constituted themselves as the left-wing rivals of the established socialists.[4] The different labels were the product of tactical differences within a European labour movement that was, at least on the level of rhetoric, in agreement as to its *goals*.[5] Even the debate on revisionism was characterised by unanimous agreement as to the 'final goal', namely the seizure of political power by the party of the proletariat and the overcoming of capitalism, with the prospect of eliminating class distinctions. It was only the question of how to get there that was controversial. None of the contending factions – not even Rosa Luxemburg, Bernstein's fiercest opponent – envisaged the formation of its own party *next to* social democracy. It was only Lenin[6] who seized upon the semantic nuance by breaking the 'Bolsheviks' away from the Russian socialists. Fifteen years later, this party's successful revolution led to a rift not only between Russia's workers' parties, but between those of all Europe. Reformist social democracy was now confronted with a communist faction that openly defended Soviet Russia.[7] The consequences were grave. Let us reconstruct the key aspects of this constellation's theoretical effects.

2.2.1 *The role of violence*

> Force [*Gewalt*] is the midwife of every old society pregnant with a new one. It is itself an economic power.[8]

> The point at which the disagreement with vulgar Marxism is most clearly expressed is the question of *violence* [*Gewalt*].[9]

First, there is the changed attitude to the role of violence, which will here be taken to mean simply the use of physical force. Marx in no way glorified the apex of the use of violence, namely *war*, but rather openly condemned it.[10] However, he was sufficiently pragmatic to recognise that war *is* an instrument of political confrontation, and one that

---

4. 'Communism refers to the uncompromising section of the social movement, which strives for fundamental solutions and is characterised by an unconditional struggle for political hegemony, as well as for a comprehensive revolution in property relations ... The definition as the radical part of the social movement simultaneously addresses another one of communism's features, namely its character as ... a potentially militant rival of social democracy'. This section of the social movement remained 'fixated on its reformist adversary' (W. Müller 2002, p. 327; Bock 1971, 1976; H. Weber 1973, H. Müller 1975, Steigerwald 1977a).

5. Lenin 1973, 1965a, 1970a; Lukács in 1975, pp. 43 ff.; Stalin 1924; Leonhard 1962, pp. 51 ff.; Lieber 1963 I, pp. 61 ff.

6. Lenin 1973.

7. Scharrer 1983.

8. *MECW* 35, p. 739.

9. Lukács 1971, p. 239.

10. *MECW* 20, p. 12 f.; *MECW* 22, pp. 7, 269 f.; Leonhard 1962, pp. 88 ff., 116, 121; Balibar 2001.

was used by the powers of his day to stifle progressive political stirrings both at home and abroad.[11]

Ever since 1789, and especially since the days of Metternich, the reaction disposed of its military alliances, with which socialist strategy needed to reckon. In particular, the German Reich, which socialists in Germany and France were confronted with, was a highly armed and thoroughly militarised autocracy.[12] As for the First World War, which was of central importance to the constitution of communism, it was instigated not by Marxists but by the ruling houses of Europe.[13] Thus taking account of relations of violence within politics was not new in itself – and the brutality of the catastrophic politics of the twentieth century was in no way engendered by the 'illusions' of Marx.[14]

While German Social Democracy had sought the road to power,[15] it lacked the requisite will at the decisive moment. Yet the Social Democrats' 1914 vote in favour of war bonds was nothing to do with a changed attitude to violence – after all, it heralded the greatest bloodshed yet. What had changed vis-à-vis Marx was the attitude toward the question of who ought to decide on the use of violence (*quis iudicat*).[16] For the majority of the Social Democrats, the War was a sort of unpredicted natural event that needed only to be responded to and that required one to shelve all of one's own plans. Marx's way of looking at such 'natural' events – his insistence on considering the social forces behind them in order not to surrender one's ability to act *independently* – had been forgotten, its codification within the International notwithstanding. The small number of socialists who opposed the War were quite helpless, at least to begin with.[17] Those

---

11. Marx reported on European and colonial wars as a newspaper commentator and discussed these wars in his correspondence with Engels (*MECW* 27, pp. 241 ff.). When the Commune seized power in Paris in 1871, Marx called on it, in vain, to stop debating the details of its programme and begin using military force to depose the government, which had fled to Versailles. Such action could have secured power for the Commune (A. Rosenberg 1939, Raddatz 1975; see Lassalle 1987, p. 143, dealing with 1848). International military alliances had been formed to counter a variety of insurrections, reformations and peasant uprisings; the last of these, in 1848, developed on a European scale. The emancipatory movements, which were on the whole not particularly bellicose, tended to be defeated militarily (such as the Montanists, Donatists, Joachimites, Catharists, Waldensians, Lollards, Taborites and Anabaptists: Farner 1985, p. 284). Marxism's endorsement of political violence fascinated many intellectuals (see Benjamin 1999d, Bohrer 1978, Joas 1989, 2000a, Sofsky 2002).

12. Engels, *MECW* 25, p. 171; *MECW* 26, pp. 453 ff.

13. See W. Bauer 1941.

14. See Furet 1999.

15. Kautsky 1908.

16. 'Sovereign is he who decides on the state of exception', said Carl Schmitt, in a brilliant simplification (Schmitt 2005, p. 5).

17. While morally honourable, the pacifism of the Second International was also politically devastating. War broke out despite the International. Once it did, the International had no more prescriptions for action and was forced to dissolve. In a decisive situation, it was unable to act. This occurred despite the fact that the approaching War had already been predicted since the 1890s, and not just by Engels. Like Arendt 1970 (see Weber 1920b, p. 28, on power and domination), Marx distinguished between power and violence. What is decisive is the degree of sociological enlightenment and political autonomy: 'The social power [*Macht*]...appears to these individuals...not

who did not wish to expose themselves to political repression in the way that Luxemburg had done were forced to flee. Many opponents of the war left for Switzerland; among them, Lenin.

The Bolsheviks, who had been familiar with the experience of emigration since 1905, displayed an attitude to violence that was new by comparison to that of the Social Democrats. Lenin was the one who did most to shape opinions on this issue, even though he did not – at the time – dispose of any dictatorial powers. By demanding the immediate signing of a peace treaty, the Bolsheviks attempted to make themselves the vanguard of the masses, who were weary of war. But the Bolsheviks treated peace like an ace up their sleeve, hoping to use it to achieve political goals. They were resolved not to surrender their capacity to act for themselves.[18] This was the real difference between them and the Social Democrats, who kept putting off the 'right' moment for the seizure of power and for political measures. In this formal respect, the Bolsheviks (like Kant) were closer to Marx than many of those who invoked his name.[19] What they most wanted to do was *act on their own account*.

This is why they directed political critiques not just at the 'social chauvinists' (Social Democrats), who had aligned themselves with nationalist tendencies, but also at 'social pacifists' like Kautsky, who were prepared to sign a peace treaty with the old powers. From the Bolsheviks' point of view, these 'social pacifists' were throwing away a unique chance to shape political developments. Their position in fact amounted to an abandonment of their *capacity* to act, regardless of the use to which they might to have put that capacity. The pacifists considered peace an end in itself, and formulated few more far-reaching demands, at least as far as politics were concerned (the pathos-laden aestheticism of expressionist currents was politically insignificant). Unlike the German Social Democrats, the Bolsheviks succeeded not just in seizing power, but also in holding it.[20] Having assumed political responsibility in a country still at war, they had to take on this challenge, whether they wanted to or not. They were soon attacked again: not by Germany, this time, but by the Western powers and by what remained of the old powers within Russia. The organisation of a 'Red Army' under Trotsky and the Bolsheviks' military self-assertion during the years that followed rank among the most widely respected

as their own united power, but as an alien force [*Gewalt*] existing outside them, of the origin and goal of which they are ignorant' (*MECW* 5, p. 48).

18. Lenin 1966, Trotsky 1918.

19. Thus Renner 1918. Rathenau is reported to have said to Radek: 'Read my books. . . . Marx only created the theory of destruction. In my books, you will find the theory of constructive socialism [see Meyer 1977]. This is the first scientific step to have been taken since Marx' (Goldbach 1973, p. 45). In fact, his books are more accurately described as vitalist diatribes against the mechanisation of spirit (Rathenau 1913; see section 2.5.2).

20. The Social Democrats were at each other's throats over their internal differences; the Party's centre under Ebert and Noske even formed an alliance with the old powers in order to vanquish its opponents. Thus the Social Democrats were soon forced to surrender their government powers. The measures they had taken to promote socialisation all petered out.

achievements of the Russian Revolution. The Bolsheviks' bellicist tendency, evident in this achievement, is not in itself a deviation from previous variants of Marxism; after all, Engels had been an active soldier in 1848. The Bolshevik attitude to violence did, however, involve some innovations that can *not* be traced back to Marx. These concerned organisational and political issues, rather than questions of principle.

What was politically fatal about communist tactics was not that the communists were prepared to use violence (unlike the Social Democrats, who castigated violence from below while approving of violence from above, but much like any other state form that claims a right to self-defence, including militant democracy), but that a minority used violence in the name of the majority, and did so in a rash and counterproductive way.[21] Unlike Sorel,[22] Lenin did not consider violence an end in itself. Following the Bolshevik seizure of power in 1917, he pushed for the immediate signing of a peace treaty, and did, in fact, negotiate such a treaty – one that involved major sacrifices, due to his catastrophically disadvantageous bargaining position. In domestic affairs, he formed numerous alliances and settled for many a compromise, such as with the peasants and the national-independence movements; he even welcomed the collaboration of former Mensheviks and opponents such as Trotsky. Yet as far as foreign policy was concerned, the political leadership – which was slow to establish itself at home – pursued the explicit goal of surrounding itself with secure bastions by 'exporting' the revolution into states already weakened by the War. Special attention was focused on Germany, which was not just the motherland of Marxist Social Democracy, but also Russia's most powerful neighbour, both economically and – despite the lost War – militarily.

According to Marx, a successful socialist revolution could take place only in a highly developed country, at least if the result was to be something other than the generalisation of scarcity, and if it was to endure politically and economically, then it needed to occur on an international scale.[23] Lenin, who believed socialism to be possible in

---

21. Attempts to stage a *putsch* in Germany, doomed from the start, led to the Social Democrats rejecting communism. What was fatal was the way that the Communist struggle focused on its Social-Democratic, rather than on its Nazi adversary (the policy of opposing 'social fascism', adopted in 1928). The collectivisation imposed by Stalin in 1929 (a genocide that led to devastating famines) and the terrorist measures by which he attacked his own comrades during the 1930s were politically senseless, if one leaves aside the role they played in maintaining and expanding his personal power. The theory of totalitarianism overgeneralises this by decontextualising it. On-principle rejections of communism that rest purely on the question of violence elide the fact that violence was also resorted to by the foundering monarchies, which initiated wars and conducted them brutally, even against their own populations. The remnant of this glorification of violence was the *Freikorps*: in fact, violence was all they had to offer in the way of a political programme. They, and not so much perverted socialist ideas, constituted the basis for fascist movements. Given such enemies, repudiating violence would have amounted to political suicide (the Social Democrats also set up a fighting squad). When the theory of totalitarianism levels this accusation at the Communists of the time, it does so because of underlying political value judgements. This does not alter the fact that out-and-out massacres did occur under Stalin, Mao, and so on.

22. See Sorel 1999.

23. *MECW* 5, p. 49.

Russia, at least retained the second of the two conditions: he considered 'proletarian internationalism' indispensable even in the case of a social revolution.[24] The Russian Revolution required outside support precisely *because* it had taken place in a country that had scarcely undergone industrial development; on this point, Lenin deliberately departed from Marx and Engels. Lenin had, however, come to lose faith in the socialists of Europe. Even during the War, when the socialist Second International became practically meaningless due to its member parties siding with their various fatherlands, Lenin made plans for the founding of a *third* international organisation, one that would break with the socialists of the period.[25] For as long as he had no state to back him, he did not play a significant role within the precursors of this International, which consisted of socialists who opposed the War (Zimmerwald in 1915; Kienthal in 1916); nor did the International have much clout within the larger political landscape. It was only when the Bolshevik Revolution set new standards that the communist alternative became more attractive.[26]

Thus, in 1919, when the Bolshevik wing of the Russian Socialist Party renamed itself the Russian Communist Party (RCP), the 'Comintern' was founded.[27] Tellingly, the very social-democratic parties whose leaders (opponents of the War) had joined the party opposition or the USPD were now especially keen to work with the new International. But Lenin, who would surely have rejoiced at such a development in 1905, was now pursuing other goals. The Comintern had little use for bourgeois-democratic parties that had already failed, in Lenin's view, back in 1914 – parties that were still not noted for their revolutionary inclinations.[28] They were ostracised from the Comintern by the introduction of new membership criteria.[29] The aim was to a create an organisation that could act concertedly on the international level, and that was capable of taking militant action if necessary.[30]

---

24. See *MECW* 5, pp. 48 f.; *MECW* 6, p. 502; *MECW* 10, p. 317 f.; *MECW* 29, p. 263 f.; *MECW* 23, p. 377; *MECW* 24, p. 39. Lenin believed a socialist revolution to be possible in Russia (Lenin 1965a; see Leonhard 1962, pp. 105–20), but he simultaneously emphasised the impossibility of socialism in one country (*LW* 15, pp. 488 ff.; *LW* 30, pp. 291 ff.; Lenin 1972a, p. 90; see H. Weber 1970, p. 140 f.).

25. Lenin 1915.

26. Radek 1919; K. Neumann 1971.

27. Lenin had called for this move in his "April Theses" and implemented it at the 1919 Party Congress (see Bukharin 1969, Protokoll 1921, Gruber 1967). According to A. Rosenberg 1965, p. 23 and Schneider 1992, p. 93, this involved a deliberate recourse to the 'early Marxism' of 1848, that of the period when the *Communist Manifesto* was written.

28. *LW* 27, p. 340.

29. *LW* 21, pp. 429–437.

30. On Lenin's development, see H. Weber 1970, Hofmann 1979, pp. 197 ff.; Arndt 1980, Reisberg 1980, Kołakowski 1976, pp. 640 ff.; Vranicki 1981, Vol. 1, pp. 407 ff.; Bergmann 1994, Wolkogonow 1994, Service 1986–1995, Žižek 2011. On the Comintern, see A. Rosenberg 1965, Borkenau 1953, Flechtheim 1967; see also Eberlein's minority opinion in Gruber 1967, pp. 87–9. There were attempts, undertaken mainly by Rathenau and Radek, but also by the National Bolsheviks (Schüddekopf 1960, Fritzsche 1976), to establish forms of economic cooperation between the revolutionary Soviet Union and the SPD-governed Weimar Republic; after all, both countries were struggling for their

For a time, the Comintern openly called for revolution in Germany. The foreseeable failure of these attempts at a *putsch* contributed significantly to the marginalisation of the Communists within German politics. Not only had they caused senseless bloodshed, but they had also all too obviously made themselves the executive organs of *Russian* interests.[31] Even the intensification of violence that began with the rule of Stalin was often uncritically accepted within Communist Parties (see section 2.2.2). The subsequent development of international communism was closely bound up with developments within Russia. It was Stalin who emerged as victor from the conflicts over Lenin's succession, after some struggle. He played the various factions off against one another long enough to become an autocrat; then, he proceeded to physically eliminate both his past and his possible future enemies.

In the literature on the subject, the question of violence is often posed in terms of principle; this allows commentators to posit a direct continuity between Marx and Stalin. Yet the difference between Lenin and Stalin is not to be determined by reference to the theoretical question of *whether* violence should be resorted to or not, but rather in the *way* that violence was used politically.[32] Both Lenin and Stalin used the political instrument of violence, domestically and abroad. Lenin used violence against foreign invaders and domestic military adversaries, but he was also capable of convincing his opponents within the Party of the sagacity of his political decisions. He did so in a

---

economic and political survival. Having been in Germany in 1918–19, Radek was aware that a revolution was out of the question, as the German communists lacked the requisite structures; he was thus willing to compromise. He advised the German communists to think in the long term, and devote themselves to building up their organisation rather than engaging in rash putschism – but to no avail (see Levi 2009, Goldbach 1973, Heym 1995). Would the envisaged cooperation have been possible in the absence of a German revolution? Not for as long as the Soviet Union and imperial Germany were at war, but Germany's transformation into a republic governed by the Social Democrats rendered it conceivable. The reasons why the plans for economic and political cooperation were never realised are numerous. Aside from the ideological reservations of the old élites, it seems that the invectives launched by the victorious powers were to blame (People's Commissar Haase refused an offer of bread shipments, pointing out that he had already received such shipments from Wilson: Goldbach 1973, 18; Heym 1995, p. 216 f.). The disastrous policies of the German communist parties also rendered cooperation impossible. The possibility was not realised until the Hitler-Molotov-Ribbentrop-Pact – and then, it was realised in a perverted form (see Leonhard 1958, Haffner 1967, Koenen 1998a).

31. The executive secretary of the Comintern, Karl Radek, who fell victim to the 'purges' in 1938, strongly advised against an attempted *putsch* both in 1919 and in 1923. The fact that bloody sacrifices were made despite this warning must be attributed, at least in part, to the behaviour of the German 'comrades'. On the German Communist Party (KPD) during the Weimar period, see Flechtheim 1969, H. Weber 1969, Mallmann 1996, W. Müller 2002.

32. As far as the question of violence is concerned, Lenin is to Stalin what the legal offence of gross negligence is to that of premeditated multiple murder. With regard to the use of violence, one might trace an abstract trajectory from Marx to Lenin and on to Stalin; they all reckoned with violence as an instrument of political confrontation. But this commonality is so vague, that its explanatory power is almost nil. Moreover, one would have to include all states and political groups prepared to wage war and combat dangerous opponents; virtually all states and groups meet this criterion.

transparent manner, presenting arguments or pointing out the successful outcome of his actions. By contrast, Stalin used intrigues within the state apparatus to eliminate such opponents, and he did so from the outset. Unlike Lenin, Stalin had virtually *no* political successes to which to point. There resulted a cruel spiral of violence that ultimately extinguished entire peoples.

What has emerged so far can be summarised as follows. In contrast with Marx, who had sworn workers to political autonomy, Social Democracy surrendered its capacity to act. In order to regain it, the Bolsheviks revised this attitude to violence and created organisational structures capable of engaging in concerted and sometimes violent political action; this development took a gruesome turn under Stalin. While one can describe the development of the concept of violence in this way, there are some principal distinctions to be made and considered more closely. For one, there is the question of the *subject* of violence. Who is to practice violence in theory, and who does in fact practice it? To answer this question, we need to examine the Leninist notions of the party (2.2.2) and of dictatorship (2.2.3). Another question that needs to be raised is that of ends, or of what is held to constitute a *justification* for violence. This question will lead us to consider the changing function of the underlying theory (2.2.4).

2.2.2 *The organisation of the party*

The party, the party, it's always right.[33]

One of Lenin's decisive innovations vis-à-vis Social Democracy concerned the *question of organisation*. His notion of the party – as strongly disciplined in its internal affairs and closed off to the outside world, but nonetheless called upon to represent the interests of the proletariat – had already caused a split within Russia's newly-constituted Social-Democratic movement in 1902. Former Komsomol member Wolfgang Leonhard pointed out, during the Cold War, that the Leninist doctrine of the party stood 'in a stark contrast to the views of Marx and Engels'.[34] Thus Bolshevism is characterised primarily by its stance on the party.[35] What precisely was new about this stance? The old Social Democracy stemmed from two sources: the efforts of the working classes to improve

33. Ernst Busch.

34. 'The true significance of the 'doctrine of the Marxist-Leninist party' lies in the fact that it . . . provides an ideological foundation for the quasi-military character of those communist parties that are in the thrall of Moscow. Marx and Engels never thought of the party as an advance guard, vanguard or elite; on the contrary, they favoured a loose organisational structure. They spoke out against faith in authority and were far from endorsing any sort of 'democratic centralism' (Leonhard 1962, p. 47; see *MECW* 6, p. 497; *MECW* 23, p. 7; *MECW* 26, pp. 120, 321; *MECW* 38, p. 290; *MECW* 45, p. 288 f.; *MECW* 46, pp. 7 ff.; *MECW* 49, pp. 129 ff.).

35. Lenin also picked up on the key aspects of measures formerly associated with his political opponents. He distributed land to the peasants as demanded by the Narodniks or 'Populists', and the NEP or 'New Economic Policy' borrowed from the market economy, much as the right to national self-determination was taken from 'bourgeois' theory.

their lot through association and the achievements of bourgeois liberalism. In imperial Germany, the latter included the creation of a parliament that the labour party – however politically disadvantaged – could use as a political platform. Thus the First International was able to state in 1872 that 'against [the] collective power of the propertied classes the working class cannot act, as a class, except by constituting itself [*sich selbst*] into a political party, distinct from, and opposed to, all old parties formed by the propertied classes' and that 'the combination of forces which the working class has already effected by its economical struggles ought at the same time to serve as a lever for its struggles against the political power of landlords and capitalists [*muss in den Händen dieser Klasse auch als Hebel in ihrem Kampf gegen die politische Macht ihrer Ausbeuter dienen*]'.[36]

Thus the party was conceived of as an organ of the entire class, which uses democratic means to achieve its 'great end', 'the economical emancipation of the working classes'.[37] This emerges especially from the expressions '*sich selbst*' ('itself') and '*in den Händen dieser Klasse*' (literally 'in the hands of this class'). The notion of autonomy invoked in these passages, which is quite Kantian, and which is further emphasised in the statement that 'the emancipation of the working classes must be conquered by the working classes themselves' is retained throughout the programme. Lenin, by contrast, did *not* display this faith in the capacity of the working class to act autonomously; he did not even do so in his theory. According to Lenin, the working class cannot represent itself:

> We have said that *there could not yet be* Social-Democratic [meaning, in this context, revolutionary] consciousness among the workers. It could only be brought to them from without.... The theory of Socialism, however, grew out of the philosophic, historical and economic theories that were elaborated by the educated representatives of the propertied classes, the intellectuals. According to their social status, the founders of modern scientific Socialism, Marx and Engels, themselves belonged to the bourgeois intelligentsia.[38]

The phenomenon of members of the bourgeoisie joining the workers' camp was interpreted by Marx and Engels not as disenfranchising workers, but as strengthening them.[39] Yet Lenin concludes from this that a revolutionary party cannot be a workers' party in the sense of being a democratic mass party;[40] he holds, instead, that it must be a small, conspiratorial and elitist party of professional revolutionaries. This externalisation of the capacity for insight into the 'true' interests of the proletariat already contains the germ of the paternalism that was to flourish so strongly under Stalin.[41] Under Stalin, the Party's

36. *MECW* 22, p. 427; see *MECW* 24, p. 340.
37. *MECW* 23, p. 3.
38. Lenin 1902, p. 37; see Milner 1999, pp. 15 ff.
39. *MECW* 6, p. 494.
40. *LW* 6, p. 237.
41. The speculative concept of 'imputed class consciousness' in Lukács 1971 is one source of what Plessner 1928 abstractly terms 'excentric positionality'.

vast range of powers was ultimately passed on to the bureaucratic apparatus: the secret police, the Cheka, the People's Commissariat for Internal Affairs and, most importantly, Stalin himself. These powers expanded enormously.[42] The *basic idea* used to gloss over all of this derives from Lenin's political metaphysics, although the proletariat was now no longer 'embodied' in an élite of hand-picked and specially qualified cadres, but in its wise leader alone:

> The Party rallied under the banner of Lenin around its Leninist Central Committee, around Comrade Stalin[43] ... Purging and consolidating its ranks, destroying the enemies of the Party and relentlessly combating distortions of the Party line, the Bolshevik Party rallied closer than ever around its Central Committee.[44]

Those who apply a crude yardstick to history will be reminded of Polybius's cycle of government. Marx's democratic concept, which involves the working class (that is, the majority of the population) determining its own fate, is transformed, under Lenin, into the aristocratic empowerment of the proletariat by its 'vanguard' and then, under Stalin, into a monolithic dictatorship. The Marxian emancipation of the working class is stood on its head; theoretically, this is reflected in the reversal of base and superstructure in the late Stalin.[45]

Soon after the German Communist Party lost Luxemburg and Liebknecht, independent minds such as Levi, Brandler, Thalheimer and Korsch began to be isolated, while cadres fully in the thrall of Moscow, such as Ruth Fischer, Maslow and later Ernst Thälmann (whose only distinguishing feature was his subservience to Stalin) were placed at the helm. As a result, the Party was as ill-equipped to train itself to act in a self-determined way as it was to do justice to its own political and economic circumstances.[46] The Moscow leadership's failure to set a consistent course for the Comintern proved especially ruinous. The Communist International created by Lenin in 1919 and shut down by Stalin in 1943 did not pursue the interests of the Europe-wide movement and its representatives, but only those of Soviet Russia. And yet, paradoxically, its positions were often contrary to Soviet foreign policy. The Comintern became an instrument of domestic disputes and caused confusion within the Communist Parties of Europe. It pursued a veritable zig-zag course and always made sure to arrange for some loophole by which to extract

42. The Central Committee held fewer and fewer Party conferences and meetings (Leonhard 1962, p. 48). Even control of the Party apparatus seemed precarious. The response to this consisted in a series of 'blood replacements'. At first, they were brought about 'only' through the exclusion of older members; later, whole groups of personnel were murdered (Koenen 1998, pp. 225, 231).

43. Commission of the Central Committee 1939, p. 279, on 1924.

44. Commission of the Central Committee 1939, p. 329, on 1935.

45. Communism's political superstructure was supposed to eliminate what remained of the old superstructure (Stalin 1972, p. 33 f.). While it does not explain much, the ancient cyclical model of Polybius nevertheless provides a stimulating perspective. If one accepts the model, then one has to assume that post-1991 Russia has become 'democratic' once more. And it has, *in principle* (see Leonhard 1997).

46. H. Weber 1969a, Winkler 1984–5.

itself from a given situation.[47] Having become increasingly dependent on Moscow, the Communist Parties were vulnerable to the power games played by the various forces within Russia, for better or for worse. Mad shifts from an offensive strategy to ever new alliances with social democrats and fascists – from 'social fascism' to the 'united front' – thoroughly discredited the German Communist Party.[48] Measures intended to render the Party more homogeneous and disciplined, initially implemented to strengthen the movement while the Bolsheviks struggled for power in Russia, were maintained *after* the revolution and imposed on European parties; the effect was the very opposite of what had been intended.

Thus a movement that aspired to self-administration found itself in a situation in which the creativity of its members, and with it the long-term political competence of the Party, were systematically undermined. Moreover, the Communists failed time and again to achieve the political goals they set themselves. Not only did they not achieve any real electoral successes,[49] but they did not succeed in forming genuine alliances either. The only option left for such a party was to attempt to institute one-party rule *violently*. Violence thus went from being a last resort to becoming communism's central axis.

---

47. In 1919, the Comintern described 'the active defense of Soviet Russia by the proletarian masses of every country' as a 'duty to be fulfilled regardless of the sacrifices demanded by the struggle. Every newly emerging proletarian state will be able to assert itself more easily against the capitalist states if Soviet Russia emerges from the struggle undefeated and strikes the first blow at the capitalist state system' (*Die Kommunistische Internationale* 4/5, 1919, p. 13, quoted in Goldbach 1973, p. 56; see Gruber 1967 and Leonhard 1981). The Comintern constituted itself in March of 1919, at the very moment when the revolutionary uprisings in Europe began to ebb. Nonertheless, its 1920 Second World Congress was held under the motto 'World Revolution'. The precipitous insurrections of 1921, which the Comintern had called for, but which were swiftly crushed like those of 1919, were given a dressing down at the Third Congress, where a new, post-revolutionary epoch was announced. 'Thus the situation in Europe and that of the world at large had not altered in any way between the Second and the Third World Congress. Soviet Russia alone had changed' (A. Rosenberg 1939a, p. 165).

48. It is worth recalling the changes of course which the German Communist Party engaged in during the Weimar Republic. The revolt of 1919 was followed in 1920 by the exclusion of the Party's left (about half the Party's members). Next came the *putsch* of 1921, the united front of 1922 and the 'German October' of 1923. 1924, the year of Stalinisation (which involved the Party losing sixty percent of its members) was followed by a right turn in 1925 (against 'Luxemburgism'), a left turn in 1927 and the ultra-left doctrine of 'social fascism' in 1928, the year that Thälmann, who had been voted out of office, was reinstated by Stalin. The 'popular-front' directive was not issued until 1935. In 1939, the Molotov-Ribbentrop Pact was signed (Müller 2002). Borkenau satirised this as follows: '[a] Communist orator... would state that the Social-Democrats, traitors to the interests of the proletariat and allies of the *bourgeoisie*, were unable to defend even the simplest working-class interests; and the orator would proceed by saying "therefore we invite the leaders of the Social-Democratic Party to co-operate with us in an honest fight for a more steeply graded income tax and for a general wage raise of fifteen percent"' (Borkenau 1952, p. 54). On the German Communist Party's alliances with fascists, see Flechtheim 1969, p. 178; Nolte 1968, p. 151; Wippermann 1986.

49. And yet they might have. The mood of the population was not always hostile to communist currents, particularly during times of crisis (such as in 1919, 1929, and 1945).

2.2.3 *The dictatorship of the proletariat*

> Our party programme is the programme of the dictatorship of the proletariat.[50]

Under Stalin, who perceived himself as 'leading' the transition from the 'period of reconstruction' to the 'period of industrialisation', and thus as realising socialism, the anticipated withering away of the state did not occur. On the contrary: the longer Stalin remained in power, the more the state apparatus ballooned. The military, the security service, the police and the bureaucracy all expanded. Stalin was an unproductive thinker, and usually only reproduced what others had said before him. Thus the 'dictatorship of the proletariat' had already been a central notion in Lenin.[51] 'Leninism', fashioned into a dogmatic doctrine by Stalin following Lenin's death, was blatantly structured around the tenet of the 'dictatorship of the proletariat'.[52] But what had been the vague term for a hoped-for transitional stage in Lenin, now became a form of domination that did not seem to want to end.

Marx and Engels had envisaged a different development; this was true even of Lenin, at least as far as his writings are concerned.[53] And yet the reign of violence justified itself by reference to them. How did this happen? Marx and Engels began their political careers as democrats; for example, the subtitle of the *Neue Rheinische Zeitung* was '*Organ der Demokratie*' ['Organ of Democracy']. Given that wage-dependent workers constituted the majority of the population,[54] Marx and Engels considered the words 'democracy' and 'socialism' to be synonymous.[55] They did not become more radically socialist until they realised that capitalism allowed for 'political emancipation' only within narrow limits.

---

50. Bukharin 1969.
51. Lenin 1918.
52. Stalin decreed: 'Leninism is the theory and tactics of the proletarian revolution in general, the theory and tactics of the dictatorship of the proletariat in particular'. (Stalin 1954a, p. 3; see pp. 38–52). 'Is Lenin's thesis that the dictatorship of the proletariat is the "root content of the proletarian revolution" [*LW* 25, 557] correct? It is unquestionably correct. Is the thesis that Leninism is the theory and tactics of the proletarian revolution correct? I think it is correct. But what follows from this? From this it follows that the fundamental question of Leninism, its point of departure, its foundation, is the question of the dictatorship of the proletariat' (Stalin 1954, p. 163 f.; see pp. 168–78). In 1937, the building of socialism was considered to have been brought to 'completion', and the 'Constitution embodying the victory of Socialism' called the country a 'workers' and peasants' democracy' (Commission of the Central Committee 1939, p. 346). On Stalin's 'theory' and its 'reception', see Hedeler 1994, pp. 33–74; A. Schaefer 1997.
53. See Engels: '[s]o long as the proletariat still *makes use* of the state, it makes use of it, not for the purpose of freedom, but of keeping down its enemies and, as soon as there can be any question of freedom, the state as such ceases to exist' (*MECW* 45, p. 64). Lenin still expressed this view in 1917. In his last writings from 1922–3, he was especially inclined to admit that the road from the revolution to socialism was a very long one (Schneider 1992, p. 175). Benjamin's remark can be applied to the dictatorship of the proletariat: '[t]he tradition of the oppressed teaches us that the "state of emergency" in which we live is not the exception but the rule' (Benjamin 2003, p. 392).
54. This category includes journeymen, servants working in agriculture and commerce, and so on (Losurdo 1993).
55. A. Rosenberg 1937, pp. 59 ff.; see Femia 1993.

The bourgeoisie was not, after all, particularly willing to stand up for 'democracy', even if this fact is often glossed over today. The proletariat had already acted on behalf of the bourgeoisie by fighting for the republic in 1848, and it was still a minority.[56] If it were to seize power, it would be forced for the duration of a 'transition period'[57] to consolidate its power in a 'dictatorial' manner. This would allow it to implement the planned measures against capital, which might still be politically and economically *powerful* despite its demographic inferiority, and against other ruling classes.[58]

Marx discerned in the Paris Commune of 1871 'the political form at last discovered under which to work out the economical emancipation of labor'.[59] The features he attributed to the Commune needed simultaneously to be read as requirements for a possible future 'dictatorship of the proletariat'. In substance, they were as follows:

a) The new society is headed by a body elected by universal suffrage, which... exercises legislative and executive functions.
b) The oppressive power of a centralised government, military and bureaucracy are overturned.
c) The political police is stripped of its political functions.
d) The deputees of the elected body and the civil servants employed in the various branches of the administration receive a salary that does not exceed a worker's wages.
e) The deputees can be deposed at any time, by being recalled by those who elected them. According to Marx and Engels, the goal of the dictatorship of the proletariat ought to consist in transforming government bodies from masters of society into servants of society. The development, after a socialist revolution, of a new bureaucracy or a new social stratum were to be prevented.[60]

---

56. The proletariat was a minority in Germany, which was still essentially an agrarian country (see *MECW* 20, p. 74 f.; *MECW* 24, p. 93 f.).

57. *MECW* 24, p. 95.

58. See *MECW* 6, p. 350; *MECW* 6, pp. 496, 504 f.; *MECW* 7, pp. 204, 431; *MECW* 10, p. 118; *MECW* 21, pp. 93 f.; *MECW* 17, pp. 28 ff., 73; *MECW* 27, p. 190; *MECW* 23, p. 371; *MECW* 24, pp. 12, 94; *MECW* 27, p. 227; *MECW* 39, pp. 62 ff. The failure of the Weimar Republic can be read as confirming the fears expressed by Marx and Engels. While the Kaiser had been overthrown, the judiciary, the civil service, the military and capital still disposed of considerable influence. The democratic measures taken by the social democratic governments, measures that aimed at a compromise, were virtually powerless in the face of this, and they were rescinded in 1933 (Gay 1968). Following the experiences of 1848, Marx raised an uncomfortable question: What does democracy actually base itself on? If it does *not* base itself on the bourgeoisie, then it does not stand a chance. But if it *does* base itself on the bourgeoisie, then capitalism cannot be overcome democratically. For this reason, he felt the French republic of the day displayed features of a 'dictatorship of the bourgeoisie' (*MECW* 10, pp. 69, 76, 126; *MECW* 7, pp. 168 f.; Schmitt 1994, p. 201).

59. *MECW* 22, p. 334.

60. Leonhard 1962, p. 162.

These features were intended to manoeuvre the new form of government past the Scylla of a violent counterrevolution and the Charybdis of a new bureaucratic rule. Marx's reflections on the 'dictatorship of the proletariat' can therefore in no way be interpreted as the germ of totalitarianism.[61] They were, in fact, directed *against* the possible reactionary counterrevolution that later imposed itself in National Socialism, and against the perverted reign of bureaucracy that was characteristic of Stalinism. The very expression was an ironic jab at Blanqui's putschist 'dictatorship of the few'.[62] Marx and Engels were quite aware of the possibility of taking power by democratic means; after all, the struggle for the franchise and for popular legislation was one of the cornerstones of socialism.[63] The socialists differed from the liberals (2.1.2) in that they did not consider democracy to be necessarily bound up with a particular economic order, namely the existing one. A 'dictatorship of the proletariat' makes sense only within the context of a democratic social order:[64]

> If one thing is certain it is that our party and the working class can only come to power under the form of a democratic republic. This is even the specific form for the dictatorship of the proletariat, as the Great French Revolution has already shown. It would be inconceivable for our best people to become ministers under an emperor.[65]

In the thought of the young Marx, democracy involves the state ceasing to be 'the governing moment'; thus, he maintained, 'democracy is the resolved mystery of all constitutions'.[66] Marx held that the 'self-legislation' of citizens would have to bring about a situation in which the state apparatus no longer stands opposed to society, as in Prussian and Bonapartist practice or in the thought of Hegel, but *subordinates* itself to it.[67] Marx thereby established the modern prospect of shaping society in a democratic and practical way. Yet unlike the reductive account offered by the theory of 'civil society', an account that factors out economic matters,[68] Marx also paid attention to the conditions that needed to be met if this prospect was to be realised; he was aware that mere resolutions and debates on norms would not be enough. The German notion that one

---

61. Löw 2002.

62. *MECW* 24, p. 13; Schneider 1992, p. 25.

63. In 1847, Engels held that the socialist revolution would have to 'inaugurate a *democratic constitution* and thereby, directly or indirectly, the political rule of the proletariat' (*MECW* 6, p. 350). In 1891, he felt that 'the old society may develop peacefully into the new one' (*MECW* 27, p. 226). During its brief heyday, "eurocommunism" attempted to act in accordance with this notion. The endpoint of these efforts is marked by Mitterrand's 1983 shift to more liberal policies, prompted by the impossibility of implementing rigorous measures in the absence of a more far-reaching transformation of property relations (and without violence).

64. The link between socialism and democracy proved impossible to sever. It emerges, albeit negatively, in Stalin's rhetoric of 'people's democracies'. States like the German Democratic Republic still needed to *call* themselves democratic.

65. Engels, *MECW* 27, p. 227.

66. *MECW* 3, pp. 29, 31.

67. *MECW* 22, p. 332 f.; *MECW* 49, pp. 179 ff.

68. See section 3.2.3.

has established control over social reality as soon as one has grasped its principles – a notion that rests on the assumption that these principles are what engenders reality in the first place – persists from Fichte to Habermas.[69] Marx's critique of German idealism within political philosophy can be summarised in the statement that changes in form do *not* affect 'content', at least not automatically, because genuine development always occurs on the level of content, not on that of form.[70]

This turning point or *Kehre* is nominalist in the sense that while form is not eliminated altogether (as in anarchism), it is *subordinated* to content.[71] Generally speaking, the political sphere is not fully autonomous in capitalist democracy; the economic sphere is primary with regard to it. To say this is not to point out anything mysterious, but only to refer to a phenomenon that even conservatives are lamenting these days, namely the waning of the power of politics. States no longer decide which firms invest in them; firms decide in which states they invest, and they impose their conditions upon the states they choose. Idealist philosophy was all the less convincing to Marx and Engels as the particular state of *Prussia* did not even meet the criteria stipulated within the 'concept' of democracy. Marx and Engels considered Prussia, and hence imperial Germany, 'a police-guarded military despotism, embellished with parliamentary forms, alloyed with a feudal admixture, already influenced by the bourgeoisie, and bureaucratically carpentered',[72] 'where the government is almost omnipotent and the Reichstag and all other representative bodies have no real power'.[73] It was delusional to hope that this monarchy, constitutional only in appearance, would allow a parliamentary majority – unlikely in itself – to act effectively.[74] The power of form to impose itself on content was doubtful. Had they won a majority in imperial Germany, the Social Democrats would have been little more than a 'fig-leaf' for absolutism.[75]

---

69. See section 2.5.2.

70. See *MECW* 5, p. 90; *MECW* 10, p. 68 f.; *MECW* 22, p. 334; *MECW* 35, p. 94 and elsewhere; see also Böhm 1998; 2.5.2, 3.1.5. Formally, the notion persists even in Adorno's *Negative Dialectics*, without its political origins being reflected upon. Even critical theory contains elements of Fichteanism (2.6.1, 3.1.5).

71. On Marx's nominalism, see K. Hartmann 1970; Krahl 1971; Althusser 1994, p. 217; and Backhaus 1997; for different assessments, see Popper 1957 and Maurer 1975. Pike 1999 compares Marx to Aristotle: Aristotle's critique of Plato's pure forms is similar to Marx's critique of Hegel and the 'purely' liberal party. Kant's 'thing in itself' was intended to help establish the notion that content is not determined by form. Engels already refused to acknowledge this (*MECW* 26, p. 367 f.; for a more in-depth discussion, see 2.5.2).

72. *MECW* 24, p. 96.

73. *MECW* 27, p. 226.

74. A parliamentary majority was prevented less by Social Democracy's lack of popularity than by electoral legislation and the arbitrary redefinition of electoral districts in favour of the government. Saxony, the cradle of Social Democracy, was doted with a 'reactionary three-tier electoral law' that barred the majority of workers from voting. The Social Democrats nevertheless received 58.8 percent of the vote in 1903 (Szejnmann 2000, p. 7).

75. Liebknecht, *MECW* 27, p. 226; 2.1.1.

Lenin did *not* reiterate the critique of pure form; he merely substituted one form for another. He retained the conviction that this would have an effect on content. Instead of exploring the conditions for a 'dictatorship of the proletariat' *within* democracy, he replaced the form of parliamentarianism with that of dictatorship.[76] The genitive 'of the proletariat' thus becomes political metaphysics: it merely suggests that the Party represents the proletariat's 'authentic' interests. Not only did the Russian proletariat not make up the majority of the population (the peasants were the decisive social stratum), but the Party did not even genuinely represent the proletariat, being controlled by a minority whose background was blatantly non-proletarian. Nor was there the institutional option of taking power legally.[77]

Thus Lenin no longer shaped the 'dictatorship of the proletariat' on the model of the French republic, but on that of imperial Germany's postal service.[78] Critics of Marx[79] would later argue that if the 'proletariat' became the 'subject of history' in Marx's writings around 1843, this was because, as a Left Hegelian, he was desperately *searching* for such a subject, to which he then attributed an exaggerated world-historical mission. This criticism was really aimed at actually-existing socialism. In late nineteenth-century Europe, the proletariat was not some scholarly concoction, but a social-revolutionary mass movement. Marx wanted to support and theoretically enlighten this movement. It is true that, in doing so, he was initially guilty of rhetorical exaggerations; they were due to the spirit and circumstances of the time.[80] Lenin's struggle against the European social democrats, taken up in 1914, saw him accusing them of representing only the interests of a treacherous 'labour aristocracy'. His legitimating construct 'proletarian interests' – meaning interests that can be correctly identified and represented only by professional revolutionaries from the elitist cadre party – indicates the distance separating him from actual workers and their organisations, both in Russia and elsewhere.[81] Lenin's theory according to which the monopolistic surplus profits of the Western European

76. In 1920, Lenin said: 'The scientific concept of dictatorship means nothing more nor less than completely unrestricted power, absolutely unimpeded by laws or regulations and resting directly on the use of force' (*LW* 25, p. 441). 'The dictatorship of the proletariat does not fear any resort to compulsion and to the most severe, decisive and ruthless forms of coercion by the state. The advanced class, the class most oppressed by capitalism, is entitled to use compulsion, because it is doing so in the interests of the working and exploited people' (*LW* 31, p. 497; see Leonhard 1962, p. 164; for a critique, see Löw 2002).

77. '"Either the dictatorsip of Kornilov... or the dictatorship of the proletariat – there can be no question of a different way out for a country... broken up so terribly by this most tortuous of all wars" [Lenin]. There is no denying that this was in fact the dilemma faced by Russia in 1917' (H. Weber 1970, p. 118). This sort of 'determination' made an impression on the political Right (Schmitt 1994, p. 201; Schmitt 1996a, p. 63).

78. Lenin 1970b, p. 59.

79. Such as Hartmann 1970.

80. Such as the 'resurrection of nature' (*MECW* 3, p. 298; *MECW* 29, pp. 261, 264 f.; *MECW* 26, p. 519; see sections 2.1.4; 2.4.6.

81. 17 July 1953 was a workers' insurrection, just like the 'Kronstadt Commune' that was brutally repressed in 1921. The 'Workers' Opposition' within the Russian Communist Party, a current that

bourgeoisie allowed it to bribe working-class leaders, thereby creating a docile labour aristocracy that made the Western labour parties into opportunists and turned them against revolutionary Russia, must be seen as an expression of his dislike for Western European labour parties.[82] Witness the following feast of epithets: '[*In the West*], the *craft-union, narrow-minded, selfish, casehardened, covetous, petty-bourgeois "labour aristocracy", imperialist-minded, imperialist bribed and imperialist-corrupted*, emerged as a much stronger stratum than in our country'.[83]

Marx and Engels were not unfamiliar with the phenomenon of reformism, which was the basis of such rants. But they did not consider reformism a reason to place oneself above others and impose truths upon them *from outside*.[84] They were interested in circulating the results of their theoretical efforts, not in improving their political rank within the party. Lenin's externalism can be interpreted as breaking with the principle of democracy; it is certainly indicative of the considerable distance separating the Party hierarchy from the population. The gap widened over time, rather than being closed. There developed a *new* class society, divided not into labour and capital, but into the general population and the bureaucracy. Thus dictatorship was rendered permanent.[85] When Stalin *extended* the 'dictatorship of the proletariat', he did so by picking up on the distinction between form and content. He no longer intended for form to be determined by content; instead, form was to violently create content in its own image:

> In October 1917 the working class had vanquished capitalism *politically*, by establishing its own political dictatorship.... Now the main task was to proceed to build a new, Socialist economic system all over the country and thus smash capitalism *economically* as well.... Socialist industrialisation of the country was the chief link in the chain; with it the construction of a Socialist economic system must begin.[86]

After twenty years of 'dictatorship of the proletariat', loosening the reins somewhat might have seemed feasible; instead, Stalin tightened them more than ever before, in

---

also developed in 1921, was a product of the trade unions (see Hillmann 1967, pp. 54–100). See also Koenen 2001, p. 324 *et passim*.

82. Hobsbawm 1977, pp. 174–84.

83. Lenin 1970a, p. 42 f.

84. See, for example, *MECW* 40, p. 344; *MECW* 27, p. 226. 'The theoretical conclusions of the Communists are in no way based on ideas or principles that have been invented, or discovered, by this or that would-be universal reformer. They merely express, in general terms, actual relations springing from an existing class struggle, from a historical movement going on under our very eyes. The abolition of existing property relations is not at all a distinctive feature of communism' (*MECW* 6, p. 498).

85. 'Stalin abolished the limits on the salaries of full-time functionaries that Lenin had introduced. These functionaries were also granted numerous privileges related to food, the provision of commodities, medical care and vacation. These privileges created a wide rift between the bureaucracy and the people' (Bartsch 1976, p. 78; see section 3.2.2; Michel 1910, Castoriadis 1949; Cliff 1955; Bettelheim 1977; Koenen 1998, p. 232).

86. Commission of the Central Committee 1939, p. 273.

order to impose, at horrific cost, his 'despotism of industrial development'.[87] Following a series of other grievous errors,[88] Stalin blustered himself into a modernising forward leap that developed an incredible destructive power. The forced collectivisation of the late 1920s cruelly sacrificed the rural population, while the major 'purges' of the 1930s did the same with the Party bureaucracy and military leadership. The condition of civil war was then definitively rendered permanent by Stalin's 'socialist industrialisation'.[89] There is no ambiguity about the incredible atrocities involved, atrocities long passed over in silence both in the East and West. But their justification in terms of Marx had as much warrant as Eichmann's invocation of Kant or colonialist references to the Bible – which is to say, next to none. Nevertheless, the fact that such justifications were formulated takes us back, once more, to the question of the political subject.[90] The descent from the liberation of the working class, in Marx, to Stalin's bureaucratic state terror, came about by way of via Lenin's Party rule[91] – which has thereby been discredited to this day.

2.2.4 *A creative evolution of Marxism?*

> Stalinism is not guided by Marxist theory, or for that matter any theory at all, but by the empirical interests of the Soviet bureaucracy.[92]

The organisational model of Lenin's Party also had consequences for the receptions of Marx's *theories*. The unity that was required of the Party soon rendered debate impossible. The banning of political imposition in 1919 was followed by the ban on factions at the Tenth Party Congress (held in 1921, shortly after the Kronstadt uprising). Next came the expulsion of Party members and the infamous 'purges', which degenerated

---

87. Schneider 1992, p. 211.

88. The idea of 'socialism in one country', proposed by Stalin from 1924 onward, was meant to win over the peasants. Gaining their support required changing the official ideology, and the change had to be rendered dogmatically indisputable. Stalin meant to strengthen the numerous middle peasants by means of self-administration, thereby isolating the kulaks, who were hostile to him. Yet Stalin's measures allowed the kulaks to extend their power. Bukharin interpreted this bolstering of capitalism as the new socialism, thereby winning the bourgeois nationalists over to his side. This situation was unfavourable to Stalin, as the peasants and the bourgeoisie were now on his side, while the old cadres were opposed to him. On the international level, Stalin formed alliances both with the Communist minority, which had been forcibly brought into line, and with the Social Democrats of Britain, Germany and China, who were far more powerful. This two-track approach led to fiascos everywhere. Stalin isolated himself completely. Domestically, he faced the opposition of the right-wing kulaks and the left-wing Party leadership; internationally, he had virtually no powerful allies (A. Rosenberg 1939a, pp. 220 ff.).

89. Courtois 1998 describes the atrocities at length; see also Nolte 1983, pp. 524 ff.; Klotz 1999. Dutschke 1975 and Schneider 1992, p. 203 compare Stalin to the Mongol invasion (on 'modernisation', see Schneider 1992, p. 201).

90. *Quis iudicabit?*

91. According to Stalin, 'in the Soviet Union, the Bolshevik Party and the state are inseparable' (Commission of the Central Committee 1939, p. 285).

92. Trotsky 1980.

into veritable state terrorism in 1937. The policies of post-1917 Russia lacked a solid theoretical foundation; the measures taken under 'actually-existing' socialism had little to do with the theories of Marx, who had produced no blueprint for a socialist politics and economy.[93] Marx provided little more than the odd label, and yet he was made to serve as a theoretical cover for what was being done politically. This fateful development was evident not just in Soviet Russia; the course followed by pre-1933 German Social Democracy was remarkably parallel, despite significant differences in political outlook and context. Both the Russian Communist Party and the German Social Democrats treated Marx's writings as a 'political theory', an ideology by which to legitimate their policies. In both cases, Marx's alleged 'philosophy of history', which predicted the demise of capitalism and prophesied world domination for the proletariat (2.6.6), was invoked in support of a politics that no longer bothered to relate given circumstances to theory.[94] Kautskyan orthodoxy was church-like, due to its symbolic value for the mass party; Lenin's elitist radicalism was reminiscent of a religious order or sect.[95]

The sectarian character of the German Communist Party was aggravated by the arcane reprimands it received from distant Moscow, as well as by the political marginalisation that resulted from attentist tactics and the failures engendered by them.[96] Both orthodoxies were characterised by a similar relationship to Marxian theory: the leaders abused and instrumentalised Marx's theory as the 'integrating ideology'[97] of a mass party or the 'legitimatory science'[98] of a revolutionary cadre party, and eventually of a bureaucratic

---

93. Dahrendorf 1952, pp. 167 ff.; Ramm 1957, Fleischer 1993, p. 20; Flechtheim 1983, p. 234 f. (for different accounts, see Bukharin 1922 and Sik 1967).

94. Examples of how the given circumstances were ignored include Trotsky's bypassing of the peasant question and his frequent but awkward comparisons to the French Revolution (Abosch 1990), Zinoviev's putschist model for the German Communists and Stalin's demented policy of industrialisation.

95. Flechtheim 1969, p. 154; A. Rosenberg 1939a, p. 168; on the social content of the 'sect', see Troeltsch 1977. Marx described both the 'League of the Just' and the Lassalleans as sects; Engels popularised the term in his work on the Peasant War. Marx and Engels did not want their own party to assume the character of a sect under any circumstances: 'If we did not want . . . to take up the movement, adhere to its already existing . . . side and to advance it further, then there was nothing left for us to do but to preach communism in a little provincial sheet and to found a tiny sect instead of a great party of action. But we had already been spoilt for the role of preachers in the wilderness; we had studied the utopians too well for that' (Engels, *MECW* 26, p. 122; see *MECW* 10, p. 421; *MECW* 23, p. 473; *MECW* 24, p. 91 f.; *MECW* 27, p. 240; and elsewhere).

96. Attentism was a feature, in any case, of the Party's Left associated with Ruth Fischer and Thälmann (Flechtheim 1969, p. 174). The German Communist Party is a textbook case of the old 'dilemma of democratic socialism' (Gay 1954). As early as 1919, the Party, then led by Paul Levi, decided: 'Members of the German Communist Party who do not share these views on the Party's nature, organisation and action are to leave the Party' (Report on the Second Party Congress of the German Communist Party, quoted in W. Müller 2002, p. 331). It was not long before there existed a number of breakaway organisations, notwithstanding the fact that the German Communist Party was relatively small to begin with. On the 'purges', see Schneider 1992, pp. 211–21; Koenen 1998, pp. 215–70; Hedeler 2002.

97. Matthias 1957.

98. Negt 1995, pp. 7 ff.

autocracy, while the rank and file piously received the Marxist gospel as a 'scientific worldview'.[99] Marxism, which had set out to provide everyone with the possibility of taking their own interests in hand, without ideological delusions, itself became an ideology.[100] It never recovered from this development.

Lenin was certainly not outstandingly talented as a theorist; he was a clever political organiser[101] with a gift for impressive public speaking. To be sure, he also knew how to convince people in writing. But he always adapted his theory to the political exigencies of the moment. Even his main *philosophical* work[102] betrays the strategic considerations behind it. It was in this work – that is, in the field of epistemology – that Lenin developed his concept of 'the struggle of parties in philosophy'.[103] This ideologisation was noticeably aggravated by the hierarchic and centralist organisation that even the sciences were subjected to under communism. Lenin's off-the-cuff 'theory of representation' and Lysenko's abstruse theoretical efforts, undertaken at the behest of the Party and with the intention of replacing Western Darwinism, are not so far apart. What is decisive, in each case, is the conviction that even science *as such* can and ought to be partisan.[104] But that science should refrain from taking sides is shown by the very possibility of demonstrating, through the critique of ideology, the concrete partisanship of a particular science. It is not just from Marx's perspective that this is impossible. That science was nevertheless expected to be partisan merely led to scientists adopting the same attitude of subservience as was evident within the Party. In East Germany, this was evident in Walter Ulbricht's distortions of history and in the practice of expelling scientists from the Party.[105] The purges in Moscow proved lethal for many theorists,

---

99. 'Dialectical materialism is the world outlook of the Marxist-Leninist party' (Commission of the Central Committee 1939, p. 105).

100. See sections 2.4.2, 2.6.1.

101. Baecker 2002.

102. Lenin 1972.

103. Lenin 1972, p. 434. In a dispute on epistemology, the Menshevik Plekhanov accused the Bolshevik Bogdanov of 'subjective idealism' and related this to Bolshevism's voluntarist tactics, arguing that a materialist ought not to attempt an overthrow of the political order before the objective preconditions of such an overthrow have matured. Lenin was not prepared to ignore this attack. He cleaned out his stable and formulated a radical rebuttal, presenting Plekhanov with a new claim. Subjective idealism, Lenin argued, is 'necessarily' on the side of the reaction, because it favours religion, whereas materialism is militant *in and of itself* (Lenin 1972, p. 415). However, the materialism of a philosopher like Hobbes was in no way emancipatory, whereas the communism of early Christianity was highly idealist. Thomism's epistemological materialism leaves religion intact while attacking subjective idealism (Kołakowski 1976, pp. 695–723). This is why Kołakowski says of Lenin's book that '[a]s philosophy it is crude and amateurish' (p. 721).

104. Stalin 1976, a work that picks up on Lenin 1972, is included in the history of the Party. Thus even the most fundamental theories are subordinated to the Party's development (see the resolution of 1930: Gropp 1960, pp. 24 ff.). Theoretical effects pale beside the fates suffered by individuals, and yet they, too, have their place in world history's cabinet of horrors (see Wetter 1958; Kosellek 1977).

105. See H. Weber 1969; Grebing 1977; Rauh 1991; Prokop 1996; Bialas 1996; Knechtel 2000. 'The pre-eminently practical nature of the Communist Party, the fact that it is a fighting party

including David Riazanov, the editor of Marx's writings. The resulting subservience and lack of independence *in theoreticis* extended to Western scholars, as the literature shows. The loss of democracy, both within the Party and outside it, and the restrictions placed on the freedom of science, went hand-in-hand.[106]

Lenin's partisan science vacillated considerably, in response to the given circumstances.[107] 'Leninism', the product of Stalin's dogmatisation of Lenin's writings, was stillborn. Not only was Lenin himself dead, but his whole body of work was rigidified: politically committed statements formulated in response to concrete situations (statements that frequently contradict each other, such as those on with whom one should ally) were reduced to axiomatic propositions. Accurately speaking, there is no such thing as 'Leninism': there is only *Stalinism* – and it is Stalinism that is meant when people say 'Leninism'.[108] It is true that all influential Bolsheviks defined themselves as 'Leninists' following Lenin's death.[109] But Stalin was the only one who contributed no ideas of his own; in this sense, he really was the 'purest' of Leninists. This may have been why he triumphed over his rivals.[110]

---

presupposes its possession of a correct theory, for otherwise the consequences of a false theory would soon destroy it. Moreover, it is a form of organisation that produces and reproduces correct theoretical insights by consciously ensuring that the organisation has built into it ways of adapting with increased sensitivity to the effects of a theoretical posture' (Lukács 1971, p. 327; on this, see Strelewitz in Papcke 1986, p. 163). Althusser 1972 still considered theory an extension of political struggles.

106. This is evident not just in texts penned by the German Communist Party itself (see Knoche 1980; Flechtheim 1980), but even in academic philosophy (Beyer 1968; Sandkühler 1973; Tomberg 1973; Steigerwald 1980). Even where ties to the German Democratic Republic are improbable, one is struck by the lack of critical distance. Many Western Marxists well-nigh internalised this 'partisanship' (Lukács; Horkheimer 1988a, p. 56; see section 2.6.1; Althusser 1970; Haug 1972). Heinrich 2001, p. 383, draws attention to the following passage in A. Schmidt 1969, p. 203: 'In Althusser, ... interest in a better society remains external to the theoretical process itself' – a statement from which one can only conclude that even Schmidt believed science ought to be 'partisan' (see Steinvorth 1977, pp. 83 ff.).

107. According to Basso 1975, Lenin was first and foremost a strategist who refused to be identified with a specific doctrine (p. 11). In support of his point, Basso quotes Zilli: 'Every theoretical contribution that Lenin has bestowed on Marxism is the product of an engagement not so much with the texts [in this case those of the Paris Commune in *State and Revolution* – C.H.] as ... with concrete political circumstances. His originality ... consisted in his ingenuous intuition of a formula that did not break with the system but did allow for more rapid achievement of the goal pursued' (p. 41).

108. 'Leninism is Marxism of the era of imperialism and the proletarian revolution' (Stalin 1954a, p. 3), said Stalin. On the Stalinist character of 'Leninism', see H. Weber 1969; Fleischer 1973; Hofmann 1979, p. 250; Schneider 1992, p. 84; Hedeler 1993, p. 89: '1926 is an ... important year for the constitution of "Leninism"' as brought about by 'Stalin, who replaced Lenin's theory with "Leninism" in order to legitimate his personal dictatorship'.

109. See Trotsky et al. 1925.

110. Lieber 1963, p. 193 remarks 'that Stalin entered into this theoretical feud without any programme of his own ... The bureaucracy accepted Stalin as the custodian of Lenin's ideas, although Stalin did not dispose of Lenin's authority. Stalin consistently described himself as a "common man" (a self-description he often used), unambitious, without a programme of his own. For this very reason, his power continued to grow, in Lenin's shadow'.

Trotsky's 1924 remark that Stalin made reference only to the pre-revolutionary Lenin is not altogether false.[111] Trotsky himself made reference to the Lenin of the 'April Theses', who had adopted Trotsky's hypothesis on the 'permanent revolution'. Following the elimination of actual or alleged 'Trotskyists', Stalin adopted what was, in substance, a Trotskyist programme.[112] However, the *function* of theory had changed once again. Following Hans-Joachim Lieber, we can distinguish three stages in the development of Marxist theory: an orthodox phase, in which the theory had high *intrinsic value*, was followed by a revolutionary phase, characterised by the increasing *interpenetration* of theory and practice. The first phase encompasses Marx's writings, only a small part of which constitute instructions for action, as well as the deliberate Kautskyan efforts to shield Marx's theory from any sort of practice. The second phase encompasses Lenin's writings, which can hardly be isolated from their context:

> Since the bourgeois-capitalist phase of Russian development had been bypassed and everyday political practice revealed a historical-social object that was expected to assume the form dictated to it, theory had to be translated immediately into practice and practice inexorably called for theoretical reflection. Within this mechanism, classical-Marxist orthodoxy was dissolved good and proper.[113]

According to Lieber, theory's extreme orientation toward practice (Lenin) yielded eventually to a dictatorial technocracy (Stalin) that allowed for the forcible implementation of a 'theory' that was methodologically unsound: 'Theory, having been caused by the experience of revolution to lose its specific character as a product of close engagement with reality that serves, at the same time, as a super-empirical guide to political action, and having merged with violence to constitute a new 'axis of history', now becomes ... immediately practical'.[114]

This suggestion of a twofold change of theory's function – from Marx's ambitious theory to Stalin's crude command economy, via Lenin's amalgamation of theory and practice – makes it strikingly clear just how little 'actually-existing socialism' had to do with Marx's theory (although Lieber certainly overestimates theory's power to shape politics). Nobody rules by means of ideologico-strategic tracts, which are merely a symbolic expression of claims to power. They *justify* the general political course. It is not just that

---

111. Trotsky 1937.

112. Trotsky mistrusted the Russian peasants and had faith only in the proletariat. This entailed the need for a militant internationalism (by which to obtain outside support) and a ruthlessly enforced industrialisation. In 1927, Stalin sidelined this approach with the aid of Bukharin. Next, Stalin turned on Bukharin. 'Once the "Left Opposition" had been smashed, its comprehensive industrialisation programme was integrated, with some minor changes, into Stalinism's political programme ... It was eventually used to justify criticism of the "Right deviation"' (Lieber 1963, p. 194; see, too, p. 195). In Lieber's view, Stalin always rejected the suggestions of others and then took the opposite course of action. This may explain the zigzag course he followed, his constant switching from Left (1923, 1928) to Right (1925, 1938).

113. Lieber 1963, Vol. I, p. 197.

114. Ibid.

the writings of Marx and Stalin are unrelated in terms of their content; Marx and Stalin also differ strongly in terms of the character of their theories:

> Here, the core of post-revolutionary Bolshevik ideology is revealed. Largely cut off from the forces that effectively shape society, it becomes a programme that, while not of any great practical value, can nevertheless be implemented by means of force. It is only in combination with force that it becomes immediate political action.[115]

Leninism only became the buttress of a totalitarian system after Stalin set out upon the road of 'socialism in one country' – a fateful decision that is often elided in the theory of totalitarianism, perhaps in order to facilitate inferences about Marx.[116] Thus 'ideology itself becomes an instrument to be used for domination, one by which to administer, steer and control the society that one wishes to bring into line'.[117]

Marxism was instrumentalised to legitimate imperial rule, and every Marxist-Leninist manual is testament to the desolation wrought by this development.[118] *Diamat*'s rigid formulas exercised little influence on politics; they were an ideological surface phenomenon.[119] It was claimed that dialectics revealed the rules governing thought, nature and society – both objectively, as manifested in 'real' contradictions, and in the form of 'subjective dialectics'; that is, as 'mirrored' in thought and cognition.[120] Philosophy was called upon to 'constantly and vigorously reflect practice as it develops'.[121] But the practice was autocratic, and so philosophy remained dependent on authority and was never in a position to formulate its own propositions, rather than simply 'interpreting' whichever statements of authority were considered topical.[122] When independent propositions were formulated after all, the author was forced to confess his own inca-

---

115. Ibid.

116. While many great thinkers – among them Lenin, Luxemburg and Gramsci – are represented in Backes 2002 (an anthology on the theory of totalitarianism), Stalin is absent.

117. Lieber 1963, Vol. I, p. 198.

118. Gropp 1960; Buhr 1972; Fiedler 1974; Becher 1976; and Wrona 1979 make this point. Individuals reporting their experiences within 'socialist scholarship' concur (2.1.4).

119. This emerges clearly from Stalin's 1938 didactic manual (Stalin 1976). The features he attributes to 'nature' give rise to general theoretical tenets that are then used to justify his policies – policies that changed frequently, to be sure. 'Further, if development proceeds by way of the disclosure of internal contradictions . . . so as to overcome these contradictions, then it is clear that the class struggle of the proletariat [this was Lenin's term for the Civil War (*LW* 29, p. 338), as well as the term by which Stalin described his aggressive industrialisation policy (Stalin 1954, p. 187)] is a quite natural and inevitable phenomenon . . . Hence, in order not to err in policy, one must pursue an uncompromising proletarian class policy' (Commission of the Central Committee 1939, p. 111; A. Schaefer 1997). At this point, the 'appeasers' – Bukharin and his associates – had already been excluded from the Party (Commission of the Central Committee 1939, p. 295; see, too, pp. 275 f., 289 f., 324 ff.; on Bukharin, see Hedeler 1994). Bochenski 1960, pp. 35 ff. presents a polemical but accurate overview of the history of philosophy in Soviet Russia, 1917–50.

120. Bochenski 1960, pp. 86 ff.; Gropp 1960, pp. 15 ff., 58 ff.; see, too, Negt 1995; Fleischer 1973.

121. Gropp 1960, p. 22.

122. In an unintentionally ironic formulation, Sandkühler 1973 described this as a 'materialist hermeneutics'.

pacity by means of 'criticism and self-criticism', if he wanted to avoid more grievous chastisement.[123] Such show trials shocked the international public during the 1930s – although the accused were, in this case, *not* able to save themselves. Under these circumstances, a 'creative development' of Marxism was out of the question. There was probably no country where the number of intellectual Marxists to lose their lives was higher than in Russia.[124] The death toll is comparable only to those of Mao's 'Cultural Revolution' or Hitler's persecution of communists (and Hitler collaborated with Stalin on this point). Despite the absence of a proper link with Marx, Soviet Russia deluded itself into thinking it represented the 'realisation' of Karl Marx's 'ideas'.[125] The West adopted the East's self-description as 'Marxist' – perhaps because easy refutations of Marx seemed a good way to score points in the Cold War, or perhaps because it was hoped the rekindling of interest in the young Marx would strengthen the Communist movement's internal opposition.[126] The result, however, was that Soviet Russia's self-ideologisation was not exposed as such, but rather promoted. This may have been a sensible discursive strategy for fighting back Marxism within one's own country, but it did justice neither to Marxian theory nor to actually-existing socialism. This thematic complex cannot be pursued further, here, as it is relevant to the reception of Marx only in a very indirect way: writings about communism are a category unto themselves. And, in any case, once the initial euphoria was gone, most of these writings were nothing but documents of political disillusionment.[127]

---

123. Gropp 1960, p. 86 f.; compare the account of this trial in Leonhard 1958.

124. There were, nevertheless, some impressive cultural achievements; witness the works of Bukharin, Radek and Trotsky; the Marx and Engels collected works in German (*MEGA*); the economists Leontiev and Kondratiev; the aestheticians Lukács, Lunacharsky and Lifshitz; and the psychologists Pavlov and Rubinstein; to name but a few; for an overview, see Groys 1996.

125. An article published in the German weekly *Die Zeit* on 3 October 2000 entitled 'Deutsche Lebenslügen' ['German Self-Deception'] points out that Germans have long tried to convince themselves that the 'values' governing Soviet society were 'Asian' and foreign. Schneider 1992, pp. 181 ff. emphasises Russia's Asian heritage; for early examples of this approach, see Lessing 1927 and Berdyaev 1945; see also Dutschke 1975.

126. Critics respond to Marx with the facile philosophical judgement that all fanaticism in the realm of ideas must degenerate into the 'terrorism of virtue' (thus Lübbe 1995) – as if Marx had advocated normative ideals that were then implemented. This assessment was already off the mark in Hegel. By tracing the Terror of the period after 1792 back to the rationalist philosophy of the Enlightenment, he insinuates that ideas are what drives history – as if the *Critique of Pure Reason* had caused the French Revolution (Hegel 1967, p. 601). The organicism (Hegel 1967, p. 602 f.) that Hegel proposed as an antidote reduces Kant's 'freedom' to a system of thought oriented toward institutional order – long before the *Philosophy of Right* (Hegel 1991, first published in 1821). This idealist construct, with its emphasis on 'necessity' (Hegel 1967, p. 606), needs to be confronted with the *German Ideology* (*MECW* 5) in order to appreciate what Marx aimed at. The history of philosophy depends, at decisive junctures, on false assessments of empirical reality and history (see section 4.1).

127. From a Marxist perspective: Merleau-Ponty 1969; Castoriadis 1949; Koestler 1941; Marcuse 1958; Leonhard 1958; Bettelheim 1969 and 1974–7; Solzhenitsyn 1974; Heym 1995.

The only member of the old guard of Soviet Russian Marxists who succeeded in escaping the influence of Stalin for a time was Trotsky. But he, of all people, remained faithful to the old system. This makes him a peculiarly ambiguous figure, to whom we now turn.

2.2.5 *Trotskyism – a lesser evil?*

Trotsky, who conducted the peace negotations at Brest-Litovsk and successfully organised the Red Army, was later stylised as an 'alternative to Stalinism'[128] – at the very moment (that is, 1929) when he was expelled from the Soviet Union and lost all influence, and even more so after he was murdered in 1940. If this view of Trotsky became increasingly widespread, then this was at least partly due to Stalin's ever more drastic responses to the purported 'Trotskyism' of his own associates. Western audiences were all the more impressed with Trotsky as he had been a moralist with Menshevik leanings before becoming a Bolshevik in 1917. His early writings (which, however, strongly contradict his post-1917 writings and actions) seemed to represent a morally superior perspective which the Russian experiment *could have* adopted. Along with the polemics penned by Trotsky during his exile, these early writings constituted an imaginary 'alternative' for those in the West who sympathised with communism but were beginning to distance themselves from Stalin.[129]

Yet Trotsky never ventured beyond official Marxism in theory (although one may take a positive view of his historical writings); nor did he represent a political alternative. He had helped build the dictatorial Party apparatus later used by Stalin, and he never disavowed these structures. Like Stalin, he displayed Bonapartist tendencies (the Kronstadt uprising was partly provoked by his style of military command), and the modernisation he advocated was similarly as rigorous as that of the post-1928 Stalin, since he had always rejected any sort of alliance with the peasants.[130] Trotsky missed the opportunity to oppose Stalin when he still could.[131] He did not take him seriously as an opponent;

---

128. Bergmann 1993.

129. The Western Left found it surprisingly difficult to distance itself from Stalin. While the show trials and the Molotov-Ribbentrop Pact certainly raised eyebrows, the USA eventually entered the Second World War on Stalin's side. Guibot 1997 describes the way the left-wing US art scene turned its back on Stalin; see, too, Bonde 1987; Diggins 1992; Lloyd 1997. The conflict between Communists and the 1968 generation in France turned on the break with Stalinism; even the anti-Marxist surge of the 1970s was essentially anti-*Stalinist*. Mao, like Trotsky, was a surrogate role model. If his glorification within parts of the European Left seems all the more grotesque today, this is due to the fact that, unlike Trotsky, he continued to uphold the terrorist régime not just in theory, but was *directly* responsible for the massacres of the Cultural Revolution (Koenen 1992). Trotsky never shied away from massacres when he disposed of political power. In the 1990s, when Bukharin was rehabilitated, there ensued a Bukharin boom (Hedeler 1993). On the 'alternative', see Bahro 1977.

130. For general portraits of Trotsky, see: Deutscher 1963; Mandel 1979; Abosch 1990; Beilharz 1987; Bergmann and Schäfer 1993; Hedeler 1994; Bourseiller 2002.

131. Abosch 1990; G. Schäfer 1993.

instead, he turned on Bukharin and others.[132] This was presumably due to the fact that he did not object to Stalin in principle; if anything, he objected to him as a person – but even this was a relatively late development.[133] The struggle against Stalin that was staged later must be understood as a *catch-up* revolt; given the absence of differences of principle, it was little more than a competition for leadership positions: a personal farce that was, to be sure, grandly stage-managed and tragically world-historical.

Trotsky thought of the Soviet Union as a 'degenerated workers' state' as a state that disposed of the right structures but was headed by the wrong leader.[134] His insistence on a 'world revolution' was mainly about influencing the situation there to his own advantage. The attempt to build an independent Left on the basis of the mini-structures created by Trotsky (the 'Fourth International') was also problematic from the outset: as long as this left traced its existence back to Trotsky, it was as incapable of breaking politically with the model of the Soviet Union as it was of enacting a theoretical break with technocratic naturalism and historical determinism. If anything, Trotsky's reception in the West has extended the portrayal of Marx's ideas as expressing a messianic philosophy of history, a technocratic faith in progress and a terrorist ignorance of reality – for Trotsky's thought displays these features of Marxist-Leninism in exponentiated form.[135] And the notion of directing a 'world revolution' by means of scattered splinter groups was hardly indicative of a critical view of terrorism.[136] This may explain why several states barred the leading Trotskyist Ernest Mandel from entering their territory. It was only by *breaking* with Trotsky's ideas that Trotskyism was able to emerge from its sectarian isolation – as in Britain and France, where parts of the Left have a Trotskyist background. Yet by assuming such a regional character, they surrendered the very essence of Trotskyism, namely internationalism.[137]

Mao and 'Third-World communism' also remained a mere episode, as far as the history of *theory* is concerned. 'Third World communism' was also received, in the West, as a Marxist alternative to Stalinism. Maoism was picked up on around 1967 in order to describe decolonisation in Marxist terms, but its significance was not understood. Inspired by Frantz Fanon, some began to imagine themselves as a Marxist 'urban

132. Trotsky 1937.
133. Trotsky 1980.
134. Linden 1992, pp. 60 ff.
135. As early as 1905, Trotsky proclaimed: 'History is a powerful machine in the service of our ideas. It works with merciless deliberation and insensibility, but it does work! We believe in it' (quoted in Abosch 1990, p. 34; see, too, p. 164). As late as 1932, Trotsky expressed his unbroken faith in technology by calling for man to 'set to work on himself, to place himself in the mortar bowl, in the chemist's alembic' (quoted in Abosch 1990, p. 117; see also pp. 133, 137).
136. Against Kautsky and Luxemburg after 1918: Trotsky 1921; Lenin 1970a; Lübbe 1981.
137. In any case, thought was less bridled within Trotskyism than under the aegis of Moscow. Authors such as Bensaïd or Callinicos belong to a Trotskyist current that still exists today, in the form of the Fourth International, but also of parties like Britain's Socialist Workers Party. On Trotskyism, see Beilharz 1987; Callinicos 1991; Cliff 1999; Koenen 2001, pp. 276 ff.; Bourseiller 2002; Bensaid 2002. On Trotsky, see also 3.4.2, and on Mandel, 2.3.2.

guerilla' operating in the metropolises of the West. With hindsight, Western Maoism needs to be interpreted as a case of intellectuals playing with fire.[138] Due to its practicism, its paradoxical student anti-intellectualism, Western Maoism's theoretical legacy is quite meagre, apart from its orientation to the Third World. Like other non-Stalinist currents, it usually leads back to Lenin. For this reason, it is worth concluding with a more detailed analysis of Lenin's decisive theoretical move. It provided the foundation, within economic theory, for the communist fixation on the state, which extended all the way to Horkheimer's 'primacy of politics' and its consequences: the theory of imperialism.

2.2.6 Key elements of Marxian theory III: imperialism

> All this looks entirely different now in the epoch of finance capitalism.[139]

Stalinism's lack of a connection to Marx's theories raises the question of what exactly separated Marx and Stalin *theoretically*.[140] As we have seen, many of these intermediate steps were taken by Lenin. This is true, for instance, of the overvaluation of the state, the 'primacy of politics' in theory and practice, which shaped twentieth-century Marxism so strongly that it even became possible to equate socialism and statism.[141] Lenin's politicisation was, no doubt, due to political factors such as the aggressive behaviour of the old empires during the First World War and the sudden rise to power of the Communists within one of these empires.[142] As far as *theory* is concerned, a staunch statist had already presided over the birth of German Social Democracy: Lassalle, who engaged in written correspondence with Bismarck for a time, proclaimed 'state socialism' as German Social Democracy's goal. As the years went by, the results of this orientation became clear.[143]

---

138. This is the verdict not just of Koenen 2001, but also of Joscha Schmierer and Christian Semmler – who should know. See their contributions to Landgrebe 1998, pp. 49 ff. and 133 ff.; see also p. 88.

139. Bukharin 2003, p. 127.

140. A biography of Stalin published during the Cold War contains these remarks: 'The convulsions he inflicted upon his country had little do with Marxist theory, of which he was surprisingly ignorant' (Payne 1965, p. 17). 'He gives no signs of having read Marx – his quotations are always those which had appeared in Lenin's articles and pamphlets' (p. 111). 'It was not for this that Marx and Engels had worked' (p. 430). Hedeler 1994, pp. 49–68 questions this stereotype, although he ultimately arrives at the same conclusion (see also H. Löwe 2002).

141. J. Fischer 1992, pp. 168 ff.

142. The other European empires also collapsed during the war: the German and the Ottoman Empire as well as the Austro-Hungarian Empire. Britain and France were creditors of Tsarist Russia and fought Lenin, who had cancelled the Tsar's debts, by openly military means between 1918 and 1920. Following two immense war efforts, these two democracies were unable to retain their colonies much longer. It was the new states, Soviet Russia and the USA, that emerged as the genuine victors of the two world wars (see Gruber 1967, pp. 90 ff.; Hobsbawm 1995).

143. 'The great association of the poorer classes – is the state' (Lassalle 1987, p. 254). The 'working-class idea of the state' was about 'allowing individuals to achieve a level of existence that they could never achieve by themselves' (Lassalle 1987, p. 222). Bismarck implemented this from above. Before Marx, 'state socialism' was propagated by John Gray, Proudhon and Rodbertus (see *MECW* 26, p. 285; *MECW* 32–3). Open Lassalleanism is evident in Schumacher 1973 and later in

Ever since Marx, Social Democracy had pursued a strategy of struggling first to institute a democratic republic alongside the bourgeoisie, or, if need be, in its place.[144]

Because this preliminary goal was never achieved in Germany, the ability to see beyond it was lost. The 'bourgeois form' was retained not just during the period of Social Democracy's opposition to imperial Germany, but also after Social Democracy *obtained* the power it had wanted for so long. Thus the fixation on the state persisted, and Marx's approach to the issue was forgotten.[145] If Marx's invectives against this fixation[146] failed to make an impression even on German comrades, then what chances were there that the Russians would be more responsive? The two currents of the workers' movement differed not so much with regard to their relationship to the state, as in their *notions* about the state. The Bolsheviks prolonged feudal 'state socialism' more faithfully than the Social Democrats, who began to incline more toward liberal bourgeois ideas. Now, Lenin prided himself on his orthodox Marxism: his worst insults consisted in calling someone a 'former' (Plekhanov, Hilferding) or 'so-called' Marxist (Struve), or even a 'renegade' (Kautsky). Can he really have been ignorant of the Marxian critique of the state? He was not: no Marxist tract is more critical of the state than *State and Revolution*.[147] The idea,

---

Helmut Schmidt. According to Schneider 1992, 'the German Social Democrats would be especially well advised to critically examine their own theoretical history with regard to "statism and socialism", instead of . . . shifting the blame to Marx and Engels, of all people' (p. 161; see pp. 15, 23, 63, 152 ff.; 2.1.3).

144. 'In accordance with the *Communist Manifesto*'s hypotheses on the transformation of the bourgeois revolution into a proletarian revolution, German Social Democrats always felt themselves to be the executors of the bourgeois revolution' (Stephan 1974, p. 115). 'In Germany, [the Communists] fight with the bourgeoisie whenever it acts in a revolutionary way, against the absolute monarchy, the feudal squirearchy, and the petty bourgeoisie. But they never cease, for a single instant, to instill into the working class the clearest possible recognition of the hostile antagonism between bourgeoisie and proletariat, in order that the German workers may straightway use, as so many weapons against the bourgeoisie, the social and political conditions that the bourgeoisie must necessarily introduce along with its supremacy, and in order that, after the fall of the reactionary classes in Germany, the fight against the bourgeoisie itself may immediately begin' (*MECW* 6, p. 519; *MECW* 10, pp. 279 ff.; Lenin 1965a).

145. 'The state is to be transformed from a state based on class rule into a people's state' (Bebel 1969, p. 14). 'Among the social organisations in existence today there is but one that has the requisite dimensions, that can be used as the requisite field, for the establishment and development of the Socialist or Co-operative Commonwealth, and that is the modern state' (Kautsky 1971, p. 101). 'The state will become the lever by which socialism is instituted' (Renner 1917, p. 32). Kelsen identifies the reasons for this development as historical forgetfulness and a typically German inclination toward statism: 'The question of what ought . . . to happen once political power has been conquered by the proletariat was generally avoided. Thus the idea of a proletarian republic – whose constitution everyday political activity was geared to – dominated political thinking so strongly that no serious consideration was ever given to the possibility of a different political form . . . To which was added the fact that the idea of the state was held in high esteem, due to historical developments and the characteristic features of the German people [!]' (Kelsen 1965, p. 95; on German statism, see also Schulz 2004).

146. *MECW* 5, pp. 89 ff.; *MECW* 24, pp. 77 ff.; *MECW* 27, pp. 217 ff.; see, too, Hennig 1974; Basso 1975; Röhrich 1980; and Böhm 1998.

147. Lenin 1917.

formulated by Marx and Engels, that the state (*qua* independent force that separates itself from the community and places itself *above* it) would 'wither away' once its functions were performed by the general public, that is, by all citizens,[148] is also expressed in *State and Revolution*.[149] Lenin even acknowledges that democracy represents a necessary transitional stage:

> Democracy is of enormous importance to the working class in its struggle against the capitalists for its emancipation.... The more complete the democracy, the nearer the moment approaches when it becomes unnecessary.[150]

> Marx... teaches us to act with supreme boldness in destroying the entire old state machine... [*P*]*ursuing this road*, we shall achieve the complete destruction of bureaucracy. The possibility of this destruction is guaranteed by the fact that Socialism will shorten the working day, will raise the *masses* to a new life, will create such conditions for the *majority* of the population as will enable *everybody*, without exception, to perform 'state functions', and this will lead to the *complete withering away* of every form of state in general.[151]

Statements of Lenin's good intent are not lacking, then. However, he wrote his book for a Western audience, and with propagandistic, rather than programmatic, intentions. Whatever the reasons for the discrepancy between these statements of good intent and the simultaneously proclaimed necessity of radical and violent political measures, the discrepancy is reflected in Lenin's definitions of Marxian terms.[152] Marx's distinction between state and society, which is of considerable theoretical import,[153] is oddly blurred in Lenin; in fact, it virtually disappears: 'A democratic republic is the best possible political shell for capitalism, and, therefore, once capital has gained possession of this very best shell... it establishes its power so securely, so firmly, that *no* change... can shake it'.[154]

Lenin thinks as an internationalist and schematically; there is always only *one* possibility. By contrast, Marx said of the French constitution: 'from the class whose old social

---

148. *MECW* 22, p. 332; *MECW* 24, pp. 93, 519; *MECW* 25, p. 268.

149. Kelsen 1965 (pp. 78 ff.) detected an affinity with anarchism, here. Marx had already pointed out against Proudhon, and then mainly against Bakunin, that they needed an authoritarian state to realise their goals, and that they denied this only because they were not interested in in-depth theoretical investigations (*MECW* 23, p. 468 and elsewhere).

150. Lenin 1917, pp. 118, 121 f.

151. Lenin 1917, p. 140 f.

152. It could be argued that the pace of events put paid to good intentions – but Lenin was himself one of the most hurried participants in these events. The discrepancy is also rooted in Lenin's stance on the 'dual power' of the February Revolution (the Provisional Government was controlled by Constitutional Democrats and the soviets by the Mensheviks). Following his return in April, Lenin declared war on these 'bourgeois' bodies, taking even the Bolsheviks by surprise (Weber 1970, p. 109 f.).

153. *MECW* 3, pp. 117 f., 159, 184; *MECW* 24, p. 94; Basso 1975, pp. 10 ff.; Colletti 1974, pp. 219 ff.

154. Lenin 1917, p. 15 f.

power it sanctions, the bourgeoisie, it withdraws the political guarantees of this power. It forces the political rule of the bourgeoisie into democratic conditions, which at every moment help the hostile classes to victory and jeopardise the very foundations of bourgeois society'.[155]

All that remains, in Lenin, of the contingent and open character of history and of a given constellation's internal tension is pure, deliberate domination. Thus Lenin states: '[u]nder capitalism we have the state in the proper sense of the word, that is, a special machine for the suppression of one class by another'.[156] The distinction between state and society is blurred. The solution seems simple: a 'real' democracy, which is, of course, a political affair, will simultaneously resolve the social and economic issues. The relation of primacy has been reversed. Lenin can do this because he never distinguishes between political, social and economic issues in the first place – ultimately, Lenin speaks *only* of politics:

> If really *all* take part in the administration of the state, capitalism cannot retain its hold...*All* citizens become employees and workers of a *single* nationwide state 'syndicate'. The whole of society will have become a single office and a single factory, with equality of labour and equality of pay.[157]

In this, too, Lenin assumes the legacy of Kautsky. Twenty-five years earlier, Kautsky had already spoken as if social and economic success were identical with political success: '[t]he state will not cease to be a capitalist institution until the proletariat, the working-class, has become the ruling class'.[158] 'Economism' was, for Lenin, a term of abuse, since consideration of a *socialist* revolution's economic preconditions, as called for by the 'legal Marxists', would condemn the Russian Social Democrats to political inactivity, or to a 'wait and see' approach.[159] Later, the justification offered for the persistence and even intensification of the 'dictatorship of the proletariat' was that despite its political triumph, socialism had yet to triumph economically.[160] In other words, the painful lesson was learned that one needed, in fact, to distinguish between the two: a 'withering away of the state' was nowhere in sight. One might argue that the politician Lenin hailed from a country where capitalism, including 'bourgeois society', was still quite young, so that he could be forgiven for neglecting to study it – all the more so as he was interested not in studying, but in overcoming it. But the fact is that Lenin *did* study capitalism seriously, and he put some stock in being recognised as an economic

155. *MECW* 10, p. 79.
156. Lenin 1917, p. 107.
157. Lenin 1917, pp. 119 ff.
158. Kautsky 1971, p. 110.
159. Lenin 1915, pp. 54 ff.
160. Commission of the Central Committee 1939, p. 273; Lenin 1919 had already spoken of an 'epoch'.

theorist.[161] It is in his second major economic work[162] that we find the *theoretical* source of the politicisation of social and economic categories.

Lenin's statement that 'imperialism is the monopoly stage of capitalism'[163] is as important as the changing function of the dictatorship of the proletariat. In making this statement, Lenin unintentionally confirmed a hypothesis formulated by Bernstein, whom he had attacked as a 'revisionist'. In essence, Bernstein's claim was that capitalism had become less prone to crisis and more governable since Marx's death. Given a system that promised them continuous improvements in their living conditions, workers could make their peace with the bourgeois state. While Lenin certainly did not want to make his peace with anyone, and least of all with Bernstein, he shared the latter's assumption concerning a 'new stage of capitalism'. His discussion of the formation of economic trusts, the changed role of banks and the development of colonialism is reminiscent of Bernstein, as is his periodisation: *Capital*, which is read as an empirical account, is presented as a completely accurate description of the old capitalism, but this is done only so as to deny its pertinence to the present, or to the 'new' stage.[164] Lenin even believed that he could put a date on the transition: 'For Europe, the time when the new capitalism *definitely* superseded the old can be established with fair precision: it was the beginning of the twentieth century';[165] 'Neither Marx nor Engels lived to see the imperialist epoch of world capitalism, which began not earlier than 1898–1900'.[166]

For a Marxist, this is an incredible step to take, as it restricts the validity of Marx's theory to the nineteenth century, thereby neutralising Marx. What is the justification offered? 'This transformation of competition into monopoly is one of the most important – if not the most important – phenomena of modern capitalist economy';[167] 'The supplanting of free competition by monopoly is the fundamental economic feature, the *quintessence* of imperialism'.[168]

There has been much debate on the precise status of this 'transformation' in Lenin. Given Lenin's characteristically schematic way of thinking, which never acknowledges more than one possibility, his statements must, no doubt, be taken literally: the break is definitive and comprehensive; it is 'epochal': 'Competition becomes transformed into monopoly'.[169] 'In other words, the old capitalism, the capitalism of free competition... is passing away. A new capitalism has come to take its place'.[170] 'The old capitalism has had

161. Lenin 1899.
162. Lenin 1916.
163. Lenin 1916, p. 105; see Basso 1975, p. 10 f.
164. Similar verdicts on Lenin have been formulated in Jordan 1974, p. 214 f; and Neusüß 1972, pp. 32, 38, 45, 70, 93.
165. Lenin 1916, p. 18; emphasis in original.
166. Lenin 1916a, p. 111.
167. Lenin 1916, p. 14.
168. Lenin 1916a, p. 105.
169. Lenin 1916, p. 24.
170. Lenin 1916, p. 43.

its day'.[171] 'Capitalism has been transformed into imperialism',[172] which 'is the monopoly stage of capitalism'.[173] 'Imperialism, as the highest stage of capitalism ... took final [!] shape in the period 1898–1914'.[174]

Within this new, highest and supposedly final 'stage of capitalism', the 'personal union, so to speak ... between the banks and the biggest industrial and commercial enterprises'[175] provides the remaining monopolists with a power hitherto unheard of. There develops 'a *dominating position* ... which did not exist under free competition',[176] namely the 'domination of finance capital'.[177] This word indicates the origins of Lenin's theory: '"Finance capital does not want liberty, it wants domination", as Hilferding very truly says'.[178]

Lenin's economic hypotheses – which he does not argue for, but merely seeks to subtantiate by means of randomly chosen statistics[179] – derive from Rudolf Hilferding. Aside from Hobson[180] and Bukharin,[181] Hilferding – the theorist of Austro-Marxism who owed his overnight fame to an anti-critique of Böhm-Bawerk[182] – was the author who provided Lenin with his template, in the form of *Finance Capital*.[183] This work is the link between the state socialism of the German Social Democrats and Lenin's statism. But what exactly did Hilferding claim? Hilferding had read his Marx fairly carefully, and so he was familiar with the rising organic composition of capital (see section 2.1.6). The narrative that Hilferding built upon this foundation can be briefly summarised as follows: according to Hilferding, the growing share of fixed capital renders transfers of capital increasingly difficult; more and more capital is literally *fixed*. This obstructs the equalisation of the rate of profit,[184] one of the basic mechanisms of competition. The banks might remedy this by providing credit. But according to Hilferding, they have no interest in competition between firms that owe them money. Given the ruthlessness of capitalist competition, the bankruptcy of one or more firms might result – and such bankruptcies might entail a loss of money capital for the banks, which, therefore, attempt to stabilise the imbalances by means of a 'bank monopoly'.

In order to confront the colossal market power of the banks, industrial and commercial capitalists will also begin forming cartels and trusts. These, however, require money. Thus the banks obtain ever greater power over industry. Eventually, they merge with it

171. Lenin 1916, p. 51.
172. Lenin 1916, p. 20.
173. Lenin 1916, p. 105.
174. Lenin 1916a, p. 106.
175. Lenin 1916, p. 45.
176. Lenin 1916, p. 27; Lenin is quoting Fritz Kestner.
177. Lenin 1916, p. 52.
178. Lenin 1916, p. 100 f., quoting Hilferding 1981, p. 334.
179. Jordan 1974, p. 219.
180. Hobson 1902.
181. Bukharin 2003.
182. Hilferding 1904.
183. Hilferding 1981.
184. *MECW* 37, pp. 171 ff.

to form 'finance capital', giving rise to the famous 'personal union'.[185] The latter may develop to the point where there exists a single 'general cartel'.[186] Thus, what the book's subtitle calls capitalism's 'latest phase' is already characterised by Hilferding as a monolithic bloc,[187] within which there occurs a direct transition from economic domination to *political* rule: 'Thus the specific character of capital is obliterated in finance capital. Capital now appears as a unitary power which exercises sovereign sway [!] over the life process of society'.[188] 'Finance capital, in its maturity, is the highest stage of the concentration of economic and political power [!] in the hands of the capitalist oligarchy. It is the climax of the dictatorship of the magnates of capital'.[189]

This spells major changes for the role of politics within capitalism: according to this way of thinking, inter-capitalist competition is turned inside-out, so to speak: it is no longer individual capitalists who compete with one another, but nationally unified blocs of monopolies. This is Hilferding's account of the birth of imperialism out of the spirit of finance capital.[190] Bukharin, who encouraged Lenin to write his book on imperialism,[191] expresses the gist of this idea by exaggerating it: 'Capitalism has attempted to overcome its own anarchy by pressing it into the iron ring of state organisation. But having eliminated competition within the state, it let loose all the devils of a world scuffle'.[192]

If domestic power structures have changed so significantly (it is *only now* that the state has become an instrument in the hands of the ruling class),[193] then the working-class party also needs to change its approach. Hilferding introduces the 'primacy of politics' as follows: '[t]he blatant seizure of the state by the capitalist class directly compels every proletarian to strive for the conquest of political power'.[194] The politicisation of capitalism compels workers to politicise themselves. Lenin, who was in a state of desperation following the European socialists' decision to enter into the First World War, must have welcomed Hilferding's book as an unexpected rescue. For it follows from Hilferding's analysis that 'where danger is, there grows also that which will save us' (Hölderlin). 'While thus creating the final organizational prerequisites for socialism, finance capital

185. K. Kim 1999, p. 113.

186. Hilferding 1981, p. 234.

187. The tendency toward the development of a general cartel can be seen to have been 'realised' when 'a revolutionary concept can be based on the conquest of the "six large Berlin banks"' (Stephan 1974, p. 113; Hilferding 1981, p. 368). Incidentally, Gramsci also thought in terms of monolithic 'blocs'. To him, they were held together ideally – by hegemony.

188. Hilferding 1981, p. 235.

189. Hilferding 1981, p. 370; see *MECW* 35, pp. 621 ff.

190. Hilferding 1981, p. 365. Hilferding's theory of imperialism predates that of Luxemburg. The link between the two consists in the reproduction schemes, whose stability Luxemburg refused to accept, because it seemed too affirmative to her (see 2.1.5).

191. Lenin read Bukharin's manuscript during his Swiss exile. It inspired him first to pen a preface (in Bukharin 2003) and then his own treatise on imperialism (see Jordan 1974, pp. 212 ff.; R. Kraus 1991).

192. Bukharin 2003, p. 180.

193. Hilferding 1981, p. 334.

194. Hilferding 1981, p. 368.

also makes the transition easier in a political sense'.[195] 'Socialism ceases to be a remote ideal, an "ultimate aim"... and becomes an essential component of the immediate practical policy of the proletariat'.[196]

To be sure, the political seizures of power differed in orientation: Hilferding went on to become a Social-Democratic minister of finance during the 1929 world economic crisis, while Lenin would be leading a revolution within just five years. Yet both Hilferding and Lenin had considerable faith in the power of politics to shape the economy and society. The rationale behind this faith is that of an amalgamation of politics and economics. To quote Bukharin once more: '[b]eing a very large shareholder in the state capitalist trust, the modern state is the highest and all-embracing organisational culmination of the latter. Hence its colossal, almost monstrous, power'.[197] The transformation of monopoly capitalism into socialism was envisaged as a rather straightforward affair – even Hilferding called for the 'dictatorship of the proletariat'[198] as the means by which to achieve this transformation. Given one's historical periodisation, it was easy to think of oneself as having come one step closer to the final goal precisely because of the defeat just suffered (a 'dialectical' notion):

> Capitalism in its imperialist stage leads right up to the most comprehensive socialization of production; it... drags the capitalists, against their will and consciousness, into some sort of a new social order, a transitional one from complete free competition to complete socialisation.[199]
>
> [S]ocialism is merely state-capitalist monopoly *which is made to serve the interests of the whole people* and has to that extent *ceased* to be capitalist monopoly.[200]

During the 'old' stage, empiricist interpretation engendered an all-powerful economic determinism, thus causing the capacity for political action to be lost sight of ('[t]he materialist is thus a Calvinist without God');[201] by contrast, the 'new stage' involved veritable *invocations* of the capacity for political action. In the theory of imperialism, the category of 'domination' reappears, even though Marx had already considered its 'motley feudal ties' to have been dissolved into undisguised economic constraints.[202] The caprice of

195. Hilferding 1981, p. 368.
196. Hilferding 1981, p. 367.
197. Bukharin 2003, p. 138. According to Bukharin, international cartels (pp. 54 ff.) have not disappeared altogether during the 'recent phase of capitalism' (p. 96); the dominant trend, however, is that toward the 'nationalisation' of capital' (p. 81): 'Finance capital seizes the entire country in an iron grip. "National economy" turns into one gigantic combined trust' (p. 125). Bukharin is so quick to present an interpretation because there is a specific phenomenon, namely war, that he urgently wants to 'explain': '[w]ar serves to reproduce definite relations of production. War of conquest serves to reproduce those relations on a wider scale' (p. 119).
198. Hilferding 1981, p. 370.
199. Lenin 1916, p. 25.
200. *LW* 25, p. 362.
201. Bernstein 1961, p. 7.
202. *MECW* 6, pp. 482–5.

the monopolists and of the opportunists bribed by them ('flattery, lies, fraud')[203] also reappear – even though Marx had desisted from '[making] the individual responsible for relations whose creature he socially remains'.[204] In this way, Lenin introduces an element of intentionality into his analysis: we are now dealing with human *malevolence*, which is punished accordingly, instead of with economic constraints. The scaling back of scientific rationality was accompanied by a corresponding boost in the identity-establishing conviction that one was fighting on the right side: '[t]he Marxist doctrine is omnipotent because it is true'.[205] The very development by which Marx's economic theory was considered historically obsolete involved an apparently limitless extension of the political possibilities open to the Communists.[206] Marx's intention was that of engaging in a scientific critique of political economy that could then serve as a guide to political action; Lenin transformed this intention into a 'political theory'[207] that did away with rational and critical standards no less than many of its contemporaneous bourgeois tendencies (which were typically bellicist).

This constellation, the theoretical 'primacy of politics' (see Lieber in section 2.2.4), is one we will encounter again. The question that needs to be raised, here, is what is shown by a comparison to Marx's theory. What one is struck by, first of all, is the question of evolutionary 'transition'. Engels had already spoken of 'monopoly capital' and the possibility of such a transition in his old age, and Bernstein[208] had already invoked the authority of letters penned by the late Engels.[209] In Marx's writings, we also encounter a 'financial aristocracy'[210] and 'bankocracy';[211] he even described joint-stock companies as 'transitional forms' that prepare the ground for socialisation.[212] But he never allowed himself to entertain any illusions about a new stage of capitalism in which victories would come more easily because there would be only *one* opponent to confront: the politico-economic cartel ('complex') that does the socialists' work for them by creating proto-socialist institutions and reducing the number of exploiters to be combated.

---

203. Lenin 1916a, p. 117.

204. *MECW* 35, p. 10. On the identification of individual responsibility, see Borkenau 1952, p. 49.

205. *LW* 19, p. 23.

206. It seems this is why Lenin responded so viruently to the accusation levelled against Bolshevism by Plekhanov (namely that it was based on 'subjective idealism'): the truth hurts.

207. Fetscher 1986, p. 1987; Kraiker 1977; Kraiker 2000; Stammer 2001.

208. Bernstein 1961, p. 34.

209. For example: '[T]he old boasted freedom of competition has reached the end of its tether and must itself announce its obvious, scandalous bankruptcy. And in every country this is taking place through the big industrialists of a certain branch joining in a cartel for the regulation of production. [...]. Thus, in this branch [the British chemical industry; C.H.], which forms the basis of the whole chemical industry, competition has been replaced by monopoly in England, and the road has been paved, most gratifyingly, for future expropriation by the whole of society, the nation' (Engels, *MECW* 37, p. 435).

210. *MECW* 37, p. 436.

211. *MECW* 10, p. 60.

212. *MECW* 37, p. 438.

For Marx, it was a matter of dealing with a deep-seated structure that is re-established through reproduction everywhere and every day, but which is so fractured that it can hardly be overcome simply by seizing power in some central locations. Marx would not have rejected such a seizure of power – he was too much of a revolutionary to do so. But the question is to what extent such a politics could justify itself by *reference* to Marx. The catch is that Marx penned ruthless analyses not just of capitalism, but also of socialist notions of a better world and the political strategies founded upon those notions. Hilferding and Lenin treat this legacy in a rather cavalier way. They adopt only those elements of Marx's work that are useful to them in the short term (in this case, the concentration and centralisation of capitals),[213] considering everything else to be historically obsolete. This is due not so much to their 'historical' reading of *Capital*[214] than to substantive misunderstandings about political economy.

Theoretically, the politicisation described results from a certain interpretation of the reproduction schemes and the theory of crisis derived from them (see section 2.1.5). For Hilferding, expanded reproduction poses no problem, as he held that Marx's reproduction schemes had shown that 'expanded reproduction can proceed without interruption as long as these proportions are maintained'.[215] Hilferding misinterprets Marx's abstract model as a *direct* statement on reality ('[s]chematic though this analysis may be, it does full justice to the realities of the problem').[216] He ontologises the model.[217] According to Hilferding, it is the task of the state to ensure that the right proportions are maintained. This is Hilferding's 'conscious regulation' of production,[218] which he takes to have been accomplished in the 'general cartel', albeit only 'in an antagonistic form'.[219] In Marx, the right proportions are *never* maintained, or if they are, this merely represents a contingent intermediate phase. The proportions regulate themselves over time, by means of the process of crisis. Their existence *is* the crisis: it is precisely by means of the crisis that they impose themselves. Hilferding disrupts this relationship: in his theory, there is crisis *or* there is regulation.[220]

If the weal of the economy depends on a single factor, namely proportionality at a given moment X, then it seems easy to establish such proportionality by means of political regulation – after all, this would be in every capitalist's interest. The only question is why proportionality has not already been established.

---

213. *MECW* 35, pp. 621 ff.; Shaikh 1983d.
214. On the 'logical/historical' debate of the 1970s, see Kittsteiner 1977; and Rakowitz 2001.
215. Hilferding 1981, p. 256; see, too, p. 241.
216. Hilferding 1981, p. 42.
217. Rosdolsky 1977, p. 464.
218. Hilferding 1981, p. 27.
219. Hilferding 1981, p. 234.
220. 'The possibility of crises is implicit in unregulated production, that is to say, in commodity production generally, but it only becomes a real possibility in a system of unregulated production' (Hilferding 1981, p. 241 and elsewhere).

Hilferding's answer is that it has. Once again, the logic of society is elided. If the sort of 'regulation' Hilferding has in mind were at all possible, then it would be possible only for the economy as a whole – but the economy as a whole is precisely what does not constitute a subject capable of action. It would require considerable powers to make the requisite decisions and impose them against the will of individuals. Moreover, such a unified economic subject would not last long, as it would be no more able to predict the sale of its products than anyone else. It would cause misallocations similar to those of anarchic self-regulation (and require even consumption to be regulated, for example via food vouchers). Genuinely demonstrating the truth of the claim that regulation exists would be quite an arduous undertaking. In Hilferding, the claim simply rests on a theoretical reification: complex, long-term economic equilibria are replaced with straightforward political *commands*, which no longer require any intermediaries, not even money.[221] Hilferding takes the outward appearance of the colonial states, in which violence featured quite prominently, as an indication that these states *actually* performed the economic meta-function stipulated in his interpretation of Marxian models ('conscious' implementation of economic laws). But this is not a theoretical argument; it is a phenomenological suggestion.[222]

By interpreting the phenomena of his time as manifestations of a 'new logic' of capitalism, the Marxist Hilferding left behind Marxian theory.[223] In doing so, he failed to notice that his periodisation is only the result of an inattentive reception. For example, Hilferding's negligence with regard to *money* shields his approach from possible objections by leading to a circular argument. Because he discusses 'Money and Commodities' separately,[224] Hilferding arrives at new definitions (for example, 'socially necessary value in circulation').[225] These definitions make the assumption of a 'new stage' seem plausible. The separate discussion of money and commodities is then justified in terms of this new stage.[226] On closer inspection, however, we find that the principle of

221. Hilferding 1981, p. 234.

222. Hilferding took 'a hypothesis developed from concrete evaluation of a given state within a specific historical situation' and 'integrated it into Marx's analysis of capital, thereby turning it into an element of a general theory of capitalist development' (Stephan 1974, p. 114). 'Developing a theory by generalising about social phenomena is to run the risk of overestimating the importance of contemporary phenomena' (Jordan 1974, p. 216). Hilferding is 'postmodern': he operates not by means of arguments but by means of 'narratives'. This trait has persisted. Other 'stages' identified by means of associatively interpreted external appearances include Fordism (or Regulationism) and post-Fordism as well as the post-industrial, tertiary or knowledge society (see 2.4.1). Some contemporary critics of globalisation still make reference to Hilferding (see Biermann 2001).

223. 'It seems that the monopolistic combine, while it confirms Marx's theory of concentration, at the same time tends to undermine his theory of value' (Hilferding 1981, p. 228; see, too, K. Kim 1999, p. 11).

224. Hilferding 1912; cf. Wolf 1980.

225. Hilferding 1981, p. 47; see section 2.3.5.

226. Hilferding does not consider commodity and money flows (C–M–C; M–C–M') in isolation from one another; in essence, he only considers the flow of money. The mystification of 'fetish capital' (*MECW* 37, p. 390), which results when money is considered in isolation, is by no means

discussing commodity and money flows in separation is not *deduced* by Hilferding from his observations; it is one of the basic assumptions that characterise his approach. Hilferding already isolates money on the methodological level – he is concerned primarily with the money supply and with prices. He never demonstrates that they have become 'delinked'.[227] Instead, he is quick to introduce into his theory a politicisation of economic categories. Once the *theoretical* link between money and changes in the value of the money commodity is lost,[228] the only regulating force that remains is the state.[229]

Hilferding is driven to this radical reassessment by some observations on outward appearances.[230] Similar observations were already made by Marx – neither concentration nor colonial war is a phenomenon that appeared out of the blue between 1883 and 1910. Hilferding and Marx differ only with regard to their theoretical assessments of these phenomena. But different assessments of similar phenomena hardly justify the theoretical assumption that capitalism has actually entered a new stage. Where Hilferding really differs from Marx is in the way he separates disruptions from the way capitalism normally functions; in Marx, the two form a *unified* complex. Possible political motives aside, the different assessment of similar phenomena can be traced back to changes in the theoretical frame of reference. Phenomena Hilferding interprets as *deviations* from the capitalism of 'pure competition' (the concentration and centralisation of capital, as well as divergent profit rates in different industries) are simply features of that capitalism,

resolved by him; he tends, rather, to consolidate it – for instance, by his 'discovery' of 'promoter's profit' (Hilferding 1981, pp. 107 ff.), which can just as well be pocketed by productive capitalists who venture onto the stock market. A 'promoter's profit' results when stocks are sold above their value. This is possible when the dividend is higher than the usual interest. Given a dividend of 10 percent, stocks worth 1,000 units are worth twice as much as 1,000 units at 5 percent interest. Thus the stocks are sold for 2,000; there results a 'promoter's profit' of 1,000 (although there are also promoter's losses involved, making this a zero-sum game). Hilferding by no means '"discovers"', which corresponds to Marx's 'fictitious' capital (*MECW* 37, 467 ff.; Bottomore 1983, p. 100). Hilferding also fails to distinguish between values and prices (thus Stephan 1974, p. 122 f.; K. Kim 1999, p. 27), notwithstanding the fact that his critique of Böhm Bawerk turned upon this very distinction (Hilferding 1904). In Hilferding, prices cannot differ from values because commodities directly represent a part of social labour time (Hilferding 1981, pp. 37 f.).

227. Hilferding speaks of 'the dissociation and relative independence of this movement [that of financial capital; C.H.] from that of industrial and commercial capital' (Hilferding 1981, p. 21). 'Without taking account of counteracting processes such as they are already contained in Marx's analysis, Hilferding insinuates that production could be influenced or directed from within circulation' (Schimkowsky 1974, p. 174; for similar assessments, see Stephan 1974, pp. 126, 132; K. Kim 1999, pp. 11, 27, 123; Zoninsein 1990 and 2000).

228. Hilferding 1981, p. 382 f.; see Stephan 1974, p. 120.

229. This is the basis of Cora Stephan's hypothesis that Hilferding's 'theory of money' was really a state theory (1974, p. 135), developed to bolster the Social Democrats' political strategy theoretically (pp. 114, 118 and elsewhere). 'By managing the sphere of circulation, the state was to be put in a position to master society's contradictions by dominating their reified expressions. In this way, the state becomes the subject of the transition to socialism' (p. 137; for similar assessments, see K. Kim 1999, p. 123; Smaldone 2000, p. 74).

230. For example, the preponderance of state-issued paper currency vis-à-vis gold coins, which Marx had already dealt with (see *MECW* 29, pp. 349 ff.).

in Marx. The 'concentration and centralisation of capital' are enforced by competition, so that they do not so much eliminate as confirm it.[231] If Hilferding arrives at a different view, then this is because *his* conception of competition, which resembles that of neoclassical economics more than that of Marx, precludes anything of the sort.[232]

As for the new stage of monopoly that Hilferding takes to constitute the predominant characteristic of the 'general cartel', it also displays a harmonist bias that is no longer anything to do with Marx: under the general cartel, 'efforts to maximise profit would seem to become senseless'.[233] Once again, what underlies this notion is neoclassical theory, which thinks of firms as passive. 'Output becomes the only criterion of success. This, however, is the principle of socialist economic organisation'.[234] Even money appears superfluous: '[m]oney would have no role. In fact, it could well disappear completely, since the task to be accomplished would be the allocation of things, not the distribution of values'.[235] All of this is supposed to occur under capitalism – that is, under capitalism as it is portrayed in neoclassical theory.[236] It looks as if only minor rearrangements were needed to arrive at socialism. The radical political and economic changes required according to Marx[237] are simply absent.

In much the same way, the passages devoted to the 'equalisation of the rate of profit' convey the false impression that this equalisation is always given in Marx. Momentary instances of unequal distribution are then immediately interpreted as a general departure from competitive capitalism.[238] But such instances can also be found in Marx – after

---

231. Shaikh 1983d.

232. 'In Hilferding's concept of competition, emphasis is laid on the existence of a large number of small firms, the absence of collusion, and the free mobility of capital among the various industrial activities. No thought is given to the time to make this mobility feasible. Each individual industrial firm plays a passive role (as a price taker) in the process of price determination. As a consequence, Hilferding abandons the notion of competition as a struggle in which individual capitals act offensively. Once this trivial conception of competition is mistaken for a Marxian interpretation, a number of phenomena of competition, which are necessary in light of Marx's theory – begin to be viewed by Hilferding as part of a process of generalised monopolisation' (Zoninsein 2000, p. 278).

233. Hofmann 1979, p. 186.

234. Ibid.

235. Hilferding 1981, p. 234.

236. On the absence of money in this theory, see Heinrich 2001, pp. 68 ff., 251; and section 2.3.5.

237. *MECW* 37, pp. 434–5, 602.

238. According to Marx, different average rates of profit ensure that capital is transferred from less profitable to more profitable industries. This creates a tendency towards the equalisation of the rate of profit. The rates of profit do not have to be *truly* equal at any point in time, since new mechanisms of production are constantly being developed, making other industries more profitable, and since obstacles to the mobility of capital arise (for instance, longer turnover periods, restrictions on capital movements – of the kind that ATTAC has now begun calling for – and natural monopolies; see *MECW* 37, pp. 171 ff.). In Schimkowsky's view, Hilferding commits the 'error of reading the account of the equalisation of the rate of profit found in *Capital* as a model of competitive capitalism as it actually operates. This is why Hilferding feels the need to bring the 'model' closer to reality by including new phenomena in it' (Schimkowsky 1974, p. 179).

all, the tendency toward equalisation operates precisely *by means of* constant unequal distribution. Hilferding severs this link. He arrives at a distinction between two epochs – that of free competition and that of a monopoly capitalism dominated by power – by failing to distinguish between the Marxian model of competition and the neoclassical model. Departures from the harmonist neoclassical model are interpreted as a new stage of capitalism – one that is also interpreted in a harmonist manner.

Once these fundamental operations have been understood, it becomes easy to refute the various arguments that Hilferding formulates in support of his claim concerning new concentrations of power and the impossibility of unfettered competition.[239] Once Hilferding's fallacious proclamation of a new stage of finance capital has been seen through, the *theoretical* arguments offered in support of the periodisation that Lenin uses to justify the primacy of politics are also invalidated. The 'last phase' was not that of a 'monopolistic' capitalism primarily characterised by domination, nor was it that of a 'parasitic or decaying',[240] that is, a stagnant capitalism, and it was not that of a 'dying', soon-to-collapse capitalism either.[241] This last definition, in particular, needed to be corrected several times during the period of the Comintern.[242] As for the theory of monopoly capitalism, however, it was retained and extended into that of 'state monopoly capitalism'.[243]

The concept of 'state monopoly capitalism' is little more than a ramshackle attempt to retain a flawed analysis of imperialism; the fact that the collapse which the Comintern

239. This is true, for example, of the hypothesis that capitalism is now being controlled by the banks: '[o]nly a comparatively small number of a bank's credit operations involve credit being used to expand production' (Stephan 1974, p. 130). Hilferding tends toward the 'assumption that all bank capital is investable loan capital. To assume this is to greatly overestimate the influence of banks' (Stephan 1974, p. 131). 'However, there is no theoretical or empirical support for the notion that the liquid form of money-capital would provoke bank domination' (Zoninsein 2000, p. 283). 'It is no accident that Hilferding's theory on the overarching and projective power of finance capital can be countered with the very arguments that Marx used to criticise the Saint-Simonists' overblown ideas about the nature of banking' (Hardach 1975, p. 80; see *MECW* 37, pp. 611–12; see also *MECW* 28–34; on the 'power of the banks', see Kotz 1978, Ronge 1979, Pohl 1993, Barth 1995). Although they were declared obsolete, money, competition by means of price cutting, and so on, continued to exist in Hilferding's day, much as they do today. For this reason, the book *Finance Capital* is important only as a historical document – its actual content is hardly referred to these days (Biermann 2001).

240. This notion was based on the assumption that the majority of capitalists survived only on interest income, having become mere 'coupon cutters' (cf. Bukharin 1926a, but see also Veblen 1912 and Burnham 1941).

241. Lenin 1916a, p. 784.

242. In 1919, the Comintern still assumed that a 'final confrontation' was imminent (Protokoll 1921, p. 171). In 1925, it spoke of 'relative stabilisation'. In 1943, Stalin dissolved the Comintern altogether, and after the War, he instituted markedly non-communist 'people's democracies' (see Lieber 1963, pp. 279–352; Hardach 1975, pp. 97–103).

243. This did not happen until the mid-1950s. In the German Democratic Republic, the shift occurred mainly in the works of Kurt Zieschang (for a synoptic account, see Zieschang 1967, or manuals such as Autorenkollektiv 1971; IMFS 1972; Becher 1976; and such like. On this development, see Wirth 1972; and Ebbinghaus 1974, in particular the contribution by Winkelmann, pp. 45–97; Huffschmid 1975; Hardach 1975, pp. 119–130; G. Krause 1998).

had proclaimed to be imminent never occurred was 'explained' in terms of state intervention.[244] Decreed by Stalin,[245] the theory was first elaborated by Eugene Varga and others; then, in the 1960s, it became the official theory of Marxism-Leninism. The residual category of the state served as a *deus ex machina*.[246] This is why the Marxist critics of this conception were justified in demanding that the role of the state be defined more precisely in economic terms.[247] And it was one reason for the 1970s debate on Marxist 'state derivation', which does not concern us here, whose premise – it is worth knowing – consisted in Lenin's analysis of imperialism and in Leninism's desperate efforts to uphold that analysis – even when it was a matter of returning *directly* to Marx in order to *criticise* Leninism.[248]

Other central theoretical-tactical aspects of Lenin also depend on his theory of imperialism, such as his explanation for the fact that Western European workers failed to live up to his revolutionary plans – the hypothesis of the bribed labour aristocracy. In Lenin's view, the labour aristocracy was 'bought' with money from the monopolistic 'surplus'.[249] While such a surplus features in bourgeois theory (such as in Hobson) it is nowhere to be found in Marx.[250] This is another instance of an overhasty politicisation of economic categories. To put that another way, in terms of being rather than of thought: decisions that were ultimately *political* (in this case, the decision not to form alliances with moderate parties) were dressed up as economic theory. When the need arose, these decisions could be revoked. Theory and practice were amalgamated.

244. 'Much as capitalism...was born only with the aid of the concentrated violence of state power, its decline can today only be delayed by the ever more concentrated deployment of imperialist state power' (Becher 1976, p. 398). 'Lenin conceived of the stage of state monopoly capitalism and its concrete form, that of the war economy, as the final stage of capitalism [*LW* 25, pp. 395, 423]. Consequently,...the concept becomes...void of meaning once the war economy is dismantled'. The concept of the final stage cannot 'be extended indefinitely without losing its theoretical substance...The concept is applied to every post-1917 situation and thereby fails to adequately characterise any of them' (Hardach 1975, p. 96; see also pp. 119 ff.).

245. Stalin 1952.

246. Hardach 1975, p. 129.

247. Neusüß 1972; see also Tristam 1974, p. 135.

248. Flatow 1973, Gerstenberger 1973, Läpple 1973, Projekt Klassenanalyse 1973, Blanke 1974, Hennig 1974, Hirsch 1974, Hochberger 1974, Röhrich 1980 (2.3.3). International debates on the state featured more concrete arguments (Miliband 1973, Anderson 1974, Basso 1975, Laclau 1977, Poulantzas 1978).

249. 'The receipt of high monopoly profits by the capitalists...makes it economically possible for them to bribe certain sections of the workers' (Lenin 1970, p. 152; see, too, pp. 123, 125 and elsewhere). Despite appearances, Lenin's 'labour aristocracy' hypothesis actually supports the theory of immiseration by supplementing it with a conspiracy theory. The 'natural law' of immiseration (2.1.1) was eclectically maintained by interpreting the improved living standards of Western European workers as the result of deliberate political action on the part of the bourgeoisie, action that only affected the minority upper layer of workers and was intended to disarm the labour movement. The law of absolute immiseration was taken still to hold for the powerless majority of workers; this is also evident from the fact that Lenin expected a revolution in Western Europe. Thus the determinist fallacy was retained and the efforts of the trade unions were denigrated radically.

250. The 'surplus' later resurfaces in Sweezy 1966 (Hardach 1975, p. 117; see section 2.3.3).

Lenin's explanation for the fact that the revolution took place not in the most but in the least developed country can also be traced back to his theory of imperialism.[251] Even the *debate on planning* conducted during the late 1920s followed Hilferding by starting from the assumption that the 'last stage' of capitalism had already provided the Communists with centralised structures that merely needed to be put to different use.[252] In fact, it was only under Stalin that such centralisation was created – in an extremely forcible manner. In this sense, Leninism's erroneous assessment of capitalism proved problematic not just for Western Marxism, but for the 'political economy of *socialism*' as well.[253] When one considers just how much of Leninist doctrine depends theoretically on the theory of imperialism, one begins to understand why the theory was retained in spite of its limited explanatory power. The theory did not explain much of what actually existed, but it went a long way as a justification of policy.[254] The two statements are equivalent if one follows Leninism (or idealism, or pragmatism) in failing to distinguish adequately between theory and practice – but it is only then that they are equivalent.

When one considers how important Leninism was within the Marxist spectrum, and for how long it retained its importance,[255] it is hardly surprising that Marxists rarely

251. 'Imperialism was held to have merged the world into a single economic unit, such that the revolution could begin in backward countries like Russia, even if, considered in "isolation", these countries were still far from ripe for profound social transformation' (H. Weber 1970, p. 100; on Third World communism, see, among others, McLellan 1979; Sklair 1991; Neumann 2000).

252. As late as October 1917, Lenin believed it would be sufficient to seize control of the 'commanding heights' (see 'The Impending Catastrophe And How To Combat It': *LW* 25, pp. 323–69). The war communism of 1918 led to tough measures (Hardach 1975, p. 138, speaks of the 'dismantling of the monetary economy and of commodity relations'); in the *ABC of Communism* (Bukharin 1969), these were interpreted as a 'leap into socialism'. Bukharin 1971 even attempted to portray the decline in production – a consequence of the War – as a necessary step, required for the destruction of bourgeois structures. He also thought of centrally directed reconstruction as a relatively simple undertaking. Following a brief interruption in the form of the NEP in 1922 and the moderate pace of industrialisation during the period 1924–8 (Bukharin changed camps, now defending the moderate NEP position), industrialisation proceeded ever more ruthlessly under Stalin (see Preobrazhensky 1965). Feldmann 1928 attempted to provide the five-year plans with a theoretical foundation (Hardach 1975, pp. 131 ff.; on the debate on planning, see Pollock 1971; O. Lange 1938; Lieber 1964, Vol. II, pp. 263 ff.; Raupach 1968; Knirsch 1969; Kornai 1992; Merten 1999).

253. See Wirth 1972; Becher 1976; Krause 1998; Wenzel 1998; and Wiards 2000.

254. Kuhn 1970, who examined similar phenomena within the history of science, had little to say about the social function that theoretically obsolete paradigms may still retain. The auxiliary assumptions that are 'attached' to paradigms that have not yet been rejected do not necessarily need to operate on the same theoretical level; they may be of a more ephemeral (for instance, epistemological or ontological) nature. The traditional critique of ideology has proven more prescient with regard to the social functions of knowledge.

255. Even the last metamorphosis of Marxism to precede its dissolution, the so-called 'Regulation School', adhered to the Leninist notion of the primacy of politics, including in science – a notion that stood Marx's approach on its head (Aglietta 1979; Hübner 1989; in the USA, this school was known as the 'social structure of accumulation' school, SSA for short: see Bowles 1987; in Germany, 'Fordism' was the key term: see Hirsch 1986; Altvater 1991; Demirovic 1992). If it proved so easy to switch to non-Marxian theories, this was because Lenin and Hilferding had already relied on bourgeois theorems for support. Left Keynesianism, which lent itself to being fleshed out with Leninist associations, took itself to be especially 'radical' (Arestis 1994 and the *Review of Radi-*

questioned the dogma that the epoch of monopoly capitalism, imperialism or even state monopoly capitalism had dawned. But now that Leninism has lost its strongest supporting 'argument' – its political power – there is no longer any denying that this was little more than an impromptu attempt not so much to base a 'voluntarist interpretation of Marxism' on Marx, as to *shield it from Marx* theoretically.[256] Here, the term 'Marxism' has become an 'empty signifier' (Laclau), a legitimating title for something that can be given almost any content whatsoever.

In section 2.2, I have set out to demonstrate that Marx's approach, which consisted in substantively questioning philosophical and political ideologemes by means of a politico-economic analysis of bourgeois society, was de-economised and re-ideologised in the course of its Communist reception. Before proceeding to apply Marx's arguments to the critique of recent social philosophy, we need to strip away Leninism's various *sediments*; if we fail to do this, we will only get caught up in them again. These sediments are often to be found on the level of basic assumptions, even when one would not expect them there: in central sociological paradigms (section 2.4) no less than in numerous philosophical 'refutations of Marx' (2.5) or in critical theory (2.6, 3.1). Even today, the technically oriented 'stages' newly attributed to capitalism every five years (post-Fordism, digital capitalism, the knowledge or information society, and so on) betray a deep-seated Leninist legacy.

Our next stop on this road is economic theory (2.3). We have already touched upon the questions it raises. What we find in it is a mirror-inverted de-politicisation of the economy.

---

cal Political Economics; a less clear-cut case is that of Laclau 1985). The only thing radical about this approach was its abandonment of Marx in favour of 'bourgeois' theorems (see section 2.3.3).

256. H. Weber 1970, p. 27; see, too, p. 128. The West German Marxist Left made a genuine attempt to liberate itself from Leninism's overpowering influence (for instance PKA 1972; Fleischer 1973; Rahbehl 1973; Dutschke 1974; and Ebbinghaus 1974). The *post hoc* debate on imperialism in the German weekly *Jungle World* (Spring 2002) was distinctly un-Leninist in character. Other theories of imperialism (see Luxemburg 1951, Sternberg 1926) have already been criticised in section 2.1.5.

2.3 Marx in economic theory

2.3.1 *Marx between economic paradigms*

> For economic theory is concerned...with the *conditions* under which men engage in provident activity directed to the satisfaction of their needs.[1]

> The aim of capitalist production is profit.[2]

Given Marxism's disastrous 'realisation' in the Soviet Union, it seemed opportune to read Marx the way Joseph Schumpeter did: by neatly distinguishing between the fields influenced by him.[3] When one proceeds in this way, Marx's non-economic writings are relegated to the margins, much like Adam Smith's writings on moral philosophy, and Marx joins the ranks of history's major economists.[4] However, a reading based on the history of dogma shows that the economists do not build one upon another, in a chronological sequence; rather, Marx represents a major caesura. The political economists Smith, Ricardo and John Stuart Mill thought of the economy as a subject area to be inquired into with 'social questions' in mind. They saw no need to whitewash the overall phenomenon; they hoped comprehensive analysis of bourgeois society would yield insight into that society's relations – this is why the science was called 'political economy'.[5] Marx the economist picked up on the theorems of the classics in order to think their questions through to the end and use the results to criticise their epigones, whom Marx considered unsystematic 'vulgar economists'.[6] Thus comprehensive analysis of 'the process of capitalist production as a whole'[7] yielded a perspective that allowed one to transcend this totality – albeit only intellectually, for the time being.[8] Grasping the totality became an anticipation of its transcendence; it was only in this way that capitalist economic behaviour in its entirety came to be seen as a "negative totality" – according to Hegel, to recognise a limit is to already have surpassed it. Even if Marx said little

1. Carl Menger 1976, p. 49.
2. Hilferding 1981, p. 183.
3. As 'prophet', 'sociologist', 'economist' and 'teacher' (Schumpeter 1942, p. 3).
4. See Ott 1989; Krummbachner 1991; Pribam 1992; Issing 1994; Glombowski 1998; F. Söllner 1999; or Dowd 2000.
5. In Aristotle, in scholasticism and in Marx: see Polanyi 1944; Pribam 1992.
6. Vulgar economy 'sticks to appearances in opposition to the law which regulates and explains them' (*MECW* 35, p. 311; see, too, pp. 91–2). Marx considered those economists 'classical' who wrote during the period up to 1830 and militated against the aristocracy (*MECW* 35, p. 16), whereas he considered economists who had already begun to display an apologetic attitude toward the proletariat 'vulgar' (see *MECW* 32, pp. 498 ff.; Heinrich 2001, pp. 78–9).
7. *MECW* 37.
8. See Lukács 1971, p. 230. Such 'transcendence into this world' is not religious; it aims at the conceivable 'beyond' of a logic that presents itself as inescapable today (Gehlen 1956, p. 16; Ludz 1999, Habermas 1992, pp. 17 ff. and Habermas 2001, pp. 9, 23).

about possible later economic forms – in terms of reception history, it was enough for his followers to know that such a perspective had become possible.[9]

The perspective was important to Marx, because it meant the larger picture had to be kept sight of each time some small step was taken; settling for unanalysed compromises would not do.[10] Yet within social democracy, the effect was the opposite: the certainty that the downfall of capitalism was approaching led to a feeling of standing on safe ground, and this led to the stance of passive noncompliance described earlier (2.1). The prospect of a possible bridge to the other shore, one that needed first to be struggled for, once more became the utopia of a better world – one awaiting workers in the not too distant future, or one that was eventually declared, after the violent excesses of actually-existing socialism, to have been 'realised' (2.2). It was this thinking, which was hardly economic, that had an effect on the bourgeois world, as a chimera. Its effects could not but extend to the development of economic theory also. And so it was probably no coincidence that the time when Marx's economic theories were published in their mature form was also the time when a counter-utopia began to be developed in the camp of academic science, one that presented the capitalist economy in an entirely different light.

I am referring to the 'neoclassical' school of economics.[11] Neoclassical economics represents a 'caesura' within the apparent 'bourgeois' continuum, one whose effects continue to be felt today.[12] The terminologies, techniques and paradigms were radically

9. Marx was less interested in devising models for the future than in intervening in the politics of his day: from the European struggle for democracy of 1848 (*MECW* 6–8), the American Civil War of 1861 (*MECW* 19, pp. 32 ff.) and his support for trade unions and the First International in 1864 (MECW 20, pp. 5 ff.) to the Paris Commune of 1871 (*MECW* 22, pp. 307 ff.) and Russia in 1881 (*MECW* 26, pp. 119; *MECW* 24, pp. 370 ff.). After the *Manifesto* (*MECW* 6, pp. 477 ff.), Marx spoke of the future only suggestively (*MECW* 24, pp. 75 ff.), in hopeful expectation (*MECW* 35, p. 89) or by formulating the rule that the conditions for the existence of new relations of production must mature within the framework of the old society (*MECW* 29, p. 263; *MECW* 6, p. 211; see Dahrendorf 1952, pp. 167 ff.; Ramm 1957, Bensch 1995).

10. Gustav Schmoller was one who settled for such compromises: '[h]is early doubts on the self-regulating mechanisms of Manchester liberalism led him to look for solutions that could avert class struggle of the Marxian kind, which would otherwise be inevitable' (Starbatty 1989, p. 111). The solution was found in the state. Yet the models of the 'golden mean' (see Aristotle's *Nicomachean Ethics*, 1107a 1) and the 'third way' are vacuous, because they depend on the extremes at a given time. The proposal for land reform formulated around 1900 (Damaschke 1920) and the social democracy of the 1950s already described themselves in these terms (Bruch 1985).

11. Bürgin 1993; Ziegler 1998; Heine 1999. *A Contribution to the Critique of Political Economy* (*MECW* 29) was published in 1859 – a hard-to-digest 'notebook' that elicited no response, to Marx's distress (Ullrich 1976). At the same time, Walras wrote to his son that he would be sure not to address property relations in his economic theory (Grossmann 1977, p. 43). In 1867, the first volume of *Capital* was published as the International met in Lausanne, where Walras was based from 1870 onward. In 1869, the Marxist Social Democratic Workers' Party was founded in Eisenach; the 'marginal revolution' followed in 1871 (Jevons 1970, Menger 1976). The second German edition of *Capital* and a new edition of the *Communist Manifesto* were published in 1872; Walras's work was published in 1874. The connection is hardly to be denied.

12. 'The "mainstream" of contemporary economic theory still... displays this neoclassical orientation. Everything published since Jevons, Menger and Walras presents itself as a mere addition

reconfigured, in a shift that is bound up with the names of W.S. Jevons,[13] Carl Menger,[14] Leon Walras[15] and Alfred Marshall;[16] the latter, Keynes's teacher, canonised the work of his precursors. That this caesura coincided with Marx's appearance within the field of economic theory is not some spurious claim by Marxists, but a fact generally recognised in economic textbooks.[17] The caesura's triple character is an index of its historically over-determined character.

It is easy to understand just what was new in the 'neo'-classical approach when one considers the range of phenomena ignored by it. By assuming a perspective that focuses on exchange,[18] it shifts attention away from production – be it the cultivation of land, handicraft or industrial manufacturing. Neoclassical economics is at pains to avoid production.[19] One consequence of this is the loss of the historical dimension: neoclassical economics no longer treats its categories as historically specific, but as universal human categories: after all, men have always engaged in 'economic activity' in the sense of working to satisfy their needs. Yet modern capitalism displays specific features that go beyond this – and they were originally the subject matter of political economy.[20]

---

of nuances, as the ... tireless working out of the assumptions and consequences inherent in the basic model of 1870' (Ziegler 1998, p. 182; see Kromphardt 1991, pp. 120 ff.).

13. Jevons 1970, first published in 1871.

14. Menger 1976, first published in 1871.

15. Walras 1984, first published 1874.

16. Marshall 1890.

17. 'One remarkable coincidence [...] is that Jevons' *Theory of Political Economy* and Menger's *Principles of Economics* were published during the same year, 1871. Thus the year 1871 is generally taken to mark the dividing line between the paradigm of classical and that of neoclassical economics' (Ziegler 1998, p. 156; Streissler 1989, p. 194). Schumpeter 1954, p. 1083 accused the Marxists of having invented the apologetic and anti-socialist motives of neoclassical economics. But there is evidence of such motives: 'Affirmative economics interprets the subjective theory of value as a scientific advance in knowledge. But the essential propositions of value subjectivism, and in particular the principle of diminishing marginal utility, had already been formulated clearly during the 18th century; moreover, they were a staple of philosophical reflections on economic phenomena from the outset' (Zinn 1987, pp. 116 f.).

18. Bowles 1990, Thielemann 1997.

19. '[T]he analysis of the concrete process of production has been increasingly excluded as an element of theory, and has been used only to establish its preconditions and overall framework' (Grossmann 1977, p. 42). The contribution of the factors of production, labour and capital is measured by reference to what they receive *de facto* (or on the level of prices). This amounts to a tautology – given perfect competition, they will always receive the right amount, and there is no basis for demanding one's 'full wages'. For this reason, Heinrich 2001, p. 71 sees the 'theory of marginal productivity' as a reissue of the 'trinity formula' (*MECW* 37, pp. 801 ff.). Žižek has pointed out that the repression of production is also evident in film. If production is represented at all, then it typically appears as a laboratory of evil (in *James Bond, Lord of the Rings, Star Trek*, and such like; see Henning 2011).

20. Marx distinguished between major historical periods in terms of their modes of production (*MECW* 5, pp. 51–2; *MECW* 6, pp. 170; *MECW* 28, pp. 399 ff. and so on). These heuristic classifications can be useful, although one does not have to declare them a 'theory of formations' (Herrmann 2000). Who can deny that knowing something about the creators of historical artefacts is key to the proper classification of those artefacts? (On 'ahistoricism', see also Heinrich 2001, pp. 77, 82.)

Another consequence is that the problematic of economic classes, which the classics distinguished in terms of their positions within the process of production, was also lost (2.4.6). From the point of view of neoclassical economics, there exist only individuals who strive for maximum utility. They can be distinguished in terms of whether they are consumers (households) or suppliers (firms), but they all behave according to the same laws of utility maximisation. Neoclassical economics focuses, instead, on the price determination of a given good under given circumstances, that is, in exchange.

Neoclassical economics is predominantly a 'theory of prices' or microeconomics. It is also called 'marginalism' because of its view that the market value of a good is determined by the sum a consumer will be willing to pay for the last item of a given sort.[21] Neoclassical economics engages with questions of price by means of mathematical models. These models are based on three variables: demand, supply and price.[22] This way of considering exchange loses sight of other aspects: for a start, money, which mediates the exchange of one good for another, appears *only* as the mediator of exchange. It serves as a *numéraire* (unit of account): both goods are expressed through money, and it is in this way that their relation to one another is revealed. All those functions of money that were central to Marx's theory (2.3.5) are ignored; money appears only as an 'interfering factor'. But to proceed in this way is not to consider actual exchange under modern capitalist conditions; it is to consider the model of a fictitious 'natural exchange',[23] or of an act that has been generalised ahistorically. Moreover, the complex calculations required for determining the missing variable (supply, demand or price) presuppose that the other two variables are already given. The development of these remaining variables is not what neoclassical economics concentrates on. From this results the static character of this type of theory.[24]

---

21. If someone has a need for X, they will acquire it on the market, at least to the extent that they are a 'utility-maximising' creature. 'Marginal utility' is reached when there is no demand for an additional good of this kind – say, a fifth apple – at the given price. The fourth apple decides on the value of all apples (*nota bene*: its 'subjective' value for the consumer). Incidentally, Marx did not neglect 'needs'. Labour that produces commodities that do not satisfy any 'social need' cannot be considered 'socially necessary' (*MECW* 35, pp. 50–1, 95–6, 116–17 and elsewhere; Heinrich 2001, p. 241). However, this need is simply the *conditio sine qua non* for the realisation of a commodity's value (namely, the sale of the commodity at an appropriate price); this does not make need a determinant of the commodity's real value (*MECW* 35, pp. 537–8).

22. Everyone who has perused a microeconomic manual is familiar with graphs showing intersecting curves. Supply increases for as long as prices rise, while demand decreases. The fictitious 'equilibrium price' (so called because there are no other factors at play, not even a dynamic) is situated at the point where the supply curve intersects with the demand curve.

23. Heinrich 2001, pp. 68 ff., 251.

24. 'The mainstream of economic theory is essentially a static discipline which explores the behaviour of economic agents over relatively short time periods' (Norman Clark, in Arestis 1994, p. 406). 'When demand and supply are in stable equilibrium, if any accident should move the scale of production from its equilibrium position, there will be instantly brought into play forces tending to bring it back to that position' (Marshall 1890, p. 404). 'The static state which has here been pictured is the one toward which society is at every instant tending' (J.B. Clark 1915, p. 402). 'Every dynamic movement is either a disturbance of a static condition, or a series of movements

Since competition is always considered 'perfect' under the conditions of 'equilibrium' presupposed in the models by which prices are calculated from supply and demand, there is no incentive for growth – growth is neither necessary nor possible.[25] The dynamic character of Marx's theory resulted from his asking what exactly fuels a given supply or a given demand. The only way to answer this question was to take into account the process of production: its ongoing expansion under capitalism and the fact that this expansion tended to occur 'turbulently', rather than steadily. Thus dynamic growth is one of the *basic assumptions* upon which Marx's economic theory rests.[26] The neoclassical growth theory that was eventually developed is a *supplement* to a theory whose basic approach is static.[27] The elements of this 'specific' growth theory were taken from Marx: either directly or via Soviet theorists of growth.[28]

Now, when one abstracts from such decisive factors as production's historically specific form and social structure, the genesis of the parameters demand, wages, interest and profit, the relationship between these parameters and the *material* determinations of value, the only factors that remain to be 'taken into account' are 'subjective' ones –

---

by which the static condition is reasserting itself, or rather by which a new static condition is being established after the disturbance' (Thomas Carver, c. 1939, quoted in Grossmann 1977, p. 95). Modern neoclassical theory has conceptualised a 'dynamic equilibrium' (Rose 1991, pp. 37–8) that is reminiscent of Zeno's arrow paradox.

25. The 'perfect competition' conceptualised in the theory of equilibrium satisfies an 'optimality criterion': income corresponds to expenses, output is invariant, prices are ideal (nothing remains unsold), firms are conceptualised as small, uninfluential units ('price-taking behaviour') and both labour and capital are fully employed (maximum utilisation). Initially, these static assumptions were simply an expression of the simplification involved in mathematical operations and the difficulty of calculating dynamic equilibria (Grossmann 1977, pp. 67 ff.). Eventually, the static condition was theoretically codified as real (Heinrich 2001, pp. 73–4).

26. *MECW* 35, p. 587; see 2.1.6. In conventional economic theory, even growth is explained in terms of external phenomena, for instance by an assumed population growth. But why is there growth? During the next fifty years, the global economy will grow two-and-a-half times as fast as the world's population (World Bank 2003, cited in *Süddeutsche Zeitung*, 22 August 2002). What is the driving force, here?

27. The distinction between a static and a dynamic sector goes back to Comte (Kühne 1972, pp. 79–80) and John Stuart Mill (Grossmann 1977, pp. 68, 78, 99). The modern theory of growth was not developed until the late 1940s; it is associated with the names of Hicks, Harrod and Domar (Rose 1991; Rostow 1990; Solow 2000; on Lucas and Romer, who focus, like Schumpeter, on the knowledge sector, see Söllner 1999, pp. 246 ff.).

28. 'The close relationship between economic growth and capitalism was first fully seen by Marx' (Weizsäcker 1962, p. 78). The same point is made by Lay 1975 and Kühne 1974, pp. 180 ff., 288, 294 ff. (Kühne calls the neoclassical formula for growth the 'Marx-Domar-equation': p. 184.) Kondratiev directed the Moscow Institute of Conjuncture until 1938, the year he was murdered (in part because he stood up for the NEP and defended the 'counterrevolutionary' notion of a possible new capitalist boom, as against Varga; see Sommer 1993, pp. 88–93). 'Input-output analysis had been developed by Wassily Leontief in the USA in 1941. However, Leontief had already… published an article in Russia… in 1925. Curiously, Leontief forgot his own Russian article. When he was presented with it in 1960, he recognised the temporal precedence of the Gromann Group' (Kühne 1974, p. 296; Gromann, Basarov and Feldmann were the planners at Gosplan, the Soviet State Planning Committee; see Domar 1957). Unlike Spiethoff, Harrod and Samuelson, Domar, Schumpeter and Goodwin openly recognised Marx's pioneering role in the development of growth theory.

the individual utility that a fictitious rational agent expects from a certain good. Keynes added 'future expectations', which are no less subjective, in addition to being unpredictable. The effects of this subjectivistic approach can be seen to this day: fluctuating stock-market prices are explained in terms of the short-term preferences and subjective valuations of speculators, unemployment is seen to result from the 'unwillingness' of the unemployed, and the causes of economic growth are sought in the psychic condition of Schumpeter's 'pioneering entrepreneurs'.[29]

Subjective utility, however, is neither observable nor otherwise ascertainable. One can neither compare nor add together the subjective utility of different persons.[30] For this reason, the character of the theory is highly artificial; there is hardly any way to apply it to reality.[31] Neoclassical economics developed more specialised questions and a more mathematical methodology. Differently from the classics, who undertook their inquiries from the perspective of society as a whole, political issues are generally avoided.[32] Here, we encounter the effects of tendencies that are immanent to the theory, and which are best described as 'atomisation', 'psychologisation' and 'harmonisation'.

By *atomisation*, I mean not just the model's atomistically conceived 'units' (utility-maximising individuals), but also the manner of framing questions, which severs the connections between one question and others. Hardly any effort is made to grapple with the larger complex of historical and systematic problems which the classics engaged with. The legitimation of the current order aside, inquiry is no longer oriented toward questions that concern society as a whole (3.2.1). Ultimately, neoclassical theory aims to

29. According to Schumpeter, heroic 'pioneering entrepreneurs' repeatedly take the static economy to a new level (Schumpeter 1911; 1942; a similar position is found in Kalecki 1969). He argued that all they require for this, besides their aristocratic and venturesome nature, is new technologies and credit, both of which Schumpeter takes for granted (unlike Marx). But where do they come from? In this model, the economy's dynamic remains external to it; it is subjectivised and naturalised. (On racist tendencies in Schumpeter, see Piper, in Sommer 1993, pp. 42 ff.)

30. A commodity's subjective value is greater for the poor than for the wealthy. Thus the subjective total utility would be much greater under conditions of egalitarian redistribution than under conditions of inequality, although the latter (those of quantitative total utility) are objectively more effective. This egalitarian vanishing point of neoclassical economics was eliminated on the level of definitions, by establishing the basic principle that utility is not comparable (the so-called 'Arrow paradox', named after Arrow 1951; see section 3.2).

31. 'Since the beginning of the twentieth century, all significant works of [neoclassical; C.H.] value theory are written on the basis of a self-conception within which theory refers only to itself, and not to some other reality' (F. Jonas 1988, p. 144) – a 'model Platonism' (Albert 1965; see Sen 1982; A. Wolfe 1986; Etzioni 1988; Brodbeck 1998). The category of utility is tautological insofar as it merely provides an additional representation of that which needs to be explained: '[i]f... utility estimations are to be deduced from given exchange relations, the argument becomes circular.... At bottom, the theory of marginal utility says nothing more than that someone who engages in an exchange in some sense expects more from this exchange than from... one he does not engage in' (Heinrich 2001, p. 68).

32. Even the name 'political economy' was dropped: Ziegler 1998, pp. 155–6 (on Jevons) and p. 162 (on Marshall).

demonstrate the self-sufficiency of the market; at best, this aim meshes with political endeavours to eliminate distortions of the market.[33]

Psychologisation means that the causes of fundamental economic mechanisms are no longer sought in constraints that are 'objective', and thereby open to empirical verification; instead, these causes are sought in the inclination and volition of individuals who are thought of as isolated. Within the history of dogmas, this is seen as the transition from an 'objective' to a 'subjective' theory of value. The scientific models that neoclassical economics is oriented toward are those of methodologically atomistic theories of 'rational choice', that is, game and decision theories.

Harmonisation refers to the nature of the overall model. The image of society upon which neoclassical theory rests is not one of heterogeneous economic classes, as in the classics, but that of a homogeneous group of utility-maximising individuals. Apart from this excessive abstraction, by which classes are made to disappear, the absence of crises in neoclassical theory also represents a 'harmonisation'. The overall economic process is thought of as a grand exchange of given goods that is 'always already' in equilibrium. The interplay of supply and demand determines prices, and economic actors passively accept the prices that the market presents them. The atmosphere is one of peace, all the more so as the model is static; growth, often so precarious in reality, is only addressed in special supplementary theories. By contrast, the classics started from the notion of a constitutive polarity: competition within and between the classes, who participate actively in struggles over distribution, invites comparisons to the *bellum omnium contra omnes* (Hobbes). Marx's pointed emphasis on economic class struggles, whose effects extend all the way into politics, merely thought this approach through to its logical conclusion. The same is true of his sceptical view of the trends associated with continuous growth, such as the immiseration and exclusion of broad sections of the population, the periodic outbreak of crises and the destruction of nature. Compared with the sober assessment of the classics, the passive behaviour of the homogeneous individuals in neoclassical theory's stable and static model of equilibrium seems quite an idealisation. And economic 'crises' are hardly to be explained in *microeconomic* terms.

Neoclassical theory is best described as a 'counter-utopia'[34] After all, the methodological paradigm shift also marks a shift in the assessment of the economic process.

---

33. Krummbacher 1991.

34. Kühne 1972, pp. 46 ff. contrasts thought that emphasises harmony with 'Marx's processual vision'. On the term 'counter-utopia', see Mannheim 1936, p. 218 (compare the terms 'contrast ideology' in Seidel 1980, p. 137, and 'counter-ideology' in Habermas 1960, p. 278). Neoclassical economists were not blind to its negative aspects. Many were driven to engage with economic theory by the need to do something about poverty (Sommer 1993). However, a theory's effect is not determined by its underlying intention. The proponent of free trade Bastiat formulated the following confession in his 1850 *Economic Harmonies*: 'I believe that the inevitable trend of society is toward a constantly rising physical, intellectual, and moral level shared by all mankind. I believe, if only man can win back his freedom of action and be allowed to follow his natural bent without interference, that his... development is assured' (Bastiat 1964, p. xxxvii, also quoted in Kromphardt 1991,

Yet this change of assessment does not come from outside, as Max Weber suggested (2.4.6); it is already implicit in the model's basic assumptions. This means that the theoretico-historical context is not the one the history of dogmas would lead us to expect. It seems natural to represent the history of economic theory as a line of development, that of 'bourgeois' economic theory, leading from the classics to the neoclassics and on to contemporary theorists of neoliberalism and their institutionalist opponents. Marx's 'revolutionary' thought cuts across this line transversely,[35] without significantly altering its course:

Table 11: Marx in the history of economic dogmas

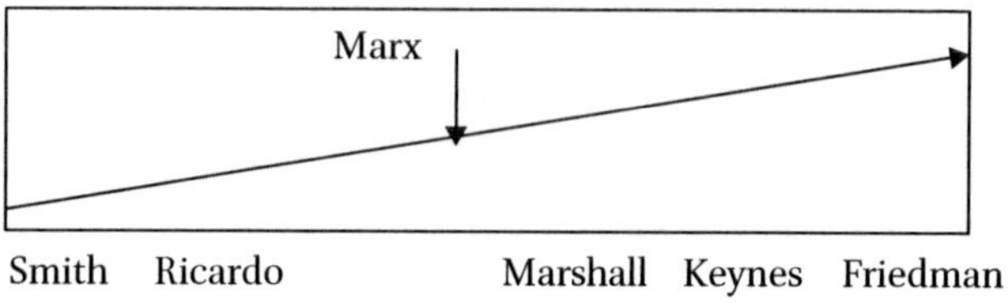

This image was reinforced both by the self-interpretations of economic theorists and by the socialist heroisation of Marx.[36] Even the term 'neoclassical', which was introduced by Keynes,[37] seems to promise continuity. Yet despite such intuitions, it turns out a chronological presentation of the relationship between Marx and other economic theorists is more appropriate. For Marx was part of the 'grand line of development': Marx the economist thought of himself as operating from within the tradition of the classics, and he *was* usually read this way, too. He reworked the theories of the classics in order to arrive at a coherent and comprehensive account of capitalism's political economy, albeit one that reaches the familiar unpleasant conclusions.

The neoclassical counter-utopia developed to counter Marx broke not only with him but also with the classical analysis of Smith and Ricardo.[38] Thus the relationship between Marx and other economic theorists ought really to be represented as follows:

---

p. 120). 'Is it not a great model that, households' notions of utility and available resources being given, savings and investments, the supply of labour, the demand for a *numéraire*, the quantities of the various factors of production employed in each firm and the quantity of products manufactured are fixed, so that the plans of every household and every firm are harmonised with one another in a simultaneous process?" (Felderer in Starbatty 1989, p. 70). That would certainly be nice, but it would seem the proper place for the theory of harmony is music (Waibl 1989, p. 197).

35. Arestis 2000.

36. Alfred Marshall's favourite word is reported to have been 'continuity' (Rieter in Starbatty 1989, p. 140). Söllner 1999 opts for precisely this mode of presentation. Marx is mentioned only as an also-ran (pp. 262 ff.). For the theorists of real socialism, the differences within 'bourgeois theory' hardly mattered (Becher 1976, pp. 393 ff.).

37. Keynes 1964, p. 177.

38. 'In demonstrating the untenability of the Classical doctrine, they [the proponents of the "dominant teaching"] can simultaneously prove the weakness of Marx's theory' (Grossman

Table 12: Marx in economic reception history

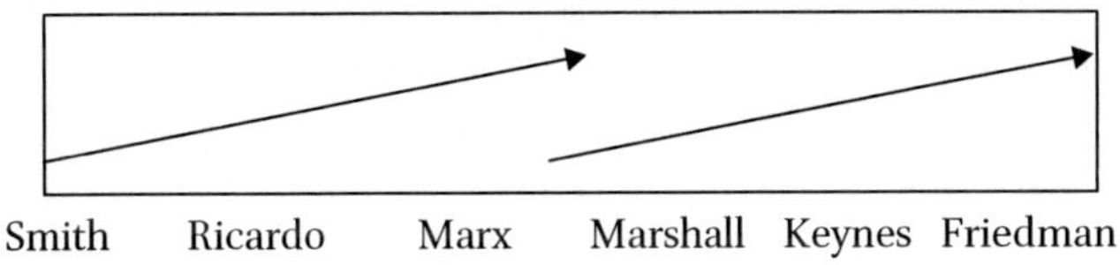

It is not the case that history is traversed by *one line* of economic thinkers, each of whom engages vertically with economic relations and horizontally with his predecessors. Rather, there is competition 'within the intellectual field'[39] as well, especially when the various theoretical currents represent different political and social camps. Neoclassical theory needs to be understood as a continuation of classical economy by altogether different means.[40] This became necessary because Marx interwove the various threads of the classical analysis in such a way that it seemed impossible to pick them up again *without addressing his work*.[41] I will not address the question of whether the marginalists actually intended to 'refute Marx'; what matters is not individual motivation, but the relationship within reception history, which is conspicuous.[42] As paradoxical as it may

1977, p. 42). This move is repeated in the field of philosophy, and in a remarkably parallel fashion (2.5.5).

39. Mannheim 1964.

40. On Marx's relationship to the classics, see Althusser and Balibar 1997, pp. 91 ff. Heinrich has difficulty situating Marx. While he notes a break between classical and neoclassical theory (Heinrich 2001, p. 75), he wants to use Marx to deny the continuity between the two (p. 18). What he is really doing is something else. He criticises the classics and Marx from a Keynesian (that is, neoclassical) perspective. He accuses Marx of continuing to 'cling to' the approach of the classics (pp. 26, 212). But that is precisely the point of Marx's work.

41. Streissler holds that 'by pointing to the tradition of German economics', one can 'definitively refute the recurrent claim that the Austrian school's subjective theory of value was developed in response to Karl Marx, as a counterrevolution against his doctrine', since 'a subjective theory of value was already developed in Germany before Marx's first writings' (Streissler 1989, p. 126). This is a *non sequitur*. There was already a subjective theory of value in the Middle Ages (Pribam 1992); the question is why the theory suddenly became so topical. 'The two basic options available to value theory – tracing a commodity's value to the labour required for its production or to the commodity's utility – had already been identified some time ago … Therefore, what requires explanation … is the fact that this theory imposed itself during the 1870s and 1880s, and not at an earlier or later time' (Heinrich 2001, p. 63; see, too, Blaug 1958, pp. 149–50; Meek 1973, pp. 97 ff.; Dobb 1977, pp. 124–5). One reason lay in the 'anti-capitalist' application of the labour theory of value by the 'Ricardian socialists' (Heinrich 2001, p. 64; cf. Kühne 1972, pp. 56, 197; *MECW* 32, pp. 397 ff.). Hodgskin 1825 formulated the right of the workers to the 'full fruits of labour'. This disconcerted bourgeois economists: 'Ricardo's system is one of discord … It has a tendency to create animosity between the classes … His book is a handbook of demagogues who seek power by the confiscation of land, war and plunder" (Carey 1848, pp. 74–5; *MECW* 31, pp. 390–1; Grossmann 1977, p. 52).

42. Even Sombart maintained that 'if the theory of marginal utility has been described as a product of the fear of socialism [Sombart is refering to Labriola; C.H.], then there is undoubtedly something in this statement that is very much valid' (Sombart 1930, p. 283). The more pointed and

seem: it is Marx who represents the hidden link between the classics, whom *he* criticised, and the neoclassics, who criticised *him*. Thus Marx's position in the history of economic paradigms is right between the dominant paradigms of the two periods.

This very general finding needs to be explained in more detail. I am not claiming that every economic theory developed since Marx's time is neoclassical. There have been other currents, such as the German historical school of Roscher, Knies and Schmoller,[43] the theory of marginal utility developed by the Austrian economists Carl Menger and Eugen Böhm-Bawerk, the resurgent institutionalism of Thorstein Veblen, Keynesianism, and, of course, monetarism and the supply-side neoliberal economic theory of past decades. But the *paradigms* worked with have been, and continue to be, those of neoclassical economics. For this reason, the term 'neoclassical economics' will be used in a broad sense in what follows: as referring to a paradigm rather than a specific school. Keynes, who – as we mentioned – introduced the term, still worked with the neoclassical model of equilibrium. He merely criticised the assumption that this model ought to be situated on the level of optimality. In his *General Theory*,[44] he discovered that there can be equilibrium on a level *other* than the 'perfect' one, for instance an equilibrium that implies high unemployment and low investment. But he retained the basic neoclassical assumptions concerning the static character of the equilibrium model and the passivity of the homogeneous market participants.[45] If anything, the static character became more pronounced when Samuelson combined Keynesian and neoclassical models in his 'great synthesis'.[46] Much the same is true of the historicists and institutionalists, who criticise specific features of the basic model, but are otherwise content to 'describe' various historical constellations; or of the monetarists, who used neoclassical assumptions about equilibrium and the quantity theory of money to contest Keynesian policies of state intervention.[47]

The observation that Marx developed his theory within the classical paradigm, that is, within a *different* paradigm than most twentieth-century economists (whatever current or school they may be affiliated with) is of central importance to the following chapters. The 'refutations' of Marx's theory developed by bourgeois economists, from Böhm-

---

dogmatic formulation of this view was, however, not very plausible: '[f]rom now on, anti-Marxism became the concentrated theoretical expression of its anti-proletarian and anti-socialist character' (Becher 1976, p. 395).

43. See Rieter 1994; Schefold 1994; Koslowski 1995 and 2000; see also the institutionalist development of this position in Reuter 1994 and Edeling 1999. The theoretical status of the historical school has, however, always been controversial. At bottom, there is no theory to speak of, here (on Roscher, see *MECW* 31, pp. 352–3; *MECW* 32, p. 502; this was also the key issue in the methodological controversy between Menger and Schmoller around 1884). Even Sombart is content to 'describe' a growing number of capitalism's features without providing any material explanation for them (Sombart 1911, 1913, 1913b; see Pollock 1926; Appel 1992; Lenger 1994; J. Backhaus 2000).

44. Keynes 1964, first published in 1936.

45. Keynes 1964; Bombach 1976; and Starbatty 1989. 'The idea that Keynes is more dynamic than Ricardo is the exact opposite of the truth' (Harrod 1948, p. 18).

46. Samuelson 1948.

47. On Reagonomics (Friedman, Hayek), see Lekachmann 1981, pp. 124–5, and Waibl 1988.

Bawerk and Keynes to Samuelson, read Marx in terms of the neoclassical paradigm.[48] Thus his analyses were removed from their internal logical context and 'transferred' to a general theoretical context that began from completely different background assumptions. Where it could be proven that, within this paradigm, Marxian hypotheses could not be retained, the claims of Marxian theory were, in fact, not done justice. Such refutations are only of limited value (2.3.2). However, many Marxist economists, particularly those in the West, accepted these 'transfers' and tried to retain Marxian hypotheses within the neoclassical paradigm, after all. Given the difficulty of this endeavour, *additional assumptions* had be made, and these led even further away from Marx's actual theories (2.3.3). Because of the dominance of the neoclassical paradigm within economic literature, and the futile attempt by many Marxists to defend Marx within it, 'economics' was increasingly taken to refer to *this* paradigm only. When philosophers speak of economics today, as in the debate on Rawls or in business ethics (3.2 and 3.3), they do so from within this paradigm – even or especially when they are criticising it philosophically (2.3.4). The political notions of the Western Left were also long based on notions derived from a neoclassically-distorted Marx. In a sense, Marxism-Leninism reinforced this trend. Due to these developments, the attempt to reconsider Marx within philosophy is saddled with a special explanatory burden. Unfortunatelty, it is not enough to try to open philosophical theory up to economic facts and theories;[49] these theories usually already contain assumptions associated with the neoclassical model. Attempts to revive one or the other older variant of 'Marxism' are even less effective, for the erroneous notions of the neoclassical model are a fixture of these past 'Marxisms' as well – one encounters them, as it were, in the toothless lion's den. If one wants to clarify just what is decisive in Marxian economics, there is no way around a critique of the economic notions of various familiar 'Marxisms'.

2.3.2 *Neoclassical refutations of Marx*

> Where two principles really do meet which cannot be reconciled with one another, then each man declares the other a fool and an heretic.[50]

The central difference between classical and neoclassical economics consists in their divergent approaches to the explanation of *commodity values*.[51] Classical economics

48. Characterisation of a certain economic theory as 'bourgeois' serves only to set it off from Marxist economic theory. As with the German term for the Civil Code [*bürgerliches Gesetzbuch – bürgerlich* meaning both 'civil' and 'bourgeois'], such characterisation is not pejorative, and is based on self-descriptions (professors of economics have described themselves to me as 'bourgeois economists').

49. See, for example, Kambartel 1998.

50. Wittgenstein.

51. 'The wealth of those societies in which the capitalist mode of production prevails, presents itself as "an immense accumulation of commodities"' (*MECW* 35, p. 45). The reason Marx chose to begin with commodities, rather than with money, is that a sum of money is not

tended toward an objective approach, whereas neoclassical economics opted for an explanation in subjective terms. To be sure, there was a controversy, within classical economics, over which element ought to be considered the source of value – the soil, as in Malthus and the physiocrats; the actual labour performed by the capitalist himself or by those working for him, as in Locke and Smith; or socially necessary labour time, as in Marx. The objective theory of value clearly distinguishes classical economics from the neoclassical theory of marginal utility, which explains value in terms of individuals' subjective considerations on utility.[52] The theory of marginal utility states that the utility an individual derives from a good decreases proportionally to ownership of this good. Thus market demand for the good correlates with the good's utility for consumers.

If the price of a good is determined only by supply and demand, it depends on the productions costs of the producers as its lower limit and the utility calculus of the consumers as its upper limit.[53] On the market, producers and consumers agree on a price, and this is the price at which the commodities are then sold. In order to illustrate this fictitious assumption, Walras invented the great 'auctioneer', who determines the prices at which entrepreneurs sell their goods *in lieu of* these entrepreneurs.[54] Here, the market becomes the subject, whereas firms are degraded to the status of its passive elements. The attacks that bourgeois economics conducted on Marx the economist started from this marked-out terrain, departure from which was already perceived as an error.[55] Now, Marx never denied that supply and demand influence the purchasing price of a given good. However, the more long-term fluctuations of the price and its real factors cannot be *explained* in this way. Marx's view was that

---

necessarily equivalent to wealth. If the money cannot purchase anything (because its purchasing power is insufficient, or because there is nothing to buy), then it is worthless. The value of money is expressed in commodities (in the famous 'basket of commodities'). This does not mean that money appears, from this point of view, as 'neutral' (after all, the elimination of money within the 'utopia of labour money' developed by Proudhon in the 1850s was one of Marx's favourite objects of criticism: *MECW* 29, pp. 322 ff.; *MECW* 35, p. 103; Rakowitz 2000, pp. 77 ff.); what it does mean is that money cannot be explained without reference to other phenomena (see 2.3.5).

52. The importance accorded to what exists objectively sometimes degenerated into a 'substantialism' that could take strange turns. Witness mercantilism's monetary theory, which assumed that money (or the money commodity) had an 'objective' value, Malthus's brutal theory of immiseration or the explanation for the falling rate of profit offered by Ricardo, which argued in terms of the deteriorating quality of newly exploited land. The 'substantialism' of classical economic theory is still criticised today (see below). Yet in Marx, 'not an atom of matter' enters into the composition of a commodity's value; the value of commodities has a 'purely social reality' (*MECW* 35, p. 57). The classical paradigm is not monolithic. It can accomodate Smith, Ricardo and Marx, just as the neoclassical paradigm can accomodate Marshall, Keynes and Friedman. Differences may persist, even where there is common ground.

53. Marshall 1890 described these two factors as 'the upper or the under blade of a pair of scissors'. This was already an attempt to mediate between classical and neoclassical theory (see Rieter in Starbatty 1989, p. 137).

54. Kromphardt 1991, p. 187; Starbatty 1989, p. 62; Hunt 1993, p. 149. Incidentally, this is more reminiscent of central planning than of the market.

55. As can be seen clearly in Mises 1936, for example.

> the change in the relations of demand and supply [explain] in regard to ... price ... nothing except its changes ... If demand and supply balance, the oscillation of prices ceases ... But then demand and supply also cease to explain anything.[56]

Ceteris paribus, prices that oscillate around a given supply and a given demand settle within an ascertainable range, which, therefore, *cannot* also be explained in terms of supply and demand. Rather, supply and demand are themselves determined by additional factors. These, however, are no longer inquired into when working with a model that focuses on the process of exchange and its given determinants during short-term periods.[57]

Marx was interested precisely in these forces that operate behind the 'determinants' and impose themselves through them in the long term. His labour theory of value examines the range within which prices are pushed upward and downward by fluctuations in supply and demand.[58] The labour theory of value was rejected by neoclassical economists because the very way in which it framed the question seemed to them to make no sense. Yet the category of individual 'utility' is hardly less mysterious than that of value. It merely has a narrower focus.[59] The neoclassical 'theory of prices' explains prices in terms of prices. It can rely only on other prices, which must be given. This approach allows one to *register* fluctuations in price, but not to explain them.[60]

Price determination was not the issue addressed by the labour theory of value. Rather, what it did was to allow one to establish the relationship between phenomena such as the decrease in the mass of profit appropriated by industrialists as determined by a larger share of 'unproductive' labour, the general fall in the average rate of profit and the investment bottlenecks associated with it, growth cycles and crises in general and the analysis of social classes and their political altercations. All of these phenomena are linked to the concept of value, and can, therefore, neither be explained nor even properly grasped by the neoclassical analysis. Marx's labour theory of value lays the groundwork for answering the question concerning the 'natural laws of ... movement'[61] that impose

---

56. *MECW* 35, p. 538.

57. The focus on the short term is reflected in Keynes's witticism that 'in the long run, we are all dead'.

58. How the 'natural price' (Smith; Marx called it the price of production) – which persists despite short-term fluctuations – is determined, 'is just the question'. This average quantity 'had naturally to be determined otherwise than by its own compensating variations' (*MECW* 35, p. 538; cf. *MECW* 37, p. 188).

59. Neoclassical theory nevertheless has philosophical offshoots that are not themselves 'economic' theories. They too now describe themselves as 'political economies' (of the state, of law, and so on; see G. Becker 1976, Behrens 1986, Buchanan 1990; see also section 3.2).

60. The development of prices can also be linked to the money supply (Friedman 1969). But this is as tautological as explaining given prices by reference to utility, since the question of what the price of a commodity will be under conditions of 'optimal money supply' is not answered; all that is said is that the price rises under conditions of inflation, and vice versa.

61. *MECW* 35, p. 10.

themselves in the capitalist economy in the long term. This question cannot even be formulated within the neoclassical paradigm; it has no 'grammatical' place there.

According to Wittgenstein, understanding the sentence 'this is blue' presupposes not just that one shares the speaker's situation, but that one also knows already what a colour is.[62] In the same way, understanding the labour theory of value presupposes that one shares the underlying question, or at least acknowledges it. To a science that refuses to do this, talk of the values at work behind prices must seem like mysticism or bad 'metaphysics', but the reasons for this are grammatical, not economic.[63] Such a refusal also has political implications: without the labour theory of value, one cannot demand wage increases, since every wage that is paid on a free market appears 'fair'; nor is it possible to retain Marx's explanations for endogenous capitalist crisis phenomena. A fall in the rate of profit will then be attributed to 'excessively high' wages rather than to the inner workings of capitalist development, such as the rising organic composition of capital (2.1.6). All unpleasant elements of Marxian theory are related to the theory of value: the collective bargaining of trade unions is related to 'exploitation', and the revolutionary rhetoric of communist parties is related to the 'theory of crisis'.[64] In this sense, focusing criticism on the theory of value was a clever move. The loss of broadly posed economic questions went hand-in-hand with a loss of political implications. Regardless of whether or not this was the intention behind the abandonment of the objective concept of value, the *effect* was politically desirable, from entrepreneurs' point of view. Relinquishment of the labour theory of value was overdetermined, and it is clear that it was partly driven by extra-theoretical motives.

There were two attempts *explicitly* to refute the labour theory of value. First, it was pointed out that the theory is empirically false: two products that contain the same amount of labour can sell at quite different prices, due to supply and demand – after all, products that contain large amounts of labour have been known to sell at very low prices.[65] This, however, is not a refutation, since Marx never denied such occurrences. The value of a single good is not determined by the labour time that was actually spent to produce it; it is determined by the amount of labour time that is 'socially necessary' at

62. Understanding the meaning of a proposition is not the same as believing it to be true; all such understanding entails is that one is in a position to identify the facts that would validate the proposition (Wittgenstein 2009, pp. 381 ff. and elsewhere). Incidentally, Wittgenstein was personally acquainted with the Cambridge economists Keynes and Sraffa (see below).

63. Philosophical critiques of the labour theory of value (see below) are off the mark as long as they do not distinguish between the various paradigms. Shaikh 1977, p. 107, compares this to trying to 'reconstruct' Einstein's assumptions on the basis of a Newtonian system, without taking account of the paradigm shift that separates the two. Such an undertaking would also inevitably produce – unnecessary – mystifications.

64. Explanations of crises in circulation (money, credit and clearance crises and the like; see Huffschmid 1999; Shaikh 1995, 1998a; 2.3.5) also involve arguments that make reference to the productive sector. That is, such explanations depend indirectly on the labour theory of value.

65. Ott 1989.

the current level of technological development.[66] If the average amount of labour time required for producing a certain good is twenty hours, the producer who takes 30 hours will not be able to sell his product at a higher price, since his price will be undercut by other producers. Hence this refutation is based on a misunderstanding.

A different refutation focused on the so-called 'transformation problem', the problem of the transformation of values into prices. From Böhm-Bawerk onward, the first and the third volumes of *Capital* were claimed to contradict one another: in the first volume, Marx assumes that commodities are sold at their values,[67] whereas in the third volume, he takes into account other factors that contribute to price determination on the market.[68] It was alleged that the theory of value aimed to explain the determination of immediate market prices. If this were the case, then the two claims *would*, indeed, contradict one another. However, the first volume deals with basic concepts (commodities, value, money, capital, surplus value, wages) and relations (exchange, production, accumulation, centralisation), whereas the third volume deals with how this logic actually imposes itself.[69] Of course, the price of commodities is formed on the market. But why is it unfortunate when prices fall (because of weak demand or because the competition is producing more cheaply)? The situation only becomes fatal when the entrepreneur sells his product 'below its value'. The purpose of the theory of value is not to determine the definite price of a definite commodity; rather, it discovers the 'golden thread' that runs through apparently chaotic market phenomena.[70]

Nor do the other theories to be found in the third volume contradict those of the first volume; instead, they show how these basic laws impose themselves on the market. Like social democracy and Leninism, academic economics also became entangled in the internal logic of Marxian economic theory. To anticipate: this entanglement was

---

66. *MECW* 35, p. 49; *MECW* 20, p. 123; *MECW* 37, p. 174.

67. *MECW* 35, pp. 177, 322; *MECW* 36, p. 32.

68. *MECW* 37, pp. 150 ff. The critique formulated in Böhm-Bawerk 1975 (first published in 1896) reappears in Robinson 1966; Samuelson 1971; Kramm 1979; and Backhaus 1997, p. 168. A hypothesis expressed in connection with this critique, namely that Marx revised the positions expressed in the first volume of *Capital* in the third volume, was retracted when it became clear that the manuscript of the third volume was written before that of the first volume (as even Samuelson admitted).

69. *MECW* pp. 27, 37.

70. 'The theory of value should … not be read as a theory of price formation but as a theory of value creation on the level of the economy as a whole, and as a theory of income distribution' (Hardach 1975, p. 48; Blaumol 1974; Zinn 1987, pp. 76 ff.). 'The labour theory of value has long been misinterpreted as a theory of price formation and criticised as such. For as the classical economists – whom Marx studied very carefully – had shown, price relations deviate from value relations … This misinterpretation of the labour theory of value as a theory of price formation can be found as early Böhm-Bawerk' – and as late as Samuelson. The labour theory of value ought, rather, to be read as 'the foundation upon which to criticise doctrines that justify capitalist income distribution, doctrines that make reference to the factors of production labour, land and capital in order to formulate a moral justification of the wage, rent and revenue incomes received by the owners of the factors of production' (Kromphart 1991, p. 136).

even passed on to philosophy. For example, Werner Becker[71] accused Marx of 'methodic irrationality'. According to Becker, Marx never defines his basic concepts; instead, he conceals his entire theory within them.[72] In pointing this out, Becker gave a correct characterisation of Marx's mode of presentation: Marx begins by introducing his basic concepts, and then progressively develops a coherent theory from their relations. As such, the meaning of the concepts lies in the function that these categories perform *within the theory*. This mode of presentation makes sense didactically: after all, every presentation of complex relations has to begin somewhere. But it is not the case that the theory can be deduced from the concepts; rather, the significance of the concepts can be deduced from the theory – and the theory is oriented toward the very reality that needs, according to Becker, to be taken into consideration. A second objection by Becker, namely that Marx never tested his hypotheses, is more serious. Of course, every empirical theory needs to be tested. It makes no sense, however, to expect the theory's *basic concepts* to stand up to such a test. How would one test the concept of 'mass' as used in physics? The only thing one can test are the hypotheses about reality that are deduced from a law that has been formulated. And Marx spent entire decades studying reality in the British Library. He developed his economic 'hypotheses' from a wealth of material and preliminary formulations, and he communicated his results once he had given them form.[73] Becker picks out two of Marx's terms and wrongly interprets them as basic *philosophical* concepts, in the manner of German deductive Marxism. By assuming that the theory is already contained in these concepts, Becker simply projects the idealist misunderstanding that is 'value-form analysis' onto Marx (see sections 2.3.5, 2.5.7).[74] Becker formulates his call for verification, which is justified in itself, at a point where it makes no sense: he expects Marx to verify his basic concepts in the first chapter of a three-volume work. He cannot have been all too serious in formulating his objection.[75] One can see, from this, that

---

71. Becker 1972.

72. Becker maintains that the categories of exchange value and use value are not to be understood, because they contradict one another (Becker 1974, pp. 70–1; 1972). Becker would have to extend this accusation to Aristotle (*Politics* I 9, 1257a; *Nicomachean Ethics* V 8; *Eudemian Ethics* 1231a, pp. 39 ff.; Bress 1974). And yet the matter is straightforward. Use value is the value a commodity has for me, for instance as a collector of bottle caps, while exchange value is the value that commodity has for others. The use value of large banknotes can be limited, for instance when I am in a hurry and dealing with a vending machine.

73. 'Marx engages in his share of social criticism and historical speculation, but . . . they . . . are relevant only to the extent . . . that they are expressions of a theory that must be . . . verifiable in principle' (F. Jonas 1976, Vol. I, p. 217).

74. The notion that Marx deduced his theory from a few 'concepts' was expressed early on: [e]ducated in Hegelian philosophy, anything whose specific features and aspects have not been "logically" deduced from a single principle had to appear unscientific to him' (P. Barth 1897, p. 631). The main point, it was argued, was that of 'presenting the general concept of capital and the dialectical development of the central categories' (Reichelt 1974, p. 40; see *MECW* 24, p. 540).

75. Becker's call for testing basic concepts (Becker 1974, pp. 63 f.) does not even do justice to the natural sciences (2.1.1, 4.3). It betrays a reductive conception of theory, a 'methodological monism' (Albrecht 1973, p. 13).

those formulating refutations of Marx have often not even bothered to read him. Becker simply adopted a standard neoclassical criticism, which was already flawed within neoclassical economics.[76]

Because of its popularity, this neoclassical 'refutation' of Marx needs to be considered more closely. One of the most controversial passages in Marx's *oeuvre* is the first chapter of *Capital*.[77] Not only was the internal logic of this introductory chapter rendered ever more enigmatic, but its position within the overall context of *Capital* was rarely considered.[78] And yet Marx had provided the key in the 1857 'Introduction' to his 'Contribution to the Critique of Political Economy', which was given the status of a dogma in Marxism-Leninism, and which is also contained in the *Grundrisse*, that text so cherished by 'Western Marxism':[79]

> It seems to be correct to begin with the real and the concrete, with the real precondition, thus to begin, in economics, with e.g. the population, which is the foundation and the subject of the entire social act of production [cf. Solow 1970; C.H.]. However, on closer examination this proves false. The population is an abstraction if I leave out, for example, the classes of which it is composed. These classes in turn are an empty phrase if I am not familiar with the elements on which they rest. E.g. wage labour, capital, etc. These latter in turn presuppose exchange, division of labour, prices, etc. For example, capital is nothing without wage labour, without value, money, price etc. Thus, if I were to begin with the population, this would be a chaotic conception [*Vorstellung*] of the whole, and I would then, by means of further determination, move analytically towards ever more simple concepts [*Begriff*], from the imagined concrete towards ever thinner abstractions until I had arrived at the simplest determinations. From there the journey would have to be retraced until I had finally arrived at the population again, but this time not as the chaotic conception of a whole, but as a rich totality of many determinations and relations... The latter is obviously the scientifically correct method. The concrete is concrete because it is the concentration of many determinations, hence unity of the diverse.[80]

---

76. See also Becker 1985, pp. 124 ff., and 1996, pp. 47 ff.
77. *MECW* 35, pp. 45–94.
78. Not even by the 'new reading of Marx' (*neue Marxlektüre*) of the 1970s – perhaps because *Capital* reading classes got bogged down in the opening passages. The first chapter remains controversial among German Marxists to this day (note Haug 1974). It was either read 'historically', in a tradition that runs from Engels to Mandel (on this tradition, see Kittsteiner 1977a; Rakowitz 2000, pp. 27 ff.), or a logical order of 'deductions' was attributed to it, in a Fichtean manner, but in such a way that even the adept no longer understood these 'deductions' (and then shifted the blame to their symbolic father figure Marx – on value-form analysis, see 2.3.5). The first chapter can, however, be skipped without any loss to the quality of the book. In an 1868 letter, Marx wrote 'that, even if there were no chapter on "value" at all in my book, the analysis I give of the real relations would contain the proof' (*MECW* 43, p. 67; Korsch 1971, p. 74; Steinvorth 1977, p. 32).
79. For a similar passage, see *MECW* 31, pp. 390 f.
80. *MECW* 28, pp. 37–8.

Marx's method consists, therefore, in formulating explanations in such a way as to 'advance from the abstract to the concrete'.[81] It is only by starting from definite abstract categories that one can arrive at theoretical relationships by which given appearances, which are 'chaotic' and sometimes contradictory, can be explained. This method is far from being uncommon in the sciences – it is no accident that Marx justifies it by reference to physics.[82] The formulation of these categories builds upon the preliminary work of earlier scholars, as well as upon Marx's own studies, to which he devoted many years.[83] Obviously, 'value' is also a fundamental category, whose origin and character need to be understood before one can begin to think of complicating the analysis and bringing it to bear more directly on reality. Since all further relations are best explained in terms of the basic mechanisms, Marx begins by presenting these basic mechanisms in isolation and abstractly, and he does so deliberately.

Marx draws the reader's attention to the fact that he begins with simplifications.[84] This is true of the assumption, made in the first and second volumes, that commodities are sold at their values, and it is also true of the assumption that there exists a specific money commodity.[85] But Marx does not aim to explain 'value'. He wants to understand the development of bourgeois society. The 'economic power that dominates everything in bourgeois society' is capital.[86] Consequently, Marx needs first to understand the way in which 'capital' operates, and he must begin not from the occasional exception, but from the normal, everyday case. What, then, is capital? It is a historically specific means of production based on ownership of money:

> The conversion of money into capital has to be explained on the basis of the laws that regulate the exchange of commodities, in such a way that the starting-point is the exchange of equivalents... [T]he formation of capital must be possible *even though the*

81. *MECW* 28, p. 38; cf. 2.1.1.

82. *MECW* 35, p. 8. That science does not necessarily have to base itself on appearances had been clear from the time of Galileo and Newton, and it was a principle that both Marx and Kant stood up for (*MECW* 35, pp. 33, 321, 537, 627; *MECW* 37, pp. 311, 804 ff. and elsewhere; see Hegel 1991, §189; 2.1.1). Althusser and Balibar 1997, pp. 83 f. also attached importance to this method.

83. *MECW* 35, p. 19.

84. *MECW* 35, p. 45.

85. German thought seems to consider simplicity a criterion of falsehood. In the age of slashed funding, the scholarly ideal is no longer clarity but opacity. It often seems to be a question not so much of achieving and circulating results as of mastering a scholarly idiom, the more complicated the better. From the perspective of the sociology of knowledge, this could be explained in terms of the attempt, prompted by dependence on extra-disciplinary examiners, to create an appearance of competence; from the perspective of the critique of ideology, it could be explained in terms of a fear of conclusions. The research conclusions arrived at in the humanities are often not just astoundingly simple, but also unpopular – and hence hardly career-enhancing. However, simplicity as such cannot be a criterion of falsehood. On the contrary, theoretical simplicity as called for by "Occam's razor" was the cradle of modern rationality.

86. *MECW* 28, p. 44.

> *price and value of a commodity be the same*; for its formation cannot be attributed to any deviation of the one from the other. If prices actually differ from values, we must, first of all, reduce the former to the latter, in other words, *treat the difference as accidental* in order that the phenomena may be observed in their purity, and our observations not interfered with by disturbing circumstances that have nothing to do with the process in question.[87]

The formation of capital and the way in which capital functions can only be understood, then, on the basis of the simplest abstractions. We are dealing with the introductory chapter of a work more than two thousand pages long. It is on this basis that it will later be possible to explain other phenomena. Marx already makes it clear in the first volume that the simplifying assumption that commodities sell at their prices does not always have to hold true: '[t]he possibility, therefore, of quantitative incongruity between price and magnitude of value, or the deviation of the former from the latter, is inherent in the price-form itself. This is no defect, but, on the contrary, admirably adapts the price-form to a mode of production whose inherent laws impose themselves only as the mean of apparently lawless irregularities that compensate one another'.[88]

Interpretations such as the one according to which the labour theory of value presents an ethical ideal cannot be understood as anything other than scurrilous.[89] Now, Marx's academic critics have used claims he makes in the third volume to question the manner of presentation he adopts in the first volume. For in the third volume, Marx writes: '[u]nder capitalist production . . . it is . . . a matter of realising as much surplus-value, or profit, on capital advanced for production, as any other capital of the same magnitude, or *pro rata* to its magnitude in whichever line it is applied. It is, therefore, a matter, at least as a minimum, of selling the commodities at prices which yield the average profit, i.e., at prices of production'.[90]

Since the price of production is calculated from the outlays for fixed and variable capital, plus an average profit, the premise that commodities sell at their values seems to be in question.[91] If this were the case, and assuming a constant rate of surplus value, different rates of profit would form in industries with different organic compositions of

---

87. *MECW* 35, p. 176; emphasis added.
88. *MECW* 35, p. 112.
89. In his list of the interpretations of the labour theory of value formulated to date, Kühne 1972, pp. 111–18 also mentions this one. It was defended by August Koppel in 1900, by A.D. Lindsay in 1925, by Rudolf Stammler in 1926, by Meek in 1958 and eventually by Kühne himself: '[t]hus values are nothing but the expression of a hypothetical 'just' distribution of surplus value among all working members of society' (Kühne 1972, p. 116).
90. *MECW* 37, p. 194; see, too, p. 156.
91. *MECW* 37, p. 173.

capital. But as Marx knew, such different rates of profit 'do not exist in reality'.[92] Thus the value calculus in the first volume appears to be either unnecessary or false: '[i]t would seem, therefore, that here the theory of value is incompatible with the actual process, incompatible with the real phenomena of production, and that for this reason any attempt to understand these phenomena should be given up'.[93]

This 'major contradiction' (Böhm-Bawerk) was precisely what the economic refutation of Marx based itself on.[94] Let us hear what Samuelson, the doyen of US mainstream economics, has to say about this so-called 'transformation problem' (what is meant is the transformation of values into prices):

> Contemplate two alternative and discordant systems. Write down one. Now transform by taking an eraser and rubbing it out. Then fill in the other one. *Voilà!*[95]

The reservations about Marx were justified mathematically. Yet on the level of content, these objections did not constitute a refutation of Marx; they simply transferred his claims to another theoretical model.[96] It was only in this model that the value calculus could not be made to accord with the 'theory of prices'. In Marx, the two *did* accord – after all, the purpose of his economic theory was to account for the interrelatedness of 'surface' phenomena. Like the vulgar economists, Marx recognised that the money form of the profit obtained *by the individual capitalist* is not determined by the surplus value produced by that capitalist, but by the magnitude of the capital he has advanced. Now, 'vulgar economy' stops at this observation,[97] whereas Marx proposes an explanation.

---

92. *MECW* 37, p. 152.

93. Ibid.

94. For the debate on the 'transformation problem', see Eberle 1973 and Nutzinger 1974 (these contain key texts such as Böhm-Bawerk 1975 and Bortkiewicz 1976), as well as King 1990, Vol. II (key English texts); see also Sweezy 1970, pp. 134–58; Kühne 1972, pp. 154–69; Meek 1973, pp. 193–212; Hardach 1975, pp. 47–51; Shaikh 1977, 1981, 1984 and 1998; Zinn 1986, pp. 76–86; Mandel 1991, pp. 21–9; Howard 1992, pp. 227–310; Hunt 1993, pp. 163–8.

95. Samuelson 1971, p. 400.

96. The Prussian statistician von Bortkiewicz (1976) found fault with Marx's model by pointing out that it considers only the transformation of values into prices, but not that of prices into values, leaving Marx's tables (*MECW* 37, pp. 154 ff.) incomplete. This problem has been dealt with in various ways; on Samuelson, see especially Mattick 1972; for general accounts, see especially Shaikh 1981 and 1984.

97. 'It is evident that the average profit can be nothing but the total mass of surplus values allotted to the various quantities of capital proportionally to their magnitudes in their different spheres of production' (*MECW* 37, p. 173). In vulgar economics, the profit made by the individual capitalist on the capital advanced by him was called 'interest on capital', but there was no explanation of from where this profit came. The statement that 'interest on capital' is a reward for the 'non-consumption' associated with waiting or hoarding is not an explanation but an attempt at legitimation. In terms of its logical form, this is simply the statement that things are as they are and that this is a good thing.

The reason for this equalisation is competition between industries.[98] This does not run counter to the labour theory of value *abstractly* introduced in the first volume,[99] as long as the peculiarities of the Marxian paradigm are taken into account. Marx is formulating an insight that is, at bottom, tautological, even though it is groundbreaking by comparison to neoclassical theory, namely that only production is productive, or that surplus value needs to exist before it can be distributed: '[i]f the commodities are not sold at their values, then the sum of the converted values remains unchanged; the plus on one side is a minus on the other'.[100]

Since exchange is an act of distribution and not of value creation – nor could it conceivably be anything else, when considered in the cold light of day – Marx is only being consistent by deducing that values and prices, or surplus value and profit, must be equal *in the aggregate*. Hence 'the sum of the prices of production of all commodities produced in society – the totality of all branches of production – is equal to the sum of their values'.[101] The laws abstractly introduced in the first volume hold true on the level of the '*totality*'. They are not descriptions; they are the specific form assumed by a law: '[u]nder capitalist production, the general law acts as the prevailing tendency only in a very complicated and approximate manner, as a never ascertainable average of ceaseless fluctuations'.[102] The law of value holds true, here, as well – or, to put this more precisely, it holds true *only* here and *only* in this way:

> Whatever the manner in which the prices of various commodities are first mutually fixed or regulated, their movements are always governed by the law of value. If the labour time required for their production happens to shrink, prices fall; if it increases, prices rise, provided other conditions remain the same.... The assumption that the commodities of the various spheres of production are sold at their value merely [!] implies,

98. 'But capital withdraws from a sphere with a low rate of profit and invades others, which yield a higher profit. Through this incessant outflow and influx, or, briefly, through its distribution among the various spheres, which depends on how the rate of profit falls here and rises there, it creates such a ratio of supply to demand that the average profit in the various spheres of production becomes the same, and values are, therefore, converted into prices of production' (*MECW* 37, pp. 194; see Mandel 1991, pp. 19–20).

99. *MECW* 35, p. 48.

100. *MECW* 36, p. 133. The 'same mass of commodities (and hence the same amount of value) exists after the sale as before. Different price relations will therefore give rise to different distributions of the total commodity-product, and of the total sum of values, but they cannot by themselves change these totals' (Shaikh 1977, p. 115). It is clear 'that if a commodity is sold above or below its value, there is merely another kind of division of surplus value, and that this different division, this changed proportion in which various persons share in the surplus value, does not in any way alter either the magnitude or the nature of that surplus value' (*MECW* 37, pp. 47); 'this always resolves itself to one commodity receiving too little of the surplus value while another receives too much, so that the deviations from the value which are embodied in the prices of production compensate one another' (p. 160).

101. *MECW* 37, pp. 159, 165, 172.

102. *MECW* 37, p. 160; cf. *MECW* 35, pp. 111–12.

> of course, that their value is the centre of gravity around which their prices fluctuate, and their continual rises and drops tend to equalise.[103]

The academic critique of Marx misunderstands the character of this law. It seeks its explanation in the individual capitalist's perception of this phenomenon (the 'participant perspective'). But for Marx, the perspectives of individuals do not seamlessly add up to society, since society is an object *sui generis*. The labour theory of value is a theory formulated from the perspective of *society*, not from that of the individual.[104] The first thing one needs, in order to arrive at the perspective of society, is science – which is by no means a 'view from nowhere'.[105] Marxian theory explicitly thematises the perspectival illusion, the 'non-identity' of part and whole – what has traditionally but ambiguously been called 'dialectics':

> The actual difference of magnitude between profit and surplus value – not merely between the rate of profit and the rate of surplus value – in the various spheres of production now completely conceals the true nature and origin of profit not only from the capitalist, who has a special interest in deceiving himself on this score, but also from the labourer [and the economists; C.H.]. The transformation of values into prices of production serves to obscure the basis for determining value itself.[106]

The academic critique of Marx is formulated from the perspective of the individual, as opposed to that of society, which remains incomprehensible to the individual.[107] The individual capitalist perceives only the average profit, which seems to come *from outside* and which tells him roughly how much profit he will make from the capital he has advanced, assuming that everything goes well. The perspective of 'vulgar economics' is the same.[108] Changes in the magnitude of this average profit, its factors and the consequences of its fluctuations, such as economic cycles or crises, remain beyond the scope

---

103. *MECW* 37, pp. 175–6.
104. *MECW* 35, p. 94; see Brentel 1989; see section 2.1.5.
105. *MECW* 37, pp. 803–4; *MECW* 42, p. 390.
106. *MECW* 37, p. 167.
107. By this, I do not mean a critique of 'society' formulated by the individual, as in the social critique of the 1960s (Helms 1969), but a critique of propositions arrived at from a different, non-individualist point of view. The neoclassical paradigm and the disciplines that follow it operate with aggregated, namely homogeneously added-up individual perspectives (on 'social choice', see 3.2.1).
108. 'Finally, since the mere transformation of surplus-value into profit distinguishes the portion of the value of a commodity forming the profit from the portion forming its cost-price, it is natural that the conception of value should elude the capitalist at this juncture, for he does not see the total labour put into the commodity, but only that portion of the total labour for which he has paid in the shape of means of production, be they living or not, so that his profit appears to him as something outside the immanent value of the commodity. Now this idea is fully confirmed, fortified, and ossified in that, from the standpoint of his particular sphere of production, the profit added to the cost-price is not actually determined by the limits of the formation of value within his own sphere, but through completely outside influences' (*MECW* 37, p. 167).

of such an approach. The neoclassical critique of Marx boils down to the accusation that Marx was not a neoclassical economist.

Yet Marx actually integrated the strong points of neoclassical theory into his own theory.[109] His effort to arrive at the 'totality' and his consideration of the 'dialectic' of perspectives ought to be interpreted not as indications of his dependence on Hegel (see part 2.5.7), but as hints as to how the relationship between the various categories is best understood: despite their 'non-identity', they refer to one another and cannot be understood in isolation from one another. This is true of conceptual pairs such as commodities and money, production and exchange, law and appearance, normality and crisis. Marx's affinity for Hegel signals the difference between his approach and that of academic economics, which considers various phenomena in an isolated fashion.[110] Marx's dialectic, which is hardly mysterious, simply consists in searching out relationships and presenting them appropriately. The appropriateness of this 'dialectical method' cannot be judged by the persuasiveness of the conceptual instruments employed (the 'categories' and their 'deductions'), but only by the explanatory power of the results arrived at.[111] The academic critique of Marx concentrated not on the results of Marx's economic theory, but on its *premises*, so it is hard to see, on the level of theory, how it could have been successful.[112] On the contrary, academic economics owes much to Marx, where it has succeeded in liberating itself from the rigid models of its neoclassical founders: the modern theories of growth and business cycles would hardly be conceivable without Marx, and phenomena such as unemployment, sales crises and financial crises would still not have been integrated into the theoretical model.

2.3.3 *Adoption of the neoclassical approach by Marxists*

In order to understand the powerful impression that the neoclassical critique of Marx has left in spite of the weakness of its arguments, one does not need to resort, like Leninism, to the notion of an 'ideological class struggle'. There are more obvious reasons. First, there is the fragmentary character of Marx's economic theory: only its basic outline is available to us, and only the smallest part of Marx's plans matured into publishable manuscripts. While Marx believed it would be easy for later theorists to build upon the foundations

---

109. Except that he did not stop there. Thus 'use value' is comparable to the concept of 'utility'. But in Marx's view, it was not possible to construct an economic theory on the basis of such a concept, let alone a theory of modern capitalism, which is not concerned with satisfying needs, but with the appropriation of profit (for a different view, see Schulze 2003).

110. It does not, however, explain the difference, for Hegel was not an economist (for a different view, see Lukács 1976).

111. In the course of the presentation, the premises reveal themselves to be results (*MECW* 35, p. 193; *MECW* 37, pp. 805–6, 859; *MECW* 28, pp. 413–14; Bubner 1972, p. 84).

112. On the academic critique of Marx, see Thier 1955; Mohl 1967; Kühne 1972 and 1974; and Bress 1975. Unrevised critiques are presented by Burchardt 1997; Warnke 1998; and Nutzinger 1998.

left by him,[113] he was largely ignored by academic economics, and the progress made by Marxist economics – which, in any case, exists only in academic niches – has been quite limited.[114] The brief *intermezzo* that followed 1968, when Marxist economics became theoretically fashionable for a time, did not last long enough to yield lasting results.[115] The intervention of communist political organs and Western Marxists' ambiguous attitude to socialist Eastern Europe did not make matters any easier. Whenever Marxists expressed their sympathies for Eastern Europe, their theories seemed no longer to require any refutation, give Eastern Europe's desolate condition.[116]

All this made it easier for the academic critique of Marx to focus on the premises, rather than on the results, of Marx's economic theory. These reasons are, however, essentially extrinsic, whereas philosophical analysis is called upon to detect reasons that are intrinsic to a theory. The most important contributions to Marxist economics to be made during the second half of the twentieth century are those of Anglophone writers. Their significance was inversely proportional to the disregard with which they were treated by German writers.[117] In the German-speaking world, the reception of Marx was characterised mainly by the fact that it developed in an environment in which the neoclassical approach was hegemonic.

Within neoclassical theory, engagement with questions of 'value' tended to be of an illustrative nature: it was not about providing reasons for one's rejection of Marxian economics, but about openly *expressing* this rejection by reference to sensitive and provocative issues. The critique of Marx was unable to demonstrate that Marx made any errors in his discussion of the transformation of values into prices.[118] It merely showed that

113. Marx believed that 'the development of the sequel . . . could easily be pursued by others on the basis thus provided' (*MECW* 41, p. 435). On the original outlines for *Capital*, see Rosdolsky 1977; Mandel 1971; Schwarz 1978; Rojas 1989; Heinrich 2001, pp. 179–195; and Shaikh 1988.

114. Howard 1989, 1992.

115. The texts in question usually begin with a ritualised display of modesty. The author announces that the bulk of the work still remains to be done and that what follows is intended only as a contribution to the requisite preliminary work (or something to that effect).

116. Marx's theory is 'explicitly anti-capitalist and in striving to understand capitalism, it means to combat and overcome it. This is probably why post-Marxian non-socialist economic theory, and in particular the neo-classical currents . . . have learned so little from Marx' (Weizsäcker 1962, pp. 78–9; see Kühne 1972 and 1974; Zinn 1987).

117. 'Marx's doctrine has been received very negatively in the German-speaking world' (Blum 2000, p. 65). It was not until the 1970s that a number of major works were translated and read by a wider audience. Even where English-language works were read (for example, within the circle of people associated with the journal *PROKLA*), their reception was often overhasty, and, therefore, uncritical. Even a relatively recent attempt to reconcile the two traditions, Bensch 1995, bears the mark of these barriers to the reception of Marx. Bensch randomly quotes English-language authors to support unquestioned German theorems.

118. The opposite has, however, been argued (Sweezy 1970, p. 140; Heinrich 2001, p. 270). The error was seen to lie in Marx's transformation table (*MECW* 37, pp. 154 ff.), which converts only output values into prices, and not input values. Mathematically, this elision does not pose a serious problem (see the 'iterative method' in Shaikh 1977); the status of Marx's substantive claim is not affected. The problem is situated not on the mathematical, but on the conceptual level.

the value calculus represented a 'detour' (Joan Robinson) within the theory of prices, which was what neoclassical theory was mainly concerned with; within the neoclassical paradigm, the need for this detour was not apparent.[119] Thus the hegemony of a certain paradigm also determines which questions are asked. To demonstrate that the theory of value is unnecessary for determining market prices is not to say anything about the theory of value as such, but this point was lost in the debate.

It has been clear at least since the theories of science developed by Kuhn[120] and Foucault[121] that dominant paradigms or discourses can be very persistent and immune to objections; this persistence and immunity extend right down to one's understanding of *basic concepts*. From this point of view, it seems possible that basic assumptions of neoclassical theory continue to be defended even when an author does not think of himself as a neoclassical theorist – simply because the terminology that author has been exposed to since his youth, and which is presented as neutral, is already heavily laden with theoretical assumptions. This is the sort of phenomenon that is at issue; we are not dealing with Marxists who 'change sides', that is, adopt a different basic theory, out of conviction.[122] One should not underestimate the significance of this kind of *unconscious* adoption of basic assumptions (mainly of the neoclassical sort) to reception history. The neoclassical critique of Marx's theory of value must have seemed so convincing to some Marxist authors that they deliberately relinquished the labour theory of value – prominent early examples include the economists Emil Lederer and Oskar Lange.[123] Since *no* Marxian theme any longer has a proper foundation once one has abandoned the labour theory of value, these authors were forced to provide ever new theoretical foundations; this is true, for example, of analytical Marxism, which turned to the theory of rational

---

In theory, the input figures consist of the previous year's prices. These figures are already average figures and they remain stable as production occurs (Mandel 1991, p. 24). The relevant difference between values and prices lies not in their numerical proportion but in the fact that prices vacillate more strongly. Previous-year average prices are considered stable both in practice (by the entrepreneur) and in theory (in Marx's example); the 'transformation problem' is less acute when it comes to inputs (*MECW* 37, pp. 162–3; on the interdependence of values and prices, see Hunt 1994, pp. 168 ff.). According to Shaikh 1981, critics of Marx often substitute model-based mathematical calculations for theoretical questions (on Samuelson, see Kühne 1974, pp. 477–8; on Böhm-Bawerk, see Kühne 1972, pp. 84 ff.).

119. The classic texts of Böhm-Bawerk 1975; Bortkiewicz 1976; Robinson 1966; and Steedman 1977 culminate in this critique (see Eberle 1973; Nutzinger 1974; Burchardt 1997). For a critique of Robinson, see Rosdolsky 1969, pp. 626–52; on Steedman and the neo-Ricardians, see Shaikh 1984.

120. Kuhn 1970.

121. Foucault 1969.

122. Of course, this has also been known to happen – aside from Liebknecht 1922, one need think only of formerly Marxist tenured professors.

123. See Lederer 1931; Lange 1977 and 1963; Robinson 1966; Steedman 1977. They were not Marxists but considered themselves part of the left-wing spectrum. The 'monetary theory of value' also abandons the labour theory of value – vague 'monetarist' reformulations are justified by the claim that every 'pre-monetary' theory of value, including that of Marx, is 'substantialist' (Heinrich 2001, p. 279; see also 2.3.5).

choice in an effort to develop an alternative theory of exploitation,[124] and it is also true of attempts to 'reconstruct' the Marxian theory of money using the conceptual instruments of late German idealism (Georg Simmel, Alfred Ammon and Bruno Liebrucks; see section 2.3.5). Such shifts in the theoretical landscape are little to do with political economy.[125]

The influence of neoclassical theory can be seen especially clearly in the way in which Marxist economists have dealt with the rate of profit. While Marx never linked his discussion of the rate of profit with a 'theory of collapse', he did accord it a special status within his theory; he spoke of 'the most important law of modern political economy'[126] and of 'a mystery whose solution has been the goal of all political economy since Adam Smith'.[127] Now, when one is operating within a family of theories that are unfamiliar with the category of 'profit', it makes no sense to speak of a 'tendency of the rate of profit to fall' – especially when the factors giving rise to this tendency are described in value terms.[128] Yet when *Marxists* abandon the tendency of the rate of profit to fall, an explanation is required. In what follows, I will not discuss the law itself again, but only the way in which Marxists have dealt with it. The purpose of this is to reveal the influence that neoclassical theory has exerted upon Marxism.

Bernstein and Kautsky already disagreed on this issue. Bernstein ignored the problem; Kautsky tried to defend the hypothesis of the tendency of the rate of profit to fall by claiming that the mass of profit can continue to grow for as long as accumulation proceeds faster than the rate of profit falls. Yet by his implicit assumption that this was actually happening, he severed the link between the fall in the rate of profit and the theory of crises, so that the latter required a *new* foundation, such as 'overproduction', disproportionality or underconsumption.

---

124. Thus there were attempts to 'reconstruct' what Marx called 'exploitation' (the proportion of total labour represented by surplus labour; in terms of the notation used in 2.1.5: $L - v = s$, s/v = rate of exploitation) without making use of any value-related concepts, such as Samuelson 1971; Hodgson 1980; Cohen 1981; Roemer 1981 and 1982; Von Parijs 1995; and Heinrich 2001, p. 275 (for critical perspectives on this, see Hunt 1986; and Steinvorth 1999, pp. 175 ff.). There resulted notions such as the one that workers 'exploit' capitalists when wages are 'too high' (a 'wage squeeze').

125. Backhaus 1997, p. 11 is concerned with philosophical interpretations of Marx. His attempted reconstructions lend support to the classical sociologists, and thereby to the neoclassical approach (Backhaus 2002, p. 117; Reichelt 2002, p. 150; see section 2.4.4). Such speculation operates 'within spaces denied it by Kant and Marx, but opened up to it by Hegel' (Liebrucks 1966).

126. *MECW* 29, p. 133.

127. *MECW* 37, p. 211; see section 2.1.6.

128. To be sure, the neoclassical school also has a concept of 'profit'. But the only claim made about it is the tautological one that profit is what remains when the entrepreneur subtracts his expenses from his revenue. Nothing is said about where profit originates or what distinguishes it from other 'incomes' (wages, rent and interest). Keynes's declining 'marginal efficiency of capital' (Keynes 1964, p. 135) corresponds to Marx's declining rate of profit, but in terms of its conceptual import, it remains a 'black box'. According to Schumpeter 1911, there is no such thing as profit; the entrepreneur only makes 'proceeds' when he departs from the usual practice by introducing technological innovation (for a similar view, see Kalecki 1969).

From then on, the law was nothing but a subordinate accessory, something one could claim or not claim.[129] What Bernstein and Kautsky had in common, however, was that they overhastily linked the level of 'abstract theory' with real phenomena: Bernstein interpreted some of what he observed as refuting the general law, while Kautsky interpreted the law in a determinist manner and was forced to smooth over, by means of *rhetoric*, those phenomena that did not immediately accord with it (see 2.1.2 and 2.1.4).[130]

Anglophone Marxists also interpreted this law as a description of empirical conditions: for example, Maurice Dobb held that while the law had not yet been in effect during the 'golden age of competitive capitalism',[131] it was valid during the current age of monopoly capitalism.[132] His student Joseph Gillman took the opposite view: the law had been valid in Marx's day, but it was 'now no longer' valid.[133] A remarkable inconsistency within Marxism. Gillman held that there had been no rising organic composition of capital, and hence no tendency of the rate of profit to fall, in the USA since 1919; Dobb held that there is a rising organic composition of capital and that it is due to excessively high wages, forcing entrepreneurs to implement labour-saving measures. This 'profit-squeeze' interpretation remained one of the dominant ones from then onward.[134] Its premises reappear in its results.

First, the lack of attention devoted to changes in of the rate of profit, which is characteristic of neoclassical theory, makes wages the only decisive factor. This means that the 'profit share' is determined by the 'wage share' alone. Yet the simple observation that wages and profits can rise and fall *in concert* already shows quite clearly that the development of these two variables has a common cause. The 'profit-squeeze' approach does not, however, pay any attention to the possibility of such a common cause; the theory is purely circulationist.[135] The influence of neoclassical theory is evident: fantasies of collapse aside, the only possible political conclusion is that wages ought to be kept low.

---

129. It was not until Grossmann 1929 that emphasis was once again placed on the law, but Grossmann's book did not receive much attention. With the exception of Paul Mattick, who corresponded with him at length, and Walter Benjamin, who turned to him for economic instruction, Grossmann's influence on Marxism was limited.

130. 'In Bernstein's hands, the variations possible within a law are transformed into a law of unlimited variation: hence his ultimate version of capitalism without limits. In Kautsky's hands, the law which emerges out of variations is transformed into a law which brooks no variation: hence his notion of the inevitable and imminent collapse of capitalism. In the end, both forms are driven by the same objective contradiction' (Shaikh 1988, p. 20), namely by the lack of mediation between the general law and appearances (Shaikh 1988, pp. 23 ff.).

131. Dobb 1937, p. 123.

132. According to Dobb, there was no rise in organic composition until the dawn of monopoly capitalism (for a critical response to this, see Shaikh 1978a).

133. 'Marx was right for the period of competitive capitalism, but wrong for the period of monopoly capitalism' (Gillman 1958, p. vii). An increase in 'capital-saving investments' is given as the reason for this (see Rolshausen 1970).

134. See 2.1.6.

135. Wright 1977, pp. 216–17.

This is a directly pro-capitalist position – which is quite unusual, at least for Marxists of the period.[136]

Another premise of this position consists in the assumption of 'Harrod-neutral' technological progress.[137] Whether such technological progress exists is a question the answer to which depends on empirical data; these data, in turn, depend on the way they are framed conceptually. The economic significance of a set of figures is not immediately apparent. When no account is taken of the fact that the very concepts of neoclassical and Marxian theory differ, because of differences between the two theories, then even Marxists get entangled in neoclassical assumptions.[138] For example, the theorists of the profit squeeze support their hypothesis that crises are *caused* by an 'excessively low' rate of exploitation (s/v) by directly equating this rate with the ratio of observable profits to wages (p'/w). To do this, they make use of conventional statistics, which have been compiled in accordance with neoclassical theories. However, the official figures do not express Marxian 'surplus value', but only the profit achieved by the individual entrepreneur, a sum that is left over after numerous deductions (p'). They fallaciously treat the ratio of 'net corporate income' to wages (p'/w) as a direct expression of the ratio, proper to the labour theory of value, of surplus value ('gross profit on sales') to variable capital (s/v).[139] The result is that the rate of exploitation appears much lower than it is, and the wage *share* much larger – all this is due simply to a fallacious transfer of the category 'surplus value' to the empirical sphere.[140]

The failure to distinguish between capital stock and capital flow betrays a similar negligence: of course, the profit rate appears much higher when one simply leaves out constant capital, which, according to Marx, is decisive for the tendency of the rate of profit to fall.[141] Yet neoclassical theorems are concealed not just in the way the figures

---

136. Classic advocates of this approach, after Dobb 1937, were Glyn 1972; Himmelweit 1974; Boddy 1975; Bowles 1983; and the commentaries on Shaikh 1978b, for instance those by Armstrong and Glyn and Steedman (in *Cambridge Journal of Economics*, Volume 4, 1980; cf. 2.1.6). In Germany, this approach was advocated by Habermas 1960; Holländer 1974; and Stammatis 1977. Heinrich believes the rate of profit falls only 'when real-wage increases are very high' (2001, pp. 274, 340).

137. According to Harrod 1948, technological innovations are both labour- and capital-saving (Rose 1991, pp. 154 ff.), such that technological progress does not entail any trend in income distribution (or in the capital/output ratio, which amounts to the same thing). This view is diametrically opposed to Marx's hypothesis as to the rising organic composition of capital.

138. Gumbel 1928.

139. On these terms, see Shaikh 1978, pp. 238–9. In Shaikh's view, the error committed by these Marxists consists in 'identifying the observed profit/wage-ratio with the rate of exploitation' (p. 237).

140. If there is a 'transformation problem', then it consists in the use of conventional statistics within 'Marxist' analysis. Once more, categories that appertain to the perspective of the individual capitalist (the 'proceeds' obtained) are seamlessly extended to the level of society (the 'surplus value' created). In Marx, unproductive industries (services such as commerce, banking and transport) are paid from surplus value, as are other fees (taxes, insurance, and so on). Moreover, re-investments are deducted from surplus value. Thus surplus value is much greater than net proceeds.

141. Okishio 1961 does not take account of fixed capital, but only of running expenses. (In the view of his student Nakatani 1980, p. 65, 'he abstracts from fixed capital'. Nakatani quotes

are compiled, but also in their assessment. A putatively Marxist account of why the rate of profit *cannot* fall was advanced in the debate on technological innovation prompted by Okishio.[142] Okishio assumed that capitalists would introduce only *those* technological innovations that raise their rate of profit (this is the so-called 'optimality criterion'). When one assumes such motivation and extends it to the social 'aggregate', one arrives at the conclusion that new technology can only raise the rate of profit. If it does fall, then the reason must consist either in overly high wages (this is where the argument is reminiscent of the theory of the 'profit squeeze') or in the price-depressing effects of foreign competition.[143]

However, the plausibility of this model depends on preliminary assumptions that make no sense within the Marxian paradigm. The first and most important of these is the assumption that entrepreneurs are passive 'price takers' operating under conditions that correspond to neoclassical theory's model of 'perfect competition'.[144] The harmonisation of competition proper to this view leads to decisive innovations, such as the introduction of the steam engine or industrial mass production, ceasing to be comprehensible ('rational').

---

a Japanese article by Okishio that begins with the words '[i]f we abstract from fixed capital...') According to Shaikh 1978a, p. 50, this means that Okishio is measuring not the rate of profit, but the 'profit margin on cost-price' (see *MECW* 37, p. 225). This profit margin is, of course, always greater than that associated with older technology; if it were not, the new technology would not have been introduced. Okishio concludes from this that the rate of profit cannot fall. In this way, Okishio misses the point of Marx's account: new technology can widen this margin while simultaneously causing the rate to fall. This time, the variable in the formula m/c+v that is fallaciously 'transformed' is not m, but c. In conventional economics, one encounters this phenomenon in the concept of 'lost costs' (Blum 2000, pp. 98, 143, 480): investment activity engaged in during the first year has an effect on the rate of profit, but not on the margin of the years that follow.

142. Okishio 1961; cf. 2.1.6.

143. Thus Brenner 1998.

144. See Sweezy 1966, p. 53; Sichel 1974, p. 158 and the articles 'Monopolistic Competition and General Equilibrium' and 'Perfectly and Imperfectly Competitive Markets' in Eatwell 1987. The formula 'at given prices' betrays this assumption. Here, prices are a function of supply and demand; firms have no power to influence them. 'Within the ideal model of perfect competition, there exist many small suppliers; they supply a specific good on a homogeneous and open market. Since every supplier is very small, he has no possibility of eliminating his competitors from the market. Hence every supplier will treat the market price as given and adjust his production in such a way as to maximise profit (so-called quantity adjustment). Competition between the suppliers takes the form of each supplier attempting to produce the homogenous product at the lowest possible cost. Profits are eliminated by competition, by virtue of the fact that all suppliers present on the market will employ the same technologies' (Weise 1991, p. 330). This model is not just questionable; it is also inconsistent: 'for any small firm to have no effect on the market when it acts, it must act alone. Thus the real secret of the story of perfect competition is that each firm is implicitly taken to believe that when it acts to change production, no other form will do so. Unfortunately such a belief contradicts two other key assumptions of the neo-classical story, which is that firms are all alike, and that they have "perfect knowledge" of the consequences of their actions. If that were so, each individual firm would know that when it acts, so will all of its brethren, so that the collective effect on the market would necessarily be non-negligible and their room in the market (their share of industry demand) would have to be taken into account' (Shaikh 1999, p. 14).

An example may serve to illustrate how Marx and neoclassical theory diverge with regard to their notions of competition. Let us assume two firms, A and B, which produce the same goods, but do so using different technologies (with different organic compositions of capital). We will call the 'leading' firm that determines the price the 'regulating' firm.[145] Let us assume that B is the regulating firm. This means that every new investment in this industry that occurs under the same technological conditions would correspond to the model of B. In our example, then, commodities are sold at the value they have in firm B:

Table 13: Formation of an Average Rate of Profit

Example I	Firm A	Firm B
Variable capital (v):	40	20
Constant capital (c):	20	50
Price (pr) of the final product, determined by B:	90	90 (s/v = 100% in B)
Realised surplus value (s) = price – (v+c):	30	20
Rate of profit (p), s/(v+c):	50%	28.6%
p' (average)	39.3%	

Now let us assume two new firms, C and D, which introduce technological innovations, namely innovations with a *higher* organic composition of capital (c/v). Let us also assume (and in so doing, we are still operating within the framework of neoclassical theory) that the increased supply *automatically* lowers the price of the commodities, so that the firms can now only sell them at the price of 80 (the price determined by C's technology). The situation now presents itself as follows:

Table 14: Effect of Technological Change on the Average Rate of Profit

Example II	A	B	C	D
v	40	20	10	10
c	20	50	60	70
pr	80	80	80	80
s	20	10	10	0
p	33.3%	14.5%	14.5%	0%
p' (average without D)			20.7%	
p'' (average with D)				15.6%

145. *MECW* 37, p. 635.

According to the neoclassical reading, there is only one response to this prognosis: because entrepreneurs are profit-maximising creatures, and because the firms C and D are obtaining lower profits despite their use of new technology, this new technology will not be 'chosen'. If the entrepreneurs acted in a highly unified manner (due, say, to monopolisation) and even took the average rate of profit (p') into account, then this would only reinforce their decision.

Thus, in the event of stagnation, one could infer that monopolisation has occurred. According to Okishio, new technologies are introduced only when they *increase* the rate of profit. In our example, this could be done by a firm E, which lowers the cost price (c+v). What new organic composition this involves is irrelevant; after all, technological progress is supposed to be 'Harrod-neutral'. Let us assume, then, that the cost price is 25c + 25v = 50. *At given prices*, this means that E's rate of profit is 37.5 percent. Only a technology of this sort would be introduced, according to the optimality criterion. This means, however, that the rate of profit and the average rate of profit increase.[146]

Marx's notion of competition differs significantly from this neoclassical notion of perfect competition.[147] If the optimality criterion were observed, most technological innovations would never have been introduced.[148] These innovations had the effect of lowering the commodity's cost price; this was achieved by greatly increasing investment in fixed capital, and, more specifically, by investing in fixed capital that performed more efficiently than earlier fixed capital. Since the new technology is labour-saving, the increased fixed costs are compensated for by a reduced wage bill.[149] The advantages of a higher organic composition only become apparent when one abandons the harmonist neoclassical image of perfect competition and considers actual competition, which occurs mainly in the form of *price competition*: each firm attempts to win new customers by actively and aggressively undercutting the prices of other firms.[150] This is only possible because greater capital intensity leads to higher productivity. Higher productivity also means that *more* can be produced. The cost price of the total mass of commodities

146. Some Marxists also take this view: 'On the level of abstraction chosen by Marx, it is impossible to provide reasons not only for a tendency of the rate of profit to fall, but also for a tendency of the rate of profit to rise' (Heinrich 2001, pp. 339 ff.; see Himmelweit 1974; Steedman 1977, 1980; Nakatani 1980; Armstrong 1980). According to Shaikh 1980, the very supposition that an *ex post* phenomenon such as the average rate of profit enters into an entrepreneur's calculation amounts to 'conceptual baggage smuggled in with the conventional techniques of mathematical economics' (p. 78). 'In the calm of a perfectly competitive equilibrium, each impotent little capital can count on directly obtaining exactly the same rate of profit as all others, so that this rate of profit is a fixed magnitude which enters directly into individual calculations' (p. 79).

147. Park 2000, 2001.

148. Shaikh 1978a, p. 52.

149. 'To put it in the language of microeconomics, capitalist production displays an inherent tendency towards lower average variable and average total costs, at the expense of higher average fixed costs' (Shaikh 1992, p. 176).

150. *MECW* 35, p. 621; compare the advertising slogan 'Thank you, dear competitors, for one million new customers'.

is now distributed over a greater number of commodities, say 10 in the case of A and B, 15 in the case of C and 20 in the case of D (the firm that has invested the most in new manufacturing technology).

The unit costs now amount to six monetary units (m.u.) in the case of A, 7 m.u. in the case of B, 4.7 m.u. in the case of C and 4 m.u. in the case of D. This allows D to wage an aggressive price war. It can lower its prices further than the other firms. What happens when D sells its commodities for the price of 5 m.u.? *All* other firms are forced to also sell at this price; otherwise, they will not be able to sell their stock:[151]

Table 15: Falling Prices and Effects of Competition

Example III	A	B	C	D
v	40	20	10	10
c	20	50	60	70
Y (output, in units)	10	10	15	20
unit price	5	5	5	5
s	(−10)	(−20)	5	20
p	(−16.7 %)	(−28.6 %)	7.1%	25%
p' (C and D)			= 16%	

Following the Marxian account of competition, which comes quite close to actual competition, the firms A and B, which are operating with older technology, are driven off the market, and even firm C has difficulty getting by.[152] While the average rate of profit has fallen markedly, firm D still has every reason to be pleased. Not only has it obtained considerable surplus value (20s – as much as firm A obtained in Example I, where firm A was selling its products far above their value and the rate of exploitation, s/v, was 150 percent); it has also eliminated several of its competitors. Consequently, it can expand production, and this will additionally increase the *mass* of surplus value it obtains. Let us now assume that firm D raises new credit in order to double production. In order to remain the market leader, the firm lowers the market price to 4.8 m.u. This creates problems for firm C. But firms A and B have merged in order to avoid bankruptcy. They are now producing with new, further improved technology that requires *even more* fixed capital. Because the massive quantities produced by D threaten to 'saturate' the market, and in order to be able to compete with D at all, A&B lowers prices still further – to

151. We are abstracting from additional complicating factors such as fixed demand (which plays a role in the theory of ground rent, where firms may be able to survive on the market even when they are operating under unfavourable conditions).

152. If the interest on the money loaned is 5 percent, the entrepreneur retains an annual net gain of only 1.5 value units, which he must use to cover additional expenses (such as those associated with the distribution of commodities, advertising, and so on; the entrepreneur also needs to set aside a certain sum for accumulation, since he will eventually have to replace his productive technology).

4.5 m.u., say. What happens? Firm A&B manages to survive, although it does so only by parting with 83.3 percent of its variable capital – that is, of its employees. Firm C is definitively eliminated from the market, and the average rate of profit has fallen further.

Table 16: Overaccumulation

Example IV	A&B		C	D
v	10		10	20
c	90		60	140
Y (output)	25		15	40
unit price	4.5		4.5	4.5
s	12.5		(−2.5)	20
p	12.5%		(−3.6%)	12.5%
p' (A&B + D only)		= 12.5%		

In the case of D, we observe a 'point of absolute overaccumulation':

> there would be absolute over-production of capital; *i.e.*, the increased capital C + ΔC would produce no more, or even less, profit than capital C before its expansion by ΔC.[153]

Firm D's new investment results in the mass of surplus value remaining constant – for the capitalist, such investment is no longer worthwhile; he will therefore refrain from it. Thus the law of the tendency of the rate of profit to fall also allows for a theory of crises and business cycles. They all result from competition as understood by Marx.[154]

---

153. *MECW* 37, p. 250. 'There would be absolute over-production of capital as soon as additional capital for purposes of capitalist production = 0'.

154. Shaikh provides a phenomenology of such crises: A 'secular fall in the rate of profit progressively undermines the incentive to invest [cf. Keynes; C.H.] and thus slows down the rate of growth of the capital stock itself...An initially accelerating mass of profit begins to decelerate until at some point it stagnates or even declines. And when total profits are stagnant, the capitalist class as a whole finds itself in the position of having invested in additional capital without getting any additional profit. This means that a portion of its capital stock is really redundant [it will be used for financial speculation; C.H.]. If the situation persists, as it would if it was the result of a long-term decline of the rate of profit, then investment is cut back, excess capacity becomes widespread, and workers are laid off in droves. This is an all too familiar picture' (1987, p. 118; cf. 1992). Crises of the real economy and crises of the monetary economy are closely related: 'Inventories pile up and profits fall, often quite sharply. Firms increase their borrowings to tide them over the bad times, and this drives up interest rates – which only makes matters worse for firms, though of course it makes banks happy. On the other hand, as businesses start to fail, they default on their debts, and this puts banks into jeopardy. The rising tide of business bankruptcies begins to trigger bank failures. Interest rates reverse themselves and begin to fall. The stock market index slides downward. For workers, matters are even worse. Layoffs and business failures give rise to widespread unemployment and increasing hardship as savings and unemployment benefits run out in the face of a persistent lack of jobs... [T]hose workers who do still have jobs come under severe pressure to make major concessions on wages and working conditions in order to save their

Such phenomena (fierce price wars, bankruptcies and mergers, unemployment, cyclical crises and the tendency of the rate of profit to fall from one business cycle to the next) are not conceivable within the framework of the neoclassical paradigm of perfect competition. That there was something wrong with this picture became clear, at the latest, during the world economic crisis of 1929. The market's capacity for self-regeneration was at a low point: despite low wages, unemployment was high and seemed not to want to fall even in the long term. This contradicted the harmonious laws of the 'labour market', according to which 'full employment' results once labour is sold at the right price. And despite an excess of commodities, there was also excess money (inflation); this was contrary to the quantity theory of money. The political response to this situation consisted in half a century of Keynesian state intervention. As for the *theoretical* response, it did not consist in a change of economic framework, not even on the Left; instead, reality was declared an impure special case, that of 'imperfect competition'.[155]

According to the model of 'perfect competition', no group has power over another and every individual disposes of all relevant information. The incongruities between this model and reality were simply explained in terms of these two conditions not being met, that is, in terms of 'imperfect competition'. While this supplementary assumption no longer denies existing economic predicaments, it also fails to trace them back to the logic of competition; instead, they are explained in terms of the *obstruction* of competition by powerful groups such as cartels, trade unions or the state (see section 2.4.1). These groups had, in fact, become increasingly active in the course of crisis management. The theoretical conjectures about these 'imperfections' coalesce around a central theme: that of the increased significance of monopoly. Where phenomena did not accord with the definitions of the harmonic models (and in most cases they do not), the conclusion drawn was that there had been an increase in monopoly power.[156]

This theory of monopoly was especially popular among Left Keynesians. 'Monopoly' was already important in Bernstein (2.1.2), and Lenin had engaged in a veritable dogmatisation of the new stage of 'monopoly capitalism' (see section 2.2.6). The increased state

jobs. In all of this, it is of course the ones on the bottom – nonwhites, women, teenagers, the non-unionized – who usually get hit the hardest. The above patterns are common to all depressions' (Shaikh 1987, p. 118).

155. Robinson 1933.

156. Shaikh responds as follows to Armstrong 1980's hypothesis that the rate of profit does not normally fall but may do so under conditions of 'oligopoly': 'the very concept of 'imperfect competition' is itself the dark side of the concept of 'perfect competition'. In perfect competition all of the tactics and strategy of real competitive battles are spirited away. Then, when faced with the unavoidable discrepancy between the fantasy world of perfect competition and the elementary facts of real competition, instead of overthrowing perfect competition orthodox theory seeks to reform it. Hence imperfect competition. Yet the real imperfection lies not in actual competition, but rather in the concept of perfect competition itself' (1980, p. 82; note the article 'Monopoly Capitalism' in Bottomore 1983).

intervention associated with Keynesianism seemed to provide a real foundation to talk of 'the power of the monopolies'.

Sweezy, who was considered an authority on the New Left, distinguished between 'imperfect' monopoly capitalism and the former 'golden age of competitive capitalism' (as Dobb put it). The way in which he did this clearly shows how neoclassical economics replaced Marxian economics:

> [S]ince market relations are essentially price relations, the study of monopoly capitalism, like that of competitive capitalism, must begin with the working of the price mechanism. The crucial difference between the two is . . . that under competitive capitalism the individual enterprise is a 'price taker', while under monopoly capitalism the big corporation is a 'price maker'.[157]

While Sweezy claims he wants to overcome Marx,[158] the narrative of the passive 'price taker' is derived from neoclassical theory alone. The widespread claim that monopoly capitalism had altered the laws of the free market was used to lend continued *support* to the neoclassical analysis of a capitalism based on perfect competition. Sweezy and Baran did not popularise Marxian ideas but those of Left Keynesians such as Robinson, Kalecki and Steindl. How is competition described within this tradition?

> Today the typical economic unit in the capitalist world is not the small firm producing a negible fraction of a homogenous output for an anonymous market [this is the neo-classical model; C.H.] but a large-scale enterprise producing a significant share of the product in an industry, or even several industries, and able to control its prices, the volume of its production, and the types and volumes of its interests.[159]

Sweezy rightly observes that the size of enterprises and their active pricing policies jar with notions of perfect competition. Yet he continues to consider this model of competition as justified; he even considers perfect competition the only possible kind of competition. Thus he concludes from the absence of perfect competition that every sort of competition has been 'abolished' ('abandonment of price competition').[160] Size and active pricing policies, the two factors that Marx considered the most important ones within *competition*, are cited as proof of *monopolisation*. This amounts to standing Marx on his head: despite the fact that Marx's laws capture the situation described by Sweezy perfectly, Sweezy considers them to have become meaningless 'today'. He believes he is describing a genuine historical transformation, but he is merely replacing, within theory, Marxian hypotheses with neoclassical ones – for example, he replaces the fall in the

157. Sweezy 1966, pp. 53–4.
158. Sweezy 1966, p. 4
159. Sweezy 1966, p. 6.
160. Sweezy 1966, p. 66.

rate of profit with an increased 'surplus'.[161] This surplus is a legacy of Hobson's theory of imperialism[162] and has nothing to do with Marx's concept of surplus value.[163]

Sweezy follows Kalecki and Steindl in interpreting greater capital intensity, which allows for higher productivity and a wider profit margin within the context of competition, as a higher 'markup' that results from greater 'monopoly power'. The limited mobility of capital in industries with a higher organic composition of capital tends to lead to firms adjusting plant utilisation rather than prices. This price inflexibility is also treated as an indication of monopoly; it is interpreted as deliberate regulation.[164] Even the period of stagnation that began during the late 1960s was traced back to monopolisation: it was claimed that monopolies were deliberately *preventing* additional technological innovation and investment so as to avoid depreciation of their capital stock.

However, inserting Marx into the stadial scheme of competition and monopoly is problematic. The Marxian account of competition accords neither with the neoclassical paradigm's harmonist notions nor with that of an 'imperfect' monopoly. This is why Gillman associated Marx with the old stage, whereas Dobb associated him with the new stage.[165] As in Lenin (see 2.2.6), the 'new stage' of monopoly capitalism was seen to be governed by new laws, whose political import was much greater than that of the Marxian laws.[166] Whether the basic assumptions of neoclassical theory were *straightforwardly* retained (as in Okishio, Steedman and Roemer) or whether they were only retained *ex negativo* – because monopoly capital was considered the index of a new era – Marxian essentials such as the labour theory of value, exploitation and the falling rate of profit were abandoned: by Marxists.

---

161. Sweezy 1966, p. 72.

162. Hobson 1901.

163. 'The "surplus" is defined by Hobson to be the excess of the total money value of the output over the strictly necessary costs of producing that output' (Shaikh 1978, p. 225; see Sweezy 1966, p. 9; Baran 1957, p. 82). 'In fact, the theory of Baran and Sweezy does not correct Marx's theory of accumulation but employs a different method to formulate a completely different proposition about a different subject' (Hardach 1975, p. 118; 2.2.6).

164. Even Mandel considers the divergent rates of profit of different industries an indication of 'monopoly power'; nothing else, he assumes, could obstruct the free movement of capital, and with it the equalisation of the rate of profit (Mandel 1975, pp. 77, 78, 85 and elsewhere). To Marx, such 'obstruction' is a matter of sheer quantity. No capitalist will casually invest the horrendous sums that are required to set up, say, a new automobile brand. Where such a large industry exists (for instance, a major car manufacturer), it is not likely to transfer all of its capital into a new industry (for instance, the New Economy) as soon as profits slacken. Moreover, the equalisation of the rate of profit only occurs over a number of 'fat and lean years' (*MECW* 37, p. 205); being a trend, it does not have to be fully realised at any one time.

165. The tendency to consider Marx to be relevant only to the nineteenth century is the dominant one (evident in Lenin's politics and in Freyer's and Sombart's sociology; see section 2.4.1).

166. For a comprehensive account, see Dobb 1937, Sweezy 1970, pp. 300–36; Gillman 1958, Mandel 1970, pp. 393–440; Rolshausen 1969, Lindbeck 1971, Braverman 1974, Wright 1977, pp. 225–6; Cowling 1982, Foster 1986, Zoninsein 1990.

German-language Marxist economic theory, which re-emerged from oblivion around 1968,[167] was more directly influenced by Leninism than its Anglophone analogues, if only because of its geographical proximity to actually-existing socialism. The hypothesis about a 'new stage' did not even need to be demonstrated by means of economic arguments. And the 'primacy of politics' was simply assumed; after all, entire publishing houses were financed by East Berlin. During the second half of the twentieht century, all variants of German-language Marxism dashed together economic and political matters to such an extent that they were taken to constitute a *single* complex. When it came to addressing this complex, Marxian economics was no longer considered relevant. The post-1968 reception of Marx in the German-speaking world involved no meaningful engagement with economic theory. When economically relevant passages of *Capital* were interpreted, this was done from the aprioristic perspective of conceptual philosophy – in what has come to be called 'German deductive Marxism'. Not being particularly interested in economics, this Marxism was all the more susceptible to the unconscious adoption of neoclassical paradigms. In Germany, 'political economy' had its centre of gravity in *politics*.[168]

This is the reason why versions of Marxism that are strongly oriented toward politics, such as regulationism, continued to meet with lively interest even when Marxism's influence gradually began to ebb. Bourgeois hypotheses on the regulatory function of the state were dressed up in Marxist terminology; it was only the assessment of this function that was reversed.[169] These atrophied stages of Marxism merely delayed the

---

167. 'Marx the political economist has ... virtually disappeared. He has not reappeared to this day. His economic theory became the symbol for various other things, which were taken to be essential' (Thier 1955, p. 18). This last statement holds true even for the period after the renaissance of Marxist economic theory.

168. See Huffschmid 1969 (*Die Politik des Kapitals*: 'The Politics of Capital'), Agnoli 1975 ('*Der Staat des Kapitals*: 'The State of Capital') or the cryptic debate on 'state derivation' (Röhrich 1980; cf. 2.2.6). On Stamokap, see IMSF 1972 and 1981; Breuer 1975; Huffschmid 1975 and 1976. Even Altvater 1975 did not really reject the notion of a 'new stage'. Non-economic Marxist works simply assume the reality of 'monopoly capitalism' (Lefebvre 1968, pp. 89 ff.; Ritsert 1973, p. 24; Jaeggi 1974, p. 61 and pp. 106 ff.; or Poulantzas 1978; see, too, Schumpeter 1942, pp. 87 ff.; Kühne 1972, pp. 331 ff.). The fixation on the state displayed by the extra-parliamentary Left (including the Red Army Faction), shows how two enemies, 'the state' and 'capital', were conflated; the opposite of this stance was a correspondingly affirmative statism, evident not just among social democrats. Marxist and bourgeois economists operated in surprisingly similar ways. They agreed that they were both 'opposed to the state', thus forming an involuntary coalition. Neoliberals opposed the state because they held that it impaired the self-regulating forces of the market; Marxists opposed it because they believed it provided monopoly capitalists with 'superprofits' and artificially maintained the purportedly bankrupt system. 'Being a Marxist' manifested itself only in extra-theoretical ways, in one's moral alignment with the working class or one or the other régime (Koenen 2001, p. 299). Ironically, this made it easy for intellectual Marxists to change sides and become neoliberals after 1990; after all, neoliberalism practised nothing but what they had long been calling for: freedom from the state (3.1.3; compare the central hypothesis of Boltanski 1999).

169. Regulationism and post-structuralism were re-importations of the 'primacy of politics' from the theoretical fashions of other countries. As bourgeois politics and theory abandoned the Keynesian regulatory model, Marxists appropriated it as their ideal. The most recent version of

transition to its disintegration. At the same time, the theory of monopoly capitalism as a static system provided the basis for theoretical production's orientation toward topical *technological* trends (Fordism, post-Fordism, the 'service society', microelectronics, the 'knowledge society', and so forth): Kalecki, Robinson, Steindl and Sweezy concur with Schumpeter and Keynes in assuming that capitalism tends toward stagnation and that growth can only be induced externally, through major inventions or political pressure. The growth observed after the Second World War – greater growth than there had ever been before – was explained by reference to external factors.[170] Thus the focus of 1970s Marxist theories on the state is still negatively dependent, at least in terms of the history of theory, on neoclassical theory and Leninism: the incongruence between their model and reality prompted the development of an obscure counter-model, one in which Marxian theories no longer played any significant role.[171] This only made it easier for the black box of 'monopoly capitalism' to accommodate theories of the 'state' and of the everyday 'microfascism' of power (as per Foucault). In this way, even Marxist and post-Marxist critics of Leninism adopted the basic Leninist model, that of an epochal politicisation of economics.

2.3.4 *Diffusion of the paradigm into neighbouring sciences*

The other group of writers who opposed the neoclassical model also failed to move beyond the neoclassical paradigm: Schmoller had already been incensed, in his methodological controversy with Menger, by the ahistoricism and excessive abstraction of the utility calculus. Yet by tending to refrain from engaging in theorisations of its own, the historicist counter-model has merely *restricted* neoclassical theory's field of application – thereby *confirming* the neoclassical approach. The theory of monopoly capitalism and the historical school supplement one another perfectly within the 'theory of formations'.[172] Neither bourgeois opponents of neoclassical theory (Keynesians and

---

academic Marxism is the thinly disguised Keynesianism of the 'monetary theory of value' (Heinsohn 1988, Heinrich 2001a; see 2.3.5).

170. Sweezy 1966, pp. 228 ff.; Kalecki 1969 and 1962; see Shaikh 1978, p. 231, Shaikh 1983a and Shaikh 1989; see also 2.4.6. The influence of the neoclassical model is evident on both sides, on that of 'perfect' competitive capitalist competition and on that of 'imperfect competition' ('incomplete competition'). Stasis is the basic feature of this 'new stage' as well. Altvater 1992a still maintained that 'oil' was what had driven economic growth, a growth that could not but seem improbable given his basic assumptions ('[t]he fossilist character of the Fordist mode of production': pp. 81 ff.). A political phenomenon such as the First Gulf War creeps into the basic assumptions of Altvater's theory. Before this, theorists of stagnation had spoken metaphorically of economic growth's need for 'fuel' (Shaikh 1983a, p. 140). This view was then ontologised.

171. Critics of this theoretical current (Neusüß 1972; Ebbinghaus 1974; PKA 1975; see section 2.2) seldom went beyond the critique of false ideas; it was only rarely that they presented analyses of their own (Huffschmid 1977; Altvater 1979).

172. See the article 'Periodization of Capitalism' in Bottomore 1983, pp. 365 ff.; Wright 1977, pp. 222 ff.; Brandt 1990. Brenner 1998 and Negri 2000 are also 'historicist' in the sense that they engage in atheoretical observation – this is why they are so quick to formulate new hypotheses.

historicists) nor Marxists had any serious objections to the basic neoclassical *paradigm*; this allowed the paradigm to dominate twentieth-century economic theory. This meant that it became more or less binding for economic theory's neighbouring sciences (law, political science, sociology, social philosophy), to the extent that they addressed the economy in a general way. It is sufficient to briefly consider works that dominated the discussions for decades, such as Talcott Parsons' *Theory of Action* (see section 2.4) or John Rawls's *Theory of Justice* (see 3.2).

Whenever 'economic' issues are addressed in these works, this is done in accordance with the neoclassical paradigm.[173] This way of thinking about the economy has taken root even where one would not expect it, for example in the theories of the Frankfurt school, which once thought of itself as Marxist (2.6), in the work of the late Habermas (3.1), in 'analytic Marxism' (1.4.2) and in modern business ethics, which thinks of itself as formulating a 'critique of capitalism' (3.3). Such phenomena call for a renewed critique of economics. By this, I mean an analysis that examines socio-philosophical theories with an eye to the presuppositions required if those theories are to seem plausible. In speaking of a 'critique of economics', I do *not* mean that economics *as such*, as a clearly defined scientific discipline, should be rejected because of its putative positivism. To call for this is merely to surrender one's capacity for sound judgement; 'critique' becomes the extraneous expression of a politically tinged judgement of taste.[174] What 'critique of economics' refers to, rather, is the critique of fallacious and ideological theorisations of the economy, a critique that bases itself on *superior* explanations.[175] No dialectic in the world can replace concrete arguments. Only economic theories that exclude the social reality of economic activity require a separate, normative social philosophy

---

Incidentally, the field of social statistics was founded, in Germany, by the historical school (Jonas 1976, Vol. I, p. 278). Thus non-conceptual figures were joined with theoretically impoverished narratives (cf. 2.4.3).

173. Talcott Parsons derived his 1937 theory of action (Parsons 1968) from Marshall and Pareto. Thus theories of 'rational choice', which were based on fictional assumptions developed for specific purposes, came to be of overwhelming importance to the social sciences. Rawls 1971 uses the 'Pareto optimum' on the level of first principles, in order to develop a criterion for a just social order; in the practically oriented part of his theory, the economy is described as functioning like a textbook neoclassical economy. The validity of the model is uncritically accepted even in Sen 1998 (see section 3.2.1).

174. In critical theory, readings of Marx that treated him as an economist were considered positivist. It was argued that Marx had criticised the very foundations of economic theory, so that engaging with it immanently was no longer necessary (see Schmidt in Euchner 1972, pp. 30 ff.; the editorials in the *Beiträge* of 1974 and *PROKLA* no. 123, 2001; see also Kambartel 1979). The 'theoretical space... within which traditional Marxism situates "Marx's economic doctrine" long remained unquestioned even within "Western Marxism".... One of the constitutive features of this Marxism... is its transformation of the critique of political economy into political economy' (Heinrich 2001, p. 152; see Behrens 1993; Backhaus 1997; Rakowitz 2000, pp. 49, 61, 255, 320; see also two more recent publications: Heinrich 2004 and Henning 2004a).

175. See Bubner 1972, p. 46.

(see sections 2.4, 2.5). In the following passage, several examples of the exclusion of the social from economics are discussed.

2.3.5 Key elements of Marxian theory IV: the theory of money

> All *derivations* of this kind are simply concerned with *diverting* attention from a problem which one is not capable of solving.[176]

By its very nature, the economy is concerned with money. Money is the element of the economy that appears on the surface of society: the 'money semblance' is quite real. Everyone knows what it means: without money, one can purchase nothing, and so everyone wants to have as much of it as possible. Money payments cast a web across all of society – and beyond.[177] This is why theories from the field of economic sociology treat money as the essence ('leading medium') of the economy. To do so is not to explain anything, but merely to *reiterate* what is obvious and plain to see.[178] Marx showed that the circulation of money involves laws that refer to something other than money. By contrast, the sociological description 'monetary economy' (as per Simmel) implies a tautological reduction of social theory to mere description – 'sticking to appearances in opposition to the law which regulates and explains them'.[179] In functional terms, this can be interpreted as a refusal of attempts at explanation,[180] which accords with the self-conception of this sort of sociology: being 'formal', it believes it can neglect the 'content' of its forms, and so leaves this issue to economics.[181]

But economists are also at a loss when it comes to answering the question of what money actually *is*.[182] Here, too, Marx's theory falls between different disciplines.

---

176. *MECW* 24, p. 542.

177. Garson 2001 once followed the money she invested around the world in person.

178. Either as a symbol and 'means of interaction', as in Simmel 1978, or as a 'symbolically generalised means of communication', as in Habermas (1984–87, Vol. II, pp. 264 ff.) and Luhmann (1998, pp. 348 ff.). Of course it is true that money is a sign; the question is what the sign is for, or to what exactly it refers. The 'code' 'payment/nonpayment' is no more than a description.

179. *MECW* 35, p. 311.

180. While Simmel's observations are original descriptions (Busch 2000), they do not explain much. Where he makes attempts at explanation (for instance by referring to the 'style' supposed to underpin both money and the modern mentality), he does no more than posit metaphysical realities. Actual history is dissolved into ideas – 'styles' are the stuff of art history.

181. 'Geometrical abstraction investigates only the spatial forms of bodies, although empirically, these forms are given merely as the forms of some material content. Similarly, if society is conceived as interaction among individuals, the description of the forms of this interaction is the task of the science of society in its strictest and most essential sense' (Simmel 1908, pp. 21–2). Thus the philosophy of money (Simmel 1978) becomes all the more potent. By his rejection of logic and 'observation', Luhmann also relinquishes explanation (Luhmann 1998, p. 69 and p. 905; see part 2.5.6).

182. Ehrlicher 1991, p. 52 admits that 'economists have not engaged in a discussion about what money is for about one hundred years' (quoted in Busch 2001, p. 115; Hahn 1982 makes a similar claim for neoclassical economic theory).

Even many critics of globalisation who have some vague recollection of Marx's theories are nevertheless convinced that the sphere of finance has 'delinked' itself and now dominates the others.[183] What this would entail for theory, however, is that money and its circulation must be explained by reference only to themselves (in a '*philosophy*' of money), in order then to explain everything else in terms of 'monetary theory' – a speculative endeavour whose questionable nature is obvious.[184]

With regard to money, Marxism has offered and continues to offer the opportunity to distinguish oneself from both bourgeois sociology and bourgeois economics. Yet German Marxism struggled with monetary issues *even more* than bourgeois economics did. This is related to its withdrawal from social philosophy. Even excursions into actually existing sociology or economics tended to be considered bold. How, then, to arrive at an engagement with Marx, who is at odds with both?

Whoever wants 'the riddle presented by money'[185] to be solved as a *philosophical* riddle will find – quite logically – that such a solution is not possible. Hence in value form analysis, a late offshoot of Adornoite social philosophy, this way of framing the question led to a farewell to Marx.[186] Yet the problems that one faces when proceeding in this way simply disappear as soon as one abandons the speculative approach. Because he treats money as the 'form' of something else, and because it is no more than *one* form, Marx prefaces his exposition of money's specific relations with remarks on the

183. Biermann 2001; see 3.3.6.

184. Though it is nevertheless undertaken (for example, Creutz 1983, Heinsohn 1996, or Lietaer 2002, following a notion first developed in Gesell 1958; see Hörisch 1983, R. Müller 1983; Altvater 1991; Jenner 1999; 3.3.2).

185. *MECW* 35, p. 58. The 'riddle presented by money' is that of how something intrinsically worthless, such as paper, can become so valuable to us – and why those who already own it continue to receive more of it. The commonplace claim that 'money is a convention' is plausible at first sight, but it explains nothing; it merely describes our everyday manner of dealing with money. If 'people' had agreed between themselves to use money, then who is it that determines the value of a currency, and who could have wanted the crises that are mediated by money (inflation, deflation, exchange rate fluctuations, stock market crashes, financial crises, and so on)?

186. Cf. 2.6.2. The editorial in Backhaus 1978 speaks openly of 'destruction' (*Gesellschaft* no. 11, p. 7). Backhaus 1970, the overture to a thirty-year debate on the 'riddle presented by money' conducted within Hegelian 'value-form analysis', levels numerous accusations at pre-Backhaus Marxists, as well as at Marx himself (the words and phrases used include 'grossly simplified', 'wholly distorted', 'lack of understanding', 'faulty reception', 'inappropriateness of the presentation', 'ignore', 'entirely unmediated', 'lack of mediation', 'no longer comprehensible', and so on). What this tone is most revealing of, however, is the author's own lack of understanding. The very question becomes increasingly obscure in the course of its various expositions. The only continuity lies in the disparagement of others (for a critical view of this, see Kittsteiner 1980, pp. 14 ff.; Kallscheuer 1986). The theoretical propositions formulated render the references to Marx arbitrary – hardly a theorem is retained. Presumably the equidistance between Marx and the sciences, and between the theoretical efforts of the student movement and the sciences, led to writers convincing themselves they were authorised to speak in the name of Marxism (for a self-critical account of this, see Koenen 2001). The very style of this reception implied a 'farewell' to Marx (see Helms 1969). On more recent texts from this current, see Y. Hahn 1999, pp. 110 ff.

'form of value';[187] these remarks offer a preview of what comes later. In the first chapters, the overall relationship is sketched in an introductory manner. This preview should not be read 'philosophically', as if one were dealing with a Hegelian self-development of the concept in which everything follows necessarily from a single principle and can thus be 'deduced' from it.[188] Rather, Marx explains the way in which he will *go on* to discuss money. Once one adopts this basic hermeneutic rule, the problems projected by value-form analysis's transcendental-deductive reading of these passages disappear. Marx's discussion of money is quite consistent and capable of answering many questions, as opposed to raising new ones. Talk of a 'pre-monetary theory of value',[189] which tends to obscure the issue, overlooks the fact that economic theory was dominated, both before and after Marx, by currents that attributed extraordinary importance to money: for mercantilists, Keynesians and monetarists, money (as gold or the optimal money supply) is what 'counts'. Money begins to present a 'riddle' only when it is posited as primary with regard to other economic phenomena, or as that which explains them. In this way, it becomes the subject of speculation.[190] One feature of this is that money is considered *exogenous*; this is typically the case in Keynesian approaches. In Milton Friedman's monetarist theory, money is even dropped from a helicopter.[191]

There is however a tradition within which money plays virtually no role: neoclassical theory. But this is precisely the tradition that is *not* decisive for understanding Marx. To insinuate, according to an either/or logic, that Marx must have thought either in a 'pre-monetary' (neoclassical) or in a 'monetary' (Keynesian) way is to label him either a theorist of finance or a theorist who is 'pre-monetary' and ought therefore to be rejected today.

---

187. *MECW* 35, pp. 45 ff.

188. Thus Backhaus 1970, p. 131, laments the absence of a 'necessary transition'. In his work, the commodity 'posits' itself 'as money'. He affirms Lenin's dictum that one needs to have studied 'the whole of Hegel's *Logic*' in order to understand *Capital*; the difference between Hegel and Marx is made to disappear (see Krahl 1970; Reichelt 1970; 2.5.7). 'Marxists who attempt to directly apply the abstract categories of Volume I of *Capital* are in a sense reverting to a Ricardian methodology. Marx is careful to point out that a basic flaw in Ricardo's method is that he "jumps" directly from the abstract (value) to the concrete (prices of production, rent, taxes) without tracing the intermediate connections [*MECW* 31, pp. 389 ff.]. It takes Marx three volumes to make that connection!' (Shaikh 1977, p. 137).

189. Heinrich 2001a.

190. This is precisely what Backhaus does. He recommends treating 'the category of money as the logically primary element of economic theory' (Backhaus 1978, p. 71; see Backhaus 2002, p. 114); alternatively, one can do the same with 'credit' (p. 75). Having explained why he remains unable, nine years after his first publication, to devote himself to Marx's texts, as opposed to secondary literature, he reiterates many secondary refutations of Marx. He 'destroys' (Backhaus 1978, p. 7) Marx by attributing insuperable contradictions to the various Marxisms and projecting them back, without further ado, onto Marx himself (pp. 28, 33). Thus alternative theories of 'modern macroeconomics' (p. 78) can be made to substitute for Marx. The only riddle associated with this monetary theory is why it still presents itself as Marxist (see Backhaus 1997).

191. Fiehler 2000, p. 126.

The implicit adoption of neoclassical paradigms that is evident in this unhappy alternative has the effect, once more, of successively dissolving Marxian theorems.[192]

As with other issues, Marx's position on money is not situated somewhere between two other positions, but beyond both of them – and this is not because he synthesises the two other positions or cannot make up his mind, but for specific reasons. Marx treats money as a central factor in the capitalist economy – given the amount of pages he devotes to money, this is a banal observation.[193] Thus Marx's 'theory of value' is 'monetary' to the extent that it takes money into account and attempts to explain its development. But it is not monetary insofar as it does not conceive of money as *autocratic*. According to Marx, money cannot be understood in isolation, as an autochtonous factor (exogenous money) capable of explaining the rest of the economy.[194] Nor is it capable, in the long term, of performing control functions of the sort Keynesians have in mind.[195] Rather, money is one form of something that is not itself money (such as gold, as the mercantilists assumed), but rather endogenous, that is, explicable in terms of something else.

This is the meaning of the distinction between 'forms'. For example, when Marx speaks about 'capital', he distinguishes between commodities, money, machines, raw materials and variable capital (labour power).[196] While these are all entirely different things, what they have in common is that they function as capital. Seen from the point of view of capital, that is, from that of the capitalist, they are all capital, albeit in different forms. If this were not so, talk of the 'circulation' of capital could hardly be made

192. Heinrich 2001 diagnoses an incomplete break with the classics in Marx. He volatilises Marx's own thought and distributes it between two other schools, classical political economy and Keynes. The only real break, here, is Heinrich's break with Marx. Neither the labour theory of value nor the fall of the rate of profit survive his 'reconstructions'. This is unfortunate, since Heinrich (like Backhaus) does little more than take Marx apart. It is in vain that one looks for a distinct theory of economic processes, beyond lectures on debates between Marxists.

193. Backhaus 1970 claims to have been the first to have seen this since Rubin 1972 (first published in 1926). (Heinrich 2001a, p. 158 accepts this claim.) But this assessment is due more to the partial nature of Backhaus's reception of Marx (see Fritsch 1968; Mandel 1970, pp. 72 ff. and elsewhere).

194. In this sense, Backhaus's forays into philosophy (such as his work on Georg Simmel, Alfred Ammon and Bruno Liebrucks) do not contribute to our understanding of money, on the contrary. They indicate that Backhaus thinks in an exogenous manner.

195. Brunoff 1976, p. 123, also notes that 'nowhere in *Capital* does the theory of money expand into a monetary theory of the economy: it remains purely a theory of the monetary economy'.

196. See *MECW* 28, pp. 95 f., 459, and so on. In doing so, he effectively translates into his own terms the reasoning of an entrepreneur who is drawing up his balance sheet. Salable commodity capital (in the warehouse), unprocessed raw materials (circulating fixed capital), the manufacturing plant (constant fixed capital) and disbursed wages all appear on the credit side. To this are added those costs that are not immediately related to production (business expenditures, interest payments, taxes, and so on). Supernumerary workers are laid off so that the capital associated with them can be employed differently.

sense of. This 'general' substance must not fallaciously be philosophised – this would be 'as if there also existed, in addition to lions, tigers, rabbits... *the animal*'.[197]

Now, money is one of these forms of capital,[198] provided that we are speaking of money under capitalism. Marx's definitions are not purely logical; they bear a historical index whose presuppositions always enter into the reflection. This was an achievement of Hegel.[199] But we have approached the issue 'from behind', so as to avoid the Hegelian fallacy of treating thought as the cause: the definition of money as a form of capital is already specific. It has the advantage of being easy to understand. But first and foremost, money is a form of *value*. This seems more difficult to understand. And yet when money and capital are understood as forms of value, they have been traced back to something that is more elementary – a basic scientific operation that is puzzling only to philosophers. In turning to what is more elementary, namely value, we can formulate propositions such as the following: the value of a commodity, which is relevant to exchange, and to which its price form is oriented, is defined (not determined) by the quantity of socially necessary labour performed.[200]

---

197. *MEGA* II.4, p. 37. This is precisely the semblance by which the 'monetary theory of value' is fooled. It takes the Hegelian idiom that Marx is caricaturing (in the *Grundrisse*, *MECW* 28–9, and in the first edition of *Capital*, *MEGA* II.4, much more than in the second edition, *MECW* 35) at face value and proceeds to ask how the substance 'perched outside the world' goes about incarnating itself in its 'form' (Backhaus 1970, p. 131; see, too, *MECW* 3, p. 175). This is to translate the neo-classical rejection of the 'tranformation' of values into prices into the realm of the philosophically inconceivable (Backhaus 1978; Backhaus 1997, p. 168). However, the substance is always-already within form (value always already expresses itself in prices); it is just that these forms change. 'There is nothing mysterious in this' (*MECW* 35, p. 68); it happens every day, starting with one's morning visit to the bakery (M–C). Substance is not situated beyond the forms; it is what they have in common. The question raised by Backhaus – how is money to be deduced? – is a 'pseudo problem'. His philosophisation is not philosophical enough; it gets stuck halfway. Wittgenstein investigated this semblance: When we leave aside vapour, ice and liquid water, where is water in itself? Where is the team spirit when we leave aside the players? How does substance achieve its form? Here, language plays a trick on philosophers (and only on them). The insight that philosophy often attempts to solve pseudo problems may have come to Wittgenstein during nightly talks with the neo-Ricardian Piero Sraffa, a friend of Gramsci (Roncaglia 2000, Sandemose 2001).

198. *MECW* 35, p. 157.

199. 'There was, however, an important fact which prevented Aristotle from seeing that, to attribute value to commodities, is merely a mode of expressing all labour as equal human labour, and consequently as labour of equal quality. Greek society was founded upon slavery, and had, therefore, for its natural basis, the inequality of men and of their labour powers. The secret of the expression of value, namely, that all kinds of labour are equal and equivalent, because, and so far as they are human labour in general, cannot be deciphered, until the notion of human equality has already acquired the fixity of a popular prejudice. This, however, is possible only in a society in which the great mass of the produce of labour takes the form of commodities, in which, consequently, the dominant relation between man and man, is that of owners of commodities' (*MECW* 35, p. 70; *MECW* 28, p. 123 and p. 158).

200. Unlike those of Lask or Luhmann, Marx's concept of form cannot be raised to a higher power ('the form of form'); rather, what is given form can be understood as the form of its counterpart, to the extent that this clarifies anything. Money is a form of capital, capital is a form of money; money, the commodity and capital are all forms of value; capital is a form of labour, and so on. (It is only on this basis that relations later posited by Marx can be understood, for instance the notion that a fall in the value of foodstuffs may lower the price of labour, thereby increasing

In this way, even far more complex terms, such as the composition of capital, can be expressed in terms of labour values.[201] Following Hegel, one could describe the relationship of the forms to one another as a relationship of 'identity and difference': while they are different, they are the same insofar as they are embodiments of value – in much the same way, the blossom cannot be said to 'be' the fruit, but it is, nevertheless, an embodiment of the same plant as the fruit. The 'transition' between them is not an aprioristic, conceptually 'necessary' one, but a *real* one (a 'complex of rules').[202] It occurs every day, although it can also be disrupted at any time, both exogenously and endogenously.[203] Thus understanding the crisis presupposes understanding the normal process. But the theory that describes this process is not already contained in the 'categories'; it is only to be found in the laws formulated.[204]

Interpreting money as one form of value can clarify its role in relation to other forms. The role of money is that of a mediator.[205] This allows for a distinction between the various functions of money. The process of abstraction by which one goes from money back to value[206] serves mainly to allow for a clear presentation: different statements about

---

surplus value). 'Value' as such does not exist for itself, but only in the form of other phenomena (such as in the form of prices). Nevertheless, one can say that its magnitude is determined by the quantity of embodied abstract labour. To say this is not any more mysterious than saying that while bacteria and plants are forms of life, "life" as such does not exist for itself. One can still formulate propositions about life, such as that metabolism is its essential feature, that elephants live longer than lizards, and so son. Marx's analysis of the form of value (*MECW* 35, pp. 45–80) is only preliminary to subsequent methodological developments. It is not 'opaque and inexplicable' (Backhaus 1970, p. 132), but rather a model of methodological reflection. Marx proceeds in a methodologically sound manner. When he relates one thing to another, he also points out why these two things can be related to one another. There has to be common ground if two distinct things are to be compared. Marx expresses this by saying that the 'substance' of value is 'abstract labour' ('substance of value': *MECW* 29, p. 307; 'social substance': *MECW* 35, p. 48). To interpret this in a substantialist manner is to be off the mark, for commodities, money, and so on develop into objective expressions of value only under capitalist social relations (Brentel 1989). '[N]ot an atom of matter enters into the composition of a commodity's value (*MECW* 35, p. 57). Nevertheless, labour needs, first of all, to be performed. The fact that Marx points this out too (he speaks of labour 'physiologically': *MECW* 35, p. 56) is too unintellectual for some (Heinrich 2001a, p. 159).

201. Marx expresses the technical composition of capital (the machine/worker ratio) in terms of value (the ratio of dead labour to living labour) and in terms of prices (the ratio of fixed costs to the wage bill; *MECW* 35, pp. 607 ff.). This is necessary because the causal force is easiest to decipher when the relationship is expressed in terms of value (2.1.6).

202. Steinvorth 1977, pp. 12, 25.

203. *MECW* 35, pp. 111–12.

204. It is true that Marx announced his intention to formulate a critique of economic "categories", and his reformulation of economic theory does imply such a critique when it comes to, say, issues of historical validity. But this does not mean that other, perhaps "normatively more substantial" concepts (or a critique of the old concepts) are sufficient. Only those who believe that 'Marx [...] introduces reality into the concept' (Reichelt 2002, p. 180) are absolved of having to engage with economic theory – a variety of 'lazy reason' (Kant).

205. *MECW* 3, pp. 322 ff.

206. In Marx's presentation, this abstraction is reversed again. It proceeds from exchange value to money. This poses some challenges to the philosophically educated. But these challenges consist simply in the fact that things are as simple as that (*MEGA* II.4, p. 28).

money refer to *different* functions of money. This is of considerable import when one compares Marx's theory to other theories, such as the IMF's credo of 'comparative advantages' through free trade (see below). But how exactly are we to understand Marx's talk of the 'money form' and the 'functions of money'? In order to avoid the fallacious philosophisations to which these expressions can give rise, the money form can be shown to be implicit in the functions of money (to proceed thusly is the opposite of 'deducing' the functions from the form).[207] Marx distinguishes the following functions of money: measure of value; medium of circulation; means of payment; universal money; depository of value; capital. Later, he adds functions related to credit.

The most basic function performed by money is that of serving as the 'measure of value'.[208] Two commodities can only be compared to one another by virtue of their common relation to money. In Marx, the proposition that the *magnitude* of a commodity's value is defined by the abstract labour embodied in it[209] does not lead to a situation where commodities are *directly* measured in terms of labour; instead, they relate to one another via the medium of money.[210] This is not due to some necessity of transcendental logic; it comes about 'naturally'.[211] This means that this fact is 'historical', but not contingent ('We can see it daily under our very eyes').[212] Many phenomena can be used to demonstrate that commodities are not exchanged directly, or at least not for long; instead, they are soon related to a third element.[213]

---

207. With reference to his efforts at 'self-clarification' (*MECW* 29, p. 261), Marx indicates the danger of a Hegelian presentation: 'It will be later necessary later... to correct the idealist manner of the presentation which makes it appear as if it were merely a matter of conceptual determinations and of the dialectic of these concepts [the dialectic of the form of value; C.H.]. Above all the phrase: the product (or activity) becomes a commodity; the commodity becomes exchange value; the exchange value becomes money' (*MECW* 28, p. 89).

208. *MECW* 29, pp. 303 ff.; *MECW* 35, pp. 103 ff.; *MECW* 28, pp. 102, 123 ff.; *MECW* 29, pp. 171 ff.

209. '[T]he value of a commodity represents human labour in the abstract, the expenditure of human labour in general' (*MECW* 35, p. 54). Heinrich 2001a disparages this as a 'theory of labour quantities' (p. 157) and invokes the link with money in order to criticise Marx. He tears the commodity and money apart; money becomes a riddle again.

210. *MECW* 28, pp. 190 ff. In the *Grundrisse*, Marx repeatedly formulated his rejection of Proudhon's 'labour money' utopia, but he only barely did so in *Capital* (on this point, see Rakowitz 2000). Marx's criticism was that either only concrete embodied labour would be measured, which would prove uneconomic in the long term, or that some institution would have to fix the rate of the labour money – which would require elements of despotism, the anarchist aims of the proponents of time chits notwithstanding (*MECW* 28, pp. 92, 97 and elsewhere).

211. *MECW* 28, p. 102.

212. *MECW* 35, p. 157.

213. Where the circulation of money has broken down and 'pre-monetary' forms of barter have re-emerged, as in Argentina, some third element (wood, tokens or something of the kind) quickly asserted itself as the measure of value – a new form of money developed. The earliest substance known to have performed this function was salt. The neoclassical '*numéraire*' corresponds to this function and is therefore not a false notion; it is simply incomplete (for a different view, see Heinrich 2001, pp. 68 ff. and p. 251).

In his preliminary studies, Marx used Hegelian phrases to describe this (the exchange value of commodities ventures forth from itself and enters into its other, and so on).[214] Behind this, there lies a basic observation.[215] What makes money a riddle is in no way dependent on money's material aspect, its substance, for it is already apparent where money assumes a crude form, such as in a money commodity like salt. It is precisely when presupposing heuristically that money is a commodity that one does not have to consider the specific material aspect of money (gold, paper bills, digital-virtual money, and so on); there is no need to come up with a new logic of money whenever the material aspect of money changes[216] – that would be a genuinely substantialist monetary theory. The criticism that considers it a limitation of Marx's theory that money, as the measure of commodity values, is itself initially a commodity, stands the matter on its head. The riddle already lies in exchange value itself, which money (of any kind) merely represents. It is precisely in order to show this – that is, in order not to be struck by the riddle of money 'in its most glaring form'[217] – that Marx defines money as the 'form' of value.[218]

The other function of money, that of being not just the qualitative measure of values, but also the quantitative 'standard of price'[219] anticipates the third volume insofar as it involves the distinction between values and prices. That values must always present themselves as prices is already clear at the beginning of the first volume.[220] For purposes of exposition, Marx begins by assuming that commodities are exchanged at their values, but he also makes it clear from the outset that this does not actually have to be the case, indeed, that it almost never is.[221] Not only do commodities reflect each other's values within the medium of money (for instance, two apples are worth as much salt as one

---

214. *MECW* 28, pp. 78 ff.

215. It can, of course, be rendered more puzzling by contrivance. But this can be done with anything, and it is not a theoretical problem but a proto-philosophical whim. Although Heinrich 1986 criticised Hegelianism, he later gives in to just this whim, claiming that the money form has not been properly 'deduced' (Heinrich 2001, pp. 223–4, 236 and elsewhere) and transferring it to a 'theory of action [!]' (to the realm of exchange: p. 231). But this is precisely where pre-monetary 'exchange' value is also situated. 'Solving the Marxian problem of money, i.e. deducing [!] an adequate form of money, thus requires one to examine the structure of the commodity in terms of the theory of action' (Hahn 1999, p. 125).

216. See below. 'Throughout this work, I assume, for the sake of simplicity, gold as the money commodity' (*MECW* 35, p. 103; also p. 128; *MECW* 29, p. 304). This assumption can be dropped once the basic mechanism it describes has been understood. To pin Marx down on his assumption that gold is the money commodity is to undermine Marx's didactic approach. Heinrich presents this assumption as necessary, against Marx's explicit advice; he imputes to Marx a 'basic' attachment to the money commodity and argues that this represents a 'defect' (Heinrich 2001a, p. 161).

217. *MECW* 35, p. 103.

218. 'In short, all the properties that are enumerated as particular properties of money are properties of the commodity as exchange value ... The exchange value of the commodity, as a special existence alongside the commodity itself, is *money*' (*MECW* 28, p. 79).

219. *MECW* 29, p. 309; *MECW* 28, p. 124; *MECW* 35, pp. 106–7.

220. 'Price is the money name of the labour realised in a commodity' (*MECW* 35, p. 111).

221. *MECW* 35, pp. 111–12.

pear), but they do this by means of *units* (one apple is worth 10 grams of salt; one pear is worth 20 grams). Thus money serves as the measure of price.[222] Those engaging in exchange do not need to actually be holding money in their hands for it to perform this function; the act of measuring is 'ideal'.[223]

Once this function of money takes on a life of its own, it results in the development of 'coins', that is, of institutionally issued forms of money.[224] This invites the perspectival illusion that money is *created* by the state or some other money-issuing institution. In fact, the state merely *takes over* these functions, which already exist.[225] Marx already spoke, in his discussion of these very tangible matters, of the 'symbolic character' of money, and especially of coins ('[r]elatively worthless things, such as *paper*, can function as symbols of gold coins').[226] Within the symbolic character of money there lurks another possibility of disruption, since symbols can always symbolise wrongly: the name given to the monetary substance's units does not have to accord with that of the money that actually develops (for instance, a pound of gold is not equivalent to one British 'pound').[227] Counterfeiting of coins and other disturbances of the monetary system – fluctuations in the price of gold, inflation – are to be situated here. Commodities, however, have a value that is merely *expressed* in money.[228] As far as this function is concerned, money only has a limited function; it is only 'valid' within a particular national economy. On Marx's

---

222. 'The measure of values measures commodities considered as values; the standard of price measures, on the contrary, quantities of gold by a unit quantity of gold' (*MECW* 35, p. 107).

223. 'Since the expression of the value of commodities in gold is a merely ideal act, we may use for this purpose imaginary or ideal money. Every trader knows, that he is far from having turned his goods into money, when he has expressed their value in a price or in imaginary money, and that it does not require the least bit of real gold, to estimate in that metal millions of pounds' worth of goods' (*MECW* 35, p. 105; *MECW* 29, pp. 314 ff.; *MECW* pp. 28, 78–9, 126). 'But, although the money that performs the functions of a measure of value is only ideal money, price depends entirely upon the actual substance that is money' (*MECW* 35, pp. 105–6) – presupposing a developed division of labour and production for the market.

224. *MECW* 29, pp. 342 ff.

225. See Stephan 1974. This is the idealism fallacy (the end of the distinction between form and content; see 2.5.2), in which a position becomes a cause (in consciousness = by consciousness, in exchange = by exchange, in the form of the state = by the state).

226. *MECW* 29, p. 348.

227. '[I]n all metallic currencies, the names given to the standards of...price were originally taken from the pre-existing names of the standards of weight' (*MECW* 35, p. 107). 'By degrees there arises a discrepancy between the current moneynames of the various weights of the precious metal figuring as money, and the actual weights which those names originally represente' (p. 109). If the state alters the rate of exchange (one pound of gold is no longer worth one pound of silver but two pounds), then it has not increased wealth but merely changed the money name ('I have merely given... another *name*': *MECW* 28, p. 129). A commodity now costs twice as much money as before, but continues to be exchanged against other commodities: 'But, both before and after these divisions are made, a definite weight of metal is the standard of metallic money. The sole alteration consists in the subdivision and denomination' (*MECW* 35, p. 110).

228. '[T]he commodity *is* exchange value, but it *has* a price' (*MECW* 28, p. 125). This is precisely what Heinrich 2001a, p. 159 ignores when he states that 'products become commodities only in exchange' (for similar claims, see Hahn 1999, p. 129; Reichelt 2002, p. 151). In fact, commodities are produced for the sake of exchange and enter into it as values. The risk that their value may not be

account, this is simply another function of money. Illusions on the economic power of the state depend on an overly hermetic understanding of this limit.[229]

Taking this relatively tangible aspect of money as his starting point, Marx arrives at the functions performed by money within simple circulation. It is here that money actually needs to be measured.[230] The formula C–M–C (commodity–money–commodity) represents this function: here, money is the *means of circulation*.[231] The trader does not simply want to measure his commodity in money; he wants actually to sell it. The shoemaker receives money for his shoes. He uses it to buy bread rolls and milk. Now, the purpose of money is to be spent. In the end, there is consumption. Money mediates the exchange of shoes for food; it appears as a mere transitional form (Hegel would say: it exists only in its disappearance). What this presupposes is a developed division of labour, and hence the possibility of comparing labour products with one another. In producing

---

fully *realised* does not mean that they do not *have* it. 'Commodities as exchange values must be antecedent to circulation in order to appear as prices in circulation' (*MECW* 29, p. 305).

229. 'Coined money assumes a *local and political character*, it uses different national languages and wears different national uniforms, just as does money of account. Coined money circulates therefore in the *internal* sphere of circulation of commodities, which is circumscribed by the boundaries of a given community and separated from the *universal* circulation of the world of commodities' (*MECW* 29, p. 342). 'The intervention of the state . . . seems to invalidate the economic law. . . . But this power of the state is mere illusion. It may throw any number of paper notes of any denomination into circulation but its control ceases with this mechanical act. As soon as the token of value . . . enters the sphere of circulation it is subject to the inherent laws of this sphere' (*MECW* 29, pp. 353–4). On the *state theory of money*, see Knapp 1921 (2.4.3), Lipietz 1985, Altvater 1991, Altvater 1997; see also Reichelt 2002, p. 187.

230. This is the very step that value-form analysis fails to take. In a reprise, Reichelt attempts once more to problematise the 'money form' in Marx. His reconstruction (Reichelt 2002, p. 145), which harks back to Hegel and Simmel more than to Marx, makes reference to what those engaging in exchange enact 'within consciousness' (p. 152). This corresponds to money's function as the measure of value in Marx, a function that is 'ideally posited' and merely transforms the commodity into money 'in the head' (*MECW* 28, p. 80). What is really presupposed in this is the social division of labour and the formal equality of persons. The value contained in the commodity is estimated (it is not that this value is 'constituted': p. 156; all that occurs is that its magnitude is *estimated*). Reichelt means to also 'reconstruct' the real presuppositions as acts of positing in the Fichtean sense ('constitutive act': p. 159). Methodologically, this is reminiscent of Hegel's elimination of the thing in itself (see section 2.5.1). However, the estimation of value that is implicit in the price refers to something (value) that already exists (in itself) beforehand. The fact that exchange may involve prices deviating from values does not mean that value *originates* in exchange. Since Reichelt, like Backhaus, presents Marx's statements as 'sheerly incomprehensible' and 'utterly inadequate' (pp. 146–7), he seamlessly adopts the notions of other authors, such as Simmel's neoclassical legend (p. 151) and Hegel's and Adorno's idealising claim that money is the 'existing concept' (p. 150). In this way, Marx's comments on the historical genesis of the form of value (a genesis that occurs long before capitalism) become epistemological processes that play out 'in consciousness', albeit it in a 'logically unconscious' manner (p. 157). This confusion is owed mainly to the failure to distinguish between the various functions of money. Yet, by failing on this point, Reichelt implicitly abandons the labour theory of value (p. 147), as do Heinrich and Backhaus. In Marx, the term 'consciousness' always refers to 'conscious being'. The tendency to view these presuppositions as 'unconscious' logical 'acts of positing' or as a 'constitution' enacted by consciousness represents a glaring and burdensome legacy of German idealism (2.5.2).

231. *MECW* 28, pp. 128 ff.; *MECW* 29, pp. 186 ff., 323 ff.; *MECW* 35, pp. 113 ff.

shoes, the shoemaker assumes that someone else is *not* producing shoes and will give him money for them; he also assumes that he will receive bread rolls in return for his money, that is, that someone else *is* producing bread rolls for the market, and such like. This direct exchange of a commodity for money (purchase) is the basis of the quantity theory of money, according to which commodity prices are determined by the quantity of money: when the quantity of money is large but that of commodities small, commodities will be expensive, but when the opposite is the case, they will be cheap. This theory is already corrected by Marx on this basic level: because money merely expresses the value of commodities, commodities are primary.[232] It follows that it is not the quantity of money that determines commodity prices, but vice versa: the value the commodities already have, and which is *expressed* in money, requires a certain amount of money for its circulation.[233] This is not the same; rather, it shows the derivative character of money, which is centrally important for understanding the financial sector (and which can be demonstrated starting from there).[234]

The formula for the simple circulation of commodities, C–M–C, may look simple.[235] But much more is implied by it than by the *direct* equation of purchase and sale that is a feature of Say's law, upon which the neoclassical theory of equilibrium rests.[236] The fact that purchase and sale do not coincide in time expresses a possibility of crisis. Commodities can remain unsaleable, and money can fail to meet with commodities.[237] Here, we already have the insight that the behaviour of money exerts influence (the 'non-neutrality' of money).[238] Where payment is deferred, we are already dealing with

232. If need be, two commodities can be exchanged without money, but money is worthless absent a commodity that can be purchased with it. Money cannot be eaten, as the Cree already knew.

233. 'Commodity circulation is the prerequisite of money circulation; money, moreover, circulates commodities which have prices' (*MECW* 29, p. 338; *MECW* 28, p. 130; *MECW* 35, pp. 127–8).

234. Shaikh 1995.

235. It does not have to be read historically, although something does correspond to it in reality (differently from what Rakowitz 2000 believes), such as the structure of the craft economy, which produces for the market, but in doing so reproduces little more than its own labour-power and that of the family – no accumulation takes place. One might also cite the economies of many traditional Third World societies. W. Becker 1974 believes the formula is so simple it expresses nothing and is, therefore, meaningless.

236. 'The metaphysical equilibrium of purchases and sales is confined to the fact that every purchase is a sale and every sale a purchase, but this gives poor comfort to the possessors of commodities who unable to make a sale cannot accordingly make a purchase either' (*MECW* 29, p. 333). On the assumption of equilibrium, see also Hahn 1999, pp. 14 ff.

237. *MECW* 35, pp. 123 f.; cf. *MECW* 29, pp. 332; *MECW* 28, pp. 132. More is required, however, for an actual crisis to occur (*MECW* 35, pp. 123–4; see Hahn 1999, pp. 130 ff.).

238. On the neutrality of money in neoclassical theory, see Hahn 1999, pp. 17 ff., pp. 40 ff. Huffschmid 1999, pp. 31 ff. describes the way currency speculation is based on the temporal lag between purchase and sale. If the exchange rate of a currency that someone is to be paid out in rises after the contract is closed, but before the commodity is delivered, he makes an additional profit. He may, however, just as likely make a loss. For this reason, entire lines of business have specialised on minimising such risks or profiting as much as possible from 'currency trading'. The underlying logic is simple; no 'new' logic is required. 'The separation of sale and purchase makes possible not only

a form of credit (trade credit),[239] which leads us to the next function of money. Where such circulation of money becomes common, money is used as *means of payment*).[240] At first glance, Marx seems to be splitting hairs by specifying this additional function of money – in fact, the banking sector depends to a large extent on just this function. Let us assume that our shoemaker regularly receives leather from a distributor. In exchange for the leather, he gives the distributor shoes to distribute. This means that commodities are circulating between the shoemaker and the distributor. If the shoemaker receives leather worth 800 dollars and provides shoes worth 1,000 dollars, the aggregate value of the circulating commodities is 1,800 dollars. In order to settle their outstanding payments, the shoemaker and the distributor can offset the values of their respective commodities. In this case, the amount of money that is circulating *as means of payment* is only 200 dollars.[241] From this one can see that – even irrespective of money's turnover rate – many commodities can circulate with little money, so that, taken by itself, the quantity of money in circulation can only exert a limited influence on prices.[242] This is also contrary to the quantity theory of money. The clearing of the balance of payments can be further 'differentiated', that is, assigned to persons who specialise on this business activity – the banks. This is the basis of 'credit money'.[243]

---

commerce proper, but also numerous *pro forma* transactions, before the final exchange of commodities between producer and consumer takes place. It thus enables large numbers of parasites to invade the process of production and to take advantage of this separation' (*MECW* 29, p. 334).

239. See Luhmann 1998, p. 348.

240. *MECW* 29, pp. 370 ff.; *MECW* 35, pp. 145 ff.

241. This presupposes a degree of trust that can only be expected once such payments occur regularly. This is still evident in terms such as 'bankers trust' (Luhmann 1973 de-economises the phenomenon).

242. 'By the currency of the circulating medium, the connexion between buyers and sellers, is not merely expressed. This connexion is originated by, and exists in, the circulation alone. Contrariwise, the movement of the means of payment expresses a social relation that was in existence long before' (*MECW* 35, p. 148).

243. 'The character of creditor, or of debtor, results here from the simple circulation' (*MECW* 35, p. 146). 'Credit-money springs... out of the function of money as a means of payment. Certificates of the debts owing for the purchased commodities circulate for the purpose of transferring those debts to others' (p. 150; see *MECW* 37, pp. 397 ff.). Similar phenomena are to be found in international trade (Brunoff 1976, pp. 99 ff.; Itoh 1999). The following example shows that the effect of the temporal lag is not eliminated by digitalisation (as argued by Altvater 1997). A is able to immediately obtain one million dollars of credit at 10 percent interest, simply by pushing a button. He invests the money in some venture that generates a profit of 200,000 dollars (that is, 100,000 dollars after interest payments). Now, bank B is able to trade in IOUs even as A sells off his property (both would be 'derivatives'). While this renders the connection to the potential profit less transparent, that connection has not disappeared. Making a profit necessarily takes time (for production of commodities, delivery, sale and receipt of payment). If the profit generated is lower than expected (say, 20,000 dollars), A faces great difficulty in paying back the credit he has received from B. This effect can be extended into a larger circuit of creditor/debtor relations by means of derivative trading (so that instead of A having problems paying B, it is now C, the buyer of A's property, who runs into problems with D, the owner of B's IOU – and D may be more than one person). But it is an illusion to think that this causes the problem to disappear. The burden has simply been shifted onto someone else's shoulders. (Even if C and D have succeeded in selling their derivatives

The functions of money that we have considered thus far all involve uncertainties. The counterfeiting of coins, other fluctuations of the money name, trade crises and the deflation or inflation they entail are all conceivable on the basis of what has been said. Complications associated with deferred payments, losses due to exchange rate fluctuations between purchase and sale and the bankruptcy of banks have now also become conceivable. The function of money as 'universal money' or 'world money'[244] already constitutes a response to these possibilities. We might rank the various forms of money according to the level of risk associated with them. Physical money can be lost, stolen or destroyed (by fire, the issuing of new bills, and so on). If I deposit it in the bank, the bank may be robbed or go bankrupt; the value of my deposit is also affected by fluctuations in the value of the local currency. A drop in the exchange rate can make a fortune disappear rather quickly. For this reason, it is safer to deposit the money in a dollar account – as many people in Argentina did. But the fact that these bank accounts were frozen during the Argentine financial crisis shows that even this option may not always be safe. The next option would be a dollar account in the United States – this would be 'universal money'. And yet it is not difficult to imagine situations that would lead to the money depreciating even in this case.[245]

This scenario illustrates the *function* that money aspires to as 'universal money': it is supposed to provide security, especially in international transactions.[246] Whether it always *performs* this function is another matter.[247] It is true that gold performed this

---

at a profit – which would give the entire situation the character of a speculative 'bubble' – all this means is that the buck now stops with E and F, who are obliged to pay.) While 'form' can modify 'content' (delay a crisis, cover up the traces, and so on), it cannot make it disappear. This semblance results from the neoclassical paradigm, in which production has always already been elided. It is not that production has disappeared 'today', because of some technological innovation; from the neoclassical point of view, production never existed in the first place. On the 'bubble', see *MECW* 37, p. 303: 'This internal dependence and external independence push merchant's capital to a point where the internal connection is violently restored through a crisis'.

244. *MECW* 35, pp. 153 ff.; *MECW* 29, pp. 381 ff.; cf. *MECW* 28, pp. 158–9.

245. The example is taken from a talk given by Anwar Shaikh in November 2002. The horrendous US trade deficit makes depreciation of the dollar seem advisable.

246. 'Finally, as international money the precious metals once again fulfil their original function of means of exchange: a function which, like commodity exchange itself, originated at points of contact between different primitive communities and not in the interior of the communities' (*MECW* 29, p. 381). 'Part of the accumulated hoards is consequently used by every nation as a reserve fund of world money, a fund which is sometimes diminished, sometimes replenished according to fluctuations in commodity exchange' (p. 382). As 'tokens of value divorced from gold substance itself' (p. 351), even today's currencies need to be convertible into other currencies. This could be today's 'universal money', the dollar, or, if push came to shove, the gold reserves held by banks. Demand for such a 'money commodity' increases during crises. The concept of the 'money commodity' denotes a function, not a substance, and the concept has been formulated with an eye to long-term developments.

247. Marx exposes the possibility of crises even as he develops his basic concepts, so it makes little sense to try to falsify his theory by invoking, of all things, monetary crises. Marx described the fragility of this function. But Heinrich believes that Marx 'linked money [!] to the money commodity in a fundamental way' (Heinrich 2001a, p. 161; see above). He reaches the conclusion that

function for a long time and, to a certain extent, continues to do so,[248] but there is nothing 'conceptually necessary' about this. That the function of money as 'universal money' *exists* and has to exist is shown by the efforts to create single currencies within large economic regions – apart from the dollar, which has been performing such functions for some time, one could mention the euro, ASEAN or the plans to create a pan-Arab gold dinar. Universal money is what remains 'when the music stops'.[249] The lasting popularity of gold is due to the fact that economic and financial crises can shake entire regions. Gold is relatively safe, or at least it is risky for *other* reasons than money held in the local currency, and differently from real estate, it can be traded anywhere and anytime. This has not changed much, even if philosophical fads have led to the proclamation of ever new stages (for instance, that of digital money).

To the extent that this money has the purpose of *not* being spent, Marx calls it a 'hoard'.[250] This function developed from the pre-capitalist variant of hoarding, in which the money owner valued money for its own sake and withdrew it from circulation.[251]

'the collapse of the Bretton Woods monetary system during the early 1970s' entails a 'fundamental' change with regard to Marx. The opposite is true: Marx describes precisely this permanent uncertainty. Incidentally, the gold standard was only established internationally in 1870, that is, after *Capital* was written (Eichengreen 1996). It was a temporary response to a question that persists and that was theoretically grasped by Marx. Heinrich's 'monetary theory of value' fails to distinguish between the various functions of money, and thereby gets entangled in them. Marx is aware that 'money as gold and silver, in so far as it serves *merely* as means of circulation, can be replaced by any other *symbol*... because material money as mere medium of exchange is itself symbolic' (*MECW* 28, p. 147). However, Marx differs from neoclassical theorists in that he identifies other functions of money, within which gold may play a role. There is a kind of anti-substantialist impulse that attacks everything in Marx that is reminiscent of substance: the money commodity, abstract labour, and so on. This accords well with 'anti-essentialist' postmodernism (Callari 1995, Bonacker 2000, Martin 2002, Antonio 2003, *Rethinking Marxism*, and such like), but it fails to do justice to the meaning of Marx's terms. To attack them in this way is to abandon their meaning, which Marx defined quite precisely.

248. For example, Kolesnikov 2002 reports that Asian central banks have begun reducing their dollar reserves and increasing their gold reserves in response to the likelihood that the dollar will become an unstable currency. Gold continues to be a reliable form of money that is not exposed to exchange rate fluctuations (although it is exposed to price fluctuations), making it relatively resistant to inflation. The reason the United States were forced to decouple the value of the dollar from gold was that their central bank's gold reserves were no longer sufficient to cover the dollar. The dollar itself has, nevertheless, retained the status of 'universal money'; one can still use it as a means of payment in many different parts of the world.

249. Thus Hicks; see Chick 2001, p. 228.

250. *MECW* 29, pp. 359 ff.; *MECW* 28, pp. 162 f.; *MECW* 35, pp. 140 ff.; Keynes was able to explain 'hoarding' only by reference to psychological motives: 1964, p. 208.

251. In order for hoarding to occur, money 'must be prevented from circulating, or from transforming itself into a means of enjoyment. The hoarder, therefore, makes a sacrifice of the lusts of the flesh to his gold fetish. He acts in earnest up to the gospel of abstention' (*MECW* 35, p. 144). Max Weber's work on the spirit of capitalism (Weber 2003, first published in 1904) describes a pre-capitalist situation (cf. 2.4.6, and 2.6.6). 'The appropriation of wealth in its general form therefore implies renunciation of the material reality of wealth... The hoarder of money scorns the worldly, temporal and ephemeral enjoyments in order to chase after the eternal treasure which can be touched neither by moths nor by rust, and which is wholly celestial and wholly mundane'

Under capitalism, the hoard performs a different function, namely that of a 'buffer': when the aggregate price of all commodities determines the quantity of money required for circulation (allowing for turnover) and not vice versa, 'superfluous' money can be used for hoarding. Since capitalism is production 'on a hunch', the quantity of saleable commodities is always changing; this necessitates considerable flexibility within circulation. An unexpected need for additional money causes the hoard to contract, whereas superfluous money causes it to expand.[252] This is a third aspect that is elided by the quantity theory of money: instead of being thrown onto the market, where it would then raise commodity prices (and depreciate), superfluous money is more likely to be taken abroad and invested or spent on luxury goods – or it will be hoarded. It escapes domestic circulation – and the quantity theory.

There is something else that only becomes possible when large amounts of money have been accumulated, and it cannot be conceptualised on the basis of the quantity theory of money: the transformation of money into *capital*.[253] Even before society differentiates itself into capital-owning and working classes, there is an unequal distribution of wealth: it is the historical basis for the ongoing reproduction and exacerbation of this inequality under capitalism ('primitive accumulation').[254]

Here, the theory of money is already complete. It leads into something far more important: the theory of capital.[255] Stylistically, the transition is masterly, since capital is already implicit in simple circulation, albeit 'inversely'. The circulation of commodities (C–M–C) ends with consumption; it therefore constantly requires new 'input'.[256] To the extent that this is the case, one can say that, in the long term, simple circulation always presupposes at least simple reproduction. However, every individual act has its perspectival counterpart (C–M corresponds to M–C on the buyer's side, and M–C corresponds

---

(*MECW* 29, pp. 362–3; see Engels in *MECW* 3, p. 422). Marx considered this appropriation of wealth one of the preliminary conditions for the development of capitalism: 'The prehistory of the development of modern industrial society opens with a general greed for money, on the part of both individuals and states... The hunt for gold in all countries leads to their discovery; to the formation of new states; first of all, to the expansion of the range of commodities which enter into circulation, creating new wants, and drawing remote parts of the world into the process of exchange and interchange of matter' (*MECW* 28, pp. 157–8).

252. It is never clear in advance how many commodities will be sold; this must be anticipated. For this reason, it is not only commodities that are stocked, but also money. 'We have seen how, along with the continual fluctuations in the extent and rapidity of the circulation of commodities and in their prices, the quantity of money current unceasingly ebbs and flows. This mass must, therefore, be capable of expansion and contraction' (*MECW* 35, p. 144).

253. *MECW* 35, pp. 157 ff.; *MECW* 28, pp. 171 ff.

254. *MECW* 35, pp. 704 ff.; see Perelman 2000.

255. 'Money recurs in all later relations; but then it does not function as mere money' (*MECW* 28, p. 176). For this reason, the concrete form that money assumes from one instance to the next is never of more than secondary interest.

256. Money is spent by the buyer of a commodity; it 'vanishes'. Commodities also exit circulation, since they are 'eaten up' sooner or later (either literally, or in the metaphorical sense of being destroyed, as in 'the machine ate my card').

to C–M on the seller's side). This means that the same process can also be considered inversely (M–C–M): this time, it is not money that vanishes, but the commodity – not because it is eaten up, but because it is sold. Here, commodities do not circulate by means of money; money circulates by means of commodities. Money is no longer a means but an end. When it appears in this form, it is already capital – merchant capital.[257]

From the point of view of monetary theory, however, the expanded formula of capital (M–C–M': money bcomes *more* money) remains puzzling. The question of where this 'more' comes from remains unanswered. Terms such as abstinence, waiting or 'risk premium' and the observation that money becomes more money merely *reiterate* the question in the form of a mystification.[258] Even if a single merchant capital obtains surplus value (ΔM = M' – M) from pilferage, on the macroeconomic level, profit on one side must correspond to *loss* on the other (this does not mean that entire nations cannot be robbed by other nations).[259] Here, 'monetary theory' does not get us anywhere.

Within Marx's *own* theory, 'monetary theory' has the character of a propaedeutics; its main purpose is to prevent misunderstandings about the nature of money. Everything that is essential about Marx's monetary theory has been said, here. By comparison to *other* economic theories, however, Marx's definition of money is controversial. This can be shown by reference to three basic notions of textbook economics that are rendered

---

257. In Marx and Kant, the shift from one perspective to another does not pose any theoretical problem; what does pose such a problem is the shift between different spheres of being, which is what perspectives become in erroneous readings of Kant and Marx. The monetary theory of value struggles with a 'problem of transition' (Hahn 1999, 49) that concerns the shift from the life world (the world of action) to the system.

258. This is the basis of Rakowitz 2001's objection (see also Bonefeld 1995) to theories associated with the journal *Bahamas* and the Freiburg-based 'Initiative for a Socialist Forum' (*Initiative Sozialistisches Forum*, ISF) (ISF 2000; 2.6.4).

259. Shaikh illustrates the conservation of value as follows: when someone sells their stereo for 1,000 dollars, they create 1,000 dollars of 'value added' on the macroeconomic level. If, however, the stereo was stolen beforehand, the 1,000 dollars of 'value added' are cancelled out by a 1,000-dollar loss, such that the amount of 'value added' is zero. Earlier theories of 'unequal exchange' were based on a similar notion (Emmanuel 1972; see McLellan 1979 and Shaikh 1979). Trading with pre-capitalist societies allows one to purchase commodities for less than they are worth, in order to then sell them at considerable profit. This is because pre-capitalist societies employ other standards of value in their exchange practices than those that apply in the country where the commodities are sold (for example, they may accept glass pearls as payment). Yet under capitalism, commercial capital cannot sustain itself by pilferage; even if it did 'pilfer', what it pilfers would have to come from somewhere. If it were freely accessible, nobody would be willing to buy it. Marx explains the surplus value obtained by a single merchant in terms of value being transferred from production to trade (*MECW* 37, pp. 266 ff.). The consumer does not purchase a commodity whose price of production is 80 value units directly from the producer for 100 value units; instead, the producer sells it to the merchant for 90 value units, and the merchant then charges the consumer 100 value units. The producer and the merchant share the surplus value. Trade does not produce this share of surplus value, but merely appropriates it, as can be seen from the fact that producers make efforts to eliminate intermediary trade (such as by selling directly on the Internet). Backhaus 2002 believes the notion of value conservation is fallaciously adopted from physics (p. 120). If anything, this anti-positivist affect confirms the mystification of money.

nonsensical by Marx's understanding of money.[260] Marx can be used to criticise these 'monetary' hypotheses. I am referring to propositions about foreign trade ('comparative advantage'), inflation (the 'Phillips curve')[261] and the self-propagation of money (the 'multiplier'). The first hypothesis states that an economically disadvantaged country may benefit from trade with an economically advantaged one. This amounts to a justification of *free trade*, which, as is well-known, constitutes one of the basic features of the neoliberal world picture (even if powerful nations only act in accordance with it for as long as doing so acts to *their* advantage; as soon as it is not, they adopt protectionist measures). The following model from Ricardo[262] is often used to illustrate the hypothesis: countries A and B both produce cloth and wine; however, country B produces them at unit prices of 45 and 40 units of universal money (gold), whereas the economically disadvantaged country A produces them at the prices of 50 and 60 m.u.:

Table 17: Comparative Advantage

	Country A	Country B
Cloth (price of production)	50	45
Wine (price of production)	60	40

It is clear that country A will import *both* commodities. As a result, gold flows in the opposite direction, from country A to country B. According to the quantity theory of money, this leads to prices rising in country B, but falling in country A. There is a *balancing* tendency, on this model. The model is called 'comparative' because the assumption continues to be made that country A may begin, despite its initial disadvantage, to export a commodity to country B, as soon as the *smaller* difference in price has been reversed by the price shifts (45/50 = a 10 percent difference in the price of cloth, compared to 40/60 = a 33.3 percent difference in the price of wine). Thus country A will begin, sooner or later, to export cloth to country B, since it enjoys a 'comparative advantage' there.[263] Moreover, each of the two countries has maximised its 'total utility', since both now obtain a commodity for less than it would cost to produce it – a harmonic view of foreign trade.

---

260. This incompatibility seems to have disconcerted German followers of Marx. Instead of using Marx to criticise such theorems, his theory was reconstructed in 'monetary' terms, that is, it was Keynesianised (not just by Backhaus and Heinrich, but also by Altvater 1991, Hahn 1999 and Gerlach 2003, pp. 108–45). The resulting hybrid is, however, not particularly useful for criticising mainstream economics; it is always Marx who ends up being criticised. Thus Germany is going through a belated replay of what Anglophone Left Keynesians accomplished in the 1950s: bidding Marx farewell.

261. Named after Phillips 1958.

262. Ricardo 1992, pp. 82 ff.

263. This also explains why the IMF and the World Bank frequently recommend not just free trade, but also currency depreciation (Blum 2000, pp. 431–2; Stiglitz 2002).

If, however, one applies *Marx's* understanding of money to this narrative, things change dramatically: country A does not enjoy a comparative (relative) advantage; it is *absolutely disadvantaged.* It is producing both commodities on worse terms, and because it is importing, it is also losing gold. The fact that country B, which is already in a better position, is increasing its supply of gold does not have to lead to a rise in prices, according to Marx, because the gold does not have to enter into circulation.[264] It can just as well perform other functions of money. Hoarding can – and will – result. Such hoarding has two possible effects. If it remains in the hands of the producer, the 'hoard' can increase productivity by being invested in additional fixed capital. Rather than reducing the difference in prices between countries A and B, this will *increase* the difference, as country B can now produce even more cheaply. Or the money can be hoarded by banks. This would lead to a drop in interest rates, thereby prompting *further* investment in country B. Once again, the situation is aggravated. The productivity of country A is lagging behind, and at the same time, country A is losing universal money (that is, purchasing power on the world market, or foreign currency, a development that causes interest rates to *rise* in country A). Let us now assume that country A attempts to counteract this trend, while interest rates are low in country B, where there is also 'superfluous' money. It is easy to see that the money market will allow for *additional* monetary flows from country A to country B: country A will borrow (universal) money from country B at a high interest rate. Of course, the borrowed money and the interest will have to be repaid in universal money, even though universal money is precisely what is becoming increasingly scarce in country A. This scenario anticipates the debt crisis of the Third World and the inequalities of globalisation. When considered from the perspective of Marx's monetary theory, the theory of comparative advantage can be shown to be a whitewash of the enforcement of unequal development.[265]

Marxian monetary theory has similarly astonishing implications for our understanding of the mechanisms underlying the wondrous propagation of money in Keynesian theory. Keynes held that the level of equilibrium – which was presupposed by him, as in neoclassical theory – could be raised (leading to greater utilisation of labour and capital) by injecting additional money into the market. Keynes argued that this would increase demand, thereby stimulating production and leading to a new equilibrium at a higher level of capacity utilisation. Keynes's teacher Denis Robertson had already raised the question of where the additional money was supposed to come from. Keynes's answer simply defined the problem away: the money was to be provided by unlimited bank

264. It could also increase demand for luxury goods, thereby boosting production.

265. On this argument, see *MECW* 37, pp. 542 ff.; *MECW* 29, pp. 247–8; Arnhold 1979, Wassina 1983, Girschner 1999, pp. 133 ff. and Shaikh 1979, 1980b and 1995. It makes no difference to the argument whether exchange rates are fixed or flexible; all that is meant by 'fixed' is 'fixed within certain limits' (temporally and financially). Periodical adjustments of fixed exchange rates are only another form of flexibility.

credit at fixed interest rates.[266] Keynes insinuated the possibility of this variable being regulated *politically*. According to this model, money is literally exogenous; growth stimulation is deficit-financed.[267]

Keynes responded to this problem by assuming a 'multiplier'. He assumes that by passing through the hands of several people, money can circulate a high number of commodities, that is, 'create' many times its own value, thereby allowing for repayment of the debt.[268] But what is the relationship between the two sums? Keynes neglected the relationship between deficit financing and the development of interest rates. When additional demand is deficit-financed, *not* financed from savings, this leads to a tightening of monetary reserves, and hence to rising interest rates, increasing the overall debt. While artificially increased demand may induce additional growth initially, the pressure exerted by the growing debt and rising interest rates will eventually curb growth and return the economy to its 'normal' growth path (namely, growth *without* additional demand). On the microeconomic level, increased demand will induce a firm to invest, but the rising interest rate will simultaneously provide a disincentive for investment, and the two trends can balance each other out in the long term. On the macroeconomic level, the one-off increase in the level of equilibrium is countered by the progressively growing debt.[269] According to Marx, internally financed growth is possible. When additional demand develops, it is integrated into the dynamic of the system without altering the system's behaviour.[270] Thus when money is conceptualised as endogenous,

---

266. Asimakopulos 1983. I rely on Anwar Shaikhs lectures here.

267. Total demand consists of demand in Departments I and II, both for consumer goods and investment goods (D = C + I; total demand = consumption + investment). The additional demand by which Keynes hoped to promote growth is the difference between supply and demand (E = D – Y; excess demand = demand – supply). The formula E = (C + I) – Y can be reformulated as E = I – (Y – C). Since supply minus consumption is simultaneously defined as savings (Y – C = S; supply – consumption = savings), it follows that E = I – S. This means that additional demand requires external deficit financing, since savings (S) have already been subtracted from investment by definition. This is, of course, the case during any period, so debt is inevitably accumulated.

268. Assuming a 25 percent savings rate, 100 units of external input are expected to generate a demand increase not of 100, but of 100 + (75 + 56.25 + 42.2 + 31.7 + 23.7 . . . = 300) = 400 (100 × 1/¼). Savings (0 + 25 + 43.75 + 57.8 + 68,3 + 76,3 . . . = 400) are expected to cover debt (Keynes 1964, p. 115; Lekachman 1966, p. 62; Bhaduri 1988, pp. 46 ff.; Majer 1991, pp. 97–8). However, debt also accumulates – and it increases further due to the rise in interest rates (see Shaikh 1991). During the crises of the 1970s, attempts to revive the economy by means of state intervention failed.

269. For a more comprehensive discussion of this argument, see Shaikh 1979, p. 33; 1989, p. 71; 1991, p. 2; 1992.

270. Majer 1991, p. 87. In Marx's model of extended reproduction, it is not credit (bank loans) that is used to finance investment but the savings of capitalists, which are made available via the money market (see section 2.1.5). For this reason, increased investment goes hand in hand with a lack of consumption on the part of capitalists. In the long term, investment induces no additional total demand (E = O), that is, it has no multiplying effects but merely effects transfers from one department to another. Marx does not treat psychological factors (the savings rate, the propensity to invest) as 'autonomous', as Keynes does; he relates them back to the overall system (Shaikh 1991, p. 7).

state-induced additional demand does *not* result in a long-term stimulus to growth. It is no accident that Keynesian policies ended with a debt crisis.[271]

The monetarist critique of Keynes, according to which additional public spending leads to inflation, can also be criticised from the perspective of Marx. Apart from the quantity theory of money, which underlies this assumption, one can question the relationship between inflation and unemployment suggested by the so-called 'Phillips curve'. Keynesians and monetarists both assume that inflation results when additional demand can no longer be met by adjusting the quantity of goods, so prices have to be adjusted instead. When *all* prices increase, the value of money decreases. The increased demand can no longer be met as soon as the 'factors of production', and, in particular, labour, are being utilised to capacity. Thus, the closer one gets to full employment, the more likely inflation becomes. And when there is inflation, it can be attributed to 'excessively high' wages. In spite of being shaken by the *simultaneity* of inflation and unemployment during the 1970s, this assumption continues to be made in conventional theory.[272] When money is introduced as autonomous in this way, the underlying structures are rendered invisible. When we follow Marx in understanding money as endogenous, as the form of *something else*, it becomes clear that unemployment and inflation do not cause one another but have a common cause. For economic growth, upon which *both* depend, is limited by the rate of profit, according to Marx.[273]

The above considerations have begun to show that there is a consistent theory of money in Marx, one that differs significantly from conventional monetary theories, but plays hardly any role in the German Marxist debate on money. In Marx, socio-theoretical *topoi* are directly thematised within political economy, as the example of unequally developed economic regions has shown. From the perspective of Marxian monetary theory, it also becomes clear why Keynesianism, a standard scientific foundation of normative social philosophy that posits the possibility of an 'ethical' regulation of the economic process, is inconsistent.

It has also become clear that the basic assumptions of neoclassical economics contain certain value judgements, for instance when a direct relationship between wage levels and inflation is suggested, such that the responsibility for inflation is clearly attributed to the factor *labour*. Marx criticises notions of money (not money itself, for it is by no means 'merely' a semblance) as fetishistic when they do not involve the attempt to understand money in terms of its own complex relations, but rather treat it as *causa sui*,

271. O'Connor 1974.
272. Rowthorn 1984; Bhaduri 1988, pp. 196 ff.; Majer 1991, pp. 203 ff.
273. This explains why lowering interest rates does not eliminate unemployment, as long as the rate of profit remains too low. See Shaikh 1995.

and as the cause of other things as well. This parallels his critique of fetishistic notions of religion, the state and law.

This chapter interpreted the reconfiguration of the theoretical groundings of economics as constituting, in functional terms, an effort to avoid Marx. Even though this paradigm shift is crying out for a critique, it remains hegemonic to this day. In bidding Marx farewell, economic theory created a serious lacuna with regard to its theoretical grasp of bourgeois society, the central theme of classical political economy. It could be shown that, ironically, many Marxist economics *accepted* the effort to place economic theory on new, non-Marxian foundations. This is one reason why the present attempt to rehabilitate Marx's theory must refer to such a wide range of issues. The content of Marx's theory is not 'available' in the sense of having been deposited somewhere; it is not simply waiting to be put to use. It needs, rather, to be excorticated by means of a negative critique. The present chapter has begun to do this for economic theory; the next chapter will archaeologically consider the theoretical consequences of functional avoidance of Marx for the 'fallback discipline' of sociology.

2.4 Marx in (German) sociology

> Sociology without political economy is 'blind', but it is just as certain that political economy without sociology is 'empty'.[1]

> Modern Sociology arose in the course of a critical encounter, first with the Enlightenment of the eighteenth century and then with its true heir in the nineteenth century, Karl Marx.[2]

The history of sociology is written in different ways, depending on what it is one wants to historicise.[3] There has been thinking about men's communal existence for as long as they have existed communally – witness the contractualism of the Sophists. Yet sociology as an academic discipline is barely over a century old.[4] These age determinations mark the liminal points of a possible historicisation.

The historiography of Friedrich Jonas[5] is still the most plausible one. He gives two conditions for the development of sociology. First, society must have *differentiated* itself from the social body hitherto previously referred to as 'the state'. Second, society must be considered as an object *sui generis*, not from the perspective of moral or state philosophy. This was achieved around 1750.[6] According to Jonas, originary sociology differed from 'state philosophy'[7] from the outset, because it did not share the view 'that people's communal activity and communal existence presupposes a master that gives this activity a law and organises it'.[8] But sociology also differed from the moralism of a mere 'cultural criticism'.[9] State philosophy resurfaces in French socialism, according to Jonas,[10] while cultural criticism resurfaces in German idealism.[11] This diagnosis can be extended: twentieth-century German sociology was still dominated by state philosophy

---

1. Eisermann 1964, p. 127.
2. Zeitlin 1981, p. V.
3. Klingemann 2001.
4. Stölting 1986.
5. Jonas 1976.
6. 'The history of sociology begins with the separation of society and state' (F. Jonas 1976, Vol. 1, p. 15). The 'problem of social integration' is first posed, 'as a sociological problem', by Montesquieu (Montesquieu 1977, p. 24; Aron 1965, Kuczynski 1975 and Althusser 1987 agree with this view). Rousseau 1950 still theorised in a moralistic manner; Smith 2009 was 'the first to describe, within a fully developed theory, society as a self-regulating and hence free interrelationship of action' (p. 105; see also Quesnay 1965, Locke 1988).
7. Jonas 1976, Vol. 1, pp. 15, 27, 59.
8. Jonas 1976, Vol. 1, p. 244.
9. Jonas 1976, Vol. 1, p. 78. According to Jonas, the 'motives and ideals' of the Enlightenment were those of 'educated and sometimes powerful social groups' that 'developed … principles by which to organise society' (Jonas 1976 I, p. 22). 'If the problem of social integration is discussed as a moral problem, then this is because, as Taine remarked, no one is thinking of actually acting on this notion' (pp. 23 f.). It is clear that Jonas is, among other things, taking a sideswipe at German critical theory.
10. Jonas 1976, Vol. 1, pp. 178, 187.
11. Jonas 1976, Vol. 1, p. 143.

and cultural criticism.[12] Since Marx, who thought of society as his object of inquiry (see section 2.1.5), focused much of his criticism on both, Marx assumes a rather prominent place in Jonas' discussion.[13] But instances of Marx so freely being accorded a place within the history of sociology are quite rare.

Within the history of *economics*, Marx's position is central: modern economic theory can be divided into classical economics, which is pre-Marxian, and neoclassical economics, which is post-Marxian (see section 2.3.1). This is why Georg Lukács thought of sociology as a by-product of the transition from classical to neoclassical economics.[14] Even though this is to underestimate the significance of pre-Marxian sociological thought, and to overestimate the significance of Marx's work, it does indicate the considerable (if not universal) importance of Marx *and* neoclassical theory for the development of sociology. What would a *more precise* description of Marx's status within the history of sociology look like? Authors such as Auguste Comte, John Stuart Mill, Herbert Spencer and Lorenz von Stein, who wrote around 1850 (that is, a century *after* the authors cited by Jonas), are generally considered the 'founding fathers' of sociology, whereas authors active around 1900, such as Simmel, Max Weber, Durkheim and Pareto, are considered 'classics' of modern sociology.[15] The founding fathers were startled by the growing social grievances and political restlessness in the wake of the French Revolution, especially by the 'social question' raised by industrialisation.[16] Their assessment and theoretical processing of these phenomena occurred in a freestyle manner, as there existed no consistent self-articulation of the rebellious groups,[17] nor had the established social strata produced a hegemonic and coherent interpretation. Thus borrowings from other disciplines and elements of emotion, opinion and utopianism (in brief: 'value judgements') were strongly in

---

12. Rehberg 1986, p. 8, identifies the fixation on the state that characterised German politics and the German churches as one cause of the hostile attitude displayed toward sociology, which focuses on 'bourgeois society'. However, sociology itself was soon subject to the 'primacy of politics' in theory (see 2.2 above).

13. Jonas 1976, Vol. 1, pp. 215 ff. 'Marx expands the canon of sociological theory... in an important and consequential way... Marx is the first to explicitly pay attention to the progress of industrialisation... and the emergence of the industrial proletariat' (p. 240; see also Krätke 1996). The greatest praise Jonas, a conservative, can bestow on Marx is to say that Marx was, at bottom, a conservative himself (p. 227). Jonas focuses less on Marx's political views than on his scientific achievements (pp. 217, 223). A 'conservative affinity with Marx' (Kühne 1972, pp. 62 ff.) is also evident in Schumpeter, Hayek and Gehlen (see Rehberg 2000).

14. Lukács 1981, pp. 585–6. A similar claim can be found in Schumpeter: 'Sociology is... the *mixtum compositum* that remains when one substracts economics' (Schumpeter 1953, p. 9; Papcke 1986, p. 80).

15. Lepenies 1985 includes Mill, Riehl and Durkheim among the 'founding fathers'; Kaesler 1976 and Münch 2002 describe Marx, Simmel, Durkheim and Weber as 'classics'. Kaesler 1984, pp. 446–76 distinguishes various 'generations', from great grandfathers to great grandchildren. Müller-Doohm 1991 (pp. 48 ff.) reverses this terminology.

16. Quesel 1989.

17. A 'subjective sociology' (König 1975). Early socialism had theoretical ambitions, but its influence was limited.

evidence in the works of these authors.[18] By contrast, the classics were confronted with an internationally constituted labour movement that knew how to articulate itself not just politically, but also theoretically. It was led, at least in theory, by Marx. Thus Marx was positioned, once again, *between* two decisive groups of theorists. However, his influence was much greater in Germany than in England or France – not because he wrote in German, but because there was in Germany a major workers' party that invoked his authority. This political influence intersected with the theoretical influence of the new economic paradigm.

In Kaesler's view, socialism is one of the sources of German sociology.[19] Marx becomes still more important when one assumes the perspective of discourse analysis, rather than that of milieu-oriented analysis. While in 1934 (the last year examined by Kaesler), Marx plays only a marginal role in the self-interpretation of German sociologists (as is hardly surprising),[20] there is no overlooking the fact that he was a crucial source of ideas for German sociology as a whole, and not just because German sociologists attempted to set themselves off from Marx. Here too, Marx influenced other theorists *ex negativo*, as the hidden fulcrum of their theoretical efforts.[21] And, once again, it was a matter of *specific* readings of Marx exerting an influence.

---

18. Jonas presents Comte as a philosopher of history who reasoned aprioristically (Jonas 1976, Vol. 1, p. 266) and metaphysically (p. 271); Spencer is portrayed as a biologist who failed to comprehend sociability (pp. 257 ff.) and Riehl as a rustic bard (p. 173). Jonas's verdict on Lorenz von Stein, who anticipated the welfare state, is more lenient, although Von Stein is not accorded the status of sociologist either; according to Jonas, Von Stein was a philosopher of the state (pp. 301–2). Nietzsche was another central influence on German sociology. His 'anti-sociology' (Lichtblau 1997, pp. 82, 111) considered even theoretical engagement with the social question a form of 'cultural decadence' (p. 86; see also G. Adler 1891, Breysig 1896, Tönnies 1897, Hammacher 1909, Winterfeld 1909; see 2.5.2).

19. Kaesler 1984 distinguishes the following currents in early German sociology: a 'critical Marxism' (p. 400; Max Adler and Alfred Meusel, a 'party sociologist' from Aachen who was a member of the East German parliament until 1960); 'confused' socialists (Michels or Breysig; Simmel sympathised with the Social-Democratic Party before 1914, as did A. Weber after 1945; p. 432); a liberal 'socialism without Marx' (Geiger, Oppenheimer, Goldscheidt, Tönnies, A. Weber. 'In the Wilhelmine era, "lectern socialism", "university socialism" or "scholarly socialism" did not under any circumstances want to be associated with the "party of subversion"': p. 442); and finally a 'vehement anti-Marxism' (p. 422) that sought to 'dethrone historical materialism' (p. 417; for example Spann 1932 or Sombart 1934; on this current, see also Pollock 1926).

20. See Kaesler account of the US sociologist E.E. Eubank's travels through Germany (Kaesler 1985). The German Society for Sociology (*Deutsche Gesellschaft für Soziologie*), then headed by Freyer, disbanded in 1934 (see König 1987, pp. 343 ff.; Rammstedt 1986, Klingemann 1996).

21. This was all the more true after 1933: 'The odds-on favourite Marxism has long been overtaken by the fascist courser', Rothacker declared (quoted in Lepenies 1985, p. 404). In 1933, Plenge preached 'the relentless, inner and principled overcoming of Marxism out of the spirit of German idealism… I already identified Marx's primary trait when I characterised him as a 'Jew' in 1911' (quoted in Kaesler 1983, pp. 411–12; for a general account of National Socialism's stance on Marx, see Nolte 1963, not Nolte 1983). It was not just in the Third Reich that Marx served as a negative point of comparison. Borrowing the terminology of psychoanalysis, one might describe Marx as an absent object (or 'abject') that surfaces repeatedly as a repressed 'trauma'. 'The history of sociological research can largely be described in terms of engagement with and rejection of Marx's class theory. At times it even seems as if sociology derived its academic right to existence from its refutation of a theory that once questioned the stability of bourgeois society' (Berger 1998,

In what follows, I will discuss some representative basic features of the traces left, within various sociological paradigms, by the relationship between the political bugbear that was Marxism and the theoretical ideal that was neoclassical theory (2.4.1). I will suggest possible reasons for this development (2.4.2). Its result was that theory assumed an increasingly normative character, until it had been comprehensively ethicised (2.4.3). Thankfully, specific interpretations of Marx referred back to what he had actually written; this invites us to verify our hypotheses (2.4.4). Finally, two examples, technology (2.4.5) and classes (2.4.6), will be used to shed light, in an exemplary manner, on the consequences of this misguided basic orientation within the development of theory.

2.4.1 *The division of the world into norm-free functions and normative frames*

The 'classics' of sociology were often celebrated political economists: take, for example, Max Weber, Werner Sombart, Franz Oppenheimer and Vilfredo Pareto, to name but a few. Since the hegemonic representation of the economy, within post-Marxian economics, was that of neoclassical theory or the 'marginal utility school', these sociologists were exposed to the influence of that representation. In this way, a specific interpretation of Marx was passed on from one discipline to another.[22] And this was not without consequences.

With regard to its relevance to sociology, the neoclassical representation of the economy (2.3.1) can be summarised as follows. The market regulates itself by means of the equilibrium of supply and demand, which is inherent and necessary. Hence unpleasant epiphenomena of capitalist modernity result not from this economic form *itself*, but from its imperfect realisation; they are due to 'external' factors that *obstruct* the market. Actual circumstances are interpreted as an impure manifestation of the model: the model assumes perfect competition, but in the real world, with all its problems, we find only an 'imperfect' form of competition, 'incomplete competition'. By and large, the sociologists were critical of the social relations of their time. Yet within an interpretive

p. 29). 'Reponses to the Marxist concept of class pervade the history of sociology as a consistent sideline' (Krysmanski 1989, p. 155; see Schelsky 1961, p. 350). The Marxist hypothesis that modern sociology is nothing but a 'bourgeois' response to Marx (Salomon 1945, Lukács 1981, Krysmanski 1989) distorts a partially justified hypothesis on historical parentage into a claim about the content of the progeny. This specious polemic fooled no one into overlooking the often feeble condition of Marxist-Leninist sociology (Kiss 1971, Ludz 1971, Hahn 1974, Sparschuh 1997). And yet it was conducted within every current, from the bourgeois centre (König 1987) to the right-wing fringe (Freyer 1964).

22. Simmel 1978 clearly replicates the subjective theory of value. Weber's orientation toward neoclassical theory has been diagnosed, among others, by Stefan Kalber (in: Böckler 1987, pp. 122 ff.). Pareto is a neoclassical theorist himself ('Pareto optimum': see section 3.2). Sombart was at least compatible with neoclassical theory, by virtue of his historicism (Sombart 1903, 1930; on the complementarity of historicism and neoclassical theory – one features concepts without apperception, the other apperception without concepts – see section 2.3.1). Lukács clearly identifies German sociology's neoclassical thrust (Lukács 1981, pp. 452–3, 592–3, 605–6; see below).

context that considered social reality a *hybrid*, the question of *which* of the hybrid's components was to be blamed for society's ills remained open: were these ills due to the logic of the system, or were they due to the factors impeding that logic?

For Marx, there could be no question of such an opposition: what neoclassical theorists considered 'distortions of the market' were, in his view, part and parcel of the market. Social inequalities and other manifestations of crisis are *inherent* to the logic of the system itself. There was no need to assume market-*distorting* factors. Marx held that the struggle for market advantages, conducted with dishonest means by various interest groups, was emphatically a part of the competitive system. Where there is monopoly, the monopolies are also subject to the logic of the competitive system, and there is no reason to conclude from their existence that a *new stage* of capitalism, which functions according to new laws, has begun (the conclusion reached by the revisionists: 2.2.6). Nor ought one to interpret these elements as *interfering* with the logic of the market or distorting the results of the allocation process (in the manner of neoclassical theorists: 2.3.2).[23] From Marx's point of view, neither interpretation is sustainable, since the overall representation is wrong. Distortions and their consequences are *endogeneous* and should be included in the analysis.

But the Platonic image of 'pure forces' plus material, empirical impurities was the dominant one within the economics of the time. Many sociologists subscribed to it, and even Marx was interpreted on the basis of it (2.3.3).[24] For this reason, it is crucial to distinguish between Marx's own arguments and those of historical Marxism. Yet as long as one remains *within* the dualism of pure forces and their distortions, there is no way to theoretically settle the question of which of the two gives rise to society's ills – it becomes a matter of deciding between one of the two options. How one 'chooses' to interpret this representation of society partly depends on extra-theoretical factors such as one's social background and political self-conception. Thus authors with an agrarian background are more likely to 'opt' for a negative verdict on the laws of the market.[25] From the point of view of Marx, the interests of clearly defined social strata (in this case, the remnants of a social stratum associated with a declining era) are not to be overlooked. The negation of the present that such strata engage in is abstract, and for

23. Around 1900, there were fierce debates about the 'agrarian question': participants in these debates included Kautsky, Lenin and Weber (P. Anderson 1978, p. 23). However, rural flight as induced by the industrialisation of agriculture, declining prices, and so on, are all easily explained within Marxism.

24. Because of this situation, Marx was often rejected, for instance on account of considering only the logic of the 'pure' economy ('economism') and overlooking the power of market distortions, or for underestimating the possibility of a welfare state and overlooking the dangers of organised capitalism. And yet, according to Marx, both phenomena have socio-economic origins and limits that can, in principle, be explained.

25. One need think only of W.H. von Riehl, Otmar Spann, Artur Damaschke, the head of the Reich Food Corporation (*Reichsnährstand*) R. Walter Darré or right-leaning agrarian parties, such as exist in contemporary Poland. To this day, the EU's farmers are shielded from the market by horrendously high subsidies and protective tariffs (*MECW* 6, p. 494).

this reason they are quite capable of employing the abstract theoretical model described, albeit it in an inverted manner.[26] By contrast, those whose 'market position' is associated with favourable 'income opportunities' (to use Max Weber's terminology) are more likely to adopt an *affirmative* position on the laws of the market, placing the blame for the occasional problem on the distorting factors. But is this enough to constitute a 'theory of society'? The belief that once a 'pure' market had been established, it would produce a just society, was at least as utopian as popular socialism's hopes for the future: in *both* cases, what was being described was an *utopos*, a place that does not exist. The need to determine the author's 'class position' by means of the critique of ideology arises not just with regard to theoretical origins (2.3.1), but also with regard to the author's basic *decision* in favour of one the two possible perspectives on the representation of society.[27] Which option does sociology 'choose'?

Let us consider the example of Franz Oppenheimer, a socially critical author from sociology's early period who was a cofounder of the Frankfurt School and one of the fathers not just of 'liberal socialism', but also of the Zionist *kibbutz* movement and the 'social market economy'. He held that 'social inequality results not from economic relations, but from their distortion through political force':[28]

> Oppenheimer did not believe in the possibility of a 'neutral' politics and strictly opposed the myth that the state is responsible for optimally shaping economic life. Freedom, prosperity and justice can be achieved only through freedom of competition, according to Oppenheimer – provided that existing 'distortions' are eliminated. Oppenheimer distinguished between the 'pure' market economy, in which land is freely available,[29] and the 'political' economy, in which the monopolisation of land by large landowners impedes settling. This, according to Oppenheimer, is the cause of every ill associated with capitalism.[30]

Although in 1934 Oppenheimer was the only one to even mention Marx as a sociological author, apart from Hans Freyer, he aggressively asserted the neoclassical notion that the cause of disturbances must be 'external'. His basic economic theory is imbued with

---

26. The individualism and atomism of the neoclassical model are accepted as a correct description of the present and merely judged to be unfortunate; by contrast, the 'distortions of the market', judged to be 'bad' within the other reading (such as agrarian feudalism or monopolies), are assessed as positive, here. Thus despite their differences, the Catholic, corporatist or *völkisch* variants of 'anticapitalism' shared the basic assumption that there exist pure forces and empirical impurities (cf. 3.3.5).

27. Lieber 1985 (pp. 37–8) reiterates the claim that for Marx, every phenomenon related to the superstructure amounts, per se, to 'ideology', and, therefore, to 'false consciousness', without providing any examples (see K. Lenk 1961, Ludz 1976). For a more accurate account, see Eagleton 1993 (refer also to section 3.1.6).

28. Vogt 1999, p. 247.

29. This is to attribute historical reality to Locke's legitimatory model (see Gesell 1958). Incidentally, Vogt is quoting Oppenheimer 1913 and 1938.

30. Vogt 1999, p. 245.

neoclassical assumptions; its theoretical superstructure is that of a 'state-philosophical' sociology. Factors similar to those that shaped Bernstein's theory may have played a role in this (2.1.2).

For example, the East Elbian landed aristocracy was quite influential in imperial Germany, and it was still able to influence Hindenburg, the president of the Weimar Republic; major corporations such as AEG (of which Rathenau was the chairman) wielded tremendous economic power. The state companies and bureaucracies of imperial Germany seemed to be imposing tight restrictions on the pure market economy. Thus, aside from the role played by the history of ideas, there were also real historical reasons for neglecting Marx's theory.[31] Yet contrary to Oppenheimer's diagnosis,[32] the laws of capitalism were still in effect within these institutions: imperial Germany had yet to develop a domestic economy and an infrastructure comparable to those of the major powers England and France. The institutions mentioned were far from curbing the forces of the market; they were working to *create* the market in the first place. Imperial Germany responded to the social costs this entailed, as well as to the rise of Social Democracy, by providing its subjects with basic legal and welfare guarantees.[33] By no means did this constitute an 'overcoming' of capitalism within the welfare state.

If Oppenheimer's analysis differed from that of Marx, this was not so much due to real changes as to the adoption of a different economic theory. Oppenheimer followed the neoclassical paradigm and took too narrow a view of capitalism, ultimately losing sight of it. It was only for this reason that he was able to develop the idea that capitalism needed to be *re-established* in the form of small agrarian communities.[34]

---

31. 'The reasons why German sociology objected, during the first third of the present century, to the notion of general historical laws are not just theoretical, but also socio-historical' (K. Lenk 1986, p. 177). To say this was neither to inaugurate a 'class analysis of the intelligentsia' (Kostede 1974) nor to claim that reality had changed fundamentally. What was new was simply that even well-meaning contemporaries saw little need to overcome the blindness to capitalism that resulted from the neoclassical bias of sociology's economic presuppositions. Twentieth-century German capitalism was politically 'bridled' in various ways (see Rosenberg 1955, Wehler 1969, Hobsbawm 1987 or B. Barth 1994). This is as true of imperial Germany as of the republics of Weimar and Bonn; it is also true of National Socialism, which 'bridled' capitalism – in the twofold sense of 'restraining' it and 'putting it to use' – by placing itself at the helm of the capitalist dynamic and pacifying workers through public provision of employment and 'welfare policies'. However, to shape capitalism politically is not to overcome it (*MECW* 43, pp. 68–9). For Marx, such efforts to impose a certain political form are part and parcel of capitalism; they follow a logic that is in no way 'beyond' capitalism (Beck 1983). Bismarck was closer to the insights of classical economy than Oppenheimer, for whom instances of state intervention were nothing but distortions.

32. See Dahrendorf 1968, p. 49.

33. 'Social legislation on health, accident and disability insurance, as well as on old-age security... was accompanied by laws on occupational safety and factory inspections' (Baier 1988, p. 48). This significantly improved the condition of the working classes, and it did so in ways that ran contrary to the interests of trade and industry. See Wehler 1985, 1979; Kocka 1986, 1990; Metzler 2003. This development ought not, however, to be interpreted as a new, 'moral' stage of capitalism.

34. Marx already criticised this idea in Proudhon and the Left Ricardians (*MECW* 6, pp. 105 ff., 143–4; *MECW* 28, p. 180; *MECW* 32, pp. 373 ff.; see also Rakowitz 2000, pp. 53 ff.; below, 3.3.4).

Concrete observations on society entered into direct competition with the explanatory patterns of a theory, and so the theory was dropped. We already noted this development in Bernstein (see section 2.1.1). But how does such an unfortunate relationship of competition come about? The answer to the question of how observations are to be related to theory depends on the theory applied. In the neoclassical paradigm, the relationship between surface phenomena and 'essence', or empirical facts and theory, is configured differently than in Marx. In the neoclassical paradigm, utility-maximising individual interests are treated as the basis of the economy as a whole.

However, relating this theoretical model to the reality one encounters is quite difficult, for reality consists of much more than harmonious exchanges between subjective 'interests'. Here, the analysis of surface phenomena is scarcely related to the model theory; given appearances are simply *legitimated*.[35] By contrast, Marx's theory seeks to *explain* appearances. This is why it also makes reference to phenomena that are not immediately apparent: contexts, correlations, relations of dependency, movements and their trends. Marx's theory calls for the interpretation of given phenomena by means of the successive introduction of intermediate terms, until a coherent explanation of the overall development, of essence *and* appearance, has been formulated.[36] In the process, one's interpretation of what one is able to observe directly may change. It is only by means of this cleavage between observation and theory that one can be related to the other; this is what constitutes their dialectic.[37] Thus theory and the empirical facts are disjunctive in both economic theories, but it is only in neoclassical theory that they are wholly unconnected. Those who believe they can refute Marx by means of simple observations are implicitly alleging that *he, too,* is operating on the basis of the neoclassical model.

Now, Marxist sociology has often suffered from a lack of such 'mediation'.[38] Yet Marx's theoretical approach should not be reduced to such attempts. Marx's approach requires one to ground analysis of an economic society's surface phenomena in a comprehensive analysis of the capitalist economy; the comprehensive analysis is undertaken before one

---

See the concept of 'freeland' in Gesell 1958. Alexander Rüstow still cherished such agrarian utopias in 1957 (Jonas 1976, Vol. 2, p. 216).

35. One could, in fact, justify any given situation in this way: by formulating an ex post 'explanation' of it in terms of the 'utility considerations' of the individuals involved (3.2.2, 3.3.3). The situation then appears as one that has been desired by the (homogeneous) individuals themselves. Disadvantages are traced back either to the personal negligence of individuals (disinformation, inflexibility, immobility, and so on) or to external influences. Such a theory is largely immune to facts.

36. Bubner 1972, p. 71.

37. Thus phenomena such as the 'fetishism' of the commodity (*MECW* 35, pp. 83–4) and of money (*MECW* 37, pp. 389–90) become explicable, as do pseudo-explanations such as the claim that price increases are caused by wage increases (*MECW* 20, pp. 137–8). Systems theory still benefits parasitically from the fact that this disjunction once proved fertile, namely in Marx.

38. See Masaryk 1964, Adler 1930 or the 'class analyses' in Haug 1970, Ritsert 1973, Tjaden 1973, PKA 1973 ff., IMFS 1973 ff., Bischoff 1976; for critical responses, see Kostede 1974 and Krämer 1983. Rather than deriving them from the statistical material itself, these authors impose their concepts of class upon that material.

engages with the specific configurations that exist at a given time. Marx would have viewed sociology as one *element* of a developed political economy, rather than as an unrelated supplement.[39] He would have looked upon in-depth engagement with sociological issues not as a rival pursuit, but as a welcome concretisation of political economy. Sociology becomes 'bourgeois' in the pejorative sense only when it treats the negative aspects of modern capitalism as factors that are not economically determined, but that impede the laws of the economy and need to be understood *independently* of them. Such sociology replaces analysis of a *single* social totality (which has many advantages, but also considerable disadvantages) with a radical rupture, the nature of which can be ideal-typically and approximately described as follows. Those contemporary phenomena that are *good* are due to the market economy; sociology has no business looking into economic laws, which are the object of economic theory (an economic theory that is also bourgeois, that is, neoclassical). Those phenomena that are bad are due to something *other* than the economy, and constitute the object of sociology.

This basic operation was necessary so that it would henceforth be possible to engage in sociology *instead of* engaging in political economy.[40] Sociology's privileged objects of inquiry now included such factors as morality and religion, power and domination, milieux, lifestyle and culture, or even rationality 'as such'. It was assumed that pathogenetic analyses of these factors could yield insight into the causes of social ills. Thus Weber and Michels examined the logic of what they perceived to be a bloated bureaucracy and the instrumental rationality that manifested itself within that bureaucracy.[41] Comte[42] and Durkheim[43] examined society's forces of emotional cohesion, which they considered to be at risk and which they saw as having to effect a 'moral' transition from traditional mechanical to 'organic solidarity'.[44] In a similar way, Tönnies[45] presented a 'community' [*Gemeinschaft*] that was, by definition, non-economic, as the ideological counterpart to a cold 'society'.[46] Simmel examined the effects of cultural milieux on the

39. See *MECW* 37, pp. 870–1; see also 2.4.6. Section 2.3.5 demonstrated the social relevance of various theories, such as theories of inflation or the rate of profit. Bourgeois theories trace these phenomena back to wages, thereby effecting a direct translation of the class struggle into theoretical terms. Marx provides far more nuanced explanations.

40. Comte thought of sociology as the 'science of stabilisation' (Lieber 1985, p. 52; Spaemann 1998). He meant to use funds from the budget of the economics department to pay for his chair of sociology (Lepenies 1985, p. 19).

41. See Foucault 1972, Michels 1978, Weber 1984, pp. 3–4. Within this fixation on the state, the separation of state and society (Kramm 1979, Koslowski 1982) that Jonas took to be constitutive of sociology was to a considerable extent revoked theoretically.

42. Comte 1830.

43. Durkheim 1994.

44. See Joas 2000.

45. Tönnies 1979.

46. See Walzer 1983.

'lifestyle' of modern individuals[47] and lamented the 'tragedy of culture', which consisted, in his view, in people failing to live up to their inventions 'subjectively'.[48]

As a 'subsystem', the economy ceases to appear other than as part of hyphenated sociological terms.[49] It is true that the sociological theories mentioned were sometimes quite critical of their surroundings: they gave rise to insights that are still topical today.[50] But they all share the feature of focusing on how the economic process is politically and culturally *embedded* – despite the fact that economic theory had ceased to address the social aspects of economic activity.[51] It seemed that if one succeeded in making improvements to this extra-economic field, the economic process would bring about improvements in social conditions as if by itself. While it was not immediately apparent, the neoclassical paradigm diffused into sociology to such an extent that the disadvantages that are structurally immanent to capitalism were blanked out. The object of inquiry 'capitalism' slipped through the gap between economic theory's and sociology's spheres of competence.[52]

---

47. Simmel 1950; see Bourdieu 1982.

48. Simmel 1916, p. 99; see Anders 1961. Lukács 1981, derided by scholars for its positive reference to Stalin, is an instructive work with regard to sociology. Lukács was familiar with the sociological scene, and once he had changed sides, he spared no one. In his trenchant diction, Lukács characterises the above-mentioned theorists as follows: Simmel 'proceeded in a radically subjectivist manner. What interested him in economics was only the subjective reflex of definite, economically conditioned situations' (p. 452; see Busch 2000). Tönnies 'volatilized concretely historical social formations into supra-historical "essences" '; 'the objective economic basis of the social structure was replaced by a subjective principle – the will' (p. 594; see Rudolph 1991). 'Weber's line of thought continually led him into ascribing to ideological (religious) phenomena, more and more strongly, an "immanent" development arising out of the phenomena themselves. Then this tendency was always so reversed that the phenomena received causal priority in respect of the entire process' (p. 604; Böckler 1987; see above).

49. Luhmann 1988, p. 8; Ulrich 2000.

50. Müller-Doohm situates Horkheimer within this context (Müller-Doohm 1991, p. 50; Lichtblau 1997, p. 44; Schäfer 1994). German critical theory is an offshoot of classical sociology, not of Marxism. It processed Weber's hypothesis on rationalisation and Simmel's 'tragedy of culture' as well as Spengler and Bergson, but not Marx's economic theory (see section 2.6.1).

51. Zinn 1987, p. 115, speaks of 'neoclassical theory's socio-theoretical dilution of bourgeois economic theory'; see Bürgin 1993. This is to overlook the view that taking note of contemporary economic theory could have rendered intellectuals immune to fascist tendencies (a view widely endorsed at a conference in Jena: see Kodalle 2000). Even those writers who did engage with economic theory failed to learn anything meaningful about their time.

52. German sociology, in particular, lost its grasp on its object of inquiry (Jonas 1976, Vol. 2, pp. 167 ff., 220, 239; Eickelpasch 1987, Schwinn 2001). Schelsky considered sociology to be both an 'empirical science that engages in the analysis of functions' (Schelsky 1959, p. 19), although it knows ever more about ever less, and a form of 'social philosophy' that seeks to establish a 'universal context of meaning' (p. 21), although it fails to do more than rehash 'the unquestionable residual values of so-called Western society, or more precisely of Western European and American society' (p. 23). He traced this dualism back to sociology's origins in 'economics and philosophy' (p. 12). Schelsky considered the absent centre to consist in the theme of 'subjectivity and the institutions' (p. 105). Yet this 'state-philosophical' consideration also left a lacuna: in circling the empty centre, it started from the points of view of the individual and the state. 'Sociological theory either exhausts itself in the process – important, to be sure – of clarifying meta-theoretical issues and/or constructing and

The resulting 'loss of the object' was even felt within sociology itself, although sociologists did not quite know how to interpret it. Dahrendorf ventured the explanation 'that many German sociologists lack a social model because, as citizens, they have no proper image of society'.[53] Schelsky and Adorno shifted the causes of theoretical impoverishment to real history.[54] Even today, authors associated with their theories believe that sociology's 'loss of the object' is to be explained not in terms of the theoretical deficits of their own discipline, but in terms of real transformations – a case of overhastily drawing conclusions about reality on the basis of theory.[55]

Before inquiring into the consequences that such a 'loss of the object', suffered by an entire discipline, has for that discipline (2.4.3), it is worth reflecting on how this anti-sociological transformation of sociology became possible (2.4.2). This transformation has become second nature to sociologists, to the extent that they seldom problematise this aspect of their own theoretical history. Why we can do no more than conjecture.

2.4.2 *Whence the predominance of the neoclassical approach in sociology?*

'It is the Marxian system which has formed the central focus of the German discussion of capitalism'.[56] However, the reception of Marx left much to be desired. A more comprehensive reception of Marx would probably have led to a different situation for sociological theory in Germany.[57]

---

reconstructing general systems of concepts, or it disintegrates into the particularism of specialised sociological research fields and limits itself, within the domain of practically oriented empirical research, to the narrow horizon of definite, heterogeneous projects' (Müller-Doohm 1991, p. 50). 'The playground of topical, feature-column cultural criticism on the one hand – and data production for the purposes of short-term planning on the other' (p. 52; see, too, p. 89).

53. Dahrendorf 1959, p. 144; see, too, Dahrendorf 1968, p. 7.

54. 'The irrationality of today's social structure prevents its rational exposition in theory. Society's regression is paralleled by that of the thoughts devoted to it' (Adorno 1976a, pp. 359–60). Schelsky, the seeker of reality (Üner 1994) speaks of man's 'loss of reality' (Schelsky 1979, pp. 394 ff.). 'Not a single work of recent German sociology attempts to depict our society "as a whole"' (Schelsky 1959, p. 149). The classics, it has been argued, did engage in such attempts (Habermas 1984–7, Vol. 1, p. 20). Müller-Doohm vacillates between lamenting this loss (Müller-Doohm 1991, p. 60) and presenting it as inevitable (p. 56; see Giesen 1991).

55. It is 'determined by the state of the object realm, by social reality itself and/or by the general condition of the epoch' (Müller-Doohm 1991, p. 71). Paradoxically, to say this is to implicitly claim a knowledge about one's object – even though the point is to demonstrate the impossibility of such knowledge. This view rests on an ontologisation of theoretical models: no distinction is made between real and theoretical objects. Thus the loss of the theoretical object is traced back to a development within the given reality. Bude 1988 draws attention to this non sequitur: 'Here, the social is taken to be the most general determination of the object [?] of sociology' (p. 119). One symptom of this consists in the tendency to formulate inflationary definitions of society 'as such', on the basis of random observations (Schulze 1992, Kneer 1997, 2001, Ponks 1999 ff.).

56. Parsons 1968, p. 488.

57. König 1987, pp. 343 ff. suggests that such a development occurred from 1928 onward, and that it was induced mainly by Karl Mannheim. The role played by the reception of Marx is elided altogether in Jonas 1976, Vol. 2, an otherwise critical analysis of 'sociology in Germany' (see

Clarifying underlying economic background assumptions would have been especially important. How are we to understand the fact that nothing of the kind was done during German sociology's formative period, a time when Marx was the object of much debate? Aside from the *theoretical* filiations explored in the present philosophical work, one could give socio-historical reasons. Dirk Kaesler has specified the social background of early German sociology: the milieux of the 'property-owning bourgeoisie', the 'Jewish community' and 'socialism'.[58] If sociology were to examine itself (in terms of the sociology of knowledge),[59] it would have to identify the reasons why none of these groups managed a more comprehensive reception of Marx: 'choosing' Marx, and hence a different representation of society than that of neoclassical theory, would have entailed considerable social disadvantages. What reservations might the milieux identified by Kaesler have had about Marx?

The *property-owning bourgeoisie* enjoys obvious advantages over other social strata, due to its economic power.[60] According to Marx's economic theory, poorer social groups remain relatively poor not because of their laziness or stupidity, but because of the very same mechanisms that make the property-owning bourgeois wealthy. Members of the property-owning bourgeoisie will not be able to accept this theory without going through some conflict. Exceptions, such as Horkheimer, confirm this rule. Other sons of industrialists, such as Simmel and Rathenau, took note of Marx but limited the impact of his theories by adding to them an intellectual foundation.[61] The *Jewish community*,

---

pp. 160–254). According to Kaesler 1981, the Tönnies/Von Wiese 'duo' sabotaged such tendencies for decades. Hence if the new development was interrupted in 1933, this was due not to the discipline's internal exhaustion, as suggested by Schelsky ('the tunes had all been played, and the opposing positions were beginning to rigidify': Schelsky 1959, p. 37; see Jonas 1976, Vol. 2, p. 216; Hans Joas was still leaving out the 1920s in a lecture delivered in New York in 1996; see Joas 1993), but rather to the active elimination of Marxist theories by National Socialist sociologists.

58. Kaesler 1984; 1999, p. 16.

59. Conservatives have often warned against this (Schelsky 1959, pp. 5 ff.; see Meja 1982, Vol. 2). Everything remains on the level of conjecture. Without further ado, Müller-Doohm 1991 turns the sociological necessity of speaking about oneself into a virtue (p. 56). But this is not very convincing, since he goes on to lament said necessity (p. 60; see, too, p. 51).

60. Economic power is associated with a higher standard of living; generally speaking, it is also associated with a greater ability to survive crises (due to the diversification of capital assets) and a power to command the labour-power of others. According to Bourdieu 1984, this implies greater social capital (connections, influence) and greater cultural capital (education and reliably sound judgement in matters of taste, style and bearing, something that greatly improves one's chances as a newcomer to the labour market; see Eder 1989, Gall 1989, Milner 1999, Hartmann 2002). Heilbronner also embellishes Marx's analysis socio-phenomenologically, pointing out that wealth bestows not just power but also sex appeal (Heilbronner 1985, pp. 33 ff.).

61. Simmel meant to 'construct a new storey beneath historical materialism such that the explanatory value of the incorporation of economic life into the causes of intellectual culture is preserved, while these economic forms themselves are recognized as the result of more profound valuations and currents of psychological and even metaphysical pre-conditions' (Simmel 1978, p. 56; Rathenau expressed a similar intention, as did Freyer, notwithstanding the fact that the latter was neither a Jew nor a child of the property-owning bourgeoisie. On Simmel's 'depth', see Lukács 1981, p. 452; Lenk 1986, p. 15; on Schütz, see Jonas 1976, Vol. 2, p. 215). The following remarks by non-

which was struggling for political equality, kept its distance from the Social Democrats, who also had a marginal position in society and were also treated with hostility, for reasons of political prudence.[62] The theoretical origin of *socialist* statism lay in the socialist reception of Marx, which has been described above (see sections 2.1 to 2.3). This reception involved the socialists coming surprisingly close to an ethical condemnation of Marx. One 'opted' only for the other side, in order then to struggle on the state front (this was as true of Lenin as it was of Bernstein); and if one did not struggle with the state, then one struggled against it, like the New Left, one of sociology's key clients. Even for socialists affiliated with political parties, making reference to Marx was dangerous: Social Democrats ran the risk of being labelled obstinately orthodox, whereas for Communists the danger was that of being seen as Marxological revisionists.[63]

Two examples can help show just how consequential more serious engagement with Marx could be for sociologists. Werner Sombart struggled for some time to find employment because his thought had initially moved in a Marxist direction.[64] And Karl Mannheim managed to fall between two stools, so that he was attacked by bourgeois and Marxist theorists at the same time – the attacks were fierce, even if the arguments were spurious.[65] It seems likely that he had touched a sore point – the 'problem of Marxism'.[66] Bourgeois theorists rejected Mannheim for not being idealist enough; they considered him too 'Marxist' (this was the view of Wiese and Tönnies, Curtius, Plessner, Arendt, and Jonas: a panorama of the thought of the time). And yet Mannheim's sociology of knowledge[67] had done little more than ask whether Marxism might be an ideology – an operation that had in many ways been provoked by the Marxism of the period.[68]

---

sociologists are also revealing: 'Marx's passion seems to me impure at its root, itself unjust from the outset, drawing its life from the negative, without an image of man, the hate incarnate of a pseudo-prophet in the style of Ezechiel . . . I can't see anything else in him but an "evil" person' (Karl Jaspers on 7 January 1951, in Arendt and Jaspers 1992, p. 163). 'A strange scientific superstitition has taken the place of wit . . . Marxism – the absence of wit!' (Landauer 1967, pp. 76, 93; see below).

62. Mosse 1985, p. 108; Berlin 1979, p. 244. Jews did not find much favour with socialists either (Silberner 1983, Heid 1982). From 1933 onward, the German Jews could not but see the repression to which they were subjected as originating in the state (Schoenberner 1991, Karady 1999).

63. Beyer 1968.

64. Sombart 1894 had been praised by Engels personally: *MECW* 37, p. 881; see Appel 1992, pp. 133 ff. On Sombart, see also Pollock 1926, Lenger 1994, J. Backhaus 2000. He says retrospectively about his first years as a civil servant, and in defense of Mannheim: 'I was a Marxist at the time and needed freedom from value judgements in order to be able to continue working as a Prussian civil servant' (quoted in Kaesler 1984, p. 390). The Social Democrat Robert Michels suffered a fate similar to Sombart's, a fact that greatly angered Max Weber (Ringer 1987, p. 133).

65. See Mcja 1982, Vol. 2; Lepenies 1985, pp. 380 ff.; König 1987, pp. 353 ff.; Hoeges 1994.

66. König 1987, p. 354.

67. Mannheim 1936.

68. On the one hand, many claims and actions of the Communists were, indeed, questionable (see 2.2.2). On the other hand, Lenin, Gramsci and others had themselves declared Marxism to be an ideology (Eagleton 1993, pp. 107, 139; Lenin 1973, p. 50; cf. 2.1.4, 2.2.4, 2.6.1). 'Historical materialism both can and must be applied to itself' (Lukács 1971, p. 228). It could no longer simply be taken for granted.

Of course, a theory that is itself in question cannot be used to answer questions (see section 1.4.1). If Mannheim wanted to avoid the usual dogmatism, he had no choice but to refrain sceptically from hypotheses on the economic background of a particular class position – he went no further than the sociology of the time, stopping at consideration of the lifestyles and world pictures specific to certain milieux.[69] Thus the accusation levelled at Mannheim was off the mark. But it had an effect, nevertheless – some mud always sticks. Mannheim had provided a platform on which to put aside one's partisan differences in order to allow for *theoretical* engagement. Instead of using the opportunity to demonstrate, for once, that their 'superior' theory was, indeed, superior, many Marxists (Neurath, Lukács and Horkheimer; see section 2.6.1) attacked him for being so 'idealist' as not to declare from the outset that Marxism was right. Only Lewalter[70] seemed to see through the situation: Mannheim's sociology of knowledge might have been turned into a more sophisticated Marxism, if only the right arguments had been formulated.[71] But the mere fact that Mannheim displayed a certain *affinity* for Marx was sufficient to isolate him completely, at least for a while.

2.4.3 *Normativity as a placeholder for incomplete worldviews*

The neoclassical economic model naturalises the economy, as if it were a 'mechanism' entirely distinct from us.[72] When the social, which remains in the form of a residuum, is then regarded by the human sciences as a 'normative frame', the two levels are separated not just insofar as each falls within the province of a different discipline, but also with regard to the theory of validity: one side can be examined separately from the other.[73]

69. Barboza 2002.

70. Lewalter 1982.

71. Mannheim's 'reservations about Marxism are ultimately purely scepticist – subtract them (and Mannheim himself explicitly rejected scepticism) and what remains is an embellished but essentially 'Marxist' position. German sociology's path has led from Dilthey to Scheler only to arrive at Marx after all' (Lewalter 1982, pp. 579–80) – not quite, one should add, but certainly in a latent way. Since Mannheim was not primarily concerned with rehabilitating Marxism, and focused on altogether different issues during his exile, his interpreters continue to agree that his positions ought to be rejected; on this point, Stalinists such as Lukács 1981 (and, following him, K. Lenk 1986) agree with conservatives such as Jonas 1976.

72. It is not the search for 'laws' governing society that should be criticised, but the fact that these laws are equated with those governing nature (which is understood in a determinist sense). 'When social behaviour is interpreted in the manner of the "natural" sciences, the question of social integration remains wholly unaddressed – precisely *because* the interpretation is formulated in the manner of the "natural" sciences' (Jonas 1976, Vol. 1, p. 249, on Bentham; p. 259, on Spencer; p. 264, on Saint-Simon; pp. 270–1, on Comte: 'The attempt to establish sociology as a natural science did not mean that delusion was subordinated to observation; this was what Comte had intended, but the ideal was not realised any more than in utilitarianism. On the contrary, observation was subordinated to delusion').

73. 'The social as such' is 'the logical act of reason' (Spann 1903, p. 589). 'All society is mind and all mind is society' (Sombart 1936, quoted in Kaesler 1984, p. 425; see Freyer 1998; Lukács 1981, p. 348; see also Nörr 1994 and Acham 1995; on mentalisation, see 2.5.2).

This allows for a number of positions: one can declare either side to be more important, 'prior' to the other or even the only one, and in posing different questions, one can arrive at different results (see 2.4.1). The totality of these different theories can then be called 'relativism' or 'pluralism'. From Marx's perspective, *both* sides need to be criticised – not for mysterious dialectical (or 'philosophical') reasons, but because his analysis of the economy adheres to a different scientific standard. Ignorance of this alternative social theory, paired with eloquence, is a remarkably persistent feature of the science of society.[74] And it was precisely because of the lack of a comprehensive analysis that 'ethics' was increasingly brought in. Early sociologists felt challenged by pressing social issues on the one hand, and by an economic theory that was coherent but out of touch with reality on the other. It was no accident that their inquiries were labelled 'moral science' (in Spencer, Durkheim, Simmel and others). Comte criticised the methodological individualism and the 'coldness' of political economy in a way that was reminiscent of the historical school of economic theory.[75]

Yet this 'normative critique' of the economy entailed a loss of the theoretical object 'economy' (see sections 2.3.4, 3.2.3). Efforts to improve on existing economic analyses were few and far between (with the exception of Sismondi).[76] Instead, one turned to *other* objects, said to have been inadequately grasped by economics, and to be capable of 'directing' the economy, if the need arose; one such object was the ethical state. This has changed little over the decades. The projection of anonymous structural laws onto tangible entities such as the state or the disposition of individuals has coalesced in existentialism. The major counter-hypothesis developed by structuralism, the 'death of the subject', dealt a powerful blow to this personalism, but at the cost of falling into the opposite extreme of a subjectless processuality of power or 'meaning'. Foucault focused on the sphere of power, whose natural centre is the state, as well as on pathologies such as madness, suffered by individuals when there is too much power. Sociological categories remained as centred on ethics and politics as before, and even the economy itself was analysed in terms of *domination*.[77]

---

74. Lange still reproaches Marx for his putative 'idea of unity' (Lange 1980, p. 133). This is to dismiss as a mere 'idea' the complex character of Marx's analyses and their understanding of society as a complex structure of relations. The economy, that is, the logic that governs this structure of relations, is not considered in Lange's conceptual analyses.

75. See König 1958, pp. 308–9; Morel 1999, p. 14; for criticisms, see Deppe 1971, pp. 11–12, Fisching 1993.

76. See Jonas 1976, Vol. 1, p. 218.

77. Weber 1968, pp. 184 ff., adopts Knapp's 'victorious' state theory of money, developed in 1905. He describes rational economic activity as involving 'deliberate planning' (pp. 62, 69–70) and speaks of a 'power of control and disposal' [*Verfügungsgewalt*] (p. 67), 'regulation of the market' (p. 82), 'power' (p. 110) and 'organization' (p. 165; see Rehberg 1979). His brother Alfred worked on the sociology of the state (A. Weber 1927). Important periodicals were called *Zeitschrift für die gesamte Staatswissenschaft* ('Journal for State Science in its Entirety') or *Der Staat* ('The State'), whereas Hilferding's magazine was called *Die Gesellschaft* ('Society'). In 1935, Mannheim proclaimed the 'age of planning'. Freyer thought of the class struggle as a 'tension within domination'

Yet for the political superstructure to be thought of as autochthonous, the neoclassical paradigm has to remain valid. Thus a two-level model is presupposed: an automatically functioning *system* provides the base for an unrelated normative 'superstructure'. (The hierarchy may be reversed, so that 'spirit' is considered 'basic'). It was not Marx who advocated such a model; the first to advocate it were his normative *critics* – as when Max Weber examines society by means of the 'subjective meaning' of the participants (see section 2.4.6).[78] Both of the two diametrically opposed schools that developed out of Weber's approach adopted this dualist model. Parsons provided sociology with a methodological model comparable to that of neoclassical economics and adopted many of neoclassical theory's features. In his famous 1937 work,[79] he even starts out directly not just from Weber and Durkheim, but also from the economists Marshall and Pareto. The economy slips through the gap between the ethically understood 'freedom' of the individual and a structure that is thought of as 'order', and construed in a manner analogous to the neoclassical approach – and once the economy is lost, everything that might give rise to conflict and institutional change also disappears.[80] The 'social integration'

[*Herrschaftsspannung*] (Freyer 1930, p. 234). The 'conflict of domination' [*Herrschaftskonflikt*] is central to Dahrendorf 1959a, where, in a context of consummate de-economisation, every interest group constitutes a class, even rabbit breeders. A complementary politicisation of the economy (for a late example, see Habermas 1984–7) was evident in so-called 'radical' economics, which spoke of 'domination' by monopolies or the state or of 'regimes of accumulation' (Arestis 1994). Thus the left had also forgotten about economics. This is reflected in films such as *Orden für die Wunderkinder* or Fassbinder's *Welt am Draht*, as well as in the ultra-Left obsession of seeing 'fascism' at work everywhere. The situation was similar in France: poststructuralism's origins within a specific Marxism are hardly to be overlooked (Milner 1999, pp. 121 ff.; 1.4.2). Schiwy 1969 and 1978 examine a revealing intermediate stage on the path to postmodernity, the 'New Philosophers', who were openly anti-Marxist: see Frank 1984, Frank 1993, Ferry 1987; Taureck 1990. It is revealing that works from this theoretical context always use the phrase 'the politics of…' (identity, difference, and so on; see Barett 1991, Taylor 1992).

78. Habermas also rigidly separates the forces of production from the relations of production (see section 3.1.3). Marx's heuristic 'base-superstructure' concept precisely did not allow for the autonomy of either of the two spheres (A. Maihofer 1992; see section 3.2 below). Here, the 'frame' is not provided by the 'normative' structure, but by the real structure, from which norms develop in the first place.

79. Parsons 1968.

80. The model of a 'system' that is always already in a state of equilibrium derives from neoclassical economics. Parsons 1968 considers the neoclassical model to be part of an overarching model of practical reason, which however is also based on utility calculi (Joas 1992, pp. 225–6; Esser 1999). Harmonism would go on to become even more dominant later, in systems theory (Parsons 1951; Luhmann 1995, pp. 488 ff.). The fact that Coser 1956, Dahrendorf 1959a and others responded to this by introducing the theme of 'conflict' is symptomatic. They did not do so with any ulterior motives of the 'Marxist' sort (see Gouldner 1970, Krysmanski 1971). Parsons's attempt to mediate between the micro and the macro level is Hegelian. Hegel also operated on the basis of an ultimately harmonious analysis of the economy, assuming that the economy's external consecutive effects would be compensated for by the state. But is it sociologically meritorious to define away the actual object of one's analyses?

of individuals[81] is achieved by means of 'values' – the 'normative', not the economic kind, of course.

Even class stratification, which the neoclassical perspective elided, is explained ethically by Parsons: the 'central criterion of the ranking involved in stratification' is the 'moral evaluation' of individuals, he writes.[82] The only economic criterion retained in the analysis of social stratification, the hierarchy of incomes, is not only given an *ex post* ethical legitimation; it is also given an *ex ante* ethical *explanation.* Parsons claims that this hierarchy corresponds, on the whole, to direct valuation – those workers who rank highest normatively will also be the best paid. This is to stand the matter on its head: no one except for pop stars is rich because they are respected; as a rule, one is respected when and because one is rich.[83]

This quietist view of the economy was adopted not just by Niklas Luhmann, but also, from the 1970s onward, by Jürgen Habermas. In his writings, the economy is strangely inactive (see section 3.1). Habermas comes from the *other* school that developed out of Weber's approach, critical theory (2.6). Critical theory inherited the dualism that we have identified, insofar as it does not genuinely return to the lost Marxian theme, even if it speaks frequently about it. Critical theory discusses cultural aspects such as aesthetics, authority and the family, anti-Semitism, the dominance of 'instrumental reason' – in brief: moral pathologies of everyday life. But in so doing, it also starts from the reductive model of economic activity that has little connection to reality as it is actually experienced. While this model now *invoked* Marx, it also adopted many features of neoclassical theory (2.6.2). Ralf Dahrendorf, a precursor of the ethicised critique of systems theory, was also a former associate of the Institute of Social Research. The theory of conflict that he proposed as an alternative to the harmonism of systems theory was normativistic as well. Dahrendorf followed Marx in holding that social change occurs by means of group conflicts.[84] But he stops at the observation that groups cohere primarily in normative ways, and treats this as an explanation.[85] In a development that would later

81. Lockwood 1970.

82. Parsons 1940, p. 70; see Heimann 1926. Parsons went to university in Germany.

83. 'Money's properties are my – the possessor's – properties and essential powers. Thus, what I *am* and *am capable of* is by no means determined by my individuality... Money is the supreme good, therefore its possessor is good... I am therefore presumed honest' (*MECW* 3, 324). Parsons's critique of Marx explicitly rejects the labour theory of value (Parsons 1968, pp. 107 ff.; see Weber 1968, pp. 63–4). 'Parsons' functionalist theory of stratification vindicates... relations that quite obviously exist in reality. This is ideological insofar as the existing inequalities of American society are not denied but... buttressed scientifically, as a functional necessity' (Krämer 1983, p. 59; see section 3.2.1 below).

84. Dahrendorf 1959a.

85. 'Human society always means that the behaviour of humans... is regulated by unmistakable, i.e. consolidated expectations. The binding character of these... norms is due to the effect of sanctions' (Dahrendorf 1967, p. 368). This description of norms would no doubt be rejected by stauncher normativists – because it is still formulated from an 'observer's perspective', that is, it is 'regularist' (Brandom 1994, pp. 26 ff.). But is the key question not where these 'norms' originate (Krämer 1983, p. 66)?

also be evident in Habermas, Dahrendorf's efforts to develop a theoretical countermodel brought him closer to functionalism.[86]

In a case of contrasting monisms, systems theory treated the micro level as a mere effluence of the system, while the works of critical theory were spiced up with hints of its former economic theory. Yet both started from the same dualist model; they simply focused on different aspects of it.[87] When one presupposes the dualism of pure laws and adulterating epiphenomena, one is forced sooner or later to *decide*, in one's efforts to explain the ills of the present, between one of the two 'contending gods' (Max Weber). In most cases, the decision has 'always-already' been made by one's social background and position, and one will try to justify the decision ethically. When sociology is thus treated as a normative theory, the transition into prescriptive ethics is fluent.[88] Sociologists tend to treat ethics with reverence, even when they do not explicitly refer to it. Both the diagnoses of one or the other form of social anomie and the remedies proposed are ultimately ethical, no matter with which interpretation of the model we are dealing.[89] Conservative proponents of the 'retentive forces' tend toward an ethics of the 'moral life' [*Sittlichkeit*]. The underlying assumption is that 'modernity', meaning modern *society*,

---

86. Dahrendorf 1967a announces an 'essential correction' of his position, namely the conversion of two perspectives (domination and integration) into one: stratification, he argues, is 'simply a consequence of the structure of domination, whereas integration is a special case of coercion' (p. 27; see Schelsky 1979, p. 391; Krysmanski 1971, pp. 137 ff.).

87. The empirical research being conducted at the same time (with a clear focus on opinion polling) was far removed from the themes discussed in the prose of the sociologists. In the course of the controversy over the purpose of sociology, René König spoke (disparagingly) of empirical 'fellaheens'; Schelsky 1959 spoke of the 'accuracy of a knowledge of banalities'. Of course, both of them also engaged in empirical research (even Adorno did this); the problem was simply that there was no link between empirical and theoretical work. 'Empirical research and humanitarian pathos are . . . the two poles that German postwar sociology revolves around', two poles that 'confront one another as strangers' (Jonas 1976, Vol. 2, p. 239; see, too, p. 280). Systems theory followed in the footsteps of 'pure' or 'formal' sociology, which existed side-by-side with empirical research in Simmel and Tönnies (pp. 167, 171, 202). Jonas distinguishes between three fractional parts of sociology: 'empirical research, theory and cultural philosophy' (p. 168). Empirical research and systems theory share a sociological habitus, the 'pursuit of security, the search for a terrain upon which one can move unchallenged while feeling at the same time that one is re-establishing one's connection to sociology's history' (p. 238).

88. In the work of Carl Schmitt and Hans Freyer, Max Weber's analysis of the normative becomes a prescriptive theory in its own right: 'The economy is unruly and must be seized more firmly' (Freyer 1925, p. 177; see, too, Freyer 1931; Schmitt 2005 and 1932). The living state is expected to abolish the dead economy ('overcoming of class antagonisms'; 1930, p. 306). He goes back from Marx to Hegel (Lichtheim 1971), from social theory to the philosophy of the state and to ethics. A more recent example of this is Foucault, whose last work was an ethics of the self (Foucault 1990). Following Foucault, Bude also arrives at the conclusion that sociology, devoid of an object, ultimately becomes ethics (Bude 1988, p. 113; see, too, Müller-Doohm 1991, pp. 83 ff.). Beck 2000 also diagnoses sociology's lack of an object (because of the 'disappearance' of the nation state: pp. 23–4, 162–3); in the end, he has nothing to offer but normative advice.

89. See Parsons's ethics of class. Comte considered sociology a sort of technique of domination, employed for the purpose of preventing conflict: '*voir pour savoir, savoir pour prévoir, prévoir pour prévenir*' (quoted in Müller-Doohm 1991, p. 48).

cannot create its own foundations.[90] In this view, the cause of modern ills has always been seen to lie in bourgeois society's orientation toward progress.

The possible salvation from growing economisation is seen to lie in putatively *non*-economic forces. These forces, which are welcomed and 'ethicised', can be of various kinds (see section 2.4.1).[91] A subset of these conservative theorists holds that the economy, understood in neoclassical terms, is not stable. These theorists fear more than merely cultural decline; they believe the stability of the economy is at risk. The remedy they propose is that of boosting the economy, or maintaining its momentum, by means of extra-economic factors; this approach was eventually institutionalised in the form of the 'social market economy'.[92] Even this German variant of Keynesianism rests on a neoclassical foundation. The morality advocated is limited to the *political* cultivation and preservation of the 'framework' and the 'entrepreneurial spirit' (see 3.3.4). Both efforts are opposed by radical proponents of the Enlightenment who consider traditional milieux and political regulation to be nothing but obstacles to reason or growth, and hence a cause of possible grievances. They advocate an ethics of self-responsibility, of economic 'liberty' and autonomy – the notion of 'Me Incorporated' ('Everyone his own entrepreneur': 3.3.3).[93] This counter-ethics culminates in Max Weber's call to endure the

90. Hence the Schmittian paradox of Böckenförde 1991, p. 112 (2.6.6). Schumpeter 1943 extended this paradox ('in opposition to Marx': Jonas 1976, Vol. 2, p. 235) by arguing that capitalism is not only unable to legitimate itself but also increasingly destroys its own foundation (Offe 1974, Habermas 1976a).

91. One might speak of an 'ethics of self-renunciation' (Bude 1988, p. 114), which is, however, addressed only to other members of society. On sociological conservatism, see Jonas 1976, Vol. 1, pp. 117 ff., 283 ff.; Klages 1972; on political conservatism, see Mannheim 1986, Greiffenhagen 1971, Schildt 1998. We already encounter this sort of thinking in the estates-based enemies of the French Revolution, who presented either the aristocracy and the monarchy (Edmund Burke and Malthus) or the peasants (Adam Müller and the land reform movement) as the 'better' side. This current runs from Hegel, who thought of the putatively extra-economic state as the ultimate embodiment of morality, to Comte and his priesthood of sociologists (Lieber 1985, p. 52), from Comte to the National Socialist Heidegger, who glimpsed in the telluric forces of 'the movement' an opportunity to 'master' the 'leaderless' [*führerlos*] character of modern technology (Heidegger 2000), and from Heidegger to the new conservatives, who place their faith in the 'retentive forces' (Freyer 1955) of the state (Forsthoff 1971), the family (Schelsky 1955a), the Church (Nell-Breuning 1980), high culture (J. Ritter 1961) or the bond with nature (Gruhl 1978). The most recent expressions of this tendency are communitarianism (in theory; 3.2.3) and the new nationalism and fundamentalism (on the streets). Nominally, what unites these groups is their *externalism:* Their critique of capitalism is simplistic, because the forces invoked are stipulated, in a purely thetic manner, to be extra- or 'non-economic'. Given that the powers of former times (the aristocracy, the family, the community, the Church) also depended on an economic foundation, one should really say 'non-capitalist' – but in the majority of cases, this is hardly justified any longer.

92. 'Revisionist' socialists consider even distortions of the market a overcoming of capitalism to be welcomed (on Bernstein, see 2.1.2; on Hilferding, 2.2.6).

93. See Henning 2005a. This 'ethics of self-invention' (Bude 1988, p. 114), an aesthetic and simplistic 'self-realisation', is evident in a range of people, from the individualists Simmel and Beck to the agents of privatisation in the economy and in society (Baier 1988), but also in Habermas and Luhmann, who eliminate 'old European' remnants because they take them to be of no more than historic value. Simmel meant to combat the 'discordances of modern life' by developing 'subjective

present just as it 'is', namely just as it is perceived in the pure model, without succumbing to daydreams about yesterday or tomorrow.[94]

Finally, there is 'liberal', *neo*-normativistic 'state philosophy', which seems to share the hope expressed in the old normative state philosophy (the theory of natural law and contractualism), namely that domination, which must, after all, be personified somewhere, can be impressed by superior arguments. Armed with 'good reasons', these theorists try to convince the rulers to rule more normatively. By considering domination superfluous and even harmful, they also uphold the paradigm of the 'pure' laws of the market, even if they only do so implicitly (see 3.3.2).

Their critique of the idealisation of the past and future notwithstanding, both sociology-free economics and economics-free sociology take a markedly uncritical view of the forces at work in the present. *Wherever one looks*, an ethics is formulated; the activity of the social sciences now consists in producing comprehensive formulations of these ethics, providing them with a 'foundation' and exploring every detail of these foundations. However, such 'normative theories' have two blind spots. First, because of the dualism within which they operate, they can only ever critically examine one of the two sides. And even the attempt to grasp this one perspective may fail, because of the 'fissuring' of perspectives.[95] Second, normativity is merely a substitute for more concrete analyses. Behind political ethics, there lie concrete interests; when we 'translate' *one* of these ethics into sociological terms, giving it the form of a 'normative theory', we are still a long way from having formulated a sociological theory. Each of the two sides of the representation focuses on certain aspects of reality; we cannot make these aspects disappear simply by declaring one of the two sides superior and using a normative theory to justify the 'colonisation' of the other.[96] *Both* realities exist, and both ethics constitute real forces within those realities.

---

culture',for instance through education (Simmel 1957, p. 97, written in 1908; see also Simmel 1916). 'Objective culture' seems, then, to be just as it should be.

94. '[T]he prophet for whom so many of our younger generation yearn is not among us' (Weber 1972, p. 153). 'The morning cometh, but it is night still' (Weber 1972, p. 156 – note the echoes of *Isaiah* 21:12 and Nietzsche, but also of Weber's students Lukács and Bloch). Kracauer's attitude was similar. While he meant to sociologically access 'the new-old areas of divinely imbued reality' (Kracauer 1978, p. 11), he also believed this could be achieved only by awaiting them (see Wiggershaus 1988, pp. 67–70).

95. Jonas 1976, Vol. 2, p. 168.

96. Habermas 1984–7 gives both the system and the lifeworld its due, but finds fault with their mixture ratio. The inadmissible colonisation of the lifeworld is to be warded off by means of 'politicisation' (a position already anticipated in Habermas 1989, first published in 1962). What the content of this politicisation ought to be remains an open question. The norm-free 'subsystems' (the state and the economy) are described in rather positive terms, as long as they remain within their bounds – which, however, are illusory. Habermas 1999b begins to find the real lifeworld uncanny. The hegemonic contents of politics (the predominant idea of the nation state and patriotism) are now replaced by the rationalist constructs of 'deliberative democracy' and 'constitutional patriotism', which legitimate themselves purely by formal rules of procedure. The distinction between system and lifeworld is retracted. Thus the state and the economy, elements initially described as

A normative theory can neither penetrate the totality of reality nor 'transcend' it, since one of the two sides would always be left out. Following the example of Parsons,[97] Habermas[98] produced a 'socio-theoretical' synthesis; he was able to do this because both schools *share* the basic assumptions of the model and argue primarily in 'normative' terms, even if each does so from a different side. But a synthesis of erroneous developments does not produce new insights.[99] The gap created between economics and sociology and its replication in the division between systems theory and culturalism[100] cannot be bridged by an 'interdisciplinarity' that simply juxtaposes the two perspectives without genuinely relating them to one another. A thematic field that is not explored by either of the two sciences, nor by either of the two sociological schools, will not be grasped any better when the two are *combined*. To put this polemically: instead of being a sociology that is 'nothing but sociology',[101] this sociology tends, rather – and I am exaggerating slightly – to be 'nothing but ethics'.[102]

2.4.4 *The flaws are projected onto the symbolic figure Marx*

Transformed by the negative centre of force that was *Marx*, economic science exerted a decisive influence on the theoretical architecture of nascent sociology. Sociology then

---

systemic, are given an even more uncritical treatment. The lifeworld is no longer 'reconstructed' rationally, but patronised rationalistically (see 3.1.5).

97. Parsons 1968.

98. Habermas 1984–7.

99. Dilthey (2.5.2), Troeltsch (2.6.6), Von Wiese 1954 (pp. 111, 117), Mannheim 1964b and A. Weber 1927 all already struggled to achieve 'synthesis'. A. Weber constructed an eclectic sociology that dealt separately with civilisation, society and culture (this gives it a distant resemblance to the 'three worlds' of Habermas 1984–7, Vol. 1, pp. 76 ff.). This only renders permanent the theoretical elimination of the social embeddedness of the 'spheres'. The naturalism and technicism evident on one level are 'supplemented' by the consummate idealism evident on the other.

100. Sociology incorporates both perspectives. This could be described, in Luhmann's vocabulary, as a 're-entry' of difference into the system.

101. König 1958, p. 7.

102. Lichtblau 1997 shows how Nietzsche's influence was especially important in promoting the ethicisation of sociology. Tönnies was inspired by Nietzsche to become an active member of the 'Society for Ethical Culture' (p. 92; see Tönnies 1893; König 1984, p. 403), Simmel praised Nietzsche as the herald of a new ethos of lordliness (p. 100; see Simmel 1907, Lichtblau 1984a) and Weber's *Protestant Ethic* (Weber 2002) needs to be read as a sequel to the *Genealogy of Morals* (p. 129; prior to this, Weber meant to mould the Germans into a 'master race': p. 135; see Weber 1994). Scheler and Sombart worked to develop a new Nietzschean ethos by which to combat the decadence of the bourgeois (p. 159; see Sombart 1913, Scheler 1999). Weber's reservations about 'value judgements' (see 2.4.6) make no difference to this; nor does the fact that Nietzsche's stance was really closer to being anti-ethical. In both cases, it was a question of opposing a specific ethics. Jonas 1976 Vol. 2 notes, with regard to the periods before (pp. 173 ff.) and after Max Weber (pp. 217 ff.), that the place of sociology had been taken not only by an 'inconsequential' form of empirical social research (pp. 169, 172, 239), but also by an ethicised cultural science ('ethos science': p. 176). He accords with Schelsky 1957, p. 19, in considering even the sociology of his own day 'merely an indirect moral doctrine' (p. 251). Jonas also notes the role that Fichte played in this (pp. 224, 251; see pp. 196, 214, 249–50 and elsewhere; see also sections 2.5.2, 3.1.5).

picked up, in its own way, on Marxian themes such as alienation or class formation. But sociology's economic preconceptions already indicate that this reception of Marxian themes was not without presuppositions. The tendency for the disciplines of sociology and economics to exclude one another had as its premise a certain economic paradigm, and so it comes as no surprise that such a perspective *results* in certain interpretations of Marx. As long as the name 'Marx' was still associated, in Germany, with real forces and groups (with trade unions and students, as well as with the 'other Germany'), sociology repeatedly focused on Marx as an object of critique; by refuting him, one could remind oneself, in an exemplary fashion, of the purpose of one's own theoretical activity. (Among Marxists, this produced the perspectival illusion that sociology is *nothing but* a response to Marx.)

For this reason, the literary genre of sociological comments on Marx is especially significant. While a concealed 'effective history' (as per Gadamer) must be distinguished from a conscious reception, the consistently vibrant response that such works met with shows that these explicit formulations tended to make visible the presuppositions at work within sociological practice. I will, therefore, use them to verify my reflections on sociology's loss of its theoretical object and its disintegration into unrelated theories of a sterile, technoid base and a purely normative superstructure. Marx, who propelled philosophy beyond itself and toward politics and science, is treated in these writings as an exponent of whatever socio-philosophical paradigm the author happens to be opposed to: he is portrayed either as a crude empiricist or as a daydreamer. Both sides of the dualism I have described, and both sides of its 'appraisal', project their specific negative image onto Marx. But the only reason for this is that economic theory's *reaction* to Marx caused the two halves to fall apart.

For instance, René König considered Marx's theory a superfluous 'philosophy of history and society'.[103] This is a familiar accusation, and one that recurs throughout the history of sociology.[104] While it applies to many of König's Marxist contemporaries (and especially

103. König wanted to establish 'sociology *tout court*' by eradicating, 'in particular, the philosophies of history and of society' (König 1958, p. 7). This included philosophers such as Tönnies (p. 91) and Adorno (p. 336), as well as Marx, even if König griped at abandoning the latter: 'On the one hand, he develops a metaphysical system of the "right society"... which is, however,... altogether devoid of content and remains a mere promise' (p. 92; this is precisely why it is not a metaphysical system). 'On the other hand, he attempts to reconstruct the "anatomy" of bourgeois society. This could, at first sight, be understood as an attempt to develop a positive science of the social. But since he took his concept of society... from the Hegelian dialectic, he remains... caught up in all sorts of abstractions related to natural law' (p. 93; see, too, König 1984, pp. 101 and 127). Hidden behind this accusation is the opposite one, which outdoes Hegel in terms of ethicisation, namely that Hegel's thinking about society is too-closely bound up with social contract theory and utilitarianism (König 1984, pp. 101, 127; König 1987, p. 64). König formulates both accusations simultaneously, much as Parsons 1968 held that Marx was both a utilitarian (p. 107) and an idealist (p. 495; Joas 1992, p. 36; see, too, Gouldner 1980).

104. It can be found in Dilthey (*GS* I, p. 108), Simmel 1989 and P. Barth 1897. 'Sociology has developed out of the philosophy of history' (Freyer 1959, p. 294; see, too, Freyer 1930, p. 125). 'To the extent that what was then developing was sociology, it was historical sociology, i.e. a sociology

to Bloch and Adorno), König fails to properly grasp the character of Marx's theory when he describes it as an 'eschatology'.[105] It was not until neoclassical economics that 'philosophical' issues were excluded from economic theory. König replicates this exclusion for sociology. Otherwise a progressive spirit, he sides with scientism on *this* point, even though he combated it in other contexts.[106] Other authors considered Marx a romantic,[107] a metaphysician[108] or a moral rigorist.[109] In characterising him thusly, they were mainly referring to his political hope for the future. But this is hardly a justification for rejecting his analyses of the present, which, after all, constitute the bulk of Marx's work. They are rejected even when Marx's 'philosophical' hypotheses, such as that regarding alienation, are endorsed.[110]

Here, the 'young' Marx was already seen as the real one, and Marx's later work as an aberration.[111] Those social philosophers who latched onto the normative side of the

---

that assumed the tasks of the previous sociology in an empirical form' (A. Weber 1931, p. 285). The expression 'philosophy of history' referred primarily to Marxism: 'The possibility of such sociology is widely rejected today, even though one such sociology, the materialist conception of history, itself became a force shaping world history' (Weber 1931, p. 285; see also Von Wiese 1954, p. 107). The accusation found its way back into philosophy and theology via Popper and Löwith (see section 2.6.6).

105. König 1987, pp. 90 ff.; König 1975. König was acquainted with Löwith (König 1984, p. 8), and Taubes's 1947 dissertation (Taubes 2009) developed 'from my lecture on Marx' (König 1984, p. 140; see also König 1987, p. 435).

106. The condemnation of König found in Kruse 1999 passes over König's achievements as a sociologist – the investigation of a distinct range of objects using distinct methods – by dissolving them into the dichotomy of 'hard' and 'soft' science (the natural sciences and the humanities). Scientism was already criticised by König 1987 (p. 350). Yet unlike Kruse, who endorses the positions of Dilthey and Rickert, König did not formulate his criticism from the perspective of vitalism, but from that of sociology. 'It hardly commends the psychology of understanding that it repeatedly proves an abject failure when it comes to understanding rationalism' (König 1981, p. 36; 2.5.1).

107. Woibl 1989, Frank 1992.

108. Popper 1965.

109. Parsons 1968, p. 495; Dahrendorf 1953.

110. For instance, Nolte 1952, Popitz 1953, Israel 1972, F. Becker 1972, Mészáros 1973 or Schrey 1975. Popitz attributes to Marx a 'theoretically unsurmounted allegiance' to Hegel (Popitz 1953, p. 58). Where Marx's thoughts do not 'venture beyond' Hegel (p. 129), the economy is simply left out. Israel 1972 does not directly reject the late Marx (since 'humanist ideals . . . can be found in every "period" of his life': p. 33), but his analysis focuses on the claims of the young Marx (pp. 48 ff., 106 ff.; see Fromm 1963). F. Jonas remarks that Weber's rationalisation hypothesis 'generalises' the Marxian concept of alienation (Jonas 1976, Vol. II, p. 207; see also pp. 200–1) while simultaneously assuming the 'primacy of the political' – hardly a surprising assumption for a civil servant to make (p. 225; see sections 2.2.6, 2.6.2). According to F. Jonas, Weber interpreted Marx as an 'ethicist' and rejected him mainly on this count (p. 190).

111. This hypothesis, last propounded by Göhler 1980, was subjected to smiting criticism early on, namely by Habermas: 'The notion that Marx simply failed to properly understand Hegel, and that Hegel had already thought through everything that Marx believed himself to have discovered in his confrontation with Hegel, is the taboo formula by which one is spared the specific problematic of a revolutionary philosophy of history that is concerned with empirical verification' (Luhmann and Habermas 1971, p. 402). Aside from the meaningless phrase 'revolutionary philosophy of history', one can only concur with this assessment. Marx's theory can 'only be disproven scientifically' (p. 413), but not 'philosophically'.

dualism refused to see Marx as anything *other* than a positivist[112] or a utilitarian.[113] The accusation that Marx does not satisfyingly elaborate the 'foundation' of a 'normative theory' (see 3.1) derives from this context.[114] There were also positive verdicts, and they clashed similarly. Thus the technocrats *praised* Marx for his 'technical humanism',[115] and in fact, it is plain to see that the planning called for by many sociologists[116] is directly derived from Marxism.[117] Meanwhile, hotheaded neo-Marxists considered Marx's strong point to consist in the *non*-technical, putatively utopian element of his work.[118] But neither of these two opposing views constitutes an adequate characterisation of Marx, who refuses to fit into this dualism. He explored the workings of the economy in such a way as to explain negative phenomena in terms of *their own* logic, and not in terms of an additionally assumed overworld of 'values'. To do this, he needed neither to liberate his model from the sociology inherent in the classical doctrine of economic classes, nor to detach his considerations on cultural and political matters, and on the ills to be found in those fields, from economic issues. If the analysis were conducted in a sufficiently stringent way, there would be no need to lament the absence of normative implications or call for additional foundations.[119] The various sociological 'refutations of Marx' did not really engage with Marx at all; they were the site of proxy wars that remained *internal to sociology*. Each camp discovered its counterpart in Marx and thought it could criticise it in him, and so each camp went astray, for Marx incorporates both sides – although he

---

112. Wellmer 1969.

113. Parsons 1968, p. 107; Gouldner 1970, Alexander 1982, Honneth 1987. Or else simply as a materialist (Schwarz 1912; Heimann 1926; Ringer 1987, p. 159).

114. This accusation reflects the explanatory difficulties encountered by a theory that never quite touches reality. It tells us little about Marx, who never propounded any normative theory that would require a foundation (perhaps a foundation that is itself also 'normative'). Still, social philosophers criticise Marx for not propounding an ethics, for propounding a poorly justified ethics or for propounding the wrong ethics (3.1.4). Sociologists who had learned Dilthey's lesson on the bond between the social sciences and life were able to apply this critique, which is really a critique of socialism, directly to science, without distinguishing clearly between theory and reality – a form of German idealism (2.5.2).

115. Klages 1965; see 2.4.5.

116. Mannheim 1940, Willms 1969, Klages 1971, Luhmann 1971.

117. H. Klages assumed 'that it would be possible to integrate the economy into an overarching social policy without first revolutionising it on its own institutional terrain' (Klages 1971, p. 51; see section 2.6.2, on Pollock). Marx's goal is adopted; the elaborate polemic merely concerns the question of how that goal is to be achieved.

118. Bloch 1918, 2.5.4, 2.6.6. Freyer combines both affirmations. A technocrat in the 1950s, he had previously celebrated Marx as the founder of the idealist 'science of reality' (Freyer 1964, p. 100). To Freyer, the people needed to achieve 'cognisance' of itself in the state (rather than the proletariat achieving cognisance of itself in the party). According to Habermas 1971a, the theologisation of Marxian theory's utopian surplus is a result (in Bloch and others) of a technologically reductive reading of that theory.

119. In this spirit, Fleischer advocated a response to philosophy's 'normative gesticulations' that consists in 'modestly and unobtrusively naming the issues, thereby drawing attention to the mode of the normative that concerns reality, in such a way as to render superfluous the entire array of imperatives, values, norms and principles' (Fleischer 1980, p. 422).

does so not by means of a mere 'synthesis' of pre-existing theories, as in Alfred Weber, Parsons and Habermas, but by means of an economic theory that is systematically *prior* to the division.[120]

These paradoxically mirrored interpretations of Marx are another indication of how German sociology was characterised by a gap between 'base' and 'superstructure', where the 'base' was interpreted in a technicistically reductive way and could be seen, whenever it was explicitly described, to be derived from neoclassical economics, while the 'superstructure' was thought of as 'ethical' and tended to be interpreted in terms of the humanities alone.[121]

2.4.5 *Critique of the technocracy-hypothesis and of industrial sociology*

> We will have to gradually get used to the idea that the difference between a stable and reglemented capitalism and a technologised and rationalised socialism is not so great.[122]

> Political economy, however, is not technology.[123]

The paradoxically mirrored nature of sociological interpretations of Marx can be illustrated by an example. The 're-philosophising' of sociology[124] involved the art of refuting Marx, previously practised within economics and sociology, becoming a theme of social *philosophy*. The refutations of Marx formulated within social philosophy were also mutually contradictory.[125] However, both sides interpreted Marx as a 'philosopher of

---

120. These sociologies have dated more rapidly than Marx, such that such proxy battles are merely of historical interest. Zygmunt Baumann remarked during a lecture held in Dresden in 2001 that systems theory's assumption of a stable state and a stable society is no longer warranted after 1989 (and even less so after September 11; see 2.5.6). Similarly, at a conference on Foucault held in Frankfurt in 2001, Nancy Fraser applied Foucault's critique of power to the paternalist welfare state, but added that this state has virtually ceased to exist (now in Honneth 2003). Theoretical fashions change rapidly. The question is whether every 'medium-range' theory requires a new paradigm.

121. This 'division' is evident even in Marxist debates. Subjectivity and intersubjectivity are 'excluded from the process of production' by the 'objectivist' Althusser (Hauck 1984, p.191; Althusser and Balibar 1997, pp. 111, 174, 180); the 'subjectivist' Habermas denies that social labour has 'any significance for social development' (Hauck 1984, p. 205; for a similar view, see Gormann 1982; see above, under 2.3.2).

122. Werner Sombart.

123. *MECW* 28, p. 24.

124. See section 2.5.

125. Arendt 1969, Habermas 1987 and Wellmer 1969 felt that Marx was a positivist and utilitarian who did not properly take account of the human condition and failed to provide his theory with an epistemological or moral-philosophical 'foundation'. By contrast, Löwith, Popper and others held that Marx argued in terms of human essence and a better future, that is, metaphysically. In fact, in the course of its political 'implementation' in East Germany and theoretical dogmatisation *qua* 'oppositional science' (Brinkman) in West Germany, Marxism did increasingly come to understand itself as a comprehensive 'worldview' (a philosophy of history and nature, historical and dialectical materialism; see section 2.2.4).

history' (2.6.6). While Marx formulated historical observations, he was, like Weber, careful to refrain from predictions.[126] Neither of the two would have welcomed the attempt to distill from pure concepts and some uncontrolled observations any general insights about 'the' concept of history. But the late-nineteenth-century debate on the nature of the historical sciences, a debate whose effects are not to be underestimated, had left a canon of methods by which historical questions were quickly transformed into *philosophical* ones; after all, it seemed that there was no choice but to proceed speculatively when addressing questions such as how the general condition of the world was developing, what the ultimate causes of this development were and what remedies might be available. In this way, quasi-substances such as history 'itself', the West, culture and even life, being, reason or modernity became the subjects of development. Situated within a narrative framework, they were all given their very own 'history',[127] whose contemporary effects one then believed oneself to have grasped philosophically. Thus philosophy came to be understood as producing knowledge and orientation within a situation of general crisis, even though it perceived the pertinent reality only in a mentalised – that is, ideologically distorted – form.[128]

One of these grand sociological narratives needs to be considered more closely, here, because it proved consequential. I mean the narrative of technology ('as such'). A technocratically reductive conception of socialism was already heralded by Lenin's declaration that electrification would bring communism.[129] The West accepted the challenge, and so technological progress became a symbolic site of systemic competition. The 'Sputnik shock' saw the Soviet Union scoring some points; even the arms race needs to be seen in this context. Now, this real antagonism is reflected in German social theory. During the 1950s, there emerged a worldview that rivalled Marxism (which was intepreted as a philosophy of history): the 'industrial society' hypothesis. This worldview took itself to be 'post-ideological'[130] by virtue of speaking only of facts and the constraints imposed by them. Yet, at the same time, it presented a speculative narrative, according to which the freeing of the natural sciences initiated a triumph of technology[131] that gave rise, in turn, to modern industry. The expansion of industry around the year 1800 was claimed to have initiated a period of transformation for humanity, one comparable only to the neo-

126. 2.2.4; 2.3.1; 2.6.6, Excursus.

127. They were provided with *Geschichte*, both in the sense of Lyotard's narrative and in that of the mythified history of Being.

128. A characteristic result of the spread of this view is the narrow focus on certain of Marx's texts, mainly his early works. Moreover, attention is paid only to those aspects of these early works that lend themselves to being integrated into such 'human science' narratives (such as the hypotheses on 'alienation' and on 'reification' that were attributed to Marx – see section 2.5.4). On the role that philosophy played, here, see Horkheimer 1990, Adorno 1988a.

129. 'Communism is Soviet power plus the electrification of the entire country' (*LW* 31, p. 516; Kesting 1959, p. 209). On the occasion of the 1928 launch of the Five-Year Plan, Stalin called for 'tractorisation' ('automobilisation': p. 214). 'In the period of reconstruction, technology decides everything' (Stalin 1976a, p. 530; translation modified).

130. Bell 1962.

131. According to Walter Gerlach, this occurred around 1600 (in Freyer 1965, pp. 63 and 77).

lithic revolution. 'Industrial society' was described as transforming one area of life after another, even man's psychic structure. Man was taken to be standing on a 'threshold of the ages'.[132] This was itself a first-rate philosophy of history.[133]

Two disparate views thus intersect in the industrial society hypothesis: a pathos of sobriety and a bold metaphysics of history. The hypothesis is best described as a *world-view*. It only appeared to be compatible with Marx – in fact, it relativised him to the point of neutralising him. It was argued that Marx had perceived some aspects of the historical change but failed to understand its proper meaning, the role of technology as subject.[134] According to Marx, technology performs a specific function under capitalism: that of rationalising production so that more can be produced, and at lower cost. Producers have no choice but to implement such measures if they want to survive; what forces them to engage in rationalisation is the competition, which, as is well known, never sleeps. Thus technology's rapid development and its sometimes harmful consequences are not brought about by technology itself, or even by some 'Faustian compulsion' (as per Spengler), but by the necessity, *under capitalism*, of constantly employing it to intensify and extend production (2.1.6). The industrial society hypothesis has nothing to say about this: technology's embeddedness in the specific social order of capitalism lies outside its range of vision (and the results are felt to this day).[135]

While the industrial society hypothesis had its precursors in utopians such as Saint-Simon, these regarded 'industrial society' as a static final stage at which the dynamic present, with its social struggles, had yet to arrive.[136] The authors writing during the 1950s believed this final stage had now been reached. There was speculation about '*post-*

---

132. Freyer 1965a.

133. For formulations of this view, see, for instance, A. Weber 1935 and 1946, Freyer 1955 and 1965, Gehlen 1961, p. 129, and Schelsky 1961a, pp. 450, 461, 483 ('total separation from previous history due to man's metaphysical change of identity'). The sequence 'natural science – technology – industrial society' appears logical and necessary. As a philosophy of history, this type of thinking is, however, ahistorical; social structures are elided.

134. Spengler 1976; F. Jünger 1993, p. 208; Dessauer 1956, p. 15; Forsthoff 1971, p. 36; for later examples of this position, see Halfmann 1996 and recent actor-network theories.

135. Forsthoff 1971, p. 164 deliberately resists such a contextualisation: '[t]he hard core of today's social whole is no longer [!] the state but industrial society' (here, he comes close to Marx's critique of Hegel), which is 'characterised by full employment and rising total output. In the face of this, class antagonisms become … meaningless' (see Schelsky in section 2.4.6). This is an odd conclusion. After all, the 'compulsion' to achieve full employment was nothing but the antagonism of class (and of the system), crystallised into the welfare state (see Metzler 2003).

136. Walter Benjamin's *Arcades Project* explores the 'promise' associated with technology during its age of triumph, the nineteenth century: namely that it might be employed in everyone's best interest (Aristotle, *Politics* 1253 b 39; *MECW* 35, pp. 410 ff.). On Saint-Simon, see Salomon 1919, Ramm 1955, Kesting 1959, pp. 32 ff.; Buber 1967, Niederwemmer in H. Lenk 1973, pp. 21 ff.; Höppner 1975, Lepenies 1985, Euchner 1991. 'Saint-Simon already stated that the domination of man by man would be replaced by the administration of things. But he failed to add that the things administrated would be men themselves' (Jonas 1976. Vol. 1, p. 271).

histoire'[137] and the 'perfectibility of history'.[138] Even though they referred to international specialist literature, the fact was that, after interpreting Marxism as a philosophy of history, these authors went on to outdo him in that field.[139] If there existed *only* the three stages of primitive, agrarian and industrial society (with the latter displaying features of re-primitivisation – a mark left by the heroisation of agrarian life under National Socialism), then there was no room for 'utopias'. Like Simmel's cultural philosophy before it, this was a historico-philosophical *counter*project that treated the key features of the age[140] as historically constituted but fixed for all time – an eternal recurrence of the same. Thus philosophy of history was neutralised not by 'pure' anthropology, as Marquard[141] believed, but by the industrial society hypothesis, which *contained* an anthropology within it.[142]

By the references to early socialism, whose promised land was claimed, in a Pauline manner, to have been reached (even if the claim was made in a melancholy way, rather than euphorically), Marx was bypassed once more. This move against Marxism was successful only because of Marxism's problematic theoretical reception history. After all, many of the specific claims associated with the industrial society hypothesis had developed from Marxism itself. Authors such as Hilferding and Lenin had recognised the validity of Marx's theories but restricted it to the nineteenth century, claiming that entirely different principles were at work in the 'new stage' of monopoly capitalism (2.1.2, 2.2.5, 2.3.3). This was already a 'historico-philosophical' neutralisation of Marx, even it

137. Gehlen 1961, p. 134.

138. Freyer 1955, pp. 62 ff. See Kojève 1980, Gehlen 1963, Freyer 1987, pp. 85 ff.; Niethammer 1989, Fukuyama 1992, Meyer 1993 and Rohbeck 2000, pp. 92 ff. Each of these authors was referring to something in history that was interpreted as history's driving force ('main contradiction'). Hegel theorises the end of art, Kojève and Gehlen theorise the end of class struggle (in accordance with the convergence hypothesis) and Fukuyama theorises the end of socialism – these end points are all quite different from one another.

139. Reference was made to Veblen 1921, Burnham 1948, Fourastie 1949, Aron 1964 and Galbraith 1968. While these were all speculations about history, Marxism was considered 'the quintessence, the *summa* of all prior European philosophy of history' (Kesting 1959, p. 77; Herrmann 2000). 'What immediately occurs to one with regard to 'Marx and technology' is the theory of history known as "historical materialism"' (H. Klages, in Freyer 1965, p. 137). That the industrial society hypothesis is itself bound up with a philosophy of history is suggested by titles such as *Weltgeschichte Europas* ['European World History']: Freyer 1948, *Urmensch und Spätkultur* ['Primordial Man and Late Culture']: Gehlen 1956, *Stellungnahmen zur geschichtlichen Situation* ['Statements on the Historical Situation']: Freyer 1965, *Schwelle der Zeiten* ['Threshold of Ages']: Freyer 1965a. and *Standorte im Zeitstrom* ['Positions in the Current of Time']: Forsthoff 1974. Rügemer, then himself an adherent of '*Diamat*', spoke of a 'historicising negation of historicity' (Rügemer 1979, p. 117); the young Habermas spoke of a 'counterideology' (Habermas 1973, p, 251). 'A system of natural and historical knowledge, embracing everything, and final for all time, is a contradiction to the fundamental laws of dialectic reasoning' (Engels, in *MECW* 25, p. 25).

140. The subjective role of technology and 'alienation': Gehlen 1963, pp. 232 ff.

141. Marquard 1973.

142. 'The historical changes undergone by social systems in their entirety cannot be understood as resulting from efforts at practical orientation', but only as 'resulting from adaptations' – on the part of the systems themselves (H. Lübbe, in H. Lenk 1973, p. 102).

still presented itself as Marxist. In principle, it became possible for non-Marxists also to interpret Marx in this manner, and this was precisely what Hans Freyer did. In his book *Revolution from the Right*,[143] he argued that Marx's analyses were accurate for the nineteenth century, but that the key historical issue had changed since – in his view, *völkisch* issues were what mattered now.[144] The structure of the argument remained the same after 1945, when *völkisch* issues were replaced with industrial society: Freyer argued that a century defined by the economy[145] had now been succeeded by the century of technology.[146]

This counterphilosophy of history, which rather arbitrarily proclaims the advent of a new stage of development, one coinciding with the twentieth century, can be found throughout the 'conservative revolution'. While it takes different forms, its theorists all start from the assumption of a 'becoming universal of technology'.[147] While this does not always involve a glorification of technology 'as such', technology is considered the transcendental feature of the epoch, to which one had to respond, for better or for worse.[148] In other words, the conflictual reproduction of which Marx took technology to be the means[149] was not what needed to be addressed. Those defending this hypothesis differed only with regard to its *assessment*. Some technocrats held that technology was capable of solving the problems it had created, by means of planning.[150] Conservative critics of culture believed that something else was needed: 'retentive forces' (Freyer), an 'intellectual and moral' embedding of technology or the strengthening of archaic institutions.[151]

143. Freyer 1931.

144. Üner 1981; for critical accounts, see Lange 1977, Saage 1983, Remmers 1994, Rehberg 1999.

145. Freyer 1966.

146. Freyer 1955, pp. 38 ff.; see, too, Remmers 1994.

147. Schelsky 1961a, p. 455. See Spengler 1931, E. Jünger 1982, F. Jünger 1993, Gehlen 1957, F. Jonas 1960, Deege 1996. Heidegger took the rule of technology to be a consequence of the West's 'forgetting of Being'. After 1945, 'technology' remained the subject of history. Schmitt 1985 (pp. 85, 89) expanded the catalogue of historical stages by attributing theology to the sixteenth century, metaphysics to the seventeenth, morality to the eighteenth, economics to the nineteenth and technology to the twentieth.

148. On 'transcendental' sociology, see Schelsky 1959, p. 95 and Nolte 1963, pp. 521 ff.

149. *MECW* 35, pp. 387–8; Park 2001.

150. Veblen 1921, Popper 1957 ('social technology'), Klaus 1961, Schelsky 1961a, p. 465; H. Klages 1971, Luhmann 1971; critically: Willms 1969, Glaser 1972, pp. 67 ff.; see, too, Meynaud 1964, Tenbruck 1967, Senghaas 1970 and H. Lenk 1973.

151. In 1929, Freyer thought of technology as a 'decisively important reality-force' (Freyer 1987, pp. 8–9; Remmers 1994, p. 107). Like Heidegger and Adorno, he associated technology, in an overly generalising manner, with a specific, modern type of rationality; the latter was seen by him as 'the embodiment of a historical will' (Freyer 1987, p. 15; Remmers 1994, p. 111). Freyer argued that this will needed to be embodied in the powerful 'framework of a historical determination of aims', and that only the *völkisch* state could achieve this. After 1945, Freyer maintained that tradition needed to be shielded from 'secondary systems', which he took to be devoid of all meaning; in his view, tradition is the only force capable of instituting meaning: 'There are retentive forces that support progress without consuming themselves' (Freyer 1987, p. 82; Remmers 1994, p. 183). The later 'functional equivalent' of heroism, neo-Aristotelianism (Schnädelbach 1986), also lamented the rule of unadulterated purposive rationality, and contrasted it with something more sublime,

From this perspective, futurist-fascist heroism was perceived as a 'synthesis' of morality and technology. For a time, it was believed that the dangers associated with technologisation could be dealt with by means of telluric forces such as the people [*Volk*], the state, the community, blood and soil. Technology was to be used for a higher *end*, one superior to and more valuable than 'technology' as a pure means, which the opposite poles Russia and America were seen to embody.[152] When this project failed, due to the superior power of the two opposite poles, substitutes were found, such as family values, religious values or proven virtues. But the subject role of technology ('as such') was treated as practically necessary and theoretically given. After 1945, technology was countered, in a purely 'compensatory' way, only with culture and the humanities.[153]

This redistribution of roles also involved a new interpretation of Marx. While Marx had already denounced such 'divisions' in his youth, he was associated, in the course of the redistribution of roles, with one camp only: in the work of Klages, Marx became a proponent of the industrial society hypothesis, like Klages himself. In fact, Marx attributed great importance to the development of technologies associated with social reproduction, since they are what creates the *leeway* required for social change. But Klages never mentions that Marx did not regard technology as an end in itself, but as a means. As such, it can be used for the all-round development of individuals: the available *technological* means allow for the production of more than enough food for everyone, with minimal labour effort, thereby making a life free of constraints possible. In Marx's view, the fact that this possibility is not realised is due not to the insufficient development of the forces of production, as Klages suggests, but rather to capitalist relations of production and appropriation.[154] The motive behind this economic form is not to provide for human needs but to but make a profit. It is this, and not some 'inability to make use of the additional possibilities for development associated with the forces of production',[155] that constitutes the scandal of capitalism, according to Marx. Marx hoped that a pos-

---

without, however, engaging purposive rationality on its own terrain. Incidentally, the analysis of institutions has grown more sophisticated in the meantime.

152. In 1935, Heidegger spoke of the 'inner truth and greatness of this movement', because in his view it was the first movement that confronted technology and did so on a 'planetary' scale (Heidegger 1953, p. 152/*GA* 40, p. 208). G. Wünsch, also formerly an ardent proponent of National Socialism, still distinguished, in 1962, between 'intensity of value' and 'magnitude of value' (p. 17). Gehlen later characterised the virtues that had been lost as 'martial' (Gehlen 1961, pp. 136–7; in the same passage, Gehlen distances himself from America and Russia).

153. On the role played by the humanities in the 'Ritter group' (Joachim Ritter, Manfred Riedel, Odo Marquard, Hermann Lübbe, Günter Rohrmoser and others), see Ritter 1961, Seifert 2000. The origin of this view lies, however, in Freyer's work: because values are compensatory, that is, 'staying' forces, they need to be shielded from destructive 'reflection'.

154. During the world economic crisis of 1929, foodstuffs were destroyed on a massive scale in order to halt the price slump; meanwhile, the population went hungry. When this structural argument is repersonalised, it comes dangerously close to a conspiracy theory – as in Marcuse, according to whom technological possibilities are not employed for good purposes 'solely because existing society mobilises all its resources against the possibility of its liberation' (Marcuse 1970, p. 14; quoted in Willms 1969, pp. 55, 58).

155. Klages in Freyer 1965, p. 139.

sible 'proletarian revolution' would be followed by additional increases in productivity. To what extent the majority of the population would benefit from democratic control of technological development remains an open question. Things turned out differently in 'real socialism'; then again, there was no trace of 'democratic control' there. Marx perceived the open character of human nature more clearly than anyone before him. To him, reproduction was a necessity whose meaning could only be that of allowing for a fulfilled life. It is indispensable, but it must not dominate men. Only after meeting basic needs can then they begin to address *other* issues. There is a deep humanism in this view.[156] But Klages sees nothing in it except the totalisation of technology:

> In the post-revolutionary situation, labouring man ... will cease progressively to be a 'mere appendix' of machinery, as in capitalism. The logic that has been freed of its economic restraints will draw him into the rapid process by which labour becomes more intellectual and scientific.... Propelling himself, as the productive force behind the productive force of machinery, into the space of science and technology, labouring man thus necessarily confronts himself with nature in an 'all-round' manner.[157]

Thus Klages suggests that Marx meant to radicalise the technological aspects of industrial society. In this way, Marx becomes an enemy of culture and humanity, the prophet of 'technological humanism'[158] and the 'technological eros'.[159] The very feature of technology that gives it such a dialectical character under capitalism, namely that it is reifying, alienating and anti-human despite its usefulness,[160] is redefined by Klages as the condition to which Marx *aspires*, and even wants to totalise. This horrific vision hardly did justice to the theoretical substance of Marx.

What it did, rather, was zero in on polytechnical education under GDR's real socialism, while presenting itself as a critique of Marx.[161] This somewhat metaphorical critique can be read in two ways. Either the present has already revealed itself as the paradise

156. What ought to be aspired to is a social order that 'makes it possible for me to do one thing today and another tomorrow, to hunt in the morning, fish in the afternoon, rear cattle in the evening, criticise after dinner, just as I have a mind' (*MECW* 5, p. 47). Labour and technology always remain 'a realm of necessity. Beyond it begins that development of human energy which is an end in itself, the true realm of freedom, which, however, can blossom forth only with this realm of necessity as its basis. The shortening of the working day is its basic prerequisite' (*MECW* 37, p. 807).

157. Klages in Freyer, pp. 141–2.

158. Klages 1964.

159. Hommes 1953. See Arendt 1969, Habermas 1971b. E. Lange worked first on Freyer and then on Marx (Lange 1977 and Lange 1980, pp. 122, 156).

160. *MECW* 35, pp. 341 ff., 374 ff.

161. '*All* citizens become employees and workers of a *single* nationwide state "syndicate".... The whole of society will have become a single office and a single factory, with equality of labour and equality of pay' (Lenin 1970b, pp. 120–1). The notion of a new culture of working man is found not only in Russia's Proletkult (of which someone like Gramsci was a representative, too), but also in Italian futurism and the work of Ernst Jünger (see Jünger 1982).

announced by Marx – in which case Marx is to blame for present ills.[162] Or Marx's vision of a different future is simply discredited as a technoid nightmare. In both cases, the question of property relations, so central to Marxian theory, is elided. After all, Marx himself describes technological progress as problematic, because it is tied up with economic antagonism. Instead of resulting in more comfortable working conditions, machines used to rationalise production represent a threat to workers. Jobs are put at risk (hence Luddism), wages drop and work becomes mindless. Entrepreneurs are also forced to constantly update their facilities so as to be able to survive competition. Even financial sectors are affected, since a falling rate of profit leads to a drop in the demand for money, thereby lowering the rate of return. Thus, under capitalism, the entire economic society depends, like it or not, on technological development ('growth'), despite the fact that it proves harmful to so many.[163] A highly abstract, de-economised and sociologically blind concept of technology leads to *philosophical* theories being resorted to as placeholders. In a case of overhasty and fallacious reasoning, conclusions about the social effects of technology are drawn directly from anthropological categories (a 'volition of the soul' in earlier versions, and a 'rationality type' in later ones). The social philosophy of technology has also lost sight of Marxian theory's main object of inquiry, capitalist society and its laws of motion.

In light of frequent references to Marx, particularly in industrial sociology, this claim may seem exaggerated. But industrial sociology's reception of Marx[164] also involved decisive philosophical filters, which rendered the object of inquiry nebulous in spite of the references to Marx; at times, industrial sociology's version of 'Marxism' even caused 'capitalism' to be lost sight of. The older industrial sociology had dealt mainly with the cultural *embeddedness* of the economic process. Economic, industrial and workplace sociology[165] imported theories from Chicago and elsewhere, for instance on the Hawthorne Experiment and wildcat strikes. The aim pursued at the Hawthorne works was explicitly that of increasing productivity by making minor improvements to working conditions. There was hardly any affinity with Marx in this. It was only the industrial sociology of the period after 1968 that was shaped by the student movement's reception of Marx. At the time, vacant university positions abounded.[166] But student Marxism's

162. This notion is found, for example, in Becker 1972 ('justification': p. 140), in Khella 1995 and in Hardt and Negri 1997.

163. See *MECW* 35, chapters 15 and 25; *MECW* 37, chapter 13. Science-fiction films often portray machines as threatening: they take the place of humans (*Blade Runner, Terminator, Star Trek: First Contact, The Matrix*; cf. 2.1.5). The conjectures about whether computers might develop self-consciousness fail to address this crucial problem. Nor does the problem of genetic engineering reside in the technology as such; it resides in its commercial use and in the problems resulting therefrom (see Enzensberger 2001). On the critique of growth, see Meadows 1972, Harich 1975, Bahro 1991.

164. Herkommer 1979.

165. Briefs 1959, Schelsky 1955, Dahrendorf 1956, Fürstenberg 1961.

166. W.D. Narr has remarked in conversation that he was suprised how easy it was for members of the 1968 generation to obtain academic positions. '[t]he complicated and time-consuming analysis of reality is replaced by desktop deductions about the "self-limitation of capital", in order

'voluntarist expectation of revolution'[167] was soon disappointed. Because it was not possible to distance oneself from Marx immediately, this was done in a more subtle, and sometimes even in a 'Marxist' way:

> When working class action was lacking, the analysis of consciousness became the preferred object; when class consciousness was lacking, it became a distillate of deductions associated with the critique of ideology ... A class-theoretical necessity was turned into a virtue of industrial sociology.[168]

Hirsch blames these trickle-down effects on 'neglect of the real economic base'.[169] This neglect can be at least partly traced back to the philosophical distortions to which Marx's theory was subjected. There were influential dualisms such as that of work and interaction, which simply took for granted that the system would function without crises during the twentieth century, even as social theory's focus shifted more and more to the field of 'pure' interaction (see section 3.1.1). This 'critical Marxism'[170] completely severed its connection to the critique of political economy – it was even candid about not being *Marxism* any longer.

A different current continued to use Marxian categories to describe this caesura. Yet those who invoked subsumption in order to turn their backs on Marxism's 'production-based model'[171] were enacting the same break, by which Marx's own *theories* were rendered ineffective. The distinction between a subsumption-based and a production-based model was more than questionable: the distinction between real and formal subsumption[172] is not a theory about the historical succession of social formations *within* capitalism.[173] In speaking of 'relative' and 'absolute' surplus production, Marx was distinguishing between a form of exploitation based on the lengthening of the working day, already known to slaveholders and 'feudal barons', and increases in the productivity or intensity of labour, such as exist only under capitalism.[174] When, following Brandt, the nineteenth century is attributed a pre-capitalist model and the twentieth century declared already to be post capitalist, the result is that capitalism disappears, even if Marxist vocabulary is still used.

Some authors *criticised* Marxism's 'metaphysics of labour',[175] claiming the new formation of 'Taylorism' or 'Fordism' was no longer governed by the logic of capital and labour,

to evade the difficulty of confronting the stress associated with middle-class upward mobility' (Bress 1975, p. 145).

167. Diettrich 1999, p. 12.
168. Hirsch 1986, p. 184.
169. Ibid.
170. Gouldner 1980.
171. Arnason 1976, p. 200.
172. *MECW* 35, pp. 510–11.
173. 'Two phases of capitalism': Brandt 1990, p. 181; see also Aglietta 1976.
174. *MECW* 35, pp. 704 ff.
175. Breuer 1977, Sieferle 1979, Lange 1980, Honneth 1980b, Lange 1980, Gorz 1989, Kurz 1994.

but by that of the 'economics of time'[176] or by the logic of a particular technology.[177] In Marx, real subsumption was a feature of the capitalist mode of production (where no alternatives exist, the worker can work only for capital); now, it was interpreted as a form of *political coercion*, as deliberate 'regulation'.[178] Interpreted as a sociological category, 'abstract labour' also seemed to presuppose some disciplinary, coercive measure, by which objectivistically interpreted 'concrete' labour is converted into 'abstract' labour in the first place.[179] The effects of the Leninist primacy of politics can still be felt, here (see 2.2.6, 2.6.2): to the extent that the Marxism of the subsumption-based model was a critical one, its critique was directed at the state.[180] All that was left for Marxist industrial sociology to do was to register the various *technological* transformations of the 'system'[181] and their psychological effects on 'worker consciousness'.[182] As for systems theory and social psychology, they hardly had any use for Marx. Like other hermetic discussions of the 1970s, Marxist industrial sociology remained an intermezzo.

2.4.6 *The sociological approach to social classes*

> Compared to the hopes associated with the reappropriation of the Marxist theory of class, fifteen years later the results are disappointing.[183]

The litmus test for sociology is the question of classes. Within the classical economics of Smith and Ricardo, social classes were central categories. There was debate on how classes contributed to the 'wealth of nations'. This was highly relevant to political issues. How great was the contribution of the peasants, and how great that of landowners?

---

176. Sohn-Rethel 1972.

177. Vahrenkamp 1973, Brandt 1978, Oetzel 1978, pp. 169 ff.; Offe 1984. See also Hirsch 1986.

178. Offe 1974, Mückenberger 1976, Steinert 1980.

179. Breuer 1977, Oetzel 1978, Altvater 1992. 'Marx's doctrine has been abandoned by most of his followers – perhaps for propagandistic reasons, or perhaps because they did not understand him – and a vulgar Marxist conspiracy theory has in many cases taken its place. It is a depressing case of intellectual decline' (Popper 1944, Vol. 2, p. 127).

180. In functional terms, adhering to this theory amounted to becoming an advocate of neoliberalism, which was constituting itself during the same period. The adherents of the theory also entered into a strange coalition with cultural criticism, which likewise put little stock in the welfare state (Forsthoff 1968, Klages 1979). Those who 'objected to welfare patronage' (Baier 1988) could cite Max Weber in support of their position, since he was one of German critical theory's warrantors when it came to the primacy of politics (2.6.1). 'In any case, the neo-Marxists, who . . . oppose workers' asset acquisition with all their might, are the most effective defenders of capitalism-as-we-know-it (Nell-Breuning 1974, p. 111; on asset acquisition: Preiser 1967, pp. 161 ff.; on shifting frontlines: Koenen 2001, p. 400). The electoral posters of the 1930s are already quite revealing (Hennig 1976, p. 292). Breuer 1977, Oetzel 1978, Lange 1980 and Khella 1995 misinterpret Marxism as a theory that merely describes the 'system', thereby supporting it). Thus Marxism was still objected to in postmodernism, in the interest of a vague 'emancipation' (Laclau 1993) – therein lies postmodernism's conservatism.

181. Popitz 1957, Pollock 1964; cf. 2.3.3.

182. Kern 1970, Deppe 1971, Schumann 1977; I have related these thoughts to the current debate in Henning 2005a.

183. Hirsch 1986, p. 183.

What share of wealth was due to entrepreneurs, and what share was due to workers? How much political influence did each of these groups deserve? These distinctions were derived from the basic logic of economic activity. We have seen that classes are highly relevant to theoretical engagement with such issues as unemployment, inflation or stagnation. As a rule, bourgeois theories blame excessively high wages for such phenomena. Hence the claim that classes no longer play any role within theoretical economics 'today' is false – the concept of class is merely not made explicit. The concept is first and foremost an economic one, and irreducibly so, because it is anchored within each economic structure in a constitutive way. It is only via this mediation that it becomes political, as can – increasingly – be seen in everyday life.[184]

The founding fathers of German sociology, Marx and Lorenz von Stein, began from these facts and proceeded to examine the social and political effects that rapid changes in the economic structure entailed over time, as well as the sometimes catastrophic way that these effects made themselves felt. What has become of this central and substantive issue, which was and probably had to be raised at the dawn of sociology, in the course of sociology's further development? The question of classes is a suitable theme by which to illustrate, in an exemplary fashion, the changes within post-Marxian German sociology that have been described so far. To do this, I will examine representative examples from different generations: Weber wrote about half a century after Marx, and Schelsky wrote about half a century after Weber. In conclusion, I will also consider Luhmann, who is sometimes portrayed as the high point in the history of German sociology, despite the fact that his *substantive* claims seldom go beyond those of his precursors.

Key elements of Marxian theory V: classes

> What he [Ricardo] forgets to emphasise is the constantly growing number of the middle classes, those who stand between the workman on the one hand and the capitalist and landlord on the other. The middle classes maintain themselves to an ever increasing extent directly out of revenue . . .[185]

Marx did not systematically present his theory of classes, because he presupposed it as something to be taken for granted.[186] This was to have dire consequences, since,

184. The franchise was linked to landed property, from ancient Athens to the Prussian state. The question of how economic structures ought to be reflected in politics was debated by Hobbes, Locke, Montesquieu (Fenske 1997, p. 334: 'What kinds of tax laws are needed to stabilise a democracy?'), Rousseau and Smith (J. Ritter 1961, Euchner 1969, Macpherson 1974, Rittstieg 1975, Finley 1980, Steinvorth 1981). The question of how different incomes ought to be taxed is still topical today. Workers are taxed more heavily than corporations, because the latter are thought to 'contribute' more to the national economy. There is a fear that higher taxes would slow growth or induce capital flight. Yet in the media, the only thing that is denounced as 'class struggle' is the attempt by unions to *challenge* from below this party political consensus.

185. Marx, *MECW* 32, p. 198.

186. The manuscript on classes breaks off (*MECW* 37, pp. 870–1). 'Now as for myself, I do not claim to have discovered either the existence of classes in modern society or the struggle between

differently from the theory of value, the theory of classes really did need to be 'reconstructed' on the basis of Marx's writings. Marx's claims are situated on various levels of abstraction, which seem incompatible at first glance. This is especially evident in the way that Marx uses a dual model in his militant writings (labour vs. capital), whereas he distinguishes up to eight different classes in his historical writings.[187] His most influential comments are from the *Communist Manifesto*. While the political rhetoric of this early work displayed a tendency toward exaggeration,[188] even these extreme formulations acknowledge facts that would later often be invoked to *criticise* Marx: the existence of middle classes, intermediate strata, intra-class fractioning, the overdetermination of class distinctions by other distinctions (such as nationality and gender) or the principally undecided character of a given class structure's political effects.[189] By no means does class structure lead deterministically to 'class consciousness'.[190]

---

them. Long before me, bourgeois historians had described the historical development of this struggle between the classes, as had bourgeois economists their economic anatomy' (*MECW* 39, p. 62). On this point, see especially Gubbay 1997, Ritsert 1998, Diettrich 1999, and Milner 1999.

187. In keeping with the descriptive intention of his historical 'writings on France', Marx expanded his conceptual toolkit. He distinguishes between large landowners and the peasant class, between the financial, the industrial and the petty bourgeoisie and between the proletariat, the lumpenproletariat and intellectuals (*MECW* 10, pp. 48 ff.; *MECW* 11, pp. 103 ff.; *MECW* 22, pp. 3 ff.). These all adopt certain 'ideal-typical' positions in political struggles; power groups such as the given state administration, the military and the clergy also play a role. Bader 1998 (in his preface) still finds himself slightly puzzled by this 'complexity'.

188. Cf. 2.1.4. 'Society as a whole is more and more [!] splitting up into two great hostile camps, into two great classes directly facing each other – Bourgeoisie and Proletariat' (*MECW* 6, p. 485). 'The lower strata of the middle class – the small tradespeople, shopkeepers, and retired tradesmen generally, the handicraftsmen and peasants – all these sink gradually into the proletariat' (p. 491). Marx was not yet thirty and had still to begin his life's work. Empirical investigations with a wider temporal and spatial focus confirm this trend (Sassen 1988, p. 136; Sassen 1996, pp. 135 ff.).

189. Thus, next to the old middle classes ('the small manufacturer, the shopkeeper, the artisan, the peasant': *MECW* 6, p. 494), there exists a 'new class of petty bourgeois' (p. 509), as well as the lumpenproletariat ('that passively rotting mass thrown off by the lowest layers of old society': p. 494). The category of the lumpenproletariat is not a residual one; on the contrary, this is the very social stratum that often proved influential in the form of a 'mob'; witness the 'Mobile Guards' of 1848 (*MECW* 10, p. 62), the *Freikorps* of 1919, or today's skinheads. These were all strata that became homeless in confusing times of change. On the question of gender: 'The bourgeois sees his wife a mere instrument of production... He has not even a suspicion that the real point aimed at is to do away with the status of women as mere instruments of production' (*MECW* 6, p. 502; cf. *MECW* 4, p. 195; *MECW* 3, p. 294; Bebel 1971). 'National differences and antagonisms between peoples are daily more and more [!] vanishing, owing to the development of the bourgeoisie, to freedom of commerce, to the world market, to uniformity in the mode of production and in the conditions of life corresponding thereto' (*MECW* 6, p. 503).

190. 'Now and then the workers are victorious, but only for a time. The real fruit of their battles lies, not in the immediate result, but in the ever expanding union of the workers.... This organisation of the proletarians into a class, and, consequently into a political party, is continually being upset again by the competition between the workers themselves' (*MECW* 6, p. 493). 'Economic conditions had first transformed the mass of the people of the country into workers. The combination of capital has created for this mass a common situation, common interests. This mass is thus already a class as against capital, but not yet for itself. In the struggle... this mass becomes united,

So what distinguishes Marx's class analysis from more recent analyses of 'social stratification', which think of themselves as more 'pluralist'?[191] In addressing this question, one is struck by something odd. Even though Marx's theory of classes is unanimously considered to be of central importance to the history of sociology, it is hard to find a sober account of that theory. Theories addressing Marx's 'theory of class' often overhastily attempt to refute it or claim that it continues to be valid.[192] And yet the basic idea distinguishing Marx from later sociology is simple: when one starts from a basic understanding that men do not live on air,[193] one is led to the observation that human communal existence is structured, in a central way, according to particular, historically specific economic *divisions of labour*. Individuals do not have to be 'aware' of the division of labour; it can still be studied scientifically.[194] Under capitalism, which has done away with the earlier cultural embeddedness of material reproduction and now treats reproduction as an end in itself,[195] the 'pure' forms of the capitalist division of labour are superimposed upon the older, 'motley' variants.[196] Thus, one would expect the division of labour to be clearly reflected in class structure – and, in fact, it is, to the extent that trade unions, employers' associations and popular political parties constitute themselves along this faultline. But Marx also explains that the process of reproduction appears to its participants in an inverted form, and he explains why this is so. For at the same time,

---

and constitutes itself as a class for itself. The interests it defends become class interests' (*MECW* 6, p. 211; see also Tugan 1905).

191. Goldthorpe 1980, Goldthorpe 1985, Beck 1983 or Hradil 2001.

192. Dahrendorf 1957, Parkin 1979, Schelsky (see below), Berger 1998 and Schroer 2001 oppose Marx overhastily. Jung 1968, Poulantzas 1975, Krysmanski 1989 and approaches from the 1970s (Haug 1970, Meschkat 1973, Tjaden 1973, IMSF 1973 ff., PKA 1973 ff., Bischoff 1976 and 1980; for critical responses, see Kostede 1976, Krämer 1983) number among those defenders of Marx who lack critical distance. According to Kostede 1976, Marxist theories of class lapse into a 'rigid schematism' by 'imposing the categorial starting points of the Marxian theory of class on West Germany's empiricial class relations in an unmediated manner' (p. 126). They limited themselves to producing an annotated catalogue of 'socio-statistical aspects' (p. 129); thus 'historical analysis became the arena in which confirmation of one's particular interpretation of Marx was sought' (p. 119). Programmes were outlined, but never implemented (p. 125). At least the ground was broken; after all, some recent works were penned by veterans (compare Ritsert 1973 to Ritsert 1998, Bischoff/Herkommer 2002 to Bischoff 1976 and Herkommer 1979 or Bader 1976 to Bader 1998).

193. 'Men can be distinguished from animals by consciousness, by religion or anything else you like. They themselves begin to distinguish themselves from animals as soon as they begin to *produce* their means of subsistence' (*MECW* 5, p. 31; cf. *MECW* 29, p. 262 f.; *MECW* 35, p. 92 f.).

194. 'In the social production of their existence, men inevitably enter into definite relations, which are independent of their will, namely relations of production appropriate to a given stage in the development of their material forces of production' (*MECW* 29, p. 263). This is a 'classic' insight; see Rousseau 1950, Smith 1999 or Durkheim 1994.

195. Polanyi 1944.

196. *MECW* 6, p. 487.

in a development that is prior to all deliberate obfuscation by means of general claims,[197] the class structure is *concealed*.[198]

Moreover, the economic base always exists within a certain cultural superstructure. While this superstructure does not overturn the economic structures, it does *model* their manifest appearance.[199] But science would be superfluous 'if the outward appearance and the essence of things directly coincided'.[200] Thus economic classes, which are central to the 'anatomy of this civil society',[201] do not appertain directly to the 'outward appearance'.[202] One can find any number of classifications of the people living in a society, both nominal classifications (that is, classifications imposed from outside) and self-descriptions; they are based on anything from local identity (East Frisian, Swabian) and hobbies (football fan, wine connoisseur) to religion and skin colour. Even people's economic differences are multiform: wage workers in car factories have as little in common with bank clerks as with student waiters or hotel owners. How such differences are dealt with is a question of the local culture. The differences may be refined, habitualised and enacted symbolically, as in France,[203] or they may act in synergy with ethnic differences

---

197. 'For each new class which puts itself in the place of one ruling before it, is compelled [...] to represent its interest as the common interest of all the members of society, that is, expressed in ideal form: it has to give its ideas the form of universality, and represent them as the only rational, universally valid ones' (*MECW* 5, p. 60). In 1914, Kaiser Wilhelm famously expressed this in his statement: 'I no longer recognise political parties; I recognise only Germans!'

198. Sennett 1972. The fetishism of commodities and money (*MECW* 35, pp. 81 ff.; *MECW* 37, pp. 389–90) leads to this being perceived differently 'in people's heads' than in theory (*MECW* 5, p. 374; *MECW* 37, p. 311; *MECW* 31, pp. 390–1). Social relations appear as properties of things – it appears as if producing more money were a 'natural' property of money. How could the final distribution of the national product, which involves numerous transfers and ramifications, be immediately transparent, when such transparency is not even a feature of the structure of revenues? In his concept of phenomena being 'covered up' [*verdeckt*], Heidegger 1962 (p. 60) adopted the formal structure of this argument (clearing and concealedness); however, he also divorced this structure from its original content, generalising and subjectivising it (2.5.5; see Henning 2004).

199. 'It is always the direct relationship of the owners of the conditions of production to the direct producers... which reveals the innermost secret, the hidden [!] basis of the entire social structure... This does not prevent the same economic basis – the same from the standpoint of its main conditions – due to innumerable different empirical circumstances, natural environment, racial relations, external historical influences, etc. from showing infinite variations... in appearance, which can be ascertained only by analysis of the empirically given circumstances' (*MECW* 37, p. 778).

200. *MECW* 37, p. 804.

201. *MECW* 29, p. 262.

202. This is suggested by the very word 'anatomy' (see 'physiology': *MECW* 31, p. 390). A person's bone structure can only be roughly intuited, and their internal organs cannot be seen at all – except under conditions of 'crisis', that is, when an injury occurs. It took considerable time for this inward gaze to become a matter of course. Foucault 1970 holds that the transition from visible similarities to conceptual relations occurred during the seventeenth century. A similar transition occurred in biology. There, the trend was to abandon morphology in favour of the analysis of 'invisible' genetic codes.

203. Bourdieu 1984.

and tear a society apart, as in Brazil.[204] They may also be busily glossed over, as in post-war Germany, where no one dared to speak about money.[205]

Normally, the social structure of the economy is revealed only within economic *theory* – namely within classical economic theory. The 'anatomy' becomes perceptible on the surface of society only during times of crisis and transition.[206] According to Marx, what people have in common is something quite basic: the nature of their 'revenue' or income. The logic of capitalism's economic sphere allows for only four typological possibilities: I can and must support myself either by means of the ground rent I receive as the owner of assets, by the profit I make as an entrepreneur or merchant, by the wages I receive as a blue- or white-collar worker, or by the redistribution of wealth. Economically, there is nothing else. Those who do not own means of production or other assets (land, real estate, stocks, and so on) will be forced, sooner or later, to sell their labour power. It is from these three revenues that the major social classes derive their income (profit, rent, wages).[207] Whatever does not take the form of such an income must at least represent a form of income redistribution: for example, the revenue of civil servants (teachers, policemen, professors, and so on) is financed out of taxes imposed on the three types of income; 'non-productive' capitals and workers (banks, services, artists, and so on) receive part of the surplus value obtained by the productive sectors.[208] Lifestyles and milieux make no difference to this.

This account roughly covers the three *types* of income sources. During prosperous, quiet times, these strata may befriend or feud with one another; they may break away or regroup. This is a *cultural* question. In times of crisis, however, when their material reproduction is at risk, they may quickly be thrown back upon themselves,[209] and the cyclical nature of growth makes it quite likely that there will in fact be such times. Marx's theory is not meant to provide a momentary description of a given society (see 2.1.2). For this reason, the cultural aspects of class are especially ill suited as evidence by which to refute his theory of classes. The theory is not 'objectivist'; it provides a basic framework

204. Altvater 1986.

205. Huster 1993, U. Neumann 1999; on this approach, see Thompson 1968, Vester 2004.

206. It takes a disruption of the normal state of affairs, such as the breaking of a bone, to raise awareness of 'anatomy' (3.3). US sociologist Richard Hofstadter suspected that class issues predominate in times of crisis, while status issues take centre stage in times of prosperity (thus Bottomore 1967, p. 112; this is reminiscent of Kautsky's response to Bernstein: 2.1.2). On the 'class in itself', which can still be modelled, see above.

207. *MECW* 37, pp. 801 ff.

208. On the analysis of transfers of value within the (US) national economy, see Shaikh 1996. 'Unproductive' does not mean that nothing is accomplished individually; it simply means that surplus value is consumed rather than created. For example, if A disposes of a high income, he can employ B as a cleaner. While this allows B to earn an income individually, through her labour, nothing is added on the level of society, since B lives off a part of A's income. Armaments or conspicuous state expenditure are similar cases (see 2.1.6).

209. When the savings of the petty bourgeoisie, which is often invoked to argue against the theory of class, suddenly melted away in 1929, there ensued a political radicalisation of these strata; their 'class constitution' took the form of fascism.

by which to understand, represent and – if possible – *explain* phenomena associated with political transitions during periods of crisis. Concrete phenomena can be 'ascertained only by analysis of the empirically given circumstances'.[210] What underpinned this was no doubt the cognitive interest of helping the working classes, in particular, to arrive at an understanding of their own situation, so that they would act more appropriately during future crises than in 1848 and 1871. As long as a distinction is drawn between theory and practice, the existence of such an interest cannot lessen the value of the insights obtained.[211]

It is worth recalling that the other great sociology to emerge at the time, French positivist sociology, was *also* developed in a context of political upheaval.[212] Its theories also had certain political implications (the ideal of a technocratic and quietist corporatism), which rested on a particular, partly economic assessment of this upheaval.[213] Here, it was the state that was emphasised, although it was not analysed so much as political wishes were addressed to it. This was what Jonas called 'state philosophy'. In contrast with this domination-centred and statist sociology, Marx meant to show that the state is far from having the upper hand within this play of forces; it is simply the prey of the various parties – whose interests he was therefore concerned to understand.[214]

Classes (and more) in Max Weber

The other great theorist of classes, Max Weber, has also left us only fragments.[215] His analysis of stratification seems to constitute a sociological supplement to the class theory of classical economics, for he *adds* to the description of the economy a description of the political sphere. Strictly speaking, he merely prepares the ground for such a description by developing the requisite 'categories'.[216] The only thing that might be criticised,

---

210. *MECW* 37, p. 778.

211. Max Weber also considers science to rest on 'presuppositions' (1972, pp. 151–2) that do not influence its content. Marx formulated insights rather than orgiastically venting the hatred felt by social *déclassés*, as suggested by Topitsch and Löw (2.6.6, Excursus). This can be seen from the fact that recent enyclopaedias still cite his works on France as standard references (thus M. Krätke, speaking in Berlin in April of 2002; see Vollgraf 2003). Nor is there any trace of objectivism in these works.

212. Kaesler 1976, pp. 19 ff.

213. All sociologists operate with certain presuppositions (Kittsteiner 1977, p. 160). 'Comte's real analogue is Fichte with his totalitarian leanings, as Windelband already pointed out' (Jonas 1976, Vol. I, p. 267; Windelband 1905).

214. When engaging with Hegel, Marx attempted to do this philosophically (*MECW* 3, pp. 5 ff., 175 ff.). In his writings on France, he was careful to provide historical evidence to show that the state was far from keeping aloof of the struggles and that it took sides, contrary to what conceptual philosophy and positivism claimed (*MECW* 10, pp. 45 ff.; *MECW* 11, pp. 99 ff.; *MECW* 20, pp. 5 ff.). On positivism's authoritarian corporatism, see Spaemann 1998, Negt 1974, Jonas 1976, Vol. I, pp. 264 ff., Jonas 1976, Vol. II, pp. 31 ff.; Lepenies 1985, pp. 16 ff.

215. Edgell 1993, p. 11.

216. 'Classes, status groups and parties' (Weber 1968, pp. 641 ff.); 'status groups and classes' (pp. 302 ff.).

here, is that this does not yet amount to an explanation of the relationship between these two domains, but providing such an explanation is not the task of a description, and much less that of a 'categorical framework'. Weber's claims contradict those of Marx only insofar as Weber's abstract description of social reality departs from the model of classes found in the *Manifesto*. But as we have seen, Marx did the same. A description of social reality has a different thematic focus than an economic analysis of the groups participating in the process of production and distribution and their behaviour during times of crisis. As long as one remains on the level of descriptions, one can still smooth over the differences between Weber and Marx.[217] Unlike Marx, Weber did not mean to 'lay bare the economic law of motion of modern society'.[218] He was interested, rather, in providing an 'overview of the obvious historical multiplicity of forms, with an eye to their ideal-typical interrelatedness'.[219] From this, one cannot necessarily deduce a relationship of rivalry. Like Marx, Weber made use of economic indicators. He also examined the condition of workers[220] and the criterion upon which his theory of 'class position' rested was similar to Marx's: the property of the 'propertied class', as opposed to the propertylessness of the 'income-dependent class'.[221]

To discover the fundamental difference between Weber and Marx, one has to look beyond their descriptions of surface appearances. Like many other members of his generation, Weber took marginalism as his starting point in economics.[222] Neoclassical theory abandoned economic differentiation and social classes. In it, there exist only buyers and sellers (with it being assumed that everyone switches from being a buyer to being a seller and vice versa) and their aggregates, firms and households. This basic theoretical choice has consequences for Weber's sociology. Classes are no longer distinguished from one another in terms of their position within the process of *production*, but in terms of their 'opportunities'[223] within the sphere of distribution, that is, on the goods or labour market.[224] Bernstein had already[225] phenomenalistically misinterpreted and rejected Marx's concept of class as a description of momentary surface appearances (see section 2.1.2). Sociology adopted this categorial transformation of the concept of class.

217. See, for example, Löwith 1988, Roth 1964, Kocka 1972 and 1977, Bader 1976, Mommsen 1974, pp. 144–81; Löwenstein 1976, Zander 1978, Weiß 1981, Münch 1992a, Antonio 1985, Böckler 1987, Lauermann 1989, Diarra 1990 and Gubbay 1997.

218. *MECW* 35, p. 10.

219. Jonas 1976, Vol. II, p. 204.

220. Weber 1924.

221. Weber 1968, p. 177.

222. Böckler 1987, pp. 122 ff.

223. Weber 1968, p. 177.

224. Weber 1968, p. 531. See Zlozlower in Böckler and Weiß 1987, p. 60. The fixation on exchange is still shared by the 'Weberian Marxist' Adorno. Horkheimer even idealised exchange when confronted with the 'total state' (see 2.6.1). Max Weber consulted Bernstein on issues related to seventeenth-century England (K. Lenk 1986, p. 220; see Weber 1894, pp. 80–1: 'Ethicisation of Class Struggle').

225. Bernstein 1968.

The phenomenalism of this economic sociology runs contrary to Marx's 'essentialism'.[226] Even though sociologists such as Weber understood the concept of 'economic class' to be an economic concept, the socio-structural analysis of the classical economists – and hence the theme of classes – was neglected for as long as economics was conducted as neoclassical economics.

Aside from this categorial transformation within economic sociology, Weber introduced, via the concept of status, the notion of social 'prestige'.[227] It was functionally equivalent to honour in estates-based society; 'estate' as the historical precursor of class was defined in terms of honour.[228] This reflected the residual feudal structure within Wilhelmine Germany.[229] Having grown wealthy thanks to victory in war and the *Gründerzeit*, imperial Germany sometimes permitted itself anticyclical political features characterised by a touch of state socialism. In response to this, Weber made an effort to distinguish his descriptive categories from those of Marx (such as with regard to the role of bureaucracy).[230] The categories of economic sociology had already become reductive due to the neoclassical influence; now Weber's analysis of social stratification was rendered extra-economic by the additions he made to it over time. This was precisely what made it so popular with later 'pluralist' theorists.[231] Neoclassical theory's influence on Weber is not limited to the elimination of classes. It can also be briefly illustrated by reference to basic Weberian concepts such as 'understanding sociology' (1) 'freedom from value judgements' (2), 'spirit of capitalism' (3), 'rationality' (4) and 'disenchantment' (5).

(1) Weber's methodology already displays a neoclassical thrust. Weber's decision to start from 'action' is innovative by comparison to organicist models, because it allows for empirical investigation. But because it is also strictly individualist, it is only of limited scope within sociological analysis. More still: it is also *subjectivist*, for Weber is not concerned with individuals as such, but only with their notions and the 'subjective meaning' that underlies their action; it is only this meaning, in his view, that can be 'understood'.[232] This makes Weber a precursor of theorists of 'rational choice'. The fact

226. The accusations of 'essentialism' and 'objectivism' are often handled as if they unmasked the true colours of the accused (Habermas 1987, p. 252; Negt in Euchner 1972, p. 44). But this unmasking of the accused relies only on the fact that his position lies crossways to the consensus within his discipline (Ritsert 1998). Sociology cannot obtain its categories from a 'consensus theory of truth'. The sociological concept of consensus was launched by Comte (1974, p. 83; see Fenske 1997, p. 662) and is indicative of the spirit of the times.

227. Weber 1968, p. 578.

228. Weber 1968, p. 149.

229. Milner 1999, p. 69.

230. Weber 1968, pp. 125 ff., 551 ff.; Weber 1921, p. 26.

231. Diettrich 1999, pp. 27 ff.

232. 'Sociology... is a science concerning itself with the interpretive understanding of social action and thereby [!] with a causal explanation of its course and consequences. We shall speak of "action" insofar as the acting individual attaches a subjective meaning to his behaviour... "Meaning"... may refer to... subjective meaning... In no case does it refer to an objectively "correct" meaning or one which is "true" in some metaphysical sense' (Weber 1972, p. 4). Weber discovers 'objective' meaning only in 'jurisprudence, logic, ethics, and esthetics' (ibid.); political economy

that Weber distinguishes various grades of consciousness, from the full consciousness characteristic of purposive action to the preconsciousness associated with mechanical behaviour, makes no difference to his subjectivism.[233] The parallel with atomistic neoclassical theory is not to be overlooked. Marx held that while 'the social' is open to scientific inquiry, it tends to remain inaccessible to the everyday consciousness of the individuals involved. Analysis of their subjective intentions cannot yield much insight into social processes and institutions – although the individuals can be familiarised with the results of scientific inquiry.[234]

(2) The call for *freedom from value judgements* is also a step forward, compared to, for instance, the open moralism of the historical school.[235] But Weber is overhasty in claiming that his own position is free of value judgements. When the barrister Weber insinuates that comprehensible reasons for an individual's actions can only be found in that individual's volition, he is invoking a juridical figure of thought – one that has

---

makes no appearance, here. Sklair argues that 'modernisation theory', which goes back to Weber, remains subjectivist in its approach (Sklair 1991, p. 34).

233. On industrial sociology in Weber 1924, see Jonas 1976, Vol. II, p. 201; see Weber's typology of action (Weber 1968, pp. 24 ff.: instrumentally rational, value-rational, affectual, traditional). Since empirical cases of 'subjective meaning' are seldom encountered, Weber replaced his typology with ideal types, which are constructed by the scholar: 'In the great majority of cases actual action goes on in a state of inarticulate half-consciousness or unconsciousness of its subjective meaning.... But the difficulty need not prevent the sociologist from systematizing his concepts by the classification of possible types of subjective meaning. That is, he may reason as if [!] action actually proceeded on the basis of clearly self-conscious meaning' (Weber 1968, pp. 21–2). Meaning is imputed. The theory of 'rational choice' isolated Weber's rationality of ends (and/or means) (3.2.1). The chimera of a meaning that is subjective and yet unconscious could now also refer to a function. Such a function can however no longer be determined without considering objective structures. For this reason, Weber's criticism of Marx – namely, that Marx ontologises his 'ideal types' – misses the mark (Weber 1952, p. 205; the criticism can still be found in Münch 1992a, pp. 533, 567 and 575). Unlike Weber, Marx does not begin with the subject.

234. Marx neither dissolves what is social into what is individual, nor does he divorce the individual from the social. He maintains that the social is rationally accessible, even if it is not immediately transparent. Social relations are usually 'independent of their will' (*MECW* 29, p. 263; see above and 2.1.5). 'We are not aware of this, nevertheless we do it' (*MECW* 35, p. 85; see, too, pp. 69–70; *MECW* 11, p. 103). 'How is it that personal interests always develop, against the will of individuals, into class interests, into common interests which acquire independent existence in relation to the individual persons, and in their independence assume the form of *general* interests? How is it that as such they come into contradiction with the actual individuals and in this contradiction, by which they are defined as *general* interests, they can be conceived by consciousness as *ideal* [!] and even as religious, holy interests?' (*MECW* 5, p. 245). 'Thus there are innumerable intersecting forces, an infinite series of parallelograms of forces which give rise to one resultant – the historical event... For what each individual wills is obstructed by everyone else, and what emerges is something that no one willed' (Engels, *MECW* 49, p. 35).

235. The disagreement turned on the controversial but 'essentially quite trivial demand that the scholar and writer distinguish between empirical facts... and his own... practically evaluative position under all circumstances' (Weber 1952, p. 486; see Jonas 1976, Vol. II, pp. 189–90; Jonas 1976, Vol. I, pp. 290 ff.; Ringer 1987, pp. 134 ff.). Nietzsche already used the term 'value judgement' (Nietzsche 1998, p. 139; see 2.6.3, motto).

served, since Locke, as a justification for the bourgeois concept of property.[236] Despite its contrafactual nature, this figure of thought is considered legitimate *within the field of law*. Yet its translation from the language of civil law into that of sociology is not free of value judgements; it is decidedly 'bourgeois'. With a certain degree of hermeneutic skill, one could read Weber's individualist methodology as directed against the 'communal action' of workers.[237] The controversy about value judgements is not without its presuppositions.

It is only within a model that allows for multiple 'interpretations', and which provides no *theoretical* guidance as to which 'interpretation' ought to be 'chosen', that Weber's problem arises. Far from promoting theoretical pluralism, such a model rests upon a theory of pure market forces and empirical impurities (see section 2.4.1). It is this model that calls for an ethical judgement. In Marx, there is no need for a value judgement on which of the two aspects gives rise to society's ills, since they are both aspects of one and the same phenomenon. For instance, historicist and neoclassical economics conform with one another insofar as they both start from the same model; they merely formulate different judgements on it.[238] Marx did not need to distinguish dualistically between good and bad factors; he describes a mechanism that gives rise to *both*. His model touches upon relationships the dualist model fails to grasp – and it is only because it does not grasp these relationships that the dualist model requires value judgements. Marx can be in favour, like Weber, of proceeding in an utterly scientific manner, without therefore needing to deny his sympathies for one side. The difference between Marx and Weber is best seen as residing in the fact that Marx provides a theoretical account of his sympathies, whereas Weber's sympathies are concealed in his basic concepts.[239]

---

236. Hegel 1991, §§ 34 ff.

237. Weber 1968, p. 531. This would be the accusation that social democracy is 'ideological', because it argues in terms of group interests, whereas economic liberalism is 'free of value judgements', because it considers only the individual. According to Rehberg 1979, Weber's subjectivist basic concepts (domination, life opportunities, and so on; see Lukács 1981, pp. 612–13; Baier 1988) were developed by reference to specific, namely 'upper-class' individuals. 'I am a member of the bourgeois classes. I feel myself to be a bourgeois, and I have been brought up to share their views and ideals' (Weber 1994, p. 23). Emphasis on the 'valuations' of individuals made it difficult for contemporaries to understand why one ought to refrain from formulating 'value judgements' of one's own (Jonas 1976, Vol. II, pp. 185, 201, 213 ff., 239). There is, however, no need for additional value judgements when they are already inherent in the theory. Jonas also sees in Weber's approach a dualism of 'blind techno-economic driving forces' and 'motives', where the latter alone are taken to be comprehensible (p. 204). This dualism is usually invoked by critics of Marx (see section 2.4.4).

238. According to Kittsteiner 1977, p. 160, Weber wanted to mediate between the two. Marx is antecedent to both. Marxism was unable to resolve the controversy on value judgements, the reason being that it also neglected economic theory, on the basis of which the requisite arguments might have been formulated. It chose a voluntaristically 'partisan' approach, 'valuing' such partisanship more highly than science (2.2.4). Here, Weber's call for restraint was justified.

239. W. Blumenberg 1962, p. 49 points out Marx's 'intellectual integrity'. Whoever criticises something must do so not 'on the basis of superficial flashes of thought, but only after long and profound study' (*MECW* 1, p. 220). Weber had Marx in mind when he wrote about value judgements: 'From scholasticism to Marxian theory . . . the notion of something 'objectively' valid,

(3) Since Weber's analysis limits itself, even at the level of its methodological approach, to the notions of individuals, it comes as no surprise that such notions are all one encounters in his genealogy of the *spirit of capitalism*. If it is clear from the outset that one is searching for something spiritual, then it is just as clear that what one is searching for can only be 'in the head', like the 'Protestant ethic'.[240] But this says less about capitalism than it says about Weber's method. In light of this spiritualism, Marx's critique of religion, which was directed not so much at religion as at the specifically *German Ideology*, appears remarkably topical.[241] Social philosophy's 'theological niceties' have only become more pronounced in Weber's followers.[242]

(4) While Weber did not think of himself as the representative of a philosophy of history, he did, in fact, develop his basic methodological choices into such a philosophy: the *disenchantment* hypothesis.[243] Here, we discover a classic syllogism: Weber has prescribed himself the methodological asceticism of formulating propositions about the world of actors only (a). However, he also observes changes in the social world, which he sees as having become ever more factual and objective (b). From this he draws the conclusion (c), at least in certain key passages, that b has been *caused* by a (c: a → b). Thus the subjectively inward moment of 'rational cognition' becomes the historically decisive factor; it becomes the subject of history: 'Wherever... rational empirical cognition has... consistently implemented [!] the disenchantment of the world, there results an open conflict with the ethical postulate that the world is a... cosmos organised in an *ethically* meaningful way'.[244] According to this idealist philosophy of history, the changes associated with modernity are due primarily to *cognition*. More still: what is genuinely unfortunate about these changes is that they no longer accord with traditional ethics.

---

i.e. of something that exists because it ought to, blends with an abstraction derived from empirical development' (Weber 1989, p. 100; Weber 1952, p. 196). 'It [an interpretation] can present a certain value judgement to us as the only "scientifically" permissible one only where – as in... Marx's *Capital* – norms (in this case of thought) come under consideration. But even here, an objectively valid 'valuation' of the object (... the logical "soundness" of Marxian forms of thought) is not one of the necessary aims of "interpretation"' (Weber 1989, p. 153; Weber 1952, p. 246). Does this not amount, once we strip away the roundabout formulations, to a kind of Husserlian *epoché*, namely to the claim that neither Marx nor anyone else was justified in judging Marx's thinking to be sound?

240. Marx spoke ironically of the 'spirit of capital' (*MECW* 35, p. 284) and of 'asceticism' (p. 589; see 2.3.5, 2.6.6), but in doing so he nevertheless identified material causal forces. Weber wants neither to 'causally explain... the phenomenon of capitalism, nor to... illustrate... the interaction of two spheres' (Jonas 1976, Vol. II, p. 203); he 'searches for the fulcrum from which capitalism's self-assertion becomes comprehensible' and discovers it in 'disciplined volition' (p. 205). Sombart 1951 was then able to blame the Jews; and Groeythusen 1927, Catholicism. The question is whether it is possible to 'understand' everything in this manner.

241. 2.6.4; see E. Wood 1986.

242. See Bolz 1989, 2.6.3.

243. Weber 1968, p. 308; Weber 1988, pp. 236, 1 ff., 536 ff. On this Weberian interpretation, see Tenbruck 1975. Hegel and Marx already spoke of Christianity having effected a 'despiritualisation' (*MECW* 5, p. 153).

244. Max Weber 1988, p. 564.

The origins of this philosophy of history are Nietzschean. It can be found not just in Weber, but also in Heidegger and Adorno.[245]

5) Disenchantment's main feature, *rationalisation*,[246] closes the circle and brings us back to neoclassical theory. This 'type' is not based on an economic-capitalist, but on a bureaucratic-administrative or even 'upper-class'-lordly perspective.[247] Weber advocates a state-centred 'container theory of society'.[248] This perspective is incapable of grasping the key constituent of *capitalism*: the blindly anarchic raging of market forces.[249] From the perspective of the sociology of knowledge, the faith in the 'primacy of politics' that was so popular among the scholars of Wilhelmine Germany[250] looks more like professoral self-persuasion than like a reliable description.[251] Within the de-economisation of basic sociological notions, we can discern the influence of Leninism (as is well known, Weber learned Russian in 1905). But it has little to do with Marx's approach. It is only within the neoclassical paradigm that politics confronts the economy as an outside force. It is only within a thought that separates the two spheres categorially – that is, aprioristically – that political categories no longer need to be related back to economics. Weber's 'rationalisation' has been described as an excessive generalisation of Marx's 'alienation'.[252] It ignores political economy, where rationalisation had a concrete theoretical place,[253]

---

245. 'Rational insight...autonomously crafted...a cosmos of truths' (Weber 1988, p. 569). This mixes up theory and reality. Or did he mean to say that theory has become more sober? That would amount to a gross simplification of the disenchantment hypothesis. On the allusion to Nietzsche, see Jonas 1976, Vol. II, p. 188; Bendix 1964, Hennis 1987, D. Kim 1999. Lichtblau 1997, pp. 77 ff. considers Nietzsche to be cultural sociology's main reference point (2.5.2). Only a form of idealism would trace 'vital need' [*Lebensnot*] (Husserl 1970, § 2) back to epistemologists like Descartes and Kant. It was Jaspers who drew Heidegger's attention to Weber. Husserl, Heidegger 1962 and Adorno 1997 then elaborated upon this philosophy of history.

246. Weber 1968, *passim*.

247. Rehberg 1979.

248. Beck 2000, pp. 23 ff. 'Beyond all their differences, such theorists as Émile Durkheim, Max Weber and even Karl Marx shared a territorial definition of modern society, and thus a model of society centred on the national state' (p. 24). They are accused of 'equating society with the national state' (p. 25). Beck disposes of no theoretical instruments by which to address the period that followed – perhaps because he himself has relied too strongly on this approach. He makes a conspicuously high number of passing references to Marx and Marx's analysis of society, which adopted a different approach from the beginning (pp. 2, 22, 153). But Beck shrinks back from Marx's analysis (pp. 24, 98, 122).

249. Calculability is not a feature of capitalism; market developments are anarchic and warlike. Weber's 'principal step was to de-economize and "spiritualize" the nature of capitalism. This he presented as a rationalizing of socio-economic life, the rational calculability of all phenomena' (Lukács 1981, p. 606; the same can still be said of Horkheimer). In making this point, Lukács is also subtly criticising himself.

250. Jonas 1976 II, p. 225.

251. 'Politics is penetrating into the economic order at the same time that economic interests are entering into politics' (Weber 1968, p. 299).

252. Hughes 1958, p. 317; Jonas 1976, Vol. II, p. 207.

253. Namely the mechanisation of production (see section 2.1.6), which is what the word 'rationalisation' is still used to refer to (*MECW* 35, pp. 374 ff., 616 ff.). Marx even uses the word once himself (*MECW* 37, p. 612).

and turns it into the 'mental' signum of the entire epoch, which is even supposed to have caused that epoch – if only because it preceded it historically, in the form of religion.

The motive behind Weber's investigations can thus clearly be seen to be *socio-philosophical*: modernity, which is so confusing, is to be re-incorporated into the subject (or 'understood').[254] But 'knowledge' is not just addressed to the subject; the subject is also treated as the criterion for 'knowledge'. (Later, it would become theory's only *content*: see section 2.5.2). Certainly there is no way of developing a theory of classes on this basis. 'Modernity' has become confusing not just in real history, but also in the history of ideas, and this is at least partly due to the fact that sociology – including Weber's sociology – has failed adequately to theorise its decisive object of inquiry: capitalism and the anatomy of capitalism, of which classes are a feature.

Classes in Helmut Schelsky

> The relatively homogeneous lifestyle proper to the levelled middle-class society... fulfils itself in the form of homogeneous participation in the material and spiritual goods of civilisational comfort.[255]

In West Germany during the period after the Second World War, when the horrors of the Third Reich were fully known and perpetrators and victims attempted to live once more within a single country, Helmut Schelsky characterised the need of the age as being for a 'neutralist background ideology of a non-antagonistic character'.[256] Neoclassical *economics* had always provided such an ideology. For this reason, it was an especially suitable background paradigm for the West-German sociology of the postwar period – all the more so as it had already been the preferred model of the sociological classics. Various forms of 'integration with the West' may also have played a role, for this was the period when neoclassical economics achieved its conclusive codification.[257] For this reason, after 1945, the methods of sociology continued, in Germany as elsewhere, to move even closer to those of neoclassical theory. A subjectivist drift was evident in the fact that empirical research made use mainly of polls, interviews and sympathy scales.

---

254. Kittsteiner 1977, p. 161 speaks of 'metaphors of chaos' in Weber. On 'confusion' [*Unübersichtlichkeit*], see Habermas 1985.

255. Schelsky 1953.

256. Schelsky 1959, p. 22; see Schelsky 1979, p. 375. By formulating the theory of the 'levelled middle-class society', he satisfied this very need. As for sociology's 'funereal silence' (Schelsky 1959, p. 32; a quotation from Dahrendorf), he explains it in terms of collegial concern for the outward appearance of a discipline that had still to be properly recognised, but mainly by invoking the risk of 'ideological-biographical suspicions'. It needs to be added that at the time, one could render one's opponents unpopular with one or the other section of the population by identifying them either as National Socialists or as emigrants.

257. In the bestseller by Samuelson 1948; Henderson 1983, Debreu 1976 (Zinn 1987).

These allowed one to gather exact measurement data, but they also reflected nothing but *moods*.[258]

Yet the legacy of Marxian sociology, and more specifically that of the theory of classes, continued to be felt. In light of the approaching Cold War, it needed to be dealt with by sociology. But the sociological theories of class developed after 1945 either blanked out the economy altogether, or thought of it only according to the neoclassical model. With this basic theory in the background, the concept of class went through the transformations already described in the discussion of Weber: it went from being primarily economic and functional to being subjective and phenomenal. Investigation of society's class-specific structure now looked to non-economic categories, examining factors such as education, areas of residence, recreational activities, general moods, the 'habitus', and so on. It comes as no surprise that Marx's claims could not be confirmed from this point of view – not even for his own time. After all, the justification for political economy as a distinct scientific discipline consists precisely in the fact that the structures of the economic process are not immediately apparent to those participating in the process. When the broadening of sociological inquiry is understood not as supplementing economic analysis, but as *replacing* it, and when Marx's theory of class is simultaneously misinterpreted as a 'description' of the current condition of society, it begins to seem as if Marx's assessments were wrong. To support this claim, people usually invoked the development of a broad, culturally interpreted 'middle class' (it was described in terms of consumption, or in terms of its 'lifestyle'),[259] the development or expansion of the 'new' middle class of 'clerical workers',[260] increased (social, not spatial) 'mobility' within society and people's declining willingness to describe themselves as belonging to one of the traditional classes.[261]

Many theorists treated such perspectives not just as empirical *observations*, but as constituting, in and of themselves, refutations of Marx's theory – without noticing the decisive difference in thematic focus and level of analysis (like Oppenheimer, see above,

258. This was a critique of empirical social research formulated by Adorno (1972a). Weber's industrial sociology already investigated the 'mood' of workers (Jonas 1976, Vol. II, p. 201).

259. Schelsky 1956, p. 336.

260. See Kracauer 1998, Grünberg 1932, Croner 1954, Bell 1975, Laclau 1977, Speier 1977 or Haupt 1998. Today, it has become more common to speak of the 'service sector'; something similar is meant by this. One might speculate about whether the percentage of people working as attendants (menial servants or service workers) is indicative of a high rate of exploitation (capital has money to spare and remunerates unproductive labour also; unemployed persons are constrained to take up such menial service work). The number of such workers was relatively high in 1861 (*MECW* 35, pp. 449–50; 202–3). In 1951, it was low (Bottomore 1967, pp. 45–6). During the mid-1990s, there once more began to be talk of a 'service society' (Kneer 1997; see, too, Ringer 1987, p. 204).

261. Stages in the theoretical renunciation of 'class' included Geiger 1949, Dahrendorf 1959a, Schelsky 1961, Bergmann 1969, Offe 1972, Beck 1983, Hradil 1987 and 2001; see Ritsert 1998, pp. 88 ff. ('German Post-War Sociology's Five-Fold Elimination of Classes'), and Diettrich 1999, pp. 21 ff. ('On the Disappearance of Class and Stratification Analysis in German Sociology'). For the English-speaking world, see Gubbay 1997 and Milner 1999.

section 2.4.1). The works on the 'concept of class' that Schelsky published during the 1950s are representative of this way of proceeding. They have the additional advantage of explicitly referring back to Marx. For this reason, they will be analysed here.

According to Schelsky, the question 'Do we still live in a class society?'[262] provoked 'one of the few theoretical debates' that were 'conducted at all within the German social sciences of the post-1945 period'.[263] For this reason, he posed the question himself, and he did so repeatedly over a period of several years. Schelsky defines sociology's task as that of arriving at a 'descriptive grasp of society'.[264] He then attributes the same descriptive intention to Marx. According to Schelsky, Marx's 'dualist' doctrine of class was intended as a representation of a 'total, all-encompassing structure' that expresses itself in 'all [!] ... phenomena of social existence'.[265] Marx's propositions on economic classes are read by Schelsky as the sociological *description* of a concrete state of society. In this way, he attributes to Marx the goal of contemporary sociology.[266] This carries to extremes the phenomenalisation of Marxian theory we have already encountered in Bernstein and Weber. And yet Schelsky had once known better: only five years earlier, he had written that Marx had known about the existence of other classes and had meant to formulate not a 'diagnostic observation' but a 'law of development'.[267] But for Schelsky, a 'law of development' has to someday be realised; he cannot think of Marx's thought, which distinguished between effective essential forces and irreducibly anarchic 'surface' phenomena, other than as a representation *in instalments*. Yet in 1961, even this concession seemed to him to be going too far – he limits himself to the deliberately misleading suggestion that Marx's intention was a descriptive one, citing as evidence the blatantly polemical passages of the *Communist Manifesto*.

Next, this putative 'description' of Marx is radically historicised in the manner of Schelsky's teacher Freyer: Marx is characterised as a 'nineteenth-century thinker'.[268] He was right for the nineteenth century,[269] Schelsky claims, but his theory no longer holds true today. Due to fundamental changes in society's structure, his theory is 'no longer' valid (this figure of thought, which has been popular among sociologists since Freyer, has origins in Hilferding and Lenin: see section 2.2.6). Freyer suggests 'that the doctrine

262. Schelsky 1956, p. 333.
263. Schelsky 1961, p. 350.
264. Schelsky 1961, p. 368; see Kneer 1997 and 2001.
265. Schelsky1961, p. 358.
266. Marxist sociology may have invited this.
267. Schelsky 1956, p. 334.
268. Freyer 1964, pp. 306 ff.; Freyer 1931; cf. Remmers 1994, pp. 72 ff.; on Schelsky's relationship to Freyer, see G. Schäfer 1999 and Rehberg 1999. Historicisation could be one reason why Schelsky revoked the concession he made originally. A theory that is interpreted as an anticipation does not allow itself to be historicised as elegantly as a description. Even language fails one in this endeavour ('Marx's belief that this would soon happen was real').
269. Schelsky implicitly describes Marx's analysis as 'correct' (Schelsky 1961, p. 390), although he simultaneously accuses Marx of idealism, theologism and reductionism (p. 359).

of class refers to a historically determinate social reality':[270] 'This industrial class society *once existed*, and there can be no doubt that our German society also increasingly assumed such a class character during the nineteenth century'.[271] 'It *was once the case* that "society as a whole is . . . splitting up into two . . . hostile . . . classes" (Marx)'.[272]

What Freyer suggests is incorrect: there was no 'all-encompassing' division of society into two classes in Marx's day, and Marx did not intend to formulate such a 'description'. Marx's 'theory of class' states only the following (see above): the capitalist mode of production is spreading all over the world. A powerful economisation of all areas of life is inherent to it. Its logic allows for only two possibilities: whoever owns no means of production and no assets will be forced sooner or later to sell his labour power. Ever-greater sections of the population are experiencing this first hand. Now, when Marx described certain stages of a particular social development, he began heuristically from this basic economic structural principle, but he never claimed that only two classes exist, or that they confront each other in such a way that each of them is 'homogeneous in itself'.[273] Schelsky, too, elides the fundamental, economic level of Marx's theory, its centrepiece.[274]

There is one claim in Schelsky upon which everything turns: namely that society's structure has changed *from the ground up*, so that Marx's theory is 'no longer'[275] valid.[276] To support this claim, Schelsky refers to all sorts of phenomena: improvements in the condition of the workers and the *declassé* status of refugees, 'generalised consumption', the development of a 'unified lifestyle', and welfare and taxation policies.[277] He also refers to a 'consensus within the social sciences',[278] namely an agreement no longer to speak of class structure – the 'best people' in science and politics consider the concept to have been discredited, Schelsky says, citing Schumpeter.[279] These are all *observations*

270. Schelsky 1961, p. 360.

271. Schelsky 1956, p. 334; emphasis added.

272. Schelsky 1961, p. 360; emphasis added.

273. 'To Marx, "class" is a socially homogenous social constitution in itself' (Schelsky 1961, p. 359). This statement contrasts with what Marx wrote in 1850: 'the struggle of the industrial wage worker against the industrial bourgeois . . . is in France a partial phenomenon, which . . . could so much the less supply the national content of the revolution, since the struggle against capital's secondary modes of exploitation, that of the peasant against usury and mortgages or of the petty bourgeois against the wholesale dealer, banker, and manufacturer – in a word, against bankruptcy – was still hidden in the general uprising against the finance aristocracy' (*MECW* 10, p. 57).

274. Schelsky even claims that this elision is 'deliberate' (Schelsky 1961, p. 350).

275. Schelsky 1961, p. 355.

276. An 'overcoming' of the class structure: Schelsky 1961, pp. 326, 337 – a formulation used in Freyer 1964, p. 306.

277. Schelsky 1961, pp. 327, 328, 336.

278. Schelsky 1961, p. 337.

279. Schelsky 1961, p. 352. See Weber 1968, p. 284. This is a form of magical thinking – theoretical discourse about an object becomes an indicator of the state of that object itself. According to Schelsky, 'class consciousness' developed only thanks to theory (Schelsky 1961, p. 370); later it was maintained, its loss of plausibility notwithstanding, by large organisations ('mass providential organisations') and by essentially functionless intellectuals (pp. 398–9, 414 – note the implicit demonisation of Schelsky's theoretical opponents). But Schelsky did not retain this position for long.

that may have been accurate at the time. But they will not do as arguments against the theory of classes. They have the status of what Marx called 'infinite variations and gradations in appearance'.[280] In order to 'overcome' the theory of classes, more needs to be done than merely enumerate opinions. But Schelsky never ventures onto the level of theory. When he writes that 'the sociologist' can analyse social transformations 'only on the level of the consciousness of the immediate actors',[281] his statement reiterates the methodology of Max Weber, which Schelsky makes use of. What this means for the theory of classes is that the verdict on it is formulated primarily in terms of feelings ('the feeling of no longer being at the very bottom')[282] and 'consciousness'.[283] But both are situated on a different level than the one Marx operates on.

Schelsky provides no *substantive* arguments in support of the claim that an 'entirely different'[284] reality has developed. But he also gets under the feet of modern subjectivist sociology, even though he means for it to bolster his claims: the sociological polls of the time show that many workers continued to use the terminology of class.[285] And so Schelsky *himself* has still to overcome the 'social consciousness' by which he meant to demonstrate that the class society has been transcended. He does this by declaring it a residue from the days of class domination, one retained only by dubious institutions and persons. This does not make the hypothesis of total transformation any more substantive. Rather, Schelsky is forced to move away from subjectivist sociology, which at least has the merit of documenting real moods and opinions (something for which he coins the neologism '*Meinungsideologie*' [ideology of opinion],[286] and into a speculative *social psychology*. Thus the matter to be investigated lies neither in the object nor in the subject, but in the social subconscious. This is a rather arbitrary level on which to advance sociological claims.[287] Schelsky gives various reasons why 'new social realities continue to be understood in terms of outdated social concepts',[288] such as 'ceremonialisation'[289] or the putative fact that even in a dynamic society, 'deep-seated, basic human drives'[290] make people subordinate themselves to 'static hierarchies'.[291] This still does not amount to substantive evidence. Schelsky's hypothesis has merely led him to develop a bold socio-psychological construct, and it has gotten him caught up in inconsistencies.[292]

280. *MECW* 37, p. 778.
281. Schelsky 1961, p. 370.
282. Schelsky 1961, pp. 328, 337, 343.
283. Schelsky 1961, pp. 329, 336, 354.
284. Schelsky 1961, p. 338.
285. Schelsky 1961, pp. 338, 357; see Popitz 1957a.
286. Schelsky 1961, pp. 369, 390.
287. Jameson 1993, Assmann 1999.
288. Schelsky 1961, p. 338.
289. Shelsky 1961, pp. 340, 367.
290. Schelsky 1961, p. 330.
291. Schelsky 1961, pp. 329, 343.
292. Schelsky vacillates between different claims. He says there once was a class society (Schelsky 1979, pp. 334, 360), and yet at the same time, class is supposed to be 'merely a mental synthesis' (p. 360). The debate on classes is a 'purely academic affair' (p. 352), and yet 'class consciousness

At no time did a real process of levelling occur.[293] But even if the 'levelled middle-class society' had in fact existed as a momentary state, this would have had few consequences for the theory of class – conceivably, economic analysis would still have faced the task of revealing the forces at work behind the scenes. Yet not much can be said about such forces on the basis of an analysis that deals only with a momentary state or brief period of time, bases its verdicts mainly on subjective assessments and considers only the sphere of the market, but not that of production, or even limits itself to extra-economic factors. The claim about a 'overcoming of class oppositions through social levelling'[294] jumps overhastily and unduly from surface phenomenon to essence, from observation to theory. An analysis that refrains from economic inquiry is ill-equipped to refute economic propositions. Thus the question arises what exactly *motivated* Schelsky's struggle against the theory of class and his repeated claims about a new, opposition-free reality. The answer is something to do with Germany's very own 'melting pot of the class society'[295] – National Socialism. Schelsky only ever refers to it in passing; he does not thematise or theorise it, even though he attributes considerable explanatory power to it: in his biographical introduction, Schelsky claims it was *National Socialism* that accomplished the great transition from a society divided into classes to a levelled society. More specifically, he expresses the view 'that the social transformations that National Socialism, the war and the consequences of war have prompted within our society were so sweeping that they rendered entire sociological libraries obsolete'.[296]

In his 1953 and 1956 books, Schelsky makes only passing references to the loss of class position suffered by the persons displaced from Germany's prewar eastern territories [the '*Heimatvertriebene*'],[297] a loss he attributes to what he calls the 'collapse',[298] and he only briefly mentions the 'rise of technical, commercial and administrative employees', without asking how they were able to rise so quickly. In 1961, he speaks more clearly, describing the 'idea of the *Volksgemeinschaft*' as 'unmistakably egalitarian'.[299]

---

exists to a considerable degree' within society (p. 361). Once more, theory and reality are not distinguished. Refuting Marx becomes an obsession. The obsession leads to a series of overemphatic statements, each of which neutralises the other ('I never ate any cake' – 'I didn't eat the chocolate cake' – 'I didn't eat it by myself').

293. 'Given the considerable differentiations in the distribution of income and more still of assets, and given the differences in lifestyle, housing situation and working relations, the hypothesis on the tendency towards levelling that H. Schelsky formulated in 1950 appears . . . historically obsolete'. In fact, 'the distribution of productive assets objectively divides society into a small group of proprietors and a large number of non-proprietors' (Rytlewski 1979, p. 115; see Greffrath 1976). Other social statistics indicate much the same.

294. Schelsky 1956, p. 337.

295. Geiger 1949.

296. Schelsky 1979, p. 12.

297. Schelsky 1979b, pp. 327, 336.

298. Schelsky 1979b, p. 400.

299. Schelsky 1979, p. 375. In 1955, Schelsky stated more openly that 'National Socialism, war, the country's collapse and the policies of the Allied Forces transformed the social structure ever

Long-standing admiration for a longtime fellow combatant[300] blends with a covert apology for the publicly accused perpetrator.[301] And yet *sociologically*, Schelsky places that which he concedes to National Socialism and to the losses consequential to it within a larger context. He thereby morally absolves National Socialism (and with it, himself):

> The rise... of nationalist ideas... originates... in changes within the social structure, particularly in the growing importance of a 'new middle class'.... This social development ought to be understood as a prerequisite of the rule of the National Socialist system, rather than as a consequence of it.[302]

Here, he is moving in a circle. The social transformation National Socialism is supposed to have caused now constitutes its prerequisite. While this strips National Socialism of the honour of having accomplished the great transformation all by itself, it also retrospectively provides it with a democratic legitimation.[303] Regardless of whether National Socialism caused the transformation or vice versa, the claim that classes disappeared in the Third Reich does not hold up.[304] All one can say is that class was no longer *spoken about*. Even if Schelsky denies it[305] – there were real reasons for the academic 'disappearance of class analysis', except that they were less to do with the objects of theory than with its subjects, the social scientists themselves.[306] Even the *post hoc* critique of the Third Reich's welfare measures fails to understand that the '*Volksgemeinschaft*'

---

more violently and radically, reconfiguring it and heading it towards new, irreversible... developments' (Schelsky 1979, p. 412; see pp. 12, 399).

300. Schelsky 1979, p. 11.

301. 'Every "movement" becomes internally conservative, and even [!] communism or National Socialism would only be conceivable, in our society, in the form of restoration efforts' (Schelsky 1979, p. 417). Schelsky lamented 'the way political volition, often characterised in the same breath and in an imposing manner as 'commitment', is attributed to the sociologist' (p. 370). Schelsky normally gives ontological precedence to ideas, but in this case he refuses to hold those who develop certain ideas responsible. König resented this: König 1984, p. 189; König 1987, p. 345.

302. Schelsky 1979, p. 352.

303. 'The administration of totalitarian states, which seeks to eliminate sections of the nation that have lost their contemporary relevance, merely implements economic verdicts issued long ago' (Adorno and Horkheimer 1997, p. 206).

304. While there was a 'welfare policy' (the German Labour Front, 'Strength Through Joy', and so on) which strove to integrate workers (Mason 1993, Recker 1985, Lauermann 1998), it can by no means be said to have abolished class differences. Some of the first measures taken in 1933 included breaking up trade unions and lowering wages. If some people were able to 'rise up' quickly, this was due to party and military hierarchies, as well as to the 'Aryanisation' of Jewish property (see Neumann 1943, Hennig 1976, Caplan 1995). War losses aside, capital and labour emerged from the war relatively unchanged; 'restoration' came very soon (Huster 1972; see Schelsky 1979, pp. 410 ff.).

305. Schelsky 1961, p. 252.

306. 'This special development of German sociology has a political history:... class theory, which was already rejected by most sociologists in the Weimar Republic, was eliminated from linguistic usage in the Third Reich. The "economic miracle" and "social partnership" replaced the National Socialist "*Volksgemeinschaft*". During the Cold War, any affinity with Marxism was suspicious' (Diettrich 1999, p. 11).

was created neither socially nor economically, but only symbolically.[307] The 'community, a people' [*Gemeinschaft des Volkes*][308] was created not by 'prosperity of the people' [*Volkswohlstand*],[309] nor by the Volkswagen (which benefitted not the people but the military frontline); if anything, it was created by Heinz Rühmann.

The *Volksgemeinschaft* was *staged*.[310] While it presented itself as anti-modern ideologically, National Socialism was quite modern when it came to aesthetics. It made widespread use of the modern mass media for the first time. From the role party newspapers and the media mogul Hugenberg played in the seizure of power to the stabilisation of National Socialist rule by means of radio and newsreel, from Riefenstahl's stagings of party conferences to ambitious projects such as the film *Kolberg*, the National Socialists handled the media so masterfully that even foreign commentators were fascinated.[311] It was not just by means of terror, but also by means of its aesthetics that National Socialism reached broad sections of the population – and there was more to this aesthetics than its backward-looking variant, that of Alfred Rosenberg and torchlit processions. It is an aesthetic synthesis of this sort that Schelsky continues to have in mind during West Germany's early years – his use of the word 'uniform' in his discussion of mass consumption is symptomatic. He 'yearns' for a return to this aesthetic synthesis.[312] Both before and after 1945, the putative 'overcoming of class structure' was nothing but a 'beautiful semblance'.[313] Schelsky, however, takes it at face value. That there was a *willingness* to let oneself be deluded by such semblance was already indicated by Schelsky in his remark, quoted above, on the 'need of the age'.[314]

---

307. The National Socialists did not rule because of their social policies (see, however, Aly 2005). The element of domination most tangible for everyone was probably the party's gentle enforcement of participation (Neumann 1943, Reibel 2002).

308. Heidegger 1962, p. 436.

309. Schelsky 1956, p. 346.

310. Ehalt 1996.

311. They were fascinated by more than just the Olympics (H. Schäfer 1981, p. 121; Fest 1973, pp. 513, 700; on the use of the media: Hofmann 1988, Donner 1995, Dröge 1995, Welzer 1995, Hanna-Daoud 1996, Ohr 1997).

312. 'Let us not forget that the Weimar Republic also suffered from... overharshly emphasised class conflicts and that a totalitarian movement... raised itself into the saddle... by the stirrups of a widespread desire for the overcoming of class conflict' (Schelsky 1961, p. 348). Schelsky is still in the thrall of this 'desire' (see pp. 326, 337, 361); what he misses in 1965 is a 'sense of order' (p. 343).

313. Reichel 1991. Like every illusion, this one also has a *fundamentum in re* – for example, in the state-owned media corporations that monopolised the new mass media in Germany during the 1950s. As far as TV is concerned, Schelsky is right – everyone watches the same programme. It is only with hindsight that this is understood to be something that cannot be taken for granted. Today, the media landscape is clearly marked by class differences, from so-called 'underclass TV' (Harald Schmidt) to upmarket video recordings of theatre performances. If so much stock is put in 'king soccer', then is this not because it is considered the last TV event to be enjoyed across class divisions?

314. Schelsky 1959, p. 22.

We have said all there is to say about the 'anti-class-theories' of this 'anti-sociologist';[315] the actual *object* of Marx's theories of class is never addressed.[316] This avoidance of Marx is also interesting for systematic reasons, for it is symptomatic. Not only does it express a certain view about the relationship of *theory and practice*, science and politics, within the science of society; it also departs from the covert value judgements of Weber's sociology by explicitly describing itself as a normative theory, or as an 'indirect moral doctrine'.[317] For even though Schelsky ultimately arrives at the same question as political economy,[318] he fends off economic questions by suggesting that everything has changed. Instead of confronting such questions, he regularly concludes his essays with moral appeals: 'This is not the issue here. The issue is the moral appeal'.[319]

> The task [of the sociologist], our genuine educational effort ought [!] to be seen to consist in our participation in the procedures and experiments by which the individual struggles to recreate his own unique and unmistakeable social reality as a person;[320] it ought [!] to consist in our participation in efforts to sustain the small group and the personal human relationship within matrimony, the family, friendship, collegiality, the professional community, etc.[321]

---

315. Schelsky 1981.

316. This is also true of Dahrendorf 1959a, who interprets the theory of class as a theory of 'domination' and is thus taken in by the notion of the 'primacy of politics' that was current at the time. Popitz 1957 is a similar case; he interprets 'class' as a distinction between intellectual and physical labour (see Sohn Rethel 1972). Some 'anti-class-theories' are criticised by Schelsky himself, such as the 'disappointment, sometimes evident in Dahrendorf, over the fact that none of the more recent theories of the social structure has fully refuted the theory of class' (Schelsky 1961, p. 359).

317. The class consciousness of workers is traced back to the unexpected longevity of socialist ideology (Schelsky 1961, pp. 365–6), the need for orientation among younger sociologists (pp. 354–5) and the influence of 'large organisations' (p. 414). Thus, while it is supposed to be 'no more' than a residue and a suggestion circulated by intellectuals, Schelsky states elsewhere that 'scientific-analytic insights always degenerate into immediate social consciousness' (pp. 369–70). If class, which is assumed to once have existed (pp. 334, 360), was nevertheless 'no more than an intellectual synthesis' (p. 360), then it seems to lie in the power of the social scientist to influence his environment as he sees fit, by means of a 'self-fullfilling-prophecy' (p. 390) (this notion is underpinned, in Freyer, by a veritable nihilism: 2.5.1). One can, however, go about this in the right way or in the wrong way – something that Schelsky evaluates politically (to him, the class theorists are apparently going about it the wrong way). It is via this evaluation that ethics is brought in, in an *ex machina* manner. In his introduction to Riesmann 1968, Schelsky wrote: 'The most... sociology can achieve is simply to formulate an indirect moral doctrine' (p. 19). Jonas 1976, Vol. II, p. 251 fails to notice that Schelsky means this affirmatively; he repeats the statement emphatically in 1965 (Schelsky 1979, p. 16). All one needs to do is learn to distinguish between false 'moralism' (Schelsky 1959, p. 108; Schelsky 1975) and the right moral doctrine as represented by Schelsky.

318. 'Our social constitution is determined by the distribution of wealth' (Schelsky 1956, p. 346 – the *Wealth of Nations*, Smith 1999). He even notes that 'economic distribution conflicts are dominant' (Schelsky 1961, p. 384).

319. Schelsky 1956, p. 348.

320. Schelsky is already speaking as an anti-sociologist. The social world, which is depicted as lacking reality, is devalued. Scheler had already lamented that Max Weber's sociology lacked the 'depth' of the 'person' (Jonas 1976, Vol. II, p. 215).

321. Schelsky 1979, p. 409.

This quotation is not taken from a training manual for future pedagogues, but from a theoretical essay. This is a veritable ethicisation and aestheticisation of sociological theory.[322] Here, ethics no longer serves as a post hoc surrogate for a lost economic theory, as in Bernstein; it serves to *actively* replace that theory. Thus the texts examined confirm my observation that Marxophobic German sociology tends toward a dualism that uses 'ethics' to supplement a technoid base,[323] and in extreme cases, to replace it. This ethicisation of reflection on society needs to be considered further, up until the present (see Chapter 3).

Classes in Luhmann

Niklas Luhmann, who is often presented as one of the most important sociologists to have written in German, has next to nothing to say about the question of class society. Ultimately, he was content to compile a catalogue of current theorems.[324] He says of this 'semantics' – which is all it is, in his view – that it belongs to 'old Europe', meaning that it now has museal value only. He refers his readers to the 'investigation of inequality', which compiles statistics on existing inequalities.[325] Hence, what is important in Luhmann is not the little he has to say about classes but the *reason* he gives for having so little to say. Luhmann has crafted a meta-narrative, currently considered valid, by which talk of classes can continue to be described, within sociology, as being topical 'no longer'. However, this narrative is not a *sociological* theory. The German 'philosophising' of sociology culminates in Luhmann.[326] Luhmann has left us a systems philosophy – and a 'philosophy of the system' – that is comparable only to that of Hegel in terms of the number of pages it fills, the hermeticism of its language and the recipe according to which it has been produced. For this reason, it makes sense to postpone discussion of this system to the next section (2.5.6).

---

322. The aestheticist desire to provoke 'first-hand experiences' (Gehlen) within science (Schelsky 1979, p. 408; see Üner 1994) could not have been expressed any better by postmodernism's pop theory, since it too is concerned with the aesthetics of existence and (self-)dramatisation. Max Weber already spoke of an 'ethicisation of class struggle' (Weber 1894, pp. 80–1).

323. Schelsky 1979, pp. 99 ff., 449 ff.

324. Luhmann 1998, pp. 1055 ff.

325. See Goldthorpe 1985, Kreckel 1983, Kreckel 1992, Hradil 1987, Hradil 2001 and, for a critical discussion, Diettrich 1999. 'No one will deny the existence of continuing distribution problems. No one will deny that workers require organised representation of their interests' (Luhmann 1986, p. 171). Then why ignore Marx's theory? Luhmann even diagnoses a fall in the rate of profit: 'The ratio of turnover to equity is becoming more and more risky' (p. 167). The distinction between 'militant semantics' and theory needs to be interpreted as a self-description (this is where his own theory becomes self-referential). He is himself conducting a 'semantic' struggle for a political recoding.

326. A 'shift from theory to *Weltanschauung*' [*Verweltanschaulichung*] (K. Müller 1996, p. 41; Schwinn 2001; 2.5.6).

The question is whether reformulating specific issues on the highest possible level of abstraction[327] is to say anything substantive about those issues. Luhmann seems to have assumed this, for how else could he have justified writing entire books about economics, law, art and religion without compiling his own data? His abstract reformulations involve the unwarranted claim that they simultaneously provide an account of real processes such as the 'differentiation of systems'.[328] Once again, it is assumed, in an idealist manner, that form creates its own content, or at least corresponds to it, in and of itself.[329] But Marx's approach requires that, rather than blindly accepting this, one search out the arguments by which Luhmann explains *why* 'the semantics of labour and capital must be abandoned'[330] – and with it that of 'social classes'.[331] As far as content is concerned, there is hardly anything new in this. Luhmann repeats point by point the argument advanced by Schelsky, his precursor at Bielefeld University, although he never mentions Schelsky's name.

Like Schelsky, Luhmann reduces the theory of class to the *description* of a momentary state, which he situates in the past.[332] The theoretical mode he thereby attributes to the theory of class replicates the vitalist reduction of theory to an expression of practice (2.5.4). Luhmann speaks of a 'militant semantics'[333] intended to 'organise sympathies'[334] and 'stimulate ... expectations of change'.[335] But today, he argues, the concept of class needs to be 'thoroughly historicised',[336] and thus relativised.[337] In Luhmann as in Schelsky,

327. 'This account forces us to formulate an account from an unusually abstract angle. The flight has to be above cloud level' (Luhmann 1995, pp. 12 f.; cf. 2.5.7).

328. Luhmann 1995, p. 25.

329. Grimm 1974, Sens 1979 and others judge sociological systems theory to be an extension of the aprioristic and 'formal sociology' of Simmel. Simmel, however, was still aware that such a theory can be formulated only in a 'purely' formal way, namely that no claims can be made about content: 'Geometrical abstraction investigates only the spatial forms of bodies, although empirically, these forms are given merely as the forms of some material content. Similarly, if society is conceived as interaction among individuals, the description of the forms of this interaction is the task of the science of society in its strictest and most essential sense' (Simmel 1908, pp. 21–2; see Sens 1979, p. 21).

330. Luhmann 1986, p. 170.

331. Luhmann 1985.

332. Like Freyer, Luhmann believes the concept of class was appropriate for 'certain societies' (Luhmann 1985, p. 150; a 'relative historical congruence of idea and reality': Luhmann 1986, p. 163).

333. Luhmann 1986, p. 165.

334. Luhmann 1986, p. 158.

335. Luhmann 1986, p. 161; Luhmann 1985, p. 123.

336. Luhmann 1985, p. 152.

337. The vitalist claim about the identity of theory and practice gets Luhmann tangled up in the same contradiction as Schelsky. On the one hand, 'ideas become social reality' (Luhmann 1986, p. 170). They dispose of a constructive power, and it is because of this power that the theory of class was once correct (p. 163). But that the theory of class is 'no longer' correct (p. 171) is something Luhmann can only suggest – by invoking claims about society and its 'major problems' (p. 171). Such claims presuppose a theory of society that Luhmann does not himself provide, and which he describes as obsolete or nonexistent ('The following investigations ... provide ... no theory of society': Luhmann 1995, p. 18; 'We do not know this society': Luhmann 1987, p. 134; 'We lack a theory

this view is due to a speculative philosophy of history that posits a total transformation. And like Schelsky, Luhmann merely presupposes this *total transformation* and tries to make it seem more plausible by the occasional foray into the lifeworld ('one need only ask housewives').[338] No reasons for it are given, just as no argument is offered in support of the hypothesis that the transformation renders obsolete the 'semantics' of capital and labour, as well as that of class. Luhmann merely points out that *other* theorists have also ceased to speak about class.[339] In doing so, he proceeds as idealistically as Schelsky: from the thought he encounters, he draws a conclusion about social reality.[340] But this is based only on a *particular* theory – on neoclassical theory's ideological division of the world into norm-free functions and functionless norms.[341] Luhmann does not discuss

---

of society; not even the outlines are visible': Luhmann 1989, p. 435; 'Sociology has... not been able to elaborate a theory of society that is even remotely satisfactory': Luhmann 1998, p. 17; on this point, see also Schwinn 2001).

338. 'But this situation is no longer our own' (Luhmann 1985, p. 152), since 'the social system has... now shifted to functional differentiation' (p. 149). 'This situation has changed decisively', and – just as in Habermas – it has done so because of 'state intervention' (Luhmann 1986, p. 163). While Luhmann does not want to deny the existence of inequalities, he ends up doing just that: he states that his theoretical model of 'functional differentiation', which he is far from offering a justification for, is 'foiled' by stratification (p. 119). Whether a terminology such as that of class is 'appropriate' (Luhmann 1986, p. 170) can be decided only by a regular theory, not by a political decision or value judgement. This is to reduce the significance of systems theory – its relationship to other theories is parasitic, as it merely processes their results or gives their content a new 'form' (to use the terminology of old Europe). In the case of the economy, the theory Luhmann has in mind is clearly the neoclassical one. Its class-free, price-regulated system, which knows nothing of production and tolerates no regulation, is fitted by Luhmann with the trappings of his technoid 'supertheory'.

339. Luhmann 1986, p. 152.

340. And yet he is himself (Luhmann 1985) one of the other theorists. After all, his theory allows for self-referentiality. He suggests that it was Marx the theorist who created the class struggle by transforming a tertiary into a binary model: different constellations result 'depending on whether one works with a binary or a tertiary model' (Luhmann 1985, p. 124). After Marx, things looked as follows: 'Then [after this theoretical operation], the unity in the direction of which the individual can project its individuality *qua* generality is simply its class... which is in conflict with the other class' (p. 127). Luhmann passes over the social realities of the time and mistakes conceptual history for real history. This is the very reduction of theory to the 'self-interpretation of a practice' that we encountered in Freyer, Korsch and Gramsci (2.5.1, 2.5.4).

341. He claims that 'the' economy is 'interested... only in the abstract difference between property and non-property' (Luhmann 1998, p. 367). This is true only of neoclassical theory. In the real economy, many other factors also matter, such as the rate of interest or wage levels, which are especially important. Luhmann reinvokes the notion of pure market forces and political adulterations: 'The difference between rich and poor is... left to politics' (ibid.). He means to 'replace the input factor labour... by the concept of the coding of communication' (Luhmann 1988, 46). Even money becomes a 'medium of communication'. While Luhmann knows, after just a few pages, how 'the economy' 'reproduces' itself (p. 58), the reader is told nothing about this process – the 'self-reproduction of payments by means of payments' (p. 71) does not tell us where the money comes from. Here as elsewhere, Luhmann does no more than provide redefinitions.

Marx's theory. As with many other theorists, this leads to the adoption of highly conventional critiques of Marx.[342]

Luhmann's characterisation of the 'new' age is also similar to Schelsky's; he argues that what is 'decisive' for social differentiation 'today' is *consumption*.[343] As true as this is when one means to describe the surface of society ('whether one lives in a house one has inherited or pays rent'), the theorist of difference Luhmann elides the crucial difference that exists within consumption, namely the question of what I use to pay for what I consume: a wage, a 'pension from capital yield' (profit, interest and rent) or reallocated wealth. These distinctions, which are quite tangible and of considerable import to any theory of society, remain hidden under a heavy cloud cover of abstractions, even though Luhmann otherwise has a weak spot for distinctions.[344] The fact that 'classes' continue to be *spoken* about, even though they are supposed to have been rendered obsolete by 'upward and downward movements',[345] is explained by Luhmann in much the same way that Schelsky explained it: in terms of the inertia of the 'legitimation schemes of organisations',[346] which continue to misinterpret 'unjust distribution'[347] class-theoretically. Thus Luhmann does not deny his political sympathies; he openly introduces them into his theory, as thetic positings.[348]

---

342. What is adopted is the suggestion that Marx intended to 'describe' society by means of class theory (Luhmann 1986, p. 157), that he effected a 'reduction to only two classes' (p. 161 – in spite of the denial on p. 163) and even the putatively Marxian theory of immiseration (p. 166). It is not the case that 'the capitalist takes no existential risk' according to Marx (p. 166); on the contrary, Marx describes inter-capitalist competition as a veritable 'war' (*MECW* 9, p. 222 and elsewhere). The view that 'this model does not do justice to the role of the worker as a consumer' is not accurate, either: in the reproduction schemes, Marx extensively discusses effective demand, which consists of investment and consumption (by the capitalist and the workers, on the basis of surplus value and wages). Luhmann 1985 criticises Marx by reference to the 'confusion' evident in the work of his followers (pp. 119, 144) and resorts to applying the semantics of class to issues of distribution – as neoclassical theory does (p. 128). As far as money is concerned, Luhmann is unaware that Marx developed a sophisticated theory of this phenomenon (Luhmann 1986, p. 171; Luhmann 1988, pp. 230–271; see 2.3.5). The list could be extended. Luhmann is another theorist who replaces Marx's economic theory by another theory, interprets the latter as proof that reality has changed and then uses this to subsequently justify the break with Marx – an idealist circular argument (see 2.3.1).

343. Luhmann 1986, p. 165.

344. Luhmann 1995, p. 13.

345. Luhmann 1986, p. 163; Schelsky's 'mobility'.

346. Luhmann 1986, p. 164; 'trade unions', p. 165.

347. Luhmann 1985, p. 152.

348. 'Historical analysis of the concept of social class implies that one take a stand on these issues' (Luhmann 1985, p. 151). Namely: 'The trade unions cannot genuinely change the worker's situation by struggling for general improvements' (Luhmann 1986, p. 165). Why not? Luhmann never tells us. This position is in conformity with the radical socialist critique of trade unions (p. 168) and might also render the concept of class more robust. This ambiguity ('contingency') is not problematised; it is decisionistically 'reduced'. Luhmann's partisan stance is already evident in the way he sees the concept of class as nothing but an expression of the partisanship of the 'other side'. 'Dualisation makes the concept of class a militant concept; the appropriate theoretical construct can be found in *Capital*' (Luhmann 1985, p. 124; Marx 'transforms the semantics of order into a

In this way, Luhmann's theory gets caught up in the performative contradiction of being involved in the very 'class struggle' it means to declare obsolete, by means of the magic formula 'no longer... today'.[349] This all rests on a weak argumentative and empirical basis. In this respect as in others, systems theory's plausibility rests not on a substantive-concrete demonstration but on an oppressive meta-narrative, a 'supertheory'.[350] Here as elsewhere, avoidance of Marx has crystallised into a consensus among experts, without valid arguments ever having been provided.

It is time to summarise our findings thus far. Using the theory of classes as an example, I aimed to show that German sociology has been characterised, from Max Weber to Luhmann, by hostility toward the content of Marx's theory.[351] And yet our pre-theoretical everyday consciousness indicates clearly – in fact increasingly clearly – that we do live in a class society.[352] Within linguistic communities less directly exposed to the Cold War, this pre-theoretical observation is common knowledge, including within social theory.[353] Measured against these two corrective instances, the German reception of the theory of classes is extremely reductive.

---

semantic of struggle, and the order of the estates into an opposition between classes') – things begin to look as if Marx had created reality from his theory. The accusation of 'translating theoretical uncertainty into political opposition' (Luhmann and Habermas 1971, p. 399) is self-referential.

349. Luhmann 1986, p. 164.

350. Luhmann 1995, p. 19; on this, see 2.5.6.

351. Dahrendorf reports that when he told Horkheimer and Adorno he meant to write his dissertation on Marx, they replied that this was not politically opportune (interview in German weekly *Der Spiegel*, 2 June 2001). He ended up writing a dissertation on Marx after all – about Marx's theory of justice (Dahrendorf 1953; 1999).

352. 'The number of the poor is growing, and so is the wealth of the rich' (German daily *Frankfurter Rundschau* on 27 February 2001, commenting on the results of a report on poverty commissioned by the German federal government). Another article calls for 'more class consciousness' ('Our Class Society': *Die Zeit*, 4 January 2001). According to a survey by the Prognos Institute, wealth is distributed very inequitably between the upper and the lower classes and between East and West Germany (*Berliner Zeitung*, 3 September 2002). For a time, the ticket envelopes of the German train service Deutsche Bahn featured the words 'Surplus Value: Travel First Class' in large red letters (this was an expression of the policy of disinvesting in short-distance transportation and investing in expensive 'Inter-City Express' trains instead; see also the way the German word for 'class' [*Klasse*] is used in the German health system). These are precisely the sorts of everyday phenomena that systems theory has immunised itself against (Halfmann 1996a, pp. 13–14, 44–5; cf. 2.5.7.

353. 'Social class is part of capitalist society' (Scase 1992, p. 99). This is why discussion of class issues comes more naturally to non-German authors (of which I have considered Bottomore 1967, Poulantzas 1975, Carchedi 1977, Wright 1979, Giddens 1979, Anderson 1980, Bourdieu 1982, Kaye 1984, Goldthorpe 1992 and 1996, Edgel 1993, Crompton 1993 and 2000, Sitton 1996, G. Marshall 1997, Milner 1999 and Sklair 2001). On the historicisation of the Bonn republic: Huster 1972, Berghahn 1985, Rammstedt 1992; for class theories since 1989. see Bader 1998, Ritsert 1998, Diettrich 1999, Kößler 2001, Bischoff 2002 and Vester 2004.

This chapter on sociology has shown that the 'theory of society' was also unable to reverse the development by which bourgeois society, the object of Marx's theory, was lost. We first encountered this loss in the Social-Democratic dualism of technology and ethics (2.1); it was exacerbated in Leninism's de-economised political theory (2.2) and in neoclassical theory's de-sociologised economics (2.3). If anything, ethicised German sociology reinforced it. The occasional socio-historical conjecture aside, I have looked for the causes of this development mainly in the history of ideas, that is, within theory – and it has turned out the causes reside in the reconfiguration of economic theory examined in the preceding section (2.3). When one begins from neoclassical-technicised notions of the economic base (as German theorists did, in spite of Marx), it becomes virtually impossible to establish any sort of link to cultural phenomena. But since the division of labour between scientific disciplines was such that sociology was expected to examine these very cultural phenomena, the fundamental reconfiguration had grave consequences for sociology: it was de-economised. While it was good at describing individual phenomena, it was scarcely able to explain them by reference to the rest of society. Nevertheless, German thought is characterised by a strong tendency toward closure (2.5.2). Thus the foundations of sociality that economic theory could have provided were increasingly replaced with attempts to arrive at *ethical* foundations. This was the point at which normative philosophy, which German sociology had once had to emancipate itself from, reintroduced itself into the theory of society. The discussion of normative philosophy found in the next chapter is intended to explain why developments that belong to the history of theory are often misinterpreted, in Germany, as real developments, even as real developments are turned into mental developments, situated within the heads of men and theorists. Once again, we will find this tendency to have been shaped by factors immanent to theory.

2.5 'From Marx to Heidegger': Social Philosophy

> Spirit is alone Reality.[1]

> Social philosophy does not examine the concrete reality of society but the social norms from which this reality ought to be derived.[2]

There is a reason why this work of philosophy has not addressed German twentieth-century philosophy sooner, namely the critical insight that philosophy is not without its presuppositions. To begin directly with philosophy would have been to bypass important junctures in the development of the German reception of Marx. Venturing a definition of philosophy, one might say that it aims to provide an orienting overview of the whole. Because of the distance this requires, philosophy is quite far removed from the real world. This makes it especially susceptible to the many distortions that may insert themselves between real states of affairs and their philosophical interpretation. Such distortions may even lead to doubt as to whether the world exists at all.[3] Thus philosophy is very good at soliloquising.

Not wanting to operate on the basis of overhasty historico-philosophical theories about the development of a certain discursive universe,[4] the present work limits itself methodologically to considering the effects of *texts*. If the philosophy of the period examined has a range of presuppositions, then the only such presuppositions analysed here are those that are *theoretical*. The theories analysed are mainly those of the labour movement (2.1, 2.2) and those of neighbouring disciplines that exerted a strong influence on philosophy (2.3, 2.4). It was the heyday of neo-Kantianism, and the neo-Kantians (at least those of the Marburg School) held that philosophy needed to refer to the sciences. In this view, the sciences provide philosophy with its 'material', and philosophy's task is merely that of inquiring into the 'conditions of validity' proper to that 'material'. For the neo-Kantians, there was no longer any question of critically discussing *content*. This is why *topoi* associated with the areas examined reappear within philosophy, although the perspective and the style change in ways that are typical of the 'field' of philosophy.[5]

---

1. Hegel 1967, p. 86.
2. Stepina 2000, p. 15.
3. See 3.4.2.
4. I am thinking of narratives such as that of the universal 'context of deception' [*Verblendungszusammenhang*], which German critical theory treated as a factor in the history of ideas, or the transformation of 'all [!] the objective forms of bourgeois society together with all the subjective forms corresponding to them' into the commodity form in Lukács 1971 (p. 83; see Sohn-Rethel 1978). Other Marxist 'explanations' of intellectual history have included the 'class character' of 'bourgeois philosophy' and its hostile stance toward the 'Great October Socialist Revolution' (Zweiling 1958, pp. 7 ff.). Such default explanations proved detrimental even at the stage of compiling one's material. Providing a substantive demonstration is quite an undertaking, and it can be done only after the material has been compiled, not before. In searching for morphological parallels, we have not yet said anything about dependencies, causal relations or chronologies.
5. Bourdieu 1991.

What are the systematically relevant findings of the preceding chapters? Examining the debates within Social Democracy (2.1) revealed, between the currents associated with Kautsky and Bernstein, a duality of 'economic fatalism and 'ethical' utopianism'.[6] This duality is also evident in the Communist variant of Marxism, where a mechanistic theory of crisis (Lenin's 'dying capitalism') coexists with political voluntarism (2.2). I have defined this as a loss of the object of inquiry 'bourgeois society', as well as of the crucial characterisation of that object as 'capitalist'. Such a loss of the object was also noted in later sections, which examined attempts to counteract it by means of a dual perspective (technicised theories of the base and ethicisations of the superstructure). Within economics, there developed a duality of abstract neoclassical model theories and moralising but largely atheoretical historiographies (2.3). Within sociology, one finds a surprisingly similar theorisation of sterile systemic automata and subjective 'moral' epiphenomena (2.4). There also occurs a transformation of theories *about* ethics (the everyday, 'value-laden' world of actors and individuals) into theories that are *themselves* ethical and prescriptive – this is the grand ambiguity surrounding the keyword of 1990s philosophy, the 'normative'.

These *topoi* now recur in the 'field' of philosophy. Twentieth-century German philosophy's basic architecture displays a similarly ruptured structure: formal consideration of select aspects in neo-Kantianism and in burgeoning analytic philosophy coexists with the decidedly 'non-analytic' theories of hermeneutics, vitalism, phenomenology and existentialism.[7] When these 'non-analytic' theories take the form of 'cultural criticism', they tend to involve strong value judgements.[8] I cannot recount the entire history of philosophy here. Nor is it an option to renew Georg Lukács's hypothesis that the division was *caused* exclusively by Marx being forgotten or repressed, and by insistence on the 'bourgeois standpoint'.[9] The hypotheses formulated since Lukács have, however, tended strongly toward the opposite view.

It is remarkable how theory's dissolution into technology and ethics *correlates*, in all areas examined thus far, with Marx being forgotten. Before beginning to survey social philosophy for exemplary traces of Marx's visible and invisible influence, it is important to equip oneself with adequate methods. In determining the criteria by which to

---

6. Lukács 1971, p. 196. A disintegration into 'the empirical and the utopian' ('natural laws and imperatives': p. 197). The 'totality' that Lukács proposes as a solution (the consciousness of the proletariat as the 'identical subject-object of history': ibid.) has more in common with vitalism than with Marx (2.5.4). Nevertheless, it needs to be recognised that Lukács perceived the problem brilliantly.

7. Wuchterl 1995, p. 15.

8. This can be seen, for example, in the appendix to Hügli 1992–93, which consists of one volume on 'hard' and one volume on 'soft' twentieth-century philosophy.

9. An 'overall knowledge' could only be achieved if philosophy focused on the 'concrete material totality', as Marx did. '*But a radical change in outlook is not feasible on the soil of bourgeois society*' (Lukács 1971, pp. 109 ff.). Lukács is searching for a *Weltanschauung* (see 2.5.4). Lukács' later, more elaborate presentation of this idea (Lukács 1981) is similarly constructed; read in a purely historiographical way, however, it testifies to Lukács's unusually thorough grasp of his material.

demonstrate that the theories of the period examined respond – openly or covertly – to Marx, I will employ a more neutral and less reductive variant of Lukács's hypothesis. I mean René König's early, 1937 attempt to interpret the latent 'irrationalism' of the social philosophy of the period as an incomplete reception of Marx and a mentalising reaction to him.[10] To render this hypothesis more plausible, I will give it greater historical depth of focus, even if I can only do so in a cursory manner (2.5.2). The hypothesis will then be used to examine the relationship between Marx and three paradigmatic philosophers of the period. I will begin with the now forgotten Rudolf Eucken, who was influential at the time and received the Nobel Prize in Literature (2.5.3). Next, I will turn to the forefather of 'Western Marxism', Georg Lukács (2.5.4). And finally, I will address the grand master of twentieth-century German philosophy, Heidegger (2.5.5). König's hypothesis can be confirmed for all three of these philosophers.[11] I will conclude with two additional sections on Hegel and Luhmann (2.5.6, 2.5.7).

2.5.1 *A categorisation attempt by René König*

> Might statistics demonstrate that there could be laws in history? Laws? Yes, statistics prove how coarse and disgustingly uniform the masses are. Are we to call the effects of the force of gravity, stupidity, mimicry, love, and hunger – laws? Now, we are willing to concede that point, but by the same token the principle is then established that, as far as there are laws in history, they are worth nothing and history is worth nothing.[12]

In Germany, historians dealing with the development of scientific disciplines sometimes consider sociology a breakaway product of philosophy. According to this argument, when social issues became more (de-)pressing, philosophy ('the branch of knowledge that deals with man'), which had opened itself up to reality after Hegel, was '*sociologised*'.[13] However, one can also make the opposite observation: when sociology had finally established itself within the academy, many eminently 'social' issues were relegated to philosophy. Early cultural sociology, for example, was really a *philosophy* of culture.[14] To put this in a catchy

---

10. König 1975; section 2.5.1.

11. Other chapters discuss additional authors (2.4: Gehlen and Freyer; 2.6: Horkheimer and Adorno, Löwith, Tillich and Benjamin; 3.1: Habermas and others). There exist in-depth analyses of each of these authors. Here, it is a matter of exploring the aspect mentioned, which is usually overlooked.

12. Friedrich Nietzsche.

13. Rehberg 1981; Lukács 1981, p. 475; Schelsky 1959, p. 22; Fisching 1993. This was more a reaction of the *milieu* associated with the humanities than a self-interpretation of what occurred.

14. Simmel and A. Weber ventured in this direction. In his opening speech at the first German sociology conference in 1910, Tönnies declared that sociology is 'first and foremost a philosophical discipline' (Tönnies 1926, p. 125 ff). Jonas exaggerates the role that philosophy played in this: 'It is the goal [or at least the effect] of the critique of sociological cognition to radically restrict sociology's concept of science in order to then occupy the space thus cleared... with a different, i.e. "higher" science, i.e. the philosophy of culture or of history, or the doctrine of *Weltanschauung*

formula, there occurred a *'re-philosophising'* of sociology.[15] Established philosophy had long played down the 'social question', refusing to grant it access to the sacred halls of self-cognition.[16] One believed oneself to already dispose of the right answers, or to be able to deduce them effortlessly, so that it was now only a matter of disseminating these answers among the people or the ruling classes in an 'educative' manner.[17]

A Weberian sociology would not have been able to allow itself this sort of moralism, which consisted almost entirely of 'value judgements'. It was no accident Weber *withdrew* sceptically from the German Sociological Society he had co-founded: sociology was assuming the heritage of the very 'mandarins' he had combated.[18] Thus, there developed, via the detour of sociology, a 'social philosophy' that was indifferent to disciplinary divisions and explicitly considered itself normative. To be sure, those engaging with social issues in this way might still have been sociologists, and to this extent, the activity continued to be described as 'sociology'.[19] But philosophy was the genuine heir – it gratefully picked up on the themes addressed. The major guiding hypotheses were in any case taken from philosophy's repertoire. René König was never properly forgiven for wanting to banish such theorems, which he described as a 'philosophy of history and society', from sociology. And yet this would have been a consistent course of action in light of the proliferation of sweeping hypotheses within this eclectic field.[20]

---

that Rickert called for as a result of his work' (Jonas 1976, Vol. II, p. 165; see p. 180). Lichtblau 1997 and Kruse 1999 confirm this assessment, although they welcome the anti-scientific 'cultural turn'.

15. On this concept, see Habermas 1984–7, Vol. I, p. 454; Schnädelbach 1983, p. 86. On the thing itself, see P. Anderson 1978, pp. 49 ff.; König 1958, p. 91 ('a philosophy, instead of sociology'), as well as K. Müller's 'shift from theory to *Weltanschauung*' [*Verweltanschaulichung*] (Müller 1996, p. 41).

16. Lübbe 1963, Ringer 1987. Works on the 'social question' such as Von Stein 1850, A. Lange 1865, A. Wagner 1871, Ludwig Stein 1897, Masaryk 1964, Oppenheimer 1912 were political.

17. After Fichte ('educating the educators': Bergmann 1915 and 1928; Langbehn 1922; see Henning 1999), many philosophers opted for a pedagogical focus – for example, Rudolf Eucken, Eduard Grisebach, Paul Natorp (1920) and Hermann Nohl (see Lübbe 1963, pp. 194 ff.; Oelkers 1989; Pascher 1997, pp. 46 ff.; Wuchterl 1995, Kodalle 2000). An exemplary expression of the anti-sociological and socio-philosophical stance is to be found in the popular series 'Social Philosophy' [*Gesellschaftsphilosophie*], which was published by a group of philosophers associated with Ottmar Spann, and in which all sorts of philosophers (Meister Eckhart, Schelling, and such like) were considered 'social philosophers'. Here, sociology's tendency to substitute ethics for analysis is extended into philosophy. In a bitterly ironic self-portrayal, Lion Feuchtwanger reports that in the course of his education, 'Plato's name was mentioned 14,203 and that of Frederick the Great 22,641 times, but the name 'Karl Marx' was not mentioned once' (quoted in Sternburg 1999, p. 56).

18. F. Jonas 1976, Vol. I, p. 211; see Lübbe 1963, p. 184.

19. Classical German sociologists such as Simmel and Weber, but also later ones such as Gehlen and Adorno, frequently feature in textbooks on the history of philosophy. For example, Max Weber and Simmel make appearances in a German dictionary of 'Great Twentieth-Century Philosophers' (Lutz 1999) that fails to mention the founders of major currents, such as Cohen and Rickert. Gehlen's and Adorno's generation had often been trained as philosophers by the time they began lecturing in sociology; the same is true of Mannheim or Elias. The preceding generation had been trained in political economy (Weber, Sombart, Oppenheimer; see 2.4.1).

20. König 1959, pp. 7 ff., 88 ff., 336. Lyotard 1989 also meant to do away with 'grand narratives', although he thereby only instituted a new one. Kruse 1999 still polemicises against König.

König's analysis attributed a key role to Marx's theory. A second-generation student of Dilthey,[21] König had been thoroughly educated as a philosopher. It is therefore worth briefly recounting how he arrived at his assessment. The habilitation thesis he submitted to Zürich University in 1937 allows us to trace the development of his efforts to set himself off from social philosophy. König begins by acknowledging the achievements of the historico-hermeneutic disciplines. Aside from the substantive results of their concrete research into specific thematic fields, the methodology of these disciplines guards against reductively naturalist conceptions of man. However, König objects to the practice of deducing a phenomenon's mode of being from its genesis; he considers this to be a mere inversion of philosophical idealism. Idealism lapsed into an 'ontologisation of methodological rationalism',[22] and hermeneutics retains this ontologisation, merely replacing 'reason' with 'life'.[23] This way of reasoning continues the tradition of Empedocles, according to whom like can only be known by like, and so it ends up with a 'philosophy of identity'[24] – be it of the naturalist, the idealist or the existentialist variety. In systematic terms, this means that *theory and reality* are no longer distinguished. König argues that in the case of existential hermeneutics, the monism is due to a flawed reception of Hegel.[25] What distinguishes Hegel from hermeneutics is not his idealism but the importance he attributes to the non-identical. There is nothing of the sort in hermeneutics. In Heidegger's case, the non-identical is absent even in the extreme case of death.[26]

König interprets this vitalist idealism as responding to and processing hypotheses that were originally Marxian. It is only in the crisis that 'life suddenly demands a new degree

---

21. König was a student of Dilthey's publisher Groethuysen (see König 1981).
22. König 1975, p. 62.
23. The type of non sequitur that consists in deducing an object's mode of being from its genesis is 'exactly the reverse of the deduction proper to dogmatic rationalism, which starts from the procedural mentalism of the philosophical humanities in order to arrive at the claim that the object of cognition must be that which can be grasped intellectually, i.e. the rational' (König 1975, p. 62). 'Our view of man has certainly been rendered more profound by the notion that man's artistic, religious, legal, social, economic, political activity is not the work of isolated 'faculties'..., but that in all of these forms of activity, man is active and real in the mode of concrete doing and hence of temporal occurrence' (p. 61). Nevertheless, 'there is no guaranteed validity to a reasoning that deduces from active man's existential condition within art, religion, law, etc. the existentiality of the cognition proper to that sphere' (p. 62). Following Tugendhat 1993 (p. 202), I will henceforth use the expression 'genetic fallacy' as shorthand for this sort of reasoning.
24. König 1975, p. 27.
25. 'At the very least, this assumption requires a justification, like the one grandly provided by Hegel. But it is odd to see existentialism, which developed out of a hostility to Hegel, adopt in its destruction of the Hegelian system that system's critically justified premise concerning the unity of thought and reality, or at least the formal structure of that premise. Existentialism replaces the pan-logism it militates against with a pan-existentialism' (König 1975, p. 62).
26. König accuses Heidegger of reiterating 'the position of the 'philosophy of identity'... already overcome by Hegel in the *Phenomenology*. In Heidegger, the effort to suppress every dialectical transition goes so far... that even death ceases to be for him something other or something that negates' (König 1975 p. 65; see Sternberger 1934).

of consciousness'; hence there develops a 'philosophy of the crisis'.[27] In Marx, the crisis was still at the thematic centre of the theory. It was only after Marx that the intra-theoretical hierarchy of consciousness and life was reversed.[28] The writings of Dilthey and Yorck, Freyer and Heidegger share the same basic thrust.[29] They differ from Marx only in that the existentialist systematics 'seized upon what can only be regarded as an... extreme exception in order to uncritically reinterpret it as life's primordial form of movement, and as the foundation of the humanities'.[30]

König accuses social philosophy of enlarging upon Marxian hypotheses in an excessively abstract manner, thereby philosophising them beyond recognition. 'Irrationalism' lurks within the results. Marx did not consider the scientific analysis of the present as it had developed up until his own time to be free of errors (he exposed and corrected such errors in a concrete way), but he held that scientificity itself ('thought') was *unaffected* by the crisis. Idealist vitalism, however, attempts to give greater 'depth' to theory and loses the ability to distinguish between theory and reality. For this reason, it sees the crisis in reality as affecting all of theory as well; this inevitably leads to the 'crisis of philosophy'.[31] The Diltheyans also situate the genesis of theory within a practical process, except that this practice is no longer one that could itself be meaningfully understood. As 'life', it is prior to every expression of consciousness and cannot itself become an object of theoretical consideration – which leads to it being interpreted in rather arbitrary ways.[32] König considers this a reinterpretation and distortion of Marxism; while it remains dependent on Marxism, it also voids it of meaning.[33]

When science has been reinterpreted in this way and goes on to posit what it examines as that which is always already familiar, it ceases to be *science*. Such a positing occurs when science considers its object of inquiry to be of the same essence as the inquirer, or as being grounded in the inquirer's own being. König considers Dilthey, Heidegger and Freyer prime examples of this approach.[34] (There are others, however.) They fail to

27. König 1975, pp. 74, 75.
28. König 1975, p. 76.
29. König 1975, p. 77.
30. König 1975, p. 81.
31. König 1975, p. 75.
32. 'Differentiation of special sciences of society accordingly did not take place through some device of theoretical understanding... life itself produced that differentiation' (Dilthey 1988, p. 99; König 1975, pp. 28–9). Freyer intends to rescue 'sociology *qua* science of reality' by attributing to science and even to the humanities (the 'sciences of the logos') 'eternally valid norms', namely a 'scheme that is entirely out of touch with life' (p. 86). This approach, at once intellectual and anti-intellectual, was also famously championed by Ludwig Klages (see Klages 1929).
33. 'In [Freyer's] theory, the pale notion of historical existence takes the place of a real crisis. Thus the principle of starting from the present is rescued for science, but the acute philosophy of crisis is depotentiated. Freyer thereby becomes part of the philosophical process of abstraction that we have attempted to outline by reference to its two outermost poles, Marx and Heidegger' (König 1975, p. 94; hence the title of section 2.5).
34. 'Here, life grasps life' (König 1975, p. 54). Heidegger, it is claimed, 'fastened the guiding thread of all [!] philosophical interrogation to the point... from whence it originates and to which

distance themselves from the object, an act that is indispensable to science, and they fail to even recognise the object *as* object.[35] According to König, who is reiterating a basic insight of the early sociology of 'distance', it is not helpful to ethicise the object,[36] since this leads precisely to it not being recognised. For if it is the case that '[t]hat which exists is that which we seek',[37] then nothing exists any longer, at least as far as philosophy is concerned:[38] neither a world that one might presuppose,[39] nor a past[40] that one might *accomodate oneself to*, nor even principles that one might *orient onself toward*.[41] According to König, the subjectivism of vitalism's grounding of science formally adopts the Marxian philosophy of crisis, but it pays no attention to that philosophy's material foundation in the 'positive sciences',[42] and this leads to a form of *nihilism*.

In the theories König discusses, the 'total absence of Being'[43] gives rise to a compensatory 'primacy of the political'.[44] This sort of philosophy inevitably lapses into an activist stance, which, however, remains limited to the 'beer-bench politics'[45] of pure self-assertion.[46] König considers the search for an 'active proof' (Fichte's *Tatbeweis*) a feature that revolutionary socialists like Sorel share with National Socialists like Freyer and Heidegger.[47] The nihilism induced by idealism produces a political voluntarism that is literally 'groundless'. König's key points can be summarised in the following formulaic statements, each of which I will go on to verify by reference to Rudolf Eucken, Georg Lukács, Martin Heidegger and Niklas Luhmann:

---

it returns' (König 1975, p. 55; Heidegger 1962, p. 38). 'Here, the light of cognition is cast, like a spotlight, on an occurrence of which the subject of cognition partakes existentially'. In sociology, 'we always find ourselves' (Freyer 1964, pp. 82 ff.; König 1975, p. 31).

35. König 1975, p. 105.
36. König 1975, pp. 33, 102.
37. König 1975, p. 33.
38. König 1975, p. 132.
39. König 1975, p. 131.
40. König 1975, p. 106.
41. König 1975, p. 133. 'Thus the path to practice does not involve the detour of 'pure' theory, as the 'sociology of distance' would have it. Rather, sociology contains within it, by virtue of its very structure, the possibility of becoming practical, insofar as it always starts from the intentions and actions of what actually occurs socially' (König 1975, p. 50; following Dunkmann 1929; on 'deducing Being from intention', see also Lübbe 1963, p. 184; on the 'Fichte renaissance': Lübbe 1963, p. 199).
42. König 1975, p. 95. König holds that the 'scientific' part of Marxism has been refuted (p. 94). As far as the passing on of formal structures, regardless of their content, is concerned, this is of no consequence. 'The crisis is downplayed by depriving it of its sting; at the same time, the notion of the development of modern life that is thereby obtained is . . . treated as a general explanatory principle'. According to König, 'the bourgeois way of representing Marxism' consists only in this (p. 95).
43. König 1975, p. 134.
44. König 1975, p. 131.
45. König 1975, p. 129.
46. Everything 'drowns in a . . . mire of aimless volition' (König 1975, p. 135; Löwith 1984b).
47. König 1975, p. 195. Gehlen spoke of 'National Socialism's active demonstration': Rügemer 1979, p. 88.

1. Social philosophy is a distortive reaction to Marxism.
2. As a distortion of Marx, social philosophy remains dependent on Marx.
3. Its origins reside in an interpretation of Hegel that eliminates the non-identical.
4. The idealist philosophy of identity is inverted and becomes existentialist.
5. Social philosophy fallaciously infers the mode of being from the genesis, and being from thought.
6. Theory is problematised *in toto*; this results in a crisis of philosophy.
7. Loss of objectivity and of the character of scientificity.
8. To compensate, social philosophy develops a vacuous 'politics' of identity and self-assertion.

König's diagnosis can be rendered still more plausible by fleshing it out with some facts from the history of philosophy. Here, this can only be done in a cursory way. The main point is to indicate the origin of the concepts and modes of thought proper to 'idealism' and the 'philosophy of identity'. This is necessary because, as we will see, Hegel is centrally important not only to pre-Marxian, but also to post-Marxian German thought; in fact, he remains central to German philosophy to this day.

2.5.2 *Confronting the philosophical history of idealism*

> There must be a genuine totality in which the opposition of thinking and being has been superseded.[48]

The influence of Fichte

When König speaks of 'idealism', he is referring primarily to the epistemological notion that the objects of consciousness are constituted by consciousness itself. From the correct insight that objects in the world can be accessed only *via* consciousness, a conclusion about the genesis of those objects is drawn: namely, that they originate *in* consciousness. This hypothesis, which is ultimately ontological, goes back to Fichte.[49] When the thinker *creates* what he thinks, as in Fichte, the two are identical – hence the term 'philosophy

48. Hermann Schwarz.
49. Fichte does not deduce, but simply equates the propositions that 'A ... is posited *in* and *through* the Ego' (Fichte 1868, p. 66). Idealism is contained in the very premises (Habermas 1987, pp. 12 ff.). This 'deduction' becomes even more explicit later: no thing 'can be anything other [!] than what is posited in the Ego ... For everything else, ... it must be shown that reality was transferred to it from the Ego' (Fichte 1868, p. 19). 'The Ego of the *Science of Knowledge* perpetually hovered between a merely epistemological (and subjectivist) procedure and a principle of objective reality' (Lukács 1981, p. 136). According to Lask 1902, pp. 80 ff., 99, Fichte later moved beyond this 'emanationism' (Glatz 2001, p. 235; for comprehensive accounts, see Rohs 1991, Hogrebe 1995, Gamm 1997).

of identity'.[50] König's analysis has historical depth of focus: 'the non-identical', which Kant wisely introduced as 'X',[51] did in fact disappear from post-Kantian philosophical reflection. The Kantians were quick to eliminate the 'thing in itself' from their philosophy; it had always been a source of irritation.[52] This gave rise to the very 'empirical idealism' that Kant had been at pains to avoid.[53]

This 'empirical idealism' can be expressed formulaically by saying that in it, *form fully impacts on content*:[54] there is no longer any 'something' that exists beyond cognitive activity, and to which it might direct itself, for the content of cognition is also primordially created – not just its aesthetic and conceptual form, but its very substance.[55] A knowledge of how thoughts *about* objects come about is fallaciously equated with knowledge *of* the objects themselves. The property of a concept (it originated there) appears as the cause of that which is conceptualised; the 'where' becomes a 'because'.[56] As in psychologism and vitalism, the mode of being is fallaciously inferred from the genesis. This is as if one wanted to predict who will take whom to court over what and how the case will be decided, on the basis of one's knowledge about the precise location of the courthouse and the underlying legal prescriptions. This type of overhasty deduction of content from form, character from place, validity from genesis or being from thought

---

50. By 'identity', Fichte means that even the non-I, the 'non-identical', is 'identical' with the I (Hegel's mind), since it only becomes possible by a self-limitation of the latter. Identity is already taken to be the 'identity of identity and non-identity', or of subject and object, in Fichte, that is, before Hegel: 'The Ego opposits in the Ego a divisible Non-Ego to a divisible Ego' (Fichte 1868, p. 84). The second (1802) edition calls this the 'identity of the subject and the object: subject-object' ['Identität des Subjekts, und Objekts: Subject-Objekt'] (p. 18): this can be traced back to the influence of the notion that mind and nature are one (Schelling 2009).

51. Kant 1998, p. 348.

52. A thing in itself, it is argued, cannot be thought (this is in fact the definition of the 'thing in itself', which is to say the criticism is tautological); therefore, the argument continues, there can be no thing in itself (thus Jacobi, Fichte and H. Cohen, among others; see Seidel 1972).

53. Kant 1998, p. 511. Kant was concerned to avoid this at all costs (Kant 1998, p. 539; Zeltner 1974). Idealists such as Schopenhauer or Heidegger preferred the earlier edition of the *Critique of Pure Reason*, which was more vague on this point. Lukács also concludes that 'Fichte, in removing Kant's 'thing-in-itself' from transcendental idealism, was directly converting his philosophy epistemologically into subjective idealism' (Lukács 1981, p. 135).

54. 'The activity of form determines matter' (Fichte 1868, p. 113). While Fichte intends to 'modify' (p. 114) this 'idealist' manner of deduction, he never gets beyond it. This is due, once again, to his premises: 'the ideal and the real ground are one and the same' (p. 115). Even Fichte's 'realism' remains idealist.

55. 'Thus, without any consideration for perception, the science of knowledge deduces, in an *a priori* manner, that which it wants to appear within perception, which is to say it deduces *a posteriori* appearances' (Fichte, *Werke* II, p. 355). It 'constructs *a priori* the entire shared consciousness of all rational creatures' (p. 379). Plessner, who, like many of his generation, was taken with Fichte (Pietrowicz 1992, pp. 58 ff.; see Lübbe 1963, pp. 194 ff.; Willms 1966, W. Schrader 1997), picks up on this idea as follows: 'The I does not extend beyond itself and its sphere. What is given to it is given to it.... Appearance' is 'equivalent to the content of consciousness and... identical with it' (Plessner 1928, p. 49).

56. See 3.1.5.

is 'speculative'. The motive behind such thought is to make the mind calm by means of intra-theoretical definitude.[57]

A rough distinction can be drawn between two styles of philosophy. One is more scientific and oriented toward cognition of the real world, to which it seeks to accomodate itself, even at the risk of giving the theory an unpleasant and incomplete form.[58] By contrast, the other, more idealist style is primarily concerned with obtaining as closed and consistent an image of the world as possible: here, thought is first and foremost an end in itself. The advantage of this second mode of thought lies in the elegance and closure of the systems it allows one to construct, as well as in its suggestion that the subject's position is an exalted one, above the world.[59] In this way, one can interpret anything – and *everything* – in terms of the independent movement of thought, the paradigmatic example being Hegel. Yet paradoxically, idealism fails to achieve the definitude it seeks. For when the two poles, thought and being, are brought too close to one another, the resulting 'one world' ends up oscillating constantly between theory and reality.[60]

The early idealist Kantians already believed they could draw *closer* to reality, and finally understand it in its entirety, by eliminating the 'thing in itself'. Now theory was complete and harmonious: 'What unity and self-perfection!'.[61] In fact, they were working to perfect an idealism that was characterised by its *distance* from reality, and which triumphed in Schelling and Hegel. In doing so, they prepared the ground for

---

57. Spinoza already meant to 'make the mind entirely calm' (Spinoza 2000, Book II, Proposition 49, Scholium; see the motto to section 3.2). Rothacker defines this as the idealism of liberty's 'demand for unity' (along with Dilthey: *GS* VIII): 'For the pressure of the manifold that besets us is what motivates the demand for unity' – a unity that Rothacker characterises as 'ethical' (Rothacker 1948, p. 138).

58. Examples include Locke, Hume and – Marx. Rothacker accuses 'naturalism' of 'getting so caught up in the manifold as to forget unity' (Rothacker 1948, p. 138). But even Rothacker's naturalism is conceived of as a *Weltanschauung* in search of a 'last instance' (p. 41). Rothacker's distinction between *Weltanschauungen* is a mentalisation of the Diltheyan sort. 'Dilthey's irrationalist, 'vitalist' tendency is... expressed most clearly in Rothacker' (Lehmann 1943, p. 233).

59. Plessner 2002, p. 61 cites the desire for community as the motivation for 'mentalisation': individuals think of their corporeality as the cause of their separation and hence as something that needs to be superseded; community is taken to be possible only 'in the realm of mind'. Yet Plessner 2002 also fails to transcend mentalisation. He does not describe the social world of his day in terms of real oppositions, but forces it into the mold of two abstract ethical concepts: Tönnies's dualism of 'community' [*Gemeinschaft*] and 'society' [*Gesellschaft*].

60. See Lukács 1981, pp. 136, 419 ff.; Taureck 2000, pp. 21 ff. (on Nietzsche). This oscillation is evident in the failure to clearly identify the referents of terms such as 'being' or 'normativity'. These terms refer both to phenomena that are immanent to theory (being as the first and most general predicate; 'normativity' as a feature of certain propositions, namely prescriptive ones) and to something that is real (being as what is ontically primary; the 'normative' as the object of ethics, such as codes of behaviour, sanctions, and so on). We have already encountered this oscillation in section 2.4, and will encounter it again in section 3.1.

61. Fichte 1987, p. 91.

the nihilism inherent in this idealism.[62] This idealism *sive* nihilism is not limited to epistemology, which merely renders it explicit; one also encounters it where one would not expect it: twentieth-century German sociology still failed to distinguish adequately between theory and reality, and the result was what one would expect: a nihilating loss of the object.[63] The philosopher of identity whose influence in Germany was greatest, J.G. Fichte, took this quest for unity to an extreme: he did not stop at eliminating matter from theoretical philosophy; he also eliminated the difference between theoretical and practical philosophy. It is only through moral action, Fichte claims, that the objects of our consciousness obtain objective reality.[64]

The empirical world is brought into the system as the material one has a 'duty' to address. Theoretical philosophy is moralised as well: it is made dependent on the *will* even on the level of premises. Yet the will is not going to accept anything that is foreign to it.[65] This amounts to a 'speculative primacy of practical reason'.[66] Such Fichteanism was quite widespread, in neo-Kantianism and beyond.[67] Meanwhile, moral philosophy

---

62. Gawoll 1989 uses Fichte as an example to show how 'the construction idealism of reason ... necessarily leads to an impaired grasp of reality': 'All of reality transforms into a wonderful dream, without a life' (p. 67, on Fichte, *Werke* I.6, pp. 251 ff.). 'Consciousness of *the object* is only a consciousness of my production of a presentation of the object' (Fichte 1987, p. 44). 'We raise ourselves out of this nothingness ... only through our morality' (p. 79). This, and not Kant's restriction of the range of cognition, is the germ cell of nihilism. Hegel 1977a perfected Fichteanism, and with it nihilism (Gawoll 1989, p. 72). A distinction needs to be drawn between two opposing nihilisms, which depend on the underlying ontology. From a Platonic perspective, the loss of the overworld is a form of nihilism; the accusation of nihilism is directed at people who care only for facts and lack all awareness of 'ideas' or 'values'. From the materialist point of view, it is, on the contrary, the idealist who is nihilist, since he places himself outside the real world. For example, a person to whom a human life is worth nothing, because they want to realise an idea, is nihilist. It is this second sense that the word is used in here (see W. Neumann 1989, Kähler 1997). Internal contradiction is a risk associated with many general concepts, including that of 'realism'. The position of someone who holds that conceptual content is real is the opposite of that of someone who believes that things are what is real. It only causes unnecessary confusion to describe both ways of thinking as 'realism', in order then to reason abstractly about whether realism is preferable to 'anti-realism', or vice versa (C. Wright 1992, Kutschera 1993).

63. See 2.4.1. It is one symptom of this kinship that Lichtblau does not hesitate to compare early German sociology to the systematic philosophy of German idealism (1997, pp. 69 ff.).

64. In his anthropology – where it was a matter of dealing with genetic issues, rather than with epistemological ones – Kant 2007 also developed a pragmatic perspective. But this is something quite different from morals (see 3.4.1).

65. Gadamer unintentionally – but consistently – gives this philosophy of identity a xenophobic twist: '[T]he structures of meaning we meet in the human sciences ... can be traced back to ultimate units of what is given in consciousness, unities which themselves no longer contain anything alien' (Gadamer 2004, pp. 56 ff.). Here, an ideological criterion of exclusion is formulated. Nothing is to be considered except what we already know or want to know (a form of 'cognisance of the known': Rodi 1990). Within this self-affirmation of the group, we deal only with ourselves. The consequence of nationalism within science was already drawn by Fichte (see Fichte 2008).

66. Kroner 1921, p. 362.

67. Aside from Riehl, who retained the 'thing in itself', Lask was the only one to reject the 'primacy of the ethical in theoretical matters' (Lask 1923, Vol. I, p. 349). After Riehl and Lask, Adorno was the next philosopher to concern himself with the non-identical 'thing in itself', although he

loses its formalism, since it now posits its own objects. Even God become 'thinkable' again – and this was something else that pleased the builders of philosophical systems. Thus this approach has only a 'philosophy of unity'[68] by which to address the various areas of reality. This means that in addition to being, ontologically, a philosophy of identity, it is *methodologically* monist.[69]

The influence of Nietzsche

But a monism of this sort has its pitfalls. For idealist monism, which oscillates between theory and reality, can easily be turned around and stood on its feet (as the late Schelling already attempted to do). One thereby arrives at a monist *naturalism*.[70] In it, 'nature' becomes that which is primary, at the ontological expense of 'mind'. Examples include Nietzsche and Haeckel, or Vaihinger and Lange within Kantianism. Thus monism can take two forms: it can be a monism of mind or a monism of matter – a mere reversal.[71] (What links the two is the 'will', which is accorded primary importance in Fichte and Nietzsche.) Since, on the level of content, one of the two aspects is always relegated to a secondary status, one monism may provoke the other.[72]

Methodologically, each of the two monisms is a case of idealism: the monist begins from a principle (whether it be conceived of as nature or mind, real or 'cognitive') and deduces everything else from it. Nietzsche's reductive naturalism was welcomed as an 'idealism':[73] his thought also displayed a top-down structure and led ultimately to an ethics.

---

did not intend the concept in this way. Lübbe 1963 and Willms 1966 estimate that Fichte's influence was greater in political philosophy. On Rickert's reference to Fichte, see Rickert 1923 and 1938; see also Windelband 1905, Schrader 1997 and Fulda 1999.

68. Kodalle 1998.

69. Gawoll already sees such a 'methodological monism' at work in Fichte 1989 (p. 59).

70. Naturalism should be distinguished from the older materialism, which did not necessarily deny ontological differences between mind and nature or different philosophical methods but struggled against theology as the doctrine of an overworld that illegitimately intrudes on the sensible world. The idealists paid little attention to Kant. After all, it was precisely 'systems' such as theirs that he had meant to render impossible (Kant 1998, pp. 366 ff., 426 ff., 326 ff.).

71. 'Both theories operate... according to the same principle. They posit one sphere as absolute – the physical sphere in the one case and the mental one in the other – and assume the other sphere to be dependent on the first' (Plessner 1928, p. 5; see Dilthey, *GS* V, pp. 346 ff.). Heidegger accused Nietzsche of a 'reversal of Platonism' (*GA* 6.1, p. 153; *GA* 43). Idealism even anticipated its own pragmatic abolition. Fichte spoke, in passages central to his theory, of 'acts' [*Tathandlungen*] ('When I act I will without doubt know that I act': Fichte 1987, p. 68. This is why Marx remarked that 'the *active* side was developed by idealism' (*MECW* 5, p. 6). Such pragmatism fails to transcend idealism's basic approach (on this, see 3.4).

72. As in Jena around 1900 (Kodalle 2000): Haeckel's monism and Eucken's philosophy of mind (2.5.3) are to be seen as counter-conceptions (Lübbe 1963, p. 177). Kautskyanism's naturalist determinism was already no more than a reversal of idealism: 'The language of determination and even more of determinism was inherited from idealist and especially theological accounts of the world and man' (Williams 1980, p. 31; see Colletti 1977).

73. Lichtblau 1997, p. 74.

Nietzsche's popularity was absolutely central to the development of social philosophy.[74] The term 'social philosophy' [*Sozialphilosophie*] became popular thanks to Nietzsche.[75] For the scholars of the time, the 'Nietzsche experience'[76] tended to be more important than reading Marx (if they did). Thus, in Weber's considerations on the sociology of religion, he openly expresses a Nietzschean philosophy of history: the price to be paid for the ubiquitous spread of rationalisation is the cruel 'disenchantment' of all areas of life,[77] which Weber says it will lead into an 'iron cage'.[78] This hypothesis about disenchantment and rationalisation has become part of social philosophy's canon, like Nietzsche's theories of decline. Thus certain philosophemes dominated the re-philosophising of sociology – especially those of Nietzsche and Fichte.[79]

They constitute the two poles of long-lived German idealism, which sublated the theoretisation of *society* into a 'normative social philosophy'. It is characterised by a pre-

---

74. On Weber, see Bendix 1964 and Hennis 1987; on German sociology in general, see Baier 1981, Rath 1987, Brose 1991, Schluchter 1996, pp. 166 ff.; Lichtblau 1984 and 1997, pp. 77–177; D. Kim 1999, Ester 2001 (see 2.4). 'The forthrightness of a contemporary scholar, and all the more so of a contemporary philosopher, can be assessed by the stance he takes on Nietzsche and Marx. Anyone who refuses to admit that he could not go about a considerable part of his work without . . . these two is lying to himself and to others. The world we exist in mentally is a world that has largely been shaped by Nietzsche and Marx' (Weber, quoted in Baumgarten 1964, pp. 554 ff.; Gneuss 1987, pp. 102, 294). Nietzsche shifted the focus of social philosophy, from the explanation of social processes to their aesthetic appraisal. He took a negative view both of positivist sociology and of socialism, since he held that they threaten to undermine the elitist foundations of 'culture' (capitalism was disregarded in this assessment; see Lukács 1981, pp. 319, 334, 354 ff.). Nietzsche used the term 'value judgement' in this context ('Our socialists are décadents, but Mr Herbert Spencer is also a décadent – he sees the triumph of altruism as desirable!': Nietzsche 1998, p. 64; see the motto to section 2.6.3). To this day, assessments of Nietzsche are dominated by judgements of taste (on this, see Cancik, Riedel and Taureck 2000). But his rejection of socialism and sociology can hardly be denied – and it was this that his influence on sociology rested on. Lichtblau 1997 and Kruse 1999 welcomed this development, since they took the only alternative to consist in a reductive positivism. The positing of such an alternative is indicative of sociology's loss of its object (2.4.1).

75. Adler 1891, Winterfeld 1909, Brose 1990.

76. An expression coined by Thomas Mann (Mann 1986, p. 283; see Bloch 1983). 'The fundamental error committed by Marxism, and by Marx himself, consists in considering decadence a form of capitalism, instead of considering capitalism a form of decadence' (H. Fischer 1932, p. 31). According to Levenstein 1914, workers' reading habits also favoured Nietzsche. However, the view that Nietzsche merely rejected social democracy's excessive bureaucracy, and not socialism as such, is not convincing (Riedel 2000, pp. 54–68; see Rentsch 2000a). For Marxist interpretations of Nietzsche, see also Lukács 1981, pp. 309–99; Gedö 1991; Harich 1994.

77. Weber 1988, pp. 262, 571.

78. Weber 1988, pp. 3, 203 ff.; on Nietzsche: pp. 204, 241; see Bolz 1989; 2.4.6. Here, too, Marx was considered a 'philosopher of history', but one with a limited perspective. A. Salomon called Weber the 'bourgeois Marx'.

79. The origins of the term 'social philosophy' are associated with M. Hess 1843, a Fichtean (Röttgers 1995, p. 1217; Lukács 1968a, pp. 36 and 647; *MECW* 5, p. 483; Lehmann 1931). The 'social philosophy' of the period around 1900 was still influenced by Fichte (Schrader 1997). Röttgers notes an 'elementary ambiguity of descriptivity and normativity' (p. 1219). Simmel's '*Social-Philosophie*' (1894) is an appendix to his 'science of morals'; Stammler 1896 argues prescriptively. On philosophy's hegemony over research, see Horkheimer 1990 and 1989a (2.6.1). 'Social philosophy' is still referred to affirmatively by Honneth (1990, 1994, 2007), Wirkus 1996, Gamm 2000.

carious 'ambiguity' between analysis and ethics,[80] such that it cannot really be said to be one or the other. It mentalises phenomena and moralises theory in an uncontrolled manner. Taking a sceptical view of the consequences of this way of thinking does not necessarily make one an amoralist. The price paid for the advantage of theoretical unity is that the 'residuum' – that for which there is no place in such aprioristic constructs (and due to the limited nature of each individual perspective, this can be any number of states of affairs) – is either omitted theoretically or relegated to a marginal region of being. This is why I speak of 'reductionism'. In *practical* terms, the residuum risks being misconstrued or crushed by those who think in this way ('the one [world] has to subordinate the other').[81]

The influence of Hegel

> Reason is negative and dialectical, because it resolves the determinations of the understanding into nothing.[82]

In Germany, the common response is to refer to Hegel as the one who sublated this particularity by breaking through into philosophical consideration of the totality. In fact, Hegel did develop a standpoint allowing the integration and interpretation of every earlier view of the world. He believed he would thereby be able to overcome the division between formal philosophy and an ungraspable material,[83] between an outer, alien world and a philosophy that limits itself to what is subjective. Philosophically, such a standpoint is highly attractive – at least if one is working in the idealist branch of philosophy, which aspires to such total interpretations.[84] Yet the difficult question is how to achieve

80. Röttgers 1995, pp. 1219, 1222.

81. Eucken 1921, p. 29; 2.5.3. 'Armed Fichteans will come onto the scene, who, with fanatic will, will be untamable by self-interest or fear; for they live in the spirit.... Indeed, such transcendental idealists would be even more inflexible in a social upheaval than the first Christians' (Heine 2007, p. 115). This conclusion was also arrived at by some 'analyses of fascism' that situated it primarily in a certain way of thinking (Glucksmann 1980). While they are reductive, they are not altogether mistaken. More generally, the postmodern dismissal of theory derives its plausibility from pseudo-philosophical degenerative forms of theorising that are not understood for what they are but interpreted as normal and projected back onto Kant, Hegel and Marx. This gives them some resemblance to 'existentialist sociology'. A similar comparison was drawn by Habermas 1987a and Frank 1993, pp. 119 ff.

82. Hegel, *Science of Logic*.

83. In Kant, the 'material' to be grasped conceptually consists of concrete apperceptions that cannot be deduced from reason. When Hegel uses the term, he intends something altogether different: the thing in itself, the norm and God himself (qua 'the infinite'). Hegel simply accused Kant of failing to address these.

84. Plessner 1928 gives expression to the idealistic style when he demands that philosophy 'ought to render visible those final depths of what exists... without consciousness of which all human endeavours lack their backdrop and remain meaningless'. Marquard interprets such formulas as degenerative forms of theodicy (in Hogrebe 1995, pp. 225 ff.). Another attempt to reconciliate the two monisms consisted in their eclectic juxtaposition and in the construction of an ontological hierarchy of worlds, neo-Kantian regions of being or a dualism of technology and morality (2.4.1).

such a standpoint. Roughly speaking, Hegel's answer also consisted in treating one of the two aspects as absolute: he may have accused Fichte, throughout his life, of doing just this, but ultimately, his 'absolute mind' did not get beyond an idealist monism. Whatever else one may think of Hegel – his system would have been altogether unthinkable if it had not been idealist, that is, a philosophy of identity and a methodological monism.[85]

Hegel is set off from his precursors Fichte and Schelling neither by the style of his philosophy nor by its aim, but by his thoroughness and methodological reflectedness. He implemented, concretely and comprehensively, what Fichte had called for: bringing everything that was alienated and not I back into the absolute subject.[86] This involved the willingness to acquire much specialist knowledge (which is not so 'absolute' at all). Hegel had an encyclopaedic grasp of the knowledge of his day.[87] His specific achievement was not that of breaking through to 'absolute knowledge' (this had already been done in religion and art, as well as in Fichte and Schelling) but that of working out what exactly it means to have such knowledge.[88]

This includes the insight that to achieve the absolute standpoint is not to increase actual knowledge. Hegel made life difficult for philosophers. His philosophy knows no *privileged* way of accessing the absolute: 'absolute mind' is always the whole, so that it cannot possibly be usurped by a single party. Nor is there any way of accessing this standpoint *immediately*; it can be accessed only by painstakingly working through every objection and doubt. Moreover, what has been processed by mind remains effectual: 'suffering'[89] remains and is 'sublated' only in the sense that it is integrated into a totality of meaning – by no means does one genuinely get rid of it. Even Hegel took a long time to arrive at these insights – he certainly had not yet reached this standpoint in

---

By proceeding thus, one is left not with two perspectives on a single world, as in Kant, but with two worlds (Schelling 1985; Habermas 1984–7, Vol. I, pp. 48 ff.).

85. 'Every philosophy is essentially an idealism' (Hegel 1929, § 316). The difference between Hegel and Fichte consists in the way they implement their common programme. Hegel also held that 'the absolute' is necessary for all cognition, except that he felt the theory of knowledge was meaningless in this regard (Hogrebe 1987, p. 90; Hegel 1967, p. 134 calls the theory of knowledge a 'deception'). Thus, as far as epistemology is concerned, he remained a Fichtean all his life, as can be seen from the way he deals with the thing in itself. Hegel's discussion of the thing in itself is Fichtean, that is, there is no 'thing in itself' for Hegel: 'Reason is the conscious certainty of being all reality' (Hegel 1967, p. 273; see pp. 170 ff. and Hegel 1977a, p. 74; on moral philosophy, see Wildt 1982). Hegel was outraged that Kant, as a philosopher of 'finitude', did not dare advocate 'cognition of the Absolute' (1977a, p. 68; see Pascher 1997, p. 24; see also 2.1.5).

86. See 2.4.6.

87. 'The truth is the whole' and the absolute is 'essentially a result' (Hegel 1967, p. 81).

88. König's verdict on this: 'In the end, one finds only what was already there to begin with . . . Yet in Hegel, the way from the beginning to the end (and hence to the whole) leads through the mediation of the dialectic. And the identity of subject and object is not an immediate, unconscious one but one that is mediated "through reflection of the otherness within oneself", i.e. an identity that has accommodated difference and negativity within itself' (König 1975, p. 64).

89. Hegel 1967, p. 81.

1801.[90] Since the 'absolute standpoint' can only be a subsequent one,[91] Hegel's own positions could not be retained for long – if only because the world described and the knowledge about it were changing rapidly. As a serious thinker, Hegel included only serious thoughts about the world in his system (where in his system he included them is another question). But he no longer has any criterion by which to decide which thoughts actually are serious.[92]

The system's plausibility depends on the topicality of the excursions into the regular sciences by which it seeks to illustrate its relevance. This was one reason why Hegel's system abruptly lost its persuasiveness after his death. Its disappearance tore a hole in German philosophy. The difficult legacy consisted in Hegel's *aspiration* to the totality. To claim that such a totality existed at a certain point in time (in Hölderlin, 'the Greeks', the pre-Socratics, and so on) is to lapse into melancholy dreams of a primordially idealist position. But even this position would have had to repress an unrecuperated residuum (thus a blind spot in Aristotle was his presupposition of slave labour, like the speculative 'sublation' of bourgeois society in Hegel).

Thus the question after Hegel was whether the aspiration to the totality ought to be retained, and if so, how one might do this. The Young Hegelians retained the aspiration (otherwise they could not have wanted to transpose their completed theory into reality, to 'realise' it, which is what Marx accused them of), but they failed to live up to it within theory.[93] During the early twentieth century, when everyone talked about overcoming the 'subject-object division', Hegel became fashionable again.[94]

---

90. Gawoll 1989, p. 72; see Siep 2000.

91. As a determination of reflection, it does not serve a regulatory purpose but rather achieves the 'aesthetic synthesis' of resumptive consideration. 'The owl of Minerva spreads its wings only with the falling of the dusk' (Hegel 1991, p. 13).

92. See *MECW* 4, pp. 60 ff. This is how the call for 'intellectual forthrightness' (Weber 1972, p. 443; Habermas 1984–7, Vol. I, p. 66; see Nietzsche and Jaspers) originates. One lacks external support and believes oneself to be 'objective' only because of moral self-commitment or the peer pressure of the scientific community. This 'morality', that of a specific group at a specific time, can very well be superseded theoretically with the aid of Marx.

93. The range of philosophical currents that erroneously took themselves to be anti-philosophical (Schnädelbach 1983, p. 21; Landmann 1977, p. 11) was broad. The Young Hegelians already made reference to Fichte (Hess 1843; see Löwith 1965, p. 87; Hogrebe 1987, p. 112; for general accounts, see McLellan 1969, Essbach 1988, Draper 1990, and Fellmann 1996).

94. For prominent examples, see Dilthey 1906, Nohl 1907, Windelband 1921, and Levy 1927; see, too, Topitsch 1967, Kiesewetter 1974 and 1995, Helferich 1979, pp. 151 ff., Losurdo 1993. Note also Adorno's understanding of Hegel (see 2.5.7, 2.6.3). What was at stake was the 'overcoming of the subject-object division that Max Weber had taken as his starting point' (Jonas 1976, Vol. II, p. 213). For analyses of various 'subject-object relations', see Lukács 1971c (the notion that ethics involves a 'destruction of the object': pp. 137 ff.), Mannheim 1964a, pp. 205 ff.; see Petrowicz 1992, pp. 45 ff.

Vitalism and the philosophy of Weltanschauung

You interpret the new conception as the seeing of a new object.[95]

The next major philosophical school to constitute itself after Hegel, neo-Kantianism, was characterised at first by its avoidance of the aspiration to totality.[96] And yet it was in the neo-Kantian context that there began, around the turn of the century and in connection with a return to Hegel, a search for a new philosophical 'worldview' [*Weltanschauung*].[97] König interpreted this as a reaction to Marxism. Is this plausible?

It would be difficult to prove that neo-Kantianism's original orientation toward the physical sciences was a response to political developments.[98] Indications that neo-Kantianism was genuinely influenced by politics can only be found during a later period, when Social Democracy had become a significant factor in imperial Germany: during the last third of the nineteenth century, idealism once more became popular. Eduard von Hartmann, Philipp Mainländer and Eugen Dühring displayed a need for a wide-scale orientation. Notwithstanding its focus on the sciences and its positivist beginnings, neo-Kantianism also turned toward idealism.[99] Various explanations have been proposed to account for this collective search for meaning. One explanation points to imperial Germany's lack of substance: the country had been unified by force alone and could offer its subjects no possibilities for 'mental' [*geistig*] identification.[100]

While other factors were, no doubt, involved, one can also regard the philosophical search for a worldview as a *tendency that reacted to Marxism*, insofar as it involved the development of the first alternatives to the materialist way of looking at the world, which had become popular.[101] 'Materialism' was understood as claiming that history and politics

---

95. Wittgenstein, *Philosophical Investigations*, aphorism 401.

96. Thus the very title of Köhnke 1986 situated neo-Kantianism between idealism and positivism. 'The search for exclusionary principles that cannot be formulated any other way (or that must be formulated in accordance with the dicta of the system's founder) is to be abandoned altogether, in favour of a comprehensive representation of what really exists' (Beneke 1832, p. 88; quoted in Köhnke 1986, p. 82). A.F. Lange declared in an 1858 letter: 'I consider every type of metaphysics a form of insanity that is justified only aesthetically and subjectively' (quoted in Köhnke 1986, p. 233).

97. See Griffioen 1998, Glatz 2001, pp. 51–154; see also Rohbeck 1999.

98. With the exception of A. Lange 1887 and 1870, where Marx is, however, only mentioned in passing. Lange died too soon to still be able to quarrel with Social Democrats.

99. See Köhnke 1986, pp. 257, 272 ff., 404 ff.; Pascher 1997, pp. 46 ff.; Kittsteiner 2001 and F.J. Schmidt 1908.

100. What was lacking, according to this argument, was a 'consolidated national idea of the state' (Plessner 1992, p. 192; Lübbe 1963, p. 180; Hermand 1977, p. 77). This was no more than a call for symbolic communitisation.

101. According to Jost Hermand, 'around the turn of the century, the power-political field was determined by two poles: the excessive nationalism of the Wilhelmine leadership and the constantly growing working class, which had created an official advocacy group for itself in social democracy' (Hermand 1977, p. 7). According to A. Weber 1931, cultural sociology (which had been influenced by Dilthey) was especially called upon to 'engage decisively with the materialist conception of history, which currently... reigns supreme and unchallenged [!]' (p. 292).

are shaped only by material factors, and this was taken to entail utter meaninglessness.[102] What seemed to be especially at risk was the ethos of the state, which was highly valued in the newly constituted country.[103] That Social Democracy was a major object of fear and hostility is evident: the newly forming humanities could not have referred more clearly to the social dislocations caused by the labour movement, for example.[104] In the search for a new worldview, then, the question was not whether there had ever been a closed and universally binding worldview *in the past.* The insuperable class boundaries of 'traditional' societies make this quite unlikely, unless one wants to return to a mythical prehistory. It was the contemporary labour movement that displayed such a worldview (2.1.4). Thus developing a *different* worldview, one contrary to materialism, was an implicit functional task that social philosophy needed to perform against Marxism, which had become well established.[105]

And yet by becoming fashionable, vitalism failed to achieve the very thing it wanted: the creation of a new, unified and binding worldview. For the time being, all it could do was gather and catalogue existing *Weltanschauungen.* As with Simmel and Mannheim after him, what motivated Dilthey to engage in this endeavour was the Fichtean quest for unity: he hoped that by compiling the various worldviews, he would be able to extract from them what they had in common, thus synthesising a new worldview that bridged existing divisions.[106] For Dilthey, discovering the commonalities within

102. The distinction between materialism and idealism is certainly not 'the' key issue in philosophy (Joas 1992, p. 229). At the time, the issue was, however, taken quite seriously (Köhnke 1986, pp. 257 ff.). Even in contemporary analytic philosophy, realism and constructivism contend with one another (C. Wright 1992; Hügli 1993, Vol. II; Kutschera 1993). At the time, 'materialism' was understood in a vague and mentalised way, as a *Weltanschauung* or direction followed by science ('positivism – psychologism – historicism': Wuchterl 1995, pp. 17, 70; see Lübbe 1963, pp. 124 ff.; Ringer 1987, pp. 202 ff.; see also Lange 1865 and Schwarz 1912). But even Rothacker saw this as a smokescreen for 'the founders of the radical party' (Rothacker 1948, p. 44). Heimann similarly viewed positivism as the 'attitude of the worker' (Heimann 1980, p. 55).

103. D. Schulz 2003, pp. 180 ff.

104. On this argument, the science of society owed its genesis to 'the loss of all inhibitory apparatuses between state power and the working class' after 1789 (Dilthey, *GS* V, p. 32). 'Rapid growth of industry and of communication links confronted state power with a daily increasing mass of workers bound together through community of interests transcending individual state boundaries and ever more clearly conscious of their interests through the progress of the Enlightenment' (Dilthey 1988, p. 126; see König 1975, p. 28).

105. 'A lesson for politicians! ... It is not just from the natural power of emotions, but also from a coherent system of thought that social democracy and ultramontanism derive their preponderance over all other political powers of our day' (Dilthey, *GS* II, p. 91; see Schäffle 1885, Eckart 1910, Eucken 1920, Ringer 1987, pp. 53, 133, 202). As early as 1873, Dilthey wrote a review of Marx's *Capital.* He criticised the lack of attention devoted to the 'real needs of individuals' and argued that Marx 'fails to recognise the significance of the type of mental [!] activity that makes work accord with need: action': *GS* XVII, pp. 186 ff.; see Orth 1985, p. 10; Arendt 1969 and Habermas 1984–7 still write in this vein).

106. Dilthey's typology of *Weltanschauungen* (*GS* VIII) merely catalogued existing *Weltanschauungen* (Lukács 1981, pp. 435 ff.). Yet the intention behind such catalogues was that of constructing a new worldview, as Hegel had done in 1807 (Hegel 1967). See Jaspers 1919, Spranger 1921, Mannheim 1936, but also less well-known works such as Hart 1899, Kroner 1914, Schlunk 1922 (*'Eine Einführung*

the 'superstructure' of worldviews required one to consider the underlying 'base'. Yet Dilthey's presuppositions hindered him from considering the *real* base, namely 'real man',[107] his conditions of existence and relations. For as a '*Geisteswissenschaftler*', a 'scientist of the mind', Dilthey refuses to acknowledge anything that is not mental ('[e]verything here derives from acts of human spirit').[108] Nevertheless, he aspires to grasping a totality, and even to founding a new one. The worldview he searches for is to be characterised by its 'totality', but he wants it to be a whole that is exclusively 'mental' [*geistig*] and individual, for Dilthey begins with consciousness.[109] Thus what Dilthey searches for *cannot* be anything other than a 'mental totality'. It cannot transcend the world of human actors: it derives from the individual perspective (that of the 'participants'), but it is nevertheless supposed to ground everything else.[110] The label he put on what he was searching for was 'life'.

Life is intuitively accessible to everyone, and it mysteriously grounds and supports everything.[111] In this sense, Dilthey is a *philosopher of identity*: life understands life[112] – as in Fichte, 'I' and 'not-I', subject and object, life and experience [*Erlebnis*] are ultimately – that is, ontologically – identical. Because of the interminability of this idealist monism, 'life' oscillates constantly between idealism and naturalism.[113] It occupies the position

---

für Suchende' – 'An Introduction for Searchers'), Heußner 1927, Wenzl 1935 and Wyneken 1940, pp. 177 ff. ('*Das geistige Erlebnis*': Mental Experience).

107. *MECW* 3, p. 181; see pp. 39 ff. and elsewhere.

108. Dilthey 2002, p. 169.

109. If ever there was a philosophy of consciousness in the sense intended by Habermas (1984–7, 1987a, 1989), then it owed its existence not to Kant but to Fichte, and was passed on to Dilthey and Husserl (and further). Dilthey was concerned with 'the entire range of empirical consciousness' (*GS* V, p. 346; see p. 386 and elsewhere). While what is dealt with is the whole, this whole is an individual, intellectual one: 'This whole is life' (*GS* V, p. 200). 'Life is the internal relationship of psychic accomplishments within the person' (*GS* V, p. 408; see Bollnow 1936; Lukács 1981, pp. 417 ff.; Ineichen in Bärthlein 1983; Orth 1985).

110. Nothing more was aimed at than the mental, individual perspective: 'If one could imagine a solitary individual making his way in the world, that individual would develop these functions [philosophy, religion and art] out of his own resources' (Dilthey 1988, p. 333). 'All that Dilthey did was to replace the false abstraction of that which is governed by mere understanding with an irrational, putative totality of experienced life' (Lukács 1981, p. 424). What was idealist was the assumption that this would allow one to state something about 'historical reality'.

111. 'Now, life is the basic fact that must serve as philosophy's point of departure' (Dilthey 2002, p. 359); 'thought cannot venture back behind life' (*GS* V, p. 5). This is 'the old procedure of hypostatising a product of abstraction from the concrete and treating it as the ontological foundation of the concrete, thereby presenting an 'explanation' that is in fact no more than a tautology' (Lübbe 1963, p. 185) – a 'very cheap method to produce the semblance of being profound and speculative in the German manner' (*MECW* 5, p. 481). What was sought was not found. One did no more than place demands on oneself – until the becoming fashionable of such demands was taken to constitute a 'theory' (not a rare phenomenon; see 2.6.1).

112. Dilthey 2002, p. 157.

113. 'As a broad category encompassing body and mind, culture and nature, the concept of 'life' allowed one to attempt to overcome the separation of the natural and the human sciences' (Rehberg 1981, p. 178; see Plessner 1928, p. 3). 'Life' oscillated between proximity to the subject and proximity to the object (Lukács 1981, pp. 419 ff., 430 ff.), much like the 'hybrids' in contemporary actor-network theory.

that consciousness occupied in neo-Kantianism, which is to say it produces the world, and there is only this one world.[114] But life not only 'perceives'; it also 'feels' and 'wills'.[115] There is a biologistic flavour to it.[116] While Dilthey starts from 'mind' [*Geist*], the transition to the contrary monism is fluent, as can be seen clearly in students of Dilthey such as Spranger and Rothacker, or in Plessner. As is well known, National Socialism still understood itself to be a *Weltanschauung*.[117]

Dilthey's search for a mental totality makes use of Hegel, who is given an idealist interpretation.[118] Like Fichte and Schlegel, Hegel already spoke of 'life'. But when Hegel's absolute standpoint is given a name that is understood to be the *proper name* of an entity with which one is 'always already' identical,[119] the genuine achievements that set Hegel off from his precursors (and from his own early writings) are lost: not only does the absolute standpoint not actually gather together the knowledge of the age; Dilthey also fails to understand that what is absolute about this knowledge is something *subsequent*, something that adds no further knowledge. Under the heading of 'life',[120] Dilthey randomly claims to have discovered a comprehensive standpoint; at most, he justifies his claim in terms of intense 'sensations'. Here, Hegel's subjectivism takes its toll. The prob-

---

114. 'Only through the idea of the objectification of life do we gain insight into the nature of the historical. Everything [!] here derives from acts of human spirit and bears the hallmark of historicity. As a product of history, everything gets interwoven with the world of sense' (Dilthey 2002, p. 169). 'Previously, life used to be conceived on the basis of the world. But the only route possible is to proceed from the interpretation of life to the world' (p. 311). Dilthey divided the world into 'the demonic power of the individual being and the hallowing, persistent power of mental forms' (Hofmannsthal qtd. in Fellmann 1993, p. 108).

115. Dilthey 1988, p. 73.

116. 'Instinct, emotion, passions, volitions are central to that which we call life' (*GS* V, p. XC). Dilthey considered Nietzsche's blonde beast, the Teuton, to be the prototype of life (2002, pp. 195 ff.; see Rickert 1911). This much was understood about life: that one could give it a thoroughly nationalist inflection. 'The facticity of race, of space, and of power-relations provides a matrix that can never [!] be spiritualized' (2002, p. 307).

117. In *Mein Kampf* (Hitler 1942, p. 315), we read: 'Without human beings, there exists no human idea in this world... In fact, certain ideas are linked to certain human beings... But if this is the case, then preserving these specific races and human beings is the precondition for preserving these ideas' (quoted in Hogrebe 1987, pp. 140 ff.). 'The absence of a tragic worldview... has contributed considerably to the political weakness of the German people. National Socialism has considered it one of its main tasks to overcome this condition of weakness. It creates a bond between all Germans in the form of a unitary worldview' (*Der Neue Brockhaus: Allbuch in vier Bänden*, Vol. 4, Leipzig: F.A. Brockhaus, 1938, pp. 68 ff., quoted by Rehberg in Rohbeck 1999; see Schwarz 1933; see also 2.4.6, on Schelsky).

118. *GS* IV.

119. If 'life' is 'that which is known from within' and 'beyond which one cannot venture' (Dilthey, 2002, p. 359), then the proper maxim is 'Know thyself' (Spann 1935). 'A living reality knows itself' (Freyer 1964, p. 82). Lukács also speaks vitalistically of the '*self-knowledge of capitalist society*' (Lukács 1971, p. 229; see 2.5.4). Hegel already began (*Werke* I, p. 378 and elsewhere) and ended with 'life' ('But the immediate Idea is Life': Hegel 1929, p. 401; see Hogrebe 1987, p. 7). In this sense, vitalism's references to Hegel are not altogether unjustified – all the worse for Hegel.

120. For later philosophies of life, see Simmel 1910 and 1918, Misch 1930, Messer 1931, Lersch 1932, Bollnow 1933, 1936 and 1958, Feifel 1938 or Glockner 1944; for analysis, Lieber 1974, Dahms 1987, Baumgartner n.d., Ebrecht 1991, Fellmann 1993, K. Albert 1995 and 2000.

lem is not that Hegel sometimes 'lent a helping hand' to make everything in his system fit.[121] It is that as far as epistemology is concerned, he remained a Fichtean all his life. This meant that a philosophical approach like Dilthey's would henceforth be possible: if all that philosophy is interested in is the self-development of thoughts *about* the world, then it will never be able to find any real footing in the outside world. This opened the door to thinkers who were less disciplined in philosophical matters. They could take whatever *they* considered important and place it wherever in their surrogate systems they thought it belonged.[122]

Thus Lukács was not exaggerating when he described this as a form of 'irrationalism'. After all, these currents themselves increasingly rejected the 'cold' rationality of science.[123] One thought one had discovered the source of what was going awry in the modern world: it was the objectifying standpoint of the positive *sciences* that was to blame. Moreover, the sciences were beginning to venture onto the terrain of philosophy, in the form of psychology.[124] Subjectivism already inhered in this approach: German thought alleged that 'the world' (the one construed in the sciences *and* the one experienced by man) was constituted by means of cognitive activity. Hence it was a matter of finding a standpoint from which to once more 'think' the world as a whole.[125] Unfortunately, these

---

121. 'The transition of the family and civil society into the political state is, therefore, this: the mind of these spheres, which is *implicitly* the mind of the state, now also behaves to itself as such.... The transition is thus derived, not from the *particular* nature of the family, etc., and from the particular nature of the state, but rather from the *general* relationship of *necessity* to *freedom*. It is exactly the same transition as is effected in logic from the sphere of essence to the sphere of the concept. The same transition is made in the philosophy of nature from inorganic nature to life. It is always the same categories which provide the soul, now for this, now for that sphere' (*MECW* 3, p. 10; see Ilting in Riedel 1975). Hegel 'does not develop his thinking from the object, but expounds the object in accordance with a thinking that is cut and dried – already formed and fixed in the abstract sphere of logic' (*MECW* 3, p. 14). Lask (1902), whom Heidegger and Lukács looked up to, still emphatically criticised Hegel's 'leaps'.

122. Schopenhauer and Nietzsche posited the 'will' as first principle: the late Schelling and Heidegger opted for 'Being', and historicism for 'history' (on historicism's kinship with Hegel, see Schnädelbach 1983, pp. 59 ff.). Dilthey posited 'life' as first principle; the late Simmel followed Bergson in according this status to the 'vital impetus'; Klages accorded it to the 'soul' and Lukács to 'class consciousness'. Contemporary discourses of structure, system, communication or difference still display an idealist top-down structure. The arbitrariness of such constructs can be seen from the way that Heidegger (speaking in one of his late seminars, which Gadamer visited with his best students) rejected each and every interpretation of his work. Even the interpretation is subjectivist; it often legitimates itself by virtue of a charismatic authority that is not transferable. Instead of students, Hegel, Nietzsche, Heidegger and Luhmann have only epigones.

123. 'Life cannot be judged in the court of reason': Dilthey, 2002, p. 359. Even Plessner speaks of a 'liberation [!] from the categories that have dominated the interpretation of our thinking, acting and hoping since Greek antiquity' (Plessner 1928, p. 25; see Klages 1929). It is only when life and reason are posited as identical that life 'cannot be judged in the court of reason'.

124. N. Schmidt 1995.

125. Theorists from southwestern Germany adopted Dilthey's concepts of 'totality', 'intellectuality' [*Geistigkeit*] and 'intuition' (Windelband 1921, p. 291; Rickert 1921, pp. 265 ff., 412). In Rickert, a world of objects that is 'existent' [*seiend*] is supplemented by an overarching sphere of values that is 'meaningful' [*geltend*]; in this way, Rickert arrived at 'consciousness as such'. Husserl's phenom-

overcomings also occurred nowhere but in the subject. In the succession of schools, a basic pattern recurs: the preceding system is judged to be too subjective and replaced with a more objective system, which is then trumped by a system that is still more objective, and so on.[126] Within this development, Heidegger's ontologism (2.5.5) marked no more than a temporary endpoint – Arendt, Anders, Löwith and Marcuse tried to outdo Heidegger by being more concrete.[127] But it was impossible to get rid of Fichteanism in this way, for it inhered in the very premises.[128]

In keeping with this approach, Dilthey interpreted even political economy as a human science [*Geisteswissenschaft*]. As a result, after Dilthey, political economy was radically mentalised [*vergeistigt*] – a development exemplified by Freyer.[129] This meant that entire regions of being, still addressed by Hegel, were now exempted from the aspiration to totality. They included nature, the investigation of which Dilthey meant to set himself off from, as well as society's non-mental underside, which had originally been the object of sociology – an eliminative idealism. From this perspective, all that remains is one's own 'self', which is, moreover, mentalised.[130] This is reminiscent of Fichte, to whom Dilthey refers in key passages.[131]

It can in fact be shown that Dilthey's early work is already characterised by a Fichtean quest for unity. In 1860, he spoke enthusiastically about Schleiermacher's hermeneutics, in which 'the rules by which to understand texts are derived from insight into the genesis

---

enology anatomised experiential contents assumed to be anterior to the split between an outer and an inner world. Vitalism sought to regain this standpoint through 'experience' [*Erleben*] (see Lehmann 1943, Hügli 1993, Wuchterl 1995).

126. The escapism of Stirner and Kierkegaard was followed by Mach's positivism, which was, however, worldless. The search for a more objective subjectivism was then taken up by neo-Kantianism, vitalism, existentialism and finally philosophical anthropology (on the latter's idealist origins, see Rehberg 1985). Even the doctrine of race can be considered an attempt to provide subjectivist relativism with a biologistic foundation.

127. Rentsch 2001, p. 215.

128. 'Thus Hegel was traced back to Fichte.... "The object is wholly and fully a knowing" [Ebbinghaus]. That was, at best, a modernized Fichte' (Lukács 1981, p. 553). Fichteanisms can be found even where one would hardly expect them: 'The separation of content from form is either impossible or inaccurate' (Horkheimer 1972b, p. 141; Brandom 1994, p. 635 speaks of 'norms all the way down' and rhapsodises about 'absolute knowledge'; see 4.3). Epistemology merely makes this assumption explicit.

129. Freyer turns Weber's hypothesis on ideal factors in history (2.4.6) into one on the character of reality; he ontologises the model. It is only this mentalisation even of the economy that makes it possible, in theoretical terms, for Freyer to believe in a will-based, ethical overcoming of the economy: 'The theory of capitalism and its development has, as is well known, traced back with great success the elements of its worldview.... [T]he innermost meaningful content of the capitalist form of life is determined by a definite morality, metaphysics, and doctrine of life' (Freyer 1998, p. 48). 'The dissolution of economic 'things' into human functions... tends to lead to a breaking apart of categories, such that only the pure subject... remains' (Freund 1932, p. 335; see Schefold 1994a, Acham 1995).

130. See Lukács 1981, pp. 421, 430 ff. Habermas inherited this division (Habermas 1987, pp. 140 ff.; 3.1).

131. Dilthey 2002, pp. 179, 300, 353 ff.; Glatz 2001, p. 230.

of those texts'. In 1865, he wished to overcome the formalism of Kant's ethics by adjusting it to theoretical reason.[132] How are we to account for the fact that Dilthey, of all people, developed such a philosophy of identity? Was he not the first to distinguish between the natural sciences and the humanities? The answer lies not in Dilthey's stated intentions, but in the basic assumptions by which he was guided. In an age of proliferating theories, one of philosophy's indispensable tasks consists in working out the various logics proper to different areas of human action and thought.[133]

Dilthey was aiming at something of this sort when he attempted to provide a solid methodological foundation for separating the historical from the natural sciences in much the same way as they had already been separated from philosophy. He transposed notions associated with neo-Kantianism, which had provided a philosophical 'foundation' for the practice of the successful natural sciences (neo-Kantianism developed the discipline of epistemology for this very purpose), to the practice of the historical sciences, which he meant to also provide with an epistemological 'foundation'. Although Dilthey objected to the practice of distinguishing between the sciences on the basis of their objects of inquiry,[134] he only did so because he held that there are *no objects* within historicity. Dilthey considered historicity a region of being that is *co-present* in everything that surrounds us.[135] Thus he assumed the existence of a distinct mode of being, of a 'historical' and a 'mental world'.[136] Idealism's genetic fallacy manifests itself in his assumption that only 'mind' [*Geist*] can be the object of the humanities [*Geisteswissenschaften*]. While living mind is not objective, its crystallisations allow one to develop a subsequent 'understanding' of older, 'objective mind'. All of these *background assumptions* are present in Dilthey. The historical sciences, which had long since constituted themselves,[137] were not genuinely provided with a 'foundation' by Dilthey's effort to attribute 'objective

---

132. Ineichen (in Bärthlein 1983, p. 153) quotes Dilthey's 1860 essay on 'Schleiermacher's Hermeneutic System' [*Das hermeneutische System Schleiermachers*] and his 1865 habilitation, 'An Attempt to Analyse Moral Consciousness' [*Versuch einer Analyse des moralischen Bewusstseins*] in Dilthey, *GS* XVIII.

133. One need think only of Aristotle's distinction between the various parts of the soul in *De Anima*, or of reason's internal distinctions in the *Nicomachean Ethics*. There have always been such fundamental philosophical reformations, especially in situations characterised by an excess of philosophical currents. Aristotle's ways of knowing, Kant's separation of the theoretical from the practical use of reason, Husserl's phenomenological distinction between specific modes of existence, Weber's distinction between different value spheres and Wittgenstein's remarks on the different grammars proper to various language games are only the most important examples.

134. *GS* V, LXXIX.

135. Dilthey 2002, p. 91.

136. Dilthey, *GS* V. What Dilthey calls 'historic-social reality' (Dilthey 1988, p. 90), Freyer 1998 calls 'objective mind'; N. Hartmann 1933 speaks of 'mental being'. What is meant is a distinct 'mental world' [*geistige Welt:* Dilthey, *GS* V]. It is no accident that Dilthey's 'Critique of Historical Reason' relegated Kant's thing in itself to cognition of nature, arguing that historical cognition knows nothing of the kind since it concerns ourselves. Here, too, the claim to cognition of the totality is forced to abandon Kant's critical objection.

137. On their earlier history, see Troeltsch 1922, Mannheim 1964b, Schnädelbach 1983, pp. 51–87.

mind' to them as their object; rather, they were remodelled and ideologised. For why should the historical disciplines concern themselves only with 'mental' things (philosophy, religion, art)? The suggestion sounds all too much like the class prejudice of an educated civil servant.[138]

Vitalism ended up with an *aporia*: it was busy *fending off* the objectifying effects of the natural sciences, but at the same time, it was struggling for *its own* specific object of inquiry, which was supposed to comprehend what is individual in history, the 'singular totality' (Simmel), one's own first and foremost.[139] Bourgeois society fell through the gap between the two. Dilthey gives a principal character to the loss of the object of inquiry that was already evident in sociology (2.4.1). Which of the two developments occurred first, whether there was a common cause or whether one development induced the other – these questions cannot be decided here. What is important is that the relevance of the loss of the object in various theoretical fields be *appreciated*. The loss of objectivity was diagnosed and promoted even in the art of the time.[140] Art's relationship to its environment was not a 'critical' one; art failed to keep its distance from the bourgeois intellectual currents of the time.

The theoretical loss of substance was preceded by the call for a comprehensive, primoridally active spontaneity of the antecedent subject-object (the self, existential living, being, the people, language or the class-conscious proletariat). The assumption was that this spontaneity needed only to be liberated from dead objectifications or 'reifications'.

---

138. Why should one not be able to understand something antecedent? It seems that 'mind' is considered 'primordial' for no other reason than because it vouches for one's group identity. The genetic fallacy is at work here. Marx also discussed religion, law, philosophy, and so on, but without mentalising them. Following Lask 1993, one can describe the apprehension of non-mental objects (social structures, processes, and so on) by the social sciences as the rational apprehension of a non-rational material. Working within the neo-Kantian approach, Lask went so far as to make form dependent on material. For this reason, Ernst Bloch called him a 'materialist St. Nicholas'. But he died too early to become influential within neo-Kantianism. Karl Lamprecht's cultural history and Mannheim's sociology of knowledge were also coolly received by contemporaries. Today, the sociology of knowledge and economic and social history are recognised as foundational disciplines. While interest in the symbolic dimension has recently been revived in the historical sciences (Francois 2000), it cannot and does not intend to replace basic considerations; it is intended merely to supplement and clarify them. 'One needs... first to get to the bottom of objective reality as it exists beyond symbols. Only then can one assess whether the symbolic representation of that reality is appropriate or of an ideological nature' (Baumgart 1991, p. 150).

139. Freyer characterises the meaning of the 'revolution in the philosophical sense of the word' as follows: 'Life... faithfully confesses to itself (however, this confession is made through fortified form) that it establishes absolutely its meaningful content for the epoch that has allowed that content.... Life lives with the awareness that culture is only *its* culture' (Freyer 1998, p. 134). It was, therefore, a matter of 'Germanness' (Mann 1919, Troeltsch 1922, Schnädelbach 1983). Ebrecht traces the concept of the 'lifeworld' back to the Diltheyan Freyer (1991, p. 85; Freyer 1998, pp. 150 ff.).

140. See Kandinsky 1986 (see Wyss 1996) or Musil's *Man Without Qualities* (on this work, see Rentsch 2000, pp. 292 ff.). Colletti critically traces this 'destruction of things' back to Hegel. Via Engels and Bergson, it influenced even Lenin, Lukács and Marcuse (Colletti 1976, pp. 157 ff.). Sartre's nihilist existentialism merely caused this atmosphere to persist, much as the abstract painting of the second decade of the twentieth century only became popular in the 1950s.

When one effects such an idealist totalisation within one's thinking, there remains nothing, no 'not-I' that one should, or can, orient oneself to in one's efforts to understand oneself. What was eventually perceived as an 'intellectual crisis' was simply the flipside of what one had once aspired to: it is the idealist, immodest claim to total cognition of reality that entails nihilism.[141] If the nihilism implicit in total 'historicisation' was not understood to be dangerous, this was only because idealism came so naturally at the time. This way of thinking was tailor-made for the aggressive politics of the day.[142] Heidegger was not the only one to sense what a brusque rejection of Marx and Kant – but not of Fichte, Hegel and Nietzsche – this was.[143]

Is it the case that *every* 'historicisation' produces a relativism, and does this mean that one should insist on the preservation of some supra-historical region?[144] Or is nihilism produced only by *idealist* historicisation, which believes itself capable of understanding everything ('totality') and thereby ends up unable to make any distinction at all, or to perceive anything other than itself? The developments I have described suggest the latter is the case. Without the premises of the philosophy of identity, one cannot infer from a certain genesis how something should be *treated* or what ontological worth it has.[145] But

---

141. Like Fichte, Dilthey does not distinguish 'between an object that is perceived and the eye that perceives it' (*GS* V, LXXIX). Dilthey eliminates the criterial distinction between subject and object; of lived experience [*Erlebnis*], he says that 'its existence is indistinguishable from what in it is there for me' (Dilthey 2002, p. 161). That this leads to nihilism ought not to be surprising – nihilism appears in the form of relativism. For various conceptualisation of the crisis see Singer 1921, H. Heller 1991, Smend 1928, p. 1; Heimann 1980, pp. 5 ff.; Mannheim 1936, p. 76; Fried 1931, pp. 139 ff.; Wenzl 1935, pp. 373 ff.; Husserl 1970; Lukács 1951, p. 7; Koselleck 1988; Habermas 1973a, pp. 195 ff.; Türcke 1987, Steil 1993, pp. 197 ff.; Lichtblau 1997, pp. 392 ff.; Kodalle 2000 and Savage 2002. On parallels in art, see Wyss 1995.

142. See recent analyses of the German philosophy of the period around the First World War (Flasch 2000, Joas 2000). In the Third Reich, many considered this idealism too soft (Lehmann 1943, pp. 120 ff., 410). Nevertheless, National Socialism also had idealist features, and it accommodated idealist thinkers such as Heidegger (Tertullian 1990), Gadamer (Orozco 1995), Rickert (Fulda 1999) and Hermann Schwarz (Henning 1999). See Kapferer 2002, Tilitzky 2002.

143. Like Dilthey, Lersch 1932 strove for the 'non-objective immediacy of the experiential experience [*Erlebniserfahrung*]' (p. 5): 'If experience, in its intimacy and immediacy, becomes for vitalism the prototype of an adequate knowledge of reality, then this means that the knowability of phenomena is not sought in the only place where it is possible according to Kant, who brought about a self-limitation of discursive knowledge' (p. 6).

144. It is 'self-evident that only an extraordinarily small part of what occurs in the world is of a historical nature' (Windelband 1908, p. 265). K. Lenk 1986 (p. 80) still holds that Mannheim, differently from Marx, retains a basic logical framework (a 'thin logical layer'). This betrays vitalism's influence on Lenk, for the opposite is true. It is Marx who presupposes and practices a reliable scientificity, while Mannheim – who sought, in his early period (Mannheim 1964b), to suspend the 'subject-object division' in a Diltheyan manner – no longer has faith in such scientificity and intends to re-establish its preconditions (2.6.1).

145. Thus, neither Kant nor Marx drew such nihilating conclusions from their empirical (and properly 'scientific') investigations. They merely insisted that the results of further investigations should not contradict empirical findings. Kant did not allow his studies on the origin of the cosmos to tempt him into a devaluation of morality or religion. To Marx, the superstructure's dependency on the economic base did not mean that the superstructure as such is null and void; nor did it

when one operates on the basis of a homogenising thought, historicisation gives rise to a free-wheeling historicism that absorbs *all* solid knowledge, even the sense of certainty upon which the natural sciences base themselves. It is only when each individual act of cognition is preceded transcendentally by an ineluctable 'effective act' of the historical subject that *everything* formerly secure and certain appears radically uncertain.

This is the only reason for the impression that one is dealing with an 'intellectual crisis'. The situation described does, in fact, amount to a crisis of theory, but the only reason for it is that theory has *abandoned* its objects, and hence itself *qua* theory. Mentalisation is already contained in the preliminary choices, which are Fichtean (and do not have to be made explicit in the form of a 'theory of knowledge'). Social philosophy ultimately cannot explain *anything*, much less 'understand' it descriptively – not even itself.[146] It has nothing to say on the *real* crises that may underpin it, for it has lost touch with reality; it has lost its footing. This is what the crisis of philosophy goes back to (Chapter 3). It becomes especially relevant when the subject of knowledge perceives itself as being exposed to political dangers or threatens to dissolve into irreconcilable groups and worldviews. Mannheim has provided a revealing account of this state of mind.[147] Let us now proceed to consider individual cases.

2.5.3 *Rudolf Eucken as precursor*

Rudolf Eucken was a Nobel Prize-winning philosopher who picked up on the proliferating 'hunger for a worldview'[148] in its pure form. He defined the universally perceived 'crisis', its causes and its remedy as purely *mental* phenomena.[149] By the closed character of this representation, he hoped to achieve a 'New Foundation for a Worldview'; he conducted a 'struggle for a mental life purpose'.[150] Eucken's pioneering achievement displays the basic features of this undertaking in an unadulterated form. For in this early variant of

---

entail that both superstructure and base ought to be engaged with by means of the same method (for a more in-depth discussion, see section 4.2).

146. Hegel, Mead, Buber and Levinas have shown that one can develop and understand oneself only with the aid of others. This requires one to accept the other's otherness, without overhastily declaring him to be 'identical' to oneself. Many recent theories still have trouble accepting this (thus Rawls adopts the reductive image of humanity proper to neoclassical economics: 3.2; similarly, Habermas acknowledges only parlamentarians who stand 'above every opposition': 3.1).

147. Mannheim 1964b and Mannheim 1936, p. 31, believed the problem of the age was that everything had already been subjected to interpretation.

148. Windelband 1921, p. 278.

149. 'From the days of my youth [Eucken was born in 1846], I was imbued with the conviction that contemporary humanity is suffering a deep crisis' (Eucken quoted in Lehmann 1943, p. 139). Eucken sensed 'an intellectual crisis more massive than any ever seen in the past' (Eucken 1908, p. 43). He received the Nobel Prize in 1909 and influenced Scheler, Grisebach, Gehlen, Schwarz, Simmel and Husserl. Examining marginal personalities is a promising way to develop a thorough understanding of a paradigm: 'form . . . becomes evident precisely in the lean body of the inferior work [conceptual poetry] as its skeleton, so to speak' (Benjamin 1977, p. 58).

150. Eucken 1921.

the undertaking, what was later formulated much more subtly (without anything substantially different being intended) is still remarkably clear, and often bluntly stated. This makes Eucken representative of the quest for a *Weltanschauung* that was developing at the time, including in neo-Kantianism. He is not the only one to be affected by the *aporiai* of this quest, but they are especially visible in his work.

Eucken starts from the assumption that his age is characterised by a critical lack of orientation (point six in König's hypotheses). Since he also makes the assumption, characteristic of normative social philosophy, that the coherence of the community is of an 'intellectual and moral' kind, he expects this lack of orientation to entail grave consequences.[151] He ventures forth to confront this 'intellectual gloom of the present'.[152] His main opponent is 'naturalism'.[153] In a typically idealist manner, Eucken refuses to distinguish between being and thought; thus he takes 'naturalism' to consist both in a reductive *way of thinking* and in the phenomenon of 'technological and industrial culture' itself.[154] He argues that, in a dialectic of enlightenment, nature has subordinated man in the form of technology; something needs therefore to be opposed to technology (point eight).[155] Eucken's definition of nature reveals that socialism is at least *part of* what he means by 'naturalism' (König's first point):[156] in Eucken's view, nature cannot create order by itself; it can do so only by placing itself 'in the service of the intellectual world'.[157] It is ironic that this opposition is introduced under the heading 'Society',[158] for it shows how Eucken manages to elide society as an object of inquiry: following the Hobbesian model, Eucken perceives nature as consisting only of individuals.[159] The very next region within the hierarchy of reality is 'mind'. And yet Aristotle's theory of natural law already posited the self-organisation of society; such self-organisation was also posited and examined, in a different form, within the political economy of Adam Smith and his successors.

Consequently, Eucken argues, those who invoke such self-organisation (and in Germany, this was done not by the bourgeoisie, but by the socialists) are to blame for the

---

151. 'It is being felt increasingly clearly that today's cultural life lacks an all-permeating and cohesive [sic!] central conviction, a common ideal' (Eucken 1921, p. IV).

152. Eucken 1921, p. V.

153. Eucken 1921, p. 7.

154. Eucken 1921, p. 5.

155. 'Technological work ... is becoming the measure of our entire life.... Thus nature has defeated us on our terrain; meaning to subordinate it, we have been defeated by it' (Eucken 1921, pp. 5 ff.)

156. 'Man, it is said, belongs entirely to nature.... Behind these opinions, ... there lies a world-historical movement' (Eucken 1921, pp. 3 ff.).

157. Eucken 1921, p. 185.

158. Eucken 1921, pp. 183 ff.

159. 'For the natural process grants a distinct life ... only to the individual.... Inner subordination to a whole', that is, self-organisation, presents itself, from this perspective, as an 'incomprehensible wonder' (Eucken 1921, p. 11; see p. 185). It is worth pointing out that this parallels neoclassical theory's atomistic point of view.

'intellectual' crisis, because they elide mind. There can be no doubt that in part, this claim expresses the resentment of mandarins who feel they have been unjustly ignored. The socialists take the order prescribed by 'mind' and reverse it, standing it on its feet.[160] According to Eucken, socialism suffers mainly from its 'insufficient engagement with the problem of life';[161] for this reason, he argues, it cannot 'achieve a mental life purpose'.[162] It is as if Eucken felt socialism had wronged him; he shouts back at it: 'The wrongness of the matter itself is compounded by the inauthenticity of the attitude'.[163] Because Eucken has defined the crisis as an intellectual one, socialism provides no way out from it. Indeed, it is driven by the same forces as industrialisation.[164] Its 'rational and abstract way' of thinking derives from the 'Enlightenment';[165] thus, instead of representing a solution, socialism remains part of the problem (a variation on König's seventh point). But Eucken seems to also address social issues:[166]

> When we consider the problems associated with the distribution of economic goods and ... the injustices resulting from the contingencies of birth, ... the traditional division of society into higher and lower classes, etc., then we can see that many problems persist, and that much remains to be done.[167]

Who is this 'we'? Is it – as the quest for 'community',[168] for 'unity' and the 'whole' would seem to suggest[169] – the entire people, which addresses the issues invoked by means of democratic self-legislation? No – Eucken means to 'join Luther, Kant and Goethe, those heroes of intellectual liberation', in 'resolutely' *objecting* to 'political democracy'[170] and 'staunchly combating this Enlightenment tendency'.[171] Why? First, because his diagnosis is based not on the existence of *capitalism*, but on that of a pre-modern, estates-based feudal structure, as the terms 'birth' and 'traditional' reveal ('how aristocratic society's

160. 'Treatment of its [society's] condition as a conclusive and exclusive end in itself leads to grave deficiencies, to an inversion of life' (Eucken 1921, p. 183 – note the ambiguity of the word 'treatment' [*Behandlung*], which may refer to theory, but also to politics). When this becomes a 'property of the whole' (which is only the case when the 'independent estate of workers' has obtained 'growing influence within society': p. 288), there necessarily results 'an inner aversion' (p. 186).

161. Eucken 1921, p. 290.

162. Eucken 1921, p. 289.

163. Eucken 1921, p. 184.

164. See also 2.4.5.

165. Eucken 1921, p. 289.

166. The 'revolution of labour' is said to have 'engendered significant transformations of life' (Eucken 1921, p. 288 – note the causal order: does 'life' not appear as a 'superstructure'?) Yet Eucken does not discuss these transformations until the 'Descending Part' of his work, after the completion of his theory. He deduces its applications, but they no longer entail anything for the theory itself (see above).

167. Eucken 1921, p. 288.

168. Eucken 1921, p. 267.

169. Eucken 1921, pp. 12, 23, 40, and so on.

170. Eucken 1921, p. 319.

171. Eucken 1921, p. 316.

outward organisation can be').[172] He takes from the conservative apologists of the feudal period their positive assessment of 'organic' wholes, without realising that capitalism also involves collective actors (classes).

He adopts the atomistic description of the market society as found in neoclassical theory, except that it serves him as the basis for normatively rejecting society as a whole. He does not engage with the *theory* of society either, since he does not distinguish between that theory and its object.[173] Instead, he calls on his readers to 'turn on society',[174] notwithstanding the fact that he has hardly anything to say about it. A philosophical ethics substitutes for sociological analysis. This makes Eucken a social philosopher *par excellence*. Within Eucken's 'normative social philosophy', those active on the political stage must not come from within *society*:

> When man is as strongly dominated by natural instincts, when his intellectual impulses are as feeble and his moral attitude is as insufficient as we have found [in the 'discussion' of society, that is, of the theory of society], the mere aggregation of such elements [the mass] is wholly incapable of creating a new order, a new stage of reason.[175]

While social issues are real, they must not under any circumstances be addressed by those affected by them, even if the group of those affected is in the majority (otherwise the downfall of 'our entire culture' may result).[176] Eucken's critique of socialism culminates in the imperative that the workers (and, one might add, their 'instrumental reason') must not proceed to take political action *themselves*: 'For now, the social movement is at the forefront of life, but it urgently needs to be supplemented with the fortification of intellectual forces'.[177] 'Intellectual forces' appear in the form of those persons who are distinguished by their ability to 'rise above the average'[178] and perform 'intellectual labour',[179] which has, after all, become more and more central ('Labour is also increasingly oriented toward thought').[180] In other words, 'intellectual forces' manifest themselves in civil servants.[181] While Eucken speaks of a *gathering*, it is only one of

---

172. Eucken 1921, p. 184; see Sontheimer 1994, pp. 114 ff.

173. This is another instance of a super-idealist conflation of theory and reality. Eucken's elision of society has a twofold background. One the one hand, he rejects society as an object of inquiry ('here, [...] intellectual life' – which is to say Eucken himself – 'finds itself on unknown terrain': p. 188) and therefore does not theorise it. On the other hand, his rejection of atomist theories of society entails that he does not perceive society as an object of inquiry.

174. Eucken 1921, p. 187. Compare Eucken's positive view of community [*Gemeinschaft*] (p. 267). Tönnies 1979 was probably the work from which Eucken obtained his knowledge of Marx.

175. Eucken 1921, p. 185.

176. Eucken 1921, p. 320.

177. Ibid.

178. Eucken 1921, p. 36.

179. Eucken 1921, p. 16.

180. Eucken 1921, p. 9.

181. Steps in the direction of an 'intellectual' labour theory of value can also be found in Simmel 1878 and Habermas 1973; see also Habermas 1971b, p. 79. Talk of a 'knowledge economy' continues

minds.[182] As for everyone else, the 'mass', he recommends 'inner subordination'[183] to the 'right of the whole of the state'.[184] Eucken does not, however, elaborate substantively on his apotheosis of the civil service, his noocracy;[185] it merely serves as the basis for a 'normative' critique of socialism. If there must be socialism – in 1918, it seemed virtually inevitable – then it should be an 'idealist' socialism.[186]

The 'path of salvation' eventually proposed by Eucken[187] comes as a disappointment: he seeks to demonstrate the existence of a 'transcending intellectuality' by means of a 'noological treatment'[188] that reduces Hegel's painstakingly achieved insight into the identity of reason and reality to mere introspection (König's third point).[189] The solution develops '*beyond* the world of contradictions'[190] and within itself only, in a purely subjective manner. This leads to an ontological fissuring of reality ('two realities go their separate ways').[191] Thus, vitalism's *aporia* recurs in Eucken: because of its mentalisation, the whole that was aspired to ends up being only half of reality; it constitutes a 'unity', but the unity is only one of 'intellectual life' (1885, 1925), or of the 'realm of truth' (1918).[192] Instead of overcoming the crisis, Eucken merely leaves it behind and *remains* where he is: he slams the door shut behind him. His solution consists in an exalted apotheosis of the private sphere.[193] Everything that is contrary to the private sphere, such as Hegel's

---

to hark back to this. Here, it will suffice to point out the collapse of the New Economy. When intellectuals praise themselves as 'productive', this is transparent enough. If intellectuals really were economically 'productive', then surely the human sciences would not be facing such budgetary pressures these days.

182. Eucken 1913.

183. Eucken 1921, p. 11.

184. Eucken 1921, p. 318.

185. See Henning 1999, p. 89.

186. Eucken 1918; see Natorp 1920; on 'ethical socialism', see 2.1.3.

187. Eucken 1921, p. 214.

188. Eucken 1921, pp. 216, 218.

189. Eucken's noological intellectual life 'encompasses' the opposition of world and 'soul' (p. 216). He already developed this watered-down version of German mysticism in 1885/88.

190. Eucken 1921, p. 224.

191. Eucken 1921, p. 29. 'Life' is to 'achieve closure in itself, beyond all conflict' (p. 218). The 'world of being by oneself' is described as a 'special way of being' in 'one area only' (p. 224). This involves a 'separating out both of the world and of life', although this 'duality... should not be found frightening', because it is simply the way the world is 'truly constituted' (p. 215). Hegel, however, deeply despised such division (2.5.2; 4.2.2).

192. In a trenchant analysis, Lehmann shows that Eucken thereby consolidates an ontological dualism of nature and mind that he fails to overcome 'intellectually' (by means of a 'nature that has been renewed in the mind') (1943, p. 142).

193. The spatial metaphors allude to the homely parlour, where the world is still as it should be: 'Here, a self-supported interiority begins to display a content of its own, and to assert it against all things foreign and hostile' (Eucken 1921, p. 218) – against the world outside the front door. 'This creation... forms a distinct realm and presents this as the soul of the whole' (p. 218). We are to 'take up our position within it' and experience 'everything else from its vantage point' (p. 219), withdrawing into this realm 'as into a safe home' (p. 222). Eucken celebrates the 'world of being by oneself, doted with secure self-ownership, beyond the world of contradictions' (p. 224; on the critique of the 'bourgeois interior': Benjamin, *GS* IV, p. 88; Adorno 1979; *MECW* 3, p. 314; but see

'civil' or 'bourgeois society' [*bürgerliche Gesellschaft*],[194] is simply ignored. Eucken's ethics covers for his denial of reality.

Eucken blends together his borrowings from German idealism in a questionable way. His exposition follows that of Hegel's *Phenomenology*.[195] Eucken rejects Kant's distinction between the spheres of validity proper to the natural sciences and to ethics,[196] introducing a 'division of worlds',[197] instead. Within the protected 'realm', there occurs a 'rebirth and exaltation' of subjectivity,[198] giving rise to a 'new world'.[199] This amounts to the return of a genetic idealism of the Fichtean sort, although the idealism returns in a bisected form: the old, pre-existing and the new, created world are juxtaposed, without any mediation between them ('one must subordinate the other').[200] In order to smooth over the dualism inherent in this Fichtean ontologisation of Kantian spheres of validity, Eucken has recourse to Schelling's philosophy of nature: the 'rebirth' within intellectual life[201] needs itself to be recognised as an 'unfolding of the world process', and this recognition must occur in a dogmatic form, that of a 'basic conviction'.[202]

This eclecticism combines mutually contradictory elements: the highly complex results of methodologically elaborate speculations are treated as if they were mere propositions *about things*, which can be strung together without any problems arising. Eucken's efforts lead ultimately to an *aestheticist* conclusion: it is only the 'being-by-itself of life'[203] obtained by means of seclusion from the world that gives the world its 'soul'.[204]

---

also Marcuse 1964, p. 244). 'Almost everything in his book culminates in the description of this authentic turn from the exterior to the interior' (Lehmann 1943, p. 141). 'When man thus ventures into the realm of truth', he is 'by himself', and the malicious exterior can no longer harm him', Lehmann says mockingly of Eucken's 'illusory unconcern' (pp. 143 ff.). Tönnies's concept of 'community' [*Gemeinschaft*] (Tönnies 1979) already implied such 'homely cosiness'. The desire for it replaces the attempt to understand 'society'.

194. 'An inner subordination to a whole [Hegel's morality], recognition of a foreign right [Hegel's state], love and sacrifice [Hegel's family] become inconceivable wonders within this [naturalist] context' (Eucken 1921, p. 11). Society is absent. Where it appears, it displays the trappings of the state: 'Society pressures and constrains the individual in a tyrannical manner [!], but is there any way its natural inertia could be overcome without recourse to powerful means?' (p. 188).

195. Lehmann 1943, p. 140.

196. For 'where a single concatenation encompasses the entire course of time, . . . there is no individual action' (Eucken 1921, p. 219).

197. Eucken 1921, p. 220.

198. Eucken 1921, p. 218.

199. Ibid.

200. Eucken 1921, p. 29. 'Intellectual life does not engage with a world [the pre-existing world] from outside'; rather, it 'extends itself, from the inside outward, in the direction of a world' (p. 216; see pp. 37 ff.) – a second, imaginary world, that of 'intellectual being'.

201. Eucken 1921, p. 218.

202. Eucken 1921, p. 216. Lübbe 1963, p. 181 and Lehmann 1943, pp. 140 ff. also note the hybrid influence of Kant, Fichte, Hegel and Schelling. In discussing this, Lübbe identifies a 'principle of selection'; Lehmann also makes reference to a forgotten classic of philosophy, Krause.

203. Eucken 1921, p. 218.

204. Eucken 1921, p. 219.

In order that this might be achieved, Eucken goes so far as to posit a 'new world'.[205] This 'overworld', immediate access to which is certain,[206] is not meant to overcome the world, but to cast it 'in a different light'.[207] Here, *Weltanschauung* needs to be understood literally: what is at issue is nothing but a different way of *looking at* the world.[208] The ultimate goal of this philosophy is to provide the 'point of contact' between the two worlds,[209] that is, everyday life, with an 'intellectual life purpose', or meaning. Eucken is a German ideologue, and he has no qualms about it.[210]

The above analysis of Eucken amply confirms the points made by König. Eucken can be seen to be reacting to Marxism (1) insofar as he starts from the 'crisis' and repeatedly addresses socialism, which he considers to be a major part of the problem. His aestheticist countermodel's continued dependence on Marx (2) can be seen from his use of terms such as 'labour',[211] 'contradiction'[212] and 'society',[213] but especially from the practicist inflection he gives the underlying dualism by theorising the 'free act' [*freie Tat*]:[214] 'man's entire essence is called upon to act and make a decision'.[215] That Eucken is working with a flawed interpretation of Hegel (3) emerges not just from the structure of his work, but also from his 'noological method', which assumes that Hegel's 'absolute standpoint' can be achieved as easily as Hegel accused his precursors of believing; moreover, one encounters questionable interpretations of Fichte and Schelling. Eucken's existential reading of idealism (4) is evident in his position that while 'freedom' is worldly, the 'world' remains an ideal construct.[216] The principle of construction is idealist, but oddly bisected: it limits itself to 'mind', which it also totalises rather *forcefully* (this is reminiscent of the 'dictum

205. Eucken 1921, p. 220.

206. We can 'become capable of a direct relationship to the source of all life' (Eucken 1921, p. 219; see p. 241). This 'direct turn toward absolute life' (p. 220) – a 'non-sensory immediacy' (p. 320) – is credited with establishing access to the new world.

207. Eucken 1921, p. 224.

208. On the aestheticist context of neo-Kantianism and the philosophy of *Weltanschauung*, see Hermand 1977, Vol. IV; Lichtblau 1997, pp. 178–279; and Krijnen 1998.

209. Eucken 1921, p. 220.

210. In 1914, Eucken became a warmonger, 'elevating the steel helmet and the uniform . . . to the rank of the intellect' (Lübbe 1963, p. 185). Yet despite being a National Socialist, Lehmann 1943 (pp. 137 ff.) remains unimpressed by Eucken's advocacy of war and the 'German way' (Eucken 1921, pp. 319, 331 ff.; Eucken 1914, pp. 22 ff.; on 'German freedom': Eucken 1919).

211. Eucken 1921, pp. 22, 32, 219, 288.

212. Eucken 1921, pp. 18, 214.

213. Eucken 1921, pp. 183 ff.

214. Eucken 1921, p. 48.

215. Eucken 1921, p. 53. The '*Tatkreis*' was also based in Jena (see Fritzsche 1976; on the activism of the *Tatkreis*, see Linse 1983).

216. Eucken 1921, pp. 48, 116, 234. Lübbe detects in this an 'existentialisation of philosophical thinking' (Lübbe 1963, p. 184). The way of engaging philosophical problems has been tailored to fit the purposes of concrete 'self-help'. But this affects philosophical content, as philosophy now concerns itself with the individual's life purpose. Like Heidegger, Eucken also speaks of two 'ways of living' (Eucken 1921, p. 29; 2.5.5).

of reason': 'There must not be any not-I').[217] Eucken acknowledges Dilthey's separation of the realm of the natural sciences from that of the humanities. In doing so, he fallaciously infers the mode of being from the genesis in the way described above (5): he treats the realms of the natural sciences and the humanities as separate 'worlds'. One also finds in his work a problematisation of theory (6), as he claims that the rational thought of the 'Enlightenment' is especially to blame for the crisis.[218]

The 'crisis of philosophy' is particularly evident in the fact that Eucken does not notice how the crisis is provoked by his very rejection of theory. Insofar as he elides society and represses and subordinates nature, Eucken is also subject to the loss of the object (7), which his 'noology' merely expresses in the form of a principle.[219] The loss of the object and the rejection of scientificity depend upon and mutually reinforce one another. Finally, as a result of his theory, Eucken advocates a politics of identity (8): he invokes the 'German way',[220] which *opposes* the 'right of the whole of the state'[221] to 'democracy'.[222] The bellicist overtones are obvious.[223] Eucken's book is an early and typical example of 'social philosophy'. The problems of the age are perceived through a philosophical 'filter' that systematically excludes non-mental and non-normative factors. In this way, social issues, their causes *and* remedies are falsely defined as 'intellectual'. Since Hegel and Fichte, the discursive 'field' proper to this style of German philosophy has *required* that only what is 'intellectual' or 'mental' be considered.

Since Dilthey, Simmel and Freyer, the new 'object' that theory has 'constituted' for itself has been called 'objective mind'. In Eucken, the 'new world' (a 'superior realm and a . . . safe home')[224] is still freshly hatched, and so 'objective mind' still strikes one as an oxymoron; if it no longer does so today, then it is only because we have gotten used to the sound of it.[225] Instead of taking such theories at face value and participating, even

217. Fichte 1868, p. 26; see p. 65. Unlike Fichte and Schelling, who attributed an intellectual character to nature as well, Eucken aims at a break with nature (Eucken 1921, p. 13; see pp. 29, 107 ff., 170 ff.). This may be due to a rivalry between Eucken and Haeckel.

218. Eucken 1921, pp. 289, 319. 'The character of life urgently requires a liberation from intellectualism' (p. 127; see Eucken 1908, p. 70). Eucken genuinely achieves this goal – unlike Hegel, he no longer makes any effort to integrate other scientific disciplines.

219. There is a nihilist quality to the way Eucken, like Fichte recognises nothing outside his priggish intellectual world except 'yawning emptiness' (Eucken 1921a, p. 66; on 'inner emptiness', see Eucken 1908, p. 43). Social processes are mentalised: 'All this [the 'German way'] is now thrust aside in favour of abstract templates' (Eucken 1921a, p. 319).

220. Eucken 1921, pp. 319, 331.

221. Eucken 1921, p. 318.

222. See Henning 2001.

223. In the 'struggle for world power [!] in intellectual life' (Eucken 1921, pp. 169 ff.), it is a matter of 'becoming common' (p. 222). This tendency openly played itself out during the First World War, and not just in Eucken (see Lübbe 1963, pp. 176 ff., 233 ff.).

224. Eucken 1921, p. 222.

225. Freyer 1998 held that 'the innermost meaningful content of the capitalist form of life is determined by a definite morality, metaphysics, and doctrine of life' (p. 48). It should be noted that on this view, the doctrine of the good life is not secondary but primary with regard to metaphysics. Objective mind is described as 'a most profound a priori [!], from which the elements of

today, in the mentalisation they effect (after all, Simmel and Heidegger are often read as if they were our contemporaries), this insight should make us question the adequacy of this style of philosophy *as a whole* – which is what Marx already did in the 1840s. Every child knows the difference between a hundred imagined coins and a hundred actual coins.[226] But the lofty German mind often takes itself to be above such childish distinctions.[227]

Following Lask,[228] one can regard Marxism as a case of 'matter' (a rapidly changing reality) penetrating the 'form' of thought, or *philosophia perennis*. It was only when they had a political party and theorists of their own that workers became 'audible' to intellectual ears.[229] It was only when he appeared in this guise, as spirit of their spirit, that German thinkers were able to respond to Marx. This should be seen as an inverted reception, especially in the case of Eucken. The shifts that Marxism had brought about on the *philosophical* scene were recognised as such and seized upon by Eucken; he treated them as negative templates and provided them with a new meaning. Thus he was negatively dependent on the existence of a movement that harked back to Marx, even though he did not engage with Marx directly.

Marx's problematisation of such mentalised engagement with social issues is never addressed, even though 'social philosophy' is concerned precisely with social issues.[230] Instead, Marx is situated within a larger intellectual panorama, and hence 'dealt with' only implicitly.[231] This inverted reception and the standpoints it gives rise to recur in later authors. The notion of a nature vanquished by man taking revenge on him in the

---

this *Weltanschauung* are derived and on which they are based' (p. 49). This mentalisation will be referred to as 'supernormativism' below.

226. Kant 1998, p. 567/A 599; *MECW* 5, pp. 23 ff.; *MECW* 43, p. 68; see also the praise of childlike thought in Nietzsche and in the New Testament.

227. See 2.3.2. Chapter Three provides exemplary critiques of recent versions of such thought and elaborates on the methodological issue of how adequate this style of philosophy is as a 'self-reflection of philosophy'. When imagined money is declared real or real money declared to exist only in the mind, the chances are that something is awry with the German mind. Two criteria by which to decide this question are international scholarship and common sense (see 4.1).

228. Lask 1993, pp. 60 ff.

229. Marxism pointed this out, and was blamed for its ill tidings (see 2.4.5). After all, Marxist thought was also a form of Enlightenment thought (2.1.2). But it was a representation of capitalism only to the extent that it respected no taboos in analysing and thematising capitalism, unlike bourgeois theories.

230. *MECW* 5, pp. 148 ff. Marx criticised mentalisation in the following words: 'Reality is not expressed as itself but as another reality' (*MECW* 3, p. 8). Along with Engels, Marx meant to 'ridicule and discredit the philosophic struggle with the shadows of reality, which appeals to the dreamy and muddled German nation' (*MECW* 5, pp. 23 ff.; see *MECW* 4, pp. 57 ff.). They succeeded in this endeavour, even if the *German Ideology* remained casuistic. It has not, however, become obsolete along with the thought of Bauer, Stirner, and such like. For in light of the 'dependence on Hegel' (*MECW* 5, pp. 28, 100), so evident in Eucken, the Marxian critique remains topical (see E. Wood 1986), even if Marx himself considered it no more than a preliminary stage (see 2.5.7).

231. Eucken 1921, pp. 181, 215.

form of technology[232] became a commonplace of cultural criticism; it recurs in Rathenau, Simmel and Klages, and later in Heidegger and Adorno. The notion can already be found in Marx,[233] except that he attributes a definite and therefore limited function to technology (namely that of continuously working to cheapen and expand the factors of production: 2.1.6, 2.3.3). This, however, was ignored by cultural criticism – perhaps because Marx expressed his position not in philosophical verse, but in economic prose (2.4.5).[234]

Social and individual 'pathologies' are also a major theme in the work of the social philosophers. They follow Marx in believing that something needs to be done about such pathologies, but the causes they identify are largely ideal ('intellectualism';[235] or 'instrumental reason'). Finally, they express contempt for the political forms of Western Europe, which they causally relate to crisis phenomena. Eucken's formulations anticipate even the nuances of Heidegger's rants about the 'they'.[236] A critique of formal democracy can also already be found in Marx. But again, his arguments were not taken notice of: where Marx started from the notion that democracy was principally desirable and had for a time been realised in France, in order to then show up its *limits*, cultural criticism *flatly* rejected democracy, in a case of 'abstract negation' (3.2.3).

This interim conclusion on Eucken is sobering. Where the German philosophy of the period picked up on Marxian *topoi* at all, it transformed them into the language of philosophy, thereby rendering them critically toothless. What remained was a historiography of *mental* processes, whose formulation had an altogether different thrust than that of Marx: now, it was no longer a matter of reversing anything except the way that individuals think. Such interpretations have persisted within philosophy for a century, so that the difference between them and Marx has become virtually imperceptible.[237] This interpretation has become a *consensus omnium* spanning several generations of philosophers. And where if not in Marx would one have expected the interpretation to be rebuffed? We have already seen that Marxism itself had degenerated into a *Weltanschauung* in the later Marxists. It is time to examine whether this inverse reception of Marx, the philosophising distortion of his thought, can also be shown to characterise the work of more important authors.

---

232. Eucken 1921, pp. 5 ff.

233. *MECW* 35, pp. 507 ff.

234. 'That the magnificent achievements of physics and chemistry have benefited only capital is something about which thinking people are no longer in doubt' (Klages 1929, p. 33). This rare gesture toward a critique of capitalism is as ornamental in Klages as it would later be in Adorno (on their affinity, see Honneth 1983; see 2.6.1, 2.6.3).

235. Eucken 1921, pp. 127, 319.

236. Heidegger 1962, pp. 163 ff.

237. Eldred 2000.

2.5.4 *Georg Lukács as mediator*

'Most men no longer live, but merely exist'.[238] This pithy formulation identifies the 'problem of life' (Eucken) that philosophy took itself to be confronting at the turn of the century. There did, in fact, occur an existentialisation of inquiries: philosophers were concerned, paradoxically enough, with finding *general* answers to the *individual* 'meaning of life'.[239] This inquiry, which strikes one as rather odd today, indicates the 'epoch's need for salvation'.[240] As could be seen in Eucken, Marxism was hardly equipped to come to philosophy's aid in answering this question.[241] On the contrary, it represents the 'mass' whose noisy claims seemed to be putting the status of scholars at risk.[242] It is all the more remarkable that someone who came from a good family and therefore had no particular inclination toward the 'mass', and who concisely formulated this 'problem of life', still managed to become a Marxist. This was the case of Georg Lukács, who was profoundly influenced by Dilthey, Simmel and Weber.[243]

It was only with a certain reluctance that his version of Marxism, virtually foundational for 'Western Marxism', was examined with an eye to these *questionable* origins;[244] perhaps because the *other* authors writing within this tradition were themselves too heavily indebted to bourgeois philosophy to be able to perceive such indebtedness as

---

238. Klages 1929, p. 29.

239. This was one effect of the belated discovery of Kierkegaard. Heinemann 1929 identifies 'existence' as a synthesis of the previous paradigms 'mind' and 'life' (paradigms associated, respectively, with the eighteenth and nineteenth centuries). The difference between 'life' and 'existence' is, however, negligible – the philosophy of existence can also be considered part of vitalism. Dilthey already meant to distinguish himself maximally from the 'masses' by means of a *Weltanschauung* (see Schulenburg 1923). On the role of Kierkegaard, see Lukács 1974b, p. 13; Lukács 1971b, p. xiii; Rentsch 1990, pp. 139 ff.

240. Rentsch 1990, p. 97; see Bry 1979, Lukács 1981, p. 462; Cancik 1982, Linse 1983, Bolz 1989. As we now know, thanks to Freud and 1968, the individual meaning of life resides within the individual life. Generally speaking, there is hardly anything meaningful to be said about 'mineness' [*Jemeinigkeit*]. Of course, some help may be necessary in the formation of an autonomous personality, but not so much from philosophy than from disciplines that are equipped to consider individual cases (as far as theory is concerned, psychology and pedagogy are examples of such disciplines). When the search for one's individual meaning of life is transferred to the field of philosophy, it leads to distortions – authors become entertainers in search of a trademark. Perhaps this was why Aristotle held that only mature adults should devote themselves to philosophy. As for the formal question of what makes human life meaningful in general, that is another matter. Those posing this question no longer have themselves in mind, at least not primarily. Rickert accused vitalism of blurring the distinction between theory and biography: 'Within the vital swamp of fashionable philosophies, one all too often encounters only worm's-eye views' (Rickert 1921 p. 33). The philosopher 'must stand above that which he seeks to penetrate theoretically, and this includes himself' (Rickert 1934, p. 8).

241. See Rolfes 1971, Ehlen 1975 and the *Jugendweihe* book (Buschendorf 1954).

242. The Parnassus is empty: L. Klages 1929, p. 29; see Tillich, *GW* II, p. 40; Gasset 1930, De Man 1952, Canetti 1960.

243. On Lukács, see the biographical preface to Lukács 1971c from 1963, Rosshoff 1975, A. Heller 1977, Keller 1984, Beiersdörfer 1985, Dannemann 1987, Jung 1988 and Luckhardt 1994.

244. Except by doctrinaire communists, whose critique exhausts itself in proving that Lukács strayed from the party line (Rudas 1924, Steigerwald 1980, Lukács 2000).

a deficit.[245] For Lukács's early writings are characterised by the fact that they are on an equal footing with the culture of the time. Compare the bigoted manner in which Eucken speaks of two 'ways of life':

> to one side, the average of the human species and situation as measure; to the other, intellectuality [*das Geistige*], raised above that level and opposed to man as measure and norm. To one side, the ubiquitous and constringent limitations of natural particularity; to the other, a living and a creating that draw on infinity[246]

with Lukács's version, which is on a par with the art of the period:

> Life is an anarchy of light and dark: nothing is ever completely fulfilled in life... [N]othing ever flowers into real life. To live is to live something through to the end: but *life* means that nothing is ever fully and completely lived through to the end.... One has to fall back into numbness. One has to deny life in order to live[247]

Lukács held that high art offers the possibility of solving this problem of life: 'For a character in a tragedy, to be there at all – to exist – is to be perfect'.[248] This made it all the more unlikely that he, of all people, would go on to affiliate himself with Marxism, which is not necessarily known for being keen on culture.[249] But appearances are deceptive. It is precisely because of his background that Lukács was the 'consistent executor'[250] of vitalism and the philosophy of existence.[251] Siding with Marxism was a radical decision for Lukács, and it is best understood in terms of the aesthetic philosophy of existence – after all, 'decision' is virtually existentialism's primordial term.[252]

---

245. Horkheimer, Adorno and Marcuse also came from well-to-do families. From 'Lukács to Althusser, Korsch to Colletti', there is an 'overwhelming predominance of professional philosophers' (Anderson 1976, p. 49). There was a 'progressive relinquishment of economic and political structures as the central concerns of theory' (ibid.). 'Western Marxism as a whole thus paradoxically inverted the trajectory of Marx's own development itself. Where the founder of historical materialism moved progressively from philosophy to politics and then economics, as the central terrain of his thought, the successors... increasingly turned... to philosophy' (p. 52; see Lichtheim 1971). At bottom, the situation is even worse. In most cases, there was no economic theory for them to abandon, and their philosophy fell back behind the early Marx, who had been a critic of Hegel, whereas they were Hegelians. This constitutes a 'return to objective idealism' (Wellmer, in: Honneth 1977, p. 478).

246. Eucken 1921, p. 29; see p. 215.

247. Lukács 1974b, pp. 152 ff.

248. Lukács 1974b, p. 156.

249. Unless one interprets it as having been, from the outset, an aesthetic experiment (see Groys 1988). It is true that communism attracted numerous artists and that there were many attempts to build a proletarian counterculture, since affiliating oneself with Marxism usually entailed being excluded from bourgeois culture (Negt 1972; Gorsen 1981, pp. 83 ff.). But the underlying intention was not an aesthetic one (Bohrer 1978).

250. Luckhardt 1994, p. 259.

251. Luckhardt 1994 emphasises the role of Simmel. Jung 2001 holds that the transition to Marxism was a 'consistent decision' (p. 18), pointing out that Lukács himself was of the same opinion (pp. 23 ff.; for a general discussion of this issue, see Lukács 1981).

252. Compare Eucken 1921, pp. 53, 215; Krockow 1958. Sartre presented a similar argument (Sartre 1964).

The version of Marxism that Lukács developed was heavy on culture and aesthetics; it displays a certain continuity with his upper-class and anti-bourgeois early period. Despite the rupture represented by Lukács's decision to become a Marxist, his extensive oeuvre is of one piece: for example, his later aesthetic theory[253] extends the theory he developed between 1914 and 1918.[254] But what kind of thought was it on the basis and by means of which Lukács affiliated himself with Marxism, and to which Marxism was transposed by him? Lukács began, in 1908, with a 'philosophy of history';[255] it was already oriented toward the history of aesthetic genres. Shortly before his conversion, he described his time as an 'age of absolute sinfulness',[256] from which he hoped to arrive at a 'new world',[257] a new 'totality' – which, however, was to be situated, as in Eucken, in a 'pure soul-reality'.[258] Thus the young Lukács accepts the premises of '*Geisteswissenschaft*' – of which the *Theory of the Novel* is a typical example, as Lukács himself would later note. To express this in terms of König's hypothesis:

Like others, Lukács begins with Hegel (point three),[259] whom he reads in existentialist terms (point four).[260] In doing so, he also diagnoses an intellectual crisis ('transcendental homelessness')[261] and loses touch with reality (point six).[262] The last point, the transition to ethics and/or politics, is only suggested (by the reference to a 'new world'). The point about Lukács is that, behaving in the spirit of Wittgenstein, he did not talk much about this transition, although he would soon implement it.[263]

Thus in Lukács, life and work are of one piece, just like the various parts of his work. This begs the question of whether Lukács's new, Marxist standpoint was not itself merely

---

253. Lukács 1963.
254. See Michel 1972, Jung 1989, pp. 30 ff.; Pasternack 1990.
255. Lukács 1981a.
256. Lukács 1971c, p. 157, following Fichte.
257. Lukács 1971c; see pp. 15; Lukács 1974b, p. 45; see also Eucken.
258. Lukács 1971c, p. 157. Since Jay 1984 sympathises with the young Lukács, he overlooks the role that Dilthey played in the development of Lukacs' concept of 'totality' (pp. 77 ff.; see p. 155): Dilthey spoke of the 'totality of the forces of the human disposition' [*Totalität der Gemütskräfte*], which 'can never quite be penetrated by the intelligence' (Dilthey 2002, p. 401; see Jung 1988). Jay goes back as far as Parmenides (p. 25) and Spinoza (p. 28). In the end, Habermas takes the stage to rescue the totality (p. 462) – that of Dilthey, not that of Marx (Habermas 1976, pp. 178 ff.).
259. See Lukács 1971c, pp. 15 ff.; Lukács 1971b, pp. ix ff.
260. Lukács 1971c, p. 18 speaks of a '"Kierkegaardisation" of the Hegelian dialectic of history'.
261. Lukács 1971c, p. 41; see p. 12; point seven.
262. '[N]othing, even at the level of the most abstract intellection, helped to mediate between my subjective attitude and objective reality' (Lukács 1971c, p. 12). To his statement that there no longer exists any 'spontaneous totality of being' (p. 38; see p. 32), he later added a quotation from Gottfried Benn: '... there was no reality [!], only, at most, its distorted image' (p. 18, after Benn's 1933 'Confession of an Expressionist'; see 2.6.1).
263. Aside from the occasional anti-Kantian outburst ('Ethics! The order that comes from the outside! The law imposed upon us, the law we cannot transcend!': 1974b, p. 148; 'The "should be" kills life': 1971c, p. 48), Lukács's remarks on ethics date from the period subsequent to his decision to become a socialist (see Tillich 1933). In 1917, he speaks of ethics only in passing and in abstract epistemological terms. As late as 1918, Bolshevism appeared to him to be 'a moral problem' (Lukács 1975, pp. 27 ff.).

another variant of '*Geisteswissenschaft*'.[264] Are there continuities between Lukács' early vitalism and his later Marxist works? To pose the question thusly is almost to have answered to it. After all, the mature Lukács extended his critique of his own early works to include even *History and Class Consciousness* (an 'out-Hegeling of Hegel').[265] What precisely were the features of Lukács's early work? As we saw above, the early Lukács was one of those thinkers who begin from the notion of a 'crisis' that is primarily intellectual. Within this crisis, there arises the problem of life, namely, the question 'how can life become essential?'.[266] Lukács is far from being concerned only with himself; he is also concerned with the individual in the abstract (this is the paradox inherent to the problem of life). The 'positive meaning' upon which 'life' is 'based' is provided by 'the totality'.[267] By this, Lukács means the closed character of an individual's world picture. The affinity with Dilthey is not to be overlooked.[268] The problem from which Lukács begins is, at first, an individual and intellectual one – it is eminently 'bourgeois'. Lukács uses Simmel (who modernised Mandeville on this point) to establish a relationship betweeen sociation and individualisation. However, in Lukács, the relationship is reversed: for Simmel,[269] as for Marx before him,[270] sociation is one of the prerequisites for individualisation, whereas Lukács regards consummate individualisation as the prerequisite for a higher form of sociation. Thus, he writes of the Romantics (and this can be read autobiographically, like so many passages in Lukács): 'They hoped that the intense unfolding of the personality would in the end bring human beings really close to one another'.[271]

---

264. A period of idiosyncratic thinking (from his time as people's commissar and his early political essays to his newly discovered 1925 self-defense and the Blum Theses; see Kammler 1974) is usually distinguished from the time when Lukács adopted the prescribed dialectical materialism. But Lukács the independent thinker resurfaced repeatedly; the distinction is artificial. Colletti holds that Lukács discovered in 'Diamat' a Hegelianism much like the one he started from (Colletti 1976, p. 190; see H. Gente in Stalin and Narr 1972, pp. 80 ff.).

265. Lukács 1971b, p. xxiii. 44 years later, Lukács described this strained application of Hegelían ideas as 'an edifice boldly erected above every possible reality' that 'attempts objectively to surpass the Master himself' (ibid.). On Lukács' self-criticism, see also Lukács 1978–80, p. 645. Lukács' 1981 settling of accounts was already quite self-critical, but only implicitly; in fact, many of Lukács' texts display a biographical dimension (Jung 2000, pp. 23 ff.; see Grunenberg 1976). This is another sense in which Lukács remained an existentialist.

266. Lukács 1971c, p. 35.

267. Lukács 1971c, p. 34.

268. See Jung 1988. Lukács's 'totality' is the coherence of a work: 'For totality . . . implies that something closed within itself can be completed' (Lukács 1971c, p. 34). The 'dialectical conception of totality' (Lukács 1971, p. 10) – how it might be achieved is something Lukács was as unable to explain as Adorno – is tailored to the basic idea of the idealist system: the greatest 'antinomy of bourgeois thought' consists in the fact that it fails to constitute itself as a system (Lukács 1971, p. 116; on Lukács's affirmative attitude to systematic thinking, see also Lukács 1974b, p. 16).

269. Simmel 1908.

270. *MECW* 4, pp. 119 ff.; *MECW* 5, p. 75; *MECW* 28, p. 17.

271. Lukács 1974b, p. 49.

Yet this totality, the closed character of the individual's horizon of life, is precisely what has been lost – presumably because of *intellectual* processes, as Lukács, an idealist on this point also, suggests.[272] But there is one force that could turn things around: *art* is capable of providing the individual life with meaning. For, at least according to Dilthey's hermeneutics, the totality is 'the formative prime reality of every individual phenomenon'.[273] Following the putative disintegration of 'unity',[274] nothing but art remains capable of revealing totalities – this aestheticist hypothesis on the compensatory function of art would later be adopted by the theorists of the Frankfurt School.[275] For art contains wholeness, or to put this more precisely: different works of art contain different individual wholenesses. Lukács would later go on to say the following about the theoretical procedure he, Mannheim and others had developed: 'It became the fashion to form general synthetic concepts on the basis of only a few characteristics – in most cases only intuitively grasped – of a school, a period, etc., then to proceed by deduction from these generalisations to the analysis of individual phenomena'.[276]

Karl Mannheim called this 'stylistic analysis'. It was no coincidence the procedure was borrowed from art history.[277] Yet it also contains within it the problem the modern 'style of stylelessness' took itself to be faced with: that of relativism.[278] For 'today', what art cannot do is precisely create a totality – and it is only here that reality begins to be considered, starting from the subject and mediated by art –, because 'the world' no longer allows for this: 'Totality of being[279] is possible only where everything is already homogeneous before it has been contained by forms; where forms are not a constraint'.[280]

Thus a 'new world', whatever it may look like, is the ultimate goal. The only way to achieve it is via a 'new culture', whose 'only possible basis' is 'art'.[281] Here, Lukács gets caught in a circle, one that will later recur in a different form: the people who might create the requisite art and culture are the ones who are faced with the problem of life,

---

272. Lukács 1971c, pp. 30 ff.

273. Lukács 1971c, p. 34. The 'totality of the transcendent world-structure is the pre-determined sense-giving, all-embracing *a priori* of each individual destiny' (p. 60). This dogmatic priority of a transcendentally active mega-subject is something one re-encounters in Heidegger (2.5.5; see the early example of Freyer's 'a priori' of the intellect). This tradition is still alive, even if contemporary theorists speak euphemistically of the 'normative framework' (see 3.1.3).

274. Lukács 1971c, p. 38.

275. On critical theory's 'bourgeois' character, see Willms 1969, pp. 82 ff.; Riedel 1994.

276. Lukács 1971c, p. 13.

277. Barboza 2002 explores the importance of art history for Mannheim. Lichtblau 1997, pp. 178 ff. and Luckhardt 1994 describe the general significance of the aesthetic dimension within the cultural sociology of the period. Michel 1972 argues that Lukács's entire work is framed by aesthetics.

278. Simmel 1978, pp. 429 ff.

279. Here, this means within the artwork, and therefore within the horizon of individual existence, which is shaped by art. 'Being' in the sense of what actually exists is addressed by the 'all'. It is worth noting, incidentally, the obvious influence of Emil Lask (see Rosshoff 1975).

280. Lukács 1971c, p. 34.

281. Lukács 1974b, p. 49.

namely that the 'unfolding of the personality'[282] presupposes the very art they are supposed to create in the first place. For the 'totality' (that is, the world picture of people capable of creating a 'new world') to be constituted, a 'new art' (one capable of revealing a totality) would first need to be created. But the 'new world' is precisely what is needed for the creation of a new art and a new culture.

There is no way of getting out of this vicious circle except by a miracle that appears from outside, a *deus ex machina*. Much as in the case of the class-unsconscious proletariat, the miracle takes the form of a self-proclaimed 'vanguard', which disposes – for whatever reason – of the means and the knowledge to break out of the circle. This is an expression of the sense of foreignness that society inspires in intellectuals when they can no longer find their place within it – and in formulating arguments of this sort, they are of course tailor-making the role of the vanguard for themselves.[283] To be sure, Lukács's pessimistic assessment distinguishes him from right-conservative thinkers who imply that art continues to be the vehicle of a totality *after all* (such as Stefan George), or who wish to bring about such homogeneity by force (such as Carl Schmitt).[284] Yet, at the same time, we can see in this to what extent Lukács's approach accorded with that of *Geisteswissenschaft*: a prescriptive aesthetics inserts itself into and shapes the analysis ('forms' *must not* be a 'constraint'); assessment of when forms have become constraints and when 'everything' has become 'homogeneous' are left to the aesthetic judgement of taste. At the end of Lukács's early work, we finds a 'normative social philosophy'. But this is hardly an achievement that contemporary philosophy should aspire to. The method of stylistic analysis referred to above was later correctly judged by Lukács to rely on 'arbitrary intellectual constructs'.[285] Much as in Bernstein and Schelsky, the role of ethics is essentially that of a placeholder (see 2.1.2, 2.4.6, 2.4.3).

Lukács would not have been Lukács had he not noticed this. He already expressed his dissatisfaction with his own early works in his essay about the essay. He admitted that

---

282. Ibid.

283. 'It was becoming more and more difficult and problematic for the great men of the age simply to exist, to belong to life, to occupy a place, to take up a stand' (Lukács 1974b, p. 45). The brothers Jünger, the *Georgekreis* and other self-proclaimed 'anti-bourgeois' personalities believed themselves capable of rising above the unsophisticated masses (Bourdieu 1991, pp. 9 ff.; Bering 1978; Bergsdorf 1982; Lepenies 1992).

284. See Gangl/Raulet 1994. This rather liberal judgement of taste may have contributed to Lukács's popularity in the West.

285. Lukács 1971c, p. 17. He would later call it an 'aggressive and paradoxical idealism' (1971b, pp. x, xiv). It is worth recalling that Nietzsche shared the early Lukács's motive – the desire to renew the (individual) meaning of life by means of a renewal of art – but drew the opposite political consequences from it: he did not advocate a new 'community', but a new slavery: 'In order that there may be a broad, deep, and fruitful soil for the development of art, the enormous majority must, in the service of a minority, be slavishly subjected to life's struggle, to a *greater* degree than their own wants necessitate. At their expense, through the surplus of their labour [!], that privileged class is to be relieved from the struggle for existence'. For Nietzsche, there can be no question 'that slavery belongs to the essence of a culture' (Nietzsche 1930, pp. 211 ff.). Hayek and Friedman still considered the existence of high culture an argument in favour of inequality (Friedman 1962, p. 168; 3.2.1).

the verdicts pronounced by the essayist are pronounced, as it were, on credit; they lack a genuine theoretical justification and amount to 'thoughts occasioned by...':[286]

> He is delivered from the relative, the inessential, by the force of judgement of the idea he has glimpsed [by reference to the criteria of judgement] but who gives him the right to judge?[287]
>
> [The essayist is] 'a John the Baptist who goes out to preach in the wilderness about another who is still to come... And if that other does not come – is not the essayist then without justification? And if the other does come, is he not made superfluous thereby?'[288]

The conception of this early philosophy was deeply bourgeois: a normative social philosophy presents us with the prospect of a 'new world'.[289] This 'new world' is necessary so that *art* may once more achieve a closed world picture. And art is necessary so that the *individual* may essentialise himself (an 'ethic of genius').[290] Lukács' attitude during the Hungarian Revolution of 1919 confirms this hierarchy: politics is 'merely a means; culture is the goal'.[291] Does this gospel of art not enormously exaggerate the significance and the effective power of art? By comparison to Marx, the character of art is stood on its head. The mature Lukács renounced the gospel, even if he only did so implicitly – via a critique of Schelling.[292]

How does this mentalised basic orientation manifest itself in Lukács's Marxist writings? The Diltheyan orientation toward a 'mental' or 'intellectual' totality remains central, the difference being that Lukács now believes himself to have *discovered* such a totality. Within the early Marxist *oeuvre*, the 'system' that Lukács claims to dispose of is still hidden behind the vacuous formula 'dialectical conception of totality'.[293] The mature Lukács then referred affirmatively to dialectical materialism (the spirit of Hegel received from the hands of Engels, Lenin and Stalin),[294] even though he sought to modify it one more time within his own systems, his later aesthetics and his ontology.[295] The speculative identity of idealism and materialism is palpable: the system that Lukács embraces is

286. Lukács 1971c, pp. 15, 191.
287. Lukács 1974b, p. 16.
288. Ibid.
289. Lukács 1971c, pp. 141 ff.; see 1974b, p. 45.
290. Lukács 1974b, p. 46. An ethics of 'essentialisation' (on Lukács, see Keller 1984) resurfaces, with *völkisch* overtones, in Heidegger (Bourdieu 1991, pp. 46 ff.), before becoming widespread under National Socialism (see Henning 1999, VI.4).
291. Lukács 1975, Vol. I, p. 94; see pp. 132 ff. (*'Alte und neue Kultur'* ['Old and New Culture'], written in 1919). In the midst of events, co-revolutionaries were told they 'ought first to read *The Brothers Karamazov*' (Jung 1989, p. 82; see p. 84). The later Lukács also made a case for the bourgeois art and aesthetics of the nineteenth century.
292. Lukács 1981, pp. 142 ff.
293. Lukács 1971, p. 10.
294. On Diamat's affinity with the natural philosophy of Hegel, see Colletti 1976, pp. 7–67.
295. Lukács 1963 and 1978–80.

materialist *in name*, but the method it employs is as aprioristic and deductive as those of idealist systems.

This systematic philosophy has next to nothing in common with 'Marx's method',[296] which, like every scientific procedure, begins by devoting itself to the underlying material and/or our apperceptions of that material, attributing to it only those forms which it can be demonstrated to actually possess.[297] Even Lukács's neo-Kantian teacher Emil Lask knew more about the necessity of referring back to empirical facts. Lukács continued to cleave to idealist systematic thought even after he became a Marxist. His most famous work criticises the bourgeoisie by pointing out that its *philosophy* is no longer capable of a conception of the totality [*Weltanschauung*].[298] According to Lukács, this is not due to correctable errors of content; in what amounts to a reversal of the genetic fallacy, he extends the accusation to the *subject* of science.[299] Conclusions about being are drawn from theory, in a way that is possible only on the basis of a philosophy of identity, even if Lukács no longer considers being to be homogeneous; it is now divided into two hostile camps, those of the classes. If bourgeois philosophy no longer perceives the 'totality', this is not because it commits philosophical blunders, but because its false 'being' renders it *incapable* of thinking in any other way:

> Such a synthesis would only be possible if philosophy were able to change its approach radically and concentrate on the concrete material totality of what can and should be known. Only then would it be able to break through the barriers erected by a formalism that has degenerated into a state of complete fragmentation.... It is clear that the philosophy of bourgeois society is incapable of this.... [*A*] *radical change in outlook is not feasible on the soil of bourgeois society*.[300]

The reason for this impossibility consists in the fact that thought and being are identical in *Lukács's* mind. In other words, a vulgar Marxist determinism cannot be transcended by means of a mentalising Hegelianisation, even if textbooks on Lukács often suggest the opposite. *History and Class Consciousness* culminates in the claim that the concrete bearer, the 'identical subject-object of history',[301] capable of overcoming thought's division into subject and object,[302] has finally been discovered – or that the task German idealism struggled with in vain has now been accomplished. The idealist approach is revealed by the fact that a 'bearer' [*Träger*] is brought in.[303] Lukács develops his approach

---

296. Lukács 1971, p. 1; see Bernstein 1961, p. 17; 2.3.2.
297. Kołakowski 1977, Vol. III, pp. 324 ff.
298. Lukács 1971, pp. 110 ff.
299. 'Bourgeois thought judges social phenomena... consistently from the standpoint of the individual. No path leads from the individual to the totality' (Lukács 1971, p. 28).
300. Lukács 1971, pp. 109 ff.
301. Lukács 1971, p. 197.
302. Lukács 1971c, pp. 122, 164.
303. Thus Kammler in Lukács 1975, Vol. I, p. 22; Anderson 1976, pp. 61 ff.; Jung 1989, p. 86; Jung 2001, p. 87.

intra-theoretically. What matters most to him, the theoretical '*aspiration towards society in its totality*',[304] is really only attributed, or 'imputed' to the proletariat.[305] The decisive factor is not the real proletariat, but its 'consciousness' ('*Only the consciousness of the proletariat can point the way that leads out of the impasse of capitalism*').[306] Lukács stresses that this consciousness is not to be confused with the actual, 'psychological consciousness' of the proletariat.[307] Class consciousness lives within the 'Communist Party'.[308] Within this construct of absolute mind, idealism goes head over heels: the identity of thought and being is 'posited' in advance; it is a matter of one half of the totality (the proletariat) finally 'positing' the *complete* totality within its thought – the totality that it already is, albeit only in a negative way (in itself, but not for itself):

> The totality of an object can only be posited if the positing subject is itself a totality; and if the subject wishes to understand itself, it must conceive of the object as a totality. In modern society only the *classes* can represent this total point of view.[309]

For the workers' movement, class consciousness is important because it allows it to act in a unified manner, and to continue being perceived as a legitimate movement by its members. But this is only the beginning of the actual political conflict. By contrast, Lukács believes that this is already the point on which everything else turns. It is in this, and not merely in his taking account of the 'proletariat', that the messianic character of his thought consists: he is still concerned with the advent of *mind* (with a 'transformation').[310] For mind has not yet arrived – just as in Fichte, the merging of thought and being is attributed to a theoretically mythified 'practice', whose advent is imminent (in 1923, one such attempt had just failed bloodily). For the purposes of this study, what we most need to consider are the grave consequences this bold construct entailed for the conception of *theory* (König's seventh point). On the level of content, and aside from the call to engage in revolution for its own sake, Lukács was less concerned with politics (the seizure of power by the proletariat and the socialist organisation of the state and the economy are only an intermediate stage, he writes)[311] than with an intellectual turnaround just as in Eucken. The main problem with which the book begins is an *intellectual* problem: 'reification'. And it is here of all places, where the very heartpiece of Marx's theory is at stake, that Lukács departs from Marx and makes reference, instead, to Simmel and Weber.[312]

---

304. Lukács 1971, p. 174.
305. Lukács 1971c, p. 74. 'Fichte's task, therefore, is to exhibit the subject of the 'action' and, assuming its identity with the object, to comprehend every dual subject-object as derived from it, as its product' (Lukács 1971, p. 123). The question to which the answer is 'the proletariat' (as 'identical subject-object': p. 197) is a question raised by Fichte.
306. Lukács 1971c, p. 76.
307. Lukács 1971c, p. 74.
308. Lukács 1971c, p. 75.
309. Lukács 1971c, p. 28.
310. Lukács 1971c, pp. 204 ff., 207 ff.
311. Lukács 1971c, p. 227.
312. Lukács 1971c, pp. 88 ff.; Jay 1984, p. 109.

Marx uses the term 'reification' twice, and he uses it to refer to precisely defined phenomena, namely the false ideas about the economy that are proper to the bourgeois *science* of economics:[313]

> [C]apital – interest, land – rent, labour – wages, in this economic trinity represented as the connection between the component parts of value and wealth in general and its sources, we have the complete mystification of the capitalist mode of production, the conversion of social relations into things.... It is an enchanted [not disenchanted! C.H.], perverted, topsy-turvy world, in which Monsieur le Capital and Madame la Terre do their ghost-walking as social characters and at the same time directly as mere things.[314]

Lukács turns this into a general proposition about everything: The 'commodity form' is 'dominant, permeating every [!] expression of life', the 'universal category of society as a whole'.[315] This is in keeping with Simmel's attempt to give greater depth to Marxism, which Lukács would later criticise so sharply.[316] What has happened? Lukács has transposed Marx's definition from theory to reality (he has ontologised it). Yet at the same time, he has idealised reality by taking it to be 'constituted' by a single principle – he speaks, in a Fichtean manner, of a 'deduction of categories'.[317] This mentalisation (attention is distracted from real problems and directed toward thought) establishes the fixation on 'consciousness' even on the level of basic conditions. In proceeding thusly, Lukács ends up with a new dilemma: how can a redeeming 'class consciousness' still be possible in a totally reified world?[318] 'Lukács was ultimately unable to resolve this dilemma'.[319] Fifty years later, Stefan Breuer still thought he could deduce from this a 'crisis of revolutionary theory'.[320] Breuer was not altogether wrong: the crisis is, indeed, one of *theory* (König's sixth point). The dilemma concerns theory *as* theory. In Lukács, theory appears, from the outset, only in the form of *philosophical* theory. He attempts to make everything in it fit perfectly, using only the means provided by theory itself. But it is precisely by proceeding in this way that he renders theory impossible.

---

313. The second remark seems more in line with Lukács' hypothesis: 'Furthermore, already implicit in the commodity, and even more so in the commodity as a product of capital, is the materialisation [*Verdinglichung*] of the social features of production and the personification of the material foundations of production, which characterise the entire capitalist mode of production' (*MECW* 37, p. 867). But nothing is said, here, about the universality of the commodity form either. In fact, such philosophical hypotheses would have seemed abstruse to the mature Marx.

314. *MECW* 37, p. 817.

315. Lukács 1971, pp. 84, 86.

316. Lukács 1981, p. 359.

317. Lukács 1971, p. 206.

318. Lukács 1971, pp. 86 ff., 207 ff.

319. Jung 2000, p. 21; Jung 1989, p. 102.

320. Breuer 1977. As the term 'revolutionary theory' [*Revolutionstheorie*] indicates (it already shifts the problem onto an intra-theoretical level), Breuer is as credulous a reader of Lukács as Habermas, whose frequent use of the phrase 'no longer' suggests that there was once, in Lukács's day, such a thing as 'class consciousness' (2.4.5; 3.1.3; see *MECW* 28, pp. 100 ff.).

Within Lukács' theoretical architecture, class consciousness is not required for political purposes.[321] Instead, the 'transformation',[322] the 'elimination of reification in all its forms'[323] that the proletariat achieves by engaging in the 'genuinely practicable',[324] is necessary for theory itself. The *system* requires the proletariat as the 'creator of the totality of content':[325] the theoretical 'system', which becomes possible only now, is what allows us to 'arrive at the concrete totality of the categories with which alone true knowledge of the present is possible'.[326] But how is 'knowledge of the present' possible *before* this?

This is the precise point at which Lukács waters down Marx's theory until it becomes something philosophical and intangible,[327] and he does so by thinking that his idealist identification of 'thought and being'[328] will render the theory more concrete. For how is reification to be responded to? Lukács is concerned with '*practical* efforts to disrupt the reified structure of existence'.[329] This dramaturgy follows the model of Fichte's philosophy and ends up with the very problems that Fichte faced.[330] There results the very same vicious circle that Lukács was already struggling with in his early philosophy.[331] It is only the proletariat that can disrupt the reified structure of existence, although it cannot do so on the basis of its own, 'psychological' consciousness, but only as the executor of the theoretically constructed absolute mind that is 'class consciousness'. This, in turn, presupposes the very theory that the redeeming action of the proletariat is supposed to render possible in the first place.

Here, Luxemburg's *political* spontaneity is transposed to the construction of theory,[332] much as, in a contrary movement, the theoretical phenomenon of the reification of social categories is projected without further ado onto reality. But because Lukács no longer distinguishes between thought and being, they obstruct one another. This is, indeed, a veritable crisis of theory (something Lukács himself called 'irrationalism'), but – and this

---

321. Lukács 1971c, pp. 207 ff.

322. Lukács 1971c, p. 204.

323. Lukács 1971c, p. 206.

324. Lukács 1971c, p. 205.

325. Lukács 1971c, p. 123.

326. Lukács 1971c, p. 206. On fulfilment within the 'great, redeeming system', see Lukács 1974b, p. 29; Lukács 1971, pp. 115 ff. The 'will to the system' still shapes Lukács's *Aesthetics* (Lukács 1963) and his *Ontology* (Lukács 1978–80).

327. Kołakowski also held that Marxism assumed, in Lukács, 'a form that is irrational and hostile to science' (Kołakowski 1977, Vol. III, p. 327). He discovers in Lukács a circular argument that moves between 'totality' and the 'dialectical method'.

328. Lukács 1971c, pp. 123, 202, 204.

329. Lukács 1971c, p. 197; translation modified; emphasis added.

330. Rosshof 1975 holds that 'no theoretico-systematic difference is to be discerned between Lukács and Fichte' (p. 90, with reference to Lud). Thus inflated, theory's goals can no longer be realised. Instead, a feigned 'practice' is invoked to solve the problems of theory – instead of giving each its due (see Habermas 2001c, pp. 482 ff.; Habermas 1987a, pp. 60 ff., 327 ff.).

331. See Fichte 1868, pp. 64 ff.

332. Luxemburg was interested in the institutions that would emerge spontaneously during the mass strike (Luxemburg 1971; see Lukács 1971, pp. 27 ff., especially pp. 40 ff.; see also pp. 272 ff.; on Luxemburg, see the article in Neumann 1942).

is what is important about it – it does not go back to Marx. What did Marx say about reification? 'It is the great merit of classical economy to have destroyed this false appearance and illusion,...this religion of everyday life'.[333] Thus, differently from what one would expect on the basis of Lukács' construct, economic theorists *have* seen through reification – much as natural scientists like Copernicus and Newton have quite obviously been capable of going beyond immediate appearances (and their 'class standpoint'). Marx is *himself* one of the theorists who engaged in this 'critical enterprise' (which is why *ad personam* accusations, such as the one that Karl Marx was really a 'bourgeois', are so devoid of content).

To what extent is Lukács' philosophical Marxism informed by such insights? 'It might be claimed...that the chapter dealing with the fetish character of the commodity contains within itself the whole of historical materialism'.[334] This is precisely what can be declared with certainty not to be the case – on the contrary, it is familiarity with Marx's substantive theories that allows one to better understand the chapter on the fetish character of the commodity.[335]

The fact that Lukács is not substantially interested in theoretical content can be seen from his remark that the criterion for 'Marxism' is 'exclusively' that of '*method*'.[336] Lukács consolidates developments examined in the preceding chapters: the loss of the object of inquiry and a farewell to Marx that occurred at the very heart of Marxism.[337] He reduces theory to *philosophical* theory, wants to construe it as a system ('to achieve a unified mastery of the whole realm of the knowable')[338] and needs then to ground it in a utopian and mystical 'praxis'. By proceeding thusly, Lukács abandoned Marx's economic theory, idealised philosophy and saddled consideration of real praxis with speculative ballast, thereby causing praxis to be lost sight of. He was not interested in Marxism's theoretical structure, and his 'decision' in favour of Marxism was grounded neither politically nor theoretically; instead, it tacitly adhered to an ethic of *Geisteswissenschaft*.

Much like Eucken, Lukács is driven by a yearning for 'communion',[339] one that strives to leave existing relations and institutions behind and is taken by him to be possible only in a strangely incorporeal form. Hence, much as Eucken is forced to repress nature and society, Lukács aims, in what is, at bottom, a mystical book, to get rid not just of the

333. *MECW* 37, p. 817,

334. Lukács 1971, p. 170.

335. According to Steinvorth 1977, pp. 6, 32 ff., this chapter is a sort of preface that merely anticipates, in an introductory way, what is then thoroughly developed in the rest of the book (in two-and-a-half thousand pages). The conclusion that 'the theory is therefore contained in there too' is not legitimate in the case of Marx, since *Capital* is not a philosophical book that merely deduces categories in the manner of a system (see *MECW* 6, pp. 161 ff.; I. Hunt 1993; 2.3.4; 2.5.7).

336. Lukács 1971, p. 1.

337. Lukács writes that any 'serious...Marxist' could safely 'dismiss all of Marx's theses *in toto*' (Lukács 1971, p. 1). The mature Lukács, otherwise so self-critical, continued to adhere to this position (Lukács 1971b, pp. xxv ff.).

338. Lukács 1971c, p. 120.

339. Lukács 1974b, p. 49.

'commodity form' (this would be an impossible undertaking in itself) but also of objectivity as such.[340] It was precisely in this that Colletti discerned a Hegelian legacy.[341]

At the end of this act-mystical contemplation, the yearned-for 'society of love',[342] or rather the new 'community', is finally attained.[343] In this, Lukács hardly differs from Bloch. The very criticism that Lukács directed at the Romantics also applies to him:[344] 'The actual reality of life vanished before their eyes and was replaced by another reality, the reality of poetry, of pure psyche.'[345]

---

340. Lukács 1971, pp. 174 ff. He further speaks of the *'transformation of the objective nature of the objects of action'* (p. 175) – objects 'become fluid: they become part of a process' (ibid.) – and reflects on how 'the rigidly reified existence of the objects of the social process will dissolve into mere illusion' (p. 179). He also speaks of the '[elimination of] reification in all its forms' (p. 206). The quotations from Marx are illustrative and essentially interchangeable. Behind this, there lies the German idealist tradition: 'since consciousness here is not the knowledge of an opposed object but is the self-consciousness of the object *the act of consciousness overthrows the objective form of its object*' (p. 178). Lukács had previously engaged intensely with Meister Eckhart (Keller 1984, pp. 133 ff.; Jung 1989, p. 56). In his 1967 self-critique, he traces his 'messianic utopianism' (Lukács 1971b, p. xviii) back to the absence of a distinction between alienation/reification (terms he claims are synonymous: pp. xxiv ff.) and objectification (pp. xxiii ff.). Lukács writes that the distinction only occurred to him in 1930, when reading Marx's 1844 Manuscripts (*MECW* 3) (pp. xxxv ff.). The 'fundamental and crude error' (p. xxiv) consisted in the assumption that Marx did not allow for the possibility of objectification being 'abolished' (compare the motto of section 2.5.7).

341. Colletti 1973, p. 185. '[T]he realization of the principle of idealism implies the *destruction of the finite and the annihilation of the world*' (Colletti 1977, p. 112). Colletti is one of the few philosophers who were not so professionally blinkered as to overlook German idealism's tremendous nihilism. He traces the history of the 'destruction of the intellect' (Colletti 1976, p. 139), or of the German hostility to science (see Callinicos 1983, pp. 99 ff.), from Jacobi to Marcuse.

342. Lukács 1919, in Lukács 1975, p. 87.

343. Lukács' notions very much display the regressive features implicit in the concept of *Gemeinschaft*, even if he hardly employs the concept (1974b, p. 49; see Kammler 1974, p. 87; Jung 1989, p. 87). Similarly, Bloch spoke very ambivalently about the new 'Kingdom' (*Reich*: Bloch 2000, p. 278). Mannheim 1936 traced Bloch's and Lukács' transposition of mysticism into politics back to the peasant wars, where it once had its proper place. Lukács 1971b, p. xviii remarks critically that his concept of 'praxis', not being grounded in real developments, led to a new form of 'contemplation' – one, however, that was no longer theoretical. After all, the concept of praxis was introduced to counter theory (and in particular 'economic' theory as understood by the Second International) (Lukács 1971, pp. 27 ff., 159 ff.; see Gramsci 1975). Here, Lukács addresses his role as founder of 'Western Marxism' (Anderson 1976). Lukács even refers to the role that Sorel played in his development (Lukács 1971b, p. x). Later, Sorel was *persona non grata* (Lukács 1981, pp. 30 ff.).

344. Lukács 1974b, p. 50.

345. This preemptive self-criticism also touches on Lukács's own problem, which he struggled with all his life: the 'search for wholeness' (Harrington 2002) risks alienating itself from life to the extent that it announces itself in art or in a philosophical system. And it is then precisely *not* a totality. Unlike epistemological idealism, which can declare whatever contradicts the conclusion reached by the system to be unreal ('so much the worse for reality'), materialism cannot do without reality, which however it will never gain access to for as long as it proceeds in this way. Therein lies materialism's disjointedness. While discussing a different political and theoretical context, Koenen confirms that the decision to adhere to Marxism does not save one from escapes into romantic superworlds. According to Koenen, the worldview of the radical students of 1968 displayed a 'largely monological, almost autistic character and aimed neither at knowledge nor at understanding in the narrow sense. It was rather the urge to give a metaphorical or formulaic expression to an attitude toward life and the world that was still undefined, by creating for

Lukács turned the objects of Marxian theory into 'spiritual' or 'mental' [*geistig*] ones ('*the strength of every society is in the last resort a spiritual strength*').[346] And in an effective move, he gave to his rhetorically brilliant balancing act the monicker of '*Marxist dialectic*'. Yet such a 'dialectic of the superstructure' (Benjamin) is little to do with Marx. This paved the way for a cultural criticism that referred to Marx even though it meant Lukács, and whose instances range from Adorno's aesthetic theory to Habermas's disembodied 'ideal communicative community'. It also paved the way for Heidegger, who transposed the 'Marxist dialectic' back to vitalism.[347] It was only with Lukács that Marx became a philosopher again, and it was only in the form given them by Lukács that his ideas found their way into German philosophy. Yet this philosophising of Marx eliminated all *content*: after all, the impossibility of constructing the content of the rational form (apperception) was what had always *prevented* the closure of the system.[348] Instead of 'reason' [*Vernunft*], or the way of thinking proper to philosophical systems, Lukács abandoned 'sense' [*Verstand*] – the rationality of economic theory and of the empirical reality comprehended by it.

Nor was the mature Lukács capable of breaking with mentalising thought patterns.[349] Even his 'ontology' is a vitalistically mentalised one: it considers real history to be the history of *mind*, or of forms, categories of objects and genres of art ('History is the history of changes to categories').[350] While he lucidly called, in 1967, for an effort to ground his *own* theory in a concrete analysis of reality, he himself never provided such an analysis. Ontology became a 'philosophy of Marxism',[351] which, starting from Nicolai Hartmann, set out once more to construct a 'system'. To proceed from the real and elaborate a theoretico-systematic account of it is to engage in an altogether different type of philosophy than that which proceeds from a philosophical *concept* of the real in order to construct

---

oneself a counter-sphere of theory, history and literature – in today's parlance: a virtual reality that transcended and largely replaced the empirical present' (Koenen 2001, p. 46 – above, I called this 'objective spirit'). In retrospect, Koenen considers this a 'New Left doctrinairism whose efforts to achieve 'totality' went far beyond the doctrinairism of the old left' (p. 52). In fact, Dutschke was an enthusiastic reader both of Heidegger (p. 46) and of Lukács' early communist texts (p. 50; see also the biographical preface in Krahl 1971, pp. 19 ff. This unworldliness reached a tragic climax in the Red Army Faction: Koenen 2001, pp. 362, 407).

346. Lukács 1971c, p. 262; see Lukács 1971b, pp. xviii ff.

347. The abstract rejection of 'modernity as such' was first formulated by Nietzsche, i.e. it originated in the very niche to which it returned in Heidegger (see 2.5.5).

348. Lukács 1971, p. 118.

349. While in fact his 'abstract utopianism' (1971b, p. xii) results from his philosophical approach, Lukács himself believed the reason lay in the narrowness of his subject matter. Hence Lukács decided to set to work on the 'object' 'nature'. He hoped to prevent economic theory from being conceptualised in an overly 'narrow' way, or in a way that ignores nature (and the concept of 'labour'), as in 1923 (1971b, p. xvi ff.). By proceeding thus, Lukács failed to find his way out of the woods: he remained a (social) philosopher. As far as its structural principle is concerned, his dialectical materialism remains an idealism.

350. Lukács 1974, p. 237; see Lukács 1971, pp. 186 ff.; Lukács 1981a; Jung 2000, p. 25; against this view, see *MECW* 6, p. 482.

351. Lukács 1971b, p. xi.

a philosophical system upon it.[352] Habermas's critique of Marxist 'productivism'[353] is on the mark only as a critique of *this* philosophical Marxism.

And yet Lukács also ranks among the most brilliant critics and analysts of 'bourgeois' thought, precisely because he was so bound up with it.[354] Where he criticises others (including himself), his writings are among the best that philosophical Marxism has produced. Those features of his work that are vulnerable to criticism are also evident in the work of other authors from the tradition of Western Marxism. For example, Gramsci also began with a dismissal of Marx's economic theory.[355] Where Lukács built upon the work of Dilthey, Simmel and Weber, Gramsci built upon that of Croce, Bergson and Sorel, developing a new variant of their culturalism.[356] Within such idealist systematic thought, 'Marxism' represents little more than the decision in favour of a certain *style* (which has now gone out of fashion). The vitalist destruction of the world and 'self-reflection'[357] was also incisively expressed by the young Ernst Bloch: 'for this world is an error, and void... The unknowing around us is the final ground for the manifestation of this world';[358] 'while inside, in the Gothic sanctum of the Self-Encounter [compare Eucken's sitting-room metaphors] this entire,... apparently so very real world will itself one day just hang on the wall like the image of some innocuous memory'.[359]

---

352. *MECW* 3, pp. 176 ff.

353. Habermas 1987a, pp. 63 ff., 75 ff.

354. Lukács cites his own bourgeois background as a reason why he has no illusions about the bourgeoisie (Lukács 1971b, p. xi), despite the fact that numerous critics of capitalism with a different social background continued to strive, up to a point, to live in a bourgeois manner (see Lukács 1981, pp. 30 ff.). One of Lukács's most grievous accusations was that of being 'drawn on to the territory of the bourgeoisie' (Lukács 1971, p. 196). But the manner in which he determines somebody's class position is simplistic: whoever sides with the communists thinks as a proletarian, and whoever thinks in a politically reformist manner is thereby bourgeois. Yet it is precisely this voluntarism, which disregards the substance of what somebody says and takes into account only what they 'will', which links him to the bourgeois philosophy of his time. Just like vitalism, he blurs reason's distinctions and the 'immediacy' of real objects, which is indispensable to positive science, in order to operate from a 'higher' plane. '[W]hen the individual confronts objective reality he is faced by a complex of ready-made and unalterable objects... Only the class can relate to the whole of reality in a practical revolutionary way.... And the class, too, can only manage it when it can see through the reified objectivity of the given world to the process that is also its own fate' (Lukács 1971, p. 193). Mastering 'immediate reality' requires one to 'abandon the standpoint of immediacy', according to Lukács (p. 194). Engels's and Lukács's distinction between reified and processual thinking (*MECW* 24, pp. 298 ff.) is closely related to Bergson's vitalism.

355. Lukács 1975.

356. See Anderson 1976, p. 56; Kołakowksi 1977, Vol. III, pp. 243 ff.; Milner 1999, pp. 47 ff. Gramsci was opposed to empiricism and in favour of 'achievement of a higher consciousness'. 'Man is primarily mind' (Gramsci 1916, in Gramsci 1987, p. 26). He praised Croce for rejecting 'economism' and compared him to Lenin in this respect Gramsci 1971b, p. 258). Gramsci was revered posthumously; one reason for this may have been that he prevented one from losing face as a Marxist when engaging with a culture understood as autonomous (Laclau 1985, Milner 1999, pp. 116 ff.). Unlike German culturalism, from Lukács to Adorno, he also lent arguments a more international touch (Haug 1985, pp. 127 ff.; Haug 1996).

357. *MECW* 5, p. 477.

358. Bloch 2000, p. 229.

359. Bloch 2000, p. 277.

In 1923, the German Left Communist Karl Korsch, who was to become widely known in 1926 for his hypothesis that capitalism had returned to Russia,[360] produced another vitalist depotentiation dilution of Marxist theory, comparable to that by Lukács. He presented even the existence of a Marxian economic *theory* as a result of alienation. In his view, Marxism was merely the 'expression' of the real proletarian-revolutionary movement, that is, of a certain 'social practice'.[361] Unfortunately, this 'inclusive whole', an 'unbreakable interconnection of theory and practice' existed only during the period between 1843 and 1848, according to Korsch.[362] Lenin also glorified this period, contrasting it with the 'economism' of Marx's later years. After 1848, the 'various components' of Marx's approach were 'further separated out', according to Korsch.[363] Thus it was not just 'bourgeois' philosophy that preferred the young Marx.

In 1923, Korsch did not read Marx's later economic writings as a scientific theory, but merely as part of a philosophical and praxeological 'system'.[364] And yet, shortly thereafter, he blamed the 'crisis of Marxism' on nothing other than Marx's scientificity. Korsch went on to call for a fundamentally new theory – as Bernstein once did.[365] For Korsch, the crisis of Marxism was not due to neglect of Marx's theories; on the contrary, it was due to the fact that Marxism wrongly took itself *to be a theory*. Having made the political decision to ally himself with socialism, Korsch was opposed to every form of political reformism – and he accused theory as such of 'lapsing' into revisionism.[366] Korsch is

360. This led to him being quoted by Stalin: Linden 1992, pp. 44 ff.; Kołakowski 1977, Vol. III, pp. 337 ff.

361. Marxism, Korsch argued, is the 'general expression of the independent revolutionary movement of the proletariat' (Korsch 1970, p. 42), the 'theoretical expression of a revolutionary process' (p. 62; for late examples of this view, see H. Fleischer and W. Schmied-Kowarzik). 'Expression' [*Ausdruck*] is a fundamental concept in Dilthey's *Geisteswissenschaft*, with which Korsch was familiar (p. 37): 'This complex of life, expression and understanding encompasses the lasting intellectual creations in which the creator's depth opens itself up to the recipient, or the persistent objectivations of mind in social formations.... It is by the process of understanding that life is enlightened, in its own depths, about itself' (Dilthey, quoted in Gerlach 1991, Vol. III, p. 122). Thus Korsch also sought 'depth'.

362. Korsch 1970, pp. 53 ff.; this view already amounts to a romantic glorification of the events.

363. Ibid.

364. 'In the writings of its creators, the Marxist system itself never dissolves into a sum of separate branches of knowledge' (Korsch 1970, p. 53). In a bizarre distortion of the distinction between philosophy and science, Korsch writes: 'To accord theory an autonomous existence outside the objective movement of history... would simply be an idealist metaphysic' (p. 52). In fact, what rests on an idealist metaphysics is his belief that he has no need of a scientific theory; Korsch assumes that the 'self-awareness' of the revolutionaries, which he conceives of in vitalist terms, already contains all knowledge.

365. Kołakowski 1977, Vol. III, pp. 339, 351; Korsch 1938, p. 1972. 'The ideological and doctrinaire separation of 'pure theory' from the real historical movement... is itself an expression of the present crisis' and therefore a 'crisis of Marx's and Engels' theory' (Korsch 1971; written in 1931).

366. '[A] unified general theory of social revolution was changed into criticism of the bourgeois economic order, of the bourgeois State.... These criticisms no longer necessarily develop by their very nature into revolutionary practice; they can equally well develop, into all kinds of attempts at *reform*" (Korsch 1970, p. 57). Korsch claimed he meant to make '"the subjective behaviour of

willing to accept nothing but 'theory' in the *philosophical* sense, and more precisely in the sense of 'German idealist philosophy'.[367] In the spirit of Dilthey, he acknowledges theory only as 'expression' [*Ausdruck*], which is to say he does not accept it as theory. But party programmes that contain not a grain of theory are also an expression of real historical developments. Because he disregards Marx's theory from the outset, Korsch takes what is revolutionary in that theory – the breakthroughs within political economy, namely the only thing that remains of Marx in the twenty-first century – to be something extraneous. Political action is the only thing Korsch is willing to accept as revolutionary. He holds that where no such action occurs, theory is obsolete as well. This *reduction of theory to practice* prepared the ground, within philosophy, for a certain kind of behaviour: that of swiftly abandoning a theory as soon as 'practice' makes it seem inopportune. This is what the critical theorists did during their exile, and what German social philosophy did, at the latest, in 1989.

This blending of theory and practice, thought and being, at the expense of economic theory, requires further examination; we need to see how it developed in Western Marxism (2.6) and beyond (3.1, 3.3). But first, we need to consider the final stage in the 'philosophical process of abstraction ... from Marx to Heidegger'.[368] Heidegger's philosophy also needs to be interpreted as a response to Marxian hypotheses, one that consists in transforming those hypotheses into philosophemes. But in Heidegger's case, Marx is philosophised less directly than in Lukács. Heidegger was responding to a Marx who had already been transformed (by Lukács) into a social philosopher, and so the philosophical refutation that Heidegger formulates 'implicitly' in *Being and Time*[369] can be related to Marx only inversely. And yet it is a central component of Marx's reception history.[370] Heidegger radicalises the mentalisation of Marx to the point where it turns into its own political opposite.[371]

---

the working class" the object of theory, rather than the economic laws of capitalism' (Kołakowski 1977 III, p. 346). This of course means that 'a "purely theoretical" capitalism is ... principally impossible' (p. 343). According to Kołakowski, Korsch is 'entirely unreceptive to empirical arguments' (p. 350): 'There are ... no longer any rational knowledge criteria'; this, Kołakowski argues, constitutes Korsch's 'hidden anti-intellectualism' (p. 350).

367. Korsch 1970, p. 42.

368. König 1937, p. 94.

369. Rohrmoser 1974.

370. Students of Heidegger such as Marcuse, Löwith or Arendt have strongly shaped twentieth-century philosophical Marxism (Rentsch 2001, p. VII; Wolin 2001).

371. An '(artificial) *overcoming through radicalization*' (Bourdieu 1991, p. 94). It 'provides conformism with its most water-tight justification' (p. 68; see Simmel 1978, p. 56; see also chapter 2.4.2).

2.5.5 *Martin Heidegger as offshoot*

> Philosophy and the study of the actual world have the same relation to one another as onanism and sexual love.[372]

Eucken's reception of Marx was shown above to have been a limited and inverted one. Yet hardly anyone still considers Eucken a serious philosopher. Lukács, who enjoys a better reputation, displayed great openness toward Marx, although he also shared many features with Eucken. Both mentalised Marxian hypotheses (and the entire 'immediate' world of things, while they were at it). Both ended up with a philosophical struggle for a 'new world' that oddly bypasses the 'real world', the one Marx considered philosophy and its negation to have an obligation to (3.4.3). In this, they resemble not just Fichte and Hegel, but also mysticism. Lukács, however, was not officially a philosopher, but rather a literary critic. More importantly, he was a communist, and hence an outsider within philosophy.

The hypothesis that twentieth-century social philosophy should be read as engaging with Marx, sometimes openly and sometimes covertly, in such a way as to de-economise and mentalise him, will now be verified by reference to another 'full-blown philosopher', who continues to strongly influence philosophy to this day: Heidegger. He was both deeply familiar with the philosophy of his day and an original thinker. Now, Lukács, who left the German academic scene in 1919 (although he would later return to it), can be said to link Heidegger to Marx, even if this is not immediately apparent,[373] much as Tönnies links Eucken and others to Marx. Before Marxian ideas were received by these thinkers, they had to be pre-digested philosophically ('reconstructed'). Marx seems to have anticipated this mentalisation; it was because of *it*, and not because he was a positivist, that he 'abandoned' philosophy.[374] Lukács, however, did not 'sublate' philosophy; he 'sublated' Marx *into* philosophy. Heidegger followed him in this, and with him large parts of social philosophy.

Eucken's diagnosis of crisis (2.5.3) was no isolated case. The historian of philosophy Fritz Heinemann noted the overarching mood of crisis within the philosophy of the time and considered 'crisis' to be *the* defining feature of the age. To be sure, Heinemann defines the crisis somewhat too broadly, as a 'crisis of man'.[375] But he is more precise in stating the cause of the crisis: namely Marx as 'philosophy's critical turning point'.[376]

---

372. *MECW* 5, p. 236.

373. See Gudopp 1983, Goldmann 1975 and, on Adorno, Mörchen 1980.

374. Brudney 1998; 2.5.7. 'Here we are, in the heart of Germany. We shall now have to talk metaphysics' (*MECW* 6, p. 161; see 3.1.3). Marx quotes Stirner: '"*Yes*, ghosts are teeming in the whole world . . .". . . . "Only *in* it? *No*, the world itself is an apparition . . . , it is the wandering pseudo-body of a spirit, it is an apparition."' (*MECW* 5, p. 153). For this reason, Marx called German philosophy 'religious' (p. 154; see 2.6.4) – and here, for once, his position really does resemble that of Nietzsche, although of course Nietzsche was writing forty years later.

375. Heinemann 1929, p. 5.

376. Heinemann 1929, p. XI.

Heinemann writes that Marx continues to be the most dangerous author of the time.[377] What is interesting about this is that he identifies Marx and Heidegger as the two most important 'interpreters of the age'.[378] Heinemann is certain that Heidegger was referring back to Marx. But should the relationship between the two be described in harmonist terms (Heidegger critically developed Marxian *topoi*)[379] or should Heidegger be seen as combating Marx?[380] Before answering the question, we need to take a closer look at Heidegger's covert engagement with Marx – which played a part in his 'decision' in favour of the *other* extremism (1). To avoid the biographical trap of considering this a mere private political 'value judgement' that is in no way related to his philosophy, I will go on to sketch Heidegger's vitalist background; it is only against this background that the motives and methods of his struggle with Marx can be deciphered philosophically (2). This will also shed light on the *theoretical* reasons for Heidegger's tremendous 'nihilism', which left him so unprotected against the National Socialist self-decapitation.

Heidegger and Marx

> We no longer want ideas and principles, we want ourselves. Hence we now face the task of liberating German socialism from Marx.[381]

What Martin Heidegger held against the currents of his age, even materialism, was their subjectivism. He believed one needed first and foremost to assure oneself of the 'foundations' of genuine philosophising. This was hardly original; it sat well with the neo-Hegelian *quest for reality*. Much as Hegel had historicised Kant's abstract philosophy of reason, Heidegger responded to the philosophy of the Kantians Rickert and Husserl by attempting a more concrete determination of the active subject. However, Heidegger's contemporaries already found this less reminiscent of Hegel's treatment of Kant than of Marx's critique of Hegel.[382] For even Hegel had remained an intellectualist who merely *observed* the self-development of thoughts from his armchair, whereas Heidegger's version of the active subject, *Dasein*, was far more practical; it even seemed to live through all the sufferings of real life. Since Heidegger nowhere indicates that he is making reference to Marx, we need to speak of a negative reception.

---

377. Heinemann 1929, p. 53.
378. Heinemann 1929, p. 393.
379. Marcuse 2005, Marcuse 1987, Alexos 1966, Maurer 1975, Fräntzki 1978, Eldred 2000, Servais 1998; see Demmerling 2003.
380. For example, Lukács 1989, 1951 and 1981, Bourdieu 1991, Gudopp 1983, Tertullian 1990. Ironically, socialist works that consider Heidegger 'an ideological agent of monopoly capital' (Zweiling 1958, p. 45; Zweiling 1961, p. 25) fail to notice the link to Marx and exhaust themselves in schematic identifications of class allegiance.
381. Spengler 1967, p. 3.
382. See, in addition to König 1975: Beck 1928, Marcuse 2005, Heinemann 1929 and Marcks 1929.

A hidden dependence of Heidegger on Marx has been claimed more than once – be it a direct dependence or one mediated by Lukács.[383] Assuming that Marx was falsely reinterpreted within philosophy allows us to search for traces of Marx even where his name is never mentioned. Yet it only makes sense to look for traces where they *can* in fact be left. The influence of some particular current is easy to claim but it remains immaterial for as long as it is not associated with decisive influences or distortions. An evident revocation of Marxian hypotheses can be found both on the polemical level of worldviews and on the 'strictly' philosophical level. Much of Heidegger's worldview is conveyed by his manner of expression and his choice of examples. They might conceivably be ignored. One would then have to distinguish between Heidegger's 'actual' philosophy and the additions he made to it for reasons related to his worldview and his time. This, however, is precisely the distinction that Heidegger eliminates in his main work, by assigning philosophy the terrain of the everyday self-understanding, where *one is never encountered without the other.*[384]

There is some disagreement over which passages in Heidegger are systematically relevant; this controversy does not interest us, here.[385] We will take Heidegger at his word and *not* draw the distinction. When one looks at the range of themes discussed in the 'patchwork' that is *Being and Time*[386] and asks the question of how they relate to Marx, one finds there are several Marxist themes among them (alienation and salvation, the critique of idealism, the search for the totality, theory's reduction to a more fundamental base, an emphasis on history, and so on).

There are also the following parallels. The critique of religion with which Marx began his critical career was also the starting point for Heidegger. Himself in conflict with his Catholic origins, his destruction of basic concepts[387] inspired his colleague in Marburg, Bultmann, to begin engaging critically with religion. Marx and Heidegger also both criticised epistemological subjective idealism, with which Marx was confronted in Bauer and Stirner, and Heidegger in neo-Kantianism and phenomenology, retaining, however, the 'active side' of the subject as developed in that approach. Idealism is responded to by positing the primacy of life with regard to form: it is form that adapts itself to changing contents. Analysis searches out these contents on a concrete level, which however is not vulgarly thought of as 'given', but rather as actively created. This active practice is none other than the factual one of lived life, which turns particularly on everyday 'care' for

383. See Lukács 1981, pp. 489 ff.; Lukács 1951, pp. 164 ff.; Rohrmoser 1974; Goldmann 1966 and 1975; Bourdieu 1991; Gudopp 1983, pp. 212 ff.; Ebeling 1993a, pp. 69 ff. I have criticised Kittsteiner 2003's claim concerning an affinity between the two, in Henning 2005.

384. Heidegger 1962, pp. 62 ff., 114 ff., 153 ff.

385. See Rentsch 2001.

386. Bast 1986.

387. Heidegger 1962, pp. 224, 271 ff.

survival. Considered from this point of view, the subject-object distinction, and with it the entire theory of knowledge, comes to be seen as a 'purely scholastic question'.[388]

With some degree of good will, one could define the basic features of Marx and Heidegger, and the common ground between them, in this way, as was in fact done, with 'Western conciliation', in the Heideggerian Marxism of Marcuse, Sartre or Kosik.[389] Yet this would be to overlook the decisive differences in the way that Marx and Heidegger concretely implemented their theoretical projects – not a trifling matter, since we are dealing with thinkers who emphasised the concrete. Here, the two could not be more different: the themes Heidegger adopts from Marx are not *engaged with* in the way intended by Marx but subjected to a more 'originary' interpretation. Heidegger promises a more 'radical' interpretation of these phenomena. But what *is* the 'root'[390] of man? What is more 'originary' than the origin of man's 'conscious being'[391] in his 'existence' – that is, his historically specific and concrete material and social conditions? As we will see, Heidegger responds to materialism by dissolving all genuine being and every other conceivable instance into nothing, with incomparable radicality. It is more appropriate, then, to speak of a 'covert enmity':[392] Marx and Heidegger 'exclude one another by their very nature'.[393]

Marx's criticisms of philosophers were aimed at philosophers who had *themselves* already criticised Hegel – and in a way that comes very close to Heidegger.[394] By contrast, Heidegger's destruction of metaphysics started with Aristotle and Plato and implied that to criticise them was to deal with Marx as well, since he was seen as a late offshoot of their thought. This approach is evident, for example, in the following note: 'Theory of ideas premise of Marxism and theory of ideologies. "*Weltanschauung*" as ideology, abstraction, superstructure of society's relations of production. Overcoming of Marxism?!'.[395]

The enmity can be seen clearly by considering how Marx and Heidegger address the same theme in different ways. The contempt for the 'public'[396] and the value judgement contained in it, both of which were to be found on *all* sides in Heidegger's day, is reminiscent of Marx's distinction between essence and appearance (2.4.6): things are not really what they are commonly taken to be; knowledge of them requires a more considered approach. For Marx, the road to knowledge was that of *science* (see the metaphor

388. In Marx's 1847 'Theses on Feuerbach': *MECW* 5, pp. 3 ff. See Heidegger 1962, p. 247.
389. Thus R. Prewo in Böckler and Weiß 1987, p. 198, on Löwith 1988; see Demmerling 2002.
390. *MECW* 3, p. 182.
391. *MECW* 5, p. 36.
392. Ebeling 1993a, p. 75.
393. Vosskühler 1996, p. 420; see Rohrmoser 1974.
394. Grondin 1994.
395. Heidegger, '*Vom Wesen der Wahrheit*': *GA* 34, p. 325. The role of Plato is ambiguous in Heidegger; perhaps Heidegger projected so much onto Plato because he felt such an affinity with him. See Safranski 1994, pp. 244 ff.; Brach 1996.
396. Heidegger 1962, pp. 163 ff., 211 ff.

of the '*camera obscura*').[397] In keeping with vitalism's 'idealist reaction against science', Heidegger places the emphasis on a more in-depth understanding of *oneself*.[398] This approach can only be taken to be more 'originary' for as long as one follows Dilthey and Fichte in regarding the individual subject as the 'origin' of the world.[399] Moreover, and leaving aside the First World War,[400] the pretentions to 'resoluteness'[401] are vaguely reminiscent of the 'struggle' within modern society that Marx described, the 'class struggle', as well as of Lenin's absolute discipline (one need think only of Lukács's 'decision'). Yet for Heidegger, what one needs to be 'resolute' about is 'being *oneself*' (individually in 1927, and as a 'people' [*Volk*] in 1933). The inverted echo of Marx becomes even clearer in the analysis of 'fallenness',[402] where Heidegger uses the word 'alienation'.[403] While Heidegger considers 'falling' to be irreversible,[404] he does hold that one should at least limit its effects, by means of a genuine practice, once its causes have been thoroughly diagnosed. A veritable revolution is required – although in Heidegger, it is only an individual one, and occurs only within thought. It presupposes an adequate degree of resoluteness and must shy away from struggle, or even from death.[405] This can only be achieved by a strong and unified collective, or at least this is what the later sections of

397. *MECW* 5, p. 36.

398. His 'existential solipsism' (Heidegger 1962, p. 233) is evident whenever *Dasein* is confronted with its freedom. Here, the identity of world and self is transformed into that of *Dasein* and Being-in-the-world ('the disclosure and the disclosed are existentially selfsame': p. 233). The abandonment of morality aside (Ebeling 1993a, pp. 31 ff.), this amounts to an exact replica of German idealism, which also mixed up theoretical and practical reason (p. 34). Authenticity *qua* 'possibility which it [*Dasein*] always is' (Heidegger 1962, p. 232) is reminiscent of Lukács's 'class consciousness'. In Lukács, it is also a matter of something that is 'objectively possible' (Lukács 1971, p. 75) becoming an object of consciousness, and thereby real.

399. Lukács 1981, p. 496, accuses Heidegger of a 'subjective-idealistic' approach.

400. Rentsch 1990, p. 144.

401. See Heidegger 1962, §§ 60 and 62.

402. Heidegger 1962, §38, §68c; Henning 2001a.

403. Heidegger 1962, pp. 222, 399. The word 'reification' also comes up (pp. 72 and 487: 'It has long been known... that there is a danger of "reifying consciousness"'; but see p. 165: 'Overnight, everything that is primordial gets glossed over as something that has long been known'). Goldmann 1975, pp. 27 ff. compares Lukács's critique of reification with Heidegger's critique of thought in the present tense. On Heidegger's familiarity with Lukács, see Gudopp 1983, pp. 130 ff. Heidegger later returned to the theme of 'estrangement': 'What Marx recognized... as the estrangement of man has its roots in the homelessness of modern man. This homelessness is specifically evoked from the destiny of Being in the form of metaphysics [!], and through metaphysics is simultaneously entrenched and covered up as such. Because Marx by experiencing estrangement [?] attains an essential dimension of history, the Marxist view of history is superior to that of other historical accounts. But since neither Husserl nor... Sartre recognizes the essential importance of the historical in Being, neither phenomenology nor existentialism enters that dimension within which a productive dialogue with Marxism first becomes possible' (Heidegger 1947, p. 243). At the time, Heidegger was utterly isolated and struggling to find his footing (Safranski 1994, pp. 388 ff.). It seems he was trying to recommend himself as someone capable of conducting the 'productive dialogue' he speaks of. The dialogue never took place, as he once more found supporters on the Right (Heidegger's correspondent Jean Beaufret would later go on to deny the Holocaust).

404. Heidegger 1962, pp. 219 ff.

405. Heidegger 1962, §§ 58, 62.

the book suggest.[406] This 'practice' introduces a historical dimension that needs, in its turn, to be examined.[407] Marx's reflections had also led him to the theme of history.[408] In Heidegger, however, even 'history' is rooted in 'historicity',[409] that is, in an attribute of the notional, abstract individual [*Dasein*].[410]

Moreover, Heidegger questions (as Lukács did) the 'thingness' of things, which was so unpopular in vitalism, and he does so by means of the distinction between 'readiness-to-hand' [*Zuhandenheit*] and 'presence-at-hand' [*Vorhandenheit*]. This is similar to Marx's distinction between use value and exchange value.[411] Both are distinct modes in which identical objects can be present, the one they display 'when we deal with them by using them and manipulating them'[412] and the one proper to a more complex practice, whose greater removal from everyday life does not, however, cause it to be annulled (because of its 'necessity'),[413] although the latter mode is thought of as deriving from the former.[414]

But Heidegger believes that this more abstract form, which recalls Kant's 'objectivity as such' (much as in Lukács), is enough to allow him to *explain* something – namely falling and all the phenomena that follow from it, whose error consists in accepting things as they appear, without perceiving the non-objective process behind them –, whereas Marx is not content with the 'concept' but rather uses it to analyse the actual movement of what is subsumed *under* it. Marx does not denounce exchange value in moral terms, as Adorno would later do; he treats it as something that is given and that one has to 'take into account'. In Heidegger, Marx's analysis of the real process is idealised (Heidegger stops at the analysis of concepts), *and* it is subjectivised (an altered self-understanding is a sufficient remedy). Simmel, Freyer, Lukács and others had for some time been preparing the ground for this.[415]

---

406. Heidegger 1962, § 74.
407. Heidegger 1962, §§ 72–7.
408. *MECW* 3, pp. 303 ff.; *MECW* 5, pp. 41 ff.; hence the term 'historical materialism'.
409. Heidegger 1962, § 74.
410. 'Dasein factically has its history, and it can have something of the sort because the Being of this entity is constituted by historicality' (Heidegger 1962, p. 434). This parallels the historicity of classes in Lukács 1971.
411. Lukács already treated the 'commodity fetish' as the main index of reification (Lukács 1971, p. 83; *MECW* 35, pp. 81 ff.).
412. Heidegger 1962, p. 98.
413. Heidegger 1962, p. 479.
414. Heidegger even describes 'readiness-to-hand' as the 'in itself' (Heidegger 1962, p. 101). This is reminiscent of Lukács' discussion of the practicist reading of the 'thing in itself' in Engels (*MECW* 26, pp. 367 ff.): Lukács formally adopts the approach of Engels, but he alters its significance by applying it not to 'industry' but to the 'totality' (Lukács 1971, pp. 131 ff.) – like Heidegger. The critique of Engels is justified, but Lukács's solution is not 'critical'; it is itself a return to idealism.
415. Simmel extended the 'Marxian scheme ... far beyond the field of economics' and thereby de-economised it (Simmel 1916, p. 98; in economic theory, Simmel was a follower of the marginal utility school; see 2.4.1; Großheim 1991, Luckhardt 1994). Lukács posited the commodity form as a 'universal category' (Lukács 1971, p. 86) and attributed to it the philosophical paradoxes that already had been troubling him for some time (Jay 1984, p. 109; see Pashukanis 1983, Sohn-Rethel 1978, Haug 1971).

Finally, one is struck by the parallel ways in which Marx and Heidegger understand theory. Marx examines its genesis within actual social practice; ultimately, a theory is only comprehensible to him when it has been read from within this context, and can only be properly developed when it thoroughly assures itself of it. The vitalist Heidegger[416] also situates theory within practice – but in an irrational one, that of 'life' as an occurrence that cannot be questioned, and/or in existence as the unassailable and 'pseudo-concrete' personalisation of life.[417] As in Nietzsche and Eucken, all these more 'originary' interpretations had the effect of making the thought of others, and hence Marxism as well, appear as a thought that has gone astray, a symptom of the crisis.[418] When the *philosophy of the crisis* was itself interpreted as the symptom of an overarching crisis, the result was a 'crisis of philosophy'.[419] Methodological monism prevented one from distinguishing sufficiently between the level of mind and that of reality.

Anti-modernists in imperial Germany already traced crises of reality back to a false philosophy in this way. Not only did this allow one to believe that one had discovered the true culprit;[420] it also had to make one doubt the very possibility of a crisis-free theory.[421] If philosophy is grounded in the explication of *Dasein* and *Dasein* goes into crisis, then philosophy can remain unaffected by the crisis only to the extent that it disposes of a 'relative autonomy' vis-à-vis *Dasein*'s concrete enactment. This was precisely what vitalism declared impossible; such an approach was rejected as dualistic and removed from life. After all, this was precisely the type of thought that one meant to identify as having *caused* the crisis – and whether in doing so one invoked Nietzsche, Dilthey or Marx was merely a matter of personal preference.

The question that needs now to be raised is *why* so many questions that were posed within Marxism reappear in Heidegger, albeit in an altered form. Was not Dilthey, and later Nietzsche, more to his liking? Why should working through Marxism be more important than addressing themes from other traditions, such as Kantianism (see Heidegger's remarks on the constitution of space and time)?[422] The reason resided partly in social reality. The world in which *Being and Time* was written and read was a shifting and disconcerting one; it was experienced as being in crisis. Many young men had lost

416. Fellmann 1993, pp. 187 ff.

417. Anders 1947.

418. Ebeling 1993, pp. 69 ff.

419. 'Philosophy does not *undergo* fundamental crises; it is itself the crisis of foundations in an institutionalised form' (Spaemann 1978, p. 92).

420. Enlightenment thought was identified as the culprit abroad; within Germany, one pointed to Social Democracy and, increasingly, to the Jews: Ringer 1987, p. 203, Sontheimer 1994. Hügli 1993, Wuchterl 1995 pass over this in silence.

421. A time without crises requires no theory, or at least no theory of society: 'That is why the happy ages have no philosophy' (Lukács 1971c, p. 29; see Hegel, *Werke* 12, p. 42: 'Periods of happiness are empty pages' in history). In Heidegger, the relationship is reversed – and this argues against his often claimed affinity with pragmatism (3.4.4): according to his worldview, a time of crisis is incapable of developing a theory.

422. Heidegger 1962, pp. 135 ff., 99, 93 ff.

their lives, and many families their property. Germany had lost its political form, and – many believed – its 'honour' (because of Versailles, not at the outbreak of the War). There was no longer anything that instituted meaning authoritatively; Heidegger too had turned his back on the church. Instead, there spread a 'hunger for a worldview';[423] attempts to satisfy it proliferated, and they were often amateurish. Much was expected from philosophy.[424] Now, Marxism provided answers to many of these questions. Moreover, it claimed to have sublated into itself the flower of philosophy, German idealism.[425] Such a claim had to be responded to, and the response required a *decision*.[426] It was not enough that Marxists were threatening to overthrow the old relations (they had been shaken anyhow – and what's toppling should be pushed over). If one became convinced that this philosophy was correct, one could not avoid drawing political consequences from it, since practice was not only an important *explanans* within it, but also its central aim. This question had 'hardness and weight'.[427]

Programmatic statements by Heidegger show he was aware of this situation. Thus Heidegger prefaced his 1914 habilitation with a motto taken from Hegel and concluded by remarking that his philosophy 'faced the major taks of engaging... with Hegel in a principal manner'.[428] *Being and Time* also closes with a reference to Hegel (and with one to Lukács).[429] If Heidegger considered reading and responding to Hegel such a major task, there was hardly any way for him to avoid saying something about Hegel's greatest critic, Marx. And that it was, in fact, Marxism that Heidegger had in mind is shown by an essay from the same period, whose conclusion is that 'there is now no law that determines how the ages succeed one another', differently from what Engels, Kautsky, Lenin and others had claimed.[430] It is shown even more clearly by Heidegger's 1932 note on Plato.[431] From this and from his statement, favourably received after 1945, that what he had hoped for from National Socialism was 'deliverance... from the dangers of communism', one can see that Heidegger engaged with Marxism and decided *against* it.[432] This explains the comprehensive adoption and reworking of Marxemes in Heidegger: because their persuasiveness was not to be denied, they had to be outdone by means of an alternative explanation. This assumption also makes the numerous stylistic borrowings more plausible. Since a mentalisation of the objects of inquiry and a philosophising of the

423. '*Hunger nach Weltanschauung*': Windelband 1921, p. 278.
424. Henning 1999, p. 12.
425. Engels, *MECW* 26, pp. 353 ff.
426. Weber, Lukács and Sartre were not the only ones who held that one's stance on Marx was an existential decision (Krockow 1958).
427. Franzen 1988.
428. Heidegger, *GA* 1, pp. 193 and 411; on this, see Gudopp 1983, pp. 87 ff. and 83.
429. Heidegger 1962, pp. 484 ff., 487.
430. Heidegger, *GA* 1, p. 431; see Heidegger 1962, pp. 470 ff.; Barash 1999.
431. Heidegger, *GA* 34, p. 325.
432. See the letter to Herbert Marcuse dated 20 January 1948 (in Kellner 1998, pp. 165 ff.; see Heidegger 1962 p. 457).

method was already evident in Lukács, with whom he shared a number of influences (Rickert, Lask, Dilthey), it was quite easy for Heidegger to reap the fruits of this labour.

It could be objected that this argument is based on superficial biographical evidence. But there is also a theoretical opposition between Heidegger and Marx. Hegel's improvement on Kant had consisted in a *historicisation*, and that of the Young Hegelians on Hegel in a *concretisation* of thought, while Marx faulted the Young Hegelians for their fixation on *thought* alone: he argued that men's consciousness is determined by social *being*, which he thus went on to place at the centre of his own analysis.[433] Heidegger's relationship to this development is one of extreme opposition. While endorsing historicisation and concretisation, he also radically subjectivises the being that emerged from this development: 'world is "subjective"'.[434] Entities such as nature, history or truth are ontologically reduced to *Dasein*.[435] And this *Dasein* is affected by a radical historicism.[436] It cannot shake it off, but it can choose between an authentic and a false historicism. Marxism and all of sociology – this is how the massively value-laden connotations of what Heidegger says should be deciphered – represent the false historicism, because they are inauthentic.[437] While Heidegger begins with everyday life,[438] the verdict he passes on it is ultimately negative.[439] What is at stake, therefore, is something extraordinary and great that has to be shielded from everyday life's 'vulgar' way of looking at things. This could conceivably have been ethics.[440] But ethics is also eliminated. While 'Being-with'

433. This development in the history of philosophy was neither necessary nor fortuitous; while it was contingent, it was also strictly consistent. Comte, von Stein, Moses Hess and Ciezowski thought alike on this point.

434. Heidegger 1962, p. 418. The world is what the subject takes it to be: 'but even in this "Being-outside" alongside the object, Dasein is still "inside"' (p. 89). Heidegger draws attention to his 'subjective idealism' (Gudopp 1983, pp. 74 and 78) himself, by equating the claim that 'Being is "in the consciousness"' with the claim that Being is 'understandable in Dasein' (Heidegger 1962, p. 251).

435. 'Hence only Dasein can be meaningful' (Heidegger 1962, p. 193). 'If no *Dasein* exists, no world is 'there' either' (p. 417). Where wholeness in inquired into, it is the wholeness of *Dasein* (p. 424). Heidegger subjectivises truth (turning it into a 'truth of existence': p. 264), nature (pp. 100, 128, 141, 184, 254, 432), history (pp. 432 ff.) and the 'doctrine of signification' (p. 209). In brief: 'all the modes of Being of entities within-the-world are founded ontologically... upon the phenomenon of Being-in-the-world' (p. 254).

436. Every 'totality of involvements' [*Bewandtnisganzheit*] is always already explicated, from its form down to its content: 'The "they"... determines what and how one "sees"' Heidegger 1962, p. 213). It is symptomatic that Heidegger hyphenates the German word '*Voraussetzung*' ['*Voraus-setzung*'], in a manner reminiscent of Fichte (p. 362; see Lafont 1994, pp. 41 ff.).

437. On economics: 'In terms of that with which inauthentically existing Dasein concerns itself, it first computes its history' (Heidegger 1962, pp. 441, 412 ff.). The 'question of how one is to establish a "connectedness" of Dasein' is 'grounded in... irresoluteness' (p. 442). 'So we need not resort to powers with a character other than that of Dasein' (p. 323). This is to reject questions that transcend the horizon of the individual subject. 'The question is not about everything that still can happen' (p. 378).

438. See Einstein 1918 for an earlier example of this approach.

439. Heidegger 1962, p. 383.

440. On the link between the experience of the sublime and ethical insight, see Vollmann 2002.

is said to be constitutive, its mode of being is consistently defined in a negative way (Being-with is fallen and guilty in and of itself).[441]

Not even the 'conscience' can help. This absence of ethics in Heidegger has reasons that are immanent to theory. Kant elaborated a formal definition of the conscience, something Hegel always held against him. According to Kant, what *exactly* the conscience will assert cannot be inferred in advance; this is comparable to the impossibility, in the theory of knowledge, of deducing content from form (2.5.2). Since Heidegger, like Fichte and Hegel, believes he can provide content, but fails to do so because of the destruction of the world, he concludes that *the conscience* asserts 'nothing'.[442] Once again, a deficit within his own theory (an 'impossible task')[443] is projected onto the underlying reality – that is, being is inferred from thought. The inference of existence from activity that Heidegger criticises in Descartes is also evident in his own theory, and in an exacerbated form: he begins from the individual conscience's 'character as a call' and infers not just that the caller/called is, but also that he ought to be (the self is 'summoned to itself').[444] Thus conscience loses its moral character.[445] Being and sense are rendered equally void; theoretical and practical reason are left undistinguished and delivered up to a practicist nihilism. The *revolution* called for remains one within the way of thinking: having worked through Heidegger's analysis of *Dasein*, the reader is free to no longer understand himself in the manner characteristic of 'fallenness' – namely, in terms of what exists – in other words, he is free to adopt a different self-interpretation.[446] The philosopher is left with the 'theoretical practice' of critique. Throughout its history, philosophy has overlooked the essential issues; it is to blame for the fallen explication of Dasein proper to the present. It must be destroyed *in toto*.

Thus Heidegger's 'escape' from materialism leads to a universal irrationalism, since the realm of *Dasein*, which everything else has been traced back to, falls outside the purview of the 'common sense' [*Verständigkeit*] of the 'logic of consistency' [*Konsequenzlogik*].[447] The result is a total nihilism: this approach no longer knows anything of nature, history,

441. 'Being-with is an existential constituent' (Heidegger 1962, p. 163). In other words, and differently from the 'they', it is not an 'existentiale' (p. 167). The mode of Being proper to Being-with is not ethics but – inauthentic – 'idle talk' (p. 221).

442. Heidegger 1962, p. 318.

443. Lafont 1994, pp. 106 ff.

444. Heidegger 1962, p. 318.

445. Consequently, 'ownness' involves the 'freedom to *give up* some definite resolution' (p. 443); it is therefore permissible to lie (see Kant 1949a, A 156, 165). Conscience is also subjectivised: Heidegger claims that it becomes objective only by virtue of its subjectivity (1962, p. 324: 'Experience of conscience'). By contrast, the 'world-conscience' (Schwarz 1919) is described as the voice of the 'they' (Heidegger 1962, p. 323).

446. Rohrmoser 1974 perceives in this 'the fascination of a radical critique, whose abstract character simultaneously guarantees that no practical consequences will have to be drawn' (pp. 75 ff.; the same position can still be found in Rohrmoser 2002).

447. Heidegger 1962, p. 363.

society, morality or theory. The 'Nothing' that Heidegger evokes[448] denominates his own thought more than anything else. The success of *Being and Time* was at least partly due to the fact that Heidegger took a way of thinking that was widespread in Germany to its logical conclusion. When one situates him in this context, he can be seen to have drawn from this way of thinking consequences that were no doubt radical, but also *consistent* and populist.

Heidegger and nihilism

> Heidegger's attractiveness was also based on a productive dismantling, namely *'Destruktion'*.[449]

The popular way of thinking just referred to was German idealism (2.5.2). One has not properly understood the pathos of *Being and Time* as long as one overlooks the fact that Heidegger aspired to provide *all* areas of knowledge with a philosophical grounding. The revealing keyword associated with this undertaking is 'originary' [*ursprünglich*], an adjective that Heidegger believes applies to no philosophy but his own. Heidegger is the heir of Dilthey, and thereby of Fichte, insofar as he unquestioningly assumes that one can infer what is logically and ontologically primary from what is *temporally* prior.[450] Because *Dasein* does not engage in science 'initially', the methodological principles of science must be 'derivative modes'.

Heidegger grounds the areas of knowledge simply by tracing them back to the formal-concrete constitution of the active subject, namely the pre-theoretical one. In this, Heidegger re-enacts Dilthey's effort to give all cognition greater 'depth', to ground and relativise it in 'life'. Heidegger, who felt himself to be writing 'in the service of Dilthey's work',[451] considered life 'as the possible *object* of the humane [sic] sciences, and especially as the *root*' of historiography.[452] An idealist reduction to the active subject [*Dasein*] and the associated homogenisation of the world are evident throughout *Being and Time*, as when Heidegger claims that the 'totality of involvements' [*Bewandtnisganzheit*] is 'prior' to all 'stuff' [*Zeug*].[453] Things in the world have no independent worth related

448. Heidegger 1962, p. 331.

449. Karl Löwith quoted in Lutz 1999, p. 280.

450. Heidegger's demonstration (Heidegger 1962, p. 187) that 'all sight is grounded primarily in understanding' is a genetic observation. But Heidegger immediately derives from it the claim that 'we have deprived pure intuition [*Anschauuen*] of its priority', or that '"[i]ntuitition" and "thinking" are both derivatives of understanding, and already rather remote ones' – that is, they are only of secondary validity (see Rauti 1999).

451. Heidegger 1962, p. 455.

452. Heidegger 1962, p. 450; see *GA* 59, pp. 15 ff.

453. Heidegger 1962, pp. 116 ff. This was already the case with Heidegger before his existential turn: in his habilitation, he developed a hermetic, identity-philosophical conception of the world that left no room for reason. Given such an all-encompassing metaphysical meshing of category and material, 'thinking can do no more than confirm what exists' (Gudopp 1983, p. 59). Epistemology and ontology are integrated into logic (p. 73).

to their own being; they are, as it were, absorbed by a whole that is temporally 'prior' *and* ontologically primary: 'But the totality of involvements goes back ultimately to a 'towards-which'... The primary 'towards-which' is a 'for-the-sake-of-which'. But the 'for-the-sake-of' always pertains to the Being of *Dasein*'.[454]

We can see in this a fallacious reduction of genesis to validity, accompanied by a subjectivist narrowing down of all conceivable contents to a being-oneself that is declared ontologically absolute. The identity-based way of thinking and the existential monism are obvious. In the passages of *Being and Time* that deal with the theory of science, Heidegger sublimely draws the relativist consequences – not just for the human sciences, but even for physics. How does he go about this?

Science is a human activity, as no one will deny. But if the mode of being proper to humans is *substantially* 'historical', then nothing is exempt from historicism. A mental 'totality' is ontologised and dogmatically declared primary – a radicalisation of the Diltheyan legacy. The sciences also have a history. This is no problem as long as a sufficiently clear distinction is drawn between genesis and validity. But when this is not done, the natural sciences are relativised in terms of historicity. How does Heidegger define mathematical physics? 'What is decisive for its development does not lie in its rather high esteem for the observation of 'facts', nor in its 'application' of mathematics... it lies rather in the *way in which Nature herself is mathematically projected*'.[455]

Heidegger contrasts two perspectives, that based on intra-physical criteria (verification by means of verifiable observation and explanation by means of mathematical formulae) and the one based on the historical development of physics. However, he does not separate them from one another, but combines them into something else in a fallaciously monistic way: he is concerned with the 'ontological genesis'.[456] Thus the originary foundation of physics is found neither in its own logic, nor in the history of its origins, but in the existential enactment of the science on the part of its subjects. But these subjects are not autonomous.

'In this projection something constantly present-at-hand (matter) is uncovered beforehand, and the horizon is opened so that one may be guided by looking at those constitutive items in it which are quantitatively determinable'.[457] The scientific subjects cannot discover the structures of an immediately given reality, for these structures have always already been projected *in a certain way*, and this has occurred 'beforehand'. Thus the individual physicist says nothing about reality; he is, as it were, drip-fed an explication of the world that is *prior* to what he says – an explication that is total and hence 'philosophical'. Heidegger has enormously expanded the purview of philosophy by universalising hermeneutics and relativising the natural sciences. He has thereby elegantly

454. Heidegger 1962, pp. 116 ff.
455. Heidegger 1962, pp. 413 ff.
456. Heidegger 1962, pp. 408, 413; compare 'transcendental-ontic'.
457. Heidegger 1962, p. 414.

divested himself of centrally important standards of rationality: the specific 'exactitude' required in the natural sciences is *not* anything to aspire to, according to Heidegger.[458] The philosopher does not need to take account of particular sciences; all he needs to do is engage in a 'working out' of the 'basic concepts'[459] of the preceding projection, which determines everything else. Within this genetic idealism, the principle creates *everything.*[460] The criterion by which to assess the *truth* of scientific propositions is not to be found in intersubjectivity (it is not 'binding for "Everyman"') or verification of the facts ('in principle there are no "bare facts"'),[461] but in the active subject: science 'has its existential basis in a resoluteness by which Dasein projects itself towards its potentiality-for- only half-heartedly Being in the "truth". This projection is possible because Being-in-the-truth makes up a definite way in which Dasein may exist'.[462]

But Heidegger distinguished two modes in which *Dasein* may exist, authenticity and inauthenticity.[463] He criticises the predominance of the semantics of presence, which is indispensable in the natural sciences, and considers it a result of fallenness and hence of inauthenticity. Hence his remark that 'science has its source in authentic existence'[464] provides a hidden clue to *his* diagnosis of the crisis and the remedy that follows from it: the crisis of the present consists in the loss of what is originary [*Ursprünglichkeit*]. It can be explained in terms of large groups of people (the 'public') succumbing to a way of looking at the world that is characterised by the semantics of presence (it is thinglike) and obstructs access to the important aspects of life. But this way of looking at the world is itself grounded – and only the philosopher can discern this, by means of his analysis of basic concepts – in a prior explication, a definite 'project' that has become inescapable – and that is traced back by Heidegger to antiquity and Descartes.[465]

This project, in turn, is grounded in a case of inauthenticity (Descartes thinks of substance as something that 'is substantially' – this corresponds to the definition of inauthenticity – thereby establishing 'Thing-ontology'); but, this time, it is the predominant

---

458. Ibid. While 'Dilthey always inclined toward recognising the equiprimordiality of the natural sciences and the human sciences… Heidegger simply reverses the naturalist prioritisation of the natural sciences vis-à-vis the human sciences, turning the natural sciences into a secondary, inauthentic, 'deficient' way of looking at things' (König 1975, p. 57).

459. Heidegger 1962, p. 414.

460. What seems absurd in this remains a feature of German philosophical critiques of Marx to this day: a rejection of scientific standards (those of the natural sciences) in favour of a methodological approach that operates by means of transcendental and conceptual analyses.

461. Heidegger 1962, p. 414.

462. Heidegger 1962, p. 415. See Tugendhat 1970. A National Socialist critic already faulted Heidegger for his existential enfeeblement of truth (Lehmann 1943, p. 402; see Gudopp 1983, p. 191). In his critique, Lehmann seized on Heidegger's characteristic 1914 statement: 'It is only by living within the normative that I know about what exists' [*'Nur indem ich im Geltenden lebe, weiß ich um Existierendes'*] (Heidegger, *GA* 1, p. 280).

463. Heidegger 1962, pp. 67 ff., 163 ff., 219 ff., 296 ff.

464. Heidegger 1962, p. 415.

465. Heidegger 1962, pp. 89 ff.

'understanding of Being' that is inauthentic.[466] It remains for the philosopher to 'guide' people to a different understanding. But how he is to do this *as a philosopher*, having jettisoned the criteria of scientific rationality, remains unclear.[467] Thus it is only consistent that being itself assumes this task in Heidegger's late philosophy. This anticipates central features of Heidegger's later political activity: the searched-for 'other beginning' was seen by Heidegger to be approaching in the form of the Third Reich, to which he proceeded to offer his services. The new 'project' could only be ventured by a resolute, 'authentic' historical collective equipped with the proper, and properly 'guided', understanding of being. This required the previous understanding of being to be destroyed root and branch.[468] In any case, on this conception, not much remains of what theory was before. Theory provokes and aggravates the crisis of philosophy. Heidegger did not abandon this view later.[469]

But let us avoid the frequent mistake of relating philosophy and politics to one another *too soon*; let us remain immanent. I have already mentioned the fact that Heidegger refers to Hegel in key passages. After all, it was a question of rescuing the legacy of systematic philosophy from the later errors. As far as Hegel's reception history was concerned, however, there was no way of ignoring the vitalist reductionism of believing one could adopt the absolute standpoint all too easily. This point of view shines through in a student of Heidegger when he interprets Dilthey as the theorist who completed the work of Hegel. According to this argument, Dilthey returns to an issue that was 'already' engaged with by Hegel, namely the 'historical unity of man and world, consciousness and being. Dilthey supersedes the banalisation of this living relationship…, its interpretation as an abstract subject-object relation…, and restores ontological unity'.[470]

Historicism is totalised to the point where 'all is one' [*panta rei*], including ontologically, only because it originates in the fertile ground of life and history. By means of this unity, Dilthey 'overcomes' the odious subject-object division, playing living unity off against dead duality. But the way in which he does this runs counter to Hegel's approach: he opposes unity and difference to one another, as if unity supported no difference but rather excluded it by definition.[471] This unity has not been recognised through reflection; nor has it been extrapolated in advance; it is an ontological unity whose existence

466. Heidegger 1962, pp. 127, 133, 413.
467. See Lafont 1994, pp. 253 ff.
468. 'We will then have to resolve to count Newton and Leibniz among the Jews', Heidegger wrote in 1938, objecting only half-heartedly to this putative necessity (Heidegger, *GA* 65, p. 163; see Stark 1937, Kather 1995, K. Fischer 1998).
469. Science 'does not think': Heidegger 1971a, p. 349.
470. Marcuse, *Schriften* 1, p. 485; this was written in 1931.
471. Marx criticised political economy as it had developed until his time for its inability to conceptualise anything other than opposites without unity or unity without opposites (*MECW* 35, p. 123). Dilthey's 'life' also seems unable to tolerate oppositions: 'By defining the relationship between man and world, consciousness and being, nature and history as one of unity from the outset, he never considers the "abstract" question concerning their causal or functional relationship' (A. Schmidt 1990, p. 169, with reference to Marcuse, *Schriften* 1, p. 482).

is simply claimed. It is introduced too soon, in the sense in which Hegel faulted Schelling for simply *starting* with the absolute.[472] The rediscovered unity is an aprioristic one that was always already there ('from the outset'). Thus there is hardly anything left for reason to do. In fact, in Dilthey, all further questions become 'obsolete', as Schmidt says. Philosophy believes itself to have no need for scientific rationality – 'reason' dismisses sense. But this unity is a 'living' one only where it first occurs, in everyday life.[473] To avoid unwanted abstractions, one should simply take everyday life as it is and relinquish all varieties of science.[474]

There is an analogy between this philosophy and its 'negating' precursors Fichte and Lukács: it has a practicist vanishing point. *Dasein* has to radically extricate itself from the inauthentic historicity out of which a prior but irresolute Being-with has pre-projected the world, and it must join a 'community of struggle' (thus Heidegger to Jaspers in 1922)[475] that creates a 'new world' (Eucken) in 'authentic historicality'[476] and 'authentic Being-with'.[477] But how is a new world to be created in the midst of a radical historicism?[478] At least Heidegger followed Hegel and the Young Hegelians in theorising the historicity and concreteness of reason.

The creation can occur neither within an isolated and merely cognitive subject nor within an ahistorical space, as was the case in Eucken. Here, nihilism becomes fatal, as theory no longer admits of an independently existing world, fellow men, a theory or a morality (they all need to be created in the first place, as 'authentic'). How is this miracle performed?[479] 'The resoluteness in which Dasein comes back to itself, discloses current factical possibilities of authentic existing, and discloses them *in terms of the heritage* which that resoluteness, as thrown, takes over'.[480] Thus *Dasein* must embrace, with atheoretical resoluteness, something that already exists, and to do this it must join an 'authentic' community. Entering into everyday life would seem the natural thing to do, but it is not an option, because of the fallenness of everyday life. Yet within the legacy, there lie hidden, during the late 1920s, currents that are hostile to irresolute common

472. Hehel 1967, pp. 71, 78 ff.

473. See Lefebvre 1977.

474. 'The attitude of the German philosopher to science is not always one of indifference. It is often a matter of open hostility' (Hook 1930, p. 147, following Callinicos 1983, p. 100; see Hook 1930, pp. 70 ff.). Marcuse was himself not above the anti-scientific vitalism that he describes with reference to Dilthey: 'The world is an estranged and untrue world so long as man does not destroy its dead objectivity and recognize himself and his own life "behind" the fixed form of things' (Marcuse 1941, p. 113; see pp. 105 ff., 143 ff., 155 ff., 320 ff. and Marcuse 1964, pp. 144 ff.). Marcuse's ill-conceived analysis of capitalism as a 'totalitarian society' (Marcuse 1964, pp. 158 ff.) also derives from the totalisation of a conceptual *a priori* adopted from the thought of Heidegger.

475. Quoted in Biemel 1992, p. 29.

476. Heidegger 1962, p. 442.

477. Heidegger 1962, p. 450.

478. See Lukács's two circular arguments.

479. Heidegger 1962, p. 435.

480. Ibid.

sense. These are precisely the currents that must be unearthed through 'repetition of the heritage of possibilities by handing these down to oneself in anticipation'.[481] Is this to be understood as a 'formal indication'? Such an indication assumes the existence of that *to which* it refers. What might that be, in this case? If we decode the above passages by relating them to the political context of the time, we get the following:

– *anticipation*: pre-reflexive, without thinking. Prejudice is given in to;[482]
– *handing down*: abandoning freedom in favour of the type of bond the Right Hegelians described as positive 'freedom to';[483]
– *repetition of the heritage*: Politically, to assume the German heritage meant revanchism, especially after Germany lost the First World War;[484]
– *of possibilities*: such as the former German aspirations to becoming a world power, indicated by the frequent equation of Germany with 'the West'. A return of the people to German 'self-assertion' would also be conceivable.[485]

This reading is not the only possible one, as the existentiell level stakes a claim, differently from the existential one, to adopting formal structures. But many terms imply that Heidegger unambiguously sided with a certain party.[486] This sort of procedure, by which partial aspects of something are presented as the whole, is *ideological* – after all, a political ideology represents a group's claim to speak for everyone.[487] Heidegger was not unaware of this. But what he says about it is clear:

> Is there not, however, a definite ontical way of taking authentic existence, a factical ideal of Dasein, underlying our ontological [*existentiell* = formally structural] interpretation of Dasein's existence? That is so indeed [!]. But not only is this Fact one which must not be

---

481. Heidegger 1962, p. 442.

482. 'Reversing this transition from immediate and direct to reflexive intention seemed to us to be the way out: it promised liberation from the inescapable circle of reflection' (Gadamer, *GW* 3, pp. 200 ff.; on the rehabilitation of prejudice, see also Gadamer 2004, pp. 277 ff.; 3.4.1).

483. Heidegger 1962, pp. 443 ff.

484. 'But taking over thrownness signifies *being* Dasein authentically *as it already was*' (Heidegger 1962, p. 373): 'Become what you are' (p. 186).

485. Heidegger 1933.

486. Terms and expressions such as 'loyalty', 'revering', 'authority', 'steadiness' (Heidegger 1962, p. 443), 'push' (p. 316), 'destiny', 'struggling' (p. 436), 'choose its hero', 'struggle of loyally following in the footsteps of that which can be repeated' (p. 437), 'the community, a people' (p. 436), 'motion' (p. 444), and so on are National Socialist jargon (see Bourdieu 1991, Ebeling 1991, Marten 1991, Fritsche 1999). Heidegger attacks 'the modern' (p. 444), and more precisely modern society – that is, liberalism – as well as the 'idea of a business procedure that can be regulated' (p. 340) – that is, socialism (Fritsche 1999, p. 163). Hardly any distinction is made between the two. Jünger expressed this in the following words: 'Marxism . . . is the capitalism of the workers' (Bourdieu 1991, p. 29; see Landauer 1967). Lafont also discerns in Heidegger's 'detranscendalization' the tendency to present what is contingent and factual as necessary (1994, p. 256; see below).

487. *MECW* 5, pp. 59 ff.

> denied and which we are forced to grant; it must also be conceived in its *positive necessity*, in terms of the object which we have taken as the theme of our investigation.[488]

Marxism also claimed to be both scientific and partisan (2.2.2; see also 2.4.6). This feature of Marxism is adopted by Heidegger. Yet Marx rigorously justified his partisanship within his economic theory. Here, proneness to crisis was no 'special case',[489] for Marx continued to take for granted the criteria of scientific rationality. Marx is no reductive monist: he confronts the real crisis in a scientifically disciplined way, since the two areas are relatively autonomous from one another.[490] But Heidegger offers no reasons for his partisanship; he simply declares it to be necessary. He means to elenctically undermine the possibility of criticising his argument as ideological:

> When it is objected that the existential Interpretation is 'circular', it is said that we have 'presupposed' the idea of existence and Being in general, and that Dasein gets interpreted 'accordingly', so that the idea of Being may be obtained from it.' This is correct. But Heidegger continues: 'We cannot ever 'avoid' a 'circular' proof in the existential analytic, because such an analytic does not do *any* proving *at all* [!] by the rules of the 'logic of consistency'. What common sense wishes to eliminate in avoiding the 'circle', on the supposition that it is measuring up to the loftiest rigour of scientific investigation, is nothing less than the basic structure of care.... *Like all research*, the research which wants to develop and conceptualize that kind of Being which belongs to existence, *is itself a kind of Being which disclosive Dasein possesses*; can such research be denied this projecting which is essential to Dasein?[491]

This passage on the 'hermeneutic circle', which is central to the justification of Heidegger's entire project, contains a number of incongruities.[492] To begin with, the notion that science casts out life or even 'wishes to eliminate it'[493] is an irrational legacy of vitalism. Has Heidegger himself not demonstrated that the logic of consistency originates in *Dasein*? Then how can he reject it as being hostile to *Dasein*? Once again, it is because of his vitalist standpoint that Heidegger postulates a hermetic identity of subject and object, in this case of *Dasein* and the alternative method. If research is 'itself a kind of Being which... Dasein possesses', then research must *be* like *Dasein* – in this case, irrational.

---

488. Heidegger 1962, p. 358.

489. König 1937, p. 88. Compare Carl Schmitt's 'State of Exception' (Schmitt 2005, p. 1; Heidegger 1962, p. 168).

490. With regard to the succession of philosophical systems, Marx was a historicist, but not a relativist: science was capable of freeing itself from ideology. The latter, and not merely class position, is the criterion for the ideological character of cultural phenomena. The world economic crisis of 1857 (H. Rosenberg 1974) did not drive Marx to formulate a 'critique of reason'; rather, it spurred his scientific activity (*MECW* 40, pp. 224 ff., 226 ff.).

491. Heidegger 1962, pp. 362 ff.

492. See Gadamer 2004, pp. 267 ff.; see already Fichte 1868 and the 'circle' in Hegel 1967, pp. 93, 386, 767 and so on).

493. See Lessing 1924, Klages 1929.

This fallacy is fatal. Other scientists have tended to emphasise that an appropriate degree of *distance* from one's object is a necessary aspect of all research ('by virtue of which theory first becomes theory, as opposed to practice').[494] This is all the more true for the human sciences, precisely *because* their object concerns us more immediately. Heidegger eliminates this distance, condemning it as 'fallen'.[495]

So far, '*Dasein*' has been misdefined as irrational and 'method' has been fallaciously posited as *Dasein*'s identical mode of being. At least Heidegger has struck a point with his remarks on the pre-structure of projection, due to which comprehension [*Verstehen*] always proceeds in a circular manner, including in the natural sciences. But this determination is purely formal. It does nothing to weaken the objection that his argument is ideological. The full relevance of this objection could be expressed as follows: '*One* (definite, partial, partisan) idea of existence and of being *tout court* is assumed in order to obtain from it *the* (general) idea of being'. This procedure is impermissible even if the formally circular structure is openly acknowledged. Properly understood, it is better described as a spiral, as there could otherwise be no advances in knowledge.

From the outset, the theory of knowledge was developed as a *criterial* one. Its purpose was to identify genuine knowledge [*episteme*] within a multitude of opinions [doxai]. But how does Heidegger define knowing? '[K]nowing is a mode of Being of Dasein'.[496] From this state of affairs, which is free of possibilities for subreption only if one substitutes 'way of behaving' for 'mode of Being',[497] Heidegger infers that the theory of knowledge is superfluous: 'what is left to be asked if one *presupposes* that knowing is already 'alongside' its world, when it is not supposed to reach that world except in the transcending of the subject?'[498] The question one would have to ask is how one is to distinguish, within this knowing, between knowledge and opinion.

But Heidegger does not pose himself this question. To know, in his sense of the word, is not to make *advances* in knowledge, but only to grasp more acutely what one is already aware of – a totalisation of Plato's maieutics. The authenticity of the cognitive subject is the criterion for truth (a charismatic legitimacy), and the meaning of cognition is *self-assertion*: 'in knowing, Dasein achieves a new status of Being [*Seinsstand*] towards

494. Lübbe 1963, p. 203.

495. Like Marx, Heidegger uses the term 'vulgar', although he gives it the opposite meaning: Marx used it to describe the point of view that fails to look beyond momentary phenomena (2.3.1), whereas Heidegger denounces detached scientificity and objectivity as 'vulgar' (Heidegger 1962, §§ 73, 81). On his early 'lack of detachment', see Gudopp 1983, pp. 59, 73. 'Cognition requires not just attachment to being, but also detachment from being' (Tillich, *GW* II, p. 232; Nietzsche's 'pathos of distance': *KSA* 5, p. 286; Simmel 1908, pp. 402 ff.; Lieber 1974, p. 45; Elias 1987).

496. Heidegger 1962, p. 88.

497. From this, one may derive the heuristic rule of interpretation that where Heidegger uses the words being, existent, ontic or ontological without any clear referent, it could be that he requires them for subsequent subreption. The key expression for ontologistic 'subreption' is 'based upon' (Heidegger 1962, p. 371): it blurs the distinction between ontology and logic (Gudopp 1983, p. 59). Transforming substantive into functional concepts would be helpful (Cassirer 1953).

498. Heidegger 1962, p. 88.

a world which has already been discovered in Dasein itself'.[499] No provision is made for diversity of opinions, standpoints, perspectives. Cognition cannot incorporate anything foreign (there *is* nothing foreign); it merely serves to consolidate existing prejudices.[500] Heidegger's ideologisation, his absolutising of partial views is grounded in his existentiell 'theory of knowledge'. Such 'truth' requires the homogeneity of the *body* of truth, to be obtained, if necessary, by excluding and combating what contradicts it. Heidegger drew this consequence in 1933. Here, the often drawn parallel between the different totalitarianisms is confirmed for philosophy.

Heidegger imitates a model in which auratic leaders discover the truth, which is then acted upon within a conspirative community – this corresponds to Lenin's 'new type of party' (2.2.2). If Communism became totalitarian because it considered the means more important than the end, then Heidegger did so because he underdetermined reason. The dominant *topoi* are the same as in Eucken and Lukács: the *a priori* of a mental 'totality', 'objective spirit', sucks theory into 'life', thereby neutralising it. Critical analysis of the real world is replaced with 'normative social philosophy' – a mixture of theoretically disguised value judgements, appellative ethics and directly practicist commitment. This process should be understood not as a 'repetition' of the grounding that Marx provided philosophy with (and which has frequently inspired the parallelisation of Marx and Heidegger),[501] but rather as a *rejection* of this grounding and its political consequences. It led to the intermediate form of a retained idealism that wanted desperately to no longer be one. Not only did it become vulnerable, because of this blind volition, to reactionary political currents; as a philosophical version of 'self-assertion'[502] that did away with reflection, it was itself such a current. Heidegger carried through the 'conservative revolution in philosophy'.[503] *Philosophically*, this was essentially a reactive response to Marx. While socio-philosophical theories cannot simply be reduced, in the manner of vulgar Marxism, to the political interests that may lie behind them, what one can do is show up the political implications of basic theoretical choices. This is especially true of a philosophy that means to overcome just such 'dualistic' separations. What has been shown here is not new. It was a matter of demonstrating that social philosophy involved a philosophical processing of Marx, especially in Heidegger's case.

---

499. Heidegger 1962, p. 90.

500. 'That which deepens the bond of life is historical; what dissolves this bond is ahistorical' (F. Kaufmann on Ludwig Yorck von Wartenburg, quoted in Jonas 1976, Vol. II, p. 176; see above). One might substitute the word 'true' for 'historical' – Heidegger's pragmatism, for which he has frequently been praised recently, is quite dubious.

501. For example, in Marcuse 2005, Sartre 1976, Axelos 1966, Servais 1998; see Bourdieu 1991, p. 94; Schmidt 1990.

502. Heidegger 1933.

503. Bourdieu 1991, p. 55; see Breuer 1993.

2.5.6 *Niklas Luhmann's philosophy of systems*

> This so-called consideration from the point of view of society means nothing more than to overlook precisely the *differences* which express the *social relation* (relation of civil society).[504]

Luhmann's systems theory also belongs in *this* context: it has less in common with sociology than with vitalist social philosophy and its 'hunger for wholeness'.[505] The shared motive of 'refuting Marx' does not need to be tiresomely exposed, for Luhmann's relationship to earlier theories shines through all by itself.[506] Thus Luhmann's theory also constitutes a distortive reaction to Marxism (König's first point), even if it is strongly mediated (by vitalism and its technicised replication in Freyer and Schelsky).

Several aspects of Luhmann's theory can be used to show that this socio-philosophical distortion also remains dependent on Marx (point two). To begin with, the direction of inquiry is the same, amounting to what was once called 'structural functionalism' – that is, a 'macrosociological' perspective on social structures, processes and laws.[507] This superficial parallel led to Habermas replacing his formerly semi-Marxist substructure with a systems-theoretical one.[508] This melange was further promoted by East-German Marxism's temporary interest in 'cybernetics'.[509] Thus many Marxists 'changed sides' and became systems theorists, and for a time, systems theory retained its thematic congruence with Marxism.[510]

---

504. Marx, *MECW* 28, p. 195.

505. Gay 1968, pp. 70 ff.; Müller 1996, pp. 38 ff.; Harrington 2002.

506. Luhmann's theoretical testament states that his 'ambition of formulating a theory of society was obstructed by neo-Marxist precepts' (Luhmann 1998, p. 11). This means that the goal of formulating a 'theory of society' [*Theorie der Gesellschaft*: a term coined by Horkheimer] was prescribed by neo-Marxism. (In Luhmann 1995, p. 4, he writes that he is deliberately not providing a 'theory of society'). He was thus constrained to engage theoretically with Marxism. Digs at neo-Marxist theories recur throughout his work ('Today, Marxists survive almost entirely on the basis of dissatisfaction with their own theory': Luhmann 1986, p. 163; see Luhmann 1967 and 1985), although his numerous allusions to more recent opponents, and in particular to Habermas, soon begin to predominate. Luhmann's style treats potential opponents as if they were already 'finished', although it would be up to him to 'finish' them: 'Our flight must take place above the clouds, and we must reckon with a rather thick cloud cover.... Occasionally, we may catch glimpses below [!]... glimpses of a larger stretch of landscape with the extinct volcanoes of Marxism' (Luhmann 1995, p. 1).

507. See Halfmann 1996a.

508. Habermas 1984–7; in Habermas 1996, pp. 66 ff., he still refers to the two in the same breath (3.1.3).

509. See Klaus 1961 and 1968, Heidtmann 1977. Systems theory's plausibility waned following the onset of the economic crises of the late 1960s and early 1970s, since, in keeping with spirit of the 1940s, it had placed its trust in the possibility of planning. (Systems theory's 'public influence' is to be explained 'in terms of its promise of socio-technological and administrative applicability': Müller 1996, p. 311; see p. 340). Once again, German thought lagged behind social reality (see 2.4.4).

510. Benner 1966, Tjaden 1971, Maciewski 1973, Schürmann 1974, Greven 1974, Giegel 1975, Sens 1979, Kiefer 1991.

Aside from their direction of inquiry, systems theory and Marxism also have a similar mystique about them: much like the student Marxism of 1968, systems theory is surrounded by a mystique of esoteric secret knowledge about 'the whole', while hermetic language ensures that the initiated vanguard remains closed off to the outside world.[511] Systems theory's kinship with Marxism is a kinship with a Marxism that has *already been transformed* socio-philosophically. Here, I am interested in systems theory's points of contact with this problematic social philosophy, and even with the way it can be said to have developed out of it. The parallels begin with the orientation of the undertaking. What Luhmann's thirty-year research project[512] aimed at was a 'theory about everything'; this can already be seen from the sheer number and the thematic range of his publications. Far from modest, he says of his systems theory that it has 'universalist' aspirations[513] and brings about nothing less than a 'paradigm shift'.[514] This change of perspective extends to *everything* that can be considered within sociology ('*everything* social').[515] Thus what Luhmann aimed at was a new system in the second sense of the word: a closed, comprehensive body of knowledge like the one idealism had aimed at.

Yet Luhmann and Hegel are related not just in terms of their aspirations, but also in terms of their method. Both Hegel and Luhmann developed a new language, in which they attempted to newly express all existing knowledge.[516] The advantage of a new theoretical language is not just that everything can be expressed in it (a 'naming game'),[517] but also that no one really understands it, so that sceptics can be silenced (in this context, there definitely is such a thing as a 'private language'). Both Hegel and Luhmann make the fallacious assumption that what can be spoken of everywhere must also constitute the *foundation* everywhere. The model is ontologised.[518] Even the basic building block, the *arché* of the system is similar: everything appears as communication – as 'spirit of

511. Thus, according to K. Müller, recent systems theory is 'living out its schismatic individual existence in a jargon that in no way ranks behind the escapades of certain old-style "dialectical derivations of concepts"' (Müller 1996, p. 353; see Göbel 2000).

512. Luhmann 1998, p. 11.

513. Luhmann and Habermas 1971, pp. 378 ff.; Luhmann 1995, pp. xlvii ff.

514. Luhmann 1995, pp. 4 ff.; Luhmann 1998, p. 60.

515. Luhmann 1995, p. xlvii.

516. 'All theory adds to this is greater degrees of abstraction' (Luhmann 1982, p. 10). In Hegel, talk of mind permeates all areas of knowledge; in Luhmann, autopoeisis, difference and communication do the same. Luhmann sidesteps the problem Hegel encounters when dealing with the 'dialectic of nature' by defining nature and mind ('life' and 'consciousness') as systems that sociology is simply not interested in.

517. Rehberg 1994a, p. 55.

518. In Hegel, speaking about everything in the terminology of mind became talk of how everything is a self-realisation of mind (2.5.2). Since 'very heterogeneous functional areas such as science and law, economy and politics, the mass media and intimate relationships' can all be 'described' in his language, Luhmann immediately concludes from this (without questioning the adequacy of his description or seeing that a description is not an explanation from which something might be inferred) that they 'display comparable structures' (Luhmann 1998, p. 12). Thus the first thing posited is 'that systems exist' (Luhmann 1995, p. 39). All areas could just as well be 'described' ethno-methodologically or in verse – but nothing follows from this alone.

the spirit'.[519] Within this system of the self-development of the concept, theology is even distinctly 'prior' to the economy – as in Hegel.[520] In any case, achieving knowledge of the particulars *of the world* requires no more than its 'concept'. It is hard to imagine a thought more typical of old Europe than Luhmann's.[521]

Now, it can certainly not be assumed that Luhmann's theory descends directly from Hegel, even if he alludes occasionally to him and received the Hegel Prize.[522] Between Hegel and Luhmann there lies a 'reception history' – namely vitalism and its effects on twentieth-century German social philosophy (König's third point). I will not discuss the

---

519. *MECW* 5, p. 54. According to Luhmann, society is 'composed of' communication (Luhmann 1995, p. 138; communication is 'the only genuinely social... operation': Luhmann 1998, p. 81). The 'production' and 'reproduction' of society occur by means of communication and distinctions (Luhmann 1998, pp. 96, 98). Luhmann believes himself to have avoided substantialism simply by virtue of the fact that this structural element is not a 'thing' but a 'process' (Luhmann 1995, pp. 139 ff.) – like Engels and Bergson. Is the reason that he has to polemicise so strongly against old Europe not that he himself undauntedly prolongs it? The way the word 'system' oscillates between thought and being, between 'system of theory' and 'theory of systems', is implicit in the basic idealist approach with its assumption that thought and being no longer need to be distinguished (Luhmann 1998, pp. 32, 867).

520. The economy is never mentioned except in Luhmann's book about it (Luhmann 1998, pp. 559 ff.). As early as the introductory chapter, he poses the question that is central to any universal system of world transformation: 'And then what will become of God?' (Luhmann 1998, p. 158). The first thing to be produced by the 'language' born from page 205 onward is 'religion'. Once it has been made flesh, 'engendering' the rest of the world is no longer a problem (p. 155), since religion is 'decisive for the way in which the... social system establishes itself in a cosmopolitan manner' (p. 232). *The Function of Religion* was published in 1997 (see Luhmann 2000), his book on the economy in 1988 (see Luhmann 1970). Luhmann turned to religion in his old age.

521. 'Accordingly, everything presupposes a clarification of the concept of communication' (Luhmann 1995, p. 139). With regard to the various functional systems, Luhmann's 'theoretical technique' consists in determining a guiding difference (such as 'payment/non-payment' in the economy; in the case of art, there are two such differences: the code of 'beauty' and the hidden subcode of an artwork's market value), from which 'everything else' can then be deduced. Thus, to understand 'social structure', it suffices to engage with society's 'semantics'. But here as in every other system, there arises the issue of form and content (Lukács 1971, p. 116; see Luhmann 1998, pp. 60 ff.). Here, there is only the following 'distinction'. Either Luhmann believes he can produce (engender, deduce, construe, or whatever one wants to call it) content from form (and there is much to suggest that this is what he believes) – this would make him a subjective idealist. Or he has yet to say anything about the content of the forms, in which case his system would amount to a purely aprioristic 'formal sociology' along the lines of Simmel 1908 and Von Wiese 1954, which provides and discusses a number of 'categories', but says nothing about 'society' as such. *Tertium non datur.* There is no use in trying to evade this alternative by claiming, in an irrationalist manner, that binary logic is 'long since obsolete' (Luhmann 1998, p. 32; see pp. 419, 495).

522. 'Truth appears in the process' (Luhmann 1982, p. 11). The theory of knowledge, which is always also a critique of knowledge, ought to ask: how and from where does Luhmann take all these insights? The hustle and bustle over his legendary claim to 'third-level' observation reveals the confusion that reigns here. The answer is simple: Luhmann does not know; he merely asserts ('posits'). He denies even the criteria required for verification (a validation of thought by being, of theory by reality). The blending of thought and being (Luhmann 1998, p. 32) merely provides a post hoc justification for the elimination of the theory of knowledge (see Gripp-Hagelstange 1995).

exact development of the various currents within this reception history; it is enough to note that there are distinct commonalities.[523]

To begin with, there is the general focus: vitalism already put aside consideration of objects in order to examine itself (and the absence of every object led to 'self-cognition' becoming 'self-*assertion*');[524] similarly, in Luhmann, everything turns on 'self-description' and observation 'in action'.[525] He turns the methodological problems ('paradoxes') that he takes this self-reference (autology) to entail into the axis around which the history of the failure of all earlier sociology revolves. This prelude, which is part of the liturgical *invocavit* of many works, resembles Hegel's 'showing forth' of 'God as he is in his eternal essence before the creation of Nature'.[526] Before he can 'reconstruct' another part of reality as a system, Luhmann has to invoke the need for such an undertaking. It is only his bold claim on the *necessary* failure of all earlier sociological efforts that can give plausibility to his breath-taking 'leap' outside of the old European rationality. (Although it cannot justify it.)[527]

This 'leap'[528] outside of rationality is the second feature that links Luhmann to vitalist social philosophy.[529] Like Dilthey before him and Heidegger after him, Lukács strove for cognition of the 'totality' by abandoning the standpoint of common sense, or of objective thought, in favour of the 'dialectical method' associated with an emphatically glorified 'reason'. As in vitalism, this entailed a 'destruction of the intellect'.[530] Something similar occurs in Luhmann, and because thought and being are treated as one[531] it occurs both on the level of things *and* on that of logic. Luhmann is factually a critic of reification,[532]

---

523. The debate on technocracy prompted by the works of the former vitalist Freyer and his students Gehlen and Schelsky presumably played an important role (2.4.5). By contrast, Parsons followed the neo-Kantians (2.4.1).

524. This is overlooked by vitalism's apologists (Fellmann 1993, Wuchterl 1995, Albert 2000).

525. Luhmann 1998, pp. 15, 69; 866–1150. The Fichte of 1801 believed that the I was equipped with an eye that see itself (Henrich 1966, pp. 25 ff.); as is well known, in Freyer a 'living reality' perceives and understands itself (Freyer 1964, p. 83).

526. Hegel 1929, p. 60.

527. See Luhmann 1995, pp. 32 ff.; Luhmann 1985, p. 119; Luhmann 1988, pp. 44 ff., 83 ff.; Luhmann 1998, pp. 16 ff., 80 ff. 'A society that describes itself... observes itself *qua* object of its own cognition, but it cannot make such observation part of its object while performing this operation' (Luhmann 1998, p. 15; see pp. 20, 57; keywords: 'paradox' and 'self-observation'; see below). This derives its plausibility from the fact that sociology has lost its object. Whether it did so for the reasons cited by Luhmann is doubtful.

528. Luhmann 1998, p. 57.

529. Müller 1996, p. 353: autopoiesis *qua* 'mythic subject of the system... "leaps" over the rules of logic thanks to a homemade theory of knowledge'.

530. Colletti 1976, p. 139.

531. Luhmann 1998, p. 32.

532. He alludes to Bergson: 'The temporal dimension prevents the thinglike consolidation of the social dimension' (Luhmann 1998, p. 45). And to Heidegger: In the 'ontological metaphysics of tradition', the 'world' and 'the existent were conceptualised in the form of things' (Luhmann 1998, p. 56). 'World society is the coming about of world by means of communication' (p. 150). The critique of reification is not in itself progressive (Henning 1999, p. 83).

and he means to get beyond the thought that operates by means of a 'binary logic'.[533] He fallaciously applies discoveries in physics[534] and brain research[535] to logic *and* ontology, in a way that reveals the monistic and identity-philosophical thrust of his entire system. Kant and Wittgenstein already insisted that the boundaries separating the grammars of different languages should be respected. This is done by all sciences, insofar as findings from chemistry are not treated as propositions of information science, or even of jurisprudence or sociology. It is only when I fail to distinguish between the various levels of locution that the paradoxes of which Luhmann speaks actually become paradoxes.[536] Luhmann's onto-historical insinuation misses reality.

In fact, the rules of logic do not become null and void simply because a creature that is equipped with a brain begins to think about this brain, inspects it, measures electrical currents within it and conducts experiments on it. All of this is done within the framework of binary logic. Why should I not speak *about* a room when I am *in* it? I came into it from outside, I can look at the construction plans and I can take samples. I can speak about it even when I am *in* it. The same holds true with regard to our planet, Earth, which I cannot leave, or with regard to social relations that I cannot extricate myself from, such as family relations. Similarly, the fact that I am '*in*' sociology (in the sense that I am inside a university building that belongs to the sociology department, or in the sense that I am a professor employed by that department) does not prohibit me from thinking *about* sociology (its history, the adequacy of its questions or the forthrightness of its authors); no paradoxes result. It is only when the meanings of words such as 'sociology', 'relation', 'brain', 'space' or 'society' is fixed so erratically that all non-identity and every difference between their various aspects is eliminated (in the manner of formal logic, where a = a holds true) that the existence of a paradox is suggested. But this is

533. K. Müller also holds that 'Luhmann's theory of autopoeisis inserts itself into a tradition that is very much old European, that of a meta-politics that translates actions and political processes into a language whose feature is precisely that it closes itself off against action-theoretical and political reflection' (Müller 1996, p. 355). This may even be a typically German phenomenon: '"Worse than Parsons", was the outside view of James S. Coleman' (Müller 1996, p. 356).

534. Luhmann 1995, pp. 480 ff.; Luhmann 1998, pp. 867, 1115.

535. Gripp-Hagelstange 1995, pp. 36 ff.

536. While Luhmann claims to observe the distinction between different levels within his own analysis (Luhmann 1998, pp. 79 ff., also with regard to two 'levels' of observation), he also believes the plethora of paradoxes he encounters 'cannot be resolved by Russell's and Tarski's distinction between levels' (p. 181; see p. 58). This rejection of the otherwise so frequently invoked 'distinction' renders impossible the existence of an 'environment', or of something that would constitute an outside vis-à-vis systems theory. This is, indeed, paradoxical, as Luhmann himself states that every system comes with an environment. Thus the only theory that cannot describe itself is Luhmann's systems theory. A similar immunisation can be attempted for Hegel, by saying that Hegel cannot be negated because he is the theorist of negation, such that every negation is already 'Hegelian'. But Hegel can, of course, be negated: he can be refuted, criticised, rejected or simply ignored. Luhmann's case is much the same.

an artificial and inappropriate 'operation'.[537] 'This scheme collapses... once one probes it more deeply'.[538]

The putative paradox of 'society' engaging in self-observation has as its specific prerequisite Luhmann's definitional, *a priori* exclusion of human beings (individuals, subjects, actors or whatever). It creates the impression that rather than persons thinking about their society, 'society' as such reflects upon itself.[539] It is only by means of this questionable operation that Luhmann can stake a claim to having overcome the paradoxes of the philosophy of consciousness. As Luhmann candidly indicates, the result that this 'new' thought claims to have achieved is the overcoming of the 'thought/being, cognition/object, subject/object distinction'.[540] This renewed bid for 'totality' echoes vitalism's social philosophy.[541]

Luhmann's systems theory speaks not of things, but of processes, takes itself to be above common sense logic, revolves around itself[542] and gets rid of bothersome opponents by relocating those phenomena whose existence cannot be denied to a deeper level, in a putatively 'radical' manner.[543] Even the basic principles 'life' and 'autopoiesis' are very closely related. And the differences in the construction of the narrative framework are quite minor:[544] the features of the whole are inferred, without any mediation,

---

537. This is one reason why Luhmann speaks of a 'world society' (Luhmann 1995, pp. 585 ff.; Luhmann 1998, pp. 145 ff.). He defines 'society' so erratically that the factual existence of several societies (English society, Spanish society, the Sociological Society, and so on) is spirited away into the hypothesis that at bottom 'there can be only one society' (Luhmann 1998, p. 156) – after all, there is only one concept of society (he believes that 'this analysis constrains [!] us to assume a single world social system': p. 78). In other words, Luhmann is not formulating a proposition about globalisation. What Luhmann means is the 'world picture' (p. 156), Dilthey's intellectual 'totality' within the thought of an individual.

538. Luhmann 1998, p. 27.

539. *MECW* 5, p. 481; 2.5.7.

540. Luhmann 1998, p. 32; see p. 867.

541. Luhmann's treatment of other sociologies – 'self-descriptions' (Luhmann 1998, pp. 866 ff.) he means to 'overcome' – is reminiscent of the way that, in Bloch, 'this entire,... apparently so very real world will itself one day just hang on the wall like the image of some innocuous memory' (Bloch 2000, p. 277). They have been neutralised as being 'long since obsolete'.

542. The only object that the hypothesis of self-referentiality fully applies to is German sociology itself. It is only German sociology that is constantly engaged with itself (Göbel 2000) – precisely because of the questions that systems theory raises. German sociology alone is the mythical '"self" of self-reference' (Luhmann 1995, p. 459; Luhmann 1985, p. 148). This could be one reason why so many sociologists (but hardly anyone else) find Luhmann's hypotheses plausible – they recognise themselves in them.

543. Luhmann attaches the attribute 'radical' to himself (Luhmann 1998, p. 35). According to Habermas 1987a (pp. 378 ff.), the subject philosophy rejected by Luhmann returns in full force on the level of the system; once more, Luhmann has simply submerged the problems, or rather raised them by one level of abstraction (2.4.6). Müller 1996 recognises that 'Parsons's original interest in the stability and reproductive conditions of modern capitalism has been translated into the generalised systems-theoretical question concerning the conditions of social order *tout court*' (p. 284). Thus Parsons already 'approached the issue too abstractly' (p. 285).

544. Instead of 'worldview' [*Weltanschauung*], Luhmann says 'world semantics' [*Weltsemantik*] (Luhmann 1998, p. 156), and, instead of 'dialectical method', he says 'second-order observation', although he does speak openly of 'sublation' [*Aufheben*] (Luhmann 1998, p. 93; see Wagner 1994).

from specific cases (one's own 'lived experience' in vitalism, radical constructivism in Luhmann), so that nothing but a 'worldview' [*Weltanschauung*] can result.[545] The elimination of 'Western' rationality allows those who know how to play this game to smuggle their value judgements past the usual criteria for assessing scientific propositions – and hence past 'critique', which Luhmann treats with derision.[546] In Luhmann, we find propositions that are as uncontrolled as those that Freyer, Lukács and Heidegger believed they could pass off, by means of their narrative frameworks, as serious science.[547]

Luhmann's political conservatism emerges from many of his theoretical statements; one example has already been discussed (2.4.6).[548] What Luhmann has to say about specific topics is, nevertheless, original and a testament to his literary erudition, as in the case of his popular 1982 book *Love as Passion*. He shares this seriousness, as a person within academic life, with Hegel. But the point about Luhmann is that he could just as well have said these things without his metanarrative.

2.5.7 Key elements of Marxian theory VI: Marx and Hegel

> *Object!* Horrible! There is nothing more damnable, more profane, more mass-like than an *object* – *à bas* the object![549]

The anti-Hegelian considerations in this chapter beg the question: Was Marx not himself a Hegelian, so that the critique of Hegel should be applied to him as well? Criticisms of Marx have, in fact, often been formulated as criticisms of Hegel, and many a defence of Marx has been understood to simultaneously constitute a defence of Hegel. I will begin

---

545. Weber already held that such a 'conversion of a discipline's 'world picture' into a worldview' (Weber 1922a, p. 401) was tantamount to 'philistinism' (p. 414). Habermas says of Luhmann's systems theory that it is 'like those metatheoretical projects that fill the function of world views' (Habermas 1987a, p. 384; 2.4.6).

546. Luhmann 1998, pp. 32, 36, and so on (see p. 1157). Here, too, Luhmann's claims derive their plausibility from real weaknesses of critical theory. But critical theory is not weak for the reasons cited by Luhmann (see 2.6.1–3).

547. 'The idealisations associated with the terminology of systems theory, and later with that of evolutionary theory, lead to a theory that is caught up in its own constructs and can assure itself of its link to reality only intuitively' (Müller 1996, p. 285). For this reason, Müller speaks of 'arbitrariness' with regard to the results of Luhmann's theory (p. 355); this judgement is all the more serious insofar as Müller is an expert on regular scientific systems theories, whose reputation Luhmann benefits from parasitically. For a classic account of how political judgements are translated into philosophy, see Bourdieu 1988. Sens 1979 draws an instructive parallel to dialectical materialism, which was able to justify any and every political judgement by its overly abstract, naturalist metatheory.

548. The rejection of every political intervention in the economy, practically implemented by Thatcher at the time, is especially striking, as is the implicit approval accorded to Helmut Kohl's 'spiritual and moral turnaround' [*geistig-moralische Wende*]; Kohl publicly advocated (family and other) 'values'. 'Unity consists in the fact that politics cannot solve the problems of the economy, just as science cannot solve those of politics or law those of the family' (Luhmann 1985, p. 150; on Luhmann's conservatism, see also Münch 1992, Wagner 1994, and Müller 1996, p. 349).

549. *MECW* 4, p. 21.

by describing Marx's stance on this issue (1), in order then to explore this stance with an eye to the history of theory (2).

Marx as a critic of Hegel

Marx owed valuable insights to Hegel, but they concerned scientific *practice* more than anything else. Thus the coherent mode of presentation proper to science is an achievement of Hegel, as is reflection on the historicity of categories. The mature Marx placed considerable stock in clarifying both a category's concrete referent and its conditions of development; he also wanted his book (or at least those parts of *Capital* that were published during his lifetime) to be something other than piecework or a motley smorgasbord of propositions, namely a work that makes factually existing relations theoretically recognisable *as* relations.[550] This can be *described* as 'Hegelian'.[551] But it simply amounts to the attempt to describe a given complex of relations as tangibly as possible. Making such an effort can hardly be interpreted as being dependent on Hegel. It is, rather, a question of style. No such effort is ever made in many publications by authors working within a particular science – nor does it have to be made, as the authors are addressing a specialist audience. But that audience should at least be able to understand the text.[552]

As soon as substantive issues were at stake, or even just the method by which Hegel arrived at his results, Marx ranked among Hegel's most severe critics – precisely because he understood him so well.[553] Marx begins criticising Hegel early on. Even during his most speculative phase, the one preceding *The German Ideology*, he criticises the critique of reification. For it was Hegel himself who 'annihilated' 'things' and the laws of common

---

550. Showing that interest and entrepreneurial profit have a common source, that is, surplus value, requires discussing the latter first. The categories 'profit' and 'surplus value' are situated on different levels of abstraction, although they can refer to the same phenomenon (just as different propositions can be applied to identical states of affairs). In order to illustrate the difference between the two, Marx begins by presenting what is more general (the 'law of value'); this then enables him to explain modifications that occur within what he has presented (such as the tendency toward the equalisation of rates of profit and the formation of a market price; see 2.1.6, 2.3.1, 2.3.5).

551. Henrich 1971, p. 192 perceives in this an 'unswerving adherence to Hegel's idea'; see Arthur 2002, Rockmore 2002.

552. Macrosociology stands in a parasitic relationship to this when it takes counterintuitiveness to be a *criterion* of scientificity (Halfmann 1996a, pp. 13 ff., 44 ff.). This leads to a situation in which sociological texts are no longer even understood by sociologists. In philosophy, choice of the mode of presentation is an especially precarious exercise, because philosophy's themes ('transcendental deduction', 'eliminative materialism', 'explanatory deficit', and so on) are far more dependent on the definitions given than those of other sciences. Here, too, something real constitutes the basis, but the process of mediation by which reference is made to the object is more protracted than where it is simply a matter of examining a certain thing (and be it the brain) to discover whether that thing displays certain features. The fact that many philosophies never bother to clarify the way they refer to their object is one of the reasons why there is talk about philosophy undergoing a crisis caused by its lack of comprehensibility.

553. *MECW* 4, pp. 57 ff.

sense by sublating them into absolute knowledge.[554] Behind this, there lies a certain way of thinking, to which Marx objects. Hegel is aware – and this is what makes him so attractive to the critics of positivism – that the things encountered in the world and the cognitive subject cannot be thought of as entirely unrelated; both are always already related to one another, and what relates them to one another is an activity, a *practice*. Marx appreciated this idea as much as pragmatism would later do.[555] But Hegel's idealism within the theory of knowledge was not adopted by Marx. This was not an immanent critique of Hegel, but an objection to his theological *premises*.[556] For this practice, whatever its character might be (whether it be the practice of 'knowing', as in Hegel, or a 'real, corporeal' praxis, as in Marx)[557] does not alter the mode of being of things. The practice exists, but the things also continue to exist ('[i]n the *actual world* these things' – the family, and so on – 'remain in existence'.[558] Yet Hegel sublates things;[559] reason strikes down common sense and sense perception.

This operation has two prerequisites: first, a way of thinking that links thought and being so closely together that a change in thoughts about thought must entail a change in thoughts about things (or in the 'mode of being' of things) – this is the method of sublation; second, the definition, also assumed from the outset, of man as a '*spiritual* being'[560] – this is the motive for sublation.[561] Because the mere 'presence' [*Vorhandenheit*) of things runs counter to Hegel's notion of what it is to be human, he considers

---

554. In the *Logic*, being becomes nothingness (as in mysticism, '[p]ure Being and pure Nothing are ... the same' (Hegel 1929, p. 95). Prior to this, 'consciousness has found "seeing" and "hearing", etc., pass away' (Hegel 1967, p. 180; 'the thing collapses': p. 174; see pp. 787 ff.). On the 'annihilation of the world', see Rohrmoser 1961, and Colletti 1977, p. 112.

555. Marx proclaimed that 'the *active* side was set forth ... by idealism' (*MECW* 5, p. 3).

556. *MECW* 4, pp. 84 ff.; *MECW* 5, pp. 41 ff. and elsewhere.

557. *MECW* 3, p. 336.

558. *MECW* 3, p. 340. 'And because thought imagines itself to be directly the other of itself, to be *sensuous reality* – and therefore takes its own action for *sensuous, real* action – this superseding in thought, which leaves its object in existence in the real world [!], believes that it has really overcome it' (p. 341). However: 'The real subject remains outside the mind an independent of it' (*MECW* 28, p. 38). 'This misunderstanding can only be corrected from outside' (Bubner 1990, p. 18).

559. Following Hegel's 'sublation', the object is nothing but 'the negative' (Hegel 1967, p. 787), 'spiritual reality' (p. 790) or even 'consciousness itself' (ibid.). Epistemological idealism notwithstanding, the term 'sublation' [*Aufhebung*] and its invocation by Hegelians lay claim to doing justice to the thinghood of things. But prior to all further operations, Hegel has already made a decision that makes just this impossible, despite his good intentions: he equates thought and being (that 'Being is Thought' is already posited by Hegel in the Preface: Hegel 1967, p. 113; see Hegel 1929, pp. 48 ff.). Hegel's talk of 'thinghood' being posited by means of the 'externalization of self-consciousness' is Fichtean (Hegel 1967, p. 789; see *MECW* 3, pp. 334 ff.). He provides no arguments in support of his claim; he simply assumes it to be true – and hence formulates it not in his investigation proper, but in the Preface. It is hardly possible to get to grips with this by means of arguments. Here, criticism is forced to come from outside – and the existence and character of this 'outside' is precisely what is at stake. This is the criterion of external consistency – the examination of whether or not he really apprehends his objects (see 4.1). 'Man must prove the truth ... of his thinking, in practice' (*MECW* 5, p. 3).

560. *MECW* 3, p. 334; *MECW* 24, pp. 537 ff.

561. 'Spirit is alone Reality' (Hegel 1967, p. 86; see Hegel 1929, p. 7).

'[*o*]*bjectivity* as such ... an *estranged* human relationship which does not correspond to the *essence of man*';[562] and this is why Hegel's philosophical efforts are directed at the '[r]eturn of the object into the self' and at 'incorporation into self-consciousness'.[563] Marx observes this in order to oppose to it a different notion of what it is to be human: man is not a spiritual but a natural being. It so happens that there are objects in nature; thus human practice is a natural and hence an objective practice.[564]

The practice by which man confronts things does not affect the mode of being of objects, even though it may alter their form, as in the case of labour.[565] For this reason, a thought that means to dissolve all things, in the spirit of the critique of reification, is vulnerable to Marx's critique – as even Lukács recognised.[566] Yet Marx was not a positivist. He did not think of things and of the categories he encounters as being simply given and altogether unrelated to human life.[567] Instead, he went further than any previous thinker in reflecting upon the practice that *actually* lies behind these things and these categories, examining it in its changeable, concrete historical constellation. But he was not an idealist either: his awareness of this practice – of the *genesis* – did not lead him to claim that the mode of being of things must be a different one, as claimed by Hegel and the vitalists, and it did not lead to him neutralising the validity of our knowledge about things.[568] Marx was a philosophically enlightened scientist, aware both of the fact that his concepts developed at a particular point in time and of the circumstances under

562. *MECW* 3, p. 333.

563. *MECW* 3, p. 334. According to Marx, Hegel strives to 'annul' objectivity, 'because it is [the objective character of the object] that is offensive and constitutes estrangement for self-consciousness. The object is therefore something negative, self-annulling – a *nullity*' (*MECW* 3, p. 338). This was vitalism's motive until Lukács.

564. One could call this Marx's anthropology. It is not a fully elaborated doctrine; it merely reproduces the notion of man that most people probably entertain since Darwin ('the common man': *MECW* 3, p. 25): man is a product of nature, he cannot overcome nature and he is constantly engaged with objects that he requires to eke out his existence, and which he puts to use, from the hand axe to the computer: he is a 'living, natural being equipped and endowed with objective (i.e., material) essential powers' (*MECW* 3, p. 335). There is 'nothing incomprehensible ... in this' (ibid.), even though man is also much more than this.

565. '[Man] can work only as Nature does, that is by changing the form of matter. Nay more, in this work of changing the form he is constantly helped by natural forces. We see, then, that labour is not the only source of material wealth, of use values produced by labour ... [L]abour is its father and the earth its mother' (*MECW* 35, p. 53). The reader will recall our discussion of the confusion surrounding 'form' in section 2.3.5.

566. Lukács 1971b. Marx criticises Hegel for not seeing that '*reappropriation ...* denotes not only the annulment of *estrangement*, but of *objectivity* as well' (*MECW* 3, pp. 333 ff.). (The older Lukács would later formulate the same criticism of the young Lukács.) The Hegelians adopt this misconception: 'Everything that is real and living is un-Critical, of a mass nature, and therefore 'nothing'; only the ideal, fantastic creatures of Critical Criticism are *"everything"*' (*MECW* 4, p. 19).

567. In fact, he criticises 'Hegel's *false* positivism' (*MECW* 3, p. 339): in providing a philosophically inflated account of what exists, Hegel accepts it as it is rather than questioning it.

568. Thus Lukács, speaking with the wisdom of old age, opined that when it is not grounded in reality, the concept of 'praxis' inevitably leads into renewed contemplation – one directed against theory as such (Lukács 1971b, pp. xviii ff.). This observation is correct, notwithstanding the fact that Lukács's own grounding, insofar as it is conceptual ('ontological'), remains 'philosophical'.

which they developed, but who did *not* therefore speculatively limit their validity or expressiveness.[569]

Thus Marx worked with two premises that differ from those of Hegel: man is not a purely spiritual, but also and in fact primarily a natural being, and thought and being are not one. This second premise is related to the first: if man were a 'spiritual' [*geistig*] being, then one would have to think of all his objects as being 'mind' [*Geist*], as in Hegel.[570] Then there would in fact be no distinction to be made between thought and being. But man is *not* a 'spiritual' being. Consequently, objects are something more than simply the act of thinking about them – after all, it is *man* who is 'posited' by *them*.[571] This, however, has implications for one's notion of what it means to know: in order to turn thoughts into true thoughts, thought has to begin by assuring itself of being. The *adaequatio intellectus et rei* is by no means guaranteed in advance, by virtue of some sort of identity.

Turning thoughts into true thoughts requires *intuition* – on this point, Marx is in complete agreement with Kant.[572] For this reason, Marx abandons idealist philosophy in favour of empirical science (and, *pace* Brudney,[573] this 'attempt' was successful). This is apparent even in the most speculative phase of Marx's development, during which he does not yet dispose of an approach of his own, but merely formulates abstract calls for its development.[574] Where philosophy does not open itself up to the world in this way, it becomes a closed system, 'total in itself', and one can only 'leap out of it' if one still wants to achieve genuine knowledge.[575] Historically, this is what happened to the *discipline* of philosophy. What this means for the interpretation of Marxian texts is that they contain no Hegelian 'concepts' from which something might be 'deduced' – neither 'the state', as suggested by the deductive Marxism of the 1970s, nor an 'ethics' of the sort that some are trying to construct even today.[576] Marx's theory is a scientific theory about objects

---

569. 'Labour seems to be a very simple category.... Nevertheless, considered economically in this simplicity, "labour" is just as modern a category as the relations which give rise to this simple abstraction' (*MECW* 28, p. 40). 'The example of labour strikingly demonstrates that even the most abstract categories, despite their being valid [!]... are... a product of historical conditions' (p. 42). For this reason, to grasp the historicity of this category is not yet to have formulated a 'critique of political economy', as German Marxists believed (Euchner 1972, Reichelt 2002; 2.3.5). The theoretical labour only begins after this propadeutic insight.

570. 'But what is "thing" in this case is self-consciousness': 1967, p. 369.

571. *MECW* 3, p. 335.

572. 'The abstract idea, which without mediation becomes *intuiting* [§ 244 of Hegel's *Encyclopaedia*], is indeed nothing else but abstract thinking that gives itself up and resolves on *intuition*', that is, 'to have a look at nature *free* of abstraction' (*MECW* 3, p. 344). On the proximity of the positions of Marx and Kant on this point, see Colletti 1976, pp. 113 ff.

573. Brudney 1998.

574. Critical theory seldom went beyond this gesture (see 2.6.1, 3.1.2).

575. 'The world confronting a philosophy total in itself is therefore a world torn apart. This philosophy's activity therefore also appears torn apart and contradictory' (*MECW* 1, p. 491). 'One has to "leave philosophy aside"... one has to leap out of it and devote oneself like an ordinary man to the study of actuality' (*MECW* 5, p. 236; *MECW* 3, pp. 180 ff.; 4.1).

576. The normativity inherent in the 'concept' of labour is sought by Gürtler 2001 and Krebs 2002 (see 3.1.2). This socio-theoretical approach still proceeds from notions of the individual *qua*

and structures that are quite real. It needs to be approached, first and foremost, via its *results*, not via its premises. If for no other reason, Marx was not a Hegelian because he was not a philosopher.

Aside from this very general Marxian critique of Hegel's *premises*,[577] which comes from outside,[578] we can also find more specific, immanent criticisms, and they, too, can already be discerned in the earliest period of Marx's theoretical activity. The identity that Hegel assumes – but never proves – allows him to stand states of affairs on their head. This is a 'dialectical' operation that Marx frequently objects to. He even presents it as the basic error of the Hegelian 'method': 'It is important that Hegel everywhere makes the idea the subject and turns the proper, the actual subject, such as 'political conviction', into a predicate. It is always on the side of the predicate, however, that development takes place'.[579] This is the *specific* meaning of Hegelian idealism as a narrative about 'ideas', which are made plausible to the reader by means of linguistic substitutions, and which are intended to establish continuity between the various elements of the doctrine. (They are, however, only plausible for as long as they are underpinned by a philosophy of identity that warrants this interchangeability.) First, the subject of the proposition, 'substance', is derived from the predicates – an exchange that occurs within the proposition. Then, the grammatical subject becomes the historical subject – a leap from thought into being.[580] Marx objects to these substitutions, evident in countless Hegelian formulations, because he starts from different premises.[581] He caricatures Hegel's substitutions as follows:

> First of all, an abstraction is made from a fact; then it is declared that the fact is based upon the abstraction. A very cheap method to produce the semblance of being profound and speculative in the German manner. For example: *Fact*: The cat eats the mouse. *Reflection*: Cat – nature, mouse – nature, consumption of mouse by cat = consumption

---

constitutive element, except that these notions are now intended to also encompass the 'concept of labour'. This, however, runs contrary to Marx's approach.

577. *MECW* 3, pp. 180 ff.

578. *MECW* 5, p. 236.

579. *MECW* 3, p. 11.

580. 'Hegel gives the predicates an independent existence and subsequently transforms them in a mystical fashion into their subjects . . . Hegel transforms the predicates, the objects, into independent entities, but divorced from their actual independence, their subject. Subsequently the actual subject appears as a result . . . Precisely because Hegel starts from the predicates of the general description instead of from the real *ens* (*hypokeimenon*, subject), and since, nevertheless, there has to be a bearer of these qualities, the mystical idea becomes this bearer' (*MECW* 3, p. 23).

581. Marx translates Hegel 1820 into plain language, thereby extracting the 'rational kernel' from the 'mystical shell' (*MECW* 35, p. 19): '"Necessity in ideality is the *development* of the idea within itself. As *subjective* substantiality it is *political conviction* [patriotism], as *objective* substantiality, in distinction therefrom, it is the *organism* of the state, the strictly *political* state and its *constitution*." . . . In plain language *political conviction* is the subjective and the *political constitution* the *objective substance* of the state' (*MECW* 3, p. 10).

> of nature by nature = self-consumption of nature. *Philosophic presentation of the fact*: Devouring of the mouse by the cat is based upon the self-consumption of nature.[582]

Hence Marx's idiosyncrasy of frequently reversing formulations: these formulations all refer to other things in his work than in Hegel, things that need, therefore, to be given new names.[583] The young Marx's twofold critique of Hegel – a critique of Hegel's premises, that being and thought are identical and that man is pure spirit; and a critique of Hegel's method, which stands relations on their head – can still be found in Marx's mature work. The difference is that it is no longer just a formal critique; rather, Marx is able to reject specific Hegelian propositions (for instance, on the state) on the basis of his own research. Nearly thirty years after the *Contribution to the Critique of Hegel's Philosophy of Law*,[584] he writes:

> My dialectic method is not only different from the Hegelian, but is its direct opposite. To Hegel, the life process of the human brain, i.e., the process of thinking, which, under the name of 'the Idea', he even transforms into an independent subject, is the demiurgos of the real world, and the real world is only the external, phenomenal form of 'the Idea'. With me, on the contrary, the ideal is nothing else than the material world reflected by the human mind, and translated into forms of thought.[585]

Here, too, the necessity of conducting empirical research, which results from the separation of thought and being, is palpable.[586] In the year 1857, midway between the two texts quoted, he formulated – for purposes of 'self-clarification',[587] as it were – a precise description of his method, which is also that of the classical economists (on this, see also section 2.3.2):

> The concrete is concrete because it is a synthesis of many determinations, thus a unity of the diverse. In thinking, it therefore appears as a process of summing-up, as a result, not as the starting point, although it is the real starting point, and thus also the starting point of perception and conception ... Hegel accordingly arrived at the illusion that the real was the result of thinking synthesising itself within itself, delving ever deeper into itself and moving by its inner motivation; actually, the method of advancing from the abstract to the concrete is simply the way in which thinking assimilates the concrete

582. *MECW* 5, p. 481.

583. The 'criticism of the weapon' is not identical with 'weapon of criticism' (*MECW* 3, p. 182). Or: 'Democracy is the truth of monarchy; monarchy is not the truth of democracy' (*MECW* 3, p. 29). What is important, in this, is the word '*not*'.

584. *MECW* 3, pp. 3–129, written in 1843.

585. *MECW* 35, p. 19; from the 1873 *Afterword* to the second German edition.

586. '[Inquiry] has to appropriate the material in detail, to analyse its different forms of development, to trace out their inner connexion. Only after this work is done, can the actual movement be adequately described' (*MECW* 35, p. 19).

587. *MECW* 29, p. 261.

> and reproduces it as a mental concrete. This is, however, by no means the process by which the concrete itself originates.[588]

After what has been said, Marx's frequent use of Kantian terms, directed against Hegel, comes as no surprise. It reveals Marx's profound understanding of philosophy.[589] Philosophy's role is limited, much as it later is in Wittgenstein, to warding off misunderstandings and ensuring the possibility of a 'perspicuous presentation'.[590] But these *remain* necessary undertakings, as our history of misunderstandings shows (see 4.2.3).

Another controversial question simply answers itself when one begins from Marx's premises, namely the question of whether there is a 'real dialectic' in Marx, and whether it is what constitutes the difference between him and Hegel's 'idealist' dialectic. As Colletti has shown, Hegel and the dialectical materialism of Engels and Leninism hardly differ in this respect, although Marx differs from *both* of them. For to eliminate the distinction between thought and being, as Hegel *and* Engels do, is to claim that in formulating theoretical definitions, one is at the same time saying something about reality – regardless of which of the two is considered primary (on Fichte and Nietzsche, see above, 2.5.2), or, to put this still more clearly: regardless of whether this 'dialectic' is called idealist or materialist. But when one follows Kant and all practical science in distinguishing between being and thought, theoretical propositions about reality need to be verified by comparison with reality, as their truth is not guaranteed beforehand.[591]

Relatively little follows from the method alone, aside from the odd heuristic indication. Making the method a criterion of truth can only be described as idealist: form engenders content. It is true Marx describes real phenomena as 'contradictions'. But this does not mean contradiction is 'the' principle of motion governing nature or society; it simply means that Marx thought it would be helpful to the reader to think of conflicts as contradictions. For instance, the 'contradiction between commodities and money'[592] is meant to describe something real (something it would seem *all* categories are supposed to do), but (following Tarski's dequotation axiom) it does not describe the contradiction between commodities and money, because 'commodities' and 'money' are abstract definitions that *nothing* corresponds to directly. They do not refer directly to things at all; they refer to states of affairs and regularities.

The same is true of the proposition 'Capital and labour contradict one another'. The proposition does not mean that there is a thing called 'labour' that stands in a real contradiction to a thing called 'capital' ('real pugnancy');[593] it means that real conflicts are

---

588. *MECW* 28, p. 38.
589. Colletti 1976, pp. 113 ff.
590. *Philosophical Investigations*, aphorism 122.
591. When it came to demonstrating 'empirical truth', Kant also referred to experience. This was precisely what irked Hegel. For him, observation of objective reality was 'merely subjective'. Marx meant to 're-adjust' this distorted view.
592. *MECW* 35, pp. 113 ff.
593. See Ruben 1975, Holz 1995.

better described when one considers not just wage disputes and street battles, but also the social and economic force fields that operate *behind* them. To do so is precisely not to engage in a 'metaphysics' that assumes the existence of ulterior things behind real things; it is to engage in self-reflexive science, which does *not* wrongly take its own categories to be the names of things.[594] The fact that Marx likes to refer, in his methodological digressions, to physical laws shows that he had a solid understanding of how regularity is expressed in the natural sciences (of its grammar, as Wittgenstein would say); it was in any case a more adequate understanding than that of his critics.

This does not mean that he subordinated himself slavishly to the 'methodological ideal' of the natural sciences, which is so unpopular with German thinkers; rather, he realised that the natural sciences had succeeded in explaining real phenomena by means of constructs that did not correspond to any real thing. For example, the natural sciences use 'forces' to describe the *behaviour* of things, as when the force of gravity is invoked to explain why the apple drops. The force of gravity does not 'describe' the dropping of the apple, for if that were the case, all apples would have to be dropping all the time. In the normal case, they remain peacefully attached to the tree. Thus the relationship between theory and empirical facts has to be a mediated one in physics as well. The science of physics simply liberated itself from the prejudices of dogmatic and metaphysical thought sooner than economics and 'social philosophy'. Within the latter, the 'critical' insight that something has been 'constructed' still invites the conclusion that it does not allow one to grasp anything real, or that *all* attempts to grasp reality are constructions, which is to blur the distinction between thought and being once more. While Hegel criticised the empiricism of wrongly taking words to be the names of things, he also went on to newly close the gap between thought and being, thereby *preventing* genuine knowledge of being.

Hegelian Marxism: semantic displacements

The follow-up question that arises is why Hegel was so popular for so long. The reason for this is a semantic *displacement*: in the 1960s, 'Hegel' and the 'dialectic' became one of

594. Steinvorth 1977 shows what the dialectic can mean as a 'method of presentation' (p. 47): it conceives of reality as something whose description requires several levels of presentation. Each time he wishes to effect the transition from one level to another, Marx construes a contradiction that is 'illusory' insofar as it has, in most cases, already been resolved. Thus commodities are normally exchanged without any trouble. Arndt has appositely pointed out that this contradiction is nevertheless 'real' and loses its illusory character in the crisis (Arndt 1985, pp. 246 ff.). And yet the crisis does not really involve single commodities and a sum of money 'contradicting' one another. Instead, the claim that they do so is a proposition situated in the specific context of an explanation of something real (considered in isolation, it would only be a 'metaphor' – but this word poses further problems, rather than explaining anything), something that would have to be called 'inflation' or 'commercial crisis' if one wanted to describe it empirically, and whose specific instances need to be considered in far greater detail. The word 'contradiction' is an explanatory formal indication: 'There is nothing mysterious in this' (*MECW* 35, p. 68).

the sites on which the proxy war against 'Marx' was waged, 'Marx' being shorthand for the student movement and the Frankfurt School, on the one hand, and Eastern Europe on the other.[595] This 'second Hegel renaissance' (as Riedel put it) was inaugurated by the foundation of two Hegel societies: the International Hegel Society [*Internationale Hegel-Gesellschaft*], which was founded in 1958, inclined toward Marxism and was soon dominated by East Germany, and the more conservative and Western-oriented International Hegel Association [*Internationale Hegel-Vereinigung*], founded in 1962. The affirmative references to Hegel evident in critical theory during the positivism dispute contributed to the term 'dialectic' becoming more symbolically charged. Kautsky[596] had already invoked the 'dialectic' against Bernstein, without being able to say what exactly he meant by the word, *aside from* the natural 'development' that Bernstein also postulated (2.1.4).[597]

Adorno's case was similar. Since the 1930s, he had rendered his analyses of a range of artworks 'thoroughly dialectical' – that is, imbued them with elements of a philosophy of history that was never more than hinted at. There was no way of discerning just what the 'dialectical' social theory invoked during the positivism dispute was actually supposed to look like – after all, it had not been formulated; the Frankfurt School, like others, had contented itself with *calling for* the development of such a theory (2.6.1).

The 'dialectic' was out of place in the positivism dispute insofar as critical theory's position was 'undialectical': Horkheimer's call for the 'right form of human coexistence' was not linked in any discernible way to concrete sociological research, and Adorno abstractly opposed the 'experiences of individuals' to science.[598] The insistence on the 'dialectic' was empty and formulaic; behind it there hid a late idealist thought that placed its hope in 'reason', as opposed to 'mere common sense', without being capable of explaining what exactly this entailed.[599] Adorno's 1966 book *Negative Dialectics*[600]

595. This link, which seems far-fetched when considered from an outsider's position but was obvious to those involved in the discussion, is confirmed not just by the Marxist Oskar Negt. Löwith, a conservative, also recognised that the 'new philosophical interest in Hegel' was 'not emerging within and from philosophy, but being forced upon it from outside (by Marx and Marxism)' (in *Frankfurter Allgemeine Zeitung*, 11 July 1970, quoted in Negt 1970, p. 10). Topitsch criticised the dialectic inherent in the materialist construction of history as a form of subreption, invoking Petrus Damiani (Topitsch 1975, p. 24) and Eduard von Hartmann (Topitsch 1967) in support of his argument. Kelsen 1948 and Merleau-Ponty 1974 also denied that the dialectic expressed anything in and of itself and noted that it was vulnerable to political instrumentalisation.

596. Kautsky 1976.

597. Kautsky 1976; see Bernstein 1961, pp. 46, 52 ff.: the dialectic as snare and pitfall.

598. In 1959, Horkheimer argued with König during the 14th German Conference of Sociologists [*Soziologentag*]; in 1961, Adorno argued with Karl Popper at a workshop held by the German Sociological Association in Tübingen; Habermas later engaged in a feud with Hans Albert (thus Wiggershaus 1994, p. 574; see Adorno 1976, Dahms 1994).

599. Willms 1969 suspected that this was the expression of a thoroughly 'bourgeois' thought that was concerned about personal liberties and wrongly took itself to be anti-bourgeois. A semi-Fichtean opposition of common sense [*Verstand*] and reason [*Vernunft*] was also posited in Theunissen 1976 and 1992. On the concept of 'reason' [*Vernunft*], see Steinvorth 2002a.

600. Adorno 2007.

offers no way out; it tends rather to obfuscate the admission of critical theory's inherent weaknesses, which had become evident in the positivism dispute, and which would really have required intellectual forthrightness.[601]

There resulted a bizarre constellation: Karl Popper, critical theory's antipode in the positivism dispute, expressed himself much more fully on Marx than the critical theorists, and acknowledged the importance of Marx's work more clearly than they did.[602] But since the token of the 'dialectic' had become one move in the (theoretico)political language game, the act of positioning oneself within two camps could be symbolically performed within it. There was the bourgeois camp, which interpreted the dialectic idealistically and opted for Hegel by declaring the dialectic to be a purely *philosophical* affair, and there was the Marxist camp, which advocated a 'materialist dialectic' that was taken to also apply to politics and the sciences. This coding accounts for the proliferation of publications featuring 'Hegel and Marx' in their title.[603] A special point of contention concerned the question of where the *young* Marx was to be situated: he could be invoked in anti-Marxist demonstrations that the real, namely the young Marx had been an idealist,[604] or to show that materialism had appropriated even Hegel,[605] or (an intermediate position) to advance Western Marxist efforts to rejuvenate an overly rigid party-political Marxism.[606]

What this served to conspicuously extend into theory was not so much a class struggle as an antagonism of systems. One of the two parties, the more thorough one, used Hegel for the purposes of short-term political altercation, by claiming he could not be brought up to date and treating him in a purely antiquarian manner.[607] The other side used Hegel to legitimate its current politics, but never confronted him historically or philosophically, contenting itself with frequently quoted formulaic statements on the 'dialectical method' that remained devoid of meaning.[608] If the bridgehead 'Hegel' could be shifted

---

601. See Wiggershaus 1994, pp. 564 ff. Perhaps this was what left some critics so embittered (Steinert 1989, Morgenstern 2001).

602. While the account of Hegel in Popper 1945 is reductive, the presentation of Marx is largely accurate. This is confirmed by the fact that Wellmer 1969, pp. 69 ff. described Marx as a positivist. Accusations of ignorance were often unfounded; Hans-Martin Schleyer knew as much about Marx as his kidnappers and assassins.

603. Thus Bekker 1940, Hommes 1953, Landgrebe 1957, Fetscher 1960, Apel 1973a, Barion 1963, Benner 1966, Hillmann 1966, Reichelt 1970, Riedel 1973, Kaminski 1978, Wolf 1979, Coster 1983; see Rohrmoser 1994, pp. 55 ff.

604. Thus Popitz 1953, Bockmühl 1961, Israel 1972; see also Habermas 1957, pp. 394 ff.

605. See Marcuse 1932 and 1941, Lukács 1942, Bloch 1962, Beyer 1970, Ley 1972.

606. For example, Korsch 1970, Marcuse 2005a, Sartre 1976 or Negt 1970.

607. See Heimsoeth, Gadamer, Riedel, Henrich and Pöggeler in Helferich 1979, p. 194.

608. Helferich 1979, pp. 192 ff. quotes from East-German standard works, according to which Hegel's dialectic is 'the greatest achievement of classical German philosophy' and 'one of the most important sources of dialectical materialism' (Buhr 1972, p. 243). 'Marx, Engels and Lenin directly adopted the dialectical method developed by Hegel, upended it and released the rational kernel from its mystical shell' (Fiedler 1974, p. 165). From then on, the dialectic was the 'science of the most general laws of development of nature, society and thought' (Buhr 1972, p. 239). While Helf-

in the direction of 'idealism' (which was not difficult to do, since Hegel himself had done just that), then one had already triumphed over the 'Marx' of Hegelian Marxism, as his references to Hegel could be shown to rest on a 'reductive' or misguided interpretation.[609] As for Marxist attempts to materialise Hegel, they tended to end either in acceptance of the naturalised form of the dialectic prescribed by Engels, Kautsky and Hegel[610] or in the above-mentioned *aporiai*, which could not be resolved, despite this being attempted for several decades.[611] Critical theory presented itself as an independent third party, comparable to the Eastern-European philosophers of the 'Praxis School', and, of course, there was a lively exchange with those philosophers.[612] But it failed to develop a distinct position; by invoking Hegel in support of the 'radical practice' it called for, it was prompted to intellectualise Marx in a way that led to the possibility of practice becoming ever more *remote*. Because critical theory mixed up Hegel with Marx, engagement with Hegel became just as academic as it was in the 'bourgeois' camp. Left-wing critical theory was distinguished from the 'bourgeois camp' only by its consistently interposed invocation of a vague 'emancipatory interest' – which thereby became, more than anything else, the index of a particular style.[613] Wanting to abandon philosophy in favour of practice, one

---

erich also refers to approaches within East-German scholarship that deserve credit, it is obvious the authorities were unwilling to tolerate the development of independent thought – one need think only of the fate of persons such as Wolfgang Harich, Robert Havemann or Peter Ruben (the latter worked explicitly on the dialectic; see Havemann 1964, Ruben 1975 and Ruben in Horstmann 1978, pp. 70 ff.). Helferich refers to the antithesis of a '"bringing to mind" that shies the exertion associated with detailed historical studies and a form of "historical research" that... is incapable of apprehending its subject matter in a genuinely philosophical manner'; he calls this antithesis 'crude', but adds that it is 'apposite' (Helferich 1979, p. 194, as discussed in a book review by Helmut Schneider, in *Hegelstudien*, 7/1972, p. 262).

609. Göhler 1980, Coster 1983. Efforts (e.g. in Gadamer und Pöggeler) to trace 'dialectics' back to the ancient meaning of the term (the 'art of conversation') often yielded the same result, even if that was not the intention. For a comprehensive discussion of Hegel's reception, see Beyer 1970, Henrich 1975, H. Fulda, in Horstmann 1978, pp. 34 ff.

610. In East Germany, this was virtually inevitable for institutional reasons (Kapferer 1990, Eichler 1996, Gerhardt 2001; 2.2.4).

611. Sartre 1976 was probably the most significant attempt to redefine the materialist dialectic, but he was as unable as others to mediate between his subjectivist point of departure and the political option. By invoking an anthropological 'deficit', his dialectic begins at too basic a level. Incidentally, authors as diverse as Hans Kelsen, Joseph Schumpeter and Rosa Luxemburg held that the dialectic is irrelevant to *Capital*.

612. Negt 1970, p. 9, calls critical theory a 'dialectic-revolutionary reception of Hegelian thought within Marxism's intellectual left opposition' as it developed after Korsch and Lukács; he distinguishes two other camps, that of 'bourgeois' thought and that of 'Soviet Marxism'. The 'philosophy of praxis' (Kołakowski 1960, Kosik 1976, Markovic 1968, Petrovic 1967 and 1971, Bloch 1970, Stojanovic 1970, Zivotic 1972, Flechtheim and Grasssi 1973, Schmidt 1988, Vranicki 1983) was less significant after the suppression of the Prague Spring; major personalities such as Agnes Heller went into exile.

613. The way out of Hegel's dilemma, the 'discrepancy between concept and reality', was taken to lead 'into description of how social reality ought to be arranged if it is to be rational' (Schnädelbach in Negt 1970, pp. 79 ff.). 'According to Marx, the only way out of this immanence of consciousness consists in the creation of social relations within which categories such as value are no longer dominant, and within which thought's very structure of abstraction has been transformed' (Krahl

remained bound up with philosophy, and the less willing one was to admit this dilemma, the more one lost control both of philosophy and of practice. This development finds its clearest expression in Adorno, who eventually described himself as a Left Hegelian.[614]

Marxist discussions about the dialectic were usually *defensive* in character; they were products of distress, even if this tended to be forgotten quite quickly.[615] With hindsight, it becomes clear. The futility of this can be observed in the fate of German 'deductive Marxism', which developed out of the student movement's engagement with Hegel. It traced itself back to Adorno and Sohn-Rethel and still counts some adherents today (see 2.3.5, 2.4.5). Marx's remarks on the twofold character of the commodity were read according to the model of Hegel's *Logic*, as the 'germ cell' of the entire theory.[616] This 'value-form analysis' was thought of as a toolkit by which to 'deduce' everything else:

> The form of the separation needs itself to be deduced from the determinate form of the worldly foundation, meaning the base. The same holds true... for the form of the political state, for morality, philosophy, theology, etc.... All forms are to be... deduced, in their determinateness, from the central, essential reversal.[617]

Here, the material grounding that Marx meant to provide for political activity is overcome ideally: the 'base' is claimed to dispose of a form that achieves itself in the *concept*. Thus it seemed that if one disposed of the concept, one was in a position to comprehend everything else. Such a view was already championed by Freyer.[618] Marx, however, was a sharp critic of such Hegelianism: 'If one finds in logical categories the substance of all things, one imagines one has found in the logical formula of movement the *absolute method*, which not only explains all things, but also implies the movement of things'.[619]

---

in Negt 1970, p. 150). 'At most, dialectics offers a perspective within which true domination is also sublated' (Theunissen in Horstmann 1978, p. 356).

614. Adorno 2007, pp. 144 ff.; Adorno 1976, p. 151; Wiggershaus 1994, pp. 570, 599; Rohrmoser 1970, pp. 30 ff.; Koenen 2001, p. 115; see 2.6.3. A fourth group consisted of those who rejected Hegel altogether; it included Marxists such as Althusser and Colletti as well as bourgeois theorists such as Topitsch 1967, W. Becker 1969, Kaltenbrunner 1970, Kiesewetter 1974.

615. Defensiveness was a feature of, among others, Kautsky's 1899 response to Bernstein, Lenin 1961 (following the collapse of the International), Lukács 1971 (following the defeated revolts of 1920) and Adorno in the positivism dispute (Anderson 1976, pp. 42 ff.).

616. Lenin had already discovered a link between Hegel's *Logic* and the method employed by Marx in *Capital* (*LW* 38, p. 180; Helferich 1979, pp. 129, 172). The question concerning the influence of Hegel's *Logic* on Marx's method was then explicitly debated in the 1970s: conflicting interpretations of the first chapter of *Capital* were formulated (Zeleny 1968, Krahl 1970, Euchner 1972, Haug 1974; for 'value-form analysis' in the narrow sense, see Reichelt 1970, 1974, Sohn-Rethel 1978, Müller 1981, Behrens 1993, Backhaus 1997, Heinrich 2001; for critical views, see K. Holz 1993 and Hafner 1993). Kallscheuer 1991, p. 51, sees the will to formulate a system as the reason for the left-wing dogmatism of the 1970s. Maihofer 1992, p. 177, calls this 'idealism'. Marx described the commodity as the 'cell form' of capitalism because it was its smallest unit (*MECW* 35, p. 8), but not in order to 'deduce' anything from it.

617. Reichelt 1974, p. 33.

618. Freyer 1923.

619. *MECW* 6, p. 164.

Thus the school of 'value-form analysis' has more in common with German idealism and social philosophy than with Marx, as the following quotations also show: 'The absolute... develops as capital'; 'value is the absolute'.[620] 'In Hegel, men are puppets.... The existence of a metaphysical consciousness superordinate to man is... capital..., the actual phenomenology of mind..., real metaphysics'.[621]

In this experimental chain of thetic positings, Krahl mixes up concepts from the various traditions of German idealism and from Marxism, without even having adequately developed these concepts.[622] Their amalgamation hardly makes this any better. Similarly, Reichelt[623] follows Fichte's idea of a basic philosophical 'science of knowledge' rather than Marx, for in his view, 'materialist science' aspires to nothing less than

> not juxtaposing itself indifferently to other sciences and philosophy, but rather... obtaining its particular quality through its engagement with the sciences as they separate out into a system that displays its own division of labour, or more precisely, by criticising not just the content of the sciences, but also their form.

The Fichtean notion that form determines content is at work here; it allows Reichelt to assume that 'bourgeois science' and philosophy ('Its content is pre-determined')[624] can be criticised from the point of view of this lofty *self-cognition*, without any need for an immanent engagement with the objects of criticism. This is the very assumption we also find in vitalism (2.5.2, 2.5.5). Here, too, validity is denied on the basis of nothing but putative knowledge about the genesis: 'As philosophy, it is determined both in its form and in its content [!] by the reversal – unperceived by the theorist – of the bourgeois form of reproduction, i.e. of its own material presupposition, into a natural form'.[625]

H.G. Backhaus also means to *deduce* 'why essence assumes this particular phenomenal form, rather than another';[626] he takes essence to be a 'historical category'. German idealism and vitalism failed because they were overly ambitious, and value-form analysis was likewise unable to achieve its goal: it asked too much of philosophy as much as it neglected science.[627] Yet, instead of attributing its failure to its own flawed appraoch, it blamed *Marx*.

---

620. Krahl 1970, p. 142.

621. Krahl 1970, p. 140.

622. In Hegel, men are not puppets: the metaphorical 'world spirit' asserts itself by means of their freedom. Marx's concepts are also employed incorrectly: 'Capital is the concept of the commodity as it develops within time. Time becomes the concept of the absolute, time becomes money' (Krahl 1970, p. 140). If this were true, then: capital = (commodity + time) = money. But what Marx had in mind is better expressed as: capital = (commodity + money) over time.

623. Reichelt 1974, pp. 35 ff.

624. Richelt 1974, p. 36.

625. Reichelt 1974, p. 36.

626. Backhaus 1970, p. 132. See below, section 2.3.5

627. During the German *Soziologentag*, Popper made reference to neoclassical political economy. Adorno responded in purely philosophical terms (Adorno 1976; see Habermas 1963c).

This amounted to a twofold misinterpretation of Marx. One began by noting that Marx 'in no way diposed of an adequate awareness of his own manner of proceeding'[628] and that his way of expressing himself had been 'utterly misleading'.[629] But what this was really about was the fact that Marx's manner of proceeding did *not* amount to the alleged deduction of the entire culture from the 'concept of value' and its historically specific form.[630] When 'reconstruction' of Marx's theory failed to lead to the desired hyper-deduction, one began to 'doubt the sustainability of the foundations'[631] – meaning not the foundations of *one's own* approach, but those of Marx's theory.[632] Later offshoots of this family of theories went on to reinterpret their own failure as a 'disappearance' of the *objects* examined, or of revolutionary theory,[633] use value[634] and even society 'as such'.[635] A theory that fails to grasp its objects ends up declaring them non-existent (2.4.5). Thus the philosophically overloaded *Hegelianisation* of Marxism prepared the way for the transition to postmodern fatalism.[636]

In this chapter on older variants of normative German social philosophy, I aimed to show that, on the level of content, there was a dependence on the proto-philosophical processing of the subject matter within the disciplines examined earlier. The economy was inadequately defined as a techno-automatic system, and its implications for the social world were relegated to a *separate* 'normative' realm, which – it was supposed – might be capable of 'guiding' the economy. Now, the field of social philosophy has a grammar of its own, which we examined in section 2.5.2, by means of a genealogy of

628. Reichelt 1970, p. 75.
629. Negt in Euchner 1972, p. 32; see p. 43.
630. Marx's theory cannot satisfy the expectation of allowing political strategies or a total explanation of the world to be 'deduced' from it, since the non-deducibility of concrete reality, the intelligible (but not exclusively intelligble) freedom of man and the open character of history constitute its philosophical core (Fleischer 1973).
631. Backhaus 1978, p. 28.
632. Backhaus 1978, pp. 23, 32, 81. A similar projection occurs in Althusser, who began by noting that Marx 'lacked an adequate concept with which to think what he produced' (Althusser and Balibar 1997, p. 29;. Kittsteiner 1980, p. 21) and then, following his personal failure, let it be understood that Marx did not really matter to him (Althusser 1992, pp. 205–26).
633. Breuer 1977.
634. Pohrt 1976.
635. Breuer 1992.
636. The conclusion was essentially that there can be no revolution without use value, and no critique without revolution. In France, the philosophical 'reconstruction' of Marxism (not Hegelian but structuralist) also paved the way, via its predictable failure, for postmodernism. Postmodernism is at once *the result and the heir* of the futile attempt to intellectualise Marxism as a deductive science. Ironically, the Hegelianisation and the structural semiotisation of Marxism survived their object by years. On postmodernism's Marxist roots, see Ryan 1982, Meistner 1990, Barrett 1991, Marsden n.d., Callari 1995 and the rather cryptic jour-fixe 1999. Postmodernism's Marxist roots are apparent in Debord 1968, Baudrillard 1993, Deleuze and Guattari 2009, Castoriadis 1998, Foucault 1991. The desire to wind one's way out of Marxism is already evident in postmodernism's precursor, the 'new philosophers' (Schiwy 1970, Glucksmann 1976). Derrida then effected a *post hoc* 'spiritualisation' of Marx (Derrida 1994, p. 142; Henning 2005c).

German idealism (in the broad sense). We have seen that one legacy of the philosophy of identity as it has developed from Fichte to Luhmann consists in the tendency to draw virtually no distinction between theories and reality. This allowed for the intepretation of the results of theoretical history as *representations* of real history, even when those results tended rather to be due to deficits immanent to theory. The response to the philosophised diagnosis found in Eucken and Heidegger consists in a remedy that has also been philosophised: Eucken und Heidegger called for a different kind of *thought* – one that was ethicised and thereby undermined the very distinctions that are indispensable to a critique of political economy in the Marxian sense, but also to the proper functioning of a normal science such as physics.

A similarly idealist irrationalism could also be seen in the work of the Marxist Lukács, and in that of the post-Marxist Luhmann. This idealism makes the critique of Marx's reception history a challenging task, as the deviations from Marx appear in a form that is philosophical and impalpable. The present chapter was able to remedy this situation by tracing the method of mentalisation back to its German idealist background, thereby exposing the underlying contentual distortions. These distortions can often be traced back to contexts of debate examined in earlier chapters.

2.6 Critical theory or the dissolution of critique in religion

Before we discuss the consequences of German theoretical Marxism's final implosion (Chapter Three), we need to consider the most abstract of all receptions of Marx – the theological one, to which critical theory also belongs. In an irony of history, it was Marx's theologisation that preserved the memory of him over and beyond the rupture. Theology's remoteness from social reality proved to be to its advantage. Another factor contributing to theology's importance is its ability to arrest speculative thinking. The purpose of theology is not to construct theoretical systems but to allow man to enter into an appropriate relationship to God and the world. This relationship cannot itself be a theoretical one. Where speculative social philosophy gets lost in hopeless theoretical elaborations, consideration of theology can prove helpful. In a sense, everything here is very simple. Moreover, theology keeps open the road to straightforward, charitable action, whose effects can prove such a blessing – even for social philosophy. This is another reason why theology merits special consideration, here.

> It seems to me to be no exaggeration to say that there are greater intellectual affinities to be discerned between Aquinas and Marx than between Marx and Adorno.[1]

As shown by the plethora of receptions of Marx already discussed, it had become virtually impossible to engage scientifically with Marx's work within a single discipline. To remedy this situation, in 1923, an 'Institute for Marxism' [*Institut für Marxismus*] was founded.[2] Conceived during the revolutionary troubles that followed the end of the First World War, it was intended to prepare people for socialism intellectually, by means of engagement with Marx's theories. Formally, it lived up to this mandate: 'critical theory' and 'Marxism' remained virtually synonymous until the period of late Marxism,[3] up until the late 1970s. Hence the Institute played a decisive role in the reception of Marx within the German-speaking world. Marx has, however, been largely disavowed by its present heirs (3.1). Between critical theory's emphatically Marxist beginnings and today's residual stages, there lies a period characterised by the ongoing enfeeblement of the truly critical theories of Marx and Kant. This volatilisation was taken so far that its former proud claims to be the guardian of reason needed, in the end, to be disguised as religion: when one still encountered them, now only in a nebulous form, neither theoretically nor practically tangible – like religion.

How are we to account for this transformation of an 'Institute for Marxism'? Is this reference to religion justified, or does invoking religion not for its own sake, but as a stopgap, not amount to renouncing religious reason as well? Here, it is a question of examining the reasons behind the successive abandonment of Marx. No one denies that

1. Hösle 1990, p. 63.
2. This was the purpose of the Frankfurt Institute as intended by its founder Felix Weil, approved by the ministry and defended by its director Grünberg (Wiggershaus 1994, p. 19).
3. Jameson 1990.

Marx was in fact abandoned; this development is usually explained in terms of the general history of the period: proletarian defeat (coinciding with the accession to office of the Institute's new director), the perversion of communism by Stalin, and of all civilisation by Hitler, seemed to have rendered the retention of Marxism impossible. But to point this out is not to *explain* the transformation; it is merely to reiterate the Institute's self-interpretation, which is precisely what is in question. Are there not reasons for the successive dissolution of Marxism within critical theory (and beyond)[4] that are immanent to theory? In what follows, the reasons for its dissociation from the very Marxism that had initially been advocated so vociferously will be exposed by reference to three central representatives of critical theory (2.6.1–2.6.3). It will be seen that their affinity for theology needs to be seen more as a loss than as a gain. This will lead us to consider theology itself and its relationship to Marx's thought (2.4.4–2.4.6), which turns out to be far more complex than one might expect.

2.6.1 *Horkheimer's vitalism*

> [I]t would not be enough to unite the special sciences mechanically; they would have to be transformed inwardly by an inwardly synthesising philosophical method.[5]

Carl Grünberg, the first director of the Institute, took office in 1924; the Institute's founder Felix Weil appointed him because he was both a renowned scientist and an avowed Marxist. He did not develop meta-models to deal with Marxist theory but straightforwardly applied that theory itself, by empirically documenting the history of the labour movement and socialism. To be sure, within the academic landscape of the day, this sort of activity was as unusual as it was unpopular. The Institute was, however, able to exist in this form for several years, thanks to the open-mindedness of the Social-Democratic Prussian authorities and the notable scientific results it achieved.[6] While the Institute's members did not engage directly in political activity, many of them were communists, and the Institute collaborated with the Marx-Engels Institute in Moscow.[7] The Institute's profile changed markedly under its second director, who took office in 1930. It now no longer aimed to empirically investigate the present and the recent past from a Marxist perspective; instead, it aspired to a general theory of society, to be formulated through the interdisciplinary work of scholars from a range of social sciences, and by means of the philosophical elucidation and coordination of that work.

At first, this was little more than a lofty goal.[8] In fact, philosophical 'guidance' not only obstructed the envisaged interdisciplinary research, but also increasingly rendered

---

4. See Albrecht 1999

5. Lukács 1971, p. 109.

6. See *Grünbergs Archiv* (1910–30). Korsch 1970 was published by Grünberg, where he and Lukács lectured (Reijen 1990).

7. See Strelewicz in Papcke 1986, pp. 150 ff.; see also Wiggershaus 1994, pp. 14 ff.

8. Horkheimer 1989a. The programme of conducting interdisciplinary social research was implemented by Neumann and Kirchheimer rather than by the 'inner circle' (Schäfer 1994, p. 65).

it impossible. I do not mean to recount the entire history of the Institute one more time,[9] but only to describe one consistently problematic feature of that history (and its consequences): Marxian theory was further philosophised. Several of the misreadings of Marx discussed thus far entered into the new understanding of Marx, which had now become a *philosophical* one. Due to the 'primacy of philosophy', the claims associated with these misreadings were given the status of principles, making it almost impossible to discern the concrete occasions for formulating them. Ultimately, the only form of reason this new understanding of Marx allowed for was a theologised one – an atrophied stage of reason.[10]

The paradoxical combination of interdisciplinary research and philosophical guidance made itself felt in the scholarly policies and habits of the Institute: most of the new members associated with Horkheimer had been trained as philosophers. Horkheimer himself had just habilitated himself in philosophy,[11] and Adorno and Marcuse had at least attempted to do the same, although their professors had failed them.[12] Erich Fromm and Leo Löwenthal practised a type of humanistic psychology, as well as literary studies. Grünberg's long-standing associates Pollock and Grossmann (and Mandelbaum, although the link was less direct in his case) were the only remaining professional economists. The ratio of the guides to the guided was itself revealing. On the institutional level, the primacy of philosophy was ensured by the 'dictatorship of the director'.[13] Yet the Institute did not participate in the forms of interdisciplinary collaboration that already existed at Frankfurt University.[14] Thus its ambitious interdisciplinary programme was a pithy slogan rather than a genuine practice.

At no point in the Institute's history was there some fall from grace that compelled these developments through outside pressure; rather, the constellation described was

---

9. There is no lack of such historical accounts; see, inter alia, Jay 1996, Dubiel 1978, Honneth 1991, Gmünder 1985, Benhabib 1986, Sahmel 1988, Wiggershaus 1994, Reijen 1990, Bolte 1994, Kraushaar 1998, Albrecht 1999, Claussen 1999, Demirovic 1999 and How 2003.

10. It was already well developed conceptually before it was resorted to as a theoretical lifebelt – by indirect fathers of the Institute such as Bloch, Kracauer or Tillich and by Löwenthal 1990 and Fromm 1989 (see Thier and Delektat 1954, Habermas 1957, pp. 416 ff.).

11. Horkheimer's advisor, the epistemologist Hans Cornelius, already held that only thinking could provide salvation from the misery of the epoch (Wiggershaus 1994, p. 59; see the self-characterisation in Schwarz 1931).

12. Marcuse was failed by Heidegger, presumably for political reasons (Wiggershaus 1994, p. 104); Adorno 1973 was failed by Hans Cornelius, like Benjamin and Löwenthal (Dahms 1994, p. 23). Cornelius seems to have seen through Adorno's overly strategic theoretical alignment with Cornelius's own positions (Wiggershaus 1994, p. 82). Adorno eventually obtained his habilitation from Tillich, in 1931 (Wiggershaus 1994, p. 91).

13. Horkheimer meant to 'institute...a dictatorship of planned labour over social science's juxtaposition of philosophical construction with empiricism' (Horkheimer 1989a, p. 42/*GS* 3, p. 31). The term 'dictatorship' had positive connotations, just as in Lenin (Wiggershaus 1994, pp. 38, 161, 266).

14. With the exception of Tillich, to whom the Frankfurt theorists owed much, no collaborators were to be found, despite the fact that progressive thinkers such as Adolph Löwe, Carl Mennicke, Karl Mannheim, Hugo Sinzheimer, Martin Buber (with whom only Fromm was in contact) and Hendrik de Man lectured at the university (Wiggershaus 1994, pp. 109–10).

evident from the beginning of Horkheimer's directorship. This emerges from the first issue of the Institute's journal, *Zeitschrift für Sozialforschung* (ZfS). Apart from articles by unaffiliated authors such as Grossmann and Borkenau, the volumes published in 1932 contain mainly calls for the application of Marxism within individual disciplines such as economics, psychology, music, literary studies and philosophy. In the articles by Pollock, Löwenthal, Fromm, Adorno and Horkheimer, one is struck by an imbalance between their Marxist trappings – all authors called unanimously for an unleashing of the repressed 'productive forces' – and the way they otherwise dealt with their material. These two features coexisted 'in an astonishingly unmediated way'.[15]

Not only did the philosophical *interventions* in the material examined remain extraneous to it; they also led to a distortion of the Marxism imputed to them. The unmediated introduction of Marxist categories (such as 'forces of production' or 'breaking the chains') into discussion of cultural phenomena caused those categories to lose their closely circumscribed meaning. They became abstract philosophemes with unclear referents, that is, 'social philosophy' – and this was in fact Horkheimer's stated goal.[16] Even during this early period of critical theory, prior to emigration (and Auschwitz), when certified economists and legal experts were still on the boat and ties to the university had not yet been severed, there developed a type of theory typical of 'Western Marxism'. It is characterised by the view, evident throughout the Institute's convoluted history,[17] that a philosophy that takes its keywords from Marxism is thereby authorised to intervene in and coordinate the social sciences. This is the secondary meaning of 'intervening thought':[18] the phrase stakes a claim to dictating the relationship between scientific disciplines.

15. Dubiel 1978, p. 126. In Wiggershaus 1994's polemical formulation, pp. 119 ff., Pollock 1975 and 1975a 'did not make the slightest attempt' to substantiate his hypothesis that the anarchy of production renders a socialist planned economy necessary. Fromm 1932's hypothesis that capitalism causes the forces of the libido to rise up against it in the course of time 'remained an ungrounded, dogmatic assertion'. Horkheimer 1989a called for a liberation of theory from the strictures of class, but his references to the radical changes in theory's real conditions that this required remained a 'stereotyped accompaniment' (Wiggershaus 1994, p. 121), since they were never examined by him. Löwenthal 1932 increasingly inclined towards Lenin's theory of reflection, without examining real developments within society or relating them to the literature on the subject. Adorno 1984 displayed a 'lack of concern' for the real tendencies of the social transformation he called for; he transposed Marxism directly into music (asserting, for example, that Schönberg's music is 'virtually irreconcilable with the present constitution of society': Wiggershaus 1994, pp. 121–2. Adorno even adopted the communist doctrine of 'monopoly capitalism' as the string puller of 'fascism'). Adorno 'did not attempt to analyse any concrete sociological mediations between music and society' and couched aesthetic judgements in Marxist formulations (Wiggershaus 1994, p. 91; for a milder judgement, see Jay 1996, pp. 22 ff.).

16. Horkheimer 1989a.

17. Benhabib 1986, pp. 149–50 distinguishes three phases (1932–7, 1937–40, 1940–5) and argues that the transitions between them occurred for political reasons (cf. Dubiel 1978, Söllner 1979, Bonß 1982).

18. Adorno 1963a; Kneist 2001.

It was this ostentatiously Marxist theory of culture that caught on, rather than the results of the actual interdisciplinary research.[19] Nor did this constellation change in the course of later projects, those developed during the period of emigration.[20] In the end, it was surrendered altogether, in favour of an *exclusively* philosophical cultural criticism.[21] But what was the underlying conception of philosophy? The call, formulated within the homogeneous theory of the Institute's closest associates, for abolishing the capitalist subjugation of various entities described as 'forces of production' (science, character, music, literature) aims at a liberation of the soul from overly constricted forms – that is, its background is essentially vitalist. Vitalism had lacked a clearly defined opponent.[22] 'Monopoly capitalism' now seemed to fully meet the conditions for serving as such an opponent. In this, one is struck by the affinities with Lenin (see 2.2.6), even if his name was not mentioned; such affinities are far from incompatible with a vitalist interpretation of Marxism.[23]

The vitalist background of the later works, and in particular of *Dialectic of Enlightenment*, has often been noted.[24] Yet this vitalist background goes back further. The vitalist

---

19. There were some results, some of them presented in model form (Horkheimer 1936, Adorno 1950). Honneth 1991, however, points out that grievous 'socio-theoretical deficits' were already in evidence then. There was a Marxist flavour to the parenthetic, abstractly formulated calls for a 'rational society' and a theory adequate to it, to the formal discussion of the features such a theory ought to display (Horkheimer 1972c; cf. Adorno 1963a) and to the claim to be such a theorist oneself (Adorno 1977, pp. 131–2). Perhaps the self-assessment that one was 'bourgeois' (Schäfer 1994, pp. 37 f.; cf. Willms 1969) was more apposite. Korsch and Lukács, the forefathers of German critical theory, were still involved in politics. Their writings actually had practical relevance (P. Anderson 1976).

20. See Wiggershaus 1994, p. 151 (on Horkheimer 1936), p. 176 (on the failure to publish Fromm's 1938 study on white-collar workers and Wittvogel's study on China), pp. 223 ff. (on the refusal to collaborate with the political scientists Neumann and Kirchheimer) and elsewhere. Wiggershaus 1994, Schäfer 1994 and Dahms 1994 lament the fact that theory and empiricism remained unconnected.

21. This was the case, at the very latest, once the hypotheses on the 'culture industry' were formulated (Adorno and Horkheimer 1997, pp. 120 ff.); cf. Horkheimer's statement that contemporary post-bourgeois culture reduces itself to 'an auxiliary of production' (1987a, p. 107/*GS* 7, p. 101). By their elitist prejudice against popular modernity, Horkheimer and Adorno perpetuated their upper-class background; the same is true, incidentally, of Günther Anders (Steinert 1993).

22. Bergson, Heidegger and many others viewed the 'mechanist world picture' as a fundamental evil, although they had little to say about its origins (cf. the various remedies proposed in Simmel 1978, Weber 2003, Rathenau 1913, Groethuysen 1927, L. Klages 1929, Husserl 1970, Horkheimer 1985b). Jay 1996 (pp. 29 ff.) describes vitalism's influence on Horkheimer. In Paris, the Institute was directly sponsored by Bergson.

23. Horkheimer engages in the identification of class positions (Horkheimer 1972c, p. 11); he speaks of the 'opposition between materialism and idealism' (p. 13), criticises Lenin's 1908 opponents (Mach: p. 36) and cites transformation as the ultimate goal (p. 46; cf. the references to Lenin's 'dictatorship' and to 'monopoly capitalism' in Horkheimer and Adorno: see Wiggershaus 1994, pp. 39, 161, 122, 266 and 269). Both Lenin and vitalism effected an overhasty rapprochement of thought and being, theory and practice, thereby undermining not just Marx's theory, but also the rationality of reason (Colletti 1973; see 2.2.4, 2.5.4).

24. Jay 1984, Rentsch 2000, p. 266; see below. One source of this development resides in the very term 'social philosophy' (see Röttgers 1995).

frame of reference is evident, for example, in an instance of Horkheimer criticising someone else as vitalist: his critique of Karl Mannheim's *Ideology and Utopia* (first published in 1929). Horkheimer's critique of Mannheim never engages concretely with the issues; he simply discredits Mannheim's approach as 'idealist'.[25] Horkheimer accuses him of abandoning a militant standpoint in favour of a metaphysical one.[26] But this does not do justice to Mannheim's posing of the question. Mannheim had noted that Horkheimer's partisanship could no longer be straightforwardly advocated within theory, without becoming ideological – since the very 'reality' that Horkheimer invoked had become controversial, and this had occurred in virtually *all of* the social sciences.[27] Horkheimer refuses to confront this problem. He believes that, unlike Mannheim, and as a philosopher, he is associated with a practice, so that he can claim that his is a theory of positive 'science and practice', even as he accuses Mannheim's theory of remaining purely philosophical.

In doing so, Horkheimer is himself drawing on Dilthey's marginalisation of theory as the expression of a practice (see section 2.5.4, on Korsch). But what 'practice' does he have in mind? Horkheimer was not affiliated with any political party. Nor was he otherwise politically active, and he did not work empirically within any specific scientific discipline either. The only conceivable explanation for his claim was that he thought of his theorising as also constituting a *really* liberating practice. But he could only do so by thinking of real problems as problems to be solved primarily by means of theory. Such an approach is only possible within a vitalist framework, but not within Marxism. Theory is declared to be practice and practice is understood as theoretical practice.[28] (But this could just as well have held true for Mannheim.)

---

25. Horkheimer 1993, pp. 136, 139, 144. Only his criticism of Dilthey, whom he suspects of being behind everything (p. 135), is on the mark. He dwells on concepts used by Mannheim ('humanisation'), which, however, stood in no relation to the intention of Mannheim's inquiry. Mannheim was more interested in a dialogue between the two camps, whose feud was growing ever harsher (p. 145). Mannheim knew perfectly well that history is 'not the effect of struggles between mere attitudes' (p. 139). Even when the later Horkheimer *himself* inclined towards the religious position here attributed to Mannheim (pp. 137, 140–1), he did not retract his harsh judgement on him (see Tae-Kook 1984).

26. Horkheimer 1993, pp. 147–8.

27. References to reality had become mere set phrases. What Carl Schmitt, for example, 'passes off as objective reality is... a partisan construct of 'reality' determined by subjective preliminary decisions, and thus... a scientific myth' (Groh 1998, p. 251; cf. Mannheim 1936, p. 226; section 2.5.4; on the parallel in physics, see K. Fischer 1998). This being the situation, it was no use engaging in self-adulation by stressing one's 'materialism': the simplistic writings that presented themselves as 'scientific socialism' and the declarations that Marxism is a worldview (Kautsky) or an 'ideology' (Gramsci and Lenin) (Eagleton 1991, pp. 89–90, 117–18) had diminished Marxism's scientific value. This was hardly Mannheim's fault (Horkheimer 1993, pp. 144–5). In any case, and in spite of his declarations (p. 148), Horkheimer contributed little to the empirical illumination of reality himself.

28. 'Thought itself is already a sign of resistance' (Horkheimer 1982, p. 116) – a 'practice *in abstracto*' (*MECW* 4, p. 40), as in Althusser. Adorno held that '[t]oday, practice... has made great inroads into theory' (Adorno 1963, p. 4; see Rohrmoser 1970, p. 46).

This conceptual approach has a vanishing point that clearly reveals its vitalist character: where theory is conducted *for its own sake*, Horkheimer recognises it neither politically nor scientifically. This does not put him in the company of Marx, as he seems to have hoped, since Marx did not regard the crisis as one of thought. It puts him, unexpectedly, in the company of vitalism, for it was not until vitalism that the crisis was conceptualised as extending into thought (2.5.1). What Horkheimer accused Mannheim of – remaining on a purely theoretical level, not taking real struggles into account, proximity to vitalism – also applied to himself, and in fact more so.[29] Horkheimer also remained within theory; he never arrived at a 'practice' himself. The difference was simply that Mannheim was quite aware of this (after all, he was concerned with knowledge),[30] whereas Horkheimer, in suggesting that theory is closely bound up with practice, effected a reduction of theory's peculiarity. If there was something in this that amounted to the 'expression' of a certain 'worldview', then it was this social philosophy, but not 'theory' as such. The only link between theory and practice to be found, here, is Horkheimer's decisionist abandonment of *both*. Just a few years later, Horkheimer would himself advocate the very insistence on philosophy of which he had previously accused Mannheim.[31] He also ended up rejecting Marx altogether.[32] In doing so, he made his vitalist beginnings, to which he had always remained faithful, explicit.[33] The possibility of a scientific critique of society was largely eliminated. The Marxist frame of reference that Horkheimer employed to criticise Mannheim was clearly no more than a superficial feature of his own thought.

2.6.2 *Pollock's hermetic analysis of state capitalism*

The state regulated the economy[34]

What needs to be problematised next, aside from the general type of theory foisted on the Institute's 'interdisciplinary' research, is the specific content that was turned, within

29. It is not Mannheim who is 'reminiscent of *Lebensphilosophie*' (1993, p. 141) but Horkheimer. The aim of Horkheimer's theory is theoretical: materialism 'tries to replace the justification of action with an explanation of it through an historical understanding of the agent' (1972c, p. 23). What is unfortunate is not so much this as Horkheimer's misconception about himself: pure theory is precisely what Horkheimer does not recognise (Horkheimer 1993b/*GS* 4, pp. 174 ff.).

30. Mannheim did not aim to apply Marx's theory politically; he created the conditions for demonstrating its validity (Mannheim 1964b, Lewalter 1982). By virtue of this, Mannheim was both closer to positive science than Horkheimer and more useful to Marxism. Mannheim was one of the few who recognised the threat posed by the rise of National Socialism, which Horkheimer was still ignoring, only to later make it the central theme of his philosophical endeavours (see Jay 1980). Mannheim 1936 also engaged intensely with vitalism.

31. Horkheimer held that 'the critical theory of society has continued to be a philosophical discipline even when it engages in a critique of the economy' (Horkheimer 1988a, p. 173).

32. Horkheimer 1970a.

33. Horkheimer 1987a, 1980.

34. Horkheimer 1982, pp. 100–1.

this philosophy, into a matter of principle ('sublated'). I am referring to the specific reading that Marxian economics was given within the thought of Friedrich Pollock. The only reason why the massive shifts that occurred, here, were able to slip undetected into the Institute's philosophical framework was that most members of the Institute had little knowledge of economics.[35] To be sure, one person associated with the Institute was a Marxist economist of high standing, namely Henryk Grossmann, whose study on the *law of collapse* constituted a veritable (albeit not the definitive) achievement within the theory of crisis since Luxemburg and Hilferding (2.1.6).[36] Yet the close personal relationship between Horkheimer and the less significant economist Pollock led to *the latter* becoming the Institute's economist.[37]

The consequences were grave, especially since the members of the Institute's inner circle had received virtually no training in economics. Pollock followed Hilferding, but not Grossmann, in assuming that the economic problem that capitalism would one day prove unable to solve was the anarchy reigning between the various sectors of the market.[38] This involved a fundamental departure from Marx's economic theory: while Marx had noted that anarchy does indeed reign on the market, he had not considered this anarchy to be the cause of serious crises, but rather part and parcel of how markets normally function. He demonstrated, in his reproduction schemes, that in the long run, there develops within the permanent turbulence of the market a dynamic equilibrium (2.1.5). Tugan-Baranowski and Hilferding had read this as the claim that crisis-free growth is guaranteed as long as the correct proportions between the various divisions of industry are observed – and such observance was understood by them as a *political* option. Pollock turned this flawed description of capitalism into a description of National Socialism,[39] claiming that National Socialism had succeeded in overcoming the capitalist tendencies toward crisis by 'organising' capitalism and wholly abolishing the chaotic market.[40] Much as Lenin had announced the stage of an imperialist monopoly capitalism governed by new laws (2.2.6; the Frankfurt School's theorists had hitherto endorsed this analysis), Pollock now announced *another* new stage:

---

35. How Franz Neumann resisted this is described by M. Schäfer 1994, pp. 64–5. Yet Adorno adopted the hypothesis without considering it more closely (on this, see Johannes 1995).

36. Grossmann 1929; on the circumstances of Grossmann's affiliation with the Institute, see Jay 1996, p. xxxiv; Wiggershaus 1994, p. 29.

37. Horkheimer and Pollock had closed a contract of friendship as children – in their case, friendship came before scholarship (Wiggershaus 1994, pp. 42, 283).

38. Pollock 1975 and 1975a; see Wiggershaus 1994, pp. 61, 119, 123 and 280.

39. On this, in addition to Gangl 1987, see Wilson 1982, Postone/Brick 1982 and M. Schäfer 1994, pp. 56 ff.

40. Hilferding 1927.

> [A]ll basic concepts [!] and institutions of capitalism have changed their function; interference of the state with the structure of the old economic order has . . . transformed monopoly capitalism into state capitalism.[41]

Since he took this new phase of 'state capitalism' to have overcome the anarchy of the market *politically*, replacing the chaotic profitseeking of individual economic actors (and hence the cause of economic crises) with state planning of the economy, Pollock predicted that it would remain stable indefinitely. This transformation of the foundations of economic theory, the need for which was fallaciously inferred from a particular political development, meant that Marx's theory was no longer applied to capitalism's current phase.[42] Whatever the previous reasons for its neglect of Marx's economic theory, critical theory now disposed of a properly economic justification for that neglect.[43] To be sure, it was not very convincing, since Pollock[44] had already advocated his Hilferdingian reading of Marx before 1933. But because of the deliberately homogenised stucture of the Institute's guiding theory, Pollock's reading of National Socialism as state capitalism proved an incisive development.

One of the consequences was that, there no longer being any prospect of crises ('absence of crises'),[45] the Institute's already pessimistic stance became even more so. Pollock had conceived of 'state capitalism' as a conflict-free automaton that could continue operating forever.[46] If one was to remain able to distinguish between 'reformism, Bolshevism [and] fascism', all of which attempted to intervene in the crisis-wracked

---

41. Pollock 1941, p. 445. '[T]he sphere of circulation . . . is being liquidated' (Horkheimer 1982, p. 95).

42. 'We may even say that under state capitalism economics . . . has lost its object (Pollock 1941a, p. 217; 2.4.1), as 'in a command economy the "theoretical laws of classical economic theory . . . are eliminated"' (Pollock 1941, p. 454; Pollock is quoting a National Socialist economist: Dubiel 1984, p. 125). The law of value has therefore been suspended, according to Pollock (Saage 1983, p. 143; Schäfer 1994, p. 60). It will suffice to point out this assumption rested on a Hegelian intermixture of being and thought.

43. It had a precursor in the claim, formulated unanimously by Bernstein and Lenin, that Marx's economic theory is irrelevant to the present. Horkheimer never mentioned Marx, allegedly for reasons of 'strategy' (Wiggershaus 1994, p. 145), and he thought he required empirical data only to illustrate his own philosophemes (ibid., p. 177). Hardly any economic treatises were produced during the Institute's later history; the closest thing to such treatises are the studies in industrial sociology produced during the 1950s (pp. 479 ff., 721 f.; see 2.4.6).

44. Pollock 1971, 1975a.

45. Horkheimer 1982, p. 102.

46. Pollock 1941a, pp. 215 ff. Members of the Institute closely affiliated with him objected only in strategic, but not in economic terms. Horkheimer was concerned to 'avoid the error of taking sides with the "totalitarian answer"' (letter dated 30 May 1941, quoted in Wiggershaus 1994, p. 282); Adorno deduced that 'the assumption that a non-antagonistic economy might be possible in an antagonistic society' was false (p. 282 – notice the direction in which the conclusion aims). These authors already demonstrated the 'seamlessness of their functionalism' (p. 125) in 1932, prior to their exile. Neumann was the only one to criticise, in a formulation whose pointedness rivals its clarity, that Pollock's approach 'clearly implies a farewell to Marxism . . . State capitalism as conceived by Pollock is set to become millenial' (Schäfer 1994, p. 80).

economy,[47] this mechanistic assumption needed to be supplemented by an additional level of analysis. It was only by means of an *ethical valuation* that National Socialism's totalitarianism could be distinguished from the others. The result was a methodological dualism whose architectonics resembles those of Bernstein's misunderstood Kantianism and anticipate Habermas. The 'farewell to Marxism' (Franz Neumann) was now justified not just economically, but also in terms of the putative 'primacy of politics'.[48] Yet the prominent status accorded to ethics contrasted with the stated aim of developing a *theory of society*.[49]

Given National Socialism's 'malice', so apparent to outside observers, it became virtually impossible to account for why it existed at all. The Institute resorted to the intermediate factor of psychological mediation.[50] The *psychological* analysis of fascism amounted to the allegation that the German people suffered from serious character defects, due, for example, to the disintegration of the nuclear family – a hypothesis that, while perhaps innovative, was not particularly helpful in light of the family relations in other countries.[51] Ironically, it seems this was precisely the hypothesis by which the Institute hoped to bolster its Marxism. Normally, it would have been up to the *proletariat* to rise up against the new rulers, since this would have been in the proletariat's 'objective interest'. But the proletariat had *failed*. This was the view later shared by all members of the Institute, notwithstanding the fact that, under Horkheimer, the Institute had not devoted much attention to the proletariat. A necessary and total class antagonism, nowhere to be found in Marx (2.4.6), was alleged to exist and *simultaneously* declared to have been suspended, with putative social pathologies offered as the reason for this suspension. The 'seamlessness' of the theoretical representation of economic processes was thus provided with a speculative and psychologico-theoretical superstructure.[52]

The same conclusion is reached in other investigations undertaken by Institute members, for instance aesthetic ones.[53] The overhasty psychological supportive argument crucially reinforced the suggestion of a *hermetics of fascism* that a flawed economic analysis

---

47. Horkheimer's (1982, p. 101; Wiggershaus 1994, p. 280) theory of totalitarianism.

48. It is important to note, as Schäfer does, that Horkheimer operated with an instrumentally narrow definition of 'politics' (1994, pp. 41, 54, 63). Incidentally, the expression 'primacy of politics' was coined by Hitler, in the context of a self-characterisation (p. 61; cf. Huhn 1970).

49. Horkheimer charges the 'will' (1982, p. 102) with the task of effecting the 'leap' (p. 107) into the 'new' (p. 105). On Adorno's late ethics (Adorno 2000), see Schweppenhäuser 1993, Kohlmann 1997, Knoll 2000.

50. Horkheimer 1932a, 1936; Pollock 1941, pp. 448 ff.; Jay 1996, pp. 62 ff.

51. Wiggershaus 1994, pp. 59, 137 and (on Horkheimer 1936) 149 ff.

52. Wiggershaus 1994, pp. 121, 141 f., 151 ff. One reason for the break with Fromm, which occurred around 1939, was Fromm's insistence on 'goodness', a category that remained hopeful in spite of everything (pp. 265 ff.). The 'principle of hope' was not very popular with the inner circle.

53. Marcuse, Horkheimer and Adorno even projected it into their taste judgements on Hollywood and jazz (on the 'culture industry', see Horkheimer 1947, *passim*; Adorno 1956, *passim*; Marcuse 1964, pp. 56 ff.; cf. Steinert 1993).

had prompted; it also reinforced the concomitant pessimistic stance. Reality seemed to be moving ever further away from the 'true' goals of human progress. Moreover, the ethicisation involved the problem that the only available ethics – that of the bourgeoisie, 'liberalism' – had previously been defined as fascism's trailblazer.[54]

Thus the 'negativity' by which theology slips into the analysis becomes recognisable as the result of a quandary. Horkheimer had often invoked 'reason' as the guarantor of a better world.[55] He treated it as a container whose contents, 'ideals' or 'values',[56] needed to be 'realised'. The error of 'liberalism' was taken to consist in the fact that it had regarded reason in a purely formal manner, thereby 'bisecting' it.[57] But what might constitute a fuller reason, or a 'rational society'? Set phrases on the 'realisation' of bourgeois ideals aside, answers to this question were only ever suggested. And when such suggestions were made, they were instrumental, as when it was claimed that what would be rational would be 'to regulate and direct the social work process and thereby human relations generally in a reasonable way, that is, according to a unified plan in the interests of the generality'.[58] This ethics could only be socialist in the sense of the 'planned economy'.[59] Now, on Pollock's reading, National Socialism (and Stalinism) had *achieved* just such a 'planned management of production'.[60] The description of National Socialism accorded perfectly with the definition of 'reason' that the Institute had itself once advocated.[61] Thus, in addition to personal catastrophes, National Socialism also caused theoretical difficulties for the Institute. This may have been one reason why the Institute's theorists were so quick to attribute to it a destruction of reason; it had rendered the Institute's own theory impossible.[62]

There were now three options: criticising one's own former ideas, retaining those ideas while transposing reason to the realm of the transcendent or retaining one's propositions

---

54. 'Liberalism' is what '"produces" the total-authoritarian state out of itself' (Marcuse 1968a, p. 19). 'But whoever is not willing to talk about capitalism should also keep silent about fascism' (Horkheimer 1989, p. 78). 'The whole span of German culture was languishing, precisely where it was most liberal, for its Hitler' (Adorno 2005, p. 35).

55. 'Bourgeois thought begins as a struggle against the authority of tradition and replaces it with reason' (Horkheimer 1936a, p. 72); cf. *GS* 2, pp. 229 f.; *GS* 5, pp. 320 ff.; *GS* 7, pp. 241 ff.; Marcuse 1937).

56. *GS* 7, pp. 230, 228.

57. Habermas 1967, pp. 45 ff.; 3.2.4.

58. Horkheimer 1936a, p. 92. Reason is defined as the capacity to 'grasp the idea of what is objectively rational' (1985b, p. 50/*GS* 7, p. 25). In 1935, Horkheimer calls for a 'social order adequate to the present level of human development. The realisation of this order is the concrete form of reason' (*GS* 12, p. 243). 'The great merit of the technocrats consists in ... [revealing] the technical possibilities of the present' (Pollock 1975, p. 57).

59. Pollock 1975a.

60. Horkheimer 1982, p. 107.

61. In 1935, Horkheimer held that 'authority' is actually 'more rational [!] ... than the liberty of the liberalism from which it developed. The totalitarian state is not to be blamed for the fact that people submit to a dictatorship ... but for the fact that this dictatorship runs contrary to the popular interest' (*GS* 12, p. 242).

62. 'The root concepts of Western civilisation ... are disintegrating' (*GS* 5, p. 320).

while giving them a new reading, rejecting the kind of 'reason' that had now 'realised' itself in National Socialism.[63] The first option was only introduced subsequently, by Habermas. He failed, however, to overcome the basic architectonic dualism, since he merely renovated the normative theoretical superstructure.[64] I will discuss the second option shortly, by reference to Adorno and Benjamin. It was the third option that presented itself as the most viable one to Horkheimer and Adorno during their exile, in light of world war and genocide: 'The new, fascist order is that type of reason [!] within which reason reveals itself to be irrational'.[65] Fascism is the 'truth of modern society'.[66] The view underlying these statements is that capitalism, itself already the embodiment of a 'bisected reason', leads necessarily to fascism. This view does not contain a critique of Horkheimer's and Adorno's own former Kautskyan faith in progress, but merely the reversal of that faith: historical progress as driven by the realisation of reason now appeared as the abiding progress of *irrationality*, up to its complete unfolding in fascism.[67] But if this was so, then it was no use to invoke 'reason' against fascism.[68] This idea would be fully elaborated in the *Dialectic of Enlightenment*. It was with this disavowal of political practice, at the latest, that Marx ceased to play any role for 'critical theory'; his place was definitively taken by Nietzsche and Schopenhauer.[69] The state capitalism hitherto assumed to have caused the catastrophic development was generalised, and its features were turned into basic principles: the blame was now placed on a 'principle of control',[70] taken to have held sway throughout the history of the West; a levelling 'thought of iden-

---

63. A fourth option consisted in affirmatively acknowledging the 'rationality' of National Socialism. Astonishingly, Horkheimer conceded to this interpretation that 'such voices, of which there are plenty, are not the most foolish, nor even the most dishonest' (1982, p. 34/*GS* 5, p. 319).

64. The economic theoretical substructure remained as mechanist in Habermas as it was in Pollock, except that Habermas decked it out in a new, systems-theoretical fashion (3.1.1).

65. Horkheimer 1987b, *GS* 5, p. 348.

66. Horkheimer 1989, p. 78.

67. A reversal of Hegel's philosophy of history (thus Schnädelbach 1988, p. 26 and Schäfer 1994, p. 82). 'Enlightenment is totalitarian' (Adorno and Horkheimer 1997, p. 6).

68. 'To appeal today to the liberal mentality of the nineteenth century against fascism means appealing to what brought fascism to power' (Horkheimer 1989, p. 91; cf. Schäfer 1994, pp. 52–3). Even the war against Hitler's Germany made little sense to him, since he held that the root of the problem lay not in this single regime but in instrumental rationality, which he viewed as being no less dominant in the USA ('Even his defeat will not necessarily halt the avalanche': *GS* 5, p. 232; cf. Schäfer 1994, pp. 105–6).

69. This was apparent in the way Horkheimer and Adorno responded to Marcuse's 1947 Marxist exposé (Wiggershaus 1994, p. 388), but also in the failure of Heinz Maus' emphatic engagement for Horkheimer and Adorno to prompt any response (p. 393) or their rejection of Dahrendorf's dissertation on Marx (Dahrendorf 1953; cf. 2.4.6). Nietzsche is more central to the *Dialectic of Enlightenment* than Marx (Rohrmoser 1971; Koch 1973, p. 7; Honneth 1983; Habermas 1987a; Rath 1987; Wiggershaus 1994, pp. 182, 215). Horkheimer turned informally from Marx back to Schopenhauer, whom he had long revered (1980/1972e, pp. 68 ff.; 145 ff./*GS* 7, pp. 240 ff.; Post 1971, Ebeling 1980).

70. Horkheimer 1982, p. 103; cf. Rohrmoser 1970, p. 14. It has already been shown (2.2.6) that the repolitisation of what had formerly been economic concepts, in this case 'domination' (the term 'contract' was also replaced, in many Institute texts, by 'command'; cf. Pollock 1941a, p. 208; Pollock 1941, p. 450; Gangl 1987, p. 226; Schäfer 1994, p. 62), was due, in both Hilferding and Lenin, to a flawed analysis of monopoly. This 'primacy of politics' was now given the status of a principle.

tity', identified as the principle's cause (thus science was also blamed – recall the vitalist laments about reification); and the 'principle of exchange', identified as having given rise to the 'thought of identity'.[71]

The result was a hermetic fatality: domination was total and thus not to be abolished. There was not even any way of *thinking* about possible solutions, as normal thought remained bound up with domination, even reinforcing it.[72] The remedy could consist only in a *different* thought, but this presupposed the abolition of the principle of exchange. Yet this was impossible as long as domination was total – a gigantic vicious circle. To be consistent, Horkheimer and Adorno would have had to fall silent, become seriously religious or express themselves only in ways *contrary* to reason, like Heidegger.[73] In a sense, that is just what they did (witness the hermetic style of Adorno's late writings), and it won them the approval of postmodern critics of reason. Yet there was no way to persevere endlessly with such a total critique, and so after the war they were quick to backpedal.

For example, during the positivism dispute, the 'concept of reason' was once more invoked (this time, reason was 'dialectical'). Yet this only made sense if one chose the *second* option, that of basing one's critical interventions on a reason somehow construed as 'transcendent'. Nevertheless, total critique kept shining though (the final instance being *Negative Dialectics*). It is by virtue of this constant oscillation that theology now enters the horizon of our considerations.

2.6.3 *Adorno's quietist utopianism*

> My objection to the whole of English and French sociology remains the fact that it knows by experience only the structures of decay in society and, in all innocence, takes its own instincts for decay as the norm for sociological value judgements.[74]

When the Institute was refounded in Frankfurt in 1950, it sided with the powers of reconstruction but refused to let itself be muzzled.[75] The popular *Dialectic of Enlightenment* had no political alternatives to present and did not endorse political intervention, yet Horkheimer, Adorno and later Marcuse did in fact comment on many social matters, and displayed considerable organisational talent and eloquence in the process. In doing

---

71. 'The self-movement of the concept of the commodity leads to the concept of state capitalism' (Horkheimer 1982, p. 108) – an amputated and speculative Marxism.

72. Horkheimer held that freedom could no longer be conceived of, nor even spoken about (Horkheimer 1982, p. 116). He formulated this claim during his US exile. 'But why go abroad at all, unless one intends to crowd on sail? Abroad, there's nothing to prevent this being done' (*MECW* 24, p. 262).

73. Similarities between Horkheimer/Adorno and the late Heidegger are discerned by, inter alia, Rohrmoser 1970, pp. 36 ff.; Mörchen 1980, Ebeling 1983 and Kittsteiner 2004 (on this, see Henning 2004).

74. Nietzsche 1888, p. 64.

75. Wiggershaus 1994, pp. 431 ff. On the 'intellectual founding of the German Federal Republic' (Albrecht 1999), see also Koenen 2001, p. 115.

so, they were compelled to revive the critique of positivism and liberalism that had preceded their total critique of reason. The critique of a fully developed but catastrophic reason was scaled back, becoming once more a critique of positivism's reductive concept of reason.[76]

The critical theorists were again claiming that their critique made use of the abundant resources of the other half of a bisected reason, of which they were now at least able to say it was 'dialectical'. Critical theory's popularity goes back, it would seem, to this period, when its exponents could be expected to have something critical to say on virtually any topic.[77] How important this was for West Germany's cultural development can already be seen from the fact that almost all of the human sciences developed an offshoot inspired by critical theory, from Klaus Holzkamp's 'critical' psychology, Hartmut von Hentig's 'critical' pedagogy and Peter Szondi's 'critical' theory of drama to 'critical' theology.[78] Critical theory's influence also extended beyond academia; witness Alexander Kluge's auteur films or the 'Union of Critical Policemen' [*Gewerkschaft kritischer Polizisten*]. In a sense, the accusation that critical theory had spurred on the student movement was not altogether wrong.[79] This all adds up to an overwhelming success, one I do not mean to deny. The only thing wrong with critical theory was that it was not a *theory*. Its intervention lacked an argumentative grounding. A theory that sets out to criticise everything but refuses to answer the question of how one might improve on it, invoking the 'prohibition on images', is a theory facing a problem of justification.[80] This problem was a result of the critical theorists' reductive reception of Marx. They continued to attribute a state-capitalist determinism to the base, including for the period after National Socialism, and insisted that this meant there were no possibilites for improvement (the student movement was denounced as rushing headlong into 'pseudo activity');[81]

76. Except for occasional pronouncements such as 'The whole is the false' (Adorno 2005, p. 50), which flirted with the former faith in totality.

77. Schöttker 2000 see the condemnation of the mass media as contradicting critical theory's skilful 'organisation of philosophical success'; he also shows how the repatriates 'attempted to repress' their Marxist beginnings (Schöttker 2000, pp. 447–8: the volume *Kritische Theorie* was not published until 1968; prior to its publication, Horkheimer was concerned to gloss over the Institute's origins). Schöttker rejects the hypothesis that critical theory did not begin to take shape until 1949 (Demirovic 1999, Albrecht 1999).

78. Oudenrijn 1972.

79. This accusation, raised by the politicians Filbinger and Dregger, was formulated in philosophical terms by, among others, Rohrmoser (obstruction of the path from theory to practice renders 'practice devoid of theory': 1970, pp. 30 ff.). Koenen 2001, pp. 115–16, confirms the accusation *ex post*; cf. Wiggershaus 1978; Wiggershaus 1994, pp. 656 f.; Negt 1995, Kraushaar 1998.

80. 'One can not determine what a free society will do or permit' (Horkheimer 1982, p. 108; cf. 1*972a, p. 150/*GS* 8, p. 331; Adorno 1998, pp. 141–2; Adorno 1975, pp. 207, 394; Wiggershaus 1994, p. 502). Freyer 1959 took a surprisingly similar view (Lukács 1981, p. 650; Grimminger 1997). Habermas identified the problem of establishing a proper foundation (Habermas 1984–7, Vol. I, pp. 366 ff.; Habermas 1984–7, Vol. II, pp. 378 ff.) and attempted an alternative solution (cf. 3.1.1).

81. According to Krahl, Adorno displayed the 'ambivalent political consciousness of many critical intellectuals... who project the notion that in combating fascist terror from the right, socialist action from the left releases the potential of that terror in the first place. Yet this is to aprioristically

because of their decision in favour of materialism, they did not want to invoke any 'normative' spheres either.

Horkheimer and Adorno were aware of this deficit to varying degrees. Horkheimer, who eventually opted for a resigned liberalism of reason, was depressed by it.[82] By contrast, Adorno repeatedly attempted to make a virtue out of necessity. His thought retreated into the realm of aesthetics, and he was not at all unhappy about this 'breathing spell',[83] since it suited his interests. The entities used to compensate for the justificational deficit were: psychoanalysis (Fromm and, to an extent, other members of the Institute), pleasure (Horkheimer and Marcuse),[84] art and religion (Adorno),[85] ethics and language (Habermas). None of the theorists named was led by these repercussions to ask whether the gap needing to be closed might have been left by the emphatic Marxism of *his own* younger years. After all, this *Marxism* and the possibilities it had promised were what had prompted the Institute's critical avoidance of all premature 'mediations' in the first place. And it was Pollock's hermetic interpretation of Marxism that had created the dualism of the technocratic structures of the base on the one hand and the unaccomplished legitimation of cultural claims on the other. Once Marxism has become a dualistically dissociated *technological* affair, whether it continues to be formally endorsed or not makes no difference to the autonomised theory of culture.[86] Thus the Frankfurt School almost said 'farewell to Marxism' (F. Neumann).[87] But even if Marx no longer

---

denounce all practice as blindly action-oriented, thus boycotting every possibility of political critique' (quoted in Kraushaar 1998, Vol. II, p. 674).

82. Quoting the correspondence between them, Wiggershaus 1994, p. 271, notes that, unlike Adorno, Horkheimer was concerned about the 'weakness in positive formulations' (Horkheimer to Adorno, 21 June 1941). In 1968, Horkheimer said: 'I avow myself a critical theorist; this means that while I can say what is wrong, I cannot define what is right' (Horkheimer 1972a, p. 150/*GS* 8, p. 331).

83. Adorno 2007, p. 245.

84. Horkheimer 1988, Wiggershaus 1994, pp. 180 ff.; Marcuse 1937 and 1966, Jay 1996, p. 38.

85. Adorno's path leads *from Marx back to Hegel* (Lichtheim 1971) and even back behind Hegel; for the latter, art and religion merely prefigured absolute knowledge (3.1.5). The notion that salvation comes through art, not through knowledge, can already be found in Schopenhauer (Ebeling 1980; see Haug 1971, Rohrmoser 1972, Gorsen 1981).

86. There was always something formulaic about the endorsements of Marx (of which the last is to be found in Adorno 1969); Johannes 1995 aptly spoke of an 'absent centre'. The attempt to once more establish a relationship between Marx and German critical theory only occurred post mortem, after 1989 (Dubiel 1990, Postone 1993, Bolte 1995). The changes made to the *Dialectic of Enlightenment* between 1944 and 1947 are revealing: 'exploitation' became 'suffering', 'forces of production' became 'possibilities', 'class society' became 'society', 'capitalism' became 'what exists' and 'monopolism' became the 'culture industry' (Horkheimer 1989, p. 303; Van Reijen 1987).

87. If Marx continued to be discussed within the Institute, then it was as a philosopher, and this was only consistent. Habermas read the thought of the young Marx and the young Lukács 'not as a critique of capitalism but rather as a theory of reification, which he looked at from the standpoint of philosophical anthropology' (Wiggershaus 1994, p. 540). Schmidt 1960 was also concerned with the 'dialectical thinking' of the young Marx, and with how it might be employed against facts that had overhastily been declared 'natural', as in the positivism dispute. In this case as in others, it was Hegel, rather than Marx, who tended to be foregrounded (see Negt 1970, and the late examples of Honneth 1996 and 2001).

played any constitutive role in its theories, it continued invoking him – at times only by remaining auspiciously silent – like some lost saint.

But what image of Marx did the Institute convey after the Second World War? Adorno's late statements can be interpreted as follows. Marx boldly attempted to sublate philosophy into science and practice. But he failed in both undertakings. The comprehensive 'theory of society' that critical theory had set out to formulate did not exist; in fact, according to Horkheimer's and Adorno's late statements, it was *impossible*.[88] Neither the societies of the East nor West could be said to be rationally organised,[89] and the likelihood of such a rational organisation was diminishing. In light of this basic situation, nothing seemed more natural than reversing the sublation Marx had attempted.

This was what Adorno did in the famous opening passage of *Negative Dialectics*: 'Philosophy, which once seemed obsolete, lives on because the moment to realize it was missed'.[90] In his defence of the Young Hegelians *against Marx*,[91] one discerns his former, vitalist and Leninist understanding of philosophy: philosophy represents the events of his time, but it disposes of no autonomy with regard these events. Thus, not having been 'realised' (this is already a Young Hegelian way of thinking), it is condemned to continue existing. But it cannot achieve closure, since its object 'no longer' displays such closure either. All this serves as an ex post justification of the way 'social theory' had always been conducted within the Institute: by means of *philosophical fragments*. In this way, Adorno drew the consequences from Horkheimer's 1937 statement of principles 'Traditional and Critical Theory',[92] an essay written on the occasion of the fiftieth anniversary of the publication of *Capital*.[93] In 'Traditional and Critical Theory', Horkheimer attempts

88. 'The irrationality of the present social structure prevents its rational unfolding within theory . . . Parallel to the regression of society, there occurs a regression of thinking about society' (Adorno 1969, pp. 359–60; see Horkheimer 1967, p. 165; Wiggershaus 1994, p. 628). In 1955, Horkheimer spoke of the 'absence of an adequate theory of society' (1972e, p. 71). 'Univocal theory presupposes . . . the unity of its object' (Horkheimer). 'The increasing irrationality of society . . . is irreconcilable with rational theory. Theory can now hardly continue to take society at a worked that society itself no longer speaks' (Adorno; both quotations are from the 1963 draft preface to *Sociologica II*, quoted in Wiggershaus 1994, p. 565). 'The notions of subjective and objective have been completely reversed' (Adorno 2005, p. 69; see Marcuse 1964, p. 148). Marcuse's attempt at a legitimation in terms of the philosophy of history was rendered impossible by Pollock's hermeticism (Benhabib 1986, p. 178).

89. In 'Nannied Music' (1953), Adorno criticised the 'dictatorships' in power 'on the other side of the [inner German] border' (quoted in Wiggershaus 1994, p. 510; cf. Adorno 2007, p. 322). The late Horkheimer defended Western 'freedom', which he had previously viewed as being nothing but a precursor of fascism (Wiggershaus 1994, p. 444; cf. Horkheimer 1972e, p. 109/*GS* 7, pp. 145 ff.).

90. Adorno 2007, p. 3.

91. For late examples, see Schmidt 1988 and Fraser and Honneth 2003, p. 239. On the accusation of Young Hegelianism, see Bubner 1969; Rohrmoser 1970, p. 46; Lichtheim 1971: 'bourgeois' philosophers defend Marx against Adorno, for he 'did not consider the Marxist concept of transcending philosophy through praxis to be relevant; instead, he sought a new philosophy' (Wiggershaus 1994, pp. 535–6; see Adorno 1963a, 1993, 1976, pp. 128–9, and so on).

92. Horkheimer 1988a.

93. Grossmann had originally proposed the publication of a volume on Marx (Wiggershaus, p. 186).

to resituate Marx's impulses within philosophy: he argues that 'interest in the abolition [*Aufhebung*] of social injustice' was 'the materialist content of the idealist concept of reason',[94] thereby retaining that concept.

Marx had meant something else by '*Aufhebung*': he was concerned with making good, within *science*, on philosophy's claim to knowledge, and with transposing emancipatory desires from the idealistically glorified surrogate level of theory to active *politics* (3.4.4). The yearning for immediacy was precisely what he had tried to make the Young Hegelians abandon. Because they blended being and thought, they took themselves to be practical by virtue of their theoretical activity, when that activity was not even genuinely theoretical, since (as German thinkers) they continued to search for the ideal system. The only unity of theory and practice was that both were spoilt. Philosophers can certainly *protest* against the 'weight of the world'.[95] But if they want to achieve something more, they must go beyond philosophy. For this reason, Marx became politically active and engaged with economics. His basic idea was simple: it is only when philosophy succeeds in 'sublating' itself into science in this way that it can hope to 'realise' itself politically.[96] To be sure, philosophy *qua* critical reflection remains indispensable – it was only by bringing his philosophical perspective to political economy that he was able to formulate a *critique* of the latter. But philosophy needs to prudently limit itself to such critical reflection.[97] Political wishes or normative claims have no business interfering with science; there is no place within science for philosophical 'leadership'. For this reason, Marx vehemently opposed party programmes that advocated any sort of 'positive' philosophy.[98]

This is precisely the theoretical development that Horkheimer revokes in his direction-setting essay: 'Philosophy has not provided a teaching on national economy'.[99] Instead of venturing down into the lowlands of science himself,[100] Horkheimer took the *results* obtained by sciences he had pre-selected and integrated them directly into philosophy – and in doing so, he proceeded quite uncritically. Thus, neither a philosophical critique

---

94. Horkheimer 1988a, p. 56/*GA* 4, p. 219.
95. Bourdieu 1999.
96. This faction 'saw *only the critical struggle of philosophy against the German world*... Critical towards its adversary, it was uncritical towards itself when... proceeding from... philosophy' (*MECW* 3, p. 181). Philosophy has to be 'realised' and 'sublated'. Marx was as little satisfied with scientification as with activism. On these passages, see Hartmann 1970, Fleischer 1970 and 1988, Braun 1992, Brudney 1998; see sections 3.4.4, 4.2.3.
97. But philosophy has no rights 'outside critique' (Habermas 1973a, p. 119). It does not follow from this that one requires a 'philosophy of history', as Marcuse believed (Marx's categories 'present a negative state of affairs in the light of its positive solution': Marcuse 1941, p. 295; Wiggershaus 1994, p. 503); nor does it mean that one needs 'normative foundations' (3.1.4).
98. Marx mocked the philosopher who, having 'at his elbow a magic formula,... thought he could dispense with going into purely economic details' (*MECW* 6, p. 178). Calls for 'fair distribution', a 'free state' and 'equal elementary education' remain 'phrases' for as long as one passes over in silence 'the conditions that alone give them meaning' (*MECW* 24, pp. 75 ff.).
99. Horkheimer 1988a, p. 173, p. 59. See also the parallel in Marcuse 1937.
100. Wiggershaus 1994, p. 183.

of science nor a scientific analysis of politics is developed (nor even an original political proposal); instead, reason is abstractly opposed to reality.[101] Horkheimer stops at ideal demands that would probably be endorsed by anyone.[102] Because Horkheimer mistakenly thinks of his theory as a 'liberating practice', he fails to recognise and consistently advocate the idealism inherent in his approach; instead, idealism is sometimes evoked and sometimes criticised, with Hegel usually serving as its representative.[103] It is the tragedy of critical theory that it had to go down in history as a philosophy but could never be brought to completion. Within this constellation, it remained dependent on *philosophical* justifications that it could, for the time being, merely announce (3.1).

Unlike Ernst Bloch and Paul Tillich, Adorno did not attempt to find a firm footing in metaphysics. Rather, the utopian digressions featured in his remarks on the most varied topics brought about a rapprochement with theology.[104] Philosophically, a religious standpoint has the advantage of having to be neither explicable nor justifiable – and it is in this refusal of explication and justification that the systematic result of *Negative Dialectics* essentially consists.[105] Horkheimer also resorted to playing with religious motifs in this way.[106] Thus, within the reception of Marx that occurred in German theology during

101. Horkheimer 1990. Horkheimer starts from the tension between 'the awareness of ends, to which the individual is predisposed, ... and the relations associated with the labour process, which are fundamental to society' (Horkheimer 1988a, p. 30/*GS* 4, p. 183). He correctly traces this 'tension between a finite human being and the ego as infinite obligation' (Horkheimer 1989a, p. 26) back to Fichte; it is only Hegel's transposition of Fichte's 'self-reflection' from 'introspection' to 'objective mind' that lends supports to the assumption that this is to say something substantive about the world: '[T]he philosophical understanding ... is now simultaneously [!] knowledge of the meaning of our own being' (Horkheimer 1989a, p. 26; on the reduction of theory to self-cognition, see 2.5.2).

102. Türcke 1990, p. 10.

103. 'The difference between concept and reality [...] is the foundation for the possibility of revolutionary praxis' (Horkheimer 1982, p. 109). Adorno both invoked Hegel to criticise positivism (1976) and critically dissected him (Adorno 1993).

104. Collaboration with Lazarsfeld on the 'Radio Research Project' yielded few results, since Adorno saw to it that the requisite empirical research 'was connected in a confused way with the question whether there should be reform or revolution' (Wiggershaus 1994, p. 243; on Lazarsfeld's letter, see p. 242). Adorno eventually spoke out against the transmission of radio symphonies (p. 244) and concluded the 1941 essay 'Popular Music' with the following utopian subterfuge: 'man needs that energy which might possibly achieve his tranformation into a man' (p. 246; cf. Dahms 1994, pp. 232 ff.).

105. '[T]he mere thought of hope is a transgression against it' (Adorno 2007, p. 402).

106. Prior to the foregrounding of the total critique of reason, Horkheimer reenacted the utopian dismissal of Marxism. He did so during a period of resurgent hope and under the influence of Benjamin, in whose memorial volume the essay was published: 'The doctrine of midwifery [*MECW* 35, p. 10] degrades the revolution to mere progress' (Horkheimer 1982, p. 107). In formulating this claim, Horkheimer extends Benjamin's criticism of Kautsky (see the opening quotation in 2.1) to Marx. But: 'For the revolutionary, conditions have always been ripe' (p. 106). Economics is interpreted as a testament to degeneration (p. 113), and Marx's theory is reduced, in a historicist manner reminiscent of Korsch, to the expression of a specific historical situation: 'It formulates the adequate consciousness for a definite phase of the struggle' (p. 106). Men, it is argued, need do no more than enact the 'leap' (p. 107) by their will; then everything will be done 'through free agreement' (p. 114) and 'in solidarity' (p. 116) (see the references to 'dreams', 'yearnings' and 'the hope for

the 1960s, 'Marxism' tended to refer to adaptation of *these* residual forms of social theory. The groundbreaking works of Moltmann and Metz show that Marx was scarcely read, and that his ideas were received only in a philosophically diluted form.[107] In this situation, critical theory's tendency to theologise tended to hinder, rather than to advance, adequate *worldly* engagement with sociological and philosophical issues. Not even the first part of Marx's *oeuvre*, his critique of religion, was retained.

Adorno had already detected a covert religiosity in his role models Kracauer and Bloch.[108] When asked about his affinity for theology, Adorno always referred to Walter Benjamin; in a division of labour of sorts, Gershom Scholem also spoke of Benjamin as being primarily a religious thinker. Benjamin does, in fact, play a key role within the process of Marx's theological enfeeblement, but it is not the role attributed to him in the standard interpretation, which treats him as a *precursor* of Adorno and Metz. The opposite is in fact the case: Benjamin is one of the few religious thinkers who concur with Marx's critique of religion and his worldly turn. Yet before Benjamin can be adequately assessed, we need to at least trace the basic features of professional theology's reception of Marx.

2.6.4 Key elements of Marxian theory VII: Marx's critique of religion

> Religion is the sigh of the oppressed creature.[109]

Theology is another discipline within which Karl Marx has gone through remarkable developments in the twentieth century. However, it was only rarely that theologians engaged with his actual theoretical message, the critique and analysis of modern society beyond and behind religion. It was more common for him to be read a *social* critic of religion. The church regarded him as a *philosophical* critic of religion who needed to be refuted in the way it had addressed and 'refuted' worldly philosophers throughout its history. Radical critiques of religion were formulated long before Marx; in fact, they have existed for almost as long as religion itself.[110] Thus conflict between the Christian

---

a classless condition', as well as to 'the other' and to a 'better possibility': pp. 102, 104, 111, 116; see Lutz-Bachmann 1988a and 1997, Amos Schmidt 1993, Pangritz 1996, Liedke 1997).

107. Most works start with Benjamin and Adorno, as if this were a matter of course (see Koch 1973, Spülbeck 1977, Türcke 1990, Deuser 1980, Neuhaus 1985, Arens 1991, Brumlik 1994, Schulte 1994, Reikerstorfer 1998, Manemann 1999 and Langthaler 2000). Helmut Gollwitzer is an exception; he also stands out by virtue of the fact that his reading of Marx did not lead to him abandoning his faith (see the critique of Sölle 1967 in Gollwitzer 1967).

108. Wiggershaus 1994, pp. 68 ff. (on Bloch and Kracauer) and pp. 83 ff. (on Benjamin); unlike them, Adorno was oriented less toward the Jewish faith (he disparagingly called Fromm a 'professional Jew') than toward Catholicism (p. 72).

109. *MECW* 3, p. 175.

110. There was a total critique of religion long before Marx, associated with the Sophists and Epicureans, the Enlightenment and the French materialists (Ley 1966, MacIntyre 1969, Niewöhner 1999, Minois 2000). Use of the term 'religion' is far from self-evident among theologians (see Kraus 1982, Link in Gräb 1999, and Ruster 2000).

religion and the critique of religion began long before Marx entered the stage of history. Much the same is true of the church's relationship to *socialism.*

Differently from radically atheist critics of religion, who meant simply to do away with heaven and all its trappings, or at least declared heaven to be irrelevant, socialism had many points of contact with revealed religion. Its egalitarian perspective had a corrollary in the egalitarian currents and interpretations of Judaeo-Christian doctrine, which were as old as Judaeo-Christian religion *itself*, even if the churches tended to repress these currents and interpretations. The Biblical call for justice in human interaction and God's promise of a better world were sufficiently rooted in human memory for socialism's variations on them to be recognisable as such. Many found this spirit was more evident in socialism than in the nominally 'Christian' policies of the European monarchs.[111] Socialism called out powerfully to religion: *tua res agitur!* Many socialists were aware of this affinity, and they did not shy away from it.[112] It was not until Marx that these flirtations were abandoned. He established a link between socialism and the radical *critique* of religion.[113] How did this turnaround come about?

In Germany, the strongest impulses toward the critique of religion, after those of the Enlightenment, were those of the Young Hegelians – a milieu to which Marx also belonged, initially.[114] The decisive difference between Marx's critique of religion and that of his precursors was that the latter, from Heraclitus to d'Holbach to Feuerbach, set up a *theoretical* antithesis and then contented themselves with calling for 'good actions' – just as religion had done. Marx's went beyond this theoretical antithesis and addressed, both theoretically *and* practically, the action that both sides did no more than call for. He is therefore a 'post-atheist'.[115] What he thereby achieved theoretically can be described as

---

111. The prophetic books of the Bible and the Book of Job address human suffering. When God eventually speaks through Elijah, he does not take action himself; instead, he urges Job's friends to help him (thus P. Stekeler-Weithofer in a lecture held in Leipzig in April 2001). Questions concerning where, when and how the 'kingdom of God' will be are secondary *vis-à-vis* the constant hope that it will indeed come about (see Bloch 1970, Farner 1985; see Corinthians 1:13). Early Christianity was also quite egalitarian with regard to the role of women, as can be seen from the Gospel of Luke.

112. Early socialists such as Cabet, Saint-Simon or Weitling (1967) struggled to establish a 'new Christianity' (Uertz 1981, p. 112; cf. Gerlich 1920, Ramm 1955, Höppner 1975, Opitz 1988, Euchner 1991). Even within social democracy, there was a struggle over who was the true 'heir', although this struggle was now conducted against religion (Dietzgen 1903; Lannert 1989, pp. 98 ff.).

113. See Marx's criticism of the religious socialists: 'Nothing is easier than to give Christian asceticism a socialist tinge. Has not Christianity declaimed against private property, against marriage, against the State? Has it not preached in the place of these, charity and poverty, celibacy and mortification of the flesh, monastic life and Mother Church? Christian socialism is but the holy water with which the priest consecrates the heart-burnings of the aristocrat' (*MECW* 6, p. 508; *MECW* 5, pp. 531 ff.). It is a matter, for Marx, of '[establishing] the *truth of this world*' once 'the *world beyond the truth* has disappeared' (*MECW* 3, p. 176).

114. The most important Young Hegelian critics of religion were Strauß (1835), Bauer (1985) and Feuerbach (1842); see Löwith 1965, Post 1969, McLellan 1974.

115. Thus Walter Kern, in: Rolfes 1974; see A. Schmidt 1960, pp. 28 ff. Marx distinguished himself from Feuerbach by considering theoretical atheism *passé* as early as 1844: 'Atheism, as the

a dissociation of politics from religion. Hence it of no import what Marx himself may or may not have believed.[116] This Marxian achievement needs to be briefly discussed, because it has so seldom been understood.

Marx's point of departure was the philosophy of Hegel,[117] which culminated in theology.[118] By this, I do not mean that the *content* of Hegel's philosophy was 'theological'; I mean that he gave to the content of his philosophy the 'Christological' form that he was familiar with from his Christian background. The self-development of mind, its self-alienation and its return to itself have *Tübinger Stift* written all over them, as Nietzsche, himself the son of a pastor, once noted venomously. Nor did Hegel make any secret of this; witness his frequent – often illogical – talk of 'father', 'son' and 'spirit'.[119] Marx knew how to distinguish between stylistic devices and substantive propositions, and so he was less bothered by this than by the presupposition that underlies Hegel's philosophy (2.5.7): Hegel posited man as a purely spiritual being *from the outset*, and so he had no difficulties in obtaining spirit [*Geist*] as his result.[120] To put it reductively, but consistently with what Hegel meant: within such a representation, 'everything is one', insofar as all contents are presented within a single form, a single language. Because thought and being are posited as identical, this involves the insinuation that each linguistic and logical transition

---

denial of this unreality, has no longer any meaning, for atheism is a *negation of God*, and postulates *the existence of man* through this negation; but socialism as socialism no longer stands in any need of such a mediation. It proceeds from the *theoretically and practically sensuous consciousness* of man and of nature as the *essence*. Socialism is man's *positive self-consciousness*, no longer mediated through the abolition of religion' (*MECW* 3, p. 306; see also pp. 297–8) – and hence free to believe once more. Thus religion is relieved of the responsibility of accounting for the state of the world. While this position does not depend on the truth of Christianity, it is nevertheless congruent with the message of Jesus (see below). This may explain why so many Christians have at times sympathised with Marxism.

116. Ollenhauer's Godesberg Declaration posed no restrictions on the motives behind someone's affiliation with the party, considering them secondary (Wehner 1985, p. 91). The Erfurt Programme declared religion a 'private matter'.

117. Marx's theory can be described as 'critical' (Bolte 1995) to the extent that it always developed from tenacious and persevering engagement with its precursors: first with Hegel, then with political economy.

118. Hegel, *Werke* 12, pp. 540, 559; Löwith 1949, pp. 52 ff.; Iljin 1946, Theunissen 1970, Küng 1970, Weischedel 1985, pp. 283 ff. (a classic). It shows on almost every page.

119. 'The Christian, in spite of logic, has only one incarnation of the *Logos*; with the philosopher there is no end to incarnations' (*MECW* 6, p. 163; *MECW* 4, pp. 57 f.). Hegel's reading of Christian religion amounted to a 'transformation of mythology into anthropological constitutional analysis' (Rentsch 2000, p. 244); as such, it anticipated demythologisation. But the fact that something makes sense as an interpretation of religion does not justify interpreting everything as religion. Internally, the claim to universality applies to 'everything', but this does not mean that other ways of considering reality become superfluous. Physics, for example, also applies to 'everything': nothing exists physically that might not be considered by physics (there is nothing 'meta-physical'). Modern theology's insight that physics and theology can exist side by side as long as one distinguishes between their specific modes of validity (instead of trying to use the Bible to 'refute' Darwin) is absent in Hegel's discourse of unity.

120. The premises recur in the results, as Hegel's thought hardly admits of empirical falsification.

denotes a real transition. In the course of such a comprehensive presentation, one can literally represent 'everything'. No empirical research is required; all that is required is an adequately consistent 'mental', that is linguistic, presentation. When push comes to shove, one can always resort to etymological tricks, as done by the late Heidegger. Marx held that this habit of philosophising purely on the basis of 'mind', which allows one to demonstrate virtually anything, had been adopted by Hegel's students.

Thus what Marx's critique of 'religion' aimed at primarily was not so much what Hegel had asserted[121] as what the *Young Hegelians* were asserting.[122] The difference was that Hegel had used his method to formulate propositions that Marx had to respect (Hegel had not formulated these propositions because of, but *in spite of* his method), whereas this was not the case in most of his students, with the possible exceptions of Eduard Gans and Feuerbach, who recognised Hegel as being a theologian as far as the content of his philosophy is concerned, and who criticised him for this. Marx acknowledged the substantive critique of religion that the Young Hegelians had elaborated.[123] But he accused them of overlooking the fact that Hegel's *genuine* theology inhered not so much in the content of what he said than in his 'presuppositions', which the Young Hegelians had yet to abandon.[124]

What Marx referred to as 'theological' was not so much the actual discipline of theology than a philosophical mode of demonstration that is reminiscent of theology.[125]

---

121. He criticised the *substance* of Hegel's pronouncements (such as the transitions in the *Philosophy of Right*, the *Phenomenology* and the *Logic*; see 2.5.2).

122. *MECW* 5, p. 56.

123. 'For Germany the *criticism of religion* is in the main complete' (*MECW* 3, p. 175). The only 'results' achieved by the Young Hegelians that Marx acknowledged were 'elucidations of Christianity from the point of view of religious history' (*MECW* 5, p. 30).

124. 'The dominance of religion was presupposed' (*MECW* 5, p. 29); more still: 'in truth religion does not form a *true* opposite to philosophy' (*MECW* 3, p. 89). Bauer 1941, for example, fights Hegel with Hegel, by donning the inquisitor's mask and demonstrating that Hegel is in fact an 'atheist and antichrist'. He adopts Hegel's method and turns it against the content of Hegel. In doing so, he does not truly break with Hegel and remains a 'theologian' in the Marxian sense.

125. *MECW* 4, pp. 64–5, 106–9; *MECW* 5, pp. 28–9, 97–8, 114–15; *MECW* 20, p. 105. The point is that theology knows no rigorously scientific proof (at best, it disposes of proofs of authority from scripture or from the head of the Church). It is true that for centuries, efforts have been made to develop a rational 'proof of the existence of God'. But this is to misunderstand the status of religious locution: when someone has faith – makes the *sacrificium intellectus* and presupposes the existence of God – then God proves his own existence (and he does so in a practical rather than in a logical way). But this has no probative force for someone who does not already agree with the presupposition. Faith can only be demonstrated by way of example; it cannot be deduced. This does not mean that theology is not a science – it is important for rendering possible an understanding of central texts and important traditions, and thereby rational worldly action. It is just that it cannot 'prove' anything outside its scope. It is up to the individual to have faith. If one wants to understand faith, one needs to consider the practice that is characterised by a given way of speaking about 'God'. It is in this sense that Marx stated: 'Kant's critique means nothing in this respect' (*MECW* 1, p. 104). A given notion may generate practical results or play a major role in some practice, even though it is nothing but a notion. But it would be nonsensical to claim that this demonstrates the 'existence' of what is imagined: 'The proofs of the existence of God are ... mere *hollow tautologies*. Take for instance the ontological proof. This only means 'that which

The speculative-'theological' demonstration only works when one has chosen beforehand to think of man as a purely spiritual being and presupposes the identity of thought and being. These are already idealist, speculative or, as Marx would say, 'theological' presuppositions. Thus Marx does not deal with historical religion itself; he criticises something else for appearing *in the guise of* religion.[126] In Marx, 'critique of religion' does not refer primarily to the critique of religion; it refers to the critique of the religious appearance of things that are in fact highly worldly. This is something we also find in Judaism and Christianity – even if we should not draw the conclusion that Marx was motivated by Judaism or dependent on Christianity.[127]

Theories were the first object of Marx's critique of religion – first those of the Young Hegelians, then those of the economists.[128] This can be described as the first stage of critique: the critique of things such as the 'state' or 'money', which appear to be religious when in fact they are not. This needs to be distinguished (at least if one follows Marx in keeping being and thought apart) from the second stage of critique, which addresses the question of *how* these things can appear to be religious in the first place.[129] This question no longer pertains to the *critique of religion*, since what is 'religious' about the state and

I conceive for myself in a real way (*realiter*) is a real concept for me" (ibid.). Talk of 'religious' objects is only valid within the context of a specific practice: 'Bring paper money into a country where this use of paper is unknown, and everyone will laugh at your subjective imagination. Come with your gods into a country where other gods are worshipped, and you will be shown to suffer from fantasies and abstractions' (ibid.). One needs to consider the underlying practice in order to understand what is meant. In 1844, Marx compares God to money. Money is also something that can only be explained by reference to real practices (after all, money is a 'social relation': *MECW* 6, p. 145), but not by philosophical ruminations on the 'meaning' of the 'category' (2.3.5). In this way, Marx anticipates post-Wittgensteinian culturalism.

126. 'Historical materialism says nothing at all about God, the world, the soul, eternity, sin, salvation, etc. Historical materialism is not a worldview but... a working method' (Eckert 1927, p. 18).

127. This overblown conclusion is drawn by Türcke 1987 and ISF 2000 (a group of theologians); both are delighted with their discovery. Yet talk of Marx as a 'prophet' was usually polemical (Schumpeter 1943, pp. 5 ff.; Popper 1945, II, pp. 164–5; Löwith 1949, p. 42; Klages 1972, p. 83; 2.4.2). The Judaeo-Christian religion is itself the first seculariser – after all, the prophets were critics of religion (*MECW* 4, pp. 129–30). For this reason, an anonymous 1842 article described 'Feuerbach' (literally: 'stream of fire') as the 'purgatorium of the present' (cited in Post 1969, p. 89).

128. Marx criticised the Young Hegelians by exaggerating their hypotheses and thereby demonstrating that these hypotheses are in fact 'theological' – in the sense that they start from Hegel's premises and go on to demonstrate anything and everything, including that the world is an 'apparition', a 'spirit' (*MECW* 5, pp. 132, 152–3, and so on; see Derrida 1994). The way Marx and Engels employ Christian language shows they were highly familiar with it (Buchbinder 1976). The later critique of the fetishism of money, commodities and capital (*MECW* 35, pp. 81 ff.; *MECW* 37, pp. 388 ff., 816; *MECW* 32, p. 451) is a critique of economic theories that raise everyday 'appearance' to the status of 'theory'. Appearances do, however, have a real foundation, and it is this real foundation in which Marx is interested.

129. 'It is, in reality, much easier to discover by analysis the earthly core of the misty creations of religion, than, conversely, it is, to develop from the actual relations of life the corresponding celestialised forms of those relations. The latter method is the only materialistic, and therefore the only scientific one' (*MECW* 35, p. 375).

money is only their 'appearance', not their 'essence'.[130] The question pertains to science and concerns underlying structures. If we calls these structures religious, we are fooled by the very appearance that Marx was concerned to penetrate theoretically:

> As, in religion, man is governed by the products of his own brain, so in capitalistic production, he is governed by the products of his own hand.[131]

> Thus, the criticism of heaven turns into the criticism of earth, the *criticism of religion* into the *criticism of law* and the *criticism of theology* into the *criticism of politics*.[132]

When Marx describes certain capitalist phenomena as trinitarian, he does not do this because those phenomena *are* supernatural, but because they can *appear* to be supernatural and become a 'fetish', an object of semi-religious reverence, as long as one does not properly understand them.[133] For instance, it 'appears' as if money multiplied itself, assuming 'an automatically active character'.[134] To understand Marx's choice of language, one needs to know he took the critique of religion to be 'in the main complete':[135] he did not want to reiterate it, but rather presupposed it. The trinity is one of the most inconceivable formulae in Christian doctrine – a 'mystery of faith'.[136] Thus to represent something *as* trinitarian is to take to an extreme the absurdity that results when a phenomenon is roundly declared to be its own essence, or when a partial observation is overhastily generalised. In this way, Marx meant to convey to his readers that this understanding is flawed.[137]

Thus the appearance of a wondrous proliferation of money is theoretically dissolved by Marx: he does this by showing how that appearance comes about in reality and by

---

130. After all, according to Feuerbach, the 'essence' of religious 'appearance' is man himself.
131. *MECW* 35, p. 616.
132. *MECW* 3, p. 176.
133. *MECW* 35, pp. 165 f.; *MECW* 37, p. 801; for similar passages, see *MECW* 3, pp. 14 f.; *MECW* 4, p. 9; *MECW* 5, p. 124. On the concept of the fetish, see R. Schröder, in Fleischer 1994, pp. 138 ff.
134. *MECW* 35, p. 164.
135. *MECW* 3, p. 175.
136. 'For the rest, the theoretical profession of faith in the divine nature in this threefold quality belongs to the mere classical formula of an ecclesiastical faith, to distinguish it from other forms derived from historical sources – a formula to which few human beings are in a position of attaching a clear and distinct concept... its examination pertains rather to teachers in their relation to one another... while mere literal faith hurts rather than improves the true religious disposition' (Kant 1998, p. 147).
137. Even those who continue to use religious expressions today can really only apply those expressions to God (and even this can only be done in an approximate way), not to anything else. Hegel took a different view: in a circular argument, he applied such expressions to all phenomena in order to then conclude that God exists. This could also be regarded as an impiety, and many believers were indeed disturbed by it: Hegel holds that a 'proof' for the existence of God is necessary, and he believes he can provide this 'proof' by means of cognition. In this way, he places philosophy above religion – and above God. It was precisely this reflection that allowed the Young Hegelians to formulate their critique of religion, 'exposing' God as a product of thought. Hegel did religion a disservice.

indicating the error within fetishising theory.[138] Hardly anything more needs to be said about Marx's critique of religion. It largely leaves religion as it is, but it seeks to elucidate the religious appearance of non-religious states of affairs, both within theory and within reality.[139] By virtue of this, Marx is part of the Enlightenment tradition (2.1.2). If one wants to get rid of this appearance, it is not enough to identify it as an appearance; the structures behind it need to be recognised and altered.[140] But there are better reasons for doing this than a critique of *religion*, of all things.

Religion for its own sake was something Marx was quite indifferent to. It was precisely because he had made this choice that he regarded freedom of religion as a valuable political liberty; this was a central aspect of his critique of Bruno Bauer.[141] He assumed that people would be less religious if they one day achieved not just political, but also 'human emancipation'.[142] But neither was such freedom from religion his motive, nor does anything depend theoretically upon the validity of this assumption. What seems in any case to be correct about it is that while religion has not disappeared in the emancipated and wealthy societies of the West, it has changed fundamentally. It has lost its

---

138. On the level of reality, there is the phenomenon that owners of money receive more money (M–C–M'). When such observations on partial phenomena go hand in hand with the failure to consider other phenomena (namely the question of what might be the nature of this 'C', which accomplishes such miracles) and are passed off as an 'essential' quality of M (one that it displays independently of the relation it has entered into, M–C–M'), money is fetishised theoretically, as in mercantilism (*MECW* 35, pp. 165–6; see Rakowitz 2001; 2.3.5).

139. For more comprehensive discussions, see Reding 1957, Bockmühl 1961, Gollwitzer 1962, Rich 1962, Post 1969, Bosse 1970, Kadenbach 1970, Oudenrijn 1972, Kröner 1977, Frostin 1978, Brechtkern 1979, H. Hirsch 1980, Monz 1995 and Gross 2000, pp. 215 ff.

140. 'But if it be declared that the social characters assumed by objects, or the material forms assumed by the social qualities of labour under the régime of a definite mode of production, are mere symbols, it is in the same breath also declared that these characteristics are arbitrary fictions sanctioned by the so-called universal consent of mankind. This suited the mode of explanation in favour during the 18th century. Unable to account for the origin of the puzzling forms assumed by social relations between man and man, people sought to denude them of their strange appearance by ascribing to them a conventional origin' (*MECW* 35, pp. 101–2). Marx calls for the Enlightenment to proceed to the second stage (this is what d'Holbach achieved for anthropology). 'The religious reflex of the real world can, in any case, only then finally vanish, when the practical relations of every-day life offer to man none but perfectly intelligible and reasonable relations with regard to his fellowmen and to Nature' (*MECW* 35, p. 90) – or: 'the point is to *change* it' (*MECW* 5, p. 5). 'Criticism has torn up the imaginary flowers from the chain not so that man shall wear the unadorned, bleak chain but so that he will shake off the chain and pluck the living flower' (*MECW* 3, p. 176).

141. 'The *privilege of faith* is a *universal right of man*' (*MECW* 3, p. 162). Marx's Jewish background may have reinforced his insight that man frees himself through 'an *essential intermediary*' when 'freeing himself *politically*' (*MECW* 3, p. 152). 'The *decomposition* of man into Jew and citizen, Protestant and citizen, religious man and citizen, is neither a deception directed *against* citizenhood, nor is it a circumvention of political emancipation, it is *political emancipation itself*' (p. 155).

142. *MECW* 3, p. 151. 'We no longer regard religion as the *cause*, but only as the *manifestation* of secular narrowness.... We do not assert [as Bauer asserted of the Jews; C.H.] that they must overcome their religious narrowness in order to get rid of their secular restrictions, we assert that they will overcome their religious narrowness once they get rid of their secular restrictions. We do not turn secular questions into theological ones' (*MECW* 3, p. 151; this is to be compared with Bonhoeffer: see below).

political relevance insofar as it has become a private matter – in Marx's day, this was the case only in the USA, the 'country of complete political emancipation'.[143] The factual differentiation of language games is resisted only by fanatical sects who boycott Darwin or endorse crusades. Various religions do, however, remain highly popular in poorer parts of the world.[144]

It remains to address one possible reservation: did Marx really leave religion as it was, criticising only its degenerate forms? Was he not an atheist after all, as many of his critics accused him of being? One thing that would seem to support this accusation of atheism was Marx's functional consideration of religion. In a methodological critique, he noted that historiography had hitherto limited itself to the chronology and glorification of political rulers ('the ideas of the ruling class':[145] or, as in Germany, philosophical ideas)[146] overlooking that both can be properly understood only by considering them within their context. Just as the characteristic features of ruling persons have not been properly understood until one knows why they *ruled* in the first place, why *they* were the ones to rule and not someone else, whom they ruled and, most importantly, *how*, the characteristic features of ideas have not been understood until one knows what was understood by means of them, *who* employed them and *who* the resulting knowledge was intended for. The inquiry needs to start from the 'real premises',[147] not from the interpretations that people formulated of themselves, their relations and the world, or that were formulated by those charged, within the 'division of labour', with developing and cultivating such interpretations.[148]

This functional approach led Marx to take roughly the following view: 'at first', within early religion, the totality of social life, which was still easy to survey, was represented

---

143. Ibid.
144. See Bielefeldt 1998.
145. *MECW* 5, p. 59.
146. *MECW* 5, pp. 56–7.
147. *MECW* 5, pp. 31, 41.
148. *MECW* 5, pp. 43–4, 51 ff.; Heym 1970. 'Just as one does not judge an individual by what he thinks about himself, so one cannot judge such a period of transformation by its consciousness, but, on the contrary, this consciousness must be explained from the contradictions of material life' (*MECW* 29, p. 263; *MECW* 5, p. 55). 'Consciousness can never be anything else than conscious being, and the being of men is their actual life-process' (*MECW* 5, p. 36). This is not the 'participant perspective' that Habermas wants to deploy against the functionalist 'reductions' he suspects Luhmann and Marx of effecting. Both Habermas and Marx invoke Vico's principle '*verum et factum convertuntur*' (*MECW* 35, p. 375); Habermas, however, applies it only to ideas ('norms': 3.1.5). When one limits the application of the principle in this way, one will be constrained to once more 'share the illusion of [the] epoch' (*MECW* 5, p. 55; cf. pp. 59–60), especially when it is one's own epoch. Marx takes the '*factum*' more seriously: 'Even the objects of the simplest "sensuous certainty" are only given . . . through social development, industry and commercial intercourse. The cherry-tree, like almost all fruit-trees, was, as is well known, only a few centuries ago transplanted by commerce into our zone, and therefore only by this action of a definite society in a definite age it has become "sensuous certainty"' (p. 39). Incidentally, Vico intended to discover 'laws of history' (Vico 1744; Fenske 1997, p. 332); he is therefore far more speculative than Marx.

in an ideal form.[149] Over time, this ideal form became autonomous, to the point where religion could even begin to '[come] into contradiction' with the rest of society.[150] This view was subsequently confirmed by the sociology of religion.[151]

When a sociological functionalisation is interpreted as an attempted *refutation* of religion, this is often due to a political desire to shield one's religion from historical critique. It was not for nothing that Marx developed his most incisive criticisms of religion in the course of his engagement with the Prussian censorship.[152] The latter attempted forcibly to repress critical inquiry – although the inquiry concerned not religion but the practice of dressing repressive *policies* up religiously.[153] Theology has changed considerably in the meantime, and this is partly due to its reception of Marxism. Today, the notion that religion must tolerate historical reflection is hardly controversial. Such reflection includes the historical exegesis of the Bible, which was only beginning to develop in Marx's day (especially in the work of the Young Hegelians); it also involves acknowledging the more inglorious episodes in the history of the Church, as well as socio-anthropological inquiry into the functions religion has exercised since the dawn of humanity, functions it doubtless continues to exercise today.[154]

---

149. *MECW* 5, p. 36. 'Religion is the general theory of that world, its encyclopaedic compendium, its logic in a popular form' (*MECW* 3, p. 175). Marx knew what he was talking about: he was highly familiar with the Bible and Luther, and his work as a journalist involved him engaging with other religions as well (Marx and Engels 1976).

150. *MECW* 5, p. 45. Marx annotated this passage by adding the word 'religion'. The 'contradiction' is not of a purely 'intellectual and moral' kind (although such a contradiction is possible in principle: p. 55); it becomes weighty only when it is grounded in real conflicts, when the groups that rebel against 'social relations' are socially powerful, and their power will, in most cases, be economically grounded (pp. 43–4). Engels calls attention to such a constellation when he explores the context of the German peasant war (*MECW* 10, pp. 397 ff.). Not even the Bible can be understood without such background knowledge (for instance of the periodical enslavement of the Jewish people).

151. There have been attempts to demonstrate the existence of other 'irreducible' functions, besides instrumental ones: witness the 'symbolic' in Gehlen or 'solidarity' in Durkheim. But it would be a mistake to read Marx so reductively as to create a need for supplementing him with such notions (in his discussion of ideology, Marx speaks of a particular interest being 'represented' as the general interest: *MECW* 5, pp. 46–7). In fact, such functions must also remain incomprehensible for as long as one does not begin with the question of how the society under consideration reproduces itself in the first place. The hermetic solidarity proper to early forms of society was necessary to their survival. Even if solidarity is 'generated symbolically', this does not alter the fact that it exercises an economic function (one need think only of the cohesion of a group of humans hunting a mammoth, or of Gehlen's 'taming of the primoridal bovine'). Sociability does not supplement a pre-existing functionality; rather, reproduction has always already been socialised.

152. *MECW* 1, pp. 109 ff., 184 ff.

153. 'Christianity precludes the possibility of 'any new decline', but the police must be on their guard to see that philosophising newspaper writers do not bring about such a decline... Christianity is sure of its victory, but... it is not so sure of it as to spurn the aid of the police' (*MECW* 1, p. 191).

154. What Marx stated with regard to this is now considered self-evident. Fanatical forms of religion such as they occur in the non-Western world are quite easily grasped from the Marxian perspective: old elites fear for their privileges, which are not likely to survive the 'purgatory of Feuerbach'; potential counter-elites couch their demands in religious terms. At the same time,

It would, in any case, be odd if a historicisation of religion that also understands itself 'historically' were to become dangerous. The accusation that the functional approach meant to destroy religion may apply to the practice of the socialist states. But there are several reasons why it misses the internal logic of Marx's theory. Because Marx took religion to be no more than a symptom, he was simply not interested in abolishing it. In fact, he suspected that if it were abolished but everything else remained the same, it would immediately resurface – much like money. Its *theoretical* 'sublation', undertaken within Marx's fragments on the critique of religion, is precisely not a 'destruction', like that of Hegel,[155] for things that are merely sublated theoretically 'remain in existence'.[156] Thus Marx also historicises the natural sciences,[157] but he is a long way from wanting to deny their 'validity'. The accusation that Marx meant to destroy religion rests on the very identification of thought and being that Marx criticised as a *fallacious* theologisation (2.5.7).

There is a second reason why one might suspect Marx's critique of religion of attacking religion itself. His notes from 1844, which were not intended for publication, contain a passage that seems to question 'creation' itself.[158] Is Marx not attacking religion itself in this passage?[159] The answer is no. As a later passage shows, Marx was aware that men cannot 'create' anything new; they can only modify what already exists. It is not a matter of providing men with divine attributes.[160] Marx rather points out two things that are also relevant to theology. In his first argument, Marx notes that talk of creation makes little sense for as long as one regards creation as a physical act: it then challenges physics (unsuccessfully);[161] moreover, when 'God' is given a physical status in this way, he ceases

religion is an '*expression* of [the] real suffering' that often reigns in such countries. '[*P*]*rotest* against real distress' (*MECW* 3, p. 175; see Bosse 1970) may be constrained to express itself religiously, because the political path of democratic or socialist modernisation has so frequently and visibly failed (see Riesebrodt in Bielefeldt 1998, pp. 67 ff.) – what caused it to fail is another matter.

155. Colletti 1975.

156. *MECW* 3, p. 340; cf. *MECW* 3, p. 7.

157. '[W]here would natural science be without industry and commerce?' (*MECW* 5, p. 40).

158. *MECW* 3, pp. 304 ff.

159. This claim is formulated in the apologies for Catholicism found in Voegelin 2000a, pp. 22 ff., Ehlen 1982, Senge 1985 and Hofmann 1987. What is ideologically 'decisive and incompatible with the Christian belief in creation... is Marx's doctrine that man creates himself through..."social labour"' (Nell-Breuning 1985, p. 262).

160. '[Man] can work only as Nature does, that is by changing the form of matter. Footnote: 'All the phenomena of the universe, whether produced by the hand of man or through the universal laws of physics, are not actual new creations, but merely a modification of matter'' (*MECW* 35, p. 53; Marx is quoting a 1771 statement by Pietro Verri; see *MECW* 5, pp. 51–2). The old accusation of apotheosising man has newly been levelled at Marx by Kuenzlen 1997, pp. 109 ff.; against Kuenzlen's position, see inter alia Reding 1957, Horský 1972, Buchbinder 1976, Kröner 1977.

161. 'The creation of the *earth* has received a mighty blow from *geognosy* – i.e., from the science which presents the formation of the earth, the development of the earth, as a process, as a self-generation. *Generatio aequivoca* is the only practical refutation of the theory of creation' (*MECW* 3, pp. 304–5).

to be *God*.[162] This sort of cosmological understanding of God has been criticised for some time, including by theologians; the debate on the 'God of the philosophers' has been going on for millennia.[163] Is the God of the Greeks, who can be devised theoretically and hence also refuted, the same as the loving and active Jewish God, who can only reveal himself?[164] The critique of the physics-based understanding of God is not necessarily an attack on religion as such.

The other key point in Marx's early note concerns the social form displayed by religion as Marx encounters it: servitude, which is due to worldly factors, is ideally and spiritually perpetuated within religion.[165] The ruler-subject model is projected onto the relationship between God and his creation.[166] This critique is not so much aimed at God as at the church and others who rule 'by the grace of God'. What the worldly role of Christianity ought to be is also the subject of a protracted and still unsettled controversy. Ought religion to lend support to worldly powers or ought it to follow up on the egalitarian demands of its revelation? This is another question that does not need to be decided for one to see that Marx's critique of *servile* Christianity is not necessarily an attack on religion as such. Marx attacks the practice of instrumentalising religion for purposes of political repression – there is a difference.[167]

---

162. 'For example, let us assume *God*, insofar as he is determined as object, 'as the *real foundation* of our cognition, then he belongs *himself*, insofar as he is object, in the *sphere of our cognition*, and therefore cannot be for us the ultimate point on which this entire sphere is suspended'' (*MECW* 1, p. 103; see Schelling, *Ausgewählte Werke*, 1, p. 55).

163. Corinthians 1:18 ff.; Colossians 2:8; Acts 17:16.

164. This distinction was also drawn by Moses Hess 1862 (see Gollwitzer 1957). On de-mythologisation, which is also de-cosmologisation, see (besides Kant) Bultmann; see Rentsch 2000, pp. 180 ff. Marx invokes Tertullian and the 'most capable and consistent section of Protestant theologians' (*MECW* 1, p. 190).

165. 'A man who lives by the grace of another regards himself as a dependent being. But I live completely by the grace of another if I owe him not only the maintenance of my life, but if he has, moreover, *created* my *life* … my life has necessarily a source of this kind outside of it. The *Creation* is therefore an idea very difficult to dislodge from popular consciousness. The fact that nature and man exist on their own account is in*comprehensible* to it, because it contradicts everything *tangible* in practical life' (*MECW* 3, p. 304).

166. While there are passages that speak of the 'servant of God' (Moses 5:32, 36; Psalms 34:23), even they contain a progressive element, as obedience to God exempts from obedience to humans (Acts 5:29, 1 Corinthians 7:23). Other passages speak not of 'servitude' but of the relationship to a benign father (Matthew 23:9), or of love both of God and of other people (Matthew 5:44; Romans 13:8). This is not especially compatible with worldly relations of servitude (Sölle 1968, Türcke 1990, pp. 112 ff.).

167. 'Not atheism, but the idols are … the enemy of God' (Ernesto Cardenal, in Thomas 1993, 236). '*Religious* questions of the day have at the present time a *social* significance. … Only the *theologian* can believe it is a question of religion as religion' (*MECW* 4, p. 108). 'The so-called Christian state, on the other hand, has a political attitude to religion and a religious attitude to politics. By degrading the forms of the state to mere semblance, it equally degrades religion to mere semblance' (*MECW* 3, p. 157). 'The so-called Christian state is the *imperfect* state, and the Christian religion is regarded by it as the *supplementation* and *sanctification* of its imperfection. For the Christian state, therefore, religion necessarily becomes a *means* [!]; hence, it is a *hypocritical* state' (ibid.). 'The social principles of Christianity justified the slavery of antiquity, glorified the serfdom

Those who want to read Marx's observations as constituting a fundamental critique of religion are implicitly claiming to be the only ones who can speak for religion; they are also operating with a cosmological idea of God and an understanding of religion that is based on the model of domination. Marx does not 'destroy' religion as such; but he has formulated some criticisms that deserve to be taken seriously by theology. How have the religions handled these criticisms? Could they not be seen as doing religion a service? Do those who resist them not create the impression that worldly things are being deified? These are questions that religion needs to settle for itself. Let us now consider how this was done.

2.6.5 *The critique of religion as a political issue*

> Was it not Christianity above all that separated church and state? Read St. Augustine's *De civitate Dei*, study the Fathers of the Church and the spirit of Christianity, and then come back and tell us whether the state or the church is the 'Christian state'![168]

The conflicts between Marxism and religion did not develop for necessary reasons;[169] they were contingent. In formulating his '*categorical imperative to overthrow all relations* in which man is a debased, enslaved, forsaken, despicable being',[170] Marx was advocating a politics the authorities of his day were not pleased with. And those authorities included the church, which thereby brought itself into contradiction with its own origins and doctrine.[171] Although the theory of natural law, the modern theory of the state, the Enlightenment and political reforms and revolutions had increasingly forced religion out of politics, the church had nevertheless reclaimed some ground in the course of various counterrevolutions. Monarchies all over Europe used the 'divine right of kings' and the 'Holy Alliance' under Metternich to resist political emancipation in the name of God. This was the reason why so many people began to dissociate themselves from the church and why Christian critics of the church began to turn to Marxism: the church was siding with the rulers, including the most repressive ones.[172]

---

of the Middle Ages and are capable, in case of need, of defending the oppression of the proletariat, with somewhat doleful grimaces' (*MECW* 6, p. 231) – and even National Socialism (Scholder 1977). This criticism cannot be deflected by arguments; the only way to deflect it would be to position oneself politically (Gollwitzer 1962). Differences between Europe and the USA are also relevant to this issue.

168. *MECW* 1, p. 198.

169. Marx provided legal support to the Jewish community of Trier (*MECW* 1, p. 400; H. Hirsch 1980; Monz 1995, pp. 146, 153).

170. *MECW* 3, p. 176.

171. 'Are not most of your court cases and most of your civil laws concerned with property? But you have been told that your treasure is not of this world' (*MECW* 1, p. 199; see, for example, Matthew 6:19, Matthew 19:24, Matthew 22:21, Luke 6:20, John 18:35, Romans 14:17; see Troeltsch 1977, Farner 1985).

172. See, inter alia, Luxemburg 1971, Dirks 1947, Fuchs 1955, Gollwitzer 1962, Lochmann 1974, Reisinger 1985.

Marx did not attack the Christian religion in the religious sense, as Weitling had done and as Eugen Dühring would later do; what he criticised was the fact that it had allowed itself to become the legitimating ideology of the 'Christian state' that was Prussia. His attack on the Christian religion was precise and political. While some Christians were open to calls for social improvements, because the discrimination of the workers was so obvious,[173] the political theology of the Protestant state church and of Catholic Ultramontanism could not accept a movement that insisted on *self-determination*.[174] The Christian reaction to social democracy was consistent: some of social democracy's demands were given a 'Christian social' formulation, so as to take the sting out of social democracy. The main goal was to lead the lost sheep back into accepting the tried and tested alliance of crown and altar.[175] This reaction on the part of the churches shows they understood socialism correctly: they perceived it as a *political* threat.

Even the charitable activities of the churches were imbued with an abstract negation of socialism, whose motivation was not at all theological, but rather highly political: the churches sided with the Kaiser and the authorities of the time, as if this were natural; they considered the relations of authority within society to be 'willed by God' and declared them to be thus. The Inner Mission of Johann Hinrich Wichern, often cited as evidence that the Church was taking social issues seriously, openly called itself the 'Association for Fighting Social Democracy' ['*Verein zur Bekämpfung der Sozialdemokratie*'] from 1875 onward.[176] Thus the motives for Christian engagement with Social Democracy were no so much theological as political – and they were not democratic but rather nationalist, monarchist and feudalistic.[177] Marx recognised this early on, and responded by transforming his critique of religion into an analysis of politics. For Christianity, the crucial issue raised by socialism was not that of 'social justice' (calling for it was easy), nor that of its immanent or transcendent 'justification', but rather the question of who would bring it about: the church, perhaps to bolster its threatened hegemony, the patrimonial state (which ended up playing this role, from Bismarck to Helmut Schmidt) or the workers themselves, as called for by Marx (2.2.2). The last option presupposed political changes, and *they* were ultimately the source of contention. The church refused to endorse political reforms. During the nineteenth century, crown and altar allied themselves so closely

173. The social encyclical *De rerum novarum* (1891; BKAB 1991, Baader 1865) is proof of this.

174. The Vatican's invectives were directed mainly against attempts at practical self-administration that undermined the clerical hierarchy, as in the case of the layman's eucharist. The Vatican's hostility to liberation theology was a matter not just of the latter's affinity for socialism, but also of its infringement upon the clerical hierarchy. Is the polemic against modern 'self-empowerment' (Schmitt 1970) not a front for the ideal of clerico-political paternalism?

175. See Lindt 1957, pp. 211 ff.; Sorg 1974, Goeggelmann 1987; see also Kral 1920, Brunstäd 1926; on Catholicism specifically, see Höffner 1949 and Dülmen 1989, pp. 174 ff.

176. Beuys 1982, p. 481; Fuchs 1955, pp. 17 ff., Eckart 1910; see also F. Bodelschwingh.

177. Contemporary Christian anti-Marxism (Rohrmoser 2000) must either content itself with a mere semblance of continuity or endanger the commitment to democracy. Historically, the Christian anti-Marxist polemic was fundamentally anti-democratic.

that they became virtually indistinguishable.[178] *This* church did not strike Social Democracy as a suitable interlocutor.

Moreover, there was little reason to negotiate one's political differences within the field of religion. This was the lesson learned first-hand by clergymen such as Adolf Stoecker or Paul Goehre, who were bold enough to attend workers' assemblies in order to campaign for new political parties. Wichern, Stoecker, Goehre and Naumann campaigned, in the name of Christianity, for parties that promised social reforms but otherwise displayed a monarchist and in some cases an imperialist orientation (2.1.2). Social Democracy saw through the *political* attack that lay behind this. August Bebel generalised: 'Christianity and socialism are opposed like fire and water. The so-called good core of Christianity... is not Christian but an expression of general humanity'.[179]

From the very beginning of the confrontation with socialism, and later Marxism, the official representatives of the theology and the church were at pains to draw a clear dividing line, in accordance with the time-proven model of distinguishing between 'friend and foe'.[180] But they often ended up unwittingly exposing their own position to critical examination, so that what had been intended as an external dividing line became an internal one: socialism reappeared within the Christian camp (much as there were and continue to be secular anti-socialists), both in the form of historical forerunners such as the Franciscans and in that of worker priests, very much a phenomenon of the time.[181] The criticisms that Christian ritual was becoming devoid of meaning and that the Church was neglecting its social duties cut to the quick. Thus religion had a substantive interest in engaging with the critique of religion – whether it did so to ward off that critique, and the loss of estates-based privileges it threatened, or to revitalise itself, to the extent that intellectual and spiritual barrenness were felt within Christianity. Thus theology and the church engaged in a decades-long 'dialogue' with socialism, ranging from no-holds-barred fighting to friendly encounters – the latter, however, only took place in the 1960s – and involving the most varied episodes (the dialogue has only ended, it seems, because one of the interlocutors is absent).[182] We can now identify some of the basic features of the positions on Marx that were defended during this dialogue.

---

178. Clerics 'were considered agents of the authorities, and they were feared as the "black police"' (Beuys 1982, p. 481; see Stahl 1853). When it was a matter of taking a definite stand, in 1914 and 1933, the church consistently and interdenominationally opted for the throne, with few exceptions. The result was a 'German church' (Scholder 1977).

179. Bebel 1874, quoted in Beuys 1982, p. 482; see also Gollwitzer 1977, p. 40. Religion 'will not be abolished'; it will 'disappear' (Bebel 1971, p. 296; Kautsky 1903). The Catholic preacher Wilhelm Hohoff (1908), whom Bebel attacked, modified Bebel's assertion by stating that Christianity and *capitalism* exclude one another like fire and water.

180. This model (Schmitt 1932) has a forerunner in E.M. Arndt's 'Popular Hatred' ['*Volkshass*'] (1813).

181. A sort of 're-entry' (Luhmann) of the system-environment difference into the system.

182. See Heimann 1955, Fuchs 1956, Garaudy 1966, Girardi 1968, McIntyre 1968, Duchrow 1969, Nell-Breuning 1969, Stockmaier 1970, Rolfes 1974, Soelle 1974, Kern 1976, Bienert 1979, Reisinger 1983.

2.6.6 *Four theological views of Marx*

Rejection of 'atheism'

> Marxism is not atheism.[183]

> Today there is only one position that could take on Marxism, and that position is Christianity.[184]

Theologians critical of the church noted the liaison with the German state had not done cultural Protestantism and its theology much good. In 1873, Basle-based church historian Franz Overbeck flatly denied that theology was still Christian in character.[185] But the official church was a long way from taking this view. A large number of its members defined themselves in terms of their common rejection of the *atheism* they attributed to Marx. We have already seen the accusation of atheism was scarcely justified. Marx started from the real circumstances he encountered. While these circumstances needed to be ordered theoretically, the order had to be derived from its material, not vice versa. Marx never started from theoretical 'principles'; deducing something from first principles was a type of theory that was foreign to him, as it is to all empirical sciences. But an ordo-philosophy whose origins lie in the Middle Ages,[186] and which does start from first principles, proceeding deductively from them to matter and on to nothingness in a downward movement, had to take a theory that does *not* begin by assuming God's existence to be a theory that assumes God's *non-existence.* And by virtue of this alone, that theory had to seem unacceptable. Economic theory had to get by without God. But this grammatical difference between economic and theological theory was ignored. Thus the accusation of 'atheism' rests on the surreptitious attribution of a homogenising model of theory.[187]

183. Max Adler 1974.

184. Lay 1975, p. 419.

185. It was only his friend Nietzsche who rejected Judaism, Christianity and socialism by deducing the latter from the former (see Cancik 2000). He accused Christianity of celebrating a cult of weakness while *simultaneously* buttressing Wilhelmine culture. What could he have had in mind, as an opponent of both Bismarck and Bebel?

186. The pope declared Thomism binding in 1879 (*Aeterni patris*, reiterated in 1931; see W. Eucken 1948). But it would have been quite possible to derive a more progressive politics from Thomas (Farner 1985, pp. 77 ff.; Fenske 1997, pp. 212 ff.).

187. 'The basic error committed by this 'Christian' criticism is that the final expectations of Christians and Marxists are situated on the same level' (Wünsch 1962, p. 89). Whether or not a physician is also a Christian is irrelevant to the validity of his theory. Even if Marx had *remained* Jewish or Christian, this would not have made the least difference to his theory. The question would be relevant only to his biographical motives. *Ad personam* statements do not, however, constitute a critique of the theory. Marx lamented 'the fact that all the philosophies of the past without exception have been accused by the theologians of abandoning the Christian religion, even those of the pious Malebranche and the divinely inspired Jakob Böhme, and that Leibniz was accused of being ... an atheist' (*MECW* 1, p. 190). Early Christians such as Celsus and Julianus were

While other features of Marxism – such as its endorsement of democracy, the emancipation of women and freedom of religion, and its rejection of the nation state, the remuneration of the clergy from public funds and religious education – may have been decisive motivationally, the accusation levelled against it was always that of 'atheism'.[188] To be sure, second-order political concessions (usually of a programmatic nature) were sometimes made, depending on the strength of the labour movement or the socialist states. But it was not just the churches that ranted against materialism (formulating arguments that would have been less off the mark as criticisms of the Monist League). Social Democracy picked up the gauntlet and attempted to demonstrate the illegitimacy of the churches, in continuity with the French Enlightenment. The churches were aggressively declared to be both untimely and backward *by their very nature*.[189] Accusations of atheism were virtually invited by Marxism's self-interpretation as a comprehensive 'worldview' (2.1.4, 2.2.4) that would suffer none beside it. *Both* sides followed Engels, Kautsky and dialectical materialism in interpreting Marxism as a naturalist system by which to explain the world.[190] When Marx is read as the author of a worldview, it becomes easy either to reject him,[191] or to endorse him for questionable reasons.[192]

But it is not just Marxian theory that cannot be correctly interpreted as a worldview. Christianity also raises the question of whether it can be understood in this way or ought rather to be considered a radical practice, at least in those cases in which it is taken seriously. Egalitarian variants of Christianity have tended to fail – because of the church. It was interested in a theology that favourably stabilised the status quo, and it strongly adjusted itself to feudal states.[193] 'Dissenting' groups could expect to be banned and persecuted as

---

accused of atheism. Marxists compared themselves to natural scientists who had been accused of heresy (Bruno, Galilei; MacIntyre 2002).

188. This is the accusation formulated in *Ex cathedra Quadragesimo anno* (1931; cf. Reisinger 1985); for philosophical versions of the accusation, see Wetter 1952, Koch 1961, Ehlen 1961, Bienert 1979, pp. 45 ff.; Senge 1985. To Herbert Wehner (1985, p. 58), the founding of the Christian Democrat Union (CDU) was an attempt to use Christianity for an 'ideological gathering against Marxism', in continuity with National Socialism (see Uertz 1981 and the 1910 'modernist oath'). Nell-Breuning's polemic focused on atheism, although his economic theory was strongly dependent on Marx: 'Marx is the main opponent whom Catholic social doctrine must confront. The confrontation concerns not Marx the economist... but Marx the philosopher' (Nell-Breuning 1985, pp. 262–3).

189. Bebel 1874, Dietzgen 1908, Steigerwald 1973; see Fetscher 1973a, pp. 58–78; Schlette 1975. Voltaire, the church's most venomous opponent, was by no means an atheist: 'If there be atheists, who are to blame? who but the mercenary tyrants of our souls, who, while disgusting us with their knavery, urge some weak spirits to deny the God whom such monsters dishonour?' (Voltaire 1843, pp. 162–3). He invokes Jesus in support of his argument against the church (283 ff.). Franz Mehring wrote noteworthy essays on this subject (1983, pp. 241–288); he had once meant to become a priest and was initially a follower of G.E. Lessing.

190. Fetscher 1971, McMurtry 1978, Ehlen 1982, A. Woods 1995, Steigerwald 2000.

191. Senge 1985, Thomas 1993.

192. Hoffman 2000.

193. In the case of the Catholic Church, these were Spain and France, first and foremost; see Duve 1976, pp. 13 ff., Hanson 1987 and Kallscheuer 1994, pp. 19 ff.; the Protestant churches adapted themselves to England and Germany.

the Albigenses were, or to exist in the 'seclusion' of marginality, like the mendicant orders.[194] Christianity's self-adulation and concomitant sureness of victory recall this imperial self-assertion. Christianity practised what it accused the Marxists of: dogmatic prejudice and 'lack of scientificity'.[195] Prophets, apostles, church fathers, reformers and Christian laymen all struggled with rigid hierarchies. This is perhaps the most tangible parallel with Marxism.

Tolerance in spite of 'atheism'

> Karl Marx's lasting achievement consists in his bold denunciation of the man-slaying countenance of the capitalist world, or, to put this theologically, in his insight into social sin *in concreto*.[196]

In the German-speaking world of the late nineteenth century, only exceptional and marginal theologians such as Wilhelm Hohoff, Rudolf Todt or Christoph Blumhardt took note of Marx.[197] While this small, moderate group had theological reservations about some decisive aspects of radical practice, it nevertheless tolerated the politics of the workers' movement, at least in part.[198] Some Social Democrats had given proof of their willingness to engage in a dialogue early on. It was argued that Social Democracy had been forced, since Rosa Luxemburg's time, to treat the church as an enemy, since the church had consistently sided with the authorities. The church should remember its commitment to justice and finally act in accordance with it.[199] Thus Social Democracy neither combated nor endorsed the church, but merely invited its *cooperation*.

---

194. Troeltsch 1977, Bloch 1970, Farner 1985; on the middle ages: Cohn 1988; Deschner 1989. 'The danger threatens both the content of the tradition and those who inherit it. For both, it is one and the same thing: the danger of becoming a tool of the ruling classes.... According to traditional practice, the spoils are carried in the procession. They are called "cultural treasures"... There is no document of culture which is not at the same time a document of barbarism' (Benjamin 2003, pp. 391–2).

195. Wetter 1952 declared Marxism unscientific because it did not heed his 'proofs for the existence of God' (Wünsch 1962, pp. 61, 73; for a reply, see Klaus 1958. The parallel between Diamat and scholasticism was diagnosed by Wetter himself.) Wünsch called such polemics an 'escape into what is Christian' (p. 85) and spoke of the 'false superiority of Christian eschatology' (p. 92): 'But why bring theology into it?' (p. 84).

196. Arthur Rich.

197. On Blumhardt see Thurneysen 1926; for an overview, see Sorg 1974, pp. 67 ff.

198. These reservations were dropped when social democracy began to display greater openness toward the church (and closed itself off against Marx). The Godesberg Programme marks the turning point (see Prümmer 1965, Wehner 1985). During socialism's strongest periods, theologians even pondered the fact that the church was not committed to a single economic system. In doing so, they were not so much beginning to accept the idea of socialism as recognising its role as the next potential potentate. Recent political theology's celebration of abstract 'remembrance' usually lacks this Machiavellian background.

199. Luxemburg 1971; for a similar position, see Max Adler 1974. Within the church, this intermediate position was taken by Friedrich Heiler, Gottfried Naumann and later Fritz Lieb (cf. Kambas 1985; Faber 1994, pp. 84 ff.).

This option was usually condemned to marginality.[200] In Germany, the situation did not change until the collapse of the monarchy, when church and state were separated for the first time. There was now no longer any compelling institutional reason to oppose socialism (if one continued to do so, then only 'for the sake of tradition').[201] Rather, Social Democracy's growing significance encouraged many theologians to engage more closely with it. In the meantime, theology had learnt some lessons about modernity, both from modernity's critics Kierkegaard and Nietzsche and from its systematisers Kant and Weber. It began to be understood that one could not theologise in a top-down manner, both because this is to pervert the Christian message, which always already *is* 'below', and because the world is not constructed hierarchically or according to aprioristic principles. Why should a Christian not be able to decide secular issues for himself? People ought to be able to decide worldly matters in worldly ways ('So give back to Caesar what is Caesar's').[202]

This sort of interpretation led to the Christian critique of the church and the socialist critique of religion coalescing in *social critique*. It was now possible for Christians to be socialists and vice versa.[203] After all, the question of 'atheism' was unimportant to Marx: he had started with the insight that scholastic treatment of this question made no difference to reality. He had not answered the question one way or the other and drawn the consequences from his answer; he had let the matter rest and considered worldly questions autonomous. One can almost always answer them without reference to the philosophical question concerning the existence of God.[204] Because one can very well arrive at divergent political judgements on a secular basis, there were some Christians who inclined toward socialism out of *secular* considerations. The question was a worldly one, including for Christians and Jews. Theirs was not a religious or 'Christian' socialism, for the world had come of age.[205] Thus it became possible to engage with Marxism

---

200. See 2.1.3. Later, however, the 'church in socialism' thrived on it (Thumser 1996).

201. Duve 1976.

202. Matthew 22:21.

203. Erwin Eckert cut to the chase of the matter in a 1926 pamphlet: 'What Germany's religious socialists... really mean to do is express their conviction... that there is a road leading from the gospel to socialism, and that there is a road from socialism to the gospel' (quoted in Balzer 1993, p. 68).

204. What Marx said was not so much 'There is no God, therefore...' but rather 'No matter what your answer to the question concerning God, it won't help us in this matter. In any case, we cannot expect those who jauntily invoke the authority of God to improve the situation. So let us put this matter behind us.' He held that even 'atheism is beginning to show signs of wear and tear' (*MECW* 3, p. 457).

205. Bonhoeffer 1949, letters written in June 1944. See Kraus 1982, Gräb 1999. Acceptance of this is in keeping with the nature of a monotheistic religion of the book: the lesson one had been forced to learn from Nietzsche (via Weber) was that the unleashing of a godless world within human reason was, among other things, a world-historical achievement of Biblical religion itself. According to Nietzsche, Christianity exposed everything in the world to reason until it finally came time for Christianity itself to be judged – and it was found wanting (*MECW* 4, pp. 129–30; Gogarten 1970, Bosse 1970, Tenbruck 1975). It would be paradoxical to claim this secular standpoint is itself

independently of the meaningless question of atheism.[206] As a result, there began to be theologians who read Marx in productive ways, including outside of theology.[207]

Religious socialism

And yet a theologian remains a theologian, even when he is not theologising. A different group held that the radical practice rejected by moderate theologians accorded not with secular reason but with Christianity, and attempted to mediate between the two for *this* reason. After all, some writings by socialists created the impression that socialism was the true 'heir', especially as far as the teachings of Jesus (Matthew 19:24),[208] the communism of early Christianity (Acts 4:32)[209] and the Reformation were concerned.[210] One could follow Kutter in taking this position *regardless* of the SPD's self-conception.[211]

Thus, a new 'religious socialism' was advocated, both by Christians ('liberation theology') and by Marxists (Bloch, Metzger).[212] This exalted conception led, however, to an 'elliptical' theology (Barth): it now disposed of two centres, God *and* the world, and the relationship between them was not always defined satisfactorily. In case of doubt, one of

---

'Christian' (or Protestant, as Stahl and Tillich claim) because of its genesis; this would be to abolish its secularity again, just as it amounts to a methodological failure to distinguish between genesis and meaning. Islam and Judaism have achieved their own secular Enlightenments; in fact, they did so before Christianity, even if their Enlightenments are in the defensive today.

206. The philosophical category 'nonsense', which Wittgenstein applied to questions that cannot be answered (*Philosophical Investigations*, aphorisms 17 and 32), sits well with Marx's remarks on the question of God's existence: 'Ask yourself how you arrived at that question. Ask yourself whether your question is not posed from a standpoint to which I cannot reply, because it is wrongly put. When you ask about ... creation ... you are abstracting, in so doing, from man and nature. You postulate them as *non-existent*, and yet you want me to prove them to you as *existing*. Now I say to you: Give up your abstraction and you will also give up your question.... Don't think, don't ask me, for as soon as you think and ask, your *abstraction* ... has no meaning' (*MECW* 3, p. 305). 'Of course there are then no questions left, and this itself is the answer' (Wittgenstein 2010, 6.52); 'don't think, but look!' (*Philosophical Investigations*, aphorism 66). Voegelin 2000a, p. 22 considered this a mere 'ban on questions' (although he also presented Marx as a gnostic). It would be more accurate to speak of a re-actualisation of the differentiation of various levels of meaning within philosophical discourse: Kant already suggested that one could employ 'speculative' statements about the origins of the world only in a 'regulative' way – nothing more can be deduced from them (Kant 1998, A 509, A 672 ff.). Marx considers the answering of such questions to be of no practical relevance, since nothing follows from them. In fact, they distract from 'worldly' issues, and there is even the danger of losing oneself in them as in a 'fly-bottle' (Wittgenstein 2009, p. 378; cf. *MECW* 4, pp. 57–8; *MECW* 5, p. 55; see below).

207. For instance Heimann, Fuchs, Wünsch or Gollwitzer; see 2.6.7.

208. See Machovec 1972, Fetscher 1974, Rolfes 1974. 'Jesus is the social movement' (Barth, in Gollwitzer 1972, p. 7).

209. See Farner 1985 and, for a more detailed account, Martin Leutzsch, in Faber 1994, pp. 77 ff.

210. See Engels in *MECW* 10, pp. 397 ff.; Kautsky 1947 and 1908, Bloch 1921.

211. Hermann Kutter, the first 'religious and social' theorist besides Leonard Ragaz and a key reference point for Barth, wrote in *Sie müssen* ('They Must', 1903) that Social Democracy was 'unconsciously driven by the living God, arisen to spur the flagging church to superindividual work for the kingdom of God' (RGG2, Vol. III, 1442; Kutter 1965, Zademach 1973).

212. See Breipohl 1970, Balzer 1973, Deresch 1977, Ewald 1977, Peter 1995 or Bai 1996.

the two had to be sacrificed, and there was no way of telling beforehand which of them it would be. It was as easy for Tillich's friend Eugen Hirsch to become a nationalist and a National Socialist as it was for Barth's friend Gogarten. Religious socialism was *essentially* not much different from the former alliance of church and crown or the new theologisation effected by *völkisch* movements. Thus, it was precisely the most radical of the religious socialists who inadvertently continued the legacy of the 'bourgeois revolution' (Metz) by sacralising culture. This was something one could do with *any* culture: liberal (Harnack, Troeltsch), socialist (Tillich, the early Barth) or nationalist (Gogarten, Hirsch). Worldly oppositions benefit little from sacralisation. They are merely rigidified.

What was ironic about the sacralisation of Marxism, of all things, was that it was prepared by the rejection of Marxism. Ernst Troeltsch, a theologian who was familiar with sociology due to his friendship with Max Weber, followed Weber in partly adopting 'historical materialism' as a *method*, even though he felt that as a *worldview*, he needed to formulate a theological refutation of it[213] – a pursuit to which he devoted more effort than to actually using the method he had accepted. His case is reminiscent of the way German social scientists like to conduct 'methodological debates' before any results have been obtained. A leading exponent of cultural Protestantism, Troeltsch combined Christianity and modern rationality in a 'European cultural synthesis'.[214] In doing so, he theologised 'culture', but he also prejudiciously pre-selected its contents: Marxism was exempted from sacralisation from the outset, because it was not considered part of 'culture' – a legacy of Nietzsche.

Theologically, Troeltsch's rejection of Marxism as a worldview was grounded in his idealist theology. He situated religion in an autonomous mental overworld,[215] the likes of which were nowhere conceptualised in the Marxist worldview – reason enough for

---

213. Bosse 1970, p. 17.

214. See Zahrnt 1966, p. 54. Ernst Robert Curtius and Max Scheler took a similar view.

215. As a student of Ritschl, Troeltsch acknowledges only intellectual causes of intellectual effects, just like Bultmann after him (Bosse 1970, p. 76). The 'ideal and independent existence of the soul' (p. 83) is a 'metaphysical principle' (p. 75). This ontological dualism concedes to the intellect its own domain, even if it is only a limited domain. The existence of religion is accounted for in objective genetic terms, while its 'truth' is explained in psychic terms (p. 138). Religion is independent, the argument goes, because the need for religion cannot be deduced from anything material; on the contrary, matter is transcended. (Following Marx, one might say worldly *scarcity* is what gives rise to religion.) Given that 'culture' usually combats religion (see Weber 1988, pp. 544 ff.), it cannot be the mother of religion (p. 73). Troeltsch holds that Marx knows nothing of religion, due to his economic reductionism (p. 106). In fact, Marx considered religion a '*protest* against real distress' (*MECW* 3, p. 175), which he rejected only because he held that it achieves nothing by itself (and that when it does, things frequently take a turn for the worse). Stähli 1976 also notes this dualism in Troeltsch: a purely rational world is juxtaposed with a worldless Christianity ('*Kultur und Askese*': Troeltsch, *GS*, Vol. II, p. 625). Nothing social remains of Christianity in reality; Christianity submits to the law that might makes right (as in Naumann; see Wünsch 1962, p. 12; Göggelmann 1987). Religious protest perished along with worldliness. 'Religious subjectivism is a good supplement to a general ethics' (Stähli 1976, p. 35). *Qua* juxtaposition of disparate phenomena, such 'supplementation' has no effects; it simply acts as a sedative, despite the assurance that 'the hereafter is the power of this world' (Troeltsch 1977, p. 979).

the metaphysical theologian to reject this worldview. While man's prospects were bleak in Protestant thought as well,[216] Troeltsch interpreted this as a *theological* palace coup: 'The dialectic and the law of nature have taken the place of God, and they have not just done away with, but also replaced it'.[217]

Thus the flawed non-wordly interpretation of Marxism led to Marxism being faulted both for its worldliness and for its otherworldliness. It was not until 1919 that Troeltsch was prompted by his work on historicism to read Marx more thoroughly;[218] he failed, however, to distinguish between Marx and the naturalist determinism of Engels and Kautsky.[219] He rejected Marxism because, like Kautsky, he took it to be a quasi-religious worldview that was illegitimately trying to rival Christianity. Thus Marx was labelled a theologian. It was orthodox Marxism's totalising way of thinking that turned Marxism into a rival of Christianity's 'absoluteness' (Troeltsch) in the first place. This way of thinking had its counterpart in the unwillingness of theologians to give non-theological questions a 'non-religious interpretation' (Bonhoeffer). In other words, religious socialism's valorising sacralisation of Marxism needs to be understood in terms of the liberal theology of culture's earlier devaluation of Marxism: the religious interpretation of culture facilitated Marxism's *positive* sacralisation to the extent that Marxism was becoming ever more 'culturally relevant'. It was enough to replace the negative assessment of Marxism with a positive one. This was precisely what Paul Tillich went on to do.[220] Tillich situated Marx within the tradition of Jewish prophets and was interested in him only to the extent that he could be thus interpreted.[221] Toward the end of the Weimar Republic,

---

216. According to Kant, there is no 'freedom' to be found in the world for as long as one considers it only from the perspective of the natural sciences. Kant holds that morality and religion are not ontologically distinct – they are not concerned with different worlds. The distinction between them is due to their different perspectives ('transcendence is the same – seen in a different way': Luhmann 1989, p. 313). As in many German thinkers, and due to the imposition of a unitary perspective in Fichte and Hegel, the distinction between different perspectives became an ontological distinction in Troeltsch (see 2.5, 3.1). Yet it was precisely the conversion of freedom into something metaphysical that rendered it easily 'falsifiable'. The Fichtean equation of freedom in action with the being of spirit is not Lutheran: the 'whore reason' does not escape creatureliness (Luther 1525; Pohl 1999).

217. Tillich, *GS*, Vol. III, p. 341.

218. Bosse 1970, p. 92.

219. Bosse 1970, p. 96.

220. Like Troeltsch, Tillich sacralised culture ('sanctification of cultural life': *GW*, Vol. II, p. 27) and aspired to 'synthesis' (p. 129): 'A new era of unity is beginning' (p. 16).

221. 'I said yes to the prophetic, humanist and realist elements in his analysis, pamphlets and propaganda, and no to the coldly calculating and materialist elements, as well as to those dictated by resentment' – in other words, he said no to the economic theory in its entirety (Tillich, *GW*, Vol. XII, p. 68; quoted in Wehr 1979, pp. 39–40). This is also true of Leonard Ragaz (Stähli 1976, p. 98; for the hypothesis that Marx was a 'prophet', see Fromm 1963, p. 15, and later Monz 1995). For Wünsch, 'calling Marx a prophet is a form of recognition, at least when it is done the way Tillich does it.... And yet it is here the critique begins to assume a derogatory character and becomes polemical. The polemic operates by showing that Marx is not really who he claims to be: he is not a scientist, but a prophet, and a false one at that' (Wünsch 1962, p. 80). The comparison between the Christian and the Marxist 'image of man' (Rich 1962, Bienert 1979) is also framed in theological

Tillich observed with concern that *two* modern religions were confronting one another: the 'prophetic' religion of socialism and the 'telluric' one of nationalism. He hoped to promote a 'Socialist Decision' by deducing its plausibility in *theological* terms. Thus Marx was once again brought into a proximity with Christianity that bordered on dependence. While this sheds some light on Tillich's personal motives, the political effects had to remain limited, for two reasons (the book was pulped anyhow). First, National Socialists were not impressed, since they rejected both Christianity and Marxism (as is often the case). Second, Christians were not necessarily convinced either, since Marxism's alleged proximity to Christianity could just as well be held *against* it. To the extent that something more was offered than the blanket accusation of atheism, Marx's interpretation of history was rejected as being a 'salvation history' without God; his interpretation of alienation was rejected for not taking account of inexpugnable original sin; his interpretation of labour was rejected for ignoring the divine creator; his anthropology was rejected for leaving no room for 'spiritual values'.[222] Thus, conservative theologians also treated Marx as one of their own, except they insisted his theology was deficient and *therefore* needed to be criticised.[223] In proceeding thus, both sides were oversimplifying matters. They hardly engaged with the relevant aspects of Marx's theories, which are secular.[224] In this way, the Marxian approach was bypassed both in religious socialism *and* in the work of its theological adversaries: there had been Christian socialists before Marx (Cabet, Saint-Simon, Weitling, and so on), and now there were socialist Christians as well (Blumhardt, Ragaz, Mennicke, Tillich). Thus one could delete the worldly Marx from one's lists of ancestors.

From our discussion of theology, it emerges that important elements of Marx's methodology sometimes found their way into theology, even when Marxism was rejected as a worldview. This was the case, for example, in Troeltsch's works on the sociology of the

---

terms: to draw such a comparison is to suggest, once again, that Marx starts from first principles, like theology ('Man is thus, therefore ...'; see 4.3.4). Incidentally, we are only speaking here of the theory of the 'religious socialists', not of their political and charity efforts.

222. The dadaist Hugo Ball (1919) became an extreme Catholic, a socialist and a polemical anti-Marxist (and anti-Semite). This was due, in part, to Marx's persistent worldliness.

223. 'Almost all Christian theologians who have dealt with Marx perceive him as a rival ... The result is ... an exaggerated caricature. There is talk of a titanic dynamism that aspires to occupy the vacant throne of God, of the 'mysticism' of labour, of expectations of an ultimate redemption of man and the ensuing worldly bliss ... of the final resolution of all historical conflicts within classless society. The subject of this development is 'collective man' qua saviour and redeemer of the world. ... This expectation, the argument goes, must fail in the face of reality, since it is fantastic, and the result is disappointment. ... Religious persons have difficulty imagining an atheist stance without declaring it to be a religion – a false one, of course' (Wünsch 1962, p. 76; see pp. 50, 81). F. Naumann heavy-heartedly rejected both Christianity and socialism in favour of his 'realism', thereby confirming the relationship *ex negativo* (pp. 20–1; compare Nietzsche).

224. 'Religious socialism's endorsement of Marx's sociological analysis of capitalist society does not necessarily entail its endorsement of his economic theory' (Tillich, *GW*, Vol. II, p. 167). How can one endorse one without the other? Tillich takes account only of Marx's early writings (Tillich 1966, p. 151).

church and in Nell-Breuning's economic theory. The opposite was also sometimes the case: theologians who endorsed Marxism as a worldview failed to engage with Marx's actual theories; this was the case of Tillich or Moltmann. In both cases, the 'forced, artificial theologisation of Marx'[225] prevented sober reflection on Marx's theories. Within such posthumous theologisations, the stance taken toward Marx remained a 'decision' – the political 'decision' had usually already been made prior to Marx's theologisation and was hardly affected by it.[226] In theory, this constellation has proven hard to dissolve – and as far as practice is concerned, political groups who claim to be able to speak in the name of Christianity still exist today. But before we begin to consider how the elements of this amalgam were separated (to separate = Greek *krinein*, hence 'critique'), we need to examine its effects. The secularisation hypothesis was one important philosophical aftershock of the theologistic amalgamation described.

Excursus: critique of the theory of secularisation

> All significant concepts of the theory of the modern state are secularized theological concepts.[227]

German philosophy aspired to be the science that defines basic concepts before the other sciences interpret them.[228] Often, however, it adopted *recently* sedimented interpretations from the discourses of particular sciences and mystifyingly declared those interpretations to be 'basic concepts'. Marx's theologisation was also passed on from theology to philosophical theories of secularisation in this way. These theories identified reflections on world history as reflections on a salvation history.

Within history, the word 'secularisation' has a precise meaning: it refers to the transfer of landed property from the church to wordly proprietors as it occurred especially in the aftermath of the French Revolution.[229] Yet once the term is transposed to philosophy, it becomes vague. After all, philosophical theories of secularisation do not content themselves with the claim, familiar from sociological textbooks, that 'modernity' involves everything becoming increasingly secular (an observation that already rests on an overly abstract generalisation); they also offer various interpretations of the meaning of this truism, interpretations informed by personal value judgements. The very generalisation involved in applying the word 'secularisation' to cultural processes implies that the 'everything' in question – that is, the social totality – was religious *prior* to modernity, in traditional societies. But what is this supposed to mean? Religion is attributed an originary instituting power; it is taken to have produced 'everything' out of itself – the social

225. Wünsch 1962, pp. 86 ff.
226. The question concerning one's stance on Marx became an unnecessary war of opinions. It would have been more important to combat the 'German Christians' within the church.
227. Schmitt 2005, p. 49.
228. Heidegger, *GA* 18, 22, 29, 51; see 2.5.5.
229. Lübbe 1965.

relations between masters and servants are taken to have been religiously coded, and to have undergone 'differentiation' only in the course of modernity.[230] When this narrative about the loss of an original unity[231] makes use of the word 'secularisation', it involves the suggestion that the original proprietor of 'everything' was the *church*. The clearly defined word becomes a philosophical myth of origins, a 'category of historical wrong'.[232]

This is to obfuscate, rather than to elucidate, the following questions. Did everything really appear in a religious form? Surely this is more than doubtful. But even on the assumption that 'everything' *was* articulated religiously, does it follow the 'substance' was also religious? Even granting the idealist assumption that men once lived on religion,[233] why should every later stage be seen as dependent on this origin? Granting even that to regard history in this way is correct, is the accusation levelled against later kinds of thought, namely that they are 'merely' secularised forms of religious thought, not rendered senseless, since it must also apply, for methodological reasons, to *every* later thought (to liberalism and democracy no less than to socialism)? Finally, this critique of Marx, which does not so much separate out as amalgamate, also raises the question of what direction it aims in: is Marx faulted for having 'secularised' excessively, for not having remained Jewish or Christian, or is he faulted for not having 'secularised' enough, for not having developed a sufficiently radical critique of religion?[234] These two possibilities are often not distinguished. The *philosophical* formula 'secularisation' turns out to be imprecise. Its substantive content is rendered intangible by numerous identity-philosophical identifications and chains of association. This is not the way to solve philosophical problems, but the way to bypass them. The accusation that Marx secularised religious ideas involves a whole sequence of non sequiturs. It rallies the motley crew of Marx's opponents around a politically charged term whose content is contradictory.

---

230. Systems theory, which flouts the 'participant perspective' methodologically (Halfmann 1996a, p. 30), remains all the more indebted to it on the level of content: changes in self-conception are what it usually describes. This can constitute a valid 'description' of reality only if thought and being are identical.

231. This is nothing but the projection of a generalisation onto an antediluvian state, in the manner of the Romantics. In fact, earlier societies were so divided ('stratified') there was hardly ever any 'communication' between their members. Under such conditions, how could there be any further 'differentiation'?

232. Blumenberg 1983, p. 1.

233. 'This much, however, is clear, that the middle ages could not live on Catholicism, nor the ancient world on politics' (*MECW* 35, p. 93; see *MECW* 5, pp. 55, 60; but see also C. Schmitt 1932a). 'Not to presume *Substance* in any domain ... means therefore ... not to recognise any *being* distinct from thought, ... any *object* distinct from the *subject*, any *practice* distinct from *theory*' (*MECW* 4, p. 141). 'This sum of productive forces, capital funds and social forms of intercourse, which every individual and generation finds in existence as something given, is the real basis of what the philosophers have conceived as "substance" and "essence of man" and what they have deified and attacked; a real basis which is not ... disturbed, in its effect and influence on the development of men, by the fact that these philosophers revolt against it as "self-consciousness" and the "unique"' (*MECW* 5, p. 54; see *MECW* 3, pp. 17–18; G. McCarthy 1992; Pike 1999).

234. Would the unity of religion and politics (thus Schmitt and Voegelin; cf. Kiel 1998) actually be desirable? The question concerns more than the Islamic veil.

The philosophical secularisation hypothesis was first formulated by Carl Schmitt. Where Max Weber had spoken only of structural analogies between the Protestant ethic and the 'spirit of capital',[235] Carl Schmitt interpreted this as a change in the form of an identical 'substance', which he considered to be genuinely religious ('theological') and which he believed needed once more to be interpreted and advocated in a 'politico-theological' sense (see 2.6.7).[236] A whole group of theorists exiled in Switzerland during the 1930s adopted the hypothesis developed by the National Socialist Schmitt. The Catholic theologian Hans Urs von Balthasar, the sociologist René König and the philosophers Karl Löwith and Jacob Taubes examined the relationship between the modern 'philosophy of history' and Judaeo-Christian eschatology.[237] As in theology, Marx was looked upon, from the outset, as a false political 'prophet'.

The presuppositions involved in this kind of thought can be shown up, in an exemplary fashion, by reference to its best-known version, Löwith's book on the 'Theological Implications of the Philosophy of History'. Löwith adopts Schmitt's substantialist

---

235. *MECW* 35, p. 284. Marx also did this ('*cultus* of abstract man': *MECW* 35, p. 90). But he saw more than Weber: Christianity has not just adapted itself perfectly to capitalism, but also to other, earlier forms, and it would adapt itself to socialism if it were constrained to do so (*MECW* 6, p. 231; *MECW* 6, p. 508). The judgement that religion is the cause of capitalism (which was not the judgement Weber considered correct, although he unwittingly promoted it) is due to a perspectival illusion and idealist premises (2.5.7). In baptising innerworldly asceticism the 'spirit of capitalism', Weber describes a pre-capitalist formation: the function of money that is 'hoarding' (*MECW* 35, pp. 140 ff.; *MECW* 36, pp. 491 ff.). 'The hoarder, therefore, makes a sacrifice of the lusts of the flesh to his gold fetish. He acts in earnest up to the Gospel of abstention' (*MECW* 35, p. 144; 2.3.5, 2.4.6). The asceticism of expanded reproduction (accumulation has to be financed out of surplus value: *MECW* 35, pp. 584–5) is no longer the same under capitalism: it yields high revenue, at least in the best possible case, so that talk of 'asceticism' or 'abstinence' (*MECW* 35, p. 593) is no longer to the point: 'Here, production and reproduction on a progressively increasing scale, go on their way without any intervention from that queer saint, that knight of the woeful countenance, the capitalist "abstainer"' (*MECW* 35, p. 594; on luxury consumption, see *MECW* 36, pp. 401 ff.). Oddly, Kurz 1994, p. 172, accuses Marx of adhering to a Protestant work ethic.

236. Schmitt's claim involves the assumption that the church is divine (it 'represents Christ': Schmitt 1923, p. 31). It is this divine substance ('the supernatural dimension of the church: Senge 1985, p. 312) that has secularised itself in the state, according to Schmitt ('The "omnipotence" of the modern lawgiver… is not only linguistically derived from theology': Schmitt 22, p. 38; see pp. 42, 5 – but then what is the relationship between the two, if it not one of substance?). For criticisms, see Kodalle 1973, Faber 1975 and 2001, Mehring 1989, Bröckling 1993, Wacker 1994, Groh 1998, Kiel 1998, Pircher 1999 or Gross 2000.

237. Schmitt 2005, Balthasar 1936, Taubes 2009, Löwith 1949, König 1987, pp. 90 ff.; see Voegelin 2000, pp. 158 ff., 235; Kröner 1977, Vondung 2000. Taubes' doctoral adviser König was a friend of Löwith. Encouraged by him, he had held lectures on Marx in Zürich. (Balthasar was also in Zürich.) Taubes referred back to them (König 1984, pp. 8, 140; König 1987, p. 435). The secularisation hypothesis derived its legitimacy from exalted forms of Marxism (both the prophetic Western variant and the Eastern cult of the state). The hypothesis has now become commonplace (cf. the conservative paradox that 'modernity' rests on premises it cannot itself guarantee: Böckenförde 1991, p. 112; 2.4.3). The way Marx was referred to was, however, questionable. On Schmitt's view, there were two secularised religions ('*nemo contra deus nisi deus ipse*'): messianic socialism (Behemoth), which he condemned, and the 'Catholic' state (Leviathan), which he endorsed (Schmitt 1985, Gross 2000, pp. 155 ff., 225 ff.; 2.6.7).

interpretation, without however referring explicitly to it.[238] He describes Marx's theory as a 'pseudo-morphosis of Jewish-Christian messianism'[239] – and seems not to be bothered by the fact that this conflation is reminiscent of Nazi talk of a 'Jewish-Bolshevist world conspiracy'; Löwith even situates Marx's unconscious messianism in his 'race'.[240] Löwith also shares with the apologists of Catholicism their idealist top-down way of thinking: everything is deduced from a first principle, he argues, and the question is only what this first principle is.[241] Since Marx was not a theologian, his first principle *had* to be 'atheism', by which his thought and behaviour were thus pre-determined.[242] The only question is: what is a 'Kingdom of God, without God'?[243]

How can atheism be messianic? It is only because Löwith himself retains the structure of theological thought that Marx's historical 'messianism' appears to him as being driven (or controlled) by the 'spirit of prophetism': 'The *Communist Manifesto* is, first of all, a prophetic document… The fundamental premise of the Communist Manifesto is… that the one class is the children of darkness and the other the children of light'.[244] The theologistic premise of Löwith's thought[245] is so powerful he integrates even Marx's *critique* of religion into his narrative,[246] even though this flatly contradicts what Marx states in that critique.[247] The rigidity of this view is evident in the way Löwith refuses, from the

238. Löwith was quite familiar with Schmitt's writing: see Löwith 1935.

239. Löwith 1949, p. 46.

240. Löwith 1949, p. 44. In this respect, Löwith resembles Plenge, whom he only refers to in his discussion of Hegel. 'I already identified Marx's innermost character as "Jewish" back then, in 1911' (Plenge, ca. 1933, quoted in Kaesler 1986, pp. 411–12; see Berlin 1994).

241. For example, the premise on which Voegelin intends to construct his 'new' science of politics is a 'thoroughly elaborated ontology, which recognises the reality of all realms of being, and especially of the otherworldy, divine realm' (Voegelin 2000, p. 16).

242. 'On the basis of this… atheism… Marx undertook his radical criticism… His whole enterprise of changing the world by a world revolution has as its negative presupposition [!] the denial of man's dependence on an existing order of creation' (Löwith 1949, p. 47). Materialism has an 'atheistic motivation', according to Löwith (ibid.). Like Nietzsche, Löwith poses the following alternative: 'Is the ultimate standard and pattern of our existence the classical view of the world as an eternal cosmos… or is it the Christian view of the world as a unique creation out of nothing, called forth by the omnipotence of a non-natural God?' (Löwith 1949, p. 215). *Tertium datur*: Marx is no more theoretically dependent on such a 'supreme measure' than Newton's physics (Newton was very pious, but he practised a methodological atheism: *etsi deus non daretur*, as Grotius stated for the doctrine of natural law) or Kant's ethics – even if, biographically, Marx considered 'Prometheus… the most eminent saint and martyr in the philosophical calendar' (*MECW* 1, p. 31).

243. Löwith 1949, p. 42.

244. Löwith 1949, pp. 43–4.

245. While Marx is not sparing with allusions to the Bible (he generally uses them to denounce his opponents' positions as absurd, rather than to praise his own: Buchbinder 1976), it is Löwith who introduces the terms terms 'original sin' (p. 43), 'last judgment' (p. 44), Christ, cross, resurrection and salvation (pp. 44 f.; shifts without hesitation from Judaism, which Marx is associated with 'racially', to Christianity). Nietzsche already struggled against 'latent Christianity (e.g. in music, in socialism)' (1967a, aphorism 1021, where the expression 'my struggle' is used five times).

246. Löwith 1949, pp. 46 ff.

247. In substance, and to put it in exaggerated terms, the critique of religion formulated by Löwith amounts to the claim that historical thought leads to Marx, while Judaism leads to histori-

outset, to recognise Marx's theory as a *science*.[248] In this respect, Löwith is a child of his times: he adopts the German bourgeoisie's typical contempt for Western politics and 'Western' science. Thus Marx, to whom the 'becoming worldly of philosophy'[249] was the starting point, was read as a speculative theologian. Marx's early writings were the only ones Löwith ever studied, and yet their achievements – the critique of religion and philosophy – seem to have made no impression on him; in this respect, he was like many members of his generation.[250] Karl Löwith, who set out to combat philosophies of history, helped to newly bolster its popularity.

Marx had spoken about things *in* history, and starting from there, he had identified heuristic regularities. He called for seizing on the opportunity to develop a different economic order. But he decidedly rejected philosophies of history.[251] Löwith, by contrast, has nothing to say about historical events; instead, he separates their form (history) from their content (historical events), in order to engage in aprioristic considerations, via the

---

cal thought, so that from the bourgeois point of view it is more prescient not to become religious, or at least not to opt for the Judaeo-Christian variant of religion. This is a prudential rule of wise conduct with Catholic-atheist features (see Gross 2000, pp. 155 ff.; Faber 2001), but it is not a theoretical critique.

248. 'Marxism needs to be situated in the context of the history of the church and of heresy, not in that of the history of science' (Hofmann 1987, p. 12). Löwith considers only the *Manifesto* (2.1.1, 2.4.6), stating that it is 'not at all a purely scientific statement based on the empirical evidence of tangible facts' (Löwith 1949, p. 43). Löwith claims that Marx's putative 'messianic faith' has merely been 'perverted into secular prognosticaton' (p. 44; this notion of perversion merely shows that Löwith's reading cannot accommodate Marx's theory): 'It would have been quite impossible to... inspire millions of followers by a bare statement of facts' (p. 45). This applies to Sorel and Gramsci, and the accusation was also levelled at Kautsky (2.1.4). As far as Marx is concerned, however, the statement indicates that Marx cannot be read as a 'messianic' author. Löwith senses that his reading of Marx as an eschatological thinker is at odds with the textual evidence, but he projects his own problem onto Marx: 'Marx's solution of this difficulty is by no means convincing' (p. 46). The difficulty never arises for Marx. While agitation plays an important role in the *Manifesto*, its ultimate aim is secular.

249. *MECW* 1, p. 85.

250. Löwith reads Marx as a prophet, but also as a Hegelian philosopher: 'The abstract principle with Marx is still what it was with Hegel: the unity of reason [*Vernunft*] and reality [*Wirklichkeit*]' (p. 50). If there is any continuity in Marx's body of work, then surely it is his struggle against this very idealist, Hegelian premise (2.5.7). But for Löwith, Marx is and remains a philosopher ('but even as a "materialist", Marx remained a philosopher': 1949, p. 34; this is reminiscent of Horkheimer 1988a, p. 173) who anticipated 'the future philosophy [!]' (Löwith 1949, p. 35). Besides, Löwith claims, Marx argued in moral terms (p. 47) – which does not quite accord with the Hegelianism that Löwith also attributes to Marx, but which continues a traditional reading of Marx that is still popular today (see Spengler 1928, Vol. I, pp. 367–8; Popper 1945, Vol. II, pp. 199 ff.; Wildt 1997; see 3.1.4).

251. Marx unambiguously opposed the 'all-purpose formula of a general historico-philosophical theory whose supreme virtue consists in being supra-historical' (*MECW* 24, p. 201; see *MECW* 28, p. 18; F. Jonas 1976 I, p. 217; see 2.1.4; 2.4.5). About his 'most general results' (*MECW* 5, p. 37; *MECW* 3, p. 231; *MECW* 29, pp. 261–2), he said: 'These abstractions in themselves, divorced from real history, have no value whatsoever. They... by no means afford a recipe or schema, as does philosophy, for neatly trimming the epochs of history' (*MECW* 5, p. 37). On this, see Vollgraf 1996 and 1998, Behrens 1997.

interpretation of other philosophies of history. Like the Young Hegelians, whose hagiographer he became, he was stuck in the fly-bottle of 'mind' and couldn't get out.[252] If anyone can be described as a theologian, it is Löwith, not Marx.[253]

As the child of a wealthy bourgeois family, Löwith had never established any rapport with the political struggles of his time.[254] He considered the upheavals of his time – and there were many – less serious than those of *mind*: 'historicism' seemed to him and his student friend Leo Strauß to be the problem of the age. It is true that Marx played an important role in the development of this paradigm within the human sciences. Like the young Marx, they had turned away from Hegel's construct of history in order to address 'real' history.[255] But the historicism practised at German universities, a version of it that already constituted a reaction to Marx, did away with the materialist linking of theory to a politico-economic base and substituted it with the irrational base of 'life' (2.5.2). While this nihilism went along with historical relativisation of 'mental constructs' formerly regarded as autonomous, it failed to *relate* those constructs to a history of the base that could be reconstructed in a historiographically stringent way.[256] The imbuing of historicism with *Geisteswissenschaft* that occurred in Dilthey and Heidegger recognised 'meaning' nowhere but within an emphatically 'historical' horizon – within a superstructure considered in isolation (2.5.2). Working from within this perspective, Löwith had the impression the constant changes historicism observed, but could not explain, no longer had any 'meaning'. Marx's thematisation of historical events and future possibilities was read idealistically by Löwith, as a *metaphysics* of history 'as such', and in such a way as to elide the base.

---

252. The philosophical fly-bottle of the Hegelians led, as late as Löwith, to a view similar to the one described by Marx: 'my true religious existence is my existence in the *philosophy of religion*; my true political existence is my existence in the *philosophy of law*; my true natural existence, existence in the *philosophy of nature*; my true artistic existence, existence in the *philosophy of art*; my true *human* existence, my *existence in philosophy*. Likewise the true existence of religion, the state, nature, art, is the *philosophy* of religion, of nature, of the state and of art' (*MECW* 3, p. 340). The list might be extended to include history and the philosophy of history. The German debates on history were already rendered explosive by the lack of clarity surrounding the scientific-theoretical status of the historical sciences (Dilthey 1988, Rickert 1896). But Löwith, a student of Husserl, does not pose the question concerning the mode of existence of the object 'history'.

253. Marx (*MECW* 5, p. 56) mocked 'the important question which has been under discussion in recent times: how exactly one "passes from the realm of God to the realm of Man" – as if this "realm of God" had ever existed anywhere save in the imagination, and the learned gentlemen were not constantly living in the "realm of Man"'.

254. Löwith left Munich in 1919, because the revolution had grown 'too noisy' for him. The 1941 Japanese air raid on Pearl Harbour also left him cold (although he had just moved from Japan to the USA) (Lutz 1999, pp. 280 ff.).

255. Löwith 1983; Lutz 1999, p. 279. On the 'overcoming of historicism', see Mannheim 1964b, Schnädelbach 1974, pp. 160 ff.

256. On Ranke, Droysen, Treitschke, and so on, see Schnädelbach 1974. Troeltsch 1922 is himself still a historicist. 'The relativity of every type of human conception of the interrelatedness of things is the historical worldview's last word, with everything flowing processually and nothing remaining' (Dilthey, *GS* V, p. 9; see Lukács 1981, pp. 440–1).

When one proceeds in the manner of Löwith and ignores not just the centrally important empirical aspects of Marx's theory but also his reflections on the relationship between his modified form of theory, its contemplative precursor and political practice, as well as the special character of the political rhetoric found in some of the texts by which Marx intervened in politics, citing certain passages without indicating their context, *then* the theory does begin to resemble a mythic philosophy of history.[257] No one will deny there this is such a distant analogy on the textual level, but it proves little and is never examined more closely. The fact that Marxism formally resembles certain religious myths when it is given a one-dimensionally philosophical reading is used to roundly proclaim Marxism's dependence on those myths, without any additional evidence being provided.[258] The textual level is the only one Löwith considers. Like Carl Schmitt, he insinuates a change in the form of an identical substance. To counter this bugbear of a Marxist metaphysics of history, Löwith means to strip history of *each and every* expectation of meaning.[259] He rejects every proposition about history that speaks of more than 'coincidences'.[260]

Faced with his 'withdrawal from history' and into nature,[261] *all* theories that deal in any way with history – ancient historiography, Jewish prophecy, mythic medieval salvation histories, Enlightenment historiography, its radicalisation in historical materialism and the occasional sketch for a 'universal history' (Herder, Condorcet, Hegel) – melt

---

257. This is why schoolbooks and introductory textbooks that present Marx as a philosopher of history are partly right; introductory textbooks and schoolbooks have to simplify (see Ständeke 1981, Angehrn 1991, Schaefler 1991). But such a view is nowhere near satisfactory when it is a matter of adequately grasping Marx philosophically.

258. Similar views expounded by Toynbee (*A Study of History*, Vol. II, p. 178) are criticised by Popper (1975, Vol. II, p. 253): '"The distinctively Jewish . . . interpretation of Marxism . . . is the apocalyptic vision of a violent revolution . . . [T]he salient features of the traditional Jewish apocalypse protrude through this threadbare disguise . . ." Now there is certainly not much in this brilliantly phrased passage with which I do not agree, as long as it is intended as nothing more than an interesting analogy. But if it is intended as a serious analysis . . . then I must protest.'

259. In dramaturgical terms, the metaphysics of history reaches its climax in Marx, just before Burckhardt takes the stage to set everything aright (Löwith 1949, pp. 33 ff.). The socialist and fascist movements in Löwith's three home countries – Germany, Italy and Japan – are never mentioned.

260. Löwith asks: '[F]or is history not very casual and contingent compared with the eternal revolution of the heavenly bodies and its cosmic necessity?' (Löwith 1949, p. 215). Nature also has a history. Marx made reference to Darwin, but also to P. Trémaux's theory of geological formations (cf. Irrlitz in Fleischer 1994, p. 113). Löwith adopts Feuerbach's opposition of nature and history, which had already been criticised by Marx (*MECW* 5, pp. 55, 39; see Löwith 1965). The imperative of not imbuing history with one's expectations of meaning ('it is mainly purpose which constitutes meaning for us': Löwith 1949, p. 5) can only signify that one should not insert value judgements into one's description of what occurs; it cannot signify that one should cease considering historical processes altogether. But Löwith rejects even the 'empirical method of Voltaire', the first scientific 'theory of "real" history' (Löwith 1949, p. 1). Does this not resemble a rejection of every approach to history in favour of a melancholy *amor fati* that wishes not to have to deal with the details?

261. See Bolz 1989. If ever there was a *theologoumenon* in the philosophy of history, then surely it is this exodus, the promised end (Niethammer 1989, Meyer 1993).

into a single erratic bloc. Consequently, Löwith loses sight of reality.[262] His *excessively* generalising way of thinking prevents him from recognising his enemies: he had once criticised the theologising decisionism inherent in the German philosophy of the inter-war period.[263] But when he believes himself to have struck at the root of this thought in *Marx*, he overlooks the fact that theologising decisionism was already directed against Marx (2.5.2). Thus Löwith ends up in an ambiguous position: he is opposed *both* to Marx and to Marx's conservative revolutionary opponents. Because he can no longer distinguish adequately between them, it becomes difficult to pin down his own position. This makes that position as 'pseudo-concrete' as Anders accused their common teacher Heidegger of being.[264]

Löwith's role model Jacob Burckhardt had already gotten stuck in a similarly ambiguous position: an opponent of philosophies of history, he nevertheless advocated such a philosophy himself; it just happened to be a different one.[265] Declaring himself to be principally opposed to religion, Löwith nevertheless ends up glorifying it – like Nietzsche or 'religious socialism' before him.[266] When the primacy of mind already inheres in one's first premises, there can be no escape from the fly-bottle of mind: when the historical catastrophes that constitute the tacit background of Löwith's remarks are considered merely to be the effluence of a certain *faith*, the remedy can only consist in a *different* faith (or in a different, sceptical philosophy, of the kind proposed by Odo Marquard).[267] Consequently, Löwith was at pains to develop a 'different thought' – like his teacher Heidegger, although Löwith's variant was the more modest one. It was presumably due to Löwith's purely mental perspective that he failed to see how his attempts at a solution brought him back into the vicinity of Marx: like his basic Epicurean stance, Löwith's

---

262. 'Compared with Marx, the greater realist is Hegel' (Löwith 1949, p. 51).

263. Löwith 1984b. Löwith remained a critic of Heidegger after 1945 (Löwith 1984 and 1986).

264. Anders 1947.

265. The 'thin thread of mere continuity' in Burckhardt (Löwith 1949, p. 26) is itself open to an interpretation in terms of the philosophy of history, or even to a theological interpretation – namely as the position of the Counter-Reformation. The latter was concerned with rendering impossible the 'state of exception' of worldly transformations (2.6.7). Löwith ignores the 'state of exception', even though it had long since come about: 'If a radical crisis really disrupted history's continuity, it would be the end of a historical epoch' (Löwith 1949, p. 21). At the time, talk of such a crisis never ceased (2.5.2). Löwith 1987 also adopted Nietzsche's 'eternal recurrence of the same', a concept that is historico-philosophical to an extreme degree.

266. Much as Jacob Burckhardt praised early Christianity's asceticism and could think of no other remedy for the 'general unrest' (Burckhardt 1943, p. 170; compare Löwith 1984a; Martin 1947), Löwith arrived at a reverence for nature that displayed features of stoicism (Habermas 1991, pp. 195 ff.). Löwith's concluding words are as follows: 'The modern mind has not made up its mind whether it should be Christian or pagan . . . Hence its vision is necessarily dim in comparison with either Greek or biblical thinking' (Löwith 1949, p. 207). The option of a radical Christianity is left open. Löwith decidedly does not acknowledge a specifically modern thought. He is trapped within 'mind'; his classical education alienated him from social reality (see Cancik 2000 on Nietzsche).

267. Löwith 1950 assumes a modern 'faith' in science and history. Communism was perceived by him, first and foremost, as a 'faith' (Löwith 1949, p. 49). This makes Löwith's argument 'theological'.

anthropological sketches and his call for a 'scientific' treatment of history (in the manner of the ancient historians)[268] had already been anticipated and *implemented* by Marx.[269] Marx, however, was led by this approach to abandon pure philosophy – and hence to move beyond Löwith's horizon.

The narrative of secularisation was shared by many authors who differed merely in their assessment of it: Löwith called for an ancient-pagan elimination of history[270] and attacked the 'Jewish messianism' that he saw at work everywhere, whereas Taubes pronounced himself *in favour* of this same messianism. Carl Schmitt held that the transposition of theological categories into politics becomes illegitimate only when *domination* has been stripped of theology (or when a theology of liberation dares to make use of domination),[271] whereas Hans Blumenberg[272] responded to this by claiming the 'self-assertion' of modernity was quite legitimate. Another variant of this narrative consisted in attributing a gnostic *dispositif* to Marx; this led to Marx being condemned either on Christian grounds (the Christian approach was quite willing to tolerate a religious politics, as long as it was Christian and Catholic)[273] or on those of a critical rationalism (which was not prepared to tolerate *any* blend of religion and politics).[274] This range of religious readings of Marxism is itself an index of how imprecise this approach is. Blumenberg stands out from these polemical texts insofar as he is at pains to avoid religious prejudice. But he also regarded the continuity within this rupture purely in terms of *intellectual history*, arguing that periods of transition had grappled with 'great questions' and the impossibility of answering them, whereas modernity had finally succeeded in formulating superior answers.[275] Only texts are considered, and they refer to nothing

---

268. Löwith 1949, p. 6

269. Löwith developed an anthropology in his habilitation thesis (1981), as well as in his later writings, where 'nature' plays a prominent role. But this was hardly the way to get rid of Marx.

270. There is already a hermeuntic deficit implicit in this, since 'antiquity' does not allow itself to be thus reconfigured. It too featured historiography and historical speculation, even systems of thought based on the idea of historical progress (Cancik 1983).

271. Schmitt endorsed such a transposition for as long as it allowed a 'theological' justification of the theology of the Counter-Reformation – one that ignored Bodinus' principle of confessional neutrality as it had already been implemented by Hobbes (Kriele 1994, pp. 55, 96 ff., 105). He opposed the secular Protestant political transformations within liberalism and the Jewish-messianic transformations within Marxism, but not the Catholic notion of a universal, 'regulatory' empire. Schmitt was a political confessionalist. In 1934, he justified the new '*Reich*' in trinitarian terms (as state, movement, people). Marx uses theological concepts to caricature politics; Schmitt uses them to sacralise it.

272. Blumenberg 1983.

273. Voegelin 2000a.

274. Topitsch 1961.

275. A comprehensive critique (see Faber 1984) would have to focus on the interpretation of Luther: Blumenberg 1983 suggests Ockham's nominalist transcendentalisation of God and Luther's doctrine of predestination relocated God to such a remote position that a worldly recommencement became inevitable. This reduction of history to the history of religion blinds Blumenberg to the twofold increase in liberty the operation entailed: on the level of the individual, a personal relationship to God was rendered possible, rather than deformed, and on the political level, the

but other texts. The way these texts refer synchronically to reality is not addressed, nor the reality *behind* the texts.[276] Thus the philosophers of history also turn Marx into a theologian. But to perceive religion everywhere is not to give proof of a more profound understanding of religion.[277] And Marx was less inclined to perceive religion everywhere than his historico-philosophical critics.

Nevertheless, the monicker 'philosophy of history' has been used, sometimes disapprovingly and sometimes approvingly, as a codeword for 'Marxism' from the 1890s until today.[278] Philosophies of history have indeed played a role in some historically influential variants of Marxism, but they served a compensatory function even there: in the orthodox Marxism of Kautsky (2.1.4) and Lenin (2.2.6), and, similarly, in the Frankfurt School (2.6.2). They were *also* used, in each of these cases, to 'reconciliate' the 'final goal' with a tactics or mode of research contrary to it. The philosophical debates on the philosophy of history were characterised by a twofold displacement: not only were they a way of engaging with Marxism by proxy, but Marxism's own philosophies of history had been developed as a way of avoiding critical objections.[279]

A related field, in which the same sort of engagement by proxy occurred, was the debate on myth and science within Marxian theory. This topic had the advantage of being controversial within Marxism itself.[280] Here, too, the historico-philosophical bias is

---

oppressive and repressive 'political theology' of the Middle Ages and the Counter-Reformation was deprived of its foundations. If a worldly recommencement was indeed provoked, then this was due to the failure to claim God politically (2.6.7), not to God's remoteness.

276. Leo Strauss had the courage to openly endorse this approach and describe himself as a Platonist (Lutz 1999, p. 428; see below).

277. Picking up on an argument formulated by Bonhoeffer, one might say that whoever knows both the workings of religion and their proper place will not take every trifle for evidence of possible 'religious premises' and will not be compelled to mix everything up. On the religious view, it is precisely because God is great that he does not depend on the world; and because he is good, he grants men the freedom to handle their affairs independently (Kraus 1982, Link 1999). 'Today, the world has become worldly' (Metz 1968, p. 1). A newspaper article notes approvingly: 'Even Catholic theologians are beginning to understand that secularisation, or the disentangling of religion from claims to authority, very much accords with the core of the Christian message' (letter to the editor published in *Süddeutsche Zeitung*, 21 December 2002; cf. Steinbüchel 1950). Nevertheless, cultural criticism still likes to present itself as a critique of religion (Luckmann 1963, Jacob 1996).

278. The two terms are used synonymously from P. Barth 1897, Freyer 1964 and O. Marquard 1973 to Rohbeck 2000. Some Marxists have approved of this, such as Conrad Schmidt or the Frankfurt School (Horkheimer 1993, Schmidt 1976, Lutz-Bachmann 1988a, Bolz 1989, Bialas 1994, Wegerich 1994, Behrens 1996, Herrmann 2000). On Russian historical speculation (Dostoevsky, Solovyov, Berdyaev), see Meyer 1993, pp. 70 ff., and Groys 1996.

279. In all three cases, the turn toward the philosophy of history can be understood as an abstracting escape from the injunction to provide an apposite justification of one's claims. Such a direct or indirect injunction had been addressed to Kautsky (by Bernstein), Lenin (by the 'economists') and Horkheimer (by Mannheim), in the form of a problematisation of the reality they took for granted (see 2.6.1).

280. See, for instance, Wetter 1958, Topitsch 1961, Zeleny 1968, Negt 1969, A. Schmidt 1970, Tomberg 1973, Büsser 1974, Szczesny 1975, Callinicos 1983, Sandkühler 1983, Sheehan 1985 or Kitching 1994.

not to be overlooked. Popper opened the debate in the postwar period. He rejected Marx as unscientific, but not because of Marx's economic theory; what Popper objected to was Marx's 'historicism' and his putatively determinist 'philosophy of history'.[281] In doing so, he adopted the practice, already evident in Bernstein and Sorel, of dividing Marx's work into two parts, one pertaining to particular scientific disciplines and one mythicising. And yet philosophers and scholars working within the human and social sciences seldom agreed on what their specific scientificity consisted in: they disagreed within their own disciplines and within the larger field of the human and social sciences, and they also disagreed with scholars working in the natural sciences.[282]

Thus the apparently weighty accusation of being 'unscientific' could mean different things, and its meaning could be altered rather arbitrarily. Wetter levelled the accusation against Marx for refusing to accept the philosophical proofs of the existence of God.[283] Popper accused Marx of being unscientific because of what he took to be Marx's *affinity* to Plato; Leo Strauss formulated the same accusation on the basis that Marx *differed* too strongly from Plato.[284] Accusations of being 'mythicising' were also formulated by theologians. For instance, Heinz-Horst Schrey says the following about scientificity and its relationship to history:

> We take the view that Marx's relationship to history does not originate in scientific objectivity, but amounts to a mythology in the service of a social doctrine of salvation. While this mythology subjectively [?] requires a scientific justification, such a justification is by no means constitutive of it.[285]

Sorel's mythicising Marxism had regarded Marx's considerations on history not as myths, but as science.[286] Sorel *opposed* to them the myth of the general strike, which was intended to demonstrate to the proletarian masses their own power.[287] In doing so, he resorted to a deliberate de-intellectualisation and to open praise of violence.[288] This could indeed be criticised as mythicising.[289] But the accusation of mythicising history was specifically German, and it seems to have become so explosive because Germany

281. Popper 1945, Vol II, p. 101; Popper 1957.
282. On this, see, inter alia, Apel 1979, Mittelstrass 1979, Oelmüller 1988, Plümacher 1996.
283. Wetter 1952.
284. Compare Strauß 1956, 1975 (Gawoll 1989, p. 126). As an advocate of progress, Marx was the counterpart to Plato, the advocate of changelessness (*stasis*); nevertheless, Popper argued that Marx was linked to Plato via Aristotle and Hegel and shared with him features such as 'essentialism' (Popper 1945, Vol. II, p. 174) and hostility to the 'open society'.
285. Schrey 1954, p. 145.
286. Sorel 1999, pp. 85, 148, 161.
287. Sorel 1908, pp. 143 ff.
288. On Sorel, see Lichtheim in Sorel 1999, Freund 1932 and H. Barth 1959.
289. See the steps in this dirrection in Lukács 1989 and König 1975. Sorel was more important than Marx both to the young Lukács and to König (Lukács 1971b, p. x; König 1984, p. 101, see 4.4).

was already *struggling with the philosophy of history*.[290] That philosophy was now projected onto Marxism. For how does Schrey account for his 'view' that Marx mythicises history? 'If Marx were concerned with objective truth, his guiding question would be: what can one learn from history? In fact, however, he is guided . . . by the notion of a final goal'.[291] Despite the call for historical objectivity, discussion of Marx takes as its point of departure a historical period that already involved serious *distortions* of Marx's theory, namely Bernstein's remarks on the 'final goal' (2.1.2).

Schrey's way of considering Marxism divides it into two halves, one scientifically sound but irrelevant, the other politically influential but irrational.[292] By proceeding thus, one could criticise Marxism politically without having to say anything about its scientific content. The context of such interventions is clear: the Cold War. The communist iconography of domination did indeed practice a political mythology.[293] One could of course have attacked Soviet communism directly, without the detour of discussing Marx. But this critique of Soviet communism, which presented itself in the guise of a critique of Marx, functioned only by virtue of *amalgamating* the two.[294] Perhaps this was an attempt to be diplomatic. In any case, the result was that theory and reality were once more brought into close proximity.

Ernst Topitsch's demythologising pamphlets were also addressed not so much to Marx than to the Soviet Union. Having participated in Germany's campaign of destruction against the Soviet Union in 1941, Topitsch concluded his philosophical career with an anti-Russian pamphlet that makes his earlier remarks on Marx appear questionable.[295] Topitsch regarded Marx as a religiously disguised and power-hungry person who had sought to become 'emperor' and even 'God' by means of a mythology. According to Topitsch, Marx placed himself, as 'saviour',[296] at the centre of his aprioristic world-historical construct. Science only served him as a way of retaining his naive and optimistic 'faith' following the disappointments of 1848.[297] By science, Topitsch means only

290. Both actual history and the methodological foundations of its theoretical reflection caused problems in Germany: witness the debates on the status of historical science that followed Droysen, Windelband, Rickert and Dilthey (Rickert 1896, Theodor Lessing 1927, Koselleck 1977; 2.5.2).

291. Schrey 1954, p. 146.

292. The mythology attributed to Marx resembles the theology of revolution: Tillich's *kairos*-like 'now' (Schrey 1954, p. 150).

293. On the aesthetics of 'totalitarianism', see Damus 1981, Groys 1988 or Tabor 1994.

294. Marxism's mythologising self-enfeeblement, for instance in 'Proletkult' (Gorsen 1981, pp. 83 ff.), encouraged critics to extend the accusation to Marx himself.

295. Topitsch 1985 holds that 'the political centrepiece of the entire war was the Soviet Union's attack on the Western democracies, an attack in which Germany and Japan merely served the Kremlin as military instruments', and that 'we owe much to the sacrifice made by Germany's soldiers', and so on (quoted in Kahl 1999, pp. 426 ff.). By contrast, Topitsch 1990 picks up on hypotheses first expounded in Topitsch 1958.

296. Topitsch 1975, p. 18.

297. Topitsch characterises Marx's personality as follows: 'The dominant motive was a veritably Caesarian will to power, combined with a messianic sense of mission, an ungovernable appetite for

the self-legitimation of Stalinist potentates, which has been stylised into laws of history, that is, 'dialectical materialism' (Popper's 'historicism'). This is to project Stalinism onto Marx.

The effect of such a projection is unfortunate, for three reasons. It does not do justice to the political situation under real socialism, because it only engages with it by proxy. It does not do justice to Marx, because he is forced into an interpretive framework that makes him appear as the founder of Stalinism (passages from Marx are hardly discussed in detail). And finally, the concept of myth is not reflected upon, despite the fact that it has been the object of close scrutiny during the twentieth century.[298] The diffuse accusation of 'mythology' allowed one, precisely *because* of its diffuseness, to avoid the concept of 'ideology', which was still associated with Marx.[299] The problem of Marx was dealt with by discrediting him and, ideally, by no longer bothering to read him at all.[300] This technique was also used against the student movement, when Marxism was no longer relevant except as an obsolete or coerced form of mind from beyond the inner German border.[301]

However, the Cold War can only serve as a partial explanation for the popularity enjoyed by philosophies of history in post-1945 Germany. There were other reasons: The question concerning the meaning of history was painfully topical in Germany, which had just lost another war, and committed monstrous atrocities in the course of it.[302] The question's topicality derived in part from the fact that the National Socialists had gone to great lengths to stylise the German past while promising a future 'Thousand Year

---

destruction and an unmistakeable tendency to self-adulation.... Thus Marx... created an ideology that... allows one to reach for total power and domination... under the guise of liberation' (Topitsch 1975, p. 13); Napoleon, Topitsch adds, was Marx's great idol. Similar *ad personam* abuse is to be found in Schwarzschild 1954, Künzli 1966, Pilgrim 1990, Löw 1996 and *Bild Dresden* ('Marx & Co.: So waren sie wirklich' ['Marx & Co.: What They Were Really Like'], 14 November 2002).

298. See, inter alia, Cassirer 1997, Bohrer 1983, Frank 1988. The deciphering of Biblical myths undertaken by Bultmann and psychoanalysis does not extract the rational kernel from a mystical shell; it formulates an existential interpretation that obtains a rational sense from the myths themselves (even from gnosticism, of which Voegelin 2000a and Topitsch 1961 accused Marx; see H. Jonas 1988). Myth may be deliberately used as a narrative device.

299. Direct criticism of Soviet communism could refer approvingly to Marx. For example, a common criticism was that class society persisted under actually-existing socialism (see Cliff 1955, Marcuse 1958, Leonhard 1962, Hillmann 1966 and 1967; see 2.2.3; a parallel can be found in Nolte 1982, pp. 86 ff., on the student movement).

300. See Tucker 1963, Albert 1969, Topitsch 1969, Senge 1985, Thomas 1993, Khella 1995, Löw 1996 or Kelpanides 1999. In 1998, Helmut Kohl stated during a TV show that he had never read a single line of *Capital*.

301. Ralf Dahrendorf, whose father had been part of the social democratic wing of the antifascist resistance, was irritated not by the student movement's confrontation with the Nazi generation but by the dressing down it gave a contemporary institution, namely the university; to his generation, this institution was a dream come true (*Der Spiegel*, 2 June 2001).

302. It was because of these atrocities that defeat was so dolorous: as victor, one could have passed over them in silence, but by losing the war, one was humiliated twice: first by the defeat itself, and then by the confrontation with one's guilt.

Reich'; their present actions (under the 'greatest military commander of all time') defied all comparison. Did one not have to ask what the worldly improvements achieved by Germany between 1871 and 1933 were good for? Had they – and much more – not been lost the very next moment? People had an interest in formulating such questions as philosophically as possible (an escape into abstraction), for such generalisations afforded some *distraction* from the worst of what had occurred. One did not ask: what exactly happened? Who is responsible for it? How was it possible? Those who asked such questions were seen to be airing the nation's dirty laundry. One asked about the meaning of it all, *details apart*. 'The subject of inquiry is the essence of history. This inquiry does not concern itself with individual historical events'.[303]

The debates on the philosophy of history had a crucial advantage: because of their religious connotations and the impossibility of deciding the issue, and because of the philosophy of history's oscillating relationship to 'eschatology', one could continue the discussion endlessly, without ever moving on to other issues. The meaning of some questions is simply that they are *not* answered. But even they can be answered, once the question is posed differently. One promising way of doing this, albeit one that has often been rejected, consists in Marx's 'reformulation', by which the question becomes one of why something appears to be philosophical, or even religious, in the first place. To proceed thus is to subject philosophy to a radical slimming cure: many of its questions resolve themselves, because they can be answered in a different way. One might welcome this as a purification of philosophy, for *pace* Engels,[304] plenty of philosophical questions remain.[305] The procedure amounts to a critique in the original sense of the word: a separation.

The separation of religion and politics

Silete Theologi in munere alieno![306]

During the 1960s, there developed a 'dialogue' between Christianity and Marxism that was eyed with suspicion by the hardliners in each of the two camps. This 'dialogue' involved a dilemma: Marxism could criticise the Christians and those Marxists who were approaching Christianity by pointing out their piety was worldless, or that it *spoke* of

303. Taubes 2009, p. 3. What was generalised by means of this question was not just the object but also the inquiring subject: instead of individuals questioning one another, 'one' posed the question – without addressing anyone in particular. The exercise did not take much of a toll on anyone. One newspaper article interprets this as an indication of the persistence of the '*Volksgemeinschaft*'-mentality ('Deutsche Lebenslügen', *Die Zeit*, 3 October 2000; see Koenen 2001, pp. 13 ff.).

304. *MECW* 25, pp. 25–6; *MECW* 5, p. 37.

305. There is as little hope of refuting freedom of the will neurologically as there is of refuting the existence of God astronomically; biology cannot determine the 'good life', etc.

306. Alberico Gentili.

what is good but failed to implement it; in fact, theology was preventing such implementation. The Christians responded that Marxism and all Christians approaching it were effecting an amalgamation, untenable from a religious perspective, of worldly and otherworldly affairs, as a result of which worldly matters were being sacralised excessively. A wholly worldless Christianity and a consummate sacralisation of worldly life seemed to be the only options. Those who negotiated the space *between* these two options could be accused of actually having chosen one or the other.[307] And in fact, politico-theological authors had often vacillated between contradictory claims.[308]

But some theologians had developed a more differentiated point of view. One of them was Karl Barth, the chief exponent of dialectical theology. Like Tillich, Barth attempted to build a theological bridge between religion and socialism.[309] One disagreement between them was due to the fact that in Tillich, the theologisation of socialism proceeds from culture, whereas Barth theologised socialism because it *overcomes* the world – by what he called a 'revolution of God' ('Jesus is the social movement').[310] Barth inclined toward socialism because the Bible prompted him to, but Tillich perceived sacral elements within socialism *itself*. This was unthinkable to Barth; he had already criticised Kutter and the religious socialists for imbuing social democracy with religious meaning.[311] He held that while socialism was willed by God, it was not itself the 'Kingdom of God', but only its 'reflection', its 'analogy'.[312] His second commentary on the Epistle to the Romans

307. Garaudy, who debated with the theologians Rahner and Metz in the Paulus Society, was expelled from the French Communist Party (and later became a Muslim). The Vatican condemned the liberation theologist Gutierrez to a year of penitential silence as late as 1985 (this was done on Ratzinger's initiative: Thomas 1993, pp. 193 ff.).

308. 'From these two dimensions proper to the idea of the Kingdom of Heaven, the yes and the no of all judgements about future history follow' (Tillich 1966, p. 148). Tillich held that 'the struggle for a new social order cannot lead to fulfilment in the sense of the Kingdom of God' (Tillich 1966, p. 77). *But*: 'each definite age poses definite tasks; a certain aspect of the Kingdom of God reveals itself as demand and expectation'. This means: no, but yes. The relationship is established by means of phrases. 'Theonomy is not fulfilment, but [?] it is the intra-historical image of fulfilment' (p. 149). 'The Kingdom of God will always remain transcendent, but [?] it appears as a judgement on a given form of society and as a norm for a coming one' (p. 79). What does 'no, but…' mean if not 'yes'? (Matthew 5:37; Corinthians 1:17; Jacob 5:12). Tillich champions the neutrality of the world (*GW*, Vol. VII, pp. 133 ff.), but he takes this to be a Protestant position (see Stahl 1853).

309. See Gollwitzer 1972, Marquard 1972, Schellong 1985. E. Busch 1998 and Pfleiderer 2000 tend to ignore this aspect of Barth's work.

310. Barth 1951 (*KD* III/4), orally in 1918 (according to Gollwitzer 1972, pp. 14, 7).

311. In 1923, Tillich (*GW*, Vol. VII, pp. 216 ff.) accused Barth of no longer treating the crisis as a transition, but as something absolute; Tillich missed something positive. Barth held that Tillich was overly positive: he spoke of a 'broad wheel of faith and revelation' crushing everything beneath it and blurring every distinction (Zahrnt 1966, pp. 34, 410; F. Marquard 1972, pp. 42, 257; Pangritz 1996, pp. 57 ff.). This disagreement made it impossible for the two cardinal thinkers to develop the common base of operations that both of them would have liked. Barth's Tambach lecture, which he held in 1919, as a replacement for Ragaz (even though Barth rejected Ragaz's approach in the lecture), already provoked unnecessary irritation (Ewald 1977, Introduction).

312. Barth in Safenwill (Gollwitzer 1972, p. 19) and Barth 1947, p. 21.

addressed a warning to those who believed, *like Barth himself*, that a Christian ought to be a socialist: they should not engage in 'outrageous identifications'.[313]

If Tillich's theologisation of socialism started from the world, Barth's started from God. In both cases, socialism risked being theologised. Barth, however, was consistent enough to concede to socialism that it considered the world *as the world* (Tillich made statements to that effect, but did not follow through on them). He jumped theologically onto the moving train that was political practice. His idea can be paraphrased as follows: one needs to distinguish radically between the world and God; human hands cannot build a Kingdom of Heaven on Earth. Nevertheless, the Biblical God demands justice in this world and stipulates precise conditions for entry into his kingdom.

For this reason, it cannot be wrong to work towards the establishment of a Kingdom of Heaven on Earth; after all, this was precisely what the saviour asked of the faithful. The gospel states: the Kingdom of God has already begun with Jesus Christ, and it is up to men to develop it. This does not involve the hubris of assuming that man could perfect the Kingdom of Heaven,[314] but rather the hope that the messiah will return one day and complete the work that men have begun. There is no veritable theological reason not to commit oneself to socialism, but there are many that suggest one should – if only abstractly. Thus one can be *motivated* by one's Christian faith to become a socialist, but one cannot invoke that faith as an argument within socialism. Anyone can say that 'God wills it', including the enemies of socialism; the claim adds little to the conventional arguments for and against socialism. Theology's task is that of warding off recusant sacralisations of the political: it knows that building the Kingdom of God is up to no one but God himself. No one can claim for himself the exclusive right to represent God's work: neither the communists, nor the church or the state.

Socialism must not be sacralised and the gospel must not be instrumentalised politically. And yet the two can relate to one another in a way that does justice to both. For this to be possible, it is essential that one distinguish radically between them. One could describe this 'dialectically', as a political unity that does not smooth over theological differences but allows them to persist as differences, thereby becoming capable of action. In this sense, 'dialectical theology' is very much dialectical (*pace* Rentsch),[315] but not so

---

313. 'It makes a difference whether we recognise the identity of the kingdom of heaven and socialism or identify our socialism . . . with the Kingdom of Heaven. In the first case, we follow the path of the gospel . . . in the second case, we use God for our own ends' (Gollwitzer 1972, pp. 9–10). F. Marquard 1972 shows how the socialist option functions as a premise in Barth. The formula of the first commentary on the Epistle to the Romans – 'social democratic, but not religiously socialist' (Barth 1919, p. 390) – is interpreted as follows by Gollwitzer: 'our attempts at obedience are not to be raised to the status of a religion or doctrine of salvation, for "religion is faithlessness"' (Barth 1972, p. 28).

314. 'To found a moral people of God is, therefore, a work whose execution cannot be hoped for from human beings but only from God himself. Yet human beings are not permitted on this account to remain idle' (Kant 1998, p. 111; Pannenberg 1959, Dittmer 1997, Bloch 1970, Sölle 1968).

315. Rentsch 1999a, p. 100.

much in theory as in the 'free' political practice it makes possible. This theology is in any case the only one that might engage in a 'productive dialogue with Marxism'.[316] As lucid as this conception was, it was largely ignored by theologians. These ideas needed to be developed, in a mirror-inverted form, by a highly popular Marxist before they were received within mainstream German theology – although they were then received in a distorted form. I am referring to Walter Benjamin, a Marxist who simultaneously based his arguments on theology.

2.6.7 *Walter Benjamin's political theology*

> The Logos breaks through the Ordeal in Freedom.[317]

Benjamin has already been referred to above, when I pointed out he was one of Adorno's role models (2.6.3). There is, however, a crucial difference between Benjamin's relationship to religion and Adorno's: unlike Benjamin, Adorno regarded the 'becoming smaller and invisible of theology'[318] as a blank cheque for making use of ownerless theological ideas as he saw fit.[319] In order to perceive this difference, which is crucial to the critique of theologised readings of Marx, I will conclude this chapter by considering Benjamin's thought more closely. He merely implied the difficult relationship between theology and Marxism in his image of the 'chess-playing automaton'. But he has often been interpreted (and the interpretation goes back to Adorno) as saying that historical materialism was *itself* in a hopeless situation and ought therefore to take theology 'into its service'. In fact, Benjamin never speaks of such a need to supplement historical materialism: he relied more strongly on historical materialism than on theology, and it was the latter about which he said that 'today [1940], as we know, [it] is small and ugly'.[320]

Marx's rigid critique of dominant theology as a theology of domination was applied by Benjamin in his failed habilitation thesis, suggestively titled *The Origin of German Tragic Drama*. It was applied to the *foremost* theologian of domination of Benjamin's own time, namely Carl Schmitt, who had attempted to 'theologically' legitimate the rising totalitarian states of the twentieth century by means of a reassessment of the seventeenth-century absolutist state.[321] Benjamin formulated an immanent critique of this conceptualisation,

---

316. Heidegger 1947, p. 243. See Turneysen 1923, Farner 1985, pp. 139 ff.; Gollwitzer 1962 and 1972, Plonz 1995.

317. Walter Benjamin.

318. Pangritz 1996, p. 214.

319. There is much talk in Adorno of 'reconcilation', 'salvation', 'rapture' and the like (see Wiggershaus 1994, pp. 187–8. on Adorno's 1936 'Marginalia on Mahler').

320. According to Benjamin, historical materialism can win 'with no further ado against any opponent', if it takes theology, 'which as everyone knows is small and ugly', into its service (Benjamin 2003, p. 389).

321. Schmitt 1922.

using arguments that were themselves theological.[322] But he was aware that such a critique had not yet been possible under the absolutism of the Baroque period – a brilliant example of historical consciousness. A liberating theological critique of the divinity insolently claimed by domination was not conceivable at the time: because of its literally incisive success (based not on arguments, but on wars), the Counter-Reformation was so hegemonic that God could be accessed via *its* theology alone.[323]

Hobbes and Schmitt, acting as neutral mediators, recommended a worldly version of absolute rule, but this rule and the natural law used to legitimate it were themselves still confessional.[324] According to Benjamin, worldly absolute rule succeeded in fully eliminating, in the interest of its own authority, the hopeful perspective of eschatology, within which all worldly rule comes to an end.[325] It was only a secular liberation from this rule (as it occurred following the religious wars and the eventual assertion of the Enlightenment theory of natural law) that restored the possibility of spiritual and intellectual

---

322. The 'disappearance of eschatology' from the theology of the Counter-Reformation was conditioned by the church's absolute, worldly will to power (by the church's 'authority', thanks to which it was able to 'guarantee' this disappearance: pp. 80–1 – this corresponds to the aspect of the katechonic in Schmitt; see Grossheutschi 1996). This meant that Baroque notions of the king's 'secularized redemptive power' (p. 81) were rendered theologically impossible, since they could assert themselves only on the 'level of the state of creation' (pp. 85–6), which is precisely where no such redemption exists. In German tragic drama, this lived impossibility becomes apparent in the way that tyrants, who take themselves to be divine, succumb to madness (pp. 86, 98–9). They do not escape creatureliness – not only because they are themselves creaturely, but also because they have helped eliminate transcendence by bringing about the 'disappearance of eschatology'. Heil's general critique of Schmitt's theologisation, and of the 'absolute monarch's inability to decide' (Heil 1996, p. 134), overlooks these theological and topical aspects of Benjamin's book.

323. The Protestant dramatists of the Baroque no longer had 'direct access to a beyond', and 'religious aspirations' were denied 'religious fulfilment', because 'the increasing worldliness of the Counter-Reformation prevailed in both confessions'. Thus there resulted a 'disappearance of eschatology', due to the 'vigour with which Christianity asserted its authority' (Benjamin 1977, pp. 79 ff.). This forced the opponents of absolutism to venture into the secular domain. This is original by comparison to the secularisation hypothesis: genuine secularisation resulted from the Counter-Reformation, which employed its religious power for secular ends. This secular drift of religion eliminated the option of opposing it religiously and promoted the development of secular opposition. In fact, the Protestant Pufendorf justified his claims about natural law, formulated in opposition to secular-Catholic claims, by reference to Descartes, rather than to Aquinas.

324. After all, 'Catholic' means 'universal'. This scandalous fact irked not just Protestant theorists of natural law such as Pufendorf, but even Frederick II of Prussia (who stated that everyone could go to heaven in his own fashion, but that the head of state should not privilege any particular religion). Marx also argued against the 'Christian state' by pointing out that while it professes to be Christian in a general way, it ultimately represents a particular confession (*MECW* 1, pp. 117–18, 198–9). On the extreme Catholicism of Carl Schmitt see, inter alia, Schmitt 1996a, Wacker 1994, Kiel 1998, Faber 2001.

325. This is the Luciferan aspect of the katechonic ('spirit of Satan': Benjamin 1977, p. 232). The motif can already be found in Schmitt 2005, in the figure of the 'Grand Inquisitor'; Grossheutschi 1996, p. 116, traces it back to the year 1932. While ordained by God, the end of the world is perceived as evil. Schmitt applies this demonisation to the socialists, who are working to terminate the feudal 'prehistory' of Europe. The way Schmitt invokes the authority of the Bible is questionable (cf. Leutzsch and Faber in Wacker 1994, pp. 175 ff. and 257 ff.). Schmitt sides with the power that persecuted Christianity from below and replaced it with Christianity from above – Rome (Faber 2001).

optimism. But this is known only to the historian; no one living at the time could have been aware of it. The knowledge rests on a solid historical 'practice'.[326] While theory is not itself practice, the knowledge of a time contains (or represses) the practical experiences of its own 'prehistory'.[327] The stance on politics that Benjamin is advocating for Jews and Christians is similar to that advocated by Barth: the Kingdom of God cannot be built by humans hands, as chiliastic movements and theocratic rulers believed, but *obstacles* barring the way to it, such as the state's worldly and religious patronisation of its subjects during the seventeenth century, or indeed any totalisation of worldly rule effected in the name of religion, of all things,[328] can and must be cleared away.[329]

The point about combining theology with politics, and specifically with Marxism, is that capitalism is also described by Benjamin as a religion, one that imposes itself – this is the meaning of the well-known 'Theologico-Political Fragment' – between God and man, just as the Counter-Reformation once did.[330] The theologian can hardly claim that work done by Marxists is itself sacred. But he can take the view that the political practice of socialism is pleasing to God, insofar as it means to abolish the service rendered to the

---

326. The purpose of a 'rescuing critique' consists in 'fanning the spark of hope in the past' (Benjamin 2003, p. 391), in showing up, *a posteriori*, the perspective that was absent then.

327. Benjamin was influenced by Lukács and Korsch. He applied their praxeology to religion: there too, the only way to achieve valid knowledge is through successful action. 'Knowledge of good, as knowledge, is secondary. It ensues from practice' (Benjamin 1977, p. 233; see *GS*, Vol. II, p. 304; *GS*, Vol. III, pp. 319, 350; a letter dated 16 September 1924 remarks that 'definite insight into theory . . . depends on practice': *Briefe* I, p. 355). In *The Origin of German Tragic Drama*, knowledge without praxis is called 'evil' (Benjamin 1977, p. 230). Might this not be read as an ex ante critique of Adorno?

328. This implies a condemnation specifically of political Catholicism, a condemnation evident not only in *The Origin of German Tragic Drama*, but throughout Benjamin's work: 'Catholicism – the process of anarchy coming up: the problem of Catholicism is that of (false, worldly) theocracy' (Benjamin, *GS* VI, p. 99; cf. *GS* II, p. 203; *GS* VI, p. 688, and elsewhere). Karl Barth was consistent enough to extend the 'suspicion' to Protestantism – and he was right to do so (cf. Stahl 1853).

329. Thielen 1991, Plonz 1995. There is therefore no such thing as a 'dangerous' affinity between Benjamin and Carl Schmitt (see Heil 1996, who also cites additional literature on this question), but rather an opposition. Adorno's refusal to speak about Benjamin's relationship to Schmitt overlooks this opposition as much as those remarks about Benjamin's and Schmitt's affinity that rest on the notion of extremes touching (Rumpf 1976, Figal 1992). Adorno presumably shunned the confrontation with Schmitt because his own positions were dangerously close to Schmitt's interpretation of secularisation as a substantive transformation of theology into politics. Benjamin, it seems, engaged with Schmitt (as he did with Klages: Fuld 1981) in order to refute him. The expression '*Herrschaft des Christentums*' ('rule of Christianity': *GS*, Vol. I.1, p. 258; see Benjamin 1977, p. 79) indicates that Benjamin perceived the Christianity of domination as his opponent (Oudenrijn 1970, pp. 155 ff.).

330. See Baecker 2003. Such a view was held not just by Barth, Tillich ('demonism') and Benjamin, but also by the theorist of business ethics Wünsch 1925, by Türcke 1987, by F. Wagner 1985 – and by Pope John Paul II (Nell-Breuning 1983, BKAB 1992). As mentioned, Marx did not think of capitalism primarily as a religion: one's understanding of capitalism is not improved by describing it as a religion, since religion is far more mysterious than capitalism. On the contrary, to understand modern religious phenomena, one needs first to thematise capitalism. Formulating a judgement on capitalism from the point of view of religion in the manner of the authors cited is something altogether different.

voracious idol that is capitalism and the numerous human sacrifices offered to this idol. The theologian can endorse this practice as a critique of religion aimed at false idols. In this way, religion and socialism may *coincide* without socialism being imbued with religious elements. On 29 May 1926, shortly after completing his book on German tragic drama, Benjamin wrote to his friend Scholem: 'a "just", radical politics, which for this very reason wants to be nothing but politics [!], will always work in favour of the Jews and... will always find the Jews working for it'.[331]

Benjamin was an assimilated Jew and a resident of Berlin; his understanding of Judaism will certainly not have been orthodox-tribalist, but rather the more universal one of the people of God, Israel.[332] It can be reconstructed roughly as follows: God and man are always and have always been interested in one another.[333] But because man is free, he can affirm or reject this.[334] In the state of the fallen creation, politics is a necessity in the Augustinian sense: men have to act in groups. Now, a group of people can manoeuvre itself into a situation in which the road to God is 'barred'.[335] In such God-forsaken situations, men cannot force God to act, as Job did. At most, they can create new idols and new golden calves for themselves. But they can find their way back to God by leaving everything behind in an *exodus* – like Moses when he led the people of Israel into the desert, or Jesus when he drove the traders out of the temple (Matthew 21:12). In other words, men can at least prepare themselves (or make themselves 'worthy to be happy': Kant).

In political terms, the destruction of the golden calf[336] signifies the radical critique of *every* theocracy and political theology.[337] No religiously motivated political action can go beyond such a purge and purification ('because there are no meaningful political goals'; May 1924).[338] It is only in such acts that 'the political and the eschatological

331. Benjamin 1978a, Vol. 1, p. 426.

332. The purely Judaic interpretation of Benjamin found in Scholem 1975 and adopted by Heil 1996, pp. 141 ff. restricts the applicability of his reflections to Judaism. By contrast, Faber 1985 shows that there are also Christian and pagan allusions to be found in Benjamin. Benjamin's Judaism was that of an assimilated Berlin Jew who engaged with the Jewish tradition in a retrospective and intellectually refracted manner, without however living 'within it' (Mayer 1994, pp. 388 ff.; for a different view, see Schulte 1994).

333. The Baroque was spurred by certain 'religious aspirations' (Benjamin 1977, p. 79). The 'gracious God' – a Jewish concept – is also concerned for the well-being of man.

334. The freedom obtained during the Fall is the 'freedom to say no' (Max Scheler). Regarding the freedom of the human will vis-à-vis God, one can say with Kant that whoever speaks of sin presupposes freedom. Otherwise, God appears as a gnostic monstrosity, punishing men for something they are not responsible for. Luther's *Servo arbitrio* (1525) claims that an immediate relationship to God and nature is impossible (Benjamin, *GS*, Vol. II, p. 154), but it leaves unquestioned freedom in human affairs.

335. Benjamin 1977, p. 79; also 'denied', 'confined': p. 80. Biblical examples include Sodom and Gomorrha, Nineveh, Babylon – and Rome (see Benjamin, GS, Vol. IV, p. 123; Faber 2001).

336. Benjamin, *GS*, Vol. VI, p. 99.

337. Benjamin, *GS*, Vol. II, p. 203.

338. Benjamin 1978a, Vol. 1, p. 426. What Benjamin has in mind is not the vitalist 'exodus' (Bolz 1985) *from reason and reality*, which in fact is no real option. In Schmitt, secularity is left

element interpenetrate one another'.[339] The two realms cannot be linked by 'absolute knowledge', or by proclamations of godliness like those found in the work of Benjamin's contemporaries Ludwig Derleth or Alois Dempf.

This is, at the same time, the decisive hint about the meaning of the book on German tragic drama: *officially*, the Baroque knows no eschatology,[340] but the secret of German tragic drama is that eschatology was *nevertheless* the hidden precondition of its possibility. For: 'The deterministic outlook cannot influence any art-form',[341] and differently from Spanish Catholicism, the Protestant faith would not admit of any mythic surrogate. But then what is it that determines this art-form? The hidden 'keystone' of the genre of German tragic drama is eschatology,[342] except that it could not be employed constitutively, since *all* theology had been occupied by the dominant political philosophy.[343] German tragic drama limited itself to showing up, in a negative way, the hopelessness of the situation created by the Counter-Reformation. This Protestant refusal caused hope to be lost sight of; it was an *overly* negative theology. The 'objective possibility' that the dramatists lost, and which needs therefore to be 'saved' by the critic, is this: 'The powerful design of this form should be thought through to its conclusion'.[344]

The Christian faith's objection to the mythic deification of domination needs to be taken to an extreme, in order to achieve an 'allegorical totality'. Only thus would German tragic drama have received 'at one and the same time the cue for its [mourning's] entry and exit'.[345] Since Benjamin had read Lukács, this should be read as referring to

---

behind for mythic worlds of illusion (on Schmitt's mythifications, see Kodalle 1973, Groh 1998 and Gross 2000). In Benjamin (as in Marx), one finds the opposite trajectory, away from such myths and *into reason and reality*. Likewise, Marx's silence about possible classless societies need not be interpreted 'religiously'. Marx wanted to avoid creating one more ideological castle in the air, whereas Adorno's reference to the 'ban on images' is used for the opposite purpose, namely that of warding off the queries of reason. 'The scientific certainty of Marxism, therefore, only relates to the proletariat negatively conceived, insofar as it is economically the dialectical contradiction of the bourgeoisie. In contrast, the bourgeoisie must be known positively... Because its essence lies in the economic, Marx has to follow it into the economic realm' (Schmitt, 1985, p. 62; Benjamin, Thesis XII).

339. Benjamin, *GS*, Vol. III, p. 100; Vol. II, p. 200.

340. Benjamin 1977, p. 66.

341. Benjamin 1977, p. 129.

342. This is suggested by the 'last day' (Benjamin 1977, p. 235) and by the reconstruction of the yearning for 'resurrection' (p. 233) from allegorical 'contemplation' and transience. 'Ultimately in the death-signs of the Baroque the direction of allegorical reflection is reversed' (p. 232) – it becomes eschatological. 'In God's world the allegorist awakens' (p. 232). Ultimately, God proves stronger than the worldly katechons, stronger than 'that world, which abandoned itself to the deep spirit of Satan' (p. 232; Benjamin is also referring, in a Lutheran manner, to the 'restoration-theology of the Counter-Reformation': p. 129).

343. Compare the term 'redeployment' ['*Umbesetzung*'] in the debate on secularisation. Scholem characterises the role of messianism in Benjamin as a 'regulatory idea' (Heil 1996, p. 142).

344. Benjamin 1977, p. 235.

345. Ibid.

theoretical self-consciousness *and* liberating praxis.[346] What is at stake is the 'about-turn'.[347] This secret becomes clear only 'on the second part of its [allegory's] wide arc', when it 'returns, to redeem'.[348] In his later works, Benjamin is still concerned with this 'turnaround',[349] which he also calls a 'reversal',[350] 'salvation',[351] the 'threshold' or the 'awakening of the collective'.[352] What is meant is liberating dissociation – both in theory and in practice – from all worldly domination and delusion, a dissociation based on knowledge of God's promise of salvation.

The book on tragic drama shows what happens when this practice is neglected: gnosticism returns,[353] Christians doubt whether Jesus is the Christ,[354] knowledge and politics become evil, and the resulting passivity of men ('despair') further aggravates the situation by becoming hermetic.[355] This is the triumph of myth: freedom has disappeared, and history,[356] emotion, nature and religion are all mythicised[357] – as in Carl Schmitt (and as in the *Dialectic of Enlightenment*). These aporias are not, however, the result of the Christian faith as such, but of its *amalgamation* with the political philosophy of the Counter-Reformation. Given this situation, politics and religion need to be rigorously distinguished.[358] Benjamin does this by distinguishing salvation from liberation.[359] First, however, the yoke needs to be taken from people's shoulders,[360] for there are no spiritual

---

346. 'The German Trauerspiel was never able... to awaken within itself the clear light of self-awareness' (Benjamin 1977, p. 158).

347. Benjamin 1977, p. 232. In the Bible, the eschatological turn causes a reversal even in the present: 'By drawing man's attention to the now as to his last hour, in the sense of the hour of decision, the messages concerning the advent of the heavenly kingdom and the will of God constitute a unity; indeed, they require one another' (Bultmann 1988, p. 91).

348. Ibid.

349. Benjamin, *GS*, Vol. II, p. 299; Vol. III, p. 108.

350. Benjamin, *GS*, Vol. I, p. 1232.

351. Benjamin 1977, p. 401.

352. Benjamin, *GS*, Vol. V, p. 491.

353. Benjamin 1977, p. 221; cf. Blumenberg 1983.

354. In his *Leviathan* (Hobbes 1968, first published in 1651), Hobbes repeats the words 'Jesus is the Christ' almost incantationally.

355. Benjamin 1977, pp. 183, 233, 99, 78. Implicit in this is a response to Kierkegaard (who is thereby 'sublated' historico-materialistically) but also to the Institute's later analysis of fascism, which got bogged down, once more, in hermeticism (2.2.6).

356. 'The essence of the mythical event is return' (Benjamin 1999, p. 119).

357. Benjamin 1977, pp. 47, 99, 94, 205.

358. 'The order of the profane should be erected on the idea of happiness' (Benjamin 1999–2003, Vol. 3, p. 305).

359. 'Will these people liberate themselves? One catches onself feeling that for them, as for poor souls, there is only one salvation left' (Benjamin, *GS*, Vol. III, p. 538). In *The Sorrows of Young Werther* by Goethe, the protagonists also feel they have been saved, but not liberated (*GS*, Vol. III, pp. 709, 552, 589; on the later 'liberation theology', which argued in similar terms, see Gutiérrez 1973, Buhl 1989, Löwy 1990, Thielen 1991, Kern 1992).

360. Benjamin, *GS*, Vol. II, p. 438.

things without material things.[361] If this is not done, every proclaimed salvation is *kitsch*, ideology, myth.[362] That is why the Baroque Protestants had no eschatology. The worldly rule of the Counter-Reformation, which claimed God for itself, was too oppressive.[363] It is true that sanctification is not a human possibility, as Barth says; but what men need most is *liberation*. And they must achieve it themselves. Only by bringing about the 'real state of emergency' – the one that Schmitt[364] meant to avoid, on Benjamin's reading[365] – can one get a clear view of God again.

Thus liberation and salvation are related, and in fact it is impossible to conceptualise one without the other.[366] But what is decisive is that only *God* can relate them to one another.[367] This renders impossible every totalitarian claim and every aestheticisation. There is no direct link between worldly history and eschatology. The latter has in any

---

361. 'Class struggle ... is a fight for the crude and material things without which no ... spiritual things could exist' (Benjamin 2003, p. 390). 'Therefore if thou bring thy gift to the altar, and there rememberest that thy brother hath ought against thee; Leave there thy gift before the altar, and go thy way; first be reconciled to thy brother, and then come and offer thy gift' (Matthew 5:23). Buber, whom Benjamin was acquainted with, expressed himself in similar terms: 'Does this mean that God cannot redeem the world without our help? It means that this is just what God does not want to be able to do' (Buber 1935, p. 55). This approach is also compatible with Kant.

362. This was one reason why the Enlightenment theorists of natural law, like many Marxists after them, took themselves to be atheist: a new path to God needs first to be cleared. This can be done only by radically secular means, beyond theological hyperbole. Benjamin illustrates the senselessness of a religious revolt in theologically bleak times by reference to Kafka, who postpones decisions for such a long time that heaven eventually becomes as bleak as the world (*GS*, Vol II, p. 681; Vol. III, p. 528; on Benjamin's essays on Kafka, see Faber 1985 and Pangritz 1996, pp. 138 ff.).

363. Benjamin also discovers this idea in Baroque images of dark and cloudy skies (Benjamin 1977, p. 79). He may himself have experienced something similar during the Third Reich, before taking his own life.

364. Schmitt 1922, p. 6.

365. Benjamin 2003, p. 392

366. 'In other words, the idea of happiness is indissolubly bound up with the idea of redemption' (Benjamin 2003, p. 389); 'but just as a force can, through acting, increase another that is acting in the opposite direction, so the order of the profane assists, through being profane, the coming of the Messianic Kingdom. The profane, therefore, although not itself a category of this Kingdom, is a decisive category of its quietest approach' (Benjamin 1999–2003, Vol. 3, p. 305). Thus Benjamin rejects the identification of liberation and salvation found in the religious socialists and in Bloch, but he does not separate the two in the manner of Catholic apologetics either; for the latter, the secular and the divine only encounter one another in Catholic rule itself (in Catholicism's 'theocratic claims': Benjamin 1977, p. 65), while autonomous human action is condemned – for Catholicism, 'so-called "human emancipation" ... is still the exact opposite [!] of the Biblical concept of liberation, which makes do without any such notion of liberation' (Hofmann 1987, p. 8). In the Old Testament, one finds almost only liberations of this kind, but not salvation. 'The age of the messias is brought closer not by waiting for God to take the initiative from above, but by political activity' (H. Cohen 1915, quoted in C. Schulte 1994, p. 203).

367. This is all the Hegelian dictum cited by Benjamin means: 'Seek for food and clothing first; then shall the Kingdom of God be granted to you' (Benjamin 2003, p. 390). In the religious language game, God is always involved, even when one is dealing with the secularised world – otherwise, he would not be God.

case never been the 'goal' of history, since it descends upon the world from above. But those who *are* religious can assess historical events in eschatological terms, albeit only negatively: the rule of God renders impossible every 'salvation' by which worldly domination seeks to establish itself as absolute and beyond the reach of human reason. Thus the message contained in Benjamin's letter to Scholem, quoted above, is as follows: during *this* historical period, Judaism and Marxism share the same motives. By allowing us to understand what is responsible for modern mythologemes, Marx promises to provide us with the best possible means for getting rid of them, and thus for liberating humanity. If this is not achieved, the danger is that of an all-dominating mythology, which involves the risk of a mythology of domination. This is why the art critic Benjamin still made use of the 'revolutionary chance in the fight for the oppressed past' during the 1930s:[368] he takes the aporias of *his* age to an extreme so as to bring about an 'allegorical totality', provoking the decisive turnaround in the spectator.[369]

Let us now return to the difference between Benjamin and Adorno. The problem that condemned the authors of German tragic drama to a radical but hopeless worldliness was that of worldly powers claiming religious insignia for themselves.[370] Living in the age of a renewed worldly absolutism that likewise made use of religious trappings (National Socialism), Benjamin also radically *eschewed* all *theologoumena* (the situation was analogous to that of German tragic drama: there is no point in talking about salvation when there is not even liberation),[371] whereas Adorno tried, in the very same situation, to make Benjamin more acceptant of religious ways of speaking.[372] This amounted to a distortion of the meaning of religion in Benjamin's thought: writing in the *particular* contexts of a certain age, Benjamin touched upon theological problems that could only be solved politically.

Adorno adopted this and made it his *general* method.[373] He spoke henceforth of 'salvation', 'redemption' and 'breaking out' as if this were a universally recognised practice

---

368. Benjamin 2003, p. 396.

369. On the method of 'rescuing critique', see Faber 1985.

370. The case is similar in the *Arcades Project* (Benjamin 1999), where the promise of a better world that originates from technology is held in check by the persistently unjust social order. This is how technology first develops mythic-demonic features. Benjamin held that there was a road out of this aporia, as yet untravelled: the proletariat needed to 'take possession' of technology, 'an act that was seen to be more and more necessary' ('Eduard Fuchs', 1937, quoted in Wiggershaus 1994, p. 201). As long as this is not done, all talk of 'salvation' is nothing but mythic subreption, as when Adorno sees salvation being anticipated, 'dialectically' and in a model form, in elitist artworks ('On the Fetish Character in Music and the Regression in Listening', 1938; see also Wiggershaus 1994, p. 239).

371. In the *Arcades Project*, Benjamin set out to accomplish something 'analogous' to what he had accomplished in the 'book on the Baroque' (1999, p. 459).

372. Wiggershaus 1994, pp. 191–2; see. Pangritz 1996, pp. 169 ff.

373. This elision of the historical context has a formal counterpart in the abandonment of the category of the particular in *Negative Dialectics* (Rentsch 2000, pp. 262 ff.). Adorno already engaged in theologisations in his 1931 habilitation thesis, despite the fact that Kierkegaard was already a

within the human sciences, and as if the theological content he thereby laid claim to but never explicated were freely available.[374] But the way that he related his own thought to Benjamin's was questionable. Benjamin had not tried to overhastily stir religious ingredients into a theoretical stew; he had aspired to a rigorous distinction between religion and theory. He had recognised theology's historico-political conditionality, including the possibility of religious 'one-way streets' that necessitate a radical worldliness – *ad maiorem dei gloriam*. Benjamin became politically active because theology had become impossible;[375] Adorno, by contrast, judged politics to have been rendered impossible and escaped into 'theology'.

Benjamin always welcomed everything that resembled worldly liberation (including anarchism, surrealism and popular culture); like Tillich, he was able to perceive in it a reflex of religion only because of its radical worldliness.[376] Adorno *rejected* all such elements: the rapprochment with the proletariat, popular culture and, eventually, the student movement.[377] His rejection of worldliness was based on value judgements rather than on arguments; both this rejection and the aesthetic interpretations of selected modern artworks by which he formulated it were supplemented with a dash of religion. Religion served him as a theoretical 'working hypothesis' of the kind that Bonhoeffer would have refused to accept. By contrast, Benjamin's theological inclinations allowed him to actively endorse a radically secular Marxism – one more radical even than the communist unity front policy of his Paris exile.[378] Religion had the opposite effect in Adorno: the utopian veneer of his call for a 'better society' – so lofty and abstract no practice was

---

theologian and thus did not need to be 'rescued'. While Benjamin, in writing about the Baroque, separated the secular from the religious, Adorno did the opposite and transferred transcendence into immanence; he also already conceived of aesthetics as the site of 'reconciliation' in 1931 (Wiggershaus 1994, p. 92; Pangritz 1996, pp. 136 f.). The conclusion of *Minima Moralia* introduces religion in a manner that renders science impossible: 'Knowledge has no light but that shed on the world by redemption' (Adorno 2005, p. 247).

374. Adorno wrote that it was the 'motive of longing for universal justice . . . that led him . . . to employ theological categories' (letter to Horkheimer, 25 January 1937, quoted in Pangritz 1996, p. 162). New music, he claimed, had 'taken upon itself all the darkness and guilt of the world' (Adorno 2006, p. 132; see pp. 128–9). 'Adorno's essays always closed by surveying the prospects for salvation' (Wiggershaus 1994, p. 313; see also pp. 312, 502).

375. This struggle became especially evident during his Paris exile (see Kambas 1985). Gogarten identified the essence of Barth's approach: 'A space was cleared for questions concerning God' (quoted in Kambas 1985, p. 285).

376. In his essay on Goethe's *Elective Affinities*, Benjamin shows that if the 'reconciliation' of the lovers fails, this is because they do not resolutely opt for practice: they 'never gathered strength for battle' (Benjamin 1999e, p. 356). For one needs only to 'be serious about love in order to recognise a "profane enlightenment" in it as well' (Benjamin, *GS*, Vol. II, p. 298). See Tillich, '*Prinzipien des Protestantismus*' (1942): 'When the profane spheres touch upon their own foundation and goal, they cease to be profane' (*GW*, Vol. VII, p. 138).

377. On this difference, see Wiggershaus 1994, p. 192: Adorno rejected Benjamin's 1934 essay 'The Work of Art in the Age of Mechanical Reproduction' (Benjamin 1978) because it featured a call for alignment with the proletariat.

378. See 'The Author as Producer' (1934; *GS*, Vol. II, p. 701) and Kambas 1985, p. 268.

adequate to it – hindered even the postponed elaboration of his social theory. This contrast between Adorno and Benjamin – evident in the fields of theory, religion *and* politics – was obscured by the fact that Benjamin's relationship to Adorno was always one of dependence. Benjamin had to moderate his views when communicating with Adorno, and it was only thanks to Adorno that Benjamin later became well-known. Adorno was, therefore, in a good position to impose his own interpretation of Benjamin's work.[379]

Benjamin only became famous after his death: he was received first in the student movement,[380] and then in recent political theology. Within the latter, Benjamin is often referred to in the context of talk about 'remembrance', 'dangerous recollection' and different conceptions of time, but concrete political issues are rarely addressed. It seems as if everything depended on having the right 'concept of time' – once again, one starts from first principles, on which everything else seems to depend, so that considering them is considered 'political' in and of itself.[381] It was precisely this sort of idealist thought that Marx referred to as 'theological' (2.6.4). Thus even the *fundamental premise* of Marxian thought, the critique of religion, was abandoned, in the name of Marxism.

This chapter has shown that critical theory also – and quite uncritically – adopted the unfortunate theoretical contents it encountered, and in particular neoclassical theory's economic avoidance of Marx and the de-economisation involved in the Leninist notion of a 'primacy of politics'. Moreover, it escaped theoretically into theology, via the detours of psychology and aesthetics. By an irony of history, it was precisely this last possible form of abstraction, the theological residuum of a critical thought once inspired by Marx, which proved resilient in the face of the intellectual attacks associated with the epochal change of 1989. For out of the numerous variants of German normativist thought, only theological business ethics has retained some *recollection* of Marxian ideas and patterns of argument (3.3.2).[382]

This may be due to theology's greater proximity to 'real people', a result of the charitable activities the church engages in at home and abroad. Other socio-philosophical

---

379. Adorno 1970, Wiggershaus 1994, p. 211; Jay 1996, p. 199.

380. Interest in Benjamin within the student may have been prompted by surrealist and other experiments (Bohrer 1970).

381. The Benjamin of 'On the Concept of History' (Benjamin 2003, written in 1940) speaks of political matters (class struggle, defeat, contempt and the willingness to make sacrifices, revolutions, and so on), proceeding to reflect on the relationship to the historical legacy and the underlying 'concept of history', but recent political theology has been interested only in his reflections on time, independently of what occurs within it. When these reflections are considered in isolation, without their political background being taken into account, they remain speculative and dilatory (see above, on Löwith; see also Moltmann 1967, Metz 1972, Manemann 1999). Hugo Assmann has criticised the fact that 'Marx and Hegel... have not yet been digested by theology'. The result is plenty of beating around the bush; the issues themselves are never addressed (in: Feil 1969, pp. 218, 221–2; see Thomas 1993, p. 190; Türcke 1990, pp. 9 ff.).

382. Marxism 'appears... to be taken seriously by almost no one but theologians these days' (Hofmann 1987, p. 11; for a recent comment on this, see Baecker 2003).

attempts to conceptualise the present, including those of critical theory, have lost their reference point (Marx) since 1989, and with it they have lost much of their sense of reality. For when social theory's normative superstructure loses its material base, normativism becomes an overarching feature of the theory, no matter how technicistically reductive a view of the base was formerly taken. What results is 'supernormativism' (4.2.5). Let us now examine the development of this thought, which the post-1989 failure to make reference to Marxian theory has left free-floating.

Chapter Three
Marx Today: Critique of Contemporary Philosophy

Marx is dead, Jesus lives.[1]

Here we are, in the heart of Germany. We shall now have to talk metaphysics while talking political economy.[2]

The political sea change that occurred with the fall of the Berlin wall entailed major changes not just for the people who had lived under real socialism. The victors of the Cold War – the democratic market economies of the West – have also undergone immense transformations. The discussion on globalisation is an attempt to take account of them. One does not need to be a Marxist to recognise in globalisation the triumphal return of the old capitalism: the aggravation of ecological problems and international conflicts goes hand in hand with the withering away both of social security and of the possibilities for state intervention in the economy. So far, there is no end in sight.[3] The explanations offered by the protagonists of this development are so blatantly based on the primacy of the economy (such as on notions of the competitive pressures of the 'world market')[4] as to obviate the need for substantiating the hypothesis that the theoretical and socio-philosophical response to this situation can only consist in a return to Marx's comprehensive analysis of capitalism (section 1.2).[5]

Yet according to Marx, base and superstructure do not constitute an *unmediated* whole. Because of the relatively

---

1. Norbert Blüm, ca. 1990.
2. Marx, MECW 6, p. 161.
3. Brecher 1994 speaks of a 'race to the bottom'.
4. Cf. Altvater 1987.
5. Especially once the phantasm of a 'communist world revolution' is off the table, which merely led Marxists to disregard Marx's economic writings (2.2.6, 2.3.3, 2.6.2).

autonomous dynamics of the superstructure, arguments and approaches inherited from the Cold War constellation survive the demise of that constellation's economic base. While the economy pages of quality dailies refer regularly to Marx, post-1989 German philosophy hardly takes notice of him (excepting the traditional anti-communism that continues to project its notions onto Marx in a fallacious manner).[6] Yet as a school of thought, German Marxism was already dead before 1989. It has been demonstrated in Chapter Two of this study that philosophical Marxisms *and* refutations of Marx have largely been built on the sand of German 'spirit'. The need to explain Marx away is often already evident in the *basic approach* of the philosophical paradigms I have examined. The only reason these paradigms have proven so successful is that German Marxism did much to prepare this altercation by proxy, which occurs 'upon the terrain of spirit'.[7] The philosophical critiques of Marx I have considered have not stood up to closer scrutiny. Thus nothing really stands in the way of contemporary philosophy's engagement with Marx, apart from discursive habits. However, in philosophy, which is so far removed from practice, such habits die harder than elsewhere. The fact that philosophy has forgotten about Marx has negative consequences for its comprehension of reality. The following part of this study, Chapter Three, presents examples to show that Marx's critique of philosophy can be applied to contemporary philosophemes.

When Marx disappeared from philosophy's consciousness after 1989, many socio-philosophical models ceased to be grounded in the economic base. When such models deal *only* with norms, and when they do so on the idealist assumption that norms are what 'constitutes' or 'generates' society, the narrow focus of the normative approach is aggravated, and *normative social philosophy* results – a theoretical overloading of normativity that assumes an increasingly free-floating character the more it shuts itself off from social reality. Sections 3.1 to 3.4 show just how important it is to criticise the historical foundations upon which this occurs; this was done in Chapter Two. The further we proceeded in our exposition, the more our references to Marx's theory were mediated by that theory's reception history. This is why we did not discuss social philosophy until late in our exposition. The way social philosophy relates to its object of inquiry is *generally* problematic.

Today, social philosophy addresses an ever-changing range of themes in a methodologically haphazard way. Often, the 'method' consists simply in adopting the terminology of an author who happens to be topical. It often remains unclear what the terms employed – such as 'normativity' or 'community' – actually refer to. Social philosophy neglects the problem of how it relates to its object of inquiry, preferring to blindly let itself be taken wherever past terminological decisions lead it. Whenever social philosophy is confronted with the real world, it becomes clear just how unfortunate a state of affairs this is. In such a situation, the adoption of an approach culled from the history of

6. For recent examples, see Löw 2001 and Gehrhart 2002.
7. Mannheim 1964.

theory becomes a matter of some import: such approaches are 'categorical frameworks' and 'background assumptions' that persist with remarkable continuity thanks to the continuing influence of certain schools of thought. These frameworks and assumptions shape one's view of things and of theory – including emotionally.

Our analysis of exemplary cases of contemporary German-language social philosophy begins with a critique of Habermas, whose work represents a direct extension of German critical theory (3.1). Habermas shares critical theory's basic problem: he diposes of an ethicised superstructural philosophy that is detached from the socio-economic base and struggles unsuccessfully to 'ground' this philosophy, to reconnect it to the economic base, by means of other theories. This aporia goes through several transformations as Habermas experiments with various fashionable theories, from anthropology (3.1.1), transcendental philosophy and the theory of rationality (both 3.1.2) to a normative and *purely* ethical metaphysics of society (3.1.3). In the end, the two varieties of reductiveness evident in Habermas (one technicist, the other moralistic) converge in the construal of a model that is reminiscent of Hegel (3.1.5). This model only succeeds in 'solving' the problem by altogether removing society from theory's field of view. This can be seen from a comparison with Marx's conceptions of ethics and law, which will be examined at the end of this chapter (3.1.4, 3.1.6).

A second variant of normative social philosophy is represented by the German reception of certain *theories of justice* that were initially developed in the USA. Section 3.2 begins to address this issue by demonstrating that the approach developed by Rawls is an ethicised mirror image of neoclassical theory's reductive model of society (3.2.1). Because of its elasticity, this approach is of little help when it comes to addressing practical matters (3.2.2). As for communitarianism, which is in many ways reminiscent of German historicism, it also fails to move beyond normative considerations (3.2.3). The debate between Rawls and the communitarians is an inter-normativist debate; considered from the point of view of the archaeology of theory, it can be characterized in terms of the return of two ethicisations, that of the economic base and that of the superstructure (2.4.3). In spite or perhaps because of this, the debate has been enthusiastically received within post-Marxist Germany. As for post-1989 German social philosophy's Hegelian attempts to reconcile the two ethics, they merely confirm one more time that German social philosophy has lost touch with 'society' as an object of inquiry, for 'society' is not explicitly theorised in either of the two 'normative theories' (3.2.4).

The section on *business ethics* (3.3) demonstrates, once more, the importance of a historico-theoretical awareness of the problem. For the intuition from which business ethics starts is profoundly critical (3.3.1) – and this is hardly surprising considering that theology, in particular, has been able to preserve for itself an awareness of Marx's critique of capitalism (3.3.2). The persistent but unrecognised effects of the erroneous interpretations of Marx that we submitted to historico-theoretical analysis in Chapter Two, but also of theoretical reconfigurations that amount, functionally, to ways of bypassing Marx, are such that the originally critical intention behind business ethics is transformed into its opposite: the discipline becomes largely apologetic. This is especially true of the branch of business ethics that focuses on management issues (3.3.3), but it is also true of the historicist branch of business ethics (3.3.4). The various syntheses of technicist and normative social philosophies attempted within the field of business ethics lead to yet another revival of Hegelianism. This cannot be otherwise for as long as the field's proper object of inquiry, bourgeois society, remains outside the theoretical field of vision or enters it only in a distorted form, in the manner described (3.3.5). The response opted for by the critics of globalisation, namely to largely renounce theory, becomes understandable given this context (3.3.6). The critics of globalisation also bring Marx back in – although until now they have treated him only as an icon. Yet philosophically fertile engagement with today's real world requires analyses undertaken from the perspective of specific disciplines as much as it requires empirical analysis. Philosophy can contribute to this undertaking by identifying and removing the obstacles to Marx's reception, as this study demonstrates by its very way of proceeding.

Consideration of another theoretical fashion, the renaissance of *pragmatism* (3.4), provides an opportunity for reflecting on the basic structure and genesis of German supernormativism. A comparison between pragmatism's basic operation, reconfiguring what has hitherto been the philosophy of mind in such a way as to address human action (3.4.2), and the Marxian conception of the critique of philosophy (3.4.4), demonstrates with surprising clarity that pragmatism can also be seen to function as a strategy for avoiding engagement with Marx – precisely *because* its basic operation is similar to Marx's (3.4.3). The application of pragmatist notions to the German-speaking world's theoretical architecture, which had already largely detached itself from the Hegelian model of spirit, leads to a re-idealisation of philosophical thought and to a philosophy of unity that circumvents certain fundamental distinctions (3.4.1). Thus the various sections of Chapter Three show up a strong tendency toward the re-Hegelianisation of social philosophy. Returning to Marx – i.e. to one of Hegel's most important critics – is shown to represent a plausible option even from a perspective that remains immanent to theory.

3.1 Jürgen Habermas or the return of the philosophy of law

> This resistance to the simplest matters and most obvious demands confirms the old principle founded in experience, that no ruling class can be convinced by reasoning, until the force of circumstances drives them to sense and to submission.[8]

The lifespan of philosophical knowledge has become as brief as that of fashion, so that philosophical textbooks published during the past decades now no longer hold any interest except from an antiquarian point of view. Yet philosophical problems are hardly

---

8. Bebel 1971.

ever solved; they tend rather to be forgotten or posed in a different way. This is why historicising the philosophical present can be a salutary operation – and this is especially true with regard to the putative *philosophical* sea change of 1989. In older philosophical textbooks, discussion of Marx was a matter of course, and Jürgen Habermas was consistently cited as a promising representative of 'critical Marxism'. The twentieth century has probably seen no 'left-wing' German author capable of interpreting, discussing and stimulating others in as sophisticated a manner as Habermas. What astounds one today is not so much this – it is something one has grown used to – than the fact that he once did so in the name of 'Marxism', or in any case was interpreted thus (in China, this was still the case as late as 2000). Leaving aside the context in which Habermas received his philosophical training and the occasional affirmative references found in his early works,[9] there was hardly any basis for such an assessment. The fact that Habermas has not invoked the authority of Marx since 1989 does not represent a break with earlier tendencies, because the instances of his doing so before 1989 are few and far between (and when he did invoke Marx, he did so in order to set himself off from him).[10]

There is an obvious explanation for this, related to the highly 'osmotic' character of Habermas's work: if there had been a competent representative of Marxism, then Habermas would surely have engaged with him. In his effort to develop a philosophically adequate formulation of 'emancipatory' politics, Habermas has commented upon and incorporated almost *every* school of thought of his time. But since most of these schools of thought were not interested in Marx (or were interested only in refuting him, which was purely a matter of obligation), it is hardly surprising that little has remained of Habermas's beginnings within Marxist theory.

Habermas's main interlocutors never spoke of Marx,[11] and even his Marxist interlocutors (such as Adorno, Marcuse or Dutschke) did not really take Marx's theory seriously when it came to applying it to the present, as we have seen. (Abendroth was the only exception to this rule.) From the point of view of 'theoretical production', there was no *occasion* for engaging closely with Marx. This, however, is indicative of an indiscriminate approach to theory: whatever theory happened to be topical was considered valuable by virtue of this very fact. It is true that Habermas sometimes sharply criticises certain features of 'theory' in general; nevertheless, he seems to accept specific theories as authoritative representations of reality simply by virtue of the fact that they have been formulated. Yet to proceed thus is to overhastily conflate thought and being. This is a fundamental difference between Habermas and Marx: Marx criticised the sciences

9. Habermas 1957 and 1973.
10. Habermas 1976b, p. 1; Habermas 1984–7, Vol. II, p. 375.
11. Chronologically, they have included Erich Rothacker, Arnold Gehlen, Martin Heidegger, Hannah Arendt, Hans-Georg Gadamer, Joachim Ritter, Hans Albert, Niklas Luhmann, Karl-Otto Apel, Dieter Henrich, Ernst Nolte, Michel Foucault, John Rawls and Robert Brandom (cf. Reese-Schäfer 2000, Horster 2000).

(albeit not from the position of an outsider, as Heidegger and Adorno did, but by developing them further), whereas Habermas unhesitatingly integrates the findings of the most diverse scientific disciplines into his philosophical system. Such an approach, however, is not without its consequences.

As a disciplined thinker, Habermas made reference, during every stage in the development of his system, to precursors he judged significant, and Marx repeatedly featured among them. In what follows, these references to Marx will be used to trace the development of Habermas's thought up to the present; I will also raise the question of what effects the various stages in the development of Habermas's system had on his interpretation of Marx. In proceeding thus, our attention will be drawn to a wide range of works by other authors who share an indebtedness to Habermasian ideas. Habermas is doubly representative of contemporary philosophy: he consistently adapts his theories to the momentary situation, in which topical theoretical models paint a picture of the world; and in doing so, he has influenced an entire generation of contemporary philosophers.[12] Let us now trace the genesis of Marx's absence from contemporary philosophy in the developmental stages of this last German systematic thinker.

3.1.1 *Anthropological beginnings*

We have already seen that the theoretical cause of the hopelessness diagnosed by the critical theory of the past lay in the hermetic character of its political economy (2.6.2). In Habermas, for whom this aporia was the point of entry,[13] this tragic hermeticism

12. The word *Gegenwartsphilosophie* [philosophy of the present] is used in a twofold sense in Lukács 1923, pp. 224 f. (cf. Grisebach 1928 and Lehmann 1943): it refers both to contemporary philosophy and to philosophy that thematises and focuses on its own immediate present. For this reason, its half-life is necessarily limited: it is no longer the meaning within or behind the changing times that is of interest; instead, specific momentary states are comprehended and philosophised in isolation. The term 'modernity', which is as popular as it is imprecise, also reflects this somewhat journalistic orientation. It represents a transfer of the thought of presence to the production of philosophical theory. The 'consensus theory of truth' (Habermas 1973b) merely renders explicit the assumption that objectivity cannot be accessed, but only approximated through 'intersubjectivity'. From this starting point, every theory is worthy of being considered true by virtue of being a theory. There exists no critical instance other than the criticisms formulated by other scholars. Given the contingency of such criticism, this is philosophically unsatisfying – the 'primacy of the object' (Adorno 2007, p. 188) has vanished. The early critic Willms pointedly summarised this sophistical notion in the following terms: discourse is 'the transfer of the liberal model of the market to the quest for truth' (Willms 1973, p. 204).

13. Habermas (1984–7, Vol. I, pp. 366 ff.; Habermas 1987a, pp. 106 ff.) was himself one of the best critics of the Frankfurt School's 'foundational deficit'. Its position was aporetic due to the fact that it involved, at one and the same time, a radical critique of reason and the invocation of reason. In an analogous way, the Frankfurt School theorists consistently called for consideration of the totality (the 'view of the whole') even as they described such consideration as impossible (or as having become impossible today – 'The whole is the false': Adorno 2005, p. 50). These positions cancelled each other out. Consequently, critical theory was noted less for its results than for its polemics against various projects – including projects similar to its own (such as Mannheim, Neurath, Heidegger, Popper, König; cf. 2.6). These 'interventions' were based on a rather vague attitude. When it came to justifying its attacks, the theory displayed considerable lacunae. This

had a different background, namely an anthropological one.[14] To be sure, the result of Habermas's anthropological considerations was not unlike that at which Adorno arrived: a resignation that followed the lead of Gehlen and Freyer.[15] But Habermas's anthropological considerations also provided him with other options for escaping hermeticism. Instead of the economic critique that would have been necessary or the aesthetic subterfuges that Adorno and Marcuse opted for, he could resort to *anthropological* counter-hypotheses.[16]

Aside from the fact that he had been a student of Erich Rothacker, a Bonn-based cultural anthropologist with a questionable past,[17] Habermas's anthropological orientation owed much to the works of Arnold Gehlen. Habermas said of them that they were 'justly famous'.[18] This may have been due to a biographical parallel: like Marcuse and later Habermas, Gehlen also began with an idealist philosophy, dissociating himself from it in his early writings in order to obtain a better grasp of 'true mind' by means of an 'empirical philosophy'.[19] This Young Hegelian tendency led Gehlen to engage with Fichte, as was only consistent;[20] he then moved on to anthropology[21] and eventually to the theme of the institutions.[22] By virtue of this, he represented a philosophy that Habermas felt a certain affinity with, having broken with the late idealist philosophy of Heidegger and with Schelling: Gehlen went 'in search of truth' without negating his idealist background altogether.[23] It is no coincidence that Habermas read Gehlen in

---

quandary was then projected onto Marx, of all people (after all, Marx was not really very relevant to critical theory).

14. Rehberg 1981.

15. Gehlen's negative anthropology (1940) described 'man' as dependent on institutions that, while they might decrease the quality of life in 'industrial society' (1957), could in no way benefit, but only be endangered by 'subjectivist' criticism (1969). Gehlen therefore recommended surrendering oneself to the situation with the pathos of knowledge ('the key to true political ethics' is nothing but 'the call … to affirm the law that already exist': Gehlen 1980, p. 147; compare Freyer's 'adaptation' and Heidegger's *Gelassenheit*; Grimminger 1997). This was still the motive behind the invectives against intellectuals in Schelsky 1975; cf. Habermas 1984–7, pp. 107 ff.; Habermas 1996, p. 480.

16. Erich Fromm's trajectory was similar; it led to his break with the Institute.

17. Cf. Rothacker 1934.

18. Habermas 1981, pp. 101 ff.

19. Gehlen 1956, p. 8. Gehlen 1931; cf. Jonas 1976, Vol. II, pp. 211 ff.; Rügemer 1979, pp. 15 ff.; Böhler 1981, Üner 1994, Rehberg 1994; Thies 2000.

20. Gehlen 1935.

21. Gehlen 1988, first published in 1940.

22. Gehlen 1956. The Young Hegelians were strongly influenced by Fichte (Hess 1843; Hogrebe 1987, p. 112). Feuerbach is their anthropological, and the critique of church and state their institutional counterpart (cf. Löwith 1965, Pepperle 1985).

23. The break with Heidegger was prompted by the renewed publication of texts written during the Nazi period: 'Until the publication of Heidegger's *Introduction to Metaphysics* in 1953, my political and my philosophical allegiances were … two utterly different things – two universes that hardly touched' (Habermas 1979, p. 515). On the role of Schelling (Habermas 1954, 2004), see Keulartz 1995. On Gehlen's 'idealist' background (that of 'transcendental action' in 1931, and of 'double reflection' in 1933 – a 'ceasing of the materiality of things': 1931, p. 176) see Boehler 1973, Rügemer 1979; on Gehlen's influence on Habermas, see Glaser 1972.

Marxist terms:[24] he was virtually driven to do this by his need for a scientific and empirically substantive philosophy that emphasised action, all the more so as Marcuse, who was centrally important to the young Habermas, had followed a trajectory from Marx back to Feuerbach, or to man in general.[25]

Now, the works of Gehlen and Arendt already constituted an implicit *critique* of Marx,[26] much as Marcuse had resolutely distanced himself from Marx. Thus Habermas's originally optimistic Marx-based[27] reception of the anthropologies of Gehlen and Rothacker led, once Habermas began to follow Horkheimer in taking a more sceptical view of instrumental reason,[28] to his abandonment not of Gehlen but of Marx. Yet the anthropological critique of Marx's putative 'production paradigm'[29] worked only as a critique (*by extension*) of Gehlen, whom Habermas had adhered to until now – and continued to adhere to.[30] Habermas projected Gehlen into Marx; his use of Marxist vocabulary remained an intermezzo.

Once the aporias of critical theory had been transferred to an anthropological model, they could be *resolved* anthropologically. This was precisely what Hannah Arendt had to offer: she had in common with other German thinkers such as Gehlen and Marcuse

---

24. 'In principle', Gehlen 'describes nothing but what the young Marx described' (Habermas 1981, p. 103), namely alienation. Even Freud is given a 'Gehlensian' reading by Habermas (1987, pp. 282 f.). Harich and Lukács also developed Marxist readings of Gehlen (Rehberg 2000). Gehlen's dialectic, according to which the 'cultural sphere' belongs to man's '*natural* requirements for life' (Gehlen 1988, p. 72) was close to Lukács's position. Similarly, Habermas considered Arendt's emphatic 'concept of praxis . . . more Marxist than Aristotelian' (Habermas 1976a, p. 238; Negt 1993, Brunkhorst 1999).

25. 'Man as species being, prior to all class oppositions, is one of the conditions of possibility of a classless society' (Marcuse 1979, p. 25, quoted in Habermas 1977, p. 281; cf. Schmidt 1988). Marcuse was the most important 'critical theorist' to Habermas (cf. Habermas 1977, pp. 266, 279; Habermas 1985, p. 216; Habermas 1991a, p. 53).

26. 'The rise of anthropology to the status of first philosophy may be the most historically effective form taken by the implicit critique of Marx' (Rohrmoser 1974, p. 57 – Arendt's contribution to this was 'negligible': p. 81; cf. Marquard 1973). Rothacker criticised Marxism explicity by introducing life styles – something predominantly mental – as 'the true bases of historical events' (Rothacker 1932, quoted in Dahms 1994, p. 366). Rothacker 1934, p. 94, agrees with Fichte in considering not ability but 'the will' the 'engine of history'.

27. Habermas also refers to Rothacker and Marx in the same breath (Habermas 1970, p. 28; cf. Morf 1970, pp. 134 ff.). It is true that Gehlen recognised a second, mimetic form of action, which leads to 'cognition'. But Habermas argues that this form of action is 'mediated through labour, as Hegel and Marx already knew' (Habermas 1958, p. 28). The expressive behaviour whose existence was first emphasised by Plessner (p. 29) and the resulting constituent elements 'lifestyle' and 'world picture' (Rothacker) are 'embedded in a certain "system" of social labour, in relations of production' (p. 31). This is not to reduce something to labour but to emphasise its overarching dominance – as in Marx.

28. It is not to be found in Marx, least of all in his early writings (Arndt 1985, pp. 17 ff.; Böhm 1998). Gehlen meant to explain 'norms' by reducing them to their survival function (Habermas 1981).

29. Habermas 1987a, pp. 75 ff.

30. Gehlensian formulations can still be found in Habermas 1996, pp. 55 and 23 f., as well as in Habermas 2003, pp. 12 and 20 f. They sit well with integral normativism (4.2.5), for it is only the functionalist reduction that requires an ethical supplement.

a tendency to reduce the economy to a purely functional affair and to consider it historically unpromising,[31] by subsuming the crisis-laden phenomena of modernity under the *concept* of 'labour'. (How capitalist reality was supposed to have developed out of this concept remained an open question.) Oddly, and in a clear departure from Marx, Arendt opposed this concept to that of 'work', within which all the creativity that Arendt refused to recognise in the biologised labour process appeared to have been concentrated.[32] The privileged concept within this model was that of a consummately worldless 'action' ('without the intermediary of things or matter'),[33] which now represented the 'pure' politics aestheticistically attributed to the ancient *polis*. Habermas followed Arendt in developing a conceptual hierarchy:[34] above the putatively Marxian 'reduction of the self-generative act of the human species to labor',[35] he placed the higher storey of 'interaction'.[36] This was not so much to criticise the reductive Gehlensian anthropology that Habermas had attributed to Marx than to supplement and thereby confirm it. Habermas's references to the 'history of the species'[37] bypass Marx in the manner characteristic of earlier German social philosophy: the reductionist conception of a purely technical 'labour' is *ramped up* with higher human forms of behaviour, which manifest themselves in their corresponding 'sciences'. Yet to *synthesise* several unfortunate theoretical developments is not to reverse any of them – by merely combining reductionist 'technology' and immaterial 'interaction', social theory loses hold of its object of inquiry.[38] Habermas's critique of *Marx* is to a considerable extent informed by

31. Arendt 1969, p. 322, fears the predominance of the *animal laborans* (a term for slaves in antiquity – note the Nietzschean undertones in the notion of the 'slave revolt', which are confirmed by Arendt's definition of the final end of politics: in politics, she writes, nothing counts except the 'immortal fame' won by great deeds and words [p. 197) will lead to modernity ending 'in the deadliest, most sterile passivity history has ever known.... [M]an may be willing and, indeed, is on the point of developing into that animal species from which, since Darwin, he imagines he has come' (p. 322).

32. See Joas 1996 for a late example of this opposition. The opposition is misleading: in both cases, work is performed and something is produced. Even in etymological terms, the opposition is inappropriate (Arendt 1969, pp. 79 f.). 'Labor' refers primarily to industrial labour (which is nugatory because it 'leaves nothing behind': p. 87 – a class prejudice); 'work' refers to petty-bourgeois 'craft' (p. 81) or the upper-class 'work of art' (p. 167). Arendt vacillates: in some passages, every product is a work, and labour is merely the process of its production (p. 87); in others, labour is the production of lower-order products such as means of consumption (pp. 145 f.), and in still others, labour is the activity proper to slaves, whereas work is the activity proper to the free (p. 91).

33. Arendt 1969, p. 7.

34. It was only later that Habermas admitted: 'It was from Hannah Arendt that I learned how a theory of communicative action ought to be tackled' (Habermas 1984–7, p. 405; Habermas 1996, pp. 147 ff.).

35. Habermas 1987, p. 42; cf. 1966.

36. Habermas 1973a, pp. 142 ff.; Habermas 1971b, pp. 91 f.; 2.4.2.

37. Habermas 1968c, p. 161; Habermas 1987, p. 197.

38. The synthesis of purely technical instrumentality and worldless morality loses its grasp on the object of inquiry capitalism (2.4.1; for a similar assessment, see Türcke in Bolte 1989, p. 35). But Habermas does not compensate for the theoretical lacuna; instead, he distorts reality to fit his model. He declares the lacuna to be the representation of a changed reality: 'The root ideology

his own biography.[39] His anthropological ramping up of his own reductionist beginnings may be original, but it is hardly acceptable as a *critique* of Marx.[40]

While I do not mean to put too much stock in filiations, it is clear the tripartite division into technical, practical and emancipatory interests *corresponds* to Hannah Arendt's 'labour, work and action'. This is true insofar as labour is conceived of in purely technical terms, whereas work corresponds mainly to artistic activity (formerly 'objective mind') and its hermeneutic processing; moreover, political action was conceived of by Arendt as 'liberating'.[41] There is even a 'speech act theory' – 'communicative action' – to be found in Arendt, as she was inspired by Jaspers to define speech as the medium of political action.[42] As far as Habermas's understanding of Marx was concerned, this anthropological approach entailed distortions. To begin with, the unmediated juxtaposition of various forms of action consolidated the problematic features of each of them. The content of 'labour' remained underdetermined, since it was taken to be a closed technical system, in the manner of Hilferding, Pollock and Gehlen; Marxian theories were no longer brought to bear on 'labour'. The categorial analysis of 'labour' (which went beyond mere matters of definition, in the young Marx) was taken to be sufficient;[43] economic analyses are in

---

of just exchange...collapsed in practice' (Habermas 1971b, p. 101; Habermas 1976a, p. 36). This historico-philosophical reconstruction needs to be understood as meeting a requirement immanent to the theory. Even decades later, the lacuna is declared necessary: the social sciences, Habermas argues, 'are unable to grasp social reality' (Habermas 1991a, p. 204) – Habermas is rather hasty when it comes to turning his observations into 'necessities' (in this, he is not unlike Heidegger; cf. Lafont 1994, p. 337).

39. Habermas was initially himself the defender of a 'labour-dialectical' perspective, but then rejected this approach (Keulartz 1995, pp. 146 f., 170): 'As a labourer, man owes his *Dasein* to himself; his history is the history of his labour' (Habermas 1958, p. 22); 'it is only when everything created by human hands is at the disposal of men that those things of which one cannot dispose are set free – only the consummate rationality of what is necessary to life makes possible the irrationality of abundance in life' (Habermas 1957, p. 442).

40. This 'reflection, which was originally intended merely as a critique of positivism', was subsequently projected onto Marx (Honneth 1980, p. 215). The technocrats had judged Marx to be an early positivist (H. Klages 1964; cf. 2.4.5, Wellmer 1969 and Simon Schäfer 1974). Early forms of the distinction can be found in Habermas 1967, pp. 15 ff.: 'Individuals who dispose only of technologically relevant knowledge and can expect no rational self-edification...lose their identity', Habermas responds to his discussion partner Albert – who was certainly not a Marxist (p. 72). In light of the formality of this dualism within the critique of Marx, Willms 1973 already noted that 'clinging to this problematic primary dualism...either takes one back to one's initial framing of the problem, or it leads one to simply ignore divergent results' (p. 178; cf. pp. 33 ff., 70 ff., 138 ff., 162). See Sensat 1979, Heller 1982, Cerruti 1983, Bolte 1989, Rockmore 1989, Roderick 1989, Bohmann 1999, McBride 2000.

41. Dahms 1994, 370 sees an affinity with Max Scheler's forms of knowledge (as does Hans Albert). Scheler distinguished between knowledge of domination, educational knowledge and knowledge of salvation (Scheler, *GW* 9, p. 114; for a comprehensive exposition, see *GW* 8).

42. The idealist fallacy of inferring content from form (cf. 2.5) is already evident in Arendt: the mere fact that speech deals with politics does not entail that it must therefore be kept 'pure' of 'labour' and 'work'. A politics that omits these *topoi* is no politics at all.

43. On the philosophisation of the concept of labour, see Marcuse 2005b, Honneth 1980b, Lange 1980, Gürtler 2001, Krebs 2002. As far as 'German social philosophy' is concerned, 'the *concept* of labour...is quite sufficient' (*MECW* 5, p. 483; 2.5.7).

fact never formulated in the work of Habermas's associates and followers. Moreover, the hermetic interpretation was *perpetuated* by closing it off to criticism: in an almost Diltheyan dualism, where mind is addressed only by mind, labour was left to the 'specialised sciences' (neoclassical theory),[44] leaving philosophy free to engage with loftier intellectual matters – 'without the intermediary of things or matter'.[45] If Marx became an objectivist, it was not so much due to his 'limited philosophical self-understanding'[46] or the Second International than to this interpretation. Habermas once rightly lamented the fact that *philosophical* interpretations of Marx remain unsatisfactory.[47] This defect is hardly corrected by making philosophy lose sight of Marx altogether – and not just of him, but also of significant parts of material, 'non-normative' social reality, which it had once been interested in comprehending.[48]

3.1.2 *Transformation into rationality types*

The multi-level anthropological model could easily be transformed into a terminologically modernised 'rationality theory' once the philosophical fashion changed. In fact, it had to be thus transformed, since it was unable to explain very much, apart from the most elementary forms of sociation.[49] The transsubtantiation occurred in *Knowledge*

44. The position of Arendt 1969 is ultimately neoclassical, insofar as she unhesitatingly assumes that fully developed society is capable of 'smooth functioning': it is 'indeed [!] ruled by an "invisible hand"' – and this, she claims, is precisely '[w]hat Marx did not... understand' (p. 44). In a bizarrely confused assertion, she describes bourgeois society as a 'communistic society' (ibid.) – modern oppositions are rendered unclear by Arendt's crude antimodernism (cf. Brunkhorst 1999, p. 91).

45. Arendt 1969, p. 7. This constellation can still be found in the controversy with Luhmann, whose arguments are uncritically accepted, within their ostensive area of validity, by Habermas; they are simply supplemented by a higher-level form of action, 'communicative' action (Habermas 1971a; cf. Habermas 1984–7).

46. Habermas 1987, p. 42.

47. Habermas 1957, p. 402.

48. Marx is lost sight of even where he is thematised: Habermas 1973 uncritically accepts hypotheses on 'organized capitalism', the supplanting of exploitation by 'alienation' and the disappearance of the proletariat, without reflecting upon the genuine Marxian meaning of these categories, which hardly allows for such hypotheses (pp. 195 f.; phrases such as 'no longer' are an index of such historico-philosophical hypotheses). Economic theory is hardly addressed, while 'empirical data' feature only in the form of developmental psychology, linguistics or systems theory (notwithstanding the fact that the latter knows nothing of empirical research). Commenting on Habermas's retrospective enumeration of the fields he has discussed, Dahms notes the absence of a 'pragmatic interpretation of the natural sciences' – it simply does not feature, no more than 'understanding' [*Verstehen*] or 'self-reflection' (Dahms 1994, p. 363; Habermas 1967, p. 9).

49. Mead, Durkheim and Gehlen had attempted to explain society anthropologically, but they hardly got any further than speculations on society's beginnings. 'Stratification of the personality' was something Rothacker 1938 was already familiar with. Along with Plessner, Habermas was aware that the stadial model 'cannot be reapplied' within a single stage, since the unity of the single stage precludes further differentiation (and hence a dualism of body and soul): even the most elementary human impulses (laughter, crying) are intellectually configured (and vice versa; cf. Habermas 1958, p. 24). Has Habermas retained this insight?

and Human Interests.[50] Rothacker's anthropology had already featured the notion that cognition is guided by interests.[51] His 'cultural anthropology' differed from Gehlen's instrumentalist variant insofar as it proceeded in the manner of *Geisteswissenschaft.* This involved a distinction between various object realms.[52] Thus Habermas became the heir of neo-Kantianism, jazzing up the old distinction between world and value terminologically.

Rothacker had turned Dilthey's cognitive psychology into a culturalist anthropology;[53] Habermas now shifted the centre of gravity to the history of science. But his distinction between the interests guiding cognition was not derived from personality types or strata, as in Dilthey, nor was it based on the assumption of self-contained cultures, as in Rothacker;[54] it rested on an 'attempt to reconstruct' the various sciences.[55] Habermas meant to thereby lay the groundwork for a 'theory of society' – one whose 'critical' character (in Horkheimer's sense) can be seen from the fact that does not yet exist . Yet by declaring the 'self-reflection' of the sciences[56] to constitute a *theory of society*, Habermas not only asked too much of the theory of science; he also lost touch with social reality in three ways. First, he recognises it only through the lens of the sciences available to him (and as we have seen, they fail to take capitalism into account). Second, the results of these sciences are uncritically accepted.[57] Third, he concerns himself only with subjective aspect of the research process.[58] The motto of the Preface, 'that a radical [?] critique of knowledge is possible only as social theory'[59] thus needs to be read in reverse: the critique of society is dissolved into the theory of knowledge. (Whether the theory of

---

50. Habermas 1987, first published in 1968.

51. On the role Rothacker played for Habermas, see the comprehensive accounts in Dahms 1994, 361 ff. and Keulartz 1995, pp. 106 ff. Apel 1988, p. 98, touched on this issue when he remarked about Habermas 1987 that 'we were both familiar with the cognitive-anthropological insights from our student days in Bonn'. On this period, see also Habermas 1990.

52. 'While the natural sciences deal with natural objects, the human sciences deal with human works' (Dahms 1994, p. 268, paraphrasing Rothacker). Methodology becomes ontology.

53. Rothacker 'no longer grounds the basic attitudes that are constitutive of worldviews in man's psychic structure; instead, he considers them the pith of cultural lifestyles' (Keulartz 1995, p. 109).

54. Rothacker spoke of 'negroes' or 'the Greeks' ('a splendid humanity contending for the prize of its measured and disciplined perfection': Rothacker 1948, p. 71), as well as of foresters and bards (Rothacker 1948, p. 161).

55. Habermas 1987, p. vii.

56. Habermas 1987, pp. 113 ff., 161 ff., 214 ff.

57. Habermas once restricted the role of philosophy to that of accepting and interpreting the results of the sciences (Habermas 1958, p. 20). By now considering 'reflection' to be independent of its material, he circumvents this initial position: reflection remains pure 'self-reflection' (Habermas 1987, pp. 63, 198), and it is no coincidence that its protagonist is Freud (pp. 214 ff.).

58. 'Interests' already functioned as a theoretical subterfuge in Horkheimer (1988a; 2.6.1); there is something intentional and subjectivistically reductive about them. They are an attempt to formulate a transcendental justification for wish lists.

59. Habermas 1987, p. vii.

knowledge is not also rendered impossible by such speculative overburdening is a question that would need to be posed separately.)

The motives for this transcendental detour to the justification of emancipatory 'interests' are no doubt to be found in the positivism dispute.[60] But instead of polemicising, in a concrete way, against the positivists whom he really has in mind,[61] Habermas reconfigures entire branches of science, an operation that goes far beyond what any polemic might justify. The consequences of this reinterpretation are especially relevant to Habermas's understanding of Marx: although Habermas has not engaged more closely with the content of Marx's theory, he now accuses him not so much of reductionism[62] as of an epistemological deficiency: 'He [Marx] considered unnecessary an epistemological justification of social theory'.[63] Nor did Marx require such a justification, for his political and economic theory – which Habermas does not discuss – relies only on its own explanatory force.[64] It was critical theory that required a 'justification', having been forced into a corner, and once again, it projected its own weakness onto Marx.[65] The theory of knowledge was no more able to help it out than psychoanalysis, evolutionary biology or moral philosophy. Instead of accounting for its critico-theoretical *content* by reference to the issue under scrutiny, attempts were made to deduce that content from oddly interchangeable theoretical superstructures, constructed for that very purpose. This was done on the idealist premise that form determines content. It was not just that the meta-theories employed as guarantors of a transcendental justification were

60. Even in Habermas 1996, one still finds traces of the positivism dispute, such as the bugbear of a 'functionalism that neutralizes anything that, from the participant perspective, appears obligatory or at all meaningful' (p. 3).

61. Cf. Habermas 1985, pp. 15 ff. 'That we disavow reflection *is* positivism' (Habermas 1987, p. vii). And in this work, even Dilthey is subsumed under the category of positivism (pp. 140 ff.).

62. The accusation formulated in Habermas 1973a was 'that Marx does not actually explicate the interrelationship of interaction and labor, but instead, under the unspecific title of social praxis, reduces the one to the other, namely: communicative action to instrumental action' (pp. 168 f.; for a different formulation, see Habermas 1987, pp. 52 f.).

63. Habermas 1987, p. 45.

64. Why should Marx have replaced the transcendental logic with a 'synthesis [that] takes place in the medium of labor' (Habermas 1987, p. 31; cf. p. 358)? It was not until Sohn-Rethel that anyone thought in these terms (Sohn-Rethel 1978, pp. 83 ff.). This philosophisation tempts one to engage in speculation: 'the barter principle ... is fundamentally akin to the principle of identification' (Adorno 2007, p. 146). Marx's polemic against this sort of thinking remains topical.

65. Its problem was that it often did no more than formulate value judgements, such as on a vaguely defined 'positivism', but was seldom able to provide objective criteria by which to assess its verdicts (Dahms 1994, pp. 138 ff., 318, 392). This was simply another attempt to rectify the problem of 'critical theory', the lacuna in its content (Habermas 1973a, p. 142), in a purely formal manner: by seeking to demonstrate epistemologically that its politico-aesthetic verdict was justified (on this kind of epistemology, see also Adler 1936, Sohn-Rethel 1978, Sandkühler 1973, Halfmann 1976, Kerber 1981, Pabst 1992 and Behrens 1993).

instrumentalised and interpreted in overly wilful ways;[66] content also benefited little. And there was no way for it to remain unaffected.

3.1.3 *The myth of 'normative foundations'*

> What . . . are we to think of a science which *airily* abstracts from this large part of human labour and which fails to feel its own incompleteness, while such a wealth of human endeavour, unfolded before it, means nothing . . . to it.[67]

Let us summarise the distortions of Marx we have encountered thus far. In a first step, it was claimed the interactive dimension is absent from his theory; the second step consisted in faulting him for this. Thus the false instrumentalist interpretation of Marx was consolidated. And this in turn caused his theory to lose its virulence. If there are cases in which it makes little sense to take a 'normative view' of things, this may be due to the reality examined.[68] But when one operates from the lofty heights of the 'transcendental', one tends to lose touch with that reality.

Finally, a dependence on the *critique of knowledge* was attributed to Marx's theory. That the ex post reconstruction of the 'radical' critique of knowledge failed to yield a 'theory of society' can be seen from the fact that the theoretical lacuna later necessitated recourse to additional philosophised disciplines: developmental psychology,[69] speech act theory[70] and moral theory.[71] Thus critical theory became entirely worldless and de-economised. Instead of defending its critical interventions against objections, it passed the blame on to Marx: *his* critique had never been justified, the argument went, because he had presented it in the form of the natural sciences.[72] The accusation reduces itself

---

66. Habermas self-critically admits: 'I believe that, in hermeneutical terms, I brutally appropriate the speech of others' (Habermas 1985, p. 206).

67. *MECW* 3, p. 303.

68. Such as when atrocities are committed in full accordance with the law – not despite, but because of and in the name of normativity – a case whose existence Foucault was not the first to point out (3.1.6). Theoretical insistence on a 'higher' human sphere is constrained either to glorify such realities or to counter them with utopian normative wish lists. Neither option seemed very sensible to Marx.

69. Habermas 1976b.

70. Habermas 1984–7.

71. Habermas 1990b and 1993.

72. Habermas 1987, p. 62. When the theory of society loses contact with reality, because it is only in this way that it can remain 'self-reflection' (Habermas 1987, pp. 214 ff.) and avoid confronting its epistemological deficiencies (4.1), then all that can still be formulated is a purely formal epistemological critique of the general practice of the sciences (Marx was not interested in this – Heidegger was; cf. 2.5.5) and an abstract moralism (which Marx was not interested in either, since it is precisely what precludes an understanding of morality). A critique based on specific, substantive arguments is no longer formulated – it would be too 'positivist'. *Knowledge and Human Interests* merely aggravated critical theory's aporetic character: still greater aspirations are accompanied by still fewer concrete results.

to that of not having distinguished dualistically between the human sciences and the natural sciences, or rather: to not having been Gustav Schmoller.

Instead of bidding Marx farewell, which would have been the normal thing to do, Habermas attempted to *integrate* him into his theoretical model – as a deficient precursor. This, however, necessitated 'reconstruction' in a different 'theoretical language'.[73] At first, this reconstruction concerned only the 'dialectical relationship between the forces of production and the relations of production'.[74] Its effect, however, was to make this very relationship disappear: the self-sufficient system of labour[75] was *juxtaposed* with an equally self-sufficient institutional framework.[76] From then on, Habermas focused only on this residual category of 'communicative action',[77] discussing it independently of its complementary category 'control'.[78] This emerges clearly from his considerations on 'discourse ethics'.[79] Between the anthropological assumptions that continue to shape the theory[80] and the formal ethical principles that regulate discourse lies the discourse itself, conceived of as open-ended. Yet its result is always already anticipated by Habermas: in an 'eternal conversation', it refers only to itself, in order to guarantee its own conditions

73. Habermas 1976b . . . Why reconstruct at all, if not to alter content? But if content is altered, then why refer back to Marx? The proper response to this is to recall an observation by Wittgenstein: in reconstruction, 'everything is on the same level'. One description has simply been replaced by another. Moreover, the new description radically shifts the concepts' system of reference, and with it their horizon of meaning. This tends to render the concepts less clear; they may even be led *ad absurdum* (cf. Rorty 1989, pp. 53 f.) – a '*kaputt* reconstruction' (Bolte 1989, p. 16).

74. Habermas 1973a, p. 169.

75. In the conceptual world of antiquity, the end of *poiesis* is external to it; only *praxis* is an end in itself. Under capitalism, the worker produces for the capitalist, but the system reproduces itself. Luhmann's 'autopoiesis' reflects this transformation – Marx's 'reproduction' in disguise (Brunkhorst 1999, p. 76).

76. Hahn 1970, p. 73, faulted Habermas for abstracting from the 'social character of production'. According to Hahn, this forces Habermas to develop an anthropologised 'historical dualism', within which domination and ideology are explained 'only' (Habermas 1987, p. 42) on the basis of 'interaction', that is, idealistically (see also Rüddenklau 1982).

77. Habermas 1987, p. 53.

78. Habermas 1987, pp. 47, 61. 'Control' [*Verfügung*] originates in Habermas's idealist early writings (Roderick 1989, pp. 181 f.). Later terms for this were 'synthesis through labour', 'technically exploitable knowledge', 'instrumental action' or 'systems integration'. The reconstructed relations of production (minus production) figured under such names as 'interaction', 'dialectic of ethical life', 'lifeworld' or 'social integration'. The rigorous separation of the two had been inaugurated as a category. But the objects under description varied considerably – in the end, Habermas described hypostatised realms, as became manifest in his talk of 'subsystems of purposive-rational action' (Habermas 1971b, p. 90) and 'institutional frameworks' (Habermas 1973a, p. 168). The distinction developed into the 'historical dualism' of system and lifeworld (Habermas 1984–7).

79. Habermas 1978, 1990b, 1993.

80. Honneth 1980a, Honneth 1996, Habermas 2003, pp. 27 f.

of possibility. Content is hardly provided for.[81] Here, discourse ethics severs its link to the world entirely.[82]

The ethicisation and psychologisation that compensated for the loss of concretion did not, however, amount to a break with critical theory – which had already attempted to gloss over the cracks in its theoretical edifices by means of 'social psychology' (2.6.2). Habermas's falsifiable claims about the 'system of labour' also see him adopting the legacy of the Frankfurt School: by assuming the primacy of politics, he relativises Marx's claims about the economy – which he has in any case already classified as deficient – and suggests that they are no longer relevant to the present.[83] The 'dialectical relationship' yields to an antagonism of various abstract logics, presided over by Gehlen on the one side, and by Piaget on the other.[84]

---

81. 'Communicative action' is neatly distinguished from instrumental and strategic action. Much as in Arendt, this recalls the ancient *polis* (the model of a legal community that practises self-determination via the collective practice of its citizens: Habermas 2003, p. 89), where the affairs of life have already been put in order (repressively) by the time discourse begins. See also Habermas's affirmative references to Freyer (1964), who openly propagated such vacuous self-recognition (Habermas 1973a, p. 461; Habermas 1967, pp. 82, 109). Discourse ethics, which wants to allow everyone involved to participate, leaves nothing substantial on which a decision might be taken.

82. Habermas's adoption of Piaget's and Kohlberg's distinction between different stages of cognitive development was not a step toward empirical work but one toward greater abstraction (Habermas 1976b, pp. 167 f.).

83. According to Habermas, technology has become a 'force of production', so that 'capitalism' has now been replaced by technocracy. The argument advanced in support of this claim was that of 'state interventionism', which was not analysed but taken as the ultimate sign of the times. This implies an uncritical adoption of Pollock's 'state capitalism' (2.6.2) and the technocracy hypothesis (2.4.5) – after all, Habermas did not take these two, but rather 'science' to be 'ideology' (Habermas 1971b, p. 111). 'If society no longer [!] "autonomously" perpetuates itself through self-regulation as a sphere preceding and lying at the basis of the state [...], then society and the state are no longer [!] in the relationship that Marxian theory had defined as that of base and superstructure. Then, however, a critical theory of society can no longer [!] be constructed in the exclusive form of a critique of political economy' (p. 101; note the philosophy of history here, of the 'no longer' variety; cf. 2.4.6, on Schelsky). 'Thus technology and science become a leading productive force, rendering inoperative the conditions for Marx's labor theory of value' (p. 104; cf. Habermas 1973, pp. 226 f., and Habermas 1987, p. 48). Capitalism has always involved science and technology – not because they are 'forces of production', but because they increase productivity. The 'forces of production' are not to be understood as a technological system that receives everything else from outside (G.A. Cohen 1978, pp. 28 ff. and 128 ff., still conceptualises the 'forces of production' in isolation from the relations of production; cf. Wildt 1977; on 'forces of production', cf. 2.6.1; Habermas 1976b, p. 184; Habermas 1996, pp. 38, 147, 151).

84. In an interim report on the progress of his theoretical project, Habermas formulates what seems to be a response to Hahn 1970 by drawing a distinction between 'labour' and 'social production' (Habermas 1976b, pp. 145 ff.). But in doing so, he merely bolsters his initial assumptions, made for reasons of 'theoretical strategy', by means of a wealth of newly introduced material. This emerges from gruff formulations such as: 'We must, however, separate the level of communicative action from that of... strategic action' (Habermas 1976b, p. 160). Why must we do this? Because Marxism, having been reduced to a 'history of technology' (p. 185, with reference to Gehlen), 'requires a structural analysis of the development of world pictures' (p. 186). In other words: because consciousness ('cognitive structures') determines social being. (Habermas 1971a, p. 491, still described 'world pictures' as 'ideology'.) The apparently empirical excursions into the

Thirteen years after *Knowledge and Human Interests*, we find another integrating and reductive discussion of Marx. This time, he is described as a 'theorist of rationality'. Marx is juxtaposed with Weber, Lukács, Horkheimer und Parsons. He now appears as someone who attempted to develop an abstract 'theory of action'.[85] This is once more preceded by the diagnosis that the real problem is 'no longer' that of 'immiseration' (although Habermas thinks it once was),[86] but that of the risk posed to freedom and meaning by 'rationalisation'.[87] Habermas thereby picks up not so much on Marx's theory of capitalism as on Weber's Nietzschean cultural critique of bureaucratisation.[88] The only aspect of Marx Habermas is interested in is the critique of commodity fetishism;[89] everything else is rejected. What this rests on is Habermas's dualism, which has now gone from being a 'supplement' to being a 'substitute':

> It is only [!] this communicative rationality, reflected in the self-understanding of modernity, that gives an inner logic – and not merely the impotent rage of nature in revolt – to resistance against the colonization of the lifeworld by the inner dynamics of autonomous systems.[90]

Habermas's critique of Marx accords with this: because Marx does not distinguish between 'system and lifeworld'[91] and totalises purposive rationality, he is unable to account for the problems associated with the new stage of 'late capitalism', Habermas argues. Marx

---

theory of evolution are meant to justify the abstractly moral 'organisational principles' (Habermas 1976b, p. 168) and 'learning mechanisms' (p. 173). They, too, are radically separated from economic theories, which are marginalised; moreover, 'organisational principles' and 'learning mechanisms' are described as having become the decisive factors 'today': 'A society's identity is determined normatively [!] and dependent on the society's cultural values' (p. 189). 'We should [?]...search' for these values 'nowhere but in the basic structures of linguistic communication' (ibid.). Notwithstanding the fact that Marx is still referred to positively (Habermas 1987, p. 53), this amounts to an ethicisation and psychologisation of social theory. It is reminiscent of the older critique of Marx formulated by Rudolf Stammler 1896, who meant to make the economy dependent on law, and law on the ethical life of the people (Henning 1999, p. 92).

85. Habermas 1984–7, Vol. II, pp. 332 ff.

86. Habermas 1977, p. 304.

87. The theory of immiseration, which states that wages are always only slightly above the subsistence minimum, was already abandoned by Marx in 1846. According to Marx's more nuanced concept of exploitation, real wage increases remain inferior to increases in profit (and productivity). Thus 'exploitation' is in no way linked to 'immiseration'; nor does it require recourse to an 'alienation' understood in social-psychological terms.

88. From this, one may conclude that, firstly, Habermas 1984–7 shares the old Frankfurt School faith in a 'new stage' of capitalism; he assumes that politics has become primary with regard to the economy and that Marx's economic theory is now of historic interest only. Secondly, this constellation renders Habermas's position strangely proximate to aestheticised conservative cultural criticism (Gehlen, Arendt, Forsthoff, and so on) which always lamented that political regulation leads to a loss of greatness and martial virtue, to 'estrangement'.

89. Habermas 1984–7, Vol. I, pp. 357 ff.

90. Habermas 1984–7, Vol. II, p. 333.

91. Habermas 1984–7, Vol. II, pp. 338 f.; the new terms for nature and mind, work and interaction, instrumental reason and communicative action.

is accused of having overlooked 'differentiation', and consequently of having overlooked the role of the state, which has solved the problems of former times and created new ones, according to Habermas.[92] Economic problems are assumed to 'no longer' be primary, and Marxism is accused of failing to account for the 'new type of reification effect' that 'arises in class-unspecific ways';[93] this replicates the industrial society hypothesis of former times (2.4.5). Habermas's critique was convincing as a critique of actually-existing socialism[94] – but it was not an analysis of Western countries, whose reality was not to be grasped by means of a few action-theoretical differentiations and their integration into an overarching systems theory.[95] Unfortunately for Habermas, the reality of Western countries is situated right in the gap *between* reductive functionalism and the totalised ethics of principles, a gap that cannot be closed by merely linking one to the other.

Habermas's hypothesis on the 'colonization of the lifeworld'[96] involves the assumption that the problematic dimension is 'no longer' the economy, but rather the socio-psychological phenomenon of the individual's possibilities for development being restricted excessively by the politico-economic 'complex'. By formulating this interpretation, Habermas unwittingly set the course for a coalition of interests with neoliberalism, which had always criticised real socialism for its lack of freedom and called for greater (economic) freedom.[97] When the socialist regimes collapsed, the oppressive 'system' disappeared, and the newly won freedom led to an onslaught of deregulation and privatisation not just in Eastern Europe, but in the West as well. Did this not seem like the *project of modernity*[98] was being accomplished?

The new constellation paralysed not just what was left of the Marxist left, but also those parts of the left that had been influenced by Habermas – after all, how was one to object to what had one had demanded for so long? A long-underestimated opponent was coming back in force: capitalism. Under the code name of 'globalisation', Habermas's erstwhile socio-psychological demands radiate out into reality: at last one is able to lead a free and self-fulfilled life – as a dynamic young entrepreneur.[99] The traditional values of the 'lifeworld' (the family, the village community) are coming back into their

92. Habermas 1984–7, Vol. II, pp. 343 ff. Habermas 1976b, p. 182, speculates that value, formerly a 'scarce resource', no longer poses a problem 'today': after all, he argues, social movements have achieved 'their goal ... in welfare-state mass democracies'. Power and security, he continues, are what has become scarce 'today', and the 'resources' motivation and meaning will likely become scarce in the future.

93. Habermas 1984–7, Vol. II, p. 349.

94. Cf. Michels 1978, Marcuse 1958 and A. Heller 1979.

95. Habermas 1984–7, Vol. II, pp. 153 ff.

96. Habermas 1984–7, Vol. II, p. 355.

97. See Willms 1973. Rolf Johannes quotes an approving 1982 verdict from the *Frankfurter Allgemeine Zeitung* (in Bolte 1989, p. 63).

98. Habermas 1990a, pp. 32 ff.

99. Neoliberal authors like to give their pamphlets a touch of Marxist chic (cf. Baer 1999, Hamel 2001, Levinson 2002; for a critique, see Boltanski 1999). The centrepiece of critical theory was the bourgeois individual (Willms 1969, Riedel 1994).

own – they have to, because the welfare state's guarantees are increasingly being abolished. Confronting this new-old capitalism would have meant rethinking the premises of several decades of theory.

Yet what was practised within the self-professed progressive philosophy of the post-1989 period was neither unreserved observation of real events nor a correction of one's own initial assumptions; instead, and paradoxically, one chose to place even *more* emphasis on 'normative foundations' than before 1989.[100] In light of this, one needs to do what always needs to be done when something seems odd about philosophy, namely ask a simple question: what exactly are the 'normative presuppositions' supposed to ground, theory or reality? Both 'groundings' are questionable operations: to try to ground reality is a pointless endeavour – unless one decides to engage in transcendental philosophy, something social theory will hardly want to be seen as doing.[101] Which leaves the claim to grounding a theory. But it is not so much theories *about* something that need to be grounded (they are verified) as moral demands and claims: the expectant stance of an entire family of theories, which has here congealed into an anthropological 'interest'. And yet it was only within the development of German theory that social theory was once more rendered 'normative' (2.1.2).[102]

Habermas set the course for later developments by defining social theory first in terms of the critique of knowledge, and then as a moral theory. It was only this conglomerate of transcendental claims and political wishes that required a distinct philosophical 'grounding'. Even in the writings of the later Habermas school, it seems that theory and reality are hardly distinguished,[103] but rather fused idealistically. But instead of these

100. See Benhabib 1992, Baynes 1992, Holz 1993, Honneth 1996, and 2000, Koorsgard 1996, Brunkhorst 1999a, Gosepath 1999 or Cannon 2001; for earlier formulations, see Schneider 1976, Wellmer 1979 or Lohmann 1980, See also below, 3.1.6.

101. Sociability's conditions of possibility (as addressed by Simmel or Alfred Schütz) reveal nothing about a given society at a given time. It seems, however, that Honneth 1980, p. 197 has just such a 'transcendental theory of society' (Schelsky 1959, p. 95) in mind: 'Marx can ... merely [!] provide an account of how the proletariat learns to hone and strategically ... deploy its ... emancipatory consciousness. Yet what renders the constitution of this emancipatory consciousness' possible in the first place appears to Honneth to be the really important question. Thus Honneth's intention can only be that of explaining reality (for a critique of this, see Kersting 1997, pp. 123 ff.) – hence his affinity for social philosophy (Habermas 1990 and elsewhere; cf. 3.2.4).

102. Habermas 1987a succinctly expresses the fact 'that the emancipatory perspective proceeds precisely not from the production paradigm, but from the paradigm of action oriented toward mutual understanding. It is the form of interaction processes that must be altered' (p. 82). It is a matter of justifying a political democracy whose citizens are formally free (with regard to Eastern Europe, this was a meaningful demand at the time); it is 'no longer' a matter of rising up against substantive exploitation and its complex consequences, or of exposing the conditionality and limits of concrete democracies. Habermas has changed theory's theme and ethicised the way the theme is addressed (it is a matter of 'normative contents' and of the 'normative use' of distinctions: pp. 81 f.).

103. Habermas's deep-seated dualism refuses to be situated: it is located on the anthropological level (in human interest), in various categories (participatory or observatory, evaluative or analytic), in individual modes of action and/or thought (instrumental or communicative), in social

questionable theoretical choices being critically scrutinised, they were adopted and used as the *standard* by which to judge Marx and reality – not exactly to the benefit of one's understanding of either. Thus one began to project problems onto Marx only because one had previously blanked out one's own theoretical history. There was no need for this. Marx had never conceived his theory as a 'normative' one, so that the search for its higher-level normative groundings is a simple matter: they do not exist – no more than epistemological, action-theoretical or semiological 'groundings'. Before we proceed in our examination of Habermas's work and its development, we need to consider this point in more detail.

3.1.4 Key elements of Marxian theory VIII: Marx and ethics

> Marxism is not ethics, but it teaches us to recognise in what sense ethical forces become forces that shape society.[104]

Virtually no one, and certainly no one on the left, would base their theory on the assumption that 'charismatic leaders' or a 'cult of personality' have any special role to play. And yet Jürgen Habermas *has* played such a role for German social philosophy. In a way comparable to the effects of the nineteenth-century Bismarck cult as criticised by Max Weber, this was detrimental to the independent-mindedness of more than one professional philosopher (something for which Habermas is certainly not to blame). This is especially the case when it comes to assessments of Marx. For it was Habermas who, in developing critical theory, believed himself unable to obtain sufficient orientation from Marx's theories. This farewell to Marx presupposed a number of developments: a historical *relativisation* of Marxian theory, its instrumental *reduction*, a moral-theoretical *transformation* of emancipation and, finally, a philosophising re-focusing on the *grounding* of the latter.

The history of theory is not a philosophically satisfying endeavour. But when social philosophy fails to relate to its own history, critique has to do this for it. The task is an urgent one, as almost all German-language contributions to the topic 'ethics and Marx'[105]

---

spheres of action (the dialectic of ethical life vs. the dialectic of labour, systems integration or social integration) and in discrete realms of being (system and lifeworld). It is located everywhere at once; it is 'transcategorial'. The various positions contradict one another; the dualism cannot be found in all of them at once (for example, it is quite possible for me to act instrumentally within the lifeworld, and such like). This can be the case only if theory and reality constitute a unity. Honneth 1980 also passes over the real background of Marx's work: he believes Marx set his hopes on the proletariat because he was led to do so by a 'labour-philosophical' 'compulsion' (pp. 191, 197). Like Lange 1980, he is preoccupied with 'concepts' and believes that by discussing them, he can simultaneously say something about reality (see above, 2.3.5).

104. Adler 1928, p. 41.

105. Fetscher 1972, Honneth 1977, 1980, Angehrn 1986, Lohmann 1991, Wildt 1997 and 2001. The forays undertaken by Arnason and Honneth (in: Jaeggi 1980) get stuck halfway: they adopt Habermas's 'categorial framework' and merely enrich it. For English-language works, (see Brenkert 1983,

start from assumptions that go back to Habermas, notwithstanding the fact that these assumptions hardly do justice to Marx. These contributions do not go very far in terms of helping one develop an adequate understanding of Marx; rather, they are symptomatic of the fatal reading of Marx whose elaboration has, for endogenous reasons, been discontinued since 1989. Following Habermas, one strayed so far from the object of inquiry 'capitalism' that one no longer knew how to say anything about it when it returned triumphantly. Despite the assumption that Marx's theory could 'no longer' be worked with, one insisted on continuing to refer back to it.[106] Following M. Hess and Bernstein, Sorel and Spengler – and Habermas – Marx's 'critique of society' was read as a 'normative' one. Now, Marx had explicitly rejected any moralising critique.[107] Consequently, one was faced with the following dilemma:

> On the one hand, Marx nowhere says that capitalism ... is unjust ... On the other hand, Marx speaks of capitalism as a system of coercion, bondage, servitude and despotism and repeatedly characterises ... exploitation as fraud, theft, robbery ... These terms obviously refer to something unjust.[108]

This dilemma resolves itself rather straightforwardly in Marx: of course the facts do not accord with our natural sense of justice. But apart from the taste for ribald language that Marx shares with Luther, he held that it is little use calling them unjust for as long as the given 'idea of justice' does not transcend the given circumstances, but rather *arises* from them in the first place. Authors who mean to ground the facts in a different 'logic' assume that the 'idea of justice' does transcend the given circumstances, but historians will usually concede that it arises from them. To invoke the 'idea of justice' against economic realities simply amounts to duplicating those realities ideally.[109] One can certainly *call* grievances unjust, but doing so is not the same as formulating a critique. It does not

---

Lukes 1985, Miller 1989, Kain 1991, West 1991 or Churchich 1994; cf. Kamenka 1962), Rawls is more important.

106. Thus Wildt 1977, p. 207, concurred with Korsch, Habermas and Castoriadis in assuming that a 'historical continuation of Marxism' would most likely be successful only if one abandoned Marxism in favour of a new 'system of thought'.

107. *MECW* 24, p. 535; *MECW* 35, pp. 185 f.; *MECW* 37, p. 493, and so on.

108. Wildt 1986, p. 150.

109. 'But don't wrangle with us so long as you apply, to our intended abolition of bourgeois property, the standard of your bourgeois notions of freedom, culture, law, &c. Your very ideas are but the outgrowth of the conditions of your bourgeois production and bourgeois property, just as your jurisprudence is but the will of your class made into a law for all, a will whose essential character and direction are determined by the economical conditions of existence of your class' (*MECW* 6, p. 501). 'Marx's critique of economic and social reality is not intended as a moral critique that judges reality by the standard of eternal human values or some normative idea: it merely means to express, within the realm of scientific thought, a critique that is present, qua virtuality, in the examined reality itself' (Goldmann 1966, p. 315; Fleischer 1973, p. 118; Fleischer 1980; Lukes 1983). 'Normative critique' makes it easy for those in power to act as if demands had already been fulfilled. For example, Helmut Kohl stole the thunder of the 1997 student strike by siding with its abstract demands. The normative duplication proved harmless.

get one any further within social theory, nor within politics – for every side can express such judgements. Rather, the given circumstances can count bourgeois morality on their side.

It was the discomfiture provoked by this incongruity that motivated Marx to go down the road to *Capital*. There, Marx shows (as Hegel did before him) that the abstract law of contract reigning on the level of exchange treats men as free and equal, which they in fact are *qua* men. In this sense, bourgeois law – including its crowning achievement, the rights of man – is ineluctable.[110] But men are, first and foremost, 'real, individual' men,[111] and under capitalism, this means they are either sellers of labour power *or* owners of means of production (and/or recipients of redistributed assets). And there are radical differences in the 'use value' of what they obtain by means of the 'just' exchange of equivalents: the worker gets his labour-power replaced, whereas the capitalist gets the value created by labour, and pockets the surplus product (after deducting his expenses for the fixed and variable capital consumed, including wages).[112] This surplus product is used to finance not just additional investments (thus extending the capitalist's power of control), but also a life that tends to be far more luxurious than any the waged worker can ever hope to enjoy, wage increases notwithstanding.[113] Ultimately, this is what explains the gigantic – but 'rightful' – disparities that exist both nationally and globally. This state of affairs is sufficiently clear even when it is *not* additionally described by such epithets as 'evil', 'unethical' or 'unjust'.

Marx does not trace evaluative ('normative') concepts back to something empirical – in other words, he is not a 'reductionist'. He simply does not require them, since he is speaking about something else. In fact, according to Marx, it makes no sense to try to rectify matters by means of the *concepts* – or a 'theory' – of law or justice, since bourgeois law corresponds precisely to the inequalities he describes.[114] Insistence on a moral

---

110. This makes it difficult to start from Marx in order to then draw conclusions about the show trials or other, more devastating events – as done (playfully) by Wildt 1977, p. 392, and (in the form of a post hoc polemic) by Lohmann 1999 (cf. Brenkert 1999, Fleischer 1997).

111. *MECW* 3, p. 168.

112. 'The law of exchange requires equality only between the exchange values of the commodities given in exchange for one another. From the very outset it presupposes even a difference between their use values and it has nothing whatever to do with their consumption, which only begins after the deal is closed and executed' (*MECW* 35, p. 582).

113. In Western countries, wages have increased in absolute terms (monetary wages), but they have not done so in relation to total output (real wages). They would need to be compared to productivity increases and/or to the rise in 'returns on capital employed' in order to verify that exploitation is increasing or decreasing. Outward appearances are not much help.

114. Being oriented toward conceptual determinations, morality is rather powerless in the face of such issues – they lie beyond its 'conceptual' level (in bourgeois morality, exploitation is not characterised as 'good'; it is not mentioned at all – on an exception from this rule, see 3.3.3). Lohmann 1999 fails to grasp the substance of Marx's critique of law: as in 1986 and 1991, he seeks a true 'concept' of law that is not 'blind' toward injustices. But blindness toward particularities is an essential aspect of law; without such blindness, it would not be law. Moreover, law has the explicit

or legal understanding of these conflicts is too quick to divert attention from the object under examination, which simply does not feature within ethical theories.[115] To Marx, genuine improvement could be achieved only by abolishing the entire state of affairs, something he took to be both possible and desirable. This standpoint is an uncomfortable one, but it can hardly be described as 'paradoxical'.[116]

Marx's theory can be endorsed or rejected. But it cannot be declared inconsistent on the basis of one's *decision* in favour of ethics as the 'last resort',[117] especially when the arguments for this verdict are purely 'conceptual' – to proceed thus is to fall back behind Marx's critique of Hegel. The demonstration that normative concepts are powerless against a reality that is structured in accordance with them cannot be countered by simply invoking the concepts *one more time*. Those making such a move may be able to rely on the support of the scientific community – but this does not make their arguments any more valid.[118] Even on the counterfactual assumption that the subjects *have* negotiated their 'normative standards' in a communicative context free of domination, they will be powerless against reality's ills to the extent that their standards need to be understood as surface phenomena associated with the *same* process. They reiterate the same

---

purpose of maintaining the public order. When this order is itself the cause of grievances, the law, which sanctions the public order, cannot simultaneously be invoked against it. It is true there might be another law – but only once there exist other social relations, which it expresses. Prior to this, the formulation of such a 'law' (such as on free healthcare) would amount to a utopianism with no prospect of achieving legal validity. '*Ideas* can never lead beyond an old world order but only beyond the ideas of the old world order. Ideas *cannot carry out anything* at all' (*MECW* 4, p. 119). Lohmann, by contrast, holds that the response to globalisation must be a 'normative' one (1999, p. 4). This is reminiscent of a joke popular among environmentalists: a sign in the forest reads 'Forest Dieback Prohibited – The Government'.

115. Practical advocacy of legal settlement is another matter: Marx was rigorously in favour of it, e.g. when it came to trade union and occupational safety issues. Christian Schefold 1970 and Böhm 1998 draw attention to a period in the life of the young Marx, ca. 1842, when he specifically called for improvements in the legal situation of outsiders (such as *MECW* 1, p. 230). But even then, Marx perceived the limits of law: 'The form is of no value if it is not the form of the content' (*MECW* 1, pp. 260 f.; cf. *MECW* 6, p. 500, and *MECW* 35, p. 94).

116. Wildt 1997.

117. Apel's 'ultimate grounding' of ethics can be understood as a counter-programme to Engels's assertion that, under capitalism, cultural phenomena are 'ultimately' economically determined (*MECW* 49, p. 34; *MECW* 50, p. 264). The way Habermas 1996 operates betrays a similar frame of reference. There, the opposing positions appear in a very clear light: it is by means of communicative action that society is integrated 'in the final analysis' (p. 26; this is not a qualification but a very strong statement); similarly, communicative action is the 'source' of law (p. 33; law issues from communicative action via the detour of 'solidarity').

118. See Habermas's consensus theory of truth (Habermas 1973b). 'If you have an appletree in your garden and attach a sign to it that reads: "This is a fig tree!" – has it then become a fig tree? No, and if you … assemble all residents of the country and let them declare loudly and ceremoniously: "This is a fig tree!" – the tree remains what it was, and the truth will come out next year, when it bears apples, not figs' (Lassalle, '*Über Verfassungswesen*' ['On the Constitutional System'], 1862; Habermas 1987, p. 145).

'content' one more time, taking it 'to a higher level'[119] in a normatively obscured way.[120] To proceed in this way is not to strike at the root of the real problems – of course every party takes itself to be the 'good' one. Only a paradigm that draws a hermetic distinction between different worlds (in this case, between forces of production and relations of production)[121] can consider normativity something that is *independent* and autonomous by nature. Once again, Habermas provides no justification for this dualism – he merely attempts to demonstrate the validity of normativism on the basis of normativism.[122] But this gets him nowhere in terms of improving on Marx.

Marx required no moral value judgements ('normative contents') for his theory, and so he did not need to elaborate a foundation for such value judgements (2.4.6). His theory deals with a different *theme*. Does this explain why Marx avoids moral vocabulary so consistently?[123] His doing so can perhaps be explained in terms of his knowledge of the inertia proper to politico-philosophical discourses: since socialism had a tendency to conceive of itself as 'ethical'[124] and since hegemonic 'bourgeois' thought would attempt to bring socialism back into the 'national' camp by means of 'ethics', it seemed prudent to avoid this vocabulary altogether.[125] Had Marx been a tenured professor of philosophy,

---

119. *MECW* 28, p. 176.

120. 'The moral ideals in terms of which we judge capitalism arise from capitalism as an idealised version of what actually is there. Then, when we judge what is actually there . . . against those ideas, capitalism will approximate them and thus appear as good and justified' (Reiman 1991, p. 159). Wildt 2002 sees a 'smokescreen' here, too (p. 429).

121. On the 'two realms' (Pohl 1999, pp. 102 ff.), see Habermas 1987, p. 55; Habermas 1971b, p. 46; Habermas 1971a, pp. 500 f.; Habermas 1976b, pp. 157 ff.

122. Formal 'communicative ethics' represents a solution to social conflicts only if one accepts the German idealist assumption that the effects of form extend all the way down to content ('all the way down': Brandom 1994, p. 635).

123. Marx certainly permitted himself value judgements: 'Owing to the fact that in the credit system the *moral recognition of a man* . . . take[s] the form of *credit*, . . . the *immoral* vileness of this morality . . . become[s] evident' (*MECW* 3, p. 216; *MECW* 3, pp. 158 f.). He could have done this more excessively. It is only when a theory that formulates value judgements goes on to declare its own object of inquiry to be something 'moral' that a dilemma arises.

124. *MECW* 6, pp. 220 ff.).

125. 'The phrase "proceeds of labor" [or, for that matter, 'equal distribution'; C.H.], objectionable even today on account of its ambiguity, thus loses all meaning' (*MECW* 24, p. 85; cf. Menger 1886). 'Edifying words by which to by-pass certain questions apologetically!' (*MECW* 4, p. 111; cf. 2.1.4). Von Stein also avoided moralising his subject matter: 'By virtue of his effort to interpret the social movement as the logical result of certain historical circumstances, Stein places himself in opposition to the spirit of the times, which was oriented toward the moralistic denunciation of radical theory and practice' (Quesel 1989, p. 143). In Marx's view, those who 'spell out' social conflicts in moral terms are caught within a restrictive perspective that refuses to see beyond even the surface appearances of the present. A moral discourse can of course attempt to liberate itself from such prior determinations (cf. Steinvorth 1999, pp. 245 ff.; Wildt 2002a). But the limits of this approach have to be clear: the resulting theory will not be a social theory but an ethical appraisal, namely one opposed to hegemonic value judgements. The reasons are not theoretical – which is why 'rational discussion' is not likely to lead, in such a case, to anything more than the founding of a small, sectarian group – but hard-and-fast, material, and they re-assert themselves globally every day.

he would perhaps have proceeded differently and searched for a 'comprehensive concept of justice'.[126] But to point out that he did not do so is not to formulate a valid criticism: Marx was not a moral philosopher but a theorist of bourgeois society; moreover, he was interested in exerting a political influence.

Perhaps it was simply political 'prudence' that made Marx eschew moral valuations of his subject matter. For not only were such valuations not suitable for proving anything within his theory; they also involved the risk of the theory's results immediately being distorted within the reader's mind.[127] Attempts to introduce such valuations subsequently[128] often involved juxtapositions of world and value as unmediated as those of neo-Kantianism, thereby falling back behind the degree of reflection achieved by Hegel and Marx. Such attempts do little to improve our understanding of Marx. The transcendental ethical transformation Marx was subjected to by Habermas was so hegemonic the only possible alternative seemed to be that of renouncing 'bourgeois' morality in favour of Marxism.[129] But as mentioned above, this alternative presupposed four things: a historical *relativisation*, a mechanistic *reduction* and an aesthetic *supplementation* of

---

126. Lohmann 1986, pp. 178 f. The young Marx already understood that abuses of 'true' morality – the kinds of abuses Lohmann is interested in – were hegemonic within moral philosophy and would emerge as the victors in the fight over words, simply because they were the morality of the time: 'The ideas of the ruling class are in every epoch the ruling ideas, i.e. the class which is the ruling *material* force of society, is at the same time its ruling *intellectual* force' (*MECW* 5, p. 59). 'Hence this *true community* does not come into being through reflection, it appears owing to the *need* and *egoism* of individuals' (*MECW* 3, p. 217). This can be paraphrased as follows: whereof one cannot speak, thereof one must be silent. Modern moral philosophy is a theoretical exercise that becomes increasingly aporetic to the extent that it withdraws from its proper place. But as soon as one considers its proper places, one understands clearly what is right and what is wrong (it 'appears'). At least as far as moral issues are concerned, the imperative formulated by Wittgenstein (and Levinas) is appropriate: 'don't think, but look!' (*Philosophical Investigations*, aphorism 66). Incidentally, Marx's brother-in-law Ferdinand of Westphalia was a Prussian minister of the interior.

127. Writing on German tragic drama, Benjamin also described the way the terminology associated with a position seen as being in and of itself correct had to be abandoned – because the position was adopted by a group with which one could under no circumstances continue to be associated (2.6.7; see also Böhm 1998, p. 85; *MECW* 4, pp. 162 ff.; *MECW* 5, pp. 240 f.; *MECW* 11, pp. 103 ff.; *MECW* 25, pp. 85 ff.).

128. Lohmann 1980 believes he can discern within the 'narrative' passages of *Capital* a 'hermeneutic' view of the 'lifeworld' from the 'observer's perspective', a view that needs merely to be translated into a modern 'theoretical language' (cf. Lohmann 1991, pp. 78 f.) – as was then done by Habermas, who referred to Lohmann in the process (Habermas 1984–7, Vol. II, p. 338). This aestheticisation misunderstands Marx's treatment of 'belles lettres': he tears to shreds a socialist novel (*MECW* 4, pp. 162 ff.; cf. Böhm 1998, p. 64).

129. For theoretical perspectives, see Wood 1981, Haug and Wood in Angehrn 1986, Steigerwald 1977, Holz 1987, Klenner 1987 (political immorality *à la* Stasi and Red Army Faction is not what is meant here). Wildt speaks of 'riddles' (1997, p. 211), as he bypasses the 150-year reception history that he is himself a part of and jumps without further ado from contemporary moral philosophers to Marxian texts. By proceeding thus, he himself creates the riddles that baffle him. His three interpretations (1997, p. 214) never venture beyond the domain of philosophy. Wildt is confronted with the old riddle of how to get from philosophy to reality (*MECW* 4, pp. 57 f.; *MECW* 5, pp. 55 f., 99 f. and elsewhere): 'The problem of descending from the world of thoughts to the actual world is turned into the problem of descending from language to life' (*MECW* 5, p. 446).

Marxian theory, as well as a *philosophisation* of the supplementary entities. As soon as the critique ventured beyond theory, it ceased to be a critique of capitalism and became a critique of the state, of bureaucratisation, of the system – a political critique.

To Marx, this was the preliminary stage of every social and economic critique.[130] While his early hope for an 'all-round development of individuals'[131] involved 'humanism' (see 2.4.5), this humanism performs no foundational function within his theory. We encounter it in those passages of his early writings that were written for self-clarification – that is, it is *antecedent* to his theory.[132] When the meaning of Marx's writings is no longer grasped or socialism assumes perverted forms, this antecedent humanism needs to be recalled. It was no accident the re-actualisation of Marxian 'humanism' came from Eastern Europe, where it was a matter of criticising not capitalism but an autocratic ossification, and from France, where there existed a dominant communist party whose structures had however become overly rigid.[133] Moreover, humanism can also serve to motivate people who do not think of themselves as Marxists and who are not workers to ally themselves with Marxists and workers (this was what 'ethical socialism' attempted; social democracy failed, however, to make good on this opportunity: 2.1.3). All these things are possible, as long one does not believe that one is thereby saying anything about Marx's *theory*. Other valuations do not affect it, since *they* are also antecedent to it; one does not have to be a revolutionary to understand it.[134]

'Intellectual honesty' would have required theorists with other evaluative standards than those of the humanism of 'all-round development' to say something like the following: 'I reject the radical consequences of this theory and therefore the theory itself. This is a decision. I can subsequently justify my decision in favour of what exists, by demonstrating that what exists is relatively good. In order to do this, I invoke the principle that to discuss concepts is to say something about the world.' Some nineteenth-century neo-Kantians had the will to explain themselves in this way. But no twentieth-century German philosopher did.

---

130. *MECW* 1, pp. 234 ff.

131. *MECW* 5, p. 439.

132. Cf. 2.6.6; 2.5.7. If Marx had provided humanist-normative 'foundations', *Capital* would have consisted of exactly one page, containing a summary of what the workers demand – a 'just' wage, 'regulated' working hours and a 'good' life – and the 'justification' that all this is 'moral' (cf. Adorno 2007, pp. 148 f.). In this case, there would be a foundational deficit in Marx, since he would still have to provide principles ('the ethical law calls for equality' or something of the sort). Yet these or similar principles were very much in effect, without benefiting those in distress.

133. Such as Merleau-Ponty 1957, Kołakowksi 1960 and 1979, Vol. III, pp. 496 ff.; Schaff 1965 and 1992, Massiczek 1968, Garaudy 1969, Horský 1972, Zivotic 1972, Sik 1979 and Vranitzky 1983, pp. 731 ff.; more recently Schlette 1991, Petersen 1997, Sayers 1998.

134. The tendency to discuss Marx under the heading of 'ethics' betrays the legacy of Heidegger, to whom everything antecedent disposed of a force that was literally fatal (2.5.5). If ethics decides everything, theory itself becomes unimportant: it is 'refuted' ethically. This is only possible, however, within Fichtean-hermetic thought (4.2.2).

It would have made sense to 'discourse' on the *substantive* question of how far a coalition of interests would get one, or of whether the conceptual principle can even be defended against Marx's theory.[135] Neither issue was addressed in the debates on 'Marx and ethics': one proceeded with the philosophy of concepts and said nothing about concrete issues. To decide against Marxism *before* considering the arguments in its favour is something other than decisionism only when there are good reasons to be invoked. But when one's decision *on* a theory is projected onto that theory itself, theory and decision are no longer distinguished sufficiently – all that remains is the decision, which is 'justified' subsequently, after the theory has been distorted by a different paradigm. It is only this that constitutes decisionism (2.4.1). Such decisionism is more evident in Habermas than in the ethical socialism of the neo-Kantians: Habermas's decision in favour of something particular that is immediately presented as universal is guided by 'interest', and thereby threatens to escape 'rational discussion'.[136] The only way that Habermas responds to Marxian arguments is by opting for a different 'categorial framework', within which those arguments no longer feature. This is not rational discussion but – monological – avoidance of it. Marx is truer to Kant than Habermas, for Marx separates theoretical claims from claims about moral positions (4.2.1).

This raises the question of the criteria by which the categorial framework is chosen. Who has chosen it and why, and how is the adequacy of the framework to be assessed? One possible criterion might be the degree to which it allows for a theoretical grasp of the reality experienced in everyday life. Of course, this reality can only be grasped so long as it is not artificially obscured by a fashionable theoretical framework. Rather, one can justifiably assume, and one should indeed assume, that in these parts, every reasonable person knows how things are going in the world. The 'background knowledge' associated

---

135. Hösle takes this to the conclusion of openly advocating a renewal of 'objective idealism'; in his view, nothing else allows for an a priori social philosophy (Hösle 1990 and 1996). Social philosophy always presupposes objective idealism, according to Hösle. The diagnosis is correct, although this way of thinking things through to their conclusion might also prompt a revision of the entire approach.

136. Claims to universality were rejected in Habermas 1970, but Habermas 1978a makes just such a claim for his own theory. 'Interest' is consistently presupposed as something that is universal and prior to everything else. The legacy of Heidegger's anti-scientism (2.5.5) is as evident in the young Habermas as it is in the young Marcuse. Both hold that 'certain ways of posing questions can never be refuted by means of scientific data … Scientific data dispose of no decisive probative force with regard to philosophical models, Habermas writes as late as 1960, in his essay on Ernst Bloch' (Keulartz 1995, p. 133). 'With the introduction of cognitive interests, there arises the risk of decisionism' (p. 131). 'Reason takes up a partisan position in the controversy between critique and dogmatism … [I]t does not define the moment of decision as external to its sphere' (Habermas 1973a, p. 254; cf. Habermas 1976a, pp. 194 ff.; Habermas 1996, p. 323). But then what – or who – is this reason? McBride 2000 even discerns in Habermas 1999 a fatal affinity with Schmitt: Habermas 'decides' in favour of the strongest and surrounds him with an aura of 'morality' and 'democracy'. In this way, McBride argues, a tragic plight becomes a cool triumph of reason – and this is the end of critique. McBride explains this by reference to Habermas's elision of the 'economic base' (now see Habermas 2003a and Habermas and Derrida 2003; cf. 1.4.1).

with the 'lifeworld' does not so much concern moral-psychological stadial frameworks and transcendental-philosophical chains of reference than real, everyday developments – such as that the rich are getting richer and the poor poorer, that natural resources are dwindling, and so on (see 1.2, 4.1).

By contrast, the Habermas school seems to operate with criteria such as the novelty of the theory and the question of who endorses it within the scientific community. If the theory is discussed in strategically important places, it will be received.[137] The question of whether social theory has a specific object of inquiry and of whether it is doing justice to that object are no longer posed. In fact, by focusing on formal procedures, critical theory no longer claims to have a specific object of inquiry at all.[138] But has the object really disappeared 'today', as suggested by the fallacious procedure of inferring features of reality from features of theory (2.1.4)? Or has it been lost sight of because of choices taken within theory?[139]

3.1.5 *Procedural structures*

> To save his system, he consents to sacrifice its basis.[140]

Habermas's central field of inquiry is 'social action'. The main elements perceived from the perspective of a theory of action are the normative notions of active *individuals* (see 2.4.6 on Weber). Social or communicative action as specific subset of individual actions relates to the actions of other individuals, and it is thereby guided by certain moral ideas,

---

137. Texts penned by members of the Habermas school typically do not begin by addressing a factual issue; instead, they make reference to theoretical 'debates' that they wish to participate in, usually by proposing some mediation. These are debates from Berkeley or Harvard, not from Mexico or India. This urge to be topical results in the short-lived nature of the theories ('philosophy of the present' in both senses of the word).

138. Habermas 1958, p. 14; Habermas 1991a, p. 204; Habermas 1996, p. 287. The loss of the object of inquiry is compensated for by the introduction of a *new* object, namely procedure. Has its role been determined correctly when its ideal is simply posited as real? 'Habermas's proceduralism is a poor way of evading the task of providing a substantial definition of equal freedom. For the rational discourses by which norms are legitimated . . . do not exist' (Steinvorth 1999, p. 79).

139. There is a peculiar imbalance, in the work of Habermas's younger students, between the elaborate 'foundation', 'justification' and 'deduction' of certain formal principles on the one hand and the uncritical acceptance of given conditions on the other (after all, these conditions are the reason why the operations of 'foundation', 'justification' and 'deduction' are undertaken in the first place). One consistently unquestioned starting point has consisted in the distinction, proper to the history of ideas, between the fields of ontology, philosophy of consciousness and (following the 'linguistic turn': Rorty 1967) linguistic theory. This 'narrative' has been discretely swept under the carpet ever since the 'rediscovery of mind' (Searle 1992). With regard to practical philosophy, by contrast, it is assumed there once 'existed' substantial values regulating the life of communities (a comfortable and 'idealist' assumption – as if there existed only a history of *ideas*), whereas these 'no longer' exist today. For example, Forst 1999, pp. 107 f. holds that 'unquestionably valid, substantial principles of what is right and good have been lost'. Forst takes this narrative from the 'contemporary debate' (p. 105; cf. Honneth 1996, p. 7, and Honneth 2007, p. 76), without verifying its present or past accuracy (2.6.6).

140. *MECW* 6, p. 131.

which are 'generated' intersubjectively. While these norms are social by nature, they are of interest only insofar as they provide the 'frame' for an action that is conceptualised from the point of view of individual actors. Thus norms make 'social sense' only on the premise that society is conceptualised as the aggregate of individual, norm-guided actions. Parsons[141] was especially important in the reimportation of this amalgam of neo-Kantianism and neoclassical economic theory into sociology.

The main difference between Marx's approach and that of Parsons and Habermas consists in the fact that Marx starts from objective, supra-personal structures and their effects, including on individuals, while Parsons and Habermas give primacy to the actor-centred perspective. Within Marx's structuralism, norms have no *explanatory* value: the socio-theoretically relevant variables are social and economic classes and the real forces driving their behaviour. Their members are subject to constraints that are not primarily moral in nature. It is only up to a point that the consequences of individual actions can be thought of as intentional – the social structures that channel action are already in place before an empirically observable individual begins to act or think – even if they change constantly due to the behaviour of such individuals.[142]

Thus there are three reasons why 'communicative action' is unsuitable as the foundation of a social theory: it narrows the focus to *individuals*, it considers only the *ideas* of those individuals and it refuses to consider other ideas than those that are *normative*.[143] Now, Habermas has himself objected to the 'philosophy of consciousness'. Like Heidegger

141. Parsons 1968.

142. Cf. 2.4.6. Giddens comments on the assertion that '[m]en make their own history, but they do not make it … under circumstances chosen by themselves' (*MECW* 11, p. 103) by adding drily: 'Well, so they do' (Giddens 1984, p. xxi). 'The egoistic individual in civil society may in his non-sensuous imagination and lifeless abstraction inflate himself into an *atom*, i.e., into an unrelated, self-sufficient, wantless, *absolutely full*, blessed being. Unblessed *sensuous reality* does not bother about his imagination, each of his senses compels him to believe in the existence of the world and of individuals outside him … But since the need of one individual has no self-evident meaning for another egoistic individual capable of satisfying that need, … each individual has to create this connection; it thus becomes the intermediary between the need of another and the objects of this need. Therefore, it is *natural necessity*, the *essential human properties* … and *interest* that hold the members of civil society together' (*MECW* 4, p. 120). 'Thus it is quite obvious … that there exists a materialist connection of men with one another, which is determined by their needs and their mode of production, and which is as old as men themselves. This connection is ever taking on new forms, and thus presents a 'history' irrespective of the existence of any political or religious nonsense which would especially hold men together' (*MECW* 5, p. 43). Ideas may modify this connection, but it has to be understood what it is that is being modified – exceptions cannot substitute for the rule (2.1.2). On 'structuralism', see Althusser 1996, pp. 200 ff., and Descombes 1980, pp. 127 ff.

143. Willms 1973, p. 164, formulated the following criticism: 'The starting point for the whole theory is the bourgeois reflexive subject, from the perspective of which all thinking remains focused on the level of action. The theories of the Enlightenment and of the Young Hegelians provide a concept of critique that … is incapable of confronting the level of subjective action with the … "level of the system" … other than negatively. In this sense, the achievements of Hegel and historical materialism are side-stepped'. Habermas 1987 still thought of institutions as pathologies (p. 276) and examples of distorted communication (p. 283).

1961 before him, he accused it of mentalism and atomism.[144] Having learned the lessons of 'post-metaphysical' philosophy, Habermas means to 'no longer' make reference to the elements of the philosophy of the subject (isolated individuals and putative overworlds and inner worlds); he intends to reflect upon procedural structures instead. (Self-consciousness, however, tended also to be conceptualised in procedural terms: see Frank 1991.) While these procedures involve the actions of individuals, it nevertheless appears as if one were dealing with hard facts, with 'institutions'. Is it the case, then, that Habermas ultimately resorts to structures, as Balkenhol and Gimmler argue?[145] A closer look shows that this is not the case. Having dealt with the main elements, theoretical and practical reason, Habermas goes on to proceduralistically 'liquefy' law as well.[146] What does he do this for?

Let us recall his cognitive interests. Habermas's reconstructions are meant to reformulate, for 'modernity', insights from the philosophical tradition, in such a way as to make them 'accessible'. Whether or not such a reconstruction is seen as necessary depends on one's assumptions about tradition and modernity. Thus the now dated discourse ethics assumed that 'the' tradition involved certain metaphysical background assumptions that are 'no longer' tenable today, that modernity is characterised by scepticism about each and every heritage and that no object of inquiry can be straightforwardly related to any longer. Habermas meant to 'save' Kant's universalist ethics, and he believed that to do so, he needed to free it from its putative 'metaphysical corset' and reconstruct it in a 'modern' way.

Within the debates on discourse ethics, these assumptions were rarely questioned, even though they were what made reconstruction seem necessary in the first place. But they are problematic. By no means did Kant posit an intelligible 'beyond'.[147] And why

---

144. Habermas 1984–7, 1987a and 1995.

145. Balkenhol 1991 and Gimmler 1998.

146. Habermas 1996. See Habermas's theory of truth (Habermas 1973b; 4.2.3) and his discourse ethics (Habermas 1983a and 1991b). The idea of 'liquefaction' is not new: Kant, Hegel and even Plato already defined reason as the activity of taking account, rather than as a substance (see also Cassirer 1911, Luhmann 1969, Stekeler-Weithofer 1995, Steinvorth 2002). Within this process, however, reason requires concrete and substantiated arguments. For a critique, see Narr 1994.

147. Kant's transcendental philosophy was fully aware of its own status: it was a criterial philosophy and understood itself to be just that. Habermas attributes to Kant the 'idealist background assumption' of an 'intelligible world' (Habermas 1991, p. 84; Habermas 1996, p. 10; Habermas 2003, p. 9). Kant was concerned with demonstrating that objectivity exists as such – that there is something that is prior to culturally specific 'invariant structures' (these being merely the 'empirically universal form': Habermas 2003, p. 20). Habermas is in search of the same but fails to perceive the Kantian query implicit in his undertaking ('If an interpretation that was rationally acceptable under certain epistemic conditions is to be recognizable as an error in a different epistemic context, then the phenomenon to be explained must be preserved in switching from one interpretation to the other': Habermas 2003, p. 33. This was the purpose of Kant's 'thing in itself', which Habermas has just rejected: Habermas 2003, pp. 21 f.). Kant required no 'transcendental subject', as Fichte did, and his 'transcendental idealism' did *not* postulate some otherworldly realm (Habermas 2003, pp. 21 f.; Kant 1998, p. 326/B 275). The roots of this understanding of Kant would seem to lie

should social theory no longer be able to access content? It was not until *discourse ethics* that the meaning of concepts such as 'good' or 'just' was dissolved into features of the concept's genesis. The legitimacy of a given norm was now assured only by the formula that all participants must be able to approve it. Neither in Kant nor in Habermas do individuals *really* vote on norms. But Kant's subject still disposed of rational criteria upon which to base its decision, whereas Habermas rejected just this as being metaphysical and monological, attributing the deliberation process to a fictitious and disembodied community. The result was an extreme formalism; it is doubtful whether one can ever obtain information about ethical issues in this way. Hegel's objections do not apply to Kant, but they do apply to discourse ethics.[148]

Thus Habermas is interested only in structures insofar as they are relevant to communicative action – to mental, and more specifically *normative* structures. They are the only structures that make 'sense' within his actor-centred and normativistic model.[149] The only thing intersubjective about this is the genesis of norms: they are *generated* socially.[150] But the abstract individual remains their reference point. The theory's self-description as 'intersubjective' rests on the German idealist fallacy of inferring the mode of being from the genesis. The procedural nature of the normative structure replicates the content of the earlier term 'interaction': communication-oriented actions of individuals remain the

---

in the objective-idealist interpretation of Kant formulated by Schelling (1985), on whom Habermas wrote his dissertation thesis (1954). Since Habermas wishes to continue 'casting the issue in transcendental terms' (Habermas 2003, p. 28), he retains the misinterpreted features of subjectivity and the overworld: the 'lifeworld' replaces objective reality (inter-)subjectively, and it displays a peculiarly 'quasi-transcendental' character' (Habermas 2003, p. 30). This takes the explanatory ambitions of transcendental philosophy too far: Habermas's 'detranscendentalisation' (Habermas 2001) is really more like a retranscendentalisation (4.2.5). Habermas bears a considerably greater burden of proof than Kant. In ethics too, Habermas attributes additional justificational burdens to Kant ('why be moral?') No 'overworld' (Habermas 1991, p. 84) can contribute to resolving this issue, since it would contradict autonomy.

148. See Habermas 1991b, p. 9. Hegel criticised Kant by remarking that the mere absence of contradiction is not sufficient for generating ethical content (Hegel 1991, § 135). He overlooked the fact that maxims always already exist: the 'categorical imperative' is a principle by which to assess ethical maxims, but they are not deduced from or generated by it. It makes recourse to instances such as reason and human dignity – something that becomes impossible only in Habermas (all substantive norms must be 'made to depend on ... discourses': Habermas 1973a, p. 94). He interprets a knowledge of where or how a norm originates ideally (or of where and how it is agreed on) as a knowledge of the content of the norm.

149. Thus Luhmann's subjectless redefinition of the word 'meaning' (Luhmann 1995, pp. 59 ff.) cut to the quick of Habermas's system. Habermas's counter-criticism was that, in Luhmann, the subject reappears in the form of the system (Habermas 1987a, pp. 353 ff.).

150. In theorising this, Habermas (1984–87) refers back to Mead and Durkheim. He could just as well have referred back to Marx: 'If man is social by nature, he will develop his true nature only in society' (*MECW* 4, p. 131). 'My relation to my surroundings is my consciousness' (*MECW* 5, p. 44; cf. *MECW* 28, p. 18). The emergence of norms (Joas 2000), however, occurs in a concrete and material way, not by virtue of a fictitious transcendental genesis.

starting point, and they continue to be the only starting point. Discourse ethics continues to cater to the philosophy of the subject.[151]

Habermas withdrew his attention from real subjects and objects and the structures within which they relate to one another, focusing instead on the fictitious surrogate object of 'ideal discourse'. But this ideal model had the deficiency of being no more than a model. Neo-Aristotelians always criticised it by pointing out that nothing of the kind exists in reality. The constitutional state now provided a response to this critique. On the one hand, it (or rather: the guarantee of freedom of speech, association, assembly and the press *by means of* the state of law) is the institutional precondition for the occurrence of unfettered discussions, as Aristotelians and Kantians must concede.[152] On the other hand, specifically legal arguments *actually* presuppose the freedom and equality of legal subjects.[153] The demonstration that everyday life involves the presupposition ('anticipation') of a domination-free condition always seemed artificial; not only is it hardly ever acted upon intentionally, but people constantly behave in ways that are contrary to it. Yet within legal theory, the notion merely refers to the condition under which law is *valid*. This pre-supposition is an actual move within the legal 'language game'. It is only there that the revealed linguistic anticipations and suppositions play the role accorded them by Habermas and Apel. Thus discourse theory *corresponds* to the formal law of modern constitutional states. In it, the principles reconstructed are actually in effect: it is an instituted reality that disposes of rational structures, and from a legal perspective, the law has even been authored by citizens themselves.

Thus it was a developmental dynamic within Habermas's work that prompted him to situate the validity conditions of rational discourse, which he had been analysing for decades, within the legal framework of the democratic and constitutional state.[154] Find-

---

151. This may shed some light on why Habermas opposed it so vehemently. Benhabib's accusation that Habermas is engaging in 'philosophy of the subject' (Benhabib 1986, pp. 330, 351 f.) was already anticipated by Willms, who described Habermas as an 'extremely bourgeois subject' (Willms 1973, p. 32) that displays a 'suggestive reflexivity' and yet remains 'oddly conservative' (Willms 1973, p. 8). The 'participant perspective' also refers to individuals and overlooks the fact that the perspective of participants is often dominated by semblance (2.4.6). Habermas may find the observation odd (Habermas 1999b, p. 253; Habermas 2000), but his theory of law is closely related to his earlier works. The hierarchy of work and interaction recurs in the 'double perspective' (Habermas 1996, p. 66) of systemic and normativistic views. The hostility toward technocracy (Habermas 1996, pp. 50 f.) and the tripartite order of pragmatic, ethical and moral questions (pp. 159 ff.; Habermas 1993, pp. 1 ff.) renew the distinction between natural, hermeneutic and critical science (Habermas 1987).

152. Aristotle linked the necessary practice of virtue to the existence of a community from which virtue can be learned. This is why the Nicomachean Ethics transitions directly into the Politics, where political forms are examined with an eye to the question of which one allows for the good life. To Kant, morality is law's ground of validity, but law is the real life-prerequisite of morality. In this sense, law is primary in Kant as well.

153. Alexy 1978.

154. It seems clear he was inspired to do this by the criticisms formulated in Wellmer 1986 (cf. Benhabib 1986, p. 291). Forst smoothens over this development when he says that discourse ethics was supplemented with a 'theory of democracy' (Forst 1999, p. 120).

ing itself in distress, discourse theory discovered a sheet anchor in law. Law is not so much examined for its own sake as used to try to close the gap, deeply rooted in Habermas's approach, between sense-free technology and immaterial interaction, system and lifeworld.[155]

Critical theory, which had been aporetic for decades, now achieved 'systemic closure', but it was a closure that replicated, once again, the dualism inherent in Habermas's basic approach. Habermas effects a rapprochement between discourse theory and law, integrating law between system and lifeworld, as a 'transmission belt'.[156] He examines law both from a normativistically reductive participants' perspective and from a systems-theoretically reductive observer's perspective; from this 'double perspective' of his own theory,[157] he draws conclusions about the nature of the object of inquiry. Within law, he claims, the two worlds, *facts and norms*, achieve the synthesis sought after. One might read Habermas's discussion of facts and norms as one of 'society and law'. But he means only the facticity and normative validity of law *itself*.[158] Instead of a theory that probes law socio-theoretically, we are presented with an explication of the self-understanding of law. All that is new is that this self-understanding is rendered 'compatible' with functionalist perspectives.

The failure to consider law from the perspective of society had, however, already been a feature of systems theory, which never related law to society, much less to the economy.[159] If nothing is said about society, neither in the functional theory of law, which is the theory of an autopoietic system, nor in the alleged normative self-understandings of legal individuals, then simply synthesising the two will not yield a 'social theory'.[160]

---

155. 'Not the logic of the matter, but the matter of logic is the philosophical element. The logic does not serve to prove the state, but the state to prove the logic' (*MECW* 3, p. 18). Discourse ethics posed itself questions such as the one whether the decision to be rational can itself be rationally grounded. It lost touch with ethically relevant issues within reality. Habermas himself has said that '*unfettered* communicative action can neither unload nor seriously bear the burden of social integration [!] falling to it'. He adds that law might be a 'plausible solution to the puzzle', since it thrives on communication but is nevertheless coercive in nature (Habermas 1996, p. 37). 'A morality that depends on the accommodating substrate of propitious personality structures would have a limited effectiveness if it could not engage the actor's motives [!] in *another* way besides internalization, that is, precisely by way of an institutionalized legal system that *supplements* postconventional morality in a manner effective for action' (p. 114). The defect of discourse ethics was that it said nothing definite, but merely evoked an integral moralism (2.5.2). But if the discourse principle was prior even to law, then one was free to once more provide moral-philosophical 'groundings' for all sorts of claims (Habermas 1996, p. 122; cf. Gosepath 1999, Burckhart and Reich 2000, Kersting 2000, pp. 202 ff., and Nida-Rümelin 2000).

156. Habermas 1996, pp. 76, 81, 448.

157. Habermas 1996, p. 66.

158. Habermas 1996, p. 24.

159. For Luhmann, law constitutes an autonomous subsystem that is 'autopoietic' and whose capacity to 'communicate' with other systems is limited (Luhmann 1969, 1972, 1983 and 2004). This is a long way from being a 'socio-theoretical' examination of law. To proceed in this way is not to make normativism 'more social' (thus Gephart 1993).

160. Habermas 1996, p. 5.

Whereas I have started from Marx and identified the object of inquiry 'capitalism' as social theory's absent centre, in Habermas, *law* takes this place.[161]

Law ousts society from theory: law itself is conceptualised as a mode of sociation, within which the functional and the normative perspectives unite.[162] The theoretical lacuna is relocated to law: it is a 'safety net' providing the social integration[163] that other systems fail to bring about. It no longer makes sense to ask about the function that law performs for sociation, since law *is itself* sociation. The only thing it provides a deficiency guarantee for is the theory of communicative action, which failed to provide an account of this sort of integration. In becoming the intra-theoretical buttress of morality, law simultaneously acts as a lifebelt for the social theory that depends on a philosophised morality. However, this involves law being overburdened and distorted. Law may be *one* medium of 'social integration' (even if this dualist distinction is questionable),[164] but that does not make it its effective cause. 'Mechanisms' of 'systemic integration' intrude severely upon the realm of law; after all, economic and political conflicts make up most of the content appearing within the form of law.[165]

---

161. Both Marx and law make reference to 'bourgeois society' [*bürgerliche Gesellschaft*], although they do so from different perspectives: law understands itself as 'bourgeois law' [*bürgerliches Recht*], while political economy examined the anatomy of bourgeois society.

162. Habermas 1996, pp. 31–2. The legal theory that Habermas opposes to normative philosophy (Habermas 1996, pp. 42 ff.) is also an ethicised one – and sociological systems theory has been normativist since Parsons (Habermas 1984–7, Vol. II, pp. 204 ff.).

163. Habermas 1996, p. 73.

164. Lockwood's distinction (1970) presupposes neatly separated functional domains, which are nowhere to be found except in Parson's models (Habermas 1996, p. 26). There are limited cases in which integration is systemic but not social (such as prison inmates) or social but not systemic (such as a church or asylum). Generally speaking, however, the social implications of what is described as 'systemic' are so far-reaching it makes little sense to distinguish theoretically between the two. And what might a social system be, other than a case of social integration?

165. The theory of consensus was already criticised in these terms by Steinvorth: he argued that the theory treats something as justified not just when, but because it merits universal approval (Habermas 1990, pp. 88 ff.; Habermas 2003, pp. 10 f.). 'The juristic forms... cannot, being mere forms, determine... content' (*MECW* 37, pp. 337 f.). Talk of 'juridification' (Kübler 1985) still makes reference to something that needs to be juridified. Habermas interprets this relationship as one of annihilation. According to Habermas, one need not dwell on Marx when considering the development that leads from Hobbes to Luhmann, since Marx reduced law to a 'mere illusion' (Habermas 1996, p. 46). Once again, something unwelcome (associated, in this case, with systems theory) is projected onto Marx (functionalism 'neutralizes' everything: p. 3). And yet law is not mere illusion in Marx; in fact, as a form of intercourse [*Verkehrsform*] proper to production, it is part of the economic base. However, its formality does not give rise to new contents; it merely processes pre-existing contents. While Habermas identifies such contents (Habermas 1996, p. 40), his theory does not account for them. Habermas alleges that normative and intentional implications are evident throughout law (he faults Luhmann for not mentioning this: p. 50), when in fact this ought only to be the case at the switchpoint linking law to the resource 'solidarity', but not at those linking it to the resources 'money' and 'power', which are systemic in and of themselves, although they are nevertheless legally regulated (p. 40). It is here that Habermas's excessive normativism becomes inconsistent. Habermas assumes that law, which is driven by normativity, has detached itself from other systems (the economy and politics) (p. 75). Hence he is not interested in 'negative liberties and social entitlements' (p. 78), but only in the de-economised and depoliticised

The family (relatives) and society (professional training and occupation, as well as basic functions mediated by these, such as social relationships, food, clothing, shelter and entertainment) are more important 'mechanisms' of 'social integration' than coercive law. Habermas describes the interconnections between various sub-domains from the perspective of law, but it is doubtful whether they can be *explained* in terms of law alone. Whoever thinks of law in this way and posits it as the final arbiter thereby assumes the free-floating autopoietic existence of normative ideas – this is the only 'metaphysical background assumption' in sight.[166] But what if we follow Marx in understanding law as the form of a content that is not itself normative (2.3.5)? Habermas ends his career doing what Marx, who had studied jurisprudence, began with: he examines law. The juridical *view* of society, which no doubt exists and which is justified within legal discourse, is fallaciously perceived by Habermas as the *cause* of society. That the normative view of society exists within law is a tautology; to interpret it as a 'theory of society', a misunderstanding.

Habermas champions a juridically reductive social philosophy.[167] In order to be able to do this, he needs first to provide a reductive and ethicised account of law, formulated from the perspective of conceptual philosophy. When the law has an egalitarian thrust, as is the case in the German constitutions of 1919 and 1949, it can be politically progressive to insist on the formality of law.[168] But Habermas interprets the normative sphere as being itself material – an echo of the philosophy of objective mind.[169]

---

liberties of 'civil society', the 'rights enjoyed by citizens' (p. 83; cf. pp. 75 f., 79, 82 ff.), namely the ones that rest on communicative action (this corresponds to Hannah Arendt's 'pure politics'). But these rights seldom feature in everyday jurisdiction, since they concern law-making, which tends to be historically prior. The result is simply this: one does not really have to be the author of one's rights; it is enough to be allowed to perceive oneself as their author. This formula lends itself to instrumentalisation.

166. Rehberg 1994a, p. 65.

167. Böhm 1998, p. 15.

168. When the (politically marginal) German Communist Party was banned in 1956, this was justified by reference to a 'liberal-democratic basic order' that was interpreted in substantive terms. National Socialist legal theory already invoked substantive law (values, ethnicity, and so on; Rüthers 1991). I. Maus distinguishes between a pre-legal substantiveness, which cannot be taken account of without dissolving law, and a post-legal substantiveness, which is compatible with equality of rights ('social rights': 1987, p. 251). Behind this lies the distinction between the labour movement, which wanted a 'substantive' realisation of the principle of equal rights, thereby remaining oriented toward procedure, and the conservatives of the 1930s and 1980s, who sought to abolish procedure in favour of real inequality.

169. The welfare state, which 'can no longer be annulled' (Habermas 1988, p. 235) 'has emerged from the confines of class' (p. 308 – the argument concerning the irreversibility of this development is moral-psychological: Benhabib 1992, pp. 275 f.). From the fact that class distinctions play no role in law, Habermas concludes that they do not exist. He can do this because he has previously chosen to bracket social conflicts 'conceptually', *a priori* (cf. Beer 1999). This bracketing is the point about legal equality: judgement is passed without distinction of person. But this legal language should not be misunderstood as an empirical description of reality: 'The welfare states of Europe and other OECD countries have in fact [!] largely compensated for the socially undesired effects of a highly productive economic system. Capitalism has, for the first time, not

Here, we need to recall Marx's objections to Hegel (2.5.7): 'sublating' social conflicts into law does not in itself amount to resolving the juridified issues; the conflict is merely taken to another level. A legal *theory* is even less capable of resolving such issues. 'The material life of individuals ... is the real basis of the state and *remains* so at all the stages'.[170] As with Hegel's, Habermas's system needs to be criticised less for its counterfactual claims than for its *reality*. In it, little remains to be 'realised', even though reality itself in many ways deserves to be criticised. The fixation on the grammar of the legal sphere impedes recognition of substantive problems.[171] For this reason, law ought to be an object of critical theory, not a replacement for it. After all, Hegel's philosophy already culminated in the apotheosis of constitutional law. Thus Habermas's development should be seen as paralleling that of Hegel.[172]

In Habermas, it is law that first provides not just 'objective mind', but also other idealist concepts with a tangible meaning. This is the case, for example, with the 'reality

---

obstructed but made possible the fulfilment of the republican promise of the equitable inclusion of all citizens' (Habermas 1999a). Habermas blurs not just the distinction between law and reality, but also that between procedural and substantive law: democracy and the welfare state are rendered 'conceptually' coextensive: 'when we read the text of our constitutions in this substantive sense, that of the realisation of a socially just society' (Habermas 1999a). What was achieved in the welfare state was to do not just with the 'idea [!] of self-legislation', but also with the antagonism between the capitalist and the socialist systems, as well as with concrete struggles over the distribution of wealth. Such struggles are hard to avoid; at best, 'ideas' can invite people not to conduct them in a militant way. The 'instrumental' and 'strategic' reasons for the granting of social rights (e.g. ensuring social peace domestically and political peace internationally) are derided normativistically. 'Today we realise that this idea has hitherto only been realised within the framework of the nation state' (Habermas 1999a). But the sought-for 'political closure' (Habermas 2001b, p. 111) of a European legal code can only be achieved when legal relations (and the real relations that underpin them) allow for it. Juridification alone cannot improve anyone's situation. Nor does it go back to an 'idea': 'In developing the welfare state, post-war European politicians of all stripes were guided by this dynamic conception of the democratic process' (Habermas 1999a). Once again, the place becomes the cause. 'It has been seen that these minutiae ... were not at all the products of parliamentary fancy. They developed gradually out of circumstances ... Their formulation, official recognition, and proclamation by the state, were the result of a long struggle of classes' (*MECW* 35, pp. 287 f.).

170. *MECW* 5, p. 329, emphasis added; cf. *MECW* 3, pp. 339 f., and *MECW* 35, p. 113; from a methodological perspective: Steinvorth 1977, pp. 12 ff.

171. McBride 1999a, Fraser 2003.

172. Cf. Habermas 1996, p. x. Jan Ross calls Habermas the 'Hegel of the German Federal Republic' (*Die Zeit*, no. 42, 2001), and Habermas himself named his Peace Prize speech after Hegel's *Faith and Knowledge* (Habermas 2001a; cf. Hegel 1977a). In both thinkers, an ebullient early period was followed, first, by an epistemogenetic overview of all available knowledge (Hegel's *Phenomenology*; compare Habermas 1987), then by a *Logic* (in Habermas's case, the theory of 'truth' and/or discourse, as a set of formal instruments: Habermas 1973b and 1983a), then by a 'system' (compare Hegel's *Encyclopaedia* with Habermas's mammoth *Theory of Communicative Action*) and finally, by a *Philosophy of Law* (Habermas 1996). By an irony of history, Habermas's discovery of the constitutional state, the capstone of his system, occurred at the very moment when that state experienced its 'downfall': by ending the containment of capitalism that was the welfare state, the 1990s eliminated the constitutional state's precondition. Thus Habermas re-enacted the tragedy of Adorno, who believed he was writing too late (Adorno 2007, pp. xix, 408).

of the idea', which Hegel had opposed to Kantian moral philosophy, and with 'reflection', namely self-clarification by reference to decisions and actions already taken.[173] But reflection is not yet 'self-reflection', even if this is what it calls itself. Human finitude having been painfully integrated into the philosophical canon, and with it the perspectival and relative nature of cognition,[174] one should not expect such self-reflection to provide meta-justifications, but only humbling insights. If we take 'self-reflection' to refer to thought about what one is actually doing when one is engaging in reflection, then we can say that it allows for a topics: it allows us to situate various theories within their relationship to reality, which self-reflection (properly understood) teaches us we must always assume as given (4.1).[175] This is precisely what is missing in the social philosophy produced by Habermas and his followers.[176] To the outside observer, its complex framework of conceptual interrelationships, principles, postulates and 'justifications'[177] appears oddly free-floating. The link to reality is not secured methodologically; it is either suggested (such as by means of 'background knowledge' associated with the 'lifeworld') or established fallaciously.

Thus a representative essay by Rainer Forst speaks unmediatedly of 'justice' – as if he were holding the key to a just society in his hands. In fact, all he does is compare various theories that have attempted to codify select social practices in the form of principles, in order then to attempt to justify these principles. Forst's undertaking cannot possibly yield more than an assessment of the theories he examines, which operate at a considerable remove from social reality. As long as the evaluative standard abstains from considering experience (or remains 'aprioristic'), the analysis remains in a kind of philosophical vacuum. The distinction between theory and reality is blurred.[178]

---

173. The sense of finally having found what he was looking for may have prompted Hegel to claim that philosophy had reached its conclusion. Marx's criticism was essentially that Hegel had cheated along the way (Böhm 1998, pp. 32 ff.). Marx conceded that political emancipation reached its fulfilment in democracy ('the solved *riddle* of all constitutions': *MECW* 3, pp. 29) – but he held that there is more to emancipation than political emancipation (pp. 159 ff.).

174. The process was a painful one because Freud and Marx were resisted for some time. There was less resistance to Nietzsche, presumably because he failed to retain his modest demeanour and surrendered to his predilection for 'philosophising with the hammer' (Nietzsche 1888; cf. Heidegger 1962, p. 196) – the pure self-assertion of a blind will to power (2.5.2). Habermas considers Nietzsche the 'turning point' of postmodernity, (Habermas 1987a, pp. 83 ff.).

175. Cf. Bubner 1990.

176. By contrast, Habermas 1987, pp. 214 ff., saddles 'self-reflection' with a burden of proof that prevents it from engaging with substantive issues (cf. his self-criticism: Habermas 2000). This is the idealist germ of the notion that the basic structure of practical reason is to be found in language itself, independently of its content. Post-Hegelian philosophy has not made Habermas more modest (Habermas 1984–7, Vol. II, pp. 396 f.; cf. Habermas 1990b, pp. 1 ff., and Habermas 1984–7, pp. 15 ff.; 4.2.4).

177. Burckhardt 2000.

178. Although Forst 1999 only means to clarify some aspects of the 'debate on the possibility of grounding a theory of political and social justice' (p. 105), he fallaciously objectifies the concept of justice. His argument proceeds by leaving behind it (in this order) the social world (1), the

The called-for self-reflection might be seen as an exercise that one can perform or not, without it making any difference to the theory.[179] But this is where the confrontation with Marx becomes relevant. According to Marx, Hegel's philosophy has something to be said for it (it has a 'rational kernel'),[180] although it misunderstands its own position in the world. What distinguished Hegel from other philosophers was the fact that he *did* engage in self-reflection. In his considerations on the relationship between theory and reality, he accorded primacy to the 'concept' – in a roundabout manner, to be sure, but very deliberately. What Marx appreciated in Hegel were the mediations between concept and reality, and so he did not simply claim – from an outside perspective, as it were – that Hegel's position is wrong; rather, he engaged with the object itself (with Hegel's philosophy, as later with political economy) in order to demonstrate that when one *situates* oneself thus, a distorted view of reality results.[181] Hegel's reflections may have involved him making correct observations about his object of inquiry, but the way

---

action-directing notions called 'justice' that are at work within the social world (2), theories about 'justice' (3), their justifications (4) and the problematisation of these justifications (5); Forst then goes on to consider even the debates about this (6) from a meta-perspective (7). It is difficult to see why Forst believes he makes can inferences about 'justice' (1/2) based on what he observes from his meta-perspective (7). Forst does admit that his 'conception of justice' also depends 'on scientific analyses of social reality' (p. 167), but he only does this in the postscript, after he has elaborated his 'autonomous' justification' (p. 112). The 'also' betrays a subtle elimination of experience: Forst makes it seem as if there were a way for philosophical theory to access these phenomena without scientific analysis; other sciences are merely tolerated as auxiliary disciplines. He gives one chapter the title 'Non-Metaphysical vs. Post-Metaphysical Justice' (p. 112). In light of what he does, the title ought really to be: 'Non-Metaphysical vs. Post-Metaphysical Theory of the Principles of the Deduction of Principles Within Notions of Social Justice'. This idealist non sequitur (Forst calls it 'constructivist') is only possible because Forst does not reflect upon what he is doing here. To do so is not to move onto a higher level of abstraction (it is hard to top the level of abstraction on which Forst is already operating; he describes it as 'prior to every justification of principles of justice': p. 107); it is to *situate* what one is saying: what is the object of inquiry, on what level of abstraction is one operating, how does one move from one level of abstraction to another, and where does one distinguish between the various levels of abstraction? What corresponds to these levels in reality, and what do the claims made tell us about reality? 'A philosophical problem has the form: "I don't know my way about"' (Wittgenstein, *Philosophical Investigations*, aphorism 123; cf. aphorism 109).

179. This is a description that applies to Habermas's activity ('reconstruction' or 'reflection'): those who feel compelled to engage in it should do so, but this makes no difference to the object of inquiry. Here, reflection is 'recursive' (Forst 1999, p. 109): the ideal object, the 'concept' (of virtue, of justice, of the good, of tolerance), serves as the starting point for questions about its implications and conceptual presuppositions.

180. *MECW* 35, p. 19.

181. Marx's critique of Hegel did not limit itself to concepts; it also addressed what had been subsumed under them. Faced with the claim that the concept effects mediation, Marx was able to provide a substantive demonstration that mediation in fact does not come about by virtue of concepts. The 'poor' fall outside the purview of the law (*MECW* 1, p. 230); the 'proletariat' escapes the 'concept' of society (*MECW* 3, p. 186; *MECW* 4, pp. 35 f.; *MECW* 5, p. 60 and elsewhere); production cannot be grasped by the concepts of exchange-based society, and so on (2.5.7).

he situated that object, by identifying it with the self-development of the concept, was an error. It could be demonstrated *ex post* that Hegel's self-reflection was flawed.[182]

The consequences are all the more serious when a situating self-reflection no longer occurs at all. Unlike Hegel, Habermas does not explicitly formulate his claim to mediation on the conceptual level; he simply practises such mediation.[183] According to Marx's critique of Hegel, it is not enough to simply claim that Habermas has neglected to engage in self-reflection, or that the structure of his entire theory is 'idealist'.[184] One needs rather to demonstrate that this normative conceptual philosophy fails to grasp key aspects of reality, even though there is such a thing as a pre-conceptual awareness of those aspects (1.2). And here we are: The elided objects are bourgeois society and real history. The way the constitutional state and democracy are discussed is reminiscent of the older neo-Hegelianism, which was already criticised for introducing the methodological chimera of an 'ontological genesis' or 'genetic grounding' that causes theory and practice to contaminate one another (2.5.5). While Habermas does inquire into the genesis of validity, he does not address the *actual* development of a specific legal system but contents himself with discussion of an abstract 'generation' of 'validity' – a transcendental history ('logical genesis').[185] Key facts such as social struggles are elided and substituted for by an imaginary transcendental history of the development of norms. At the same time, however, the validity that has been historicised in this manner is mixed up with its transcendental genesis in such a way that *actual* validity is lost sight of – after all, every concrete case of validity appears timeless when considered internally.[186]

---

182. Recognising the achievements of reflection while simultaneously criticising its overblown claims, Marx spoke of 'division' (*MECW* 1, pp. 490 f.; 2.5.7).

183. The dialectic, which was intended to perform a situating function (Bubner 1990), disappeared from Habermas's vocabulary in the course of the positivism dispute ('Let us try to get by with a little less dialectics': Habermas 1990a, p. 223; cf. Habermas 1970 and 1976, and especially Dahms 1994, pp. 373 ff.). Where in reality Habermas's positionings are actually situated remains an open question.

184. Habermas even partly admits to his idealism (Habermas 1996, p. 41; cf. Habermas 1973a, pp. 259 f.; Habermas 1987, p. 287; see also Marcuse 1937).

185. Habermas 1996, p. 121. There is nothing but a history of the concept: the developments filed under 'no longer' are conceptual (practical reason, for example, is said to have 'shattered': Habermas 1996, p. 3), but they are treated as if they were real developments: as in Heidegger, conceptual history seems to coordinate real events transcendentally (a 'deficit' in Marx's theory determined the real history of Russia: Habermas 1996, pp. 478 f.; Adorno's 'resignation' is projected onto the entire Federal Republic of Germany: p. 480, for example). Habermas's surrogate transcendental history first becomes manifest in his claim about an independent historical 'evolution' that follows the stages distinguished by Piaget and Kohlberg (Habermas 1976b, pp. 63 ff., 129 ff.). Here, real history is replaced by theory. Habermas transforms critical theory from a critique of society back into a critique of theories (for Marx, the latter was no more than a preliminary stage). This only makes sense on the assumption that theories contain reality in and of themselves (Habermas 1976b, pp. 184 f.; Habermas 1996, p. 41).

186. Established law cannot simultaneously assert its own relativity. Either it is valid, in which case it remains so until replaced by a new law, or it is not valid. It cannot be 'a little bit' valid. Similarly, the history of mathematics should not feature in actual mathematical calculations. That would not be a permissible move within the mathematical language game.

The absence of an explicit self-reflection – which might have provided answers to the questions of what exactly falls within the purview of the law, what it means for it to fall within that purview, where in reality the theorising of law is situated and what assessment is derived from such theorising – constrains us to expose Habermas's *implicit* positionings archaeologically.[187] To do this, we need to backtrack a little. A change in the political orientation of critical theory occurred with Claus Offe's statement that '[t]here is no practical alternative to the constitutional programme of liberal and welfare state democracy'.[188] When Habermas, building upon Offe's preliminary work, addressed late capitalism's legitimation issues,[189] he had changed his position vis-à-vis his beginnings as a cultural critic: he no longer followed early critical theory by acting as the bourgeois subject's advocate *against* the state and its bureaucracies, conceived of as excessively powerful and as depriving people of their liberties; instead, he began to consider the very same state as a bulwark against systemic imperatives threatening to bring about cultural impoverishment. Habermas was now concerned with the legitimacy resources of the given state (governed by the Social Democratic Party at the time).[190]

Habermas's endorsement of the democatic constitutional state puts him in the company of the young Marx, who considered the US constitution a model to aspire to. Marx accorded with the few democrats of his age in holding that political emancipation was necessary.[191] The differences begin '[w]here speculation ends'.[192] Habermas believes that such demands already amount to a social theory. This presupposes the idealist assumption that society is *constituted* by norms. By contrast, Marx diverted attention from the state and focused it on society. If one thinks of the state as the form that society gives itself, as done within social contract theory, then 'autonomy' does not refer to the self-legislation of the political, but to self-determination *by means of* the political.

---

187. Habermas once openly expressed himself in favour of valuations within theory (Habermas 1973a, p. 253; Habermas 1976a, pp. 142 ff.); later, he still held that philosophy is immediately political (Habermas 2003, pp. 263 f.). It ought therefore not to be overly difficult to detect such valuations. This way of proceeding is similar to a theory of coherence. The notion that reality ought to serve as the touchstone for theory only seems odd for as long as one is philosophising. In normal life, everyone knows what is real, and denying it would amount to a performative fallacy. For this reason, Marx concluded that one ought to begin with reality – but not with reality as it presents itself to the individual 'within consciousness' (this was Husserl's starting point) or as we would like it to be (this was what the Young Hegelian Freyer tried to take as his starting point; cf. Über 1994).

188. Offe 1974, p. 53.

189. Habermas 1976a.

190. Habermas 1984–7, Vol. II, p. 327; H. Berndt in Bolte 1989, p. 95. The 'norms formulated within today's political theories have been... recognised by most contemporaries' (Steinvorth 1999, p. 77). Then why are they not fully asserted? 'This could partly be due to a deficit of... normative theory itself: it has not formulated a satisfactory account of how equal freedom is to be concretely understood and implemented.... This is a purely normative task; in addressing it, one must not get side-tracked by asking which interests might provide ideas with the requisite support. Otherwise... the theorist would merely be "applauding the rising powers"' (p. 78, quoting M. Weber).

191. *MECW* 4, pp. 115 f.

192. *MECW* 5, p. 37.

But the underlying society is no single subject.[193] It develops by means of antagonisms that traverse the state, both nationally and internationally. In the worst case, which however is not rare, the state can become a class state which smashes labour organisations and combines industry and the state to form an authoritarian regime. A juridical perspective (the 'idea of communicative freedom', which Honneth[194] sees as having the – questionable – advantage, vis-à-vis Marx, of blanking out disadvantages) has difficulty grasping this and other problematic processes, since they may occur *legally*, within the form of law. Law makes such processes possible, too.

Habermas's theoretical background assumptions facilitated his *Kehre*.[195] If it is clear, because of one's 'conceptual' preliminaries, that the state *qua* manifestation of pure politics rests on communicative action, then threats originating within the state are less likely to be addressed than threats that can be traced back to other imperatives. The mere act of concerning oneself with non-communicative issues had to appear as such a threat, even on the conceptual level. Thus the welfare state was interpreted as a burden upon the constitutional state's legitimacy.[196] The state's legitimacy already seemed to have suffered from the erosion of culture (or of the lifeworld); state intervention into the economy further increased the state's need for legitimation. Now, Habermas's systems-theoretical perspective prevents him from concretely addressing this political diagnosis: within the system's environment, no distinctions are drawn; the mass of 'citizens' is regarded as a mass of unified *political* subjects (*citoyens*). Habermas means to democratise law, but he avoids the requisite concretion. 'Legitimacy' is a four-part predicate: person A addresses person B in order to legitimate a state of affairs C by reference to a state of affairs D. Habermas never answers the question of who performs the role of B: who is it that the welfare state needs to present itself as legitimate to?

---

193. 'Moreover, to consider society as a single subject is wrong: a speculative approach' (*MECW* 28, p. 31). 'Now this view can be expressed again in a speculative-idealistic, i.e. fantastic, way as 'self-generation of the species' ('society as the subject'), and thereby the consecutive series of interrelated individuals can be regarded as a single individual, which accomplishes the mystery of generating itself' (*MECW* 5, p. 52). Marx was not a philosopher of consciousness (Habermas 1987a, pp. 62 f.).

194. Honneth 1999a, p. 295.

195. The extreme left's precarious hostility to the state (which sometimes led to a paradoxical endorsement of East Germany and to terrorist assassinations) was of course part of the general context within which Habermas developed this approach (cf. Koenen 2001), as was the fact that Marxist ideas were publicly discredited by the behaviour of the extreme Left.

196. This Right Hegelian discussion had been going on since the introduction of the 'social market economy' [*soziale Marktwirtschaft*]: Forsthoff 1968, Tohidipur 1978. Habermas had originally called for 'asceticism' (in Habermas 1970; see Kreulartz 1995, p. 60; cf. Gehlen 1949, p. 54); in 1992, he referred to the 'undesirable [for whom? C.H.] effects of welfare-state provisions' (Habermas 1996, p. 391; cf. Habermas 1984–7, Vol. II, pp. 361 ff.). Opposition to the welfare state was seldom motivated by a democratic ethos (authors such as Forsthoff, Huber, Gehlen and Schmitt had often enjoyed successful careers under National Socialism); more frequently, such opposition was motivated by a fear of losing one's social status, and/or by a fear of politically more far-reaching demands (cf. H. Klages 1979).

Habermas is not so much thinking of the recipients of housing, child, child-raising, health and unemployment benefits, of Federal Training Assistance Act [*Bundesausbildungsfördergeld*, BAFöG] and welfare assistance, of pensions and transitional funds for pensioners [*Altersübergangsgeld*], who make up a large part of the population; he is thinking of entrepreneurs, who risk being burdened with higher expenses (ancillary wage costs, taxes, and so on). Thus his theoretical abandonment of Marx leads functionally to political partisanship. Habermas thereby surrenders the further possibilities for a critique of capitalism. All he offers by way of explanation is his overarching historico-philosophical hypothesis that a critique of culture can 'no longer' be formulated today. According to this hypothesis, under 'late capitalism', technocracy[197] and the welfare state[198] have solved the problems of former times.[199]

Habermas provides no justification for his general hypothesis, upon which the disappearance of capitalism as an object of inquiry rests. He operates on the basis of unverified assumptions. Thus he has a 'justification deficit' of his own, except that it is situated on the empirical level.[200] His convincingly argued discussions of democracy, law and justice take themselves to be progressive. Yet terms such as 'radical democracy' or 'political culture' have no definite referent. The question of what exactly they refer to remains unanswered. Habermas analyses the implications of normative concepts derived from the *self-understanding* of the democratic constitutional state, in what amounts to a 'hermeneutics of democracy'.[201] Habermas provides a transcendental deduction of the German Federal Republic.[202]

The questions of what these normatively reconstructed concepts mean in political reality and where in it the author situates himself can no longer be posed on the basis of the concepts themselves, but only on the basis of reality. Only a naive materialism or

---

197. Habermas 1971b.

198. Habermas 1976a.

199. Instead of private capitalism, we have 'today' the primacy of politics (Habermas 1976a, p. 5), a new complex of the economy and the state that 'no longer' involves problems such as the systematic discrimination against entire sections of the population (cf. Habermas 1971b, pp. 100 f.; Habermas 1970; Habermas 1976a, pp. 33 ff.; Habermas 1976b, p. 182; Habermas 1984–7, Vol. II, pp. 343 ff. and elsewhere). 'Only in an egalitarian public of citizens that has emerged from the confines of class [...] can the potential of an unleashed cultural pluralism fully develop' (Habermas 1996, p. 308). Why do class barriers 'no longer' exist today? Because they have been abolished by 'equal rights of citizenship' (p. 308). Habermas interprets this juridical expression as a description of empirical reality. 'Historically speaking, liberal rights crystallized around the social position of the private property owner' (Habermas 1996, p. 78). This is 'no longer' the case either. Rather, these rights and the 'paternalistically bestowed' 'social entitlements' promote a 'privatistic retreat from the citizen's role' (ibid.). The 'social question' is taken to have been solved, and the new problem is declared to be that of rights. Habermas even uses the Schelskyan term 'levelling' (p. 79; cf. 2.4.6).

200. Aprioristic social philosophy is not informed by such 'empirical, and not conceptually necessary, relationships' (Habermas 1996, p. 78). Nor does Habermas intend to 'dwell on' semi-empirical theories (p. 288; Honneth 2003).

201. Höffe 1996, p. 137.

202. See Benhabib 1992, p. 285. Scheyli 2001 regrets the absence of a deduction of the Swiss Confederation.

idealism would wholly deny the existence of one of the two dimensions, concept and reality. Their relationship can be defined in two ways: either one alleges, by means of a logic of realisation, that ideas are primary and that reality is *modelled* on them. We may call this 'weak idealism'. Or reality already disposes of a certain structure, which is *replicated* one more time in the realm of ideas – this is the 'weak materialism' of Marx, which regards normative ideas as one part of reality. It is only on the basis of 'weak materialism' that the question concerning the *relationship* between concept and reality can be posed at all. By contrast, 'weak idealism' engages in a form of social critique that amounts to lamenting the fact that ideas have 'not yet' – or not *fully* – been realised. It is faced with an additional problem of justification, as it needs to explain where 'normative contents' come from if they are not to be found within material social reality. This is the Young Hegelian model of critique, which critical theory still adhered to (2.6.3). In Habermas, it has become apologetic. Apology was always the flipside of Hegelianism.[203]

In terms of the history of theory, this development has its background in German social philosophy (2.5). In Habermas, theory and practice, between which Kant drew a clear methodological distinction, fuse into a 'unity', as they did in Fichte. This leads to the unfortunate expectation that theory should derive everything from a single principle.[204] Like Freyer 1964, Habermas assumes that social reality is not pre-given but *lived* by us and hence open to rational reconstruction. To support this assumption, he invokes Vico ('*verum et factum convertuntur*').[205] Everything encountered in the human world appears as having been created by humans, whether historically or according to a plan. Consequently, there is no instance that could stand opposed to communicative action and the theoretical compilation of its results; this possibility is already ruled out on the 'categorial' level.[206] Men give themselves the law; *therefore* they must also act

---

203. Lübbe 1962.

204. On Fichte, see Habermas 1973a, pp. 256 ff.; Habermas 1987, pp. 295 ff. 'Insight' and 'emancipation' (Habermas 1973a, p. 9), knowledge and interest constitute a 'unity' (Habermas 1987, p. 187; cf. pp. 198 and 209; Habermas 2003, p. 238; Jonas 1976 II, pp. 213 and 250; cf. Jonas 1976 I, pp. 135 ff.; Joas 1980, pp. 55 and 219; Hösle 1986; Schönrich 1994, pp. 171 ff.). The 'quasi-transcendental' anthropologism ('Kant with Darwin': Habermas 2003, p. 9) mixes up theoretical questions with practical ones. Habermas misunderstands the 'purity' of Kant's definition of principles as the general absence of an object of inquiry. But there can be no question of such an absence in Kant. At least Habermas still provides reasons for what is due only to negligence in others: failure to take account of reality.

205. Habermas 1973a, pp. 242 f. and 45 ff; Habermas 1996, p. 46; cf. 2.6.4.

206. As in Fichte, love of freedom was taken so far that even theoretical philosophy no longer disposed of any 'nature': in the consensus theory of truth (Habermas 1973b), propositions are 'true' simply by virtue of being unanimously accepted within the scientific community. Kant was concerned with transcendental truth, with the relation to objects as such, whereas Habermas is concerned with the question of empirical truth. For Kant, the latter continued to be a matter of the '*adequatio rei at intellectus*' (Kant 1998, p. 197/A 58). Habermas transcendentalises even the empirical (although he later qualifies this somewhat; cf. Habermas 2003, pp. 8 f.). Objects are absent even from his 'weak naturalism' (Habermas 2003, pp. 22, 219 f.); it merely adopts a different procedure (the socio-evolutionary 'learning' of cognitive anthropology).

in accordance with it.[207] In retrospect, the 'ideal communicative community' and 'discourse without domination' reveal themselves to be the somewhat exalted precursors of the later 'democratic procedure',[208] except that the latter leaves nothing to be realised. Theory becomes hermetic – and ideological. As accurate as some of the descriptions provided within this model are, it does not pass muster as a 'critical theory of society'. For society itself is hardly theorised within it. Let us now consider law one more time.

3.1.6 Key elements of Marxian theory IX: Marx and law

> The materialist determination of cultural traits is only possible if it is mediated through the *total social process*.[209]

Between Facts and Norms inaugurated a new theoretical fashion. Later theories were oriented primarily toward legal discourse (the most recent example being that of Honneth).[210] These theories all followed the same pattern, that of exposing the normative implications of various concepts. Such concepts are of little use, however, except when it comes to formulating normative *evaluations*. Even jurisdiction involves more empirical information than this 'juridically focused' social philosophy.[211] Before a verdict is reached, evidence and witnesses need to be presented, and there is the controlling instance of the jury. In Germany, however, a lack of empirical data has seldom hindered the development of philosophical systems. Thus the third generation of Frankfurt School theorists placed greater emphasis on 'normative foundations':[212] it discussed 'radical democracy',

---

207. This is the maximum claim to be derived from Habermas's propositions. It is, however, never formulated, for it amounts to an idealisation (one that is at least deliberate): citizens are autonomous not because they themselves author the law, but because they 'may ... understand themselves' as authoring it (Habermas 1996, p. 33; on the concept of the 'author', see *MEGA* I.6, p. 179). A law is just when all those affected by it can be thought of as approving it. They need do no more than imagine that they might be in a position to do so. Ultimately, it is enough for the 'authors' of such transcendental deductions to imagine that the subjects can imagine this. 'Just those action norms are valid to which all possibly affected persons could agree as participants in rational discourses' (Habermas 1996, p. 107). When would this be the case? *Quis iudicat?* Compared to the limits on freedom that present themselves as 'acknowledgements of necessity', this reduction has the potential to be even more ideological, since it describes necessity (that of 'coercible laws': p. 31) as freedom. Habermas defends himself against the accusation of idealism (Habermas 1999b, pp. 335 ff.), but the common sense of 'substantive reasons' (Habermas 1996a, pp. 1507) that he suddenly invokes contradicts his basic assumptions. 'There is still much work to be done in this area' (Habermas 1996a, pp. 1518). Habermas's most recent critique of his own theoretical foundations goes quite far (Habermas 1996a, pp. 1507 and 1517; Habermas 2003, pp. 8 f. and 239 f.; Habermas 2000, pp. 12 ff.). What, however, does this entail for his more recent theories?

208. Habermas 1996, pp. 301 ff.

209. Adorno to Benjamin, 10 November 1938.

210. Honneth 2010.

211. Böhm 1998, p. 45.

212. Philosophical 'groundings' are typically German. The following witticism is attributed to Richard Bernstein: 'The Germans are always obsessed with "the ground"'.

'recognition', 'double recognition', 'mutual respect', 'tolerance', law, human rights, justice (3.2) and other, similarly desirable things.[213]

Some of the reasons for this were no doubt endogenous, such as the popularity of John Rawls's social philosophy and of communitarianism; the two engaged in a dispute about these same foundations.[214] But this popularity is itself in need of explanation. Perhaps German theorists sensed that legal achievements would be subject to a process of erosion. But the general tone of the works published during the period was also informed by the neoliberal spirit of the East German *Gründerzeit*. When Honneth[215] continued his moral 'critique of power', this was reminiscent of the call for tax cuts, and when Joas praised the 'creativity of action',[216] one could have been forgiven for thinking he was handing out credit to entrepreneurs.

The procedure of looking to law for orientation is nothing new (one need think only of Kant's 'court of justice for all controversies of pure reason').[217] Yet law-oriented social theory was less interested in the procedures by which evidence is assessed than in 'normativity' as such. This focus on 'validity' is a legacy of neo-Kantianism. Now, law *can* be understood as a normative representation of society – it considers social relations from the perspective of their legal relevance. The normativistic social theory that has developed on the basis of Habermas's work is so fascinated by this perspective that it seldom pauses to recall its specifically juridical *background* and grammar. Thus the term 'recognition', which Honneth places such high hopes in,[218] is taken from the legal sphere. There, it means little more than that the law *presupposes* individuals 'recognising' one another as legal subjects. This assumption is also made when individuals act in ways that run contrary to such recognition. When it is recalled that this is the function performed by 'recognition' within the legal language game, trying to 'realise' recognition begins to look like a futile undertaking. It always already *is* real ('intersubjective social relations ... always already guarantee a minimal normative consensus in advance'),[219] since it is one of the basic rules governing entry to the legal game. Discourse theory ontologises these rules, such that society now appears to *actually* rest on its members mutually recognising one another, in an act that is situated nowhere. If they happen to overlook a few details, such as recognising 'the Other', critical theory will step in to make up for this. This may be laudable in certain situations; the question is what it does to theory.

213. Habermas 1996, p. xliii; Honneth 1996, Wingert 1993, pp. 190 ff.; Gosepath 1999, Brunkhorst 1999a, Forst 2000.

214. Honneth 1999a, p. 282.

215. Honneth 1996.

216. Joas 1996.

217. Kant 1998, p. 649/A 75.

218. Honneth 1996; cf. 3.2.4.

219. Honneth 1996, p. 42.

It seems as if legal fictions already labelled idealist by Marx were being transferred to social theory without anyone noticing.[220]

In their dissertation theses, Andrea Maihofer[221] and Andreas Böhm[222] have examined Marx's conception of the role of law in greater detail.[223] They break with conventional critiques both of Marx *and* of various Marxisms by representing this conception as follows: Marx defines law as a specific sphere consisting of various legal discourses; this sphere is not *independent*, and it only depends on the economy in the last instance. This conception makes it prohibitive to think of law as being monocausally dependent on *single* elements such as the commodity form, exchange, production or specific ruling interests. Conventional legal theory was justified in rejecting this sort of reductive view, found within *Marxist* theories of law.[224] But it threw the baby out with the bath water. Marx's position constitutes an alternative to *both* positions, reductionism and normativism.[225] How should this be understood?

On Marx's view, law is bound up with social relations in their entirety. These relations encompass not just the economic sphere (which involves more than merely exchange 'as such' and production 'as such')[226] but also other cultural areas. Law reacts to changes within the economic sphere (witness patent law or cartel law), but it also reacts to changes within its own sphere[227] or within the cultural sphere (that of morality, religion, art or philosophy). These domains should not, however, be misinterpreted as self-sufficiently closed-off subsystems; they should rather be understood in terms of

220. 'But society is not founded upon the law; that is a legal fiction'. The 'Code Napoleon ... has not created modern bourgeois society. On the contrary, bourgeois society, which emerged in the eighteenth century ..., merely finds its legal expression in this Code' (*MECW* 8, p. 327). 'For him the law is first, and then comes commerce; in reality it is the other way round: first there is *commerce*, and then a *legal system* develops out of it' (*MECW* 24, p. 553).

221. Maihofer 1992.

222. Böhm 1998.

223. For other German works, see Renner 1965, Negt 1995, C. Schefold 1970, Rottleuthner 1975, Mückenberger 1976, Steigerwald 1977, Tohidipur 1978, H. Holz 1987, Klenner 1987, Maus 1986 and Harms 2000; for non-German works, see Wolff 1971, Tigar 1977, A. Hunt 1981, Spitzer 1983, Stone 1985, Ghai 1987, Kryzier 1990, C. Varga 1993, Czarnuta 1994 and Rokumotom 1994.

224. Maihofer formulates critiques of Pashukanis 1983, Negt 1975 and Poulantzas 1979.

225. By normativism, I mean theories that assume the law to be wholly independent of other areas of society. This includes systems-theoretical as well as discourse-analytical theories. The latter concord with systems theory in assuming that law is independent by virtue of its differentiation, although they simultaneously attribute to it the effect of regulating society (hence 'normativism'). Thus, to understand norms is to understand the society that is organised in accordance with them. Parsons represents an intermediary between these two forms of normativism.

226. Maihofer 1992, p. 150.

227. Law also has a specific temporality (Maihofer 1992, pp. 160 ff.). 'Every ideology, however, once it has arisen, develops in connection with the given concept-material, and develops this material further; otherwise, it would not be an ideology, that is, occupation with thoughts as with independent entities' (*MECW* 26, p. 394).

their *specific* relationships to the economic sphere. They have themselves already been influenced by the *mode* of production.[228]

In describing these interrelationships, Marx does not make use of mechanical metaphors, as if the economy 'generated' its superstructure;[229] rather, the metaphors he uses are organic: the economy is the 'source' or the 'ground' of law, much as a tree springs from the soil. If one regards the economy as society's 'metabolism', then the development of individual organs is by no means predetermined, although the *range of possibilities* is limited (2.1.5, 2.1.6, 4.3.2), in the sense in which one speaks of a person's physical 'constitution'.[230] Moreover, law is not mere ideology; it is itself a practice, specifically one that is concerned with regulating other practices and/or with ensuring their *self*-regulation. Since it refers to these *other* practices from the outset and is also historically subsequent to them, it can neither be elevated to the status of a constitutive force, nor reductively conceptualised as 'mere semblance'.

> To Marx, the notions found within the philosophy of law are by no means 'nothing but the idealised market' [Pashukanis]... They are – and this is what is lost sight of from the perspective of the *critique* of ideology – historically determined reflexive elaborations of social relations and forms of consciousness, and hence descriptions of how social relations are lived, conceptualised and experienced as legal relations... Not only do traditional conceptions of law accord with social relations; they are the way in which a society's legal relations are *lived*![231]

Critical theory's basic assumption, namely that bourgeois norms are the touchstone by which to assess bourgeois social relations, does not accord with Marx's theoretical intentions. For legal relations are *themselves* nothing other than social relations; they are simply social relations taken to 'a higher level', as Marx says, citing Schelling.[232]

---

228. The letters of the late Engels (*MECW* 49, pp. 33 ff.) confirm Marx's early writings (*MECW* 5, pp. 51 f.; Röhrich 1980, pp. 56 ff.). If normative social theory rejects this as 'objectivist', it should take a look at disciplines such as history, ethnology, historical anthropology or political geography; there it will find not just overwhelming evidence, but also an interdisciplinary consensus (cf. Tigar/Levy 1978 and Reuber 2001). The claim is quite basic: in forms of society based on agriculture, one will tend to encounter laws that concern the cultivation of land (for example, agrarian laws were hotly contested in Rome), whereas nomadic peoples have other matters to put in order, for which reason they develop other legal forms and contents. Once women had been drawn into military production, their legal emancipation was hardly to be avoided. The influence of the pill on sexual morality is well known. The list could be extended.

229. This would be a mere reversal of the genetic idealism practised by value-form analysis (2.5.7). Such distortions account for the accusation that Marx is a 'philosopher of consciousness'.

230. Simmel's metaphor of the rose blossoming on the dunghill (Rentsch 2000, p. 196) is not a valid objection to Marx. Aside from the fact that dung is an excellent fertiliser, the influence of climate and natural conditions on a culture has been a topic of social theory since Montesquieu and Herder, and it would be odd to backtrack on this. It certainly makes a difference to the rose whether or not the dung has been chemically or radioactively polluted (cf. the example of the cherry-tree: *MECW* 5, p. 39).

231. Maihofer 1992, pp. 198 f.

232. *MECW* 28, p. 176.

Marx accorded such importance to Hegel's dialectic because it was capable of 'representing' these relations, capturing the way two realms of being may be distinct and yet identical, in a unity of opposites. Habermas, by contrast, is a philosopher of identity in the *Fichtean* sense: form affects content; identity is unmediated. In Habermas, it seems as if society represented itself within law, as if 'social integration' did not merely occur within, but *by means of* law. Thus Marx takes law more seriously than the normativists: it is because law disposes of its own logic and its own temporality that translating social relations into legal terms involves a displacement. Something non-identical remains; not everything can be taken to a higher power; the 'content' that is given a certain 'form' does not remain unaltered (2.5.7).[233] Freedom and equality, the essence of law, are given a far more substantive grounding by Marx than by normativism: Marx considers them both within the context of their *historical* development during the emancipation of the bourgeoisie and in terms of their synchronic, constantly renewed groundedness in a *material* social practice.[234] It is because he pays attention to how law rests on social practice that Marx is able to make critical statements about the purview of law.

For example, law is not capable of 'doing justice' to what has not been subsumed under it. In describing this, Marx resorts to metaphors of 'form' and 'content'.[235] Under capitalism, the specific feature of the content antecedent to the form of law is to be

---

233. Habermas 2003, p. 260, claims the opposite. This is one difference between Marx and Adorno: Marx also speaks of the 'non-identical', but in his theory, it can be clearly identified, and it does not necessitate an abandonment of reason or law in favour of aestheticist 'mimesis'. Lohmann 1991 uses Simmel and Adorno to reduce Marx's theory to an analysis of exchange. The very essence of Marx's theory of law, namely its tendency to inquire into what lies beyond a given set of laws, is described by him as the 'collapse of critique' (Lohmann 1991, pp. 26, 278 ff.). But then what is critique supposed to be? If Lohmann were right, critique would only be possible as legal critique – the critique of law would be impossible (cf. Reiman 1991).

234. 'In normative philosophies, law is what guarantees the link [between freedom and reason], whereas in Marx, the forces of production and the relations of production become the most important bearers of universality, and it is upon them that the link between freedom and reason rests' (Böhm 1998, p. 106). 'Thus, if the economic form, exchange, in every respect posits the equality of the subjects, the content, the material... which impels them to exchange posits *freedom*. Hence equality and freedom are not only respected in exchange... but the exchange of exchange values is the real productive basis of all *equality* and *freedom*. As pure ideas, equality and freedom are merely idealised expressions of this exchange; developed in juridical, political and social relations, they are merely this basis at a higher level' (*MECW* 28, p. 176). '[R]egulation and order are themselves indispensable elements of any mode of production, if it is to assume social stability and independence from mere chance and arbitrariness. These are precisely the form of its social stability and therefore its relative freedom from mere arbitrariness and mere chance. Under backward conditions of the production process as well as the corresponding social relations, it achieves this form by mere repetition of their very reproduction. If this has continued on for some time, it entrenches itself as custom and tradition and is finally sanctioned as an explicit law' (*MECW* 37, pp. 779 f.; *MECW* 5, pp. 89 f.; *MECW* 35, pp. 94 f. and 185 f).

235. 'This *actual* relation, which only arises through and in the exchange, is later given *legal form* in the contract, etc.; but this form neither creates its content, the exchange, nor the *relationship between the persons inherent in it*, but vice versa' (*MECW* 24, pp. 553 f.). 'The juristic forms... cannot, being mere forms, determine this content' (*MECW* 37, pp. 337 f.). 'It is this economic relation that determines the subject-matter comprised in each such juridical act' (*MECW* 35, pp. 95).

found not in the sphere of distribution but in that of production. The exploitation that occurs there, an exploitation that is subject to ongoing expanded reproduction, does *not* enter into bourgeois law and the legal ideas derived from it,[236] nor do the consequences of exploitation do so (3.2.3). In fact, bourgeois law cannot be informed by them, since its purpose is precisely that of liberating economic subjects. A comprehensive normative 'regulation' would be incompatible with the principle of legal equality; it would therefore entail the dissolution of bourgeois law.[237] Thus the 'contents' of the sphere of production remain invisible for as long as one interprets it juridically (on the model of the exchange of equivalents).[238] Yet as soon as exchange value and use value are distinguished, it can be seen that there exists a commodity within which the two do not coincide, namely labour-power.[239] On Marx's view, theories that are incapable of taking this step are apologetic. For the crux of the matter is that

> in monetary relationships simply conceived, all immanent contradictions in bourgeois society appear to be extinguished. Bourgeois democracy therefore falls back on this in its apologetics for existing economic relationships.[240]

> Hence, we may understand the decisive importance of the transformation of value and price of labour-power into the form of wages, or into the value and price of labour itself. This phenomenal form, which makes the actual relation invisible, and, indeed, shows the direct opposite of that relation, forms the basis of all the juridical notions of both labourer and capitalist, of all the mystifications of the capitalistic mode of production, of all its illusions as to liberty, of all the apologetic shifts of the vulgar economists.[241]

A theory of society that wants to be something *more* than an apology must therefore at some point go beyond the perspective of exchange (as important as that perspective is). For it is only on 'leaving this sphere of... exchange of commodities, which furnishes the 'Free-trader Vulgaris' with his views and ideas, and with the [normative; C.H.] standard

---

236. 'Capital is concentrated social force, while the workman has only to dispose of his working force. The *contract* between capital and labour can therefore never be struck on equitable terms' (*MECW* 20, p. 191); it is 'a hiding' (*MECW* 35, p. 186). Improvements in the standard of living are due not so much to 'social rights' issued from above (Marshall 1963) than to enormous increases in productivity and to the struggles over distribution waged by the workers' movement (2.1.1, 2.4.1). Rights were a subsequent expression of this and an attempt to render one's achievements permanent, to institutionalise them (Luhmann 1972).

237. Kambartel follows Silvio Gesell in advocating the abolition of interest (Kambartel 1998, p. 20; cf. 3.3.2; 2.3.5), and he misinterprets the 'rate of profit' in a politicised and de-economised way (2.2.6), describing it as a 'social variable that is determined in particular by the policies of central banks' (p. 55). The measures he proposes are dissolved within this (cf. 4.4).

238. Habermas 1984–7, Vol. II, p. 257.

239. 'The ever repeated purchase and sale of labour-power is now the mere form; what really takes place is this – the capitalist again and again appropriates, without equivalent, a portion of the previously materialised labour of others, and exchanges it for a greater quantity of living labour' (*MECW* 35, pp. 582 f.).

240. *MECW* 28, p. 172.

241. *MECW* 35, p. 540.

by which he judges a society..., [that]...we can perceive a change in the physiognomy of our *dramatis personae*'.[242]

As late as the 1990s, Habermas felt compelled to set himself off from Marx.[243] In fact, he had to do this, for if it should be the case that Marx's theory is valid in the present, then some of the most important basic assumptions made by Habermas would 'no longer' hold true – specifically, that class antagonism has been abolished by the welfare state, that the key political problem is that of protecting citizens from state intervention and that juridical and moral norms can be the basis of a theory of society. When Habermas's theories are topologically situated within social reality, they are seen to suffer from the same loss of the theoretical object that already characterised the older German sociology and social philosophy (2.4–2.6). In making his social philosophy a normative one, Habermas performs an operation similar to that performed by his sociological and socio-philosophical precursors: he declares real structures to be the epiphenomena of a more basic, 'mental' cause (the intentions of speaking subjects). The difference vis-à-vis older versions is that it is no longer particular mental contents but 'universal normative contents' that are thought of as generative. By virtue of its underdetermination as a self-sufficient system, the base was blanked out for decades – until it too was conceived of as 'spirit of their spirit':[244] systemic structures were eventually thought of as sediments of normativity. This amounted to a return of the oxymoron 'objective mind' (4.2.6).[245] Real problems of the present, whose roots are largely economic under global capitalism,[246] are hardly to be grasped from such a perspective.

One reason for Habermas's theoretical development would seem to lie in his reductive reception of Marx. He adopted unfortunate interpretations of Marx, characterised by (a) a neoclassical understanding of the economy that is oriented to the market as the site of exchange, thereby already failing to grasp these interrelationships on the economic level (2.3.1); (b) a reverse idealist conception of law as a 'generated' product of the economy (cf. 2.5.7) that prompted an excessively normativistic countermovement, within which the interrelatedness of law and the economy was overlooked; and finally (c) a tendency to relativise Marx by regarding his theories as relevant to the nineteenth century only, thereby allowing the newly declared primacy of politics to attribute excessive influence to law (qua 'medium of control'). This ultimately created the appearance

242. *MECW* 35, p. 186.

243. Habermas makes use of arguments developed by Popper, Arendt and Löwith (Habermas 1996, pp. 47 f. and 478 f.; Habermas 2003, pp. 256 ff.; cf. 2.6): history cannot be predicted, and a planned society would be totalitarian. He even makes use again of one of his earliest concepts: 'control' ['*Verfügung*'] (Habermas 1996, p. 552; cf. Habermas 1954 and Kreulartz 1995, pp. 35 f.).

244. *MECW* 5, pp. 51 f., 57 f., 107 f.

245. In the end, norms and organisations 'issue from' from law (Habermas 1996, p. 153; cf. p. 25), much as 'institutions' were previously produced by communication (Habermas 1987, p. 283).

246. Sassen 1988.

that the *form* of law, and the newly formalised reflections upon this form, no longer needed to be confronted with the content of law.

Habermas channelled critical theory's old dilemma through various sets of categories until it disappeared as a problem, because articulating criticisms of it became virtually impossible. But it was only critical theory that had difficulty grounding its moral demands, because it failed to adequately grasp Marx's object of inquiry, bourgeois society; critical theory issued its invectives without bothering to provide them with any normal scientific basis. Instead of going back behind critical theory to Marx, Habermas attempted to make social criticism accord with whatever theory of reality happened to be topical at the time, notwithstanding the fact that these theories were themselves problematic. He attempted to *reformulate* the problem in anthropological, epistemological, rationality-theoretical, moral-philosophical and eventually legal-theoretical terms. But content cannot be given a different form without being altered, and so Habermas's project ended up – by the time he formulated his 'philosophy of law', at the latest – as an apology that is hardly second to Hegel's. Let us now consider the second normative socio-philosophical supertheory.

3.2 John Rawls or the apotheosis of ignorance

> One can see that there is no interest in investigating the real causes of objects. All that matters is the tranquility of the explaining subject.[247]

The normativism evident in the Habermas school has been identified and criticised as a juridical social philosophy. The same can be done for the philosophy that was a *second* major subject of debate during the 1990s: John Rawls's theory of justice. It, too, refers primarily to law,[248] although its perspective on law differs from that of Habermas in two ways. First, Rawls sets out to consider law not in a reductively normative way, but from within legal reality itself.[249] Second, he focuses not on the legitimating advantages of law,

247. *MECW* 1, p. 45.

248. Terminologically, 'justice' is essentially a standard used within codified and case law (Kelsen 1960, 1985, Rüthers 1991, Wesel 2003). Rawls treats the concept as a model of sociability in its entirety.

249. Habermas accuses Rawls of not doing justice to 'reality' ('social facticity', or the 'base' [!]: Habermas 1992a, pp. 89 f.). To Habermas, the latter is represented by systems theory (Habermas 1992a, p. 88), which is really quite far removed from reality. To Rawls, 'the primary subject of justice is the basic structure of society, or more exactly, the way in which the major social institutions distribute fundamental rights and duties and determine the division of advantages from social cooperation' (Rawls 1971, p. 6; cf. p. 47; see also Steinvorth 1998 and issue no. 2, 2003, of *Deutsche Zeitschrift für Philosophie*).

but on its structurally immanent disadvantages, which need to be minimised.[250] Rawls does not examine the internal structure of normativity, nor does he seek a justification for it; rather, he is interested in the features that *institutions* need to display in order to bring about greater social justice. This is what he declares, in any case. The question is whether he comes closer to social reality than Habermas.[251] Common criticisms of Rawls have focused on his guiding conceptions of normativity (the discourse-ethical criticism) and on the notion of man presupposed by him (the communitarian criticism). Yet what is more problematic is Rawls's idea of *reality*. 'By major institutions I understand the political constitution and the principal economic and social arrangements'.[252] It is difficult to say something about social reality, or even to criticise it, on the basis of a few condensed ethical 'principles'.[253] To derive normative contents from the 'basic structure'[254] of social reality while deriving this reality itself from the 'constitution' is circular reasoning. Moreover, one's assessment of 'economic and social arrangements' will differ depending on how closely one examines social reality. Rawls relies uncritically on the claims of neoclassical economics (3.2.1). It seems he is concerned, like Habermas, with legitimating existing 'structures'.[255] But the legitimation could just as well be used to justify the 'basic structures' of far worse societies (3.2.2). Rawls's concept has nonetheless strongly determined the development of the debate. The reactive and temporarily quite influential current that is communitarianism can hardly be understood without reference to Rawls's *Theory of Justice* (3.2.3).

3.2.1 *John Rawls as a neoclassical theorist*

Rawls's two 'principles of justice' state the conditions that he believes a 'well-ordered society'[256] must satisfy:

(1) 'each person is to have an equal right to the most extensive scheme of equal basic liberties compatible with a similar scheme of liberties for others',[257] and

---

250. 'In this way the institutions of society favor certain starting places over others. These are especially deep inequalities.... It is these inequalities, presumably inevitable..., to which the principles of social justice must... apply' (Rawls 1971, p. 7). 'Habermas wrongly defines the relationship between normative politically theory and descriptive sociological theory. He is interested in the conditions that promote the realisation of norms, yet what requires attention are the conditions that hinder such realisation' (Steinvorth 1999, p. 77).

251. The changes made by Rawls (1993, 2003) concern the justification of his hypotheses, not the hypotheses themselves. Since they are what is at issue, I will focus on the 1971 original.

252. Rawls 1971, p. 6.

253. Rawls 1971, pp. 47 ff.

254. Rawls 1971, p. 8.

255. 'Many of the traditional activities of government, insofar as they can be justified, can be accounted for in this way' (p. 236; cf. pp. 6 f., 15, 506 ff.).

256. Rawls 1971, p. 8.

257. Rawls 1971, p. 53; cf. pp. 220, 53.

(2) 'social and economic inequalities are to be arranged so that they are both (a) reasonably expected to be to everyone's advantage, and (b) attached to positions and offices open to all'.[258]

These principles contradict one another: either there is equality – of rights, liberties, basic assets or whatever – or there is not.[259] The exposition of a contradiction from which everything further develops could be intended as a 'dialectical' move.[260] But this is not at all what Rawls has in mind. He simply presupposes that these principles *hold true* (Plato's hypothetical method) and asks what must be the case for them to be *effective* as well.

According to Rawls, these principles can be interpreted in various ways. He distinguishes between: (a) a Manchesterist interpretation,[261] on which 'everyone's advantage' is understood as a utilitarian optimal aggregate utility that is 'open to all', the principle of merit being applied under the given social circumstances; (b) an ordoliberal variant,[262] in which an effort is made to minimise the socially determined inequalities in people's starting conditions; (c) a genetocratic interpretation that involves the 'natural' differences between people being used to everyone's advantage; and (d) a 'democratic' variant, in which natural differences are compensated for.[263] Rawls 'chooses' this last option. His choice is value-dependent; he offers no more than a conditional justification for it and it is by no means a necessary choice.[264] What is decisive for this choice (Nozick and Buchanan would prefer the first option, while others would prefer egalitarianism) is the way reality is grasped conceptually. How does it inform Rawls's account of justice?

---

258. Rawls 1971, p. 53; cf. pp. 72 f., 266 f.

259. 'The principle of liberty may also be called the principle of unconditional equality, because it guarantees everyone unconditional equality within the basic liberties, and the principle of equality may also be called the principle of conditional inequality, because it allows for social inequalities on one condition' (Steinvorth 1999, p. 100).

260. Thus the second principle, which qualifies the first, but is also subject to qualification itself, may be understood as a 'negation of the negation'. This could also be read as a representation of the 'contradiction' between the state and society.

261. Rawls 1971, pp. 87 f.

262. Rawls 1971, p. 93.

263. Rawls 1971, p. 95.

264. His choice is only valid, Rawls argues, 'once we try to find a rendering ... which treats everyone equally as a moral person, and which does not weight men's share in the benefits of burdens of social cooperation according to their social fortune or their luck in the natural lottery' (Rawls 1971, p. 65). In light of the fact that he is formulating a 'theory of justice', it is difficult to see how Rawls can get away with presenting these central assumptions as 'preliminary remarks', without any further justification. This is the only variant with social democratic features: 'Justice is prior to efficiency and requires some changes that are not efficient in this sense [that of Pareto optimality]' (Rawls 1971, p. 69). But material circumstances remain marginal. Rawls continued working on this typology, although he did not himself publish the results (Pogge 1994, p. 131). A compensation of natural inequalities (e.g. an hourly wage that is inversely proportional to one's degree of professional training) can only be effected by a strong state, which thereby violates the private sphere, both conceptually and legally. Habermas, Nozick *and* Sandel object to this (Forst 2002, pp. 14 f.).

According to Rawls, 'ethical principles depend on general facts'.[265] The core of his theory is contained within this formulation: ethical principles do not express an *a priori* 'fact of reason', as in Kant, but they are not based on concrete apperception either, as in the Scottish moral philosophers;[266] they occupy an *intermediate* position. This can only mean that Rawls means to base his principles on a *theory*, for it is only theories that deal with 'general facts'. And it is a specific theory that he bases his principles on.[267] There are numerous indications of this: his choice to examine social justice by engaging only with the 'basic structure'[268] is partisan in the sense that it favours a certain theoretical paradigm. Neoclassical theory and neoliberalism always objected to socialism and Keynesianism that state-issued precepts should be limited to the 'basic structure', so as to preserve the liberty of citizens, which would otherwise be at risk.[269]

The second principle involves the assumption[270] that social inequalities turn out to be to everyone's advantage by resulting in greater productivity. This assumption is also one of the basic elements of neoclassical theory, even if Rawls attempts to introduce an egalitarian perspective by means of his 'maximin criterion' (distributive relations are to be assessed not in terms of their aggregate utility but in terms of the improvements they entail for those who are worst off). Thus justice is understood in utilitarian terms, just as in neoclassical theory:

> The second problem, then, is to select from among the procedural arrangements that are both just and feasible those which are most likely to lead to a just and effective legal order. Once again this is Bentham's problem of the artificial identification of interests [!], only here the rules (just procedure) are to be framed to give legislation (just outcome) likely to accord with the principles of justice rather than the principle of utility.[271]

---

265. Rawls 1971, p. 234.
266. Rawls 1971, p. 40.
267. Rawls hints at his dependence on a specific theory: 'The various conceptions of justice are the outgrowth of different notions of society.... Fully to understand a conception of justice we must make explicit the conception of social cooperation from which it derives' (Rawls 1971, p. 9; cf. Pogge 1994, pp. 129 ff.). This is just what we are doing.
268. Rawls 1971, p. 8; Rawls 1977, pp. 159 ff.
269. For a popular version of this criticism, see Milton Friedman 1962, p. 200: 'The central defects of these measures [governmental reforms; C.H.] is that they seek through government to force people against their own immediate interest in order to promote a supposedly general interest [this is already the structure of the later communitarian critique of Rawls]. They seek to resolve what is supposedly a conflict of interest... not by establishing a framework [sic!] that will eliminate the conflict, but by forcing people to act against their own interest' (p. 200); for a German counterpart to this approach, see W. Eucken 1965, among others (cf. 3.3.4).
270. Rawls 1971, p. 53.
271. Rawls 1971, p. 173.

Marx situated utilitarianism within capitalism's core ideological framework.[272] Rawls holds 'that the principles of justice may serve as part of a doctrine of political economy'.[273] This is indeed what they are within his work. He derives them tautologically from a theory that is presupposed by him.[274] The economic literature he refers to is clearly based on the neoclassical paradigm (he cites Arrow, Buchanan, Edgeworth, Jevons, Olson, Pareto, Sen, and so on). His indebtedness to this paradigm is betrayed by his very use of such words and expressions as 'market', 'equilibrium' and 'perfect competition'. Rawls himself hints at the origins of his theory: 'we have to ascertain which principles it would be rational to adopt given the contractual situation. This connects the theory of justice with the theory of rational choice'.[275]

The theory of rational choice (also known as the theory of collective, social or public choice)[276] is a sociological generalisation of the basic neoclassical assumption of utility-maximising individuals. Another fundamental model assumption of neoclassical economics, 'perfect competition' (cf. 2.3.3), serves Rawls as 'an ideal scheme which shows how the principles of justice might be realized'.[277] Neoclassical theory had essentially already done Rawls's work for him: rational choice theories had been used to conceptualise a 'just' state, namely one based on the principles of neoclassical economics. Rawls merely laments the fact that these theories neglect issues of justice in favour of efficiency issues.[278] He means to make up for this *without* making any serious changes to the basic paradigmatic assumptions.[279] In his theory, the social order continues to be decided on by individuals who act in accordance with their interests. The only difference concerns his *construal* of the decisional context: There are some things individuals do not know, but they do have an additional 'sense', namely that of justice.[280] The basic assumptions are retained. Rawls's work needs therefore to be seen as a philosophical explication of the fundamental fictions guiding neoclassical theory. It is only when his theory is

---

272. 'Freedom, Equality, Property and Bentham': *MECW* 35, p. 186; cf. *MECW* 5, pp. 408 ff.

273. Rawls 1971, p. 228.

274. Höffe perceived this tautology without being able to identify its origins: 'There is a sense in which Rawls's principles of justice are tautological. For they are nothing more than an explication of the rational attributes that inform his earlier definition of the original position' (Höffe 1979, p. 187). Rawls was not the first theorist to proceed in this way.

275. Rawls 1971, pp. 15 f.; cf. pp. 129 f., 229 f.

276. For classic formulations, see Neumann 1944, Arrow 1951, Downs 1957, Buchanan 1962 and 1968, Baumol 1965 or Sen 1970. Ever new variants of these approaches continue to be discussed today (Becker 1976, Behrens 1986, Pies 2000).

277. Rawls 1971, p. 272.

278. Rawls 1971, pp. 19 ff.

279. Rawls does not reject these works; he means to expand on them. 'Thus despite certain resemblances between markets and elections, the ideal market process and the ideal legislative procedure are different in crucial respects.... So far at least there does not exist a theory of just constitutions as procedures leading to just legislation which corresponds to the theory of competitive markets as procedures resulting in efficiency' (Rawls 1971, pp. 316 f.).

280. Rawls 1971, pp. 41, 274 f.

thus interpreted that otherwise puzzling features of it become surprisingly meaningful. The theoretical model of neoclassical economics interpreted the economy as a grand exchange (2.3.1). *Within this model,* all participants are 'equal' – that is, they are individuals who are concerned with their utility and exchange their commodities on the market. They are also 'free', since they act out of purely economic motives, without political or other outside influences. For want of external impediments, there will result an 'equilibrium' of supply and demand, which determines prices. This 'procedure' and its result are 'just' because all participants are treated equally (whoever has money can use it to purchase commodities, regardless of whether they are black or white), and the result can be interpreted as 'democratic' (by definition, no one is cheated within exchange).

Neoclassical theory and procedural justice share the same paradigm, that of 'equal exchange'; they merely emphasise different aspects of it.[281] But as an account of the *entire* economy, this model suffers from several weaknesses. To cite only the most obvious: it ignores not just the sphere of production, its specific relations and developmental tendencies, but also competition and its effects.[282] Rawls models not just the entire economy on the paradigm of equal exchange, but the social totality as well. His indebtedness to the paradigm is already evident in the definition he gives to the object under examination. Rawls posits 'cooperation' as the basic mode of sociation.[283] While this is more realistic than Habermas' 'consensus', it still does not do justice to social reality. Instead, it ontologises theoretical assumptions, albeit not those of legal theory (as in Habermas), but those inherent in the ideologically reductive models of neoclassical economics.[284] Rawls assumes that 'satisfaction of needs' is the economic motive driving cooperative societies. To Marx, the owners of capital were the relevant units of capitalist economic motivation; they are concerned, of necessity, not with satisfying society's needs but with obtaining ever greater profit.[285] The problems that the political controversy on justice seeks to address arise from the conflict between private appropriation and the satisfaction of social needs (or between private appropriation and all those who

281. Rawls uses this market model affirmatively (1971, pp. 239 ff., especially p. 242). This dependence is still evident in Höffe, although in his work, it appears in a specifically German guise: Höffe speaks of 'transcendental exchange' (Höffe 1998; cf. Höffe 1991).

282. 'Perfect competition' (Rawls 1971, p. 240; see above) is precisely the absence of competition: all suppliers passively accept market prices and none of them engage in cost-saving investment (cf. 2.2.6, 2.3.3).

283. Rawls assumes that 'society' is a 'self-sufficient association of persons who in their relations to one another recognize certain rules of conduct as binding'; 'these rules specify a system of cooperation designed to advance the good of those taking part in it. Then ... society is a cooperative venture for mutual advantage' (Rawls 1971, p. 4). On the deep-seated notions of equal exchange evident in the concept of 'cooperation', see Axelrod 1984, Honneth 1999a (on Dewey).

284. After all, Rawls is aiming for an even 'higher level of abstraction' (1971, p. 10) than that found in Locke, Rousseau and Kant.

285. The distinction between economic motives is not an isolated psychological, but a social (structurally functional) distinction. On 'economic styles', see Sombart 1912, Müller-Armack 1938, Schefold 1993.

dispose of no productive assets, between the owners of capital as *human beings* and the community as such). Rawls blanks out this problem even on the level of premises.[286]

As a model-oriented theory, neoclassical economics is especially concerned with consistency: in and of themselves, its mathematical models are in no way connected to any economic reality.[287] Rawls constructs a four-stage sequence that corresponds precisely to the way such a theory is applied to reality. The 'original position'[288] corresponds to the first stage of theory, that of the model: in it, the parties know only 'particular facts'; they are familiar with everyday observations, but they know nothing about their own position. They are however also familiar with 'the first principles of social theory'.[289] This unmediated juxtaposition of particular *and* general knowledge, without any knowledge of anything specific, can hardly be understood on its own terms. Marx held that human interests are bound up with the immediate reality of everyday life.[290] In Rawls, knowledge about particulars is accompanied by familiarity with an abstract theory that has nothing to do with those particulars. The theory has not been developed by reference to empirical data; it has been developed 'aprioristically' (it is an 'ideal scheme').[291] The notion that the participants can 'know the relevant general facts about their society, that is, its natural circumstances and resources, its level of economic advance and culture, and so on',[292] even though they 'do not know their own social position',[293] suggests that pure spirit hovers above the world and assumes one form or another for contingent reasons only. This odd assumption becomes comprehensible when it is interpreted as reflecting neoclassical theory, which Rawls began studying as a young man.[294] *Its* basic assumptions sidestep empirical reality by diverting attention away from capitalism and toward the putatively timeless 'nature' of economic activity (2.3.1; 2.4.1). Rawls's claims on liberty, equality and justice are already implicit in the assumptions of the neoclassical model.

---

286. 'When one... defines societies as cooperative enterprises that aim at the mutual benefit of all, one is ignoring the very aspect of all hitherto existing societies that prompted complaints about their injustice' (Steinvorth 1999, p. 97). Rawls touches on the 'regulatory framework' only sporadically and with an eye to issues in the theory of distribution (Rawls 1971, p. 272). Marx is only mentioned in passing (pp. 229, 268).

287. On neoclassical theory's Platonism, see 2.3.1. Economists have always confirmed this to me in conversation. 'A conception of justice cannot be deduced from self-evident premises [as in Kant] or conditions on principles [as in Marx]; instead, its justification is a matter of the mutual support of many considerations, of everything fitting together into one coherent view' (Rawls 1971, p. 19).

288. Rawls 1971, pp. 15 ff., 102 ff.

289. Rawls 1971, p. 175.

290. *MECW* 4, pp. 80 f. and elsewhere.

291. Rawls 1971, p. 272.

292. Rawls 1971, pp. 172 f.

293. Rawls 1971, p. 172.

294. Pogge 1994, p. 22.

The determination of the principles of justice, which Rawls treats as occurring in the 'original position', corresponds to the abstract verdicts on reality that are issued on the basis of this aprioristic theory.[295] The principles chosen are stated by Rawls: he fixes the *result* of the deliberative process, even though it is supposed to be a question of 'reconstructing' (Kantian) freedom – a contradiction that discourse theory also suffers from (3.1.3). Rawls is no clairvoyant, equipped with psychic skills that allow him to predict what these oddly constituted individuals would decide in the 'original position'; like the individuals in his model, he takes his principles from the 'socio-scientific theory' of neoclassical economics. The 'veil of ignorance', meant to reconstruct the neutrality of the law, corresponds to neoclassical theory's blanking out of the sphere of production. For it is there that the 'general facts' that remain hidden behind the 'veil of ignorance' are to be found.[296]

The next two stages, those of the drafting of the constitution and of legislation, involve knowledge of such 'general facts about society, such as its size and level of economic advance, its institutional structure and natural environment'.[297] As in neoclassical economics, knowledge of these facts does *not* enter into the social sciences; it is merely used to *apply* and concretise the valuations derived from an abstract theory. For Rawls, it is not specific relations that are just or unjust, but concrete, specific institutions and laws. Rorty would later express the content of such theories in the phrase 'I'm just an American'; in doing so, he was very much speaking in the spirit of Rawls.[298] While Rawls increasingly retracted his universal intentions in his later writings, it was already quite clear in the early and most powerful version of his theory (the 1971 edition of *A Theory of Justice*) that he was thinking of the USA, whose institutions are glorified by means of the alleged universality of his theory. The moment the individuals in the originary position begin to make concrete decisions, the institutions they create resemble those of the

295. Discourse theory also got bogged down in such verdicts. I can use my 'normative schemes' to formulate propositions such as 'slaves are unfree' or 'It is unjust for people in Africa to be starving'. In doing so, I express the common sense of my age, which my theory can only elide at the risk of appearing extremely naive. Rawls has to presuppose morality in his 'sense of justice' (Rawls 1971, p. 397). No theoretical progress is made by proceeding in this way. 'Such a primordial condition explains nothing; it merely pushes the question away into a grey nebulous distance' (*MECW* 3, 271).

296. For this reason, the 'veil of ignorance' would be better described as 'mystification through ignorance' [*genitivus subiectivus*]. Rawls rehashes the value judgement proper to social contract theory. 'Critics of the market such as Marx spoke of an unsconscious process that plays out "behind the backs of the producers", "whose inherent laws impose themselves only as the mean of apparently lawless irregularities that compensate one another", "after the manner of an overpowering natural law"... [*MECW* 35, pp. 116, 112, 490]. Precisely because of its blindness, which disregards people's origins and knows no distinction of person, just like the blindfolded Lady Justice, this phenomenon appeared to Hobbes as that which guarantees the justice of the market' (Steinvorth 1998, p. 317). Yet this is to blur the distinction between economics and politics.

297. Rawls 1971, p. 175.

298. Richard Rorty, oral communication 1985, reported by K.O. Apel, in Blasche 1988, p. 122.

USA down to the smallest detail.[299] *A Theory of Justice* needs therefore to be read as a 'transcendental deduction' of the USA.

3.2.2 *Justifying Stakhanov*

Hennecke, you lead the way![300]

What is unfortunate about such deductions of modern states is not that (differently from what their authors claim) they apply only to specific countries; it is the fact that they are (quasi-)transcendental.[301] A society's real structures are hardly to be grasped from this kind of aprioristic perspective, which deduces everything from first principles and seeks to aprioristically 'construct' even those principles. At best, such an approach allows one to reconstruct the internal structure of a specific society's *self-interpretation*, albeit only from a normative-juridical perspective and only on the basis of certain bold assumptions.[302]

This reconstruction of the normative self-understanding of certain political institutions within American society was the point of attack for communitarianism, which felt itself to not have been properly represented (3.2.3). But the theory also encounters difficulties when one takes seriously the generative pathos of its author and does *not* posit the corresponding society as 'given'. For the principle of difference can also be used to justify altogether different societies. The 'real socialist' states, which were not particularly egalitarian, *also* adhered to this principle, and the most extreme forms of unequal capitalist distribution can just as well be justified by it.[303] On Ulrich Steinvorth's strong

299. Thus, we find in Rawls's theory a constituent assembly (Rawls 1971, pp. 172 f., 194), political parties (p. 120), delegates (pp. 172 f., 197), electors (p. 196), freedom of religion (p. 180 – the USA were forced to 'invent' freedom of religion in 1776 because of the heterogeneous composition of the country's population), freedom of speech (p. 197), cartel laws (p. 240), consumer taxes (p. 246) and the economic and political liberalism that Rawls's critics went on to attack. 'The idea of a four-stage sequence is suggested by the United States Constitution' (p. 172; cf. p. 6 f.).

300. East German proverb.

301. Cf. 3.1.5 on Habermas. 'Deduction' is semantically coextensive with 'foundation' and/or 'justification': in both cases, it is a question of demonstrating the legitimacy of something (Kersting 1997, pp. 121 ff.). The 'constructivism' of moral philosophy resembles an aprioristic philosophy of first principles.

302. The 'social contract' and/or 'discourse' are intended to generate conceptually what the theories of natural and rational law sought to implement in practice. Steinvorth 1999, p. 92, speaks of an 'embarassing misunderstanding'. In fact, and despite the claim to being 'postmetaphysical' (Habermas 1995, Rawls 1971, pp. 187 f.; Rawls 1993: 'political, not metaphysical'), the transcendental philosophy that Kant made use of in a limited and well-considered way (it served him as the basis for criticising hypertrophic expectations with regard to reason) is non-sensically applied to empirical issues (3.1.5). The attempt to take social contract theory 'to a higher level of abstraction' (Rawls 1971, p. 10; cf. Habermas 1976b, pp. 167 f.) eliminates the promising possibilities for differentiation still to be found in Kant; what results is a diffuse 'philosophy of unity' (for a comprehensive discussion, see 2.5.2 and 4.2.5).

303. That inequality is better for everyone was the assumption governing the socialist New Economic Policy (2.2.2), as well as the Stakhanov system and the Soviet activists' movement

reading of this fact, it constitutes a falsification of the theory; on a weaker reading, it at least demonstrates the theory's tremendous elasticity.[304]

Thus we are either dealing with an interpretation of the normative self-understanding of existing institutions. If that is the case, the approach chosen is roundabout and misleading, and its claims to universality are unjustified. Rawls's theoretical rivals, libertarian social contract theorists such as Buchanan and Nozick, are closer to the truth than he is, because they do not resort to fictions, which is to say they adhere more closely to the 'general facts'.[305] Or Rawls's claim to universality is retained. On a weak reading, this means his theory is over-inclusive; on a strong reading, it means it is simply false, because its basic assumptions have repeatedly been falsified. In either case, *A Theory of Justice* becomes ideological. In spite of his egalitarian intentions, Rawls relies on a theory that turns the result and the thrust of his work into its opposite. If he really wanted to improve the rights or the situation of the lower classes, as sometimes appears to have been the case and is often emphasised in defence of Rawls, he would have been better advised to consider the *concrete* situation of those classes: in the USA, if they were what his theory meant to concern itself with, or in the world, if that was what it aimed at.[306] In either case, a theory that means to speak for the 'less favoured',[307] cannot rely on the mechanisms of the market, since the market is precisely what is creating the new poverty (or at least it is what has aggravated it).

(Dittrich 1987). 'Higher wages and other privileges ... are thought of as leading to greater aggregate output ... The increased national product can be used ... to provide the lowest wage group with higher wages ... The socialist states relied on this principle when they ... provided "labour heroes" with bonuses and rewarded officials with dachas, intershops and trips abroad' (Steinvorth 1999, p. 84). Under capitalism, wages do not increase as rapidly as productivity (cf. 2.1; see also 2.3.3). In Rawls's theory, the – realistic – scenario of productivity increasing by ten percent and entrepreneurial profit by fifty percent while wages only increase by two percent is 'just'. Such value judgements are common today.

304. 'A principle of justice that can be used to justify incompatible actions is unable to distinguish between just and unjust. This makes it useless as a theory from which contradictory propositions can be deduced' (Steinvorth 1999, p. 85).

305. In formulating the neoliberal ('libertarian') response to Rawls 1971, Nozick 1974 and Buchanan 1975 deliberately began with existing relations and the notions of the people living in those relations. Since Nozick and Buchanan were also strongly guided by the assumptions of neoclassical theory ('To Buchanan, economic exchange is the archetype of free interaction': Kersting 1994, p. 327; in Nozick, 'all political organisational forms have been absorbed by the structures of the market': p. 316), they ended up explicitly defending the status quo and endorsing policies that benefit capital. One can justifiedly claim that 'Buchanan's radically democratic decision rule for public goods [everyone must be able to approve; CH] amounts to a veto principle with a conservative drift: the political petrification of the given property relations is its covert consequence' (Kersting 1994, p. 341; cf. Koller 1987 and Kley 1989).

306. Rawls 1994 and 2002, Pogge 2002.

307. Rawls 1971, p. 90, but also: 'less advantaged': p. 68.

3.2.3 *The communitarian response*

Rawls's theory was egalitarian insofar as it called for a 'more just distribution'. This is why Rawls's Anglophone Marxist critics were on the wrong track when they tried to trump his demands: as *demands*, they are hardly to be trumped.[308] The thrust of Marx's critique was different: their apparent progressiveness notwithstanding, such demands can lead one to make one's peace with existing conditions, since they are already lawful.[309] 'Social justice', which sounds so desirable, already exists within the 'basic structure', as does 'radical democracy'. The theories of Rawls and Habermas do not aim to explain real inequalities, much less to alter them; what they aim for is a change of perspective.[310] For as long as they do not go beyond the normative, mere changes of perspective are easily recuperated by the other side; it is enough for it to demonstrate in skilfully written treatises that the present relations and measures are lawful and that there is no alternative to them (3.1.4). Marx's critique of law has not been properly taken account of for as long as law continues to be thought of as the place where theory can deposit its normative demands, so that they then need only to be implemented: according to Marx, law *has* already incorporated the demands for equality, liberty and justice, at least in the Western states. Those who continue to call for equality, liberty and justice end up formulating an apology for what exists.[311]

---

308. Rawls explicitly leaves open the question of whether the laws of the market (the 'well-ordered society') might also be applied under socialism (Rawls 1971, p. 228; under real socialism, experimenting with market sectors was tantamount to heresy; cf. Sik 1972). For English leftist critiques of Rawls see Wood 1980, Miller 1977, DeMarco 1980, Francis 1980, Young 1981, A. Buchanan 1982, DiQuattro 1983, Reiman 1991 and Fraser 1997. Kymlicka raises the question of whether one can be any more left-wing than Rawls (Kymlicka 1990, p. 169). This is an effect of the 'veil of ignorance', which goes back to neoclassical theory's orientation toward the model of exchange (and social philosophy's orientation toward the legal sphere): because Kymlicka does not problematise the legal sphere, he stops at the observation that Rawls and his Marxist critics formulate the same demands. It would have been important to ask what Rawls and the Marxists go on to do with these demands.

309. *MECW* 6, pp. 143 f.

310. Rawls says of his 'conception of justice' that it ought to 'transform our perspective [!] on the social world and to reconcile us to the dispositions of the natural order' (Rawls 1971, p. 448). 'It is only when human rights have found their 'place' in a worldwide democratic legal order... that we will be able to assume, on the global level, that those to whom these rights are addressed will simultaneously be in a position to think of themselves as their originators' (Habermas 1999; cf. Honneth 1999a, p. 283). To guarantee human rights the world over is an honourable goal, but even if it were achieved, individual human beings would not be the 'originators' of those rights. They can already think of themselves as the originators of human rights today; the aspect of what one thinks of oneself makes little difference to the matter. Marx criticised the Young Hegelians for merely effecting a change of perspective (2.5.7). On deconstruction's goal of modifying the perspective of 'everyone', see Fraser 1997, p. 24.

311. On the parallel in Habermas, see 3.1.5. Law can only juridify those relations that already exist, at least in a rudimentary form, and that are therefore capable of existing as juridified relations (3.1.5). When it is a question of juridifying the protection of minorities or of the environment, one needs therefore to argue in material terms. Those who mean to strengthen fundamental human rights outside the Western hemisphere should try to develop those rights from given

For this reason, the form of law subsequently provoked a critique that seemed to want not just to sublate, but to *abandon* it: communitarianism, which constituted itself as a critique of Rawls.[312] This response to theoretical liberalism focused on problematising the theory's abstract character. In doing so, it made use of arguments already found in Hegel and Marx.[313] For them, however, the 'form' of law was an achievement of modern society. The communitarians' abstract negation mirrors Rawls's undialectical conception of law and society, turning it into its opposite: in Rawls, 'law' is thought of as fully congruent with society; in the communitarian critique, it is thought of as being not at all congruent with society, at least initially.

This dispute between two US currents of thought, liberalism and communitarianism, is misunderstood when it is regarded as a conflict between idealist 'normativists' and more down-to-earth 'realists'. It is really a conflict between different conceptions of the normative. Communitarianism problematised the adequacy of Rawls's model by opposing to it a *different* normative model. Ultimately, this is no more than a conflict between different convictions: 'One barren assurance, however, is of just as much value as another'.[314] The intra-normativistic dispute concerns the level upon which society's cohesive forces and central 'mechanisms' ought to be conceptualised theoretically. The communitarian critics shared Rawls's view that society is the product of a contract; they merely held that the contract does not have to be a legal one.

According to the communitarians, it is the *notions* of those entering into the contract that are decisive. Are these people driven by egoistic interests plus a sense of justice[315] or by a warm-hearted sense of community?[316] But this critique already conceded so much to Rawls that the critics either wanted only to correct internal details or did not problematise the theory itself, but only the objects it aimed at. Thus the communitarian critique of Rawls introduced *new* notions, which mainly concerned the concept of the 'person' and its implications,[317] the question of the primacy of what is substantively good

---

relations and traditions, in order to avoid merely imposing them imperially. This ought to be feasible in most regions.

312. Thus Honneth 1993, p. 8; Reese-Schäfer 1994, pp. 13 ff.; Kallscheuer 1994, p. 126; Krebs 2000, p. 7. Of course there were different standpoints within the communitarian current – some of its representatives even cheekily distanced themselves from it (e.g. Taylor and Walzer). But it is only where there is common ground that specific differences can appear. This common ground is the critical response to Rawls, which emphasises an (ethnic, cultural or even sexual) 'community'. Because this community derives its identity from a 'difference', theories of difference should also be seen as pertaining to the communitarian paradigm.

313. Taylor 1975; Walzer 1990, p. 159.

314. Hegel 1867, p. 135; cf. p. 273.

315. Rawls 1971, p. 17.

316. Sandel 1982 was concerned about the cohesion of the kind of atomistic society he discovered in Rawls's conception: 'Sharing presupposes the . . . community of sharers' (Reese-Schäfer 1994, p. 18; for earlier formulations, see Taylor 1975 and MacIntyre 1981). Walzer 1983, p. 133, calls the social contract a 'moral bond' – one that is not merely utility-oriented. On the link to Tönnies, see Rehberg 1993.

317. Sandel 1984a, Taylor 1988.

vis-à-vis what is formally just[318] and the form of law.[319] The critics correctly observed that the law is blind to certain entities, especially membership in cultural, religious or sexual minorities. They argued that the subject assumed by social contract theory needs to be 'thought' more substantively, and that one needs to acknowledge the way it is situated in irreducible social contexts – an anti-liberal argument that goes back to Burke and Hegel. Real problems such as material inequality and social discrimination cannot, however, be eliminated merely by being 'recognised', no matter how carefully this recognition is distinguished from both ethics and law. There is in fact the risk of inequalities and discrimination being consolidated.[320] For this reason, liberals objected to the critique by insisting that the constitutional state's granting of social liberty is prior to all diversity within the body politic, so that the 'identity' of a certain group cannot be invoked against it. This somewhat more considered form of liberalism seems to mark the end of the debate, as many communitarians have agreed with it.[321]

The road to this compromise formula involved the critique of overly abstract liberalism adopting many elements of its former opponent, including keywords such as 'autonomy' or 'recognition'[322] – primarily legal categories that were applied to extra-legal problems.[323] The hope was that this would bring about *legal* recognition, such as the legal codification of gender equality and same-sex partnerships, or the linguistic autonomy of cultural minorities such as the French Canadians.[324] This transfer of theoretical liberalism's legal categories to other domains actually ran contrary to the communitarians' concretistic

---

318. MacIntyre 1981.

319. Forst 2002, pp. 30 ff.

320. '[A]ssimiliation is the cardinal sin against the ideal of authenticity' (Taylor 1992, p. 38). Slavoj Žižek has mocked the way indigeneous peoples are given museal, socially disadvantaged picture-book roles, roles that are consolidated by insistence on identity and recognition (oral communication, New York, 1997; cf. Altvater 1992). Feminism also suffers from this ambiguity: either it aspires to the legal equality of the sexes, which entails structural disadvantages for women, or it calls for the legal recognition of 'specifically female' traits, in which case women are stereotyped. 'The theorists of recognition are wrong to invoke Hegel, … not [only] because Hegel does not use the expression 'struggle for recognition', but because … such a struggle is virtually impossible' (Luckner 1995, p. 145; this view is confirmed by Stekeler 2003, p. 211). The struggle 'is not about recognition; it is itself a form of recognition'. The expression 'struggle for recognition' suggests 'that this struggle is over as soon as mutual recognition is achieved' (Luckner 1995, p. 145). See also Siep 1979, Wildt 1982, Amengual 1990 or Girndt 1990.

321. Walzer 1996.

322. Walzer 1983, pp. 356 ff.

323. Charles Taylor has pointed out that the political discourse of the present turns essentially on rights (Taylor 1990, p. 94). Walzer also admits: 'our situation is largely captured by that vocabulary' (Walzer 1995, p. 14). 'In the history of philosophy, recognition is the concept by which Fichte and Hegel replaced Hobbes' social contract as the foundation of law and the state. Recognition refers to the process of reciprocal interaction by which individual consciousness constitutes itself simultaneously with the general will through which it is treated as a person, i.e. as a bearer of rights' (Amengual 1990).

324. Taylor 1992.

intentions. But once one has ventured into the domain of the normative, law remains the victor, insofar as it is the necessary buttress of all modern morality (3.1.5).

Thus liberalism was countered by considering more concrete levels, but the merits of the political sphere were quickly imposed on them, too. For example, the communitarian concept of *civil society*[325] takes the concept of 'normative' integration from the politico-legal sphere, where it belongs, but then transfers it from law and the state, which seemed overly abstract, to the community (and/or to ethics, its philosophically diluted placeholder). In this way, formalism and deliberate 'blindness' to the economy were not overcome but rather *extended* to the social sphere.[326] This is partly due to the lack of clarity about what theory is supposed to achieve. If the aim was to call for political activity, then the choice of theory as a medium was doubtless unfortunate. If the aim was to formulate a critique, it would have been better achieved by a detailed exposition of ills. By trying to formulate alternative theories of justice or of the good, the communitarians replaced one 'embellished shadow' of society[327] with another.

The result could be neither scientific nor a critique; it was merely an evocative avowal. If things are the way communitarianism says they are, there is no need to worry. If they are *not*, if it is articulating grievances, then what is required is an analysis of the causes (which communitarianism does not provide) and sober reflection on political strategies. The observation that the body politic is subject to erosion in many areas is correct. But merely formulating ethical appeals[328] tends to have the effect of distracting from the possible real causes, especially since such appeals can hardly be intended to be practically political for as long as they *simultaneously* mean to deliver a 'theory of society'. It is not universalist morality alone that transcends context and the collective self-understandings of participants (it would simply justify moral demands differently): they are already – and more effectively – transcended within causal inquiries. But neither of the two sides engages in such theorisation.

Ironically, the communitarian response is characterised by the gradual adoption not just of legal categories, but also of theoretical liberalism's implicit apology for the market, despite the fact that its original impulse was one of scepticism toward modernity, and

325. Walzer 1995, Taylor 1990.

326. Walzer 1995, p. 20, hopes that 'civil society' will do what only the absolute state was able to do during the seventeenth century: end religious wars. State tasks are projected onto society. This is true even with regard to the welfare state, which is to be replaced or supplemented by a 'social society' (Reese-Schäfer 1998, p. 96). The concept of 'civil society' considers citizens only as *citoyens*, not as *bourgeois* (Cohen 1995, p. 36); it is de-economised. To use an image of which Walzer is fond (Walzer 1987, pp. vii, 20 f., 93): it remains within the Platonic 'cave'. Thus the theoretical liberals are not the only ones for whom social reality is hidden behind a 'veil of ignorance'. On 'blindness', see Steinvorth 1999, p. 98.

327. *MECW* 6, p. 144.

328. 'Join the associations of your choice' (Walzer 1995, p. 25). 'Get involved!' (Etzioni 1995, p. 277).

hence toward the market.[329] German conservatism had already enacted a 'turn' from general anti-modernism to a rejection of *socially* modernising currents that was accompanied by the endorsement of *technological* modernisation (including the relations of production).[330] Similarly, the second major statement of the communitarian position already saw the critique of market atomism degenerate into the cultural-critical spoilage of an otherwise affirmative theory:[331] in his alternative *theory of justice*, Michael Walzer tried to grasp social reality by means of the paradigm of 'distribution', considering various interrelationships such as friendship, social security, washing machines, administrative bodies, job vacancies, leisure time, education, love, religion and power as 'goods' (as existing in the form of commodities). The market paradigm becomes the guiding idea in Walzer's social theory as well, except that Walzer's theory features *more than one* market. He adopts the optimistic interpretation of the market. At bottom, the market model upon which the entire theory depends, with distributive principles serving as a common denominator, is positively assessed: 'one might almost say that goods distribute themselves'.[332] In particular, Walzer judges the *economic* market to be unproblematic. Ronald Reagan or Bill Gates might have said what he says:

> It is in the market that money does its work, and the market is open to all comers.[333]

> And once we have blocked every wrongful exchange…, we have no reason to worry about the answers the market provides.[334]

> The market… is without doubt the economic formation most consistent with the civil society argument.[335]

---

329. 'In order to secure the survival of democracy, it was necessary to confront the concentration of economic power with a comparable concentration of political power' (Sandel 1984, p. 92; cf. Bellah et al. 1991) 'If the destructive energies of the capitalist economy are not tamed…, the liberal and democratic societies of the West have no future' (Wellmer 1993, p. 189).

330. See Schmitt 1919, Mannheim 1986, Greifenhagen 1971; see also Mohler 1989, Faber 1981, Breuer 1993. This parallel suggests a comparison (cf. Rehberg 1993 and Joas 1993). No one is denying that notions of community were perverted by the National Socialists. But, interestingly, the anti-modernism of the period was driven by very similar motives: then as now, the cold market was rejected in favour of warm sentiments – from a normative point of view, there is nothing inherently bad about this. However, good and bad cannot be distinguished from a purely 'conceptual' perspective; it is only reality that can put theory to the test (in the case of nationalism, the theory is quite close to reality). The theory of Marxism – one that many insist has been falsified historically – is something far more complex than those aspects of it that were implemented. By contrast, National Socialism realised many of its (horrible) goals.

331. Sandel 1982 was the first, and Walzer 1983 the second major statement of the communitarian position. This social utopia *corresponds* to the self-conception of the USA (Sandel 1982, p. 318; Sandel 1984a).

332. Walzer 1983, p. 7.

333. Walzer 1983, p. 104.

334. Walzer 1983, p. 107.

335. Walzer 1995, p. 17.

Instead of following Rawls in regarding market forces as the forces by virtue of which society coheres, Walzer attributes this function to the moral 'community', even on a purely descriptive level. The 'community' is the only opposing force that can sensibly be invoked. This is to turn an 'ought' into an 'is'; society appears to be *constituted* by ethics (2.4.3). Walzer does insist that the effects of the economic market sphere on other areas of life should be limited;[336] he argues for *boundaries* between the various 'markets'. A society is just when the boundaries of its 'spheres of distribution' are respected: 'Good fences make just societies'.[337] Yet when the boundaries are already drawn within theory, many social problems become virtually invisible, such as the unbridled expansion of the economic market sphere and the occultation of the sphere of production that lies beyond it.[338] The differentiation of theoretical spheres is ontologised, becoming one of society; the possibility of formulating a critique of capitalism is thereby eliminated.

While Walzer's intentions are emancipatory, the effect of his separation of the various 'spheres of justice' is the opposite. The question remains: who fixes such boundaries, and on the basis of which criteria? Despite his talk of 'community', the only foundation for the *general* social bond Walzer is able to identify is 'membership' in the one overarching association, namely the state. Common membership in the state is the only thing that unites all members of a society (citizenship is the highest good).[339] No one but the state can impose the 'limits' Walzer calls for.[340] But the way it does this is not what Walzer has in mind. Real borders such as the protectionist lines of razor wire along the Mexican border are abstracted from in his ethicisation.

Liberalism still took account of the market's overarching significance for modern society – even if it only did so implicitly (Rawls) or apologetically (Buchanan). But to postulate in opposition to it, within theory, other, equivalent spheres is either a demand that is *even more* normative and worldless than liberalism, or it is a description, in which case it

---

336. 'But were the markets to be set firmly within civil society, politically constrained, . . . limits might be fixed on its unequal outcomes' (Walzer 1995, p. 19). This is the wish that is passed on from the state to society. It is not market inequalities that should be abolished, but their extension to other areas of society. The boundaries are, however, 'ethical': associations and 'ideas' are expected to deal with the disadvantages.

337. Walzer 1983, p. 319.

338. Lohmann 1994, p. 231, criticises this as an ethicisation of Luhmann's division of society into distinct functional systems. Moreover, Walzer's theory of spheres remains 'dependent on the nation state' (Reese-Schäfer 1998, p. 87). This is hardly an improvement on Rawls's state-focused single-principle approach; like Rawls, Walzer can merely formulate demands about how plural distribution ought to occur. His ethical discussion of the distribution of 'hard work' is content to list suggestions (Walzer 1983, pp. 165 ff.: higher wages, conscription, rotation; cf. Walzer 1988). The market sceptic Bellah regards the market as originating not in production but in morality: 'Opportunities for taking a responsible part in the shared life sustain the life not only of families but of schools, communities, religious organizations, business enterprises [and] nations' (Bellah 1992, p. 93). He calls for 'self-cultivation' and greater 'morality' – how these things ought to be brought about remains an open question.

339. Walzer 1983, p. 29.

340. Walzer 1983, p. 282.

whitewashes real relations. For discrimination against ethnic, religious, gender or sexual minorities often has economic implications as well.[341] Hegel's insight into the materiality and crudeness of 'bourgeois society' (2.1.1) has here become a normativistic cross-fading of these very features. As in the older, toothless cultural criticism of normative social philosophy (2.5), it is not material constraints that are identified as the cause of pathologies, but an ethical decline. Unlike Rawls, Walzer situates the link between the different spheres not in the abstract realm of law but in the apparently more concrete 'shared understandings' of citizens.[342] Both regard social integration as 'normative'; the dispute is only about what exactly constitutes its (equally and in fact even more 'normative') 'foundation'. The difference is that Walzer wants normative regulation to be effected not from a central perspective (Thomas Nagel's 'view from nowhere') but from particular contexts. Unlike Plato, Walzer wants to stay in the cave:[343] he does not want to transcend the self-understandings of those situated in particular contexts – despite the fact that they themselves do this all the time, by virtue of their particular roles. If there existed a principle of distribution that could only be understood from an internal perspective, then how would it be possible to criticise it without transcending its context?[344] Exclusive contextualism clearly fosters relativism.

Once again, this blindness is an 'abstract negation', or the flipside, of Rawls's liberal 'veil of ignorance': Rawls is so obsessed with principles he loses sight of reality; Walzer is so obsessed with identity he loses sight of supra-contextual factors. Liberalism's faith in principles is not overcome, but merely pluralised: each domain should function only according to its own principle. To understand one of these domains, it is enough to be familiar with its proper principle. The basic conception of philosophy and society remains normativistic. In functional terms, both reductions lead to similar results. The reason for this is not only philosophical: within reality, the market is expanding further and further, and in doing so, it creates the problems without which hardly anyone would be writing works of social philosophy in the first place. The capitalist economy is the meta-institution of modern societies. Since 1989, during the new stage of unbridled 'globalisation', capitalism, which has always shaped modern societies, has become the decisive factor. Theories that do not adequately take it into account risk doing its work. This is a challenge to social philosophy.

---

341. Persons who have no rights to assert are more easily exploited (cf. Fraser 2003). The wave of post-Marxist texts published during the 1980s has led to such implications being overlooked (cf. Hirsch 1990). Economically privileged groups have often been the ones to conspicuously demonstrate their 'difference' in extra-economic ways. But this was mere self-description: an apartment in Greenwich Village is something one needs to be able to afford in the first place (Milner 1999, pp. 145 ff.).

342. Forst 2002, p. 160.

343. Walzer 1988, p. 7.

344. To Walzer 1987, every non-ethical criticism is an 'asocial criticism', an 'external intervention' (p. 64). Like Rorty, he believes '[i]t is better to tell stories' (p. 65).

But theoretical liberalism does not perceive this systematic and real undermining of its principles, because of its unrealistic normativism. And communitarianism does not seem to be able to grasp the structural disadvantages of market sociation,[345] because of its rejection of every supra-contextual perspective. In functional terms, communitarianism's practical demands are identical with those of neoliberalism: the provision of welfare should be handed from the state to private groups.[346] Either the communities take welfare into their hands – the communitarians approve of this because it promotes the community's social forces, and the neoliberals approve of it because it reduces the ratio of government expenditures to gross national product; or, if the communities are not up to the task, a private corporation steps in. The population's sense of 'identity' could conceivably be strengthened in both cases, as the history of Germany during and after the Second World War has shown. But at what price? Greater material inequality between the 'community' of the impoverished and the profiteers of privatisation is to be expected, as are diminished protection against forms of exclusion and the aggressive rejection of minorities.[347] There remains the question of what justice and its theory stand to gain from this.

---

345. On average, net income in the USA has increased by 0.5 percent since 1980, but within the top percentile, it has increased by 157 percent (Assheuer 2003). The wealthiest 13,000 US citizens own more money than the 20 million poorest (a ratio of 1:1540). CEOs of major corporations have an average annual income of 37.5 million dollars (Paul Krugman, in *Die Zeit*, no. 46, 2002). By the end of the 1980s, the top percentile – 834,000 US households – owned 5,700 billion dollars more than the remaining 90 percent, who had 4,800 billion dollars to their name (Suvin 1998, p. 79, citing Philipps 1990 and Chomsky 1993). The highest tax rate for chief executives has dropped from 94 percent in 1945 to 28 percent in 1991. Between 1980 and 1988, the number of millionaires in the USA has more than doubled, from 574,000 to 1.3 million. Ten percent of Germans live in poverty (their monthly net income is inferior to 1,200 euros per household; an executive director of Daimler/Chrysler earns four million euros a year – a ratio of 1:178. Efforts to force executive directors to publish their incomes are ongoing). In Germany, 17 percent of adolescents live in financially precarious circumstances (Assheuer 2003). Globally, an estimated 40 million people starved during the 1980s (UNDP 1996, p. 20).

346. 'Communitarianism, by contrast, is the dream of a perfect free-riderlessness' (Walzer 1990, p. 16). Communitarianism lends itself to 'ideological window-dressing 'and to the justification of welfare cuts'; 'strategies of exclusion' are implicit in it (Reese-Schäfer 1998, p. 98; Reich 1992; cf. Kersting 2000, p. 251). His sympathies for socialism notwithstanding, Walzer (1983, pp. 25, 113, 122, 318) also operates on the basis of a neoclassical conception: 'the more perfect the market, the smaller the inequalities of income will be' (p. 116).

347. 'Dogmatic insistence on retaining the concept of closed identities that encompass people's entire lives leads... to a situation in which the de facto erosion of fundamental constitutive factors such as profession, family and matrimony... can be confronted only by forms of culture-critical rejection. What is overlooked in this is that the experiences of suffering associated with the dissolution of traditional sources of meaning often result from the fact that the spaces opened up, in principle, by the abandonment of traditional patterns of orientation tend, in practice, to be accessible only to a privileged minority, while the majority is propagandistically pacified by means of surrogate identities. Thus possibilities for fostering identities turn into threats to identity, because social change... occurs, in actual fact, by means of massive processes of exclusion. It is because of this that a return to traditional patterns of orientation can then be effected only by means of authoritarian regulatory policies' (Steinfath 1994, p. 89).

It is clear that only a minority will be able to enjoy a 'good life' under such circumstances. In conclusion, one can say that communitarianism and the discourses that build on it have had the effect, during the past two decades, of generalising sceptical intuitions that have for a much longer time been formulated with regard to the Western state form – the democratic constitutional state and its guiding theory, liberalism. Communitarianism stands upon the shoulders of Hegel and, as far as its emancipatory pathos is concerned, upon those of Marx. But unlike Marx, it is no longer capable of ascertaining anything substantive; it remains on the level of alleged normative self-understandings. In light of political Marxism's global hopelessness, it needs to be seen as a 'surrogate ideology'. Its function is the same as that of postmodernism in France and of critical theory in Germany (3.4.3).

What this discursive context lacks is not so much philosophical 'mediation' as substantive criteria. This absence is partly rooted in social philosophy's false belief that it does not require such criteria at all.[348] The call for a politicisation of the community and a 'moralisation of politics' (Etzioni), or the allegation that they have already occurred, attempted to bridge the gap between two normativisms. In Germany, this was done under the headings of 'democratic morality' and 'constitutional patriotism'.[349] Due to their transposition to the language of law, the various discourses could even be integrated into a full-fledged system, as aspects of 'recognition'.[350] While this renewed

348. On Habermas, see 3.1.4; 4.1. Reese-Schäfer 1998, p. 102, accuses the theoretical liberals of holding that they can 'devise their models of what is to be regarded as just at the drawing board, without being disturbed by the unsatisfying... political discussion'. This is at least as true of communitarianism.

349. Rawls 1993 aims at an 'overlapping consensus' that takes seriously the 'fact of pluralism' and does not transcend the actual moral notions of various groups. On this point, Rawls and Walzer supplement one another. Honneth also posits the alternative as an intra-normative one, by raising the question of 'which moral motives and bonds need to be regarded as necessary in order to preserve the liberty-vindicating institutions of a modern democracy' (in: Zahlmann 1994, p. 119). The compromise formula of 'democratic morality' is intended to satisfy the moral-theoretical expectations of both camps.

350. The theoretical edifice that Forst 2002 means to incorporate the debate in proceeds by the equivocation of various ways of speaking about recognition. His '"abstractly" justified theory' (Forst 2002, p. 200) consists, apart from discussions of the literature, of the definition that justificatory reason should be 'reciprocal and general' (p. 227). Despite the highly general character of his theory, Forst does not want to be 'abstract in the wrong way; the basic structure [!] it argues for represents a framework in which persons are recognized intersubjectively in different ways: as ethical persons in their ethical self-determination of the good life; as legal persons in their rights claim to "equal concern and respect" (Dworkin); as politically autonomous and equally entitled citizens of a political community; and, finally, as moral persons, as human beings "per se"' (Forst 2002, p. 200; cf. pp. 291 f.). Theory provides the framework for practical recognition, which however has always already occurred. This sort of notion is only possible when one is operating on the basis of idealist assumptions (3.1.4). Within the various synthesised theories, practical political problems appear either as having already been solved (ethical communities recognise one another: as a definition, this is tautological; as a proposition about reality, it is in many cases false), or they do not appear at all. It is difficult to see what substantive proposition is supposed to be advanced by the theory of the framework and its intra-theoretical synthesising operation. The 'patterns of intersubjective recognition' are taken from Honneth. In his work, the grammar of law already

'synthesis' of two debates has resolved a meta-theoretical disagreement, it has done little for our understanding of legal and social *reality*. On the contrary, there is the risk, when one is operating from this perspective, of normatively blanking out society's material problems. Moreover, the point about law's formality, its promise of liberty, is lost. Once again, the German 'philosophy of unity' has perfected theory by totalising it and *removing* it from reality.[351]

3.2.4 *Responses within post-1989 German philosophy*

The dispute between US philosophy's two camps became an export hit. How is this to be explained? Was the situation in Europe not a different one, given Europe's much stronger welfare state and its relatively homogeneous population?[352] Because of greater historical awareness, the arguments were not perceived to be new; there had been similar theoretical conflicts between theories based on Kant and theories based on Hegel or Aristotle.[353] In Germany, a significant reception only occurred after the fall of the Berlin Wall and actually existing socialism's disappearance from the world stage: during the 1990s, after a ten-year delay, there was a veritable wave of communitarianism.[354] The fact that none of the protagonists of this reimported 'debate' made reference to Marx, at least not in significant ways, sat well with the incrimination of Marxism that followed the latter's palpable and universally welcomed failure.[355]

The dispute about what was primary, universal and formal principles or substantive but relative definitions of the 'good', could be engaged in *without* having to engage with the new reality. It seemed to be enough to seek a 'synthesis' between the two theoretical conceptions of normativity – or a 'middle road', as one began to say now, more pragmatically. Eastern Europe's dissident movements were treated as crown witnesses

---

predominates: the patterns are those of legal recognition (the only form of recognition that is called by that name), and of emotional and solidary attention (Honneth 1996, p. 94; see also Honneth 2010; on the role of Hegel, see Kojève 1947, Siep 1974, Wildt 1982 and Luckner 1995).

351. Cf. 2.5.7. The 'philosophy of unity' also appears in the guise of 'difference', by providing a concept that incorporates every difference. What use is a 'theory about everything' that has nothing to say about anything specific (2.5.2)?

352. See Nida-Rümelin 2000, pp. 348 f., who follows Esping-Andersen 1990 and Schmid 1996.

353. See for example J. Ritter 1969, Arendt 1974 or Schnädelbach 1986. On the history of the concept of justice, see Nell-Breuning 1980, Kramer 1992, Huber 1996 and Steinvorth 1998.

354. Cf. Brumlik 1993, Honneth 1993, Zahlmann 1994, Forst 2002.

355. Rawls sometimes mentions Marx (Rawls 1971, pp. 249 and 271), and Rawls's critics also sometimes refer to him (A. Buchanan 1982, Brenkert 1983, Nussbaum 1999 or Sheldon Wolin. During the 1970s, Charles Taylor was host to the 'analytical' Marxists). Early readings of Rawls thematised Marx (Wood 1980, Miller 1977 in Höffe 1977; in Höffe 1998, every trace of Marx has been effaced). Communitarianism's putative Marx renaissance began before its 'second phase' (thus Honneth 1999, p. 644). It would be more precise to speak of the gradual dissolution of German reception barriers (Honneth 1989a, Honneth 2002). Honneth's view that everything worth examining had already been examined during the academic reception of Marx in 1970s Germany is to be rejected. These works (Honneth mentions E. Lange, G. Lohmann, Wildt and Zimmermann) tended to be quite one-sided.

of 'civil society', but with an eye not so much to their *real* contexts as to their 'contextualism', which was considered in a formal and thus performatively contradictory way. In the German reception, the unquestioned premise of these debates – the view that all societies achieve integration 'normatively' – lost the innocence it may still have had in the USA.[356]

With hindsight, it seems as if the search for more modest surrogate narratives that characterised German social philosophy after 1989 was not so much about *limiting* oneself to the normative perspective out of necessity than about proving that this perspective is the *only* one social theory can sensibly adopt. The other, darker half of social theory, which Habermas had hitherto treated as secondary by applying systems theory to it, but which he had simultaneously denounced as 'instrumental' or 'strategic', was now lost sight of for good. When one examines how significant works from recent years deal with this material side, one is struck by the way the authors consistently opt for a purely normative view – regardless of whether they advocate a liberal, a communitarian or a libertarian variant. I will conclude by discussing how this normativism manifests itself in the work of three influential exponents of German social philosophy.

Otfried Höffe

Otfried Höffe attempts to oppose a 'normative' interpretation of the state and law to reductive positivist accounts of these phenomena.[357] His longstanding interest in Rawls[358] seems however to have made him believe that normative philosophy deals with norms. By no means does this have to be the case. It is the often crude material facts – suffering, disease and death; hunger, exclusion and oppression – that tend to prompt us to engage in normative considerations, not existing norms, which are by and large quite satisfactory. These unsavoury *facts* 'ought' not to be. No one would disagree with this in the abstract – the claim requires no elaborate 'philosophical' justification. What is needed, rather, are investigations into why no improvement is in sight, despite abundant resources and no lack of good will. Höffe, by contrast, is led by years of research to conclude that 'normative' questions of political justice need to be posed in such a way

---

356. In the USA, the assumption was an innocent one insofar as significant theoretical currents (such as Parsons) actually had operated on it (cf. 3.4). Moreover, the integration of immigrants from such different backgrounds was in fact achieved by means of the values the US constitution codified for its citizens. In Europe, where the 'community of states' had a much longer history to look back upon, and where theoretical traditions that take an entirely different view (the Enlightenment, materialism, Marxism, but also fascism) had long been dominant, it is not possible to naively defend such a view.

357. Höffe 1995 and 1996.

358. Höffe 1977 and 1998. He has rendered outstanding services to the reception of the classics of practical philosophy: he has edited reference works, commentaries and the book series *Klassiker Auslegen*.

as to 'detach' them from economics.[359] Then what remains for the philosopher to do, except to present an aprioristic construct? This is what normativistic social philosophers have been doing for years (3.1, 3.2). Being original in this field requires some creativity. Thus Höffe means to explain moral norms not in terms of 'reason' but in terms of other, already existing norms: 'Human rights are underpinned by a morality, that… is content with an ethics of… just exchange'.[360]

Thus Höffe 'justifies' one form of normativity by another – but he does so in an affirmative way. This very equivalence – and the simultaneous observation that little has changed for the better, *in spite of* the validity of law – prompted the 'classical' theorist Marx to transcend the purely normative sphere theoretically. Höffe does nothing of the sort. His self-confidently presented philosophy concludes with a call for 'global charity'.[361] Who apart from Carl Schmitt would not sign his name to this *demand*? There remains the question, however, of what sort of 'world republic' this might be,[362] considering that it can already be justified in terms of a global 'exchange society', and considering further that all other economic relations are simply blanked out.[363] In functional terms, such deliberately 'blind' thought is tantamount to a 'normative' glorification of global free trade. While Höffe says next to nothing about free trade,[364] his way of speaking about 'norms' as if they simply existed, and as if everything had been achieved once they are valid, tends to divert philosophical attention from the *examination* of real occurrences. In the end, he is content to call for the realisation of still more norms; the catalogue he presents is a document of left-liberal common sense: a global competitive order, a global economic policy, a global welfare policy, global solidarity and global environmental protection. This simply replicates one more time the old dualism of a functionalist and neoclassically reductive conception of the economy and its supplementation with normative or aesthetic idealisations. Should social philosophy not rather ask how these two levels actually relate to one another?

---

359. 'The legitimation [of human rights; C.H.] needs for example to be detached from the debate on economic prerequisites' (Höffe 1998, p. 30). Thus the biggest problem is spirited away at the outset.

360. Höffe 1998, p. 37.

361. Höffe 2007, p. 297.

362. Höffe 2000; cf. Höffe 1995, pp. 249 ff.

363. 'A sober theory of justice [one that renounces more far-reaching claims; C.H.] invokes […] just exchange as its new [?] paradigm' (Höffe 1998, p. 38, with references to Marcel Mauss, Levy-Strauss and Axelrod 1984). The sceptics are told theirs is an 'overly restricted, […], 'impatient', […], 'pettifogging' concept of exchange' (p. 41). At the Berlin Conference on Kant in 2000, Höffe attempted to 'justify' social rights not externally but in terms of the norms themselves. Onora O'Neill asked him why he said nothing about the atrophy of the state. The reason would seem to be that it is not a 'normative' phenomenon.

364. Höffe 2007, pp. 287 ff., speaks of a 'global regulation of competition' – without noticing that he is calling for existing structures one more time, in a normatively inflated way. For a critique of these structures, see e.g. Ziegler 2002.

Wolfgang Kersting

In contrast to Höffe, Wolfgang Kersting takes the view that anyone who cares for the *efficacy* of existing norms ought not so much to compile 'normative' wish lists than to minimise his catalogue of demands, trimming it down to the most basic norms.[365] Thus state intervention to compensate for income differentials is rejected as a paternalist restriction of libertarian civil rights and communitarian virtues of citizenship. Writing in the spirit of communitarianism,[366] Kersting argues that it is more important to vindicate the pre-political status of being a citizen ('democratic virtue').

In reflecting on what this might entail, Kersting also blanks out the economy, such that autonomy can be guaranteed only 'ethically', but not materially. This ethic deliberately runs counter to the frequently invoked 'social rights'.[367] In seeking to limit the individual's social rights vis-à-vis the state, Kersting not only implicitly provides economic interests groups with philosophical support, like Höffe; he also *explicitly* endorses the tendency toward cuts in social services, which is asserting itself anyhow.[368] The final aim of this sort of 'citizens' virtue' is that of ensuring that 'supported' persons become 'market-competent' once more. But what would this entail in concrete terms? One can easily predict that these persons (the poor, the elderly, the infirm, the handicapped, students, mothers, the long-term jobless, unskilled workers, and so on) will stand a chance only on the low-wage labour market, if at all.

The situation that Kersting begins from was already the starting point for modern political philosophy: a 'war of all against all' (Hobbes), waged over 'naturally' scarce resources. However, philosophy once aspired to *not* be deceived by the dominant semblance, but to probe beyond it and grasp the underlying realities. By operating with a suggestive notion of 'nature', Kersting abandons this quest for elucidation: 'We will leave it up to the private charity of the ant whether or not it wants to share its hearth and its

---

365. Although Kersting has also published on classics of philosophy (Kersting 1988, 1992 and 1993), he focuses on recent contractualist theories (Kersting 1994, 1997, 2000 and 2000a). He also discusses the work of Höffe (Kersting 1996).

366. Kersting 1997, pp. 397 ff.

367. Marshall 1963.

368. Kersting 2000 objects to the 'monetarism of social democracy' (p. 254), which he takes to be 'ethically blind' (p. 255). Working hard for little money would seem, then, to be 'ethical'. Kersting calls for 'measures to eliminate the irresponsible labour-market logjam created by collective bargaining cartels', on the grounds that 'job creation [is] the most effective social policy' (p. 250). He criticises the welfare state's 'machinery of support and disenfranchisement' (ibid.), whose 'cushioning of existence' he regards as making it 'an institution for preventing and endangering citizenship'. Welfare cuts are explained neither in terms of budgetary constraints, as in politics, nor in terms of job creation, as entrepreneurs' associations are wont to do. They are ethicised: 'moral convictions are part of what calls for a minimisation of... welfare-state bureaucracy' (p. 249). The purpose of social policy is to 'bring about market-competence', for '[t]he market does not exist to support the welfare state;... the welfare state exists to support the market' (p. 247). Recall the statement by Weber cited in 3.1.5.

provisions with the cricket in the wintertime. It cannot be just for the crickets to force the ants to provide for them'.[369]

The very example is paradoxical: either the differences in the behaviour of the ant and the cricket are due to 'nature', in which case the ants have no reason to be proud of their diligence; or the differences are freely chosen and thus 'deserved' – but then this sort of naturalisation is inappropriate. Sociality, a *sui generis* domain situated *between* nature and morality, is misunderstood from the outset – not to speak of the specific social formation of present-day modern capitalism. Those who believe that social inequalities are due to *natural* inequalities and can therefore not be corrected – so that wealth is always 'deserved', in and of itself – fall back behind the insights of 18th century sociology and economics (2.4.1).

It is only consistent that Kersting justifies his principles not sociologically but by reference to neoclassical theory. His 'ethic of merit' follows Böhm-Bawerk[370] in attempting to legitimate profit as the long-term reward for renouncing consumption in the short term. The welfare equality advocated by egalitarians like Dworkin would lead, according to Kersting, 'to hardworking people supporting the dropouts and to seltzer drinkers subsidising champagne drinkers'.[371] His 'merit-ethical naturalism',[372] the 'merit-ethical undramatising of the difference between nature and freedom',[373] stands the old dualism of nature and freedom on its head: it means to legitimate advantages that derive from *social* nature as advantages that derive from freedom or 'merit', whereas 'moral' demands are rejected, before this Hayekian 'nature', as non-existent: 'welfare equality would also eliminate those inequalities that derive from differences in the willingness to work, in ambition and in commitment'.[374]

Kersting believes rejection of this principle already amounts to a socio-philosophical analysis. This is to rank the importance of norms to social philosophy very highly. When social philosophy makes itself 'dependent on… normative principles within the theory of justification', as Kersting demands,[375] there is no longer any need for it to consult reality. This sort of thought transposes seemingly natural semblance directly to theory, thereby aggressively asserting the interests of the strongest. Marx's pointed pen might have polemically described this as 'vulgar philosophy' (2.3; 2.5.5).

Axel Honneth

Differently from such tendencies, Axel Honneth still sees himself as a 'progressive'. He means to use the conceptual apparatus of the Frankfurt School – which he does not need

369. Kersting 2000, p. 223.
370. Böhm-Bawerk 1921.
371. Kersting 2000, p. 223.
372. Kersting 2000, p. 237.
373. Kersting 2000, p. 233.
374. Kersting 2000, p. 223.
375. Kersting 1997, p. 138.

to go out of his way to evoke, as the successor of Horkheimer[376] – in order to arrive at a 'normatively substantive theory of society'.[377] But the question of how a philosophy can be both normative and substantive never occurs to him either. Instead, one finds in his work an inflationary use of the words 'conceptual' (a priori), 'normative' (meaning propositions not about reality but about wishes and claims) and 'moral'.[378] The goals this allows him to set himself are 'normatively more substantive' *concepts*, such as 'work'[379] or 'recognition'.[380] Such concepts might be used to elaborate more differentiated formulations of wishes or claims than those found, for example, in Adorno, who rarely demanded anything more than that the world finally be 'saved'.[381] But like Höffe, Honneth believes that by compiling catalogues of wishes, he is already making propositions about reality – namely, elaborating a 'critical theory of society'.[382] In systematic terms, this can only work if the objective idealist assumption is made that normative concepts constitute social reality.[383]

Like Kersting, Honneth is one of the authors who have done most to promote the reception of communitarianism. Honneth also resembles Kersting in that he largely neglects to pay attention, in a systematic way, to reality – even if this is precisely what he often *calls for* programmatically.[384] The only empirical reality subjected to closer examination is situated within the domain of morality: Honneth aims to 'justify' universal moral principles in terms of *developmental psychology*. In setting out to do this, is Honneth not succumbing to the naturalist fallacy? Why should social theorists have to 'constructively justify' existing norms and claims one more time? After all, they already exist. What one would need to do, first of all, is compile them empirically (who is demanding what from whom and in what situation); following that, one could inquire into their relationship to social reality (to what end, with what effect). But this presupposes an adequate empirical and theoretical grasp of social reality itself. This primary task of social theory has still not been performed. And moral-psychological philosophising does nothing to change this.[385] Even the empirical compilation of pre-given normative claims ('feelings of social

376. Honneth 2007, pp. 28 f., 64 ff.
377. Honneth 1996, p. 68.
378. Much is reinterpreted 'normatively', e.g. the 'morally motivated [!] struggles of social groups', by which 'the normatively directional [!] change of societies proceeds' (Honneth 1996, p. 93). In one section of Honneth 2003, the words 'normative' and 'moral' are used no less than thirty-three times (pp. 110–117).
379. Honneth 1980.
380. Honneth 1996 and 2003.
381. On this, see Honneth 1991.
382. Honneth 2007, pp. 63 ff.
383. Hösle 1990; 3.1.4.
384. Honneth 1996, pp. 69 f.; Honneth 2007, pp. 80 ff.; Honneth 2003, p. 110; in this, Honneth is the heir of the older critical theory; cf. 2.6.3; Habermas 1987, p. vii.
385. It is no coincidence that one also finds a neoclassically reductive account of the economy: what Hegel still called 'labour and enjoyment' (Hegel 1805, p. 213) becomes 'consumption and exchange' in Honneth (Honneth 1996, pp. 50 f.). See the critique in Fraser 2003.

injustice')[386] is prevented by the aim chosen, that of using these claims to systematically resolve the dilemma of critical theory.[387]

In Honneth, the influence of communitarianism[388] and Foucault[389] leads to Habermas's existing normative theory[390] being filled with 'material', that is, more substantive *norms*. Thus Honneth is operating one level of abstraction above Höffe, since Höffe still engaged directly with pre-given normative claims. Honneth's 'normative social philosophy' demands not just 'equal freedom', or a fair procedure for elaborating formal principles, but also 'substantive' guarantees, seen as necessary for the development of a sound personality. These theoretical demands ('claims'), addressed to no one in particular, are rendered *still more* abstract within theory. For this reason, they require an additional 'justification', at least on normativism's understanding.

Honneth intends to provide this 'justification' by an operation that is surprisingly analogous to Apel's ultimate justification: he means to show, by a procedure he considers empirical, that substantive claims have 'always already' been anticipated.[391] The result of this phenomenology of normative spirit[392] is that a 'minimal normative consensus' is 'always already' guaranteed 'in advance'.[393] What is achieved by this reference to 'original intersubjectivity'?[394] Either it is itself expected to solve all problems – in which case those problems would merely be concealed theoretically. Or it does *not* solve them – this begs the question of what the argument is supposed to achieve theoretically, besides

386. Honneth 2007, p. 87.
387. Honneth 2007, pp. 80 ff.
388. Honneth 1993.
389. Honneth 1986, pp. 121 ff.
390. Cf. Honneth 2007, pp. 41 f., 70 f., 83.
391. Where Habermas referred to Piaget and Kohlberg, Honneth 1996, pp. 98 f., refers to Donald W. Winnicott (like Wild 1982 before him). But the question is what there is to 'prove' about love (it is bad to harm people because…?). With regard to law, Honneth follows Marshall 1963 (a 1950 lecture that was popular during the postwar period) in claiming that the introduction of 'social rights' has ended the struggles over distribution seen during the nineteenth century; these struggles are interpreted as having been primarily about 'membership'. This is reminiscent of the way Walzer refashions social struggles into a tussle over the right to association (Walzer 1983 and 1995). Hegel's state dimension of 'solidarity' is reinterpreted as a social dimension, that of 'appreciation'. It too is never demonstrated, but merely called for (Honneth 1996, p. 179). Social theory cannot select from the empirical manifold whatever 'proof' fits its hypotheses (anything could be 'proven' in this way); it ought, instead, to eliminate possible falsifications of those hypotheses.
392. Honneth 2003, p. 114.
393. Honneth 1996, p. 42. Brumlik has spoken, in a manner that was initially critical, of a 'phenomenology of moral conflicts' (in: Edelstein 2000, p. 81). 'Built into the structure of human interaction there is a normative expectation that one will meet with the recognition of others, or at least an implicit assumption that one will be given positive consideration in the plans of others' (Honneth 1996, p. 44). Since Habermas, the concept of interaction has involved material reproduction being systematically ignored. As in neo-Kantianism, 'society' is conceptualised as being 'constituted' by deliberate, value-oriented ('normative') acts of individuals. This 'subjectively intended meaning' yields the 'material' by which Apel's ultimate justification is enriched.
394. Honneth 1996, p. 30.

justifying the 'normative claims'[395] of a critical theory, without it ever being stated what these claims actually consist in. Like the communitarians, Honneth wants a 'communicative basis' upon which 'individuals, who have been isolated [!] from each other by legal relations, can be reunited'.[396] This is an appeal for the ideal duplication of legal relations: a demand that has always already been implemented, like those of Rawls and the communitarians.

For social philosophy, this is where the real questions begin. Who is formulating demands, and who are they addressing them to? What real structures and processes lie behind this? What ideas and traditions are these demands informed by, and by what right are they formulated? How could they be implemented? What is their relationship to the *actual* principles of the liberal constitutional state, legal equality and economic and political liberty? What political changes would be necessary in order to implement them at least partly, and what limits should be imposed on structural change of this kind? What practical steps would need to be taken in order to effect such a transformation of the political structure? How should one respond to the theoretical opponents of such measures, and how to their political opponents? We are eager to hear how these questions will be answered. Honneth is content to expand the catalogue of demands ('Love, Rights, Solidarity') and engage in historical considerations on what the young Hegel and G.H. Mead thought about these issues. He cites fragments of Hegel's 1802 *System of Ethical Life* [*System der Sittlichkeit*], which is a more like a religious treatise than a republican manifesto (see his references to 'mutual recognition').[397] Honneth's invocation of the 'early' Hegel is reminiscent of the way Heidegger mythified 'earliness', as well as of the 'anti-Marxist Hegel strategy'[398] of 1950s German philosophy (2.5.7). His invocation of Mead is also not very convincing sociologically: as a psychologist, Mead was interested primarily in the genesis of consciousness. When society comes up in his work, he tends to be interested in the effect that the *notion* of society has on the behaviour of individuals. What is sociological about this is also idealist ('the ideal society').[399]

So where is the promised 'empirical' implementation[400] of normative demands? Where Honneth's theory makes progress is in its negative deduction of the *theory's* normative claims from a real 'violation of implicit rules'.[401] This move is original, but on

395. Honneth 2007, pp. 90 and 112.
396. Honneth 1996, p. 24.
397. Honneth 1996, p. 16. Hegel corrected Hobbes by pointing out that persons already recognise one another in the state of nature. They do the same things as in Hobbes; it is just that the explanation for what they do is more 'normatively substantive'. In this way, the state is given one more theoretical support. Hegel is concerned with reconciliation – his own reconciliation with the state, in this case. Basing a critical theory or even an 'emancipatory' politics on this would likely prove a difficult undertaking. Hegel ought rather to be interpreted as a philosopher of religion (2.6.4).
398. R. Mehring 1989.
399. Mead 1934, p. 317; cf. 3.4.2.
400. Honneth 1996, p. 1.
401. Honneth 1996, p. 160; Honneth 2007, pp. 63 ff.

closer consideration, it is also tautological (on the affirmation of circular reasoning in German thought, see 2.5.5). A violation of rules can perhaps serve as a *ratio cognoscendi* of the violated rules, but it can hardly 'explain' them. A theoretical list of claims that are attributed to individuals as their intentions can only constitute a social theory on the assumption that societies are *generated* and develop by virtue of such norms. It is only consistent, then, that Honneth evokes the image of a purposive evolution of society, produced by the transcendental mechanism of the moral 'struggle for recognition'.[402] Like Luhmann's claim that 'society' consists of communication (2.5.6), this is a classic case of generative idealism. Intersubjectivity is posited as transcendent. Honneth is in line with Fichte's and Hegel's procedural idealism, except that he calls the result 'normative' (this is also the difference between his theory and Luhmann's).[403] Marx's critique of Hegel applies to Honneth as well. In fact, it applies to Honneth even more than to Hegel, since Hegel accorded more room to the economy and did not treat individuals as the *explanans* of an overblown intentionality.

Axel Honneth's long-time associate Hans Joas[404] performed a similar theoretical operation, although Joas moved in a slightly different direction: following the normativistic course set by Habermas, he also attempted to formulate a more 'substantive' presentation of the normativistic position by taking account of other theoretical currents (such as G.H. Mead and John Dewey). One outcome of this effort was a book on the 'genesis of values'.[405] It describes theories by which *other* authors, from Nietzsche to Charles Taylor, have attempted to conceptualise the way humans arrive at their *notions* of what is morally valuable. Since then, he has also focused on religion. Both Joas and Honneth attribute great theoretical importance to a transcendental 'intersubjectivity' that is prior to every individuation and every formal sociation – despite the fact that they set them-

402. History becomes the history of the explication of norms: 'in every historical epoch, individual, particular anticipations of expanded recognition relations accumulate into a system [!] of normative demands, and this, consequently, forces societal development as a whole to adapt to the process of progressive individuation' (Honneth 1996, p. 84). The 'basis' is 'communicative' (p. 24; cf. 1.3). Honneth unabashedly assumes a moral evolution of society, one that is identity-philosophical insofar as the ethical structure is 'always the same' (p. 16). Normative concepts and principles yield knowledge because they are what constitutes society: on Honneth's view, 'social struggles' are conducted with arguments, and decided by them (p. 115). Honneth has inherited this normative Vicoism from Habermas (cf. 2.6.4).

403. While Honneth criticises Fichte and Hegel as 'philosophers of consciousness', this is his only criticism. It rests on the hermeneutic reduction that Habermas effected before Honneth (3.1.5). Luckner 1995 situates Honneth (and Taylor) on the level of Fichte and Hegel. And in fact, everything does develop from the 'prior' ethics [*Sittlichkeit*] of recognition, except that it is not the old Hegelian 'ethical state' that coordinates everything, but a civil 'community of citizens'. Hegel's principalist construction of history is also actualised by Honneth (and in doing so, he makes significant use of Marxian terminology). C.B. Macpherson and even the conservative J. Ritter knew more about the prominent role the capitalist economy plays at the heart of bourgeois law.

404. See Honneth and Joas 1980, 1986 and 1987.

405. Joas 2000.

selves off from Habermas.[406] Because of this, they tend to lose sight somewhat of real conflicts. To be sure, examination of the genesis of self-consciousness yields such gratifying and theoretically important discoveries as the creativity of action[407] and 'practical intersubjectivity'.[408] But it would be a genetic fallacy (2.5.1) to argue that one can use this to attenuate current conflicts. Unfortunately, holding norms in high esteem may block one's theoretical view of the reality that conflicts with these norms, a reality that does not exhaust itself in their 'genesis' (3.3).[409]

This section (3.2), which has examined various theories of justice that were developed in the USA and dominated German academic social theory during the first post-Marxist decade, has confirmed the result of section 3.1: excessive emphasis on normative phenomena has hindered consideration of the normative's real foundations in multiple ways, even largely *replacing* theoretical engagement with those foundations. The debate between Rawls's theoretical liberalism and the more Hegelian approach that is communitarianism has been seen especially clearly to be an intra-normativistic one in which little is said about the social world's real structure – about where the normative is situated. At the same time, it has become clear that the role of theory has shifted from that of providing a distanced 'explanation' of social processes to that of providing a justification of the results of those processes. Before we examine the methodological origins of this 'pragmatic' conception of philosophy (3.4), we need to consider one more discipline in which the revival of the normative within philosophy has manifested itself: business ethics (3.3). Business ethics lends itself to an additional demonstration of the relevance of my

406. Honneth 1986, pp. 144 ff.; Joas 1992, pp. 171 ff.

407. Joas 1996.

408. Joas 1980.

409. Honneth rewrites the history of social struggles as the self-explication of moral concepts, in a Hegelian manner. Marx described the 'process of opposing good to bad, ... and of administering one category as an antidote to another' as follows: 'There is no longer any dialectics but only, at the most, absolutely pure morality' (*MECW* 6, p. 169). Honneth 1988a means to continue Sartre's reflection on negativity, in order to ward off possible threats to the 'idea of communicative freedom' (p. 74). He claims that Sartre 'was only forced to construe human interaction negativistically because he already excludes the possibility of personal identity on the level of basic concepts' (p. 80). The analysis proceeds on a purely conceptual level and remains oddly extraneous to the reality of 'human interaction' – fundamental negativity is one of the basic features of such interaction, one that remains in effect no matter how successfully people interact (Rentsch 2000, pp. 11 ff. and 109 ff.). Joas 1993, pp. 43 ff., means to dispel scepticism about the negative connotations of the 'rhetoric of community' by pointing out that historically, many things developed quite differently in the USA (this may explain the preference for US authors; cf. 3.4). Joas 2000a's unequivocal condemnation of the Kosovo War left nothing to be desired. And yet from his *theoretical* perspective, wars seem to be interesting primarily because they drive people to endorse human values, i.e. they are interesting when they are over. Honneth 1996 circumvents the antinomy of social and political rights (3.1.5) by regarding it simply as a 'successive expansion' (p. 177). Bismarck tended to bestow rights to passive participation *instead of* rights to active participation; the latter were even paternalistically restricted by him (Metzler 2003; cf. 2.4.1). Normativism desensitises one to the decisive legal antinomy of liberty and equality, as the struggle over these norms only becomes noticeable beyond the normative sphere.

criticisms, as it uses a number of the philosophical and proto-philosophical approaches considered thus far for its own ends. It is only on closer consideration that one discovers what purpose this serves, beyond the mere usage of ethical *vocabulary*. The authors examined in the following chapter pursue lofty goals, but once again, those goals are turned, functionally, into their opposite, as a result of conceptual choices.

3.3 Business ethics: a 'normatively substantial' social theory?

3.3.1 *Reasons for the rise of this discipline*

> Competition is more solidary than sharing.[410]
> [E]nrichment as such as the purpose of production[411]

Even back in the 1980s, Marxism played next to no part in the rise of the 'new social movements'. This was probably due to the ossified structures of the communist parties, but also to the dogmatism of Marxist groups whose obstinacy was matched by their lack of theoretical results.[412] This tendency to leave Marx behind intensified considerably after 1989. While it was politically liberating to break with patronising, self-declared vanguards (a break that occurred somewhat earlier in the West than in the East), the abandonment of Marxism also left a *theoretical* gap. Notwithstanding the fact that its numerous variants had grave internal deficiencies (Chapter Two), Marxism formulated the most in-depth 'critique of capitalism', as most were willing to concede. The peace and environmental, the feminist and gay-rights movements deliberately warded off theorisation and theoretically disguised paternalism, holding that they would restrict the movement's diversity: this is still a feature of contemporary critics of globalisation such as ATTAC. Due to its internal deficits, the Marxism of the period would in fact have been unable to act as a theoretical leader; it seldom formulated the called-for 'concrete analysis of the concrete situation' (Lenin), and when it did, the results tended not to be convincing. And yet it was concrete situations that the new social movements were responding to (the NATO Double-Track Decision, the building of the Runway West at Frankfurt on the Main Airport, the plans to build a nuclear fuel reprocessing plant in the Bavarian municipality of Wackersdorf). The place of the absent overarching theory was taken by various other narratives: in the environmental movement, straightforward indignation was soon coupled with esoteric tendencies;[413] the peace movement always had a certain affinity

410. Karl Homann.
411. *MECW* 36, p. 64.
412. See J. Hirsch 1980, Thompson 1980, Haug 1982, Habermas 1985 and R. Roth 1987.
413. These were some serious philosophies of nature (Jonas 1984, Meyer-Abich 1984, Schefold 1988, Hösle 1991), but there was also a tendency toward degeneration into airy romanticism or

with religion, because of the role that church conventions had played in its development;[414] finally, the sexual liberation movements began to be informed by the poststructuralist discourse of identity.[415]

Yet none of these narratives was capable of providing an overarching explanation for the current state of the world, not to speak of rendering an account of its relationship to the present. Philosophically considered, the new demands thereby turned into an 'ought' that was opposed to reality as something foreign to it.[416] While this tendency toward moralisation did meet with its deriders in the academic world, one can nevertheless speak of philosophical ethics going through a veritable boom period.[417] Thus, at the very moment when Marxism seemed to disappear for good, there emerged a new discipline that drew even 'the economy' into the domain of the ethical once again, or at least subjected it to an ethical interpretation: business ethics.[418]

While the groundwork for the rise of business ethics was already done during the mid-1980s, there was nevertheless a veritable flood of business ethics publications around 1989.[419] One reason for this may have been that there was a time following the opening

---

nationalism (Gruhl 1978, Bahro 1991, Geden 1996, Ditfurth 1997, Markovits 1997). On the origins of the ecological critique of capitalism, see Waibl 1989, pp. 119–55.

414. Such as Weizsäcker 1977, Schulte 1987 or Drewermann 1991. There was also a Marxist current of peace studies (Senghaas 1979), Psychology was often invoked, too, and for good reason, it seems. On how non-Marxist currents split off from movement Marxism, see the inside account of Koenen 2001.

415. Poststructuralism enjoyed no more than a marginal reception in Germany; it was especially popular in France and the USA. There, one can see clearly how Marx was replaced: Baudrillard, Lyotard and Foucault, for instance, came directly from one or the other variant of Marxism, from which they then sought to extricate themselves. Their theories are beyond the scope of this book and have already been subjected to in-depth criticism (Ferry 1987, Taureck 1988, Habermas 1987a, Frank 1983, 1993, pp. 119 ff.). Derrida has little to offer on Marx besides plays on words (Derrida 1995 and 2004; cf. Henning 2005c).

416. This tendency had its precursors and parallels within the Marxist camp (2.1.4, 2.6.3). Bourgeois sociology was essentially moralistic (2.4.3). Moreover, the dominant *zeitgeist*, that of the 'Kohl system' (Friedbert Pflüger), was hardly open to new ideas (Hess 1988). Commune members and members of alternative rural communities did attempt to live their ideals, but in doing so they abstracted from the rest of the world. The films *The Idiots* and *Together* deal appositely with this subject.

417. On the ethics boom, see Türcke 1989, Hösle 1991, Taureck 1992, Piper 1998 and Thurnherr 2000. Deriders of this tendency include the Right Hegelians Ritter 2003a, Marquard 1973, Gehlen 1973 and Lübbe 1987, as well as Luhmann 1978 and 1989.

418. In Ulrich 2001, for instance, 'economics … is integrated not with, but *in* ethics' (Korff 1999, Vol. I, p. 871). Koslowski 2001 also includes business ethics in an overarching 'ethical economy' (see above, 3.3.4).

419. Apart from Koslowski 1982, Sen 1987 and Rich 1987, see, for example, Enderle 1988, Hesse 1988, Koslowski 2001, Molitor 1989, Pappi 1989, Waibl 1989, Rich 1990, Schauenberg 1990, Ulrich 1990, EKD 1991, Hengsbach 1991, Steinmann 1991, Furger 1992, Homann 1992, 1992a, Rich 1992, Spiegel 1992, Enderle 1993 or Wieland 1993. Following a 1985 conference in St. Gallen, a work group was founded in 1986; in 1989, a permanent committee on 'economics and ethics' was established within the 'Association for Social Policy' [*Verein für Sozialpolitik*]. In the meantime, several chairs of business ethics have been established at German universities; a 'German Business Ethics

of the inner German border when it seemed as if East Germany's future was still undecided, so that academics felt it might be necessary to do some promotional work for the social market economy. After all, traditional business ethics was little more than the attempt to provide an ex post philosophical legitimation of the basic regulatory decision in favour of the 'social market economy' [*soziale Marktwirtschaft*] against socialism.[420] But before long it was clear the fall of the Berlin Wall would bring major changes for West Germany as well. In retrospect, the various post-1989 variants of business ethics give the impression of wanting to newly codify, or even invoke, the spirit of the pre-1989 Federal Republic.[421]

When this fundamental decision had been taken for the acceding territories as well, the political dispute between the overzealous apologists for this order and those who had begun to develop a more critical view, due to the growing number of wrongs associated with it,[422] began increasingly to be argued out within the medium of business ethics, now an established discipline; this did not, however, involve the formulation of a critique of capitalism as radical as the one that had been widespread during the 1970s. The new discipline's popularity culminated eventually in a 3,000 page *summa*.[423] Meanwhile, the critique of capitalism has returned in the form of the critique of globalisation. Business ethics persists within it, for the arguments formulated by the critics of globalisation have tended, so far, to be ethical, and there is a certain abstinence from theory (3.3.5). The following examination of the brief spring of business ethics focuses not so much on its sometimes meritorious details than on its basic argumentative choices, for it is they that are symptomatic.

Why is it not until the extra-economic critique of globalisation that Marx is remembered? How should the phenomenon of inflationary variants of business ethics be assessed from a perspective that does *not* ignore Marx? After all, the seemingly powerful arguments invoked by business ethics are far from new (3.2.3); in substance, they derive from contexts of debate that we have already encountered in our discussion of historical responses to Marx: mainly religion and theology (2.6), neoclassical economics (2.3) and historicism (2.5). These contexts are, however, partly incompatible: business ethics was soon characterised by an aporia between a theologising abstract critique of 'the economy' (3.3.2) and a forerunning, management-oriented and professionally blinkered apology for it (3.3.3). A third, Hegelian current held that while the 'concept' of ethical business practices is real, it has yet to be fully realised (3.3.5). But the 'integration' of

---

Network' [*Deutsches Netzwerk Wirtschaftsethik*] has also been created (see the journal *Forum Wirtschaftethik*).

420. See Müller-Armack 1990, Eucken 1965, Heimann 1955, Erhard 1957, Grosser 1988, Rich 1990 and Zinn 1992.

421. For a late example, see Merkel 2000; cf. Reuter 2001.

422. Rising unemployment, poverty, welfare cuts, xenophobia, growing public debt, the aggravation of domestic and international inequality, the destruction of the environment, the resurgence of wars and of nationalist and religious fanaticism (cf. 1.2).

423. Korff 1999.

otherworldliness and affirmation leads beyond neither of them. On the contrary, it involves the additional disadvantage of the theorists of business ethics no longer knowing what exactly they are saying: talk of the 'economy', coupled, as the case may be, with 'critique', leaves it open whether what is being addressed is the economy itself or the theory of the economy. This makes a major difference to the thrust of a critique. But this is never even perceived as a problem. Thus the lack of clarity that characterises business ethics on the level of content is compounded by a similar lack of clarity in methodological matters. Most German-language variants of business ethics are caught within this quandary, but it is most evident in the historicist ones (3.3.4). The more detailed examination that follows is intended to answer the question of whether further elaboration of normative contents yields a superior social theory.

3.3.2 *Theological business ethics*

In Germany, early, prescriptively oriented business ethics publications had a religious background. Within religion, social democracy had been engaged with relatively openly, and in some cases, there had even been an affirmation of 'socialism', albeit one that tended *not* to involve the adoption of Marxian theorems (2.6.6).[424] This can be explained in terms of the Christian religion's equidistant position: because of its 'eschatological proviso', Christianity's attitude to bourgeois society was as reserved as that long displayed by the proletariat. 'Ye cannot serve God and Mammon'.[425] It is only by considerable hermeneutic efforts that the social-revolutionary implications of large parts of the Bible can be incorporated in a market apologetic view. Because of its scriptural principle [*sola scriptura*], Protestantism was especially affected by this problem. But West German Catholics were also forced by the key imperative of actively loving one's neighbour[426] to orient themselves toward redistribution and public welfare.[427]

To be sure, this rapprochement tended to have a tempering effect on the greater part of the labour movement prompting its condemnation by Marxists. But after 1989, one observes a contrary 'dialectic of moderation': when one of two poles (a, c), whose mediation (b) was sought, disappears entirely, the mediating instance (b) may in the meantime have absorbed so much of (a) that it becomes its (a's) placeholder vis-à-vis the remaining extreme (c). This is not just the case where the disappearance or suppression of socialist aspirations leads to similar demands being formulated in the name of Catholic social doctrine, as happened recently in Argentina; it is also the story of German business ethics. Like a thermal storage system, theology became the functional equivalent of the very critique of capitalism it had sought to 'refute', once the socially and economically

424. See Scheler 1919, Wünsch 1927 and Heimann 1931. Heimann 1980 'had to make use of ... the Marxian perspective, even if he rejected specific Marxian or Marxist theories' (p. 308).

425. Matthew 6:24.

426. 3 Moses 19:18; Matthew 5:44; Romans 13:8.

427. Uertz 1981.

disadvantaged had lost their intercessors. Thus the key impulses for the invigoration of business ethics ca. 1989 came from the context of *theological* social ethics.[428]

Theological ethics was quite willing to engage with Marx, even if it usually discussed him as a moralistic 'theorist of alienation'.[429] There was, however, the problem of a lack of focus. Ethical imperatives derived from religion can be applied to the present, but this kind of application often appears strangely extraneous to present-day circumstances. To apply the imperatives one has obtained to a certain object, one needs first to have developed an adequate understanding of that object. But because of its apparent ethical superiority, a pontifically self-assured ethics will tend to assume it does not need to consider its object more closely. In this way, the abstractness of the *applicandum* ('ethics') is aggravated by the lack of a precise definition of the *applicans* ('business'). An application does not create its own *applicans*, but needs rather to accept it as something pre-given (3.2.2). No matter how good an ethic is, it may still be defining its *object* wrongly – a problem familiar from genetic ethics and other fields of application.

The fact that theological business ethicists tend not to be professional economists does not have to be a disadvantage, as professional economists have become blinkered due to the dominance of the neoclassical paradigm (see 2.3.1). Because of its greater willingness to engage with the critic of capitalism, Marx, Christian business ethics has the chance to describe capitalism more accurately than professional economics. But how does it actually deal with capitalism?

> We commonly call the economist who advocates the right to ownership of capital a capitalist. This designation is used by idealistically oriented sermonisers to refer to a greedy profit gambler. By contrast, the teleological ethicist starts from experience and looks for the original definition, namely the one that applies to the status for which one cannot yet speak of established property relations. This is an empirically obtained

---

428. This is evident in Rich 1987/1990, EKD 1991, Hengsbach 1991, Herms 1991, Furger 1992, Spiegel 1992, Duchrow 1994, Utz 1994, Erfurt 1997 or Schramm 1997.

429. For early examples, see Rich 1951 and 1962, and Duchrow 1969. Duchrow 1994 cites Altvater and Kurz, as well as Marx (Duchrow 1994, pp. 30 ff.). Spiegel makes reference to some Marxian arguments (Spiegel 1992, p. 177 and elsewhere). Hengsbach, Nell-Breuning's successor as chair of business ethics, acknowledges the workers' movement's civilising effects, even if he takes them to have been unintentional: 'From a long-term perspective, one has to recognise that the old and new social movements have tamed and perhaps even re-oriented European capitalism' (Hengsbach 1992, p. 80). The very term 'capitalism' is indicative of a willingness to engage with Marx; professional economists tend to speak of the 'market economy'. The 'market' and/or the 'market economy' are mentioned from a business-ethical perspective in the titles of Kapp 1979, Rich 1990, Koslowski 1991, *Forum für Philosophie* 1994, Thielemann 1997, and from the perspective of the critique of globalisation in the titles of Saul 1997 and Klein 2001 – that makes one theologian per six non-theologians; 'capital' and 'capitalism' are mentioned in the titles of Waibl 1989, Furger 1992, Duchrow 1994, Jacob 1996 and Walk 2002 – three theologians per two non-theologians. The word 'capitalism' is even used by businessmen (Breuer 1999); it is only apologetic *theory* that shuns it. Koslowski 2001 mentions 'capitalism' in the title but otherwise speaks of the 'market'. Abstract talk of the 'economy' betrays a certain undecidedness (Horn 1996, Karmasin 1996, Ulrich 2001).

> concept that is nevertheless abstract: a means of increasing the productivity of labour with an eye to satisfying human needs.[430]

This is an astonishing definition, and as is well known, astonishment is the beginning of philosophical reflection. For we have here a plethora of contradictions. Let us analyse this passage more closely.

'We commonly call the economist who advocates the right to ownership of capital a capitalist.' The word 'capitalist' is commonly used to refer not to the *economist*, but to the owner of capital. A confounding of theory and reality is evident in this sentence.

'This designation is used by idealistically oriented sermonisers to refer to a greedy profit gambler.' This was no doubt written with Marx in mind. A harsh critic of idealism and morality, he is presented here as a sermoniser, and as an idealistic one at that. This misperception is due purely to the writer's *own* mentalisation of phenomena, such that nothing is perceived by him other than 'spirit of the spirit' (2.5.2, 3.4.3). Even a cursory reading of *Capital* shows that Marx was far from wanting to accuse individuals on anthropological grounds ('mania for possession').[431]

'By contrast, the teleological ethicist starts from experience and looks for the original definition, namely the one that applies to the status for which one cannot yet speak of established property relations'. References to empirical data and experience are always praiseworthy. But 'original definitions' are not to be found in experience – this was precisely the problem that gave rise to modern philosophy in Kant. But Utz's starting point is not so much philosophy as teleology: the 'teleological ethicist' already has an a priori knowledge of what is 'good' and therefore no longer needs to distinguish between means and ends, dispositions and consequences. The basis of this is not experience but a theological 'thought experience'. The 'abstract concept' that is provided in advance by teleological ethics is in no way 'empirically obtained', as historical reality is abstracted from. After all, there are always 'established property relations' of one kind or another; the 'mutual relations' of the labourer and the capitalist (the '*Kapitalverhältnis*')[432] *are* themselves historically established property relations. How is one to discover anything about them by situating oneself in an imagined 'originary state' and abstracting even from what one is looking for?

Utz takes himself to be beyond all established property relations, but this does not prevent him from making quite precise statements about capital in the next sentence: it is 'a means of increasing the productivity of labour with an eye to satisfying human needs.' Proceeding in an abstract-empirical way, the teleological ethicist stumbles upon

430. Utz 1994, p. 6.

431. Kant 2007, pp. 374 ff. As early as the *Preface* [!], Marx explains: 'But here individuals are dealt with only in so far as they are the personifications of economic categories, embodiments of particular class-relations and class-interests. My standpoint ... can less than any other make the individual responsible for relations whose creature he socially remains' (*MECW* 35, p. 10; 'personifications' ['*Charaktermasken*']: p. 95; cf. Gamm 2001, pp. 52 ff.).

432. *MECW* 35, p. 399 and elsewhere.

'the original definition' of capital that he has himself hidden. The ethicisation of capital is accomplished by isolating one of its functions (to the extent that capital is invested in new technologies, it increases productivity) and declaring that function to be its sole purpose. It accords perfectly with the purpose of the economy as posited by teleological ethics, 'satisfaction of needs'.[433] Nothing remains of the critique of capitalism. Utz even polemicises against a church memorandum[434] because it fails to criticise trade unions:

> Oddly enough, the memorandum does not criticise the policies of the German Federation of Trade Unions[435]... Is it not one cause of this undesirable development that households have too much money? Wages are driven up without larger economic and social developments being taken into account[436]... [they are driven up by] outside pressure, mainly from the trade unions[437]... In particular, the public sector strike is intended to torment peaceable citizens.[438]

As can be seen from these statements, the theological business ethicist Utz's position is openly neoliberal.[439] Theoretical negligence also leads more critical theological business ethicists to defend positions directly contrary to their intentions. The basic concept of religiously inspired business ethics, 'subservience to life' [*Lebensdienlichkeit*], already leads to a serious dilemma: either the concept is understood as stating the actual purpose of economic activity, the way 'fulfilment of demand' is understood in neoclassical theory. Then business ethics necessarily becomes apologetic, for how could an economy that is, by definition, subservient to life simultaneously be harmful to life?[440] Or the concept is understood as a counterfactual 'normative precept' (Rich) – in which case it remains unclear how business ethics will ever get beyond formulating pious wishes.[441]

---

433. Utz 1994, p. 6.
434. EKD 1991.
435. Utz 1994, p. 47.
436. Utz 1994, p. 158.
437. Utz 1994, p. 144.
438. Utz 1994, p. 223.
439. It culminates in the patent remedy 'Sober living, hard work and saving' (Utz 1994, p. 160). Moral theology has been familiar with this remedy 'throughout the centuries' (ibid.), and so Utz can simply bypass the present.
440. 'Subservience, namely subservience to life, is the primary and God-given purpose of the economy' (E. Brunner 1932, p. 387; Ulrich 2000, p. 204; Rich 1990, pp. 23 and 140). That satisfaction of demand is the purpose of 'the' economy is taken for granted by: Molitor 1989, p. 36; Utz 1994, p. 6; Horn 1996, p. 24; Wieland 1996, p. 54 ('satisfaction of needs'/'allocation of scarce resources'); Korff 1999, Vol. I, p. 30; Reuter 2000, p. 342; Ulrich 2001, p. 11. The neoclassical definition of a concept (see the motto of 2.3) is fallaciously taken as a description of reality – this is one of the sources of idealism. The definition is completely unspecified: is it descriptive or normative? How has it been obtained? Is it historically indexed? Marx provided such a historical index specifically for the capitalist economy: in it, 'enrichment as such' is considered 'the purpose of production' (*MECW* 36, p. 64), not satisfaction of needs (cf. 2.3.1). The criterion by which to choose a definition should be its explanatory force.
441. When Rich (1987, p. 173) invokes 'co-humanity [*Mitmenschlichkeit*], creatureliness [*Mitgeschöpflichkeit*], participation' as 'normative precepts', it remains unclear what this is supposed to

Professional economists can then reject the demands formulated by business ethics as 'otherworldly'.[442] Aware of the unworldliness of theological ethics, Georg Wünsch once judiciously insisted that the logics of economics and theology should be mediated in a more sophisticated way – which would presuppose, first and foremost, that they be distinguished.[443]

A premature intermingling of the two perspectives is also evident in the work of Ulrich Duchrow.[444] He uses a critical, but second-hand, definition of capitalism, thereby arriving at a fatal opposition of 'money' and 'life'. I will comment on one passage: 'What was decisive in the transition to the market economy of industrial capitalism was that... not only goods, but also labour, land and money... became commodities'.[445] Here, contrary theoretical currents are dashed together: the concepts 'market economy' and 'goods' are taken from neoclassical economics, whereas the concepts 'commodities' and 'industrial capitalism' are taken from Marxism. They run counter to one another and cannot be juxtaposed with impunity (2.3.3). As emerges from the following: 'This, however, is a colossal abstraction or fiction. For it is quite obvious that concretely considered, labour, land and money are not commodities, viz. produced for sale or purchase'.[446] Duchrow wants to concretise his critical impetus. But his 'concrete consideration' causes him to overlook the fact that these things do indeed become commodities *under capitalism*. What he seems to want to say is that they do not have to be commodities by virtue of some timeless necessity. There have been epochs during which they were not commodities, and it might be worthwhile to aspire to something of the kind again. But 'concretely considered', the present state of affairs in one in which the worker sells his labour power on the labour market, money is traded on the money market and land on the real estate market: Marx refers to the prices of these commodities as wages, interest and rent.

---

mean and how one might implement it. The same is true of the 'guiding business ethical hypotheses' listed in Spiegel 1992 (satisfaction of primary needs, redistribution, health, the right to work, the humanisation of work, participation and control, preservation of natural resources and the environment, limits to growth, an end to waste, adherence to human measure) and Hengsbach 1991 (women's equality, humane job design, the eco-social rebuilding of society, worldwide justice, love, dignity, participation). What is being said by this, unless these are simply catalogues of demands that are confronted with reality in an unmediated way?

442. In fact, the theological business ethicists accuse one another of 'otherworldliness': Homann (1994, p. 11), not one to make accusations sparingly, accuses Kant, H. Jonas, Ulrich, Steinmann, Honneth and Kambartel of an 'ethical imperialism' that remains 'abstract' and 'fruitless'. Ulrich (2001, pp. 102 f.) passes the accusation on to Steinmann, but especially to Koslowski; the latter would probably also refuse to accept it (at least his 'ethics of capitalism' is based on the theory of natural law, so that normativity is 'in the nature of things'). The accusation is by no means refuted by the fact that it travels full circle – it is justified in the case of all the authors mentioned.

443. The 'entelechy of economic activity' should 'not be judged by the standards of Christian ethics [...], otherwise both are debased' (Wünsch 1932, column 1969; cf. 2.6.6). The author of the classic work of modern ethics also rejected efforts to ground ethics religiously, as he felt such efforts are always limited in scope (H. Jonas 1984, pp. 47 f.).

444. Duchrow 1994.

445. Duchrow 1994, p. 28.

446. Ibid.

It is simply wrong to claim that these goods are not produced to be sold. Methodological negligence leads to capitalism being degraded to the status of a fiction; it becomes a mental phenomenon.

Taking this view, one would ultimately have to assume that capitalism does not really exist at all: 'This is indicative of the fundamental problem of the capitalist market economy [sic!]: it is deeply abstract; it does not begin with concrete life but imposes upon it the iron law of the money-increasing mechanism'.[447] Unlike Marx, who observed natural forces at work on the market, Duchrow abstractly opposes 'life' and 'money' to one another. How capitalism, an unnatural phenomenon, came about in the first place remains as mysterious as its fictionalised existence. Moreover, Duchrow risks slipping into a social Darwinist glorification of life. This becomes manifest when he refers positively to the *völkisch* merchant and man of letters Silvio Gesell,[448] who advocated 'breeding' the human race to perfection and devised a worldview in which interest dominates everything. According to Gesell, it is enough to abolish interest in order to restore 'natural' competition between capitalists. This position was inconsistent and highly susceptible to political instrumentalisation. The National Socialists adopted many elements of the thought of the 'Free Land Movement' (such as the 'breaking of interest slavery'); Gesell may not have wanted this, but it was only consistent.[449] While Duchrow wants to adopt a critical stance toward the 'market economy', his insufficient grasp of the subject matter causes him to end up in questionable company.

---

447. Ibid.

448. Duchrow 1994, pp. 38, 248.

449. The idea goes back to the social reform that saw John Ruskin et al. invoke 'life' against the negative effects of capitalism. It was therefore easy to interpret it in social Darwinist terms (on Gesell, see Senft 1990, Bartsch 1994, Ditfurth 1997 and Geden 1996, pp. 152–67). In modernity, a 'market economy without capital' is a contradiction in terms: the commodities exchanged on the market have to be produced somewhere. If they are produced capitalistically, under conditions of competition, then capital is required – and the more cheaply the commodities need to be produced, the more capital is required. This leads 'naturally' to an increasing demand for money, which of course is met via the money market. Thus neither capital nor interest can be abolished within a 'market economy'. The notion is based on a reductive participant perspective: the small trader is suffering from a lack of demand. He limits himself to asking how people might spend more money (in his store). When one imagines one factor (such as interest, as in Gesell 1958, or money, as in Proudhon) disappearing at a given time, there seems to result a one-off opportunity for exchanging existing commodities on more favourable terms (more favourable for one of the two parties, that is). Several questions remain unaddressed in this, such as those of where the commodities come from, how they and the people engaging in exchange reproduce themselves and what role money and interest play over and beyond simple exchange. Marx criticised this 'philistine utopia' at length (*MECW* 6, pp. 138 ff.; *MECW* 28, pp. 90 ff.; *MECW* 29, p. 323; *MECW* 35, pp. 78 f., 94 f. According to Rakovitz 2000, pp. 77 ff., this theme is what determines the structure of the *Grundrisse*, *MECW* 28–30). When this notion is rehashed nowadays, this is usually done in an attempt to use interest and compound interest to explain material inequalities between 'money owners' and ordinary mortals (Creutz 1983, Kennedy 1991). This is to overlook the fact that the greatest payers of interest are corporations: their wealth must therefore originate elsewhere. According to Marx, interest is a share of profit, not its cause (*MECW* 37, pp. 336 ff.; 2.3.5).

These examples show that theological business ethics fails to refer in a satisfactory way to Marxian theory. It limits itself to applying neoclassical theorems, including Keynesian theorems.[450] These writings lead back into the market apologetic camp. They differ only with regard to the degree of intervention they believe to be permissible at present. Not only does this ethics never get beyond mere suggestions, and not only does it prove extremely flexible in practice,[451] but the fact that it wants more state guarantees to be introduced in the age of globalisation also reveals its 'cloistered spirit' (Hegel). It is not its *own* time that it gives conceptual expression to; rather, it expresses the ideals of the immediate postwar period. Where its mentalisation of the phenomenon becomes critical, it leads to capitalism being interpreted as a religion.

Marx's passage from the critique of religion to the critique of political economy is reversed.[452] While Marx recognised that capitalism displays religious features, he did not treat these features as an *explanans*, but as an *explanandum*. To restrict oneself to the surface structure of a 'religion', or even to consider it the 'basis' of material structures, appeared to him to be a form of mysticism. When money, for example, is considered in this way, it becomes a thing with features that are no longer comprehensible.[453] A religious critique can lament the power of money in ethical terms; *theoretically* speaking, it thereby affirms this perspective. The features that theologians criticise money for are the ones they have themseves attributed to it.[454] Understood in this way, money caricatures the paradox of Christianity: a *malum* is lamented and simultaneously declared necessary – *credo quia absurdum*.[455]

---

450. This applies not just to Utz and Duchrow but also to Rich 1990, Hengsbach 1991, Furger 1992 and Schramm 1996.

451. See 3.2.2. Neoliberals such as Buchanan 1962 want a 'minimal state'.

452. 2.6.3; cf. Wagner 1985, Jacob 1996 and Binswanger 1998.

453. 'The standpoint at which people are content with such tales about spirits is itself a religious one, because ... people who adopt it regard religion as ... *causa sui* [its own cause] ... instead of ... showing how definite relations of industry and intercourse are necessarily connected with a definite form of society, hence, with a definite form of state and hence with a definite form of religious consciousness' (*MECW* 5, p. 154). Marx retained this position: 'It is, in reality, much easier to discover by analysis the earthly core of the misty creations of religion, than, conversely, it is, to develop from the actual relations of life the corresponding celestialised forms of those relations. The latter method is the only materialistic, and therefore the only scientific one' (*MECW* 35, p. 374; cf. 2.6). The *theologoumena* found in the work of Marx and Engels serve no explanatory or justificatory purpose; they should be interpreted – like the 'dialectic' – as a dramaturgical means of exposition and as heuristic metaphors (Buchbinder 1976; cf. 2.5.7, 2.6.4).

454. Delektat 1953, Hörisch 1983, Türcke 1983, Wagner 1985.

455. Normally, the fall of man and the death of Christ are considered examples of *felix culpa* (cf. *MECW* 3, pp. 212 and 322 ff.). Faced with the deficiencies of 'modern economy' (*MECW* 35, p. 93), Marx said: 'for a society based upon the production of commodities, ... Christianity ... is the most fitting form of religion' (p. 90). The notion of capital as the absolute, 'greater than itself' (p. 166), equipped with an 'automatically active character' (p. 164) was not one that Marx defended; he criticised it as an example of 'fetishism'. The comparisons drawn in ISF 2000 are misleading: 'One needs to pay attention to his theologising metaphors ... to recognise what the scandalous cusp and the denunciative heart of the critique of political economy consist in: simply in the fact that that which entire centuries were able to picture only nebulously, as "God", has become, in the

Theological business ethics became a placeholder for the critique of capitalism, but because it wrongly defined its object, the economy, mentalising its features to the point of theologising them, it was torn back and forth between an extraneous moralism ('ethics') and an unintentional apology (for 'business'). Business ethics oscillates undecidedly between these two poles. While theological business ethics has raised important questions, the answers to those questions need to be sought elsewhere.

3.3.3 *Managerial business ethics*

> The ethics of political economy is *acquisition*.[456]

Thus the discipline traditionally concerned with economic matters was able to step in and take the initiative by attempting to develop a more adequate form of business ethics. The gesture by which Molitor 1989 begins is characteristic: he makes it clear that he needs to straighten out the 'basic facts' about economic activity before ethical matters can be addressed ('Food is the first thing, morals follow on', as Brecht wrote in the *Threepenny Opera*). The project of traditional 'business ethics' is continued: a regulatory hypothesis for legitimating the institutions of the market economy, it started from the basic assumptions of neoclassical economics (the 'basic facts' that the purpose of the economy is the satisfaction of needs and its basic force that of exchange) in order to legitimate the market economy vis-à-vis its external rival while simultaneously working to curb state intervention. The market economy was claimed not only to be the more efficient model, but also to grant people more liberty. The classic arguments, which go back to Locke and were given well-known formulations by Hayek, Friedman and Walter Eucken,[457] are supplemented, in the new business ethics, with economic considerations to which an *additional* moral quality is attributed:

> The market economy is distinguished not only by the degree of liberty it allows for and its capacity for productivity increases. The moral character of this type of order consists in the fact that it gives priority to consumer interests and automatically ensures that households benefit from productivity increases.[458]

This argument is by no means meant to oppose purely efficiency-oriented considerations. Productivity increases mean that more can be produced with means of production of the

---

concept of capital and in actual capital, reality's law of movement – it has assumed an "automatically active character". This easily used phrase... is incomprehensible in itself and objectively; it is objectively as non-rational as befits a "crazy form"' (p. 21). Here, the fetish is affirmed (cf. 2.6.4; Rakowitz 2001).

456. *MECW* 3, p. 310.

457. John Locke held that an Indian chief lives more miserably than the poorest Englishman, because his people does not work: 'a king of a large and fruitful territory there feeds, lodges, and is clad worse than a day-labourer in England' (*Second Treatise*, 1681, § 41). Mandeville moralised this argument (*Fable of the Bees*, 1714; cf. Steinvorth 1981 and Waibl 1988).

458. Molitor 1989, p. 73.

same initial value – that is, the profit margin increases. Now, this additional profit could be passed on to 'consumers' by increasing their wages. This would be to reduce morality to efficiency – for passing the productivity increase on to consumption is not any more 'moral', in and of itself, than the productivity increase itself –, but one could at least speak of the additional profit being *distributed* 'justly' between entrepreneurs and workers. But this is not what Molitor has in mind. Rather, the way he envisions productivity increases being passed on involves a jibe at the labour movement.

This is not an ideology-critical allegation, for Molitor says as much himself: productivity increases can only be 'passed on to the household' on condition that wages increase *more slowly*;[459] otherwise the price reduction effect is offset, he argues. Hence it is morally right that profits should increase while wages do not – the 'consumer' benefits only from the fact that commodity prices fall. But that is something companies also benefit from, since the prices of means of production will fall as well. What Molitor is really advocating is the intensification of exploitation. This used to be called the 'bourgeois class standpoint'. It is already implicit in the underlying basic assumptions. They are associated with the neoclassical model of the economy, which allows one to see that production has become *less costly*, but not that *more is being produced*. Overall supply increases; this is one of the reasons why trade unions call for an increase in the purchasing power of the masses, to be brought about by higher wages. Molitor does not mention the fact that it is not just reinvestment and wages that may increase, but also corporate profits – as has increasingly been the case since 'Reaganomics'. The 'Ackermann case', for example, seems inconceivable from his point of view.

His position also becomes clear from the roles he attributes to 'morality' and 'nature': 'natural' competition requires no morality, he claims. Morality only becomes necessary, on Molitor's view, when the natural equilibrium – Hayek's 'spontaneous order' – has been disturbed, such as by the rise of trade unions. It is only then that morality is needed – in order to temper the unions:

> When the price of labour does not form on the market like other prices but is ... fixed in periodical negotiations, specific economic problems result.[460]

> Where the economic domain is not regulated by competition ..., the morality of the participants is ... called for. This is obviously true where price formation occurs by means of the negotiations of established labour market organisations.[461]

Why do trade unions disturb equilibrium, in Molitor's view? What sort of equilibrium does he have in mind? Capital considers the activity of trade unions a violation of the rules because, for once, society's 'total capital'[462] is not buyer and seller in one, but buyer

459. Molitor 1989, p. 118.
460. Molitor 1989, p. 117.
461. Molitor 1989, p. 121.
462. *MECW* 35, p. 408.

only, such that it is naturally constrained to pay a price. This is far from contradicting the rules of the market: after all, the market is itself nothing other than a 'periodical negotiation' (one need only think of the stock market). Here, it is no longer the rules of the market that Molitor considers natural (wages can be higher or lower, depending on market conditions) but only what is in the interest of entrepreneurs: low wages.[463]

Molitor's putative 'basic facts' are nothing but the assumptions inherent in the neoclassical model. They only seem to 'exist' as facts because Molitor treats them as being beyond criticism. Once again, theory and reality become indistinguishable; thought and being are one. Differently from theological business ethics, managerial business ethics does not involve a flawed reception of Marx's critique of capitalism; it ignores that critique altogether.[464] Rather than mentalising features of capitalism, like the theological variant, the managerial variant of business ethics does the opposite: it ontologises theoretical models. In Molitor, the 'solution' to ethical problems consists simply in defining them away: within this context, they are not conceivable (this is quite true); *therefore* it seems they do not exist.[465] It would be more appropriate, however, to treat these problems as an occasion for verifying the theory (in accordance with the criterion of external consistency; cf. 1.5; 4.1).

Managerial business ethics fails to capture the distinctive features of capitalism; moreover, it stands ethics on its head. It 'wants to be the synthesis', but it is only 'a composite error'.[466] Let us verify this hypothesis by considering other exponents of managerial business ethics. The position of Karl Homann, the former nestor of business ethics at the Catholic University of Eichstätt-Ingolstadt, is symptomatic. He is an exponent of traditional regulatory ethics – he also attributes objective reality to the axioms of a certain theory: 'The market economy is... the best means for realising universal solidarity that

463. It needs to be stressed, as done by Koslowski 1982, that the institutional framework of the market, including trade unions, is subject to the same evolution as the market itself. Thus it makes little sense to play nature off against social institutions.

464. A special case within managerial business ethics is represented by corporate ethics. It concerns itself not with the regulatory framework but with the behaviour of firms and with behaviour within firms. Given its frame, this theory cannot provide an apology for the market economy; consequently, there is less reason to lament the absence of reflections on the critique of capitalism. Since this field is praxis-oriented, its use value is greater, both for entrepreneurs and for potential critics of capitalism. Even from a Marxist perspective, there is probably nothing to be said against a corporate ethics that works to improve the climate at the workplace and promotes customer-friendly, sustainable or environmentally friendly business strategies (cf. Steinmann 1994 and 1998; Wieland 1996, 1998 and 1999; *Bank und Umwelt* 2002). The question of how market rules are implemented should, however, not be confused with that of whether they are good.

465. In his discussion of globalisation, Molitor (1989, p. 64) confronts real problems with theoretical axioms. The latter are treated as a higher reality, behind which the actual reality disappears: 'It is hard to see why the so-called 'social dimension' would have to suffer from a fully developed common market. Private households qua consumers would in any case benefit most. But factor utilisation also increases, with positive consequences for average wages in particular. Moreover, free movement of labour allows those who make use of it to improve their individual maximum utility'.

466. *MECW* 6, p. 178.

we know of'.[467] 'The pursuit of profit is conducive to universal solidarity'.[468] If this were indeed so, then it would be difficult to account for the problems that led to the development of 'business ethics' in the first place. If one does not want to ignore these problems altogether (Homann is quite willing to admit the existence of 'deficiencies'), then they must be seen as resulting not from the logic of the market, but from something else, something external (2.4.1).

Homann ascribes this 'something else' to individual morality. In functional terms, this corresponds to the damning verdict on the trade unions in Utz and Molitor: 'Communicative action... ruins the economy when the attempt is made to impose it... by means of law and planning (socialism)'.[469] According to Homann, who invokes the authority of Luhmann on this point,[470] individual ethics can 'no longer be Kantian' today, or in 'modernity',[471] since it is a feature of the market economy (just as claimed by the neoclassical axiom) that prudence comes to be moral in and of itself, whereas the old morality becomes harmful: 'During the past decades, the separation of morality and prudence, which goes back to Kant, has blinded us to the fact that all morality needs to be grounded in social control'.[472] In this way, the level of Kantian morality is eliminated. It is 'drowned... in the icy water of egotistical calculation'.[473] The fundamental practical distinction between donating fifty euros to charity 'out of a sense of duty' or prudently depositing them on a high-interest Internet bank account (or a Swiss number account) can no longer be drawn. In a bold historico-philosophical construction, Homann seeks to deprive individual morality, which interferes with the market, of its basis; and yet he *calls* this anti-moralistic operation 'ethical'. With regard to 'theoretical strategy',[474] this may be a smart move, but it distorts the meaning of the word 'morality'.[475] This is a 'transvaluation of all values' that follows Nietzsche[476] in attributing the predicate 'good' only to those who prove stronger in the struggle for survival.[477] Habermas' super-normativism,

467. Homann 1994, p. 14.
468. Homann 1994, p. 15.
469. Ibid.
470. Homann 1993; cf. Wieland 1996.
471. Homann 1994, p. 22.
472. Ibid.
473. *MECW* 6, p. 487.
474. Homann 1994.
475. 'Corporate ethics of the Homann variety should openly admit it is no corporate ethics at all' (R. Pfriem, in Maak 1998, p. 484). Even a colleague of Homann's says about his thought that it 'rests on a static neoclassical model of the market' (Korff 1999, Vol. I, p. 846). Since Homann has no concept of modern ethics, his 'claim to formulating an ethical theory' is 'questionable' (p. 847). Homann clearly falls prey to his own hierarchical model: the dominance of the economy over ethics (Homann 1994, p. 11).
476. Nietzsche 1967a.
477. See 3.2.4, on Kersting. On this move's premise within the history of theory, the impossibility of distinguishing between good and bad within the dualist neoclassical model, see 2.4.1. Marx escaped this Nietzscheanism by not using the language of morality at all (3.1.4). He was quite aware that real relations and developments make a mockery of morality. But neither did he close his

which treated the system as *emanating* from morality, is followed here by a decapitation: the superfluous head (morality) rolls, and the system itself becomes the genuine depository of ethics.

How did this turnaround come about? Homann provides no answer to this question. He merely ontologises another theoretical construct – this time, it is the prisoner's dilemma, popular within theories of rational choice.[478] Although this dilemma was conceived of as a timeless one (in keeping with neoclassical theory's ahistorical approach: cf. 2.3.1), Homann presents it as *the* signum of our age[479] – an age in which moral action is 'no longer' possible, because a *single* norm-violating action, or even its possibility, makes it impossible to adhere to a universal moral norm. But the possibility of violating a norm has never been an argument against moral norms, nor is it one 'today'. Here, Homann departs not just from Kant, but also from Luhmann: even in the latter's work, normativity displays the feature of being *resistant* to disappointments.[480]

Homann makes the 'ought' resemble a 'can': 'A moral norm has no validity for as long as its enforceability is not warranted' (Homann 1993, p. 37).[481] This is a reversal of the naturalist fallacy: instead of an 'ought' being inferred from an 'is', an 'ought not' is inferred from a 'cannot'. The 'ought' is shattered by a possible 'cannot' – the end of morality. As is well known, it is always easy to find reasons why something cannot be done. Kant took the opposite view: you can, therefore you ought to.[482] By contrast, Homann advocates a consummate reductionism: 'Integration is not possible without a "pragmatic reduction"'.[483] This conceptual transvaluation renders the moral perspective impossible.[484] What remains is a 'pure' regulatory doctrine that is as void of

---

eyes to reality, nor did he glorify what he saw morally – he simply took note of it. Fetscher 1999, p. 136, interprets Marx's assessment of British rule in India as sacrificing the individual (*MECW* 12, pp. 132 f.). This is to wrongly project back onto Marx the anti-individualist Leninist 'ethic' that shines through in Brecht's *The Measures Taken*. Marx's putative amorality was simply due to his describing what exists ('This class has always to sacrifice a part of itself in order not to be wholly destroyed': *MECW* 3, p. 237).

478. Homann 1994, p. 23; cf. Blum 2000, pp. 392 f.

479. Cf. Homann 1997.

480. 'Cognitive expectations […] are characterised by […] preparedness to learn, whilst normative expectations signify the determination not to learn from disappointments' (Luhmann 1972, p. 33; Habermas 1992a, p. 70).

481. Suchanek 2001 calls this 'making our moral intuitions harmonise […] with reality [!]' (p. viii). The argument is similar to the one found in Gehlen 1973, except that here, it is not the state that is defended, but the market.

482. Kant 1998, pp. 537 ff./A 542 ff.; Kant 1949a, pp. 140 f.

483. Homann 1994, p. 20 – what is meant is the 'integration' of ethics and economics; cf. Ulrich 2001. 'Pragmatic reduction' is from Suchanek 1994.

484. Homann takes a different view. To him, there is no such thing as 'economic imperialism': 'I have never defended this position' (Homann 1994, p. 11; but see Homann 1990, pp. 105 f.). He nevertheless describes this perspective as 'rewarding' and encourages 'more work in this direction' (Homann 1994, p. 27). Homann claims he is not a reductionist, because he erroneously identifies reductionism with a dualist position. He concludes: 'I do not advocate dualism; therefore I do not advocate any economic reductionism either' (p. 19). But what is reductionist is the form of monism

'normative contents' as it is of empirical economic data: '*individual ethics* offers no solution; only *regulatory* ethics, which is based on individual *interests*, does so'.[485] What needs to be done, according to Homann, is to 're-orient ethics, replacing the small and easily surveyed group... with a different regulatory mechanism'.[486] These rules of the game are 'of course' the tried and tested ones of the unqualified market economy. Like Molitor's, Homann's view is more than merely market apologetic; he is directly expounding an 'ethic of capital'. This is betrayed by the fact that he resorts to the vocabulary of repression ('regulatory mechanism'; 'control mechanism'; 'social control'),[487] in spite of his constant assurance that everything will regulate itself.

In other authors, one's finds variations of this market-transcendental argument. Thus Ilse Horn does not regard the basic fictions of neoclassical theory as abstract theoretical models but as actual features of reality; at the same time, she considers them to be proof of that reality's 'morality':[488]

> After all, neoclassical theory's self-interest hypothesis is, at bottom, an ethically valuable postulate, as is the assumption that economic subjects behave rationally. The market limits the possibilities for self-interested behaviour, for competition is survived only by those whose actions are also useful to others [!]. Self-interest, materialism [!], immorality – these are aberrations... The market derives its ethical value from its inherent ability to handle these unvirtuous forms of behaviour in such a way as to make them yield social valuable results.[489]

Even Hayek admitted that the market is, at best, neutral about what is 'good and bad'.[490] If anything, one would have to say it *promotes* 'self-interest, materialism, immorality'. For bad things are easily sold on the market, precisely because of its indifference to morality; they can even be sold *as* 'good' things. This is true in a practical sense – commodities such as weapons, horror films, drugs, criminal services and even human beings can be

---

that eliminates one aspect by reducing it to the other – as in Homann: moral norms are 'pragmatic shorthand for more elaborate economic calculations' (p. 18). 'Dignity, humanity, duty... are categories of (moral) philosophy...; they cannot directly inform economics... in this form. They have no place in economics unless they are translated into its paradigm' (p. 17).

485. Homann 1994, p. 23.
486. Homann 1994, p. 13.
487. Homann 1994, pp. 13, 18 and 22 respectively.
488. Horn 1996, p. 137.
489. Horn 1996, p. 82.
490. 'The term "social justice" does not belong to the category of error but to that of nonsense, like the term "a moral stone"' (Hayek 1973, Vol. II, pp. 98 f.). For this reason, one should not speak of a 'social' market economy, Hayek argues. This is intended both as a descriptive and as a prescriptive claim: 'It is precisely because in the cosmos of the market we all constantly receive benefits which we have not deserved in any moral sense that we are under an obligation also to accept equally undeserved diminutions of our incomes' (p. 94) – as if one 'we' were the same as the other! Classes are already eliminated by Hayek on the level of definitions. Redistribution is disadvantageous even to the losers, according to Hayek, because violating the 'rules of the game' reduces their chances of one day being winners.

sold very profitably on the market ('Money is the supreme good, therefore its possessor is good')[491] – and it is true in a theoretical sense: managerial business ethics reduces what is 'morally good for someone' to what is 'quantitatively useful for the numerically defined collectivity'.[492] This reversal is effected by Horn:

> Morally 'good' behaviour reduces the transaction costs of economic exchange. Economic subjects *ought to* behave in a way that conforms to the system, for the rules of the market economy use economic incentives to influence people's behaviour in *morally desirable* ways, and only the unimpeded [!] operation of competition on merit can lead to *ethically desirable* macroeconomic efficiency.[493]

The only problem with this reinterpretation is our common usage of the terms 'ethics' and 'morality'. Here too, Homann's historico-philosophical reduction is invoked to redress the situation: 'the perspective of social ethics also has the purpose of elucidating individual ethics'.[494] In Horn, the conceptual elimination of all prior morality leads to the market being eulogised, to a degree not seen even in Hayek, by means of the capitalist ethic. The 'elucidation' consists in attributing to the market the features of which individual ethics has previously been stripped: 'By the criteria of social ethics, the market economy represents the best economic form of society – of this there can be no doubt'.[495] 'The regulatory framework is morality's systematic place within the market economy'.[496] But as is well known, the purpose of the regulatory framework is to ensure 'the unimpeded operation of competition on merit'.[497]

Andreas Suchanek's also adopts Homann's reversal. He proposes the following definition: 'Economic ethics concerns itself with the (empirical) conditions of possibility for making morality and self-interest compatible with one another when they enter into conflict, or for making their relationship a fruitful one'.[498] 'The fundamental problem of corporate ethics is that of… contributing to the resolution of the conflict between profit and morality'.[499]

---

491. *MECW* 3, p. 324; cf. 2.4.3.

492. Mandeville 1714 still had the grandeur to call these 'private vices' by their name, treating them not as an 'error' but as the rule. In spite of the 'invisible hand', Adam Smith also attributed to the 'wealthy' excessive self-estimation, avidity, presumption and all-consuming ambition (Smith 2009, pp. 296 f.). The young Marx lamented the fact that political economy and morality apply an 'opposite yardstick' (*MECW* 3, p. 310). Money corrupts; it dissolves morality, he argued: 'I am bad, dishonest, unscrupulous, stupid; but money is honoured, and hence its possessor' (p. 324); a 'world upside-down' (p. 326; cf. Helmich 1980). Shakespeare's diagnosis (pp. 323 f.) is still largely apposite.

493. Horn 1996, p. 127; emphasis added; cf. Sen 1985.

494. Horn 1996, p. 53.

495. Horn 1996, p. 135.

496. Horn 1996, p. 127.

497. Ibid.

498. Suchanek 2001, p. 30.

499. Suchanek 2001, p. 104.

The juxtaposition of 'empirical' and 'conditions of possibility' makes one sit up and take notice – the underlying non sequitur already announces itself semantically (on quasi-transcendentalism, see 3.1.5 and 3.4.4). In fact, Suchanek answers none of the 'empirical' questions he raises.[500] Instead, he fixes the 'conditions of possibility'[501] of such a conflict becoming *unthinkable* (cf. the parallel in 3.1.4). No part of this transcendental operation is empirical. How does he proceed? He begins by formulating an 'imperative of economic ethics'[502] – whose appellative character jars oddly with his previously expressed intention of focusing on 'rules of the game' rather than on individual ethics: 'Act in such a way that your [entrepreneurial; C.H.] action always simultaneously represents an investment in the improvement of the conditions for mutually beneficial social cooperation'.[503]

What is the purpose of this 'always simultaneously'? In light of the world-historical 'transition'[504] from individual ethics to the ethics of institutional frameworks that Homann already claimed was occurring, its purpose can only be that of insinuating that this is always already the case on the market. The transcendental empirical 'condition of possibility' of the conflict being resolved, in the sense of it becoming unthinkable, consists in an ontologisation of the neoclassical model (2.4.1). And so this 'deduction' is nothing but a reiterative explication of the neoclassical *premise*: 'To date, the market economy represents the best instrument of mutually beneficial (economic) cooperation, insofar as every actor is given incentives to invest in such cooperation'.[505]

Within this unqualified market economy, the demands of the 'economic imperative' have *always already* been satisfied. Suchanek merely reiterates them in an a priori manner. His business ethics also champions a neoliberal position; its critique of state intervention[506] is *de rigueur*. Where something over and above this is 'recommended',[507] the recommendation's lack of applicability and practicality is as pronounced as that commonly attributed to Peter Ulrich's suggestions.[508] What distinguishes this form of business ethics from older exponents of the same argument, such as Locke, Mandeville,

---

500. Such as: 'An industrial corporation produces a primary product that can also be used to produce armaments. Should it renounce a lucrative business agreement with a Middle Eastern "crisis region"?' (Suchanek 2001, p. 103). Thereafter, Suchanek gradually ceases to provide empirical examples. His view 'that corporations are given responsibilities they may not be able to fulfil adequately' (p. 104) is revealing of his 'solution'. The conflict becomes a transcendental semblance. For does it not follow from this that the industrial corporation will enter into the business agreement, and that there is nothing wrong with this from the point of view business ethics (everything is 'in order')? Not entering into the agreement would in any case not be a good 'investment in relations' (p. 114). After all, the ethos of business relations is based on discretion, or on sidestepping public opinion, which places 'crisis region' under a taboo.

501. Suchanek 2001, p. 30.
502. Suchanek 2001, p. 16.
503. Suchanek 2001, p. 69; cf. the alternative formulations on pp. 68 and 70.
504. Suchanek 2001, p. 16; cf. p. 75.
505. Suchanek 2001, p. 80.
506. Suchanek 2001, pp. 84 ff.
507. Suchanek 2001, pp. 24, 69.
508. Suchanek 2001, pp. 105 f.

Smith and Hayek is the fact that the profit principle is distorted into a 'moral' or 'ethical duty':[509] 'Long-term profit maximisation is not a privilege that entrepreneurs should have to constantly apologise for; it is their moral duty'.[510]

This position reduces itself to a 'pure' apology for the market. Its use of the terms 'economy' *and* 'ethics' is illegitimate: the economy hardly features, aside from the sparse model assumptions that are perpetually eulogised morally, without their applicability to empirical reality ('objective reality' in the Kantian sense) being demonstrated. Kantian ethics, declared obsolete, is underdefined. For when Suchanek claims that 'modern society is no longer value- but rule-integrated',[511] and consequently demands for 'today' that 'men need to collectively set themselves the rules by which to govern their coexistence',[512] he is expressing nothing other than Kant's position, which Kant called human 'autonomy'.[513] But this human autonomy is exposed to ever greater threats 'today', and they issue from the very instance that Suchanek glorifies: the market and the capitalist mode of production that underpins it. It is because of the problems this causes that business ethics developed in the first place.[514] Transcendental business economics à la Homann, which calls itself 'business ethics', never even reaches this level of the problem.

3.3.4 *Historicist business ethics*

These excessively apologetic tendencies, which asserted themselves in the name of ethics, provoked concern even within the camp of business ethics. But in order to sort through the reactions within the discipline, one needs to take account of the discursive refractions that occur within the specific field of academic science, and which are due to the history of the relevant institutions. In particular, German economics and the German social sciences have been characterised for some time by a smouldering conflict between the paradigms of the natural sciences and the humanities (cf. 2.4.3). This conflict is restaged within business ethics: a 're-entry' (Luhmann). The restaging is only

509. Homann 1992, p. 38.

510. Ulrich 2001 also quotes (pp. 172 and 406) an entrepreneur to whom 'entrepreneurial activity is itself the first moral duty': 'To him, what is economically necessary is not opposed to what is morally right: the two coincide' (p. 401, quoting Gert Habermann). But this 'normative glorification' does not go back to M. Friedman, as Ulrich believes (p. 400); like Hayek, Friedman described the 'ethos' of the entrepreneur as being 'morally' neutral.

511. Suchanek 2001, p. 96.

512. Suchanek 2001, p. 19.

513. Kant, however, spoke of the 'law', not of 'rules of the game'. The word 'game' is evocative of the debate on 'rule-following' in analytic philosophy. But the comparison is misleading: playing a game presupposes a degree of removal from everyday life; games are played for leisure or for company, but not for the sake of playing them (this would be a compulsion). The rules of the 'market economy' need to be taken seriously; they increasingly determine the totality of relations (Sandemose 2001).

514. For a US perspective on this, see Hartley 1993, Wieland 1993a. On 'violations of the public trust', which have become the rule, see Werner 2001, Klein 2001 and Mander 2002.

partially due to real phenomena, to the objects of these sciences; it is at least equally due to the conflict between morality and economics as *sciences*. The humanities camp was all too willing to pick up the gauntlet thrown it by a reductionist economics bold enough to festoon itself with the laurels of 'ethics'.

It is no coincidence that the institutional context within which business ethics established itself at German universities was the 'Social Policy Association' [*Verein für Sozialpolitik*]. This association, which already played an important role in Max Weber's life, originated within the theoretical framework of the historical school. Weber was also one of the first to use the term 'business ethics' [*Wirtschaftsethik*]: in his sociology of religion, he examined the 'economic ethics of the world religions' [*Wirtschaftsethik der Weltreligionen*].[515] From this perspective, the economy was situated within a larger cultural framework, which in turn was influenced by a certain 'spirit'. Thus it seemed one could discover something about 'the' economy by examining the culture, the 'spirit' of an epoch – of which ethics is, after all, a significant aspect.[516]

But if the theory fails to conceptualise ethics as a form of intercourse proper to certain real relations, and if it does not relate ethics back to those relations, then 'mental' explanations of economic crises or structural problems are only a small step away – as if the 'intellectual and moral' dispositions of individuals had any effect on their purchasing power, their employment status or the amount of wages they receive.[517] Historically considered, the struggle was therefore less about the political consequences of a reductive economics than about the intra-academic interpretive sovereignty of the phenomenon 'business ethics'. It was at least *partly* about university appointments and about young scholars' chances of making a name for themselves. A struggle between worldviews is implicit in this, as each camp presents its position in the form of 'basic facts' (Molitor);

515. Weber 1984, pp. 237 ff.

516. Due to his sense of method, Max Weber was more careful. He limited himself to analysing the motivations of subjects and the genesis of those motivations ('the practical incentives for action rooted in the psychological and pragmatic relations of the religions': Weber 1984, p. 238; 2.4.6), and he made reference to a wealth of empirical material. But the very German reception of his work involved the sociological analysis of mind quickly becoming compulsively 'philosophical' again (2.5.2). This can be seen in Freyer 1920 or in the work of Werner Sombart, who traced capitalism back to a different set of historical relations in each of his books. 'Capitalism is not primarily an economic system that regulates the distribution of property; it is an entire system of life and culture. This system stems from the aims and appreciations of a certain bio-psychic type, namely, the bourgeois' (Scheler, '*Die Zukunft des Kapitalismus*' ['The Future of Capitalism'], 1913, in Scheler 1999, p. 113).

517. In an odd reversal of base and superstructure, Scheler already meant to reconfigure capitalism 'dispositionally' ['*gesinnungsmäßig*'], against social democracy (Utz 1994 still recommends something of the sort as a 'solution to the question of unemployment': 'live frugally, work more ... and save': pp. 159 f.). Here too, neoclassical economics is one of the theoretical prerequisites for ethicisation, since neoclassical authors consider unemployment voluntary. A worker always finds work: 'It is enough for him to temper his wage demands or change his profession and workplace' (Mises 1940, p. 546).

after all, entire life plans are at stake. However, stylistic differences do not necessarily lead to a different *result*.

The philosopher of religion Peter Koslowksi is an accomplished exponent of humanistic business ethics. His *Ethics of Capitalism*, which has seen several print runs, skilfully deduces the 'metaphysics of capitalism' ['*katallaxia versus oikonomia*'] from scholastic treatises[518] and from Leibniz:[519]

> Each culture has its own social metaphysics in which its last and general principles of '*Weltanschauung*' are included. This social metaphysics exerts a decisive influence on the conception of the economic system.[520]

In this way, capitalism is already mentalised on the level of basic concepts; it turns into a 'social theory'[521] and a stage in the 'manifestation of the development of the European spirit'.[522] No wonder the guest commentator of the neoclassically reductionist style, James Buchanan, does not understand this ('I do not understand the sentence...').[523] For what is Koslowski doing on the level of theoretical strategy? He is making it clear that capitalism cannot dispense with the humanities.[524]

Koslowski stresses this again by introducing a 'value problem':[525] capitalism releases people into freedom, but it does not tell them *what* they should do.[526] To make this point is to say little about capitalism, but it is to legitimate ethics, the lifeblood of the humanities, as a discipline. But once the place of ethics has been secured, it performs the very same function the Homann school hoped to see its *abolition* perform: that of providing the 'market economy' with improved theoretical legitimation and political support. Citing Ernst Jünger (this is, again, a question of taste), Koslowski prophesises that if the

518. Koslowksi 1996, p. 20.
519. Koslowksi 1996, p. 27.
520. Koslowski 1996, p. 21; cf. Freyer 1998, p. 48.
521. Koslowski 1996, p. 54.
522. Koslowski 1996, p. 13.
523. Koslowski 1996, p. 66.
524. Cf. 3.2.4. 'Intellectual' gourmets can expect to discover genuine delicacies in Koslowski's book. For example, Weber's hypothesis that capitalism was an unintended consequence of Calvinism is normally accepted without hesitation (Ulrich 2001, pp. 134 f.), but Koslowski opposes to it the hypothesis that the motives 'private property', 'profit and utility maximization' and 'coordination of economic activities by markets and prices' needed merely to be 'disembedded' intellectually (Koslowski 1998, pp. 11 f.); this, he argues, was achieved mainly by Hobbes (p. 16) and the Jesuits (p. 18). Elsewhere, Koslowski argues that the mediation of mechanism and teleology was first achieved not by Smith but by Leibniz (p. 29). In this way, Koslowski overhastily identifies political economy as a form of theodicy (ibid.). A certain lack of mediation is also evident in his – almost Agambenian – leap from Tertullian ('economic trinity') to Marx ('economic utopia': p. 29; cf. 2.6.6).
525. Koslowski 1996, pp. 32, 34, 36.
526. Koslowski applies Kant's ethical formalism to the very historical transition by means of which Homann and Suchanek sought to leave Kant behind; after all, he argues, Kant was familiar with the work of Smith (Koslowski 1996, p. 38; cf. 1982).

market is interfered with, 'terror' will result.[527] Compared to the reductionists, Koslowski is the better ideologue; at least his arguments are more appropriate to old Europe. In functional terms, he says the same thing, but he avoids stylistic and professional taboos.[528] He does a better job of responding to the widespread reservations about a 'pure' market economy.[529] On the level of content, he does not require anything more than the minimal or 'nightwatch' state, which even the most radical reductionists regard as necessary.[530]

Its deduction can integrate the critique of capitalism by opposing to 'pure' market sociation, which no one apart from Homann and his followers advocates, an 'ethical' sociation.[531] There is nothing in this to endanger capitalism, for by a wondrous dialectic, the market and the state correspond to one another as harmonious opposites – Koslowski speaks prosaically of a 'structural relationship'.[532] The title of his book already gestures in this direction (and the titles of humanistic works are seldom thoughtlessly chosen): Koslowksi did not call his book *Ethics* and *Capitalism*,[533] but *Ethics* of *Capitalism*.

---

527. Koslowski 1996, p. 51.

528. Koslowski is a rhetor first and foremost: he uses a different style to convey the same contents as economic theory. When for instance he demands that 'subsistence' must be warranted (Koslowski 1998, p. 49), this may sound innovative, but he is only rehashing the theory of immiseration: in real terms, wage decreases and welfare cuts are compatible with this. His 'consumer sovereignty', which seems at first to counteract inequality (p. 45; equalisation via average consumption), in fact merely reiterates Molitor's argument that productivity increases cheapen commodities – an argument that involved Molitor insisting that wages must under no circumstances increase. When Koslowski says that '[o]ne needs... institutions' (p. 48), he is sure to meet with approval in Europe. But the question is: what institutions? None that might democratise the economy, Koslowksi believes: 'Under these conditions, nothing is to be gained by the transfer from the market to a plebiscitary democracy' (ibid.).

529. The Pope had also decreed: 'The position of 'rigid' capitalism [*capitalismus rigidus, capitalismus primitivus;* C. H.] continues to remain unacceptable' (*Laborem exercens*, quoted in Waibl 1989, p. 178). See also writings like Forrester 1997, Lissabon Group 1997, Saul 1997, Nürnberger 1999, Jenner 1999, Klein 2001 or Strasser 2001. What is questionable is whether the 'other', putatively more ethical Adam Smith (Meyer-Faje 1991) can be invoked to justify such a tempered capitalism. Smith did not regard his moral philosophy as limiting his economic theory; on the contrary, he held that the economy lent support to his moral philosophy (Binswanger 1998, p. 122; cf. Ballestrem 2000).

530. Thus Buchanan likes to speak, albeit misleadingly, of 'constitutions' (Buchanan 1962 and 1990, and in Koslowski 1998). Friedman, Hayek and Nozick have also advocated a 'regulatory framework' (3.2.2). Koslowski faults Hayek and Buchanan for considering only the 'impartial rules', but not the reshuffling of the deck that is part of every card game (Koslowski 1996, p. 43). But what does he mean by 're-embedding the market... into social and ethical norms' (p. 42)? Are the two not always already bound up with one another in his theory? What he means is a theoretical re-embedding. To Marx, it is a truism that capitalist relations of production and forms of intercourse sediment themselves in corresponding legal relations (3.1.6).

531. Koslowski 1996, p. 32.

532. Koslowski 1996, p. 46.

533. Cf. Scheler 1999, Waibl 1989.

Thus Koslowski's historicist business ethics does not ground the apology for market economy differently; it grounds it twice.[534] In addition to his affirmative theory of the market, Koslowski also has one of the 'social genesis and normative justification of preference..., of... social institutions... and... of political compensation of capitalist failure'.[535] The market has nothing to fear from such a harmonistic 'ethical economy', not even on the level of theory. But other historicists object to this. Here, the dilemma of theological vs. managerial business ethics reappears in a different guise. For the abstract theological critique that is disharmoniously opposed to excessive affirmation can also be reiterated in a historicist form.

This is the case of Peter Ulrich. His call for subordinating the 'profit principle' to morality, limiting it 'morally', comes no closer to the reality of capitalism than the model constructs of Homann and Koslowski, its elaborate moral philosophical 'substructure' notwithstanding.[536] The only difference is that Homann and Koslowksi posit a state of *being*, whereas Ulrich abstractly opposes a *norm* to it. He aspires to the following target state: 'The legitimate pursuit of profit is always a morally limited pursuit of profit'.[537] If he wants to avoid this sentence being given a legitimatory reading ('The pursuit of profit is legitimate, therefore it has *always already* been limited morally'), he needs to supplement this demand with another, namely that for the 'primacy of politics vis-à-vis the logic of the market'.[538] Consequently, Ulrich begins by trying to provide, in a manner that reveals his indebtedness to discourse ethics, a 'justification' for his moral demand (the first, second and sixth chapters); then, he uses a political ethics to tailor for it the requisite institutional settings (chapters seven, eight and nine).

But *neither* of these operations ventures beyond the normative.[539] Ulrich even normativistically dissolves the constraint of profit maximisation, which firms have no choice but to act upon, if they want to survive. He does this by labelling all references to this constraint positivist: such references amount to the 'empiricist reinterpretation of a... normative question',[540] he claims, speaking elsewhere of an 'end to reflection'[541] – as if one could *rise above* reality by persistent reflection.[542] The ethical dimension Ulrich

---

534. On the historicist backdrop, see Koslowski 1995, p. 2000; Koslowksi 2001, he invokes the authority of Scheler, and in 1991 that of Schmoller.

535. Koslowski 1996, p. 54.

536. Ulrich 2001, pp. 124, 429; cf. 1.3; 3.2.4.

537. Ulrich 2001, p. 415.

538. Ulrich 2001, p. 334. Ulrich speaks equivocally of the 'primacy of political ethics' (p. 267; cf. pp. 145, 147), the 'primacy of ethics vis-à-vis economics' (p. 121) and the primacy of 'moral volition' (p. 25). This is already indicative of how he oscillates between theory and reality, thought and being. Here, ethics appears to be politics.

539. The remaining chapters (three to five and ten) criticise traditional business ethics; they do not transcend the internal perspective of normativity either.

540. Ulrich 2001, p. 403.

541. Ulrich 2001, p. 100.

542. Justifications eventually lead not to a normative ultimate justification but to an endpoint at which the 'spade' is 'turned' and one can only say: 'This is simply what I do' (Wittgenstein, *Philo-*

calls for first presents itself in the guise of a dualism that belies the influence of Habermas ('What is required is ... a dualist social theory');[543] it then becomes the counterpart of a reductive economics, namely *ethical* reductionism ('There is ultimately only one principle: the ... principle of morality').[544]

This development is only possible because of Ulrich's consistent mentalisation of the phenomenon: not only does Ulrich believe he can take literally the 'primary narrative' of capitalism's mentalisation,[545] namely Weber's narrative ('The Puritan wanted to work in a calling; we are forced to do so');[546] he also believes he can reverse it, as if he were not dealing with the past or with an ideal-typical construct of the past. Where Homann transformed a 'cannot' into an 'ought not', Ulrich transforms Weber's 'forced to' back into a 'want to'. The constraints of the market, he argues, are not real constraints; they are simply the *volition* of those who want things to be this way (Ulrich repeatedly places the word 'want' in italics).[547] There are no material causes for this, according to Ulrich, but only mental reasons.[548] Ulrich claims that it is only corporate ethics that gives the 'as if' – assumption[549] of the 'profit principle' normative significance, even though the 'validity'[550] of the principle 'cannot be demonstrated rationally'.[551] Thus, everything ends up being based not on real structures but on a 'metaphysics of the system'.[552]

Once the real problem has been redefined as a conceptual one, it appears it can be solved by a philosophical operation – Ulrich's categorical and conceptual prioritisation of

---

sophical Investigations, aphorism 217; *On Certainty*, aphorisms 110, 192 and 204); in this case: 'It's the economy, stupid!' But Ulrich has a German conception of philosophy: 'Integrative corporate ethics conceives of itself as a permanent process of ... reflection' (Ulrich 2001, p. 428; cf. 3.1.5 and 3.4.3).

543. Ulrich 2001, p. 145.
544. Ulrich 2001, p. 415.
545. Ulrich 2001, pp. 134 ff.
546. Weber 2003, p. 181.
547. Ulrich 2001, pp. 138, 140, 143, 144.
548. Ulrich 2001, p. 131 – 'that which is, is that which we want'; König 1975, p. 33; cf. 2.5.1.
549. Ulrich 2001, p. 415.
550. Ulrich 2001, p. 399.
551. Ulrich 2001, p. 401.
552. Ulrich 2001, p. 142; compare Koslowski. Ulrich is readjusting history when he claims that in the past, everything was normative ('wholly and fully permeated ... with norms': Ulrich 2001, p. 132) and holistic ('no separate areas with a distinct organisation of life': p. 133). There were separate reproductive worlds in the past as well; one need think only of slavery or the oppression of women (for an overview, see Krätke 2002). History is reduced to the history of ideas: Ulrich does not investigate given problems, but theories (from Arendt to Sandel). When these theories are no longer situated in actual political discourse, theory and reality become indistinguishable. For instance, Ulrich claims that Adam Smith enacted an 'epochal break' with business ethics (Ulrich 2001, p. 132; even though Smith was not the first economist to no longer treat economics as a subsection of ethics). But a few lines further down, he writes 'that Smith's liberal political economy can ultimately only be understood on the basis of his moral philosophy'. What happened to the break? The historical specificity of material conditions, of which the normative glorifications of economic ethics and normative social philosophy are a product, has vanished. When Ulrich states that it is a question of 'restoring non-coercive politico-economic relations of communication between emancipated citizens' (Ulrich 2001, p. 124), he mixes up ethics, politics, economics and reflection somewhat opaquely.

ethical legitimacy vis-à-vis economic rationality.[553] The price to be paid for this theoretical radicalism is political naievete: the dangers associated with a 'policy of placing limits on practical constraints'[554] are hardly examined. The plenitude of power that would be required for the implementation of such a policy seems not to pose any problems. But how would such power be obtained? Ought one not to ask:

> Who decides which values are defined, in a universally binding way, as the supreme goals of economic activity? If some institution places the economy under an obligation to pursue unitary goals, then we are soon dealing with a command economy. It displays authoritarian and paternalist features, because it claims to know what is good for people and what they should all desire.[555]

The first thing Ulrich would need to call for is far-reaching political change. But he contents himself with *philosophical* operations. It is only by conceptually alleging the existence of this sort of Rousseauian general will that Ulrich can smuggle in the 'primacy of politics'. While labelling the rights and virtues of economic citizens 'republican' sounds good,[556] Ulrich passes over this decisive issue, which already split the environmental movement.[557] On the domestic level, imposed guidelines are quite easy to sidestep by means of capital flight ('exit option').[558] The possible 'validity' of such restrictions, however it may be enforced politically and whatever its 'discourse ethical' justification, could prove inefficient, since it merely displaces the 'immoral' effects of the profit principle (exploitation, environmental pollution, proneness to crises); moreover, it could prove to be short-lived: no nation state will be able to endure such capital flight for very long, and so it will either sidestep such regulations itself, or it will revoke them.[559]

---

553. Ulrich 2001, p. 428.

554. Ulrich 2001, p. 162.

555. Waibl 1989, p. 153.

556. Ulrich 2001, pp. 293 ff., cf. Lorenzen 1991, p. 63.

557. It is hard to see how this politics of placing limits on practical constraints could be implemented other than in an authoritarian manner. Ulrich does not seem to be disturbed by authoritarian tendencies; he simply calls the position he aspires to 'republican liberalism' (Ulrich 2001, p. 296), without seeing the contradiction implied in this: a speculative-'dialectical' (p. 319) coincidence of opposites. A concept cannot be rendered legitimate simply by giving it a certain name. If Ulrich were to rely instead on the 'consensus-based regulation of disagreements' (p. 314), his position would be more moderate politically, but his demands would hardly be realisable – they would condemn themselves to insignificance. Once again, 'ethics' is preceded by an erroneous definition of the object, due to which action ultimately becomes unnecessary, since 'at bottom', or on the level of basic categories, everything is already in order. The other, social Darwinist reading of Ulrich's basic concept 'subservience to life' [*Lebensdienlichkeit*] – a concept that features in the title of his book, but which he does not elaborate on – is never discussed. Ulrich's position most resembles the elitism of Habermas, whose talk of legitimation by means of arguments does not refer to actual social deliberation, but to 'critical examination' as performed by intellectuals (p. 148).

558. Altvater and Mahnkopf 1999, pp. 343 f.; Habermas 2001b, pp. 68 f.

559. Ulrich touches on these issues at the end of his book (Ulrich 2001, pp. 377–91), but his proposals are not informed by them. He claims that 'sooner or later, crash barriers . . . will need to

German supernormativism fails, then, to overcome its 'mental' self-ghettoisation in historicist business ethics; it never makes it into the real world.[560] Here too, it limits itself to compiling catalogues of demands. It is not the formulation of demands as such that is unfortunate, but the fact that what is demanded is either impossible under the given circumstances or is always already the case. What underlies this is, once again, German philosophy's characteristic underdetermination of social reality. 'Normativity' is only a small part of this reality, and the more it is isolated, the less it is understood. The dilemma of business ethics, its unmediated oscillation between the abstract critique of theology and the equally abstract super-affirmation of business economics, has not been resolved by its transposition to 'humanistic' trappings. The philosophical annexes have not solved the problem; they have aggravated it.

3.3.5 *The Hegelianism of business ethics*

In the German context, this opposition of two unreconciled theoretical positions soon prompted theorists to devote their attention to a thinker who specialised in the sublation of theoretical oppositions: Hegel. It is indeed the case that what is missing here is the middle term, the reason being that the underlying child 'capitalism' was thrown out with the bathwater 'Marx'. Given the absent 'synthesis' of the two extremes, *each* position invokes Hegel to claim that it is itself a synthesis: everyone tries to show their own variant of business ethics is the 'mediating middle term' of all the others. 'One barren assurance, however, is of just as much value as another'.[561] Invocation of Hegel makes no difference to the various positions. It is merely another expression of the struggle over interpretive sovereignty. Tellingly, Karl Homann, the least philosophical of the business ethicists, stakes the most explicit claim to being the true successor of Hegel. It is a matter, he writes, 'of avoiding dualism from the outset':[562] 'An integration of ... morality and economics that is systematic in the Hegelian sense requires ... one to deduce them from an originary unity – identity'.[563]

Homann and his followers have succeeded perfectly in this endeavour: in their work, the 'parallel discourse'[564] of economics and ethics has become a 'philosophy of identity'[565] because one of the two sides has been *eliminated* by preliminary conceptual decisions: 'Economics is – merely – ethics by other, additional means'.[566] But a reductive elimination is neither a synthesis nor a sublation. Anyone with an affinity for Hegel must judge

---

be set up' (p. 384); taking his view, global 'vital-political embedding' becomes inevitable once the real idealist reversal of cause and effect is understood (p. 385).

560. Cf. *MECW* 5, p. 56.
561. Hegel 1967, p. 135.
562. Homann 1994, p. 11.
563. Homann 1994, p. 13.
564. Homann 1994, p. 17.
565. Homann 1994, p. 12.
566. Homann 1994, p. 18.

this attempt to make use of his thought a failure. (Although the opposite could also be argued, namely that this very way of proceeding is the 'truth' of Hegel.)[567]

Koslowksi is also basking in the aura of Hegel when he immodestly claims to be providing a *philosophical* 'theory of all of reality'.[568] Due to the unprecedented mentalisation that occurs in his work, ethics is not eliminated, but it is also reconfigured so as to always already correspond to the given model of the market. His ideological glorifications of the larger social organism, directed against a purely moralising critique, are a replication less of Hegel than of *Right* Hegelianism.

Left Hegelianism also experiences its business ethical *redivivus*: proceeding in a genuinely Hegelian manner at first, Peter Ulrich states his intention of 'thoroughly sublating... the two-worlds conception of ethics and unadulterated economics'.[569] But how does he go about this? Ulrich's way of posing the problem already renders it excessively theoretical. He believes he can solve the problem by discovering ethical concepts within 'economics', which he regards as being indifferent to theory and practice.[570] If this is to be something other than open affirmation, Ulrich has to *modify* the ethical concepts. As far as the critique of real phenomena is concerned, it seems to be sufficient to denounce certain mental dispositions or rationality types, namely those that do not accord with his concepts. Like the Left Hegelians, Ulrich limits himself to the critique of concepts. The analogy is evident even in the fine points of his critique of religion: Ulrich regards 'economic liberalism' as a form of *theology*.

> The naturalist systemic perspective of the 'free' market [*qua* theory; C.H.] is therefore the 'natural' perspective [not of a materially defined group; C.H., but] of those who mean to justify an economically determined market society as normatively right and meaningful because they believe [!] in the immanent meaningfulness... of an economic cosmos kept in good order by the 'invisible hand'.[571]

The reason Ulrich has no difficulties abandoning the profit principle is that he takes it to be nothing more than a *belief*, developed by theorists such as Erich Gutenberg[572] ('It was throughout merely a question of dogmas and belief in dogmas').[573] Ulrich wants to sublate his belief into something 'higher'.[574] Thus the conceptual operation performed

---

567. The accusation of reductionism can be extended to Hegel, even if it leads back to something else. In any case, Hegel's 'syntheses' also involved him eliminating whatever refused to be 'sublated' (Kant's freedom, nature, the thing in itself) by means of conceptual operations (cf. 2.5.2; 2.5.7, 4.2.2).

568. Koslowski 1994, p. 4.

569. Ulrich 2001, p. 119.

570. Ulrich means to discover 'the normative... within economic thought and [!] activity' (Ulrich 2001, p. 117; 3,1.2). His concept of 'economic reason' encompasses theory and practice – whatever is rational is real as well.

571. Ulrich 2001, p. 143.

572. Ulrich 2001, pp. 397 ff.

573. *MECW* 5, p. 29.

574. Ulrich 2001, p. 144.

by his business ethics reduces itself to calling for a 'new thought' (on this tendency, compare Ulrich's precursors Heidegger and Löwith: 2.5.5, 2.6.6). Consequently, his critique of economism is followed by a presentation of new categories. But a more conciliatory description of the same phenomenon is merely a somewhat more covert affirmation (an 'embellished shadow').[575] Marx anticipated this sort of operation when he remarked:

> Once upon a time a valiant fellow had the idea that men were drowned in water only because they were possessed with the *idea of gravity*. If they were to knock this notion out of their heads, say by avowing it to be a superstitious, a religious concept, they would be sublimely proof against any danger from water.[576]

In light of the complexity of today's economic circuits, which even customary economic theories are unable to grasp fully, the call for a renewed modification of 'categories' is not very convincing. For this ethicisation to be something more than a prolegomenon, 'business ethics' would have to provide far more substantive information on its object. As long as it fails to do this, its facile basic concepts will not allow it to grasp a reality that is problematic – leaving that reality to practical people and to those who formulate *explicit* apologies for it.[577]

Like the critiques of capitalism once formulated by the church or the *völkisch* movement, business ethics risks becoming, because of its vagueness, the pleasing accompa-

---

575. *MECW* 6, p. 144. What is meant by 'critical reflection on the ethical premises of legitimate pursuit of profit' (Ulrich 2001, p. 395)? What is critical about 'thinking systematically about indissoluble interrelationships' (p. 396), if they are indeed 'indissoluble'? Ulrich's website (www.iwe.unisg.ch/iwe/web.nsf) calls for a 'business ethics that searches for . . . the normative within economic categories and patterns of thought'. When he continues: 'and makes it accessible to critical reflection', he is giving the lie to his claim to merely want to 'disclose' categories hermeneutically (Ulrich 2001, p. 13). He is concerned with changing them. Ulrich 1993 calls for a different way of 'thinking' about the economy (Ulrich 2001, pp. 13 and 397 ff.; Suchanek 1994). The esoteric part of the environmental movement already called for a different way of thinking: 'What is needed is an economic culture that enables us to think [!] in terms of broad and long-term relations, and which makes us capable of understanding that there is no opposition between economics and ecology, but only one between short-term and long-term economics' (Waibl 1989, p. 152). This insight has obviously already been achieved. What is a culture shaped by more deeply, an 'insight' or its material structures? What prevents this insight from asserting itself? Like the Young Hegelians, Ulrich confronts reality with its own ideals, failing to perceive their dialectical unity: 'the basic philosophical ideas [!] of political liberalism . . . are too important to . . . resign oneself to their erosion' (p. 260). Reality is already a 'realisation' of these concepts, since it is reality that they originate in. To play one out against the other is to duplicate reality in the idea (3.1.6). 'This demand to change consciousness amounts to a demand to interpret the existing world in another way, i.e. to recognise it by means of another interpretation' (*MECW* 5, p. 30).

576. *MECW* 5, p. 24; cf. p. 5.

577. Ulrich repeatedly emphasises that he is presenting no more than a programme: he says he is 'trying to develop a "line of thought"' (Ulrich 2001, p. 15; 'an integrative ethical programme . . . would ideally . . .': p. 461). A lack of material elaboration is also lamented by Korff 1999, Vol. I, p. 870 and R. Pfriem: 'Ulrich should recognise that . . . prospects for development . . . can only come about by means of contributions to the . . . development of modern societies – not by means of principled condemnations of the pursuit of profit' (in Maak 1998, p. 484).

niment to the capitalist economy's unbridled additional expansion.[578] It is only on the assumption that these theoretical operations make a practical difference that talk of 'embeddedness' (Polanyi) becomes something more than the coining of new concepts. But the assumption is problematic: both in the Right and in the Left Hegelian versions of business ethics, the preaching of morality is counteracted by an elision of the world. Ulrich and Homann resemble one another in their failure to distinguish adequately, in their use of the term 'economics', between theory and object.[579] The 'synthesis' of economics and morality is made possible by virtue of the fact that economic *concepts* can be interpreted ethically – Homann does this by 'revealing' the alleged moral implications of the market, while Ulrich subordinates the market to morality 'conceptually'. Both treat theory and practice, the normative and the factual, thought and reality as a *unity*, except that, in the identity-philosophical agglomeration that is 'business ethics', it is sometimes the concept of the economy that is treated as being *more real*, and sometimes that of ethics – a subjective subject-object is opposed to an objective subject-object.[580] Both syntheses presuppose the prior mentalisation of the phenomena. The object of inquiry 'capitalism' slips through every theoretical net in the case of business ethics as well.

3.3.6 *The critique of globalisation as a placeholder*

With thought closing itself off to reality in this way, economic reason stepped out of the seminar rooms and lecture halls and became its other (to put it in Hegelian terms): it took to the streets. Thought did not strive for realisation, but reality strove towards

---

578. Papal demands speak of an ethical 'principle of the primacy of labour over capital' (*Laborem exercens*, quoted in Waibl 1989, p. 182). 'While the free market should not be abolished, competition should be limited in such a way as to render it just and social, viz. humane' (*Populorum progressio*, quoted in Waibl 1989, p. 179). On the one hand... On the other hand... But we are never told what should be done. Politically, the church limited itself to promoting a different way of thinking. This simply amounted to a normative glorification of what exists: the 'order of professions' was to lead to 'harmonious cooperation between the professions; humans were to regard themselves as a 'higher unity', 'beyond the distinction between employers and employees' (*Quadragesimo anno*, quoted in Waibl 1989, p. 183). 'All that matters is the tranquility of the explaining subject' (*MECW* 1, p. 45). The *völkisch* movement demanded that the economy 'serve the people' (F. Nonnenbruch, quoted in Waibl 1989, p. 158). 'The people does not live for the economy...; rather, finance and the economy, the captains of industry and all theories [!] have only to serve our people's struggle for self-assertion' (Hitler, quoted in Waibl 1989, pp. 261 f.). The *völkisch* movement also turned this into a cognitive operation by means of mentalisations: 'Ownership of the economy by the people is not a material fact but one of the soul and mind' (Nonnenbruch, quoted in Waibl 1989, p. 259). To Moeller van den Bruck, the economy was 'a superstructure, while ideas, power, law and the state are the base that supports the economy' (quoted in Waibl 1989, p. 157).

579. Something 'like "cognition of reality" is not a sensible research programme' (Homann 1994, p. 21). Ulrich also does not intend to provide 'solutions to concrete problems of economic activity and/or economic policy'; he merely wants to clarify the 'form of rational thought' (Ulrich 2001, p. 14).

580. Hegel 1977, pp. 17 f., 85.

thought.[581] It was not only the practical economists who interrupted the soliloquies of the theoretical economists;[582] more importantly, this was achieved by those real human beings whom Marx had always invoked. In the form of the 'masses', they provoked and influenced the current discussions on the economic state of the world. From this perspective, it is not just the year 1989 that marks a watershed, but also 1999.[583]

The ethicisation practised during the decade between these two years,[584] and the institutions this ethicisation made use of, are described as follows (and this at least captures the *intentions* of the most radical faction of business ethics):

> Analyses that refer to interests, and to relations of power and domination, were declared obsolete following the watershed of 1989. The representatives of lobbying non-governmental organisations (NGOs) now attempt to persuade 'the economy' that it is in its 'well understood interest' to globally adopt policies that are more social and ecological.[585]

Even the author of the work that initiated the 'ethicisation' boom understood himself to be acting primarily as a political consultant.[586] In the decades that followed, this legacy was largely passed on to business consultancy.[587] Noting that it has yielded no results, the critics of globalisation straightforwardly declare ethicisation to have failed: 'Another world is possible'[588] only if we fight for it. These counterforces must not address themselves to 'the state' or 'the politicians', asking them to please work toward a politics that is more ecological and 'social'. The question that is identified as crucial is one that academic theory neglected, that of the *subject* (cf. 2.2.2, 2.6.5). Leaving aside the question of whether globalisation can be traced back to concrete agents (this is what is suggested by talk of a 'crime scene' [*Tatort*]),[589] or whether it is a product of anonymous, non-attributable 'practical constraints'[590] – in order to resist its effects, the 'losers' of

---

581. *MECW* 3, p. 183.

582. For such efforts, see Tobin 1978, Scott 1997, Gray 1998, Krugmann 1996, Soros 1998 or Stiglitz 2002.

583. 'With the 1999 protests in Seattle, at the latest, it has become clear that not only is a broad protest movement possible in the metropoles, but it can make petrified relations dance. Seattle was followed by Davos, Prague, Göteborg, Genoa in the summer of 2001. They are all synonyms for a worldwide, many-voiced awakening and for militant refusal of globalised capitalism and its disastrous effects' (*Tatort Globalisierung. Die Zeitung zum BUKO 25-Kongress*, Frankfurt am Main, 9–12 May 2002, p. 1).

584. Kuschel 1999, Weiler 1999.

585. *Tatort Globalisierung. Die Zeitung zum BUKO 25-Kongress*, Frankfurt am Main, 9–12 May 2002, p. 2.

586. H. Jonas 1984, pp. 79 ff.

587. Steinmann 1994, Wieland 1999.

588. On this slogan, coined by ATTAC, see Cassen 2002, Grefe 2002 and Löwy 2002.

589. Cf. Gray 1999.

590. Altvater 1987.

globalisation[591] have begun to constitute *themselves* as a political subject.[592] But what does this politicisation tell us about business ethics?

The twentieth-century social history of the Western hemisphere can be roughly summarised as follows. Negative social developments and the widening income gap repeatedly had the political effect of prompting those affected to engage in 'direct action'. This led the state to juridify social claims, with the purpose of taming the class struggle and opposing something to the alternative system that had constituted itself in the meantime.[593] As a result, the social situation improved, by and large, but there also resulted a paternalistic depoliticisation. Detente was in any case only possible for as long as the post-war economic boom lasted. Following a decade of crisis, 1967–77, there began a period of global 'liberalisation', of reprivatisation and of the abolition not so much of protectionist policies as of welfare services.[594] Thus the institutionalisation of social disadvantages yielded to its re-individualisation.[595] The loss of juridified structures in the socio-economic and ecological spheres means that standards can no longer be enforced there; instead, there is now reliance on 'voluntary commitment'.[596]

The concomitant loss of secure rights and of material achievements associated with the 'social democratic century' (Dahrendorf) can, however, hardly be compensated for *ethically* (3.2.3). *Functionally*, ethicisation becomes a fig leaf for institutional downsizing. As the juridification of social conflicts continues to be revoked, returning to political action constitutes one remaining possibility for change: the number of strikes and major demonstrations is on the rise again. This is the 're-politicisation' long called for by

591. Mander 2002.

592. The church had already inaugurated the decade of 'business ethics'. Tellingly, some church groups are along for the ride again. Now that it no longer acts as the representative of the disenfranchised within a purely theoretical discourse, it is able to intervene as a mediator once more; this is, in keeping with its traditional role (2.6.6, 3.3.2).

593. On 'juridification', see Habermas 1984–7 and Kübler 1985. Confronted with material improvements in the situation of working people, the Western Marxism of the postwar period also pursued an 'ethical' course: instead of calling for additional improvements, it spoke of intact identities, greater liberty and 'repoliticisation' (cf. 2.6.3, 3.1.1 and 3.2.4).

594. Huffschmid 1999, pp. 98 ff.

595. Beck 1983.

596. The business ethicists all agree when it comes to endorsing this de-institutionalisation. To Ulrich 2001 (p. 13), an 'ethico-rational practice' presupposes a changed way of thinking – but it is only individuals who can think. Ulrich puts his faith in the 'willingness to engage in autonomous moral self-commitment, based on the insight that such self-commitment is humanly important both for us and for others' (p. 25). 'Competing corporations [another way of answering the question concerning the subject; C.H.] determine... their own standards of behaviour, e.g. with regard to environmental protection.... The most important form of such collective self-constraint is voluntary self-commitment. Such self-commitments may be defined as... legally non-binding declarations' (Suchanek 2001, p. 117). They tend to be nothing more than fine words, since: 'Important prerequisites for such a strategy include:... The self-commitment must be inherently advantageous for the participating corporations' (ibid.). But the decline in state power is not a general one: 'security' tends to be enforced more vigorously, both domestically (policing, domestic intelligence) and internationally (the military, alliance policies; Hirsch 1996 and Zugehör 1998, p. 105).

German theory.[597] With hindsight, 'ethicisation' needs to be read as an interlude associated with the secular process of *de-juridification.* Even on the level of outward appearances, the situation is gradually beginning to resemble the one that Marx took as his starting point. It is no coincidence that this constellation involves a return to Marx. To date, this return has, however, been limited to Marx's name being invoked on the feature pages of newspapers and to cadre parties confronting the critics of globalisation with proprietorial claims to being his sole legitimate heir.[598] As long as Marxism refuses to confront its *own* catastrophic history, fears of its renewed dogmatic ossification remain justified. In this way, it becomes a task of *philosophy* to do something about the lack of concepts by which to address the ongoing global political transformations. Philosophy has no immediate practical relevance and is therefore above any suspicion of extremism. It is up to it to ensure the content of Marxian thought is retained.

In this section (3.3), I have analysed another branch of German normative social philosophy and shown that the older dualist division into technology and ethics (Chapter Two) became an ethical claim to sole authority following the decline of theoretical Marxism. Hegel was explicitly evoked in support of attempts to grasp the social totality from one of several ethicised perspectives, including perspectives hitherto thought of as norm-free. This has failed to make the theory more substantive. By shutting itself off from the world in this Hegelian manner, it has in fact become more vulnerable to a Marxian critique.

3.4 Neo-pragmatism or the persistence of Hegel

In our examination of the philosophies of the present, their value-judgement controversies and the various syntheses within which they have been 'reconciled',[599] we noted the odd fact that they no longer have much to say about the underlying *objects.* This could be interpreted as a return of the philosophy of principles, were it not for their 'post-metaphysical' self-understanding.[600] What sort of philosophy are we dealing with? When one considers the genesis of this post-metaphysical principalism, one soon encounters the influence of an older current, which already staked a claim to being just

597. Islamist terrorism can hardly be seen as a countermovement, since it tends to accelerate not just the loss of social achievements such as tolerance, freedom of religion and equality of rights but also the transition to a militarised 'security state'. It contributes to the unsavoury aspects of globalisation. Incidentally, it is not interested in those aspects at all. Al Qaida is ultimately interested in ending the US 'occupation' of Saudi Arabia; the movement is a classic counter-elite, relying on reasonably well educated but relatively disadvantaged young men.

598. An article in the 22 August 2002 issue of *Financial Times Deutschland* featured a portrait of Marx (cf. 1.1). Participants in the conference on Lenin that Slavoj Žižek organised in 2001 were presented with real-life satire, as leftover Marxist splinter groups battled each other for hegemony over the critique of globalisation (cf. Bensaïd 2002).

599. Habermas 1999b, pp. 49 ff.

600. Habermas 1995, Rawls 1993; see also Forst 1999.

that: pragmatism.[601] From Peirce to Brandom, pragmatism was a *still more* reflexive philosophy addressing itself to a philosophy that was itself already objectless (a philosophy-philosophy).[602] It sought to transform not the content of philosophy but the manner of philosophising. And as its name suggests, it thought of this transformation as a movement away from a 'dualist' and contemplative (Cartesian and Lockean) philosophy toward a new approach that focused on action. What this *transformation of philosophy*[603] achieved for the US tradition was the overcoming of putatively old European idealisms that were being championed at the time, and thereby the founding of 'American philosophy'. Following the gradual decline of the analytic tradition, this prototypically American philosophy resurfaced, promoted, inter alia, by Rorty.

Rather than paying tribute once more to this development, I want to raise the question of what systematic benefits this transformation yielded vis-à-vis the transformations *already* achieved in Europe (3.4.2). From the perspective of an immanent functional analysis of texts (1.4), one can see the 'renaissance of pragmatism'[604] as being – at least in part, or as far as it political and socio-philosophical aspects are concerned – a reaction to the various waves of 1970s Western Marxism, but also (after the decline of Western Marxism in the 1990s) a theoretical lifesaver for ex- or post-Marxists. Neo-pragmatism moved into the gap that the disappearance of the various Marxisms had left in the academic world after 1989 (3.4.3). This was possible because of a superficial resemblance between Marxism and pragmatism. When considering them more closely, however, one notes striking differences (3.4.4). In Germany in particular, the late reception of pragmatism presented the opportunity of not abandoning the old positions of German thought but 'reconstructing' them in a modernised form. One needs, therefore, to ask critically whether the German post-Marxist reception of pragmatism, which is more technicistically oriented, should not be understood as a normative re-idealisation. The ongoing debates on this question have in any case not ruled out this possibility. Both German and non-German neo-pragmatism can be interpreted as a reissue of Hegelianism (3.4.1).

3.4.1 *The German reception of pragmatism as the index of a problem*

German philosophy, still world-renowned in the nineteenth century, involved a rupture long before American pragmatism: the break with Hegel.[605] It became necessary because

---

601. Apel 1975 and Apel 1973, Vol. II, pp. 157 ff.; Habermas 1987, pp. 91 ff.; Habermas 1995, pp. 149 ff.; R. Bernstein 1971.

602. Raatzsch 2000; Dilthey, *GS* VIII.

603. Apel 1973.

604. Sandbote 2001.

605. See Löwith 1942. Authors such as Kierkegaard, Bakunin or Ciesowski are part of the wider context of 'German philosophy', since their thought operated within a Hegelian framework. By contrast, French and English authors were often less in need of such a rupture, since materialism and political economy were already examples of 'worldly' thought. Marx differed from the Young Hegelians in that he also engaged with such non-German texts.

of the impossibility of retaining the post-Kantian philosophy of unity, especially Hegel's. Kierkegaard, Nietzsche and the philosopher who completed the work of both, Heidegger, abandoned some of philosopher's essential standards of rationality in response (2.5.5). If there was to be philosophy after Heidegger (and this problem was often felt to be an existential one), then it had to go back to a point before the rupture, but without saddling itself with Hegel's metaphysical baggage. A 'transformation of philosophy' (Apel) had become necessary; it meant to pre-empt the 'break' with philosophy.[606]

We have already seen that Kant's philosophy was not burdened with comparable deficits. Kant examined scientific rationality in a critically reflected manner, and his philosophy was itself an example of such rationality (2.5.2). And Marx had already broken with Hegel, without simultaneously breaking with rationality (2.5.7). This transformation of philosophy stimulated German thought for a long time, even if it only ever did so in a partial or deficient way (2.4–2.6). While Marx had left philosophy behind, he could be re-integrated into it on condition that one adopted a Kantian framework, as certain Austro-Marxist approaches showed (2.1.3, 4.2.3). Pragmatism's role in the USA corresponded roughly to that of Marx in German philosophy. An influential variant of Hegelianism had developed in the USA as well, albeit with some delay, and philosophy continued to bear the marks of this Hegelianism even after it had been overcome. This was probably why pragmatism was so enthusiastically received in Germany after Marxism left philosophy's stage. But what is a renewed 'Copernican revolution' supposed to achieve?[607] Why is it considered necessary? What is the effect of the renewed 'transformation' of a philosophy that has already been transformed into a sociologically enlightened thought?[608]

In postwar West German philosophy, Anglophone thought was being seriously engaged with again. This tore many German thinkers from their dogmatic slumber. The focus was on analytic philosophy, which inserted the new instance of language between old philosophical problems and their solution.[609] In reflecting on how thought is mediated by language, one began to examine the structures of language, in the hope of gaining new insight into old questions, or at least of sorting out those questions that are 'meaningless'. The main division within this movement resembled the one between Rawls and

---

606. From the outset, Habermas read 'American pragmatism as the ... third productive response to Hegel' (Habermas 1985b, p. 215). 'The real breakthrough in the reception of Habermas ... owes itself to Karl-Ottel Apel' (Joas 2000, p. 9). Apel's prefaces to Peirce's works (Peirce 1967 and 1970) were pioneering achievements; the consequences were drawn by Apel 1973; cf. Apel 1988.

607. Pragmatism resembles a counterrevolution: Kant inquired into the conditions of possibility. Pragmatism drew attention to the effects.

608. Marx needs to be neither re- nor de-transcendentalised, since his method – like all serious science – is simply subject to the 'transcendental' presuppositions identified by Kant (3.4.4, 4.2.3). Howard 1985 and Negt 2003 examine other links between Kant and Marx (see above, 2.1.3).

609. Philosophical patriots may have found some consolation in the fact that key founders of analytic philosophy, such as Frege, Wittgenstein and Carnap, were German speakers. Much the same was true of sociology's re-importations, since US sociology regarded German-speaking thinkers such as Marx, Simmel, Weber and, oddly enough, Ratzenhofer as founding fathers (2.4.1).

the communitarians (3.2.3): one faction thought it had discovered language's central structure, upon which everything else could now be made to depend, in the proposition (Russell, the early Wittgenstein, Carnap, Brandom), whereas the other theorised the irreducible *pluralism* of language games (the late Wittgenstein, Austin, Searle). What both factions had in common was the view that the examination of language would henceforth have to be the first and the most important field of inquiry for philosophical analysis. The analysis could of course be performed in different ways; hence the results obtained also differed.[610]

Now, the question is: what conception *underpinned* this reorientation of philosophy? The most 'basic' element was the view that human reality is linguistically constituted.[611] Regardless of whether this is achieved by several different 'speech acts' or by *one* central mechanism of world constitution, speech is thereby understood less as a way of expressing thoughts or emotions than as world-creating action.[612] However, the focus on language caused language to become, within reflection, the same sort of veil between subject and object that 'representation' and 'sensation' had previously been. The question of where the subject gets its object was by no means overcome; it was merely transposed to the question of how words refer to objects.[613] Thus the reflection upon reflection – upon the premises and implications of an analytic philosophy that was itself already reflexive – soon led to attention being directed at pragmatism.

Not only had pragmatism taken important steps toward an analysis of language;[614] it had also effected the requisite change in philosophy's basic orientation. It was 'no longer' consciousness, which had ostensibly once been regarded as constitutive, that attention was focused on, as in the 'philosophy of consciousness', but rather action.[615] The role that pragmatism attributed to action and speech seemed to imply an antecedent intersubjectivity that promised both to dissolve awkward dualisms and to provide an alternative 'grounding' for social philosophy,[616] whose results had hitherto left much to be desired. But is pragmatism even able to perform this task? 'Grounding' social philosophy was the

610. For an overview, see Hügli 1992, Blume 1998 and Demmerling 2002.

611. 'Logic fills the world': Wittgenstein, *Tractatus*, 5.61; cf. Carnap 1998.

612. Lafont 1994.

613. This was what Quine 1960 did; the question was also sometimes posed as that of how 'propositions' refer to 'facts' (Wittgenstein 1984). But repositioning the question is not the same as answering it. Analytic linguistic philosophy did not escape the dualisms (of mind and body, and so on) that were so feared in Germany; for a recent discussion of this, see Demmerling 2003.

614. 'Another such deception is to mistake a mere difference in the grammatical construction of two words for a distinction between the ideas they express' (Peirce, *Collected Papers*, 5.399).

615. Pragmatism's depth consisted less in its 'pragmatic' solution of philosophical and other problems (although this is what it propagated) than in its epistemological consideration of the constitutive effects of action (Greek *pragma*), which are prior to all thought (Nagl 1998). The dominant 'philosophy of consciousness' was however not the philosophy of Kant; in Germany, it tended rather to be that of Fichte, while in the USA it was a combination of Lockean psychology and Emersonian 'transcendentalism' (see below).

616. Habermas 1987.

last thing pragmatism had set out to do. It was concerned with developing a different concept of *logic*, and it wanted to provide idealist systematic philosophy with a new, up-to-date form.[617] What proved decisive was of course the way in which pragmatism was understood. It was fatal that neither pragmatism nor its adepts distinguished adequately between Kant and Hegel: because Kantian philosophy was seen through the dim lens of Fichte and Hegel, its internal differences were no longer perceived. As a result, certain weaknesses ('psychological props', 'metaphysical background assumptions', 'idealism') that are really associated with Fichte and Hegel (3.1.5), more than with Kant, were nevertheless projected onto Kant's philosophy, which one happened to be focusing on. And yet at the same time, one expected Kant's philosophy to do what Hegel's philosophy had promised.

It was only because too much was expected of Kant, and because Kantian philosophy was perceived as more homogeneous than it is, that a 'transformation of philosophy' came to be thought of as necessary in the first place. For this reason, neo-pragmatism's world picture made it look as if there existed a philosophy of unity that needed merely to be lifted off its high overworldly-metaphysical horse and brought back to the ground, but without making it cease to be 'transcendental'.[618] The plausibility of this goal depended, however, on the overly homogenising conception and interpretation of philosophy. Unfortunate results were the outcome, as the neo-pragmatist transformation was applied equally to the various parts of a philosophy that had already been transformed by Marx (3.4.4): it was applied to scientific theory and to reflection upon it as well as to ethics and politics and reflection upon them.

The disciplines of first philosophy and social theory, clearly distinguished in Kant and Marx, are conflated so strongly that in the end both are corrupted. Thus philosophy ceases to be a reflection upon fundamentals: theory's and morality's immanent conditions of possibility are '*de*-transcendentalised', even though this operation is fatal to them – by definition, an a priori cannot be obtained a posteriori.[619] At the same time, social theory was 're-transcendentalised': the theoretical pragmatist Habermas made it dependent first on the critique of knowledge, then on ethics and finally on a transcendentalised language (3.1). Any single scientific discipline will cease to be science as soon

617. Dewey 1949, p. 60, called for a new (epistemic, not metaphysical) idealism. Peirce already regarded pragmatism as the 'true idealism' (*Collected Papers*, 8.284; 'pragmatism is closely allied to the Hegelian absolute idealism': *Collected Papers*, 5.436). But the approaches chosen were entirely indebted to the old idealism – a diamond is hard only when it is perceived to be hard (*Collected Papers*, 5.403, and Apel 1975, p. 147).

618. Popular 'detranscendentalisers' included Wittgenstein and Heidegger (Apel 1973, Rentsch 2003, Habermas 2001). But the word 'transcendental' crops up six times on the contents page of Apel 1973, Vol. II alone; cf. Rentsch 1999a and Habermas 2003, p. 20; see also Schelsky 1959, p. 95; Kersting 1997, pp. 41 ff. and 121 ff.; cf. 3.1.5.

619. Apel 1973 II, p. 163, advocated a language-analytical and semiotic 'de-transcendentalisation of the cognitive subject'; Habermas wants to use Hegel to re-insert the cognitive subject into 'worldly contexts' (Habermas 2003, pp. 179 and 175; Habermas 2001).

as it is burdened with the task of providing 'philosophical' justifications that are foreign to it (3.2.4). This sort of iterated justificatory duty does not allow one to formulate concrete verdicts.[620] Theoretical and moral judgements are conflated with one another (3.3), and their cumulative 'justifications' cause them to be lost sight of. Empirical truth and moral judgement are abstractly called into question. I have already criticised the results of such 'normative social philosophy' in the preceding chapters (3.1–3.3). I will now analyse the theoretico-historical background of this re-idealising transformation with an eye to the question of whether or not it can serve as an equivalent of the Marxian transformation, and if so, to what extent it is able to do so.

3.4.2 *A transformation of German idealism?*

> We are not aware of this, nevertheless we do it.[621]

The scientific landscape of the USA, which only began to take shape in the nineteenth century, was initially strongly dependent on European ideas. These ideas were, however, expounded in distinct ways. Because European philosophy was dominated by idealism at the time (2.5.2), certain forms of idealism served as the 'point of departure' for pragmatism.[622] It meant to distance itself from them. Its attempt to do so was only partly successful, because idealism's questions were retained; they were merely answered differently. For instance, pragmatism's 'founder' Peirce felt indebted to Kant throughout his life: he meant to develop a *new* transcendental philosophy, one that came closer to the natural sciences. Peirce can therefore be compared to the Fichtean neo-Kantianism of his day (in 1867, he compiled a 'New List of Categories'): both effected a naturalisation of the cognitive subject.[623] What was original in Peirce was his choice to venture not

620. While Habermas objects to Kant's putative 'mentalism' (Habermas 2003, p. 177), he also wants to re-introduce 'transcendental consciousness' as a consciousness that is 'simultaneously social and manifold' (Habermas 2003, p. 19). Apel already wanted to 'find a way back to Kant' (or rather to a quasi-Kant: Apel 1973 II, pp. 161 f. and 173). Kant was read as a generative idealist (Habermas 2003, p. 209). Habermas was the first to problematise what Kant had still considered certain: he wanted to 'ground' the validity of truth in discourse. He failed, because there is never a discourse that is free of domination, whereas truth 'occurs' all the time. Discourse was merely the description of a promising genesis of truth (Habermas 1973b); its 'claims' were a call for such a genesis (Habermas 1981b). Habermas wanted to provide a foundation even for the 'transformed' categorical imperative (Habermas 1990b, p. 94). According to Kant, this cannot be done, since the moral law is unconditional: it admits of no 'transcendental deduction'; it is rather that which demonstrates the reality of 'freedom' in the first place. It is a 'fact... of pure reason' (Kant 1949a, p. 157), comparable to truth and reality in science (Kant 1998, p. 427/A 371).

621. *MECW* 35, p. 85.

622. I am referring, for example, to the neo-Hegelianism of F.H. Bradley and B. Bosanquet or the transcendentalism of R.W. Emerson and Thoreau (see Tenbruck 1985, pp. 239 f.; cf. p. 198; Baumgarten 1938; for an overview, see H. Schneider 1957).

623. Peirce, *Collected Papers*, 6.545 ff.; Apel 1975, p. 78; cf. A.F. Lange 1887 or Vaihinger 1911. In Peirce, the naturalisation resides not in the redefinition of the cognitive subject but in that of

into psychology but into semiotics, and his Scotist realism.[624] Peirce is only indirectly relevant to our topic, by virtue of his notion of 'logical socialism',[625] which was what rendered 'pragmatist social philosophy'[626] and neo-pragmatist normativism possible in the first place. How did it come about?

Peirce's naturalisation already involved an abolition of the distinction between a priori and empirical knowledge.[627] This meant that there was no longer any way to clearly determine when a proposition is true. Peirce was forced to resort to the metaphysical doctrine of postulates even when dealing with the simplest of things.[628] Thus Peirce's naturalisation leads him to lose the very centrepiece of Kant's philosophy: as in the Kantians and Heidegger, the desire to get rid of the 'thing in itself'[629] leads to a loss of secure knowledge about empirical states of affairs (2.5.2). Now, common sense has little use for a theory that claims we know neither what is true nor what is real, since these words serve us quite well in everyday life. Rejection of the only *accomplished* common-

---

thought itself: Peirce noted the pragmatic genesis of theory ('irritation of doubt ... is the motive for thinking'; 'belief is a rule for action': *Collected Papers*, 5.397), but went on to also reduce thought's content and mode of validity to this genesis ('and nothing else': *Collected Papers*, 8.13).

624. On semiotics, see Schönrich 1990; on Peirce's Scotist realism, see Honnefelder 1990.

625. Apel 1973, p. 177; Apel 1975, p. 367.

626. Schlüter 2000.

627. Peirce situates the structures of thought that Kant identified as 'transcendental' within the actual process of research. This is to conflate genesis and validity: 'There can hardly be any doubt that Peirce 1877 has succumbed to a subtle version of the "naturalistic fallacy"' (Apel 1975, p. 121): 'deeply committed to analysing the conditions of the concrete research process, he does not reflect on his own epistemological analysis' conditions of possibility' (p. 123). A '"reductive" reading of transcendental philosophy' (p. 75) is evident in the way that Peirce equates the function of a priori propositions that is relevant to their validity (a function that remains in effect even when the propositions are not of a general kind) with genetic issues: 'The Kantian distinction between phenomena and noumena ... is replaced with the distinction between the factually known and the infinitely knowable.... The Kantian dichotomy of synthetic a priori judgements and a posteriori judgements ... is replaced with the virtuous circle of hypothesis ... and experiential verification' (p. 74; Kempski 1952).

628. For 'every premise we require faith ... this is overlooked by Kant and others who drew a distinction between knowledge and faith' (Peirce, quoted in Apel 1975, pp. 29 and 77; Murphey 1961, p. 27; cf. Hegel 1977a and James 1897). As in Fichte, this rendered the distinction between theoretical and practical reason obsolete. To Kant, a proposition is empirically true when it corresponds to reality. 'Transcendental truth', the objective validity of the categories, is not sufficient for producing empirical truth. If analytic philosophy encountered problems with the 'theory of truth', this was partly due to the fact that it surrendered many Kantian distinctions (such as the one between analytic and synthetic judgements: Quine 1960). Differently from Hegelianism, the present works starts from the distinction between thought and being. Drawing this distinction also allows one to grasp the difference between belief and knowledge: knowledge is directed at what exists and is principally capable of truth, because it can be verified empirically. Belief follows a different grammar (2.6.4).

629. Peirce was also guided by this desire, as shown by Apel 1975 (pp. 29 and 67; Peirce, *Collected Papers*, 5.452 and 5.525).

sense philosophy, Kant's doctrine of the 'thing in itself',[630] ultimately leads to a need for elaborate constructs – in the case of American pragmatism as much as in that of German neo-pragmatism. These constructs are not rendered any more comprehensible by their *invocation* of 'common sense'.[631]

Peirce's alternative solution made 'objective validity', the truth of propositions, but also the reality of the proposition's content, dependent on a consensus of *opinions*: 'consensus... constitutes reality'.[632] Nothing is 'real' and 'true' but what all scientists agree upon – something that is, however, 'not already' the case. In light of the persistent disagreements among scientists, the consensus was relocated to the uncertain future of a 'final opinion',[633] and thereby rendered even more abstract.[634] This amounted to an unwarranted reconstruction of the validity conditions of talk about truth, following the abandonment of the 'transcendental' distinction between thought and being. It is, however, far more speculative than its putatively 'metaphysical' precursor Kant. The 'real-

630. The same object can be considered from various perspectives. We experience this fact every day (your view is not mine, and no one knows what 'really' happened). Nevertheless, we do not question the existence of reality. This state of affairs only begins to seem problematic when one reflects upon it: the plurality of perspectives places comprehensive cognition of the object beyond our reach; the object becomes a 'thing in itself'. But this is merely to preserve what we observe every day, against the exaggerated claims of the sciences.

631. Peirce 1905 refers to 'critical common-sensism' (*Collected Papers*, 5.438; cf. James 1907, pp. 111 ff.; Mead 1968, p. 402). Peirce, James and Dewey conflate the knowledge that is given both in everyday life and in the single sciences with a putatively metaphysical 'knowledge' of overworlds and primordial principles. Thus by abandoning one, they also abandon the other. This is an explanation of the exception to the rule, a transformation of the theory of crisis into the crisis of theory (cf. 2.5.1). Kant reserved the term 'pragmatic' for the exceptional case of action needing to be taken in the absence of knowledge: 'The doctor must do something for a sick person who is in danger, but he does not know the illness. He looks to the symptoms, and judges, because he does not know of anything better, that it is consumption. His belief is merely contingent even in his own judgement; someone else might perhaps do better. I call such contingent beliefs, which however ground the actual use of the means to certain actions, pragmatic beliefs' (Kant 1998, p. 687/A 824; compare the 'hypothetical imperatives' and 'counsels of prudence' in Kant's ethics). Pragmatism transforms this exception, turning it into the rule: knowledge becomes possible only in the mode of 'belief' (Peirce 1877, in 'Fixation of Belief', *Collected Papers*, 5.358 ff.; James 1897).

632. Peirce, *Collected Papers*, 8.16.

633. Peirce, *Collected Papers*, 8.17.

634. 'Everything, therefore, that will be brought to exist in the final opinion is real, and nothing else' (*Collected Papers*, 8.13). 'The opinion which is fated [!] to be ultimately agreed to by all who investigate, is what we mean by the truth, and the object represented in this opinion is the real' (*Collected Papers*, 5.407). Unfortunately, however, 'catholic consent' (*Collected Papers*, 8.13) is a disputable assumption, including historically: social and ethical questions, for example, admit of no obvious answer. Among other things, Peirce is ignoring the transcendental dialectic: '*non entis nulla sunt praedicata*' (Kant 1998, 670/A 793). One – temporally removed – perspective is declared to be the only one. If one takes this passage seriously, it leads to a futuristic, scientio-speculative onto-monism that rivals Ernst Bloch.

ity of the outside world' was rendered problematic, much as in Berkeley (and later in Dilthey).[635] It was no accident both Peirce and James referred back to Berkeley.[636]

The 'loss of the world'[637] is especially evident in James, who popularised pragmatism. While James champions a 'natural realism' in his theory of perception, not much of it remains in his 'conception of truth', which prompted many critical reactions.[638] Peirce's reflexive definition, according to which the *concept* of a thing is identical, for us, to the notions we have about its *effects*,[639] became a reductive 'theory of truth' in James. The theory claimed that an assumption is 'true' when its long-term effects turn out to be 'good'. While this is not altogether untrue, it is not a complete definition of the concept either.[640] The incompleteness of the definition leads to what is called 'pragmatic' in the pejorative sense: when common sense is not just regarded as the foundation of all higher-level knowledge but erroneously elevated to the status of a 'theory' in its own right (4.1), it has difficulties relating *other* theories to an identical object and is forced

635. Dilthey, *GS* V, pp. 90 ff.; cf. 2.5.2.

636. 'Berkeley's criticism of "matter" was ... absolutely pragmatistic' (James 1907, p. 68). Pragmatism 'does little more than consistently carry out the "pragmatic method"' which Locke and Berkeley 'were the first to use' (James 2008, p. 5; cf. Peirce, *Collected Papers*, 5.219, 5.310, 6.481, 8.30). Lenin's apparently far-fetched comparison of pragmatism to Berkeley (Lenin 1972, p. 355) was quite apposite after all. Kant grasped the dilemma: 'The transcendental realist therefore represents outer appearances ... as things in themselves ... It is really this transcendental realist who afterwards plays the empirical idealist; and after he has falsely presupposed about objects of the senses that if they are to exist they must have their existence in themselves even apart from sense, he finds that from this point of view all our representations of sense are insufficient to make their reality certain' (Kant 1998, p. 426/A 369). Incidentally, Mead once meant to write his doctoral dissertation under Dilthey's supervision.

637. Putnam 1998, p. 30.

638. It was not until National Socialism that pragmatism was taken seriously (Baumgarten 1938, Gehlen 1988, p. 253). On the earliest German debate, see Joas 1992, pp. 114 ff. On the reception of pragmatism in Fascist Italy, see Diggins 1972. Putnam 1998 emphasises the 'natural realism' of James, and in doing so refers to the readings of James found in Russell and Austin. But James more resembles the idealism of Husserl ('natural attitude') and the 'critical realism' of Külpe and Schwarz (Henning 1999, pp. 54 ff.), since he speaks of a *Will to Believe* (James 1897), not of a 'reason' to believe.

639. What 'a thing means is simply what habits it involves' (*Collected Papers*, 5.400). In this, it is mainly concepts that are at stake: 'Consider what effects, that might conceivably have practical bearings, we conceive the object of our concept to have. Then, our conception of these effects is the whole of our conception of the object' (*Collected Papers*, 5.402; Apel 1975, p. 143).

640. The definition of a concept cannot content itself with naming examples; it has to define its object to the point where exemplary cases can be understood as applications of the concept. This is little to do with satisfaction: 'Why should truth be at the service of our interest, yield satisfaction rather than frustration, pleasure rather than pain?' (Diggins 1998, p. 220). James, by contrast, propagated the 'attitude of looking away from ... principles ..., and of looking towards ... fruits' (James 1907, p. 47). Out of the countless variations on this theory, some are doubtless better than others. But picking one of them out, making some technical improvements and then presenting it as the yardstick by which to measure the others, in order to dismiss criticisms of James as 'misunderstandings', is a questionable procedure. The fact remains that James wrote unambiguously: 'Ought we ever not to believe what it is *better for us* to believe?' (James 1907, p. 77). This epistemic voluntarism should be taken at its word; all the more so as this sort of technicised thought was precisely what prompted Peirce to rename his own theory 'pragmaticism'.

to reject them. James's 'natural realism' can therefore be opposed to the critical examination of propositions about reality. From an immanent functional perspective, this 'theoretical strategy' has the effect of shielding prejudices and ideologies *from* scientific elucidation (see 2.5.5). Despite the many differences between James and Nietzsche, the two do have one major commonality: both gave in to a vitalist notion of truth that was always able to reject 'truths' without bothering to inspect them more closely, simply by claiming that they are harmful to 'life'.[641]

In this way, other theories can easily be rejected or ignored (or adopted, if they have greater 'vital value'). To be sure, this is a certain type of pragmatic *behaviour*, not a 'theory'. But that is precisely what pragmatism wants as the yardstick by which to assess conventional theories. Consequently, pragmatism must also allow itself to be assessed by this yardstick. Kant used the word 'pragmatic' to mean 'consequence-oriented, provisional'. This was precisely how Peirce understood the term when he adopted it.[642] He wanted to use it to express the intuition that there are many things of which we can have no certain knowledge, so that we have to content ourselves with probabilities. In such cases, he argues, 'pragmatically' paying attention to the consequences of something is enough for knowing that thing. Kant would probably have agreed as far as everyday life is concerned, and Aristotle with regard to *phronesis*. But philosophy is less concerned with *producing* such certain knowledge than with determining, by means of a critique of meaning, what we mean by the words 'knowledge' and 'truth' when we use them appropriately, and how they are possible. When Peirce claims that to understand the consequences is to have obtained 'the whole "meaning" of a conception', he turns a pragmatic emergency into a pragmatic rule.[643] But when I am compiling examples of possible consequences, I need to be able to say what *makes* them consequences – thus Kant:

---

641. 'The method of 'pragmatic hermeneutics' may only lead to a consensus-contrived interpretation that reflects little more than a specific generation's subjective dispositions' (Diggins 1998, p. 224). James's notion of truth is subjectivistic (a '*satisfactory relation with other parts of our experience*': James 1907, p. 58 – a hedonist coherence), technoid ('truth in our ideas' is synonymous with 'their power to "work"': ibid.), utilitarian ('an idea is "true" so long as to believe it is profitable to our lives': p. 75; '"*The true*"... *is only the expedient in the way of our thinking*': p. 222); construed ('Truth is *made*': p. 218), superficial (the 'pragmatic method' is '*the attitude of looking away from first things*': pp. 54 f.) and irrationalist (the approach is 'anti-intellectualist' and concerned with 'vital benefits' in 'real life': pp. 54 and 78; 'if there were *no* good for life in true ideas, or if the knowledge of them were positively disadvantageous and false ideas the only useful ones, then... our duty would be to *shun* truth': p. 76).

642. Apel 1975, p. 109, refers to passages in which Peirce elaborates on how he was inspired by Kant (*Collected Papers*, 5.1, 5.412). He does not mention a passage that I take to be centrally important (pragmatic = contingent belief: Kant 1998, pp. 686 f./A 824). Hochkeppel 1989 describes our everyday usage of the word 'pragmatic' as follows: 'A politician's leadership style... is referred to as "pragmatism"' when 'he makes his decisions based on whether they prove themselves in practice, in the here and now', and when he 'gets his bearings not from an overarching theory... but from the given prospects for success'. This corresponds functionally to Bernstein's role vis-à-vis Marx (Hochkeppel 1989, p. 270).

643. The 'whole "meaning" of a conception expresses itself in practical consequences' (Peirce, *Collected Papers*, 5.2).

> If the grounds from which a certain cognition should be derived are too manifold or lie too deeply hidden, then one tries whether they may not be reached through their consequences. Now *modus ponens*, inferring the truth of a cognition from the truth of its consequences, would be allowed only if all of the possible consequences are true ... But this procedure is unusable, because to have insight into all possible consequences of any proposition that is assumed exceeds our powers.[644]

Thus, according to Kant, to consider consequences only is to underdetermine the concepts of truth and reality. This is also a critique of Berkeley, who inspired Peirce's maxim).[645] When the correct insight that science rarely *results* in certain knowledge (e.g. because it is hardly possible to genuinely isolate factors) is generalised into a *premise* of science, it ceases to be science; all that remains is occasional problem solving, a mere 'muddling through'. The endpoint of this pragmatist disempowerment of scientific rationality is marked by Dewey's agnostic statement that 'today', one should abandon the concepts of 'necessity' and the 'rule'.[646] This would render impossible even the most basic of scientific operations, namely drawing inferences from general laws and antecedent conditions.[647] Where there are no rules, violating a rule becomes inconceivable, so that the critique of knowledge is likewise eliminated. But these problems only appear to have been solved when they 'disappear' from view for the pragmatist. The only thing that really disappears is scientific rationality – this resembles a *destruction of reason* (Colletti).[648] The pragmatists have not been able to avoid becoming idealists, metaphysicians, and – as far as political philosophy is concerned – ideologues.[649]

---

644. Kant 1998, p. 669/A 790.

645. Peirce, *Collected Papers*, 6.481. The concept of 'rule-following' does not replace that of truth either; it merely provides an account of its genesis. Learning by example only yields vague knowledge; theory requires accuracy.

646. 'For just as *necessity* and the search for a *single* all-comprehensive law was typical of the intellectual atmosphere of the forties of the last century, so *probability* and *pluralism* are the characteristics of the present state of science' (Dewey 1939, p. 123). Dewey also 'suspends' the distinction between philosophy and science. He cites results obtained by science; these were never as conclusive as Dewey suggests. But in order to arrive at them, one needs to presuppose both logical necessity and the efficacy of the laws one is seeking to identify. Like Peirce, Dewey contaminates the philosophical demonstration of science's *conditions of possibility* with science's inferences.

647. Hempel and Oppenheim 1948.

648. See 2.5.4; cf. Habermas 2001, p. 21. 'We do not solve them, we get over them. Old questions are solved by disappearing' (Dewey 2008, p. 14; cf. Wittgenstein 1984, p. 85). Rorty's abandonment of the critique of knowledge (1979) is a logical consequence of the cancellations of dualism attempted since Peirce. Kant's distinctions were criterial; they were subservient to critique. The slimming down of philosophy I am calling for is the opposite of this curtailment of science.

649. Rorty laments philosophers' lack of patriotism (Rorty 1999, p. 252; Rorty in Joas 2000, p. 339). He wants philosophy to operate without any correspondence to reality, without concepts of essence and without principles; on his view, it should simply articulate political hopes and create cosy group identities ('solidarity': Rorty 1989). 'The founding of democracy through logic' (Westbrook in Joas 2000) merely calls for a democratisation of science (everyone should be able to contribute to hypotheses). This resembles the 'communism' of Feuerbach (Joas 1980, pp. 55 and 138 compares Mead to the Young Hegelians; cf. Habermas 1985b, p. 215). Dewey's concept

A theoretical occasionalism[650] is evident not just in the superficial aspects, but in the very fundamentals of pragmatist theories. Joas has noted[651] that the difference between the anthropologies of Gehlen and Mead consists in their different political stances. This is an example of theoretical relativism: philosophical anthropology, which wants to be the *foundation* of all other human sciences, is itself dependent on something – on value judgements. If what is true is what is 'good for us', then our view of what is 'true' depends, first, on who 'we' are,[652] and second, on what we take to be good. It is only subsequently that available 'objective' propositions are grouped around these decisions. This may occasionally be an accurate description of how opinions are formed in society. But it is no replacement for the absent criterion of truth. It was only consistent for many pragmatists to devote themselves *directly* to political agitation – not just for democracy, but also for socialism or Italian Fascism (see 2.5.1, point 8).[653]

What has remained of this in the minds of the neo-pragmatists is only the 'democratic' variant, which espoused a tendency that 'we' still take to be significant today.[654] This is why pragmatism's theoretical voluntarism seems to be excusable; it needs merely to be provided with additional 'justifications'. But it is only when 'pre-reflexive voluntarism' becomes aware of its foundations that pragmatism can be interpreted as a coherent whole. For example, the neo-pragmatist Rorty began by rejecting the theory of knowledge,[655] as is consistent with the pragmatist approach; he then went on to replace theory with 'democracy', in continuity mainly with Dewey. But when 'democracy' is ahistorically grounded in human nature,[656] pragmatism abolishes itself, since it had once thrived on the desire to reject such grand metaphysical propositions. The pragmatists

---

of 'democracy' is abstract (it does not describe the concrete functioning of a country's political institutions) and appellatively expectant; sometimes it becomes sermonising (Joas 1980, p. 214). Peirce and James wanted to prove the existence of God; Mead was the son of a theologian; Royce was himself a theologian. In 1939, Dewey wrote that 'he had worked all his life to make explicit the religious value inherent in the spirit of science, as well as 'the religious values implicit in our common life, especially in moral significance of democracy as a way of living together'. Democracy becomes Dewey's secularised religion' (Joas 2000, p. 157; Joas rejects the theme of the 'sacralisation of democracy': p. 17). Peirce's 'ideal society' (Peirce, *Collected Papers*, 5.311; Mead 1934, p. 317) was not particularly pragmatic either, and it displayed religious features. Perhaps Marx was right to formulate cautiously when he wrote: 'For Germany, the *criticism of religion* is in the main complete' (*MECW* 3, p. 175).

650. Cf. Löwith 1984b.

651. Joas 1979.

652. Karl Mannheim also diagnosed thought's special affinity with being (Mannheim 1936, pp. 258 ff.); although he hoped that by drawing attention to it, he would be able to mitigate its effects. Rorty's 'we' (Rorty 1989, pp. 108 and 307) is flexible and vacuous – and sometimes patriotic (Rorty 1999a).

653. Diggins (1992 and 1998) draws attention to this. The pragmatist William Y. Elliot (*The Pragmatic Revolt in Politics*) espoused fascism (Diggins 1972), whereas Dewey's student Sidney Hook was a Marxist (Hook 1933).

654. Honneth 1999a, Joas 2000.

655. Rorty 1979.

656. Dewey 1918, Mead 1934.

ended up championing metaphysical systems of their own, just like the European thinkers of the period.[657]

3.4.3 *Neo-pragmatism and Marxism as hostile brothers*

In light of the difficulty of comparing theories from different contexts, we need to begin by asking the question of what exactly major philosophical operations are supposed to achieve theoretically and, by way of theory's mediation, socially.[658] The immanent-functional understanding depends on how the actors perceive and interpret their initial theoretical situation. Kant, for example, was read in a psychologistic way both by the Kantians and by Peirce. Kant's terms were understood as the proper names of entities that had after all to 'exist' somewhere: they were situated either 'in consciousness' (an interpretation that suggested itself due to the persistence of British empiricism)[659] or in an 'overworld', as the influence of Anglophone 'transcendentalism' suggested.[660] Neither option seemed attractive. Hegel was more accessible to the pragmatists, since they shared his speculative 'need'.[661] For it seems that pragmatism was also driven by a need

---

657. See Peirce 1891 (Apel 1975, pp. 259 ff.), James 2008 or even Dewey 1929. Pragmatist voluntarism had a parallel in German thought, which devoted itself to other issues for purely contingent reasons (2.5.2, 2.5.5; Joas 1992, pp. 114 ff.; Joas 1993). Horkheimer's adage that human interests do not remain extraneous to reason was also of this kind. This is why critical theory could easily be combined with pragmatism, despite initial scepticism (Dahms 1994, pp. 191 ff.).

658. Rehberg 1985, pp. 61 f.; Tenbruck 1985. Pragmatism compared itself to the Copernican revolution (Dewey 2002, p. 13) and the Reformation (Dickstein 1998, p. 3).

659. Peirce read Kant as an exponent of 'psychological transcendentalism' (Apel 1973, Vol. II, p. 168, quoted in Murphey 1961, p. 26). His transformation was that from a solitary to an intersubjective naturalisation: Kant's 'highest point' was transferred, in a reifying manner, onto 'the future thought of the community' (Peirce, *Collected Papers*, 5.316; Apel 1973, Vol. II, p. 169). But the first reading, which is merely reconfigured in the second, is already flawed. It is not the structures of the subject that 'ground' certain knowledge, but vice versa: the certainty of empirical knowledge allows us to infer the structures of thought. 'Where' these structures 'are' is not a philosophically interesting question, and it is not a question that Kant made any claim to answering (Kant 1998, p. 273/A 141). What is important is that we ourselves institute these structures, and that we have 'always already' done so. Kant is by no means 'nothing but a... confused pragmatist' (*Collected Papers*, 5.525; Apel 1973, Vol. II, p. 169).

660. 'All philosophies of the classic type have made a fixed and fundamental distinction between two realms of existence... Over against this absolute and noumenal reality which could be apprehended only by the systematic discipline of philosophy itself stood the ordinary empirical, relatively real, phenomenal world of everyday experience' (Dewey 1949, pp. 42 f.). The normal world of human beings has never been the 'pure' world of physics, to which an overworld was opposed, as Dewey holds (Dewey 1949, p. 35; at best, this 'common sense' was the worldview of some nineteenth-century engineers: Hortleder 1970). The metaphysical tradition usually referred to the 'world' that Dewey has in mind. But in considering this 'world', it drew certain critical distinctions – which Dewey abandons, because he can no longer make sense of them. This does not prevent him from freely formulating metaphysical propositions of his own (such as 'every individual into the full state of his possibility': Dewey 1949, p. 147; 'liberating of human capacity': p. 164 – these are conventional metaphysical positions).

661. 'When the might of union vanishes from the life of men... the need of philosophy arises' (Hegel 1977, p. 91). On Hegelianism in Peirce, see Apel 1975, pp. 30 and 50; in Mead, Joas 1980,

to overcome the 'painful dualism'[662] of mind and body, subject and object, religion and science – it was characterised by a 'revolt against dualism'[663] and a need for 'unity and 'reconciliation' (2.5.2).

And genesis and validity, theory and practice, logic and ethics were in fact newly 'combined', conflated, by pragmatism – as had earlier been done in pre-Kantian philosophy and in German idealism.[664] Like the German philosophy of *Weltanschauung*, the pragmatist philosophy of unity was forced to proceed voluntaristically and be 'partisan'. Its varying degrees of popularity are related to this partisanship.[665] According to Tenbruck, G.H. Mead practised the partisanship of philosophy by holding up the flag of 'Americanism' and polemicising against Europe and, to a lesser extent, the East Coast.[666]

---

pp. 57 ff., Honneth 1996 and Nagl 1998, pp. 89 ff.; in Dewey, Rorty 1994 and Joas 2000, pp. 124 and 228. Peirce claimed a 'close affinity' with Hegel, arguing that he acknowledges an 'objective logic' and, 'like Hegel', is concerned to 'assimilate the truth to be got from many a system' (*Collected Papers*, 8.283). He believes 'the one intelligible theory of the universe is that of objective idealism, that matter is effete mind, inveterate habits becoming physical laws' (*Collected Papers*, 6.25/6.605; cf. Apel 1975, p. 20). To Dewey, Hegel was the 'quintessence of the scientific spirit' (*Early Works* 3, p. 134, quoted in Rorty 1994, p. 35).

662. Joas 2000, p. 16.

663. Lovejoy 1929.

664. Habermas shares Heidegger's aim of overcoming the 'subject-object model of the philosophy of consciousness' and identifies the 'approaches to the critique of consciousness' developed by language analysis and behavioral psychology as pragmatist (Habermas 1984–7, Vol. II, p. 11; on Peirce's 'will to the system', see Apel 1975, pp. 30 ff.). A quest for unity can also be found in James, who often speaks of 'reconciliation' (James 1907, pp. 33, 55, 172). Although he rejected an overhasty monism at the time (James 1907, p. 108), he would later adhere to it himself (James 2008). The case of Dewey is similar. His concepts of 'habit' (Dewey 2008b) and 'experience' are supposed to be above and prior to every opposition, in an approach informed by Bergson (Dewey 1929; cf. Rorty 1982, pp. 72 ff.; Shusterman 2000). Joas identifies Mead's motives as that of unifying knowledge (on the model of the 'experimental natural sciences': Joas 1980, p. 40) and 'overcoming the distinction between practical and theoretical reason' (p. 41; Rehberg 1985, pp. 63 and 83). Pragmatism was first and foremost a *Weltanschauung*.

665. The 'great systems have not been free from party spirit exercised in preconceived beliefs' (Dewey 1949, p. 41); 'what philosophy has been unconsciously…, it must henceforth be openly and deliberately' (p. 46). Thus philosophy is to be openly partisan (2.2.2). '[I]f philosophy takes for its pragmatist goal not the grounding of knowledge but the production of better lived experience, then it need not be confined to the realm of discursive truth and the language-games of their justification. Philosophy can aim more directly [i.e. non-reflexively; C.H.] at the practical end of improving experience by advocating and embodying practices which achieve this' (Shusterman 1994, p. 141). Heidegger's philosophy of unity also entailed that he could only proclaim, in 1933: 'We want ourselves!' (2.5.5).

666. Tenbruck 1985 contextualises Mead. Its conjunction with political currents such as the 'social science movement' (a group of social workers who ran the 'Hull House' in Chicago) caused American sociology to get off to an unprofessional start, as A. Small later admitted (Tenbruck 1985, p. 190). Mead championed a crude Americanism: 'Thus Mead does not present us with human beings as experience, biography and history show them to be, but as the "American community" wishes them to be' (p. 229). '"The American pioneer was spiritually stripped for the material conquest of a continent and the formation of a democratic community". He required no other justification for his actions and decisions than the palpable improvement of life in the community' (p. 197). The 'declaration of independence from European culture is followed by a song of praise in which pragmatism is glorified as the right philosophy for American democracy and the American

Theories that seemed to him not to be 'good' were excluded (according to James's theory of truth, this is legitimate); Marx's theory was among them, unsurprisingly.[667] This voluntarism renders questionable both Mead's own theory and the ethic blended into it.[668] Nevertheless, neo-pragmatists still adhere to his 'principalisation' of this choice of sides.[669]

While critics of pragmatism have seldom succeeded in attacking pragmatism on the level of content, it presented them with an open flank here: *endorsement* of one side entailed rejection of another.[670] That Marxism features as *one* of pragmatism's declared enemies should not come as a surprise to anyone. An attempt to play 'democracy' off against Marxism can already be found in Eduard Bernstein (2.1.1). How much more natural must it have seemed to weigh the two against each other in countries with a far more democratic culture?[671] Mead, Dewey and Rorty functionally *oppose* Marxism, sometimes implicitly and sometimes explicitly, by endorsing 'democracy', even declaring it to be prior to philosophy. This, however, gives their 'social philosophy'[672] an atheoretical and decisionist flavour. For their rejection of Marx is not based on *arguments*. After all, if one adheres to the pragmatist maxim, the theories of Marx cannot be distinguished from their 'consequences', the form they were given in *political* Marxism.

---

nation.... Whoever got involved with European culture was forced to surrender his American soul' (pp. 197 f.). Americanism also involved intra-American rivalry (Brooks 1958). Mead, who lectured in Chicago, was hostile to the East Coast and favoured the Midwest (Tenbruck 1985, pp. 199 and 228), whose ideals he propagated as universal reality (p. 213) or the goal of history (p. 200).

667. On Mead's reception of Marx, see Joas 1980, pp. 50, 56 and 138 f. Mead wanted to resolve the conflict of interests between 'capital and labor' by means of education ('organization of common attitudes', 'social control': Mead 1934, p. 323). Within the 'theory of the self', the term 'interest' is subjectivised in advance. Rorty later stated that he has never properly read Marx (Rorty 1999, p. 210), before going on to explain why one does not need to (p. 220; cf. Rorty 1998). Rorty has also eliminated theory in advance (for a comprehensive account, see T. Schäfer 2001).

668. Tenbruck criticises the way Mead falls back behind the way the questions had been posed in Germany, despite the fact that Mead had studied there (Tenbruck 1985, pp. 183, 203 and 206; cf. Diggins 1998, p. 216). 'Mead's ethics is hardly anything more than a committed dressing-up of his society's cultural ideals' (Tenbruck 1985, p. 213). 'Throughout, the idealised experience of the American community provides the model for man, morality and society... Mead's ethics is a relentless polemic against all positions that attribute to the individual the ability, or even the duty, to dispose of "standards and criteria" of its own. The innocent American Adam [Lewis 1955] must not be forced to make a moral choice between "conflicting ends"... Everything he wills is innocent, because it is natural, and only develops its moral dimension within the community' (Tenbruck 1985, p. 209; cf. p. 242). Compare Dewey: 'Growth itself is the only moral "end"' (Dewey 1949, p. 141).

669. Dewey 1918; Dewey 1949, p. 46; Dewey 1939; cf. Rorty 1989, pp. 84 ff.; Putnam 1992, Joas 2000; cf. Ryan 1995, Westbrook 1991, and their contributions to Joas 2000, where they make democracy and logic converge.

670. For example, Diggins (1998, p. 219) and Fraser (1998, p. 172) detect a covert racism.

671. Bernstein's argument was already based on England. He strove for a 'unity of theory and reality' (Bernstein in an 1898 letter, quoted in Lehnert 1983, p. 95). Mead's position, in turn, explicitly invoked the authority of the German revisionist (Joas 1980, p. 34).

672. Schlüter 2000.

Thus it is a striking feature of Dewey's discussion with Trotsky that Dewey[673] hardly engages with any of Trotsky's theoretical positions. He declares himself opposed, like Trotsky, to ethical 'absolutism' and, of course, to Stalin, but he wards off Marxism.[674] But what is it that he objects to in *Marx*? For one thing, he has reservations about Marx's putative determinist philosophy of history and economic reductionism. I have shown in Chapter Two that these accusations do not do justice to Marx's theories.[675]

In addition to this, Dewey objects to the claim 'that human ends are interwoven into the very texture and structure of existence'.[676] This is precisely what he himself had claimed elsewhere,[677] so that the example nicely illustrates his decisionism. In light of this, one might venture the hypothesis that pragmatism – which is, initially, nothing but the name for an unrealised programme – owes its lasting popularity mainly to the fact that it is not Marxism.[678] It allowed one to 'conceptualise' those elements of Marxian thought that seemed important for philosophy while simultaneously establishing one's independence from Marx; the relevant aspects of Marx's thought were 'reconstructed' in an alternative way.[679] Following the decline of 'grand narratives',[680] and in particular after 1989, Dewey presented himself as a fallback option to many US intellectuals: some

---

673. Dewey 2008c.

674. During the Moscow trials, Dewey lent his support to Trotsky, who was living in Mexico at the time (Deutscher 1972, pp. 371 ff., Kohlmann 2001).

675. Dewey 1939, 14, 75 ff. Wells 1954 even refutes this accusation by reference to texts by Stalin (pp. 161 f.). Dewey wants to oppose to this a 'pluralist' factor theory (pp. 23, 80). To the extent that this expresses the social scientist's impartiality prior to an analysis, it is justified. But such a theory cannot *anticipate* any results (Münch 1992a still overhastily turns this methodological consideration into a preliminary contentual decision about the 'structure of modernity'). Dewey's result is, however, monofactorial. To him, (American) society is dependent on morality 'today' (pp. 164 ff.): 'Anything that obscures the fundamentally [!] moral nature of the social problem is harmful' (p. 184).

676. Dewey 2008c, p. 354.

677. Dewey 2008c, quoted in Joas 1980, p. 141. A grounding of human ends in nature was endorsed by Dewey in his ethics (Dewey 1908 and 2008b), his theory of democracy (Dewey 1918 and 1939) and his metaphysics of nature (Dewey 1929). The position is in keeping with Dewey's characteristic combination of Hegel and Darwin (Rorty 1994; cf. Dewey 2008 and Heyer 1982).

678. On pragmatism as a counter-model to Marx, see Wells 1954, pp. 157 ff. ('Dewey's Attack n Marxist Historical Materialism') or Novack 1978, pp. 269 ff. ('Deweyism and Marxism' – this pamphlet was authored at Trotsky's request). Neither Lenin 1972 nor Wells 1954 nor Novack 1978 perceived pragmatism's strengths. As far as philosophical insight is concerned, they fell back behind it; their critique comes to nothing. Moreover, they merely oppose to its choice of sides a different choice, without accounting for this in any way. (Today, Novack is one of the signatories of Walzer 2002.) Goff 1980, Joas 1978 and Joas 1980 attempted a 'synthesis' of pragmatism and materialism. Today, a vague recollection of Dewey's affinity with Marx is evident in Honneth 1999a, as it was in Gavin 1988. For the US perspective, see Wald 1987, pp. 118 ff.; Diggins 1992; Guibaut 1997, pp. 41 ff.; Lloyd 1997. The above formulation is intended to remind readers that Apel once regarded all three as philosophically viable: only 'Marxism, existentialism and pragmatism . . . have recognised the problem of the antecedent mediation of theoretical meaning by real or future practice' (Apel 1975, pp. 61 and 138; cf. also pp. 11 ff. and Sartre 1964 and 1965). But it is only pragmatism of which there is still any philosophical awareness.

679. Dewey 1949; cf. 2.5.5, 3.1.3.

680. Lyotard 1989, pp. 31 ff.

of them Marxist, some of them post-analytical and some of them post-poststructuralist.[681] This was possible because of Dewey's numerous theoretical indeterminacies: anyone can take from him what appeals to them. But this also involves elements of the 'self-assertion' that suggests the comparison to German vitalism.[682]

But why should one compare pragmatism to Marx at all?[683] The answer is obvious: because Marx already posited a 'constitution of the world through practice' fifty years before the pragmatists, using Hegel as his starting point like they did but then relying on material investigations.[684] Then what is it that distinguishes the two elaborations of this idea *theoretically*, apart from their different choice of sides? Kant already understood that basic categories are *instituted* by men themselves.[685] Hegel historicised this insight, arguing that the concepts of pure reason are historically constituted. The question of how insight into the historicity of concepts affects their validity was left unanswered.

In Hegel, history was absorbed into the history of the *concept*, so that an adequate understanding of concepts (that is, Hegel's understanding) 'reconciled' them with history and with the rest of reality. Pragmatism recognised this 'sublation' of dualisms as its paragon; it merely wanted to avoid the intellectualist fixation. Ultimately, it also arrived at a 'philosophy of unity'; the modification vis-à-vis Hegel consisted in the Darwinisation of monism. While this ventured in the direction of dialectical Marxism, it was not the solution proposed by Marx.[686]

---

681. 'Not long before I made my break with Marxism-Leninism, I ... argued ... that Marxism should no longer be taught as the official doctrine ... What I was suggesting ... was ... a different way of thinking, one more congenial to the American spirit ... I had in mind the philosophy of John Dewey' (Ph. Selznick in Walzer 1995, pp. 128 f.). 'On my view, James and Dewey were not only waiting at the end of the dialectical road which analytic philosophy travelled, but are waiting at the end of the road which ... Foucault and Deleuze are currently travelling' (Rorty 1980, pp. xviii). Dewey was waiting, first and foremost, at the end of the road that Rorty was travelling, a road that had once started from Trotsky (Rorty 1999, pp. 3 ff.). But it is true Lyotard has nothing to replace grand narratives with, besides 'pragmatisms' (Lyotard 1989, pp. 18 ff.).

682. 'The concepts of "rationality" and "democracy" obviously afford sufficient leeway to allow people to relate to them in quite different ways. They alone cannot prevent ethics serving as an extraneous ideological argument against social movements' (Joas 1980, p. 138; cf. 3.1). America's self-assertion within philosophy was evident in Rorty's lesson that the world can only live in peace once it has been 'Westernised' (in a lecture given in Berlin in late 2001; cf. Rorty 1999, pp. 252 ff.; Rorty 1999a). Asked whether there is only one Western way, Rorty seemed discomfited. He had obviously not yet distinguished between the USA and Europe (now see Rorty 2003; on military self-assertion, cf. Walzer 2002). Incidentally, these remarks are not 'anti-American', if only because what they criticise pragmatism for is its affinity with German thought.

683. This question was already raised with regard to vitalism (2.5.2). Its proximity to pragmatism was emphasised by Joas 1996, p. 173 – without mentioning the commonality with Marxism (but see Joas 1980, pp. 41, 56, 138).

684. Dewey may have theorised the constitution of the world through practice before Heidegger and Wittgenstein (Joas 2000, p. 8, with L. Hickman), but Marx did so even earlier – and in a richer way.

685. Kant 1998, p. 273/A 141; Kaulbach 1978.

686. James prided himself on being 'anti-intellectualist' (James 1907, p. 47). Similarly, Dewey wanted philosophy to be understood not so much as a science than as 'a form of desire, of effort at action' (Dewey 1918, p. 43). This 'naturalised Left Hegelianism' (A. Ryan in Joas 2000, p. 320) was

3.4.4 *The conservation of rationality and normativity in Marx*

They therefore acted . . . before they thought[687]

Marx 'left aside' first philosophy,[688] just as he said he would. He was not interested in questions of transcendental philosophy, which was in any case not particularly important around 1840.[689] Nevertheless, Marx did not suspend Kant's propositions on the constitution of the object and on causality, as Hegel and the pragmatists did; he simply applied them by engaging in material research.[690] With regard to the foundations of scientific and practical reason, Marx distinguished between genetic issues and issues of validity; in doing so, he went from Hegel back to Kant. Marx's particular concepts differ from those of Hegel, but in principle, he does not depart from Kant. Kant always left room for empirical inquiry.[691] Marx operated within this space, that of scientific reasons, situated beyond mere value judgements. He was aware of the '*active* side' of the constitution of the world,[692] but differently from Hegel, he did not attempt to conceptualise it by means of first philosophy. Such a sublation of practice into theory leads to those products of fancy that Marx criticised so trenchantly, and which are impossible after Kant. Instead, he tried to demonstrate the pragmatic constitution of *certain* concepts in an *a posteriori*, empirico-scientific way (2.6.4, 3.1.4, 3.1.6).[693]

He found that their validity was often closely circumscribed and only transcended real relations to the extent that *every* concept transcends that which it is a concept of, without any unrealised residue remaining behind in the realm of spirits.[694] Like Hegel, Marx knew that ethical concepts also have a history. But because he distinguished between

still bound up with Hegel. What is odd is that the structural parallel between this monism and 'dialectical materialism' has not been noted more often.

687. *MECW* 35, p. 97.

688. *MECW* 5, p. 236; cf. 4.1.

689. Köhnke 1986, pp. 23 ff.

690. To Engels, it is not just the history of ideas that remains in effect, but also logic (*MECW* 25, pp. 25 f.). This was precisely what Dewey *accused* Marxism of: 'Marxism is "dated" in the matter of its claims to be peculiarly scientific' (Dewey 1939, p. 84).

691. Kant 1998, pp. 640 f./A 820.

692. *MECW* 5, p. 3; *MECW* 3, pp. 331 f.

693. Nothing can be deduced from pure concepts, without apperception. The claim of the Hegelians that Hegel's 'concepts' are saturated with experience remains just that – a claim. This can be seen in the numerous errors on minor points of detail, the points upon which everything turns in the realm of experience. It was only because Marx examined each of these points of detail independently and noted that they do not conform to Hegel's 'logic' (2.5.2) that he was able to say of Hegel's method that it stands on its head. The statement is a result, not a principle (2.5.7, 3.1.6).

694. One can prejudiciously condemn the contextualism implicit in this – but there is no argumentative mileage in doing so. Philosophical debates on realism and universalism were usually conducted by means of conceptual, but hardly ever by means of concrete, socio-historical arguments. When one proceeds in this way – blanking out the level upon which 'conceptual' operations are put to the test – 'normative philosophy' triumphs all too easily.

genesis and validity, he was able to emphasise the real history within which concepts originate, opposing it to their 'sublation' in Hegel's transcendental history of concepts, where concepts produce one another. Thus Marx made it an obligation to examine the *concrete* practice underpinning each philosophical concept and the history of the practice, without smuggling wishes and demands of one's own ('normative content') into this description.[695] In terms of his research practice, he thereby went far beyond Hegel, vitalism and pragmatism.

Marx's pragmatism did not consist in the attempt to make his own theory 'true' by means of a mysterious practice, as Lenin, Lukács and Korsch believed (2.5.4); it consisted in spelling out what remains an abstract formula in pragmatism. But Marx differs from pragmatism not just in terms of his research practice, but also in terms of his methodology. His 'transformation of philosophy' avoided two unfortunate steps: unlike the pragmatists, he did not engage in a Hegelian 'destruction' of rationality and normativity (2.5.2). He did not need to undermine *scientificity*, as pragmatism is always in danger of doing, Rorty being the best contemporary example.[696] Marx had no intention of post-metaphysically surrendering 'old European' rationality. And just as he remained within the space of reason, as far as science was concerned, he submitted to the absolute demand when it came to actions. Silence on the categorical imperative's justification corresponds to simple adherence to it.[697] Marx cleared the way for the transition from ideas

695. This is only possible within a thought that has eliminated the distinction between theoretical and practical reason – as done not just by Fichte and Heidegger, but also by Peirce (Apel 1975, p. 77) and Dewey (Dewey 1930, p. 77). Lohmann 1980 and 1991 means to supplement the world of technology in Marx (a product of his own reductive interpretation) with a lifeworld whose 'description' he hopes will yield the norms he cannot find in Marx's account. And yet Marx does sometimes write about norms; it is just that he does not do so 'normatively'. Lohmann has decided beforehand that 'critique' can only be normative. This obstructs his view of the – theoretical and socially given – material (3.1.4).

696. The criterial distinction between representation and object is a penultimate question that cannot be replaced in any given research situation or in everyday life. To reinterpret it as a 'last question' about what exactly these representations are is to undermine it. The neo-pragmatism of Rorty 1979 and Brandom 1994 means to no longer acknowledge representations ('representationalism' is identified as a flawed epistemological 'theory'), but only concrete speech acts as performed within a linguistic community. Scientific practice is not elucidated by being thus philosophised; rather, it becomes impossible to understand its internal logic. What underlies this is the unbroken idealist belief that everything depends on 'last questions' (cf. 2.6.4 and 2.6.6).

697. Kant's imperative – 'Act so that you treat humanity, whether in your own person or in that of another, always as an end and never as a means only' (*Foundations of the Metaphysics of Morals*, p. 87) – was formulated more precisely by Marx, becoming the '*categorical imperative to overthrow all relations* in which man is a debased, enslaved, forsaken, despicable being' (*MECW* 3, p. 182). Marx took the primacy of practical reason seriously: he did not talk about ideas of practical reason (except to demonstrate their 'transcendental dialectic'); he applied them. He implemented his insight into the impossibility of theorising practical moral foundations in a more fundamental way than Wittgenstein, who fled into the private 'practice' of gardening and teaching (Rubinstein 1981), and Heidegger, whose political practice was irrational (2.5.5). Common sense says: 'Nothing good happens unless you do it' (Erich Kästner). Everyone probably knows what is 'good'. Why the good is valid is an idle question; moreover, answering it makes no difference to the validity of the good. It is a matter of finding out what exactly needs to be done, in order then to do it.

of practical reason to practice by newly opening up the possibility of those ideas being applied, against theoreticist cavilling. Differently from the pragmatists, Marx provided no conjectures or appeals, but tangible analyses of *concrete* pragmatic interrelationships.[698] By making his specific analyses of the pragmatic constitution of social phenomena and conceptualities concrete, he avoided having to operate with unwarranted and ultimately ideological concepts.

Because he revealed the actual semantic range of terms such as 'practice', 'human' or 'justice', and because he also provided, whenever possible, analyses both of the practice actually underpinning these terms and of its history, he was always aware of the limits of such grand words. This prevented him from becoming an ideologue, something he would have been quite capable of being, given his magniloquence and irascibility. It also provided him with an instrumentarium by which to accuse *others* working in the same field of being ideological.[699] When has pragmatism ever achieved anything comparable? In light of all this, the unmediated application of pragmatism within contemporary, post-Marxian German philosophy appears as questionable as pragmatism's understanding of the European tradition. Ironically, neo-pragmatist 'de-transcendentalised reason' is promoting a re-*spirit*ualisation of social theory ('idealisation').[700]

Pragmatism attempted to ground philosophical activity anew. This means it focuses on the critique of methods and on the theory of science. The way it does so has been shown, in this chapter, to be flawed and to fall back behind Marx's reflections. The German reception of pragmatism had a particularly questionable effect, since German theorists used pragmatism to solve the problems of justification notoriously associated with their

---

698. Dewey's social philosophy amounted to the proposition that the project of American democracy was still 'in the making'. One needed to regain one's faith in 'human nature', such that 'men acting together may attain freedom of individuals which will amount to fraternal associations with one another' (Dewey 1939, p. 164). According to his reductive social history of philosophy, an elitist caste of philosophers has worked since antiquity to secure an outdated domination by means of 'overworlds' ('But when it comes to convincing men of the truth of doctrines which are no longer to be accepted upon the say-so of custom..., there is no recourse save to magnify the signs of rigorous thought...Thus arises that appearance of abstract definition and ultra-scientific argumentation': Dewey 1949, p. 41). This, he claims, was always opposed by a purely technical knowledge ('the matter of fact positivistic knowledge': Dewey 1949, p. 34). In actual fact, all knowledge, including technical knowledge, is embedded in holistic contexts of reference, and this is all the more true the further back in history one goes. Dewey's identification of class position is about as reductive as dialectical materialism's. Moreover, he fails to mention progressive philosophy, which never exhausted itself in purely technical knowledge.

699. Marx did not claim abstractly that no concept can transcend its context; he showed that some concepts only make sense within a particular context. Those who 'universalise' them in a way that runs counter to their meaning expose themselves to the critique of ideology and lose the ability to articulate such a critique themselves: moral universalism renders the critique of ideology impossible by assuming that the 'claims' it formulates are always already justified. 'Contextualism' allows for a critique of ideology as long as it distinguishes between thought and being, validity and genesis.

700. Habermas 2001, pp. 5, 33 ff.

'normative social philosophy' (the amalgam of an incomplete social theory and particular value judgements). The reception of pragmatism served normative German social philosophy as a – post hoc – 'justification' of its 'claims', which however were hardly rendered more 'substantive'. Following this reception, it was seldom clear what ought to be understood as philosophy and what as science, or what belongs to the theoretical and what to the practical side.[701] The 'dualisms' of theory and practice, philosophy and science, ethics and politics, thought and being were 'overcome' in a way that left an indigestible bloc. Thus Marx's critique of philosophy has not been rendered obsolete by pragmatism. I will now proceed to evaluate systematically the material examined in Chapters Two and Three.

701. 'It is…virtually impossible to distinguish clearly between genuinely philosophical and socio-scientific lines of argument in the works of…Mead or Jürgen Habermas' (H. Wenzel in Joas 2000, p. 237). H.P. Krüger high falutingly calls this 'interpenetration' (Joas 2000, p. 199). Dewey meant to liberate the 'project' of Bacon of its scruples (Dewey 1949, p. 61). Calls for the technological 'improvement' of the world can already be found in Descartes (Descartes 2008, p. 15); the difference being that Descartes was aware that this requires certain theoretical knowledge, whereas moral questions need to be dealt with differently. Dewey blurs these distinctions.

Chapter Four
Conclusion: What Philosophy after Marx?

In light of the persistence of capitalism, the present work is intended to help the social sciences and philosophy adopt a more relaxed attitude to Marx, who has developed what remains the most stringent theory of capitalism. This theory has however been so strongly distorted in the course of its political and academic reception history that it needs first to be freed of these superimpositions. It was with this in mind that I undertook a critical revision of some, usually concealed, aspects of the development of German 'social philosophy' (Chapter Two). The resulting theorico-genetic depth of focus then allowed me to criticise, by way of exemplification, some of contemporary social philosophy's more unfortunate basic categorial choices (Chapter Three). What emerged particularly clearly from this was the surprising continuity of patterns of thought associated with German idealism. This sort of casuistry could be continued. But there is one question that still needs to be answered, namely the question of what systematic conclusions should be drawn from this about the possibilities and limits of social philosophy and its relationship to Marxian theory.

This last chapter explores the concept of philosophy that is not only compatible with the critique practised in this work, but has in fact guided it. To begin with, I specify once more the proposed criterion for the critique of philosophy that the early Marx developed for the purposes of his engagement with Hegel and Feuerbach: its 'testing' by reference to the social reality that we experience every day, and which is quite present in the media (4.1; cf. 2.5.7, 3.1.5). Such a pre-theoretical and lifeworldly perspective does not yield yet another theory; rather, it allows one to critically situate existing theories with regard to other theories and social reality. I then propose this kind of 'perspicuous presentation'[1] for different variants of social philosophy (4.2). I aim to reflect systematically on the problematic ways in which the theories analysed relate thought and being, model and reality, theory and practice to one another.

In doing so, I develop a concept of philosophy that does greater justice to the present *and* to the philosophical tradition. It is no longer forced, by traditional 'cognitive constraints' or current theoretical fashions, to blank out Marxian theories, as has hitherto often been the case. Ultimately, Kant's and Wittgenstein's differentiated and lean concept of philosophy, which Marx also shared, proves superior to the German thought of unity as found in Hegel, Heidegger and Honneth. In this way, many misunderstandings can be resolved, such as on the role that 'science' and talk of 'laws' play within Marxian thought (4.3). What has proven particularly unfortunate in this respect is the neoclassical distortion of Marx. When Marx's talk of laws is misread philosophically, this leads, by way of reaction, to the sorts of re-Hegelianisations and ethicisations of theory that we have encountered numerous examples of throughout this study, and that I have criticised. They embody a continuity of German idealism that *bypasses Marx* (4.4).

4.1 The reality check as a philosophical litmus test

It has repeatedly emerged from this work that the following 1841 statement by Marx, originally formulated with Aristotle and Hegel in mind, remains apposite today:[2] 'The world confronting a philosophy total in itself is therefore a world torn apart. This philosophy's activity therefore also appears torn apart'.[3] One cause of this congruence consists in the persistence of Hegelian philosophy within German thought, even more than a hundred and seventy years after his death. Parallels with Hegel have been detected in Habermas (3.1.5), in business ethics (3.3.5) and especially in neo-pragmatism (3.4.2); communitarianism invoked Hegel, even if it failed to mediate moral appeals and reality in the way that he did (3.2.3). We saw earlier that the traditional social philosophies of Eucken, Lukács, Heidegger and Luhmann adhered to the Hegelian model (2.5.3–2.5.6). Even critical theory invoked Hegel (2.6.3); the effects of this can still be seen in the speculative philosophy of money developed by the 'monetary theory of value' (2.3.7).

These Hegelianisms do not, or at least not in every case, go back to a pronounced fondness for difficult texts from the early nineteenth century. Rather, the 'method' used by Hegel is so attractive, in Germany, that it can be used even by those who are not particularly familiar with Hegel's work. This 'method' consists in replacing *direct* engagement with an object, still widely suspected of amounting to positivism,[4] with the

1. Wittgenstein, *Philosophical Investigations*, aphorism 122.
2. See 2.5.7; 3.1.5; 3.2.3.
3. *MECW* 1, p. 491.
4. Wellmer 1969, pp. 69 ff.; Negt in Euchner 1972, p. 44.

encirclement of a phenomenon by means of a 'synthesis' of various pre-existing theories that deal more or less directly with that phenomenon (2.5.2).

Adorno already propagated such 'constellational analysis'.[5] But the true master of synthetic secondary analysis is Habermas.[6] And yet this approach is precisely what most resembles a positivist stance, except that the uncritical reception of *theories* (3.1.1; 4.3) takes the place of an uncritical acceptance of what is given.[7] Without wishing to say anything about intentions, it is clear that one functional effect of Hegelian elements within social philosophy is that of social philosophy successively closing itself off to social reality by means of the identity-philosophical belief that being already inheres in a given thought and its concepts.

German thought was characterised by a special need for Hegelian syntheses. It was seen, especially in the early chapters of this work (2.1–2.4), that the reflections on society conducted from the mid-eighteenth century until Marx's day, split up into theories of technology and theories of ethics after Marx's death. This disjointedness was first seen in the social democratic quarrel between a naturalist orthodoxy and an ethicising revisionism (2.1). It was also evident in the Leninist worldview, in which a fatalist scenario of crisis unmediatedly confronted a voluntarist mysticism of practice (2.2), and in economic theory, which was characterised by the drifting apart of technicised neoclassical models and ethicised historicist counter-models (2.3). The rupture also ran through sociology and critical theory, as neoclassically oriented, ontologised models of an automatic system confronted theories that looked primarily to the normative notions of individuals (2.4, 2.6).

When the option of directly testing such disparate claims by reference to reality, a common procedure in Anglophone empiricism, is not chosen, the only remaining option, apart from decisionistically choosing one claim over the others, is that of synthesis. Such synthesis results in a *twofold* removal from social reality. The theories engaged with were already characterised by a failure to properly grasp social reality; this is especially true of neoclassical economics, whose effects are still evident in Leninism, due to Hilferding. When these theories are philosophically reinterpreted and amalgamated with other theories, the deficiency is not eliminated but aggravated (2.4.3, 3.1.1, 3.3.5).

5. Adorno 1977, pp. 335 f.; Adorno 2007, pp. 164 f.

6. According to Habermas, whoever speaks unmediatedly about objects is failing to take account of the linguistic turn and falling guilty of realism or naturalism. 'Social theory must therefore prove its mettle on a meta-theoretical level, from which social reality cannot be accessed directly' (Habermas 1991a, p. 203). One needs now to make use of 'empirical data' and specialist terminology from other disciplines (such as moral philosophy, speech act theory, developmental psychology: p. 204). We are never told why the world cannot be accessed; Habermas merely informs us of an onto-historical caesura: following the 'linguistic turn', he tells us, we can no longer access inner or outer reality in a linguistically unmediated way (Habermas 2003, p. 20). Now that 'the subject' has been 'removed from practical reason' (Habermas 1996, p. 489), practical reason has been 'shattered' (Habermas 1996, p. 3; cf. the overhasty talk of a 'collapse' of Marxism in Honneth and Fraser 2003, p. 126; see also 4.2.4, 4.2.5).

7. Cf. Schnädelbach 1971.

This theoretical procedure is certainly possible within philosophy. But the question raised by such grand edifices is that of how they relate to social reality. There results the situation hinted at in the statement by Marx that I have quoted repeatedly. 'The world... is therefore a world torn apart'. What this means, in the present context, is that theories about the world break into two irreconcilable halves (2.4.1). Where they are reconciled within philosophy, philosophy becomes 'total in itself'. By virtue of this, philosophy further increases the distance between itself and the real world and 'also appears torn apart', since the real world is precisely what it stakes a claim to comprehending.[8] Nancy Fraser arrives at the same diagnosis. Her analysis of Axel Honneth's 'normative monism' of recognition reaches this conclusion:[9]

> Honneth, however, is unwilling to put experience to the test.... The result is a surprisingly traditional theoretical edifice: a foundationalist construction in which moral psychology grounds, and unduly constrains, political sociology, social theory, and moral philosophy, illegitimately truncating those inquiries and infringing their relative autonomy.[10]

Consideration of the normative notions of individuals – undertaken, in this case, in the form of a philosophised moral psychology – is not seen as what it is: the investigation of a closely circumscribed domain that can only be grasped empirically. Rather, it is stylised into a philosophical synthesis of the contrary perspectives of moral philosophy and social theory. While this involves changes being made to these two disciplines, they are not the changes that our analysis has shown to be necessary: moral philosophy and social theory are not tested against the social reality that underlies them. Instead, they are subjected to a Hegelian 'sublation'.

The fact that this philosophy also stakes a claim to being a *political* philosophy[11] betrays the initial identity-philosophical premise that by speculating about the theories of others, one can simultaneously say something about social reality. Fraser rightly objects to this. Honneth's 'normative monism', which I am merely using as an example here, is a variant of ethicised German social philosophy as it has developed in the wake of Habermas. I already concluded in section 3.1.5 that such monological theoretical formations lack the controlling instance of a jury that might object – perhaps naively, but emphatically – in the way Fraser is objecting here. Aside from our role as people engaging in philosophy, we are, 'firstly and mostly',[12] human beings, and as human beings, we have quite a clear knowledge of what is real. We hear about misery and war, feel natural urges and must find a way to pay our bills. This sort of anticipatory consultation of

---

8. *MECW* 1, p. 491; cf. 2.5 ff.
9. Honneth 2003, p. 3.
10. Fraser 2003, p. 206.
11. Honneth 2007, p. 3.
12. Cf. *MECW* 37, p. 5.

common sense[13] – and in an enlightened society, common sense may know more than specialised science – serves as the starting point for what follows. To proceed in this way is possible even in the absence of a detailed socio-economic theory. After all, anticipatory consultation of the lifeworld is not meant to constitute one more theory, but merely to serve as a criterion by which to assess other theories.[14]

This sort of procedure can also be found in other writers. For example, Steinvorth has something similar in mind when he recommends paying attention to our intuitions when judging the adequacy of philosophical reconstructions of ethical principles.[15] By no means are such intuitions[16] sufficient for falsifying a theory. But as pointers, they should not be ignored. When we are in doubt about a theory, they should prompt us to verify it. Hilary Putnam follows William James in also assuming that whenever we have doubts about highly abstract theories (in this case, analytic theories of knowledge), we should resort to 'direct realism' as a criterion of verification.[17] Husserl's emphasis on the 'lifeworld', which began when scientific theories ceased to be transparent,[18] was inspired by similar considerations.[19] The insight is not new. Not unlike Heidegger and Wittgenstein,[20] Marx recommended a therapeutic realism in cases in which the 'categorial framework' of other 'linguistic bedevilments' seem to cut us off from reality:

> The philosophers have only to dissolve their language into the ordinary language, from which it is abstracted, in order to recognise it as the distorted language of the actual world, and to realise that neither thoughts nor language in themselves form a realm of their own, that they are only *manifestations* of actual life.[21]

---

13. Reid 1994; 1.2; Henning 2001.

14. One medium by which to learn about such pre-conceptual understandings of social reality is the press, especially feature pages (cf. 1.1; 2.4.6; 3.2.3). The theorist of the bourgeois public sphere also makes use of it (Habermas 1962; the most recent examples are Habermas 1999, 2001a, 2003a and Habermas and Derrida 2003). 'Today, one can read about how capitalism functions and what patterns of distribution it creates in virtually any daily newspaper' (Habermas 2000, p. 15). Even if that were the case, social theory seems to immunise itself against such 'feature-page' insights. As is well known, Marx began his career as a journalist, even if he did so out of material necessity (*MECW* 1, p. 194; cf. Winkler 2003). It is also crucial to take into account observations made outside Germany and the USA.

15. Steinvorth 1999, pp. 36 f., 64.

16. Cf. Shklar 1992.

17. Putnam 1995, p. 30; Putnam 1998, p. 46; Putnam 1994, pp. 78 ff.; Bashkar 1986.

18. Husserl 1970, § 28.

19. N. Einstein 1918 already intuited this. The intuition was distorted when it was understood as a theory in its own right. Thus Husserl proceeded, in the next paragraph, to theorise and subjectivise the lifeworld (as a 'realm of subjective phenomena': 1936, § 29). Instead of serving to situate different rationalities, the lifeworld is reified as the counter-model to objective scientific rationality (this is still the case in Habermas 1984–87 II, pp. 119 ff. and 318 ff.), to the point of replacing it (cf. 2.5.5). Incidentally, the concept of the 'lifeworld' is a successor of 'mind' (Ebrecht 1991 p. 85; Wirkus 1996, p. 277; cf. Freyer 1998, p. 115).

20. Rentsch 2003.

21. *MECW* 5, p. 447; cf. Lassalle 1987, pp. 130 ff.

> Back to the rough ground![22]
>
> What is your aim in philosophy? – To shew the fly the way out of the fly-bottle.[23]
>
> And because this average everydayness makes up what is ontically proximal for this entity, it has again and again been passed over in explicating Dasein. That which is ontically closest [is that the ontological signification of which] is constantly overlooked.[24]

Philosophy has to endure being integrated into the real world. This is best done in a 'worldly' – not purely philosophical, but philosophically reflected – manner:[25] 'One has to "leave philosophy aside"…, one has to leap out of it and devote oneself like an ordinary man to the study of actuality'.[26] This procedure does not result in a reductive treatment of philosophical problems, but in their being *situated*.[27]

From the perspective of someone familiar with philosophy, who suspends the purely immanent way of seeing and considers the interrelationships between various theories, their position within contemporary reality and their possible functional trends, the core propositions of these theories can be related to one another. Because this approach involves the trends being identified on the basis of the texts themselves, and not by means of a theory of the social base to which the various theories are reduced, I have already called it the 'immanent-functional interpretation' in section 1.4.1, following Karl Mannheim.[28] This is the intention underlying the following 'perspicuous presentation' (Wittgenstein), which summarises the systematic results obtained for the various philosophical frameworks identified in the course of this work.

This sort of situating procedure does not affect Kant's philosophy of principles, since Kant liberated worldly rationality and merely compiled formal determinations, within which much remains possible. It does however have consequences for a philosophy that uses the critique of knowledge and the analysis of concepts to cobble together a social philosophy that formulates its normative propositions without taking empirical states of affairs into account, attempting instead to ground those propositions in anthropology, discourse ethics or moral psychology. This is to *bypass* the most important level of analysis, that of society, while simultaneously assuming it to be constituted in a certain way – normative social philosophy's loss of its object of inquiry (2.1.5, 2.4.1, 2.4.4, 2.5.2).

---

22. Wittgenstein, *Philosophical Investigations*, aphorism 107; cf. Engels, *MECW* 25, p. 20 f.

23. *Philosophical Investigations*, aphorism 309; cf. Nietzsche, *The Dawn*, aphorism 444; see 2.6.6.

24. Heidegger 1962, p. 69.

25. Philosophy needs first to be understood, but then it can be treated non-philosophically. On the affinity of Marx and Wittgenstein, see Rubinstein 1981, Steinvorth 1985, pp. 149 f.; Kitching 1988 and 2002; Pleasants 1999.

26. *MECW* 5, p. 236.

27. Karl Mannheim already meant to use the 'originary totality given to extra-theoretical experience' (Mannheim 1964a, p. 92; 'pre-scientific totality': p. 95) to determine the 'logical place' (p. 93) of specialised research (cf. Schelsky 1959).

28. Mannheim 1964c.

4.2 Topology of social philosophy

In Chapters Two and Three, I related the development of normative German social philosophy to Marxian theory. Attempts to integrate Marxian theory – undertaken in order to ward it off or in order to pick up on it – usually involved it being philosophised (2.5.1). In examining this, it was seen the operation has often been performed on the basis of a philosophical framework that was in some way influenced by Hegel. By contrast, it has been my hypothesis that a *Kantian* framework would have allowed Marxian theory to be fully integrated (see 2.1.3, 2.5.2, 3.1.5, 3.1.4), but that German philosophy made use of such a framework only in exceptional cases. Here, I will systematically present the difference between the sober Kantian and the various exalted Hegelian frameworks.

I begin by discussing Kant's simplified topology of philosophy (4.2.1). Here, Marxian theory does not conflict with the overblown aspirations of speculation. Next, I consider the operation of 'overcoming dualism' in Hegel (4.2.2), the different transformations of Hegelian philosophy effected by Marx (4.2.3) and pragmatism (4.2.4) and, finally, the structure of *twice* transformed philosophy in German supernormativism (4.2.5).

4.2.1 *Kant's philosophical topology*

Kant's topology can be briefly summarised as follows. The unitary, real world that is 'always already' given to us in our everyday experience is one that we relate to theoretically in science, and practically in our ethical judgements and political actions. The *Critique of Pure Reason* reflects upon the way we relate to the world theoretically and identifies its limitations. By no means does it 'ground' sciences or present scientific propositions about the world. Differently from empirical science, theoretical philosophy does not relate to the world as its object.[29] This presents no problem for as long as a distinction is drawn between philosophy and science. The *Critique of Practical Reason* reflects upon the conditions of possibility of our practical engagement with the world, without formulating particular ethical prescriptions or wrongly taking itself to be a 'politics'. Moral philosophy is not yet a practice. Thus there is a clear distinction here between theoretical and practical philosophy. Nor are they fallaciously identified with their theme – namely, scientific and practical engagement with the world.

The function of unity is proper to the world itself: a variety of propositions can be made about the world as substratum, without it ever being wholly accessible by any single approach. No theory or philosophy can provide a comprehensive representation of the world – which is not a problem as long as no claim to doing this is made. The delineating critique of knowledge serves to rule out such claims. Theoretical philosophy reflects upon the world as upon a liminal concept that can never be scientifically recuperated

---

29. It expresses itself in reflexive propositions that do not describe 'the world' but rather organise our propositions about the world (such as by revealing the implications of our talk about 'space' and 'time': Kant 1998, pp. 174 ff./A 23 ff.).

(we cannot 'know' everything) but is nevertheless always presupposed, as happens all the time in everyday life.[30] Practical philosophy reflects upon the world as upon an idea of practical reason[31] that can never be fully apprehended, but which we always presuppose in our actions. There is no total perspective from which propositions could be made about everything at once. Ways of speaking that reflect a 'worldview' [*Weltanschauung*], such as those proper to art and religion, need to be clearly classified as *non-theoretical*, as emotive-expressive, reflexive and 'subjective',[32] as group-specific expressions.

Since Marxian theory *qua* science of bourgeois society presents itself neither as an alternative theory of knowledge or moral philosophy nor as a 'worldview' [*Weltanschauung*], integrating it into this philosophical framework presents no problems. It is just another theory on the empirical level. To note this is not yet to have said anything about whether it is justified substantively. This needs to be demonstrated in factual terms – and cannot in fact be demonstrated any other way.

4.2.2 *The overcoming of dualism in Hegel*

> *Wenn Hegels Begriff das Wahre, so spart man Taten und Jahre.*
> [If Hegel's concept is true, it saves us deeds and years.][33]

Hegel felt that Kant's distinctions were dualisms, and he lamented the absence of an intra-theoretical function of unity (2.5.2, 2.5.7) On Hegel's view, the 'need of philosophy' is the need for unity.[34] Simply put, his philosophical operation consisted in eliminating as many of the 'dualisms' he encountered as possible. Starting from Nicolai and Fichte, he began by eliminating the 'thing in itself' – which however had represented the critical insight that while science has objective reality (is capable of formulating true propositions) these propositions cannot be used to elaborate a super-science of reality. Hegel only created such 'absolute knowledge' by sleight of hand: he eliminated the dualism of philosophy and science. Because philosophy is able to *reflect* upon how the various scientific opinions must refer to a unitary substratum, he argued, *it* already 'knows' this substratum.[35] In Kant, reflection is precisely what does *not* engender a new and specific knowledge of objects.[36] By a similar operation, Hegel sublated practical politics into philosophy: it is only in philosophy (of law) that it receives its genuine justification. Morality and law were merged in a still higher, speculative entity (the *state*, the 'actual God' *qua*

30. Kant 1998, pp. 466/A 419, pp. 525 f./A 519.
31. Kant 1998, pp. 678 f./A 808.
32. Kant 1952, I, pp. 155 f./A 297 f.
33. Franz Grillparzer.
34. Hegel 1977, p. 94.
35. Kant's philosophy 'does not go on... from the acknowledgement that the judgment is the appearing of the In-itself to the cognition of the In-itself'. Deducing being from thought, Hegel concludes that 'the world [!] is in itself falling to pieces' (Hegel 1977a, p. 74).
36. Kant 1998, pp. 453 ff./A 260 ff.

'actuality of the ethical idea').[37] Another 'dualism' eliminated by Hegel was the distinction between theoretical and practical reason; the two undergo a 'synthesis' in Hegel's philosophy of unity, even though that philosophy features neither a critique of knowledge nor an ethics of its own. In this sense, the distinction was never really sublated; it would be more accurate to say it was eliminated – as in Heidegger (2.5.5).

The function of unity was transferred from the 'world' to philosophy: the overcoming of opposites now occurs within philosophy – within the 'concept'.[38] Reason, in which thought and being are one,[39] became 'all concrete actuality'.[40] The intuition is understandable. Hegel may have said to himself: 'I experience 'unity' every day' (this is reminiscent of Dewey's concept of experience); 'why should I not be able to represent it?' But every attempt to describe the 'world' as it is has the disadvantage of no longer being able to say anything *definite* in a controlled manner.[41] What remains is a philosophy of unity, or a supertheory, which it is by no means a misunderstanding to describe as contemplative and mystical. Rather, it misunderstands itself when it believes it can also be something else (cf. 2.1.5; 2.5). This merely renders it ideological.

4.2.3 *The transformation of (Hegelian) philosophy in Marx*

Marx's intellectual rank is . . . hardly to be exaggerated.[42]

This total philosophy provoked an intellectual reaction. One option was that of breaking with scientific rationality altogether, as done by Kierkegaard, Nietzsche, Dilthey and Heidegger, but also by positivism. They 'leaped' unmediatedly from the philosophy of unity into the world. While they now disposed of 'reality', they were no longer able to state anything that could lay a claim to being scientific, as they had eliminated the requisite distance. But because they remained philosophers, they returned occasionally to the abandoned bosom of the absolute, in order to formulate mythic general propositions (about 'life', 'being' or the eternal recurrence of the same). In this sense, Marx's critique of the Young Hegelians applies to these thinkers as well – they *failed* to overcome Hegel. One effect of this is that empirical data and abstractions continue to be juxtaposed unmediatedly in Young Hegelian approaches. By contrast, it was Marx's strategy to simultaneously 'sublate' ['*aufheben*'] Hegelian philosophy and 'make it a reality' ['*verwirklichen*'].[43]

37. Hegel 1991, pp. 275, 279/§§ 257 f.
38. The idea, 'the absolute suspendedness of the antithesis', is 'the only authentic reality' (Hegel 1977a, p. 68).
39. Hegel 1967, p. 113.
40. Hegel 1967, p. 273.
41. What is most general is, moreover, subjective: 'What has history to do with me? Mine is the first and only world! I want to report how I find the world' (Wittgenstein 1984, p. 177).
42. J. Plenge
43. *MECW* 3, pp. 133 ff.

To put this in a less lofty fashion, it was a matter of restoring rationality's original rights within science and politics – where it is already situated in Kant and in many non-German theoretical currents. Stood on its feet, the 'sublation of philosophy' refers to its being relocated one floor down, so that it can engage with problems it is actually capable of solving – by means of science and reflection upon science ('you cannot supersede philosophy without making it a reality').[44] 'Making it a reality' means conducting political ideals such as freedom and equality toward their political implementation. This cannot succeed unless one has first examined, without any illusions, what exactly the ideals mean (such as in political economy), no matter how sobering an experience this turns out to be. Philosophy cannot be made a reality without being 'superseded'.

In his writings, Marx hardly dealt with Kant as a philosopher. But this is very much in keeping with Kant's philosophical self-understanding, since Kant's philosophy leaves the world as it is.[45] Its validity continues to be presupposed; it is not questioned (3.4.4). Marx was as wary of metaphysical subtleties and 'theological niceties'[46] as Kant, and he referred explicitly to the categorical imperative.[47] What is central in Marx is the role of scientific theory: it is open both to empirical work (observations on the world) and to abstraction (philosophemes), but its purpose is that of *mediating* between the two. For this reason, one should criticise both attempts to cobble together, on the basis of momentary observations, a new anti-Marxian theory of the epoch (2.1.2, 2.2.6, 2.4.1, 2.4.5 f.) and contrary efforts to 'justify' a given social reality on the basis of unanalysed abstractions (3.1, 3.2). Both attempts fail to do justice to the structure and place of Marx's theory.

In Marx, Kant's topology is almost completely restored: the primary role of justifications is that of *substantively* justifying moral verdicts and political acts. It was for this purpose that political economy was developed, long before Marx. Normative social philosophy, such as the theory of natural law, tended rather to take the form of moral verdicts bound up with politics. Each party to a conflict attempted to buttress its view by calling it 'natural law'. But this did not make its position any better or any more true.[48] Political science attempted to conduct such disputes by means of *arguments*. It guaranteed a decision that was justified substantively and not 'normatively' or in terms of value judgements. In this respect, classical economics was 'political' (2.3.1). Nor can the primary purpose of social theory conceivably be anything other than that of creating the

44. *MECW* 3, p. 181.
45. Wittgenstein, *Philosophical Investigations*, aphorism 126.
46. *MECW* 35, p. 81.
47. *MECW* 3, p. 182.
48. There was a version of 'natural law' that meant to protect the state from citizens (Hobbes), and one that meant to protect citizens from the state (Locke). The Hobbesian claim to 'neutrality', still heard from Hobbesians today, was itself partisan: it was impossible to concretely demonstrate its truth, and it was given the lie in practical politics (2.6.7; Mannheim 1986, pp. 102 f.; Habermas 1973a, pp. 82 ff.; Ilting, '*Naturrecht*', in O. Brunner 1972).

possibility of pacifying political conflicts in a well-informed manner. To be able do this, it needs to be objective and refrain from covert value judgements.[49]

Where social theory is practised, philosophy plays a critical role: it examines scientific and political practice to ascertain whether sense is being violated. It functions as a public judge, without itself being a specialised science or a form of politics.[50] Historically, the absence of these two critical instances was at least partly to blame for Marxism's frequent deterioration into questionable ideological systems and irrational political acts.[51] And yet the Marxian paradigm would have allowed philosophy to develop a workable self-understanding. There is no need to break with Marx for the sake of philosophy or vice versa. But neither can a critical post-Marxian philosophy sidestep common sense and the sciences, or use them only selectively, for illustrative purposes, in the name of some higher-order 'reason'. This presupposes a differentiated understanding of Kant, one that does not read him, in the manner of Fichte, as an early author of normative guarantees, but as a negative-critical instance. It also presupposes a degree of political equanimity, such that mere mention of Marx does not immediately prompt atheoretical kneejerk reactions. This is what I would like to make a case for.[52]

---

49. Kant objected to objectless 'persuasion', which relies merely upon the particular condition of the subject (such as its cultural identity); a Socratic legacy. Consensus does not establish a relation to the object; rather, it presupposes it. 'Truth, however, rests upon agreement with the object, with regard to which, consequently, the judgments of every understanding must agree ... [T]here is at least a presumption that the ground of the agreement of all judgments, regardless of the difference among the subjects [the fact of pluralism: Rawls 1993], rests on the common ground, namely the object' (Kant 1998, pp. 685/A 820 f.). Consensus is not a criterion of 'truth', but merely its index. To Mannheim, 'sociological inquiry is indispensable if we are to clarify somewhat the current state of thought ..., which often genuinely leads into desperation' (Mannheim 1964, pp. 368 f.).

50. This determination of function is not cognitivist or technocratic: it is not science itself that acts, but only politics, which is governed by a different logic. Politics is, however, becoming increasingly dependent on factual knowledge. This 'factual knowledge' is also subject to philosophical scrutiny: overblown scientism and naturalist fallacies need to be exposed regardless of the short-term consequences. Habermas aimed at a similar constellation, from his critique of positivism and his attempts to integrate Marx (Habermas 1957, 2004, 1976b and 1984–7) to his identification of the role of the critical public (Habermas 1962) and his later references to Kant's philosophy of law (Habermas 1996). Whether he achieved this goal is a matter of contention (3.1).

51. The historical reasons for the absence of philosophy in Marx and Marxism are obvious: Kant's 'Copernican revolution' was still too recent to be soberly considered and implemented – it prompted strong emotional reactions both among its opponents and among its advocates. Moreover, it was soon absorbed by Hegel's philosophical system. Socio-historically, philosophers have had major difficulties not just with the growing importance of 'science' as such, but also with their relationship to a particular science – since behind that science there stood a political movement. Steps toward a successful Marxist reception of Kant can be found in Austro-Marxism (Mozetic 1987; cf. 2.1.3).

52. See Henning 2005b.

4.2.4 *The transformation of (Hegelian) philosophy in pragmatism*

It has already become clear that this understanding of Kant and Marx was not that of pragmatism. Rather, pragmatism was concerned with avoiding 'dualisms', in order then to 'ground' as much as possible in a philosophy of unity (3.4).

This was what one *expected* of philosophy. But because it was perceived through the lens of Hegel, philosophy was unable to meet this expectation. Thus the question became that of changing philosophy. In the pragmatist 'transformation of philosophy', which only began to affect German thought in the twentieth century, although it did so all the more strongly then, the high expectations vis-à-vis philosophy, expectations that derive from Hegel, were retained.[53] They were merely withdrawn from the realm of speculation and given a more down-to-earth mode, oriented to physics and biology.[54] Neo-pragmatism is situated 'between Hegel and Darwin',[55] meaning that it seeks to live up to the claims of the philosophy of unity using the means provided by the experimental natural sciences.[56] The result is a 'naturalised Left Hegelianism'[57] that fails to distinguish adequately between theoretical and practical reason, and between philosophy and scientific theory. It falls between two stools. Not only can no additional scientific propositions about society be formulated (they immediately appear 'quasi-transcendental'), but no concrete ethical principles can be obtained either (such principles have been 'transcendentalised' and thus rendered objectless). Nor is it possible to formulate philosophical definitions, since their 'a priori' and 'necessary' character is 'no longer' in reach. The only thing that can still be done is formulate propositions *about everything* from a super-perspective, but the status of such propositions remains notoriously unclear. 'Justifications' are introduced for all manner of things, though one cannot situate them or clarify their mode of validity.[58]

---

53. 'In neo-pragmatism and Dewey scholarship, there is a consensus that Kant and German idealism, and in particular Hegel, were a constitutive reference point for Dewey's transformation of the philosophical tradition' (H.-P. Krüger in Joas 2000, p. 228) – as well as for Peirce, Mead, Apel, Habermas, Honneth and Homann.

54. According to Peirce, the principles of pragmatism are 'what Hegel's might have been had he been educated in a physical laboratory instead of in a theological seminary' (Peirce, *Collected Papers*, 8.283; cf. Apel 1975, p. 30). Dewey 1939 still considered experimental natural science the touchstone.

55. Rorty 1994.

56. For Peirce, 'cognizability...and being are...metaphysically the same', 'synonymous' (Peirce, *Collected Papers*, 5.274; cf. Apel 1975, p. 54).

57. A. Ryan in Joas 2000, p. 320.

58. One need think only of how democracy is 'justified' anthropologically or logically, the validity of truth in terms of an obstruction of action that renders thought necessary in the first place, scientificity in terms of increasing utility, and so on (3.1.5). According to Peirce, one needs 'to make a philosophy like that of Aristotle, that is to say, to outline a theory so comprehensive that, for a long time to come, the entire work of human reason...shall appear as the filling up of its details' (*Collected Papers*, 1.1; Apel 1975, p. 33; cf. Mead 1987 I, pp. 60 ff.). James wrote: 'You want a system that will combine both things, the scientific loyalty to facts..., but also the old confidence in human values...I offer the oddly-named thing pragmatism as a philosophy that can satisfy both

The totalisation of philosophical claims leads, as in Berkeley's idealism, but inadvertently, to a 'loss of the world' ('The world well lost').[59] The elimination of the difference between philosophy and science renders both Kantian and Marxian philosophy pointless: before they can become practically relevant, the sciences need to be subjected to an in-depth philosophical critique. The philosophy of unity is no longer able to do this, insofar as it defines itself by reference to the specialised sciences or allows them to dictate its results. Much the same is true for the 'translations' effected between other realms:[60] before calling on politics to implement a philosophical concept of democracy or solidarity, one ought to test the concept socio-economically. To justify it in logical terms (even though logic has itself been distorted by the philosophy of unity and has therefore ceased, strictly speaking, to be logic) is to bypass social reality and the role of democracy within social reality; it is to become – *horribile dictu* – an ideologue.[61] But who is to formulate such a critique, when science has already been 'sublated' by the philosophy of unity?

Recently, neo-pragmatism and poststructuralism have fraternised under the logo of 'postmodernity'.[62] Rather than credulously accepting the grand narrative that there 'no longer' exist any rational subjects or ways of accessing real objects (an epistemic philosophy of history), a post-Marxian philososophy recommends soberly defining the possibilities for rationality. When this is done, many problems solve themselves. Like Left Hegelianism (4.4), pragmatism then appears as a heuristic transitional phase within the nineteenth-century crisis of philosophy: when one thinks it through to its logical conclusion, one cannot *remain* a pragmatist. Thus the original pragmatists gravitated toward pre-critical metaphysics.[63] In Germany, pragmatism has mainly had the effect of reinforcing the tendency toward ethicisation – to the point of 'normative monism'. Some of its adherents have progressed to 'historical materialism' (3.4.3) – that is a wordplay in German, but it is lost in English because pragmatism promised much but delivered very little.

4.2.5 *Supernormativism: philosophy twice transformed*

The German reception of pragmatism is a case unto itself. Humanistic reservations about all varieties of naturalisation are common in Germany. Since the thought of unity had

---

kinds of demands' (James 1907, pp. 26 and 33). Dewey, who wrote not just on logic and anthropology but also on pedagogy, aesthetics, ethics and religion, ended up seeing himself as a 'systematic' thinker (cf. Lukács 1971, pp. 116, 207; Husserl 1970, § 3; Habermas 1984–7, Vol. I, pp. 396 f.).

59. Rorty 1982, pp. 3 ff.; Putnam 1995, pp. 20, 64.

60. Habermas takes this to be the main task of philosophy (Habermas 2003, p. 259). Yet this hardly amounts to a more modest and realistic conception of philosophy (Habermas 2003, pp. 258 f.); on the contrary, it adds greatly to philosophy's tasks (3.1.5).

61. For a critique of the ideologisation of 'democracy', see Diggins 1998 and 1994; Lloyd 1997.

62. Nagl 2001.

63. A recent example is Searle 1993; cf. 3.4.

some roots in Germany anyway,[64] developing a version of pragmatism that accords with the normativism of German thought was not difficult. Apel's interpretation of the 'a priori of the communicative community' as the 'foundation of ethics'[65] turned pragmatism into an *ethics* – albeit one that did not so much allow for the formulation of concrete moral verdicts (it seldom did this)[66] as it assumed the tasks of practical philosophy (such as 'ultimate justification'), social theory,[67] theoretical philosophy[68] and even 'world constitution'.[69]

Differently from in the USA, however, the topology of knowledge that pragmatism encountered here was one that *had* already been transformed by Marx. Consequently, the object of 'de-transcendentalisation' was not an idealist philosophy of unity but a differentiated framework of disciplines. These were now subjected to renewed idealistic compression. Section 3.4 demonstrated how German normativism (a focus on the ethical that treats the functional as distinct from the ethical, in order then to largely ignore it) replaced its idealist foundations with pragmatist ones. Yet because of pragmatism's idealist moorings, the transformation *remained* idealist. The universally competent philosophy of 'normative genesis' becomes a supernormativism: the functional is no longer bypassed; it is itself ethicised, declared to be 'normative'. Now, both superstructure *and* base appear as 'normative'.

While pragmatism never determined the contents of this philosophy, it accorded all too well with a social philosophy that believed it needed to deal only with transparent and pleasing issues of 'intersubjectivity' (interaction, communication, discourse, recognition, self-legislation, solidarity, and so on). Objectivity, which has largely been lost in social philosophy,[70] is in fact impossible, according to the pragmatist theory of knowledge: since nothing is 'void of signs', everything is intersubjective, meaning, on this view, that it is 'normative', and therefore only to be grasped from the participant perspective. Thus the reception of pragmatism did not correct social philosophy's loss of the world.[71]

---

64. On the role that Fichte played for pragmatism, see Joas 1980, pp. 52 and 145; Oehler 1995, pp. 172 ff. Both James's psychology and Mead's unmediated deduction of a macro subject (the community) from a micro subject (the self) display Fichtean features; the same deduction is evident in Heidegger's 'authentic' community (2.5.5; 3.1.5)

65. Apel 1973, Vol. II, pp. 358 ff.

66. For this reason, Apel 1988a felt constrained to add a 'Part B'.

67. Habermas 1987 and 1984–7; Joas 1992 and 2000; Honneth 1996 and 2003.

68. Habermas 1976a. Efforts to 'ground' logic ethically can already be found in Rickert (Lask 1923, Vol. I, p. 349). The Erlangen School also attempted a pragmatic reconstruction of logic (cf. Gethmann 1991).

69. The 'weak naturalism' of Habermas 2003, pp. 22 ff.

70. While it did not deny the existence of 'objective' facts – cf. the verdict on Mead's idealism in Habermas 1984–7, Vol. II, p. 369 –, it did lose sight of it (2.4, 2.5, 3.1). Objectivity now informs the content of the theory only in an unrecognised manner.

71. The most recent neo-pragmatist system, Robert Brandom's first philosophy, accords with this philosophy as far as its aspirations are concerned: its reconstructions depict everything as 'normative' (Brandom 1994, p. 635; Brandom 2000; Seel 2002). The debate has tended to problematise not so much the approach as the finer points of its implementation.

Other theories could be mentioned in lieu of supernormativism. There is no lack of 'theories about everything' – one need think only of systems theory (2.5.6), interpretationism, reductive materialism and the like. Here, it will suffice to draw attention to the problematic initial constellation: regardless of what is given the 'reconciling' middle position, the aprioristic attempt to elaborate such a 'supertheory' needs itself to be questioned from the perspective of Marx.[72]

4.3 The function and scope of theory after Marx

> It has often been said that those who ignore history are condemned to repeat it. To this it should be added that those who ignore theory are condemned to reconstruct it.[73]

The point about the present work is that it has identified the break with Marx as one of the main factors contributing to this development in the history of ideas. Like Kant, Marx still had a complete world in view, and he interpreted it from various perspectives.[74] By de-sociologising economic theory in response to Marx (2.3.1), neoclassical economics arrived at a purely functional theory that needed to be *supplemented* with ethical considerations (2.4.1). The technoid and normative socio-philosophical speculations that developed from this split were subsequently de-economised (2.4.3, 2.4.5).

But the problem with this intellectual division of labour was that the two perspectives could no longer be properly combined. Within this dualist framework (nature and mind, subject and object, work and interaction, system and lifeworld), which was increasingly interpreted in ontological terms as it was passed on from one thinker to the next, German socio-philosophical thought ended up concerning itself almost *exclusively* with the normative sphere, or, to put it in vulgar Marxist terms, with superstructural phenomena (2.5, 2.6; 3.1, 3.2). An anti-positivist impulse led, in most cases, to elision of what was taken to be purely technical. But each of these sides took its own position to be the only true one, and so both sides featured an 'ethics' (2.4.3), including the opposing side of technocracy, systems theory and business management (2.4.5, 2.5.6, 3.3.3). It is the structure of 'German idealism' in the wider sense to interpret everything on the basis

72. Rentsch 2003a.

73. Anwar Shaikh.

74. Even the distinction between use value and exchange value is not an ontological but a perspectival one. In actual fact, there is no exchange value without use value, but they perform different roles within social practice, and so theory considers them from different perspectives (*MECW* 35, p. 29). Whether simple circulation is perceived as C–M–C or as M–C–M is also a question of perspective (2.3.7). The predicate 'bourgeois' indicates that a theory has only grasped something from a certain perspective, thereby necessarily ignoring other phenomena (Marx used the term 'standpoint' ['*Standpunkt*', sometimes translated as 'position' or 'point of view' – translator's note]; see *MECW* 35, p. 167, as well as pp. 17, 115, 124, 137, 172, 200 and elsewhere; *MECW* 37, pp. 33, 90, 261, 312, 319, 323, 352, 492 and elsewhere; *MECW* 3, 149 f.; MECW 5, pp. 5 and 28. Max Weber 1984, p. 633, starts from the 'standpoint of state interests'). Nancy Fraser calls the dualism of redistribution and recognition 'perspectival' (in Honneth 2003, pp. 3 and 66 ff.; cf. Kaulbach 1990).

of a single principle, whether it be mind, nature or a 'higher' third instance (the will, the commodity form, communication, normativity).[75] This idealism became increasingly noticeable in German social philosophy after 1989, as considerations on functional and systemic aspects were largely neglected within post-Marxism, with even these phenomena being interpreted as 'normative' (3.1–3.4; 4.2.5). These neo-Hegelian systems, which are theoretically self-contained and as far removed from practice as can be, should be read as a return of earlier social philosophies of 'objective mind'.

I set out to demonstrate that even the most speculative socio-metaphysical systems, such as Luhmann's, remain negatively dependent on Marxism (2.5.6). What is decisive when one enacts a break with something is in what way and as what one defines this something. It is one of the results of this study to have shown that the character of Marxian theory (see the sections on 'core elements of the system') was usually misunderstood. As the above topology has shown (4.2), its manner of speaking is primarily a scientific one,[76] and its theme is bourgeois society (2.1.5, 2.4.1). In order to arrive at this manner of speaking, Marx needed however to break with hypertrophic systematic philosophy first. This is why references to speculative philosophical formulas can still be found in his texts. While these references are mostly of an ironic nature, they were sufficient for rendering the validity status of Marx's enunciations unclear within the German reception – to this day.

4.3.1 *The avoidance of theory in critiques of Marx*

In summary, four principal systematic features of the misinterpretation of Marx can be identified. *First*, Marxian theory was interpreted as examining not society but nature (2.1.4, 2.2.4, 3.1.1). *Second*, this changed the way Marx's use of the term 'law' was understood: the term was no longer taken to refer to the specific economic laws of the capitalist mode of production but was interpreted without further ado as referring to laws of nature. Such an understanding of the term does not do justice to the meaning of Marx's texts.[77] But at least Marx's theory was still understood as a science, albeit as a natural science. The *third* principal misunderstanding consisted in reinterpreting this scientific manner of speaking as a philosophically speculative one, thereby relocating it to the level upon which Hegel's propositions are situated. Thus Marxism appeared to be a naturalist 'worldview' [*Weltanschauung*], one that admitted of hardly any scientific criticism or improvement and no longer allowed for internal differentiation in the way that Kantian philosophy had done (2.5.4, 2.6.6).

The *final* step was that of applying a vitalist hermeneutics to this worldview and reading it as the expression of a practice. It thereby became bound up with a specific historical constellation. In addition to being overhastily historicised, the theory was

75. Cf. 2.5.2; Kittsteiner 2001.
76. Cf. Little 1986.
77. 2.1.5, 2.1.6; *MECW* 35, pp. 615 f.; *MECW* 37, pp. 359 f. and 393 f.

misinterpreted on empiricist lines (2.1.2, 2.4.6, 2.5.4). It was only by alleging that Marx's 'worldview' had been intended as a 'description' of its present that other momentary observations could be presented as 'refuting' it. Thus naturalisation, philosophisation and empiricism all refused to attribute to Marxian theory the status of a complex *science*.

Key motives for breaking with Marx were informed by these misinterpretations. From theological attempts to refute Marx (2.6.5) to the postmodern eschewal of 'grand narratives',[78] Marx was read as a man of letters who had elaborated a political *Weltanschauung*. He was responded to by identifying realms that do not belong to nature and are therefore not governed by 'natural laws' (4.4; cf. 2.5.3, 2.5.5, 2.6.3, 3.1.2, 3.2.3, 3.3.2), or historico-philosophical stadial models were extended by the addition of a new stage within which Marx's laws 'no longer' hold (2.2.6, 2.3.3, 2.4.4, 2.5.6, 2.6.2. 3.1.3).

This was to misinterpret Marx: he was not concerned with 'nature' but with *bourgeois society* (2.4.6), and he did not intend to describe the surface of that society, but its hidden law of movement. Such a thematisation of society has astoundingly often been absent from post-Marxian socio-philosophical considerations (2.1.5, 2.4.1, 2.5.2, 3.1.1, 3.3.5). The functional rejection of nature often relocated the site of socio-theoretical reflection to mind and to a spiritualist 'history' (2.5.5, 2.6.6) – but this did justice only to Fichte and Hegel.[79] And yet it would be possible to develop an understanding of Marx's laws that distinguishes them both from laws of 'nature' and from hermeneutic surveys of 'mind'. Nor do these laws exhaust themselves in formulating momentary observations; they aim to grasp the regularity within the permanent *transformation* of bourgeois society (see the various 'Key Elements of Marxian Theory' above). To operate on the basis of this interpretation is to take the wind out of the sails of the implicit refutations and functional avoidances of Marx that have so characterised twentieth-century normative social philosophy.

4.3.2 *Marx's theory is not a determinism*

The purpose of science is to explain as much as possible while making as few assumptions as practicable. Ever since the first reflections on scientificity in Plato, this has led to the question of how 'the one' relates to the 'many', or how unifying thought relates to the manifold of being, how scientific laws relate to the phenomena they describe.[80]

In the modern natural sciences, the concept of laws has hardly ever been understood as determining a phenomenon's behaviour down to the last detail. This view devel-

---

78. Lyotard 1989, Laclau 1985.

79. This can be seen from the very titles of Dilthey 1988, Eucken 1921, Weber 2003, Sombart 1967, Bloch 2000, Freyer 1998, Schmitt 1996a, Gehlen 1931, Jaspers 1931 or Plessner 1992; on the level of content, it is evident in Scheler 1999, Lukács 1971, Adorno 1944, Habermas 1987 and, most recently, Boltanski 1999 and Franck 2002. The anti-naturalism that inheres in talk of interaction and normativity shows them to be functional equivalents of the older asociological formula of 'mind' (see above on the 'lifeworld').

80. Cf. Plato's dialogues *Sophistes*, 137c ff., *Parmenides*, 250e ff., and *Philebos*, 11a ff.

oped when features attributed to scientific engagement with the world were transposed to a deterministic and mechanistic *worldview*,[81] in a development that leads up to contemporary naturalism. The *philosophical* categories of nature, determination and law – derivative modes of science – were what first motivated philosophical counter-movements in the name of 'mind', 'freedom', and 'normativity'.

When one considers this from the perspective of the sociology of knowledge, it is impossible to overlook that more than questions about the matter itself were at stake. Functionally, this development was also about social claims – from abstract cultural prerogatives of interpretation (of the church, the aristocracy, the bourgeoisie or a social class of 'mandarins')[82] to concrete benefits and positions. It seems likely that such pre-theoretical motives also informed engagement with Marx (2.4.2). For the accusation of determinism (the accusation of being a 'Calvinist without God')[83] did not apply to Marx. The purpose of formulating a natural law is not to predict developments down to the smallest detail but rather that of detecting regularities within phenomena, which remain manifold. A law serves to identify the range of possibilities within which phenomena operate. By no means does the validity of the law of gravity entail that apples drop *ceaselessly* onto the heads of famous physicists (2.1.1, 2.5.7).[84]

4.3.3 *Marx's topic is civil society*

The relative openness of the concept of laws vis-à-vis everyday phenomena, already a feature of this concept in properly understood natural science, increases further when what is being considered are not natural but rather social phenomena. The difference is by no means that social phenomena are *not* governed by laws because they are entirely man-made. This was a functionally understandable but substantively erroneous invective against the application of explanatory patterns from the natural sciences to the field of the human sciences – a 'spiritualisation of social theory'.[85] It overlooked that man is by no means only 'mind' or free-floating normativity. Even individuals are never so free and so transparent unto themselves that they are consistently determined only by themselves[86] – and such self-determination is even less in evidence when it comes to the primordial *coexistence* of human beings, which is traversed by external constraints

81. Borkenau 1934.
82. See Mannheim 1936, Ringer 1987 and Bourdieu 1992.
83. Bernstein 1961, p. 7; Popper 1945, Vol. I, p. 101.
84. It is 'absurd for men...to hope that maybe another Newton may some day arise, to make intelligible to us even the genesis of but a blade of grass from some natural laws' (Kant 1952, Vol. II, p. 54/B 338).
85. Wirkus 1996, p. 276; 2.5.2.
86. Rentsch 2000, pp. 81 ff.

and always historically shaped. The difference is rather that the factors political economy must reckon with are less fixed than those of nature. Economic laws are only valid in certain historical constellations.[87] They do not impose themselves in a mechanically uniform manner, but are rather violated and transformed in manifold ways. But they *remain* laws – as shown today by the vain efforts of politicians to alter social processes at the touch of a button.

Thus the philosophical rejection of Marxian 'determinism' and the reduction of Marx's theory to purely 'instrumental' aspects is doubly erroneous: it underestimates the complexity of the concept of laws even in the natural sciences and it overlooks the fact that Marx examined not nature but modern capitalist society. Culture, interaction and normativity all play out within this society. Marx thematises culture only in passing and by reference to specific cases, not by means of a theory of culture 'as such'. But his social theory is better equipped to grasp such phenomena than a model that antithetically opposes mind to nature and operates with normative notions of individuals free of natural constraints and social relations (3.1, 3.2). Marxist analyses of art and literature – from Lukács to Bredekamp – have often demonstrated this. By contrast, even postmodernity, with its stylisation of plurality and 'difference', remains dependent on its specially modelled opponent, that of a naturalisation attributed, among others, to Marx. It abstractly opposes to this naturalisation a rulelessness that merely glosses over the distinct character of bourgeois society and the fact that economic laws always afford us a certain leeway.[88] This view of the social as shaped but not determined, and as transparent to reason but not to immediate observation (2.4.6), distinguishes Marx both from the disintegration of the social into the individual, as found in hermeneutics and in theories of rational choice, and from the total separation of individual and society, as found from Spencer to Luhmann.

4.3.4 *Neoclassical redeployments within economic theory*

Now, it is not enough for social philosophy to simply engage more strongly with the positive sciences. Rather, what I am making a case for here is critical awareness of the theoretical foundations upon which philosophical edifices are erected. Philosophy needs to be critical of the sciences too, and it cannot allow all of its data to be dictated to it by whichever scientific currents happen to be hegemonic.[89] Thus it is not a matter of indifference *which* economic theories one chooses to philosophically elucidate real developments by. Most economic phenomena are better recognised from Marx's perspective than from those of neoclassical or Keynesian theory. Neoclassical and Keynesian economists

87. Marx remarked critically about Adolph Wagner that his analytic method 'does not proceed from *man* but from a given economic period of society' (*MECW* 24, p. 547; cf. *MECW* 35, p. 605; Petersen 1997, Sayers 1998, Hann 1999).
88. 2.1.6; Milner 1999, pp. 115 ff.
89. Cf. Honneth 2003, pp. 115 f.

need to make *supplementary* assumptions to explain the existence of growth and crises, the premises that Marx *starts* from (2.3.1). Whenever several theoretical approaches are available for explaining a phenomenon, the model that explains more must not be abandoned overhastily, even if it has unpopular political implications.

The most abstract modern social philosophies start from the presuppositions of neoclassical economics (3.1, 3.2). Even much of what currently presents itself as egalitarian, or even as a variant of Marxism, has been seen to be an unwitting intra-Marxist echo of earlier 'bourgeois' avoidances of Marx.[90] Marxist narratives such as the primacy of politics (2.2.6) or the technoid periodisation of Fordism and post-Fordism (2.4.5) implicitly start from the harmonist assumptions inherent in the neoclassical model of the economy, assumptions by which one once hoped to neutralise the virulence of Marxian theory (2.3.2). The neoclassical 'refutation' of Marx, with its reduction of the economy to *market* events ('exchange'), persists even in Adorno's hypothesis on fatality (2.6.3), and thereby in the numerous 'normative' countermodels (3.1). Marx's theory is rarely taken seriously *as a theory*; it tends rather to be read as a pre-modern philosopheme (as a philosophy of history, a 'metaphysics of labour' and so on) which needs 'today' to be overcome.[91] This is why the critique of philosophy presented in this study concerned not just 'bourgeois' thought, but also speculative neo-Marxism and recent critical theory.

4.3.5 *The side-play of dialectics as discursive displacement*

I could now proceed to cite authors who second my unspectactular view of Marx and philosophy.[92] But exegesis of their work would newly entangle us in the historico-textual controversies that I have been trying to avoid. Most of the more important contexts within which Marx is discussed in Germany are opposed to the rather sober view presented here. Hegelian Marxism as it has developed in the wake of value-form analysis is a case in point.[93] Marx undeniably used the word 'dialectic', albeit in an ever narrower sense.[94] But these passages can be read soberly (2.3.5, 2.5.7). Marx presents real developments that are apparently contrary to one another as interrelated. Today, one might cite the growing impoverishment of broad sections of the population in spite of social

---

90. Heinrich 2001, Gerlach 2003, pp. 21 ff.; cf. Henning 2004.

91. This view is even shared by writings *about* Marx like Backhaus 1997, Bonschab 1999, most contributions in Demirovic 1998 and Gerlach 2003, Gorz 1989, Heinrich 2001 (one of the few to present economic arguments, sometimes culled from Keynes – who is more outdated than Marx), ISF 2000, Kurz 1994, Lohmann 1991, Losurdo 1995, Van Parijs 1993 or Wildt 2002.

92. Some recent books venture in the direction outlined here (Berger 2004, Heinrich 2004).

93. On value-form analysis, see 2.3.5 and 2.5.7. Contemporary exponents of a Hegelianising Marxism include (internal controversies notwithstanding): Backhaus 1997, Behrens 1993, Braun 1992, Brentel 1989, Brudney 1998, K. Holz 1993, H. Holz 1997, ISF 2000, Rakowitz 2000, Reichelt 2002, Rockmore 2002, Wildt 1997 or Wolf 2003.

94. Göhler 1980.

prosperity,[95] rising unemployment in spite of economic growth,[96] the decline in profits in spite of rising productivity[97] and the ever more ruthless overexploitation of natural resources in spite of improved technological options. Marx did not juxtapose such phenomena as if they were unconnected; he exposed their common cause.[98] Two apparently contradictory observations, A and B, can both be true, as long as they are mediated theoretically – *explained.* It is a matter of identifying the 'conditions of compatibility' of contrary phenomena, meaning their real causes.[99] There is no reason to interpret this Marxian point as the deterioration of a conventional scientific presentation into a philosophico-speculative 'dialectic'. Marx's presentation is rather directly opposed to Hegel's: Hegel did not start from real phenomena but from their concept, which he came upon positivistically.[100] Like Backhaus, he dealt constantly with contradictions because he abstracted *excessively.*

Of course different things contradict one another when I combine them into a single concept.[101] But this does not mean that the 'concept' contradicts itself and develops; it could just as well mean that the wrong concept has been chosen. Fetishisations of the concept of abstraction, which attempt to philosophise Marx by means of concepts such as 'real abstraction' or 'abstract labour', have also been seen to be inadequate (2.4.5, 2.5.7). Marx's abstractions are something less than his theory; they only prove themselves by the way they function within the theory. These terms can also be meaningfully interpreted as non-metaphysical terms. It is only in the models of neoclassical economics and theories of justice that abstractions are unmediatedly presented as explanations (2.4.1, 3.2.1). But because the middle terms are missing, nothing is explained by this; all that is achieved is a consolidation of opinions (2.4.3). The function of this is explicitly that of a 'justification' (3.2.2) – ideologisation.

4.3.6 *The task of a critique of normative social philosophy*

Reading Marx's theory as an empirical description has been seen to be an error (2.1.2, 2.4.6). The theory is a theoretical model that stakes a claim to systematically apprehending and *explaining* some of the key social phenomena associated with modernity. The opposite error consisted in reading Marx's theory as a philosophical one (2.4.4, 2.5.4, 2.6.1, 4.2.3). Its position between everyday observation and philosophical 'description' was in both cases misconstrued.

95. Botwinick 1993.
96. Eatwell 1996, Howard 1975, Chapter 11.
97. Shaikh 1987, 1992.
98. Demirovic 1998, p. 87; cf. 2.4.1.
99. Steinvorth 1977, pp. 14 ff., 24 f.
100. *MECW* 3, pp. 331, 338.
101. *MECW* 4, p. 57; 2.5.2.

A model's justification depends neither on philosophical appreciation of some randomly chosen aspects nor on the occasional 'empirical' verification of individual propositions by reference to momentary appearances; it depends on the explanatory force of the entire theory.[102] This ought to be the starting point for anyone who wishes to criticise Marx. But since the economic critiques of Marx examined cannot be considered valid (2.3.2, 4.3.4), it was the various philosophisations that made it possible, functionally, to circumvent Marxian theory within social philosophy – this time, the arguments deployed were *philosophical*. This presupposed turning Marx into a philosopher. I have shown by way of several examples that attempts to reconstruct Marx 'philosophically' lead to him being declared obsolete (2.3.5, 2.4.4, 2.6.2, 3.1.3).

Such a verdict may just as well indicate that the 'reconstruction' has failed. The efforts to read and refute Marxian theory as a philosophical theory that have been examined in this study had to be rejected as flawed. All too often, they distorted the meaning of Marx's propositions. They presented no apposite criticisms of the Marxian theory of society, criticisms that could justify continuing to neglect Marx. (What follows from this *politically* is another matter.)

Instead of criticising Marx's theory philosophically, as has so often been done, I have been able to proceed in the opposite direction and criticise German social philosophy from the perspective of Marxian theory – without resorting to class analysis or a political economy of the present. For Marxian theory has major consequences for philosophical background assumptions; they concern the relationship between theory and empirical data. Is it even possible to reason 'conceptually' – aprioristically – about reality, in order to formulate general propositions about it? The ennobling light in which structures hitherto not critically examined are cast by the normative is philosophically inadmissible. There can be no social philosophy without an analysis of empirical data and its interpretations,[103] certainly no 'normative' social philosophy. The spark of the normative cannot be struck from a limited number of factual cases. When something of the kind is surreptitiously attempted, as in recent debates on the technological options available in medicine and food production, a methodologically enlightened philosophy needs to expose the 'normative' subreption – rather than engaging in its *own* subreption, in order then to abstractly oppose it to the original one.

102. Duhem 1954, p. 187; Callinicos 1983, p. 121; Janich 1997. Marx criticises approaches that borrowed their categories 'from every-day life... without further criticism': 'That in their appearance things often represent themselves in inverted form is pretty well known in every science except political economy' (*MECW* 35, p. 537) and philosophy.

103. Zinn 1987, p. 35.

The Marxian critique of philosophy can be summarised as follows: in terms of our Kantian topology (4.2.1), philosophy is not situated 'topmost', as in Hegel; it needs rather to descend 'below', or into the world, repeatedly (2.5.7, 3.1.5). By contrast, German idealism, which is so astoundingly persistent, holds that philosophy can solve a given set of problems intra-theoretically – by means of a new philosophical 'theory'. This leads to the iterated formation of meta-discourses and meta-meta-theories, which raise their own questions about self-justification and ultimate justification. The result is that access to salutary consideration of social reality – 'gay positivism' – is increasingly blocked. It is not just the quality of philosophical themes and hypotheses that suffers from this, but also social reality itself. Critical intelligence, whose interventions it might benefit from, tends in this way to be diverted from important real questions. Since Aristotle's day, philosophy has concerned itself, among other things, with scientific and economic issues. This perspective needs to be restored by means of Marx. A post-Marxian philosophy must not give itself the air of being a Hegelian (4.2.2) or post-Hegelian superphilosophy (4.2.4, 4.2.5). It needs rather to follow Kant in reflecting upon the science and the politics ('theory and practice') it encounters, *without* bypassing reason in the process. Such reflection involves the effort to critically situate theory and practice from the perspective of political economy. This would amount to a return to the Kantian concept of philosophy (4.2.1), except that the contents would be those of the twenty-first century.

4.4 Normative theory: Ethics as a surrogate for explanation

Ethics is booming[104]

This study tried to show that the contents and the character of Marxian theory have seldom been adequately understood either by his opponents or advocates. This had consequences for the counter-models, too. They got their orientation not from what they militated against, but from the image they had of it. Since the idea one had of Marxian theory was that of a reductive materialist worldview [*Weltanschauung*], opposing to it an ethical worldview seemed a sensible thing to do – this was the birth of 'normative social philosophy' from the spirit of a polemic gone astray. Even today, socio-philosophical conceptions continue to display this normativistic character, even when a functional anti-Marxism is no longer, or hardly, in evidence (3.1–3.4). How might the results of my Marx-oriented critique of normativistic social philosophy be summarised systematically?

The point about Marx is that he developed his theory by critically engaging with such ethical social philosophies (2.5.7). The term 'social philosophy' [*Sozialphilosophie*] was

104. Kohlmann 1997, p. 11/Knoll 2000, p. 7.

coined by Moses Hess, a temporary ally of Marx.[105] What Hess had in mind was that philosophy, formerly worldless, was now addressing worldly matters, and in particular the social question and the budding socialist movements. Ever since its origins in the work of the Young Hegelians, German social philosophy was therefore caught between a worldless philosophical idealism and direct wordly activity, with one sometimes transitioning unmediatedly into the other. In terms of the history of theory, it was situated between idealist philosophical systems and conventionally scientific sociological theory. Its characteristic manner of expressing itself, 'interpretation' [*Deutung*],[106] is also situated somewhere between a substantive proposition, an ethical valuation and a particular political appeal. It is therefore a transitional phenomenon,[107] not unlike pragmatism (4.2.4).

Thus, in today's situation, in which 'political emancipation'[108] has already been achieved in the form of the democratic constitutional state, there is no longer any theoretical gain in withdrawing from the worldly political activity and the sober scientific elucidation of that activity that are now open to us, in order to return to normative social philosophy (2.6.3). Today, morality and law may still serve as means for asserting particular interests as general interests (such as through the negative discrimination practised by means of quota systems or through certain principles of taxation). But as a rule, this form already involves a scaling back of one's aspirations – if only because its temporal horizon is posterior.[109] Law is supposed to end or at least pacify conflicts that are already playing out. For this reason, it would not be wise to articulate political and social demands in a legal or moral form *from the outset*, as bourgeois opponents of Marx have always demanded.[110] But what is even more misguided is the way social philosophy attempts to reduce such demands to normative ones in advance.[111] To proceed in this way is to forego the possibility of criticising moralistic ideologies. Moreover, material consideration of law and morality bypasses the question of the *subject*.

According to Marx, similar contents cannot be seamlessly given different forms (2.5.7, 4.3).[112] 'Normative social philosophy' overlooks the fact that autonomy does not admit of legal representation. For example, whenever the interests of workers were articulated not by the workers themselves, but by bourgeois bureaucracies who gave

105. Tellingly, 'K. Marx and F. Engels did not adopt this terminology' (Röttgers 1995, p. 1218; *MECW* 5, p. 483; cf. *MECW* 3, pp. 201 f. and 457. On Hess, see I. Berlin 1994; for a general discussion, see Löwith 1965, McLellan 1969, Essbach 1988 and Draper 1990). After Hess, Tönnies was the first to use the concept again (2.5.2).

106. Cf. Dilthey 2002, pp. 252 f.; Weber 1968, pp. 9 f.; Adorno 1977, p. 334; Rothacker 1934, p. 98; Ständeke 1981 and Rehberg 1986.

107. Freyer 1964, p. 221.

108. *MECW* 4, p. 115; *MECW* 3, pp. 140 ff.

109. Hegel 1991, p. 23.

110. A. Menger 1886.

111. 3.1.5; for the most recent examples, see Honneth 2010 and 2003.

112. Marx is situated between the optimistic conception of philosophy as universal translator found in Habermas and the postmodern rejection of translation functions (Lyotard 1987, p. 49; 3.2.3).

those interests a legal form, they ceased to be the interests of workers. If anything, this parallels the paternalism with which workers were treated by Leninist cadre parties (on autonomy, see 2.2.2, 2.6.5, 3.3.6).

By virtue of its peculiar intermediate position, the transitional discipline that is contemporary social philosophy inherits from its precursors their familiar ambiguity.[113] A discipline that reflects on ethical dispositions instead of on material states of affairs, and which takes itself, moreover, to be not descriptive but 'normative', faces a momentous dilemma. To the extent that ethics is supposed to act as a social theory, it easily gravitates toward the glorification of what exists by claiming, in a Hegelian manner, that the normative is already significantly anchored in what exists, or it becomes normative in a platonically worldless way, abstractly confronting the world without offering any point of contact (2.4.3). Karl Mannheim provided a vivid description of this precarious situation, that of liberal social philosophy. He impressively outlined its intermediate position between an ecstatic-religious utopianism that wants to create a completely new world from 'spirit', and the anti-rationalist and affirmative 'historically determined consciousness' [*Bedingtheitsbewusstsein*] proper to conservative thought.[114]

In this work, I have focused especially on normativism's conservative-quietist tendencies, which are sometimes deliberate and sometimes not.[115] But we have also encountered intimations of normativism's utopian-anarchist flipside: its 'mental' [*geistig*] tendencies, which bypass every institution, thereby becoming latently authoritarian and destructive, began to suggest themselves in our examination of Trotskyism (2.2.5), Eucken, Lukács, Heidegger and Adorno (2.5.3 ff., 2.6.3), as well as in some branches of business ethics (3.3.2, 3.3.4). Where it is not affirmative, Habermas' social philosophy also tends, at least implicitly, in the direction of an oddly placeless and elitist noocracy (3.1.5). At the very least, abandonment of socio-economic theory in favour of a 'normative' politics of identity creates the *possibility* of irrationalism.[116] This can already be seen in Georges Sorel, who was a follower of Bernstein.[117]

---

113. Röttgers 1995.

114. Mannheim 1936, pp. 226 f. 'The liberal idea is adequately intelligible only as a counterpart to the ecstatic attitude of the Chiliast which often hides behind a rationalist facade and which historically and socially offers a continual, potential threat to liberalism. It is a battle cry against that stratum of society whose power comes from its inherited position in the existing order, and which is able to master the here and now at first unconsciously and later through rational calculation' (Mannheim 1936, p. 226; cf. p. 222).

115. 2.1.2, 2.4.3, 2.5.6, 3.1.5, 3.2.1 f., 3.3.3 f.; for recent examples, see Rifkin 2000, Turner 2001, Schulze 2003.

116. Maalouf 2000.

117. 'Nothing is more removed from actual events than the closed rational system. Under certain circumstances, nothing contains more irrational drive than a fully self-contained, intellectualistic world-view' (Mannheim 1936, p. 219). Sorel's mythic neo-Marxism started from Bernstein's ethical reconfiguration of socialism (Sorel 1961, p. 216; Sorel 1999, p. 132). He used the destructive ethos of revolution, which Bernstein had meant to overcome, for his new politics of identity. And he anticipated many features of Western Marxism: he formulated a prohibition on images (Sorel 1961, p. 215; Sorel 1999, p. 135), invoked the authority of Vico (Kołakowski 1976, pp. 477 ff.), formulated a

'Normative social philosophy' operates between these two equally unfortunate poles, as if it were moving upon the smooth surface of a display cabinet, with its actual object of inquiry situated *below* the glass.[118] A third option will be available to social theory only if it moves beyond its ethicised transitional form; to have done this is a lasting achievement of Marx's pioneering effort. He made intellectual headway by ceasing to treat ethical ideas as a 'normative backdrop' and as an unquestioned 'conceptual basis', in the manner of liberal social philosophy (which is not identical with liberalism as a political movement); instead, he thematised these ideas themselves. He considered them an element of material history, and it was for this reason that they became an object of theory.[119] Almost any moral claim can *call* itself 'universal'.

But it cannot determine, by itself, what the effects of its political implementation would be – at least not in a theoretically legitimate way. Considered from the perspective of social theory, certain 'normative' presuppositions become recognisable as ideologies whose scope is limited; it also becomes evident that these presuppositions are frequently employed not to supplement concrete analysis, but to replace it (2.4.3; 3). Only when it disposes of a *material* theory can the will to political transformation navigate the straits of a moral sermonising that is affirmative, therefore ineffective, and efforts to improve the world that are out of touch with reality, therefore putschist. Moreover, intense disagreements can usually be given a more unemotional and objective form by suspending morally fossilised 'validity claims' (whose real meaning tends to be: 'The biggest slice of cake belongs to me') (4.2.3). Normativism and supernormativism surrender this advantage unnecessarily.[120]

---

pragmatic analysis of cognitive interests (Sorel 1961, pp. 249 f.) and emphasised the symbolic and the institutional: 'On the contrary, it is those symbolic portions which were formerly regarded as being of dubious worth that constitute the definitive value of his [Marx's] work' (1961, 251). '*Socialism is a philosophy of the history of contemporary institutions*' (Sorel 1999, p. 40). Sorel transforms material and concrete issues into normative and abstract ones, by inquiring into 'how to *create today the ethic of the producers of the future*' (Sorel 1999, p. 224; cf. Landauer 1967). His enthusiastic readers included Lukács (1971b, p. x) and Gramsci (Kołakowski 1976, p. 475; cf. p. 1033, on Korsch). König judges Sorel's influence on German thought to have been considerable (König 1975, p. 195): 'Seen through Sorel's glasses, Karl Marx looked to me... like the 'Jewish grandmother' of National Socialism' (König 1984, p. 101; see 2.6.6).

118. This can still be seen from the most recent discussions in the journal *Deutsche Zeitschrift für Philosophie* (no. 2, 2003, pp. 233 ff.), in which a worldless philosophical egalitarianism is weighed against an apparently more enlightened but equally normativistic anti-egalitarianism (Krebs 2000), in order then to search for a philosophical compromise formula (cf. 3.3.3). '[E]thics has outgrown its status as a subordinate moment in abstract theory. Henceforth it *is* philosophy, the other divisions being absorbed into it' (Spengler 1928 I, p. 366).

119. 'A veritable Copernican revolution occurred when man began to regard not merely himself, not merely man, but also the existence, the validity, and the influence of these ideas as conditioned factors, and the development of ideas as bound up with existence, as integral to the historico-social process' (Mannheim 1936, p. 244).

120. 'Bourgeois liberalism was much too preoccupied with norms to concern itself with the actual situation as it really existed. Hence, it necessarily constructed for itself its own ideal world' (Mannheim 1936, pp. 221 f.). Conservative thinkers often accused normative thought of devaloris-

Philosophical ethics is itself a legitimate and important discipline – more so than ever before, in fact. What is problematic is the attempt to develop a *social theory* on its basis. When this is attempted, one's particular political ethics ceases to be an object of critical analysis, becoming the transcendent measure of analysis instead. It thereby becomes a blind spot. In systematic terms, this implies an obstructive gradation: processed philosophically, a demand that 'holds with regard to' (Emil Lask) something objective in the world becomes a repetitive self-assertion of the act of demanding *qua philosophical* act, without ever reaching its object. In the optics of social philosophy, the object is lost (4.1). The intentional reference to the world no longer enters the world; it remains stuck, as it were, in philosophy. A mediating instance becomes an end in itself, obstructing access to the content originally aimed at (2.6.7; something similar occurred in neo-Marxism, which got so bogged down in Marxian texts it never found its way back to the world).[121]

Properly understood, a reassessment of Marx that breaks with current interpretive schemes promises a way out of these normativistic dilemmas. If the present work has contributed to this, it has achieved its purpose. The accusation of reductive naturalism has in any case been shown not to apply to Marx, and the normativistic German-style counter-model has been shown to be objectless and hopeless. Science has nothing to offer besides trial and error – so let's get to work, and, as Luther says: *peccate fortiter!*

---

ing its opponents not just politically, but also morally (Schmitt 1932, Gehlen 1973, Lübbe 1987, Luhmann 1978 and 1989) – which did not prevent them from formulating an ethics of their own (2.4.3, 2.5.6). By effecting a rapprochement of politics and consensual establishment of the truth, Dewey and Habermas eliminate the distinction between theory and practice. Like Schmitt, they situate the 'decision' beyond the reach of reason and within ethics – this is the opposite of the neutrality aspired to during the seventeenth century (2.6.6; 3.1.4).

121. The parallel with the church prompted accusations of 'hierocratic coercion' (Schelsky 1975, Tenbruck 1984, Weber 1968, p. 54). On the sociology of the postmodern intellectual, see Milner 1999, pp. 145 ff.; Bourdieu 1989 and 1992; Giesen 1999.

Afterword to the English Translation

Writing the book was an immense pleasure. To this day, I am grateful to those who made it possible for me to engage in this project: my dissertation supervisor, Professor Thomas Rentsch of Dresden; Anwar Shaikh from New York, who opened my eyes to economic issues; and the German National Academic Foundation [*Studienstiftung des Deutschen Volkes*]. *In spite of everything*, the book has eventually found patient readers. I continue to be surprised at how many people have made use of it. My readers have tended also to be surprised when they found me to be a comparatively normal and (at the time) young person, not a wizened bookworm (something I am now gradually becoming).

I hope the book will now prove an enjoyable read to Anglophone readers as well. I wish to take this opportunity to express my gratitude to those who have made the present translation possible. My thanks go to Frederic Jameson for a judicious review, to Peter Thomas and Sebastian Budgen of *Historical Materialism*, to Max Henninger for the monstrous labour of translation, to the Brill and Transcript publishing houses and, last but not least, to the University of St. Gallen and the German Publishers and Booksellers Association [*Börsenverein des Deutschen Buchhandels*] for their financial support.

One final remark: a recent (similarly voluminous) publication does me the questionable honour of mentioning me in the same breath as Althusser and Lukács – as a third 'anti-normativist'.[1] This is to misunderstand my book. I do not wish to claim that it is altogether senseless to speak of ethics, but rather to make the point that ethics cannot *take the place* of a theory of society,

1. Dath and Kirchner 2012, pp. 675–85.

although it has frequently done so in German philosophical thought (partly because of a sense of threat caused by Marx). The concoction called 'normative social philosophy' fails both as an ethics and as a theory of society. (The theory of recognition, already under attack when I wrote may book, has nevertheless continued to walk this road without a care.) To formulate such a criticism is not tantamount to rejecting every form of ethics. Having discussed Karl Marx's normative premises in greater detail since my book was first published,[2] I now believe Marx advocated a specific version of *perfectionism*, similar to those found in William Godwin, William Morris and John Dewey. I already gesture toward these normative premises of Marx's critique in the present work, which focuses, however, on criticising the disappearance of social theory, including in the 'critical theories' of our time. Enjoy the read!

Christoph Henning, Zürich, April 2012

2. See for example Henning 2008a, 2009 and 2010.

References

Abendroth, Wolfgang 1965, *Sozialgeschichte der europäischen Arbeiterbewegung*, Frankfurt am Main: Suhrkamp.

—— 1969 [1964], *Aufstieg und Krise der deutschen Sozialdemokratie. Das Problem der Zweckentfremdung einer Partei durch die Anpassungstendenz von Institutionen an vorgegebene Machtverhältnisse*, Frankfurt am Main: Stimme.

—— 1972 [1968], *Antagonistische Gesellschaft und Politische Demokratie. Aufsätze zur politischen Soziologie*, Neuwied/Berlin: Luchterhand.

Abosch, Heinz 1990, *Trotzki zur Einführung*, Hamburg: Junius.

Acham, Karl 1995, *Geschichte und Sozialtheorie*, Freiburg/Munich: Alber.

Adler, Georg 1891, 'Nietzsche. Der Sozialphilosoph der Aristokratie', *Nord und Süd*, 56, 97–107.

Adler, Guido 1887, *Die Grundlagen der Marx'schen Kritik der bestehenden Volkswirthschaft*, Tübingen: Laupp.

Adler, Max 1972 [1908], *Marx und Engels als Denker*, Frankfurt am Main: Makol.

—— 1913, 'Die Zukunftsfrage des Christentums. Können wir noch Christen sein?', *Arbeiter-Zeitung*, 5 January 1913.

—— 1924, *Das Soziologische in Kants Erkenntniskritik. Ein Beitrag zur Auseinandersetzung zwischen Naturalismus und Kritizismus*. Vienna: Wiener Volksbuchhandlung.

—— 1925, *Kant und der Marxismus. Gesammelte Aufsätze zur Erkenntniskritik und Theorie des Sozialen*, Berlin: Laub.

—— 1928, *Über psychologische und ethische Läuterung des Marxismus*, Berlin: Laub.

—— 1930, *Soziologie des Marxismus*, Vienna: Europa-Verlag.

—— 1964 [1922], *Die Staatsauffassung des Marxismus. Ein Beitrag zur Unterscheidung von soziologischer und juristischer Methode*, Darmstadt: Wissenschaftliche Buchgesellschaft.

—— 1974 [1913], *Marxistische Probleme. Beiträge zur Theorie der materialistischen Geschichtsauffassung und Dialektik*, Berlin: Dietz.

—— 1975 [1936], *Das Rätsel der Gesellschaft. Zur erkenntnistheoretischen Grundlegung der Sozialwissenschaft*, Aalen: Scientia.

Adler, Max and Stephan Bauer (eds.) 1971 [1931], *Festschrift für Carl Grünberg zum 70. Geburtstag*, Glashütten: Auvermann.

Adorno, Theodor W. 1950, *Studies in Prejudice 1, The Authoritarian Personality*, New York: Harper (partial reprint in *GS* 9).

—— 1956, *Dissonanzen. Musik in der verwalteten Welt*, Göttingen: Vandenhoeck und Ruprecht (also in *GS* 14).

—— 1969, *Spätkapitalismus oder Industriegesellschaft? Verhandlungen des 16. Deutschen Soziologentages in Frankfurt am Main 1968*, Stuttgart: Enke.

—— 1970, *Über Walter Benjamin*, edited by Rolf Tiedemann, Frankfurt am Main: Suhrkamp.

—— 1972–86, *Gesammelte Schriften*, 20 volumes, edited by Rolf Tiedemann, Frankfurt am Main: Suhrkamp (cited as *GS*).

—— 1972 [1942], 'Reflexionen zur Klassentheorie' in *GS* 8.

—— 1972a [1957], 'Soziologie und empirische Forschung' in *GS* 8.

—— 1973 [1927], 'Der Begriff des Unbewußten in der transzendentalen Seelenlehre' in *GS* 1

—— 1976 [1969], *The Positivist Dispute in German Sociology*, New York: Harper & Row.

—— 1977 [1931], 'The Actuality of Philosophy', *Telos*, 31, 120–33.

—— 1979 [1933], *Kierkegaard. Konstruktion des Ästhetischen* in *GS* 2.

—— 1984 [1932], 'Die gesellschaftliche Lage der Musik' in: *GS* 18.

—— 1988 [1957], *Reason and Revelation* in idem, *Critical Models: Interventions and Catchwords*, New York: Columbia University Press.

—— 1988a [1962], *'Why Still Philosophy?'* in idem, *Critical Models: Interventions and*

Catchwords, New York: Columbia University Press.
—— 1990 [1938], 'On the Fetish-Character in Music and the Regression in Listening' in *Musical Aesthetics: A Historical Reader*, Vol. III, edited by Edward A. Lippmann, Hillsdale: Pendragon.
—— 1993 [1963], *Hegel: Three Studies*, Cambridge, MA: MIT Press.
—— 1997 [1970], *Aesthetic Theory*, Minneapolis: University of Minnesota Press.
—— 2000 [1963], *Problems of Moral Philosophy*, Stanford: Stanford University Press.
—— 2005 [1951], *Minima Moralia: Reflections on a Damaged Life*, London: Verso.
—— 2006 [1949], *Philosophy of New Music*, Minneapolis: University of Minnesota Press.
—— 2007 [1966], *Negative Dialectics*, New York: Continuum.
Adorno, Theodor W. and Max Horkheimer 1997 [1947], *Dialectic of Enlightenment*, London: Verso.
Aeschbacher, Urs 1992, *Faschismus und Begeisterung. Psychologische Neuvermessung eines Jahrhunderttraumas*. Essen: Die Blaue Eule.
Aglietta, Michel 1976, *Regulation et crises. L'experiment des etats-unis*, Grenoble: Calmann-Lévy.
—— 1979, *A Theory of Capitalist Regulation: The US-Experience*, London: New Left Books.
Ahlberg, René 1974, *Das Proletariat. Die Perspektiven der Arbeiterklasse in der Industriegesellschaft*, Stuttgart: Kohlhammer.
Albers, Detlev 1987, *Sozialismus im Westen. Erste Annäherungen: Marxismus und Sozialdemokratie*, Berlin: Argument.
Albert, Hans 1965, 'Modellplatonismus. Der neoklassische Stil des ökonomischen Denkens' in *Logik der Sozialwissenschaften*, edited by Ernst Topitsch, Cologne: Kiepenheuer und Witsch.
—— 1969 [1964], 'Der Mythos der totalen Vernunft. Dialektische Ansprüche im Lichte undialektischer Kritik' in *Spätkapitalismus oder Industriegesellschaft? Verhandlungen des 16. Deutschen Soziologentages*, edited by Theodor W. Adorno, Stuttgart: Enke.
—— 1972, *Theorie und Realität. Ausgewählte Aufsätze zur Wissenschaftslehre der Sozialwissenschaften*, Tübingen: Mohr.
Albert, Karl 1990, 'Lebensphilosophie' in *Theologische Realenzyklopädie*, Vol. XX, Berlin: De Gruyter.
—— 1995, *Lebensphilosophie. Von den Anfängen bei Nietzsche bis zu ihrer Kritik bei Lukács*, Freiburg and Munich: Alber.
Albrecht, Clemens 1999, *Die intellektuelle Gründung der Bundesrepublik. Eine Wirkungsgeschichte der Frankfurter Schule*, Frankfurt am Main: Campus.
Albrecht, Reinhardt 1973, *Sozialtechnologie und ganzheitliche Sozialphilosophie. Zu Karl R. Poppers Kritik der ganzheitlichen Sozialphilosophie*, Bonn: Bouvier.
Alexander, Jeffrey 1982, *The Antinomies of Classical Thought: Marx and Durkheim. Theoretical Logic in Sociology 2*, London: Routledge and Kegan Paul.
Alexy, Robert 1978, *Theorie der juristischen Argumentation*, Frankfurt am Main: Suhrkamp.
Althusser, Louis 1972, *Lenin and Philosophy*, New York: Monthly Review Press.
—— 1977 [1970], 'The Conditions of Marx's Scientific Discovery', *Theoretical Review*, 1.
—— 1978, 'Enfin la crise du marxisme!' in *Pouvoir et opposition dans les sociétés post-révolutionnaires*, Paris: Seuil.
—— 1994 [1992], *The Future Lasts A Long Time and The Facts*, London: Vintage.
—— 1996 [1965], *For Marx*, London: Verso.
Althusser, Louis and Etienne Balibar 1997 [1968], *Reading Capital*, London and New York: Verso.
Altvater, Elmar 1975, 'Wertgesetz und Monopolmacht' in *Zur Theorie des Monopols: Staat und Monopole I*, Hamburg: Argument.
—— 1987, *Sachzwang Weltmarkt. Verschuldungskrise, blockierte Industrialisierung, ökologische Gefährdung – das Beispiel Brasilien*, Hamburg: VSA.
—— 1991, *Die Zukunft des Marktes. Ein Essay über die Regulation von Geld und Natur nach dem Scheitern des "real existierenden Sozialismus"*, Münster: Westfälisches Dampfboot.
—— 1992, 'Stammwesen im globalen Dorf', *Blätter für deutsche und internationale Politik*, 5.
—— 1992a: *Der Preis des Wohlstands oder Umweltplünderung und neue Welt(un)ordnung*, Münster: Westfälisches Dampfboot.
—— 1997, 'Geld, Globalisierung, hegemoniale Regulierung' in *Jenseits der Nationalökonomie? Weltwirtschaft und Nationalstaat zwischen Globalisierung und Regionalisierung*, edited by S. Becker, Hamburg: Argument.
Altvater, Elmar et al. 1971, *Materialien zur Kritik der bürgerlichen Ökonomie. Begründung für*

eine Lehreinheit "Politische Ökonomie", Giessen: Polit-Buchvertrieb.

Altvater, Elmar, Jürgen Hoffmann and Willi Semmler 1979, *Vom Wirtschaftswunder zur Wirtschaftskrise. Ökonomie und Politik in der Bundesrepublik*, Berlin: Olle und Wolter.

Altvater, Elmar and Birgit Mahnkopf 1999 [1996], *Grenzen der Globalisierung*, Münster: Westfälisches Dampfboot.

—— 2002, *Globalisierung von Ungleichheit. Über Arbeit im Schatten, Schwarze Kassen und informelle Politik*, Münster: Westfälisches Dampfboot.

Altwegg, Jürgen 1986, *Die Republik des Geistes. Frankreichs Intellektuelle zwischen Revolution und Reaktion*, Munich and Zürich: Piper.

Aly, Götz 2005, *Hitlers Volksstaat. Raub, Rassenkrieg und nationaler Sozialismus*, Frankfurt am Main: S. Fischer.

Amengual, Gabriel 1990, 'Anerkennung' in *Europäische Enzyklopädie der Philosophie und Wissenschaften*, edited by Hans Jörg Sandkühler, Hamburg: Lang.

Anders, Günther (as G. Stern) 1947, 'On the Pseudo-Concreteness of Heidegger's Philosophy', *Philosophy and Phenomenological Research*, VIII: 337–71.

—— 1961 [1956], *Die Antiquiertheit des Menschen. Über die Seele im Zeitalter der zweiten industriellen Revolution*, Munich: Beck.

Anderson, Kevin 1995, *Lenin, Hegel, and Western Marxism: A Critical Study*, Urbana, IL: University of Illinois Press.

Anderson, Perry 1974, *Lineages of the Absolutist State*, London: New Left Books.

—— 1976, *Considerations on Western Marxism*, London: New Left Books.

—— 1976a: 'The Antinomies of Antonio Gramsci', *New Left Review*, I/100, 5–78.

—— 1980, *Arguments within English Marxism*, London: New Left Books.

Angehrn, Emil and Georg Lohmann, Georg (eds.) 1986, *Ethik und Marx. Moralkritik und normative Grundlagen der Marxschen Theorie*, Königstein: Hain.

Angehrn, Emil 1991, *Geschichtsphilosophie*, Stuttgart: Kohlhammer.

Antonio, R.J. and R.M. Glassman (eds.) 1985, *A Weber-Marx Dialogue*, Lawrence: University Press of Kansas.

Antonio, Robert 2003, *Marx and Modernity: Key Readings and Commentary*, Malden: Blackwell.

Apel, Karl-Otto 1973, *Transformation der Philosophie*, 2 Vols., Frankfurt am Main: Suhrkamp.

—— 1973a [1962], 'Reflexion und materielle Praxis: Zur erkenntnisanthropologischen Begründung der Dialektik zwischen Hegel und Marx', in *Transformation der Philosophie. 1, Sprachanalytik, Semiotik, Hermeneutik*, Frankfurt am Main: Suhrkamp.

—— 1975 [1967 and 1970], *Der Denkweg von Charles S. Peirce. Eine Einführung in den amerikanischen Pragmatismus*, Frankfurt am Main: Suhrkamp.

—— 1979, *Die "Erklären-Verstehen"-Kontroverse in transzendentalpragmatischer Sicht*, Frankfurt am Main: Suhrkamp.

—— 1988, 'Zurück zur Normalität? Oder könnten wir aus der nationalen Katastrophe etwas Besonderes gelernt haben?' in *Zerstörung des moralischen Selbstbewusstseins: Chance oder Gefährdung? Praktische Philosophie in Deutschland nach dem Nationalsozialismus*, edited by Siegfried Blasche, Frankfurt am Main: Forum für Philosophie Bad Homburg.

—— 1988a: *Diskurs und Verantwortung*, Frankfurt am Main: Suhrkamp.

—— 1998, *Auseinandersetzungen in Erprobung des transzendentalpragmatischen Ansatzes*, Frankfurt am Main: Suhrkamp.

Appel, Michael 1992, *Werner Sombart – Theoretiker und Historiker des modernen Kapitalismus*, Marburg: Metropolis.

Appelt, Erna 2001, *Globalisierung*. Hamburg: Argument.

Arendt, Hannah 1955, *The Origins of Totalitarianism*, New York: Schocken Books.

—— 1969 [1960], *The Human Condition*, Chicago: University of Chicago Press.

—— 1963, *On Revolution*, New York: Viking.

—— 1969, *On Violence*, London: Lane.

Arendt, Hannah and Karl Jaspers 1992, *Correspondence, 1926–1969*, New York: Harcourt Brace Jovanovich.

Arens, Edmund (ed.) 1989, *Habermas und die Theologie*, Düsseldorf: Patmos.

Arens, Edmund et al. 1991, *Erinnerung, Befreiung, Solidarität: Benjamin, Marcuse, Habermas und die politische Theologie*, Düsseldorf: Patmos.

Arestis, Philip and Malcolm Sawyer (eds.) 1994, *The Elgar Companion to Radical Political Economics*, Aldershot: Elgar.

—— 2000, *A Biographical Dictionary of Dissenting Economists*, Aldershot: Elgar.

Armstrong, Philip and Andrew Glyn 1980, 'The Law of the Falling Rate of Profit and

Oligopoly: A Comment on Shaikh', *Cambridge Journal of Economics*, 4: 69–70.

Arnason, Johann Páll 1971, *Von Marcuse zu Marx*, Neuwied: Luchterhand.

—— 1976, *Zwischen Natur und Gesellschaft. Studien zu einer kritischen Theorie des Subjekts*, Frankfurt am Main: Europäische Verlags-Anstalt.

—— 1988, *Praxis und Interpretation: Sozialphilosophische Studien*, Frankfurt am Main: Suhrkamp.

—— 1993, *The Future that Failed: Origins and Destinies of the Soviet Model*, London: Routledge.

Arndt, Andreas 1982, *Lenin – Politik und Philosophie. Zur Entwicklung einer Konzeption materialistischer Dialektik*, Bochum: Germinal.

—— 1985, *Karl Marx. Versuch über den Zusammenhang seiner Theorie*, Bochum: Germinal.

—— 1994, *Dialektik und Reflexion. Zur Rekonstruktion des Vernunftbegriffs*, Hamburg: Meiner.

Arndt, Ernst Moritz 1813, *Über Volkshass und den Gebrauch einer fremden Sprache*, n.p.

Arndt, Helmut 1979, *Irrwege der politischen Ökonomie*, Munich: Beck.

Arnhold, B. 1979, 'Marx' Auseinandersetzung mit *currency principle* und Bankingtheorie in den Londoner Exzerptheften 1850–1853', *Arbeitsblätter zur Marx-Engels-Forschung*, 8: 32–47.

Aron, Raymond 1953, *Deutsche Soziologie der Gegenwart*, Stuttgart: Kröner.

—— 1964 [1955], *Die industrielle Gesellschaft*, Frankfurt am Main: Fischer.

—— 1965, *Main Currents in Sociological Thought*, 2 Vols., New York: Basic Books.

—— 1970, *Fortschritt ohne Ende?* Gütersloh: Bertelsmann.

—— 1970a: *Die heiligen Familien des Marxismus*, Hamburg: Wegner.

Aronson, Ronald 1995, *After Marxism*, New York: Guilford Press.

Arrow, Kenneth Joseph 1951, *Social Choice and individual Values*, New York: John Wiley and Sons.

Arthur, Christopher J. 2002, *The New Dialectic and Marx's Capital*, Leiden: Brill.

Asimakopulos, A. 1983, 'Kalecki and Keynes on Finance, Investment, and Saving', *Cambridge Journal of Economics*, 37: 9.

Aster, Ernst von 1929, *Marx und die Gegenwart*, Tübingen: Mohr.

Assheuer, Thomas 2003, 'Schattenboxen im leeren Ring. Mehr Freiheit? Oder mehr Gleichheit? Philosophen streiten über Gerechtigkeit', *Die Zeit*, 28 May 2003.

Avineri, Shlomo 1970, *The Social and Political Thought of Karl Marx*, Cambridge: Cambridge University Press.

Axelos, Kostas 1966, *Einführung in ein künftiges Denken. Über Marx und Heidegger*, Tübingen: Niemeyer.

Axelrod, Robert 1984, *The Evolution of Cooperation*, New York: Basic Books.

Baader, Franz von 1865, *Grundzüge der Sozietätsphilosophie. Herausgegeben von F. Hoffmann*, Würzburg, n.p.

—— 1957, *Gesellschaftslehre. Herausgegeben von Hans Grassl*, Munich: Kösel.

Backes, Uwe and Stéphane Courtois 2002 (eds.), *Ein Gespenst geht um in Europa. Das Erbe kommunistischer Ideologien*, Cologne: Böhlau.

Backhaus, Hans-Georg 1970 [1969], 'Zur Dialektik der Wertform' in *Beiträge zur marxistischen Erkenntnistheorie*, edited by Alfred Schmidt, Frankfurt am Main: Suhrkamp.

—— 1974, 'Materialien zur Rekonstruktion der Marxschen Werttheorie 1' in *Gesellschaft. Beiträge zur Marxschen Theorie 1*, edited by Hans-Georg Backhaus, Frankfurt am Main: Suhrkamp.

—— 1975, 'Materialien zur Rekonstruktion der Marxschen Werttheorie 2' in *Gesellschaft. Beiträge zur Marxschen Theorie 3*, edited by Hans-Georg Backhaus, Frankfurt am Main: Suhrkamp.

—— 1978, 'Materialien zur Rekonstruktion der Marxschen Werttheorie 3' in *Gesellschaft. Beiträge zur Marxschen Theorie 11*, edited by Hans-Georg Backhaus, Frankfurt am Main: Suhrkamp.

—— 1997, 'Materialien zur Rekonstruktion der Marxschen Werttheorie 4' in idem, *Dialektik der Wertform. Untersuchungen zur Marxschen Ökonomiekritik*, Freiburg: Ça ira.

—— 2000, *Werner Sombart (1863–1941) – Klassiker der Sozialwissenschaften*, Marburg: Metropolis, 2000.

—— 2002, 'Der widersprüchliche und monströse Kern der nationalalökonomischen Begriffsbildung' in *Emanzipation als Versöhnung. Zu Adornos Kritik der "Warentausch"-Gesellschaft und Perspektiven der Transformation*, edited by Iring Fetscher and Alfred Schmidt, Frankfurt am Main: Verlag Neue Kritik.

Backhaus, Hans-Georg and Helmut Reichelt 1995, 'Wie ist der Wertbegriff in der Ökonomie zu konzipieren?', in *Beiträge zur Marx/ Engels-Forschung:. Engels Druckfassung versus Marx' Manuskript*, Hamburg: Argument.

Bader, Veit Michael et al. 1976, *Einführung in die Gesellschaftstheorie. Gesellschaft, Wirtschaft und Staat bei Marx und Weber*, 2 Vols, Frankfurt am Main and New York: Campus.

—— 1998, *Die Wiederentdeckung der Klassen*, Hamburg: Argument.

Baecker, Dirk 2002, 'Lenin's Void: Towards a Kenogrammar of Management', *Soziale Systeme*, 8: 294–305.

—— 2002a: *Archäologie der Arbeit*, Berlin: Kadmos.

—— 2003, *Kapitalismus als Religion*, Berlin: Kadmos.

Baer, Oliver (translator) 1999, *Das Cluetrain Manifest*, available at: <www.trans-mission .de/cluetrain.com>.

Bahro, Rudolf 1977, *Die Alternative. Zur Kritik des real existierenden Sozialismus*, Cologne: Europäische Verlags-Anstalt.

—— 1991, *Rückkehr. Die In-Weltkrise als Ursprung der Weltzerstörung*, Frankfurt am Main: Horizonte.

Baier, Horst 1981/3, 'Die Gesellschaft – ein langer Schatten des toten Gottes. Friedrich Nietzsche und die Entstehung der Soziologie aus dem Geist der *décadence*', *Nietzsche-Studien*, 10/11: 6–33.

—— 1988, 'Vater Sozialstaat. Max Webers Widerspruch zur Wohlfahrtspatronage' in *Max Weber. Ein Symposion*, edited by Christian Gneuss and Jürgen Kocka, Munich: Deutscher Taschenbuch-Verlag.

Baig, Yong-Gi 1996, *Bund der religiösen Sozialisten Deutschlands in der Weimarer Republik*, dissertation, Bochum.

Bakunin, Mikhail 1972, *Staatlichkeit und Anarchie und andere Schriften. Herausgegeben von Horst Stuke*, Frankfurt am Main: Ullstein.

Balibar, Etienne 2001, 'Gewalt' in *Historisch-kritisches Wörterbuch des Marxismus 5, Gegenöffentlichkeit bis Hegemonialapparat*, edited by Wolfgang Fritz Haug, Hamburg: Argument.

Balkenhol, Nikola 1991, *Kommunikative Rationalität und politische Institutionen in der kritischen Gesellschaftstheorie von Jürgen Habermas*, Hamburg: Kovač.

Ball, Hugo 1993, *Critique of the German Intelligentsia*, New York: Columbia University Press.

Ball, Terence and James Farr (eds.) 1989, *After Marx*, Cambridge: Cambridge University Press.

Ballestrem, Henning 2000, *Adam Smith*, Munich: Beck.

Balthasar, Hans Urs von 1939, *Apokalypse der deutschen Seele. Studien zu einer Lehre von den letzten Haltungen*, Vol. 3, *Die Vergöttlichung des Todes*, Salzburg and Leipzig: Pustet.

Balzer, Friedrich-Martin 1973, *Klassengegensätze in der Kirche. Erwin Eckert und der Bund der religiösen Sozialisten*, Bonn: Pahl-Rugenstein.

Bamm, Arno et al. (eds.) 1993, *Der kalte Blick der Ökonomie. 30 Gespräche*, Munich: Profil.

Bank und Umwelt. Infodienst der Umweltbank AG 2002, *Ethik als Schlüssel zum Erfolg*, Nuremberg: n.p.

Baran, Paul 1957, *The Political Economy of Growth*, New York: Monthly Review Press.

Barash, Jeffrey Andrew 1999, *Heidegger und der Historismus. Sinn der Geschichte und der Geschichtlichkeit des Sinns*, Würzburg: Königshausen und Neumann.

Baratta, Mario von (ed.) 2002, *Der Fischer Weltalmanach 2003*, Frankfurt am Main: Fischer.

Barboza, Amalia 2002, *Die Eroberung des Formalen. Die Stilanalyse in der Kultur- und Wissenssoziologie Karl Mannheims*, dissertation, TU Dresden.

Barion, Jakob 1963, *Hegel und die marxistische Staatslehre*, Bonn: Bouvier.

Barlow, Tani E. (ed.) 2002, *New Asian Marxisms*, Durham: Duke University Press.

Barrett, Michéle 1991, *The Politics of Truth. From Marx to Foucault*, Cambridge: Polity Press.

Barth, Boris 1995, *Die deutsche Hochfinanz und die Imperialismen. Banken und Aussenpolitik vor 1914*, Stuttgart: Steiner.

Barth, Hans 1959, *Masse und Mythos. Die ideologische Krise an der Wende zum 20. Jahrhundert und die Theorie der Gewalt: Georges Sorel*, Reinbek: Rowohlt.

—— 1976 [1945], *Truth and Ideology*, Berkeley, CA: University of California Press.

Barth, Karl 1919, *Der Römerbrief*, Bern: Theologischer Verlag.

—— 1936 ff.: *Church Dogmatics*, New York: T&T Clark.

Barth, Paul 1890, *Die Geschichtsphilosophie Hegels und der Hegelianer bis auf Marx und Hartmann. Ein kritischer Versuch*, Leipzig: Reisland.

—— 1897, *Die Philosophie der Geschichte als Soziologie. Erster Teil: Grundlegung und kritische Übersicht*, Leipzig: Reisland.

Bärthlein, Karl (ed.) 1983, *Zur Geschichte der Philosophie*, Vol. 2, *Von Kant bis zur Gegenwart*, Würzburg: Königshausen und Neumann.

Bartsch, Günter 1976, *Schulen des Marxismus oder was aus Marx geworden ist*, Troisdorf: Kammwegverlag.

—— 1994, *Die NWO-Bewegung Silvio Gesells. Geschichtlicher Grundriss 1891–1992/93*, Lütjenburg: Gauke.

Basso, Lelio 1975, *Gesellschaftsformation und Staatsform. Drei Aufsätze*, Frankfurt am Main: Suhrkamp.

Bast, Rainer A. 1986, 'Ist Heideggers Sein und Zeit ein Patchwork?', *Information Philosophie*, 4: 18–30.

Bastiat, Frédéric 1964 [1850], *Economic Harmonies*, Princeton: D. van Nostrand.

Bataille, Georges 1978, *Die psychologische Struktur des Faschismus/Die Souveränität*, Munich: Matthes und Seitz.

Baudrillard, Jean 1993 [1970], *Symbolic Exchange and Death*, London: Sage.

Bauer, Bruno 1841, *Kritik der evangelischen Geschichte der Synoptiker*, Vol. 1, Leipzig: Wigand.

—— 1842, *Kritik der evangelischen Geschichte der Synoptiker*, Vol. 2, Leipzig: Wigand.

—— 1842a: *Kritik der evangelischen Geschichte der Synoptiker*, Vol. 3, Braunschweig: Otto.

—— 1843, *Die Judenfrage*, Braunschweig: Otto.

—— 1985 [1841], 'Die Posaune des jüngsten Gerichts über Hegel, den Atheisten und Antichristen' in *Die Hegelsche Linke. Dokumente zu Philosophie und Politik im deutschen Vormärz*, edited by Heinz Pepperle and Ingrid Pepperle, Leipzig: Reclam.

Bauer, Otto 1913, 'Die Akkumulation des Kapitals', *Die Neue Zeit*, 31, 23.

—— 1936, *Zwischen den Weltkriegen*, Bratislava: Prager.

Bauer, Wilhelm 1941, *Das Bild des Krieges im deutschen Denken. Der Krieg in der deutschen Geschichtsschreibung von Leopold von Ranke bis Karl Lamprecht*, Stuttgart: Kohlhammer.

Baumann, Zygmunt 1992, *Dialektik der Ordnung. Die Moderne und der Holocaust*, Hamburg: Europäische Verlags-Anstalt.

Baumgart, Ralf and Ralf Eichener 1991, *Norbert Elias zur Einführung*, Hamburg: Junius.

Baumgarten, Eduard 1938, *Die geistigen Grundlagen des amerikanischen Gemeinwesens*, Vol. 2, *Der Pragmatismus (R.W. Emerson, W. James, J. Dewey)*, Frankfurt am Main: Klostermann.

—— 1964, *Max Weber. Werk und Person*, Tübingen: Mohr.

Baumgartner, Hans Michael 1969, 'Lebensphilosophie' in *Bilanz der Theologie im 20. Jahrhundert. Perspektiven, Strömungen, Motive in der christlichen und nichtchristlichen Welt*, Vol. 1, edited by Herbert Vorgrimler and Robert Vander Gucht, Freiburg: Herder.

Baumgartner, Hans Michael and Hans-Martin Sass 1980, *Philosophie in Deutschland 1945–1975. Standpunkte, Entwicklungen, Literatur*, Königstein: Hain.

Baumol, William J. 1965, *Welfare Economics and the Theory of the State*, Cambridge, MA: Harvard University Press.

Baumol, W. 1974, 'The Transformation of Values: What Marx "Really Meant" (An Interpretation)', *Journal of Economic Literature*, 12, 1: 51–62.

Bayle, Pierre 2002 [1682], *Various Thoughts on the Occasion of a Comet*, Albany, NY: State University of New York Press.

Baynes, Kenneth 1992, *The Normative Grounds of Social Criticism. Kant, Rawls, and Habermas*, Albany, NY: State University of New York Press.

Bebel, August 1874, *Christentum und Sozialismus*, Dresden: Zentralverband Proletarischer Freidenker.

Bebel, August 1969 [1870], *Unsere Ziele. Eine Streitschrift gegen die Demokratische Korrespondenz*, Berlin: Dietz.

—— 1971 [1879], *Woman Under Socialism*, New York: Schocken Books.

Becher, Jürgen et al. 1976, *Politische Ökonomie des Kapitalismus und des Sozialismus. Lehrbuch für das marxistisch-leninistische Grundlagenstudium*, Berlin: Dietz.

Beck, M. 1928, 'Referat und Kritik von Martin Heidegger: *Sein und Zeit*', *Philosophische Hefte*, 1, 5–44.

Beck, Ulrich 1983, 'Jenseits von Klasse und Stand? Soziale Ungleichheit, gesellschaftliche Individualisierungsprozesse und die Entstehung neuer Formationen und Identitäten' in *Soziale Ungleichheiten*, edited by Reinhard Kreckel, Göttingen: Schwartz.

—— 2000 [1997], *What Is Globalization?*, Cambridge: Polity Press.

Becker, F.J.E. 1972, *Freiheit und Entfremdung bei Fichte, Marx und in der kritischen Theorie*, dissertation, Cologne.

Becker, Gary S. 1976, *The Economic Approach to Human Behavior*, Chicago: University of Chicago Press.

Becker, Theo 1977, *Der politische Erfahrungsgehalt der geschichtsphilosophischen Kritik Karl Korschs am dogmatischen Marxismus (1923–1939)*, dissertation, Hannover.

Becker, Werner 1969, *Hegels Begriff der Dialektik und das Prinzip des Idealismus*, Stuttgart: Kohlhammer.

—— 1972, *Kritik der Marxschen Wertlehre. Die methodische Irrationalität der ökonomischen Basiskategorien des Kapitals*, Hamburg: Hoffmann und Campe.

—— 1974, 'Dialektik als Methode in der ökonomischen Werttheorie von Karl Marx' in *Marx und Marxismus heute*, edited by Gerd Breitenbürger and Günter Schnitzler, Hamburg: Hoffmann und Campe.

—— 1985, *Elemente der Demokratie*, Stuttgart: Reclam.

—— 1996, 'Die Überlegenheit der Demokratie. Politische Philosophie nach dem Scheitern des Marxismus' in *Politik und Ethik*, edited by Kurt Bayertz, Stuttgart: Reclam.

Beer, Raphael 1999, *Zwischen Aufklärung und Optimismus. Vernunftbegriff und Gesellschaftstheorie bei Jürgen Habermas*, Wiesbaden: Deutscher Universitäts-Verlag.

Behrens, Diethard (ed.) 1987, *Geschichtsphilosophie oder das Begreifen der Historizität*, Freiburg: Ça ira.

—— 1993, *Gesellschaft und Erkenntnis. Zur materialistischen Erkenntnis- und Ökonomiekritik*, Freiburg: Ça ira.

Behrens, Peter 1986, *Die ökonomischen Grundlagen des Rechts*, Tübingen: Mohr.

Beiersdörfer, Kurt 1985, *Max Weber und Georg Lukács. Über die Beziehung von verstehender Soziologie und westlichem Marxismus*, Frankfurt am Main and New York: Campus.

Beilharz, Peter 1987, *Trotsky, Trotskyism and the Transition to Socialism*, London: Croom Helm.

Bekker, Konrad 1940, *Marx' philosophische Entwicklung. Sein Verhältnis zu Hegel*, Zürich: Oprecht.

Bell, Daniel 1962, *The End of Ideology. On the Exhaustion of Political Ideas in the Fifities*, New York: Free Press.

—— 1973, *The Coming of Post-Industrial Society: A Venture in Social Forecasting*, New York: Basic Books.

—— 1976, *The Cultural Contradictions of Capitalism*, New York: Basic Books.

Bellah, Robert N. et al. 1985, *Habits of the Heart: Individualism and Commitment in American Life*, Berkeley, CA: University of California Press.

—— 1992, *The Good Society*, New York: Vintage.

Bendix, Reinhard 1964, *Max Weber – Das Werk. Darstellung, Analyse, Ergebnisse*, Munich: Piper.

Beneke, Friedrich Eduard 1832, *Kant und die philosophische Aufgabe unserer Zeit. Eine Jubeldenkschrift auf die Kritik der reinen Vernunft*, Berlin: Mittler.

Benhabib, Seyla 1986, *Critique, Norm, and Utopia: A Study of the Foundations of Critical Theory*, New York: Columbia University Press.

Benjamin, Walter 1977 [1928], *The Origin of German Tragic Drama*, London: New Left Books.

—— 1978 [1934], 'The Author as Producer' in *The Essential Frankfurt School Reader*, edited by Andrew Arato and Eike Gebhardt, New York: Urizen Books.

—— 1980–99, *Gesammelte Schriften*, 10 Vols., edited by Rolf Tiedemann and Hermann Schweppenhäuser, Frankfurt am Main: Suhrkamp (cited as *GS*).

—— 1999–2003, *Selected Writings*, 4 Vols., edited by Michael W. Jennings, Howard Eiland and Gary Smith, Cambridge, MA: Harvard University Press.

—— 1999 [1927 ff.], *The Arcades Project*, Cambridge: Harvard University Press.

—— 1999a: *The Complete Correspondence, 1928–1940*, edited by Henri Lonitz, Cambridge, MA: Harvard University Press.

—— 1999b [1920], 'Theologico-Political Fragment' in Benjamin 1999–2003, Vol. 3.

—— 1999c [1921], 'Capitalism as Religion' in Benjamin 1999–2003, Vol. 1.

—— 1999d [1921], 'Critique of Violence' in Benjamin 1999–2003, Vol. 1.

—— 1999e [1924], 'Goethe's Elective Affinities' in Benjamin 1999–2003, Vol. 1.

—— 2003 [1940], 'On the Concept of History' in Benjamin 1999–2003, Vol. 4.

Benner, Dietrich 1966, *Theorie und Praxis. Systemtheoretische Betrachtungen zu Hegel und Marx*, Vienna: Oldenbourg.

Benoist, Jean-Marie 1970, *Marx est mort*, Paris: Gallimard.

Bensaïd, Daniel 2002 [1995], *Marx For Our Times*, London: Verso.

Bensch, Hans Georg 1995, *Vom Reichtum der Gesellschaften. Mehrprodukt und Reproduktion als Freiheit und Notwendigkeit in der Kritik der politischen Ökonomie*, Lüneburg: zu Klampen.

Bensch, Hans Georg and Frank Kuhne 1998, *Das automatische Subjekt bei Marx. Studien zum Kapital*, Lüneburg: zu Klampen.

Benz, Ernst 1974, *Das Recht auf Faulheit oder die friedliche Beendigung des Klassenkampfes*, Stuttgart: Klett.

Berdyaev, Nikolai 1934 [1931], *Christianity and Class War*, London: Sheed and Ward.

—— 1945 [1923], *The Meaning of History*, London: Centenary Press.

Berger, Johannes 1986, 'Die Versprachlichung des Sakralen und die Entsprachlichung der Ökonomie' in *Kommunikatives Handeln. Beiträge zu Jürgen Habermas' "Theorie des kommunikativen Handelns"*, edited by Axel Honneth and Hans Joas, Frankfurt am Main: Suhrkamp.

—— 1998, 'Was behauptet die Marxsche Klassentheorie – und was ist davon haltbar?' in *Konflikt in modernen Gesellschaften*, edited by Hans-Joachim Giegel, Frankfurt am Main: Suhrkamp.

Berger, Michael 1974, 'Theorie der Geschichte bei Karl Marx' in *Marx und Marxismus heute*, edited by Gerd Breitenbürger and Günter Schnitzler, Hamburg: Hoffmann und Campe.

—— 2003, *Karl Marx*: Das Kapital. *Eine Einführung*, Munich: Fink.

Berger, Peter L. (ed.) 1997, *Grenzen der Gemeinschaft*, Gütersloh: Bertelsmann-Stiftung.

Berghahn, Volker 1985, *Unternehmer und Politik in der Bundesrepublik*, Frankfurt am Main: Suhrkamp.

Bergmann, Ernst 1915, *Fichte, der Erzieher zum Deutschtum*, Leipzig: Meiner.

—— 1928, *J.G. Fichte, der Erzieher*, Leipzig: Meiner.

Bergmann, Johannes et al. 1969, 'Herrschaft, Klassenverhältnis und Schichtung' in *Spätkapitalismus oder Industriegesellschaft? Verhandlungen des 16. Deutschen Soziologentages in Frankfurt am Main 1968*, edited by Theodor W. Adorno, Stuttgart: Enke.

Bergmann, Theodor and Mario Kessler (eds.) 1993, *Ketzer im Kommunismus: Alternativen zum Stalinismus*, Mainz: Decaton.

Bergmann, Theodor and Gert Schäfer (eds.) 1993, *Leo Trotzki – Kritiker und Verteidiger der Sowjetgesellschaft. Beiträge zum internationalen Trotzki-Symposium, Wuppertal 26.–29. März 1990*, Mainz: Decaton.

Bergmann, Theodor et al. (eds.) 1994, *Lenin. Theorie und Praxis in historischer Perspektive*, Mainz: Decaton.

Bergmann, Theodor 1995, 'Diktatur des Proletariats' in *Historisch-Kritisches Wörterbuch des Marxismus*, Vol. 2, edited by Wolfgang Fritz Haug, Hamburg: Argument.

Bering, Dieter 1978, *Die Intellektuellen. Geschichte eines Schimpfwortes*, Stuttgart: Klett-Cotta.

Berkeley, George 2005 [1710], *Treatise Concerning the Principles of Human Knowledge*, New York: Cosimo.

Berlin, Isaiah 1979, *Against the Current: Essays in the History of Ideas*, New York: Viking Press.

Berman, Marshall 1999, *Adventures in Marxism*, London: Verso.

Bermbach, Udo and Frank Nuscheler (eds.) 1973, *Sozialistischer Pluralismus*, Hamburg: Hoffmann und Campe.

Bernstein, Eduard 1896/7, 'Probleme des Sozialismus', *Die Neue Zeit*, 25, 2.

—— 1897, 'Der Kampf der Sozialdemokratie und die Revolution der Gesellschaft', *Die Neue Zeit*, 16, 1.

—— 1899, 'Dialektik und Entwicklung', *Die Neue Zeit*, 17, 2: 353–63.

—— 1961 [1899], *Evolutionary Socialism: A Criticism and Affirmation*, New York: Schocken Books.

—— 1968 [1905], 'Klasse und Klassenkampf' (1905) in *Klassenbildung und soziale Schichtung*, edited by Bruno Seidel and Siegfried Jenker, Darmstadt: Wissenschaftliche Buchgesellschaft.

—— 1976 [1908], 'Der Revisionismus in der Sozialdemokratie' in idem, *Ein revisionistisches Sozialismusbild. Drei Vorträge*, Berlin: Dietz.

Bernstein, Richard J. 1971, *Praxis and Action: Contemporary Philosophies of Human*

Activity, Philadelphia: University of Pennsylvania Press.
Berthold, Norbert (ed.) 1999, *Globalisierung der Wirtschaft. Ursachen – Formen – Konsequenzen*, Berlin: Duncker und Humblot.
Bettelheim, Charles 1969, *Zur Kritik der Sowjetökonomie. Eine Diskussion marxistischer Ökonomen des Westens über die Wirtschaftsreform in den Ländern Osteuropas*, Berlin: Wagenbach.
—— 1976–8 [1974–7], *Class Struggles in the USSR*, 2 Vols., New York: Monthly Review Press.
Beuys, Barbara 1982, *Und wenn die Welt voll Teufel wär: Luthers Glaube und seine Erben. Fünfhundert Jahre Protestantismus*, Reinbek: Rowohlt.
Beyer, Marga et al. 1975, *Revolutionäres Parteiprogramm – Revolutionäre Arbeitereinheit*, East Berlin: Dietz.
Beyer, Wilhelm Raimund 1968, *Tendenzen bundesdeutscher Marxbeschäftigung*, Cologne: Pahl-Rugenstein.
—— 1970, *Hegelbilder. Kritik der Hegel-Deutungen*, Berlin: Akademie-Verlag.
—— 1970a: *Vier Kritiken: Heidegger, Sartre, Adorno, Lukács*, Cologne: Pahl-Rugenstein.
—— 1972, *Die Parteinahme der Wissenschaft für die Arbeiterpartei*, Frankfurt am Main: Verlag Marxistische Blätter.
Bhaduri, Amit 1988, *Makroökonomie. Die Dynamik der Warenproduktion*. Marburg: Metropolis.
Bhaskar, Roy 1986, *Scientific Realism and Human Emancipation*, London: Verso.
—— 1991, *Philosophy and the Idea of Freedom*, Oxford: Blackwell.
Bialas, Wolfgang 1994, *Geschichtsphilosophie in kritischer Absicht im Übergang zu einer Teleologie der Apokalypse. Die Frankfurter Schule und die Geschichte*, Frankfurt am Main: Lang.
—— 1996, *Vom unfreien Schweben zum freien Fall. Ostdeutsche Intellektuelle im gesellschaftlichen Umbruch*, Frankfurt am Main: Fischer.
Bickel, Cornelius 1991, *Ferdinand Tönnies. Soziologie als skeptische Auflärung zwischen Historismus und Rationalismus*, Opladen: Westdeutscher Verlag.
Bielefeldt, Heiner and Wilhelm Heitmeyer (eds.) 1998, *Politisierte Religion. Ursachen und Erscheinungsformen des modernen Fundamentalismus*, Frankfurt am Main: Suhrkamp.
Biemel, Walter and Hans Saner (eds.) 1992, *Martin Heidegger/Karl Jaspers: Briefwechsel 1920–1963*, Munich: Piper.
Bienert, Walter 1979, *Über Marx hinaus zu wahrem Menschsein. Eine kritische Analyse der Marxschen Anthropologie in ihrer Begegnung mit dem christlichen Menschenbild*, Frankfurt am Main: Lembeck.
Biermann, Werner and Arno Klönne 2001, *Globale Spiele. Imperialismus heute – das letzte Stadium des Kapitalismus?* Cologne: PapyRossa.
Bievert, Bernd et al. (eds.) 1990, *Sozialphilosophische Grundlagen ökonomischen Handelns*, Frankfurt am Main: Suhrkamp.
Bild Dresden 2002, 'Marx und Co: Wie Marx und Engels ihre Eltern erpressten', 14 November 2002.
Binswanger, Hans Christoph 1998, *Die Glaubensgemeinschaft der Ökonomen. Essay zur Kultur der Wirtschaft*, Munich: Gerling.
Bischoff, Joachim (ed.) 1976, *Die Klassenstruktur der Bundesrepublik Deutschland. Ein Handbuch zum sozialen System der BRD*, Berlin: VSA.
Bischoff, Joachim et al. 1982, *Jenseits der Klassen? Gesellschaft und Staat im Spätkapitalismus*, Hamburg: VSA.
Bischoff, Joachim, Sebastian Herkommer and Hasko Hüning 2002, *Unsere Klassengesellschaft. Zur Aktualität der Klassenanalyse*, Hamburg: VSA.
BKAB (Bundesverband der Katholischen Arbeitnehmer-Bewegung Deutschlands) (eds.) 1992, *Texte zur katholischen Soziallehre*, Bornheim: Ketteler.
Blackburn, Robin (ed.) 1991, *After the Fall: The Failure of Communism and the Future of Socialism*, London: Verso.
Blanke, Bernhard et al. 1974, 'Zu neueren marxistischen Diskussionen über die Analyse von Form und Funktion des bürgerlichen Staates. Überlegungen zum Verhältnis von Politik und Ökonomie', *Probleme des Klassenkampfes*, 14, 15.
Blasche, Siegfried et al. (eds.) 1988, *Zerstörung des moralischen Selbstbewusstseins: Chance oder Gefährdung? Praktische Philosophie in Deutschland nach dem Nationalsozialismus*, Frankfurt am Main: Forum für Philosophie Bad Homburg.

Blasche, Siegfried (ed.) 1998, *Sozialpolitik und Gerechtigkeit*, Frankfurt am Main: Campus.

Blaug, Mark 1958, *Ricardian Economics: A Historical Study*, New Haven: Yale University Press.

Bleaney, Michael 1976, *Underconsumption Theories: A History and Critical Analysis*, London: Lawrence and Wishart.

Bloch, Ernst 1962, *Subjekt-Objekt*, Frankfurt am Main: Suhrkamp.

—— 1969 [1919], *Thomas Münzer als Theologe der Revolution*, Frankfurt am Main: Suhrkamp.

—— 1970 [1968], *Atheismus im Christentum. Zur Religion des Exodus und des Reichs*, Reinbek: Rowohlt.

—— 1983 [1906], 'Das Problem Nietzsche', in *Bloch Almanach*, 3: 71–80.

—— 2000 [1923], *The Spirit of Utopia*, Stanford: Stanford University Press.

Bloch, Ernst et al. 1970, 'Karl Marx und die Revolution' in Marxismuskollektiv 1970 (lectures held at the Korcula summer school).

Blocker, H. Gene and Elizabeth Smith (eds.) 1980, *John Rawls' Theory of Social Justice. An Introduction*, Athens, OH: University of Ohio Press.

Bloor, David 1997, *Wittgenstein, Rules and Institutions*, London: Routledge.

Blum, Ulrich 2000, *Volkswirtschaftslehre. Studienhandbuch*, Munich: Oldenbourg.

Blumenberg, Hans 1983 [1966], *The Legitimacy of the Modern Age*, Cambridge, MA: MIT Press.

Blumenberg, Werner 1962, *Karl Marx in Selbstzeugnissen und Bilddokumenten*, Reinbek: Rowohlt.

Blumhardt, Christoph 1925 ff., *Predigten und Andachten*, 5 Vols., Erlenbach: Rotapfel.

Bochenski, I.M. 1960, *Der sowjetrussische dialektische Materialismus (Diamat)*, Bern: Francke.

Böckenförde, Ernst-Wolfgang 1991, *Recht, Staat, Freiheit. Studien zur Rechtsphilosophie, Staatstheorie und Verfassungsgeschichte*, Frankfurt am Main: Suhrkamp.

Böckler, Stefan and Johannes Weiß (eds.) 1987, *Marx oder Weber? Zur Aktualisierung einer Kontroverse*, Opladen: Westdeutscher Verlag.

Bockmühl, Klaus 1961, *Leiblichkeit und Gesellschaft. Studien zur Religionskritik und Anthropologie im Frühwerk von Feuerbach und Marx*, Göttingen: Vandenhoeck und Ruprecht.

Boddy, R. and J. Crotty 1975, 'Class Conflict and Macro-Policy: The Political Business Cycle', *Review of Radical Political Economics*, 7, 1: 1–19.

Boehler, Dietrich 1971, *Metakritik der Marxschen Ideologiekritik. Prolegomenon zu einer reflektierten Theorie-Praxis-Vermittlung*, Frankfurt am Main: Suhrkamp.

—— 1981, 'Arnold Gehlen: Handlung und Institution' in *Grundprobleme der großen Philosophien. Philosophie der Gegenwart 2*, edited by Josef Speck, Göttingen: Vandenhoeck und Ruprecht.

Boff, Leonardo 1985, *Kirche: Charisma und Macht. Studien zu einer streitbaren Ekklesiologie*, Düsseldorf: Patmos.

Böhm, Andreas 1998, *Kritik der Autonomie. Freiheits- und Moralbegriffe im Frühwerk von Karl Marx*, Bodenheim: Syndikat.

Bohman, James 1999, 'Habermas, Marxism and Social Theory: The Case for Pluralism in the Critical Social Sciences' in *Habermas – A Critical Reader*, edited by Peter Dews, Oxford: Blackwell.

Böhm-Bawerk, Eugen von 1921 [1884], *Kapital und Kapitalzins, Erste Abteilung: Geschichte und Kritik der Kapitalzinstheorien*, Jena: Gustav Fischer.

—— 1921a, *Positive Theorie des Kapitals*, Jena: Gustav Fischer.

—— 1975 [1896], *Karl Marx and the Close of his System*, Clifton: A.M. Kelley.

Bohrer, Karl-Heinz 1970, *Die gefährdete Phantasie oder: Surrealismus und Terror*, Munich: Hanser.

—— 1978, *Ästhetik des Schreckens. Die pessimistische Romantik und Ernst Jüngers Frühwerk*, Munich: Hanser.

—— 1983, *Mythos und Moderne. Begriff und Bild einer Rekonstruktion*, Frankfurt am Main: Suhrkamp.

—— 1997, '1968 – Die Phantasie an die Macht?', *Merkur*, 51, 12.

Boll, Friedhelm 1992, *Arbeitskämpfe und Gewerkschaften in Deutschland, England und Frankreich: ihre Entwicklung vom 19. zum 20. Jahrhundert*, Bonn: Dietz.

Bollnow, Otto Friedrich 1933, *Die Lebensphilosophie F.H. Jacobis*, Stuttgart: Kohlhammer.

—— 1936, *Dilthey. Eine Einführung in seine Philosophie*, Leipzig: Teubner.

—— 1958, *Die Lebensphilosophie*, Berlin: Springer.

Boltanski, Luc and Ève Chiapello 1999, *Le nouvel esprit du capitalisme*, Paris: Gallimard.

Bolte, Gerhard (ed.) 1989, *Unkritische Theorie. Gegen Habermas*, Lüneburg: zu Klampen.

—— 1995, *Von Marx bis Horkheimer. Aspekte kritischer Theorie im 19. und 20. Jahrhundert*, Darmstadt: Wissenschaftliche Buchgesellschaft.

Bolz, Norbert W. 1979, *Geschichtsphilosophie des Ästhetischen. Hermeneutische Rekonstruktion der Noten zur Literatur Th. W. Adornos*, Hildesheim: Gerstenberg.

—— 1989, *Auszug aus der entzauberten Welt. Philosophischer Extremismus zwischen den Weltkriegen*, Munich: Fink.

Bombach, G. et al. (eds.) 1976–1983, *Der Keynesianismus*, 3 Vols., Berlin: Springer.

Bonacker, Thorsten 2000, *Die normative Kraft der Kontigenz. Nichtessentialistische Gesellschaftskritik nach Weber und Adorno*, Frankfurt am Main: Campus.

Bonefeld, W., R. Gunn and K. Psychopedis (eds.) 1992–5, *Open Marxism*, 3 Vols., London: Pluto Press.

Bonefeld, Werner 1995, 'Das Kapital als Subjekt und die Existenz der Arbeit' in Bonefeld, Gunn and Psychopedis (eds.) 1992–5, Vol. 3.

Bonhoeffer, Dietrich 1971, *Letters and Papers from Prison*, London: Macmillan.

Bonschab, Thomas and Ralph Schrader 1999, 'Ausbeutung, Klasse und Freiheit im analytischen Marxismus', *Deutsche Zeitschrift für Philosophie*, 47, 4: 573–89.

Bonsiepen, Wolfgang 1977, *Der Begriff der Negativität in den Jenaer Schriften Hegels*, Bonn: Bouvier.

Bonss, Wolfgang 1982, *Die Einübung des Tatsachenblicks*, Frankfurt am Main: Suhrkamp.

Borkenau, Franz 1934, *Der Übergang vom feudalen zum bürgerlichen Weltbild. Studien zur Geschichte der Philosophie der Manufakturperiode*, Paris: Félix Alcan.

—— 1953, *European Communism*, London: Faber and Faber.

—— 1962, *World Communism. A History of the Communist International*, Ann Arbor: University of Michigan Press.

Borschel, Frank 1998, *Exkurs zur Marxschen Werttheorie. Das Kapital – eine Einführung in die Arbeitswertlehre von Karl Marx*, Berlin: Wünsche.

Bortkiewicz, Ladislaus von 1976 [1906], *Wertrechnung und Preisrechnung im Marxschen System*, Gießen: Achenbach.

Bose, Arun 1975, *Marxian and Post-Marxian Political Economy*, Harmondsworth: Penguin.

Bosse, Hans 1970, *Marx – Weber – Troeltsch. Religionssoziologie und marxistische Ideologiekritik*, Munich: Kaiser.

Bottomore, T.B. 1966, *Classes in Modern Society*, New York: Pantheon.

—— 1968, *Critics of Society: Radical Thought in North America*, New York: Pantheon.

Bottomore, Tom and P. Goode (eds.) 1978, *Austro-Marxism*, Oxford: Clarendon Press.

Bottomore, Tom (ed.) 1983, *A Dictionary of Marxist Thought*, Oxford: Blackwell.

Botwinik, H. 1993, *Persistent Inequalities: Wage Disparities under Capitalist Competition*, Princeton, NJ: Princeton University Press.

Boudin, Louis B. 1907, *The Theoretical System of Karl Marx in the Light of Recent Criticism*, Chicago: C.H. Kerr.

Bourdieu, Pierre 1984 [1979], *Distinction: A Social Critique of the Judgment of Taste*, Cambridge, MA: Harvard University Press.

—— 1990, *Homo Academicus*, Cambridge: Polity Press.

—— 1991 [1974], *The Political Ontology of Martin Heidegger*, Cambridge: Polity Press.

—— 1996, *The State Nobility: Elite Schools in the Field of Power*, Cambridge: Polity Press.

—— 1999, *Weight of the World: Social Suffering in Contemporary Society*, Cambridge: Polity Press.

—— 1999a: *Acts of Resistance: Against the Tyranny of the Market*, New York: The New Press.

Bourseiller, Christophe 2002, 'Doktrinärer Rigorismus und strategischer Pragmatismus – Trotzki und der Trotzkismus' in *Ein Gespenst geht um in Europa. Das Erbe kommunistischer Ideologien*, edited by Uwe Backes and Stéphane Courtois, Cologne: Böhlau.

Bowles, Samuel 1981, 'Technical change and the profit rate: a simple proof of the Okishio theorem', *Cambridge Journal of Economics*, 5, 2: 183–6.

Bowles, Samuel, David M. Gordon and T.E. Weisskopf 1984, *Beyond the Wasteland: A Democratic Alternative to Economic Decline*, London: Verso.

—— 1987, 'Power, Accumulation and Crisis: The Rise and Demise of the Postwar Social Structure of Accumulation' in *The Imperiled Economy 1*, edited by R. Cherry, New York: Union for Radical Political Economics.

Brach, Markus Joachim 1996, *Heidegger – Platon. Vom Neukantianismus zur existentiellen Interpretation des Sophistes*, Würzburg: Königshausen und Neumann.

Brakemeier, Gottfried 1988, *Der Sozialismus der Urchristenheit. Experiment und neue Herausforderung*, Göttingen: Vandenhoeck und Ruprecht.

Bramke, Werner 2001, 'Die Sozialisierung marschiert: Eigentum in Programmatik und Politik der deutschen sozialistischen Bewegung in der ersten Hälfte des 20. Jahrhunderts', lecture held before the Leipzig Philosophical Colloquium, 17 October.

Brandis, Kurt (alias K.F. Brockschmidt, K.F.) 1931, *Die deutsche Sozialdemokratie bis zum Fall des Sozialistengesetzes*, Leipzig: Hirschfeld.

Brandom, Robert 1994, *Making it Explicit. Reasoning, Representing and Discursive Commitment*, Cambridge; MA: Harvard University Press.

—— 2000, 'Facts, Norms and Normative Facts', *European Journal of Philosophy*.

Brandt, Gerhard et al. 1978, *Computer und Arbeitsprozess. Eine arbeitssoziologische Untersuchung der Auswirkungen des Computereinsatzes in ausgewählten Betrieben der Stahlindustrie und des Bankgewerbes*, Frankfurt am Main: Campus.

Brandt, Gerhard 1990, *Arbeit, Technik und gesellschaftliche Entwicklung. Transformationsprozesse des modernen Kapitalismus. Aufsätze 1971–1987*, Frankfurt am Main: Suhrkamp.

Brandt, Karl 1993, *Geschichte der deutschen Volkswirtschaftslehre*, Vol. 2, *Vom Historismus zur Neoklassik*, Freiburg: Haufe.

Brandt, Reinhard 1974, *Eigentumstheorien von Grotius bis Kant*, Stuttgart: Frommann-Holzboog.

Branstner, Gerhard 2000, 'Marxismus der Beletage', *Marxistisches Forum*, 25.

Braudel, Ferdinand 1985, *La dynamique du capitalisme*, Paris: Arthaud.

—— 1982–4, *Civilization and Capitalism, 15th–18th Centuries*, New York: Harper & Row.

Braun, Eberhard 1992, *Aufhebung der Philosophie – Marx und die Folgen*, Stuttgart: Metzler.

Braverman, Harry 1974, *Labour and Monopoly Capital: The Degradation of Work in the Twentieth Century*, New York: Monthly Review Press.

Brecher, Jeremy and Tim Costello 1994, *Global Village or Global Pillage. Economic Reconstruction from the Bottom Up*, Boston: South End Press.

Brecht, Bertolt 1977, *Arbeitsjournal 1938–1955*, Berlin: Aufbau.

Brechtkern, Josef 1979, *Die praxisdialektische Kritik des Marxschen Atheismus. Studien zum anthropozentrisch-kritischen Wirklichkeitsbegriff vom Standpunkt der geschichtlichen Praxis und zu seinen religionsphilosophischen Konsequenzen. Hegel–Kierkegaard–Marx. 2. Teil: Die Religion. Kierkegaard gegen Marx*, Königstein: Forum Academicum.

Breipohl, Renate 1970, *Religiöser Sozialismus und bürgerliches Geschichtsbewusstsein zur Zeit der Weimarer Republik*, Zürich: Theologischer Verlag.

Breitenbürger, Gerd and Günter Schnitzler (eds.) 1974, *Marx und Marxismus heute*, Hamburg: Hoffmann und Campe.

Brenkert, George G. 1999 [1986], 'Marx and Human Rights' in *Karl Marx's Social and Political Thought: Critical Assessments*, Vol. 7, edited by Bob Jessop, London: Routledge.

—— 1983, *Marx's Ethics of Freedom*, London: Routledge and Kegan Paul.

Brenner, Robert 1998, 'The Economics of Global Turbulence', *New Left Review*, I/229, 1–264.

—— 2002, *The Boom and the Bubble. The US in the World Economy*, London: Verso.

Brentel, Helmut 1989, *Soziale Form und ökonomisches Objekt. Studien zum Gegenstands- und Methodenverständnis der Kritik der politischen Ökonomie*, Opladen: Westdeutscher Verlag.

Bress, Ludwig 1974, 'Grundzüge gegenwärtiger Marxkritik' in *Marx und Marxismus heute*, edited by Gerd Breitenbürger and Günter Schnitzler, Hamburg: Hoffmann und Campe.

—— 1975, 'Der Beitrag der Marxschen Ökonomie zur Entwicklung der Wirtschaftswissenschaften' in *Marxismus – ernst genommen. Ein Universalsystem auf dem Prüfstand der Wissenschaften*, edited by Gerhard Szczesny, Reinbek: Rowohlt.

Breuer, Rolf, Jürgen Schrempp et al. (eds.) 1999, *Der Kapitalismus im 21. Jahrhundert*, Munich: Piper.

Breuer, Stefan 1977, *Die Krise des Revolutionstheorie. Negative Vergesellschaftung und Arbeitsmetaphysik bei Herbert Marcuse*, Frankfurt am Main: Syndikat.

—— 1993, *Anatomie der konservativen Revolution*, Darmstadt: Wissenschaftliche Buchgesellschaft.

Breuer, Wilhelm M. 1975, *Zur politischen Ökonomie des Monopols. Einführung in die Probleme der Monopoltheorie*, Cologne: Kiepenheuer & Witsch.

Brewer, Anthony 1990 [1980], *Marxist Theories of Imperialism. A Critical Survey*, London: Routledge & Kegan Paul.

Breysig, Kurt 1936, 'Nietzsches ethische und sociologische Anschauungen', *Jahrbuch für Gesetzgebung, Verwaltung und Volkswirtschaft im Deutschen Reich*, 20: 349–71.

Briefs, Götz 1959 [1931], 'Betriebssoziologie' in *Handwörterbuch der Soziologie*, edited by Alfred Vierkandt, Stuttgart: Enke.

Bröckling, Ulrich 1993, *Katholische Intellektuelle in der Weimarer Republik. Zeitkritik und Gesellschaftstheorie bei Walter Dirks, Romano Guardini, Carl Schmitt, Ernst Michel und Heinrich Mertens*, Munich: Fink.

—— 2000, *Gouvernementalität der Gegenwart. Studien zur Ökonomisierung des Sozialen*, Frankfurt am Main: Suhrkamp.

Brodbeck, Karl-Heinz 1998, *Die fragwürdigen Grundlagen der Ökonomie. Eine philosophische Kritik der modernen Wirtschaftswissenschaften*, Darmstadt: Wissenschaftliche Buchgesellschaft.

Brooks, Van Wyck 1958 [1915], *America's Coming-of-Age*, Garden City: Doubleday.

Brose, Karl 1990, *Sklavenmoral. Nietzsches Sozialphilosophie*, Bonn: Bouvier.

Bruch, Rüdiger vom (ed.) 1985, *Weder Kommunismus noch Kapitalismus. Bürgerliche Sozialreform in Deutschland vom Vormärz bis zur Ära Adenauer*, Munich: Beck.

Brückner, Peter 1972, *Zur Sozialpsychologie des Kapitalismus*, Frankfurt am Main: Europäische Verlags-Anstalt.

Brudney, Daniel 1998, *Marx's Attempt to Leave Philosophy*, Cambridge, MA: Harvard University Press.

Brugger, Winfried 1999, *Liberalismus, Pluralismus, Kommunitarismus. Studien zur Legitimation des Grundgesetzes*, Baden-Baden: Nomos.

Brumlik, Micha and Hauke Brunkhorst (eds.) 1993, *Gemeinschaft und Gerechtigkeit*, Frankfurt am Main: Fischer.

Brumlik, Micha 1994, 'Theologie und Messianismus im Denken Adornos' in *Jüdisches Denken in der europäischen Geistesgeschichte*, Vol. 1, edited by Eveline Goodman-Thau and Michael Daxner, Berlin: Akademie-Verlag.

Brüning, Walter 1961, *Geschichtsphilosophie der Gegenwart*, Stuttgart: Klett.

Brunkhorst, Hauke 1979, *Der Intellektuelle im Land der Mandarine*, Frankfurt am Main: Suhrkamp.

—— 1983, 'Paradigmakern und Theoriedynamik der Kritischen Theorie der Gesellschaft', *Soziale Welt*, 25 ff.

—— 1999, *Hannah Arendt*, Munich: Beck.

Brunkhorst, Hauke and Peter Niesen (eds.) 1999, *Das Recht der Republik*, Frankfurt am Main: Suhrkamp.

Brunner, Emil 1932, *Das Gebot und die Ordnungen. Entwurf einer protestantisch-theologischen Ethik*, Tübingen: Mohr.

Brunner, Otto et al. (eds.) 1972 ff.: *Geschichtliche Grundbegriffe. Historisches Lexikon zur politisch-sozialen Sprache in Deutschland*, 5 Vols., Stuttgart: Klett-Cotta.

Brunhoff, Suzanne de 1976, *Marx on Money*, New York: Urizen.

Brunstäd, Friedrich 1924, *Deutschland und der Sozialismus*, Berlin: Elsner.

Brus, Wlodzimierz 1971, *Funktionsprobleme der sozialistischen Wirtschaft*, Frankfurt am Main: Suhrkamp.

Brüsemeister, Thomas et al. 1991, *Die versteinerten Verhältnisse zum Tanzen bringen*, Berlin: Dietz.

Bry, Carl Christian 1979 [1924], *Verkappte Religionen. Kritik des kollektiven Wahns*, Munich: Ehrenwirth.

Buber, Martin 1935, *Deutung des Chassidismus: Drei Versuche*, Berlin: Schocken.

—— 1967, *Der utopische Sozialismus*, Cologne: Jakob Hegner.

Bubner, Rüdiger 1972, *Dialektik und Wissenschaft*, Frankfurt am Main: Suhrkamp.

—— 1990, *Dialektik als Topik. Bausteine zu einer lebensweltlichen Theorie der Rationalität*, Frankfurt am Main: Suhrkamp.

Bubner, Rüdiger et al. (eds.) 1978, 'Marx' Methodologie', *Neue Hefte für Philosophie*, 13.

Buchanan, Allen 1982, *Marx and Justice. The Radical Critique of Liberalism*, London: Rowman and Littlefield.

Buchanan, James and Gordon Tullock 1962, *The Calculus of Consent. Logical Foundations of Constitutional Democracy*, Ann Arbor: University of Michigan Press.

Buchanan, James 1968, *The Demand and Supply of Public Goods*, Chicago: Rand McNally.

—— 1975, *The Limits of Liberty: Between Anarchy and Leviathan*, Chicago: University of Chicago Press.

—— 1991, *The Economics and the Ethics of Constitutional Order*, Ann Arbor: University of Michigan Press.

Bukharin, Nikolai 1925, *Historical Materialism: A System of Sociology*, New York: International Publishers.

—— 1968 [1927], *The Economic Theory of the Leisure Class*, New York: Greenwoord Press.

—— 1969 [1919], *The ABC of Communism: A Popular Explanation of the Programme of the Communist Party of Russia*, Harmondsworth: Penguin.

—— 1971 [1920], *Economics of the Transformation Period*, New York: Bergmann.

—— 1972 [1926], 'Imperialism and the Accumulation of Capital' in Rosa Luxemburg and Nikolai Bukharin, *The Accumulation of Capital – an Anti-critique/Imperialism and the Accumulation of Capital*, New York/ London: Monthly Review Press.

—— 2003 [1915], *Imperialism and World Economy*, London: Bookmarks.

Buchbinder, Reinhard 1976, *Bibelzitate, Bibelanspielungen, Bibelparodien, theologische Vergleiche und Analogien bei Marx und Engels*, Berlin: E. Schmidt.

Bude, Heinz 1991, 'Auflösung des Sozialen? Die allmähliche Verflüssigung des soziologischen "Gegenstandes" im Fortgang der soziologischen Theorie' in *Jenseits der Utopie. Theoriekritik der Gegenwart*, edited by Stefan Müller-Doohm, Frankfurt am Main: Suhrkamp.

Buhl, Klaus (ed.) 1990, *Option für die Armen. Theologie der Befreiung und kirchliche Basisgemeinden in Lateinamerika*, Leipzig: Reclam.

Buhle, Paul 1987, *Marxism in the United States: Remapping the History of the American Left*, London: Verso.

Buhr, Manfred and Gerd Irrlitz 1968, *Der Anspruch der Vernunft. Die klassische deutsche Philosophie als theoretische Quelle des Marxismus*, East Berlin: Akademie-Verlag.

Buhr, Manfred and Georg Klaus 1972, *Philosophisches Wörterbuch*, Berlin: Das Europäische Buch.

Bulgakov, Sergej 1897, *The Question of Markets in Capitalist Society*, Moscow: n.p.

Bultmann, Rudolf 1940, *Theologie des Neuen Testaments*, Tübingen: Mohr.

—— 1988 [1926], *Jesus*, Tübingen: Mohr.

Bundesverband der Katholischen Arbeitnehmer-Bewegung Deutschlands (KAB) (ed.) 1992, *Texte zur katholischen Soziallehre*, Bornheim: Ketteler.

Bundesverfassungsgericht, ruling passed 17 August 1956, 1BvB 2/51, special printing, Karlsruhe 1958.

Burchardt, Michael 1997, *Marxistische Wirtschaftstheorie. Mit einem Anhang zu Leben und Werk von Karl Marx*, Munich: Oldenbourg.

Burckhardt, Jacob 1943 [1910], *Reflections on History*, London: Allen & Unwin.

Burckhart, Holger and Kersten Reich 2000, *Begründung von Moral. Diskursethik versus Konstruktivismus – Eine Streitschrift*, Würzburg: Königshausen und Neumann.

Bürgin, Alfred 1993, *Zur Soziogenese der Politischen Ökonomie*, Marburg: Metropolis.

Burke, Peter 1980, *Sociology and History*, Boston: Allen & Unwin.

Burnham, James 1941, *The Managerial Revolution*, New York: John Day.

Busch, Eberhard 1998, *Die große Leidenschaft. Einführung in die Theologie Karl Barths*, Gütersloh: Gütersloher Verlagshaus.

Busch, Ulrich 2000, 'Georg Simmels Geldverständnis in der Tradition von Karl Marx' in *Georg Simmels Philosophie des Geldes. Einhundert Jahre danach*, edited by Jürgen G. Backhaus and H.-J. Stadermann, Marburg: Metropolis.

Buschendorf, Gisela et al. (ed.) 1954, *Weltall, Erde, Mensch. Eine Sammlung zur Entwicklungsgeschichte von Natur und Gesellschaft*, East Berlin: Neues Leben.

Büsser, Fritz (ed.) 1974, *Karl Marx im Kreuzverhör der Wissenschaften*, Zürich: Artemis.

Butler, Judith 1998, 'Merely Cultural', New Left Review, I/227: 33–44.

Butterwege, Christoph 1981, *Marxismus, SPD, Staat*, Frankfurt am Main: Verlag Marxistische Blätter.

Callari, Antonio et al. (eds.) 1995, *Marxism in the Postmodern Age: Confronting the New World Order*, New York: Guilford Press.

Callinicos, Alex 1983, *Marxism and Philosophy*, Oxford: Oxford University Press.

—— 1989, *Marxist Theory*, London: Oxford University Press.

—— 1991, *Trotskyism*, Milton Keynes: Open University Press.

—— 1995, *The Revolutionary Ideas of Karl Marx*, London: Bookmarks.

Campbell, Martha and Geert Reuten 2002, *The Culmination of Capital. Essays on Vol. III of Marx's Capital*, New York: Palgrave.

Cancik, Hubert (ed.) 1982, *Religions- und Geistesgeschichte der Weimarer Republik*, Düsseldorf: Patmos.

—— 1983, 'Die Rechtfertigung Gottes durch den Fortschritt der Zeiten' in *Die Zeit. Dauer und Augenblick. Veröffentlichungen der Carl Friedrich von Siemens Stiftung*, Vol. 2, edited by J. Assmann et al., Munich: Piper.

—— 2000, *Nietzsches Antike. Vorlesung*, Stuttgart: Metzler.

Candeias, Mario (ed.) 2001, *Ein neuer Kapitalismus? Akkumulationsregime – Shareholder Society – Neoliberalismus und neue Sozialdemokratie*, Hamburg: VSA.

Cannon, Bob 2001, *Rethinking the Normative Content of Critical Theory: Marx, Habermas and Beyond*, New York: Palgrave.

Caplan, Jane 1995, *Nazism, Fascism and the Working Class*, Cambridge: Cambridge University Press.

Caporaso, James A. and David P. Levine 1992, *Theories of Political Economy*, Cambridge: Cambridge University Press.

Carchedi, Guglielmo 1977, *On the Economic Identification of Social Classes*, London: Routledge & Kegan Paul.

—— 1989, 'Classes and Class Analysis' in *The Debate on Classes*, edited by Eric Olin Wright, London: Verso.

Carmichael, Joel 1967, *Die Russische Revolution. Von der Volkserhebung zum bolschewistischen Sieg. Februar Oktober 1917*, Reinbek: Rowohlt.

Carnap, Rudolf 1928, *Scheinprobleme in der Philosophie. Das Fremdpsychische und der Realismusstreit*, Berlin: Weltkreis-Verlag.

—— 1998 [1928], *Der logische Aufbau der Welt*, Hamburg: Meiner.

Carsten, Francis Ludwig 1993, *Eduard Bernstein 1850–1932. Eine politische Biographie*, Munich: Beck.

Cassen, Bernard et al. 2002, *Eine andere Welt ist möglich! Attac: Globalisierung ist kein Schicksal*, Hamburg: VSA.

Cassidy, John 1997, 'The Return of Karl Marx', *The New Yorker*, 27 October 1997.

Cassirer, Ernst 1953 [1910], *Substance and Function, and Einstein's Theory of Relativity*, New York: Dover.

—— 1997 [1923 ff.], *Philosophie der symbolischen Formen*, 4 Vols., Darmstadt: Wissenschaftliche Buchgesellschaft.

Castoriadis, Cornelius 1949, 'Le capitalisme bureaucratique', *Socialisme ou barbarie*, 2. Reprinted in *La sociéte bureaucratique*, Vol. 1, Paris: Union général d'éditions, 1973.

—— 1998 [1975], *The Imaginary Institution of Society*, Cambridge, MA: MIT Press.

Cerruti, Furio 1983, 'Habermas und Marx', *Leviathan*, 11, 2: 352–375.

Chick, Victoria 2001, 'Über Geld und Geldtheorien', *Prokla*, 123: 227–243.

Chomsky, Noam 1993, *Year 501, The Conquest Continues*, London: Verso.

—— 1999, *Profit over People. Neoliberalism and Global Order*, New York: Seven Stories Press.

Chossudovsky, Michel 2002, *Global Brutal. Der entfesselte Welthandel, die Armut, der Krieg*, Frankfurt am Main: Zweitausendeins.

Churchich, Nicholas 1994, *Marxism and Morality: A Critical Examination of Marxist Ethics*, Cambridge: James Clarke.

Claessens, Dieter 1973, *Kapitalismus als Kultur*, Cologne: Diederichs.

Clairmont, Frederic F. 1995, *The Rise and Fall of Economic Liberalism: The Making of the Economic Gulag*, Penang: Southbound/Third World Network.

Clark, J.B. 1915, *Essentials of Economic Theory*, New York: Macmillan.

—— 1927, *The Distribution of Wealth*, New York: Macmillan.

Claussen, Detlev et al. (eds.) 1999, *Keine kritische Theorie ohne Amerika*, Frankfurt am Main: Verlag Neue Kritik.

Cliff, Tony 1955, *Stalinist Russia: A Marxist Analysis*, London: Michael Kidron.

—— 1999, *Trotskyism after Trotsky. The Origins of the International Socialists*, London: Bookmarks.

Cohen, Gerald A. 1978, *Karl Marx's Theory of History: A Defense*, Princeton: Princeton University Press.

—— 1981, 'The Labour Theory of Value and the Concept of Exploitation' in *The Value Controversy*, edited by Ian Steedman, London: Verso.

—— 2000, *If You're An Egalitarian, How Come You're So Rich?* Cambridge, MA: Harvard University Press.

Cohen, Hermann 1915, Deutschtum und Judentum, Gießen: Töpelmann.

—— 1974 [1896], 'Einleitung mit kritischem Nachtrag zu Langes Geschichte des Materialismus' in *Werke*, Vol. 5/2, Hildesheim: Olms.

—— 1981 [1904], 'Ethik des reinen Willens' in *Werke*, Vol. 7, Hildesheim: Olms.

Cohen, Jean L. 1982, *Class and Civil Society: The Limits of Marxian Critical Theory*, Amherst: University of Massachusetts Press.

—— 1995, 'Interpreting the Notion of Civil Society' in *Toward a Global Civil Society*, edited by Michael Walzer, Providence: Berghahn Books.

Cohen, Jean L. and Andrew Arato 1992, *Civil Society and Political Theory*, Cambridge, MA: MIT Press.

Cohn, Norman 1961, *The Pursuit of the Millenium: Revolutionary Millenarians and Mystical Anarchists of the Middle Ages*, New York: Harper & Row.

Colletti, Lucio 1973, *Marxism and Hegel*, London: New Left Books.

—— 1974, *From Rousseau to Lenin: Studies in Ideology and Society*, New York: Monthly Review.

—— 1975, 'Marxism and the Dialectic', *New Left Review*, I/93, 3–29.

Commission of the Central Committee of the C.P.S.U.(B.) (ed.) 1939 [1938], *History of the Communist Party of the Soviet Union (Bolshevik): Short Course*, Westport, CT: Greenwood Press.

Comte, Auguste 1830–42, *Cours de philosophie positive*, 6 Vols., Paris.

Conert, Hansgeorg 2002, *Vom Handelskapital zur Globalisierung. Entwicklung und Kritik der kapitalistischen Ökonomie*, Münster: Westfälisches Dampfboot.

Conway, David 1987, *A Farewell to Marx: An Outline and Appraisal of his Theories*, Harmondsworth: Penguin.

Coole, Diana 2000, *Negativity and Politics: Dionysus and Dialectics from Kant to Poststructuralism*, London: Routledge.

Coser, Lewis A. 1956, *The Functions of Social Conflict*, London: Routledge.

Cöster, Otto 1983, *Hegel und Marx*, Bonn: Bouvier.

Courtois, Stephane (ed.) 1998, *The Black Book of Communism: Crimes, Terror, Repression*, Cambridge, MA: Harvard University Press.

Cowling, Keith 1982, *Monopoly Capitalism*, London: J. Wiley.

Creutz, Helmut 1993, *Das Geld-Syndrom*, Munich: Wirtschaftsverlag Langen-Mueller.

Crompton, Rosemary 1993, *Class and Stratification. An Introduction to Current Debates*, Cambridge: Polity Press.

Crompton, Rosemary and John Gubbay 1977, *Economy and Class Structure*, London: Macmillan.

Crompton, Rosemary et al. (ed.) 2000, *Renewing Class Analysis*, Oxford: Blackwell.

Croner, Fritz 1954, *Die Angestellten in der modernen Gesellschaft*, Frankfurt am Main: Humboldt-Verlag.

Cunow, Heinrich 1915, *Parteizusammenbruch? Ein offenes Wort zum inneren Parteistreit*, Berlin: P. Singer.

Czarnota, Adam 1994, 'Marxism, Ideology, and Law', *Poznan Studies in the Philosophy of the Sciences and the Humanities*, 36: 173–197.

Dahmer, Helmut and Helmut Fleischer 1976, 'Karl Marx' in *Klassiker des soziologischen Denkens*, edited by Dirk Kaesler, Munich: Beck.

Dahmer, Helmut 1994, *Pseudonatur und Kritik: Freud, Marx und die Gegenwart*, Frankfurt am Main: Suhrkamp.

Dahms, Hans-Joachim 1987, 'Aufstieg und Ende der Lebensphilosophie' in *Die Universität Göttingen unter dem Nationalsozialismus*, Munich: Saur.

—— 1994, *Positivismusstreit. Die Auseinandersetzungen der Frankfurter Schule mit dem logischen Positivismus, dem amerikanischen Pragmatismus und dem kritischen Rationalismus*, Frankfurt am Main: Suhrkamp.

Dahn, Daniela 1999, *In guter Verfassung. Wie viel Kritik braucht die Demokratie?* Reinbek: Rowohlt.

Dahrendorf, Ralf 1953, *Marx in Perspektive: Die Idee des Gerechten im Denken von Karl Marx*, Hannover: Dietz.

—— 1956, *Industrie- und Betriebssoziologie*, Berlin: de Gruyter.

—— 1959, 'Betrachtungen zu einigen Aspekten der gegenwärtigen deutschen Soziologie', *Kölner Zeitschrift für Soziologie und Sozialpsychologie*, 11.

—— 1959a [1957], *Class and Social Conflict in Industrial Society*, Stanford: Stanford University Press.

—— 1961, *Gesellschaft und Freiheit*, Munich: Piper.

—— 1967, *Pfade aus Utopia*, Munich: Piper.

—— 1967a [1961], 'Über den Ursprung der Ungleichheit unter den Menschen' in *Pfade aus Utopia*, Munich: Piper.

—— 1967b [1966], *Society and Democracy in Germany*, New York: W.W. Norton & Company.

Damaschke, Adolf 1914/29, *Geschichte der Nationalökonomie*, 2 Vols., Jena: Fischer.

—— 1920, *Die Bodenreform*, Jena: Fischer.

Damus, Martin 1981, *Sozialistischer Realismus und Kunst im Nationalsozialismus*, Frankfurt am Main: Fischer.

Dangelmayr, Siegfried 1979, *Die philosophische Interpretation des Theorie-Praxis-Bezugs bei Karl Marx und ihre Vorgeschichte*, Meisenheim: Hain.

Dannemann, Rüdiger 1987, *Das Prinzip Verdinglichung. Studie zur Philosophie Georg Lukács'*, Frankfurt am Main: Sendler.

Dath, Dietmar and Barbara Kirchner 2012, *Der Implex. Sozialer Fortschritt: Geschichte und Idee*, Berlin: Suhrkamp.
De Man, Hendrik 1927, *Au-delà du marxisme*, Brussels: Églantine.
—— 1954, *L'ère des masses et le déclin de la civilisation*, Paris: Flammarion.
Debord, Guy 1967, *La société du spectacle*, Paris: Buchet/Chastel.
Debreu, Gérard 1976 [1959], *Werttheorie. Eine axiomatische Analyse des ökonomischen Gleichgewichts*, Berlin: Springer.
Deege, Michael 1996, *Die Technikphilosophie Arnold Gehlens*, Hamburg: Kovač.
Deflem, Mathieu (ed.) 1996, *Habermas, Modernity and Law*, London: Sage.
Dehnert, Detlef Immo 1997, *Die deutschsprachige Rawls-Diskussion: Systematisierung der Ziele, Argumente und Vergleich*, doctoral dissertation, Stuttgart.
Delektat, Friedrich 1954, 'Vom Wesen des Geldes. Eine theologische Marxanalyse', in *Marxismusstudien*, Vol. 1, Tübingen: Mohr.
Deleuze, Gilles and Félix Guattari 2009 [1972], *Anti-Oedipus: Capitalism and Schizophrenia*, New York: Penguin.
DeMarco, Joseph 1980, 'Rawls and Marx' in *John Rawls' Theory of Social Justice. An Introduction*, edited by H. Gene Blocker and Elizabeth Smith, Athens, OH: University of Ohio Press.
Demirovic, Alex 1999, *Der nonkonformistische Intellektuelle. Die Entwicklung der Kritischen Theorie zur Frankfurter Schule*, Frankfurt am Main: Suhrkamp.
—— 2002, *Gesellschaftliche Arbeitsteilung und Demokratie. Bezugspunkte kritischer Theorie*, Münster: Westfälisches Dampfboot.
Demirovic, Alex et al. (ed.) 1992, *Hegemonie und Staat. Kapitalistische Regulation als Projekt und Prozess*, Münster: Westfälisches Dampfboot.
—— 1998–9, 'Was hat die Marxsche Ökonomiekritik noch zu sagen? Eine Artikelserie', *Zeitschrift für kritische Theorie*, 6–8.
Demmerling, Christoph 2003, 'Heideggermarxismus' in *Heidegger-Handbuch. Leben, Werk, Wirkung*, edited by Dieter Thomae, Stuttgart Metzler.
Demmerling, Christoph and Thomas Blume 1998, *Grundprobleme der analytischen Sprachphilosophie*, Paderborn: Schöningh.
Deppe, Frank 1971, *Das Bewusstsein der Arbeiter. Studien zur politischen Soziologie des Arbeiterbewusstseins*, Cologne: Pahl-Rugenstein.
Derrida, Jacques 1994 [1993], *Spectres of Marx: The State of the Debt, the Work of Mourning, and the New International*, London: Routledge.
Desai, A.V. 1968, *Real Wages in Germany*, n.p.
Desai, Meghnad 2002, *Marx's Revenge: The Resurgence of Capitalism and the Death of Statist Socialism*, London: Verso.
Deschner, Karlheinz 1989–97, *Kriminalgeschichte des Christentums*, 6 Vols., Reinbek: Rowohlt.
Descartes, René 2008 [1637], *Discourse on the Method*, New York: Cosimo.
Descombes, Vincent 1980 [1979], *Modern French Philosophy*, Cambridge: Cambridge University Press.
Dessauer, Friedrich 1927, *Philosophie der Technik. Das Problem der Realisierung*, Bonn: F. Cohen.
—— 1956, *Der Streit um die Technik*, Frankfurt am Main: J. Knecht.
—— 1980, *Dialektische Theologie. Studien zu Adornos Metaphysik und zum Spätwerk Kierkegaards*, Munich: Kaiser.
Deutscher, Isaac 1970, *The Prophet Outcast: Trotsky, 1929–1940*, Oxford: Oxford University Press.
Dewey, John 1929, *Experience and Nature*, New York: Norton.
—— 1939, *Freedom and Culture*, New York: Capricorn Books.
—— 1939a: *The Quest for Certainty*, London: Allen & Unwin.
—— 1949 [1920], *Reconstruction in Philosophy*, Boston: Beacon Press.
—— 2002 [1899], *The School and Society*, Boston: McGraw Hill.
—— 2008 [1910], 'The Influence of Darwinism on Philosophy' in *The Middle Works, 1899–1924*, Vol. 4, Carbondale: Southern Illinois University Press.
—— 2008a [1918], 'Philosophy and Democracy' in *The Middle Works*, Vol. 11, Carbondale: Southern Illinois University Press.
—— 2008b [1922], 'Human Nature and Conduct' in *The Middle Works*, Vol. 14, Carbondale: Southern Illinois University Press.
—— 2008c [1938], 'Means and Ends' in *The Later Works, 1925–1953*, Vol. 13, Carbondale: Southern Illinois University Press, 2008.
Dews, Peter (ed.) 1999, *Habermas – A Critical Reader*, Oxford: Blackwell.
Diarra, Abdramane 1990, *Religion und frühbürgerliche Gesellschaft. Marx-Rezeption bei Weber und Versuch eines Vergleichs*, Frankfurt am Main: Fischer.

Dickstein, Morris (ed.) 1998, *The Revival of Pragmatism: New Essays on Social Thought, Law, and Culture*, Durham, NC: Duke University Press.

Diettrich, Ben 1999, *Klassenfragmentierung im Postfordismus. Geschlecht, Arbeit, Rassismus, Marginalisierung*, Münster: Unrast.

Dietzgen, Josef 1903, *Die Religion der Sozialdemokratie: Kanzelreden*, Berlin: Vorwärts.

Diggins, John Patrick 1972, *Mussolini and Fascism: The View from America*, Princeton: Princeton University Press.

—— 1975, *Up from Communism: Conservative Odysseys in American Intellectual History*, New York: Harper & Row.

—— 1992, *The Rise and Fall of the American Left*, New York: W.W. Norton.

—— 1994, *The Promise of Pragmatism: Modernism and the Crisis of Knowledge and Authority*, Chicago: University of Chicago Press.

—— 1998, 'Pragmatism and its Limits' in *The Revival of Pragmatism: New Essays on Social Thought, Law, and Culture*, edited by Morris Dickstein, Durham, NC: Duke University Press.

Dilthey, Wilhelm 1988 [1883], *Introduction to the Human Sciences*, London: Harvester.

—— 1990, 'Die geistige Welt. Einleitung in die Philosophie des Lebens. Erste Hälfte. Abhandlungen zur Grundlegung der Geisteswissenschaften' in *Gesammelte Schriften* (*GS*), Vol. 5, Göttingen: Vandenhoeck und Ruprecht.

—— 1990a [1894], 'Ideen zu einer beschreibenden und zergliedernden Psychologie' in *Gesammelte Schriften* (*GS*), Vol. 5, Göttingen: Vandenhoeck und Ruprecht.

—— 1990b: 'Die Jugendgeschichte Hegels und andere Abhandlungen zur Geschichte des deutschen Idealismus' in *Gesammelte Schriften* (*GS*), Vol. 4, Göttingen: Vandenhoeck und Ruprecht.

—— 1991, 'Weltanschauung und Analyse des Menschen seit Renaissance und Reformation' in *Gesammelte Schriften* (*GS*), Vol. 2, Göttingen: Vandenhoeck und Ruprecht.

—— 1991b: 'Weltanschauungslehre. Abhandlungen zur Philosophie der Philosophie' in *Gesammelte Schriften* (*GS*), Vol. 8, Göttingen: Vandenhoeck und Ruprecht.

—— 2002 [1910], 'The Formation of the Historical World in the Human Sciences' in *Selected Works*, Vol. 3, Princeton, NJ: Princeton University Press.

DiQuattro, A. 1983, 'Rawls and Left Criticism', *Political Theory*, 11, 1: 53–78.

Dirks, Walter 1947, 'Marxismus in christlicher Sicht', *Frankfurter Hefte*.

Ditfurth, Jutta 1997, *Entspannt in die Barbarei. Esoterik, (Öko-)Faschismus und Biozentrismus*, Hamburg: Konkret.

Dittmer, Uwe 1997, *Die Utopie des Reiches Gottes. Politik mit der Bibel*, Frankfurt am Main: Lembeck.

Dittrich, Gottfried 1987, *Die Anfänge der Aktivistenbewegung*, East Berlin: Dietz.

Dobb, Maurice 1937, *Political Economy and Capitalism*, New York: International Publishers.

—— 1974, *Organisierter Kapitalismus. Fünf Beiträge zur politischen Ökonomie*, Frankfurt am Main: Suhrkamp.

—— 1976, *Theories of Value and Distribution Since Adam Smith*, Cambridge: Cambridge University Press.

Dobb, Maurice, Joseph M. Gillmann and Paul Sweezy 1973, *Aufsätze zur Theorie des Spätkapitalismus*, Giessen: Rotdruck.

Dodge, Peter 1966, *Beyond Marxism: The Faith and Works of Hendrik de Man*, The Hague: Nijhoff.

Domar, Evsey D. 1946, 'Capital Expansion, Rate of Growth and Employment', *Econometrica*, 14.

—— 1957, *Essays in the Theory of Economic Growth*, Oxford: Oxford University Press.

Donner, Wolf 1995, *Propaganda und Film im "Dritten Reich"*, Berlin: TIP.

Dowd, Douglas 2000, *Capitalism and its Economics: A Critical History*, London: Pluto Press.

Downs, Anthony 1957, *An Economic Theory of Democracy*, New York: Harper.

Draper, Hal 1990, *Karl Marx's Theory of Revolution 6, Critique of Other Socialisms*, New York: Monthly Review Press.

Drewermann, Eugen 1991, *Die Spirale der Angst. Der Krieg und das Christentum. Mit vier Reden gegen den Krieg am Golf*, Freiburg: Herder.

Dröge, Franz and Michael Müller 1995, *Die Macht der Schönheit. Avantgarde und Faschismus oder die Geburt der Massenkultur*, Hamburg: Europäische Verlags-Anstalt.

Druwe, Ulrich and Volker Kurz (eds.) 1999, *Politische Gerechtigkeit*, Opladen: Leske und Budrich.

Dubiel, Helmut 1978, *Wissenschaftsorganisation und politische Erfahrung. Studien zur frühen kritischen Theorie*, Frankfurt am Main: Suhrkamp.

—— 2001, *Kritische Theorie der Gesellschaft. Eine einführende Rekonstruktion von den Anfängen im Horkheimer-Kreis bis Habermas*, Weinheim: Juventa.

Duchrow, Ulrich (ed.) 1969, 'Weltreligionen und Marxismus vor der wissenschaftlich-technischen Welt' in *Marxismusstudien*, Vol. 6, Tübingen: Mohr.

—— 1997, *Alternativen zur kapitalistischen Weltwirtschaft. Biblische Erinnerung und politische Ansätze zur Überwindung einer lebensbedrohenden Ökonomie*, Gütersloh: Gütersloher Verlagshaus.

Duhem, Pierre 1954, *The Aim and Structure of Physical Theory*, Princeton: Princeton University Press.

Dülmen, Richard von 1989, *Religion und Gesellschaft. Beiträge zu einer Religionsgeschichte der Neuzeit*, Frankfurt am Main: Fischer.

Dunkmann, Karl 1929, *Angewandte Soziologie*, Berlin: Reimar Hobbing.

Durkheim, Émile 1993, *Ethics and the Sociology of Morals*, Buffalo: Prometheus.

—— 1994 [1893], *The Division of Labor in Society*, New York: The Free Press.

—— 2001 [1912], *The Elementary Forms of Religious Life*, Oxford: Oxford University Press.

Dussel, Enrique and Fred Moseley 2001, *Towards an Unknown Marx: A Commentary on the Manusripts of 1861–1863*, London: Routledge.

Dutschke, Rudi 1974, *Versuch, Lenin auf die Füße zu stellen*, Berlin: Wagenbach.

Duve, Freimut (ed.) 1976, *Antisozialismus aus Tradition? Memorandum des Bensberger Kreises zum Verhältnis von Christentum und Sozialismus heute*, Reinbek: Rowohlt.

Dworkin, Ronald 2000, *Sovereign Virtue. The Theory and Practice of Equality*, Cambridge, MA: Harvard University Pres.

Eagleton, Terry 1990, *The Ideology of the Aesthetic*, Oxford: Blackwell.

—— 1991, *Ideology: An Introduction*, London: Verso.

—— 1997, *The Illusions of Postmodernism*, Oxford: Blackwell.

—— 1999, *Marx*, London: Routledge.

Eatwell, John (ed.) 1996, *Global Unemployment: Loss of Jobs in the '90s*, New York: M.E. Sharpe.

Eatwell, John and Lance Taylor 2000, *Global Finance at Risk: The Case for Regulation*, New York: The New Press.

Eatwell, John and Lance Taylor (eds.) 2002, *International Capital Markets: Systems in Transition*, Oxford: Oxford University Press.

Eatwell, John et al. (eds.) 1990, *The New Palgrave: A Dictionary of Economics*, London: Palgrave.

Ebbinghaus, Rolf (ed.) 1974, *Monopol und Staat. Zur Marx-Rezeption in der Theorie des staatsmonopolitischen Kapitalismus*, Frankfurt am Main: Suhrkamp.

Ebbinghaus, Rolf and Friedrich Tiemann (eds.) 1984, *Das Ende der Arbeiterbewegung in Deutschland? Ein Diskussionsband zum 60. Geburtstag von Theo Pirker*, Opladen: Westdeutscher Verlag.

Ebeling, Hans 1991, *Martin Heidegger – Philosophie und Ideologie*, Reinbek: Rowohlt.

—— 1993, *Die beschädigte Nation. Identität und Fremdheit in Restdeutschland*, Hamburg: Europäische Verlags-Anstalt.

—— 1993a: *Das Subjekt in der Moderne. Rekonstruktionen im Zeitalter der Zerstörung*, Reinbek: Rowohlt.

Ebeling, Hans and Ludger Lüdkehaus (eds.) 1980, *Schopenhauer und Marx. Philosophie des Elends – Elend der Philosophie*, Königstein: Hain.

Eberle, Friedrich (ed.) 1973, *Aspekte des Marxschen Systems 1, Zur methodischen Bedeutung des dritten Bandes des Kapital*, Frankfurt am Main: Suhrkamp.

Eberle, Friedrich and Eike Hennig 1974, *Anmerkungen zum Verhältnis von Theorie und Empirie. In: Gesellschaft. Beiträge zur Marxschen Theorie 2*, Frankfurt am Main: Suhrkamp.

Ebrecht, Angelika 1991, *Das individuelle Ganze. Zum Psychologismus der Lebensphilosophie*, Stuttgart: Metzler.

Eckart, Siegfried 1910, *Warum ich kein Sozialdemokrat bin*, Munich: Birk.

Edeling, Thomas et al. (eds.) 1999, *Institutionenökonomie und neuer Institutionalismus. Überlegungen zur Organisationstheorie*, Opladen: Leske und Budrich.

Edelstein, Wolfgang and Gertrud Nummer-Winkler (eds.) 2000, *Moral im sozialen Kontext*, Frankfurt am Main: Suhrkamp.

Eder, Klaus (ed.) 1989, *Klassenlage, Lebensstil und kulturelle Praxis. Beiträge zur Auseinandersetzung mit Pierre Bourdieus Klassentheorie*, Frankfurt am Main: Suhrkamp.

Edgell, Stephen 1993, *Class*, London: Routledge.

Ehalt, Hubert Christian (ed.) 1996, *Inszenierung der Gewalt. Kunst und Alltagskultur im Nationalsozialismus*, Frankfurt am Main: Lang.

Ehlen, Peter 1961, *Der Atheismus im dialektischen Materialismus*, Munich: Pustet.

Ehlen, Peter and Siegfried Rother 1975, 'Der Marxismus und die Frage nach dem Sinn des Lebens' in *Marxismus – ernst genommen. Ein Universalsystem auf dem Prüfstand der Wissenschaften*, edited by Gerhard Szczesny, Reinbek: Rowohlt.

Ehlen, Peter 1982, *Marxismus als Weltanschauung. Die weltanschaulich-philosophischen Leitgedanken bei Karl Marx*, Munich: Olzog.

Ehrenberg, Herbert 1974, *Zwischen Marx und Markt. Konturen einer infrastrukturorientierten und verteilungswirksamen Wirtschaftspolitik*, Frankfurt am Main: Societäts-Verlag.

Ehrenreich, Barbara 2001, *Nickel and Dimed: On (Not) Getting By in America*, New York: Metropolitan.

Ehrlicher, Werner et al. 1991, *Was ist Geld? Eine Podiumsdiskussion*, Wangen: FIU.

Eichengreen, Barry 1996, *Globalizing Capital: A History of the Monetary System*, Princeton: Princeton University Press.

Eichler, Klaus-Dieter (ed.) 1996, *Russische Philosophie im 20. Jahrhundert. Mit einem Anhang: Die Philosophie in der DDR zwischen Bolschewisierung und deutscher Tradition*, Leipzig: Leipziger Universitäts-Verlag.

Eickelpasch, Rolf and Burkhard Lehmann 1987, *Soziologie ohne Gesellschaft? Probleme einer phänomenologischen Grundlegung der Soziologie*, Munich: Fink.

Eidam, Heinz 1992, *Discrimen der Zeit. Zur Historiographie der Moderne bei Walter Benjamin*, Würzburg: Königshausen und Neumann.

Einstein, Norbert 1918, *Der Alltag*, Munich: Müller.

Eisermann, Gottfried 1964, *Wirtschaft und Gesellschaft;*. Stuttgart: Enke.

EKD 1991, *Gemeinwohl und Eigennutz. Wirtschaftliches Handeln in Verantwortung für die Zukunft. Eine Denkschrift der evangelischen Kirche in Deutschland*, Gütersloh: Mohn.

—— 1991a: *Verantwortung für ein soziales Europa. Herausforderung einer verantwortlichen sozialen Ordnung im Horizont des europäischen Vereinigungsprozesses*, Gütersloh: Mohn.

Eldred, Michael 2000, *Kapital und Technik. Marx und Heidegger*, Dettelbach: Röll, 2000.

Elias, Norbert 1987 [1983], *Involvement and Detachment: Contributions to the Sociology of Knowledge*, Oxford: Blackwell.

Ellul, Jacques 1958, *Leben als moderner Mensch*, Zürich: Zwingli.

—— 1964 [1954], *The Technological Society*, New York: Knopf.

Elster, John 1986, *Making Sense of Marx*, Cambridge: Cambridge University Press.

Emmanuel, Arghiri 1972, *Unequal Exchange. A Study of the Imperialism of Trade*, New York: Monthly Review Press.

Enderle, Georges 1988, *Wirtschaftsethik im Werden. Ansätze und Problematik der Wirtschaftsethik*, Stuttgart: Akademische Diözese Rottenburg-Stuttgart.

—— 1993, *Handlungsorientierte Wirtschaftsethik. Grundlagen und Anwendungen*, Bern: Haupt.

Enderle, Georges et al. (eds.) 1993a: *Lexikon der Wirtschaftsethik*, Freiburg: Herder.

Enzensberger, Hans Martin 2001, 'Putschisten im Labor', *Der Spiegel*, 2 June 2001.

Erfurter Erklärung: Bis hierhier und nicht weiter. Verantwortung für die Soziale Demokratie, 9 January 1991, available at: <www.glasnost.de/db/DokZeit/9702erfurt.html>.

Erhard, Ludwig 1957, *Wohlstand für alle. Bearbeit von Wolfram Langer*, Düsseldorf: Econ.

Esping-Andersen, Gøsta 1990, *The Three Worlds of Welfare Capitalism*, Princeton: Princeton University Press.

Essbach, Wolfgang 1988, *Die Junghegelianer. Soziologie einer Intellektuellengruppe*, Munich: Fink.

Esser, Hartmut 1999–2001, *Soziologie. Spezielle Grundlagen*, 6 Vols., Frankfurt am Main: Campus.

Ester, Hans (ed.) 2001, *Zur Wirkung Nietzsches. Der deutsche Expressionismus: Menno Ter Braak, Martin Heidegger, Ernst Jünger, Thomas Mann, Oswald Spengler*, Würzburg: Königshausen und Neumann.

Etzioni, Amitai 1988, *The Moral Dimension: Towards a New Economics*, London: Collier Macmillan.

—— 1993, *The Spirit of Community: Rights, Responsibilities and the Communitarian Agenda*, New York: Crown.

Euchner, Walter 1983, *Karl Marx*, Munich: Beck.

—— 1991, *Klassiker des Sozialismus*, 2 Vols., Munich: Beck.

Euchner, Walter and Helga Grebing (eds.) 2000, *Geschichte der sozialen Ideen in Deutschland: Sozialismus, katholische Soziallehre, protestantische Sozialethik. Ein Handbuch*, Essen: Klartext.

Euchner, Walter and Alfred Schmidt (eds.) 1972, *Kritik der politischen Ökonomie heute. Hundert Jahre "Kapital". Referate und Diskussionen vom Frankfurter Colloquium 1967*,

Frankfurt am Main: Europäische Verlags-Anstalt.

Eucken, Rudolf 1885, *Prolegomena zu Forschungen über die Einheit des Geisteslebens in Bewusstsein und Tat der Menschheit*, Leipzig: Veit.

—— 1908, *Der Sinn und Wert des Lebens*, Leipzig: Quelle und Meyer.

—— 1918, *Welt und Mensch. Eine Philosophie des Lebens*, Leipzig: Quelle und Meyer.

—— 1919, *Deutsche Freiheit. Ein Weckruf*, Leipzig: Quelle und Meyer.

—— 1920, *Der Sozialismus und seine Lebensgestaltung*, Leipzig: Reclam.

—— 1921 [1896], *Der Kampf um einen geistigen Lebensinhalt. Neue Grundlegung einer Weltanschauung*, Berlin: de Gruyter.

—— 1921a: *Lebenserinnerungen. Ein Stück deutschen Lebens*, Leipzig: Koehler.

—— 1925 [1888], *Die Einheit des Geisteslebens in Bewusstsein und Tat der Menschheit. Untersuchungen*, Leipzig: Veit.

—— 1939, *Die Grundlagen der Nationalökonomie*, Berlin: Springer.

—— 1965 [1952], *Grundsätze der Wirtschaftspolitik*, Reinbek: Rowohlt.

Eucken, Walter et al. (eds.) 1948 ff.: *ORDO. Ein Jahrbuch*, Godesberg.

Eucken-Bund (ed.) 1925 ff.: *Die Tatwelt. Zeitschrift für die Erneuerung des Geistes*, Jena.

Ewald, Günter (ed.) 1977, *Religiöser Sozialismus*, Stuttgart: Kohlhammer.

Faber, Richard 1975, *Die Verkündigung Vergils. Reich – Staat – Kirche. Zur Kritik der "Politischen Theologie"*, Hildesheim: Olms.

—— 1984, *Der Prometheus-Komplex. Zur Kritik der Politicotheologie Eric Voegelins und Hans Blumenbergs*, Würzburg: Königshausen und Neumann.

—— 1994, *Sozialismus in Geschichte und Gegenwart*, Würzburg: Königshausen und Neumann.

—— 2001, *Lateinischer Faschismus. Über Carl Schmitt den Römer und Katholiken*, Berlin: Philo.

Faber, Richard and Norbert Bolz (eds.) (1985): *Walter Benjamin: Profane Erleuchtung und rettende Kritik*, Würzburg: Königshausen und Neumann.

Faber, Richard and Jürgen Ebach (eds.) (1995): *Bibel und Literatur*, Munich: Fink.

Farner, Konrad 1985 [1969], *Theologie des Kommunismus?* Zürich: Diogenes.

Farner, Konrad and Werner Post 1972, *Marxistische Religionskritik*, Freiburg: Imba.

Fehrmann, Eberhard (ed.) 1997, *Turbokapitalismus. Gesellschaft im Übergang ins 21. Jahrhundert*, Hamburg: VSA.

Feifel, Rosa Maria 1937, *Die Lebensphilosophie Friedrich Schlegels und ihr verborgener Sinn*, Würzburg: Triltsch.

Feil, Ernst and Rudolf Weth (eds.) 1969, *Diskussion zur "Theologie der Revolution"*, Munich: Kaiser.

Fellmann, Ferdinand (ed.) 1996, *Geschichte der Philosophie im 19. Jahrhundert. Positivismus, Linkshegelianismus, Existenzphilosophie, Neukantianismus, Lebensphilosophie*, Reinbek: Rowohlt.

—— 1993, *Lebensphilosophie. Elemente einer Theorie der Selbsterfahrung*, Reinbek: Rowohlt.

Femia, Joseph v. 1993, *Marxism and Democracy*, Oxford: Clarenden Press.

Fenske, Hans (ed.) 1997, *Geschichte der politischen Ideen. Von der Antike bis zur Gegenwart*, Frankfurt am Main: Fischer.

Ferry, Luc and Alain Renaut 1987, *Antihumanistisches Denken. Gegen die französischen Meisterphilosophen*, Munich: Hanser.

Fest, Joachim 1973, *Hitler – eine Biographie*, Berlin: Propyläen.

Fetscher, Iring 1954, 'Der Marxismus im Spiegel der französischen Philosophie' in *Marxismusstudien*, Vol. 1, Tübingen: Mohr, 1954.

—— 1960, 'Das Verhältnis des Marxismus zu Hegel' in *Marxismusstudien*, Vol. 3, Tübingen: Mohr.

—— 1971 [1967], *Marx and Marxism*, New York: Herder.

—— 1972, 'Zum Problem der Ethik im Lichte der Marxschen Geschichtstheorie' in *Probleme der Ethik*, edited by G. Grau, Freiburg: Alber.

—— 1973, *Demokratie zwischen Sozialdemokratie und Sozialismus*, Stuttgart: Kohlhammer.

—— 1973a: *Der Marxismus. Seine Geschichte in Dokumenten. Philosophie, Ideologie, Ökonomie, Soziologie, Politik*, Munich: Piper.

—— 1975 [1956], *Von Marx zur Sowjetideologie. Darstellung, Kritik und Dokumentation des sowjetischen, jugoslawischen und chinesischen Marxismus*, Frankfurt am Main: Diesterweg.

—— 1985, *Überlebensbedingungen der Menschheit. Ist der Fortschritt noch zu retten?* Munich: Piper.

—— 1999, *Marx*, Freiburg: Herder.

Fetscher, Iring and Milan Machovec (eds.) 1974, *Marxisten und die Sache Jesu*, Munich: Matthias-Grünewald-Verlag.

Fetscher, Iring and Herfried Münkler (eds.) 1986, *Pipers Handbuch der politischen Ideen 4, Neuzeit: Von der Französischen Revolution bis zum europäischen Nationalismus*, Munich: Piper.

Fetscher, Iring and Alfred Schmidt (eds.) 2002, *Emanzipation als Versöhnung. Zu Adornos Kritik der "Warentausch"-Gesellschaft und Perspektiven der Transformation*, Frankfurt am Main: Verlag Neue Kritik.

Feuerbach, Ludwig 1849 [1841], *Das Wesen des Christentums* in *Sämmtliche Werke*, Vol. 7, Leipzig 1849.

Fichte, Johann Gottlieb 1868 [1794], *The Science of Knowledge*, Philadelphia: J.B. Lippincott.

—— 1987 [1800], *The Vocation of Man*, Indianapolis: Hackett.

—— 2008 [1806], *Addresses to the German Nation*, Cambridge: Cambridge University Press.

Fiedler, Frank et al. 1974, *Dialektischer und historischer Materialismus. Lehrbuch für das marxistisch-leninistische Grundlagenstudium*, Berlin: Dietz.

Fiehler, Fritz 2000, *Die Gesellschaft der Vermögensbesitzer. Über Geld, Chicago und Milton Friedman*, Hamburg: VSA.

Figal, Günter 1992, 'Vom Sinn der Geschichte. Zur Erörterung der politischen Theologie bei Carl Schmitt und Walter Benjamin' in *Dialektischer Negativismus. Michael Theunissen zum 60. Geburtstag*, edited by Emil Angehrn et al., Frankfurt am Main: Suhrkamp.

Finley, Moses I. 1973, *Democracy Ancient and Modern*, New Brunswick: Rutgers University Press.

Fischer, Hugo 1932, *Marx*, Jena: Fischer.

Fischer, Joschka 1992, *Die Linke nach dem Sozialismus*, Hamburg: Hoffmann und Campe.

Fischer, Klaus 1998, 'Jüdische Wissenschaftler in Weimar: Marginalität, Identität und Innovation' in *Jüdisches Leben in der Weimarer Republik*, edited by Wolfgang Benz, Tübingen: Mohr.

Fischer, Wolfram (ed.) 1985, *Handbuch der europäischen Wirtschafts- und Sozialgeschichte*, Vol. 5, Stuttgart: Klett-Cotta.

Fisching, Horst 1993, *Moral und Gesellschaft. Zur Soziologisierung des ethischen Diskurses in der Moderne*, Frankfurt am Main: Campus.

Flasch, Kurt 2000, *Die geistige Mobilmachung. Die deutschen Intellektuellen und der erste Weltkrieg. Ein Versuch*, Berlin: Fest.

Flatow, Sybille von and Freerk Huisken 1973, 'Zum Problem der Ableitung des bürgerlichen Staates', *Probleme des Klassenkampfes*, 7.

Flechtheim, Ossip K. 1967, *Bolschewismus 1917–1967. Von der Weltrevolution zum Sowjetimperium*, Vienna: Europa-Verlag.

—— 1969 [1948], *Die KPD in der Weimarer Republik*, Frankfurt am Main: Europäische Verlags-Anstalt.

—— 1983, *Marx heute. Pro und Contra*, Hamburg: Hoffmann und Campe.

—— 1986, *Karl Liebknecht zur Einführung*, Hamburg: Junius.

—— 1986a: *Rosa Luxemburg zur Einführung*, Hamburg: Junius.

Flechtheim, Ossip K. and Ernesto Grassi (eds.) 1973, *Marxistische Praxis. Selbstverwirklichung und Selbstorganisation des Menschen in der Gesellschaft*, Munich: Fink.

Flechtheim, Ossip K. et al. 1980, *Der Marsch der DKP durch die Institutionen. Sowjetmarxistische Einflussstrategien und Ideologien*, Frankfurt am Main: Fischer.

Fleischer, Helmut 1970, *Marx und Engels. Die philosophischen Grundlinien ihres Denkens*, Freiburg: Alber.

—— 1973 [1969], *Marxism and History*, London: Allen Lane.

—— 1973, *Sozialphilosophische Studien. Kritik der marxistisch-leninistischen Schulphilosophie*, Berlin: Olle und Wolter.

—— 1977, 'Parteilichkeit und Objektivität im Geschichtsdenken nach Marx' in *Theorie der Geschichte. Beiträge zur Historik 1, Objektivität und Parteilichkeit*, edited by Reinhart Koselleck et al., Munich: Deutscher Taschenbuch-Verlag.

—— 1980, 'Über die normative Kraft im Wirklichen' in *Arbeit, Handlung, Normativität. Theorien des historischen Materialismus 2*, edited by Axel Honneth and Urs Jaeggi, Frankfurt am Main: Suhrkamp.

—— 1987, *Ethik ohne Imperativ. Zur Kritik des moralischen Bewusstseins*, Frankfurt am Main: Fischer.

—— 1988, 'Karl Marx: Die Wendung der Philosophie zur Praxis' in *Grundprobleme der großen Philosophen. Philosophie der Neuzeit II: Kant, Fichte, Schelling, Hegel, Feuerbach, Marx*, edited by J. Speck, Göttingen: Vandenhoeck und Ruprecht.

—— 1993, *Epochenphänomen Marxismus*, Hannover: Edition Gesellschaftsphilosophie.

—— 1994, *Der Marxismus in seinem Zeitalter*, Leipzig: Reclam.

—— 1997, 'Karl Marx diesseits und jenseits des Marxismus', *Logos*, 4, 3: 173–96.

Foley, Duncan 1986, *Money, Accumulation and Crisis*, Chur: Harwood.

—— 1986a: *Understanding Capital: Marx's Economic Theory*, Cambridge, MA: Harvard University Press.

Fornet-Betancourt, Raúl 1994, *Ein anderer Marxismus? Die philosophische Rezeption des Marxismus in Lateinamerika*, Mainz: Grünewald.

Forrester, Viviane 1997, *Der Terror der Ökonomie*, Vienna: Zsolnay.

Forst, Rainer 1999, 'Die Rechtfertigung der Gerechtigkeit. Rawls' Politischer Liberalismus und Habermas' Diskurstheorie in der Diskussion' in *Das Recht der Republik*, edited by Hauke Brunkhorst and Peter Niesen, Frankfurt am Main: Suhrkamp.

—— 2000, *Toleranz: Philosophische Grundlagen und gesellschaftliche Praxis einer umstrittenen Tugend*, Frankfurt am Main: Campus.

—— 2002 [1994], *Contexts of Justice*, Berkeley, CA: University of California Press.

Forsthoff, Ernst (ed.) 1968, *Rechtsstaatlichkeit und Sozialstaatlichkeit*, Darmstadt: Wissenschaftliche Buchgesellschaft.

—— 1971, *Der Staat der Industriegesellschaft. Dargestellt am Beispiel der Bundesrepublik Deutschland*, Munich: Beck.

Forsthoff, Ernst and Reinhard Hörstel (eds.) 1974, *Standorte im Zeitstrom. Festschrift für Arnold Gehlen zum 70. Geburtstag*, Frankfurt am Main: Athenäum.

Forum für Philosophie Bad Homburg (ed.) 1994, *Markt und Moral. Die Diskussion um die Unternehmensethik*, Bern: Haupt.

Foster, J.B. (ed.) 1986, *The Theory of Monopoly Capitalism: An Elaboration of Marxian Political Economy*, New York: Monthly Review Press.

Foucault, Michel 1970 [1966], *The Order of Things: An Archaeology of the Human Sciences*, New York: Pantheon.

—— 1977 [1975], *Discipline and Punish: The Birth of the Prison*, New York: Random House.

—— 1990 [1984], *The History of Sexuality 3, The Care of Self*, London: Penguin.

—— 1991, *Remarks on Marx. Conversations with Duccio Trombadori*, New York: Semiotext[e].

—— 1997, 'What is Critique?' in *The Politics of Truth*, edited by Sylvère Lotringer and Lysa Hochroth, New York: Semiotext[e].

—— 2002 [1969], *The Archaeology of Knowledge*, London: Routledge.

Fourastié, Jean 1963, *Le grand espoir du XXe siècle*, Paris: Gallimard.

Francis, Leslie Picker 1980, 'Responses to Rawls from the Left' in *John Rawls' Theory of Social Justice. An Introduction*, edited by H. Gene Blocker and Elizabeth Smith, Athens, OH: University of Ohio Press.

Franck, Georg 2005, *Mentaler Kapitalismus. Eine politische Ökonomie des Geistes*, Munich: Hanser.

Francois, Etienne and Hagen Schulze (eds.) 2001–2002, *Deutsche Erinnerungsorte*, 3 Vols., Munich: Beck.

Frank, Manfred 1984, *Einführung in den Neostrukturalismus*, Frankfurt am Main: Suhrkamp.

—— 1988, *Vorlesungen über die Neue Mythologie II: Gott im Exil*, Frankfurt am Main: Suhrkamp.

—— 1991, *Selbstbewusstseinstheorien von Fichte bis Sartre*, Frankfurt am Main: Suhrkamp.

—— 1992, *Der unendliche Mangel an Sein. Schellings Hegelkritik und die Anfänge der marxschen Dialektik*, Frankfurt am Main: Suhrkamp.

—— 1993, *Conditio moderna. Essays, Reden, Programm*, Leipzig: Reclam.

Fräntzki, Ekkehard 1978, *Der missverstandene Marx. Seine metaphysisch-ontologische Grundstellung*, Pfullingen: Neske.

Franzen, Winfried 1988, 'Die Sehnsucht nach Härte und Schwere. Über ein zum NS-Engagement disponierendes Motiv in Heideggers Vorlesung "Die Grundbegriffe der Metaphysik" von 1929/30' in *Heidegger und die praktische Philosophie*, edited by Annemarie Gethmann-Siefert and Otto Pöggeler, Frankfurt am Main: Suhrkamp.

Fraser, Ian 1998, *Hegel and Marx: The Concept of Need*, Edinburgh: Edinburgh University Press.

Fraser, Nancy 1997, *Justice Interruptus: Critical Reflections on the "Post-Socialist" Condition*, New York: Routledge.

—— 1998, 'Heterosexism, Misrecognition and Capitalism: A Response to Judith Butler', *New Left Review*, 228: 140–149.

—— 2003, 'Distorted Beyond All Recognition: A Rejoinder to Axel Honneth' in Axel Honneth and Nacy Fraser: *Redistribution or Recognition? A Political-Philosophical Exchange*, London: Verso.

Fraser, Nancy and Axel Honneth 2003, *Redistribution or Recognition? A Political-Philosophical Exchange*, London: Verso.
Freiwald, Gerd 1999, *Marx – was bleibt?* Berlin: G. Freiwald.
Freund, Michael 1932, *Georges Sorel. Der revolutionäre Konservativismus*, Frankfurt am Main: Klostermann.
Freyberg, Jutta von et al. 1989, *Geschichte der deutschen Sozialdemokratie. Von 1863 bis zur Gegenwart*, Cologne: Pahl-Rugenstein.
Freyer, Hans 1925, *Der Staat*, Leipzig: F. Rechfelden.
—— 1931, *Revolution von Rechts*, Jena: Diederichs.
—— 1948, *Weltgeschichte Europas*, 2 Vols., Wiesbaden: Dietrich.
—— 1955, *Theorie des gegenwärtigen Zeitalters*, Stuttgart: Deutsche Verlagsanstalt.
—— 1959 [1931], 'Typen und Stufen der Kultur' in *Handwörterbuch der Soziologie*, edited by Alfred Vierkandt, Stuttgart: Enke.
—— 1964 [1930], *Soziologie als Wirklichkeitswissenschaft. Logische Grundlegung des Systems der Soziologie*, Stuttgart: Teubner.
—— 1965a: *Schwelle der Zeiten*. Stuttgart: Deutsche Verlags-Anstalt.
—— 1966 [1921], *Die Bewertung der Wirtschaft im philosophischen Denken des 19. Jahrhunderts*, Hildesheim: Olms.
—— 1970, *Gedanken zur Industriegesellschaft. Arbeiten aus dem Nachlass, herausgegeben von Arnold Gehlen*, Mainz: von Hase und Koehler.
—— 1987, *Herrschaft, Planung und Technik. Aufsätze zur politischen Soziologie, herausgegeben von Elfriede Üner*, Weinheim: VCH.
—— 1998 [1923], *Theory of Objective Mind: An Introduction to the Philosophy of Culture*, Athens, OH: Ohio University Press.
Freyer, Hans et al. (eds.) 1965, *Technik im technischen Zeitalter. Stellungnahmen zur geschichtlichen Situation*, Düsseldorf: Schilling.
Fricke, Dieter 1987, *Handbuch zur Geschichte der deutschen Arbeiterbewegung, 1869–1917*, 2 Vols., East Berlin: Dietz.
Fried, Ferdinand 1931, *Das Ende des Kapitalismus*, Jena: Diederichs.
Friedenthal, Richard 1981, *Karl Marx. Sein Leben und seine Zeit*. Munich: Piper.
Friedman, Milton 1962, *Capitalism and Freedom*, Chicago: University of Chicago Press.
—— 1969, *The Optimum Quantity of Money, and Other Essays*, Chicago: Aldine.
Friedrich, Manfred 1960, *Philosophie und Ökonomie beim jungen Marx*, Berlin: Duncker & Humblot.
Fritsch, Bruno 1968 [1954], *Die Geld- und Kredittheorie von Karl Marx*, Frankfurt am Main: Europäische Verlags-Anstalt.
Fritsche, Johannes 1999, *Historical Destiny and National Socialism in Heidegger's "Being and Time"*, Berkeley, CA: University of California Press.
Fritz, Georg 1984, *Menschliches Glück als Anliegen marxistischer und christlicher Ethik*, Frankfurt am Main: Lang.
Fritzsche, Klaus 1976, *Politische Romantik und Gegenrevolution. Fluchtwege in der Krise der bürgerlichen Gesellschaft: Das Beispiel des "Tat"-Kreises*, Frankfurt am Main: Suhrkamp.
Fromm, Erich 1932, 'Über Methoden und Aufgaben einer analytischen Sozialpsychologie', *Zeitschrift für Sozialforschung*, 1–2.
—— 1932a: 'Die psychoanalytische Charakterologie und ihre Bedeutung für die Sozialpsychologie', *Zeitschrift für Sozialforschung*, 3.
—— 1963, *Marx's Concept of Man*, New York: Ungar.
—— 1980 [1938], *Arbeiter und Angestellte am Vorabend des Dritten Reiches*, Stuttgart: Deutsche Verlags-Anstalt.
—— 1989 [1922], *Das jüdische Gesetz. Zur Soziologie des Diaspora-Judentums*, Weinheim: Beltz.
Frostin, Per 1978, *Materialismus, Ideologie, Religion. Die materialistische Religionskritik bei Karl Marx*, Munich: Kaiser.
Fuchs, Emil 1955 [1952], *Christentum und Marxismus*, Leipzig: Koehler und Amelang.
—— 1956–9, *Christliche und marxistische Ethik. Lebenshaltung und Lebensverantwortung des Christen im Zeitalter des werdenden Sozialismus*, 2 Vols., Leipzig: Koehler und Amelang.
Fuld, Werner 1981, 'Walter Benjamins Beziehung zu Ludwig Klages', *Akzente*, 28, 3: 274 ff.
Fulda, Hans (ed.) 1999, 'Schwerpunkt: Philosophie und Nationalsozialismus', *Deutsche Zeitschrift für Philosophie*, 2: 201–269.
Fukuyama, Francis 1992, *The End of History and the Last Man*, New York: The Free Press.
Furet, François 1999, *The Passing of an Illusion: The Idea of Communism in the Twentieth Century*, Chicago: University of Chicago Press.
Furger, Franz 1992, *Moral oder Kapital? Grundlagen der Wirtschaftsethik*, Zürich: Benziger.

Fürstenberg, Friedrich 1961, *Wirtschaftssoziologie*, Berlin: de Gruyter.

Gadamer, Hans-Georg 1999, *Gesammelte Werke* (*GW*), 10 volumes, Tübingen: Mohr.

—— 2004 [1960], *Truth and Method*, London: Continuum.

Gall, Lothar 1989, *Bürgertum in Deutschland*, Berlin: Siedler.

Galbraith, John Kenneth 1968, *The New Industrial State*, New York: New American Library.

Gamm, Gerhard 1997, *Der Deutsche Idealismus. Eine Einführung in die Philosophie von Fichte, Hegel und Schelling*, Stuttgart: Reclam.

Gamm, Gerhard et al. 2001, *Hauptwerke der Sozialphilosophie. Interpretationen*, Stuttgart: Reclam.

Gangl, Manfred 1987, *Politische Ökonomie und Kritische Theorie. Ein Beitrag zur theoretischen Entwicklung des Frankfurter Schule*, Frankfurt am Main: Campus.

Gangl, Manfred and Gérard Raulet (eds.) 1994, *Intellektuellendiskurse in der Weimarer Republik. Zur politischen Kultur einer Gemengelage*, Darmstadt: Wissenschaftliche Buchgesellschaft.

Garaudy, Roger 1968, *From Anathema to Dialogue: A Marxist Challenge to Christian Churches*, New York: Vintage.

—— 1969, *Marxismus im 20. Jahrhundert*, Reinbek: Rowohlt.

Garaudy, Roger, Johann Baptist Metz and Karl S.J. Rahner 1966, *Der Dialog, oder: Ändert sich das Verhältnis zwischen Katholizismus und Marxismus*? Reinbek: Rowohlt.

Garson, Barbara 2001, *Money Makes the World Go Round*, New York: Viking.

Gasset, José Ortega y 1932 [1930], *The Revolt of the Masses*, New York: Norton.

Gavin, William J. (ed.) 1988, *Context over Foundation: Dewey and Marx*, Dordrecht: Reidel.

Gawoll, Hans-Jürgen 1989, *Nihilismus und Metaphysik. Entwicklungsgeschichtliche Untersuchung vom deutschen Idealismus bis zu Heidegger*, Stuttgart: Frommann-Holzboog.

Gay, Peter 1952, *The Dilemma of Democratic Socialism: Eduard Bernstein's Challenge to Marx*, New York: Columbia University Press.

—— 1968, *Weimar Culture: The Outsider as Insider*, New York: Harper & Row.

Geary, Dick 1987, *Karl Kautsky*, New York: St. Martin's Press.

Geden, Oliver 1996, *Rechte Ökologie. Umweltschutz zwischen Emanzipation und Faschismus*, Berlin: Elefanten Press.

Gedö, András 1983, 'Die Philosophie von Marx im Kräftefeld der Wahlverwandtschaften. Zu neueren Entwicklungen der Marxismus-Diskussion' in *Karl Marx – Philosophie, Wissenschaft, Politik*, edited by Hans Jörg Sandkühler, Cologne: Pahl-Rugenstein, 1983.

Gedö, András 1991 [1988], 'Warum Marx oder Nietzsche?' in *100 Jahre philosophische Nietzsche-Rezeption*, edited by Alfredo Guzzoni, Frankfurt am Main: Hain.

Gehlen, Arnold 1931, *Wirklicher und unwirklicher Geist. Eine Untersuchung in der Methode absoluter Phänomenologie*, Leipzig: Noske.

—— 1935, *Deutschtum und Christentum bei Fichte*, Berlin: Junker und Dünnhaupt.

—— 1956, *Urmensch und Spätkultur. Philosophische Ergebnisse und Aussagen*, Bonn: Athenäum.

—— 1957, *Die Seele im technischen Zeitalter. Sozialpsychologische Probleme in der industriellen Gesellschaft*, Reinbek: Rowohlt.

—— 1961, *Anthropologische Forschung. Zur Selbstbegegnung und Selbstentdeckung des Menschen*, Reinbek: Rowohlt.

—— 1963, 'Über kulturelle Kristallisationen' in *Studien zur Anthropologie und Soziologie*, Berlin: Luchterhand.

—— 1973 [1969], *Moral und Hypermoral. Eine pluralistische Ethik*, Frankfurt am Main: Klostermann.

—— 1978, *Gesamtausgabe* (*GA*), Vol. 1, *Philosophische Schriften* I (1925–1933), Frankfurt am Main: Klostermann.

—— 1978a [1927], 'Zur Theorie der Setzung und des setzungshaften Wissens bei Driesch' in *Gesamtausgabe* (*GA*), Vol. 1, *Philosophische Schriften* I (1925–1933), Frankfurt am Main: Klostermann.

—— 1980, *Gesamtausgabe* (*GA*), Vol. 2, *Philosophische Schriften* II (1933–1938), Frankfurt am Main: Klostermann.

—— 1980a [1933], 'Theorie der Willensfreiheit' in *Gesamtausgabe* (*GA*), Vol. 2, *Philosophische Schriften* II (1933–1938), Frankfurt am Main: Klostermann.

—— 1983 [1952], 'Über die Geburt der Freiheit aus der Entfremdung. In: Archiv für Rechts- und Sozialphilosophie' in *Gesamtausgabe* (*GA*), Vol. 4, *Philosophische Anthropologie und Handlungslehre*, Frankfurt am Main: Klostermann.

—— 1988 [1940], *Man: His Nature and Place in the World*, New York: Columbia University Press.

Gehlen, Arnold and Helmut Schelsky (eds.) 1955, *Soziologie. Ein Lehr- und Handbuch zur modernen Gesellschaftskunde*, Cologne: Diederichs.

Geiger, Theodor 1932, *Die soziale Schichtung des deutschen Volkes*, Stuttgart: Enke.

—— 1949, *Die Klassengesellschaft im Schmelztiegel*, Cologne: Kiepenheuer.

Geißler, Rainer 1996, 'Kein Abschied von Klasse und Schicht. Ideologische Gefahren in der deutschen Sozialstrukturanalyse', *Kölner Zeitschrift für Soziologie und Sozialpsychologie*, 48: 319 ff.

General, Regina and Michael Jäger (eds.) 1994, *Marx MEGA out? Streitgespräche*, Berlin: Elefanten Press.

George, Susan (ed.) 1995, *The Lugano Report*, London: Routledge.

George, Vic and Paul Wilding 1985, *Ideology and Social Welfare*, London: Routledge & Kegan Paul.

Gephart, Werner 1993, *Gesellschaftstheorie und Recht. Das Recht im soziologischen Diskurs der Moderne*, Frankfurt am Main: Suhrkamp.

Geras, Norman 1989 [1985], 'The Controversy About Marx and Justice' in *Marxist Theory*, edited by Alex Callinicos, Oxford: Oxford University Press.

Gerhardt, Volker (ed.) 1996, *Eine angeschlagene These. Die 11. Feuerbach-These im Foyer der Humboldt-Universität zu Berlin*, Berlin: Akademie-Verlag.

Gerhardt, Volker 1997, 'Die Asche des Marxismus. Über das Verhältnis von Marxismus und Philosophie', *Berliner Debatte Initial*, 4.

—— 2001, *Marxismus. Versuch einer Bilanz*, Mageburg: Scriptum.

Gerlach, Hans-Martin et al. (eds.) 1988 ff.: *Philosophen Lesebuch*, 3 Vols., Berlin: Dietz.

Gerlach, Olaf et al. (eds.) 2003, *Mit Marx ins 21. Jahrhundert. Zur Aktualität der Kritik der politischen Ökonomie*, Hamburg: VSA.

Gerlich, Fritz 1920, *Der Kommunismus als Lehre vom tausendjährigen Reich*, Munich: Bruckmann.

German Social Democratic Party 1904 [1891], 'Programme of the German Social Democratic Party, Voted at Erfurt, 1891' in *Modern Socialism, As Set Forth by Socialists in Their Speeches, Writings, and Programmes*, edited by R.C.K. Ensor, London: Harper & Brothers.

Gerstenberger, Heide 1973, 'Zur Theorie der historischen Konstitution des bürgerlichen Staates', *Probleme des Klassenkampfes*, 8/9.

Gesell, Sylvio 1958 [1916], *The Natural Economic Order*, London: Peter Owen.

Gethmann, Carl Friedrich 1991, 'Phänomenologie, Lebensphilosophie und Konstruktive Wissenschaftstheorie. Eine historische Skizze zur Vorgeschichte der Erlanger Schule' in *Lebenswelt und Wissenschaft. Studien zum Verhältnis von Phänomenologie und Wissenschaftstheorie*, Bonn: Bouvier.

Ghai, Yash, Robin Luckham and Francis Snyder (eds.) 1987, *The Political Economy of Law: A Third World Reader*, Delhi: Oxford University Press.

Giddens, Anthony 1973, *The Class Structure of the Advanced Societies*, London: Hutchinson.

—— 1981, *A Contemporary Critique of Historical Materialism*, Berkeley, CA: University of California Press.

—— 1984, *The Constitution of Society*, Cambridge: Polity Press.

—— 1992 [1971], *Capitalism and Modern Social Theory: An Analysis of the Writings of Marx, Durkheim and Weber*, Cambridge: Cambridge University Press.

—— 1994, *Beyond Left and Right: The Future of Radical Politics*, Stanford: Stanford University Press.

Giegel, Hans-Joachim 1975, *System und Krise. Kritik der Luhmannschen Gesellschaftstheorie*, Frankfurt am Main: Suhrkamp.

Giesen, Bernhard 1991, *Die Entdinglichung des Sozialen. Eine evolutionstheoretische Perspektive auf die Postmoderne*, Frankfurt am Main: Suhrkamp.

—— 1999, *Kollektive Identität. Die Intellektuellen und die Nation*, Frankfurt am Main: Suhrkamp.

Gilcher-Holtey, Ingrid 1986, *Das Mandat des Intellektuellen. Karl Kautsky und die Sozialdemokratie*, Berlin: Siedler.

Gillman, Joseph M. 1958, *The Falling Rate of Profit: Marx's Law and its Significance to Twentieth Century Capitalism*, New York: Cameron Associates.

Gimmler, Antje 1998, *Institution und Individuum. Zur Institutionentheorie von Max Weber und Jürgen Habermas*, Frankfurt am Main: Campus.

Girardi, Giulio 1968, *Marxism and Christianity*, New York: Macmillan.

Girndt, Helmut (ed.) 1990, *Selbstbehauptung und Anerkennung. Spinoza–Kant–Fichte–Hegel*, Sankt Augustin: Academia.

Girschner, Christian 1999, *Politische Ökonomie und Weltmarkt. Allgemeine Weltmarktdynamik in der Marxschen Kritik der politischen Ökonomie*, Cologne: PapyRossa.

Glaser, Wilhelm R. 1972, *Soziales und instrumentales Handeln. Probleme der Technologie bei Arnold Gehlen und Jürgen Habermas*, Stuttgart: Kohlhammer.

Glatz, Uwe B. 2001, *Emil Lask. Philosophie im Verhältnis zu Weltanschauung, Leben und Erkenntnis*, Würzburg: Königshausen und Neumann.

Glockner, Hermann 1944 [1938], *Das Abenteuer des Geistes*, Stuttgart: Frommann.

Glombowski, Jörg et al. (eds.) 1998, *Zur kontinentalen Geschichte des ökonomischen Denkens*, Marburg: Metropolis.

Glotz, Peter 2001, 'Das Ende des Klassenkampfes', *Die Woche*, 11.

Glucksmann, André 1975, *La cuisinière et le mangeur d'hommes*, Paris: Seuil.

—— 1980 [1977], *The Master Thinkers*, New York: Harper & Row.

Glyn, Andrew and Robert B. Sutcliff 1972, *British Capitalism, Workers and the Profit Squeeze*, Harmondsworth: Penguin.

Gmünder, Ulrich 1985, *Kritische Theorie. Horkheimer, Adorno, Marcuse, Habermas*, Stuttgart: Metzler.

Gneuss, Christian and Jürgen Kocka (eds.) 1988, *Max Weber. Ein Symposion*, Munich: Deutscher Taschenbuch-Verlag.

Göbel, Andreas 2000, *Theoriegenese als Problemgenese. Eine problemgeschichtliche Rekonstruktion der Systemtheorie Niklas Luhmanns*, Constance: UVK.

Goff, Tom W. 1980, *Marx and Mead: Contributions to a Sociology of Knowledge*, London: Routledge & Kegan Paul.

Gogarten, Friedrich 1915, *Religion und Volkstum*, Jena: Diederichs.

—— 1970 [1953], *Despair and Hope for our Time*, Boston: Pilgrim Press.

Göggelmann, Walter 1987, *Christliche Weltverantwortung zwischen sozialer Frage und Nationalstaat. Zur Entwicklung Friedrich Naumanns 1860–1903*, Baden-Baden: Nomos.

Göhler, Gerhard 1980, *Die Reduktion der Dialektik durch Marx: Strukturveränderungen in der Kritik der politischen Ökonomie*, Stuttgart: Klett-Cotta.

Goldbach, Marie-Luise 1973, *Karl Radek und die deutsch-sowjetischen Beziehungen 1918–1923*, Bonn: Verlag Neue Gesellschaft.

Goldmann, Lucien 1959, *Recherches dialectiques*, Paris: Gallimard.

—— 1973, *Lukács et Heidegger*, Paris: Denoel.

Goldthorpe, John H. 1980, *Social Mobility and Class Structure in Modern Britain*, Oxford: Oxford University Press.

—— 1996, 'Class Analysis and the Reorientation of Class Theory: The Case of Persisting Differentials in Educational Attainment', *British Journal of Sociology*, 47.

Goldthorpe, John H. and Hermann Strasser (eds.) 1985, *Die Analyse sozialer Ungleichheit. Kontinuität, Erneuerung, Innovation*, Opladen: Westdeutscher Verlag.

Goldthorpe, John H. and Gordon Marshall 1992, 'The Promising Future of Class Analysis: A Response to Recent Critiques', *Sociology*, 26.

Gollwitzer, Helmut 1962, 'Die marxistische Religionskritik und der christliche Glaube' in *Marxismusstudien*, Vol. 4, Tübingen: Mohr.

—— 1967, *Von der Stellvertretung Gottes. Christlicher Glaube in Erfahrung von der Verborgenheit Gottes. Zum Gespräch mit Dorothee Sölle*, Munich: Kaiser.

—— 1972, *Reich Gottes und Sozialismus bei Karl Barth*, Munich: Kaiser.

—— 1974, *Die kapitalistische Revolution*, Munich: Kaiser.

Goodman-Thau, Eveline and Michael Daxner (eds.) 1994–95, *Jüdisches Denken in der europäischen Geistesgeschichte*, 2 Vols., Berlin: Akademie-Verlag.

Goodwin, Richard M. 1972, 'A Growth Cycle' in *A Critique of Economic Theory. Selected Readings*, edited by E.K. Hunt and Jesse Schwartz, Harmondsworth: Penguin.

Goodwin, William 1976 [1793]: *Enquiry concerning Political Justice*, Harmondsworth: Penguin.

Görg, Christoph (ed.) 1998, *Kein Staat zu machen. Zur Kritik der Sozialwissenschaften*, Münster: Westfälisches Dampfboot.

Gormann, Robert A. 1982, *Neo-Marxism: The Meanings of Modern Radicalism*, Westport: Greenwood Press.

Gorsen, Peter 1981, *Transformierte Alltäglichkeit oder Transzendenz der Kunst*, Frankfurt am Main: Europäische Verlags-Anstalt.

Gorz, André 1983, *Farewell to the Working Class*, London: Pluto Press.

—— 1989, *Critique of Economic Reason*, London: Verso.

—— 1997, *Misères du présent, richesse du possible*, Paris: Galilée.

Gosepath, Stefan 1999, 'Zur Begründung sozialer Menschenrechte' in *Philosophie der Menschenrechte*, edited by Stefan Gosepath and Georg Lohmann, Frankfurt am Main: Suhrkamp.

Gosepath, Stefan and Georg Lohmann (eds.) 1999, *Philosophie der Menschenrechte*, Frankfurt am Main: Suhrkamp.

Gottlieb, Roger S. 1992, *Marxism: Origins, Betrayal, Rebirth, 1844–1990*, New York: Routledge.

Gould, Carol C. 1980, *Marx's Social Ontology: Individuality and Community in Marx's Theory of Social Reality*, Cambridge, MA: MIT Press.

Gouldner, Alwin W. 1970, *The Coming Crisis of Western Sociology*, New York: Basic Books.

—— 1977, 'The Two Marxisms' in *For Sociology. Renewal and Critique in Sociology Today*, Harmondsworth: Penguin.

—— 1980, *The Two Marxisms: Contradictions and Anomalities in the Development of Theory*, London: Macmillan.

Gräb, Wilhelm 1999, *Religion als Thema der Theologie. Geschichte, Standpunkte und Perspektiven theologischer Religionskritik und Religionsbegründung*, Gütersloh: Kaiser.

Gramsci, Antonio 1967, *Philosophie der Praxis. Eine Auswahl*, Frankfurt am Main: S. Fischer.

—— 1975 [1917], 'The Revolution against Capital' in *History, Philosophy and Culture in the Young Gramsci*, edited by Pedro Cavalcanti and Paul Piccone, St. Louis: Telos Press.

—— 1987, *Marxismus und Kultur. Ideologie, Alltag, Literatur*, Hamburg: VSA.

Gray, John 1998, *False Dawn: The Delusions of Global Capitalism*, New York: New Press.

Grebing, Helga 1966, *Geschichte der deutschen Arbeiterbewegung. Ein Überblick*, Munich: Nymphenburger Verlagshandlung.

—— 1977, *Der Revisionismus. Von Bernstein bis zum "Prager Frühling"*, Munich: Beck.

Grefe, Christiane et al. 2002, *Attac: Was wollen die Globalisierungskritiker?* Berlin: Rowohlt Berlin.

Greffrath, Mathias 1976, 'Das endgültige Ende der Ideologie? Helmut Schelskys Weg von der "Technokratie" zum "Klassenkampf"', *Das Argument*, 100: 949–65.

Greiffenhagen, Martin 1971, *Das Dilemma des Konservatismus in Deutschland*, Munich: Piper.

Greven, Michael Th. 1974, *Systemtheorie und Gesellschaftsanalyse. Kritik der Werte und Erkenntnismöglichkeiten in Gesellschaftsmodellen der kybernetischn Systemtheorie*, Darmstadt: Luchterhand.

Griffioen, Sander 1998, 'Rickert, Windelband, Hegel und das Bedürfnis nach Weltanschauung' in *Sinn, Geltung, Wert. Neukantianische Motive in der modernen Kulturphilosophie*, edited by Christian Krijnen and Ernst Wolfgang Orth, Würzburg: Königshausen und Neumann.

Grimes, Michael D. 1991, *Class in Twentieth-Century American Sociology: An Analysis of Theories and Measurement Strategies*, New York: Praeger.

Grimm, Klaus 1974, *Niklas Luhmanns "Soziologische Aufklärung" oder das Elend der aprioristischen Soziologie: ein Beitrag zur Pathologie der Systemtheorie im Licht der Wissenschaftslehre Max Webers*, Hamburg: Hoffmann und Campe.

Grimminger, Michael 1997, *Revolution und Resignation. Sozialphilosophie und die geschichtliche Krise im 20. Jahrhundert bei Max Horkheimer und Hans Freyer*, Berlin: Duncker und Humblot.

Gripp-Hagelstange, Helga 1995, *Niklas Luhmann. Eine erkenntnistheoretische Einführung*, Munich: Fink.

Grisebach, Eberhard 1928, *Gegenwart. Eine kritische Ethik*, Halle: Niemeyer.

Groethuysen, Bernhard 1927–30, *Die Entstehung der bürgerlichen Welt- und Lebensanschauung in Frankreich*, 2 Vols., Halle: Niemeyer.

Groh, Dieter 1973, *Negative Integration und revolutionärer Attentismus. Die deutsche Sozialdemokratie am Vorabend des Ersten Weltkrieges*, Frankfurt am Main: Ullstein.

Groh, Ruth 1998, *Arbeit an der Heillosigkeit der Welt. Zur politisch-theologischen Mythologie und Anthropologie Carl Schmitts*, Frankfurt am Main: Suhrkamp.

Grondin, Jean 1994, 'Das junghegelianische und ethische Motiv in Heideggers Hermeneutik der Faktizität' in *Der Sinn für Hermeneutik*, Darmstadt: Wissenschaftliche Buchgesellschaft.

Gropp, Rugard Otto 1961, *Der dialektische Materialismus. Kurzer Abriss*, Leipzig: VEB Verlag Enzyklopädie.

Gross, Raphael 2000, *Carl Schmitt und die Juden. Eine deutsche Rechtslehre*, Frankfurt am Main: Suhrkamp.

Grosser, Dieter et al. 1988, *Soziale Marktwirtschaft. Geschichte, Konzept, Leistung*, Stuttgart: Kohlhammer.

Großheim, Michael 1991, *Von Georg Simmel zu Martin Heidegger. Philosophie zwischen Leben und Existenz*, Bonn: Bouvier.
Grossheutschi, Felix 1996, *Carl Schmitt und die Lehre vom Katechon*, Berlin: Duncker und Humblot.
Grossmann, Henryk 1929, *Das Akkumulations- und Zusammenbruchsgesetz des kapitalistischen Systems*, Leipzig: Hirschfeld.
—— 1977 [1941], 'Marx, Classical Political Economy and the Problem of Dynamics', *Capital and Class*, 2: 32–55, and 3: 67–99.
—— 1992, *The Law of Accumulation and Breakdown of the Capitalist System*, London: Pluto (abridged translation of Grossmann 1929).
Group of Lisbon 1995, *The Limits to Competition*, Cambridge, MA: MIT Press.
Groys, Boris 1988, *Gesamtkunstwerk Stalin. Die gespaltene Kultur in der Sowjetunion*, Munich: Hanser.
—— 1996, *Die Erfindung Russlands*, Munich: Hanser.
Gruber, Helmut 1967, *International Communism in the Era of Lenin: A Documentary History*, Ithaca: Cornell University Press.
Gruhl, Herbert 1978, *Ein Planet wird geplündert. Die Schreckensbilanz unserer Politik*, Frankfurt am Main: Fischer.
Grünberg, Emil 1932, *Der Mittelstand in der kapitalistischen Gesellschaft*, Leipzig: Hirschfeld.
Grünberg, Carl (ed.) 1910 ff.: *Archiv für die Geschichte des Sozialismus und der Arbeiterbewegung*, Leipzig.
Grundmann, Reiner 1991, *Marxism and Ecology*, Oxford: Clarendon Press.
Grunenberg, Antonia 1976, *Bürger und Revolutionär. Georg Lukács 1918–1928*, Cologne: Europäische Verlags-Anstalt.
Gubbay, Jon 1997, 'A Marxist Critique of Weberian Class Analysis', *Sociology*, 31: 73–89.
Gudopp, Wolf-Dieter 1983, *Der junge Heidegger. Realität und Wahrheit in der Vorgeschichte von "Sein und Zeit"*, Berlin: Akademie-Verlag.
Guilbaut, Serge 1983, *How New York Stole the Idea of Modern Art: Abstract Expressionism, Freedom, and the Cold War*, Chicago: University of Chicago Press.
Gumbel, Emil Julius 1928, *Klassenkampf und Statistik*, Berlin: Laub.
Gürtler, Sabine (ed.) 2001, 'Schwerpunkt: Arbeit und Gerechtigkeit', *Deutsche Zeitschrift für Philosophie*, 5, 686–760.
Gustafsson, Bo 1972, *Marxismus und Revisionismus. Eduard Bernsteins Kritik des Marxismus und ihre ideengeschichtlichen Voraussetzungen*, 2 Vols., Frankfurt am Main: Europäische Verlags-Anstalt.
Gutiérrez, Gustavo 1973, *Die Theologie der Befreiung. Perspektiven*, Munich: Kaiser.
Habermas, Jürgen 1954, *Das Absolute und die Geschichte. Von der Zwiespältigkeit in Schellings Denken*, Bonn: Bouvier.
—— 1958, 'Anthropologie' in *Das Fischer Lexikon Philosophie*, edited by Alwin Diemer and Ivo Frenzel, Frankfurt am Main: Fischer.
—— 1966, 'Knowledge and Interest', *Inquiry*, 285–300.
—— 1970, 'Bedingungen für eine Revolutionierung spätkapitalistischer Gesellschaftssysteme' in Marxismuskollektiv 1970 (lectures held at the Korcula summer school).
—— 1970a [1954], 'Die Dialektik der Rationalisierung. Vom Pauperismus in Produktion und Konsum' in *Arbeit, Erkenntnis, Fortschritt. Aufsätze 1954–1970*, Amsterdam: de Munter.
—— 1970b: 'Der Universalitätsanspruch der Hermeneutik' in *Hermeneutik und Dialektik II*, edited by Rüdiger Bubner, Tübingen: Mohr.
—— 1971, 'Eine Auseinandersetzung mit Niklas Luhmann: Systemtheorie der Gesellschaft oder Kritische Gesellschaftstheorie?' in Niklas Luhmann and Jürgen Habermas, Theorie der Gesellschaft oder Sozialtechnologie, Frankfurt am Main: Suhrkamp.
—— 1971a [1957], 'Literaturbericht zur philosophischen Diskussion um Marx und den Marxismus' in *Theorie und Praxis. Sozialphilosophische Studien*, Frankfurt am Main: Suhrkamp.
—— 1971b [1968], *Toward a Rational Society*, London: Heinemann.
—— 1973 [1960], 'Between Philosophy and Science: Marxism as Critique' in *Theory and Practice*, Boston: Beacon Press.
—— 1973a [1963], *Theory and Practice*, Boston: Beacon Press.
—— 1973b: 'Wahrheitstheorien' in *Wirklichkeit und Reflexion*, edited by H. Fahrenbach, Pfullingen: Neske.
—— 1976 [1963], 'The Analytical Theory of Science and Dialectics' in *The Positivist Dispute in German Sociology*, edited by Theodor W. Adorno, New York: Harper & Row.
—— 1976a [1973], *Legitimation Crisis*, London: Heinemann.
—— 1976b: *Zur Rekonstruktion des Historischen Materialismus*, Frankfurt am Main: Suhrkamp.

—— 1978, 'Der Ansatz von Habermas (Protokoll der Diskussion)' in *Transzendentalphilosophische Normenbegründung*, edited by Willi Oelmüller, Paderborn: Schöningh.

—— 1978a [1976], 'What is Universal Pragmatics?' in *Communication and the Evolution of Society*, Boston: Beacon Press.

—— 1981 [1956], 'Arnold Gehlen: Der Zerfall der Institutionen' in *Kleine Politische Schriften*, Frankfurt am Main: Suhrkamp.

—— 1981a [1977], 'Gespräch mit Herbert Marcuse' in *Kleine politische Schriften I–IV*, Frankfurt am Main: Suhrkamp.

—— 1981b [1979], 'Interview mit Detlef Horster und Willem van Reijen' in *Kleine politische Schriften I–IV*, Frankfurt am Main: Suhrkamp.

—— 1981c: *Kleine politische Schriften I–IV*, Frankfurt am Main: Suhrkamp.

—— 1983 [1976], 'Hannah Arendt: On the Concept of Power' in *Philosophical-Political Profiles*, Cambridge, MA: MIT Press.

—— 1983a: *Philosophical-Political Profiles*, Cambridge, MA: MIT Press.

—— 1983b: 'Die Verschlingung von Mythos und Aufklärung. Bemerkung zur Dialektik der Aufklärung – nach einer erneuten Lektüre' in *Mythos und Moderne. Begriff und Bild einer Rekonstruktion*, edited by Karl-Heinz Bohrer, Frankfurt am Main: Suhrkamp.

—— 1984–7 [1981], *The Theory of Communicative Action*, 2 Vols., Cambridge, MA: Polity Press.

—— 1985, *Die neue Unübersichtlichkeit*, Frankfurt am Main: Suhrkamp.

—— 1987 [1968], *Knowledge and Human Interests*, Cambridge, MA: Polity Press.

—— 1987a [1985], *The Philosophical Discourse of Modernity: Twelve Lectures*, Cambridge, MA: Polity Press.

—— 1988, 'Law and Morality' in *The Tanner Lectures on Human Values VIII*, edited by Sterling M. McMurrin, Cambridge: Cambridge University Press.

—— 1988a [1967], *On the Logic of the Social Sciences*, Cambridge, MA: MIT Press.

—— 1989 [1962], *The Structural Transformation of the Public Sphere: An Inquiry into a Category of Bourgeois Society*, Cambridge, MA: MIT Press, 1989.

—— 1990, 'Ein Baumeister mit hermeneutischem Gespür. Der Weg des Philosophen Karl-Otto Apel' in *Karl-Otto Apel zur Einführung*, edited by Walter Reese-Schäfer, Hamburg: Junius.

—— 1990a: *Die Moderne – ein unvollendetes Projekt. Philosophisch-politische Zeitdiagnosen, 1977–1990*, Leipzig: Reclam.

—— 1990b [1983], *Moral Consciousness and Communicative Action*, Cambridge, MA: Polity Press.

—— 1991, 'Martin Heidegger: Werk und Weltanschauung' in *Texte und Kontexte*, Frankfurt am Main: Suhrkamp.

—— 1991a: *Texte und Kontexte*, Frankfurt am Main: Suhrkamp.

—— 1991b: 'Treffen Hegels Einwände gegen Kant auch auf die Diskursethik zu?' in *Erläuterungen zur Diskursethik*, Frankfurt am Main: Suhrkamp.

—— 1992, *Faktizität und Geltung*, Frankfurt am Main: Suhrkamp.

—— 1993 [1991], *Justification and Application*, Cambridge, MA: MIT Press.

—— 1995 [1988], *Postmetaphysical Thinking*, Cambridge, MA: Polity Press.

—— 1996 [1992], *Between Facts and Norms*, Cambridge, MA: Polity Press.

—— 1996a: 'Reply to Symposium Participants, Benjamin N. Cardozo School of Law', *Cardozo Law Review*, 17: 1477–1558.

—— 1999, 'Bestialität und Humanität. Ein Krieg an der Grenze zwischen Recht und Moral', *Die Zeit*, 29 April 1999.

—— 1999a: 'Der europäische Nationalstaat unter dem Druck der Globalisierung', *Blätter für deutsche und internationale Politik*, 4: 425–436.

—— 1999b [1996], *The Inclusion of the Other*, Cambridge, MA: MIT Press.

—— 2000, 'Nach dreissig Jahren: Bemerkungen zu Erkenntnis und Interesse' in *Das Interesse der Vernunft. Rückblicke auf das Werk von Habermas seit "Erkenntnis und Interesse"*, edited by Stefan Müller-Doohm, Frankfurt am Main: Suhrkamp.

—— 2001, 'Glauben, Wissen – Öffnung. Zum Friedenspreis des deutschen Buchhandels: Eine Dankrede', *Süddeutsche Zeitung*, 15 October 2001.

—— 2001a: *Kommunikatives Handeln und detranszendentalisierte Vernunft*, Stuttgart: Reclam.

—— 2001b [1998], *The Post-National Constellation: Political Essays*, Cambridge, MA: MIT Press.

—— 2001c [1984], *Social Interaction: Preliminary Studies in the Theory of Communicative Action*, Cambridge, MA: MIT Press.

—— 2003 [1999], *Truth and Justification*, Cambridge, MA: MIT Press.

—— 2003a: 'Was bedeutet der Denkmalsturz? Verschließen wir nicht die Augen vor der Revolution der Weltordnung: Die normative Autorität Amerikas liegt in Trümmern', *Frankfurter Allgemeine Zeitung*, 17 April 2003.

—— 2004 [1963], 'Dialectical Idealism in Transition to Materialism: Schelling's Idea of a Contraction of God And Its Consequences for a Philosophy of History' in *The New Schelling*, edited by Judith Norman and Alistair Welchman, New York: Continuum.

Habermas, Jürgen and Jacques Derrida 2003, 'Nach dem Krieg: Die Wiedergeburt Europas', *Frankfurter Allgemeine Zeitung*, 31 May.

Haffner, Sebastian 1967, *Der Teufelspakt. 50 Jahre deutsch-russische Beziehungen*, Reinbek: Rowohlt.

Hafner, Kornelia 1993, 'Gebrauchswertfetischismus' in *Gesellschaft und Erkenntnis. Zur materialistischen Erkenntnis- und Ökonomiekritik*, edited by Diethard Behrens, Freiburg: Ça ira.

Hagelstange, Thomas 1976, 'Finanzkapital – Hilferdings Erklärung des modernen Kapitalismus', *Beiträge zum wissenschaftlichen Sozialismus*, 3: 52–77.

Hahn, Erich 1968, *Historischer Materialismus und marxistische Soziologie. Studien zu methodologischen und erkenntnistheoretischen Grundlagen der soziologischen Forschung*, Berlin: Dietz.

—— 1970, 'Die theoretischen Grundlagen der Soziologie von Jürgen Habermas' in *Die Frankfurter Schule im Lichte des Marxismus. Zur Kritik der Philosophie und Soziologie von Horkheimer, Adorno, Marcuse, Habermas*, edited by Johannes Henrich et al., Frankfurt am Main: Verlag Marxistische Blätter.

Hahn, Frank 1982, *Money and Inflation*, Oxford: Blackwell.

Hahn, Young Bin 1999, *Die Geldtheorie von Marx und Keynes. Ein Vergleich in Bezug auf den Krisenbegriff in der Geldwirtschaft* (digital dissertation, FU Berlin).

Halfmann, Jost and Tillman Rexroth 1976, *Marxismus als Erkenntniskritik: Sohn-Rethels Revision der Werttheorie und die produktiven Folgen eines Missverständnisses*, Munich: Hanser.

Halfmann, Jost 1996, *Die gesellschaftliche "Natur" der Technik. Eine Einführung in die Techniksoziologie*, Opladen: Leske und Budrich.

—— 1996a: *Makrosoziologie der modernen Gesellschaft. Eine Einführung in die soziologische Beschreibung makrosozialer Prozesse*, Weinheim: Juventa.

—— 1998, *Technische Zivilisation. Zur Aktualität der Technikreflexion in der gesellschaftlichen Selbstbeschreibung*; Opladen: Leske und Budrich.

Haller, Max 1989, *Klassenstrukturen und Mobilität in fortgeschrittenen Gesellschaften. Eine vergleichende Analyse der Bundesrepublik Deutschland, Österreichs, Frankreichs und der Vereinigten Staaten von Amerika*, Frankfurt am Main: Campus.

Haltern, Utz 1985, *Bürgerliche Gesellschaft. Sozialtheoretische und sozialhistorische Aspekte*, Darmstadt: Wissenschaftliche Buchgesellschaft.

Hamel, Gary 2002, *Leading the Revolution: How to Thrive in Turbulent Times by Making Innovation a Way of Life*, Boston: Harvard Business School Press.

Hammacher, Emil 1909, *Das philosophisch-ökonomische System des Marxismus*, Leipzig: Teubner.

—— 1910, 'Nietzsche und die soziale Frage', *Archiv für Sozialwissenschaft und Sozialpolitik*, 31: 779–809.

Han, Seungwan 1995, *Marx in epistemischen Kontexten*, Frankfurt am Main: Lang.

Hanak, Tibor 1976, *Die Entwicklung der marxistischen Philosophie*, Stuttgart: Schwabe.

Hann, Christopher (ed.) 1999, *Property Relations: Renewing the Anthropological Tradition*, Cambridge: Cambridge Universits Press.

Hanna-Daoud, Thomas 1996, *Die NSDAP und der Film bis zur Machtergreifung*, Cologne: Böhlau.

Hanson, Eric O. 1987, *The Catholic Church in World Politics*, Princeton: Princeton University Press.

Hardach, Gerd and Dieter Karras 1975, *Sozialistische Wirtschaftstheorie*, Darmstadt: Wissenschaftliche Buchgesellschaft.

Harich, Wolfgang 1994, *Nietzsche und seine Brüder. Eine Streitschrift in sieben Dialogen, zu dem Symposium "Bruder Nietzsche?" der Marx-Engels-Stiftung in Wuppertal*, Berlin: Kiro.

—— 1975, *Kommunismus ohne Wachstum? Babeuf und der "Club of Rome"*, Reinbek: Rowohlt.

Harms, Andreas 2000, *Warenform und Rechtsform. Zur Rechtstheorie von Eugen Paschukanis*, Baden-Baden: Nomos.

Harnack, Adolf 1908, *Das Wesen des Christentums. Sechzehn Vorlesungen vor Studierenden aller Facultäten im Wintersemester 1899/1900 an der Universität Berlin gehalten*, Leipzig: Hinrichs.

Harrington, Anne 2002, *Die Suche nach Ganzheit. Die Geschichte biologisch-psychologischer Ganzheitslehren: Vom Kaiserreich bis zur New-Age-Bewegung*, Reinbek: Rowohlt.

Harrod, Roy F. 1948, *Towards a Dynamic Economics*, London: Macmillan.

Harsch, Donna 1993, *German Social Democracy and the Rise of Nazism*, Chapel Hill: University of North Carolina Press.

Harsch, Wolfgang 1995, *Die psychoanalytische Geldtheorie*, Frankfurt am Main: Fischer.

Hart, Herbert L.A. 1961, *The Concept of Law*, Oxford: Clarendon Press.

Hart, Julius 1899, *Der neue Gott. Ein Ausblick auf das kommende Jahrhundert*, Leipzig: Diederichs.

Hartley, Robert F. 1993, *Business Ethics: Violations of the Public Trust*, New York: J. Wiley.

Hartmann, Eduard von 1963 [1868], *Über die dialektische Methode. Berlin: Duncker*, Darmstadt: Wissenschaftliche Buchgesellschaft.

Hartmann, Frank 1993, 'Wider Natur. Die Biologisierung sozialer Praxis im "naturwissenschaftlichen Monismus"' in *Nationalsozialismus und Moderne*, edited by Frank Welzer, Tübingen: Edition Diskord.

Hartmann, Klaus 1970, *Die Marxsche Theorie. Eine philosophische Untersuchung zu den Hauptschriften*, Berlin: de Gruyter.

Hartmann, Michael 1999, 'Auf dem Weg zur transnationalen Bourgeoisie? Die Internationalisierung der Wirtschaft und die Internationalität der Spitzenmanager Deutschlands, Frankreichs, Großbritanniens und der USA', *Leviathan*, 27, 1: 113–141.

—— 2002, *Der Mythos von den Leistungseliten*, Frankfurt am Main: Campus.

Hartmann, Nicolai 1933, *Das Problem des geistigen Seins*, Berlin: de Gruyter.

Harvey, David 1982, *The Limits to Capital*, Oxford: Blackwell.

Hauck, Gerhard 1984, *Geschichte der soziologischen Theorie. Eine ideologiekritische Einführung*, Reinbek: Rowohlt.

Haug, Wolfgang Fritz (ed.) 1970, 'Die Arbeiterklasse im Spätkapitalismus', *Das Argument*, 61–2.

—— 1971, *Kritik der Warenästhetik*, Frankfurt am Main: Suhrkamp.

—— 1972, 'Die Bedeutung von Standpunkt und sozialistischer Perspektive für die Kritik der politischen Ökonomie', *Das Argument*, 74: 561–85.

—— 1974, *Vorlesungen zur Einführung ins "Kapital"*, Cologne: Pahl-Rugenstein.

—— 1982, *Neue soziale Bewegungen und Marxismus*, Hamburg: Argument.

—— 1983–9, *Kritisches Wörterbuch des Marxismus*, 8 Vols., Hamburg: Argument.

—— 1985–7, *Pluraler Marxismus*, 2 Vols., Hamburg: Argument.

—— 1994 ff.: *Historisch-kritisches Wörterbuch des Marxismus*, 5 Vols., Hamburg: Argument.

—— 1996, *Philosophieren mit Brecht und Gramsci*, Hamburg: Argument.

—— 2001, *Dreizehn Versuche, marxistisches Denken zu erneuern*, Berlin: Dietz.

Häupel, Beate 1993, *Karl Kautsky. Seine Auffassungen zur politischen Demokratie*, Frankfurt am Main: Lang.

Haupt, Heinz-Gerhard and Geoffrey Crossick 1998, *Die Kleinbürger. Eine europäische Sozialgeschichte des 19. Jahrhunderts*, Munich: Beck.

Havemann, Robert 1964, *Dialektik ohne Dogma? Naturwissenschaft und Weltanschauung*, Reinbek: Rowohlt.

Hayek, Friedrich 1976, *Law, Legislation and Liberty*, Vol. 1, *Rules and Order*, London: Routledge and Kegan Paul.

Hedeler, Wladislaw 1994, *Stalin Trotzki Bucharin. Studien zum Stalinismus und Alternativen im historischen Prozess*, Mainz: Decaton.

—— 2002, *Stalinistischer Terror, 1934–1941. Eine Forschungsbilanz*, Berlin: Basis Druck.

Hedeler, Wladislaw and Ruth Stoljarowa 1993, Nikolai Bucharin. Leben und Werk, Mainz: Decaton.

Heer, Friedrich 1969, 'Jüdischer Messianismus im 20. Jahrhundert – Probleme des jüdischen Marxismus' in *Die geistige Gestalt des heutigen Judentums*, edited by Ernst Ludwig Ehrlich, Munich: Kösel.

Hegel, Georg Willhelm Friedrich 1929 [1812], *The Science of Logic*, London: Allen & Unwin.

—— 1931 [1805–6], *Jenaer Realphilosophie. Vorlesungsmanuskripte zur Philosophie der Natur und des Geistes von 1805–1806*, Hamburg: Meiner.

—— 1967 [1807], *Phenomenology of Mind*, New York: Harper & Row.

—— 1977 [1801], *The Difference Between Fichte's and Schelling's Systems of Philosophy*, Albany, NY: State University of New York Press.

—— 1977a [1802], *Faith and Knowledge*, Albany, NY: State University of New York Press.

—— 1986 [1830], *Enzyklopädie der philosophischen Wissenschaften*, 3 Vols., in *Werke*, Vols. 8–10, Frankfurt am Main: Suhrkamp.

—— 1986a: *Werke in zwanzig Bänden* (cited as: *Werke*), 20 Vols., Frankfurt am Main: Suhrkamp.

—— 1991 [1821], *Elements of the Philosophy of Right*, Cambridge: Cambridge University Press.

Heid, Ludger and Arnold Paucker (eds.) 1992, *Juden und deutsche Arbeiterbewegung bis 1933. Soziale Utopien und religiös-kulturelle Traditionen*, Tübingen: Mohr.

Heidegger, Hermann 1956, *Die deutsche Sozialdemokratie und der nationale Staat 1870–1920. Unter besonderer Berücksichtigung der Kriegs- und Revolutionsjahre*, Göttingen: Muster-Schmidt.

Heidegger, Martin 1961, *Nietzsche*, Pfullingen: Neske 1961.

—— 1962 [1927], *Being and Time*, Oxford: Blackwell.

—— 1971 [1946], 'On Humanism' in *Basic Writings*, New York: Harper & Row.

—— 1971a [1954], 'What is Called Thinking?' (1954) in *Basic Writings*, New York: Harper & Row.

—— 1983 [1933–4], *Die Selbstbehauptung der deutschen Universität. Das Rektorat 1933–34*, Frankfurt am Main: Klostermann.

—— 2000 [1935], *An Introduction to Metaphysics*, New Haven: Yale University Press.

Heidtmann, Bernhardt et al. 1977, *Marxistische Gesellschaftsdialektik oder "Systemtheorie der Gesellschaft"?* East Berlin: Akademie-Verlag.

Heil, Susanne 1996, *"Gefährliche Beziehungen"—Walter Benjamin und Carl Schmitt*, Stuttgart: Metzler.

Heilbroner, Robert L. 1993, *21st Century Capitalism*, New York: Norton.

Heimann, Eduard 1926, *Die sittliche Idee des Klassenkampfes und die Entartung des Kapitalismus*, Berlin: Dietz.

—— 1931, *Kapitalismus und Kommunismus*, Tübingen: Mohr.

—— 1955, *Vernunftglaube und Religion in der modernen Gesellschaft. Liberalismus, Marxismus und Demokratie*, Tübingen: Mohr.

—— 1980 [1929], *Soziale Theorie des Kapitalismus. Theorie der Sozialpolitik*, Frankfurt am Main: Suhrkamp.

Heinemann, Fritz 1929, *Neue Wege der Philosophie: Geist, Leben, Existenz. Eine Einführung in die Philosophie der Gegenwart*, Leipzig: Quelle & Meyer.

Heine, Heinrich 2007 [1835], 'On the History of Religion and Philosophy in Germany' in *On the History of Religion and Philosophy and Other Writings*, Cambridge: Cambridge University Press.

Heine, Michael and Hansjörg Herr 1999, *Volkswirtschaftslehre. Eine paradigmenorientierte. Eine paradigmenorientierte Einführung in die Mikro- und Makroökonomie*, Munich: Oldenbourg.

Heinrich, Michael 1986, 'Hegel, die "Grundrisse" und das "Kapital". Ein Nachtrag zur Diskussion um das "Kapital" in den 70er Jahren', *Prokla*, 16: 145–60.

—— 1988, 'Was ist die Werttheorie noch wert? Zur neueren Debatte um das Transformationsproblem und die Marxsche Werttheorie', *Prokla*, 72: 15–38.

—— 1995, 'Gibt es eine Marxsche Krisentheorie? Die Entwicklung der Semantik von "Krise" in den verschiedenen Entwürfen zu einer Kritik der politischen Ökonomie' in *Beiträge zur Marx-Engels Forschung*, Hamburg.

—— 2001 [1991], *Die Wissenschaft vom Wert. Die Marxsche Kritik der politische Ökonomie zwischen wissenschaftlicher Revolution und klassischer Tradition*, Münster: Westfälisches Dampfboot.

—— 2001a: 'Monetäre Werttheorie. Geld und Krise bei Marx', *Prokla*, 123: 151–72.

—— 2004, *Kritik der politischen Ökonomie. Eine Einführung*, Stuttgart: Schmetterling.

Heinsohn, Gunnar and Otto Steiger 1988, 'Warum Zins? Keynes und die Grundlage einer monetären Werttheorie' in *Keynes' "General Theory" nach fünfzig Jahren*, edited by Harald Hagemann and Otto Steiger, Berlin: Duncker und Humblot.

—— 1996, *Eigentum, Zins und Geld – Ungelöste Rätsel der Wirtschaftswissenschaft*, Reinbek: Rowohlt.

Heiseler, Johannes Henrich von et al. (eds.) 1970, *Die Frankfurter Schule im Lichte des Marxismus. Zur Kritik der Philosophie und Soziologie von Horkheimer, Adorno, Marcuse, Habermas*, Frankfurt am Main: Verlag Marxistische Blätter.

Heller, Agnes 1977, *Die Seele und das Leben. Studien zum frühen Lukács*, Frankfurt am Main: Suhrkamp.

—— 1979, *Diktatur über die Bedürfnisse: sozialistische Kritik osteuropäischer Gesellschaftsformationen*, Hamburg: VSA.

—— 1982, 'Habermas and Marxism' in *Habermas – Critical Debates*, edited by David Held and John B. Thomson, London: Macmillan.

Heller, Hermann 1991 [1926], 'Die Krisis der Staatslehre' in *Gesammelte Schriften*, Vol. 2, Tübingen: Mohr, 1991.

Helmich, Hans-Joachim 1980, *"Verkehrte Welt" als Grundgedanke des Marxschen Werkes. Ein Beitrag zum Problem des Zusammenhanges des Marxschen Denkens*, Frankfurt am Main: Lang.

Helms, Hans G. 1969, *Fetisch Revolution. Marxismus und Bundesrepublik*, Darmstadt: Luchterhand.

Hempel, Carl G. and Paul Oppenheim 1948, 'The Logic of Explanation', *Philosphy of Science*, 15.

Henderson, James Mitchell and Richard Quandt 1983 [1958], *Mikroökonomische Theorie. Eine mathematische Darstellung*, Munich: Vahlen.

Hengsbach, Friedhelm 1991, *Wirtschaftsethik. Aufbruch, Konflikte, Perspektiven*, Freiburg: Herder.

Hennig, Eike, Joachim Hirsch, Helmut Reichelt and Gert Schäfer 1974, *Karl Marx/Friedrich Engels: Staatstheorie. Materialien zur Rekonstruktion der marxistischen Staatstheorie*, Frankfurt am Main: Ullstein.

Henning, Christoph 1999, *Vom unselbstischen Handeln zur handelnden Ewigkeit: Der Denkweg von Hermann Schwarz: 53 Jahre Philosophie in Deutschland (1892–1945)*, MA thesis.

—— 2001, '"Deutsche Philosophie": Funktion und Begriff des "Arteigenen" in der Philosophie vor und nach 1933' in *"Entartete Musik" 1938 – Weimar und die Ambivalenz*, edited by H.W. Heister, Saarbrücken: Pfau.

—— 2001a: 'Verfallen' in *Historisches Wörterbuch der Philosophie*, Vol. 11, edited by Joachim Ritter, Basel: Schwabe.

—— 2001b: 'Vorgriff; Vorhabe, Vorsicht' in *Historisches Wörterbuch der Philosophie*, Vol. 11, edited by Joachim Ritter, Basel: Schwabe.

—— 2004, 'Zuhanden, Zeug' in *Historisches Wörterbuch der Philosophie*, Vol. 12, edited by Joachim Ritter, Basel: Schwalbe.

—— 2004a: 'Die Rückkehr des Ökonomischen. Michael Heinrich bringt das Marxsche Erbe (fast) auf den Punkt', *Literaturkritik.de*, September.

—— 2005, 'Geplänkel im Überbau. Zur Kritik neuerer Marxliteratur', *Philosophische Rundschau*, 2: 124–43.

—— 2005a: 'Messianismus aus Abstraktion', *Deutsche Zeitschrift für Philosophie*, 1: 150–52.

—— 2005b: 'Private Virtues, Public Vices? Sozialphilosophische Implikationen der Rede von Korruption' in *Unaufgeklärter Kapitalismus. Multidisziplinäre Analysen zu Funktionen und Folgen der Korruption*, edited by Birger Priddat and Stephan Jansen, Wiesbaden: VS Verlag.

—— 2007, 'Entgrenzung des Schönen – Vollstreckung der Kunst? Ästhetizistische Tendenzen in Anti- und Postmoderne' in *Die Ambivalenz der Moderne Vl. 2*, edited by Hanns-Werner Heister, Berlin: Weidler.

—— 2008, 'Vom Systemvertrauen zur Selbstverantwortung: Der Wandel kapitalistischer Gefühlskultur und seine seelischen Kosten' in *Verantwortung als marktwirtschaftliches Prinzip. Zum Verhältnis von Moral und Ökonomie*, edited by Ludger Heidbrink and Alfred Hirsch, Frankfurt am Main: Campus.

—— 2008a 'Was bleibt von der Marx'schen Philosophie? Zu Marx' moralischem Perfektionismus' in *Was bleibt? Karl Marx heute*, edited by Beatrix Bouvier, Bonn: FES, available at: <http://library.fes.de/pdf-files/kmh/06595.pdf>.

—— 2009, 'Perfektionismus und liberaler Egalitarismus: Ein Versuch ihrer Vermittlung', *Deutsche Zeitschrift für Philosophie*, 6: 845–60.

—— 2010, 'Selbsttätigkeit, gelingende Gemeinschaft, Herrschaftsfreiheit: Marxsche Motive für die politische Philosophie' in *Marx – ein toter Hund? Beiträge zur Marxrenaissance*, edited by Heinz Bude et al., Hamburg: VSA.

—— 2011, 'Glück in Arbeit und Muße: Das Spektrum der Tätigkeiten vom Denken zum Feiern' in *Glück: Ein Interdisziplinäres Handbuch*, edited by Dieter Thomä, Christoph Henning and Olivia Mitscherlich, Stuttgart: Metzler.

Henning, Friedrich-Wilhelm 1974, *Die Industrialisierung in Deutschland 1800–1914*, Paderborn: Schöningh.

Hennis, Wilhelm 1987, *Max Webers Fragestellung. Studien zur Biographie des Werks*, Tübingen: Mohr.

Henrich, Dieter 1966, *Fichtes ursprüngliche Einsicht*, Frankfurt am Main: Klostermann.
—— 1971 [1961], 'Karl Marx als Schüler Hegels' in *Hegel im Kontext*, Frankfurt am Main: Suhrkamp.
—— 1977, *Ist systematische Philosophie möglich? Proceedings of the Stuttgart Hegel Conference, 1975*, Bonn: Bouvier.
—— 1982 [1970], 'Die Grundstruktur der modernen Philosophie. Über Selbstbewusstsein und Selbsterhaltung' in *Selbstverhältnisse. Gedanken und Auslegungen zu den Grundlagen der klassischen deutschen Philosophie*, Stuttgart: Reclam.
—— 1993, *Nach dem Ende der Teilung. Über Identitäten und Intellektualität*, Frankfurt am Main: Suhrkamp.
Henwood, Doug 1997, *Wall Street: How it Works and for Whom*, London: Verso.
Herkommer, Sebastian and Heinz Bierbaum 1979, *Industriesoziologie. Bestandsaufnahme, Kritik, Weiterentwicklung*, Stuttgart: Enke.
Hermand, Jost 1977, *Epochen deutscher Kultur von 1879 bis zur Gegenwart*, Vol. 4, *Stilkunst um 1900*, Frankfurt am Main: Fischer.
Hermand, Jost and Reinhold Grimm (eds.) 1978, *Karl Marx und Friedrich Nietzsche. Acht Beiträge*, Königstein: Athenäum.
Herms, Eilert 1991, *Gesellschaft gestalten. Beiträge zur evangelischen Sozialethik*, Tübingen: Mohr.
Herrmann, Joachim et al. 2000, *Geschichtsphilosophie. Kolloquium zum 70. Geburtstag von Wolfgang Eichhorn*, Berlin: Trafo-Verlag.
Hess, Henner et al. 1988, *Angriff auf das Herz des Staates*, 2 Vols., Frankfurt am Main: Suhrkamp.
Hess, Moses 1843, 'Philosophie der Tat' in *Einundzwanzig Bogen aus der Schweiz*, edited by Georg Herwegh, Zürich: Verlag des literarischen Comptoirs.
Hesse, Helmut (ed.) 1988, *Wirtschaftswissenschaft und Ethik*, Berlin: Duncker und Humblot.
Heußner, Alfred 1927, *Die philosophischen Weltanschauungen und ihre Hauptvertreter. Eine Einführung in das Verständnis philosophischer Probleme*, Göttingen: Vandenhoeck und Ruprecht.
Heyer, Paul 1982, *Nature, Human Nature, and Society. Marx, Darwin, Biology, and the Human Sciences*, Westport: Greenwood Press.
Heym, Stefan 1995, *Radek*, Munich: Bertelsmann.
Hilferding, Rudolf 1981 [1910], *Finance Capital: A Study of the Latest Phase of Capitalist Development*, London: Routledge & Kegan Paul.
Hilferding, Rudolf 1904, *Böhm-Bawerks Marx-Kritik*, Vienna: Brand.
—— 1912, 'Geld und Ware', *Die Neue Zeit*, 30, 22.1: 773–82.
—— 1927, *Organisierter Kapitalismus. Referat und Diskussion*, Spandau: Volksblatt.
Hillmann, Günter 1966, *Marx und Hegel. Von der Spekulation zur Dialektik. Interpretation der ersten Schriften von Karl Marx im Hinblick auf sein Verhältnis zu Hegel (1835–1841)*, Frankfurt am Main: Europäische Verlags-Anstalt.
—— 1967, *Selbstkritik des Kommunismus. Texte der Opposition*, Reinbek: Rowohlt.
—— 1970, *Die Befreiung der Arbeit. Die Entwicklung kooperativer Selbstorganisation und die Auflösung bürokratisch-hierarchischer Herrschaft*, Reinbek: Rowohlt.
Himmelweit, Susan 1974, 'The Continuing Saga of the Falling Rate of Profit – A Reply to Mario Cogoy', *Bulletin of the Conference of Socialist Economists*, 2, 9.
Hirsch, Helmut 1980, *Marx und Moses. Karl Marx zur Judenfrage und zu den Juden*, Frankfurt am Main: Lang.
Hirsch, Joachim 1974, *Staatsapparat und Reproduktion des Kapitals*, Frankfurt am Main: Suhrkamp.
—— 1980, *Der Sicherheitsstaat. Das "Modell Deutschland", seine Krise und die neuen sozialen Bewegungen*, Frankfurt am Main: Europäische Verlags-Anstalt.
—— 1990, *Kapitalismus ohne Alternative?* Hamburg: VSA.
—— 1996, *Der nationale Wettbewerbsstaat. Staat, Demokratie und Politik im globalen Kapitalismus*, Berlin: ID-Archiv.
Hirsch, Joachim and Roland Roth 1986, *Das neue Gesicht des Kapitalismus. Vom Fordismus zum Post-Fordismus*, Hamburg: VSA.
Hobbes, Thomas 1968 [1651], *Leviathan, or The Matter, Forme, and Power of a Common-Wealth Ecclesiastical and Civil*, Harmondsworth: Penguin.
Hobsbawm, Eric J. 1973, *Revolutionaries: Contemporary Essays*, New York: Pantheon.
—— 1987, *The Age of Empire 1875–1914*, London: Pantheon.
—— 1994, *The Age of Extremes: The Short Twentieth Century 1914–1991*, London: Joseph.
Hobsbawm, Eric et al. 1998, *Das Manifest heute – 150 Jahre Kapitalismuskritik*, Hamburg: VSA.

Hobson, John A. 1902, *Imperialism: A Study*, New York: J. Pott.

Hochberger, Hugo 1974, 'Probleme einer materialistischen Bestimmung des Staates', *Gesellschaft*, 2: 155–203.

Hochkeppel, Willi 1989, 'Pragmatismus' in *Handlexikon zur Wissenschaftstheorie*, edited by Helmut Seiffert and Gerard Radnitzky, Munich: Ehrenwirth.

Hodgson, Geoff 1980, 'A Theory of Exploitation without the Labour Theory of Value', *Science and Society*, 44, 3: 257–73.

Hodgskin, Thomas 1825, *Labour Defended Against the Claims of Capital: By a Labourer*, London: Knight and Lacey.

Hoeges, Dirk 1994, *Kontroverse am Abgrund: Ernst Robert Curtius und Karl Mannheim. Intellektuelle und "freischwebende Intelligenz" in der Weimarer Republik*, Frankfurt am Main: Fischer.

Höffe, Otfried (ed.) 1977, *Über John Rawls' Theorie der Gerechtigkeit*, Frankfurt am Main: Suhrkamp.

—— 1991, *Gerechtigkeit als Tausch? Zum politischen Projekt der Moderne*, Baden-Baden: Nomos.

—— 1995 [1987], *Political Justice*, Cambridge: Polity Press.

—— 1996, *Vernunft und Recht. Bausteine zu einem interkulturellen Rechtsdiskurs*, Frankfurt am Main: Suhrkamp.

—— 1998, *John Rawls: Theorie der Gerechtigkeit*, Berlin: Akademie-Verlag.

—— 1998a: 'Transzendentaler Tausch. Eine Legitimationsfigur der Menscherechte?' in *Philosophie der Menschenrechte*, edited by Stefan Gosepath and Georg Lohmann, Frankfurt am Main: Suhrkamp.

—— 2000, 'Auf dem Weg zur Weltrepublik', supplement to *Süddeutsche Zeitung*, 24 June.

—— 2001 [1995], *Categorical Principles of Law*, University Park: Pennsylvania State University Press.

—— 2007 [1999], *Democracy in an Age of Globalisation*, Dordrecht: Springer.

Hoffmann, Alfred 2000, *"Mit Gott einfach fertig." Untersuchungen zu Theorie und Praxis des Atheismus im Marxismus-Leninismus der Deutschen Demokratischen Republik*, Leipzig: Benno.

Höffner, Joseph 1949, *Katholizismus und Sozialismus*, Cologne: Kiepenheuer & Witsch.

Hofmann, Hilmar 1988, *Und die Fahne führt uns in die Ewigkeit. Propaganda im NS-Film*, Frankfurt am Main: Fischer.

Hofmann, Rupert (ed.) 1987, *Gottesreich und Revolution. Zur Vermengung von Christentum und Marxismus in politischen Theologien der Gegenwart*, Münster: Regensberg.

Hofmann, Werner 1979, *Ideengeschichte der sozialen Bewegung des 19. und 20. Jahrhunderts*, Berlin: de Gruyter.

Hofmannsthal, Hugo von 1979 [1911], 'Wilhelm Dilthey' in *Gesammelte Werke, Reden und Aufsätze*, Vol. 1, Frankfurt am Main: Fischer.

Hogrebe, Wolfram 1987, *Deutsche Philosophie im XIX. Jahrhundert*, Munich: Fink.

—— 1995, *Fichtes Wissenschaftslehre 1794. Philosophische Resonanzen*, Frankfurt am Main: Suhrkamp.

Hohoff, Wilhelm 1908, *Die Bedeutung der Marxschen Kapitalkritik*, Paderborn: Bonifacius-Druck.

Holländer, Heinz 1974, 'Das Gesetz des tendenziellen Falls der Profitrate. Marxens Begründung und ihre Implikationen', *Mehrwert*, 6: 105–31.

Holloway, John 2002, *Change the World Without Taking Power*, London: Pluto Press.

Holz, Hans Heinz 1972, *Strömungen und Tendenzen im Neomarxismus*, Munich: Hanser.

—— 1984, *Marxismus–Ideologie–Politik. Krise des Marxismus oder Krise des "Arguments"*, Frankfurt am Main: Verlag Marxistische Blätter.

—— 1987, *Die Rechte der Menschen*, Cologne: Pahl-Rugenstein.

—— 1997–8, *Einheit und Widerspruch. Problemgeschichte der Dialektik in der Neuzeit*, 3 Vols., Stuttgart: Metzler.

Holz, Klaus 1993, *Historisierung der Gesellschaftstheorie. Zur Erkenntniskritik marxistischer und kritischer Theorie*, Pfaffenweiler: Centaurus-Verlag.

Homann, Karl (ed.) 1992, *Aktuelle Probleme der Wirtschaftsethik*, Berlin: Duncker und Humblot.

—— 1993, 'Wirtschaftsethik. Die Funktion der Moral in der modernen Wirtschaft' in *Wirtschaftsethik und Theorie der Gesellschaft*, edited by Josef Wieland, Frankfurt am Main: Suhrkamp.

—— 1994, 'Ethik und Ökonomik. Zur Theoriestrategie der Wirtschaftsethik' in *Wirtschaftsethische Perspektiven I*, Berlin: Duncker und Humblot.

—— 1997, 'Sinn und Grenze der ökonomischen Methode in der Wirtschaftsethik' in *Wirtschaftsethik und Moralökonomik. Normen, soziale Ordnung und Beitrag der Ökonomik*,

edited by Detlef Aufderheide and Martin Dabrwoski, Berlin: Duncker und Humblot.
—— 1999, 'Die Legitimation von Institutionen' in *Handbuch der Wirtschaftsethik*, Vol. 2, edited by Wilhelm Korff, Gütersloh: Gütersloher Verlagshaus.
Homann, Karl and U. Gerecke 1999, 'Ethik der Globalisierung: Zur Rolle der multinationalen Unternehmen bei der Etablierung moralischer Standards' in *Perspektiven der internationalen Wirtschaft*, edited by Michael Kutschker, Wiesbaden: Gabler.
Homann, Karl and Franz Blome-Drees 1992, *Wirtschafts- und Unternehmensethik*, Göttingen: Vandenhoeck und Ruprecht.
Hommes, Jakob 1953, 'Von Hegel zu Marx', *Philosophisches Jahrbuch*, 62: 359–93.
—— 1995, *Der technische Eros*, Freiburg: Herder.
Honnefelder, Ludger 1990, *Scientia transcendens. Die formale Bestimmung der Seiendheit in der Metaphysik des Mittelalters und der Neuzeit (Duns Scoutus–Suarez–Wolff–Kant–Peirce)*, Hamburg: Meiner.
Honneth, Axel 1980, 'Arbeit und instrumentelles Handeln. Kategoriale Probleme einer kritischen Gesellschaftstheorie' in *Arbeit, Handlung, Normativität. Theorien des historischen Materialismus 2*, edited by Axel Honneth and Urs Jaeggi, Frankfurt am Main: Suhrkamp.
—— 1983, 'Anthropologische Berührungspunkte zwischen der lebensphilosphischen Kulturkritik und der Dialektik der Aufklärung' in *21. Deutscher Soziologentag 1982*, edited by Friedrich Heckmann and Peter Winter, Opladen: Westdeutscher Verlag.
—— 1988, 'Kampf um Anerkennung' in *Sartre. Ein Kongress*, edited by Traugott König, Reinbek: Rowohlt.
—— 1989, 'Logik der Emanzipation. Zum philosophischen Erbe des Marxismus' in *Wege ins Reich der Freiheit*, edited by Hans Leo Krämer and Claus Leggewie, Berlin: Rotbuch.
—— 1990, *Die zerrissene Welt des Sozialen. Sozialphilosophische Aufsätze*, Frankfurt am Main: Suhrkamp.
—— 1991 [1985], *The Critique of Power*, Cambridge, MA: MIT Press.
—— 1993, *Kommunitarismus. Eine Debatte über die moralischen Grundlagen moderner Gesellschaften*, Frankfurt am Main: Campus.
—— 1993a: 'Posttraditionale Gemeinschaften. Ein konzeptueller Vorschlag' in *Gemeinschaft und Gerechtigkeit*, edited by Micha Brumlik and Hauke Brunkhorst, Frankfurt am Main: Fischer.
—— 1994, 'Pathologien des Sozialen. Tradition und Aktualität der Sozialphilosophie' in *Pathologien des Sozialen*, Frankfurt am Main: Suhrkamp.
—— 1994a: 'Individualisierung und Gemeinschaft' (16–23) and 'Die Herausforderung des Kommunitarismus (118–23)' in *Kommunitarismus in der Diskussion. Eine streitbare Einführung*, edited by Christel Zahlmann, Berlin: Rotbuch.
—— 1996 [1992], *The Struggle for Recognition*, Cambridge, MA: MIT Press.
—— 1999, 'Ungleichzeitigkeiten der Marx-Rezeption. Philosophie-Kolumne', *Merkur*, 53, 7: 643–51.
—— 1999a: 'Jürgen Habermas' in *Klassiker der Soziologie 2, Von Talcott Parsons bis Pierre Bourdieu*, edited by Dirk Kaesler, Munich: Beck.
—— 2000, 'Demokratie als reflexive Kooperation. John Dewey und die Demokratietheorie der Gegenwart' in *Das Andere der Gerechtigkeit*, Frankfurt am Main: Suhrkamp.
—— 2002, 'Schwerpunkt: Marx in der Diskussion', *Deutsche Zeitschrift für Philosophie*, 3: 393–453.
—— 2002a: *Befreiung aus der Mündigkeit. Paradoxien des gegenwärtigen Kapitalismus*, Frankfurt am Main: Campus.
—— 2003, *Michel Foucault – Zwischenbilanz einer Rezeption. Frankfurter Foucault-Konferenz 2001*, Frankfurt am Main: Suhrkamp.
—— 2007 [2000], *Disrespect*, Cambridge: Polity Press.
—— 2010 [2001], *The Pathologies of Individual Freedom: Hegel's Social Theory*, Princeton: Princeton University Press.
Honneth, Axel and Wolfgang Bonß (eds.) 1982, *Sozialforschung als Kritik. Zum sozialwissenschaftlichen Potential der Kritischen Thorie*, Frankfurt am Main: Suhrkamp.
Honneth, Axel and Urs Jaeggi (eds.) 1977, *Theorien des historischen Materialismus 1*, Frankfurt am Main: Suhrkamp.
—— 1980, *Arbeit, Handlung, Normativität. Theorien des historischen Materialismus 2*, Frankfurt am Main: Suhrkamp.
Honneth, Axel and Hans Joas 1980, *Soziales Handeln und menschliche Natur. Anthropologische Grundlagen der Sozialwissenschaften*, Frankfurt am Main: Suhrkamp.
—— 1986, *Kommunikatives Handeln. Beiträge zu Jürgen Habermas' "Theorie des*

kommunikativen Handelns", Frankfurt am Main: Suhrkamp.
—— 1987, 'War Marx ein Utilitarist?' in *Karl Marx und Friedrich Engels. Ihr Einfluss und ihre Wirksamkeit in der Geschichte und Gegenwart der soziologischen Theorie*, edited by Helmut Steiner, East Berlin: Institut für Soziologie und Sozialpolitik.
Honneth, Axel et al. (eds.) 1989, *Zwischenbetrachtungen im Prozess der Aufklärung*, Frankfurt am Main: Suhrkamp.
Hook, Sidney 1930, 'A Personal Impression of Contemporary German Philosophy', *Journal of Philosophy*, 27, 6.
—— 1933, *Towards the Understanding of Karl Marx. A Revolutionary Interpretation*, New York: John Day.
—— 1955, *Marx and the Marxists: The Ambiguous Legacy*, Princeton: Van Nostrand.
—— 1983, *Marxism and Beyond*, Totowa: Rowman and Littlefield.
Höppner, Joachim and Waltraud Seidel-Höppner (eds.) 1975, *Von Babeuf bis Blanqui. Französischer Sozialismus und Kommunismus vor Marx*, 2 Vols., Leipzig: Reclam.
Hörisch, Jochen 1983, *Gott, Geld und Glück*, Frankfurt am Main: Suhrkamp.
Horkheimer, Max 1932, 'Geschichte und Psychologie", *Zeitschrift für Sozialforschung*, 1.
—— 1936, *Studien über Autorität und Familie. Forschungsberichte aus dem Institut für Sozialforschung*, Paris: Félix Alcan.
—— 1947, *Eclipse of Reason*, Oxford: Oxford University Press.
—— 1968, *Kritische Theorie*, 2 Vols., Frankfurt am Main: Fischer.
—— 1970, *Traditionelle und kritische Theorie. Vier Aufsätze*, Frankfurt am Main: Fischer.
—— 1970a: 'Interview', *Der Spiegel*, 6 January 1970.
—— 1972 [1936], 'Authority and the Family' in *Critical Theory: Selected Essays*, New York: Herder and Herder.
—— 1972a: *Gesellschaft im Übergang. Aufsätze, Reden und Vorträge 1942–1970*, Frankfurt am Main: Fischer.
—— 1972b [1937], 'The Latest Attack on Metaphysics' in *Critical Theory: Selected Essays*, New York: Herder and Herder.
—— 1972c [1933], 'Materialism and Metaphysics' in *Critical Theory: Selected Essays*, New York: Herder and Herder.
—— 1972d [1932], 'Notes on Science and the Crisis' in *Critical Theory: Selected Essays*, New York: Herder and Herder.
—— 1972e: *Sozialphilosophische Studien. Aufsätze, Reden und Vorträge 1930–1972*, Frankfurt am Main: Fischer.
—— 1980 [1961], 'Die Aktualität Schopenhauers' in *Schopenhauer und Marx. Philosophie des Elends – Elend der Philosophie*, edited by Hans Ebeling and Ludger Lüdkehaus, Königstein: Hain.
—— 1982 [1942], 'The Authoritarian State' in *The Essential Frankfurt School Reader*, edited by Andre Arato and Eike Gebhardt, New York: Continuum.
—— 1985 [1935], 'Autorität und Vernunft' in *Gesammelte Schriften*, Vol. 12, Frankfurt am Main: Fischer.
—— 1985a [1968], 'Marx heute' in *Gesammelte Schriften*, Vol. 8, Frankfurt am Main: Fischer.
—— 1985b [1951], 'Zum Begriff der Vernunft' in *Gesammelte Schriften*, Vol. 7, Frankfurt am Main: Fischer.
—— 1985 ff.: *Gesammelte Schriften* (*GS*), 18 Vols., Frankfurt am Main: Fischer.
—— 1987 [1934], 'Dämmerung. Notizen in Deutschland', in *Gesammelte Schriften*, Vol. 2, Frankfurt am Main: Fischer.
—— 1987a [1960], 'Philosophie als Kulturkritik' in *Gesammelte Schriften*, Vol. 7, Frankfurt am Main: Fischer.
—— 1987b [1942], 'Vernunft und Selbsterhaltung' in *Gesammelte Schriften*, Vol. 5, Frankfurt am Main: Fischer.
—— 1988 [1936], 'Egoismus und Freiheitsbewegung. Zur Anthropologie des bürgerlichen Zeitalters' in *Gesammelte Schriften*, Vol. 4, Frankfurt am Main: Fischer.
—— 1988a: 'Traditionelle und kritische Theorie' in *Gesammelte Schriften*, Vol. 4, Frankfurt am Main: Fischer.
—— 1989 [1939], 'The Jews and Europe' in *Critical Theory and Society: A Reader*, edited by Stephen Eric Bronner and Douglas MacKay Kellner, New York: Routledge.
—— 1989a [1931], 'The State of Contemporary Social Philosophy and the Tasks of an Institute for Social Research' in *Critical Theory and Society: A Reader*, edited by Stephen Eric Bronner and Douglas MacKay Kellner, New York: Routledge.
—— 1990 [1928], 'Zur Emanzipation der Philosophie von der Wissenschaft' in *Gesammelte Schriften*, Vol. 10, Frankfurt am Main: Fischer.
—— 1993 [1930], 'A New Concept of Ideology?' in *Between Philosophy and Social Science:*

Selected Early Writings, Cambridge, MA: MIT Press.

—— 1993a [1930], 'Beginnings of the Bourgeois Philosophy of History' in *Between Philosophy and Social Science: Selected Early Writings*, Cambridge, MA: MIT Press, 1993.

—— 1993b [1934], 'The Rationalism Debate in Contemporary Philosophy' in *Between Philosophy and Social Science: Selected Early Writings*, Cambridge, MA: MIT Press.

Horn, Karen Ilse 1996, *Moral und Wirtschaft*, Tübingen: Mohr.

Horowitz, David 1968, *Marx and Modern Economics*, London: MacGibbon & Kee.

Horský, Vladimir 1972, 'Die Frage nach dem neuen Menschen in der theologischen und marxistischen Anthropologie' in *Marxismusstudien* 7, *Das Humanum als Kriterium der Gesellschaftsgestaltung*, Tübingen: Mohr.

Horster, Detlef 1999, *Habermas zur Einführung*, Hamburg: Junius.

Horstmann, Rolf-Peter (ed.) 1978, *Seminar: Dialektik in der Philosophie Hegels*, Frankfurt am Main: Suhrkamp.

Hortleder, Gerd 1970, *Das Gesellschaftsbild des Ingenieurs. Zum politischen Verhalten der Technischen Intelligenz in Deutschland*, Frankfurt am Main: Suhrkamp.

Hösle, Vittorio 1986, 'Die Transzendentalpragmatik als Fichteanismus der Intersubjektivität', *Deutsche Zeitschrift für philosophische Forschung*, 40: 235–52.

—— 1990, *Die Krise der Gegenwart und die Verantwortung der Philosophie. Transzendentalpragmatik, Letztbegründung, Ethik*, Munich: Beck.

—— 1992, 'Versuch einer ethischen Bewertung des Kapitalismus', in *Praktische Philosophie in der modernen Welt*, Munich: Beck.

—— 1996, *Philosophiegeschichte und objektiver Idealismus*, Munich: Beck.

How, Alan 2003, *Critical Theory*, Houndsmills: Palgrave Macmillan.

Howard, Dick 1985, *From Marx to Kant*, Albany, NY: State University of New York Press.

Howard, Michael Charles and J.E. King 1985, *The Political Economy of Marx*, Harlow: Longman.

—— 1989, *A History of Marxian Economics*, Vol. 1, *1883–1929*, Princeton Princeton University Press.

—— 1992, *A History of Marxian Economics*, Vol. 2, *1929–1990*, Princeton: Princeton University Press.

Hradil, Stefan 1987, *Sozialstrukturanalyse in einer fortgeschrittenen Gesellschaft*, Opladen: Leske und Budrich.

—— 2001 [1992], *Soziale Ungleichheit in Deutschland*, Opladen: Leske und Budrich.

Huber, Wolfgang 1996, *Gerechtigkeit und Recht. Grundlinien christlicher Rechtsethik*, Gütersloh: Gütersloher Verlagshaus.

Hubig, Christoph 1978, *Dialektik und Wissenschaftsbegriff. Eine sprachphilosophisch-handlungstheoretische Analyse*, Berlin: Campus.

Hübinger, Gandolf and Thomas Hertfelder (eds.) 2000, *Kritik und Mandat. Intellektuelle in der deutschen Politik*, Stuttgart: Deutsche Verlags-Anstalt.

Hublmann, Gerald 2002, 'Rückkehr in die Philosophie? Neue Marx-Literatur', *Deutsche Zeitschrift für Philosophie*, 3: 445–53.

Hübner, Kurt 1989, *"Theorie der Regulation". Eine kritische Rekonstruktion eines neuen Ansatzes in der politischen Ökonomie*, Berlin: Edition Sigma.

Huffschmid, Jörg 1969, *Die Politik des Kapitals. Konzentration und Wirtschaftspolitik in der Bundesrepublik*, Frankfurt am Main: Suhrkamp.

—— 1975, 'Begründung und Bedeutung des Monopolbegriffs in der marxistischen politischen Ökonomie', *Zur Theorie des Monopols: Staat und Monopole I*, Argument Sonderband 6: 9–92.

—— 1999, *Politische Ökonomie der Finanzmärkte*, Hamburg: VSA.

Huffschmid, Jörg and Herbert Schui (eds.) 1977, *Gesellschaft im Konkurs? Handbuch zur Wirtschaftskrise 1973–76 in der BRD*, Cologne: Pahl-Rugenstein.

Hughes, H.S. 1958, *Consciousness and Society*, New York: Vintage.

Hügli, Anton and Poul Lübcke (eds.) 1992, *Philosophie im 20. Jahrhundert*, Vol. 1, *Phänomenologie, Hermeneutik, Existenzphilosophie und Kritische Theorie*, Reinbek: Rowohlt.

—— 1993, *Philosophie im 20. Jahrhundert*, Vol. 2, *Wissenschaftstheorie und Analytische Philosophie*, Reinbek: Rowohlt.

Huhn, Willi 1970, 'Etatismus – Kriegssozialismus – Nationalsozialismus in der Literatur der deutschen Sozialdemokratie', *Neue Kritik*, 55–56.

Hundt, Martin 1998, 'Zur Ethik von Marx als Historiker' in *Geschichtsphilosophie und Ethik*, edited by Domenico Losurdo, Frankfurt am Main: Lang.

Hunke, Sigrid 1995, *Das nach-kommunistische Manifest*, Engerda: Arun-Verlag.

Hunt, Alan 1981, 'Marxism and the Analysis of Law' in *Sociological Approaches to Law*, edited by Adam Podgórecki and Christopher J. Whelan, London: Croom Helm.

Hunt, E.K. and Jesse Schwartz 1972, *A Critique of Economic Theory: Selected Readings*, Harmondsworth: Penguin.

Hunt, Ian 1993, *Analytical and Dialectical Marxism*, Aldershot: Avebury.

Husserl, Edmund 1970 [1936], *The Crisis of European Sciences and Transcendental Phenomenology*, Evanston: Northwestern University Press.

Huster, Ernst-Ulrich et al. 1972, *Determinanten der westdeutschen Restauration 1945–1949*, Frankfurt am Main: Suhrkamp.

—— 1993, *Reichtum in Deutschland: Der diskrete Charme der sozialen Distanz*, Frankfurt am Main: Campus.

Iljin, Iwan 1932, *Gift. Geist und Wesen des Bolschewismus*, Berlin-Steglitz: Eckart.

—— 1946, *Die Philosophie Hegels als kontemplative Gotteslehre*, Bern: Francke.

IMSF (Institut für Marxistische Studien und Forschungen) (ed.) 1972, *Der staatsmonopolistische Kapitalismus. Einführung in marxistische Analysen aus der DDR, Frankreich und der Sowjetunion*, Frankfurt am Main: Verlag Marxistische Blätter.

—— 1973, *Klassen- und Sozialstruktur der BRD 1950–1970*, Frankfurt am Main: Verlag Marxistische Blätter.

—— 1974, *Klassenstruktur und Klassenbewusstsein in der BRD*, Frankfurt am Main: Verlag Marxistische Blätter.

—— 1981, *Staatsmonopolistischer Kapitalismus der Bundesrepublik Deutschland in Daten und Fakten*, Frankfurt am Main: Verlag Marxistische Blätter.

Institut für Gesellschaftswissenschaften beim ZK der SED 1971, *Der Imperialismus der BRD*, East Berlin: Dietz.

Institut für Marxismus-Leninismus (ed.) 1979, *Das Werk von Marx und Engels in der Literatur der deutschen Sozialdemokratie (1869–1895). Bibliographie*, East Berlin: Dietz.

Iorio, Marco 2003, *Karl Marx – Geschichte, Gesellschaft, Politik. Eine Ein- und Weiterführung*, Berlin: de Gruyter.

ISF (Initiative Sozialistisches Forum) 2000, *Der Theoretiker ist der Wert. Eine ideologiekritische Skizze der Wert- und Krisentheorie der Krisis-Gruppe*, Freiburg: Ça ira.

Israel, Joachim 1972, *Der Begriff Entfremdung. Zur Verdinglichung des Menschen in der bürokratischen Gesellschaft*, Reinbek: Rowohlt.

—— 1979, *Der Begriff Dialektik*, Reinbek: Rowohlt.

Itoh, Makoto 1980, *Value and Crisis: Essays on Marxian Economics in Japan*, London: Pluto Press.

Itoh, Makoto and Costas Lapavitsas 1999, *Political Economy of Money and Finance*, Basingstoke: Macmillan.

Jacob, Willibald (ed.) 1996, *Die Religion des Kapitalismus. Die gesellschaftlichen Auswirkungen des totalen Marktes*, Lucerne: Exodus.

Jaeggi, Urs 1969, *Macht und Herrschaft in der Bundesrepublik*, Frankfurt am Main: Fischer.

—— 1974, *Kapital und Arbeit in der Bundsrepublik*, Frankfurt am Main: Fischer.

James, William 1897, *The Will to Believe*, New York: Longmans, Green and Company.

—— 1907, *Pragmatism*, New York: Longmans, Green and Company.

—— 2008 [1912], *Essays in Radical Empiricism*, New York: Cosimo.

Jameson, Fredric 1990, *Late Marxism: Adorno, or, the Persistence of the Dialectic*, London: Verso.

—— 1991, *Postmodernism, or, the Logic of Late Capitalism*, Durham, NC: Duke University Press.

Janich, Peter 1997, *Kleine Philosophie der Naturwissenschaften*, Munich: Beck.

Jánoska, Judith et al. 1994, *Das "Methodenkapitel" von Karl Marx. Ein historischer und systematischer Kommentar*, Basel: Schwabe.

Jaroslawski, Jan 1973, *Theorie der sozialistischen Revolution. Von Marx bis Lenin*, Hamburg: Hoffmann und Campe.

Jaspers, Karl 1919, *Psychologie der Weltanschauungen*, Berlin: Springer.

—— 1931, *Die geistige Situation der Zeit*, Berlin: de Gruyter.

Jay, Martin 1984, *Marxism and Totality. The Adventures of a Concept from Lukács to Habermas*, Berkeley, CA: University of California Press.

—— 1996 [1973], *The Dialectical Imagination: A History of the Frankfurt School and the Institute for Social Research 1923–1950*, Berkeley, CA: University of California Press.

Jenner, Gero 1999, *Das Ende des Kapitalismus. Triumph oder Kollaps eines Wirtschaftsystems?* Frankfurt am Main: Fischer.

Jesse, Eckhard 1999, *Totalitarismus im 20. Jahrhundert: eine Bilanz der internationalen*

Forschung, Bonn: Bundeszentrale für politische Bildung.

Jessop, Bob (ed.) 1990–99, *Karl Marx's Social and Political Thought: Critical Assesments*, 7 Vols., London: Routledge.

Jevons, William Stanley 1970 [1871], *Theory of Political Economy*, Harmondsworth: Penguin.

Joas, Hans 1978, 'George Herbert Mead' in *Klassiker des soziologischen Denkens*, edited by Dirk Kaesler, Vol. 2, Munich: Beck.

—— 1979, 'Intersubjektivität bei Mead und Gehlen', *Archiv für Rechts- und Sozialphilosophie*, 65.

—— 1980, *Praktische Intersubjektivität. Die Entwicklung des Werkes von G.H. Mead*, Frankfurt am Main: Suhrkamp.

—— 1985, *Das Problem der Intersubjektivität. Neuere Beiträge zum Werk George Herbert Meads*, Frankfurt am Main: Suhrkamp.

—— 1986, 'Die unglückliche Ehe von Hermeneutik und Funktionalismus' in *Kommunikatives Handeln. Beiträge zu Jürgen Habermas' "Theorie des kommunikativen Handelns"*, edited by Axel Honneth and Hans Joas, Frankfurt am Main: Suhrkamp.

—— 1992, *Pragmatismus und Gesellschaftstheorie*, Frankfurt am Main: Suhrkamp.

—— 1993, 'Gemeinschaft und Demokratie in den USA. Die vergessene Vorgeschichte der Kommunitarismus-Diskussion' in *Gemeinschaft und Gerechtigkeit*, edited by Micha Brumlik and Hauke Brunkhorst, Frankfurt am Main: Fischer.

—— 1996, *The Creativity of Action*, Cambridge: Polity Press.

—— 2000 [1997], *The Genesis of Values*, Cambridge: Polity Press.

—— 2000 (ed.), *Philosophie der Demokratie. Beiträge zum Werk von John Dewey*, Frankfurt am Main: Suhrkamp.

—— 2000a: *Kriege und Werte. Studien zur Gewaltgeschichte des 20. Jahrhunderts*, Weilerswist: Velbrück.

—— 2001 (ed.), *Lehrbuch der Soziologie*, Frankfurt am Main: Campus.

Joas, Hans and Helmut Steiner (eds.) 1989, *Machtpolitischer Realismus und pazifistische Utopie. Krieg und Frieden in der Geschichte der Sozialwissenschaften*, Frankfurt am Main: Suhrkamp.

Johannes, Rolf 1995, 'Das ausgesparte Zentrum. Adornos Verhältnis zur Ökonomie' in *Soziologie im Spätkapitalismus. Zur Gesellschaftstheorie Theodor W. Adornos*, edited by G. Schweppenhäuser, Darmstadt: Wissenschaftliche Buchgesellschaft.

Jonas, Friedrich 1960, *Sozialphilosophie der industriellen Arbeitswelt*, Stuttgart: Enke.

—— 1964, *Das Selbstverständnis der ökonomischen Theorie*, Berlin: Duncker und Humblot.

—— 1976 [1968], *Geschichte der Soziologie*, 2 Vols., Reinbek: Rowohlt.

—— 1984 [1979], *The Imperative of Responsibility*, Chicago: Chicago University Press.

—— 1988 [1964], *Gnosis und spätantiker Geist*, 2 Vols., Göttingen: Vandenhoeck und Ruprecht.

Jordan, Dirk 1974, 'Der Monopolbegriff im System der Kritik der politischen Ökonomie' (137–72), and 'Der Imperialismus als monopolistischer Kapitalismus: Zur Imperialismusanalyse Lenins als Basis der Theorie des staatsmonopolitischen Kapitalismus' (212–42) in *Monopol und Staat. Zur Marx-Rezeption in der Theorie des staatsmonopolitischen Kapitalismus*, edited by Rolf Ebbinghaus, Frankfurt am Main: Suhrkamp.

jour-fixe-Initiative Berlin (ed.) 1999, *Kritische Theorie und Poststrukturalismus. Theoretische Lockerungsübungen*, Hamburg: Argument.

Juillard, Michael 1981, 'The Departmental Analysis of Growth: A Brief Comparison between Postwar France and the USA', paper presented at the third Hungarian Conference on Input-Output Techniques.

Jung, Heinz 1968, 'Die Marxsche Klassentheorie und ihre Kritiker', *Marxismus in unserer Zeit*, special issue 1 of *Marxistische Blätter*.

—— 1970, 'Zur Diskussion um den Inhalt des Begriffs "Arbeiterklasse" und zu Strukturveränderungen in der westlichen Arbeiterklasse' in *Die Arbeiterklasse im Spätkapitalismus*, edited by Wolfgang Fritz Haug, Karlsruhe: Das Argument.

Jung, Werner 1988, 'Georg Lukács als Schüler Wilhelm Diltheys', *Dilthey-Jahrbuch*, 5: 240–57.

—— 1989, *Georg Lukács*, Stuttgart: Metzler.

—— 2001, *Von der Utopie zur Ontologie. Zehn Studien zu Georg Lukács*, Bielefeld: Aisthesis.

Jünger, Ernst 1982 [1932], *Der Arbeiter. Herrschaft und Gestalt*, Stuttgart: Klett-Cotta.

Jünger, Friedrich Georg 1993 [1946], *Die Perfektion der Technik*, Frankfurt am Main: Klostermann.

Kadenbach, Johannes 1970, *Das Religionsverständnis von Karl Marx*, Munich: Schöningh.

Kahl, Joachim 1999, 'Topitsch, Ernst' in *Die großen Philosophen des 20. Jahrhunderts.*

Biographisches Lexikon, edited by Bernd Lutz, Munich: Deutscher Taschenbuch-Verlag.

Kähler, Wilfried 1997, *Nichts*, Würzburg: Königshausen und Neumann.

Kain, Philip J. 1986, *Marx's Method, Epistemology and Humanism: A Study in the Development of his Thought*, Boston: Reidel.

—— 1991, *Marx and Ethics*, Oxford: Clarendon Press.

Kalecki, Michal 1969 [1954], *Theory of Economic Dynamics: An Essay on Cyclical and Long-Run Changes in Capitalist Economy*, New York: Augustus M. Kelley.

—— 1991 [1962], 'Observerations on the Theory of Growth' in *Collected Works*, Vol. 2, *Economic Dynamics*, Oxford: Clarendon Press,

Kallscheuer, Otto 1986, *Marxismus und Erkenntnistheorie in Westeuropa*, Frankfurt am Main: Campus.

—— 1991 [1977], 'Phantom Marxismus. Rückblick auf den materialistischen Glauben' in *Glaubensfragen. Über Karl Marx und Christus und andere Tote*, Frankfurt am Main: Frankfurter Verlags-Anstalt.

Kaltenbrunner, Gerd-Klaus (ed.) 1970, *Hegel und die Folgen*, Freiburg: Rombach.

Kambartel, Friedrich 1979, 'Ist rationale Ökonomie als empirisch-quantitative Wissenschaft möglich?' in *Methodenprobleme der Wissenschaften vom gesellschaftlichen Handeln*, edited by Jürgen Mittelstraß, Frankfurt am Main: Suhrkamp.

—— 1998, *Philosophie und Politische Ökonomie*, Göttingen: Wallstein.

Kambas, Chryssoula 1985, 'Wider den "Geist der Zeit". Die antifaschistische Politik Fritz Liebs und Walter Benjamins' in *Der Fürst dieser Welt. Carl Schmitt und die Folgen. Religionstheorie und Politische Theorie*, edited by Jacob Taubes, Vol. 1, Munich: Fink.

Kamenka, Eugene 1962, *The Ethical Foundations of Marxism*, New York: Praeger.

Kaminski, Winfred 1978, *Zur Dialektik von Substanz und Subjekt bei Hegel und Marx*, Frankfurt am Main: Haag und Herchen.

Kammler, Jörg 1974, *Politische Theorie von Georg Lukács. Struktur und Praxisbezug bis 1929*, Darmstadt: Luchterhand.

Kandinsky, Wassily 1986 [1912], 'Über das Geistige in der Kunst – besonders in der Malerei' in *Der blaue Reiter: Dokumente einer geistigen Bewegung*, edited by Andreas Hüneke, Leipzig: Reclam.

Kant, Immanuel 1949 [1785], *Foundations of the Metaphysics of Morals* in *Critique of Practical Reason and Other Writings in Moral Philosophy*, Chicago: University of Chicago Press.

—— 1949a [1788], *Critique of Practical Reason* in *Critique of Practical Reason and Other Writings in Moral Philosophy*, Chicago: University of Chicago Press.

—— 1952 [1790], *Critique of Judgement*, Oxford: Clarendon Press.

—— 1968 ff.: *Werkausgabe*, 12 Vols., Frankfurt am Main: Suhrkamp.

—— 1998 [1781], *Critique of Pure Reason*, Cambridge: Cambridge University Press.

—— 2007 [1800], *Anthropology From a Pragmatic Point of View* in *Anthropology, History, and Education*, Cambridge: Cambridge University Press.

Kapferer, Norbert 1990, *Das Feindbild der marxistisch-leninistischen Philosophie in der DDR (1945–1988)*, Darmstadt: Wissenschaftliche Buchgesellschaft.

—— 2002, *Die Nazifizierung der Philosophie an der Universität Breslau*, Münster: Lit.

Kapp, Karl William 1979 [1963], *Soziale Kosten der Marktwirtschaft*, Frankfurt am Main: Fischer.

Karady, Victor 1999, *Gewalterfahrung und Utopie. Juden in der europäischen Moderne*, Frankfurt am Main: Fischer.

Karmasin, Matthias 1996, *Ethik als Gewinn. Zur ethischen Rekonstruktion der Ökonomie*, Vienna: Linde.

Kaesler, Dirk (ed.) 1976–8, *Klassiker des soziologischen Denkens*, 2 Vols., Munich: Beck.

—— 1981, 'Der Streit um die Bestimmung der Soziologie auf den deutschen Soziologentagen 1910 bis 1930' in *Soziologie in Deutschland und Österreich 1918–1945. Materialien zur Entwicklung, Emigration und Wirkungsgeschichte*, edited by M. Rainer Lepsius, Opladen: Westdeutscher Verlag.

—— 1984, *Die frühe deutsche Soziologie 1909 bis 1934 und ihre Entstehungs-Milieus. Eine wissenschaftssoziologische Untersuchung*, Opladen: Westdeutscher Verlag.

—— 1991 [1985], *Sociological Adventures: Earle Edward Eubank's Visits with European Sociologists*, New Brunswick: Transaction Publications.

—— 1999, *Klassiker der Soziologie*, 2 Vols., Munich: Beck.

Kather, Regine 1994, 'Die Wahrheit der Wissenschaft: "Deutsche und Jüdische Physik"' in *Jüdisches Denken in der europäischen Geistesgeschichte*, edited by Eveline Goodman-

Thau and Michael Daxner, Vol. 2, Berlin: Akademie-Verlag.
Kaulbach, Friedrich 1978, *Das Prinzip Handlung in der Philosophie Kants*, Berlin: de Gruyter.
—— 1990, *Philosophie des Perspektivismus, Erster Teil: Wahrheit und Perspektive bei Kant, Hegel und Nietzsche*, Tübingen: Mohr.
Kautsky, Karl 1880, *Der Einfluss der Volksvermehrung, auf den Fortschritt der Gesellschaft untersucht*, Vienna: Bloch und Hasbach.
—— 1888, *Thomas More und seine Utopie*, Stuttgart: Dietz.
—— 1893, *Der Parlamentarismus, die Volksgesetzgebung und die Sozialdemokratie*, Stuttgart: Dietz.
—— 1895, 'Die materialistische Geschichtsauffassung und der psychologische Antrieb', *Die Neue Zeit*.
—— 1899, 'Bernstein und die Dialektik', *Die Neue Zeit*, 17, 2: 4–16.
—— 1902, *Die soziale Revolution*, Berlin: Vorwärts.
—— 1902a: *Die Sozialdemokratie und die katholische Kirche*, Berlin: Vorwärts.
—— 1908, *Der Ursprung des Christentums*, Stuttgart: Dietz.
—— 1909, *Der Weg zur Macht*, Berlin: Vorwärts.
—— 1918, *Die Diktatur des Proletariats*, Vienna: Wiener Volksbuchhandlung.
—— 1919, *Terrorismus und Kommunismus. Ein Beitrag zur Naturgeschichte der Revolution*, Berlin: Neues Vaterland.
—— 1921, *Von der Demokratie zur Staats-Sklaverei*, Berlin: Freiheit.
—— 1927, *Die materialistische Geschichtsauffassung*, 2 Vols., Berlin: Dietz.
—— 1947 [1895], *Die Vorläufer des neueren Sozialismus*, 2 Vols., Berlin: Dietz.
—— 1971 [1892], *The Class Struggle (Erfurt Program)*, New York: W.W. Norton & Company.
—— 1976 [1899], *Bernstein und das Sozialdemokratische Programm. Eine Antikritik*, Berlin: Dietz.
—— 1980 [1887], *Karl Marx' ökonomische Lehren. Gemeinverständlich dargestellt und erläutert*, Berlin: Dietz.
Kaye, Harvey J. 1984, *The British Marxist Historians: An Introductory Analysis*, Cambridge: Polity Press.
Keel, Othmar 1995, 'Bertolt Brecht und das erste Testament', *Bibel und Kirche*, 50: 13 ff.
Keller, Ernst 1984, *Der junge Lukács. Antibürger und wesentliches Leben. Literatur- und Kulturkritik 1902–1915*, Frankfurt am Main: Sendler.
Kellner, Douglas (ed.) 1998, *Technology, War, and Fascism: Collected Papers of Herbert Marcuse*, Vol. 1, New York: Routledge.
Kelpanides, Michael 1999, *Das Scheitern der Marxschen Theorie und der Aufstieg des westlichen Neomarxismus. Über die Ursachen einer unzeitgemäßen Renaissance*, Bern: Lang.
Kelsen, Hans 1948, *The Political Theory of Bolshevism*. Berkeley, CA: University of California Press.
—— 1960 [1928], 'Das Problem der Gerechtigkeit' in *Reine Rechtslehre*, Vienna: Deuticke.
—— 1965 [1920], *Sozialismus und Staat. Eine Untersuchung der politischen Theorie des Marxismus*, Vienna: Verlag der Wiener Volksbuchhandlung.
—— 1967, *Demokratie und Sozialismus. Ausgewählte Aufsätze (1926–1954)*, Vienna: Verlag der Wiener Volksbuchhandlungen.
—— 1985, *Die Illusion der Gerechtigkeit. Eine kritische Untersuchung der Sozialphilosophie Platons. Aus dem Nachlass herausgegeben von Kurt Ringhofer und Robert Walter*, Vienna: Manz.
Kemper, Peter (ed.) 1990, *Martin Heidegger – Faszination und Erschrecken. Die politische Dimension einer Philosophie*, Frankfurt am Main: Campus.
Kempski, Jürgen von 1952, *Charles S. Peirce und der Pragmatismus*, Stuttgart: Kohlhammer.
Kennedy, Margrit 1991, *Geld ohne Zinsen und Inflation. Ein Tauschmittel, das jedem dient*, Munich: Goldmann.
Kerber, Harald 1981, *Transzendentalismus und kritische Gesellschaftstheorie: zur Kritik der erkenntnistheoretischen Begründung der Marxschen Theorie durch Max Adler*, Osnabrück: Druckerei der Universität Osnabrück.
Kerber, Harald and Arnold Schmieder (eds.) 1991, *Soziologie. Arbeitsfelder, Theorien, Ausbildung. Ein Grundkurs*, Reinbek: Rowohlt.
Kern, Bruno 1992, *Theologie im Horizont des Marxismus. Zur Geschichte der Marxismusrezeption in der lateinamerikanischen Theologie der Befreiung*, Mainz: Grünewald.
Kern, Horst and Michael Schumann: *Industriearbeit und Arbeiterbewusstsein. Eine empirische Untersuchung über den Einfluss der aktuellen technischen Entwicklung auf die industrielle Arbeit und das Arbeiterbewusstsein*, 2 Vols., Frankfurt am Main: Europäische Verlags-Anstalt.
Kern, Lucian (ed.) 1984, *Probleme der postindustriellen Gesellschaft*, Königstein: Athenäum.

Kern, Walter 1976, *Atheismus, Marxismus, Christentum*, Innsbruck: Tyrolia.

Kersting, Wolfgang 1994, *Die Politische Philosophie des Gesellschaftsvertrages*, Darmstadt: Primus-Verlag.

Kersting, Wolfgang (ed.) 1996, *Gerechtigkeit als Tausch? Auseinandersetzungen mit der politischen Philosophie Otfried Höffes*, Frankfurt am Main: Suhrkamp.

—— 1997, *Recht, Gerechtigkeit und demokratische Tugend*, Frankfurt am Main: Suhrkamp.

—— 2000, *Politische Philosophie des Sozialstaats*, Weilerswist: Velbrück.

—— 2000a: *Theorien der sozialen Gerechtigkeit*, Stuttgart: Metzler.

Kessler, Rainer and Eva Los (eds.), *Eigentum: Freiheit und Fluch. Ökonomische und biblische Einwürfe*, Gütersloh: Kaiser.

Kesting, Hanno 1959, *Geschichtsphilosophie und Weltbürgerkrieg*, Heidelberg: Winter.

Kesting, Hanno, Heinrich Popitz et al. 1957, *Technik und Industriearbeit/Das Gesellschaftsbild des Arbeiters*, Tübingen: Mohr.

Kettner, Matthias (ed.) 2000, *Angewandte Ethik als Politikum*, Frankfurt am Main: Suhrkamp.

Keulartz, Jozef 1995, *Die verkehrte Welt des Jürgen Habermas*, Hamburg: Junius.

Keynes, John Maynard 1964 [1936], *The General Theory of Employment, Interest and Money*, New York: Harcourt, Brace and World.

Khella, Karam 1995, *Mythos Marx – Eine Geschichts- und Theorierevision*, Hamburg: Theorie und Praxis.

Kiefer, Josef 1991, *Die Marxsche Theorie als Computersimulation. Versuch einer systemtheoretischen Explikation des Marxschen Forschungsprogramms*, Frankfurt am Main: Lang.

Kiel, Albrecht 1998, *Gottesstaat und Pax Americana. Zur politischen Theologie von Carl Schmitt und Eric Voegelin*, Cuxhaven: Junghans.

Kienbaum 2003, press release from Kienbaum Management Consultants, 4 April 2003, *Aufsichtsratsbezüge: Missverhältnis zwischen Vergütung und Aufgabe*, available at: <www.kienbaum.de>.

Kiesewetter, Hubert 1995, *Von Hegel zu Hitler. Eine Analyse der Hegelschen Machtstaatsideologie und der politischen Wirkungsgeschichte des Rechtshegelianismus*, Hamburg: Hoffmann und Campe.

Kim, Duk-Yung 1999, 'Nietzsche und die Soziologie. Georg Simmel und Max Weber' in *Jahrbuch für Soziologiegeschichte 1995*, edited by Carsten Klingemann et al., Opladen: Leske und Budrich.

Kim, Kyung-Mi 1999, *Hilferding und Marx. Geld- und Kredittheorie in Rudolf Hilferdings "Das Finanzkapital" und im Marxschen "Kapital"*, Cologne: PapyRossa.

King, J.E. (ed.) 1990, *Marxian Economics*, 3 Vols., Aldershot: Gower.

Kiss, Garbor 1971, *Marxismus als Soziologie. Theorie und Empirie in den Sozialwissenschaften der DDR, UdSSR, Polens, der CSSR, Ungarns, Bulgariens und Rumäniens*, Reinbek: Rowohlt.

Kitching, Gavin 1988, *Karl Marx and the Philosophy of Praxis*, London: Routledge.

—— 1994, *Marxism and Science. Analysis of an Obsession*, University Park: Pennsylvania State University Press.

Kitching, Gavin and Nigel Pleasants 2002, *Marx and Wittgenstein: Knowledge, Morality and Politics*, London: Routledge.

Kittsteiner, Heinz-Dieter 1977, 'Objektivität und Totalität. Vier Thesen zur Geschichtstheorie von Karl Marx' in *Theorie der Geschichte. Beiträge zur Historik*, Vol. 1, *Objektivität und Parteilichkeit*, edited by Reinhart Koselleck et al., Munich: Deutscher Taschenbuch-Verlag.

—— 1977a: '"Logisch" und "Historisch". Über Differenzen des Marxschen und Engelschen Systems der Wissenschaft', *Internationale wissenschaftliche Korrespondenz zur Geschichte der deutschen Arbeiterbewegung*, 13, 1: 1–47.

—— 1980, *Naturabsicht und unsichtbare Hand. Zur Kritik des geschichtsphilosophischen Denkens*, Frankfurt am Main: Ullstein.

—— 2001, 'Deutscher Idealismus' in *Deutsche Erinnerungsorte*, Vol. 1, edited by Etienne Francois and Hagen Schulze, Munich: Beck.

—— 2004, *Mit Marx für Heidegger – Mit Heidegger für Marx*, Munich: Fink.

Klages, Helmut 1964, *Technischer Humanismus. Philosophie und Soziologie der Arbeit bei Karl Marx*, Stuttgart: Enke.

—— 1965, 'Marxismus und Technik' in *Technik im technischen Zeitalter. Stellungnahmen zur geschichtlichen Situation*, edited by Hans Freyer et al., Düsseldorf: Schilling.

—— 1971, *Planungspolitik. Probleme und Perspektiven der umfassenden Zukunftsgestaltung*, Stuttgart: Kohlhammer.

—— 1972, *Geschichte der Soziologie*, Munich: Juventa.

—— 1979, *Die unruhige Gesellschaft. Untersuchungen über Grenzen und Probleme sozialer Stabilität*, Munich: Beck.

Klages, Helmut and Helmut Quaritsch (eds.) 1994, *Zur geisteswissenschaftlichen Bedeutung von Arnold Gehlen*, Berlin: Duncker und Humblot.

Klages, Ludwig 1926, *Vom kosmogonischen Eros*, Jena: Diederichs.

—— 1929 [1913], 'Mensch und Erde' in *Mensch und Erde. Sieben Abhandlungen*, Jena: Diederichs.

—— 1929–32, *Der Geist als Widersacher der Seele*, 3 Vols., Leipzig: Barth.

Klaus, Georg 1958, *Jesuiten, Gott, Materie*, Berlin: VEB Deutscher Verlag der Wissenschaften.

—— 1961, *Kybernetik in philosophischer Sicht*, East Berlin: Dietz.

—— 1968, *Wörterbuch der Kybernetik*, East Berlin: Dietz.

Klein, Naomi 2000, *No Logo: Taking Aim at the Brand Bullies*, New York: Picador.

Klenner, Hermann 1982, *Marxismus und Menschenrechte. Studien zur Rechtsphilosophie*, East Berlin: Akademie-Verlag.

Kley, Roland 1989, *Vertragstheorien der Gerechtigkeit. Eine philosophische Kritik der Theorien von John Rawls, Robert Nozick und James Buchanan*, Stuttgart: Haupt.

Klingemann, Carsten 1996, *Soziologie im Dritten Reich*, Baden-Baden: Nomos.

—— et al. (eds.) 2001, *Jahrbuch für Soziologiegeschichte 1997/1998*, Opladen: Leske und Budrich.

Klotz, Johannes (ed.) 1999, *Schlimmer als die Nazis? Das "Schwarzbuch des Kommunismus", die neue Totalitarismusdebatte und der Geschichtsrevisionismus*, Cologne: PapyRossa.

Knapp, Georg Friedrich 1921 [1905], *Staatliche Theorie des Geldes*, Munich: Duncker und Humblot.

Knechtel, Rüdiger and Jürgen Fiedler 2000, *Stalins DDR. Berichte politisch Verfolgter*, Leipzig: Forum.

Kneer, Georg and Armin Nassehi (eds.) 1997, *Soziologische Gesellschaftbegriffe. Konzepte moderner Zeitdiagnosen*, Munich: Fink.

—— 2001, *Klassische Gesellschaftsbegriffe der Soziologie*, Munich: Fink.

Kniest, Christoph et al. (eds.) 2001, *Eingreifendes Denken. Wolfgang Fritz Haug zum 65. Geburtstag*, Münster: Westfälisches Dampfboot.

Knirsch, Peter 1969, *Strukturen und Formen zentraler Wirtschaftsplanung*, Berlin: Duncker und Humblot.

Knoche, Hansjürgen 1980, *Die DKP. Organisation, Ideologie, Politik*, Hannover: Niedersächsische Landeszentrale für politische Bildung.

Koch, Hans-Joachim et al. (eds.) 1994, *Theorien der Gerechtigkeit. 15. Tagung der deutschen Sektion der internationalen Vereinigung für Rechts- und Sozialphilosophie in Hamburg, 30. Sept.–2. Okt. 1992*, Stuttgart: Steiner.

Koch, Hans-Gerhard 1961, *Abschaffung Gottes? Das Buch über den Atheismus*, Stuttgart: Quell-Verlag.

Koch, Max 1998 [1994], *Vom Strukturwandel einer Klassengesellschaft. Theoretische Diskussion und empirische Analyse*, Münster: Westfälisches Dampfboot.

Koch, Traugott, Klaus-Michael Kodalle and Hermann Schweppenhäuser 1973, *Negative Dialektik und die Idee der Versöhnung. Eine Kontroverse über Theodor W. Adorno*, Stuttgart: Kohlhammer.

Kocka, Jürgen 1966, 'Karl Marx und Max Weber. Ein methodologischer Vergleich', *Zeitschrift für die gesamte Staatswissenschaft*, 122, 328–357.

—— 1977, 'Karl Marx und Max Weber im Vergleich. Sozialwissenschaften zwischen Dogmatismus und Dezisionismus' in *Sozialgeschichte. Begriff–Entwicklung–Probleme*, Göttingen: Vandenhoeck und Ruprecht.

—— 1986, *Arbeiter und Bürger im 19. Jahrhundert. Varianten ihres Verhältnisses im europäischen Vergleich*, Munich: Oldenbourg.

—— 1988, *Bürgertum im 19. Jahrhundert*, Göttingen: Vandenhoeck und Ruprecht.

—— 1990, *Arbeitsverhältnisse und Arbeiterexistenzen. Grundlagen der Klassenbildung im 19. Jahrundert*, Bonn: Dietz.

Kodalle, Klaus-Michael 1973, *Politik als Macht und Mythos. Carl Schmitts "Politische Theologie"*, Stuttgart: Kohlhammer.

—— 1998, 'Fichtes Einheitsphilosophie: "Erpresste Versöhnung"?' in *Bürgersinn und Kritik. Festschrift für Udo Bermbach zum 60. Geburtstag*, edited by Herfried Münkler et al., Baden-Baden: Nomos.

—— 2000, *Angst vor der Moderne: philosophische Antworten auf Krisenerfahrungen. Der Mikrokosmos Jena 1900–1940*. Würzburg: Königshausen und Neumann.

Koenen, Gerd (ed.) 1998, *Deutschland und die russische Revolution 1917–1924*, Munich: Fink.

—— 1992, *Die großen Gesänge: Lenin, Stalin, Mao Tse-tung. Führerkulte und Heldenmythen des 20. Jahrhunderts*, Frankfurt am Main: Eichborn.

—— 2000, *Utopie der Säuberung – Was war der Kommunismus?* Berlin: Fest.

—— 2001, *Das rote Jahrzehnt – Unsere kleine deutsche Kulturrevolution*, Cologne: Kiepenheuer und Witsch.

Koestler, Arthur 1941, *Darkness at Noon*, London: Macmillan.

—— 1950, *The God that Failed: Six Studies in Communism*, London: Hamilton.

Kohlmann, Ulrich (ed.) 2001, *Karl Kautsky, Leo Trotzki, John Dewey: Politik und Moral. Die Zweck-Mittel-Debatte in der neueren Philosophie und Politik*, Lüneburg: zu Klampen.

Köhnke, Klaus Christian 1986, *Entstehung und Aufstieg des Neukantianismus. Die deutsche Universitätsphilosophie zwischen Idealismus und Positivismus*, Frankfurt am Main: Suhrkamp.

Kojève, Alexandre 1980, *Introduction to the Reading of Hegel: Lectures on the Phenomenology of Spirit*, Ithaca, NY: Cornell University Press.

Kołakowski, Leszek 1960, *Der Mensch ohne Alternative*, Munich: Piper.

—— 1969, *Towards a Marxist Humanism. Essays on the Left Today*, New York: Grove.

—— 2005 [1976], *Main Currents of Marxism: The Founders – The Golden Age – The Breakdown*, New York: W.W. Norton and Company.

Kolesnikov, Sonia 2002, 'Asia Central Banks Upping Gold Reserves', Business and Economic Desk, United Press International (UPI), 13 October.

Koller, Peter 1987, *Neue Theorien des Sozialkontrakts*, Berlin: Duncker und Humblot.

Kondylis, Panjokis 1987, *Marx und die griechische Antike. Zwei Studien*, Heidelberg: Manutius.

König, René (ed.) 1958, *Das Fischer Lexikon: Soziologie*, Frankfurt am Main: Fischer.

—— 1975 [1937], *Kritik der historisch-existenzialistischen Soziologie. Ein Beitrag zur Begründung der objektiven Soziologie*, Munich: Piper.

—— 1981, 'Soziologie in Berlin um 1930' in *Soziologie in Deutschland und Österreich 1918–1945. Materialien zur Entwicklung, Emigration und Wirkungsgeschichte*, edited by M. Rainer Lepsius, Opladen: Westdeutscher Verlag.

—— 1984 [1980], *Leben im Widerspruch. Versuch einer intellektuellen Biographie*, Frankfurt am Main: Ullstein.

—— 1987, *Soziologie in Deutschland. Begründer, Verfechter, Verächter*, Munich: Hanser.

Kondratieff, N.D. 1926, 'Die langen Wellen der Konjuktur', *Archiv für Sozialwissenschaft und Sozialpolitik*, 56, 3.

Korff, Wilhelm (ed.) 1999, *Handbuch der Wirtschaftsethik*, 4 Vols., Gütersloh: Gütersloher Verlagshaus.

Kornai, János 1992, *The Socialist System: The Political Economy of Communism*, Princeton: Princeton University Press.

Korsch, Karl 1929, *Die materialistische Geschichtsauffassung. Eine Auseinandersetzung mit Karl Kautsky*, Leipzig: Hirschfeld.

—— 1970 [1923], *Marxism and Philosophy*, London: New Left Books.

—— 1971, *Die materialistische Geschichtsauffassung und andere Schriften*, Frankfurt am Main: Europäische Verlags-Anstalt.

—— 1972, *Three Essays on Marxism*, New York: Monthly Review Press.

—— 1977, *Revolutionary Theory*, Austin: University of Texas Press.

—— 1981 [1938], *Karl Marx. Marxistische Theorie und Klassenbewegung*, Reinbek: Rowohlt.

—— 1996, *Gesamtausgabe*, Vol. 5, *Krise des Marxismus. Schriften 1928–1935*, Amsterdam: IISG.

Korsgaard, Christina and Onora O'Neill 1996, *The Sources of Normativity*, Cambridge: Cambridge University Press.

Koselleck, Reinhart 1988 [1959], *Critique and Crisis: Enlightenment and the Pathogenesis of Modern Society*, Cambridge, MA: MIT Press.

Koselleck, Reinhart et al. (eds.) 1977, *Theorie der Geschichte. Beiträge zur Historik*, Vol. 1, *Objektivität und Parteilichkeit*, Munich: Deutscher Taschenbuch-Verlag.

Kosik, Karel 1976 [1963], *Dialectics of the Concrete: A Study on Problems of Man and World*, Dordrecht: Reidel.

Koslowski, Peter 1982, *Gesellschaft und Staat. Ein unvermeidlicher Dualismus*, Stuttgart: Klett-Cotta.

—— 1991, *Gesellschaftliche Koordination. Eine ontologische und kulturwissenschaftliche Theorie der Marktwirtschaft*, Tübingen: Mohr.

—— 1994, *Die Ordnung der Wirtschaft. Studien zur praktischen Philosophie und Politischen Ökonomie*, Tübingen: Mohr.

—— 1995, *The Theory of Ethical Economy in the Historical School. Wilhelm Roscher, Lorenz von Stein, Gustav Schmoller, Wilhelm Dilthey and Contemporary Theory*, Berlin: Springer.

—— 1996 [1982], 'Ethics of Capitalism' in *Ethics of Capitalism and Critique of Sociobiology*, Berlin: Springer.

—— 1998, *Ethik des Kapitalismus*, Tübingen: Mohr-Siebeck.

—— 2000, *Contemporary Economic Ethics and Business Ethics*, Berlin: Springer.
—— 2000a: *The Theory of Capitalism in the German Economic Tradition. Historism, Ordo-Liberalism, Solidarism*, Berlin: Springer.
—— 2001 [1988], *Principles of Ethical Economy*, Dordrecht: Kluwer Academic Publishing.
Kößler, Reinhart and Hans Wienold 2001, *Gesellschaft bei Marx*, Münster: Westfälisches Dampfboot.
Kostede, Norbert 1976, 'Kritik neuerer Analysen zur Klassenstruktur der BRD. Rezension der Studien des IMSF und des PKA', *Gesellschaft: Beiträge zur Marxschen Theorie*, 7: 119–32.
Koth, Harald 1993, *"Meine Zeit wird wieder kommen..." Das Leben des Karl Kautsky*, Berlin: Dietz.
Kotowski, Elke-Vera et al. (eds.) 1999, *Wirtschaft und Gesellschaft. Franz Oppenheimer und die Grundlegung der Sozialen Marktwirtschaft*, Berlin: Philo.
Kowalski, Werner (ed.) 1990, *Karl Kautsky. Referate und Beiträge der Halleschen Konferenz anlässlich des 50. Todestages*, Halle: Martin-Luther-Universität.
Kracauer, Siegried 1978 [1922], 'Soziologie als Wissenschaft. Eine erkenntniskritische Untersuchung' in *Schriften*, Vol. 1, Frankfurt am Main: Suhrkamp.
—— 1998 [1929], *The Salaried Masses: Duty and Distraction in Weimar Germany*, London: Verso.
Krader, Lawrence 1973, *Ethnologie und Anthropologie bei Marx*, Munich: Hanser.
Krahl, Hans-Jürgen 1969, 'Der politische Widerspruch in der Kritischen Theorie Adornos', *Frankfurter Rundschau*, 13 August 1969.
—— 1970, 'Bemerkungen zum Verhältnis von Kapital und Hegelscher Wesenslogik' in *Aktualität und Folgen der Philosophie Hegels*, edited by Oskar Negt, Frankfurt am Main: Suhrkamp.
Kraiker, Gerhard 1977, 'Theorie der bürgerlichen Gesellschaft bei Karl Marx und Friedrich Engels' in *Handbuch Politischer Theorien und Ideologien*, edited by Franz Neumann, Reinbek: Rowohlt.
—— 2000, 'Theorie von Karl Marx/Friedrich Engels: Gegen Dogmatisierung und Marginalisierung' in *Handbuch politischer Theorien und Ideologien*, edited by Franz Neumann, Opladen: Westdeutscher Verlag.
Kral, Josef 1920, *Der christliche Sozialismus? Die Versöhnung von Christentum und Sozialismus. System einer Gesellschaftreform nach Naturrecht und Sittengesetz*, Dillingen: Keller.
Krämer, Hans Leo 1983, *Soziale Schichtung. Einführung in die moderne Theoriediskussion*, Frankfurt am Main: Diesterweg.
Kramer, Rolf 1992, *Soziale Gerechtigkeit – Inhalt und Grenzen*, Berlin: Duncker und Humblot.
Kramm, Lothar 1979, *Politische Ökonomie. Eine kritische Darstellung*, Munich: Beck.
Krätke, Michael R. 1996, 'Marxismus als Sozialwissenschaft' in *Materialien zum Historisch-Kritischen Wörterbuch des Marxismus*, edited by Michael R. Krätke and Frigga Haug, Hamburg: Argument.
—— 2002, *Kleine Geschichte der Weltwirtschaft. Staaten und Märkte*, Hamburg: VSA.
Kraus, Chris 2001, *Hatred of Capitalism. A Semiotext(e) Reader*, Los Angeles: Semiotext[e].
Kraus, Hans-Joachim 1982, *Theologische Religionskritik*, Neukirchen-Vluyn: Neukirchener Verlag.
Kraus, Rainer 1991, *Die Imperialismusdebatte zwischen Vladimir I. Lenin und Karl Kautsky. Eine vergleichende Analyse ihrer Theorien*, Frankfurt am Main: Lang.
Krause, Günter 1998, *Wirtschaftstheorie in der DDR*, Marburg: Metropolis.
Krause, Ulrich 1982 [1979], *Money and Abstract Labour*, London: New Left Books.
Kraushaar, Wolfgang (ed.) 1998, *Frankfurter Schule und Studentenbewegung. Von der Flaschenpost zum Molotowcocktail (1946 bis 1995)*, 3 Vols., Hamburg: Hamburger Edition.
Kraushaar, Wolfgang 1998a: 1968 – *das Jahr, das alles verändert hat*, Munich: Piper.
Krebs, Angelika (ed.) 2000, *Gleichheit oder Gerechtigkeit. Texte der neuen Egalitarismuskritik*, Frankfurt am Main: Suhrkamp.
—— 2002, *Arbeit und Liebe. Die philosophischen Grundlagen sozialer Gerechtigkeit*, Frankfurt am Main: Suhrkamp.
Kreckel, Reinhard 1992, *Politische Soziologie der sozialen Ungleichheit*, Frankfurt am Main: Campus.
Kriele, Martin 1994, *Einführung in die Staatlehre. Die geschichtlichen Legitimitätsgrundlagen des demokratischen Verfassungsstaates*, Opladen: Westdeutscher Verlag.
Krijnen, Christian and Ernst Wolfgang Orth (eds.) 1998, *Sinn, Geltung, Wert. Neukantianische Motive in der modernen Kulturphilosophie*, Würzburg: Königshausen und Neumann.

Krockow, Christian Graf von 1958, *Die Entscheidung. Eine Untersuchung über Ernst Jünger, Carl Schmitt, Martin Heidegger*, Stuttgart: Campus.

Kromphardt, Jürgen 1991, *Konzeptionen und Analysen des Kapitalismus – von seiner Entstehung bis zur Gegenwart*, Göttingen: Vandenhoeck und Ruprecht.

Kröner, Ludwig 1977, *Eschatologie bei Karl Marx*, Erlangen: Palm und Enke.

Kroner, Richard 1914, *Kants Weltanschauung*, Tübingen: J.C.B. Mohr.

—— 1921, *Von Kant bis Hegel*, Vol. 1, Tübingen: J.C.B. Mohr.

Krugmann, Paul 1996, *Pop Internationalism*, Cambridge, MA: MIT Press.

Krummbachner, Josef 1991, *Geschichte der Wirtschaftstheorie*, Munich: Verlag für Wirtschaftsskripten.

Kruse, Volker 1994, *Historisch-soziologische Zeitdiagnosen nach 1945. Eduard Heimann, Alfred v. Martin, Hans Freyer*, Frankfurt am Main: Suhrkamp.

—— 1999, *"Geschichts- und Sozialphilosophie" oder "Wirklichkeitswissenschaft"? Die deutsche historische Soziologie und die logischen Kategorien René Königs und Max Webers*, Frankfurt am Main: Suhrkamp.

Krygier, Martin, et al. 1990, 'Debate: Marxism and the Rule of Law', *Law and Social Inquiry*, 15, 4: 633–732.

Krygier, Martin 1994, 'Marxism, Communism, and the Rule of Law', *Poznan Studies in the Philosophy of the Sciences and the Humanities*, 36: 137–71.

Krysmanski, Hans Jürgen 1971, *Soziologie des Konflikts. Materialien und Modelle*, Reinbek: Rowohlt.

—— 1989, 'Entwicklung und Stand der klassentheoretischen Diskussion', *Kölner Zeitschrift für Soziologie und Sozialpsychologie*, 41: 149–67.

Kübler, Friedrich (ed.) 1985, *Verrechtlichung von Wirtschaft, Arbeit und sozialer Solidarität. Vergleichende Analysen*, Frankfurt am Main: Suhrkamp.

Kuczinsky, Jürgen 1967, *Die Geschichte der Lage der Arbeiter unter dem Kapitalismus*, Berlin: Akademie-Verlag.

Küenzlen, Gottfried 1997, *Der neue Mensch. Eine Untersuchung zur säkularen Religionsgeschichte der Moderne*, Frankfurt am Main: Suhrkamp.

Kuhn, Thomas S. 1970 [1962], *The Structure of Scientific Revolutions*, Chicago: University of Chicago Press.

Kuhne, Frank 1995, *Begriff und Zitat bei Marx. Die idealistische Struktur des Kapitals und ihre nicht-idealistische Darstellung bei Marx*, Lüneburg: zu Klampen.

Kühne, Karl 1972, *Ökonomie und Marxismus I: Zur Renaissance des Marxschen Systems*, Berlin: Luchterhand.

—— 1974, *Ökonomie und Marxismus II: Zur Dynamik des Marxschen Systems*, Berlin: Luchterhand.

—— 1975, *Geschichte und Profitrate im Marxismus*, Berlin: Luchterhand.

Künzli, Arnold 1966, *Karl Marx. Eine Psychographie*, Frankfurt am Main: Europa-Verlag.

Kurz, Robert 1994, 'Fetisch Arbeit. Der Marxismus und die Logik der Modernisierung' in *Der Marxismus in seinem Zeitalter*, edited by Helmut Fleischer, Leipzig: Reclam.

—— 1994a [1991], *Der Kollaps der Modernisierung*, Leipzig: Reclam.

—— 1999, *Schwarzbuch Kapitalismus. Ein Abgesang auf die Marktwirtschaft*, Frankfurt am Main: Eichborn.

—— 2000, *Marx lesen. Die wichtigsten Texte von Karl Marx für das 21. Jahrhundert*, Frankfurt am Main: Eichborn.

Kuschel, Karl-Josef et al. (eds.) 1999, *Ein Ethos für eine Welt? Globalisierung als ethische Herausforderung*, Frankfurt am Main: Campus.

Kutschera, Franz von 1993, *Die falsche Objektivität*, Berlin: de Gruyter.

Kutter, Hermann 1904, *Sie müssen! Ein offenes Wort an die christliche Gesellschaft*, Zürich: Füssli.

Kutter, Hermann (junior) 1965, *Hermann Kutters Lebenswerk*, Zürich: EVZ-Verlag.

Kymlicka, Will 1990, *Contemporary Political Philosophy*, Oxford: Oxford University Press.

Labedz, Leopold (ed.) 1965, *Der Revisionismus*, Cologne: Kiepenheuer & Witsch.

Labica, Georges 1998, *Karl Marx–Thesen über Feuerbach*, Hamburg: Argument.

Labriola, Antonio 1966 [1896], *Essays on the Materialistic Conception of History*, New York: Monthly Review Press.

Laclau, Ernesto 1977, *Politics and Ideology in Marxist Theory. Capitalism–Fascism–Populism*, London: New Left Books.

—— 1996, *Emancipation(s)*, London: Verso.

Laclau, Ernesto and Chantal Mouffe 1985, *Hegemony and Socialist Strategy: Towards a Radical Democratic Politics*, London: Verso.

Lacroix, Jean and Henri de Lubac 1948, *Der Mensch in christlicher und marxistischer Schau*, Offenburg: Verlag der Dokumente.

Lafargue, Paul 2011 [1883], 'The Right to be Lazy' in *The Right to be Lazy and Other Essays*, Edinburgh: AK Press.

Lafont, Cristina 2000, *Heidegger, Language, and World-Disclosure*, Cambridge: Cambridge University Press.

Landauer, Gustav 1967 [1911], *Aufruf zum Sozialismus*, Frankfurt am Main: Europäische Verlags-Anstalt.

Landgrebe, Christian and Jörg Plath (ed.) 1998, *'68 und die Folgen. Ein unvollständiges Lexikon*, Berlin: Argon.

Landgrebe, Ludwig 1957, 'Hegel und Marx', *Marxismusstudien*, 1: 39–53.

Landmann, Michael 1977, *Was ist Philosophie?* Bonn: Bouvier.

Landshut, Siegfried 1932, 'Einleitung' in idem (ed.): *Der historische Materialismus*, Stuttgart: Kröner.

—— 1969 [1956], 'Die Gegenwart im Lichte der Marxschen Lehre' in *Kritik der Soziologie*, Berlin: Luchterhand.

—— 1969a [1929], *Kritik der Soziologie*, Berlin: Luchterhand.

Langbehn, Julius 1922 [1890], *Rembrandt als Erzieher. Von einem Deutschen*, Weimar: A. Duncker.

Lange, Ernst Michael 1977, *Rezeption und Revision von Hegelschen Themen im frühen Werk Hans Freyers*, dissertation, FU Berlin.

—— 1980, *Das Prinzip Arbeit*, Frankfurt am Main: Ullstein.

Lange, Friedrich Albert 1865, *Die Arbeiterfrage in ihrer Bedeutung für Gegenwart und Zukunft*, Duisburg: Falk & Volmer.

—— 1887 [1866], *Geschichte des Materialismus und Kritik seiner Bedeutung in der Gegenwart*, Leipzig: Baedeker.

Lange, Max G. 1955, *Marxismus, Leninismus, Stalinismus: zur Kritik des dialektischen Materialismus*, Stuttgart: Klett.

Lange, Oskar 1963, *Political Economy*, Oxford: Pergamon.

—— 1977 [1935], 'Marxsche Ökonomie und moderne Wirtschaftstheorie' in *Ökonomisch-theoretische Studien*, Frankfurt am Main: Europäische Verlags-Anstalt.

Lange, Oskar and Fred M. Taylor 1938, *On the Economic Theory of Socialism*, Minneapolis: University of Minnesota Press.

Langthaler, Rudolf 2000, *Gottvermissen – Eine theologische Kritik der reinen Vernunft? Die neue Politische Theologie (J.B. Metz) im Spiegel der Kantischen Religionsphilosophie*, Regensburg: Pustet.

Lannert, Berthold 1989, *Die Wiederentdeckung der neutestamentlichen Eschatologie durch Johannes Weiß*, Tübingen: Francke.

Läpple, Dieter 1973, *Staat und allgemeine Produktionsbedingungen*, Berlin: Verlag für das Studium der Arbeiterbewegung.

Lask, Emil 1902, *Fichtes Idealismus und die Geschichte*, Tübingen: Mohr.

—— 1993 [1911], *Die Logik der Philosophie und die Kategorienlehre: eine Studie über den Herrschaftsbereich der logischen Form*, Tübingen: Mohr.

Lassalle, Ferdinand 1892–3, *Reden und Schriften. Neue Gesamt-Ausgabe. Mit einer biographischen Einleitung, herausgegeben von Eduard Bernstein*, 3 Vols., Berlin: Verlag der Expedition des Vorwärts.

—— 1987 [1863], 'Offenes Antwortschreiben an das Zentralkommitee zur Berufung eines allgemeinen deutschen Arbeiterkongresses zu Leipzig' in *Reden und Schriften*, Leipzig: Reclam.

Lauermann, Manfred 1989, *Die Macht des Sozialen. Dekonstruktionen seit Max Weber*, unpublished manuscript.

—— 1998, 'Das Soziale am Nationalsozialismus', *Berliner Debatte Initial*.

Lay, Rupert 1975, *Marxismus für Manager. Kritik einer Utopie*, Munich: Wirtschaftsverlag Langen-Müller-Herbig.

Lebowitz, Michael A. 1992, *Beyond Capital: Marx's Political Economy of the Working Class*, New York: St. Martin's Press.

Lederer, Emil 1931, *Aufriss der ökonomischen Theorie*, Tübingen: Mohr.

—— 1938, *Technischer Fortschritt und Arbeitslosigkeit. Eine Untersuchung der Hindernisse des ökonomischen Wachstums*, Geneva: ILO.

—— 1979, *Kapitalismus, Klassenstruktur und Probleme der Demokratie in Deutschland 1910–1940, herausgegeben von Jürgen Kocka*, Göttingen: Vandenhoeck und Ruprecht.

Lee-Lampshire, Wendy 2001, *On Marx*, London: Wadsworth.

Lefebvre, Henri 1968 [1966], *The Sociology of Marx*, London: Penguin.

—— 1991 [1947–9], *Critique of Everyday Life*, London: Verso.

LeGoff, Jacques 1988, *Your Money or Your Life: Economy and Religion in the Middle Ages*, New York: Zone Books.

Lehmann, Gerhard 1931, 'Sozialphilosophie' in *Lehrbuch der Soziologie und Sozialphilosophie*, edited by K. Dunkmann, Berlin: Junker und Dünnhaupt.

—— 1943, *Deutsche Philosophie der Gegenwart*, Sttutgart: Kröner.

Lehnert, Detlef 1983, *Sozialdemokratie zwischen Protestbewegung und Regierungspartei 1848–1983*, Frankfurt am Main: Suhrkamp.

Lekachman, Robert 1967, *The Age of Keynes: A Biographical Study*, Harmondsworth: Penguin.

Lekachmann, Robert and Boris van Loon 1981, *Capitalism for Beginners*, New York: Pantheon.

Lenel, Hans Otto 1989, 'Walter Eucken (1891–1950)' in *Klassiker des ökonomischen Denkens*, edited by Joachim Starbatty, Vol. 2, Munich: Beck.

Lenger, Friedrich 1994, *Werner Sombart 1863–1941. Eine Biographie*, Munich: Beck.

Lenger, Hans-Joachim 2994, *Marx zufolge. Die unmögliche Revolution*, Bielefeld: Transcript.

Lenin, Vladimir 1933, *Religion*, New York: International Publishers.

—— 1960 [1899], 'The Development of Capitalism in Russia' in *Works* (*LW*), Vol. 3, Moscow: Progress Publishers.

—— 1961 [1914], 'Conspectus of Hegel's Book *The Science of Logic*' in *Works* (*LW*), Vol. 38, Moscow: Progress Publishers.

—— 1965 [1916], *Imperialism and the Split in Socialism* in *Works* (*LW*), Vol. 33, Moscow: Progress Publishers.

—— 1965a [1905], *Two Tactics of Social-Democracy in the Democratic Revolution*, Peking: Foreign Languages Press.

—— 1966 [1915], *Socialism and War*, Peking: Foreign Languages Press.

—— 1970 [1916], *Imperialism, the Highest Stage of Capitalism*, Peking: Foreign Languages Press.

—— 1970a [1920], *"Left-Wing" Communism, an Infantile Disorder*, Peking: Foreign Languages Press.

—— 1970b [1917], *State and Revolution*, Peking: Foreign Languages Press.

—— 1972 [1908], *Materialism and Empirio-Criticism*, Peking: Foreign Languages Press.

—— 1972a [1918], *Proletarian Revolution and the Renegade Kautsky*, Peking: Foreign Languages Press.

—— 1973 [1902], *What is to be Done? Burning Questions of Our Movement*, Peking: Foreign Language Press.

Lenk, Hans (ed.) 1973, *Technokratie als Ideologie. Sozialphilosophische Beiträge zu einem politischen Dilemma*, Stuttgart: Kohlhammer.

Lenk, Kurt (ed.) 1961, *Ideologie. Ideologiekritik und Wissenssoziologie*, Neuwied/Berlin: Luchterhand.

—— 1986 [1970], *Marx in der Wissenssoziologie*, Lüneburg: zu Klampen.

Leonhard, Wolfgang 1958 [1955], *Child of the Revolution*, Chicago: H. Regnery.

—— 1962, *Sowjetideologie heute 2, Die politischen Lehren*, Frankfurt am Main: Fischer.

—— 1981, *Völker hört die Signale – Die Gründerjahre des Weltkommunismus 1919–1924*, Munich: Goldmann.

—— 1997, *Russland. Gegenwart und Aspekte der Zukunft*, Hamburg: Übersee-Club.

Leontief, Wassily 1966, *Input-Output Economics*, Oxford: Oxford University Press.

Lepenies, Wolf (ed.) 1981, *Geschichte der Soziologie. Studien zur kognitiven, sozialen und historischen Identität einer Disziplin*, 4 Vols., Frankfurt am Main: Suhrkamp.

—— 1985, *Die drei Kulturen. Soziologie zwischen Literatur und Wissenschaft*, Munich: Hanser.

—— 1992, *Aufstieg und Fall der Intellektuellen in Europa*, Frankfurt am Main: Campus.

Lepsius, M. Rainer (ed.) 1981, *Soziologie in Deutschland und Österreich 1918–1945. Materialien zur Entwicklung, Emigration und Wirkungsgeschichte*, Opladen: Westdeutscher Verlag.

Lersch, Philipp 1932, *Lebensphilosophie der Gegenwart*, Berlin: Junker und Dünnhaupt.

Leser, Norbert 1985, *Zwischen Reformismus und Bolschewismus. Der Austromarxismus als Theorie und Praxis*, Frankfurt am Main: Europa-Verlag.

Lessing, Theodor 1924, *Untergang der Erde am Geist. Europa und Asien*, Hannover: W.A. Adam.

—— 1927 [1919], *Geschichte als Sinngebung des Sinnlosen oder die Geburt der Geschichte aus dem Mythos*, Leipzig: Reinicke.

Lessnoff, Michael H. 1999, *Political Philosophy of the Twentieth Century*, Oxford: Blackwell.

Lefèvre, Wolfgang 1971, *Zum historischen Charakter und zur historischen Funktion der Methode der bürgerlichen Soziologie*, Frankfurt am Main: Suhrkamp.

Levenstein, Adolf 1914, *Friedrich Nietzsche im Urteil der Arbeiterklasse*, Leipzig: Meiner.

Levi, Margaret (ed.) 1991, *Marxism*, 2 Vols., Aldershot: Elgar.

Levi, Paul 2009, 'Our Path – Against Putschism', *Historical Materialism*, 17, 3: 111–45.

Levine, Michael 1993, *Guerilla PR: How You Can Wage An Effective Publicity Campaign – Without Going Broke*, New York: Harper Business.

Levy, Heinrich 1927, *Die Hegel-Renaissance in der deutschen Philosophie*, Berlin: Pan-Verlag.

Lewalter, Ernst 1982 [1930], 'Wissenssoziologie und Marxismus' in *Der Streit um die Wissenssoziologie*, edited by Volker Meja and Nico Stehr, Vol. 2, Frankfurt am Main: Suhrkamp.

Lewis, John 1972, *The Marxism of Marx*, London: Lawrence and Wishart.

Lewis, Robert W.B. 1955, *The American Adam: Innocence, Tragedy and Tradition in the Nineteenth Century*, Chicago: University of Chicago Press.

Ley, Hermann 1966–89, *Geschichte der Aufklärung und des Atheismus*, 9 Vols., Berlin: Deutscher Verlag der Wissenschaften.

Lichtblau, Klaus 1978, *Theorie der bürgerlichen Gesellschaft. Zum Verhältnis von Ökonomie, Recht und Politik*, Gießen: Focus.

Lichtblau, Klaus 1984, 'Ökonomie, politische' in *Historisches Wörterbuch der Philosophie*, edited by Joachim Ritter et al., Vol. 6, Stuttgart: Schwabe.

—— 1984a: 'Das Pathos der Distanz. Präliminarien zur Nietzsche-Rezeption bei Georg Simmel' in *Georg Simmel und die Moderne. Neue Interpretationen und Materialien*, edited by Heinz-Jürgen Dahme and Otthein Rammstedt, Frankfurt am Main: Suhrkamp.

—— 1997, *Kulturkrise und Soziologie um die Jahrhundertwende. Zur Genealogie der Kultursoziologie in Deutschland*, Frankfurt am Main: Suhrkamp.

—— 1999, *Das Zeitalter der Entzweiung. Studien zur politischen Ideengeschichte des 19. und 20. Jahrhunderts*, Berlin: Philo.

Lichtheim, Georg 1961, *Marxism: An Historical and Critical Study*, New York: Praeger.

—— 1971, *From Marx to Hegel*, New York: Herder and Herder.

Lieber, Hans-Joachim 1974, *Kulturkritik und Lebensphilosophie. Studien zur Deutschen Philosophie der Jahrhundertwende*, Darmstadt: Wissenschaftliche Buchgesellschaft.

Lieber, Hans-Joachim and Karl-Heinz Ruffmann (eds.) 1963, *Der Sowjetkommunismus. Dokumente*, 2 Vols., Cologne: Kiepenheuer und Witsch.

Liebknecht, Karl 1922, *Studien über die Bewegungsgesetze der gesellschaftlichen Entwicklung*, Munich: Wolff.

Liebrucks, Bruno 1966, *Sprache und Bewusstsein*, Vol. 3, *Wege zum Bewusstsein. Sprache und Dialektik in den ihnen von Kant und Marx versagten, von Hegel eröffneten Räumen*, Frankfurt am Main: Lang.

Liedke, Ulf 1997, *Naturgeschichte und Religion. Eine theologische Studie zum Religionsbegriff in der Philosophie Theodor W. Adornos*, Frankfurt am Main: Lang.

Liessmann, Konrad Paul 1992, *Karl Marx 1818–1989. Man stirbt nur zweimal*, Vienna: Sonderzahl.

Lietaer, Bernard 2002, *Das Geld der Zukunft. Über die zerstörerische Wirkung unseres Geldsystems und Alternativen hierzu*, Munich: Riemann.

Lindau, Hans 1900, *Johann Gottlieb und der neuere Sozialismus*, Berlin.

Lindau, Hans and Marianne Weber 1987, *Schriften zu J.G. Fichtes Sozialphilosophie*, Hildesheim: Olms.

Lindbeck, Assar 1971, *Die Politische Ökonomie der neuen Linken*, Göttingen: Vandenhoeck und Ruprecht.

Linden, Marcel van der 1992, *Von der Oktoberrevolution zur Perestroika: Der westliche Marxismus und die Sowjetunion*, Frankfurt am Main: Dipa.

Lindt, Andreas 1957, *Leonard Ragaz. Eine Studie zur Geschichte und Theologie des religiösen Sozialismus*, Zollikon: Evangelischer Verlag.

Linse, Ulrich 1983, *Barfüßige Propheten. Erlöser der zwanziger Jahre*, Berlin: Siedler.

Lipietz, Alain 1985, *The Enchanted World: Inflation, Credit and the World Crisis*, London: Verso.

Lippi, Marco 1979, *Value and Naturalism in Marx*, London: New Left Books.

Little, Adrian 1998, *Post-industrial Socialism: Towards a New Politics of Welfare*, London: Routledge.

Little, Daniel 1986, *The Scientific Marx*, Minneapolis: University of Minnesota Press.

Lloyd, Brian 1997, *Left Out: Pragmatism, Exceptionalism, and the Poverty of American Marxism, 1890–1922*, Baltimore: Johns Hopkins University Press.

Lobkowicz, Nikolaus 1967, *Theory and Practice: History of a Concept from Aristotle to Marx*, Notre Dame: University of Notre Dame Press.

Loccumer Initiative kritischer Wissenschaftlerinnen und Wissenschaftler (ed.) 1997, *Ökonomie ohne Arbeit – Arbeit ohne Ökonomie? Entwicklungstendenzen des Kapitalismus und politische Interventionen*, Hannover: Offizin.

Lochmann, Jan Milic 1974, 'Die Herausforderung Marxscher Religionskritik' in *Karl Marx im Kreuzverhör der Wissenschaften*, edited by Fritz Büsser, Zürich: Artemis.

Locke, John 1988 [1690], 'An Essay Concerning The True Origin, Extent and End of Civil Government' in *Two Treatises of Government*, Cambridge: Cambridge University Press.

Lockwood, David 1970 [1964], 'Soziale Integration und Systemintegration' in *Theorien des sozialen Wandels*, edited by Wolfgang Zapf, Cologne: Kiepenheuer und Witsch.

—— 1982, 'The Weakest Link in the Chain? Some Comments on the Marxist Theory of Action' in *Research in the Sociology of Work* 1, edited by Richard L. Simpson and Ida Harper Simpson, Greenwich; JAI Press.

Lohmann, Georg 1980, 'Gesellschaftskritik und normativer Maßstab. Überlegungen zu Marx' in *Arbeit, Handlung, Normativität. Theorien des historischen Materialismus* 2, edited by Axel Honneth and Urs Jaeggi, Frankfurt am Main: Suhrkamp.

—— 1991, *Indifferenz und Gesellschaft. Eine kritische Auseinandersetzung mit Marx*, Frankfurt am Main: Suhrkamp.

—— 1994, 'Soziale Gerechtigkeit und soziokulturelle Selbstdeutungen' in *Theorien der Gerechtigkeit. 15. Tagung der deutschen Sektion der internationalen Vereinigung für Rechts- und Sozialphilosophie in Hamburg, 30. Sept.–2. Okt. 1992*, edited by Hans-Joachim Koch et al., Stuttgart: Steiner.

—— 1999, 'Karl Marx' fatale Kritik der Menschrechte', *Jahrbuch Politisches Denken*, Stuttgart: Metzler.

Lohmann, Hans-Martin 2001, *Marxismus*, Frankfurt am Main: Campus.

Lohmann, Hans-Martin and Ossip Flechtheim: *Marx zur Einführung*. Hamburg: Junius, 2000.

Lorenzen, Paul 1991, 'Philosophische Fundierungsprobleme einer Wirtschafts- und Unternehmensethik' in *Unternehmensethik*, edited by Horst Steinmann and Peter Löhr, Stuttgart: Poeschel.

Lösche, Peter and Franz Walter 1992, *Die SPD: Klassenpartei–Volkspartei–Quotenpartei. Zur Entwicklung der Sozialdemokratie von Weimar bis zur deutschen Vereinigung*, Darmstadt: Wissenschaftliche Buchgesellschaft.

Losurdo, Domenico 1993, *Zwischen Hegel und Bismarck. Die Achtundvierziger Revolution und die Krise der deutschen Kultur*, Berlin: Akademie-Verlag.

—— 1995, *Zukunft des Marxismus. Kolloquium der Internationalen Gesellschaft für Dialektische Philosophie*, Cologne: Dinter.

—— 1998, *Geschichtsphilosophie und Ethik*, Frankfurt am Main: Lang.

Love, Nancy S. 1995, 'What's Left of Marx?' in *The Cambridge Companion to Habermas*, edited by Steven K. White, Cambridge: Cambridge University Press.

Lovejoy, Arthur O. 1929, *The Revolt Against Dualism: An Inquiry Concerning the Existence of Ideas*, La Salle: Open Court.

Löw, Konrad 1985, *Warum fasziniert der Kommunismus – eine systematische Untersuchung*, Munich: Saur.

—— 1988, *Marxismus–Quellenlexikon*, Cologne: Kölner Universitätsverlag.

—— 1996, *Der Mythos Marx und seine Macher. Wie aus Geschichten Geschichte wird*, Munich: Langen Müller.

—— 2001, *Marx und Marxismus. Eine deutsche Schizophrenie*, Munich: Olzog.

—— 2002, '"Diktatur des Proletariats" – Marx und der Marxismus' in *Ein Gespenst geht um in Europa. Das Erbe kommunistischer Ideologien*, edited by Uwe Backes and Stéphane Courtois, Cologne.

Löwe, Bernd P. 1973, *Klassenkampf oder sozialer Konflikt? Zu den Gleichgewichts- und Konflikttheorien der bürgerlichen Soziologie. Zur Kritik der bürgerlichen Ideologie*, East Berlin: Akademie-Verlag.

Löwe, Heinz Dietrich 2002, *Stalin. Der entfesselte Revolutionär*, Göttingen: Muster-Schmidt.

Löwenstein, Julius 1976, *Marx contra Marxismus*, Tübingen: Mohr.

Löwenthal, Leo 1990 [1920], 'Das Dämonische. Entwurf einer negativen Religionsphilosophie' in *Untergang der Dämonologien. Studien über Judentum, Antisemitismus und faschistischen Geist*, Leipzig: Reclam.

—— 1932, 'Zur gesellschaftlichen Lage der Literatur', *Zeitschrift für Sozialforschung*, 1–2.
Löwenthal, Richard (alias Paul Sering) 1946, *Jenseits des Kapitalismus*, Lauf: Nest.
Löwith, Karl 1949, *Meaning in History*, Chicago: University of Chicago Press.
—— 1965 [1941], *From Hegel to Nietzsche: The Revolution in Nineteenth-Century Thought*, London: Constable.
—— 1981 [1928], 'Das Individuum in der Rolle des Mitmenschen', in Löwith 1981–6, Vol. 1.
—— 1981–6, *Sämtliche Schriften, herausgegeben von Klaus Stichweh*, 9 Vols., Stuttgart: Metzler (cited as *Schriften*).
—— 1983 [1958], 'Marxismus und Geschichte' in Löwith 1981–6, Vol. 2.
—— 1983a [1951], 'Natur und Geschichte' in Löwith 1981–6, Vol. 2.
—— 1984 [1953], 'Heidegger. Denker in dürftiger Zeit' in Löwith 1981–6, Vol. 8.
—— 1984a: 'Jacob Burckhardt. Der Mensch inmitten der Geschichte' in Löwith 1981–6, Vol. 7.
—— 1984b [1935], 'Der okkasionelle Dezisionismus von Carl Schmitt' Marx' in Löwith 1981–6, Vol. 8.
—— 1985 [1930], 'Phänomenologische Ontologie und protestantische Theologie' in Löwith 1981–6, Vol. 3.
—— 1986, *Mein Leben in Deutschland vor und nach 1933. Ein Bericht*, Stuttgart: Metzler.
—— 1987 [1936], 'Nietzsches Philosophie der ewigen Wiederkehr des Gleichen' in Löwith 1981–6, Vol. 6.
—— 1988 [1932], 'Max Weber und Karl Marx' in Löwith 1981–6, Vol. 5.
Löwy, Michael 1990, *Marxismus und Religion. Die Herausforderung der Theologie der Befreiung*, Frankfurt am Main: isp-Verlag.
Löwy, Michael et al. 2002, 'Der Geist von Porto Allegre und die Strategie der Linken', supplement to *Sozialismus*, 3.
Lübbe, Hermann (ed.) 1962, *Die Hegelsche Rechte*, Stuttgart: Frommann.
—— 1963, *Politische Philosophie in Deutschland*, Basel: Schwabe.
—— 1965, *Säkularisierung*, Freiburg: Alber.
—— 1987, *Politischer Moralismus. Der Triumph der Gesinnung über die Urteilskraft*, Berlin: Siedler.
Lübbe, Hermann et al. (eds.) 1995, *Heilserwartung und Terror. Politische Religionen des 20. Jahrhunderts*, Düsseldorf: Patmos-Verlag.
Lübbe, Peter (ed.) 1981, *Kautsky gegen Lenin*, Berlin: Dietz.
Luckhardt, Ute 1994, *"Aus dem Tempel der Sehnsucht". Georg Simmel und Georg Lukács: Wege in und aus der Moderne*, Butzbach: AFRA-Verlag.
Luckner, Andreas 1995, 'Autonomie und Identität. Zum Begriff der Anerkennung in der politischen Philosophie' in idem (ed.): *Dissens und Freiheit – Kolloquium Politische Philosophie*, Leipzig: Leipziger Universitäts-Verlag.
Ludz, Peter Christian 1999 [1962], 'Religionskritik und utopische Revolution' in *Wolfgang Harich zum Gedächtnis. Eine Gedenkschrift*, Vol. 1, Munich: Müller und Nerding.
—— 1971, *Soziologie und Marxismus in der DDR*, Berlin: Luchterhand.
—— 1976, *Ideologiebegriff und marxistische Theorie. Ansätze zu einer immanenten Kritik*, Opladen: Westdeutscher Verlag.
Luhmann, Niklas 1967, 'Positives Recht und Ideologie', *Archiv für Rechts- und Sozialphilosophie*, 4: 531 ff.
—— 1969, *Legitimation durch Verfahren*, Berlin: Luchterhand.
—— 1970, 'Wirtschaft als soziales System' in *Soziologische Aufklärung*, Opladen: Westdeutscher Verlag.
—— 1971, *Politische Planung*, Opladen: Westdeutscher Verlag.
—— 1972, *A Sociological Theory of Law*, London: Routledge & Kegan Paul.
—— 1977, *Funktion der Religion*, Frankfurt am Main: Suhrkamp.
—— 1978, 'Soziologie der Moral' in *Theorietechnik und Moral*, Frankfurt am Main: Suhrkamp.
—— 1979 [1973], *Trust and Power*, Chichester: Wiley.
—— 1981, *Ausdifferenzierung des Rechts. Beiträge zur Rechtssoziologie und Rechtstheorie*, Frankfurt am Main: Suhrkamp.
—— 1985, *Soziale Differenzierung. Zur Geschichte einer Idee*, Opladen: Westdeutscher Verlag.
—— 1987, *Soziologische Aufklärung 4*, Opladen: Westdeutscher Verlag.
—— 1988, 'Kapital und Arbeit. Probleme einer Unterscheidung' in *Die Wirtschaft der Gesellschaft*, Frankfurt am Main: Suhrkamp.
—— 1989, 'Ethik als Reflexionstheorie der Moral' in *Gesellschaftsstruktur und Semantik 3*, Frankfurt am Main: Suhrkamp.
—— 1995 [1984], *Social Systems*, Stanford: Stanford University Press.

—— 1998, *Die Gesellschaft der Gesellschaft*, 2 Vols., Frankfurt am Main: Suhrkamp.

—— 2000, *Die Religion der Gesellschaft*, Frankfurt am Main: Suhrkamp.

—— 2004 [1993], *Law as a Social System*, Oxford: Oxford: University Press.

Luhmann, Niklas and Jürgen Habermas 1971, *Theorie der Gesellschaft oder Sozialtechnologie*, Frankfurt am Main: Suhrkamp.

Lukács, Georg 1963, *Die Eigenart des Ästhetischen*, 2 Vols., Berlin: Luchterhand.

—— 1971 [1923], *History and Class Conciousness*, London: Merlin.

—— 1971a [1924], *Lenin: A Study on the Unity of his Thought*, Cambridge, MA: MIT Press.

—— 1971b [1967], 'Preface to the New Edition' in *History and Class Conciousness*, London: Merlin.

—— 1971c [1916], *Theory of the Novel* (1916), Cambridge, MA: MIT Press.

—— 1974, *Conversations With Lukács*, Cambridge, MA: MIT Press.

—— 1974a [1916–18], *Heidelberger Ästhetik*, Darmstadt: Luchterhand.

—— 1974b [1911], *Soul and Form*, Cambridge, MA: MIT Press.

—— 1975, *Taktik und Ethik. Politische Aufsätze I: 1918–1920*, Darmstadt: Luchterhand.

—— 1976 [1948], *The Young Hegel: Studies in the Relations Between Dialectics and Economics*, Cambridge, MA: MIT Press.

—— 1978–80 [1968], *The Ontology of Social Being*, 2 Vols., London: Merlin.

—— 1981 [1954], *The Destruction of Reason*, Atlantic Highlands: Humanities Press.

—— 1981a [1908], 'Entwicklungsgeschichte des modernen Dramas' in *Werke*, Vol. 15, Darmstadt: Luchterhand.

—— 1989 [1933], 'Wie ist die faschistische Philosophie in Deutschland entstanden?' in *Zur Kritik der faschistischen Ideologie*, Berlin: Aufbau-Verlag.

—— 2000 [1925], *A Defense of "History and Class Consciousness": Tailism and the Dialectic*, London: Verso.

Lukes, Steven 1983, 'Morals' in *A Dictionary of Marxist Thought*, edited by Tom Bottomore, Cambridge, MA: Harvard University Press.

—— 1985, *Marxism and Morality*, Oxford: Clarendon Press.

Lüschen, Günther (ed.) 1979, *Deutsche Soziologie seit 1945. Entwicklungsrichtungen und Praxisbezug*, Opladen: Westdeutscher Verlag.

Luther, Martin 1979 [1525], 'De Servo arbitrio' in *Kritische Gesamtausgabe*, Vol. 18, Weimar: Böhlau.

Luther, Sara F. et al. (eds.) 1995, *Diverse Perspectives on Marxist Philosophy – East and West (Proceedings of the World Congress of Philosophy, Moscow 1993)*, Westport, CT: Greenwood Press.

Luttwak, Edward 1999, *Turbo-Kapitalismus. Gewinner und Verlierer der Globalisierung*, Hamburg: Europa-Verlag.

Lutz, Bernd (ed.) 1999, *Die großen Philosophen des 20. Jahrhunderts. Biographisches Lexikon*, Munich: Deutscher Taschenbuch-Verlag.

Lutz-Bachmann, Matthias 1988 [1981], *Geschichte und Subjekt. Zum Begriff der Geschichtsphilosophie bei Kant und Marx*, Freiburg: Alber.

—— 1988a: *Materialismus und Theologie im Spätwerk Max Horkheimers* in *Perspektiven kritischer Theorie*, edited by Christoph Türcke, Lüneburg: zu Klampen.

—— 1997, *Kritische Theorie und Religion*, Würzburg: Echter.

—— 2002, 'Religion – nach der Dialektik der Aufklärung' in *Jahrbuch für Religionsphilosophie*, Vol. 1, edited by Markus Enders, Frankfurt am Main: Klostermann.

Luxemburg, Rosa 1951 [1913], *The Accumulation of Capital*, London: Routledge and Kegan Paul.

—— 1971 [1905], 'Kirche und Sozialismus' in *Internationalismus und Klassenkampf. Die polnischen Schriften*, Berlin: Luchterhand.

—— 1971a [1899], 'Social Reform or Revolution' in *Selected Political Writings*, New York: Monthly Review Press.

—— 1972, *The Accumulation of Capital – an Anti-critique*, London: Monthly Review Press.

—— 1974 [1918], 'Zur russischen Revolution' in *Gesammelte Werke*, Vol. 4, East Berlin: Dietz.

Lyotard, Jean-Francois 1974, *Economie libidinale*, Paris: Éditions de Minuit.

—— 1983, *Le différend*, Paris: Éditions de Minuit.

—— 1989 [1979], *The Postmodern Condition: A Report on Knowledge*, Minneapolis: University of Minnesota Press.

Maak, Thomas and York Lunau (eds.) 1998, *Weltwirtschaftsethik. Globalisierung auf dem Prüfstand der Lebensdienlichkeit*, Bern: Haupt.

Maalouf, Amin 2000, *Mörderische Identitäten*, Frankfurt am Main: Suhrkamp.

Machovec, Milan 1972, *Jesus für Atheisten. Mit einem Geleitwort von Helmut Gollwitzer*, Stuttgart: Kreuz-Verlag.

Maciejewski, Franz (ed.) 1973–4, *Theorie der Gesellschaft oder Sozialtechnologie. Beiträge zur Habermas-Luhmann Diskussion, Supplemente 1 and 2*, Frankfurt am Main: Suhrkamp.

MacIntyre, Alasdair 1968, *Marxism and Christianity*, London: Duckworth.

—— 1981, *After Virtue: A Study in Moral Theory*, Notre Dame: University of Notre Dame Press.

MacIntyre, Alasdair and Paul Ricoeur 1969, *The Religious Significance of Atheism*, New York: Columbia University Press.

MacPherson, C.B. 1962, *The Political Theory of Possessive Individualism: Hobbes to Locke*, Oxford: Clarendon Press.

Maier, Hans 1970, *Kritik der politischen Theologie*, Einsiedeln: Johannes-Verlag.

—— 1996, *Totalitarismus und politische Religionen: Konzepte des Diktaturvergleichs*, Paderborn: Schöningh.

Maihofer, Andrea 1992, *Das Recht bei Marx. Zur dialektischen Struktur von Gerechtigkeit, Menschenrechten und Recht*, Baden-Baden: Nomos.

Majer, Helge 1991, *Makroökonomik: Theorie und Politik. Eine anwendungsbezogene Einführung*, Munich: Oldenbourg.

Malia, Martin 1989, *Experiment ohne Zukunft? Voraussetzungen und Folgen der Russischen Revolution*, Hamburg: Junius.

Mallmann, Klaus-Michael 1996, *Kommunisten in der Weimarer Republik. Sozialgeschichte einer revolutionären Bewegung*, Darmstadt: Wissenschaftliche Buchgesellschaft.

Mandel, Ernest 1970 [1962], *Marxist Economic Theory*, 2 Vols., New York: Monthly Review Press.

—— 1971, *The Formation of the Economic Thought of Karl Marx*, New York: Monthly Review Press.

Mandel, Ernest 1975 [1972], *Late Capitalism*, London: Verso.

—— 1979, *Trotsky – A Study in the Dynamic of his Thought*, London: New Left Books.

—— 1980, *Long Waves of Capitalist Development*, Cambridge: Cambridge University Press.

—— 1989, 'How to Make no Sense of Marx' in *Analyzing Marxism: New Essays on Analytical Marxism*, edited by Kai Nielsen and Robert Ware, Calgary: University of Calgary Press.

—— 1990 [1976], 'Introduction' in Karl Marx: *Capital*, Vol. 1, London: Penguin.

—— 1991 [1981], 'Introduction' in Karl Marx: *Capital*, Vol. 3, London: Penguin.

—— 1992 [1978], 'Introduction' in Karl Marx: *Capital*, Vol. 2, London: Penguin.

Mandel, Ernest and Alan Freeman (eds.) 1984, *Ricardo, Marx, Sraffa: The Langston Memorial Volume*, London: Verso.

Mander, Jerry and Edward Goldsmith (eds.) 2001, *The Case Against the Global Economy – And For a Turn Towards Localization*, London: Earthscan.

Manemann, Jürgen (ed.) 1999, *Befristete Zeit. Jahrbuch Politische Theologie 3*, Münster: Lit.

Mann, Thomas 1919, *Betrachtungen eines Unpolitischen*, Berlin: Fischer.

—— 1986, *Aufsätze, Reden, Essays*, Vol. 3, 1919–1925, Berlin: Aufbau-Verlag.

Mannheim, Karl 1936 [1929], *Ideology and Utopia*, New York: Harcourt, Brace & Company.

—— 1940 [1935], *Man and Society in an Age of Reconstruction*, London: Routledge.

—— 1964 [1928], 'Die Bedeutung der Konkurrenz auf dem Gebiete des Geistigen' in *Wissenssoziologie. Auswahl aus dem Werk*, Berlin: Luchterhand.

—— 1964a [1921–2], 'Beiträge zur Theorie der Weltanschauungsinterpretation' in *Wissenssoziologie. Auswahl aus dem Werk*, Berlin: Luchterhand.

—— 1964b [1924], 'Historismus' in *Wissenssoziologie. Auswahl aus dem Werk*, Berlin: Luchterhand.

—— 1964c [1926], 'Ideologische und soziologische Interpretation der geistigen Gebilde' in *Wissenssoziologie. Auswahl aus dem Werk*, Berlin: Luchterhand.

—— 1964d [1925], 'Das Problem einer Soziologie des Wissens' in *Wissenssoziologie. Auswahl aus dem Werk*, Berlin: Luchterhand.

—— 1986 [1925], *Conservatism: A Contribution to the Sociology of Knowledge*, London: Routledge & Kegan Paul.

Manuel, Frank Edward 1995, *A Requiem for Marx*, Cambridge: Harvard University Press.

Marck, Siegfried 1929–31, *Die Dialektik in der Philosophie der Gegenwart*, 2 Vols., Tübingen: Mohr.

Marcuse, Herbert 1941, *Reason and Revolution: An Introduction to the Dialectical Thinking of Hegel and Marx*, London: Oxford University Press.

—— 1958, *Soviet Marxism: A Critical Analysis*, New York: Columbia University Press.

—— 1964, *One-Dimensional Man*, London: Routledge & Kegan Paul.

—— 1966 [1955], *Eros and Civilization: A Philosophical Inquiry into Freud*, Boston: Beacon Press.
—— 1968 [1937], 'Philosophy and Critical Theory' in *Negations: Essays in Critical Theory*, Boston: Beacon Press.
—— 1968a [1934], 'The Struggle Against Liberalism in the Totalitarian View of the State' in *Negations: Essays in Critical Theory*, Boston: Beacon Press.
—— 1970 [1967], 'The End of Utopia' in *Five Lectures*, Harmondsworth: Penguin.
—— 1979 [1977], *The Aesthetic Dimension*, London: Macmillan.
—— 1987 [1932], *Hegel's Ontology and the Theory of Historicity*, Cambridge, MA: MIT Press.
—— 2005 [1928], 'Contributions to a Phenomenology of Historical Materialism' in *Heideggerian Marxism*, edited by Richard Wolin and John Abromeit, Lincoln: University of Nebraska Press.
—— 2005a [1932], 'New Sources on the Foundation of Historical Materialism' in *Heideggerian Marxism*, edited by Richard Wolin and John Abromeit, Lincoln: University of Nebraska Press.
—— 2005b [1933], 'On the Philosophical Foundation of the Concept of Labor in Economics' in *Heideggerian Marxism*, edited by Richard Wolin and John Abromeit, Lincoln: University of Nebraska Press.
Markovic, Mihailo 1968, *Dialektik der Praxis*, Frankfurt am Main: Suhrkamp.
Markovits, Andrej and Philip S. Gorski 1997, *Grün schlägt rot. Die deutsche Linke nach 1945*, Hamburg: Rotbuch.
Márkus, György 1976, 'Der Begriff des "menschlichen Wesens" in der Philosophie des jungen Marx' in *Die neue Linke in Ungarn*, Vol. 2, edited by A. Hegedüs et al., Berlin: Merve.
Marquard, Friedrich-Wilhelm 1972, *Theologie und Sozialismus. Das Beispiel Karl Barths*, Munich: Kaiser.
Marquard, Odo 1958 [1954], *Skeptische Methode im Blick auf Kant*, Freiburg: Alber.
—— 1973 [1964], 'Hegel und das Sollen' in *Schwierigkeiten mit der Geschichtsphilosophie. Aufsätze*, Frankfurt am Main: Suhrkamp.
Marsden, Richard 1999, *The Nature of Capital: Marx after Foucault*, London: Routledge.
Marshall, Alfred 1890, *Principles of Economics*, London: Macmillan.
Marshall, Gordon 1997, *Repositioning Class: Social Inequality in Industrial Societies*, London: Sage.
Marshall, Thomas H. 1963 [1950], 'Citizenship and Social Class' in *Sociology at the Crossroads and Other Essays*, London: Heinemann.
Marten, Rainer 1991, *Heidegger lessen*, Munich: Fink.
Martin, Alfred von 1947, *Die Religion Jacob Burckhardts. Eine Studie zum Thema Humanismus und Christentum*, Munich: Erasmus-Verlag.
Martin, Hans-Peter and Harald Schumann 1996, *Die Globalisierungsfalle. Der Angriff auf Demokratie und Wohlstand*, Reinbek: Rowohlt.
Martin, Randy 2002, *On Your Marx. Relinking Socialism and the Left*, Minneapolis: University of Minnesota Press.
Marx, Karl 1983 [1867], *Das Kapital. Kritik der politischen Ökonomie, erster Band. Hamburg 1867, Gesamtausgabe (MEGA)*, Vol. II.5, Berlin: Dietz.
—— 1988 [1862], *Resultate des unmittelbaren Produktionsprozesses*, Berlin: Dietz.
Marx, Karl and Friedrich Engels 1956 ff., *Werke*, 42 Vols., Berlin: Dietz (cited as: *MEW*).
—— 1975–2005, *Collected Works*, 50 Vols., Moscow: Progress Publishers (cited as: *MECW*).
—— 1976, *Über Religion*, East Berlin: Dietz.
Marx-Engels-Stiftung (ed.) 1991, *Politische Theorien des Marxismus im Wandel historischer Entwicklungen*, Bonn: Pahl-Rugentsein.
—— 1997, *Die Oktoberrevolution 1917 und ihr Platz in der Geschichte*, Bonn: Pahl-Rugenstein.
Marxismusstudien. Schriften der Studiengemeinschaft der evangelischen Akademien, Tübingen 1954–72, edited by Erwin Metzge (Vol. 1, 1954), Iring Fetscher (Vols. 2–5, 1957–68), Ulrich Duchrow (Vol. 6, 1968) and H.E. Tödt (Vol. 7, 1972).
Masaryk, Thomas G. 1964 [1899], *Die philosophischen und sociologischen Grundlagen des Marxismus. Studien zur socialen Frage*, Osnabrück: Otto Zeller.
Mason, Timothy W. 1993 [1977], *Social Policy in the Third Reich*, Providence: Berg.
Massiczek, Albert 1968, *Der menschliche Mensch. Karl Marx' jüdischer Humanismus*, Frankfurt am Main: Europa-Verlag.
Matthias, Erich 1952, *Sozialdemokratie und Nation*, Stuttgart: Deutsche Verlags-Anstalt.
—— 1957, 'Kautsky und der Kautskyanismus', *Marxismusstudien*, 2: 151–97.

Mattick, Paul 1969, *Marx and Keynes. The Limits of the Mixed Economy*, Boston: P. Sargent.
—— 1972, 'Samuelson's "Transformation" of Marxism into Bourgeois Economics', *Science and Society*, 36, 3: 258–73.
—— 1983, *Marxism – Last Refuge of the Bourgeoisie?* London: Merlin Press.
Maurenbrecher, Max 1904, *Die Gebildeten und die Sozialdemokratie. Ein erweiterter Vortrag*, Leipzig: Leipziger Buchdruck-AG.
Maurer, Reinhart 1975, *Revolution und "Kehre". Studien zum Problem gesellschaftlicher Naturbeherrschung*, Frankfurt am Main: Suhrkamp.
Maus, Ingeborg 1986, *Rechtstheorie und Politische Theorie im Industriekapitalismus*, Munich: Fink.
Mayer, Hans 1994, *Der Widerruf. Über Deutsche und Juden*, Frankfurt am Main: Suhrkamp.
McBride, William 2000, 'Habermas and the Marxian Tradition' in *Perspectives on Habermas*, edited by Lewis Edward Hahn, Chicago: Open Court.
McCarthy, G.E. (ed.) 1992, *Marx and Aristotle: Nineteenth Century German Social Theory and Antiquity*, Savage: Rowman and Littlefield.
McInnes, Neil 1972, *The Western Marxists*, New York: Library Press.
McLellan, David 1969, *Karl Marx and the Young Hegelians*, London: Macmillan.
—— 1972, *Marx Before Marxism*, Harmondsworth: Penguin.
—— 1987, *Marxism and Religion*, New York: Harper & Row.
McLennan, Gregor 1989, *Marxism, Pluralism and Beyond: Classic Debates and New Departures*, Cambridge: Polity Press.
McMurtry, John Murray 1978, *The Structure of Marx's World-View*, Princeton: Princeton University Press.
Mead, George Herbert 1934, *Mind, Self, and Society*, Chicago: University of Chicago Press.
—— 1964 [1930], 'The Philosophy of Royce, James and Dewey in their American Setting' in *G.H. Mead: Selected Writings*, edited by Andrew Reck, Indianapolis: Bobbs-Merrill.
Meadows, Denis 1972, *Die Grenzen des Wachstums*, Stuttgart: Deutsche Verlags-Anstalt.
Meckenstock, Günter 1997, *Wirtschaftsethik*, Berlin: de Gruyter.
Meek, Ronald L. 1956, *Studies in the Labour Theory of Value*, London: Lawrence and Wishart.
—— 1967, *Economics and Ideology and Other Essays*, London: Chapman & Hall.
Megill, Allan 2002, *Karl Marx: The Burden of Reason (Why Marx Rejected Politics and the Market)*, Lanham: Rowman and Littlefield Publishers.
Mehring, Franz 1960 [1897–8], *Geschichte der deutschen Sozialdemokratie* in *Gesammelte Schriften*, Vols. 1 and 2, East Berlin: Dietz.
—— 1983, *Gesammelte Schriften*, Vol. 13, *Philosophische Aufsätze*, East Berlin: Dietz.
Mehring, Reinhard 1989, *Pathetisches Denken. Carl Schmitts Denkweg am Leitfaden Hegels: Katholische Grundstellung und antimarxistische Hegelstrategie*, Berlin: Duncker und Humblot.
Meistner, Robert 1990, *Political Identity. Thinking Through Marx*, Cambridge: Blackwell.
Meja, Volker and Nico Stehr (eds.) 1982, *Der Streit um die Wissenssoziologie*, 2 Vols., Frankfurt am Main: Suhrkamp.
Mende, Hans-Jürgen 1985, *Karl Kautsky – vom Marxisten zum Opportunisten. Studie zur Geschichte des historischen Materialismus*, East Berlin: Dietz.
Menger, Anton 1886, *Das Recht auf den vollen Arbeitsertrag*, Stuttgart: Cotta.
—— 1890, *Das bürgerliche Recht und die besitzlosen Volksklassen*, Tübingen: Laupp.
Menger, Carl 1976 [1871], *Principles of Economics*, Auburn: Ludwig von Mises Institute.
Merkel, Angela 2000, 'Die Wir-Gesellschaft. Über die Notwendigkeit einer Neuen Sozialen Marktwirtschaft', *Frankfurter Allgemeine Zeitung*, 18 November 2000.
Merleau-Ponty, Maurice 1969 [1947], *Humanism and Terror: An Essay on the Communist Problem*, Boston: Beacon Press.
—— 1974 [1955], *Adventures of the Dialectic*, London: Heinemann.
Merten, Stefan 1999, *Wirtschaftspolitische Leitbilder des Marxismus-Leninismus. Konzeptionen, Defizite, Folgen*, Wiesbaden: Deutscher Universitäts-Verlag.
Meschkat, Klaus and Oskar Negt (eds.) 1973, *Gesellschaftsstrukturen*, Frankfurt am Main: Suhrkamp.
Messer, August 1931, *Lebensphilosophie*, Leipzig: Meiner.
Meszaros, Istvan 1973, *Der Entfremdungsbegriff bei Marx*, Munich: List.
Meszaros, V.N. 1995, *Beyond Capital: Towards a Theory of Transition*, London: Merlin Press.
Metz, Johann Baptist 1968, *Zur Theologie der Welt*, Mainz: Grünewald.

—— 1980, *Jenseits bürgerlicher Religion. Reden über die Zukunft des Christentums*, Munich: Kaiser.

Metzger, Arnold 1979, *Phänomenologie der Revolution. Frühe Schriften*, Frankfurt am Main: Syndikat.

Metzler, Gabriele 2003, *Der deutsche Sozialstaat. Vom Bismarckschen Erfolgsmodell zum Pflegefall*, Stuttgart: Deutsche Verlags-Anstalt.

Meusel, Alfred 1925, *Untersuchungen über das Erkenntnisobjekt bei Marx*, Jena: G. Fischer.

Meyer, Martin 1993, *Ende der Geschichte?* Munich: Hanser.

Meyer, Thomas 1977, *Bernsteins konstruktiver Sozialismus. Eduard Bernsteins Beitrag zur Theorie des Sozialismus*, Berlin: Dietz.

Meyer-Abich, Klaus Michael 1984, *Wege zum Frieden mit der Natur – Praktische Naturphilosophie für die Umweltpolitik*, Munich: Hanser.

Meyer-Faje, Arnold and Peter Ulrich, Peter (eds.) 1991, *Der andere Adam Smith*, Stuttgart: Haupt.

Meynaud, Jean 1964, *La Technocratie. Mythe ou réalité*, Paris: Payot.

Michel, Willy 1972, *Marxistische Ästhetik – Ästhetischer Marxismus*, 2 Vols., Frankfurt am Main: Athenäum.

Michels, Robert 1978 [1910], *Political Parties: A Sociological Study of the Oligarchical Tendencies of Modern Democracy*, Gloucester: P. Smith.

Mies, Maria 2001, *Globalisierung von unten. Der Kampf gegen die wirtschaftliche Ungleichheit*, Hamburg: Rotbuch.

Miliband, Ralph 1973 [1969], *The State in Capitalist Society: The Analysis of the Western System of Power*, London: Quartet Books.

Miller, James 1979, *History and Human Existence. From Marx to Merleau-Ponty*, Berkeley, CA: University of California Press.

Miller, R.W. 1977 [1974], 'Rawls and Marxism' in *Über John Rawls' Theorie der Gerechtigkeit*, edited by Otfried Höffe, Frankfurt am Main: Suhrkamp.

Miller, Richard 1984, *Analyzing Marx: Morality, Power and History*, Princeton: Princeton University Press.

Miller, Susanne 1964, *Das Problem der Freiheit im Sozialismus. Freiheit, Staat und Revolution in der Programmatik der Sozialdemokratie von Lassalle bis zum Revisionismusstreit*, Frankfurt am Main: Europäische Verlags-Anstalt.

Miller, Susanne and Heinrich Pothoff 1983, *Kleine Geschichte der SPD. Darstellung und Dokumentation, 1848–1983*, Bonn: Dietz.

Milner, Andrew 1999, *Class*, London: Sage.

Minois, Georges 1998, *Histoire de l'athéisme: les incroyants dans le monde occidental des origines à nos jours*, Paris: Fayard.

Misch, Georg 1930, *Lebensphilosophie und Phänomenologie. Eine Auseinandersetzung der Diltheyschen Richtung mit Heidegger und Husserl*, Bonn: Cohen.

Mises, Ludwig von 1936 [1922], *Socialism*, London: Cape.

—— 1940, *Nationalökonomie. Theorie des Handelns und Wirtschaftens*, Geneva: Editions Union.

Mishra, R. 1999 [1981], 'Marx and Welfare' in *Karl Marx's Social and Political Thought: Critical Assesments*, edited by Bob Jessop, Vol. 7, London: Routledge.

Misik, Robert 1998, *Mythos Weltmarkt. Vom Elend des Neoliberalismus*, Berlin: Aufbau-Verlag.

Mittelman, James H. (ed.) 1996, *Globalization: Critical Reflections*, Boulder: Lynne Rienner Publishers.

Mohl, Ernst Theodor 1967, 'Anmerkungen zur Marx-Rezeption' in *Folgen einer Theorie. Essays über "Das Kapital" von Karl Marx*, Frankfurt am Main: Suhrkamp.

Mohler, Armin 1989 [1949], Die *konservative Revolution in Deutschland 1918–1932. Ein Handbuch*, Darmstadt: Wissenschaftliche Buchgesellschaft.

Molitor, Bruno 1989, *Wirtschaftsethik*, Munich: Vahlen.

Moltmann, Jürgen 1967 [1964], *Theology of Hope*, New York: Harper & Row.

Mommsen, Wolfgang J. 1974, *Max Weber: Gesellschaft, Politik und Geschichte*, Frankfurt am Main: Suhrkamp.

Monnerot, Jules 1963, *Sociologie du communisme*, Paris: Gallimard.

Montada, Leo and Melvin J. Lerner. (eds.) 1996, *Current Societal Concerns About Justice*, New York: Plenum Press.

Montesquieu 1977 [1748], *The Spirit of Laws*, Berkeley CA: University of California Press.

Monz, Heinz 1995, *Gerechtigkeit bei Karl Marx und in der Hebräischen Bibel*, Baden-Baden: Nomos.

Mörchen, Hermann 1980, *Macht und Herrschaft im Denken von Heidegger und Adorno*, Stuttgart: Klett-Cotta.

—— 1981, *Adorno und Heidegger. Untersuchung einer philosophischen Kommunikationsverweigerung*, Stuttgart: Klett-Cotta.

More, Thomas 1975 [1516], *Utopia*, New York: Norton.

Morel, Julius et al. (eds.) 1999, *Soziologische Theorie. Abriss der Ansätze ihrer Hauptvertreter*, Munich: Oldenbourg.

Morf, Otto 1970 [1951], *Geschichte und Dialektik in der Kritik der politischen Ökonomie*, Frankfurt am Main: Europäische Verlags-Anstalt.

Morgenstern, Soma 2001, *Kritiken, Berichte, Tagebücher*, Lüneburg: zu Klampen.

Morishima, Michio 1973, *Marx' Economics: A Dual Theory of Value and Growth*, Cambridge: Cambridge University Press.

Mosse, George, L. 1985, *German Jews Beyond Judaism*, Bloomington: Indiana University Press.

—— 1978, *Toward the Final Solution: A History of European Racism*, New York: H. Fertig.

Mozetic, Gerald 1987, *Die Gesellschaftstheorie des Austromarxismus. Geistesgeschichtliche Voraussetzungen, Methodologie und soziologisches Programm*, Darmstadt: Wissenschaftliche Buchgesellschaft.

Mückenberger, Ulrich 1976, 'Thesen zur Funktion und Entwicklung des Sozialrechts', *Kritische Justiz*, 2.

Muhs, Karl 1927, *Anti-Marx: Betrachtungen über den inneren Aufbau der Marxschen Ökonomik*, Jena: Fischer.

Muller, Jerry Z. 1987, *The Other God that Failed. Hans Freyer and the Deradicalization of German Conservativsm*, Princeton: Princeton University Press.

Müller, Klaus 1988, 'Analytischer Marxismus', *Prokla*, 18, 3: 39–71.

—— 1996, *Allgemeine Systemtheorie. Geschichte, Methodologie und sozialwissenschaftliche Heuristik eines Wissenschaftsprogramms*, Opladen: Westdeutscher Verlag.

Müller, Rudolf Wolfgang 1981, *Geld und Geist. Zur Entstehungsgeschichte von Identitätsbewusstsein und Rationalität seit der Antike*, Frankfurt am Main: Campus.

Müller, Werner 2002, 'Gab es in Deutschland einen demokratischen Kommunismus?' in *Ein Gespenst geht um in Europa. Das Erbe kommunistischer Ideologien*, edited by Uwe Backes and Stéphane Courtois, Cologne: Böhlau.

Müller-Armack, Alfred 1974, *Genealogie der sozialen Marktwirtschaft. Frühschriften und weiterführende Konzepte*, Stuttgart: Haupt.

—— 1990 [1946], *Wirtschaftslenkung und Marktwirtschaft*, Munich: Kastell.

Müller-Doohm, Stefan 1991, 'Soziologie ohne Gesellschaft? Notizen zum Gegenstandstandsverlust einer Disziplin' in *Jenseits der Utopie. Theoriekritik der Gegenwart*, Frankfurt am Main: Suhrkamp.

Müller-Lyer, Franz Carl 1918, *Soziologie der Zuchtwahl und des Bevölkerungswesens*, Munich: Langen.

Münch, Richard 1992, 'Autopoiesis by Definition', *Cardozo Law Review*, 13, 5: 1463–71.

—— 1992a [1984], *Die Struktur der Moderne. Grundmuster und differentielle Gestaltung des institutionellen Aufbaus der modernen*, Frankfurt am Main: Suhrkamp.

—— 2002, *Soziologische Klassiker. Lehrbuch der Theoriegeschichte*, Frankfurt am Main: Campus.

Murphey, Murray G. 1961, *The Development of Peirce's Philosophy*, Cambridge, MA: Harvard University Press.

Nagl, Ludwig 1983, *Gesellschaft und Autonomie. Historisch-systematische Studien zur Entwicklung der Sozialtheorie von Hegel bis Habermas*, Vienna: Österreichische Akademie der Wissenschaften.

—— 1998, *Pragmatismus*, Frankfurt am Main: Campus.

Nagl, Ludwig and Chantal Mouffe (eds.) 2001, *The Legacy of Wittgenstein: Pragmatism or Deconstruction*, Frankfurt am Main: Campus.

Nakatani, Takeshi 1979, 'Price Competition and Technical Change', *Kobe University Economic Review*, 25.

—— 1980, 'The Law of Falling Rate of Profit and the Competitive Battle: Comment on Shaikh', *Cambridge Journal of Economics*, 4: 65–8.

Narr, Wolf-Dieter 1994, 'Recht – Demokratie – Weltgesellschaft. Überlegungen anlässlich der rechtstheoretischen Werke von Jürgen Habermas und Niklas Luhmann', *Prokla*, 1: 87 ff. and 2: 324 ff.

Natorp, Paul 1920, *Sozialidealismus. Neue Richtlinien sozialer Erziehung*, Berlin: Springer.

Naumann, Friedrich 1905, *Demokratie und Kaisertum. Ein Handbuch für innere Politik*, Berlin: Buchverlag der Hilfe.

—— 1964, *Werke*, Vol. 5, *Politische Schriften*, Opladen: Westdeutscher Verlag.

Negri, Antonio and Michael Hardt 1994, *Labor of Dionysus: A Critique of the State-Form*, Minneapolis: University of Minnesota Press.

—— 2000, *Empire*, Cambridge, MA: Harvard University Press.
Negt, Oskar (ed.) 1969, *Deborin/Bucharin. Kontroversen über dialektischen und mechanischen Materialismus*, Frankfurt am Main: Suhrkamp.
—— 1970, *Aktualität und Folgen der Philosophie Hegels*, Frankfurt am Main: Suhrkamp.
—— 1974 [1963], *Die Konstituierung der Soziologie zur Ordnungswissenschaft. Strukturbeziehungen zwischen den Gesellschaftslehren Comtes und Hegels*, Frankfurt am Main: Europäische Verlags-Anstalt.
—— 1975, 'Zehn Thesen zur marxistischen Rechtsphilosophie' in *Probleme der marxistischen Rechtstheorie*, edited by Hubert Rottleuthner, Frankfurt am Main: Suhrkamp.
—— 1993, 'Zum Verständnis des Politischen bei Hannah Arendt' in *Die Zukunft des Politischen. Ausblicke auf Hannah Arendt*, edited by Peter Kemper, Frankfurt am Main: Fischer.
—— 1995 [1968–9], 'Produktion und Recht – ein rechtsphilosophisches Kolloquium 1968/69' in *Achtundsechzig. Politische Intellektuelle und die Macht*, Göttingen; Steidl.
—— 1996, *Marx. Ausgewählt und vorgestellt von Oskar Negt*, Munich: Diederichs.
—— 2003, *Kant und Marx. Ein Epochengespräch*, Göttingen: Steidl.
Negt, Oskar and Alexander Kluge 1972, *Öffentlichkeit und Erfahrung. Zur Organisationsanalyse von bürgerlicher und proletarischer Öffentlichkeit*, Frankfurt am Main: Suhrkamp.
—— 1992, *Maßverhältnisse des Politischen. 15 Vorschläge zum Unterscheidungsvermögen*, Frankfurt am Main: Fischer.
Nell-Breuning, Oswald von 1969, *Die Auseinandersetzung um Karl Marx*, Munich: Huber.
—— 1974, *Kapitalismus – kritisch betrachtet. Zur Auseinandersetzung um das bessere "System"*, Freiburg: Herder.
—— 1980, *Gerechtigkeit und Freiheit: Grundzüge katholischer Soziallehre*, Vienna: Europa-Verlag.
—— 1983, *Arbeit vor Kapital. Kommentar zur Enzyklika "Laborem exercens" von Johannes Paul II*, Vienna: Europa-Verlag.
Nelson, Gary and Lawrence Grossberg (eds.) 1988, *Marxism and the Interpretation of Culture*, Urbana, IL: University of Illinois Press.
Nettl, Peter 1968, *Rosa Luxemburg*, Frankfurt am Main: Büchergilde Gutenberg.
Neuhaus, Gerd 1985, *Atheismus oder anonymes Christentum? Ein Versuch transzendentaler Hermeneutik des Gottesglaubens in Auseinandersetzung mit Feuerbach, Marx, Horkheimer und Benjamin*, Annweiler: Plöger.
Neumann, Franz 1943 [1942], *Behemoth: The Structure and Practice of National Socialism*, London: Victor Gollacnz.
—— 1977 [1974}: *Handbuch Politischer Theorien und Ideologien*, Reinbek: Rowohlt.
—— 1978, *Wirtschaft, Staat, Demokratie. Aufsätze 1930–1954*, Frankfurt am Main: Suhrkamp.
Neumann, John von and Oskar Morgenstern 1944, *The Theory of Games and Economic Behavior*, Princeton: Princeton University Press.
Neumann, Karl-Heinz (ed.) 1971, *Marxismus-Archiv*, Vol. 1, *Marxismus und Politik. Dokumente zur theoretischen Begründung revolutionärer Politik. Aufsätze aus der Marxismus-Diskussion der zwanziger und dreißiger Jahre*, Frankfurt am Main: Makol.
Neumann, Udo 1999, *Struktur und Dynamik von Armut. Eine empirische Untersuchung für die Bundesrepublik Deutschland*, Freiburg: Lambertus.
Neumann, Walter 1989, *Die Philosophie des Nichts in der Moderne. Sein und Nichts bei Hegel, Marx, Heidegger und Sartre*, Essen: Die Blaue Eule.
Neurath, Otto 1979, *Wissenschaftliche Weltauffassung. Sozialismus und Logischer Empirismus*, Frankfurt am Main: Suhrkamp.
Neusüss, Christel 1972, *Imperialismus und Weltmarktbewegung des Kapitals*, Erlangen: Politladen.
Nida-Rümelin, Julian 2000, 'Die ethischen Grundlagen des Sozialstaats' in *Politische Philosophie des Sozialstaats*, edited by Wolfgang Kersting, Weilerswist: Velbrück.
Nielsen, Kai and S.C. Patten (eds.) 1981, *Marx and Morality*, Guelph: Canadian Association for Publications in Philosophy.
Nielsen, Kai and Robert Ware (eds.) 1988, *Analyzing Marxism: New Essays on Analytical Marxism*, Calgary: University of Calgary Press.
Nielsen, Kai 1989, *Marxism and the Moral Point of View: Morality, Ideology and Historical Materialism*, Boulder: Westview Press.
Nietzsche, Friedrich 1967 [1872, 1888], *The Birth of Tragedy, and The Case of Wagner*, New York: Vintage.

—— 1967a [1887], *The Will to Power*, New York: Random House.

—— 1988, *Sämtliche Werke. Kritische Studienausgabe*, 15 Vols. (cited as *KSA*), Munich: Deutscher Taschenbuch-Verlag.

—— 1998 [1888], *Twilight of the Idols or How to Philosophize with a Hammer*, Oxford: Oxford University Press.

Niewöhner, Friedrich (ed.) 1999, *Atheismus im Mittelalter und in der Renaissance. Wolfenbütteler Symposion*, Wiesbaden: Harrassowitz.

Nohl, Herman (ed.) 1907, *Hegels theologische Jugendschriften. Nach den Handschriften der königlichen Bibliothek in Berlin*, Tübingen: Mohr.

—— 1970, *Die Deutsche Bewegung: Vorlesungen und Aufsätze zur Geistesgeschichte von 1770–1830*, Göttingen: Vandenhoeck und Ruprecht.

Nolte, Ernst 1952, *Selbstentfremdung und Dialektik im Deutschen Idealismus und bei Marx*, dissertation, University of Freiburg.

—— 1963, *Der Faschismus in seiner Epoche: Action francaise, italienischer Faschismus, Nationalsozialismus*, Munich: Piper.

—— 1968, *Der Faschismus. Von Mussolini zu Hitler. Texte, Bilder und Dokumente*, Munich: Desch.

—— 1982 [1977], *Marxism, Fascism, Cold War*, Atlantic Highlands, NJ: Humanities Press.

—— 1983, *Marxismus und industrielle Revolution*, Stuttgart: Klett-Cotta.

—— 1986, *Der Europäische Bürgerkrieg 1917–1945. Nationalsozialismus und Bolschewismus*, Berlin: Propyläen.

Noske, Gustav 1947, *Aufstieg und Niedergang der deutschen Sozialdemokratie*, Zürich: Aero-Verlag.

Novack, George 1978, *Polemics in Marxist Philosophy*, New York: Monad Press.

Nozick, Robert 1974, *Anarchy, State, and Utopia*, New York: Basic Books.

Nürnberger, Christian 1999, *Die Machtwirtschaft. Ist die Demokratie noch zu retten?*, Munich: Deutscher Taschenbuch-Verlag.

Nussbaum, Martha C. 1999 [1990], 'Der aristotelische Sozialdemokratismus' in *Gerechtigkeit oder das gute Leben*, Frankfurt am Main: Suhrkamp.

Nutzinger, Hans G. 1999, 'Was bleibt von Marx' ökonomischer Theorie?' in *Der Wohlstand der Personen. Festschrift zum 60. Geburtstag von Georg Zinn*, Marburg: Metropolis.

Nutzinger, Hans G. and Elmar Wolfstetter (ed.) 1974, *Die Marxsche Theorie und ihre Kritik*, Frankfurt am Main: Campus.

O'Connor, James 1973, *The Fiscal Crisis of the State*, New York: St. Martin's Press.

O'Neill, John 1995, *The Poverty of Postmodernism*, London: Routledge, 1995.

—— 1998, *The Market. Ethics: Knowledge and Politics*, London: Routledge.

Oehler, Klaus 1995, *Sachen und Zeichen. Zur Philosophie des Pragmatismus*, Frankfurt am Main: Klostermann.

Oelmüller, Willi 1977, *Weiterentwicklungen des Marxismus*, Darmstadt: Wissenschaftliche Buchgesellschaft.

—— 1988, *Philosophie und Wissenschaft*, Paderborn: Schöningh.

Oetzel, Klaus-Dieter 1978, *Wertabstraktion und Erfahrung. Über das Problem einer historisch-materialistischen Erkenntniskritik*, Frankfurt am Main: Campus.

Offe, Claus 1972, 'Politische Herrschaft und Klassenstruktur. Zur Analyse spätkapitalistischer Gesellschaftssysteme' in *Politikwissenschaft. Eine Einführung in ihre Probleme*, edited by Gisela Kress and Dieter Senghaas, Frankfurt am Main: Fischer.

—— 1974 [1972], 'Structural Problems of the Capitalist State. Class Rule and the Political System. On the Selectiveness of Political Institutions', *German Political Studies*, 1: 31–57.

—— 1984, 'Arbeit als soziologische Schlüsselkategorie?' in idem (ed.): *"Arbeitsgesellschaft". Strukturprobleme und Zukunftsperspektiven*, Frankfurt am Main: Campus.

Ohr, Dieter 1997, *Nationalsozialistische Propaganda und Weimarer Wahlen*, Opladen: Westdeutscher Verlag.

Oihshi, Tahahisa 2001, *The Unknown Marx*, London: Pluto Press.

Okishio, Nobuo 1961, 'Technical Change and the Rate of Profit', *Kobe University Economic Review*.

Opitz, Heinrich et al. (eds.) 1988, *Philosophen-Lesebuch*, Vol. 2, East Berlin: Dietz.

Oppenheimer, Franz 1912, *Die soziale Frage und der Sozialismus. Eine kritische Auseinandersetzung mit der marxistischen Theorie*, Jena: Fischer.

—— 1913, 'Praktische Ökonomik und Volkswirtschaftspolitik', *Annalen der Natur- und Kulturphilosophie*, 12.

—— 1919, *Weder Kapitalismus noch Kommunismus*, Stuttgart: Fischer.

—— 1922–35, *System der Soziologie*, 8 Vols., Jena: Fischer.
—— 1938, *Das Kapital. Kritik der Politischen Ökonomie. Ein kurzgefasstes Lehrbuch der nationalökonomischen Theorie*, Leiden: Sijthoff.
—— 1998, *Gesammelte Schriften*, Vol. 3, *Schriften zur Marktwirtschaft*, Berlin: Akademie-Verlag.
Orozco, Teresa 1995, *Platonische Gewalt. Gadamers politische Hermeneutik der NS-Zeit*, Hamburg: Argument.
Orth, Ernst Wolfgang (ed.) 1985, *Dilthey und die Philosophie der Gegenwart*, Freiburg: Alber.
Orth, Ernst Wolfgang and Helmut Holzhey (eds.) 1994, *Neukantianismus. Perspektiven und Probleme*, Würzburg: Königshausen und Neumann.
Orth, Gottfried 1995, *Helmut Gollwitzer. Zur Solidarität befreit*, Mainz: Grünewald.
Ott, Alfred E. 1967, 'Marx und die moderne Wachstumstheorie', *Der Volkswirt*, 16: 637 f.
—— 1989, 'Karl Marx' in *Klassiker des ökonomischen Denkens*, edited by Joachim Starbatty, Vol. 2, Munich: Beck.
Ottmann, Henning 1999, *Philosophie und Politik bei Nietzsche*, Berlin: de Gruyter.
Oudenrijn, Frans 1972, *Kritische Theologie als Kritik der Theologie. Theorie und Praxis bei Marx – Herausforderung der Theologie*, Munich: Kaiser.
Overbeck, Franz 1903 [1873], *Über die Christlichkeit unserer heutigen Theologie*, Leipzig: Naumann.
Pabst, Karl H. 1992, *Transzendentale Erkenntnis und Gesellschaft. Zur Kritik transzendentaler Begründungsversuche der Gesellschaftstheorie bei Max Adler, Jürgen Habermas und Theodor W. Adorno*, Frankfurt am Main: Lang.
Pagels, Kurt 1992, *Kant gegen Marx, Engels, Lenin: Kritik der marxistisch-leninistischen Philosophie*, Meppen: Ewert-Verlag.
Pangritz, Andreas 1996, *Vom Kleiner- und Unsichtbarwerden der Theologie. Ein Versuch über das Projekt einer "impliziten Theologie" bei Barth, Tillich, Bonhoeffer, Benjamin, Horkheimer und Adorno*, Tübingen: Theologischer Verlag.
Pannenberg, Wolfhart 1969, 'Heilsgeschehen und Geschichte', *Kerygma und Dogma*, 5.
Papcke, Sven (ed.) 1986, *Ordnung und Theorie. Beiträge zur Geschichte der Soziologie in Deutschland*, Darmstadt: Wissenschaftliche Buchgesellschaft.
Pappi, Franz Urban (ed.) 1989, *Wirtschaftsethik: Gesellschaftswissenschaftliche Perspektiven*, Kiel: Presse- und Informationsstelle der Universität.
Park, Chel-Soo 2000, *Three Essays in Marxian Economics: A Study of Marxian Theory of Competition and Dynamics*, dissertation, New School University, New York.
—— 2001, 'Criteria of Technical Choice and Evolution of Technical Change' in *Marx's Capital and Capitalism. Markets in a Socialist Alternative*, edited by Paul Zarembka, Amsterdam: JAI.
Parkin, Frank 1979, *Marxism and Class Theory: A Bourgeois Critique*, London: Tavistock.
Parsons, Talcott 1928, 'Capitalism in Recent German Literature: Sombart and Weber', *Journal of Political Economy*, 36, 641–661.
—— 1951, *The Social System*, New York: The Free Press.
—— 1954 [1940], 'An Analytical Approach to the Theory of Social Stratification' in *Essays in Sociological Theory. Revised Edition*, New York: The Free Press.
Parsons, Talcott 1968 [1937], *The Structure of Social Action: A Study in Social Theory, with Special Reference to a Group of Recent European Writers*, 2 Vols., New York: Free Press.
Pashukanis, Evgeny 1983 [1924], *Law and Marxism: A General Theory*, London: Pluto Press.
Pasternack, Gerhard (ed.) 1990, *Zur späten Ästhetik von Georg Lukács*, Frankfurt am Main: Vervuert.
Paul, E. Frankel (ed.) 1986, *Marxism and Liberalism*, Oxford: Blackwell.
Payne, Robert 1966, *The Rise and Fall of Stalin*, New York: Avon.
Peirce, Charles Sanders 1891, 'The Architecture of Theories', *The Monist*, 1: 161–76. Now in *Collected Papers*, 6.8–6.34.
—— 1960–66, *Collected Papers* (cited as *CP*), 13 Vols., Cambridge: Cambridge University Press.
Pennock, J. Roland and John W. Chapman (eds.) 1983, *Marxism*, New York: New York University Press.
Pepperle, Heinz and Ingrid Pepperle (eds.) 1985, *Die Hegelsche Linke. Dokumente zu Philosophie und Politik im deutschen Vormärz*, Leipzig: Reclam.
Perelman, Michael 1987, *Marx's Crisis Theory: Scarcity, Labor, and Finance*, New York: Greenwood Press.
—— 2000, *The Invention of Capitalism: Classical Political Economy and the Secret History of Primitive Accumulation*, Durham, NC: Duke University Press.

Peter, Ulrich 1995, *Der "Bund der religiösen Sozialisten" in Berlin von 1919 bis 1933. Geschichte–Struktur–Theologie und Politik*, Frankfurt am Main: Lang.

Petersen, Thiess 1997, *Anthropologie und Ökonomie. Das Menschenbild bei Marx und dessen Bedeutung für seine Kritik an der politischen Ökonomie*, Frankfurt am Main: Lang.

Petrovic, Gajo 1967 [1965], *Marx in the Mid-Twentieth Century: A Yugoslav Philosopher Considers Karl Marx's Writings*, Garden City: Anchor Books.

—— 1971, *Philosophie und Revolution. Modelle für eine Marx-Interpretation. Mit Quellentexten*, Reinbek: Rowohlt.

Petrowicz, Stephan 1992, *Helmuth Plessner. Genese und System seines philosophisch-anthropologischen Denkens*, Freiburg: Alber.

Petry, Franz 1974 [1916], 'Der soziale Gehalt der Marxschen Werttheorie' in *Die Marxsche Theorie und ihre Kritik*, edited by Hans G. Nutzinger and Elmar Wolfstetter, Frankfurt am Main: Campus.

Petulla, Joseph 1972, *Christian Political Theology: A Marxian Guide*, New York: Orbis.

Pfabigam, Alfred 1982, *Max Adler. Eine politische Biographie*, Frankfurt am Main: Campus.

Pfleiderer, Georg 2000, *Karl Barths praktische Theologie. Zu Genese und Kontext eines paradigmatischen Entwurfs systematischer Theologie im 20. Jahrhundert*, Tübingen: Mohr.

Phillips, Kevin 1990, *The Politics of Rich and Poor*, New York: Random House.

Phillips, A.W. 1958, 'The Relation Between Unemployment and the Rate of Change in the Money Wage Rates in the United Kingdom, 1861–1957', *Economica*, 11, 283–299.

Pieper, Annemarie (ed.) 1998, *Angewandte Ethik*, Munich: Beck.

Pies, Ingo 2000, *Ordnungspolitik in der Demokratie*, Tübingen: Mohr.

Pike, Jonathan E. 1999, *From Aristotle to Marx: Aristotelianism in Marxist Social Ontology*, Aldershot: Ashgate.

Pilgrim, Volker Elis 1990, *Adieu Marx. Gewalt und Ausbeutung im Hause des Wortführers*, Reinbek: Rowohlt.

Pircher, Wolfgang (ed.) 1999, *Gegen den Ausnahmezustand. Zur Kritik an Carl Schmitt*, Vienna: Springer.

PKA (Projekt Klassenanalyse) 1972, *Leninismus – neue Stufe des wissenschaftlichen Sozialismus? Zum Verhältnis von Marxscher Theorie, Klassenanalyse und revolutionärer Taktik bei W.I. Lenin*, Berlin: Verlag für das Studium der Arbeiterbewegung.

—— 1973–4, *Materialien zur Klassenstruktur der BRD*, 2 Vols., Berlin: Verlag für das Studium der Arbeiterbewegung.

—— 1975, *Stamokap in der Krise oder das Kapital als Notanker*, Berlin: Verlag für das Studium der Arbeiterbewegung.

Plamenatz, John 1954, *German Marxism and Russian Communism*, London: Longmans.

Pleasants, Nigel 1999, *Wittgenstein and the Idea of a Critical Social Theory: A Critique of Giddens, Habermas and Bhaskar*, London: Routledge.

Plechanow, G.W. 1929, 'Bernstein und der Materialismus' in *Werke*, Vol. 11.

Plenge, Johann 1911, *Marx und Hegel*, Tübingen: Laupp.

Plessner, Helmuth 1928, *Die Stufen des Organischen und der Mensch. Einleitung in die philosophische Anthropologie*, Berlin: de Gruyter, 1928.

—— 1992 [1959], *Die verspätete Nation. Über die politische Verführbarkeit bürgerlichen Geistes*, Frankfurt am Main: Suhrkamp.

—— 2002 [1924], *Grenzen der Gemeinschaft. Eine Kritik des sozialen Radikalismus*, Frankfurt am Main: Suhrkamp.

Plonz, Sabine 1995, *Die herrenlosen Gewalten. Eine Relektüre Karl Barths in befreiungstheologischer Perspektive*, Mainz: Grünewald.

Plümacher, Martina 1996, *Philosophie nach 1945 in der Bundesrepublik Deutschland*, Reinbek: Rowohlt.

Pogge, Thomas W. 1994, *John Rawls*, Munich: Beck.

—— 2002, *World Poverty and Human Rights*, Cambridge: Polity Press.

Poggi, Alfredo 1904, *La questione morale nel socialismo (Kant e il socialismo)*, Palermo: Reber.

Pohl, Friedrich Wilhelm and Christoph Türcke 1999, *Heilige Hure Vernunft. Luthers nachhaltiger Zauber*, Lüneburg: zu Klampen.

Pohl, Hans (ed.) 1993, *Europäische Bankengeschichte*, Frankfurt am Main: Knapp.

Pohrt, Wolfgang 1976, *Theorie des Gebrauchswertes oder über die Vergänglichkeit der historischen Voraussetzungen, unter denen allein das Kapital Gebrauchswert setzen kann*, Frankfurt am Main: Syndikat.

Polanyi, Karl 1957, *The Great Transformation: The Political and Economic Origins of Our Time*, Boston: Beacon Press.

Pollock, Friedrich 1926, *Sombarts "Widerlegung" des Marxismus*, Leipzig: C.H. Hirschfeld.

—— 1941, 'Is National Socialism a New Order?', *Studies in Philosophy and Social Science*, 9: 440–455.

—— 1941a: 'State Capitalism: Its Possibilities and Limitations', *Studies in Philosophy and Social Science*, 9, 2: 200–255.

—— 1957 [1956], *Automation: A Study of its Economic and Social Consequences*, New York: Praeger.

—— 1971 [1929], *Die planwirtschaftlichen Versuche in der Sowjetunion 1917–1927*, Frankfurt am Main: Verlag Neue Kritik.

—— 1975 [1933], 'Bemerkungen zur Wirtschaftskrise' in *Stadien des Kapitalismus*, Munich: Beck.

—— 1975a [1932], 'Die gegenwärtige Lage des Kapitalismus und die Aussichten einer planwirtschaftlichen Neuordnung' in *Stadien des Kapitalismus*, Munich: Beck.

Polybius 1922–7, *The Histories*, London: Heinemann.

Pongs, Armin 1999–2000, *In welcher Gesellschaft leben wir eigentlich? Gesellschaftskonzepte im Vergleich*, 2 Vols., Munich: Dilemma.

Popitz, Heinrich 1967 [1953], *Der entfremdete Mensch. Zeitkritik und Geschichtsphilosophie des jungen Marx*, Frankfurt am Main: Europäische Verlags-Anstalt.

—— 1980, *Die normative Konstruktion von Gesellschaft*, Tübingen: Mohr.

Popitz, Heinrich et al. 1957, *Technik und Industriearbeit*, Tübingen: Mohr.

—— 1957a: *Das Gesellschaftsbild des Arbeiters*, Tübingen: Mohr.

Popper, Karl R. 1945 [1944], *The Open Society and Its Enemies*, 2 Vols., London: Routledge & Kegan Paul.

—— 1957, *The Poverty of Historicism*, Boston: Beacon Press.

Post, Werner 1969, *Kritik der Religion bei Karl Marx*, Munich: Kösel.

—— 1971, *Kritische Theorie und metaphysischer Pessimismus. Zum Spätwerk Max Horkheimers*, Munich: Kösel.

Postone, Moishe 1993, *Time, Labor, and Social Domination: A Reinterpretation of Marx's Critical Theory*, Cambridge: Cambridge University Press.

Postone, Moishe and Barbara Brick 1982, 'Critical Pessimism and the Limits of Traditional Marxism', *Theory and Society*, 11, 5: 617–58.

Poulantzas, Nicos 1975, *Classes in Contemporary Capitalism*, London: New Left Books.

—— 1978, *State, Power, Socialism*, London: New Left Books.

Preiser, Erich 1924, *Das Wesen der Marxschen Krisentheorie. In: Wirtschaft und Gesellschaft. Beiträge zur Ökonomik und Soziologie der Gegenwart. Festschrift für Franz Oppenheimer zu seinem 60. Geburtstag*, Frankfurt am Main: Frankfurter Societäts-Druckerei.

—— 1967, *Wirtschaftspolitik heute. Grundprobleme der Marktwirtschaft*, Munich: Beck.

—— 1974, *Politische Ökonomie im 20. Jahrhundert. Probleme und Gestalten*, Munich: Beck.

Preobrazhensky, E.A. 1965 [1926], *The New Economics*, London: Clarendon Press.

Pribam, Karl 1992, *Geschichte des ökonomischen Denkens*, 2 Vols., Frankfurt am Main: Suhrkamp.

Prior, Bernd 1998, 'Der Transaktionskosten- und Property Rights-Ansatz bei Marx als Grundlage für seine Kritik der Marktwirtschaft' in *Zur kontinentalen Geschichte des ökonomischen Denkens*, edited by Jörg Glombowski et al., Marburg: Metropolis.

Prokop, Siegfried 1996, *Ein Streiter für Deutschland. Auseinandersetzung mit Wolfgang Harich*, Berlin: Edition Ost.

Protokoll der Verhandlungen in Moskau vom 2. bis 10. März 1919. Der erste Kongress der Kommunistischen Internationale, Hamburg 1921. Reprinted 1967, Milan: Feltrinelli.

Prümmer, Franz von 1965, *Von Marx bis Godesberg. Geschichte, Wirklichkeit, Absicht*, Würzburg: Fränkische Gesellschaftsdruckerei.

Przeworski, Adam 1985, *Capitalism and Social Democracy*, Cambridge: Cambridge University Press.

Putnam, Hilary 1992, 'A Reconsideration of Deweyan Democracy' in *Renewing Philosophy*, Cambridge, MA: Harvard University Press.

—— 1995, *Pragmatism: An Open Question*, Cambridge: Blackwell.

—— 1998, 'Pragmatism and Realism' in *The Revival of Pragmatism: New Essays on Social Thought, Law, and Culture*, edited by Morris Dickstein, Durham, NC: Duke University Press.

Quesel, Carsten 1989, *Soziologie und soziale Frage. Lorenz von Stein und die Entstehung der Gesellschaftswissenschaft in Deutschland*, Wiesbaden: Deutscher Universitäts-Verlag.

Quesnay, Francois 1965 [1758], *Tableau économique. Remarques sur les variations de la distribution des revenus annuels dúne nation*, Berlin: Akademie-Verlag.

Quine, William V. 1960, *Word and Object*, Cambridge, MA: MIT Press.
Raatzsch, Richard 2000, *Philosophiephilosophie*, Stuttgart: Reclam.
Rabehl, Bernd 1973, *Marx und Lenin. Widersprüche einer ideologischen Konstruktion des "Marxismus-Leninismus"*, Berlin: VSA.
Raddatz, Fritz J. 1975, *Karl Marx. Eine politische Biographie*, Hamburg: Hoffmann und Campe.
Radek, Karl 1909, *Die Entwicklung des Sozialismus von der Wissenschaft zur Tat*, Berlin: A. Hoffmann, 1909.
Ragaz, Leonhard 1929, *Von Christus zu Marx – von Marx zu Christus*, Wernigerode: Harder.
Rakowitz, Nadja 2000, *Einfache Warenproduktion. Ideal und Ideologie*, Freiburg: Ça ira.
Rakowitz, Nadja and Jürgen Behre 2001, 'Automatisches Subjekt? Zur Bedeutung des Kapitalbegriffs bei Marx', manuscript of lecture held at Rote Ruhr Uni, 15 November.
Ramm, Thilo (ed.) 1955, *Die großen Sozialisten als Rechts- und Sozialphilosophen*, 2 Vols., Stuttgart: Fischer.
—— 1957, 'Die künftige Gesellschaftsordnung nach der Theorie von Marx und Engels', *Marxismusstudien*, 2: 77–119.
Rammstedt, Otthein 1986, *Deutsche Soziologie 1933–1945. Die Normalität einer Anpassung*, Frankfurt am Main: Suhrkamp.
Rammstedt, Otthein and Gert Schmidt (eds.) 1992, *BRD Ade! Vierzig Jahre in Rück-Ansichten von Sozial- und Kulturwissenschaftlern*, Frankfurt am Main: Suhrkamp.
Rancière, Jacques 1975, *Wider den akademischen Marxismus*, Berlin: Merve.
Rath, Norbert 1987, 'Zur Nietzsche-Rezeption Horkheimers und Adornos' in *Vierzig Jahre Flaschenpost: "Dialektik der Aufklärung" 1947 bis 1987*, edited by Willem van Reijen and Gunzelin Schmid Noerr, Frankfurt am Main: Fischer.
Rathenau, Walther 1913, *Zur Mechanik des Geistes oder vom Reich der Seele*, Berlin: Fischer.
Rauh, Hans-Christoph (ed.) 1978, *Ideologischer Klassenkampf und bürgerliche Gegenwartsphilosophie. Studien*, East Berlin: Dietz.
—— 1991, *Gefesselter Widerspruch. Die Affäre um Peter Ruben*, Berlin: Dietz.
Rauh, Hans-Christoph and Volker Gerhardt (eds.) 2001, *Anfänge der DDR-Philosophie. Ansprüche, Ohnmacht, Scheitern (1945–1958)*, Berlin: Links.
Raupach, Hans 1968, *Das System der Sowjetwirtschaft. Theorie und Praxis*, Reinbek: Rowohlt.
Rauti, Alessandra 1999, *Die Bedeutung der Philosophie Diltheys für den frühen Heidegger*, dissertation, University of Hamburg.
Rawls, John 1958, *Justice as Fairness*, New York: Irvington.
—— 1971, *A Theory of Justice*, Cambridge, MA: Belknap Press.
—— 1977, 'The Basic Structure as Subject', *American Philosophical Quarterly*, 14, 2: 159–65.
—— 1993, *Political Liberalism*, New York: Columbia University Press.
—— 1999, *The Law of Peoples*, Cambridge, MA: Harvard University Press.
—— 2001, *Justice as Fairness: A Restatement*, Cambridge, MA: Harvard University Press.
Recker, Marie-Luise 1985, *Nationalsozialistische Sozialpolitik im Zweiten Weltkrieg*, Munich: Oldenbourg.
Reding, Marcel 1957, *Der Sinn des Marxschen Atheismus*, Munich: Pustet.
—— 1957a: *Der politische Atheismus*, Graz: Styria.
Rees, John 1998, *The Algebra of Revolution: The Dialectic and the Classical Marxist Tradition*, London: Routledge.
Reese-Schäfer, Walter 1994, *Kommunitarismus*, Frankfurt am Main: Campus.
—— 1998, 'Kommunitaristisches Sozialstaatsdenken. Sozialpolitische Gerechtigkeitsimplikationen in der kommunitaristischen Diskussion' in *Sozialpolitik und Gerechtigkeit*, edited by Siegfried Blasche, Frankfurt am Main: Campus.
—— 2000, *Politische Theorie heute*, Munich: Oldenbourg.
Rehberg, Karl-Siegbert 1979, 'Rationales Handeln als großbürgerliches Aktionsmodell. Thesen zu einigen handlungstheoretischen Implikationen der "Soziologischen Grundbegriffe" Max Webers', *Kölner Zeitschrift für Soziologie und Sozialpsychologie*, 31: 199–236.
—— 1981, 'Philosophische Anthropologie und die "Soziologisierung" des Wissens vom Menschen. Einige Zusammenhänge zwischen einer philosophischen Denktradition und der Soziologie in Deutschland' in *Soziologie in Deutschland und Österreich 1918–1945. Materialien zur Entwicklung, Emigration und Wirkungsgeschichte*, edited by M. Rainer Lepsius, Opladen: Westdeutscher Verlag.
—— 1985, 'Die Theorie der Intersubjektivität als eine Lehre vom Menschen. G.H. Mead

und die deutsche Tradition der "Philosophischen Anthropologie"' in *Das Problem der Intersubjektivität. Neuere Beiträge zum Werk George Herbert Meads*, edited by Hans Joas, Frankfurt am Main: Suhrkamp.

—— 1986, 'Deutungswissen der Moderne oder "administrative Hilfswissenschaft"? Konservative Schwierigkeiten mit der Soziologie' in *Ordnung und Theorie. Beiträge zur Geschichte der Soziologie in Deutschland*, edited by Sven Papcke, Darmstadt: Wissenschaftliche Buchgesellschaft.

—— 1993, 'Gemeinschaft und Gesellschaft – Tönnies und Wir' in *Gemeinschaft und Gerechtigkeit*, edited by Micha Brumlik and Hauke Brunkhorst, Frankfurt am Main: Fischer.

—— 1994, 'Existentielle Motive im Werk Arnold Gehlens. "Persönlichkeit" als Schlüsselkategorie der Gehlenschen Anthropologie und Sozialtheorie' in *Zur geisteswissenschaftlichen Bedeutung von Arnold Gehlen*, edited by Helmut Klages and Helmut Quaritsch, Berlin: Duncker und Humblot.

—— 1994a: 'Institutionen als symbolische Ordnungen. Leitfragen und Grundkategorien zur Theorie und Analyse institutioneller Mechanismen' in *Die Eigenart der Institutionen. Zum Profil politischer Institutionentheorie*, edited by Gerhard Göhler, Baden-Baden: Nomos.

—— 1999, 'Hans Freyer', 'Arnold Gehlen', 'Helmut Schelsky' in *Klassiker der Soziologie*, edited by Dirk Kaesler, Vol. 2, *Von Talcott Parsons bis Pierre Bourdieu*, Munich: Beck.

—— 2000, 'Kommunistische und konservative Bejahung der Institution. Eine Brief-Freundschaft' in *Wolfgang Harich zum Gedächtnis. Eine Gedenkschrift*, Vol. 1, Munich: Beck.

Reibel, Carl-Wilhelm 2002, *Das Fundament der Diktatur. Die NSDAP-Ortsgruppen 1932–1945*, Paderborn: Schöningh.

Reich, Robert B. 1992, *The Work of Nations: Preparing Ourselves for 21st Century Capitalism*, New York: Vintage.

Reich, Wilhelm 1929, 'Dialektischer Materialismus und Psychoanalyse', *Unter dem Banner des Marxismus*, 3.

Reichel, Peter 1991, *Der schöne Schein des Dritten Reiches – Faszination und Gewalt des Faschismus*, Munich: Hanser.

Reichelt, Helmut 1970, *Zur logischen Struktur des Kapitalbegriffs bei Karl Marx*, Frankfurt am Main: Europäische Verlags-Anstalt.

—— 1974, 'Zum Wissenschaftsbegriff bei Karl Marx' in *Marx und Marxismus heute*, edited by Gerd Breitenbürger and Günter Schnitzler, Hamburg: Hoffmann und Campe.

—— 2002, 'Die Marxsche Kritik ökonomischer Kategorien. Überlegungen zum Problem der Geltung in der dialektischen Darstellungsmethode im "Kapital"' in *Emanzipation als Versöhnung. Zu Adornos Kritik der "Warentausch"-Gesellschaft und Perspektiven der Transformation*, edited by Iring Fetscher and Alfred Schmidt, Frankfurt am Main: Verlag Neue Kritik.

Reid, Thomas 1994 [1784], 'Of Common Sense' in *The Works of Thomas Reid*, Vol. 1, Bristol: Thoemmes Press.

Reijen, Wilhelm van 1984, *Philosophie als Kritik. Einführung in die kritische Theorie*, Königstein: Athenäum.

Reijen, Wilhelm van and Jan Bransen 1987, 'Das Verschwinden der Klassengeschichte in der "Dialektik der Aufklärung". Ein Kommentar zu den Textvarianten der Buchausgabe von 1947 gegenüber der Erstveröffentlichung von 1944' in Max Horkheimer, *Gesammelte Schriften*, Vol. 5, Frankfurt am Main: Fischer.

Reijen, Wilhelm van and Gunzelin Schmid Noerr (eds.) 1990, *Grand Hotel Abgrund. Eine Photobiographie der Frankfurter Schule*, Hamburg: Junius.

Reikerstorfer, Johann (ed.) 1998, *Vom Wagnis der Nichtidentität. Johann Baptist Metz zu Ehren*, Münster: Lit.

Reiman, Jeffrey 1991, 'Moral Philosophy: The Critique of Capitalism and the Problem of Ideology' in *The Cambridge Companion to Marx*, edited by Terrel Carver, Cambridge: Cambridge University Press.

Reisberg, Arnold 1980, *Wladimir Iljitsch Lenin. Dokumente seines Lebens. 1870–1924*, 2 Vols., Leipzig: Reclam.

Reisinger, Ferdinand (ed.) 1983, *Marxismus und Christentum*, Linz: OLV-Buchverlag.

—— 1985, 'Christentum und Marxismus – ein Beispiel ideologischer Auseinandersetzung' in *Funk-Kolleg Religion* 2, edited by Peter Fiedler et al., Gütersloh: Mohn.

Remmers, Hartmut 1994, *Hans Freyer: Heros und Industriegesellschaft. Studien zur Sozialphilosophie*, Opladen: Leske und Budrich.

Rendtorff, Trutz and Heinz Eduard Tödt 1968, *Theologie der Revolution. Analysen und Materialien*, Frankfurt am Main: Suhrkamp.

Renner, Karl 1917, *Marxismus, Krieg und Internationale*, Stuttgart: Dietz.

—— 1965 [1903/1928], *Die Rechtsinstitute des Privatrechts und ihre soziale Funktion*, Stuttgart: Fischer.

Renton, Dave (ed.) 2001, *Marx on Globalization*, London: Lawrence & Wishart.

Rentsch, Thomas 1999, 'Husserl, Edmund', 'Lask, Emil' and 'Simmel, Georg' in *Die großen Philosophen des 20. Jahrhunderts. Biographisches Lexikon*, edited by Bernd Lutz, Munich: Deutscher Taschenbuch-Verlag.

—— 1999a [1990], *Konstitution der Moralität. Transzendentale Anthropologie und praktische Philosophie*, Frankfurt am Main: Suhrkamp.

—— 2000, *Negativität und praktische Vernunft*, Frankfurt am Main: Suhrkamp.

—— 2000a: 'Pathos der Distanz?', *Philosophische Rundschau*, 47, 3: 234–9.

—— 2001, *Martin Heidegger: Sein und Zeit*, Berlin: Akademie-Verlag.

—— 2003 [1985], *Heidegger und Wittgenstein. Existential- und Sprachanalysen zu den Grundlagen philosophischer Anthropologie*, Stuttgart: Klett-Cotta.

—— 2003a: 'Substitute des Absoluten', lecture held in Dresden.

'Resolution der Parteizelle des Institutes der Roten Professur für Philosophie und Naturwissenschaften in Moskau, 29 December 1930' in *Unter dem Banner des Marxismus*, 5, 2: 161–70.

Reuter, Norbert 1994, *Der Institutionalismus. Geschichte und Theorie der evolutionären Ökonomie*, Marburg: Metropolis.

—— 2000, *Ökonomik der "langen Frist". Zur Evolution der Wachstumsgrundlagen in Industriegesellschaften*, Marburg: Metropolis.

—— 2001, 'Aufbruch in die Vergangenheit. Die Initiative Neue Soziale Marktwirtschaft missachtet Traditionen, auf die sie sich beruft', *Die Zeit*, 11 October 2001.

RGG: Die Religion in Geschichte und Gegenwart. Handwörterbuch für Theologie und Religionswissenschaft, 1928–32, 6 Vols., edited by Hermann Gunkel and L. Zscharnack, Tübingen: Mohr.

Ricardo, David 1992 [1817], *The Principles of Political Economy and Taxation*, London: Dent.

Rich, Arthur 1951, 'Die kryptoreligiösen Motive in den Frühschriften von Karl Marx', *Theologische Zeitschrift*, 7: 192 ff.

—— 1962, *Das Menschenbild des jungen Marx und der christliche Glaube*, Zürich: Gotthelf-Verlag.

—— 1987, *Wirtschaftsethik. Grundlagen in theologischer Perspektive*, Gütersloh: Mohn.

—— 1990, *Wirtschaftsethik II. Marktwirtschaft, Weltwirtschaft, Planwirtschaft*, Gütersloh: Mohn.

Rickert, Heinrich 1896–1902, *Die Grenzen der naturwissenschaftlichen Begriffsbildung. Eine logische Einleitung in die historische Wissenschaft*, 2 Vols., Tübingen: Mohr.

—— 1911–12, 'Lebenswerte und Kulturwerte', *Logos*, 2.

—— 1920, *Die Philosophie des Lebens. Darstellung und Kritik der philosophischen Modeströmungen unserer Zeit*, Tübingen: Mohr.

—— 1921, 'Psychologie der Weltanschauungen und Philosophie der Werte', *Logos*, 9: 1–42.

—— 1923, 'Die philosophischen Grundlagen von Fichtes Sozialismus', *Logos*, 11.

—— 1934, *Grundprobleme der Philosophie. Methodologie, Ontologie, Anthropologie*, Tübingen: Mohr.

—— 1938, 'Die allgemeinen Grundlagen der Politik Fichtes', *Zeitschrift für deutsche Kulturphilosophie*, 4.

Riedel, Manfred 1965, *Theorie und Praxis im Denken Hegels*, Stuttgart: Kohlhammer.

—— 1972, *Rehabilitierung der praktischen Philosophie*, Freiburg: Rombach.

—— 1973 [1970], 'Hegel und Marx' in *System und Geschichte. Studien zum historischen Standort von Hegels Philosophie*, Frankfurt am Main: Suhrkamp.

—— 1975, *Materialien zu Hegels Rechtsphilosophie*, Vol. 2, Frankfurt am Main: Suhrkamp.

—— 1994, *Tradition und Utopie. Ernst Blochs Philosophie im Licht unserer geschichtlichen Denkerfahrung*, Frankfurt am Main: Suhrkamp.

—— 2000, *Nietzsche in Weimar. Ein deutsches Drama*, Leipzig: Reclam.

Riesman, David 1953, *The Lonely Crowd: A Study of the Changing American Character*, Garden City: Doubleday.

—— 1968 [1957], *Die einsame Masse. Eine Untersuchung der Wandlungen des amerikanischen Charakters. Mit einer Einführung in die deutsche Ausgabe von Helmut Schelsky*, Reinbek: Rowohlt.

—— 1994, 'Historische Schule' in *Geschichte der Nationalökonomie*, edited by Otmar Issing, Munich: Vahlen.

Rifkin, Jeremy 2000, *The Age of Access: The New Culture of Hypercapitalism, Where All of Life is a Paid-For Experience*, New York: J.P. Tarcher.

Ringer, Fritz K. 1987 [1969], *Die Gelehrten. Der Niedergang der deutschen Mandarine, 1890–1933*, Munich: Klett-Cotta.

Ritsert, Jürgen and Claus Rolshausen 1973 [1970], 'Zur Sozialstruktur der Bundesrepublik Deutschland' in *Gesellschaftsstrukturen*, edited by Klaus Meschkat and Oskar Negt, Frankfurt am Main: Suhrkamp.

Ritsert, Jürgen 1988, *Der Kampf um das Surplusprodukt. Einführung in den klassischen Klassenbegriff*, Frankfurt am Main: Campus.

—— 1998, *Soziale Klassen*, Münster: Westfälisches Dampfboot.

Ritter, Gerhard A. 1959, *Die Arbeiterbewegung im Wilhelminischen Reich*, Berlin: Colloquium.

—— 1990, *Der Aufstieg der deutschen Arbeiterbewegung. Sozialdemokratie und freie Gewerkschaften im Parteiensystem und Sozialmilieu des Kaiserreichs*, Munich: Oldenbourg.

Ritter, Gerhard A. and Klaus Tenfelde 1992, *Arbeiter im Deutschen Kaiserreich*, Bonn: Dietz.

Ritter, Joachim 1974, *Subjektivität. Sechs Aufsätze*, Frankfurt am Main: Suhrkamp.

—— 2003 [1963], 'Die Aufgabe der Geisteswissenschaften in der modernen Gesellschaft' in *Metaphysik und Politik. Studien zu Aristoteles und Hegel. Erweiterte Neuausgabe*, Frankfurt am Main: Suhrkamp.

—— 2003a [1962], 'Person und Eigentum. Zu Hegels "Grundlinien der Philosophie des Rechts", §§ 34–81' in *Metaphysik und Politik. Studien zu Aristoteles und Hegel. Erweiterte Neuausgabe*, Frankfurt am Main: Suhrkamp.

Rittstieg, Helmut 1975, *Eigentum als Verfassungsproblem. Zu Geschichte und Gegenwart des bürgerlichen Verfassungsstaates*, Darmstadt: Wissenschaftliche Buchgesellschaft.

Robinson, Joan 1933, *The Economics of Imperfect Competition*, London: Macmillan.

—— 1966 [1942], *An Essay on Marxian Economics*, New York: St. Martin's Press.

—— 1974 [1958], *The Accumulation of Capital*, New York: Monthly Review Press.

Rockmore, Tom 1989, *Habermas on Historical Materialism*, Bloomington, IN: Indiana University Press.

—— 2002, *Marx after Marxism: The Philosophy of Karl Marx*, Oxford: Blackwell.

Röd, Wolfgang 1986, *Dialektische Philosophie der Neuzeit*, Munich: Beck.

Roderick, Rick 1989, *Habermas und das Problem der Rationalität. Eine Werkmonographie*, Hamburg: Argument.

Rodi, Frithjof 1990, *Erkenntnis des Erkannten. Zur Hermeneutik des 19. und 20. Jahrhunderts*, Frankfurt am Main: Suhrkamp.

Roemer, John 1978, 'Neoclassicism, Marxism and Collective Action', *Journal of Economic Issues*, 7: 85–99.

—— 1981, *Analytical Foundations of Marxian Economic Theory*, Cambridge; Cambridge University Press.

—— 1982, *A General Theory of Exploitation and Class*, Cambridge, MA: Harvard University Press.

—— 1986, *Analytical Marxism*, Cambridge: Cambridge University Press.

—— 1988, *Free to Lose: An Introduction to Marxist Economic Philosophy*, Cambridge, MA: Harvard University Press.

Rohbeck, Jonannes (ed.) 1999, *Philosophie und Weltanschauung*, Dresden: Thelem.

—— 2000, *Technik–Kultur–Geschichte. Eine Rehabilitierung der Geschichtsphilosophie*, Frankfurt am Main: Suhrkamp.

Röhr, Heinz 1962, *Pseudoreligiöse Motive in den Frühschriften von Karl Marx*, Tübingen: Mohr.

Röhrich, Wilfried 1980, *Marx und die materialistische Staatstheorie: Ein Überblick*, Darmstadt: Wissenschaftliche Buchgesellschaft.

Rohrmoser, Günter 1961, *Subjektivität und Verdinglichung. Theologie und Gesellschaft im Denken des jungen Hegel*, Gütersloh: Mohn.

—— 1970, *Das Elend der kritischen Theorie*, Freiburg: Rombach.

—— 1971, *Nietzsche und das Ende der Emanzipation*, Freiburg: Rombach.

—— 1972, *Herrschaft und Versöhnung. Ästhetik und die Kulturrevolution des Westens*, Freiburg: Rombach.

—— 1974 [1968], 'Stillstand der Dialektik. Grundpositionen expliziter und impliziter Marxismuskritik' in *Marxismus und Menschlichkeit*, Freiburg: Herder.

—— 1994, *Der Ernstfall. Die Krise unserer liberalen Republik*, Frankfurt am Main: Ullstein.

—— 2000, *Geistige Wende. Christliches Denken als Fundament des modernen Konservativismus*, Munich: Olzog.

—— 2002, *Deutschlands Tragödie: Der geistige Weg in den Nationalsozialismus*, Munich: Olzog.

Rohs, Peter 1991, *Johann Gottlieb Fichte*, Munich: Beck.
Rojas, Rául 1989, *Das unvollendete Projekt. Zur Entstehungsgeschichte von Marx' "Kapital"*, Hamburg: Argument.
Rokumotom, Kahei (ed.) 1994, *Sociological Theories of Law*, New York: New York University Press.
Rolfes, Helmuth 1971, *Der Sinn des Lebens im marxistischen Denken*, Düsseldorf: Patmos.
—— 1974, *Marxismus – Christentum*, Mainz: Grünewald.
Rolshausen, Claus (ed.) 1970, *Kapitalismus und Krise. Eine Kontroverse um das Gesetz des tendentiellen Falls der Profitrate*, Frankfurt am Main: Europäische Verlags-Anstalt.
Rolshausen, Claus et al. (eds.) 1969, *Monopolkapital. Thesen zu dem Buch von Paul A. Baran und Paul M. Sweezy*, Frankfurt am Main: Europäische Verlags-Anstalt.
Roncaglia, Alessandro 2000, *Piero Sraffa: His Life, Thought and Cultural Heritage*, London: Routledge.
Ronge, Volker 1979, *Bankpolitik im Spätkapitalismus. Politische Selbstverwaltung des Kapitals?* Frankfurt am Main: Suhrkamp.
Ropohl, Günther 1991, *Technologische Aufklärung. Beiträge zur Technikphilosophie*, Frankfurt am Main: Suhrkamp.
Röpke, Wilhelm 1958, *Jenseits von Angebot und Nachfrage*, Stuttgart: Rentsch.
Rorty, Richard (ed.) 1967, *The Linguistic Turn*, Chicago: University of Chicago Press.
—— 1979, *Philosophy and the Mirror of Nature*, Princeton, NJ: Princeton University Press.
—— 1982, *Consequences of Pragmatism: Essays 1972–1980*, Minneapolis: University of Minnesota Press.
—— 1989, *Contingency, Irony, and Solidarity*, Cambridge: Cambridge University Press.
—— 1989a: *Philosophy and Social Hope*, Cambridge: Cambridge University Press.
—— 1991, 'The Priority of Democracy to Philosophy' in *Objectivity, Relativism and Truth*, Cambridge: Cambridge University Press.
—— 1994, 'Dewey Between Hegel and Darwin' in *Rorty and Pragmatism: The Philosopher Responds to his Critics*, edited by Herman J. Saatkamp, Nashville: Vanderbilt University Press.
—— 1998, *Achieving Our Century: Leftist Thought in Twentieth-Century America*, Cambridge, MA: Harvard University Press.
—— 2003, 'Demütigung oder Solidarität? Für Amerika wäre es eine Tragödie, wenn Europa sich nicht gegen Washington behaupten würde', *Süddeutsche Zeitung*, 31 May.
Rosdolsky, Roman 1977, *The Making of Marx's "Capital"*, London: Pluto Press.
Rose, Günther 1974, *"Industriegesellschaft" und Konvergenztheorie. Genesis, Strukturen, Funktionen*, Berlin: Deutscher Verlag der Wissenschaften.
Rose, Klaus 1991, *Grundlagen der Wachstumstheorie*, Göttingen. Vandenhoeck und Ruprecht.
Rosenberg, Arthur 1939, *Democracy and Socialism: A Contribution to the Political History of the Past 150 Years*, London: Bell.
—— 1939a [1933], *A History of Bolshevism: From Marx to the First Five Year Plan*, Oxford: Oxford University Press.
—— 1955, *Entstehung und Geschichte der deutschen Republik*, Frankfurt am Main: Europäische Verlags-Anstalt.
Rosenberg, Hans 1974 [1934], *Die Weltwirtschaftskrise 1857–1859*, Göttingen: Vandenhoeck und Ruprecht.
Rosshoff, Hartmut 1975, *Emil Lask als Lehrer von Georg Lukács. Zur Form ihres Gegenstandsbegriffs*, Bonn: Bouvier.
Rostow, Walt W. 1960, *The Stages of Economic Growth: A Non-Communist Manifesto*, Cambridge: Cambridge University Press.
—— 1990, *Theorists of Economic Growth from David Hume to the Present. With a Perspective on the Next Century*, Oxford: Oxford University Press.
Roters, Karl-Heinz 1998, *Reflexionen über Ideologie und Ideologiekritik*, Würzburg: Königshausen und Neumann.
Roth, Guenther 1963, *The Social Democrats in Imperial Germany. A Study in Working-Class Isolation and National Integration*, Totowa: Bedminster Press.
—— 1968, 'Das historische Verhältnis der Weberschen Soziologie zum Marxismus', *Kölner Zeitschrift für Soziologie und Sozialpsychologie*, 20: 433 ff.
Roth, Roland 1987, *Neue Soziale Bewegungen in der Bundesrepublik*, Bonn: Bundeszentrale für politische Bildung.
Rothacker, Erich 1934, 'Geschichtsphilosophie' in *Handbuch der Philosophie IV: Staat und Geschichte*, Munich: Oldenbourg.
—— 1938, *Die Schichten der Persönlichkeit*, Leipzig: Barth.

—— 1948 [1926], *Logik und Systematik der Geisteswissenschaften*, Bonn: Bouvier.

—— 1948a [1942], *Probleme der Kulturanthropologie*, Bonn: Bouvier.

Röttgers, K. 1995, 'Sozialphilosophie' in *Historisches Wörterbuch der Philosophie*, Vol. 9, edited by J. Ritter et al., Basel: Schwabe.

Rottleuthner, Hubert (ed.) 1975, *Probleme der marxistischen Rechtstheorie*, Frankfurt am Main: Suhrkamp.

Rousseau, Jean Jacques 1950 [1762], *The Social Contract*, New York: Dutton.

—— 1984 [1754], *A Discourse on Inequality*, Harmondsworth: Penguin.

Rowthorn, Bob 1984, *Capitalism, Conflict and Inflation: Essays in Political Economy*, London: Lawrence & Wishart.

Ruben, Peter: 'Über Sozialismus und Kommunismus. Was ist gemeint? Wie wäre zu denken?' Undated manuscript.

Ruben, Peter 1975, *Widerspruch und Naturdialektik. Dissertation B*, East Berlin: Max-Planck-Institut für Wirtschaftsgeschichte.

Rubin, Isaak I. 1972 [1926], *Essays on Marx's Theory of Value*, Detroit: Black and Red.

Rubinstein, David 1981, *Marx and Wittgenstein: Social Praxis and Social Explanation*, Boston: Routledge & Kegan Paul.

Rudas, Ladislaus 1924, 'Die Klassenbewusstseinstheorie von Lukács', *Arbeiter-Literatur*, 10.

Rüddenklau, Eberhard 1982, *Gesellschaftliche Arbeit oder Arbeit und Interaktion?* Frankfurt am Main: Lang.

Rudolph, Günther 1991, 'Ferdinand Tönnies und die Lehre von Karl Marx. Annäherung und Vorbehalt' in *Hundert Jahre "Gemeinschaft und Gesellschaft". Ferdinand Tönnies in der internationalen Diskussion*, edited by Lars Clausen, Lars and Carsten Schlüter, Opladen: Leske und Budrich.

Rügemer, Werner 1979, *Philosophische Anthropologie und Epochenkrise. Studie über den Zusammenhang von allgemeiner Krise des Kapitalismus und anthropologischer Grundlegung der Philosophie am Beispiel Arnold Gehlens*, Cologne: Pahl-Rugenstein.

Russell, Bertrand 1965 [1896], *German Social Democracy*, New York: Simon & Schuster.

Ruster, Thomas 2000, *Der verwechselbare Gott. Theologie nach der Entflechtung von Christentum und Religion*, Freiburg: Herder.

Rüthers, Bernd 1991, *Das Ungerechte an der Gerechtigkeit. Defizite eines Begriffs*, Zürich: Edition Interfrom.

Ryan, Alan 1995, *John Dewey and the High Tide of American Liberalism*, London: Norton.

Ryan, Michael 1982, *Marxism and Deconstruction*, Baltimore: Johns Hopkins University Press.

Rytlewski, Ralf and Manfred Opp de Hipt 1987, *Die Bundesrepublik Deutschland in Zahlen 1945/49–1980. Ein sozialgeschichtliches Arbeitsbuch*, Bonn: Bundeszentrale für politische Bildung.

Saage, Richard 1983, *Rückkehr zum starken Staat?* Frankfurt am Main: Suhrkamp.

—— 1986, *Solidargemeinschaft und Klassenkampf*, Frankfurt am Main: Suhrkamp.

Safranksi, Rüdiger 1994, *Ein Meister aus Deutschland. Heidegger und seine Zeit*, Munich: Hanser.

Sahmel, Karl-Heinz 1988, *Die Kritische Theorie: Bruchstücke*, Würzburg: Königshausen und Neumann.

Saint-Simon, Henri de 1834 [1825], *New Christianity*, London: Cousins.

Salomon, Albert 1945, 'German Sociology' in *Twentieth Century Sociology*, edited by George Gurvitch, New York: Philosophical Library.

Salomon, Gottfried (ed.) 1919, *Saint-Simon und der Sozialismus*, Berlin: Cassirer.

Salvadori, Massimo 1979, *Karl Kautsky and the Socialist Revolution 1880–1938*, London: New Left Books.

Samuelson, Paul A. 1948, *Economics: An Introductory Analysis*, New York: McGraw Hill.

—— 1967, 'Marxian Economics as Economics', *American Economic Review*, 57: 2.

—— 1971, 'Understanding the Marxian Notion of Exploitation: A Summary of the So-called Transformation Problem between Marxian Values and Competitive Prices', *Journal of Economic Literature*, 9, 2.

Sandbote, Mike (ed.) 2001, *Die Renaissance des Pragmatismus. Aktuelle Verflechtungen zwischen analytischer und kontinentaler Philosophie*, Weilerswist: Velbrück.

Sandel, Michael J. 1982, *Liberalism and the Limits of Justice*, Cambridge: Cambridge University Press.

—— 1984, *Liberalism and its Critics*, New York: New York University Press.

—— 1984a: 'The Procedural Republic and the Unencumbered Self', *Political Theory*, 12: 81–96.

Sandemose, Jörgen 2001, 'The World as a Game in Sraffa and Wittgenstein: A Case Study in Modern Bourgeois Ideology' in *Marx's*

Capital and Capitalism. Markets in a Socialist Alternative, edited by Paul Zarembka, Amsterdam: JAI.

Sandkühler, Hans Jörg (ed.) 1973, *Marxistische Erkenntnistheorie. Texte zu ihrem Forschungsstand in den sozialisitischen Ländern*, Stuttgart: Frommann-Holzboog.

—— 1973a: *Praxis und Geschichtsbewusstsein. Studie zur materialistischen Dialektik, Erkenntnistheorie und Hermeneutik*, Frankfurt am Main: Suhrkamp.

—— 1977, 'Plädoyer für den Historischen Materialismus als Philosophie' in *Theorien des historischen Materialismus 1*, edited by Axel Honneth and Urs Jaeggi, Frankfurt am Main: Suhrkamp.

—— 1983, *Karl Marx – Philosophie, Wissenschaft, Politik*, Cologne: Pahl-Rugenstein.

—— 1995 [1991], 'Dialektik und Materialismus in epistemischen Kontexten. Über den defizitären Status des historischen und dialektischen Materialismus in der Phase seiner Konsolidierung' in *Zukunft des Marxismus. Kolloquium der Internationalen Gesellschaft für Dialektische Philosophie*, edited by Domenico Losurdo, Cologne: Dinter.

Sandkühler, Hans Jörg and Rafael de la Vega (eds.) 1970, *Austromarxismus. Texte zu Ideologie und Klassenkampf von Otto Bauer, Max Adler, Karl Renner, Sigmund Kunfi, Béla Forgarasi und Julius Lengyel*, Frankfurt am Main: Europäische Verlags-Anstalt.

—— 1974, *Marxismus und Ethik*, Frankfurt am Main: Suhrkamp.

Sandkühler, Hans Jörg et al. (eds.) 1986, *Karl Marx. Kritik und positive Wissenschaft*, Cologne: Pahl-Rugenstein.

Sannwald, Rolf 1957, *Marx und die Antike*, Einsiedeln: Benziger.

Sartre, Jean Paul 1976 [1960]: *Critique of Dialectical Reason: Theory of Practical Ensembles*, London: New Left Books.

Sartre, Jean Paul et al. 1965, *Existentialismus und Marxismus. Eine Kontroverse zwischen Sartre, Garaudy, Hyppolite, Vigier und Orcel*, Frankfurt am Main: Suhrkamp.

Sass, Hans-Martin 1980, 'Philosophie in der DDR' in idem and Hans Michael Baumgartner: *Philosophie in Deutschland 1945–1975. Standpunkte, Entwicklungen, Literatur*, Meisenheim: Hain.

Sassen, Saskia 1988, *The Mobility of Labour and Capital*, Cambridge: Cambridge University Press.

—— 1991, *The Global City: New York, London, Tokyo*, Princeton: Princeton University Press.

Saul, John Ralston 1997, *The Unconscious Civilization*, New York: Free Press.

Sauvage, Dagmar de 2002, *Die Krise der Philosophie im Zeitalter wissenschaftlich-technischer Rationalität*, Reinbek: Rowohlt.

Sayers, Sean 1998, *Marxism and Human Nature*, London: Routledge.

Schaefer, Alfred 1997, *Das Dogma – Wegbereiter der Diktatur. Analyse von Stalin-Texten. Zur dialektischen Methode in "Das Kapital I"*, Cuxhaven: Traude.

Schaeffler, Richard 1973, *Einführung in die Geschichtsphilosophie*, Darmstadt: Wissenschaftliche Buchgesellschaft.

Schäfer, Gerd 1993, 'Leo Trotzki – die Tragödie eines revolutionären Marxisten' in *Ketzer im Kommunismus: Alternativen zum Stalinismus*,edited by Theodor Bergmann and Mario Kessler, Mainz: Decaton.

—— 1994, *Gewalt, Ideologie und Bürokratismus. Das Scheitern eines Jahrhundertexperiments*, Mainz: Decaton.

Schäfer, Gerhard 1999, *Soziologe und Intellektueller. Studien zu einer Intellektuellen-Biographie*, dissertation, University of Bremen.

Schäfer, Hans Dieter 1981, *Das gespaltene Bewusstsein. Deutsche Kultur und Lebenswirklichkeit 1933–1945*, Munich: Hanser.

Schäfer, Michael 1994, *Die "Rationalität" des Nationalsozialismus. Zur Kritik philosophischer Faschismustheorien am Beispiel der kritischen Theorie*, Weinheim: Beltz.

Schäfer, Thomas et al. (ed.) 2001, *Hinter den Spiegeln. Beiträge zur Philosophie Richard Rortys*, Frankfurt am Main: Suhrkamp.

Schaff, Adam 1965, *Marxismus und das menschliche Individuum*, Vienna: Europa-Verlag.

—— 1992, *Ökumenischer Humanismus*, Salzburg: Müller.

Schäffle, Albert 1885 [1874], *Quintessenz des Sozialismus*, Gotha: Perthes.

Scharrer, Manfred 1983, *Die Spaltung der deutschen Arbeiterbewegung*, Stuttgart: Edition Corderliers.

Schauenberg, Bernd (ed.) 1990, *Wirtschaftsethik. Schnittstellen von Ökonomie und Wirtschaftstheorie*, Wiesbaden: Gabler.

Schefold, Bertram 1994, 'Nationalökonomie und Kulturwissenschaften: Das Konzept des Wirtschaftsstils' in *Wirtschaftsstile*, Vol. 1, *Studien zum Verhältnis von Ökonomie und Kultur*, Frankfurt am Main: Fischer.

Schefold, Bertram et al. 1983, *Arbeit ohne Umweltzerstörung. Strategien für eine neue Wirtschaftspolitik*, Frankfurt am Main: Fischer.

—— 1994a: *Geisteswissenschaften zwischen Kaiserreich und Republik. Zur Entwicklung von Nationalökonomie, Rechtswissenschaft und Sozialwissenschaft im 20. Jahrhundert*, Stuttgart: Steiner.

—— 1998, *Erkenntnisgewinne, Erkenntnisverluste. Kontinuitäten und Diskontinuitäten in den Wirtschafts-, Rechts- und Sozialwissenschaften zwischen den 20er und 50er Jahren*, Stuttgart: Steiner.

Schefold, Christian 1970, *Die Rechtsphilosophie des jungen Marx von 1842*, Munich: Beck.

Scheler, Max 1955 [1913], 'Versuche über die Philosophie des Lebens. Nietzsche-Dilthey-Bergson' in *Gesammelte Werke*, Vol. 3, Munich: Bouvier.

—— 1999, *Ethik und Kapitalismus. Zum Problem des kapitalistischen Geistes*, Berlin: Philo.

Schelling, F.W.J. 1985 [1800], 'System des transzendentalen Idealismus' in *Ausgewählte Schriften*, Vol. 1, Frankfurt am Main: Suhrkamp.

Schellong, Dieter 1985, 'Jenseits von politischer und unpolitischer Theologie. Grundentscheidungen der "Dialektischen Theologie"' in *Der Fürst dieser Welt. Carl Schmitt und die Folgen. Religionstheorie und Politische Theorie*, edited by Jacob Taubes, Vol. 1, Munich: Fink.

Schelsky, Helmut 1955, 'Industrie- und Betriebssoziologie' in *Soziologie*, edited by Helmut Schelsky and Arnold Gehlen, Cologne: Diederichs.

—— 1959, *Ortsbestimmung der deutschen Soziologie*, Cologne: Diederichs.

—— 1975, *Die Arbeit tun die anderen. Klassenkampf und Priesterherrschaft der Intellektuellen*, Opladen: Westdeutscher Verlag.

—— 1979 [1961], 'Die Bedeutung des Klassenbegriffs für die Analyse unserer Gesellschaft' in *Auf der Suche nach Wirklichkeit. Gesammelte Aufsätze*, Cologne: Diederichs.

—— 1979a: 'Der Mensch in der wissenschaftlichen Zivilisation' in *Auf der Suche nach Wirklichkeit. Gesammelte Aufsätze*, Cologne: Diederichs.

—— 1979b [1956], 'Gesellschaftlicher Wandel' in *Auf der Suche nach Wirklichkeit. Gesammelte Aufsätze*, Cologne: Diederichs.

—— 1981, *Rückblicke eines Anti-Soziologen*, Opladen: Westdeutscher Verlag.

Schelsky, Helmut and Hermann Boehrs 1954, *Die Aufgaben der Betriebssoziologie und der Arbeitswissenschaften*, Stuttgart: Ring-Verlag.

Schelz-Brandenburg, Till 1992, *Eduard Bernstein und Karl Kautsky. Entstehung und Wandlung des sozialdemokratischen Parteimarxismus im Spiegel ihrer Korrespondenz 1879 bis 1932*, Cologne: Böhlau.

Scheyli, Martin 2000, *Politische Öffentlichkeit und deliberative Demokratie nach Habermas. Institutionelle Gestaltung durch direktdemokratische Beteiligungsformen?* Baden-Baden: Nomos.

Schieder, Wolfgang 1991, *Karl Marx als Politiker*, Munich: Piper.

Schildt, Axel 1998, *Konservatismus in Deutschland. Von den Anfängen im 18. Jahrhundert bis zur Gegenwart*, Munich: Beck.

Schillebeeck, Edward (ed.) 1988, *Mystik und Politik. Theologie im Ringen um Geschichte und Gesellschaft*, Mainz: Grünewald.

Schimkowsky, Reinhard 1974, 'Zur Marx-Rezeption bei Hilferding. Die Bestimmungen von Konkurrenz und Monopol im "Finanzkapital"' and 'Exkurs über Hilferding: vom Generalkartell zur Konzeption des organisierten Kapitalismus' in *Monopol und Staat. Zur Marx-Rezeption in der Theorie des staatsmonopolitischen Kapitalismus*, edited by Rolf Ebbinghaus, Frankfurt am Main: Suhrkamp.

Schiwy, Günter 1969, Der französische Strukturalismus: Mode, Methode, Ideologie. Mit einem Textanhang, Reinbek: Rowohlt.

Schlegel, Friedrich 1969 [1827], 'Philosophie des Lebens. In 15 Vorlesungen gehalten zu Wien im Jahre 1827' in *Kritische Ausgabe*, Vol. 10, Munich: Schöningh.

Schlette, Heinz Robert 1975, 'Marxismus und Religionswissenschaft' in *Marxismus – ernst genommen. Ein Universalsystem auf dem Prüfstand der Wissenschaften*, edited by Gerhard Szczesny, Reinbek: Rowohlt.

—— 1991, 'Marxismus – ein Humanismus?' in *Konkrete Humanität: Studien zur praktischen Philosophie und Religionsphilosophie*, Frankfurt am Main: Knecht.

Schluchter, Wolfgang 1996, 'Zeitgemäße Unzeitgemäße. Von Friedrich Nietzsche über Georg Simmel zu Max Weber' in *Unversöhnte Moderne*, Frankfurt am Main: Suhrkamp.

Schlunk, Martin 1921, *Die Weltanschauung im Wandel der Zeit. Eine Einführung für Suchende*, Hamburg: Agentur des Rauhen Hauses.

Schlüter, Steffen 2000, *Individuum und Gemeinschaft. Sozialphilosophie im Denkweg und im System von Charles Sanders Peirce*, Würzburg: Königshausen und Neumann.

Schmid, Josef 1996, *Wohlfahrtsstaaten im Vergleich*, Opladen: Leske und Budrich.

Schmidt, Alfred (ed.) 1960, *Der Begriff der Natur in der Lehre von Marx*, Frankfurt am Main: Europäische Verlags-Anstalt.

—— 1967, 'Über Geschichte und Geschichtsschreibung in der materialistischen Dialektik' in *Folgen einer Theorie. Essays über "Das Kapital" von Karl Marx*, Frankfurt am Main: Suhrkamp.

—— 1970, *Beiträge zur marxistischen Erkenntnistheorie*, Frankfurt am Main: Suhrkamp.

—— 1971, *Geschichte und Struktur. Fragen einer marxistischen Historik*, Munich: Hanser.

—— 1974, 'Praxis' in *Gesellschaft. Beiträge zur Marxschen Theorie*, 2: 264–306.

—— 1976, *Die Kritische Theorie als Geschichtsphilosophie*, Munich: Hanser.

—— 1988 [1973], *Emanzipatorische Sinnlichkeit. Ludwig Feuerbachs anthropologischer Materialismus*, Munich: Piper.

—— 1990, 'Heidegger und die Frankfurter Schule: Herbert Marcuses Heidegger-Marxismus' in *Martin Heidegger – Faszination und Erschrecken. Die politische Dimension einer Philosophie*, edited by Peter Kemper, Frankfurt am Main: Campus.

Schmidt, Amos 1993, *Materialismus zwischen Metaphysik und Positivismus. Max Horkheimers Frühwerk: Darstellung und Kritik*, Opladen: Westdeutscher Verlag.

Schmidt, Ferdinand Jacob 1908, *Zur Wiedergeburt des Idealismus*, Leipzig: Dürr.

Schmidt, Nicole 1995, *Philosophie und Psychologie. Trennungsgeschichte, Dogmen und Perspektiven*, Reinbek: Rowohlt.

Schmidt-Soltau, Kai 1997, *Der Marxismus des 20. Jahrhunderts. Bilanz und Perspektive*, Münster: Lit.

—— 1998, *Die apathische Revolution. Grundlegung einer praktischen Philosophie nach Marx*, Münster: Lit.

Schmied-Kowarzik, Wolfdietrich 1981, *Die Dialektik der gesellschaftlichen Praxis. Zur Genesis und Kernstruktur der Marxschen Theorie*, Freiburg: Alber.

—— 1984, *Das dialektische Verhältnis des Menschen zur Natur. Philosophiegeschichtliche Studien zur Naturproblematik bei Karl Marx*, Freiburg: Alber.

—— 1985, *Die gegenwärtige Bedeutung des Marxschen Denkens. Marx Symposion 1983 in Dubrovnik*, Bochum: Germinal.

Schmied-Kowarzik, Wolfdietrich and Johannes Weiß 1992, *Aufklärung und Ideologie. Die Rolle von Philosophie und Soziologie im gesellschaftlichen Umbruch der "realsozialistischen Staaten"*, Kassel: Jenior und Pressler.

Schmied-Kowarzik, Wolfdietrich and Heinz Eidam 1995, *Kritische Philosophie gesellschaftlicher Praxis. Auseinandersetzungen mit der Marxschen Theorie nach dem Zusammenbruch des Realsozialismus*, Würzburg: Königshausen und Neumann.

Schmitt, Carl 1934, *Staat, Bewegung, Volk. Die Dreigliederung der politischen Einheit*, Hamburg: Hanseatische Verlagsanstalt.

—— 1957, 'Die andere Hegel-Linie – Hans Freyer zum 70. Geburtstag', *Christ und Welt*, 10, 3.

—— 1970, *Politische Theologie II. Die Legende von der Erledigung jeder Politischen Theologie*, Berlin: Duncker und Humblot.

—— 1985 [1923], *The Crisis of Parliamentary Democracy*, Cambridge, MA: MIT Press.

—— 1994 [1921], *Die Diktatur. Von den Anfängen des modernen Souveränitätsgedankens bis zum proletarischen Klassenkampf*, Berlin: Duncker und Humblot.

—— 1996, [1932] *The Age of Neutralizations and Depoliticizations* in *The Concept of the Political*, Chicago: University of Chicago Press.

—— 1996a [1923], *Roman Catholicism and Political Form*, Westport, CT: Greenwood Press.

—— 2005 [1922], *Political Theology: Four Chapters on the Concept of Sovereignty*, Chicago: University of Chicago Press.

Schnädelbach, Herbert 1971, *Erfahrung, Begründung und Reflexion. Versuch über den Positivismus*, Frankfurt am Main: Suhrkamp.

—— 1974, *Geschichtsphilosophie nach Hegel. Die Probleme des Historismus*, Freiburg: Alber.

—— 1983, *Philosophie in Deutschland 1831–1933*, Frankfurt am Main: Suhrkamp.

—— 1986, 'Was ist Neoaristotelismus?' in *Moralität und Sittlichkeit*, edited by Werner Kuhlmann, Frankfurt am Main: Suhrkamp.

—— 2000, *Hegels Philosophie: Kommentare zu den Hauptwerken*, 3 Vols., Frankfurt am Main: Suhrkamp.

Schneider, Herbert Wallace 1957 [1946], *Geschichte der amerikanischen Philosophie*, Hamburg: Meiner.

Schneider, Michael 1992, *Das Ende eines Jahrhundertmythos. Eine Bilanz des Sozialismus*. Cologne: Kiepenheuer und Witsch.

Schneider, Peter Karlfried 1976, *Theorie normativer Vernunft bei Karl Marx*, Munich: Raith.

Schoenberner, Gerhard 1991, *Der gelbe Stern. Judenverfolgung in Europa 1933 bis 1945*, Frankfurt am Main: Fischer.

Scholder, Klaus 1977, *Die Kirchen und das Dritte Reich*, Vol. 1, *Vorgeschichte und Zeit der Illusionen, 1918–1934*, Frankfurt am Main: Propyläen.

Scholem, Gershom 1975, *Walter Benjamin. Die Geschichte einer Freundschaft*, Frankfurt am Main: Suhrkamp.

Schöler, Uli 1999, *Ein Gespenst verschwand in Europa. Über Marx und die sozialistische Idee nach dem Scheitern des sowjetischen Staatssozialismus*, Bonn: Dietz.

Schönrich, Gerhard 1990, *Zeichenhandeln. Untersuchungen zum Begriff einer semiotischen Vernunft im Ausgang von Charles S. Peirce*, Frankfurt am Main: Suhrkamp.

—— 1994, *Bei Gelegenheit Diskurs. Von den Grenzen der Diskursethik und dem Preis der Letztbegründung*, Frankfurt am Main: Suhrkamp.

Schorske, Carl E. 1981 [1955], *Die große Spaltung. Die deutsche Sozialdemokratie 1905–1917*, Berlin: Olle und Wolter.

Schöttker, Detlev 2000, 'Die Organisation des philosophischen Erfolgs. Zur Dynamik der kritischen Theorie', *Merkur*, 5.

Schrader, Fred E. 1980, *Restauration und Revolution. Die Vorarbeiten zum "Kapital" von Karl Marx in seinen Studienheften 1850–1858*, Hildesheim: Gerstenberg.

—— 1985, 'Die Auflösung der "Politischen Theologie" Hegels. Von der nominalistischen Abstraktionskritik Feuerbachs (1843) zu Marxens Kritik der ideellen Verdoppelung (1857/58)' in *Der Fürst dieser Welt. Carl Schmitt und die Folgen. Religionstheorie und Politische Theorie*, edited by Jacob Taubes, Vol. 1, Munich: Fink.

Schrader, Wolfgang H. (ed.) 1997, 'Fichte im 20. Jahrhundert. 200 Jahre Wissenschaftslehre – die Philosophie Johann Gottlieb Fichtes', *Fichte-Studien*, 13.

Schramm, Michael 1997, 'Christliche Wirtschaftsethik' in Christliche Sozialethik interdisziplinär, edited by Hans-Joachim Höhn, Paderborn: Schöningh.

Schrey, Heinz-Horst 1954, 'Geschichte oder Mythos bei Marx und Lenin', *Marxismusstudien*, 1, 145–60.

—— 1975, *Entfremdung*, Darmstadt: Wissenschaftliche Buchgesellschaft.

Schroer, Markus 2001, 'Klassengesellschaft' in *Klassische Gesellschaftsbegriffe der Soziologie*, edited by Georg Kneer and Armin Nassehi, Munich: Fink.

Schüddekopf, Ernst 1960, *Linke Leute von rechts. Die nationalrevolutionären Minderheiten und der Kommunismus in der Weimarer Republik*, Stuttgart: Kohlhammer.

Schüddekopf, Ernst 1970, *Nationalbolschewismus*, Berlin: Ullstein.

Schulenburg, Sigrid von der (ed.) 1923, *Briefwechsel zwischen Wilhelm Dilthey und dem Grafen Paul Yorck von Wartenburg*, Halle: Niemeyer.

Schulte, Christoph 1994, 'Messias und Identität. Zum Messianismus im Werk einiger deutsch-jüdischer Denker' in *Jüdisches Denken in der europäischen Geistesgeschichte*, Vol. 1, edited by Eveline Goodman-Thau and Michael Daxner, Berlin: Akademie-Verlag.

Schulte, Günter 1992, *Kennen Sie Marx? Kritik der proletarischen Vernunft*, Frankfurt am Main: Campus.

Schulz, Daniel 2004, *Verfassung und Nation. Formen politischer Institutionalisierung in Deutschland und Frankreich*, Wiesbaden: VS Verlag für Sozialwissenschaften.

Schulze, Gerhard 1992, *Die Erlebnisgesellschaft. Kultursoziologie der Gegenwart*, Frankfurt am Main: Campus.

—— 2003, *Die beste aller Welten. Wohin bewegt sich die Gesellschaft im 21. Jahrhundert?* Munich: Hanser.

Schumacher, Kurt 1973 [1920], *Der Kampf um den Staatsgedanken in der deutschen Sozialdemokratie*, Stuttgart: Kohlhammer.

Schumann, Michael 1977, *Industriearbeit und Arbeiterbewusstsein. Eine empirische Untersuchung über den Einfluss der aktuellen technischen Entwicklung auf die industrielle Arbeit und das Arbeiterbewusstsein*, Frankfurt am Main: Suhrkamp.

—— 2003, *Metamorphosen von Industriearbeit und Arbeiterbewusstsein. Kritische Industriesoziologie zwischen Taylorismusanalyse und Mitgestaltung innovativer Arbeitspolitk*, Hamburg: VSA.

Schumpeter, Joseph A. 1934 [1911], *The Theory of Economic Development*, Cambridge, MA: Harvard University Press.

—— 1939, *Business Cycles*, London: McGraw Hill, 1939.

—— 1943 [1942], *Capitalism, Socialism, and Democracy*, London: Allen & Unwin.

—— 1951, *Essays*, Cambridge: Addison-Wesley.

—— 1954, *History of Economic Analysis*, 2 Vols., Oxford: Oxford University Press.

Schürmann, Axel 1974, *Wertgesetz und gesellschaftliche Entwicklung. Voruntersuchungen zu einer materialistischen Systemtheorie der Gesellschaft*, Gießen: Achenbach.

Schwan, Gesine and Alexander Schwan 1974, *Sozialdemokratie und Marxismus. Zum Spannungsverhältnis von Godesberger Programm und marxistischer Theorie*, Hamburg: Hoffmann und Campe.

Schwartländer, Johannes and Dietmar Willoweit (eds.) 1983, *Das Recht des Menschen auf Eigentum*, Kehl: Engel.

Schwartz, Jesse (ed.) 1977, *The Subtle Anatomy of Capitalism*, Santa Monica: Goodyear.

Schwarz, Hermann 1904, *Der moderne Materialismus als Weltanschauung und Geschichtsprinzip*, Leipzig: Dieterich.

—— 1912, *Grundfragen der Weltanschauung*, Leipzig: Dieterich.

—— 1919, *Weltgewissen oder Vaterlandsgewissen?* Erfurt: Keyser.

—— 1931, *Deutsche Systematische Philosophie in ihren Gestalten*, Berlin: Junker und Dünnhaupt.

—— 1933, *Nationalsozialistische Weltanschauung. Freie Beiträge zur Philosophie des Nationalsozialismus aus den Jahren 1919–1933*, Berlin: Junker und Dünnhaupt.

Schwarz, Winfried 1978, *Vom "Rohentwurf" zum "Kapital". Die Strukturgeschichte des Marxschen Hauptwerkes*, Berlin: Das Europäische Buch.

Schwarzschild, Leopold 1954, *Der rote Preuße: Leben und Legende von Karl Marx*, Stuttgart: Scherz und Goverts.

Schweppenhäuser, Gerhard 1993, *Ethik nach Auschwitz. Adornos negative Moralphilosophie*, Hamburg: Argument.

—— 1995, *Impuls und Negativität – Ethik und Ästhetik bei Adorno*, Hamburg: Argument.

Schwinn, Thomas 2001, *Differenzierung ohne Gesellschaft. Umstellung eines soziologischen Konzeptes*, Weilerswist: Velbrück.

Scott, Alan 1997, *The Limits of Globalization: Cases and Arguments*, London: Routledge.

Searle, John R. 1992, *The Rediscovery of Mind*, Cambridge: MIT Press.

Seel, Martin 2000, 'Review of Robert Brandom: Facts, Norms and Normative Facts', *European Journal of Philosophy*.

Seidel, Alfred 1980 [1924], *Bewusstsein als Verhängnis. Fragmente über die Beziehungen von Weltanschauung und Charakter oder: Über Wesen und Wandel der Ideologien*, Bremen: Edition Subversion.

Seidel, Bruno (ed.) 1968a: *Wege der Totalitarismusforschung*, Darmstadt: Wissenschaftliche Buchgesellschaft.

Seidel, Bruno and Siegfried Jenker (eds.) 1968, *Klassenbildung und soziale Schichtung*, Darmstadt: Wissenschaftliche Buchgesellschaft.

Seidel, Ch. and H. Herring 1972, 'Ding an sich' in *Historisches Wörterbuch der Philosophie*, Vol. 2, Basel: Schwabe.

Seifert, Jürgen 2000, 'Joachim Ritters "Collegium Philosophicum". Ein Forum offenen Denkens' in *Kreise, Gruppen, Bünde*, edited by Richard Faber and Christine Holste, Würzburg: Königshausen und Neumann.

Sen, Amartya 1970, *Collective Choice and Social Welfare*, San Francisco: Holden-Day.

—— 1982 [1977], 'Rational Fools: A Critique of the Behavioral Foundations of Economic Theory' in *Choice, Welfare, and Measurement*, Oxford: Blackwell.

—— 1985, 'The Moral Standing of The Market' in *Ethics and Economics*, edited by E.F. Paul et al., Oxford: Blackwell.

—— 1987, *On Ethics and Economics*, Oxford: Blackwell.

—— 1998, 'Soziale Gerechtigkeit und ökonomische Effizienz' in *Philosophie und Politik II: Soziale Gerechtigkeit und ökonomische Effizienz*, edited by Julian Nida-Rümelin, Essen: Klartext.

Senft, Gerhard 1990, *Weder Kapitalismus noch Kommunismus. Silvio Gesell und das libertäre Modell der Freiwirtschaft*, Berlin: Libertad.

Senge, Angelika 1985, *Marxismus als atheistische Weltanschauung. Zum Stellenwert des Atheismus im Gefüge des marxistischen Denkens*, Paderborn: Schöningh.

Senghaas, Dieter (ed.) 1979, *Kapitalistische Weltökonomie. Kontroversen über ihren Ursprung und ihre Entwicklungsdynamik*, Frankfurt am Main: Suhrkamp.

Senghaas, Dieter and Claus Koch (eds.) 1970, *Texte zur Technokratiediskussion*, Frankfurt am Main: Europäische Verlags-Anstalt.

Sennett, Richard 1972, *The Hidden Injuries of Class*, Cambridge: Cambridge University Press.

—— 1998, *The Corrosion of Character: The Personal Consequences of Work in the New Capitalism*, New York: Norton.

Sens, Eberhard 1979, *System und gesellschaftliche Organisation. Aspekte des Verhältnisses von kybernetischer Systemtheorie und Gesellschaftswissenschaften*, dissertation, Berlin.

Sensat, Julius 1979, *Habermas and Marxism*, Beverly Hills: Sage.

Servais, Günter 1998, 'Marx, Marxismus und Heidegger' in *Arbeit, Vernunft, Glück: Die Freiheitskonzeption des frühen Herbert Marcuse*, Frankfurt am Main: Haag und Herchen.

Service, Robert 1986–95, *Lenin: A Political Life*, 3 Vols., Basingstoke: Macmillan.

Shaikh, Anwar 1974, 'Laws of Agebra and Laws of Production: the Humbug Production Function', *Review of Economics and Statistics*, 51, 1: 115–20.

—— 1977, 'Marx's Theory of Value and the "Transformation Problem"' in *The Subtle Anatomy of Capitalism*, edited by Jesse Schwartz, Santa Monica: Goodyear.

—— 1978, 'An Introduction to the History of Crisis Theories' in *US Capitalism in Crisis*, New York: Economics Education Project of the Union for Radical Political Economics.

—— 1978a: 'Political Economy and Capitalism: Notes on Dobb's Theory of Crises', *Cambridge Journal of Economics*, 6.

—— 1979–80, 'Foreign Trade and the Law of Value', *Science and Society*, 43, 3: 281–302 and 44, 1: 27–57.

—— 1980, 'Marxian Competition versus Perfect Competition: Further Comments on the So-called Choice of Technique', *Cambridge Journal of Economics*, 4: 75–83.

—— 1980a: 'Laws of Algebra and Laws of Production: the Humbug Production Function II' in *Growth, Profits and Property: Essays on the Revival of Political Economy*, edited by Edward J. Nell, Cambridge: Cambridge University Press.

—— 1980b: 'On the Laws of International Exchange' in *Growth, Profits and Property: Essays on the Revival of Political Economy*, edited by Edward J. Nell, Cambridge: Cambridge University Press.

—— 1981, 'The Poverty of Algebra' in *The Value Controversy*, edited by Ian Steedman, London: Verso, 1981.

—— 1982, 'Neoricardian Economics: A Wealth of Algebra, a Poverty of Theory', *Review of Radical Political Economics*, 14, 2.

—— 1983, articles in *A Dictionary of Marxist Thought*, edited by Tom Bottomore, Oxford: Blackwell: 'Economic Crises' (a), 'Falling Rate of Profit' (b), 'Concentration and Centralisation of Capital' (c), 'Reserve Army of Labour' (d).

—— 1984, 'The Transformation from Marx to Sraffa: Prelude to a Critique of the Neo-Ricardians' in *Marx, Ricardo, Sraffa*, edited by Ernest Mandel, London: Verso.

—— 1986, articles in *The New Palgrave: Dictionary of Economics*, edited by John Eatwell, New York: Palgrave: 'Abstract and Concrete Labour' (a), 'Capital as a Social Relation' (b), 'Exploitation' (c), 'Humbug Production Function' (d), 'Market Value and Market Price' (e), 'Organic Composition of Capital' (f), 'Surplus Value' (g).

—— 1987, 'The Falling Rate of Profit and the Economic Crises in the US' in *The Imperiled Economy*, edited by Robert Cherry, New York: Union for Radical Political Economics.

—— 1987a: 'The Welfare State and the Myth of the Social Wage' in *The Imperiled Economy*, edited by Robert Cherry, New York: Union for Radical Political Economics.

—— (ca. 1988): 'The Economic Analysis of Capitalist Systems', undated manuscript, New York.

—— 1989, 'Accumulation, Finance and Effective Demand in Marx, Keynes, and Kalecki' in *Financial Dynamics and Business Cycles: New Perspectives*, edited by Willi Semmler, Armonk: Sharpe.

—— 1989, unpublished working papers, New York: 'Dynamics of the Falling Rate of Profit' (a), 'The Structure of the Falling Rate of Profit Argument' (b), 'A Retrospective on the Choice of Technique Debate' (c).

—— 1990, *Valor, Acumulacion y Crisis. Ensayos de economía política*, Bogotá: Tercer Mundo Editores.

—— 1991, 'Competition and Exchange Rates: Theory and Empirical Evidence', working paper no. 25, Department of Economics, New School for Social Research, New York.

—— 1991a: 'Wandering Around the Warranted Path: Dynamic Nonlinear Solutions to the Harrodian Knife-Edge' in *Nicholas Kaldor and Mainstream Economics: Confrontation or Convergence?*, edited by Willi Semmler and Edward J. Nell, London: Macmillan.

—— 1992, 'The Falling Rate of Profit as the Cause of Long Waves: Theory and Empirical Evidence' in *New Findings in Long Wave Research*, edited by Alfred Kleinknecht et al., London: Macmillan.

—— 1992a: 'A Dynamic Approach to Effective Demand' in *Profits, Deficits, and Instability*,

edited by Dimitri Papadimitrou, New York: St. Martin's Press.
—— 1994, 'The Analytical Structure of Classical Marxian Economics', draft manuscript, New York.
—— 1996a: 'Free Trade, Unemployment, and Economic Policy' in *Global Unemployment: Loss of Jobs in the 90s*, edited by John Eatwell, New York: Sharpe.
—— 1997, 'Explaining inflation and umempoyment: an alternative to neoliberal economic theory', paper presented at the Conference on Contemporary Economic Theory, Athens.
—— 1998, 'The Empirical Strength of the Labor Theory of Value' in *Marxian Economics: A Centenary Appraisal* (*Conference Proceedings*), London.
—— 1998a, 'The Stock Market and the Corporate Sector: A Profit-Based Approach' in *Essays in Honour of Geoff Harcourt*, edited by Malcolm Saywer et al., London: Routledge.
—— 1999, 'Explaining the Global Economic Crisis', *Historical Materialism*, 5, 1: 103–14.
—— 1999a: 'Understanding the US Trade Deficit', testimony before the US Trade Deficit Review Commission, Washington, DC, December.
—— 2000, 'Anwar Shaikh' (biographical entry) in: *A Biographical Dictionary of Dissenting Economists*, edited by Philip Arestis and Malcolm Sawyer, Aldershot: Elgar.
—— 2000a: 'Nonlinear Dynamics and Pseudo-Production Functions', draft manuscript, New York.
Shaikh, Anwar and E. Ahmet Tonak 1996, *Measuring the Wealth of Nations: The Political Economy of National Accounts*, Cambridge: Cambridge University Press.
Shaikh, Anwar and Rania Antonopoulos 1998a: 'Explaining Long Term Exchange Rate Behavior in the United States and Japan', working paper no. 250, New York.
Sheehan, Helena 1985, *Marxism and the Philosophy of Science: A Critical History*, Atlantic Highlands: Humanities Press.
Shklar, Judith 1990, *The Faces of Injustice*, New Haven: Yale University Press.
Shustermann, Richard 1994, 'Dewey on Experience: Foundation or Reconstruction?', *Philosophical Forum*, 26: 127–48.
Shute, Stephen and Susan Hurley 1993, *On Human Rights: The Oxford Amnesty Lectures*, New York: Basic Books.
Shute, Stephen and Susan Hurley (eds.) 1994, *Die Idee der Menschenrechte*, Frankfurt am Main: Fischer.
Sichel, Werner and Peter Eckstein 1974, *Basic Economic Concepts*, Chicago: Rand McNally.
Sichtermann, Barbara 1990, *Der tote Hund beißt*, Berlin: Wagenbach.
Sieferle, Rolf Peter 1979, *Die Revolution in der Theorie von Karl Marx*, Frankfurt am Main: Ullstein.
Sienra, Adolfo de la 1992, *The Logical Foundations of the Marxian Theory of Value*, Boston: Kluwer.
Siep, Ludwig 1974, 'Der Kampf um Anerkennung. Zu Hegels Auseinandersetzung mit Hobbes in den Jenaer Schriften', *Hegel-Studien*, 9: 155–207.
—— 1979, *Anerkennung als Prinzip der praktischen Philosophie. Untersuchungen zu Hegels Jenaer Philosophie des Geistes*, Freiburg: Alber.
—— 2000, *Der Weg der "Phänomenologie des Geistes". Ein einführender Kommentar zur Hegels "Differenzschrift" und zur "Phänomenologie des Geistes"*, Frankfurt am Main: Suhrkamp.
Sik, Ota 1967, *Plan and Market under Socialism*, White Plains: International Arts and Sciences Press.
—— 1976, *The Third Way: Marxist-Leninist Theory and Modern Industrial Society*, White Plains: International Arts and Sciences Press.
Silberner, Edmund 1983, *Kommunisten zur Judenfrage. Zur Geschichte von Theorie und Praxis des Kommunismus*, Opladen: Westdeutscher Verlag.
Simmel, Georg 1894, 'Parerga zur Social-Philosophie. In: Jahrbuch für Gesetzgebung, Verwaltung und Volkswirtschaft des deutschen Reiches', 18: 257–65.
—— 1907, *Schopenhauer und Nietzsche. Ein Vortragszyklus*, Leipzig: Duncker und Humblot.
—— 1910, *Hauptprobleme der Philosophie*, Leipzig: Göschen.
—— 1918, *Lebensanschauung. Vier metaphysische Kapitel*, Leipzig: Duncker und Humblot.
—— 1950 [1908], 'Sociology' in *The Sociology of Georg Simmel*, New York: Free Press.
—— 1957 [1916], 'Wandel der Kulturformen' in *Brücke und Tür. Essays des Philosophen zur Geschichte, Religion, Kunst und Gesellschaft*, Stuttgart: Koehler.

—— 1978 [1900], *The Philosophy of Money*, London: Routledge and Kegan Paul.

—— 1989 [1892], 'Die Probleme der Geschichtsphilosophie' in *Gesamtausgabe (GA)*, Vol. 4, Frankfurt am Main: Suhrkamp.

—— 1989a [1890], 'Über sociale Differenzierung' in *Gesamtausgabe (GA)*, Vol. 4, Frankfurt am Main: Suhrkamp.

Simon-Schäfer, Roland 1974, 'Karl Marx – Dialektiker oder Positivist?' in *Beiträge zur Theoriediskussion II*, edited by Georg Lührs, Berlin: Dietz.

Simon-Schäfer, Roland and Walter Zimmerli 1975, *Theorie zwischen Kritik und Praxis. Jürgen Habermas und die Frankfurter Schule*, Stuttgart: Frommann-Holzboog.

Singer, Kurt 1921, 'Die Krisis der Soziologie', *Weltwirtschaftliches Archiv*, 16: 246–61.

Singer, Peter 1980, *Marx*, Oxford: Oxford University Press.

Sitton, John F. 1996, *Recent Marxian Theory: Class Formation and Social Conflict in Contemporary Capitalism*, Albany, NY: State University of New York Press.

Sklair, Leslie 1991, *Sociology of the Global System*, London: Harvester Wheatsheaf.

—— 2001, *The Transnational Capitalist Class*, Oxford: Blackwell.

Smaldone, William 1998, *Rudolf Hilferding: The Tragedy of a German Social-Democrat*, DeKalb: Northern Illinois University Press.

Smend, Rudolf 1928, *Verfassung und Verfassungsrecht*, Leipzig: Duncker und Humblot.

Smith, Adam 1979 [1776], *An Inquiry into the Nature and the Cause of the Wealth of Nations*, Harmondsworth: Penguin.

—— 2009 [1759], *The Theory of the Moral Sentiments*, New York: Penguin.

Sofsky, Wolfgang 2002, *Zeiten des Schreckens. Amok, Terror, Krieg*, Frankfurt am Main: Fischer.

Sohn-Rethel, Alfred 1972, *Die ökonomische Doppelnatur des Spätkapitalismus*, Darmstadt: Luchterhand.

—— 1978 [1972], *Intellectual and Manual Labour*, Basingstoke: Macmillan.

Sölle, Dorothee 1967 [1965], *Stellvertretung: Ein Kapitel Theologie nach dem "Tode Gottes"*, Berlin: Kreuz-Verlag.

—— 1968, *Atheistisch an Gott glauben. Beiträge zur Theologie*, Freiburg: Walter.

—— 1968a, *Phantasie und Gehorsam. Überlegungen zu einer künftigen christlichen Ethik*, Berlin: Kreuz-Verlag.

—— 1986, 'Christentum und Postmarxismus', *Das Argument*, 156.

Sölle, Dorothee and Klaus Schmidt (eds.) 1974, *Christentum und Sozialismus. Vom Dialog zum Bündnis*, Stuttgart: Kohlhammer.

Söllner, Alfons 1979, *Geschichte und Herrschaft. Studien zur materialistischen Sozialwissenschaft*, Frankfurt am Main: Suhrkamp.

—— 1997, *Totalitarismus. Eine Ideengeschichte des 20. Jahrhunderts*, Berlin: Akademie-Verlag.

Söllner, Fritz 1999, *Die Geschichte des ökonomischen Denkens*, Berlin: Springer.

Solow, Robert M. 1970, *Growth Theory: An Exposition*, Oxford: Oxford University Press.

Solzhenitsyn, Alexander 1974, *The Gulag Archipelago, 1918–1956, An Experiment in Literary Investigation*, New York: Harper and Row.

Sombart, Werner 1886, *Sozialismus und soziale Bewegung im 19. Jahrhundert*, Jena: Fischer.

—— 1894, 'Zur Kritik des ökonomischen Systems von Karl Marx', *Brauns Archiv für soziale Gesetzgebung*, 7, 4.

—— 1903, *Die deutsche Volkswirtschaft im 19. Jahrhundert*, Berlin: Bondi.

—— 1909, *Das Lebenswerk von Karl Marx*, Jena: Fischer.

—— 1913, *Der Bourgeois. Zur Geistesgeschichte des modernen Wirtschaftsmenschen*, Munich: Duncker und Humblot.

—— 1913a: *Krieg und Kapitalismus*, Munich: Duncker und Humblot.

—— 1917 [1902], *Der moderne Kapitalismus. Historisch-systematische Darstellung des gesamteuropäischen Wirtschaftslebens von seinen Anfängen bis zur Gegenwart*, Munich: Duncker und Humblot.

—— 1924, *Der proletarische Sozialismus (Marxismus)*, 2 Vols., Jena: Fischer.

—— 1927, *Der moderne Kapitalismus*, Vol. 3, *Das Wirtschaftsleben im Zeitalter des Hochkapitalismus*, Munich: Duncker und Humblot.

—— 1929, 'Die Wandlungen des Kapitalismus', *Schriften des Vereins für Sozialpolitik*, 175: 23–41, 124–35.

—— 1930, *Die drei Nationalökonomien*, Munich: Duncker und Humblot.

—— 1934, *Deutscher Sozialismus*, Berlin: Buchholz und Weisswange.

—— 1936, *Soziologie. Was sie ist und was sie sein sollte*, Berlin: de Gruyter.

—— 1951 [1911], *The Jews and Modern Capitalism*, Glencoe: Free Press.

—— 1967 [1913], *Luxury and Capitalism*, Ann Arbor: University of Michigan Press.

Sombart, Nicolaus 1991, *Die deutschen Männer und ihre Feinde. Carl Schmitt – ein deutsches Schicksal zwischen Männerbund und Matriarchatsmythos*, Munich: Hanser.

Sommer, Theo (ed.) 1993, 'Zeit der Ökonomen. Eine kritische Bilanz volkswirtschaftlichen Denkens', *ZEIT-Punkte*, 3.

Sontheimer, Kurt 1994 [1962], *Antidemokratisches Denken in der Weimarer Republik. Die politischen Ideen des deutschen Nationalismus zwischen 1918 und 1933*, Munich: Deutscher Taschenbuch-Verlag.

Sorel, Georges 1961 [1906], 'The Decomposition of Marxism' in *Radicalism and the Revolt Against Reason: The Social Theories of Georges Sorel*, edited by Irving Louis Horowitz, New York: Humanities Press.

—— 1999 [1908], *Reflections on Violence*, Cambridge: Cambridge University Press.

Sorg, Richard 1974, *Marxismus und Protestantismus in Deutschland. Eine religionssoziologisch-sozialgeschichtliche Studie zur Marxismus-Rezeption in der evangelischen Kirche 1848–1948*, Cologne: Pahl-Rugenstein.

Soros, George 1998, *The Crisis of Global Capitalism: Open Society Endangered*, New York: Public Affairs.

Spaemann, Robert 1978, 'Kampf der Philosophen' in *Wozu Philosophie?*, edited by Hermann Lübbe, Berlin: de Gruyter.

—— 1998 [1959], *Die Geburt der Soziologie aus dem Geist der Restauration. Studien über L.G.A. de Bonald*, Stuttgart: Kösel.

Spann, Othmar 1903, 'Untersuchungen über den Gesellschaftsbegriff', *Zeitschrift für die gesamte Staatswissenschaft*, 59.

—— 1931, *Die Irrungen des Marxismus. Eine Darstellung und Prüfung seiner Wirtschaftslehre*, Berlin: Erneuerungsverlag.

—— 1934, *Kämpfende Wissenschaft. Gesammelte Abhandlungen zur Volkswirtschaftslehre, Gesellschaftslehre und Philosophie*, Jena: Fischer.

—— 1935, *Erkenne Dich selbst. Eine Geistesphilosophie als Lehre vom Menschen und seiner Weltstellung*, Jena: Fischer.

Sparschuh, Vera 1997, *Soziologie und Sozialismus: Die Gründergeneration der DDR-Soziologie. Versuch einer Konturierung*, Opladen: Leske und Budrich.

Speck, J. (ed.) 1988, *Grundprobleme der großen Philosophen. Philosophie der Neuzeit II: Kant, Fichte, Schelling, Hegel, Feuerbach, Marx*, Göttingen: Vandenhoeck und Ruprecht.

Speier, Hans 1977, *Die Angestellten vor dem Nationalsozialismus. Ein Beitrag zum Verständnis der deutschen Sozialstruktur 1918–1933*, Göttingen: Vandenhoeck und Ruprecht.

Spencer, Herbert 1970 [1851], *Social Statics, or, the Conditions Essential to Human Happiness Specified, and the First of Them Developed*, London: Chapman.

—— 1975 [1872], *The Principles of Sociology* in *System of Synthetic Philosophy (1862–1896)*, Vol. 5, Westport: Greenwood Press.

Spengler, Oswald 1928 [1923], *The Decline of the West*, 2 Vols., New York: Alfred A. Knopf.

—— 1967 [1920], 'Prussianism and Socialism' in *Selected Essays*, Chicago: Regnery.

—— 1976, *Man and Technics: a Contribution to a Philosophy of Life*, Westport, CT: Greenwood Press.

Spiegel, Yorick 1992, *Wirtschaftsethik und Wirtschaftspraxis – ein wachsender Widerspruch?* Stuttgart: Kohlhammer.

Spiethoff, Arthur 1903, 'Die Krisentheorie von Tugan-Baranowski und L. Pohle', *Schmollers Jahrbuch*, 27, 70 ff.

—— 1925, 'Krisen' in *Handwörterbuch der Staatswissenschaften*, Vol. 6, Jena: Fischer.

Spinoza, Benedict 2000 [1677], *Ethics*, Oxford: Oxford University Press.

Spitzer, Steven 1983, 'Marxist Perspectives in the Sociology of Law', *Annual Review of Sociology*, 9, 103–124.

Spoo, Eckart et al. (eds.) 2000, *Der Mensch und der Plan. Eine Jahrhundertbilanz des Kommunismus*, Hamburg: VSA.

Spranger, Eduard 1950 [1914], *Lebensformen. Geisteswissenschaftliche Psychologie und Ethik der Persönlichkeit*, Tübingen: Niemeyer.

Spülbeck, Volker 1977, *Neomarxismus und Theologie. Gesellschaftskritik in kritischer Theorie und Politischer Theologie*, Freiburg: Herder.

Sraffa, Piero 1960, *Production of Commodities by Means of Commodities: Prelude to a Critique of Political Economy*, Cambridge: Cambridge University Press.

Stahl, Friedrich Julius 1987 [1853], *Der Protestantismus als politisches Prinzip. Vorträge, auf Veranstaltung des Evangelischen Vereins für kirchliche Zwecke zu Berlin im März 1853 gehalten*, Aalen: Scientia-Verlag.

Stähli, Martin Johann 1976, *Reich Gottes und Revolution: Christliche Theorie und Praxis für die Armen dieser Welt. Die Theologie des Religiösen Sozialismus bei Leonhard Ragaz und die Theologie der Revolution in Lateinamerika*, Hamburg: Reich.

Stalin, Joseph V. 1954 [1926], 'Concerning Questions of Leninism' in idem; *Collected Works*, Vol. 8, Moscow: Foreign Languages Publishing House.

—— 1954a [1924], 'The Foundations of Leninism' in *Collected Works*, Vol. 6, Moscow: Foreign Languages Publishing House.

—— 1972 [1950], *Marxism and Problems of Linguistics*, Peking: Foreign Languages Press.

—— 1976 [1938], 'Dialectical and Historical Materialism' in *Problems of Leninism*, Peking: Foreign Languages Press.

—— 1976a [1931], 'The Tasks of Economic Executives' in *Problems of Leninism*, Peking: Foreign Languages Press.

Stamatis, Georgios 1977, *Die "spezifisch kapitalistischen" Produktionsmethoden und der tendenzielle Fall der Profitrate*, Berlin: Mehrwert.

Stammer, Theo 2001, 'Karl Marx (1818–1883)' in *Klassiker des politischen Denkens*, edited by Hans Maier and Horst Denzer, Vol. 2, Munich: Beck.

Stammler, Rudolf 1896, *Wirtschaft und Recht in der materialistischen Geschichtsauffassung*, Leipzig: Veit.

Ständeke, Helmut and Reiner Tack 1981, *Geschichte – Deutung und Erkenntnis. Kurs: Philosophie*, Düsseldorf: Bagel,

Starbatty, Joachim (ed.) 1989, *Klassiker des ökonomischen Denkens*, 2 Vols., Munich: Beck.

Stark, Johannes 1937, 'Weiße Juden in der Wissenschaft', *Das Schwarze Korps*, 15 July 1937.

Starr, Amory (ed.) 2000, *Naming the Enemy: Anti-Corporate Movements Confront Globalization*, New York: Zed Books.

Stedman Jones, Gareth (ed.) 1977, *Western Marxism: A Critical Reader*, London: New Left Books.

—— 1988, *Klassen, Politik, Sprache. Für eine theorieorientierte Sozialgeschichte*, Münster: Westfälisches Dampfboot.

Steedman, Ian 1977, *Marx after Sraffa*, London: New Left Books.

—— 1980, 'A Note on the "Choice of Technique" Under Capitalism', *Cambrige Journal of Economics*, 4: 61–4.

—— 1981, *The Value Controversy*, London: Verso.

Steenson, Gary P. 1978, *Karl Kautsky 1954–1938, Marxism in the Classical Years*, Pittsburgh: University of Pittsburgh Press.

Steigerwald, Robert 1973, *Marxismus–Religion–Gegenwart*, Berlin: Akademie-Verlag.

—— 1977, *Menschenrechte in der Diskussion*, Frankfurt am Main: Verlag Marxistische Blätter.

—— 1980, *Bürgerliche Philosophie und Revisionismus im imperialistischen Deutschland*, Berlin: Akademie-Verlag.

—— 1996, *Materialistische Philosophie. Eine Einführung für junge Leute*, Essen: Neue Impulse.

Steigerwald, Robert and Willi Germs 1977a: *Probleme der Strategie des antimonopolistischen Kampfes*, Frankfurt am Main: Verlag Marxistische Blätter.

Steil, Armin 1993, *Krisensemantik. Wissenssoziologische Untersuchungen*, Opladen: Leske und Budrich.

Stein, Lorenz von 1850, *Geschichte der sozialen Bewegung in Frankreich von 1789 bis auf unsere Tage*, 3 Vols., Leipzig: Wigand.

Stein, Ludwig 1897, *Die sociale Frage im Lichte der Philosophie*, Stuttgart: Enke.

Steinbüchel, Theodor 1950, *Gesammelte Aufsätze zur Geistesgeschichte I: Sozialismus*, Tübingen: Mohr.

Steindl, Josef 1952, *Maturity and Stagnation in American Capitalism*, Oxford: Blackwell.

Steiner, Helmut 1999, *Der Kurzschluss der Marktwirtschaft. Instrumentalisierung und Emanzipation des Konsumenten*, Berlin: Duncker und Humblot.

Steinert, Heinz 1989, *Adorno in Wien. Über die (Un-)Möglichkeit von Kunst, Kultur und Befreiung*, Vienna: Verlag für Gesellschaftskritik.

—— 1993, *Die Entdeckung der Kulturindustrie, oder: Warum Professor Adorno Jazz-Musik nicht ausstehen konnte*, Vienna: Verlag für Gesellschaftskritik.

Steinfath, Holmer 1994, 'Der Verlust der Identität' in *Kommunitarismus in der Diskussion. Eine streitbare Einführung*, edited by Christel Zahlmann, Berlin: Rotbuch.

Steinmann, Horst and Albert Löhr 1994, *Grundlagen der Unternehmensethik*, Stuttgart: Poeschel.

Steinmann, Horst and Andreas Scherer (eds.) 1998, *Zwischen Universalismus und Relativismus. Philosophische Grundlagenprobleme des interkulturellen Managements*, Frankfurt am Main: Suhrkamp.

Steinvorth, Ulrich 1977, *Eine analytische Interpretation der Marxschen Dialektik*, Meisenheim: Hain.

—— 1981, *Stationen der politischen Theorie*, Stuttgart: Reclam.
—— 1985, 'Ludwig Wittgenstein: Sprache und Denken' in *Grundprobleme der großen Philosophen. Philosophie der Gegenwart I*, edited by J. Speck, Göttingen: Vandenhoeck und Ruprecht.
—— 1994, 'Gerechtigkeit in einer Weltgesellschaft' in *Theorien der Gerechtigkeit. 15. Tagung der deutschen Sektion der internationalen Vereinigung für Rechts- und Sozialphilosophie in Hamburg, 30. Sept.–2. Okt. 1992*, edited by Hans-Joachim Koch et al., Stuttgart: Steiner.
—— 1998, 'Gerechtigkeit' in *Philosophie. Ein Grundkurs*, Vol. 1, edited by Ekkehard Martens and Herbert Schnädelbach, Rowohlt, 1998.
—— 1999, *Gleiche Freiheit. Politische Philosophie und Verteilungsgerechtigkeit*, Berlin: Akademie-Verlag.
—— 2002a: *Was ist Vernunft? Eine philosophische Einführung*, Munich: Beck.
Steinvorth, Ulrich and Ulrich Schmücker (eds.) 2002, 'Gerechtigkeit und Politik. Philosophische Perspektiven', *Deutsche Zeitschrift für Philosophie*, special issue 3.
Stekeler-Weithofer, Pirmin 1995, *Sinn-Kriterien. Die logischen Grundlagen kritischer Philosophie von Platon bis Wittgenstein*, Paderborn: Schöningh.
—— 2003, 'Normative Kulturentwicklung oder evolutiver Zivilisationsprozess? Eine Verteidigung der Vernunftphilosophie Kants und Hegels' in *Entwicklung sozialer Wirklichkeit*, Weilerswist: Velbrück.
Stephan, Cora 1974, 'Geld- und Staatstheorie in Hilferdings "Finanzkapital"', *Gesellschaft. Beiträge zur Marxschen Theorie*, 2: 111–54.
Stepina, Clemens K. 1994, *Marx und die kritische Gesellschaftstheorie heute*, Vienna 1994.
—— 2000, *Handlung als Prinzip der Moderne. Handlungsphilosophische Studien zu Aristoteles, Hegel und Marx*, Vienna: Passagen-Verlag.
Sternberger, Dolf 1934, *Der verstandene Tod. Eine Untersuchung zu Martin Heideggers Existenzialontologie. Mit einer monographischen Bibliographie*, Leipzig: Hirzel.
Sternburg, Wilhelm von 1999, *Lion Feuchtwanger. Ein deutsches Schriftstellerleben*, Berlin: Aufbau-Verlag.
Sternhell, Zeev 1986 [1983], *Neither Right nor Left. Fascist Ideology in France*, Berkeley, CA: University of California Press.
Stiehler, Gottfried 1997, *Werden und Sein. Philosophische Untersuchungen zur Gesellschaft*, Cologne: PapyRossa.
Stiglitz, Joseph 2002, *Globalization and its Discontents*, New York: Norton.
Stockmaier, Peter, Ernesto Grassi et al.: *Humanismus zwischen Christentum und Marxismus*, Munich: Kösel.
Stojanovic, Svetozar 1970, *Kritik und Zukunft des Sozialismus*, Munich: Hanser.
Stölting, Erhard 1986, *Akademische Soziologie in der Weimarer Republik*, Berlin: Duncker und Humblot.
Stone, Alan 1985, 'The Place of Law in the Marxian Structure-Superstructure Archetype', *Law and Society Review*, 19, 1: 39–67.
Strasser, Johanno 2001, *Leben oder Überleben. Wider die Zurichtung des Menschen zu einem Instrument des Marktes*, Zürich: Pendo.
Strauss, David Friedrich 1835–6, *Das Leben Jesu, kritisch bearbeitet*, 2 Vols., Tübingen: C.F. Osiander.
—— 1872, *Der alte und der neue Glaube. Ein Bekenntnis*, Leipzig: Hirzel.
Strauss, Leo 1953, *Natural Right and History*, Chicago: University of Chicago Press.
—— 1975, *The Argument and The Action of Plato's Laws*, Chicago: University of Chicago Press.
Streissler, Erich 1989, 'Carl Menger (1840–1921)' in *Klassiker des ökonomischen Denkens*, Vol. 2, edited by Joachim Starbatty, Munich: Beck.
Suchanek, Andreas 1994, *Der ökonomische Ansatz und das Problem der ökonomischen Integration*, Tübingen: Mohr.
—— 2001, *Ökonomische Ethik*, Tübingen: Mohr.
Sullivan, Stefan 2002, *Marx for a Post-Communist Era: On Poverty, Corruption, and Banality*, London: Routledge.
Sweet, Robert T. 1991, *Marx, Morality and the Virtue of Beneficience*, New York: Lang.
Sweezy, Paul M. 1970 [1942], *The Theory of Capitalist Development. Principles of Marxian Political Economy*, New York: Monthly Review Press.
Sweezy, Paul M. and Paul A. Baran 1966, *Monopoly Capital: An Essay on the American Economic and Social Order*, New York: Monthly Review Press.
Szczesny, Gerhard (ed.) 1975, *Marxismus – ernst genommen. Ein Universalsystem auf dem Prüfstand der Wissenschaften*, Reinbek: Rowohlt.
Szejnmann, Claus-Christian W. 2000, *Vom Traum zum Alptraum. Sachsen in der*

Weimarer Republik, Dresden: Sächsische Landeszentrale für politische Bildung.

Tabor, Jan (ed.) 1994, *Kunst und Diktatur: Architektur, Bildhauerei und Malerei in Österreich, Deutschland, Italien und der Sowjetunion 1922–1956*, Baden: Grasl.

Tae-Kook, Jeon 1984, *Karl Mannheims Ideologietheorie und ihr Verhältnis zur Kritischen Theorie der Frankfurter Schule*, dissertation, Frankfurt am Main.

Taps, Claudia 2000, *Bürgergesellschaft – Politische Freiheit im Zeitalter ökonomischen Umbruchs. Theoretische Konzeptionen zur strukturellen Veränderung moderner Gesellschaften und empirische Erfahrungen mit Non-Governmental Organiziations hinsichtlich gesellschaftlicher Inklusionsprozesse am Beispiel des USA*, Frankfurt am Main: Lang.

Taubes, Jacob (ed.) 1985, *Der Fürst dieser Welt. Carl Schmitt und die Folgen. Religionstheorie und Politische Theorie*, Vol. 1, Munich: Fink.

—— 2009 [1947], *Occidental Eschatology*, Stanford: Stanford University Press.

Taureck, Bernhard 1988, *Französische Philosophie im 20. Jahrhundert*, Reinbek: Rowohlt.

—— 1992, *Krisenethik – Ethikkrise. Analysen, Texte, Modelle*, Reinbek: Rowohlt.

—— 2000, *Nietzsche und der Faschismus. Ein Politikum*, Leipzig: Reclam.

Taylor, Charles 1975, *Hegel*, Cambridge: Cambridge University Press.

—— 1988 [1985], *Negative Freiheit? Zur Kritik des neuzeitlichen Individualismus*, Frankfurt am Main: Suhrkamp.

—— 1990, 'Modes of Civil Society', *Public Culture*, 3, 1: 94–132.

—— 1992, *Multiculturalism and "The Politics of Recognition": An Essay*, Princeton, NJ: Princeton University Press.

Tenbruck, Friedrich H. 1967, 'Zu einer Theorie der Planung' in *Wissenschaft und Praxis*, edited by Leo Brandt, Cologne: Westdeutscher Verlag.

—— 1975, 'Das Werk Max Webers', *Kölner Zeitschrift für Soziologie und Sozialpsychologie*, 27: 663–702.

—— 1984, *Die unbewältigten Sozialwissenschaften oder die Abschaffung des Menschen*, Graz: Styria.

—— 1985, 'George Herbert Mead und die Ursprünge der Soziologie in Deutschland und Amerika. Ein Kapitel über die Gültigkeit und Vergleichbarkeit soziologischer Theorien' in *Das Problem der Intersubjektivität. Neuere Beiträge zum Werk George Herbert Meads*, edited by Hans Joas, Frankfurt am Main: Suhrkamp.

Tertullian, Nicolas 1990, 'Seinsgeschichte als Legitimation der Politik' in *Martin Heidegger – Faszination und Erschrecken. Die politische Dimension einer Philosophie*, edited by Peter Kemper, Frankfurt am Main: Campus.

Thalheimer, August 1974 [1930], 'Über den Faschismus' in *Texte zur Faschismusdiskussion 1, Positionen und Kontroversen*, edited by Reinhard Kühnl, Reinbek: Rowohlt.

Theunissen, Michael 1969, *Gesellschaft und Geschichte. Zur Kritik der kritischen Theorie*, Berlin: de Gruyter.

—— 1970, *Hegels Lehre vom absoluten Geist als theologisch-politischer Traktat*, Berlin: de Gruyter.

—— 1976, 'Die Aufhebung des Idealismus in der Spätphilosophie Schellings', *Philosophisches Jahrbuch*, 83: 1–29.

—— 1978, *Sein und Schein. Die kritische Funktion der Hegelschen Logik*, Frankfurt am Main: Suhrkamp.

—— 1983, 'Negativität bei Adorno' in *Adorno-Konferenz 1983*, edited by Ludwig von Friedeburg and Jürgen Habermas, Frankfurt am Main: Suhrkamp.

—— 1992, *Negative Theologie der Zeit*, Frankfurt am Main: Suhrkamp.

Thielemann, Ulrich 1997, *Das Prinzip Markt. Kritik der ökonomischen Tauschlogik*, Bern: Haupt.

Thielen, Helmut 1991, *Revolution des Glaubens. Religionsphilosophische Versuche über Befreiung*, Hamburg: Argument.

Thier, Erich 1954, 'Etappen der Marxinterpretation', *Marxismusstudien*, 1: 1–38.

—— 1957, *Das Menschenbild des jungen Marx*, Göttingen: Vandenhoeck und Ruprecht.

Thiermann, Sven 2001, *Gesellschaft und Entfremdung, betrachtet von Rousseau bis zur DDR-Philosophie*, MA thesis, Dresden.

Thies, Christian 2000, *Gehlen zur Einführung*, Hamburg: Junius.

Thomas, Andreas Maria 1993, *Das Ende des Mythos Sozialismus. Vom Scheitern der sozialistischen Politik und Theologie*, Frankfurt am Main: Lang.

Thompson, Edward Palmer 1968, *The Making of the English Working Class*, Harmondsworth: Penguin.

—— 1993, *Customs in Common: Studies in Traditional Popular Culture*, New York: The New Press.
Thumser, Wolfang 1996, *Kirche im Sozialismus. Geschichte, Bedeutung und Funktion einer ekklesiologischen Formel*, Tübingen: Mohr.
Thurneysen, Eduard 1926, *Christoph Blumhardt*, Munich: Kaiser.
—— 1963 [1923], 'Sozialismus und Christentum' in *Anfänge der dialektischen Theologie II*, edited by J. Moltmann, Munich: Kaiser.
Thurnherr, Urs 2000, *Angewandte Ethik zur Einführung*, Hamburg: Junius.
Thyssen, Johannes 1936, *Geschichte der Geschichtsphilosophie*, Berlin: Junker und Dünnhaupt.
Tietz, Udo (ed.) 1997, 'Marx – Deutungen nach dem Funeral', *Berliner Debatte Initial*, 8, 1/2.
—— 1997a: 'Zur Genesis und Kritik der Lukácsschen Demokratisierungsideologie' in *Auf der Suche nach dem Citoyen*, edited by Volker Caysa, Frankfurt am Main: Lang.
Tigar, Michael E. and Madeleine R. Levy 1977, *Law and the Rise of Capitalism*, New York: Monthly Review Press.
Tilitzky, Christian 2002, *Die deutsche Universitätsphilosophie in der Weimarer Republik und im Dritten Reich*, 2 Vols., Berlin: Akademie-Verlag.
Tillich, Paul 1962, 'Christentum und soziale Gestaltung. Frühe Schriften zum religiösen Sozialismus' in *Gesammelte Werke* (*GW*), Vol. 2, Stuttgart: Evangelisches Verlagswerk.
—— 1962a: 'Der Protestantismus als Kritik und Gestaltung' in *Gesammelte Werke* (*GW*), Vol. 7, Stuttgart: Evangelisches Verlagswerk.
—— 1963, 'Der Widerstreit von Raum und Zeit' in *Gesammelte Werke* (*GW*), Vol. 6, Stuttgart: Evangelisches Verlagswerk.
—— 1966 [1962], *On the Boundary*, New York: Scribner.
Tjaden, Karl Hermann (ed.) 1971, *Soziale Systeme*, Berlin: Luchterhand.
Tjaden, Karl Hermann and Margarete Tjaden-Steinhauer 1970, 'Sozialstruktur des deutschen Kapitalismus' in *Die Arbeiterklasse im Spätkapitalismus*, edited by Wolfgang Fritz Haug, Karlsruhe: Das Argument.
—— 1973, *Klassenverhältnisse im Spätkapitalismus. Beitrag zur Analyse der Sozialstruktur unter besonderer Berücksichtigung der Bundesrepublik*, Stuttgart: Enke.
Tobin, James 1978, 'A Proposal for International Monetary Reform', *Eastern Economic Journal*, 3, 3/4, 153–159.
Todd, Emmanuel 1998, *L'illusion économique: essai sur la stagnation des économies développées*, Paris: Gallimard.
Tohidipur, Mehdi (ed.) 1978, *Der bürgerliche Rechtsstaat*, 2 Vols., Frankfurt am Main: Suhrkamp.
Tomberg, Friedrich 1973, *Bürgerliche Wissenschaft*, Frankfurt am Main: Fischer.
—— 1974, *Basis und Überbau. Sozialphilosophische Studien*, Neuwied: Luchterhand.
Tönnies, Ferdinand 1893, *"Ethische Cultur" und ihr Geleite*, Berlin: Dümmler.
—— 1897, *Der Nietzsche-Kultus. Eine Kritik*, Leipzig: Reisland.
—— 1921, *Marx. Leben und Lehre*, Jena: Erich Lichtenstein.
—— 1979 [1887], *Gemeinschaft und Gesellschaft. Grundbegriffe der reinen Soziologie*, Darmstadt: Wissenschaftliche Buchgesellschaft.
Topitsch, Ernst 1961, *Sozialphilosophie zwischen Ideologie und Wissenschaft*, Berlin: Luchterhand.
—— 1967, *Die Sozialphilosophie Hegels als Heilslehre und als Herrschaftsideologie*, Berlin: Luchterhand.
—— 1969, *Mythos – Philosophie – Politik. Zur Naturgeschichte der Illusion*, Freiburg: Rombach.
—— 1973, *Gottwerdung und Revolution. Beiträge zur Weltanschauungsanalyse und Ideologiekritik*, Pullach: Verlag Dokumentation.
—— 1975, 'Marx zwischen Mythos und Wissenschaft' in *Marxismus – ernst genommen. Ein Universalsystem auf dem Prüfstand der Wissenschaften*, edited by Gerhard Szczesny, Reinbek: Rowohlt.
—— 1985, *Stalins Krieg. Die sowjetische Langzeitstrategie gegen den Westen als rationale Machtpolitik*, Munich: Olzog.
Touraine, Alan 1971, *The Post-Industrial Society*, New York: Random House.
Tristam, Wolfgang 1974, 'Allgemeine Formbestimmung des bürgerlichen Staates. Zur Kritik des Staatsbegriffs in der Theorie des staatsmonopolistischen Kapitalismus' in *Monopol und Staat. Zur Marx-Rezeption in der Theorie des staatsmonopolitischen Kapitalismus*, edited by Rolf Ebbinghaus, Frankfurt am Main: Suhrkamp.
—— 1974a: 'Revolution und Staat. Zum Verhältnis von Analyse und Taktik bei Lenin' in

Monopol und Staat. Zur Marx-Rezeption in der Theorie des staatsmonopolitischen Kapitalismus, edited by Rolf Ebbinghaus, Frankfurt am Main: Suhrkamp.

Troeltsch, Ernst 1922, 'Der Historismus und seine Probleme 1, Das logische Problem der Geschichtsphilosophie' in *Gesammelte Schriften*, Vol. 3.1, Tübingen: Mohr.

—— 1977 [1912], 'Die Soziallehren der christlichen Kirchen und Gruppen' in *Gesammelte Schriften*, Vol. 1.3, Tübingen: Mohr.

Trotsky, Leon 1918, *Krieg und Revolution*, Zürich: Verlag der Grütlibuchhandlung.

—— 1921, *Terrorism and Communism: A Reply to Karl Kautsky*, London: Allen & Unwin.

—— 1932, *The History of the Russian Revolution*, 3 Vols., New York: Simon & Schuster.

—— 1937 [1924], *The Lessons of October*, New York: Pioneer Publishers.

—— 1969 [1938], *Their Morals and Ours: Marxist versus Liberal Views on Morality*, New York: Pathfinder Press.

—— 1973 [1940], *In Defense of Marxism*, New York: Pathfinder Press.

—— 1980 [1937], *The Lessons of Spain: The Last Warning*, London: Militant.

Tschentscher, Axel 2000, *Prozedurale Theorien der Gerechtigkeit. Rationales Entscheiden, Diskursethik und prozedurales Recht*, Baden-Baden: Nomos.

Tuchscheerer, Walter 1968, *Bevor "Das Kapital" entstand*, Cologne: Pahl-Rugenstein.

Tucker, Robert C. 1961, *Philosophy and Myth in Karl Marx*, London: Cambridge University Press.

Tugan Baranovsky, Michael 1901 [1894], *Studien zur Theorie und Geschichte des Handelskrisen in England*, Jena: Fischer.

—— 1904, 'Der Zusammenbruch der kapitalistischen Wirtschaftsordnung um Lichte der nationalökonomischen Theorie', *Archiv für Sozialwissenschaft und Sozialpolitik*, 19.

—— 1905, *Theoretische Grundlagen des Marxismus*, Leipzig: Duncker und Humblot.

Tugendhat, Ernst 1970, *Der Wahrheitsbegriff bei Husserl und Heidegger*, Berlin: de Gruyter.

—— 1993, *Vorlesungen über Ethik*, Frankfurt am Main: Suhrkamp.

Türcke, Christoph 1987 [1983], 'Die religiösen Wurzeln der Marxschen Kritik' in *Kritik und Krise. Zur Aktualität der Marxschen Theorie*, Lüneburg: zu Klampen.

—— 1988, *Perspektiven kritischer Theorie*, Lüneburg: zu Klampen.

—— 1989, *Die neue Geschäftigkeit. Zum Ethik- und Geistesbetrieb*, Lüneburg: zu Klampen.

—— 1990 [1979], *Zum ideologiekritischen Potential der Theologie. Konsequenzen materialistischer Paulus-Interpretation*, Lüneburg: zu Klampen.

—— 1997, *Kassensturz. Zu Lage der Theologie*, Lüneburg: zu Klampen.

Turner, Adair 2001, *Just Capital: The Liberal Economy*, London: Macmillan.

Tyrell, Hartmann 1994, 'Max Webers Soziologie – eine Soziologie ohne "Gesellschaft"' in *Max Webers Wissenschaftslehre. Interpretation und Kritik*, edited by Gerhard Wagner and Heinz Zipprian, Frankfurt am Main: Suhrkamp.

Uertz, Rudolf 1981, *Christentum und Sozialismus in der frühen CDU. Grundlagen und Wirkungen der christlich-sozialen Ideen in der Union 1945–1949*, Stuttgart: Deutsche Verlags-Anstalt.

Ullmann, Hans-Peter 1996, *Das deutsche Kaiserreich (1871–1918)*, Frankfurt am Main: Suhrkamp.

Ullrich, Horst 1976, *Zur Reaktion der bürgerlichen Ideologie auf die Entstehung des Marxismus*, East Berlin: Akademie-Verlag.

Ulrich, Peter 1993 [1986], *Transformation der ökonomischen Vernunft: Fortschrittsperspektiven der entwickelten Industriegesellschaft*, Bern: Haupt.

—— 1997, *Integrative Wirtschaftsethik. Grundlagen einer lebensdienlichen Ökonomie*, Bern: Haupt.

Ulrich, Peter and Thomas Maak (eds.) 2000, *Die Wirtschaft in der Gesellschaft. Perspektiven an der Schwelle zum 3. Jahrtausend*, Bern: Haupt.

UNDP (United Nations Development Programme) (ed.) 1996, *Human Development Report 1996*, New York: UNDP.

Üner, Elfriede 1981, 'Jugendbewegung und Soziologie. Wissenschaftssoziologische Skizzen zu Hans Freyers Werk und Wissenschaftsgemeinschaft bis 1933' in *Soziologie in Deutschland und Österreich 1918–1945. Materialien zur Entwicklung, Emigration und Wirkungsgeschichte*, edited by M. Rainer Lepsius, Opladen: Westdeutscher Verlag.

—— 1992, *Soziologie als "geistige Bewegung". Hans Freyers System der Soziologie und die "Leipziger Schule"*, Weinheim: VCH.

—— 1994, 'Hans Freyer und Arnold Gehlen: Zwei Wege auf der "Suche nach Wirklichkeit"' in *Zur geisteswissenschaftlichen Bedeutung von Arnold Gehlen*, edited by Helmut Klages and Helmut Quaritsch, Berlin: Duncker und Humblot.

Utz, Arthur 1994, *Sozialethik, IV: Wirtschaftsethik. Mit internationaler Bibliographie*, Bonn: WBV.

Vahrenkamp, Richard (ed.) 1973, *Technologie und Kapital*, Frankfurt am Main: Suhrkamp.

Vaihinger, Hans 1911, *Die Philosophie des Als Ob*, Berlin: Reuther und Reichhard.

Van Parijs, Philippe 1980, 'The Falling Rate of Profit Theory of Crisis: A Rational Reconstruction by Way of Obituary', *Review of Radical Political Economics*, 4, 1: 1–16.

—— 1993, *Marxism Recycled*, Cambridge: Cambridge University Press.

—— 1995, *Real Freedom for All: What (if Anything) Can justify Capitalism?* Oxford: Clarendon Press.

Varga, Csaba (ed.) 1993, *Marxian Legal Theory*, New York: New York University Press.

Varga, Eugene 1935, *The Great Crisis and its Political Consequences: Economics and Politics, 1928–1934*, London: Modern Books.

—— 1955, *Grundfragen der Ökonomie und Politik des Imperialismus (nach dem Zweiten Weltkrieg)*, Berlin.

—— 1969, *Die Krise des Kapitalismus und ihre politischen Folgen*, Frankfurt am Main: Europäische Verlags-Anstalt.

Veblen, Thorstein B. 1921, *The Engineers and the Price System*, New York: Huebsch.

—— 1965 [1899], *The Theory of Leisure Class*, New York: Kelley.

Vester, Michael (ed.) 1970, *Die Frühsozialisten, 1789–1948*, 2 Vols., Reinbek: Rowohlt.

—— 1970a: *Die Entstehung des Proletariats als Lernprozess*, Frankfurt am Main: Europäische Verlags-Anstalt.

—— 2004, 'Soziale Ungleichheit, Klasse und Kultur' in *Handbuch der Kulturwissenschaften*, edited by Friedrich Jaeger and Jörn Rüsen, Vol. 3, Stuttgart: Metzler.

Vico, Giambattista 1968 [1725], *The New Science*, Ithaca: Cornell University Press.

Vierkandt, Alfred (ed.) 1959, *Handwörterbuch der Soziologie*, Stuttgart: Enke.

Voegelin, Eric 2000 [1952], 'The New Science of Politics' in *Collected Works (CW)*, Vol. 5, Columbia: University of Missouri Press.

—— 2000a [1959], 'Science, Politics, and Gnosticism' in *Collected Works (CW)*, Vol. 5, Columbia: University of Missouri Press.

Vogel, Paul 1925, *Hegels Gesellschaftsbegriff und seine Fortbildung durch Lorenz Stein, Marx, Engels und Lassalle*, Berlin: Pan-Verlag.

Vogt, Bernhard 1997, *Franz Oppenheimer. Wissenschaft und Ethik der Sozialen Marktwirtschaft*, Bodenheim: Philo.

—— 1999, 'Franz Oppenheimer und die Grundlegung der Sozialen Marktwirtschaft' in *Wirtschaft und Gesellschaft. Franz Oppenheimer und die Grundlegung der Sozialen Marktwirtschaft*, edited by Elke-Vera Kotowski et al., Berlin: Philo.

Vogt, Winfried (ed.) 1973, *Seminar: Politische Ökonomie*, Frankfurt am Main: Suhrkamp.

Volf, Miroslav 1988, *Zukunft der Arbeit – Arbeit der Zukunft. Der Arbeitsbegriff bei Marx und seine theologische Wertung*, Munich: Kaiser.

Vollgraf, Ernst et al. (eds.) 1991 ff.: *Beiträge zur Marx-Engels-Forschung*, Hamburg.

Vollmann, Morris 2002, *Das Erhabene und die Endlichkeit. Zum kritischen Potential einer ästhetischen Kategorie*, MA thesis, TU Dresden.

Voloshinov, V.N. 1986 [1929], *Marxism and the Philosophy of Language*, Cambridge, MA: Harvard University Press.

Voltaire 1843 [1770], A *Philosophical Dictionary*, Strand: Dugdale.

Vondung, Klaus 2000 [1988], *The Apocalypse in Germany*, Columbia: University of Missouri Press.

Vorgrimmler, Herbert 1985, *Theologische Gotteslehre*, Düsseldorf: Patmos-Verlag.

Vorländer, Karl 1926, *Kant und Marx. Ein Beitrag zur Philosophie des Sozialismus*, Tübingen: Mohr.

Vosskühler, Friedrich 1996, *Der Idealismus als Metaphysik der Moderne. Studien zur Selbstreflexion und Aufhebung der Metaphysik bei Hölderlin, Hegel, Schelling, Marx und Heidegger*, Würzburg: Königshausen und Neumann.

Vranicki, Predag 1983 [1961–71], *Geschichte des Marxismus*, 2 Vols., Frankfurt am Main: Suhrkamp.

Wacker, Bernd 1994, *Die eigentlich katholische Verschärfung … Konfession, Theologie und Politik im Werk Carl Schmitts*, Munich: Fink.

Wagner, Falk 1985, *Geld oder Gott? Zur Geldbestimmtheit der kulturellen und religiösen Lebenswelt*, Stuttgart: Klett-Cotta.

Wagner, Gerhard 1994, 'Am Ende der systemtheoretischen Soziologie. Niklas Luhmann und die Dialektik', *Zeitschrift für Soziologie*, 23, 4: 292–305.

Waibl, Elmar 1988, *Ökonomie und Ethik I. Die Kapitalismusdebatte in der Philosophie der Neuzeit*, Stuttgart: Frommann-Holzboog.

—— 1989, *Ökonomie und Ethik II. Die Kapitalismusdebatte von Nietzsche bis Reagonomics*, Stuttgart: Frommann-Holzboog.

Wald, Alan W. 1987, *The New York Intellectuals: The Rise and Decline of the Anti-Stalinist Left from the 1930s to the 1980s*, Chapel Hill: University of North Carolina Press.

Waldenfels, Bernard et al. (eds.) 1977–9, *Phänomenologie und Marxismus*, 4 Vols., Frankfurt am Main: Suhrkamp.

Walicki, Andrzej 1995, *Marxism and the Leap to the Kingdom of Freedom: The Rise and Fall of Communist Utopia*, Stanford: Stanford University Press.

Walk, Heike and Nele Boehme (eds.) 2002, *Globaler Widerstand. Internationale Netzwerke auf der Suche nach Alternativen im globalen Kapitalismus*, Münster: Westfälisches Dampfboot.

Wallgärtner, Gisela 1991, *Der soziologische Diskurs im Kaiserreich. Auswertung sozialwissenschaftlicher Zeitschriften*, Hamburg: Lit.

Walras, Leon 1984 [1874], *Elements of Pure Economics, or, The Theory of Social Wealth*, Philadelphia: Orion.

Walzer, Michael 1983, *Spheres of Justice: A Defense of Pluralism and Equality*, New York: Basic Books.

—— 1987, *Interpretation and Social Criticism*, Cambridge, MA: Harvard University Press.

—— 1988, 'Socialising the Welfare State' in *Democracy and the Welfare State*, edited by Amy Gutman, Princeton: Princeton University Press.

—— 1988a: *The Company of Critics: Social Criticism and Political Commitment in the Twentieth Century*, New York: Basic Books.

—— 1990, 'The Communitarian Critique of Liberalism', *Political Theory*, 18, 1: 6–23.

—— 1994, *Thick and Thin: Moral Argument at Home and Abroad*, Notre Dame: University of Notre Dame Press.

—— 1995 [1991], 'The Concept of Civil Society' in *Toward a Global Civil Society*, Providence: Berghahn Books.

Walzer, Michael, Amitai Etzioni, Francis Fukuyama, Samuel P. Huntington et al. 2002, 'What We are Fighting for. A Manifesto for the Just War', available at <www.americanvalues.org/html/what_we_re_fighting_for.html>.

Warnke, Cornelia and Gerhard Huber (eds.) 1998, *Die ökonomische Theorie von Marx: was bleibt?* Marburg: Metropolis.

Waser, Ruedi 1994, *Autonomie des Selbstbewusstseins. Eine Untersuchung zum Verhältnis von Bruno Bauer und Karl Marx (1835–1843)*, Tübingen: Francke.

Wassina, L. 1983, 'Die Ausarbeitung der Geldtheorie durch Karl Marx in den Londoner Heften (1850–1851)', *Marx-Engels Jahrbuch*, 6, 148–172.

Weber, Alfred 1927, *Ideen zur Staats- und Kultursoziologie*, Karlsruhe: G. Braun.

—— 1931, 'Kultursoziologie' in *Handwörterbuch der Soziologie*, edited by Alfred Vierkandt, Stuttgart: Enke.

—— 1935, *Kulturgeschichte als Kultursoziologie*, Leiden: Sijthoff.

—— 1955, *Einführung in die Soziologie*, Munich: Piper.

—— 1964, *Der dritte oder der vierte Mensch. Vom Sinn des geschichtlichen Daseins*, Stuttgart: Deutscher Bücherbund.

Weber, Hermann 1969, *Demokratischer Kommunismus? Zur Theorie, Geschichte und Politik der kommunistischen Bewegung*, Hannover: Dietz.

—— 1969a: *Die Wandlung des deutschen Kommunismus. Die Stalinisierung der KPD in der Weimarer Republik*, Frankfurt am Main: Europäische Verlags-Anstalt.

—— 1970, *Lenin in Selbstzeugnissen und Bilddokumenten*, Reinbek: Rowohlt.

—— 1973, *Das Prinzip Links. Eine Dokumentation. Beiträge zur Diskussion des demokratischen Sozialismus in Deutschland, 1847–1973*, Ulm: Fackelträger-Verlag.

Weber, Hermann and Ulrich Mählert (eds.) 1998, *Terror. Stalinistische Parteisäuberungen 1936–1953*, Paderborn: Schöningh.

Weber, Marianne 1900, *Fichtes Sozialismus und sein Verhältnis zur Marxschen Doktrin*, Tübingen: Mohr.

Weber, Max 1894, *Bericht über die Verhandlungen des fünften Evangelisch-sozialen Kongresses*, Berlin: Rehtwisch.

—— 1924, *Gesammelte Aufsätze zur Soziologie und Sozialpolitik*, Tübingen: Mohr.

—— 1952 [1919], 'Science as a Vocation' in *From Max Weber: Essays in Sociology*, London: Routledge and Kegan Paul.

—— 1968 [1922], *Economy and Society*, New York: Bedminster Press.

—— 1972 [1919], *Politics as Vocation*, Philadelphia: Fortress Press.

—— 1982 [1922], *Gesammelte Aufsätze zur Wissenschaftslehre*, Tübingen: Mohr.

—— 1984 [1920a], 'Der Sozialismus' in *Gesamtausgabe*, Vol. I.15, Tübingen: Mohr.

—— 1988 [1920], *Gesammelte Aufsätze zur Religionssoziologie 1*, Tübingen: Mohr.

—— 1989, *Rationalisierung und entzauberte Welt. Schriften zu Soziologie und Geschichte*, Leipzig: Reclam.

—— 1994 [1895], 'The Nation State and Economic Policy' in *Political Writings*, Cambridge: Cambridge University Press.

—— 2003 [1904], The *Protestant Ethic and the "Spirit" of Capitalism*, New York: Dover.

Wegener, Bernd (ed.) 2000, *Social Justice Beliefs in Transition: Eastern and Central Europe 1991–1996*, special issue of *Social Justice Research*, 13.

Wegener, Bernd and Hans-Peter Müller (eds.) 1995, *Soziale Ungleichheit und soziale Gerechtigkeit*, Opladen: Leske und Budrich.

Wegerich, Ullrich 1994, *Dialektische Theorie und historische Erfahrung. Zur Geschichtsphilosophie in der frühen kritischen Theorie Max Horkheimers*, Würzburg: Königshausen und Neumann.

Wehler, Hans Ulrich 1969, *Bismarck und der Imperialismus*, Cologne: Kiepenheuer und Witsch.

—— 1979, *Klassen in der europäischen Sozialgeschichte*, Göttingen: Vandenhoeck und Ruprecht.

—— 1985 [1972], *Geschichte und Ökonomie*, Königstein: Athenäum.

Wehner, Herbert 1985, *Christentum und demokratischer Sozialismus. Beiträge zu einer unbequemen Partnerschaft*, Freiburg: Dreisam.

Wehr, Gerhard 1979, *Paul Tillich*, Reinbek: Rowohlt.

Weiler, Rudolf 1999, *Gerechtigkeit in der sozialen Ordnung. Die Tugend der Gerechtigkeit im Zeitalter der Globalisierung*, Berlin: Dunker und Humblot.

Weingart, Peter et al. 1988, *Rasse, Blut und Gene. Geschichte der Eugenik und Rassenhygiene in Deutschland*, Frankfurt am Main: Suhrkamp.

Weischedel, Willhem 1985 [1971], Der *Gott der Philosophen. Grundlegung einer Philosophischen Theologie im Zeitalter des Nihilismus*, Munich: Deutscher Taschenbuch-Verlag.

Weise, Peter et al. 1991, *Neue Mikroökonomie*, Heidelberg: Physica.

Weiss, Andreas von 1965, *Die Diskussion über den Historischen Materialismus in der deutschen Sozialdemokratie 1891–1918*, Wiesbaden: Harrassowitz.

Weiß, Johannes 1981, *Das Werk Max Webers in der marxistischen Rezeption und Kritik*, Opladen: Westdeutscher Verlag.

Weisser, Gerhard 1976, 'Philosophischer Kritizismus, Kritischer Rationalismus, Kritische Theorie und Neomarxismus im Wettbewerb um die geistige Fundierung der Programmatik der SPD' in *Kritischer Rationalismus und Sozialdemokratie II. Diskussion und Kritik*, edited by Georg Lührs et al., Berlin: Dietz.

Weitling, Wilhelm 1967 [1845], *Das Evangelium des armen Sünders*, Leipzig: Reclam.

—— 1974 [1842]: *Garantien der Harmonie und Freiheit*, Stuttgart: Reclam.

Weizsäcker, Carl Christian von 1962, *Wachstum, Zins und optimale Investitionsquote*, Tübingen: Kyklos.

—— 1977, *Der Garten des Menschlichen. Beiträge zur geschichtlichen Anthropologie*, Munich: Hanser.

Wellmer, Albrecht 1969, *Kritische Gesellschaftstheorie und Positivismus*, Frankfurt am Main: Suhrkamp.

—— 1979, *Praktische Philosophie und Theorie der Gesellschaft. Zum Problem der normativen Grundlagen einer kritischen Sozialwissenschaft*, Constance: Universitätsverlag.

—— 1986, *Ethik und Dialog*, Frankfurt am Main: Suhrkamp.

—— 1993, 'Bedingungen einer demokratischen Kultur. Zur Debatte zwischen Liberalen und Kommunitaristen' in *Gemeinschaft und Gerechtigkeit*, edited by Micha Brumlik and Hauke Brunkhorst, Frankfurt am Main: Fischer.

World Bank (International Bank for Reconstruction and Development) 2003, *World Development Report 2002*, Washington: World Bank.

Welzer, Harald 1995, *Das Gedächtnis der Bilder. Ästhetik und Nationalsozialismus*, Tübingen: Edition Diskord.

Wenzel, Siegfried 1998, *Plan und Wirklichkeit. Zur DDR-Ökonomie. Dokumente und Erinnerungen*, St. Katharinen: Scripta Mercaturae.

Wenzl, Alois 1935, *Wissenschaft und Weltanschauung. Natur und Geist als Probleme der Metaphysik*, Berlin: Hoffmann.

Werkstatt Ökonomie 2002, *Reichtum und Armut als Herausforderung für kirchliches Handeln*, Heidelberg: Werkstatt Ökonomie.

Werner, Klaus and Hans Weiss 2001, *Schwarzbuch der Markenfirmen. Die Machenschaften der Weltkonzerne*, Vienna: Deuticke, 2001.

Wesel, Uwe 2003, *Recht, Unrecht und Gerechtigkeit. Von der Weimarer Republik bis heute*, Munich: Beck.

West, Cornel 1991, *The Ethical Dimensions of Marxist Thought*, New York: Monthly Review Press.

Westbrook, Robert B. 1991, *John Dewey and American Democracy*, Ithaca, NY: Cornell University Press.

Wetherly, Paul (ed.) 1982, *Marx's Theory of History: The Contemporary Debate*, Aldershot: Avebury.

Wetter, Gustav A. 1952, *Der dialektische Materialismus. Seine Geschichte und sein System*, Freiburg: Herder.

—— 1958, *Philosophie und Naturwissenschaft in der Sowjetunion*, Reinbek: Rowohlt.

Wetzel, Manfred 1972, *Erkenntnistheorie. Die Gegenstandsbeziehung und Tätigkeit des erkennenden Subjekts als Gegenstand der Erkenntnistheorie*, Munich: Fink.

Wheen, Francis 1999, *Karl Marx: A Life*, New York: Norton.

White, James 1996, *Karl Marx and the Dialectical Origins of Dialectical Materialism*, London: Macmillan.

Wiards, Mathias 2000, *Krise im Realsozialismus. Die Politische Ökonomie der DDR in den 80er Jahren*, Hamburg: Argument.

Wieland, Josef (ed.) 1993, *Wirtschaftsethik und Theorie der Gesellschaft*, Frankfurt am Main: Suhrkamp.

—— 1993a: *Formen der Institutionalisierung von Moral in amerikanischen Unternehmen. Die amerikanische Business-Ethics-Bewegung. Why and how they do it*, Bern: Haupt.

—— 1996, *Ökonomische Organisation, Allokation und Status*, Tübingen: Mohr.

—— 1998, 'Wie kann Unternehmensethik praktiziert werden' in *Unternehmensethik in der Praxis*, edited by Josef Wieland and Peter Ulrich, Bern: Haupt.

—— 1999, *Ethik der Governance*, Marburg: Metropolis.

Wielenga, Baastian 1971, *Lenins Weg zur Revolution. Eine Konfrontation mit Sergej Bulgakov und Peter Struve im Interesse einer theologischen Besinnung*, Munich: Kaiser.

Wiese, Leopold von 1954 [1926], *Soziologie. Geschichte und Hauptprobleme*, Berlin: de Gruyter.

Wiggershaus, Rolf 1978, 'Die Geschichte der Frankfurter Schule', *Neue Rundschau*, 89, 4: 571–87.

—— 1994 [1988], *The Frankfurt School: Its History, Theories, and Political Significance*, Oxford: Polity Press.

—— 2000, *Wittgenstein und Adorno*, Göttingen: Wallstein.

Wildt, Andreas 1970, 'Hegels Kritik des Jakobinismus' in *Aktualität und Folgen der Philosophie Hegels*, edited by Oskar Negt, Frankfurt am Main: Suhrkamp.

—— 1982, *Autonomie und Anerkennung. Hegels Moralitätskritik im Lichte seiner Fichte-Rezeption*, Stuttgart: Klett-Cotta.

—— 1986, 'Gerechtigkeit in Marx' *Kapital*' in *Ethik und Marx. Moralkritik und normative Grundlagen der Marxschen Theorie*, edited by Emil Angehrn and Georg Lohmann, Königstein: Hain.

—— 1997, 'Paradoxien in der Marxschen Moralkritik und ihre Auflösungen', *Logos*, 3: 210–42.

—— 2002, 'Revolutionärer Terror und Moral bei Marx und Engels', *Deutsche Zeitschrift für Philosophie*, 3: 425–43.

—— 2002a: 'Gibt es Marxsche Kriterien der politischen Gerechtigkeit?', *Deutsche Zeitschrift für Philosophie*, special issue 3.

Wilharm, Heiner 1990, *Denken für eine geschlossene Welt. Philosophie in der DDR*, Hamburg: Junius.

Williams, Raymond 1980, 'Base and Superstructure in Marxist Cultural Theory' in *Problems in Materialism and Culture*, London: Verso.

Willke, Helmut 2001, *Atopia. Studien zur atopischen Gesellschaft*, Frankfurt am Main: Suhrkamp.

Willms, Bernard 1967, *Die totale Freiheit. Fichtes politische Philosophie*, Cologne: Westdeutscher Verlag.

—— 1969, *Planungsideologie und revolutionäre Utopie. Die zweifache Flucht in die Zukunft*, Stuttgart: Kohlhammer.

—— 1973, *Kritik und Politik. Jürgen Habermas oder das politische Defizit der "Kritischen Theorie"*, Frankfurt am Main: Suhrkamp.

Wilson, Michael 1982, *Das Institut für Sozialforschung und seine Faschismusanalysen*, Frankfurt am Main: Campus.

Windelband, Wilhelm 1905, 'Fichte und Comte' in *Congrès Internationale de Paris*, Geneva.

—— 1916, *Geschichtsphilosophie. Eine Kriegsvorlesung*, Berlin: Reuther und Reichhard.

—— 1921 [1910], 'Die Erneuerung des Hegelianismus' in *Präludien*, Vol. 1, Tübingen: Mohr.

—— 1921a [1908], 'Fichtes Geschichtsphilosophie' in *Präludien*, Vol. 1, Tübingen: Mohr.

Wingert, Lutz 1993, *Gemeinsinn und Moral*, Frankfurt am Main: Suhrkamp.

Winkler, Heinrich August 1984, *Der Schein der Normalität. Arbeiter und Arbeiterbewegung in der Weimarer Republik 1924–1930*, Berlin: Dietz.

—— 1985, *Von der Revolution zur Stabilisierung. Arbeiter und Arbeiterbewegung in der Weimarer Republik 1918 bis 1924*, Berlin: Dietz.

—— 2000, *Der lange Weg nach Westen*, 2 Vols., Munich: Beck.

Winkler, Willi 2003, 'Der Aufrührer: Karl Marx – früher Verfechter rücksichtsloser Kritik und Recherche, um politische Zustände zu "unterwühlen"', *Süddeutsche Zeitung*, 27 January.

Winterfeld, Achim von 1909, *Nietzsche als Sozialphilosoph und seine Stellung zur Gesellschaft*, Gautzsch: F. Dietrich.

Wippermann, Wolfgang 1986, 'Triumph des Willens oder "kapitalistische Manipulation"? Das Ideologieproblem im Faschismus' in *Nationalsozialistische Diktatur 1933–1945. Eine Bilanz*, edited by Karl Dietrich Bracher et al., Bonn: Bundeszentrale für politische Bildung.

Wirkus, Bernd 1996, *Deutsche Sozialphilosophie in der ersten Hälfte des 20. Jahrhunderts*, Darmstadt: Wissenschaftliche Buchgesellschaft.

Wirth, Margaret 1972, *Kapitalismustheorie in der DDR. Entstehung und Entwicklung der Theorie des staatsmonopolistischen Kapitalismus*, Frankfurt am Main: Suhrkamp.

Wittgenstein, Ludwig 1969, *On Certainty*, Oxford: Blackwell.

—— 1984, *Werkausgabe*, Vol. 1, Frankfurt am Main: Suhrkamp.

—— 2009 [1953], *Philosophical Investigations*, Chichester: Blackwell.

—— 2010 [1922], *Tractatus logico-philosophicus*, Lexington: Seven Treasures.

Wittkau-Hörby, Anette 1998, *Materialismus. Entstehung und Wirkung in den Wissenschaften des 19. Jahrhunderts*, Göttingen: Vandenhoeck und Ruprecht.

Wolf, Dieter 1979, *Hegel und Marx. Zur Bewegungsstruktur des absoluten Geistes und des Kapitals*, Hamburg: VSA.

—— 1980, *Ware und Geld*, Hamburg: VSA.

Wolfe, Alan 1986, *Whose Keeper? Social Science and Moral Obligation*, Berkeley, CA: University of California Press.

Wolfe, Bertram David 1966, *Marxism: One Hundred Years in the Life of a Doctrine*, New York: Dial Press.

Wolff, Jonathan 2002, *Why Read Marx Today?* Oxford: Oxford University Press.

Wolff, Richard D. 2002, 'The US Economic Crisis: A Marxian Analysis', *Rethinking Marxism*, 14, 1: 118–31.

Wolff, Robert Paul (ed.) 1971, *The Rule of Law*, New York: Simon & Schuster.

—— 1984, *Understanding Marx: A Reconstruction and Critique of "Capital"*, Princeton: Princeton University Press.

Wolkogonow, Dimitri 1994, *Lenin. Utopie und Terror*, Düsseldorf: Econ.

Woltmann, Ludwig 1899, *Die Darwinsche Theorie und der Sozialismus*, Düsseldorf: Michels.

Wolin, Richard 2001, *Heidegger's Children: Hannah Arendt, Karl Löwith, Hans Jonas, and Herbert Marcuse*, Princeton: Princeton University Press.

Wood, Allen W. 1980 [1972], 'The Marxian Critique of Justice' in *Marx, Justice and History*, edited by Marshall Cohen, Thomas Nagel and Thomas Scanlon, Princeton: Princeton University Press.

—— 1980a [1979], 'Marx on Right and Justice: A Reply to Husami' in *Marx, Justice and History*, edited by Marshall Cohen, Thomas Nagel and Thomas Scanlon, Princeton: Princeton University Press.

—— 1981, *Karl Marx*, London: Routledge & Kegan Paul.

—— 1986, 'Marx' Immoralismus' in *Ethik und Marx. Moralkritik und normative Grundlagen der Marxschen Theorie*, edited by Emil Angehrn and Georg Lohmann, Königstein: Hain.

Wood, Ellen Meiksins 1986, *The Retreat from Class: A New "True" Socialism*, London: Verso.

Woods, Alan and Ted Grant 1995, *Reason in Revolt: Marxist Philosophy and Modern Science*, London: Wellred.

Worldwatch Institute (ed.) 2003, *State of the World, 2003*, New York: Norton.

Worsley, Peter 2002 [1982], *Marx and Marxism*, London: Routledge.

Wray, L. Randall 1998, *Understanding Modern Money: The Key to Full Employment and Price Stability*, Cheltenham: Edwar Elgar.

Wright Mills, C. 1962, *The Marxists*, New York: Dell.

Wright, Crispin 1992, *Truth and Objectivity*, Cambridge, MA: Harvard University Press.

Wright, Eric Olin 1977, 'Alternative Perspectives in Marxist Theory of Accumulation and Crisis' in *The Subtle Anatomy of Capitalism*, edited by Jesse Schwartz, Santa Monica: Goodyear.

—— 1978, *Class, Crises and the State*, London: New Left Books.

—— 1989, *The Debate on Classes*, London: Verso.

—— 1997, *Class Counts: Comparative Studies in Class Analysis*, Cambridge: Cambridge University Press.

Wrona, Vera et al. 1979, *Zur Geschichte der marxistisch-leninistischen Philosophie in der DDR. Von 1945 bis Anfang der sechziger Jahre*, East Berlin: Dietz.

Wuchterl, Kurt 1995, *Bausteine zu einer Geschichte der Philosophie des 20. Jahrhunderts: Von Husserl zu Heidegger. Eine Auswahl*, Bern: Haupt.

Wünsch, Georg 1925, *Religion und Wirtschaft*, Tübingen: Mohr.

—— 1927, *Evangelische Wirtschaftsethik*, Tübingen: Mohr.

—— 1932, 'Wirtschaftsethik' in *RGG*, Vol. 5, Tübingen: Mohr.

—— 1962, *Zwischen allen Fronten. Der Marxismus in soziologischer und christlicher Kritik*, Hamburg: Reich.

Wygodski, Solomon L. 1972, *Der gegenwärtige Kapitalismus. Versuch einer theoretischen Analyse*, Cologne: Pahl-Rugenstein.

Wyneken, Gustav 1940, *Weltanschauung*, Munich: Reinhardt.

Wyss, Beat 1996, *Der Wille zur Kunst. Zur ästhetischen Mentalität der Moderne*, Cologne: DuMont.

Young, Iris 1981, 'Toward a Critical Theory of Justice', *Social Theory and Practice*, 7, 3: 279–302.

Zademach, Wieland 1973, *Marxistisches Religionsverständnis und die biblische Botschaft von der Rechtfertigung des Gottlosen*, Düsseldorf: Patmos.

Zahlmann, Christel (ed.) 1994, *Kommunitarismus in der Diskussion. Eine streitbare Einführung*, Berlin: Rotbuch.

Zahrnt, Heinz 1966, *Die Sache mit Gott. Die protestantische Theologie im 20. Jahrhundert*, Munich: Piper.

Zander, Jürgen 1978, *Das Problem der Beziehung Max Webers zu Karl Marx*, Frankfurt am Main: Haag und Herchen.

Zarembka, Paul (ed.) 2001, *Marx's Capital and Capitalism: Markets in a Socialist Alternative*, Amsterdam: JAI.

Zeitlin, Irving N. 1968, *Ideology and the Development of Sociological Theory*, Englewood Cliffs: Prentice Hall.

Zeleny, Jindirch 1968, *Die Wissenschaftslogik bei Marx und das "Kapital"*, Frankfurt am Main: Europäische Verlags-Anstalt.

Zeltner, H. et al. 1974, 'Idealismus' in *Historisches Wörterbuch der Philosophie*, Vol. 4, Basel: Schwabe.

Ziegler, Bernd 1998, *Geschichte des ökonomischen Denkens. Paradigmenwechsel in der Volkswirtschaftslehre*, Munich: Oldenbourg.

Ziegler, Jean 1991, *À demain, Karl: pour sortir de la fin des ideologies*, Paris: R. Déforges.

—— 2002, *Les nouveaux maîtres du monde et ceux qui leur resistant*, Paris: Fayard.

Zieschang, Kurt et al. 1967, *Zur Theorie des staatsmonopolistischen Kapitalismus*, East Berlin: Akademie-Verlag.

Zimmerli, Walter Ch. 1993, 'Die Bedeutung philosophischer Klassiker für das Gegenwartsverständnis – Der Fall Marx', lecture held in Trier.

Zimmerman, Rolf 1985, *Utopie, Rationalität, Politik. Zu Kritik, Rekonstruktion und Systematik emanzipatorischer Gesellschaftstheorie bei Marx und Habermas*, Freiburg: Alber.

Zinn, Karl Georg 1974, *Arbeitswerttheorie – Zum heutigen Verständnis der positiven Wirtschaftstheorie von Karl Marx*, Berlin: Verlag Neue Wirtschaftsbriefe.

—— 1987, *Politische Ökonomie: Apologien und Kritiken des Kapitalismus*, Opladen: Westdeutscher Verlag.

—— 1992, *Soziale Marktwirtschaft: Idee, Entwicklung und Politik der bundesdeutschen Wirtschaftsordnung*, Mannheim: BI Taschenbuchverlag.

Zivotic, Miladin 1972, *Proletarischer Humanismus. Studien über Mensch, Wert und Freiheit*, Munich: Hanser.

Žižek, Slavoj 1993, *Tarrying with the Negative: Kant, Hegel and Ideology Criticism*, Durham, NC: Duke University Press.

—— 2011, *Revolution at the Gates*, London: Verso.

Zoninsein, Jonas 1990, *Monopoly Capital Theory: Hilferding and Twentieth Century Capitalism*, New York: Greenwood Press.

—— 2000, 'Rudolf Hilferding's Theory of Finance Capitalism and Today's World Financial Markets' in *Theory of Capitalism*, edited by Peter Koslowski, Berlin: Springer.

Zugehör, Rainer 1998, *Die Globalisierungslüge. Möglichkeiten einer verantwortlichen Wirtschaftspolitik*, Bad Honnef: Horlemann.

Zweiling, Klaus (ed.) 1958, *Die deutsche bürgerliche Philosophie seit 1917*, East Berlin: Deutscher Verlag der Wissenschaften.

—— 1961, *Die deutsche Philosophie von 1917–1945*, East Berlin: Deutscher Verlag der Wissenschaften.

Person Index[1]

1. Excluding footnotes.